THE

OLYMPIC GAMES

COMPLETE TRACK AND FIELD RESULTS

1896 – 1988

THE IMPORTANT THING IN THE OLYMPIC GAMES IS NOT WINNING BUT TAKING PART. THE ESSENTIAL THING IN LIFE IS NOT CONQUERING BUT FIGHTING WELL.

BARON de COUBERTIN

The Olympic Opening Ceremony.

THE
OLYMPIC
GAMES

COMPLETE TRACK
AND FIELD RESULTS

1896 – 1988

BARRY J. HUGMAN
AND PETER ARNOLD

Facts On File
New York • Oxford

Olympic Games: Complete Track and Field Results 1896–1988

Copyright © 1988 by Hugman Enterprises Ltd

Facts on File. Inc.
460 Park Avenue South
New York, New York 10016

CIP data available on request

Facts on File books are available at special discounts when purchased in bulk quantities for businesses, associations, institutions, or sales promotion. Please contact the Special Sales Department at 212/683-2244. (Dial 1-800-322-8755, except in NY, AK, HI)

10   9   8   7   6   5   4   3   2   1

This book is printed on acid-free paper

Printed in the UK

Contents

Acknowledgements 6
Preface 7
Key to Reading the Statistical Sections 9
The History of the Summer Olympics 11

1896 Prince George Joins the Marathon 17
1900 Olympic Running in the Bois de Boulogne 21
1904 Not Many Go to the Fair at St Louis 27
1906 The Intercalated Games in Athens 33
1908 Dorando Pietri, the World's Most Famous Loser 41
1912 The Disqualification of Jim Thorpe 53
1920 War Heroes Compete in an Austere Antwerp 67
1924 Paavo Nurmi and the Flying Finns 79
1928 The First Women Track and Field Competitors 91
1932 Babe Didrikson's All-Round Performance 105
1936 Jesse Owens Mocks the Nazi Propaganda Machine 119
1948 Fanny Blankers-Koen, a Popular Heroine 135
1952 Zatopek's 38 Miles and Three Gold Medals 153
1956 The Games Go to the Southern Hemisphere 171
1960 Elliott's Electric Pace and Bikila's Bare Feet 189
1964 Telstar Brings Tokyo's Stars to Millions 209
1968 Bob Beamon Leaps into the Record Books 233
1972 Viren Gets Up to Win — Then Wins Again 261
1976 White Lightning Strikes Twice 285
1980 Coe and Ovett Shine in Moscow 307
1984 Carl Lewis Leads the American Celebrations 329
1988 Flo Jo Adds Glamour Plus Speed 355

Bibliography 384

Acknowledgements

The authors would like to thank the many people, whose help has made this book possible.

Dave Terry researched all the Games reports, producing copy of great depth and quality. Dave is a Chartered Engineer with a 30 year interest in the history of track and field and the Olympic Games. He has been associated with many other works and is an acknowledged expert in these fields. Outside of research, Dave is heavily involved in club athletics as a veteran athlete, coach, official and organiser. Dave's help was also invaluable in the attainment of pre-war photographs, having access to a magnificent picture library.

Andrew Huxtable, who works at the Sports Council, checked all the statistical material diligently and also found the time to convert manual timings to automatic for the 1952-68 Games, inclusive. Andrew has been associated with many athletics works, mainly in the area of statistics, since 1958. He has many varied interests, including literature and typography, and is the Secretary General of the Association of Track and Field Statisticians.

Bob Sparks, who is the President of the Association of Track and Field Statisticians, was a great influence and found the time to lend a hand when the going got tough. He is generally considered to be the world's leading authority on automatic timing.

Michael Featherstone, was the man chosen to put all the athletes, who have competed in the Games since 1896, into alphabetical order. He had previously assisted Barry Hugman in researching the Football League Players' Records and has proved the ideal choice for a most difficult task.

Mark Shearman, a leading sports photographer, has covered all of the Games since Tokyo in 1964 and we are extremely fortunate to have been given access to his highly personalised library.

Steve Powell and Lee Martin of All-Sport (UK) Ltd, came to the rescue in their normal helpful professional manner, when a shortfall among the earlier photos was discovered.

The British Olympic Association have always given great support to the project and over the years allowed the authors the use of their reference library along with invaluable reproduction facilities.

In a book of this statistical nature, one must not forget all of the hard work put in checking the authenticity of seemingly endless rows of figures and text, and Jennifer and Deborah Hugman must be thanked, for their great efforts.

Finally, a special thank you to Edwin Cook and Ray Hedley for their handling of design work and implementation, which once again was up to their normal high standards.

With the Olympics in Seoul not too far away, Peter Arnold, a well established sports writer and myself, Barry J. Hugman, decided to produce a book that specialised on the track and field element of the Games.

I have either compiled or am in the process of compiling, several other statistically based tomes for various sports and acknowledged that there was a place on the shelf for a work encompassing all the track and field competitors' performances, since the inception of the Modern Olympic Games in 1896.

With this in mind, it was decided to list alphabetically, in Games order, the individual record for every track and field competitor, by country, round-by-round, time, height or distance achieved and medals won. This allows the reader to analyse the complete Olympic career of any athlete. Who, for example, would remember that Mamo Wolde, the Ethiopian, finished seventh in a 800 metres heat at Melbourne, 1956, and was eliminated, long before he won the marathon gold medal in Mexico City 12 years later.

Preceding the statistical entries, again in Games order, is a comprehensive report of every track and field event participated in since 1896. The reports highlight all the drama, excitement and magic moments of not only the more recent of memories, but also of great achievements from the dim and distant past. Each final is covered in detail, with the times given for the leading athletes, and where necessary, mention is made of notable happenings in the earlier rounds.

Over 100 pen portraits covering the athletic greats of track and field are also included and are placed within the Games of their final gold medal winning performances. These are the athletes who have become household names down the years and have brought immense pleasure into the lives of both the spectators and television viewers alike.

There are over 200 illustrations spanning the years between Athens in 1896 and Seoul, 1988. Several of the earlier photographs, some rare and unpublished in this country, have a hidden depth and depict the era of the "true blue" amateur splendidly. How interesting it is to see the winner of the 110 metres hurdles in the 1908 London Games, Smithson of America, posing as in action against the background of the "timbers", Bible in hand.

Discontinued events have been included in their particular year, except for the tug-of-war. Surprisingly, track and field included cross country between 1912 and 1924, an event which no longer appears in the Olympic programme, except within the modern pentathlon. Some events have been superseded by others like the women's pentathlon by the heptathlon, for example.

Regarding the track finals, there were usually less than six competitors between 1896 and 1912, but from 1920 to 1960, six was standard. However, at Tokyo in 1964, this was increased to eight and has remained at that number of finalists ever since.

The time recording policy at the Olympics has varied over the years and in the Games before 1928 only the winner's time was considered to be official, except for 1912, where fuller times were given in the official report. From 1924, the first six finishers in the finals had their times taken, other than in the sprints, but were not necessarily recorded in official sources until 1952. The above situation has resulted in many placed times being acquired from semi-official sources or estimations of the distance the athlete finished behind the winner.

In 1931, the Kirby two-eyed camera was developed for the Los Angeles Games and automatic timing became a reality. These devices have been used ever since and allow for a continuous photograph to be taken of the runners together with a timer, although the mechanism was not used in 1948.

From 1932 to 1968, photo-finish automatic timers were used as an aid to determine the finishing positions in close races, but from the 1972 Games, they became adopted as the standard form of timekeeping to 1/100th sec.

Data of automatic times from 1932 and 1936 are largely incomplete, but archive photo-finish film from 1948 has mostly survived and fully automatic times are included within this book from 1952 to 1988 inclusive. It should be noted, that in some instances, the timer was stopped before all athletes had completed the race, or that the timer failed to function. In these cases, hand times only are shown. Sometimes unofficial hand times have been given, where official times were obviously incorrect.

It is worth mentioning, that no comparative trials have been carried out between the 1932 (Kirby) or the 1936 (Zielzeitkamera) systems and the post-1948 ones. In 1948, photo-finish prints without times have been used in certain cases to produce "adjusted" place times, based on the interval from the hand-timed winner.

In the combined events of the decathlon, heptathlon and pentathlon, no recomputations have been made using fully automatic times, either on the tables in use at the time or on the current tables.

The degree of accuracy of the timing for the first three Games was to 1/5th sec for all track events and to one second in the marathon. From 1906 to 1924 all running events were recorded to 1/5th sec, except in 1912 when the standard was 1/10th sec. In 1928 it was to 1/5th sec, with the marathon at one second.

A three stage arrangement was employed in 1932, where the two sprints, short relay and high hurdles were timed to 1/10th sec. All other events except the marathon and 50km walk were taken to the 1/5th sec, and the road events to one second. Supplementary automatic timing was to the 1/100th sec.

There was a change again in 1936 with 1/10th sec timing for 100 to 800 metres, both hurdles and short relay only. The rest of the events were timed to 1/5th sec, and automatic times to 1/100th sec.

In 1948, times were recorded to 1/10th sec for the events up to 800 metres and 1/5th sec for 1,500 metres upwards, with the exception of the marathon and 50km walk, which were timed to the second. A photo-finish camera, without timer, was used with a supplementary system of stop-watches started by the gun and stopped by a photo-electric cell at the finish.

All events above 800 metres were timed to 1/5th sec in 1952, but on this occasion a timer was used in conjunction with the photo-finish camera. Times to 1/100th sec have been obtained in most events, except for lower places in distance races. In 1956, the marathon was timed to one second, and 1960 was similar to 1952.

In 1964, all events up to and including the 1,500 metres, were now timed to 1/10th sec and all road events to the one second. The photo-finish camera had an 0.05 sec built-in delay, which, for instance, recorded 10.01 on film, but was actually 10.06 sec. All 1/100th times are known for events up to 400 metres, excluding the relays. The same situation prevailed in 1968, but automatic times are known for all track events other than the 10,000 metres.

Timing at 1/100th sec was officially introduced in 1972 for distances up to 400 metres without any built-in delay. The 800, 1,500 and 4 × 400 metres relay were timed to 1/10th sec, and the 3,000 metres and upwards to 1/5th sec. The timing structure was the same for 1976, but the official result sheets gave times for all running events to 1/100th sec.

A further change occurred in 1980 with 1/10th sec timing being extended to 10,000 metres, by rounding up the 1/100th sec automatic times.

However, in 1984, all track events were officially programmed at 1/100th sec, with road events to the full second.

It is also worth mentioning that there are three other Games included within the "Numbered Games", which are not recorded in this book, for obvious reasons. They are Berlin, 1916, Tokyo, then Helsinki, 1940 and London in 1944, all of which were cancelled due to wartime conditions.

Finally, on behalf of both myself and Peter Arnold, I wish you many hours of pleasure in examining the records of the lesser known athletes as well as those of the stars.

BARRY J. HUGMAN

Key to Reading the Statistical Sections

The statistical data is to be found in Games order, year by year, following the reports, and comprises all of the athletes in alphabetical sequence, recording their complete performances for each of the Games.

Competitor   Surnames are shown first, followed by known initials. Prior to 1928 only males competed.

Country Code   The abbreviations of the names of the countries who have competed in the Games, track and field since 1896. Certain countries have changed their names over the years and where that has happened, the current name has been used throughout to make identification easier. (See page 10 for country code key).

Event   All track events are presented in metres, other than the walks, which are traditionally shown in kilometres.

Round   Gives the round number from the prelims through to the final.
Q = Qualifying round
R = Repêchage round
SF = Semi-final
F = Final

Heat   Where applicable, heat numbers are given for the rounds in question.

Place   Shows the official positions that the respective athletes finished in their events.
NP = Not placed
DIS = Disqualified
DNF = Did not finish
DNQ = Did not qualify
DNS = Did not start

Time & Distance   In many of the earlier Games only the first two or three were timed and in later years many placings were estimated (see preface).
Hours are suffixed by   :
Minutes are suffixed by -
Seconds are suffixed by ·
Metres are suffixed by   ,

Medal   All Medallists are denoted by the following:
G = Gold
S = Silver
B = Bronze

COUNTRY CODES

AFG — Aghanistan	GUA — Guatemala	PAK — Pakistan
AHO — Netherlands Antilles	GUI — Guinea	PAN — Panama
ALB — Albania	GUY — Guyana	PAR — Paraguay
ALG — Algeria	HAI — Haiti	PER — Peru
ANG — Angola	HBR — British Honduras	PHI — Philippines
ARG — Argentina	HKG — Hong Kong	POL — Poland
ARS — Saudi Arabia	HOL — Netherlands	POR — Portugal
AUS — Australia	HON — Honduras	PRK — Dem. People's
AUT — Austria	HUN — Hungary	Rep. of Korea
BAH — Bahamas	INA — Indonesia	PUR — Puerto Rico
BAR — Barbados	IND — India	RHO — Rhodesia
BEL — Belgium	IRL — Ireland	ROC — Republic of China
BER — Bermuda	IRN — Iran	RUM — Rumania
BIR — Burma	IRQ — Iraq	SAA — Saarland
BOH — Bohemia	ISL — Iceland	SAF — South Africa
BOL — Bolivia	ISR — Israel	SAL — El Salvador
BRA — Brazil	ISV — Virgin Islands	SEN — Senegal
BUL — Bulgaria	ITA — Italy	SER — Serbia
BWI — British West Indies	JAM — Jamaica	SEY — Seychelles
CAN — Canada	JOR — Jordan	SIN — Singapore
CEY — Ceylon (now Sri Lanka)	JPN — Japan	SLE — Sierra Leone
CGO — Congo	KEN — Kenya	SMR — San Marino
CHA — Chad	KHM — Cambodia	SOM — Somali Republic
CHI — Chile	KOR — Korea	STV — St Vincent
CIV — Ivory Coast	KUW — Kuwait	SUD — Sudan
CMR — Cameroon	LAO — Laos	SUI — Switzerland
COL — Colombia	LAT — Latvia	SUR — Surinam
CRC — Costa Rica	LBA — Libya	SWE — Sweden
CUB — Cuba	LBR — Liberia	SWZ — Swaziland
DAH — Dahomey	LES — Lesotho	SYR — Syria
DEN — Denmark	LEB — Lebanon	TAN — Tanzania
DOM — Dominican Republic	LIE — Liechtenstein	TCH — Czechoslovakia
ECU — Ecuador	LITH — Lithuania	THA — Thailand
EGY — Egypt	LUX — Luxembourg	TOG — Togo
ESP — Spain	MAD — Madagascar	TON — Tonga
EST — Estonia	MAL — Malaysia	TRI — Trinidad and Tobago
ETH — Ethiopia	MAR — Morocco	TUN — Tunisia
FIJ — Fiji Islands	MAW — Malawi	TUR — Turkey
FIN — Finland	MEX — Mexico	UGA — Uganda
FOR — Formosa	MGL — Mongolia	URS — U.S.S.R.
FRA — France	MLI — Mali	URU — Uruguay
GAB — Gabon	MLT — Malta	USA — United States of
GBR — United Kingdom	MON — Monaco	America
GDR — German Democratic	NBO — North Borneo	VEN — Venezuela
Republic	NCA — Nicaragua	VNM — Vietnam
GER — Germany (but West	NEP — Nepal	VOL — Upper Volta
Germany only from	NGR — Nigeria	YUG — Yugoslavia
1968)	NIG — Niger	ZAM — Zambia
GHA — Ghana	NOR — Norway	ZIM — Zimbabwe
GRE — Greece	NZL — New Zealand	ZAI — Zaire

The History of the Summer Olympics

The modern Olympic Games share with the Soccer World Cup the distinction of being the greatest festivals of sport in the world. Despite boycotts by Eastern European countries, 140 nations were represented at Los Angeles in 1984, and over half the world's population (about 2·5 billion people) watched some of the action on television.

The Games take their name from those held at Olympia, in Elis in ancient Greece. There were other Games in Greece, but those at Olympia, the altar to Rhea, "Mother of the Gods", became the most important.

The first records of the ancient Games begin in 776 BC, but it is known that there were Games for at least six centuries before this. The Games were part of religious ceremonies. On the day of the feast to Rhea, a priest would make a sacrifice at the altar, and the young men would wait at a distance of one stade (about 192·28 metres or 210·23 yards) for a signal to race to the altar. The first to arrive would take the torch from the priest and light the sacrificial fire.

Among the legends surrounding these early ceremonies is that of Heracles, who won the sprint and announced that the race would be run every four years. He called the Games the Olympic Games and the four-year period was an Olympiad.

The first king of Elis, Aethlius, continued the tradition and from him arose the word "athlete". A later King, Iphitus, was responsible for the *ekeheira*, a truce he signed in 884 BC by which men from the cities of Sparta and Pisa, the rivals in combat to Olympia, were guaranteed safe passage to and from the Games.

For years the stadium race was the only official race of the festivities. The winner in 776 BC, the first Olympic champion whose name is recorded, was Coroebos of Elis. In 724 BC a second race was added, the *diaulus*, of twice the distance. In 720 BC came the *dolichus* of 24 stadia (about 4·4km or 2¾ miles). This was followed in 708 BC by wrestling and a pentathlon (running, jumping, discus, javelin, wrestling). Boxing was introduced in 688 BC, chariot racing in 680 BC and the *pancratium* in 648 BC, a mixture of boxing and all-in wrestling.

With these extra events, the Games lasted five days instead of one. From about 720 BC the athletes competed in the nude, and women were barred from watching. Winners received olive branches, which signified vitality, and brought great prestige to their regions. They were celebrated by the artists of the day. Gradually the athletics became more important than the religious festival. Under Pericles (490-429 BC) the Greek ideal of classical art, intellectualism and athleticism was at its highest.

The importance of the Olympic Games eventually hastened their downfall (a lesson for today?). Athletes were bribed and towns began to hire professionals. The Games went into decline. The rise of Christianity led to the physical and religious aspects losing their appeal. The sacred truce became less sacred and eventually the Roman Emperor Theodosius the Great banned all forms of pagan worship and issued a decree prohibiting the celebration of the Olympic Games. The last of the ancient Games were held in AD 393.

The ancient Olympic Games had lasted over a thousand years since 776 BC, and probably nearer 2,000 years in all. The last Olympiad was the 293rd since counting began with Coroebos. It is one of the incredible sequences in history. Olympia thereafter rapidly declined, helped by pillaging, earthquakes and floods, and soon only ruins remained of this great centre of Greek culture.

One modern memorial on the site of Olympia was erected to the memory of Pierre de Coubertin, the Frenchman who revived the Games and what is called today the "Olympic ideal".

De Coubertin was born in Paris on 1 January 1863. His aristocratic parents lived in a private hotel in the French capital, and he graduated in arts, sciences and law. He was meant for the Army, but became interested in educational reform. He wanted to help his country recover from its defeat by Germany in 1871. In 1886 he published his first article *La Reforme Sociale*, and two years later the first of many books. Visiting England, he was impressed by the ideas of Thomas Arnold, the former headmaster of Rugby School, and decided that sport should be as important in French education as it was in English.

In 1888 de Coubertin was secretary-general of a committee for the propagation of physical exercise and the following year he headed an international congress in Paris. He went to the United States and Canada, and discussed with American universities the idea that sport must be internationalised to achieve popularity, and formed the International Athletic Congress to forward his plans. On 25 November 1892 he ended a conference with a speech suggesting the re-establishment of the Olympic Games.

His proposal fell on deaf ears, but he persevered. Opening an International Athletic Conference on 16 June 1894 in Paris he made a brilliant speech to 2,000 people, and a week later 69 delegates from 12 countries voted unanimously to re-establish the Games. At this Conference the Greek "Hymn to Apollo" was sung.

Baron de Coubertin himself selected the first International Olympic Committee, the body which remains in charge of the Games.

The first of the modern Olympics, due to be held in Athens in 1896, was threatened by financial problems, but a committee was formed in Greece which raised the necessary money for the stadium and facilities. The money for the stadium came from a wealthy Greek businessman, Georgios Averoff, who lived in Egypt. A definition of amateur status was another big problem, and finances and amateurism have remained two of the most discussed aspects of Olympic organisation ever since.

A statue to Averoff was unveiled on 5 April 1896, and the Games got under way on Easter Monday, 6 April 1896, the 75th anniversary of the declaration of Greek independence. Because the Greeks were using the old Julian calendar, these dates are sometimes given as 24 and 25 March.

The first events were 100 metres heats. The first modern Olympic Champion was James B. Connolly of the Suffolk Athletic Club, USA, who won the triple jump, then known as the "hop, step and jump".

The Americans took the Games more seriously than most countries (including France) and sent a strong team. They won most of the athletics events. As well as athletics, there were events in cycling, fencing, gymnastics, lawn tennis, shooting, swimming (including a 100 metres freestyle for sailors) weightlifting (one-hand and two-hand) and wrestling. Rowing and sailing were abandoned because of severe storms.

The track was in the reconstructed Panathenean Stadium, first built in 330 BC, rebuilt 500 years later by Herodis, and excavated in the 1870s. It measured 400 metres, with two "hairpin" bends, making it unsuitable for a 200 metre race. The racing was anti-clockwise.

The climax of the Games was the marathon, an event not included in the ancient Olympics. It was the suggestion of Michel Breal, a French student of Greek mythology, to commemorate the run of Pheidippides from the plains of Marathon to Athens in 490 BC with the news of the Greek victory over the Persians. The race began at Marathon, and to the delight of the enthusiastic Greeks, was won by a 18-year-old Greek shepherd, Spiridon Louis.

Prizes were awarded on the last day of the Games. The winners all received silver medals and the runners-up bronze. There were no prizes for third. They were designed by Jules Chaplain of France. Gold medals were not awarded until 1908.

The 1900 Olympics were held in Paris, but only became "Olympic" at the last minute. An athletics programme was planned as part of the celebrations for the Paris Universal Exposition, a "World Fair". But when Baron de Coubertin was asked for advice he persuaded the authorities that the Games should carry the designation "Olympic". The quality of the competitors was far superior to Athens. Sixteen nations participated in the athletics (compared to ten in Athens) while there were 127 athletes (compared to 59).

On the other hand, the facilities were poor. The track was a 500-metre oval laid out on a horse-race course. The events were organised as sideshows for the Fair, and did not comprise a "meeting" — in fact the Olympics lasted five months. Of course, not everybody then knew what "the Olympics" were, and some of the athletes realised they had taken part in the Olympic Games only when they read what it said on the medals. It was not until 1912 that the IOC attempted to reconstruct the results, there having been little press notice at the time. Of the athletics events. all but three were won by US or British athletes (and one of those three, George Orton, a Canadian, was for many years regarded as American because he had been entered by his US university).

The star of the Games was Alvin Kraenzlein, who won four events, although he might have been lucky in the long jump, as Myer Prinstein, the world record holder,

would not take part in the finals, because they were held on a Sunday.

The 1904 Games in St Louis were even more disastrous than those of 1900. Moved from Chicago so that they could be held at the Louisiana Purchase Exposition, another World Fair, they were even more of a side-show than before. Again events were spread over a long period — 4½ months — and again the IOC had to decide later which events were Olympic events.

In practice, the Games were little more than American Games with a few "guest" runners. Few European countries took part, and even Baron de Coubertin did not bother to go. The athletics were actually better organised than in Paris, and the track at Washington University was better than that of Paris. However, only nine nations took part in the athletics, the fewest ever, although at 132 there were actually five more competitors than in Paris. In most events the USA provided the first three. In two events only was their a foreign winner. Etienne Desmarteau, a Canadian policeman, won the 56-lb weight, and the other foreign winner came in a novelty event called the "All-Around Championship", really a decathlon, which was won by Tom Kiely, a 35-year-old Irishman who paid his own way to St Louis. It was not until 1954 that he was recognised as an Olympic winner.

The Greeks had regarded the Olympics as theirs since 1896, and having overcome political and financial problems now wanted to take over the Games permanently. Baron de Coubertin agreed to a series interspersed with the main Games, to start in 1906, the tenth anniversary of the first of the modern Games. These Games would have IOC blessing but could not be numbered in the series of official Games, as an Olympiad was a four-year period.

The 1906 Intercalated, or Interim, Games were a big success compared to Paris and St Louis, with good crowds supporting a well-run programme of events standing on its own feet.

London took on the 1908 Olympics when Rome was forced to back out. The athletics were held at the new White City track, Shepherds Bush, London, and there was a big jump in the number of athletes taking part: 455 from 20 nations. With their expertise in organisation the British ran the whole show, and the Games were the best organised yet. Unfortunately the British provided all the officials, and this led to all sorts of protests over the rules. The British, who introduced most of today's popular sports to the world, naturally decided to take the Games seriously since they were hosts — in other words to win many of the events. The USA, of course, had until now dominated the Games, largely because they showed much more enthusiasm for them than anybody else. The two giants now collided with so much bickering and bitter argument that the Olympics almost ended there and then. The most famous argument came in the 400 metres, where the "final" was run by one Englishman, the Americans having refused to re-run after one of their competitors had been disqualified.

Whatever the rights and wrongs of the affair, or affairs, it marked the end of the host country controlling the competition — in future the international governing bodies of the various sports took responsibility.

On the field, gold medals were awarded for the first time, with silver and bronze for the runners-up. The remarkable Olympic career of Ray Ewry ended with his tenth win out of ten in the standing jumps, and Dorando Pietri became one of the world's most famous marathon

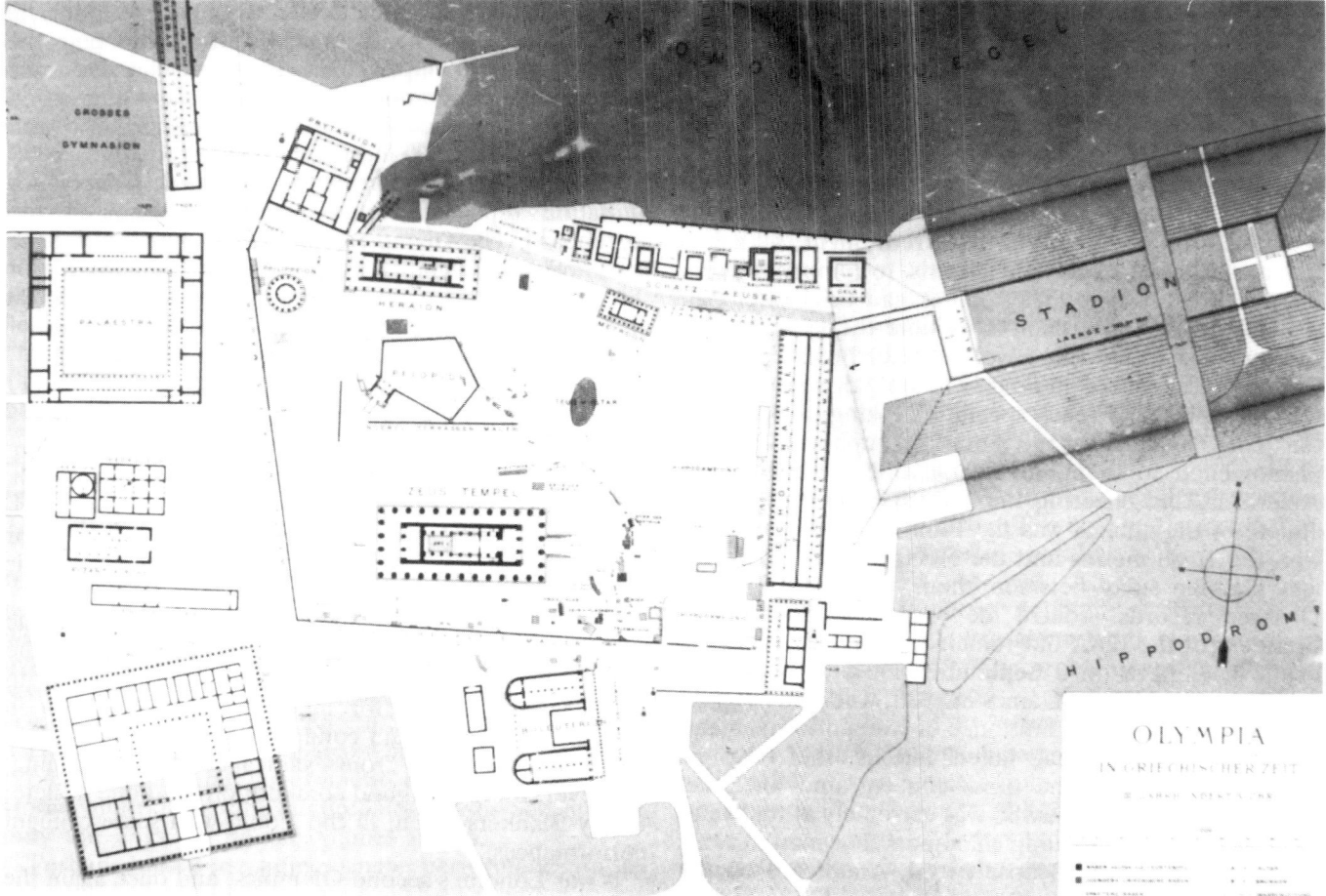

The capital of the Olympic ideal, Olympia.

runners by collapsing five times in the stadium before being helped over the line first, only to be disqualified.

De Coubertin attended a religious service in St Paul's Cathedral, London, on 19 July 1908, where the Bishop of Pennsylvania preached a sermon and used a phrase which moved de Coubertin to enlarge and repeat it in a speech: "The most important thing in the Olympic Games is not to win but to take part, just as the most important thing in life is not the triumph but the struggle. The essential thing is not to have conquered but to have fought well". These famous words now appear on the scoreboard at the opening ceremonies of Games.

The 1912 Games in Stockholm are regarded as the ones which really put the Olympics on the road to what they are today. They were well organised and without disputes. At last the athletes of the world came together in friendship, as envisaged by Baron de Coubertin. In track and field there were 556 from 26 nations.

Innovations included electric timing and photo-finish equipment. There were two stars of the Games. One was Jim Thorpe, who won the new pentathlon and decathlon events. Giving him his medals, King Gustav V called him "the greatest athlete in the world". "Thanks, King", was the much-quoted laconic reply. Sadly Thorpe was forced to return his medals next year when it transpired he had played baseball for money. He was re-instated and the medals returned in 1982, long after Thorpe's death. The other star was Hannes Kolehmainen, the first of the "Flying Finns" who dominated the long distance track events for so long. The Finns at the time were forced to compete under the Russian flag, causing Kolehmainen much anger. This was the last Games for the Russians, however, for 40 years. The Bolshevik revolution was to come before the next Games, and Communist Russia did not re-enter until after the Second World War.

Another step towards the forming of the Olympic Games of today arose from the Swedes refusing to allow boxing to take place in their country. The IOC were forced to limit from then on the power of the local organising committees.

With war threatening in Europe, the 1916 Games were awarded, on de Coubertin's advice to Berlin, in the hope that war could be averted in the preparation for friendly Games. It wasn't, but the Germans did not withdraw Berlin, expecting the war to be short.

During the war de Coubertin established the headquarters of the IOC in Lausanne, Switzerland, where he lived. The 1920 Games were given to Antwerp, Belgium, as consolation for the war that had been fought within Belgium's borders.

The defeated powers, Germany, Austria, Hungary, Bulgaria and Turkey, were not invited, and the USSR declined to take part, much to the satisfaction of the Finns.

There were three Olympic innovations at Antwerp. First of all the Olympic oath was introduced. The first sportsman to take it was Victor Boin, of Belgium. A representative of the host country holds a corner of his national flag at the opening ceremony and pronounces the oath. "In the name of all competitors, I promise that we will take part in these Olympic Games, respecting and abiding by the rules which govern them, in the true spirit of sportsmanship, for the glory of sport and the honour of our teams".

The Olympic motto was also adopted: "*Citius, Altius, Fortius*" (Faster, Higher, Stronger). There was also the first hoisting of the Olympic flag, with its five interlaced rings. The five rings represent the five continents and their colours include colours from all participating nations.

Robert Garrett, from America, the winner of the world's first international discus competition.

1896

Prince George Joins the Marathon

All the dreams of a French educationalist, Baron Pierre de Coubertin, were realised in 1896 when the first celebration of the modern Olympic Games, which he had done so much to inspire, took place in Athens. It was hardly a Games as we know them today, and many of the competitors were rather casual about it all. However, there was no doubt about the enthusiasm of the spectators when the Greeks registered their only win, appropriately enough in the marathon, taking its name from the run of Pheidippides from Marathon to Athens when bringing the news of the Greek victory over the Persians there in 490 BC.

Men's Track Events

The newly laid track at Athens was somewhat loose, which might explain the slow times recorded in the **100 metres**. On paper, Francis Lane of the USA was the fastest sprinter competing, having run 10·0 sec for 100 yards, with fellow American Thomas Burke being the next best. Burke set a Games' record of 11·8 in the heats and went on to make the final. Six sprinters qualified from three heats for the final, but only five of them ran. A comparison of the starting methods employed by the finalists is of interest. Burke used a dab start; Lane a crouching bunch position; Fritz Hofmann of Germany supported himself on props; Alajos Szokolyi of Hungary adopted the lunge attitude and Alex Chalkokondilis of Greece started with a dab. At the off, Hofmann was quickest away and led by two metres at the half-way stage, but Burke pulled away to win in 12·0 from Hofmann, 12·2, and Szokolyi, 12·6.

Because the **400 metres** track had to be fitted into an ancient stadium, the straights were long and the connecting curves hairpins. It was impossible to negotiate the bends at full speed and the loose track did not help. Thomas Burke was undoubtedly the fastest man in the field, the others having no great reputations as 400 metres runners. The American Herbert Jamison won the first heat in 56·8 sec and Burke the second in 58·4. Only four runners qualified for the finals, two from each heat. The small Fritz Hofmann of Germany headed the group of runners at 250 metres but coming off the bend Burke pounced and raced away to win in 54·2. Jamison was second in 55·2 and the German came third in 57·0.

None of the world's top middle distance runners were present in Athens and the pace was consequently slow, but the races interesting. Edwin "Teddy" Flack of Australia won the first heat of the **800 metres** in 2-10·0. He just happened to be present because he was gaining business experience in London and took his holiday at the time of the Games. Heat two was won by Albin Lermusiaux of France in 2-16·6, but he did not appear in the line-up for the final, of which two from each heat

qualified. In the final, Flack was up against Demetrios Golemis of Greece and Nandor Dani of Hungary, who had a personal best of 2-05·4. Flack cut out the pace from the start, closely followed by Dani and passed the first lap in 65·5 with Golemis trailing. Into the final straight Flack spurted to win in 2-11·0 from Dani 2-11·8 and Golemis 2-28·0.

Eight competitors lined up for the final of the **1,500 metres**, to be run in the English University fashion of clockwise around the track. From the gun, Albin Lermusiaux of France took command with Edwin Flack holding second place and the other runners being strung out. At the end of the third lap Flack went to the front, but Lermusiaux did not like this and wrested the lead back again. However, a decisive sprint from Flack took him ahead again, followed by Art Blake of the USA. Flack went on to win in 4-33·2 from Blake, 4-34·0, and Lermusiaux, 4-36·0

The **Marathon** was the idea of Michel Breal, a Frenchman of letters, who had offered to donate a cup for the winner. In 490 BC. the Greeks had defeated the Persians on the plain of Marathon and Pheidippides was selected to run the 40km to Athens and break the news. This he apparently did with such enthusiasm on a hot day, that he expired upon his arrival. The same route was now to be the course over which 18 aspirants for Olympic honors would run. The host nation had run two trial races over the course to select the 14 hopefuls who would represent Greece, and Gyula Kellner, of Hungary, who had run a 40km trial in Budapest in three hours was also competing. Unhappily, one of Italy's top distance runners, Carlo Airoldi, was refused entry to the race as there was nobody to vouch for his being an amateur. Amazingly, Airoldi completed the journey from his home in Milan to Athens on foot, having travelled a total of 1,333km. Also competing in the marathon were the track runners Edwin Flack of Australia, Art Blake of America and Albin Lermusiaux of France, all of whom had been drawn into the euphoria of the moment. Lermusiaux cut out the pace over the hard stony roads for the first 23km, which he passed in 1:34-00 with Flack following in 1:35-00. Blake 1:38-00, Charilaos Vasilakos of Greece 1:41-00 and Spiridon Louis of Greece 1:41-30. Blake dropped out at 25km and Lermusiaux shortly afterwards. Louis caught Flack at 32km and, three kilometres further on, Flack fainted and was taken up into a Geneva Red Cross carriage. Kellner was now second behind Louis with Vasilakos third and Spiridon Belokas, also of Greece, fourth. As Louis entered the suburbs of Athens, cannon were fired to alert the crowd in the stadium. A lone runner entered the amphitheatre and soon he was recognised, by his number, as a Greek, which lifted the Greeks from their seats in a tumultuous roar. Even the referee, Prince George of Greece, could not restrain himself from running half a lap alongside the victor, who finished in 2:58-50. Vasilakos was second to

17

COMPETITOR	COUNTRY CODE	EVENT	ROUND	HEAT	PLACE	TIME & DISTANCE	MEDAL
MALES							
Adler, L.	FRA	Shot put	F		4		
		Discus throw	F	1	4		
Andreou, A.	GRE	110m hurdles	1	1	4		
Belokas, S.	GRE	Marathon	F		DIS		
Blake, C.A.	USA	1500m	F		2	4-34.0	S
		Marathon	F		DNF		
Burke, T.E.	USA	100m	1	3	1	11.8*	
			F		1	12.0	G
		400m	1	2	1	58.4	
			F		1	54.2*	G
Chalkokondilis, A.	GRE	100m	1	2	2		
			F		5	12.6	
		Long jump	F		6	5,74	
		Triple jump	F		6		
Christopoulos, D.	GRE	Marathon	F				
Clark, E.H.	USA	High jump	F		1	1,81*	G
		Long jump	F		1	6,35*	G
Connolly, J.B.	USA	High jump	F		=2	1,65	S
		Long jump	F		3	6,11	B
		Triple jump	F		1	13,71*	G
Curtis, T.P.	USA	100m	1	2	1	12.2*	
			F		DNS		
		110m hurdles	1	2	1	18.0*	
			F		1	17.6*	G
Damaskos, E.	GRE	Pole vault	F		3	2,85	B
Dani, N.	HUN	100m	1	3	4		
		800m	1	1	2		
			F		2	2-11.8	S
De La Naziere,	FRA	400m	1	2	3		
		800m	1	2	5		
Deliyannis, E.	GRE	Marathon	F		6		
Doerry, K.	GER	100m	1	2	DNF		
		400m	1	1	3		
Elliott, L.	GBR	100m	1	2	4		
Flack, E.H.	ALS	800m	1	1	1	2-10.0*	
			F		1	2-11.0	G
		1500m	F		1	4-33.2*	G
		Marathon	F		DNF		
Galle, K.	GER	1500m	F		4	4-39.0	
Garrett, R.	USA	High jump	F		=2	1,65	S
		Long jump	F		2	6,18	S
		Shot put	F		1	11,22*	G
		Discus throw	F		1	29,15*	G
Gennimatas, G.	GRE	100m	1	3	5		
Gerakakis, E.	GRE	Marathon	F		7		
Gmelin, C.H.S.	GBR	100m	1	1	4		
		400m	1	2	2		
			F		4		
Golemis, D.	GRE	800m	1	2	2		
			F		3	2-28.0	B
		1500m	F		6		
Goulding, G.T.S.	GBR	110m hurdles	1	1	1	18.4*	
			F		2	17.7	S
Gouskos, M.	GRE	Shot put	F		2	11,20	S
Grigoriou, G.	GRE	Marathon	F				
Grisel, A.	FRA	400m	1	1	4		
		Long jump	F		5	5,83	
		Triple jump	F		7		
Hofmann, F.	GER	100m	1	3	2		
			F		2	12.2	S
		400m	1	1	2		
			F		3	57.0	B
		110m hurdles	1	2	3		
		High jump	F		5	1,55	

COMPETITOR	COUNTRY CODE	EVENT	ROUND	HEAT	PLACE	TIME & DISTANCE	MEDAL
Hoyt, W.W.	USA	110m hurdles	1	2	2		
			F		DNS		
		Pole vault	F		1	3,30*	G
Jamison, H.B.	USA	400m	1	1	1	56.8*	
			F		2	55.2	S
Jensen, A.V.	DEN	Discus throw	F				
Kafetzis, E.	GRE	Marathon	F				
Karakatsamis, C.	GRE	1500m	F		7		
Kellner, G.	HUN	Marathon	F		3	3:09-35	B
Lagoudakis, S.	GRE	Marathon	F		9		
Lane, F.A.	USA	100m	1	1	1	12.2*	
			F		4	12.6	
Lavrentis, G.	GRE	Marathon	F				
Lermusiaux, A.	FRA	800m	1	2	1	2-16.6	
			F		DNS		
		1500m	F		3	4-36.0	B
		Marathon	F		DNF		
Louis, S.	GRE	Marathon	F		1	2:58-50*	G
Manno, L.	HUN	100m	1	1	5		
Mossouris, S.	GRE	Marathon	F		8		
Nielsen, H.L.	DEN	Discus throw	F				
Papasideris, G.	GRE	Shot put	D		3	10,36	B
		Discus throw	F		5		
Papasimeon, E.	GRE	Marathon	F		5		
Paraskevopoulos, P.	GRE	Discus throw	F		2	28,95	S
Persakis, J.	GRE	Triple jump	F		3	12,52	B
Phetsis, A.	GRE	800m	1	2	3		
		1500m	F		5		
Reichel, F.	FRA	800m	1	1	4		
		110m hurdles	1	1	3		
Robertson, G.S.	GBR	Discus throw	F		6		
Scaltsoyannis, A.	GRE	Long jump	F				
Schmidt, E.S.	DEN	100m	1	2	5		
Schuhmann, C.	GER	Long jump	F		7	5,70	
Sjoeberg, H.	SWE	100m	1	3	3		
		High jump	F		4	1,60	
		Discus throw	F		7		
Subercaseaux, L.	CHI	100m	1	1	6		
Szokolyi, A.	HUN	100m	1	1	2		
			F		3	12.6	B
		110m hurdles	1	1	2		
			F		DNS		
		Triple jump	F		4	12,30	
Theodoropoulos, T.	GRE	Pole vault	F		4	2,80	
Tomproff, D.	GRE	800m	1	2	4		
		1500m	F		8		
Tournois, A.	FRA	100m	1	1	3		
Traun, F.A.	GER	800m	1	1	3		
Tuffere, A.	FRA	100m	1	2	3		
		Long jump	F		4	5,98	
		Triple jump	F		2	12,70	S
Tyler, A.C.	USA	Pole vault	F		2	3,25	S
Vanitakes,	GRE	Marathon	F				
Vasilakos, C.	GRE	Marathon	F		2	3:06-03	S
Versis, S.	GRE	Discus throw	F		3	28,78	B
Vrettos, I.	GRE	Marathon	F		4		
Wein, D.	HUN	Long jump	F		8	5,64	
Xydas, V.	GRE	Pole vault	F		5	2,50	

1900

Olympic Running in the Bois de Boulogne

Held in France, the 1900 Games were combined with the Paris Universal Exposition. There were many disputes among the organisers and the Games were so badly planned that Baron de Coubertin himself wondered if they would survive. Many sports were represented including such as cricket, croquet, golf and rugby, and the whole thing lasted months. Several athletics events took place in the Bois de Boulogne, where the trees got in the way of the throwing. There was controversy, too, over some finals being held on a Sunday, causing some of the American college athletes not to take part.

Men's Track Events

The **60 metres** sprint was an addition to the Paris programme in a Games where track events were held on grass with lanes marked out using string. Four qualifiers came from two heats and in the first Alvin Kraenzlein beat his fellow 17-year-old fellow American Edmund Minahan with 7·0 sec to 7·1. In heat two, Walter Tewksbury of the USA defeated Stanley Rowley of Australia 7·2 to 7·3. The final saw Kraenzlein again clock 7·0 to win with Tewksbury only inches behind in 7·1 and Rowley third in 7·2.

Arthur Duffey of the USA, the favourite for the **100 metres**, was one of the fastest starters in history. In the very first heat he set a new Olympic record of 11·4 sec, while fellow American John Tewksbury did a similar time in the next one. These performances were eclipsed in the third heat when Frank Jarvis, also of the USA, equalled the world record of 10·8 with Stanley Rowley of Australia just behind in 10·9. In the second round, it was the turn of America's Walter Tewksbury to be timed at 10·8, the other winners in this round being Duffey and Jarvis. These three qualified for the final together with Rowley, the winner of a repechage heat. The starter in the preliminary heats had been incompetent and was persuaded to allow G.F. Sandford of Britain to take over. There was a very even start in the final, but Duffey was a metre up at the half-way mark. Suddenly, Duffey was on the ground with a pulled muscle. Jarvis came through to win in 11·0 sec from Tewksbury, 11·1, and Rowley, 11·2.

In Athens the bends had been too sharp to allow the running of a **200 metres**, but the event was ideally suited to the contours of a 500-metre track with only half a bend to run around. Eight competitors only competed with the first and second from two heats qualifying for the final. These four sprinters were away together from the gun with Norman Pritchard of India setting the pace for the first 100 metres. Walter Tewksbury of the USA then made his effort and came home in 22·2 sec from Pritchard in 22·8, who just held off Stanley Rowley of Australia with 22·9.

Running around only one bend on a 500-metre track

was obviously advantageous and the standard in the **400 metres** was somewhat higher than at Athens four years earlier. Maxey Long, the US champion, was expected to win and he established a new Olympic record of 50·4 sec in the first heat. Other Americans, William Moloney and Dixon Boardman, won the other two heats which were all held on the Saturday. The final, however, was contested on the Sunday which caused pangs of conscience among many of the American collegemen and three refused to run in the six-man final, with the result that Long was joined at the start line only by Ernst Schultz of Denmark and Bill Holland of the USA. Long took the lead immediately and in his blue and white vest was mistaken by the cheering French spectators as that of a member of the Racing Club de France. He won in a Games record of 49·4, towing Holland home in 49·6 in second place, while Schultz finished third and outclassed, in 53·0.

The first heat of the **800 metres** was a good one with David Hall of the USA coming home in an Olympic best of 1-59·0 from Alf Tysoe of Britain, a short way back in 1-59·6. Henri Deloge of France took the second race in 2-00·6 and John Cregan of the USA the third with 2-03·0. The final saw Deloge control the pace over the first half of the race but with 150 metres to go, Tysoe and Cregan overtook the Frenchman and sprinted for the line. Tysoe was victorious in 2-01·2 from Cregan, 2-01·8, with Hall getting up for third in 2-03·0.

Only nine runners competed in the **1,500 metres**, held on a Sunday, which may well explain the non-appearance of the top Americans. Charles Bennett of Britain took up the running, in a race where three laps of the 500-metre track had to be negotiated. Bennett completed the first lap in 1-21·2, but slowed to record 2-56·0 on the next, with Henri Deloge on his shoulder. He hotted things up over the third circuit, which he ran in 1-10·2, to win in a new world record of 4-06·0 with Deloge reaching the finish in 4-06·6 for second place and John Bray of the USA finishing third with 4-07·2.

With the temperature at 30°C (86°F), the **marathon** took place over three laps of the Racing Club de France's grounds, before joining an oval course of 33·9km around the city walls. Then it was on to cobbled roads which were broken up in places, and finally, three more circuits of the grounds. At the gun some 17 runners set out with Georges Touquet-Daunis of France leading the way followed by Ernst Fast of Sweden. At 27·5km Daunis gave up and Michel Theato of France assumed the lead followed by Fast and Emile Champion of France. Theato was a baker's roundsman and knew the suburbs of Paris well, so he had knowledge of the best ground to run over. When he arrived at the track in first position, the appointed band struck up the "Marseillaise". He won in 2:59-45 from Champion, 3·04-17, and Fast, 3:37-14. Only four others are known

21

MALES

COMPETITOR	COUNTRY CODE	EVENT	ROUND	HEAT	PLACE	TIME & DISTANCE	MEDAL
Adler, L.	FRA	Shot put	F				
Andersen, C.A.	NOR	High jump	F		4	1,70	
		Pole vault	F		3	3,20	B
Banfi, E.	ITA	800m	1	2			
Bauer, R.	HUN	Discus throw	F		1	36,04*	G
Baxter, I.K.	USA	High jump	F		1	1,90*	G
		Standing high jump	F		2	1,52	S
		Standing long jump	F		2	3,13	S
		Standing triple jump	F		2	9,95	S
		Pole vault	F		1	3,30*	G
Bennett, C.	GBR	1500m	F		1	4-06-0*	G
		4000m steeplechase	F		2	12-58-6	S
Besse, E.	FRA	Marathon	F		4	4:00-43	
Blom, T.	SWE	High jump	F		8	1,50	
		Long jump	F		11	5,77	
Boardman, D.	USA	100m	1	6	2		
			2	1	4		
		400m	1	3	1	51·2	
			F		DNS		
Bray, J.	USA	800m	1	3	2		
			F		6		
		1500m	F		3	4-07·2	B
Bryn, Y.	NOR	200m	1	2	3		
		400m	1	2	5		
Burroughs, C.L.	USA	100m	1	1	6	11·4	
			2	1	3		
			R				
Bushnell, E.R.	USA	800m	1	2			
Champion, E.	FRA	Marathon	F		2	3:04-17	S
Chastanie, J.	FRA	2500m steeplechase	F		3		B
		4000m steeplechase	F		4	7-41·0	
Choisel, E.	FRA	110m hurdles	1	1			
			R	1	3		
		200m hurdles	1	1	2		
			F		4		
Christiansen, C.A.	DEN	800m	1	1	5		
		1500m	F		5		
Clement, G.	FRA	400m	1	1			
Colket, M.B.	USA	Pole vault	F		2	3,25	S
Colombo, U.	ITA	100m	1	3	3		
		400m	1	3			
Connolly, J.B.	USA	Triple jump	F		2	13,97	S
Coray, A.	HUN	Discus throw	F				
Cregan, J.F.	USA	800m	1	3	1	2-03·0	
			F		2	2-01·8	S
Crettier, R.	HUN	Shot put	F		4	12,05	
		Discus throw	F		5	33,65	
Delannoy, A.	FRA	Long jump	F		5	6,75	
		Triple jump	F		5		
Deloge, H.	FRA	800m	1	2	1	2-00·6	
			F		4		
		1500m	F		2	4-06·6	S
Dorry, K.	GER	100m	1	4	2		
			2	2	DNF		
Drumheller, W.E.	USA	400m	1	1			
		800m	1	1			
Duffey, A.F.	USA	100m	1	1	1	11·4	
			2	1	1	11·0	
			F		DNF		
Duhne, F.	GER	2500m steeplechase	F		6		
		4000m steeplechase	F		6		
Ewry, R.C.	USA	Standing high jump	F		1	1,65*	G
		Standing long jump	F		1	3,30*	G
		Standing triple jump	F		1	10,58*	G
Faidide, V.	FRA	400m	1	2	3		
Fast, E.	SWE	Marathon	F		3	3:37-14	B
Flanagan, J.J.	USA	Discus throw	F				
		Hammer throw	F		1	51,01	G
Gandil, J.	DEN	100m	1	4	3		
Garrett, R.	USA	Standing triple jump	F		3	9,50	B
		Shot put	F		3	12,35	B
		Discus throw	F		7		
Gonczy, L.	HUN	High jump	F		3	1,75	B
Gontier, E.	FRA	Pole vault	F		=4	3,10	
		Discus throw	F		10	32,00	
Grant, A.	USA	800m	1	1			
		4000m steeplechase	F				
Grant, R.	USA	Marathon	F				
Hall, D.C.	USA	800m	1	1	1	1-59·0*	
			F		3	2-03·0	B
		1500m	F		4		
Hare, T.T.	USA	Discus throw	F				
		Hammer throw	F		2	46,25	S
Hayes, H.W.	USA	800m	1	1	3		
Holland, W.J.	USA	60m	1	2	3		
		200m	1	1	1	24·0	
			F		4		
		400m	1	3	2		
			F		2	49·6	S
Horton, D.S.	USA	Triple jump	F				
		Standing triple jump	F				
Janda-Suk, F.	TCH	Discus throw	F		2	35,25	S
Jarvis, F.W.	USA	100m	1	3	1	10·8*	
			2	3	1	11·2	
			F		1	11·0	G
		Triple jump	F				
		Standing triple jump	F				
Kauser, J.	HUN	Pole vault	F		=4	3,10	
Keyl, J.	GER	100m	1	3	4		
Klingelhoefer, A.	FRA	60m	1	1			
		200m	1	1	3		
		110m hurdles	1	2	4		
Koppan, P.	HUN	60m	1	2			
		100m	1	2	3		
		400m	1	2	4		
		Triple jump	F				
		Standing triple jump	F				
Kraenzlein, A.C.	USA	60m	1	1	1	7·0*	
			F		1	7·0*	G
		110m hurdles	1	1	1	15·6*	
			F		1	15·4*	G
		200m hurdles	1	1	1	27·0*	
			F		1	25·4*	G
		Long jump	F		1	7,18*	G
Leahy, P.J.	IRL	High jump	F		2	1,78	S
		Long jump	F		3	6,95	B
		Triple jump	F		4		
Lecuyer, J.	FRA	110m hurdles	1	3	1		
			F		4		
Lee, H.G.	USA	400m	1	1	2		
			F		DNS		
Leiblee, C.M.	USA	100m	1	4	1	11·4	
			2	2	2		
			R		3		
Lemming, E.V.	SWE	High jump	F		5	1,70	
		Long jump	F		12	5,50	
		Triple jump	F				
		Pole vault	F		=4	3,10	
		Discus throw	F		8		
		Hammer throw	F		4		
Lewis, W.F.	USA	110m hurdles	1	2	3		
			R	1	2		
		200m hurdles	1	2			
		400m hurdles	1	1	2		
			F		DNS		
Long, M.W.	USA	400m	1	1	1	50·4*	
			F		1	49·4*	G
Lord, H.H.	USA	400m	1	1	3		
		800m	1	3	3		
Lubowiecki, C.V.	AUT	Discus throw	F				
McClain, T.B	USA	100m	1	2	2		
			2	3	2		
			R				
		4000m steeplechase	F				
		200m hurdles	1	2	3		
		Long jump	F		7	6,43	
McCracken, J.C.	USA	Shot put	F		2	12,85	S
		Discus throw	F				
		Hammer throw	F		3	44,50	B
MacDonald, R.J.	CAN	Marathon	F				
McLean, J.F.	USA	110m hurdles	1	1	3		
			R	2	1		
			F		2	15·5	S
		Long jump	F		6	6,65	
		Triple jump	F				
		Standing triple jump	F				
Marchais, A.	FRA	Marathon	F		DNF		
Mechling, E.A.	USA	800m	1	3			
Minahan, E.J.	USA	60m	1	1	2	7·1	
			F		4	7·2	
		100m	1	5	2		
			2	3	4		
Moloney, F.G.	USA	100m	1	1	2		
			2	2	3		
			R				
		110m hurdles	1	1	2		
			R	1	1	17·0	
			F		3	15·8	B
		200m hurdles	1	1	3		
Moloney, W.A.	USA	400m	1	2	1	51·0	
			F		DNS		

COMPETITOR	COUNTRY CODE	EVENT	ROUND	HEAT	PLACE	TIME & DISTANCE	MEDAL
Monnier, L.	FRA	High jump	F		7	1,60	
Nedved, K.	TCH	400m hurdles	1	1	3		
Newton, A.L.	USA	2500m steeplechase	F		4		
		Marathon	F		5	4:04-12	
Nilsson, A.	SWE	Pole vault	F		8	2.60	
		Shot put					
Novy, V.	TCH	100m	1	1	3	DNF	
Nystroem, J.	SWE	Marathon	F		DNF		
Orton, G.W.	CAN	2500m steeplechase	F		1	7-34.4	G
		4000m steeplechase	F		5		
		400m hurdles	1	2	2		
			F		3	58.5	B
Paraskevopoulos, P.	GRE	Shot put	F		5	11,52	
		Discus throw	F		4	34,04	
Pool, E.	GBR	Marathon	F		DNF		
Prinstein, M.	USA	Long jump	F		2	7,17	S
		Triple jump	F		1	14,47*	G
Pritchard, N.D.	IND	60m	1	1	3		
		100m	1	5	1	11.4	
			2	3	3		
			R		2		
		200m	1	1	2	26.6	
			F		2	22.3	S
		110m hurdles	1	2	1	16.6	
			F		5		
		200m hurdles	1	2	1	26.8*	
			F		2	26.0	S
Pukl, O.	TCH	800m	1	3			
		1500m	F				
Randall, D.F.	GBR	Marathon	F		DNF		
Rau, G.	GER	200m hurdles	1	1			
Remington, W.P.	USA	110m hurdles	1	2	2		
			R	2	2		
		200m hurdles	1	1			
		Long jump	F		4	6,82	
Rimmer, J.T.	GBR	1500m	F				
		4000m steeplechase	F		1	12-58.4*	G
Robinson, S.J.	GBR	2500m steeplechase	F		2	7-38.0	S
		4000m steeplechase	F		3	12-58.8	B
Rowley, S.J.	AUS	60m	1	2	2	7.3	
			F		3	7.2	B
		100m	1	3	2	10.9	
			2	1	2		
			R		1	11.0	
			F		3	11.2	B
		200m	1	2	1	25.0	
			F		3	22.9	B
Salomez, M.	FRA	800m	1	1	4		
Saward, W.	GBR	Marathon	F		DNF		
Schubert, E.	HUN	60m	1	2			
		100m	1	5	3		
		Long jump	F		9	6 05	
Schultz, E.L.E.	DEN	400m	1	2	2		
			F		3	53.0	B

COMPETITOR	COUNTRY CODE	EVENT	ROUND	HEAT	PLACE	TIME & DISTANCE	MEDAL
Scrafford, J.M.	USA	800m	1	2	3		
Segondi, L.	FRA	1500m	F				
Sheldon, L.P.	USA	Standing high jump	F		3	1,50	B
		Standing long jump	F		4		
		Triple jump	F		3	13,64	B
		Standing triple jump	F		4	9,45	
Sheldon, R.	USA	Shot put	F		1	14,10*	G
		Discus throw	F		3	34,60	B
Slack, H.	USA	100m	1	6	3		
		400m	1	3	3		
Smith, H.P.	USA	800m	1	2			
Soederstroem, G.	SWE	Shot put	F		6	11,18	
		Discus throw	F		6	33,30	
Spied, Z.	HUN	400m	1	3			
		800m	1	2	2		
			F		5		
		200m hurdles	1	2			
Staaf, K.	SWE	Triple jump	F				
		Standing triple jump	F				
		Pole vault	F		7	2,80	
		Discus throw	F		11		
		Hammer throw	F		5		
Steffen, W.	GER	High jump	F		6	1,70	
		Long jump	F		8	6,30	
		Triple jump	F				
		Standing triple jump	F				
Strausz, G.	HUN	Long jump	F		10	6,01	
		Discus throw	F				
Tauzin, H.	FRA	200m hurdles	1	2	4		
		400m hurdles	1	2	1		
			F		2	58.3	S
Tewksbury, J.W.B.	USA	60m	1	2	1	7.2	
			F		2	7.1	S
		100m	1	2	1	11.4	
			2	2	1	10.8*	
			F		2	11.1	S
		200m	1	2	2		
			F		1	22.2*	G
		200m hurdles	1	2	2		
			F		3	26.1	B
		400m hurdles	1	1	1	1-01.0	
			F		1	57.6*	G
Theato, M.	FRA	Marathon	F		1	2:59-45	G
Torcheboeuf, E.	FRA	Standing long jump	F		3	3,03	B
Touquet-Daunis, G.	FRA	Marathon	F		DNF		
Tuffere, A.	FRA	Triple jump	F		6		
Tysoe, A.E.	GBR	800m	1	1	2	1-59.6	
			F		1	2-01.2	G
Versis, S.	GRE	Shot put	F				
Westergren, I.	SWE	60m	1	1			
		100m	1	5	4		
Winckler, C.G.C.	DEN	Shot put	F			10,76	
		Discus throw	F		9		
Wraschtil, H.	AUT	1500m	F		6		
		2500m steeplechase	F		5		

separated the leader Spring from the last runner, Yamasini, a Kaffir from South Africa. Arthur Newton of the USA moved to the front at 10km while fellow American Fred Lorz suffered cramp at 15km and was taken up into an automobile. After one hour of running Mellor was in the lead, but at 27km Hicks passed him and he gave up. Another 5km along the road Lorz's transport broke down and he commenced running again. Meanwhile, Hicks was in a bad way over the final 10km and was being laced with sulphate of strychine, white of egg and brandy to keep him going. Cheers echoed in the stadium when Lorz arrived and crossed the line the apparent winner. But he later admitted to his lift, was promptly disqualified and banned from athletics for a time. Hicks won the race in 3:28-53, although he was too weak to be presented with the silver cup until the following day. Despite the lack of water on the way, Albert Corey of France finished strongly in 3:34-52 for second place, while Newton also looked quite perky when finishing third in 3:47-33.

The top **110 metres hurdles** experts in America during 1904 were Edwin Clapp and Thad Shideler, who had recently run 15·0 sec for a new world best only to find the record disallowed due to a faulty third watch. Hurdling was against the wind, which was reflected in the slow times, and four Americans qualified for the final from two heats. In the final, Fred Schule and Shideler raced neck and neck for six flights, but Schule's longer legs won him the day in 16·0 from Shideler, 16·3, and Les Ashburner, 16·4.

Only five athletes appear to have competed in the **200 metres hurdles** over 2ft 6in barriers, on a course laid out across the infield of the track. Harry Hillman and George Poage, the coloured runner, raced shoulder to shoulder for most of the way, with Frank Castleman lying handily. Hillman made a strong effort with 20 metres to go and won the gold medal in 24·6 sec, while Castleman finished just as fast to take the silver in 24·9, from a slowing Poage who clocked 25·2.

In America it was usual to run the 440 yards hurdles over 2ft 6in flights, and this was the arrangement for the **400 metres hurdles**. It would appear that only four

hurdlers took part, all Americans, Harry Hillman, Frank Waller, George Poage and George Varnell. From the very start, Hillman was pushed by Waller all the way to the tape, but he won in 53·0 sec, despite hitting the eighth flight and losing ground. His record could not be accepted for two reasons: the hurdles were not the regulation 3ft height and he had knocked one over. Waller was credited with 53·2 for second while Varnell tripped at the seventh flight and came last, allowing Poage to score an easy third place in 54·8.

It has been claimed that the **2,500 metres steeplechase** was in fact run over 2,590 metres. The course was laid out within the inner perimeter of the track with a lap of about 450 metres, which included three brush hurdles and a water jump at the finish of each circuit. After one lap of the race, John Daly of Ireland, who was the firm favourite, led by ten metres from Harvey Cohn and Jim Lightbody, both of America. Daly still led at the bell by at least 15 metres and it was here that Lightbody made his great effort, clearing the 10ft water jump in one bound and winning in 7-39·6. Daly was second, but accounts vary as to whether he lost by a slight margin or by 90 metres. Third man home was Arthur Newton of the USA, 25 metres behind Daly.

Men's Field Events

Sam Jones was the American **high jump** champion and expected to do well at St Louis, and he did. Both he and fellow-American Garrett Serviss were reported as scissor jumpers, while Paul Weinstein of Germany did a form of western roll, and Lajos Gonczy of Hungary jumped with a simple knee-tuck technique. With the bar at 1,75 metres only the four mentioned jumpers succeeded. Serviss and Weinstein both cleared 1,77 but failed at the next height and, after a jump-off, Serviss gained the silver medal and Weinstein the bronze. Meanwhile, Jones had cleared 1,80 for the gold and asked for the bar to be raised to 1,89, but he failed three times.

Ward McLanahan of the USA was the favourite to win the **pole vault** as co-world record holders Norman Dole of the USA and Fernand Gonder of France were not competing, leaving the overseas competition to come from Paul Weinstein of Germany. At 3,35 metres five of the Americans cleared the bar, but only Charles Dvorak went on to reach 3,425 and 3,50 to win the gold. He even tried unsuccessfully for a new world record of 3,70. Left in were Leroy Samse, Louis Wilkins, Ward McLanahan and Claude Allen, who jumped-off for the remaining positions. Samse and Wilkins tied at 3,35 and a second jump off was needed to determine that Samse got the silver and Wilkins the bronze.

In the **long jump**, the principal actors were all Americans, with Meyer Prinstein redeeming his narrow defeat in Paris with a new Olympic record of 7,34 metres in the final round. Dan Frank was expected to jump Prinstein close, but reached only 6,89 for the silver, while Bob Stangland was nudged into third with 6,88.

Defending champion, Meyer Prinstein, led the all-American entry for the **triple jump** and retained his title with 14,35 metres to achieve a unique long jump and triple jump double. Fred Englehardt was second with 13,90, while Bob Stangland took the third spot.

The three **standing jumps** of high, long and triple were competed for as in Paris four years earlier. However, the latter event was described as three standing jumps, which may or may not have been a hop, step and jump.

Thomas Hicks

Drama had already become a feature of Olympic marathons, and the 1904 race in St Louis proved no exception. being run in a sweltering 32°C (90°F) in the afternoon. Thirty-two started and in addition to an extremely dusty course with seven punishing hills, there was no water readily available.

Fewer than half the contestants completed the distance and excitement erupted in the packed stadium as the American Fred Lorz arrived to be acclaimed the winner. But before he could be presented with the gold medal it was discovered he had enjoyed a ride in a car for some ten miles of the way. Lorz was promptly given a life-ban instead of the medal. This ban was lifted the following year.

The winner of the Olympic title was the English-born Hicks, from Cambridge, Massachusetts, who would probably have been disqualified also, had today's rules been rigidly enforced. He was given reviving substances when he looked in the later stages to be incapable of continuing.

The oddest character of the event was a Cuban, Felix Carvajal who had never run a marathon before and arrived at the starting line wearing ordinary walking shoes and long trousers. He was withstanding the conditions going well until tempted to help himself to a couple of green apples from an orchard along the way.

The outstanding feat of the Games was Ray Ewry's performance in retaining the three titles, with America winning all the nine medals on offer. In the high jump he won at 1,50 metres and went on to achieve 1,60, but at the Olympic record height of 1,65 he finally failed. Joseph Stadler, a coloured athlete, and Lawson Robertson tied at 1,45 but in the jump-off both sailed over 1,475 with Stadler eventually taking second place. Three trials only were allowed in the long jump, with Ewry exceeding the world record on his last attempt with 3,47. Charles King leaped 3,27 for the silver position and John Biller took the bronze, two centimetres less. Ewry was just short of his Paris performance in the triple jump with 10,54 metres, winning from King, 10,16, and Stadler, 9,60.

On 4 July 1904 Wesley Coe had set a world record of 14,81 metres, and fellow-American Ralph Rose had thrown only a little less, so a grand competition for the **shot put** was in prospect. On his first throw, from an area now standardised as a seven-foot circle, Rose achieved 14,32 to which Coe responded with 14,02. In the final three rounds, Rose improved to 14,35 and Coe retaliated with 14,40. This fired the 6ft 7in giant Rose into launching a world record-equalling 14,81 to win the gold medal. Coe took the silver with his 14,40 throw, and Leon Feuerbach heaved 13,37 to give the United States a clean sweep. Nicolaos Georgantas of Greece, who was actually throwing and not putting the shot, had his first two attempts disqualified and promptly stormed off in disgust.

A **56-pound weight** throw from a seven-foot circle was competed for only twice in Olympic history, at these Games and in 1920. John Flanagan of the USA was the world record holder and firm favourite for the title, with the bulky Canadian, Etienne Desmarteau, the danger man. He had beaten Flanagan before, and using one turn he threw 10,46 metres for the gold medal. The more agile Flanagan, despite using two turns, was suffering from flu and reached only 10,16 for second place with James Mitchell of the USA in third position.

Martin Sheridan of the USA was the major exponent of the **discus throw** among the competitors and although Nicolaos Georgantas of Greece was greatly admired for his physique and his style of throwing the discus from the standing position, the American was still favourite to win the event. Both Sheridan and his compatriot, Ralph Rose, employed a full turn and achieved identical throws of 39,28 metres for a new Olympic record. The athletes were each allowed a further throw to break the tie and the consistent Sheridan sent his discus out to 38,96, while Rose could only manage 36,75. Georgantas's standing throw of 37,68 brought him the bronze medal.

For nine years John Flanagan of the USA had been supreme in the **hammer throw** but the pre-Games buzz was that his fellow-American, Ralph Rose, had thrown over 58 metres in practice. Flanagan, the champion from 1900, throwing from a seven-foot circle, won again with 51,23, a new Games record and another American, John De Witt, threw 50,26 to take second position. He and Flanagan used two turns, while the third placer, Rose, used one turn to reach 45,73 for the bronze medal.

The **all-around** competition held at the American championships was nominated an Olympic event, and Tom Kiely of Ireland had specifically travelled to St Louis to test his prowess. This forerunner of the decathlon consisted of 100 yards, shot, high jump, 880-yards walk, hammer, pole vault, 120-yards hurdles, 56-lb weight, long jump and one mile. All these events

Charles Dvorak, the USA champion, clinches the pole vaulting event as he flies over the bar.   Dave Terry

A rare picture of Myer Prinstein, the American double gold medallist for the long and triple jumps in both Paris and St Louis.   Dave Terry

had to be completed in one day and scoring was according to percentage tables prepared in 1892. After five events, Truxton Hare of the USA led with 3,217 points from fellow American Adam Gunn, 3,170, and Kiely, 3,064. Kiely's long 56-lb weight throw was the deciding factor and it won him the gold medal with 6,036 points from Gunn, 5,907, who took the silver and Hare, 5,813, the bronze.

An historic moment set against an unusual background, sees the American standing high jump champion, Ray Ewry, clear 1,655 metres for a new world record.
N.S. Barrett Collection

Despite being drenched with the sun and choked by road dust, Thomas Hicks is encouraged by his handlers to compete the marathon and win gold for the USA.
N.S. Barrett Collection

1906

The Intercalated Games in Athens

The Greeks believed that the true home of the Olympic Games was Athens, and that city should be the only site for them. De Coubertin supported an Intercalated or Interim Games for 1906 (and also, incidentally, for 1910, but these did not transpire).

The Games were well organised, and were valued more because they were not part of a trade fair. However they were not given official IOC patronage, and are not numbered in the series of Olympiads.

Men's Track Events

Nineteen sprinters qualified for the second round of the **100 metres** and as one athlete withdrew, three heats sufficed, two qualifying for the final from each. William Eaton of the USA clocked the fastest time of 11·2 sec on a loose track. However, Archie Hahn of the USA got away quickest in the final and led all the way to win in 11·2 although Fay Moulton, also of the States, and Nigel Barker of Australia were catching him towards the finish. Moulton eventually took second place by inches from Barker, both being timed at 11·3.

Paul Pilgrim, the American **400 metres** competitor, had not originally been selected to represent the United States, but had paid his own expenses and had been allowed to join the team. Six heats were run with the winners progressing to the final, while the runners-up in the heats competing in a repechage race, in which the winner, W.D. Anderson of Britain, became the seventh finalist. In the final, Wyndham Halswelle of Britain led Nigel Barker of Australia and Paul Pilgrim around the final tight bend, but the American produced the best finishing sprint and won in 53·2 sec. Halswelle was second in 53·8 and Barker third in 54·1.

Eight runners qualified from four heats for the final of the **800 metres**. The athletes tipped to win were Reginald Crabbe and Wyndham Halswelle of Britain and James Lightbody of America. It was a slow race with most of the runners in contention for 500 metres before Lightbody struck for home followed by Halswelle and Pilgrim. But 60 metres from the tape Pilgrim found an astonishing burst to win in 2-01·5. Lightbody fought him all the way and finished in 2-01·6 with Halswelle third in 2-03·0.

Two heats produced eight athletes for the final of the **1,500 metres**. George Bonhag of America set the pace for three laps shadowed by his compatriot, James Lightbody, with the others strung out behind. As the race drew to a finish, Lightbody sprinted off the final bend and won in 4-12·0. And although John McGough of Britain came with a terrific sprint to close the large gap between him and the winner, he had to settle for second place in 4-12·6. Kristian Hellstroem of Sweden was third in 4-13·4.

The **5 miles** race was run as a straight final with 27 competitors taking part. The race was steady until the last few laps, when Henry Hawtrey of Britain speeded up, taking John Svanberg and Edvard Dahl, both of Sweden, and John Daly of Ireland with him. Hawtrey won in 26-11·8 with Svanberg second in 26-19·4 and Dahl third with 26-26·2. Daly actually finished in the bronze medal position, inches ahead of Dahl, but was disqualified for impeding the Swede.

Fifty-three competitors for the **marathon** were sent out to Marathon the night before the race, 31 of them being Greeks. The distance was to be 40km and at 3.00 pm on a very hot day the runners set off for Athens. George Blake of Australia soon jumped into the lead with Will Frank of the USA and John Daly of Ireland in close attendance. William Sherring of Canada took over from Frank after 15 miles and shortly before the finish, John Svanberg of Sweden had moved into second place. Sherring, however, had built up a lead of seven minutes during the latter stages and won in 2:51-23·6, losing 14lb of weight on the way. Svanberg was second in 2:58-20·8 and Frank was third with 3:00-46·8.

In the **110 metres hurdles** the winners of the three heats and Vincent Duncker of South Africa, who won the repechage heat for second place men, contested the final. He had arrived in Athens from Germany with the German team. The final was a close race with Bob Leavitt of the USA and Bert Healey of Britain racing neck and neck. Leavitt got the nod from the judges for the gold medal in 16·2 sec, the same time recorded by Healey, and in third place was Duncker in 16·3, just holding off Hugo Friend of the USA.

Richard Wilkinson of Britain and Eugen Spiegler of Austria raced into the lead in the **1½ kilometres walk** and detached themselves from the other seven competitors. Wilkinson won handsomely with Spiegler second and George Bonhag of the USA third. The judges then disqualified all three for unfair walking but Prince George of Greece intervened and Bonhag was declared the winner in 7-12·6. He was an Olympic winner and had never race-walked before in his life! Donald Linden of Canada was given second place in 7-19·8 and Constantin Spetsiotis of Greece third in 7-22·0.

As in the 1½ kilometres, a similar situation arose in the **3 kilometres walk**. Richard Wilkinson of Britain won and Eugen Spiegler of Austria was second and both were disqualified. Gyorgy Sztantics of Hungary was placed first in 15-13·2 with Hermann Mueller of Germany second in 15-20·0 and Georgios Saridakis of Greece third in 15-33·0.

Men's Field Events

The **high jump** began with 18 jumpers in contention, but by the time the bar reached 1,675 metres there were only five competitors left. As it was now dusk the competition was adjourned to the next day. When the bar reached 1,72 only Con Leahy of Ireland, Lajos Gonczy of Hungary, Thmistoclis Diakidis of Greece and Herbert Kerrigan of America were left in. At the next height the last two failed and were placed equal third, while Gonczy cleared the bar at 1,75 to finish in second place. Leahy jumped 1,77 to win the competition.

Fernand Gonder of France held the world record for the **pole vault** at 3,74 metres and during the warm-up he had gone over the bar at 3,66. However, his winning jump in the competition using a bamboo pole was only 3,50. In second place came Bruno Soederstroem of Sweden with 3,40, while Edward Glover of the USA achieved 3,35. The talented Ed Archibald of Canada went out of the competition at an earlier height when his pole snapped and he lost his confidence.

On the first trial of the **long jump** Meyer Prinstein of the USA jumped 7,20 metres which eventually won the competition. An official stuck his cane in the ground alongside the jumping pit to show where the leading jump was and Peter O'Connor of Ireland exceeded it more than once. but each time he sat down in the pit and the attempts were ruled fouls. He eventually finished second with 7,02, while Hugo Friend of America was third at 6,96.

Con Leahy of Ireland was expected to win the **triple jump**, but he was taking off well before the board and was shunted into second place with 13,98. When Peter O'Connor of Ireland produced 14,075 on his last jump he was so delighted with his win that he climbed a flagpole and replaced the British flag with an Irish one. Third in the competition was Thomas Cronan of the USA with 13,70, whereas his team-mate, Meyer Prinstein, the reigning Olympic champion, could manage only 12,27.

Once again the **standing jumps** were on the Olympic agenda and consisted of separate competitions for both high and long jump. In the high jump Ray Ewry of the USA won with 1,56 metres and made an unsuccessful attempt at 1,66 to beat his own world record. There was a three-way tie for second place between Leon Dupont of Belgium, and Lawson Robertson and Martin Sheridan, both of the USA, at 1,40. It was also a clean sweep in the standing long jump for the Americans with Ewry taking gold with 3,30 metres, Sheridan the silver with 3,09 and Robertson the bronze with 3,05.

The standard in the **shot put** was very moderate, with Martin Sheridan of the USA achieving only 12,32 metres for the premier position. Mihaly David of Hungary reached 11,83 for the silver medal and Erik Lemming of Sweden attained a distance of 11,26 for the bronze. The muscular Werner Jaervinen was expected to win the contest, but his attempts were ruled fouls, as he actually threw instead of putting.

Some prodigious throwing occurred in the **stone throw** in which a rather large sphere of masonry weighing 6,4kg was thrown overarm. The winner was Nicolaos Georgantas of Greece with a distance of 19,92 metres. Martin Sheridan of the USA, who also exceeded the 19 metres mark by 3,5 centimetres, was placed second. Third was Michel Dorizas of Greece at 18,58.

Martin Sheridan of the USA, the world record holder in the **discus throw**, won the event with a distance of 41,46 metres. Second placed Nicolaos Georgantas of Greece achieved a respectable 38,06 while Werner Jaervinen threw 36,82.

In the **discus throw, Greek style**, competition Werner Jaervinen of Finland produced a standing throw of 35,17 metres while Nicolaos Georgantas of Greece reached 32,80 for second spot. Third was Istvan Mudin of Hungary with 31,91 in an event where Martin Sheridan of the USA never quite got the knack.

Erik Lemming, the Swedish expert and world record holder in the **javelin throw**, had it all his own way with a splendid mark of 53,90 metres. The lesser medallists were also Swedes, with Knut Lindberg throwing 45,17 for second and Bruno Soederstroem 44,92 for third.

The **pentathlon** events were similar to those indulged in by the ancient Greeks, that is, a standing long jump, a standing discus throw, a running javelin throw, a 192 metres sprint and a wrestling competition. Points were allocated according to the position of finishing in each event. Hjalmar Mellander of Sweden was the overall winner with 24 points, followed by Istvan Mudin of Hungary with 25 and Erik Lemming of Sweden with 29.

Dave Terry

James Lightbody

James Lightbody, born in Pittsburgh on 17 March 1882, was the Sebastian Coe of his early racing days. A shrewd 800m and 1,500m runner he won both titles at the 1904 Games in St Louis and then added for good measure the gold for the 2,500m steeplechase.

He was ever a student of his opposition. In races he would be content to place himself comfortably behind the leaders and wait for the appropriate moment to strike for victory.

In the 800m final he was in fifth place until approaching the finish when he rounded his two teammates, Howard Valentine and Emil Breitkreutz, to win in an Olympic record of 1-56·0.

Again in the 1,500m he tailed the leaders until the end of the back straight, when he swooped to win by six yards from two of his Chicago Club colleagues Bill Verner and Lacey Hearn to set a new world record of 4-05·4.

Two years later, the Greeks held their intercalated Athenian Games with the blessing of the IOC in Athens and Lightbody was there again, winning the 1,500m. But over the 800m another American, Paul Pilgrim, just beat him to the line while Lightbody, thinking he was about to win was looking round on the inside to see how the rest of the runners were placed. He died on 2 March 1953.

William Sherring, the Canadian long distance wizard, trotting home to win the marathon, accompanied by the Crown Prince of Greece.

All-Sport Photographic Ltd.

The 2,500-year-old stadium was renovated for the first modern Olympic Games. This shot shows a scene from the 1906 intercalated Games. N.S. Barrett

COMPETITOR	COUNTRY CODE	EVENT	ROUND	HEAT	PLACE	TIME & DISTANCE	MEDAL
MALES							
Abrahams, S.S.	GBR	100m	1	10	1	11·8	
			2	1	4		
			F		5		
		Long jump	F		5	6,21	
Ahlman, H.A.	FIN	Pole vault	F		=5	3,00	
		Shot put	F				
		Discus throw	F				
		Stone throw	F				
		Javelin throw	F				
		Pentathlon	F		DNF		
Alepous, I.	GRE	Marathon	F		5	3:09-25·4	
Amiras, P.	GRE	Standing long jump	F		12	2,77	
Anagnostopoulos, N.	GRE	Shot put	F				
Anastasiadis, G.	GRE	800m	1	2	4		
		1500m	1	1			
Anastasopoulos, S.	GRE	100m	1	8	3		
		400m	1	4			
Anderson, W.D.	GBR	400m	1	1	2		
			R		1	54·8	
			F		7		
		800m	1	1	4		
Andoniadis, S.	GRE	Javelin throw	F				
Andreadakis, N.	GRE	High jump	Q		DNQ		
		Long jump	F		13	5,90	
		Triple jump	F		NP	0	
Andreadis, A.	GRE	1500m	1	2			
		Marathon	F				
Anesakis, E.	GRE	Standing long jump	F		29	2,42	
		Discus throw Greek style	F				
		Javelin throw	F				
Archibald, E.B.	CAN	Pole vault	F		=10	2,75	
		Pentathlon	F		DNF		
Arvanitis, I.	GER	5 miles	F				
Bacon, C.J.	USA	400m	1	5	1	56·2	
			F		5		
		800m	1	1	2		
			F		6		
Banikas, G.	GRE	Pole vault	F		=5	3,00	
Barker, N.	ALS	100m	1	9	2		
			2	3	2		
			F		3	11·3	B
		400m	1	3	1	53·0	
			F		3	54·1	B
Baur, H.	AUT	Discus throw Greek style	F				
		Pentathlon	F		DNF		
Beckmann, M.	GER	100m	1	3	3		
		400m	1	6	3		
Belokas, S.	GRE	Marathon	F				
Bergvall, T.	SWE	Marathon	F				
Bjolgerud, H.	NOR	High jump	F		=6	1,67	
Blake, G.	AUS	1500m	1	2			
		5 miles	F		6		
		Marathon	F		6	3:09-35·0	
Bock, O.	DEN	100m	1	1	2		
			2	1	3		
		High jump	Q		DNQ		
		Long jump	F		15	5,77	
Bonhag, G.V.	USA	1500m	1	2	3		
			F		6		
		5 miles	F		4		
		1½k walk	F		1	7-12·6*	G
Bonheure, E.	FRA	Marathon	F				
Boulakakis, V.	GRE	Marathon	F				
Brambilla, E.	ITA	Standing long jump	F		16	2,72	
		Pentathlon	F		DNF		
Brustman, M.	GER	100m	1	9	3		
		Standing long jump	F		17	2,70	
		Long jump	F		14	5,85	
		Triple jump	F		NP	0	
Carlsrud, C.	NOR	Javelin throw	F		7		
Carnelley, S.	GBR	5 miles	F				
Churchill, A.R.	GBR	1500m	1	1			
		5 miles	F				
Cohn, H.W.	USA	1500m	1	2	4		
			F				
		5 miles	F				
Connolly, F.	USA	Long jump	F		25	5,28	
		Triple jump	F		6	12,75	
Connolly, J.B.	USA	Long jump	F		NP	0	
		Triple jump	F		NP	0	
Cormack, J.N.	GBR	Marathon	F		14		
Crabbe, R.P.	GBR	800m	1	3	1	2-07·6	
			F		4		
		1500m	1	2	2		
			F				
Cronan, T.F.	USA	Long jump	F		6	6,18	
		Triple jump	F		3	13,70	B
Dahl, E.	SWE	1500m	1	2			
		5 miles	F		3	26-26·2	B
Daly, J.J.	IRL	5 miles	F				
		Marathon	F				
Davaris, C.	GRE	Marathon	F		10		
David, M.	HUN	Shot put	F		2	11,83	S
		Stone throw	F				
		Discus throw	F				
		Discus throw Greek style	F				
		Javelin throw	F				
De Fleurac, L.	FRA	5 miles	F				
Demestichas, I.	GRE	400m	1	2			
Desfarges, A.	FRA	Shot put	F				
		Stone throw	F				
		Discus throw	F				
		Pentathlon	F		DNF		
Devetzis, C.	GRE	100m	1	4	=3		
Diakidis, T.	GRE	High jump	F		3	1,72	B
		Standing high jump	F		=7	1,25	
Dialektos, N.	GRE	Marathon	F				
Dionisiotis, T.	GRE	Marathon	F				
Dorizas, M.M.	GRE	Stone throw	F		3	18,58	B
		Discus throw	F				
		Discus throw Greek style	F				
Dorr, W.	GER	Discus throw	F				
		Pentathlon	F		DNF		
Drosinos, N.	GRE	High jump	Q		DNQ		
Du Coteau, M.B.	FRA	100m	1	10	3		
		400m	1	5	2		
			R		2		
			F		8		
Duncker, J.V.	SAF	100m	1	8	2	12·2	
			2		DNS		
		400m	1	2	2		
			R		3		
		800m	1	3	DNF		
		110m hurdles	1	1	2		
			R		1	17·4	
			F		3	16·3	B
Dupont, L.	BEL	High jump	Q		DNQ		
		Standing high jump	F		=2	1,40	S
		Standing long jump	F		4	2,97	
Eaton, W.D.	USA	100m	1	2	1	11·6	
			2	3	1	11·2	
			F		4		
Edgren, R.W.	USA	Shot put	F				
		Discus throw	F				
Edwards, F.M.	GBR	5 miles	F				
Ektoros, P.	GRE	100m	1	3	2		
			2		DNS		
		400m	1	4			
		800m	1	3			
		3k walk	F		4		
Ewry, R.C.	USA	Standing high jump	F		1	1,56	G
		Standing long jump	F		1	3,30	G
Ferarolakis, H.	GRE	Marathon	F				
Forshaw, J.	USA	Marathon	F		12		
Fotakis, G.	GRE	Marathon	F				
Fowler, R.J.	USA	Marathon	F				
Frank, W.G.	USA	Marathon	F		3	3:00-46·8	B
		5 miles	F				
Friend, H.M.	USA	110m hurdles	1	1	1	16·8	
			F		4	16·4	
		Long jump	F		3	6,96	B
		Standing long jump	F		NP	0	
Georgantas, N.	GRE	Stone throw	F		1	19,92*	G
		Discus throw	F		2	38,06	S
		Discus throw Greek style	F		2	32,80	S
Giannarakis, M.	GRE	Marathon	F				
Glover, E.C.	USA	Pole vault	F		3	3,35	B
Gonczy, L.	HUN	High jump	F		2	1,75	S
		Standing high jump	F		5	1,35	
Gonder, F.	FRA	Pole vault	F		1	3,50	G
Guttormsen, O.	NOR	Triple jump	F		4	13,34	

COMPETITOR	COUNTRY CODE	EVENT	ROUND	HEAT	PLACE	TIME & DISTANCE	MEDAL
Haeggman, U.	FIN	100m	1	8	4		
		Standing long jump	F		28	2,42	
		Discus throw	F				
		Javelin throw	F		4	34	
		Pentathlon	F		4	34	
Hahn, A.F.	USA	100m	1	1	1	12·0	
			2	1	1	11·4	
			F		1	11·2	G
Hahnel-Kohout, O.	TCH	100m	1	9			
		Long jump	F		20	5,57	
Halse, A.	NOR	Javelin throw	F		6	43,60	
Halswelle, W.E.	GBR	100m	1	6	2		
			2	3	3		
		400m	1	4	1	54·0	
			F		2	53·8	S
		800m	1	2	2		
			F		3	2-03·0	B
Haug, O.	NOR	Pole vault	F		=5	3,00	
Hawtrey, H.C.	GBR	1500m	1	-	DNF		
		5 miles	F		1	26-11·8*	G
Healey, A.H.	GBR	100m	1	1	8	12·2	
			2	3	6		
		110m hurdles	1	3	1	16·5	
			F		2	16·2	S
Hellmich, M.	HUN	100m	1	10			
Hellstroem, K.	SWE	800m	1	2	1	2-05·8	
			F		5		
		1500m	1	1	2		
			F		3	4-13·4	B
Hillman, H.L.	USA	400m	1	1	1	54·8	
			F		4		
		110m hurdles	1	3			
Hofmann, F.	GER	100m	1	2	5		
Horne, J.W.	GBR	400m	1	3	3		
		800m	1	3	3		
Houndoumadis, G.	GRE	Marathon	F		11		
Ioannou, C.	GRE	Marathon	F				
Isigonis, G.	GRE	110m hurdles	1	3	2		
			R		3		
Jaervinen, W.	FIN	Shot put	F				
		Stone throw	F				
		Discus throw	F		3	36,82	3
		Discus throw Greek style	F		1	35,17*	G
		Javelin throw	F		5	44,25	
Jardin, H.	FRA	Standing long jump	F		9	2,83	
Johansson, H.	SWE	Standing long jump	F		19	2,69	
Kakousis, P.	GRE	Discus throw Greek style	F				
Kaltenbach, C.	GER	Shot put	F				
		Stone throw	F				
		Discus throw	F				
		Javelin throw	F				
		Pentathlon	F		DNF		
Kantzias, D.	GRE	1500m	1	2			
		5 miles	F				
		Marathon	F				
Karvelas, C.	GRE	Marathon	F		7	3:15-54·0	
Kerrigan, H.W.	USA	High jump	F		=3	1,72	B
		Pole vault	F		=10	2,75	
		Standing long jump	F		10	2,83	
Kesar, P.	GRE	100m	1	5	-	12·6	
			2		DNS		
Kiss, I.	HUN	Pole vault	F		=5	3,00	
Kollaros, I.	GRE	Standing long jump	F		11	2,78	
Koskoris, V.	GRE	Marathon	F				
Koudouriotis, S.	GRE	Pole vault	F		=5	3,00	
Kouris, A.	GRE	1½k walk	F		6		
Kousoulidis,	GRE	Marathon	F				
Koutoulakis, A.	GRE	Marathon	F				
Koutoulas, D.	GRE	Discus throw Greek style	F				
Kovacs, N.	HUN	110m hurdles	1	1			
Kraemer, J.	GER	High jump	Q		DNQ		
Kroejer, G.	AUT	100m	1	6	3		
		High jump	Q		DNQ		
		Standing high jump	F		=9	1,12	
		Long jump	F		18	5,62	
		Standing long jump	F		24	2,57	
		Triple jump	F		15	11,98	
		Pentathlon	F		DNF		
Kwieton, F.	AUT	1500m	1	2			
		5 miles	F				
		Marathon	F				
Lahner, L.	AUT	Shot put	F				
		Stone throw	F				

COMPETITOR	COUNTRY CODE	EVENT	ROUND	HEAT	PLACE	TIME & DISTANCE	MEDAL
Lampelmayer, K.	AUT	100m	1	1			
		400m	1	5	4		
		Triple jump	F		NP	0	
		Long jump	F		23	5,38	
Leahy, C.	IRL	High jump	F		1	1,77	G
		Triple jump	F		2	13,98	S
Leavitt, R.G.	USA	110m hurdles	1	2	1	16·5	
			F		1	16·2	G
Lelokas, S.	GRE	Triple jump	F		17	11,45	
Lemming, E.V.	SWE	Standing long jump	F		26	2,53	
		Triple jump	F		13	12,19	
		Shot put	F		3	11,26	B
		Stone throw	F		4	18,21	
		Discus throw	F		4	35,62	
		Discus throw Greek style	F				
		Javelin throw	F		1	53,90*	G
		Pentathlon	F		3	29	B
Leon, L.	GRE	Long jump	F		19	5,58	
		Triple jump	F		16	11,96	
Lesage, J.	BEL	Marathon	F				
Lightbody, J.D.	USA	400m	1	3	2	53·0	
			R		DNS		
		800m	1	1	1	2-05·4	
			F		1	2-01·6	S
		1500m	1	1	1	4-19·4	
			F		1	4-12·0	G
Lindberg, K.	SWE	100m	1	4	1	11·8	
			2	2	2		
			F		6		
		Javelin throw	F		2	45,17	S
		Pentathlon	F		6	37	
Linden, D.J.	CAN	1½k walk	F		2	7-19·8	S
Ljung, A.	SWE	100m	1	7	2		
			2	3	4		
		110m hurdles	1	2	3		
		Standing long jump	F		5	2,95	
Lorentzen, V.	DEN	Standing long jump	F				
Low, N.	DEN	High jump	Q		DNQ		
		Long jump	F		22	5,47	
		Standing long jump	F		27	2,52	
		Triple jump	F		14	12,00	
Lucchi, E.	ITA	Discus throw Greek style	F				
Luntzer, G.	HUN	Discus throw	F				
		Discus throw Greek style	F		5	30,26	
		Javelin throw	F				
		Pentathlon	F		DNF		
McGough, J.	GBR	800m	1	4			
		1500m	1	2	1	4-18·8	
			F		2	4-12·6	S
		5 miles	F				
Makris, T.	GRE	Pole vault	F		4	3,25	
Malfait, G.	FRA	100m	1	2	3		
		400m	1	3	4		
Malindretos, N.	GRE	Marathon	F				
Mallwitz, A.	GER	Long jump	F		24	5,38	
		Standing long jump	F		20	2,67	
		Pentathlon	F		DNF		
Manarolakis, C.	GRE	Marathon	F				
Mandakas, M.	GRE	Marathon	F				
Marangoudakas,	GRE	Marathon	F				
Marson, A.	EGY	5 miles	F				
		Marathon	F				
Maspoli, A.	FRA	Standing long jump	F		18	2,69	
Masprone, A.	ITA	Discus throw	F				
Mellander, H.	SWE	800m	1	3			
		Long jump	F		4	6,58	
		Javelin throw	F		4	44,30	
		Pentathlon	F		1	24*	G
Milonakis, C.	GRE	5 miles	F				
		Marathon	F				
Molinie, H.	FRA	110m hurdles	1	2	2		
			R		2		
			F		5		
		High jump	Q		DNQ		
Moulton, F.R.	USA	100m	1	3	1	11·8	
			2	2	1	11·2	
			F		2	11·3	S
		400m	1	6	1	54·8	
			F		6		
Mourmouris, N.	GRE	100m	1	8			
		High jump	Q		DNQ		

COMPETITOR	COUNTRY CODE	EVENT	ROUND	HEAT	PLACE	TIME & DISTANCE	MEDAL
Mudin, I.	HUN	Standing long jump	F		15	2,75	
		Shot put	F				
		Discus throw	F				
		Discus throw Greek style	F		3	31,91	B
		Javelin throw	F				
		Pentathlon	F		2	25	S
Mueller, H.	GER	5 miles	F				
		Marathon	F		9	3:21-00·0	
		3k walk	F		2	15-20·0	S
Muller, D.	GRE	Triple jump	F		5	13,12	
Negrepontis, V.	GRE	Marathon	F		13		
Nejedly, A.	TCH	5 miles	F				
		Marathon	F				
O'Connor, P.	IRL	High jump	Q		DNQ		
		Long jump	F		2	7,02	S
		Triple jump	F		1	14,07	G
Pagliani, P.	ITA	1500m	1	2			
		5 miles	F		5		
Panagoulopou-los, I.	GRE	3k walk	F		5		
Papadakis, E.	GRE	100m	1	9			
Papachristou, G.	GRE	Stone throw	F				
		Discus throw	F				
Papageorgiou, V.	GRE	Shot put	F				
		Stone throw	F				
		Discus throw	F				
		Discus throw Greek style	F				
		Javelin throw	F				
Papazian, H.	TUR	800m	1	4			
		1500m	1	1			
Papot, J.	FRA	High jump	Q		DNQ		
Parousis, E.	GRE	Javelin throw	F				
Parsalis, C.	GRE	Triple jump	F		10	12,52	
		Pentathlon	F		DNF		
Parsons, E.B.	USA	400m	1	1			
		800m	1	3	2		
			F		7		
Patestidis, P.	GRE	100m	1	4			
Pedersen, C.A.	NOR	Triple jump	F		8	12,68	
Petersen, A.	DEN	100m	1	4			
		High jump	Q		DNQ		
		Long jump	F		21	5,55	
		Standing long jump	F		25	2,55	
Peterson, A.	DEN	400m	1	1			
Pietri, D.	ITA	Marathon	F				
Pilgrim, P.H.	USA	400m	1	2	1	55·2	
			F		1	53·2	G
		800m	1	4	1	2-06·6	
			F		1	2-01·5	G
Pohl-Polensky, B.	TCH	100m	1	4	2		
			2	1	5		
		Triple jump	F		12	12,19	
Polimenos, P.	GRE	Marathon	F				
Priftis, A.	GRE	Long jump	F		26	5,23	
Prinstein, M.	USA	100m	1	10	2		
			2		DNS		
		Triple jump	F		11	12,27	
		Long jump	F		1	7,20	G
Queyrouze, G.H.	USA	400m	1	5	3		
Rageneau, G.	FRA	5 miles	F				
Reed, R.	GBR	100m	1	7	1	12·0	
			2		DNS		
		400m	1	6	4		
Ritzenhoff, W.	GER	100m	1	6	4		
		Standing long jump	F		21	2,67	
		Stone throw	F				
		Pentathlon	F		DNF		
Robertson, L.N.	USA	100m	1	9	1	11·4	
			1	1	2		
			F		5		
		400m	1	4	2		
			R		DNS		
		Standing high jump	F		=2	1,40	S
		Standing long jump	F		3	3,05	B
		Pentathlon	F		5	36	
Roffi, A.	FRA	Marathon	F		8	3:17-49·8	
Roenstroem, G.	SWE	100m	1	6	5		
		High jump	F		5	1,70	
		Long jump	F		7	6,15	
Rossidis, M.D.	GRE	Marathon	F				
Runge, J.	GER	400m	1	6	2		
			R		DNS		
		800m	1	4	2		
			F		DNF		
		Long jump	F		12	5,90	
Santorineos, I.	GRE	5 miles	F				
Saridakis, G.	GRE	1½k walk	F		4		
		3k walk	F		3	15-33·0	B
Scheidl, T.	AUT	High jump	Q		DNQ		
		Standing high jump	Q		DIS		
		Standing long jump	F		13	2,77	
		Discus throw Greek style	F				
		Pentathlon	F		DNF		
Schick, W.A.	USA	100m	1	6	1	12·2	
			2	2	3		
Schirmer, J.	GER	High jump	Q		DNQ		
Schoeffthaler, R.	AUT	100m	1	2	4		
		110m hurdles	1	3			
Sennecke, R.	GER	Marathon	F				
Serrander, E.	SWE	800m	1	1	3		
		5 miles	F				
Sheridan, M.J.	USA	Standing high jump	F		=2	1,40	S
		Standing long jump	F		2	3,09	S
		Shot put	F		1	12,32	G
		Stone throw	F		2	19,03	S
		Discus throw	F		1	41,46*	G
		Discus throw Greek style	F		4	31,50	
		Pentathlon	F		DNF		
Sherring, W.J.	CAN	Marathon	F		1	2:51-23·6	G
Siantis, D.	GRE	400m	1	2			
Skoutaridis, G.	GRE	110m hurdles	1	2			
Skullerud, F.	NOR	5 miles	F		DNF		
Soalhat, M.	FRA	800m	1	2			
		1500m	1	2	5		
Soederstroem, B.	SWE	High jump	F		=6	1,67	
		Pole vault	F		2	3,40	S
		Javelin throw	F		3	44,92	B
Solar, F.	AUT	Shot put	F				
		Pentathlon	F		DNF		
Solidakis, G.	GRE	Marathon	F				
Somodi, I.	HUN	High jump	Q		DNQ		
		Long jump	F		8	6,04	
		Standing long jump	F		6	2,86	
Soucek, F.	TCH	Discus throw	F				
		Discus throw Greek style	F		6	27,55	
		Javelin throw	F				
		Pentathlon	F		DNF		
Spetsiotis, C.	GRE	1½k walk	F		3	7-22·0	B
		3k walk	F				
Spiegler, E.	AUT	1½k walk	F		DIS		
		3k walk	F		DIS		
Spring, M.	USA	Marathon	F				
Stamou, D.	GRE	5 miles	F				
Stamoulis, G.	GRE	Marathon	F				
Stournaras, V.	GRE	100m	1	10			
		Long jump	F		9	6,03	
		Triple jump	F		7	12,72	
Strausz, G.	HUN	Discus throw	F				
		Discus throw Greek style	F				
		Javelin throw	F				
Sullivan, D.A.	USA	Pentathlon	F		DNF		
Sullivan, J.P.	USA	800m	1	2	3		
		1500m	1	1	5		
			F				
Sustera, M.	TCH	Discus throw	F				
		Discus throw Greek style	F		7	27,08	
		Pentathlon	F		DNF		
Svanberg, J.P.	SWE	5 miles	F		2	26-19·4	S
		Marathon	F		2	2:58-20·8	S
Szegedy, G.	HUN	High jump	Q		DNQ		
		Standing high jump	F		=9	1,†2	
Sztantics, G.	HUN	1½k walk	F		7		
		3k walk	F		1	15-13·2*	G
Tison, A.	FRA	Standing long jump	F		22	2,66	
		Shot put	F		4	11,02	
		Discus throw	F		5	34,81	
Tobler, A.	SUI	Marathon	F				
Topsidelis, T.	GRE	Marathon	F				
Toernros, G.	SWE	Marathon	F		4	3:01-00·0	
Torretta, G.	ITA	100m	1	2	2		
			2	3	5		
		Long jump	F		17	5,65	
Tsatsanifos, C.	GRE	800m	1	4			
		1500m	1	1			
Tselepopoulos, A.	GRE	5 miles	F				
		Marathon	F				

COMPETITOR	COUNTRY CODE	EVENT	ROUND	HEAT	PLACE	TIME & DISTANCE	MEDAL
Tsiklitiras, K.	GRE	Standing high jump	F		6	1,30	
		Standing long jump	Q		DNQ	2,84	
Tsolias, A.	GRE	Javelin throw	F				
Tuffere, A.	FRA	110m hurdles	1	2			
		Standing long jump	F		7	2,35	
Valentine, H.V.	USA	400m	1	4			
		800m	1	2	3		
Varanakis, I.	GRE	Shot put	F				
Vargha, P.	HUN	110m hurdles	1	3			
		High jump	Q		DNQ		
		Long jump	F		10	5,97	
		Javelin throw	F				
		Pentathlon	F		DNF		
Vasilakos, C.	GRE	1½k walk	F		5		
Veliotis, S.	GRE	Marathon	F				
Vellas, S.	GRE	Discus throw Greek style	F				
Venizelos, L.	GRE	800m	1	2			
Volonakis, E.	GRE	Marathon	F				
Wagner, B.	GER	Long jump	F		11	5,95	
Wagner, J.	SUI	100m	1	1			
		Standing long jump	F		14	2,75	
		Shot put	F				
		Stone throw	F				
		Discus throw Greek style	F				
		Pentathlon	F		DNF		

COMPETITOR	COUNTRY CODE	EVENT	ROUND	HEAT	PLACE	TIME & DISTANCE	MEDAL
Walters, D.W.	GBR	110m hurdles	1	1	3		
Weber, H.G.	GBR	5 miles	F				
Weinstein, P.	GER	Standing high jump	F		=7	1,25	
		Long jump	F		16	5,72	
		Standing long jump	F		23	2,65	
		Triple jump	F		9	12,61	
		Javelin throw	F				
Wheatley, G.	AUS	800m	1	4	3		
		1500m	1	1	4		
			F		4		
Wilkinson, R.	GBR	1½k walk	F		DIS		
		3k walk	F		DIS		
Wittman, J.	AUT	Shot put	F				
		Stone throw	F				
		Discus throw Greek style	F				
Zinon, G.	GRE	100m	1	1			
		110m hurdles	1	1			

Rounding the tight turn of the track in the 800 metres, the American Paul Pilgrim (second from left), was the eventual winner.

Dave Terry

Frank Irons sails to a new Olympic record in the long jump for America.

All-Sport Photographic Ltd.

Dorando Pietri, the World's Most Famous Loser

The 1908 Games were originally intended for Rome, but in 1906 Vesuvius erupted and, among other things, ruined the Italian economy. London stepped in.

The Games were the best run so far, but there was controversy. For the first time the British competed seriously — too seriously according to some Americans, who felt that the home team were getting the benefit of some decisions. The 400 metres in particular caused bitter feelings, with the US representatives refusing a re-run and leaving the British runner to go round alone for the gold medal.

The most famous man at the Games, however, was an Italian, Dorando Pietri. First over the line in the marathon, he was disqualified for accepting help, only to be given a special gold cup by Queen Alexandra. He is remembered when all the medal-winners are forgotten.

Men's Track Events

Bobbie Kerr of Canada and James Rector of America were the two pre-race favourites for the **100 metres**. Rector had lived up to expectations when he equalled the Olympic record of 10·8 sec in the first round, although Reggie Walker of South Africa, with the same time, had also raised some eyebrows. Only the four second round winners competed in the final with Walker being fastest away and Kerr the worst. At 50 metres, Rector overtook Walker, but in the closing stages the South African found another gear and won by nearly a metre in 10·8. He was actually clocked at 10·7, but the timing was rounded up. Rector was second in 10·9 and Kerr third in 11·0.

Run without lanes around one turn, the **200 metres** appeared to suit Bobbie Kerr, who completed an extremely fast first round heat in 22·2 sec. Four only competed in the final with Kerr fastest around the bend, but the two Americans, Robert Cloughen and Nat Cartmell closed up on him in the straight. Kerr fought them off to win in 22·6, with Cloughen given the same time and Cartmell finishing third in 22·7.

The **400 metres** had promised a good competition, and in the second round Wyndham Halswelle of Britain surpassed the Olympic record with 48·4 sec. Only the heat winners lined up for the final and the positions for the draw, there being no lanes, were John Carpenter on the inside, Halswelle, John Taylor, the coloured American athlete and W.C. Robbins. From the gun, Carpenter set off at a great pace followed closely by Robbins, Halswelle and Taylor. Coming off the final bend Halswelle went wide to overtake Robbins and came up on the outside of Carpenter, who commenced to veer to the right until both he and Halswelle were running along the extreme outside of the track. The judges broke the worsted tape and waved their arms at the runners, who all stopped except Carpenter, running

through in 48·6. Carpenter was disqualified and the race declared void. A re-run was organised for the next day, but only Halswelle turned up and ran alone to win in 50·0. No silver or bronze medals were awarded.

Eight heat winners qualified for the final of the **800 metres**. Ivo Fairbairn-Crawford of Britain sprinted away at the start and by 200 metres was 15 metres ahead of Mel Sheppard of the USA, who was just up on Emilio Lunghi of Italy and Theodore Just of Britain. Sheppard led at 400 metres in 53·0 sec from Lunghi, who weakened, and won in a new world and Olympic time of 1-52·8. Lunghi finished second in 1-54·2, while the German, Hanns Braun, won the race for third position with 1-55·2.

During the British trials Harold Wilson had set a world best of 3-59·8 for **1,500 metres** and was tipped to win. In the final, Ivo Fairbairn-Crawford of Britain produced a fast pace for 500 metres and then allowed fellow Briton, E.V. Loney to run in front. But Loney let the pace drop and it was not until 300 metres from the finish, when Wilson made his burst, that the race hotted up. Off the final bend it was Wilson leading Norman Hallows of Britain and James Sullivan of the USA. However, Mel Sheppard, the winner of the 800, was biding his time and with a powerful sprint down the home straight won the gold medal in 4-03·4 for a new Olympic record. Wilson held on for the silver in 4-03·6 and Hallows the bronze in 4-04·0.

Two preliminary heats were held in the **3 miles team race** and Britain were the only team to finish with three scoring runners in the first. However, in the second heat both America and France qualified. In the final Arthur Robertson of Britain set off at a smart pace for two laps, before his team-mates William Coales and Joe Deakin took it in turns to lead. These three and John Eisele of the USA forged ahead and in the final lap Deakin sprinted home and won by 30 metres in 14-35·0 from Robertson, 14-41·0, and Coales, 14-41·6. Britain won the team event with 6 points from USA, 19, and France, 32.

A **5 miles** race was run at these Games with two each to qualify from six heats. Only ten runners started the final, with J.F. Fitzgerald of Canada soon in the lead. There were various leaders up to the four-mile mark before John Svanberg started to cut out the pace, towing the others in his wake. With 700 metres to go Emil Voigt of Britain made a decisive move and ran away from the rest to win by 65 metres in 25-11·2. His fellow-Briton, Eddie Owen, jumped Svanberg off the last bend to sprint home for the silver spot in 25-24·0. Svanberg finished third in 25-37·2.

The **marathon** had originally been planned for a 25-mile route, but the appeal of starting the race at Windsor Castle and finishing at the stadium meant that 26 miles 385 yards or 42·195km had to be traversed. The

385 yards does not refer to the distance run in the stadium, which was about 288 yards, but from the stadium entrance to the finish. It was 2.30 pm on a hot day when the 56 starters were given the signal by her Royal Highness the Princess of Wales. The leading group, running down Castle Hill, consisted of T. Clarke and E. Barnes of Britain, A. Burn and Tom Longboat of Canada, and Dorando Pietri of Italy. The first mile was reached in a fast 5-01·4 with Tom Jack of Britain now leading. Jack was still leading at 3 miles in 15-42·0, but at 10 miles, the Briton Jack Price, was in front with Pietri and Charles Hefferon of South Africa not far behind. The terrain at 15 miles was hilly and Hefferon took over the running, with Fred Lord of Britain, Pietri and Longboat two minutes down. At 20 miles Hefferon had a lead of 4 minutes over the Italian, with John Hayes of the USA a mile further behind. In the last mile Pietri passed Hefferon and although he reached the stadium five minutes in advance of Hayes, he was in a dazed state. He tried to run the wrong way onto the track and was turned the correct way, but he fell three times and was given liquid stimulants by doctors. In the end he was helped across the finishing line in 2:54-46·4 and thereby disqualified. Hayes won in 2:55-18·4 and Hefferon was a very tired second in 2:56-06. J. Forshaw of the USA was third.

Held over a grass course on the stadium infield, the **110 metres hurdles** second round heats saw Forrest Smithson of the USA equal the Olympic record of 15·4 sec, which made him the firm favourite for the final. Only the four semi-final winners competed in the final and all were Americans. Smithson made an excellent start and improved his lead throughout the race to win in 15·0, a new world and Olympic record. John Garrels was second in 15·7 and Arthur Shaw was placed third.

Three times the world record was beaten in the **400 metres hurdles**. Firstly, Charles Bacon of the USA recorded 57·0 sec in the third heat before fellow American, Harry Hillman, chopped this down to 56·4. In the final, only the four second round winners competed and both Bacon and Hillman went off at a furious pace. At 150 metres the two Britons, Leonard Tremeer and Leslie Burton were well out of it and the two leaders were together all the way. Bacon's run-in from the last hurdle was the stronger and he won in 55·0 for a world and Olympic record. Hillman finished in 55·3 and Tremeer in 57·0 for the third place.

As in the hurdles, the course for **3,200 metres steeplechase** was held on the grass infield immediately inside the cinder track and was the nearest equivalent to two miles that the organisers could achieve. In the last of the six heats James Lightbody of the USA, the defending champion, finished second and was eliminated, as only heat winners progressed to the final. Guy Holdaway of Britain led at the gun for the first lap then fellow team mate, Arthur Russell took charge. After four laps, Russell broke away with John Eisele of the USA and Arthur Robertson of Britain chasing. The three steeplechasers jostled for position until 200 metres from the finish when the two Britons sprinted. Russell just got to the tape first in 10-47·8 to Robertson's 10-48·8 with Eisele trailing in third place.

The strange distance for the **3½ kilometres walk** arose as a compromise between the previous 3 kilometres and the usual English distance of two miles. There were three heats with nine walkers qualifying for the final, where Ernie Webb of Britain set off at a smart pace followed by the pack. But on the second lap both he and

Ray Ewry

Ray Ewry was the marvel of the Olympic Games in Paris 1900, St Louis 1904 and London 1908. Born in Lafayette, Indiana, on 14 October 1873, as a boy he was confined to a wheelchair because of paralysis and he was never expected to walk. Yet during those three Olympics he won eight gold medals.

Sheer determination through exercise enabled Ewry to develop incredible strength in his legs which encouraged him to tackle the then popular standing jump events — long, high and triple. He won all three of these finals in Paris, again in St Louis and the long and high in London. His standing long jump of 11ft 4¾in (3,47m) in St Louis remained a world record until the event ceased to be recognised internationally.

He was 27 when making his first Olympic appearance and so superior were his jumping distances that in Paris he won the long jump by three inches, the high jump with five inches to spare and the triple jump by two feet.

Despite his physical handicaps Ewry captained both his track and field and football teams while at Purdue University.

He attempted to compete for the US in the Stockholm Games of 1912 but age had robbed him of much of his elasticity and he retired — with an Olympic record unlikely ever to be equalled in track and field athletics. He died on 29 September 1937.

George Larner drew away. Towards the end of the race Larner took control, passing two miles in a creditable 13-43·4 before going on to win in 14-55·0. Webb came home in 15-07·4 and Harry Kerr of New Zealand, but representing Australasia, was third in 15-43·4.

In the **10 miles walk**, six walkers qualified from two heats and every single competitor came from Britain. In the final, Edward Spencer led the field, but in the second lap George Larner and Ernie Webb "trod on the gas" and opened a wide gap. At four miles Larner surged ahead and went on to win in a world's best time of 1:15-57·4 from Webb, 1:17-31, and Spencer, 1:21-20·2.

For many years known as the Olympic relay, the **medley relay** was an innovation that did not generally catch on. It consisted of two 200 metres, a 400 metres and an 800 metres in that order. Seven countries competed in three heats, with the winner of each heat qualifying for the final. The fastest time of the day occurred in the third heat where the USA beat Britain in 3-27·2. In the final, the USA took on Germany and Hungary. William Hamilton ran the first leg for them in 22·0 sec, handing over to Nat Cartmell six metres up. He increased the lead to eight metres with 22·2, before John Taylor took over and ran his leg in 49·8, leaving Mel Sheppard to romp home in 1-55·4 for a total winning time of 3-29·4. Meanwhile, Germany beat Hungary by inches for the silver after a fine tussle in 3-32·4.

Men's Field Events

The **high jump** competition was organised in pools with the bar raised one inch at a time from 5ft 10in and the actual performances being recorded in metres. There was no tie-breaking rule, so when Con Leahy of Britain and Ireland, Istvan Somodi of Hungary and Andre of France all jumped 1,88 metres they each received a silver medal for second place. Harry Porter of the USA went on to clear 1,90 to create a new Olympic record before failing three times at 1,95.

In the **pole vault** competition the preliminaries also

Squired by his official attendant, the Italian waiter, Dorando Pietri, on his way to the stadium, and his sensational collapse.   All-Sport Photographic Ltd.

John Flanagan

One of early Irish hammer throwers to migrate to the United States, Flanagan had been born in Limerick, Ireland, on 9 January 1868. In America he joined the New York police force and became the greatest thrower of the hammer in his day. Winning his first American title in 1897, he subsequently repeated the success six times up to 1907.

He was the first athlete to win the same standard event at three successive Olympic Games. His first gold medal was won in Paris in 1900 with a fling of 167ft 4½in (51,01m). In St Louis four years later he reached 168ft 1in (51,23m) and in London in 1908, 170ft 4¼in (51,92m) to bring him a new Olympic record at the age of 36.

While world records were not officially ratified until 1913 it is accepted that Flanagan, between 1895 and 1909, improved the world's best throwing distance on at least a dozen occasions, taking it from 145ft 10½ (44,46m) in gradual stages to 184ft 4in (55,19m), which makes him the oldest world record breaker in the history of track and field athletics.

At the St Louis Games he also won a silver medal in the now discontinued-56 lb weight event. Three years after his third Olympic triumph Flanagan returned to live in Ireland, where he died in 1938.

All-Sport Photographic Ltd.

took place in pools, with Edward Cooke of the USA achieving the best vault of 3,71 metres for a new Olympic record. The American vaulters had some difficulty in convincing the British officials that they needed a hole dug in front of the jumping stands to plant their poles into, as the old English practice had been to use a spiked pole. Also it was noticeable that most vaulters used the lighter bamboo poles in preference to the solid type. In the finals only Alfred Gilbert of the USA improved to equal Cooke's earlier mark and they were both awarded gold medals. Ed Archibald of Canada, Charles Jacobs of the USA and Bruno Soederstroem of Sweden all tied at 3,58 and received bronze medals, there being no silver medal awarded.

Preliminaries settled the positions of the **long jump** medallists with only the American Frank Irons improving from 7,44 to 7,48 metres in the final three trials. Both jumps exceeded the previous Olympic record. Dan Kelly of the States secured the silver position with a leap of 7,09 and was closely followed by Calvin Bricker of Canada with 7,08 for the bronze spot. The highly rated Irishman Tim Ahearne, jumping for Britain, could only manage eighth place.

Tim Ahearne of Britain and Ireland made amends for his poor showing in the long jump with his fine win in the **triple jump**. His second jump in the qualifying rounds reached 14,73 metres for a new Olympic record and in the final he improved upon this in the last round with 14,92. The applause stimulated Garfield Macdonald of Canada to leap 14,76 with his last jump to gain second place over Edvard Larsen of Norway.

Once again the phenomenon of the **standing jumps**, Ray Ewry, continued his domination. He jumped 1,57 metres to win the standing high jump with Constantin Tsiclitras of Greece and John Biller of the USA at 1,55 each taking home a silver medal. In the standing long jump, he sprang 3,33 with Tsiclitras again second at 3,22. Martin Sheridan of America was third.

Ralph Rose, the reigning Olympic champion and world record holder in the **shot put**, was in London to defend his title, but conditions were poor, with the competitors throwing from a wet and slippery grass circle. The American Rose had been regularly reaching in excess of 15,00 metres in practice, but managed only

14,21 to win the gold. Dennis Horgan of Britain and Ireland was second, also below par with 13,62. Third place went to John Garrels of America with 13,18.

Martin Sheridan of the USA was a firm favourite to win the **discus throw** and so retain the Olympic title he had won in St Louis. The preliminaries were held in pools where he threw 40,57 metres, but his fellow American, Merritt Giffin, launched a life-time best of 40,70. Luckily for Sheridan, he managed a throw of 40,89 in the final to win the gold medal, with Merritt taking the silver and Marquis Horr of the USA the bronze with 39,45. The first four exceeded the official Olympic record.

The **discus throw, Greek style** event was held for the second and last time and consisted of a standing throw from a sloping plinth. Martin Sheridan of the USA won the contest with 37,99 metres from Marquis Horr of the USA 37,32, and Werner Jaervinen of Finland, 36,48. The first four competitors beat the best on record.

John Flanagan of the USA was one of the giants of **hammer throw**ing. He had held the world record for 13 years, had won two Olympic titles at the event, and was joint favourite with team-mate Matt McGrath. McGrath led in the preliminaries with 51,18 metres to Flanagan's 50,36, but in the final rounds the defending champion propelled his missile to a new Olympic record of 51,92 and made it three victories in three Olympics. McGrath was second and Con Walsh of Canada third with 48,50.

Although it had been held at the unofficial Games of 1906, the **javelin throw** was a new event to the Olympic programme. Erik Lemming of Sweden, the world record holder, dominated the competition in more ways than one, being 6ft 3in and 196lb. In the preliminaries he threw 53,68 metres and improved this to 54,83 in the final for victory. Second was Arne Halse of Norway with 50,57 and third Otto Nilsson of Sweden at 47,10.

In addition to the regular competition there was, for the only time, a **javelin throw, freestyle** contest which allowed the spear to be hurled in any manner the athlete desired. Erik Lemming of Sweden won this with a regular throw of 54,44 while Michel Dorizas of Greece claimed second place with 51,36 and Arne Halse of Norway threw 49,73 for the bronze.

John Hayes, of the USA, en-route to winning the marathon.   All-Sport Photographic Ltd.

American, Martin Sheridan, the eventual winner, prepares to throw the discus in the Greek style.

Dave Terry

Wyndham Halswelle

Two of the most sensational happenings in the history of the modern Olympic Games took place in London 1908. One involved Halswelle's victory in the 400m and the other the disqualification of Italy's Dorando Pietri when in the lead within yards of the finish of the marathon.

The Scottish Halswelle, who was born in 1882 and fought in the Boer War, lined up for the 400m final along with three Americans, J.C. Carpenter, J.B. Taylor and W.C. Robbins. Being no lanes in those days, there was a suspicion the Americans might work as a team against the Scot, so officials were placed at regular spots around the track.

Robbins was soon in a commanding lead but coming out of the final bend Halswelle and Carpenter moved to pass the leader on the outside. The challenge from Halswelle was resisted by Carpenter moving wide, so preventing the Scot going to the front. Official cries of "foul" were instant and the tape was broken ahead of Carpenter by officals who declared the race void and ordered a re-run without him.

After much controversy the re-run took place two days later — but with only one runner, Halswelle. Both Taylor and Robbins refused to go to their marks and it was left to the Scot merely to complete the circuit, which he did in 50 sec flat.

The 1,500 metres winner, Mel Sheppard (left) of the USA, seen breasting the tape ahead of the Englishman, Harold Wilson.   All-Sport Photographic Ltd.

Forrest Smithson, from America, the 110 metres hurdles winner, bible in hand, demonstrates his technique.   All-Sport Photographic Ltd.

COMPETITOR	COUNTRY CODE	EVENT	ROUND	HEAT	PLACE	TIME & DISTANCE	MEDAL
MALES							
Adams, P.	USA	Standing long jump	Q		DNQ		
		Standing high jump	F		=5	1,47	
		Triple jump	F		5	14,07	
Agger, H.	DEN	Hammer throw	Q		DNQ		
Ahearne, T.J.	GBR	110m hurdles	1	9	1		
			2	3	4		
		Standing long jump	Q		DNQ		
		Long jump	F		8	6,72	
		Triple jump	F		1	14,92*	G
Aitken, W.V.	GBR	Marathon	F		DNF		
Andersson, E.A.	SWE	1500m	1	3	6		
Andre, G.	FRA	Standing high jump	F		=5	1,47	
		High jump	F		=2	1,88	S
Appleby, F.	GBR	Marathon	F		DNF		
Archibald, E.B.	CAN	Pole vault	F		=3	3,58	B
Ashford, F.	GBR	800m	1	1	DNF		
Astley, A.	GBR	400m	1	9	2	51·4	
		800m	1	5	2	1-59·8	
Atlee, J.C.	USA	400m	1	11	1	50·4	
			2	4	3		
Avattaneo, U.	ITA	Discus throw	Q		DNQ		
		Discus throw Greek style	Q		DNQ		
Bacon, C.J.	USA	400m hurdles	1	3	1	57·0*	
			2	2	1	58·8	
			F		1	55·0*	G
Baker, J.M.	SAF	Marathon	F		DNF		
Banikas, G.	GRE	Pole vault	F		=6	3,50	
Barber, G.	CAN	Standing long jump	Q		DNQ		
		Standing high jump	Q		DNQ		
		Long jump	Q		DNQ		
		High jump	Q		DNQ	1,72	
Barker, H.	GBR	3200m steeplechase	1	3	DNF		
Barnes, E.	GBR	Marathon	F		13	3:17-30·8	
Barrett, E.	GBR	Shot put	F		5	12,89	
		Discus throw	Q		DNQ		
		Javelin throw free style	Q		DNQ		
Barrett, H.E.	GBR	Marathon	F		DNF		
Barrett, J.	GBR	Shot put	Q		DNQ		
Barozzi, U.	ITA	100m	1	7	4		
		200m	1	8	2	24·1	
Beale, J.G.	GBR	Marathon	F		17	3:20-14·0	
Beard, C.B.	USA	800m	1	5	1	1-59·3	
			F		DNF		
Bechler, C.	GER	100m	1	17	2	11·7	
		Javelin throw	Q		DNQ		
Beland, D.	CAN	100m	1	5	3		
Bellah, S.H.	USA	Long jump	Q		DNQ		
		Triple jump	Q		DNQ		
		Pole vault	F		=6	3,50	
Bellars, F.G.	USA	5 miles	1	2	2	28-45·0	
			F		8		
Bellerby, A.C.B.	GBR	Long jump	Q		DNQ	1,58	
		High jump	Q		DNQ		
Bengtsson, A.	SWE	Standing high jump	Q		DNQ		
Biller, J.A.	USA	Standing long jump	F		4	3,21	
		Standing high jump	F		=2	1,55	S
Bjoern, E.	SWE	800m	1	1	3		
		1500m	1	3	5		
		Medley relay	1	1	2		
Blake, G.B.	AUS	5 miles	1	1	3		
		Marathon	F		DNF		
Blasi, U.	ITA	Marathon	F		DNF		
Bleadon, W.H.	GBR	Standing long jump	Q		DNQ		
		Long jump	Q		DNQ		
Blijstad, W.	NDR	110m hurdles	1	11	2		
		Standing high jump	F		=8	1,42	
Bodor, O.	HUN	800m	1	1	1	1-58·6	
			F		4	1-55·4	
		1500m	1	1	8		
		Medley relay	1	1	1	3-32·6	
			F		3	3-32·5	B
Bonhag, G.N.	USA	3200m steeplechase	1	4	DNF		
		3 mile team race	1	2	1	10	
			F		2	19	S
Bouin, J.	FRA	1500m	1	7	2	4-17·0	
		3 mile team race	1	2	2	15	
			F		3	32	B
Braams, W.T.	HOL	5 miles	1	3	DNF		
		Marathon	F		DNF		
		3 mile team race	1	1	DNF		
Braun, H.	GER	800m	1	7	1	1-58·0	
			F		3	1-55·2	B
		1500m	1	8	3	4-18·2	
		Medley relay	1	2	1	3-43·2	
			F		2	3-32·4	S
Brambilla, E.	ITA	200m	1	11	5		
		Javelin throw free style	Q		DNQ		
Brennan, J.J.	USA	Long jump	F		5	6,86	
		Triple jump	F		8	13,59	
Breynck, A.	GER	800m	1	6	2	2-06·0	
		1500m	1	6	2	4-30·0	
Bricker, C.	CAN	Long jump	F		3	7,08	B
		Triple jump	F		4	14,09	
Bromilow, J.	USA	800m	1	7	2	1-58·3	
Brown, B.C.	GBR	3½k walk	1	1	DIS		
Buckley, F.J.	GBR	3200m steeplechase	1	2	DNF		
Buddo, D.	CAN	400m	1	6	2		
			1	5	3		
		Medley relay	1	3	3		
Buff, G.J.M.	HOL	Marathon	F		DNF		
Burn, A.	CAN	Marathon	F		24	3:50-17·0	
Burroughs, W.G.	USA	Shot put	Q		DNQ		
		Discus throw	F		8	37,43	
		Discus throw Greek style	Q		DNQ		
Burton, G.	GBR	400m hurdles	1	5	1		
			2	4	DNF		
Burton, L.A.	GBR	400m hurdles	1	12	1	60·4	
			2	3	1	59·8	
			F		4	58·0	
Butler, J.	GBR	3½k walk	1	3	5	16-17·0	
		10 mile walk	1	2	10		
Butterfield, G.	GBR	1500m	1	2	3	4-11·8	
		800m	1	1	2	1-58·9	
Caffrey, J.	CAN	Marathon	F		11	3:12-46·0	
Carlsrud, C.M.	NOR	Javelin throw free style	Q		DNQ		
Carpenter, J.C.	USA	400m	1	14	1	49·6	
			2	1	1	49·4	
Carr, E.P.	USA	3200m steeplechase	1	1	DNF		
		5 miles	1	2	2	27-24·4	
Cartasegna, M.	ITA	400m	1	10	2		
		1500m	1	3	3		
		3200m steeplechase	1	1	2		
		3 mile team race	1	1	DNF		
Carter, F.T.	GBR	10 mile walk	1	1	2	1:21-25·4	
			F		4	1:21-20·2	
Cartmell, N.J.	USA	100m	1	8	1	11·0	
			2	4	1	11·2	
			F		4	11·2	
		200m	1	4	1	23·0	
			2	2	1	22·6	
			F		3	22·7	B
		Medley relay	1	3	1	3-27·2	
			F		1	3-29·4	G
Celis, F.	BEL	Marathon	F		DNF		
Chapman, M.	GBR	100m	1	10	2	11·3	
Chavasse, C.H.	GBR	400m	1	8	2	50·7	
Chavasse, N.G.	GBR	400m	1	7	3	51·5	
Clarke, W.T.	GBR	Marathon	F		12	3:16-08·6	
Clougher, F.	USA	100m	1	5	1	11·0	
		200m	1	8	1	23·4	
			2	3	1	22·6	
			F		2	22·6	S
Coales, W.	GBR	5 miles	1	1	DNF		
		3 mile team race	1	1	1	6	
			F		1	6	G
Coe, H.L.	USA	800m	1	4	2	1-58·0	
		1500m	1	4	2	4-09·2	
		400m hurdles	1	2	1	58·8	
			2	1	2	57·0	
Coe, W.W.	USA	Shot put	F		4	13,07	
Collins, M.	GBR	Discus throw	Q		DNQ		
Conn, H.W	USA	3 mile team race	1	2	1	10	
			F		2	19	S
Cooke, E.T.	USA	Long jump	F		4	6,97	
		Pole vault	F		=1	3,71*	G
Cornish, L...	GBR	Standing long jump	Q		DNQ		
		Long jump	Q		DNQ		
Cotter, E.	CAN	Marathon	F		DNF		
Coulcumberados, G.	GRE	5 miles	1	2	DNF		
		Marathon	F		DNF		
Countouriotis, E.	GRE	Pole vault	Q		DNQ		
Coutoulakis, A.	GRE	Marathon	F		DNF		

COMPETITOR	COUNTRY CODE	EVENT	ROUND	HEAT	PLACE	TIME & DISTANCE	MEDAL
Dahl, E.M.	SWE	800m	1	5	DNF		
		1500m	1	8	2	4-10·4	
		5 miles	1	2	DNF		
		3 mile team race	1	2	3	21	
Dahl, N.	NOR	1500m	1	1	7		
Danielson, F.G.	SWE	800m	1	6	DNF		
Davies, C.C.	GBR	400m	1	12	1	50·4	
			2	1	2	49·8	
Deakin, J.E.	GBR	1500m	1	6	1	4-13·6	
			F		6	4-07·9	
		5 miles	1	4	DNF		
		3 mile team race	1	1	1	6	
			F		1	6	G
Dearborn, A.K.	USA	Discus throw	F		5	38,52	
		Discus throw Greek style	F		4	35,65	
De Fleurac, L.N.L.B.	FRA	1500m	1	1	6		
		3200m steeplechase	1	2	DNF		
		3 mile team race	1	2	2	15	
			F		3	32	B
De Keyser, J.	HOL	1500m	1	1	9		
		5 miles	1	4	DNF		
Delloye, F.	BEL	1500m	1	8	5		
Demetrios, S.	GRE	1500m	1	4	4		
Densham, J.B.	GBR	400m hurdles	1	2	2	59·2	
Den Held, C.J.	HOL	200m	1	12	4		
		400m	1	12	2		
De Selding, F.M.	USA	400m	1	15	2	50·8	
De Veenhuijsen, H.	HOL	Pole vault	Q		DNQ		
Dineen, M.D.	GBR	Triple jump	Q		DNQ		
Dorizas, M.	GRE	Shot put	Q		DNQ		
		Discus throw	Q		DNQ		
		Discus throw Greek style	Q		DNQ		
		Javelin throw free style	F		2	51,36	S
Downing, T.	GBR	3200m steeplechase	1	1	DIS		
Dreher, J.	FRA	1500m	1	4	5		
		3 mile team race	1	2	2	15	
			F		3	32	B
Drubina, E.	HUN	3½k walk	1	2	5	18-44·6	
Dubois, G.	FRA	400m	1	6	DNF		
Duffy, E.J.	SAF	100m	1	1	1	11·6	
			2	3	3		
		200m	1	2	2	23·2	
Dugmore, C.R.	GBR	Triple jump	Q		DNQ		
Dull, G.A.	USA	3200m steeplechase	1	4	2		
		3 mile team race	1	2	1	10	
			F		2	19	S
Duncan, A.	GBR	Marathon	F		DNF		
Duncan, R.C.	GBR	100m	1	7	1	11·4	
			2	3	4		
		200m	1	5	2	23·1	
Dupont, L.	BEL	Standing long jump	Q		DNQ		
		Standing high jump	F		=8	1,42	
		High jump	Q		DNQ	1,67	
Eicke, H.	GER	100m	1	7	3	11·6	
		Medley relay	1	2	1	3-43·2	
			F		2	3-32·4	S
Eisele, J.L.	USA	3200m steeplechase	1	2	1	11-13·6	
			F		3	11-00·8	B
		3 mile team race	1	2	1	10	
			F		2	19	S
Ekberg, O.R.B.	SWE	Standing long jump	F		5	3,19	
English, J.C.	GBR	800m	1	4	DNF		
		3200m steeplechase	1	2	DNF		
Evers, B.	HOL	400m	1	15	3		
		800m	1	7	DNF		
		Standing long jump	Q		DNQ		
		Long jump	Q		DNQ		
		Pole vault	Q		DNQ		
		Medley relay	1	2	2		
Ewry, R.C.	USA	Standing long jump	F		1	3,33	G
		Standing high jump	F		1	1,57	G
Fairbairn-Crawford, I.F.	GBR	800m	1	8	1	1-57·8	
			F		DNF		
		1500m	1	8	1	4-09·2	
			F		5	4-07·6	
Falchenberg, J.	NOR	Discus throw	Q		DNQ		
Fayollat, A.	FRA	3 mile team race	1	2	2	15	
			F		3	32	B
Fischer, P.	GER	100m	1	10	DNF		
Fitzgerald, J.F.	CAN	1500m	1	8	7		
		3200m steeplechase	1	6	DNF		
		5 miles	1	5	2	26-05·8	
			F		7		
Flanagan, J.J.	USA	Hammer throw	F		1	51,92*	G
		Discus throw	Q		DNQ		
Flaxman, A.E.	GBR	Standing high jump	Q		DNQ		
		Discus throw	Q		DNQ		
		Discus throw Greek style	Q		DNQ		
		Javelin throw free style	Q		DNQ		
Fleetwood, F.	SWE	Discus throw	Q		DNQ		
Forshaw, J.	USA	Marathon	F		3	2-57-10·4	B
French, C.M.	USA	800m	1	5	DNF		
Fryksdal, K.	SWE	100m	1	12	3		
		Standing high jump	Q		DNQ		
		Triple jump	F		7	13,65	
Fyffe, A.H.	GBR	Hammer throw	Q		DNQ		
Galbraith, W.	CAN	1500m	1	7	3	4-20·2	
		3200m steeplechase	1	3	1	11-12·4	
			F		6		
		5 miles	1	6	2	27-23·2	
Garrels, J.C.	USA	110m hurdles	1	2	1	16·2	
			2	4	1	16·2	
			F		2	15·7	S
		Shot put	F		3	13,18	B
		Discus throw	Q		DNQ		
		Discus throw Greek style	Q		DNQ		
George, J.B.	GBR	100m	1	2	1	11·6	
			2	4	4		
		200m	1	1	1	23·4	
			2	3	3		
Georgandas, N.	GRE	Shot put	Q		DNQ		
		Discus throw	Q		DNQ		
		Discus throw Greek style	Q		DNQ		
		Javelin throw free style	Q		DNQ		
Gidney, H.A.	USA	High jump	F		=5	1,85	
Giffin, M.H.	USA	Discus throw	F		2	40,70	S
Gilbert, A.C.	USA	Pole vault	F		=1	3,71*	G
Gillis, S.P.	USA	Hammer throw	F		7	45,58	
		Discus throw	Q		DNQ		
Giovanoli, E.	ITA	3000m	1	1	DNF		
Goetzee, J.	HOL	10 mile walk	1	1	8		
		3½k walk	1	1	7	17-37·8	
Goldsboro, W.	CAN	Marathon	F		16	3:20-07·0	
Gould, E.W.	GBR	400m hurdles	1	8	1		
			2	3	3		
Goulding, G.	CAN	10 mile walk	1	2	13		
		Marathon	F		22	3:33-26·4	
		3½k walk	1	3	1	15-54·0	
			F		4	15-49·8	
Grantham, W.	GBR	3200m steeplechase	1	6	DNF		
Greven, E.J.C.	HOL	100m	1	4	5		
		200m	1	6	3		
Groenings, O.	GBR	110m hurdles	1	3	1	16·4	
			2	1	4		
		400m hurdles	1	7	1		
			2	2	DNF		
Gunia, P.	GER	10 miles walk	1	1	7	1:26-09·4	
		3½k walk	1	1	4	16-38·0	
Gutierrez, H.	FRA	Long jump	Q		DNQ		
Guttormsen, O.	NOR	100m	1	2	2		
		200m	1	14	1		
			2	4	4		
		400m	1	5	2		
		Triple jump	Q		DNQ		
		110m hurdles	1	12	2		
Halbart, F.	BEL	110m hurdles	1	8	1		
			2	4	DNS		
		200m	1	10	5		
Hall, C.L.	USA	3200m steeplechase	1	5	4		
		5 miles	1	3	4	28-24·0	
Halligan, A.	GBR	110m hurdles	1				
Hallows, N.F.	GBR	1500m	1	3	1	4-03·4*	
			F		3	4-04·0	B
Halme, J.	FIN	Shot put	Q		DNQ		
		Javelin throw free style	Q		DNQ		
		Javelin throw	F		6	44,96	
Halse, A.	NOR	Shot put	Q		DNQ		
		Javelin throw free style	F		3	49,73	B
		Javelin throw	F		2	50,57	S

COMPETITOR	COUNTRY CODE	EVENT	ROUND	HEAT	PLACE	TIME & DISTANCE	MEDAL
Halstead, J.P.	USA	800m	1	3	1	2-01·4	
			F		6		
		1500m	1	2	2	4-05·6	
Halswelle, W.	GBR	400m	1	15	1	49·4	
			2	2	1	48·4*	
			F	2	-	50·0	G
Haluzsiusky, J.	HUN	High jump	Q		DNQ	1,72	
Hamilton, W.F.	USA	100m	1	11	1	11·2	
		200m	1	10	1	22·4	
			2	1	2	22·7	
		Medley relay	1	3	1	3-27·2	
			F		1	3-29·4	G
Hammond, T.E.	GBR	10 mile walk	1	1	6	1.23-44·0	
Hansen, R.C.	DEN	Marathon	F		26	3:53-15·0	
Harmer, F.W.	GBR	400m hurdles	1	4	1		
			2	3	2		
Harmer, H.S.	GBR	100m	1	5	DNF		
Harrison, R.	GBR	10 mile walk	1	2	2	1:18-21·2	
		3½k walk	1	3	2	16-04·8	
			F		DIS		
Hatch, S.H.	USA	Marathon	F		14	3:17-52·4	
Hawkins, G.A.	GBR	200m	1	15	1	22·8	
			2	4	1	22·5	
			F		4	22·9	
		Medley relay	1	3	2		
Hayes, J.J.	USA	Marathon	F		1	2:55-18·4*	G
Healey, A.H.	GBR	110m hurdles	1	1	1	15·8	
			1	3	2	15·9	
Hedenlund, A.	SWE	High jump	Q		DNQ	0	
Hefferon, C.	SAF	5 miles	1	1	2	26-05·0	
			F		4	25-44·0	
		Marathon	F		2	2:56-06·0	S
Hellstedt, F.	SWE	High jump	Q		DNQ	1,57	
Hellstrom, K.	SWE	800m	1	8	2		
Henderson, W.E.B.	GBR	Standing long jump	Q		DNQ		
		Standing high jump	F		=8	1,42	
		Discus throw	Q		DNQ		
		Discus throw Greek style	Q		DNQ		
		Javelin throw free style	Q		DNQ		
Henny, V.	HOL	100m	1	1	3		
		200m	1	1	2		
		400m	1	7	4		
		Medley relay	1	2	2		
Hesse, A.	GER	1500m	1	2	7	4-40·0	
Hillman, H.L.	USA	400m hurdles	1	6	1	59·2	
			2	1	1	56·4*	
			F		2	55·3	S
Hoffmann, A.	GER	100m	1	3	1	11·4	
		200m	1	13	2	23·5	
		Long jump	Q		DNQ	6,50	
		Medley relay	1	2	1	3-43·2	
			F		2	3-32·4	S
Hojme, A.H.S.	DEN	10 mile walk	1	1	DNF		
		3½k walk	1	1	6	17-23·4	
Holdaway, C.G.	GBR	3200m steeplechase	1	5	1	11-18·8	
			F		4		
Holding, H.E.	GBR	800m	-	7	3	1-58·5	
Holics, E.	HUN	Long jump	Q		DNQ		
Holmes, F.L.	USA	Standing long jump	Q		DNQ		
		Standing high jump	F		4	1,52	
Hoogveld, J.	HOL	100m	1	9	3		
		200m	1	15	3		
		400m	1	16	2		
		Standing long jump	Q		DNQ		
		Long jump	Q		DNQ		
		Medley relay	1	2	2		
Horgan, D.	GBR	Shot put	F		2	13,32	S
Horr, M.F.	USA	Hammer throw	F		6	46,94	
		Shot put	F		7	12,82	
		Discus throw	F		3	39,45	B
		Discus throw Greek style	F		2	37,32	S
Howe, L.V.	USA	110m hurdles	1	13	1	15·8	
			1	2	3		
Huff, H.J.	USA	100m	1	12	1	11·4	
			2	3	2	11·1	
		200m	1	2	1	22·8	
			2	2	3		
Huijen, J.	HOL	10 mile walk	1	2	DNF		
		3½k walk	1	3	7	17-43·0	
Hurdsfield, S.	GBR	200m	1	9	1	23·6	
			2	3	4		
Hussey, E.R.J.	GBR	110m hurdles	1	11	1	16·8	
			2	1	2		
Hutcheon, E.H.	AUS	Standing high jump	Q		DNQ		
Irons, F.C.	USA	Standing long jump	Q		DNQ		
		Standing high jump	F		=8	1,42	
		Long jump	F		1	7,48*	G
		Triple jump	Q		DNQ		
Jack, T.	GBR	Marathon	F		DNF		
Jacobs, C.S.	USA	Pole vault	F		=3	3,58	B
Jaccuemin, V.	BEL	100m	1	6	2	11·5	
		400m	1	10	DNF		
Jakobsson, E.B.	FIN	Javelin throw free style	Q		DNQ		
		Javelin throw	Q		DNQ		
Jakoosson, J.	FIN	Standing long jump	Q		DNQ		
		Javelin throw free style	Q		DNQ		
		Javelin throw	Q		DNQ		
Jardin, H.	FRA	Standing long jump	Q		DNQ		
		Standing high jump	Q		DNQ		
Jaervinen, W.	FIN	Shot put	Q		DNQ		
		Discus throw	F		4	39,43	
		Discus throw Greek style	F		3	36.48	B
		Javelin throw free style	Q		DNQ		
Jesina, F.	HUN	Discus throw	Q		DNQ		
		Discus throw Greek style	Q		DNQ		
		Javelin throw free style	Q		DNQ		
Johannsen, J.	NCR	100m	1	5	2		
		Javelin throw free style	Q		DNQ		
		Javelin throw	Q		DNQ		
Jorgensen, J.F.	DEN	5 miles	1	2	3	28-08·8	
		Marathon	F		23	3-47-44·0	
Jones, L.P.	USA	800m	1	4	3	1-58·6	
Just, T.H.	GBR	Medley relay	1	3	2		
		800m	1	6	1	1-57·8	
			F		5	1-56·4	
Kelly, D.	USA	Long jump	F		2	7,09	S
Kemp, J	FIN	Javelin throw free style	Q		DNQ		
Kerr, H.E.	AUS	10 mile walk	1	2	3	1:18-40·2	
			F		DNF		
		3½ walk	1	1	2	16-02·2	
			F		3	15-43·4	B
Kerr, F.	CAN	100m	1	10	1	11·0	
			2	2	1	11·0	
			F		3	11·0	B
		200m	1	11	1	22·2	
			2	1	1	22·6	
			F		1	22·6	G
Kiely, L.A.	GBR	110m hurdles	1	4	1		
			2	3	3		
Kinahan, C.E.	GBR	110m hurdles	1	12	1	16·8	
			1	4	2		
Kinchin, J.W.	GBR	3200m steeplechase	1	5	2		
Kiralfy, E.G.	USA	100m	1	4	4		
Kitching, F.O.	GBR	Standing long jump	Q		DNQ		
Knott, F.A.	GBR	1500	1	1	4		
Knyvett, W.A.	GBR	110m hurdles	1	7	1		
			2	2	15·6		
Koczan, M.	HUN	Javelin throw free style	Q		DNQ		
		Shot put	Q		DNQ		
		Discus throw	Q		DNQ		
Koeger, G.	FRA	Pole vault	Q		DNQ		
Kohlmey, W.	GER	100m	1	15	3	12·0	
Konings, _	BEL	100m	1	4	2	11·6	
Koops, E.	HOL	100m	1	3	4		
		200m	1	3	4		
		400m hurdles	1	1	1		
			2	1	DNF		
		Standing long jump	Q		DNQ		
		Medley relay	1	2	2		
Kovacs, N.	HUN	110m hurdles	1	10	2		
		400m hurdles	1	9	1		
			2	2	DNF		
Kovesdi, G.	HUN	Long jump	Q		DNQ		
Laaftman, S.	SWE	200m	1	6	1	23·8	
		400m	1	4	3		
		Medley relay	1	1	2		
Lagarde, C.	FRA	Shot put	Q		DNQ		
		Discus throw	Q		DNQ		
Lamotte, G.	FRA	100m	1	11	3		

Name	Country	Event	Round	Heat	Place	Result	Medal
Spencer, E.A.	GBR	10 mile walk	1	1	3	1:21-25·4	
			F		3	1:21-20·2	B
Spitzer, R.A.	USA	3200m steeplechase	1	5	3		
Stafford, L.H.G.	GBR	Standing long jump	Q		DNQ		
		Standing high jump	Q		DNQ		
Stark, J.P.	GBR	100m	1	16	1	11·8	
			2	4	3		
		200m	1	11	2		
Stenberg, R.	FIN	100m	1	7	5		
		200m	1	4	3		
Stenborg, K.	SWE	100m	1	7	2		
		200m	1	2	4		
		Medley relay	1	1	2		
Stevens, L.B.	USA	100m	1	8	1	11·2	
			2	1	4		
Stevenson, S.	GBR	5 miles	1	5	3	26-17·0	
		Marathon	F		DNF		
Stupart, D.A.	SAF	110m hurdles	1	1	3		
		Triple jump	F		10	13,40	
Sullivan, J.P.	USA	1500m	1	1	1	4-07·6	
			F		DNF		
Sustera, M.	BOH	Discus throw	Q		DNQ		
		Discus throw Greek style	Q		DNQ		
Sutton, H.	AUS	800m	1	8	DNF		
Svanberg, J.F.	SWE	5 miles	1	1	1	25-46·2*	
			F		3	25-37·2	B
		Marathon	F		8	3:07-50·8	
		3 mile team race	1	2	3	21	
Svanstroem, F.	FIN	800m	1	7	DNF		
		1500m	1	5	3	4-25·2	
Szathmary, C.	HUN	Pole vault	F		8	3,35	
Tait, J.	CAN	1500m	1	5	1	4-12·2	
			F		4	4-06·8	
		5 miles	1	4	DNF		
		Marathon	F		DNF		
Talbot, L.J.	USA	Hammer throw	F		5	47,86	
		Shot put	F		5	12,93	
		Discus throw	Q		DNQ		
		Discus throw Greek style	Q		DNQ		
Tarella, G.	ITA	400m	1	11	3		
Taylor, J.B.	USA	400m	1	4	1	50·8	
			2	3	1	49·8	
		Medley relay	1	3	1	3-27·2	
			F		1	3-29·4	G
Tewanina, L.	USA	Marathon	F		9	3:09-15·0	
Thompson, F.B.	GBR	Marathon	F		DNF		
Tison, A.	FRA	Shot put	Q		DNQ		
		Discus throw	F		7	38,30	
Toernros, G.	SWE	Marathon	F		21	3:30-20·8	
Torretta, G.	ITA	100m	1	16	2	12·0	
Tremeer, L.F.	GBR	400m hurdles	1	10	1		
			2	4	1	60·6	
			F		3	57·0	B
		Javelin throw	Q		DNQ		
Trieloff, O.P.	GER	400m	1	14	2	50·9	
		Medley relay	1	2	1	3-43·2	
			F		2	3-32·4	S
Trube, H.L.	USA	3 mile team race	1	2	1	10	
			F		2	19	S
Tsiclitiras, C.	GRE	Standing long jump	F		2	3,22	S
		Standing high jump	F		=2	1,55	S
Uetwiller, L.	GER	Hammer throw	Q		DNQ		
		Discus throw	Q		DNQ		
		Long jump	Q		DNQ	6,05	
		Standing long jump	Q		DNQ		
		Javelin throw free style	Q		DNQ		

Name	Country	Event	Round	Heat	Place	Result	Medal
Van Leeuwen, H.W.	HOL	High jump	Q		DNQ	1,63	
Voigt, E.R.	GBR	5 miles	1	2	1	26-13·4	
			F		1	25-11·2*	G
Von Bonning-hausen, H.	GER	100m	1	14	5		
Vosbergen, A.C.H.	HOL	800m	1	6	DNF		
		1500m	1	6	3	4-38·2	
		5 miles	1	5	DNF		
		Marathon	F		DNF		
		3 mile team race	1	1	DNF		
Wagner, J.	SUI	Hammer throw	Q		DNQ		
Wakker, W.W.	HOL	5 miles	1	2	DNF		
		Marathon	F		20	3:28-49·0	
		3 mile team race	1	1	DNF		
Wal, H.J.W.	HOL	100m	1	2	3		
		400m	1	14	4		
		800m	1	1	DNF		
Walker, R.E.	SAF	100m	1	4	1	11·0	
			2	1	1	10·8*	
			F		1	10·8*	G
Walsh, C.	CAN	Hammer throw	F		3	48,50	B
Walters, D.W.	GBR	110m hurdles	1	6	1	17·8	
			2	1	3		
Watson, H.	GBR	100m	1	14	3		
Watt, W.F.C.	GBR	Long jump	Q		DNQ		
Webb, E.J.	GBR	10 mile walk	1	1	1	1:20-18·8*	
			F		2	1:17-31·0	S
		3½k walk	1	2	1	15-17·2	
			F		2	15-07·4	S
Weinstein, A.	GER	Long jump	F		7	6,77	
Welton, A.R.	USA	Marathon	F		4	2:59-44·4	
Welz, E.	GER	Discus throw	F		9	37,00	
		Discus throw Greek style	Q		DNQ		
Westergaard, C.P.M.	CAN	10 mile walk	1	2	DNF		
		3½k walk	1	2	2	17-07·0	
			F		6		
Wiegant, A.J.A.	SWE	5 miles	1	5	DNF		
		3 mile team race	1	2	3	21	
Wieslander, H.K.	SWE	Long jump	Q		DNQ		
		Shot put	Q		DNQ		
		Discus throw	Q		DNQ		
		Javelin throw	Q		DNQ		
Wiesner, F.	HUN	100m	1	14	4		
		200m	1	6	2	24·0	
Wilhelm, R.	GER	2½k walk	1	3	6	17-33·8	
Williams, C.H.	GBR	Long jump	Q		DNQ		
Wilskman, L.	FIN	Discus throw	Q		DNQ		
		Discus throw Greek style	Q		DNQ		
Wilson, G.H.	GBR	High jump	Q		DNQ	1,72	
Wilson, H.A.	GBR	1500m	1	7	1	4-11·4	
			F		2	4-03·6	S
		3 mile team race	1	1	1	6	
			F		1	6	G
Winkelmann, W.F.	HOL	10 mile walk	1	1	DNF		
		3½k walk	1	2	4	17-57·6	
Withers, G.R.J.	GBR	10 mile walk	1	2	5	1:19-22·4	
Wood, W.	CAN	Marathon	F		5	3:01-44·0	
Wyatt, A.	GBR	Marathon	F		DNF		
Yeomans, A.T.	GBR	10 mile walk	1	1	DNF		
Yorke, R.F.C.	GBR	3200m steeplechase	1	4	DIS		
Young, G.W.	GBR	400m	1	16	1	52·4	
			2	1	4		
Zilliacus, B.	FIN	Shot put	Q		DNQ		
Zouras, C.	GRE	Javelin throw free style	F		4	48,61	
		Javelin throw	Q		DNQ		

The Disqualification of Jim Thorpe

New stadiums were built at Stockholm for the 1912 Games, and the enthusiastic Swedes were rewarded with fine weather throughout. There were no disputes, and a carnival atmosphere lasted to the end.

The only controversy connected with the Games came afterwards, when the great American athlete Jim Thorpe, who won both the pentathlon and the decathlon, was disqualified and his medals taken back when it was discovered he had played baseball for money. Seventy years later he was re-instated, but he had died a poor man years earlier.

Men's Track Events

The sprinting in the **100 metres** was of a high standard and only the winners of the six second round heats proceeded to the final. This was an unfair arrangement, as two eliminated sprinters had equalled the existing Olympic record of 10·8 sec. Donald Lippincott of the USA set a new Olympic record of 10·6 in heat 16, in a close finish with Willie Applegarth of Britain and along with Howard Drew, the coloured US sprinter, was favourite. Unfortunately Drew was injured and unable to run. The athletes were very nervous and it took eight starts to get them away; surprisingly nobody was disqualified. George Patching of South Africa was quickest into his running and was half a metre clear at 40 metres. However, Ralph Craig of the USA was accelerating and he edged in front at the 75-metres mark, with fellow American Alvah Meyer at his shoulder. Craig just won in 10·8 with Meyer taking second in 10·9 from a fast closing Donald Lippincott, also timed at 10·9. Patching and Frank Belote of the USA were only inches behind.

As in the short sprint, the same system of only winners qualifying for the final also prevailed in the **200 metres**, where ropes were laid down on the track to form lanes. Richard Rau of Germany had a poor start, but the rest were away together and Willie Applegarth of Britain had a slight lead entering the home straight with Ralph Craig spearheading the American contingent. Craig, with his fellow countryman Donald Lippincott on his shoulder, eased past Applegarth to take first and second places respectively in 21·7 sec and 21·8. Applegarth held on to third position and finished in 22·0 from a fast finishing Rau.

With only five races and just five qualifiers for the final, the second round heats of the **400 metres** were fiercely contested. The heats had been run without lanes, but these were provided for the final. James Meredith of America set off at a hot pace and led down the back straight pulling back the stagger on Hanns Braun of Germany who was running in the lane outside him. Braun put in a major effort around the final bend, as did Charles Reidpath of the USA, who passed the

German 15 metres from the tape to record a fine win in 48·2 sec and achieve a world and Olympic record. Braun was timed in 48·3 for second place, while Edward Lindberg of the USA came through over the latter stages to clock 48·4 for third place.

There was an unprecedented high standard in the **800 metres**. In the first heat of the second round even the seventh runner clocked 1-55·6 and was still three places away from qualifying. Emilio Lunghi, the world record holder, also missed the final after finishing fifth in his heat. Right from the gun getting the final underway, Mel Sheppard of the USA led the field at a very sharp pace and passed the 400 in 52·6 sec. Sheppard was closely trailed by his compatriot, Ted Meredith, Hanns Braun of Germany and two other Americans, Ira Davenport and Charles Edmundson. But at the finish, Meredith just squeezed past him to win in 1-51·9, a new world and Olympic record. Sheppard clocked 1-52·0 for the silver medal, just shutting out Davenport, who was given the same time.

The top Europeans faced the crack Americans in the **1,500 metres** final with Abel Kiviat, the US world record holder, starting as favourite. Henri Arnaud of France shot away and led for two laps with the rest of the field playing a waiting game behind him. At the bell, Kiviat piled on the pace, but his strike was not decisive and with 300 metres to go Arnold Jackson of Britain made his move from sixth position and began pulling back the runners ahead of him. With long powerful strides he swept by to a three-metre win in 3-56·8, a new Olympic record. Kiviat just held on to take second place from his fellow American, Norman Taber, who was catching up fast. They both stopped the watch at 3-56·9.

There were three heats in the **3,000 metres team race**, in which Hannes Kolehmainen of Finland recorded the fine time of 8-36·9. Only three teams contested the final, America winning with 9 points from Sweden 13 and Britain 23. The individual winner was Tell Berna who stretched the field over the last lap to win in 8-44·6 from Thorild Ohlsson of Sweden, also 8-44·6 and Norman Taber of the USA 8-45·2.

Run only two days after a gruelling series of 10,000 metres competitions, the **5,000 metres** is best remembered for the classical dual between two superb runners, Hannes Kolehmainen of Finland and Jean Bouin of France. In the final Kolehmainen immediately went into the lead followed by Bouin and George Bonhag of the USA, with George Hutson of Britain and Louis Scott of the USA just behind. Kolehmainen soon became tired of the company and injected a spurt to which only Bouin was able to respond, leaving Bonhag to lead the rest of the field. Then it was Bouin's turn to kick, but he could not lose his adversary. At the bell, Bouin tried again but Kolehmainen matched him stride for stride and with only 20 metres remaining, the Finn forced himself ahead to win in the stunning time of

France and James Soutter for Britain. Sheppard made a fast get-away, closely followed by Lelong, but Soutter was slow into his running and lost more than 30 metres in the first leg, due to a muscle pull he had sustained in the heats. America increased her lead during the following three laps with the help of Ed Lindberg, James Meredith and Charles Reidpath and clocked a new world and Olympic record of 3-16·6. France was second in 3-20·7 and Britain third with 3-23·2.

Men's Field Events

Earlier that year George Horine of the USA had set a new **high jump** world record of 2,01 metres using a revolutionary technique called the "western roll" and so much was expected of him at the Games. Eleven jumpers qualified at 1,83, of which seven repeated their performance the following day in the finals. At 1,87 five men were clear: Alma Richards, George Horine, Egon Erickson and Jim Thorpe of the USA together with Hans Liesche of Germany. At 1,89 Erickson and Thorpe were eliminated. The next height of 1,91 saw Liesche over first time, and Richards on his third, but at 1,93 it was Richards who jumped the bar at his first attempt for a new Olympic record before the nervous Liesche failed completely. Horine took the bronze at 1,89.

Following the preliminaries, 11 men qualified for the **pole vault** final by succeeding at 3,65 metres. Seven of these cleared 3,75 and exceeded the old Olympic record. There was a tie at 3,85 for the silver medal between the Americans Frank Nelson and Marc Wright, the current world record holder, while Harry Babcock of the USA cleared 3,90 and 3,95 to take the gold medal. Babcock then made three valiant attempts at the world record height of 4,06 without succeeding.

In the **long jump**, competitors were divided into three pools for the preliminary three jumps. Albert Gutterson of the USA led with a brilliant Olympic record of 7,60, within a centimetre of the world record, while Calvin Bricker of Canada laid claim to the silver position with 7,21. George Aberg of Sweden jumped 7,04, but then improved in the final rounds to 7,18 to clinch the bronze.

All the big jumps occurred in the three qualifying pools of the **triple jump** and was a clean sweep for the Swedes. On his very first attempt Gustaf Lindblom sprinted fast down the runway and exceeded his own expectations with a hop, step and jump of 14,76 metres to take first place. It was not long before George Aberg added the triple jump silver medal to his long jump silver with 14,51 and Erik Almlof completed Sweden's day with 14,17 for the bronze position.

The **standing jumps** consisted of a long and a high jump for which medals were awarded for each competition. The Adams brothers of America were prominent in both competitions, picking up four medals between them, with the Greek jumper Constantin Tsiclitiras taking the other two. Platt Adams won the standing high jump with 1,63 metres from brother Ben at 1,60 and Tsiclitiras at 1,55, all using a scissors technique. The long jump was effected with the toes over the edge of the sandpit. But this time Tsiclitiras won with 3,37 while Platt Adams was just one centimetre behind and Ben Adams achieved 3,28 for the bronze.

Ralph Rose of the USA was the world record holder at 15,54 metres for the **shot put**, all 6ft 5½in and 280lb of him, and it was inconceivable that he would be beaten — but he was. Rose threw 15,25 in the second round of the preliminaries against fellow American Pat McDonald's

14,78, but in the fourth round McDonald unleashed a lifetime best of 15,34 and won with an Olympic record. Well down in third place was another American, Lawrence Whitney, who threw 13,93, with Elmer Niklander, the favoured Finn, having an off day.

For the only time in Olympic history a **shot put, both hands** competition was held. Ralph Rose of the USA took his revenge on compatriot Pat McDonald by throwing 15,23 metres with his right hand and 12,47 with his left for a total of 27,70. McDonald achieved 15,08 + 12,45 for 27,53 and Elmer Niklander of Finland recorded 14,71 + 12,43 for 27,14.

The favourite for the **discus throw** was James Duncan of the USA who had only that year raised the world record to 47,58 metres. To save time, the 40 competitors were divided into five pools. Strangely, only the leading three were allowed to take three further throws — also apparently to save time! Armas Taipale of Finland won with a new Olympic record of 45,21, and Dickie Byrd of the USA surprisingly took the silver with 42,32 from his vaunted colleague Duncan, who threw 42,28.

In a one off competition, never again held at an Olympic Games, the Scandinavians dominated the **discus throw, both hands** competition. There were two pools with the best three overall receiving three further throws with each hand. Predictably, Armas Taipale of Finland won with a right hand effort of 44,68 metres and a left hand effort of 38,18 for a total of 82,86. Elmer Niklander, also of Finland, threw 40,28 + 37,68 for 77,96 and Emil Magnusson of Sweden achieved 40,58 + 36,79 for 77,37.

Matt McGrath of the USA won the **hammer throw** as he pleased. It was in the preliminary rounds of two pools that the event was virtually decided when McGrath commenced with a throw of 54,13 metres and improved to 54,74 for the gold medal. Duncan Gillis took second place with 48,39, while Clarence Childs reached 48,17, despite a twisted ankle sustained in training.

Erik Lemming of Sweden had been the master of **javelin throwing** in the world for 13 years while Juho Saaristo of Finland had recently become the world record holder, so a good competition was in prospect. Both were capable of throwing 60 metres, as was Mor Koczan of Hungary, who was also known as Kovacs. Lemming eventually secured the gold in the fourth round with a throw of 60,64, although it was only in the sixth and final round that Saaristo threw 58,66 for the silver and Koczan lofted one out to 55,50 for the bronze.

As with the shot and discus there was a **javelin throw, both hands** competition, again held only at these Games. The winner was Juho Saaristo of Finland, with an excellent 61.00 metres with his right hand and 48,42 with his left for 109,42. Two other Finns, Vaino Siikaniemi, who threw 54,09 + 47,04 to total 101,13 and Urho Peltonen, who achieved 53,58 + 46,66 for 100,24, took the silver and bronze.

Although a **pentathlon** had been held at Athens in 1906, the events had now been standardised to long jump, javelin, 200 metres, discus and 1,500 metres. The winner of this event, Jim Thorpe, an American Indian, was head and shoulders above his contemporaries. He was a brilliant athlete who shone in many sports and it was said there were only three sports he did not play: cricket, croquet and golf. He won four of the five events in the pentathlon outright to score six points. Some months after the Olympics at Stockholm he was asked to return the medals he had won in the pentathlon and decathlon, because during college vacations he had played professional baseball. The credited winner of the event thus became Ferdinand Bie of Norway with 16 points from Jim Donahue of the USA with 24 points and Frank Lukeman of Canada also 24. Second place went to Donahue as he had scored more points according to the decathlon tables.

The Olympic **decathlon** was an invention of the Swedes to discover the greatest all-round athlete. This they did in Jim Thorpe. the American Indian who won the competition with 8,412·995 points from Hugo Wieslander of Sweden with 7,724·495 and Charles Lomberg, also of Sweden, with 7,413·51 points. Following Thorpe's disqualification for professionalism, the lesser medallists were promoted one place, and third position given to Gosta Holmer of Sweden.

Pat McDonald, from New York, the surprise winner of the shot put.

Dave Terry

COMPETITOR	COUNTRY CODE	EVENT	ROUND	HEAT	PLACE	TIME & DISTANCE	MEDAL
Caulle, J.	FRA	800m	1	1	5		
Charkov, N.	URS	1500m	1	5	7		
Childs, C.C.	USA	Hammer throw	F		3	48,17	B
Chisholm, G.A.	USA	110m hurdles	1	1	1	15.3	
			2	4	2		
Choultz, A.	URS	Long jump	F		21	6,15	
		Decathlon	F		10	6134.47	
Christiansen, L.	DEN	Cross country	F		14	49-06.4	
Christiensen, J.	DEN	Marathon	F		29	3:21-57.4	
Colbacchini, D.	ITA	110m hurdles	1	8	2	16.1	
			2	2	2	16.0	
Cooke, C.C.	USA	200m	1	7	1	22.2	
			2	3	2		
		4×100m relay	1	2	1	43.7	
			2	1	DIS		
Corkery, J.J.	CAN	Marathon	F		DNF		
Cortesao, A.Z.	POR	400m	1	3	3		
		800m	1	3	2		
			2	2	9		
Cottrill, W.	GBR	1500m	1	7	3		
		Cross country	F		DNF		
		3000m team race	F		3	23	B
Courtney, J.I.	USA	100m	1	3	1	11.2	
			2	1	2		
		200m	1	3	1	22.7	
			2	1	3		
		4×100m relay	1	2	1	43.7	
			2	1	DIS		
Coyle, F.J.	USA	Pole vault	F		=8	3,65	
Craig, R.C.	USA	100m	1	17	1	11.2	
			2	4	1	10.7	
			F		1	10.8	G
		200m	1	2	1	22.8	
			2	1	1	21.9	
			F		1	21.7	G
Dahl, J.	SWE	Javelin throw	F		15	45,67	
Dahl, N.	NOR	Cross country	F		DNF		
Dahlberg, H.	SWE	Marathon	F		27	3:13-32.4	
Dahlin, J.	SWE	400m	1	8	2	51.0	
			2	1	DNS		
		4×400m relay	1	3	2	3-25.0	
Danild, F.	DEN	Cross country	F		DNF		
D'Arcy, V.H.A.	GBR	100m	1	5	1	11.2	
			2	5	4		
		200m	1	10	2		
			2	6	2		
		4×100m relay	1	3	1	45.0	
			2	1	1	43.0*	
			F		1	42.4	G
Davenport, I.N.	USA	400m	1	12	2		
			2	5	2		
		800m	1	5	1	1-59.0	
			2	1	4	1-55.9	
			F		3	1-52.0	B
Decoteau, A.	CAN	5000m	1	1	2	15-24.2	
			F		8		
Delaby, M.F.L.	FRA	100m	1	10	3		
		110m hurdles	1	6	1	16.0	
			2	2	3	16.2	
Delloye, F.	BEL	1500m	1	3	6		
De Mar, C.H.	USA	Marathon	F		12	2:50-46.6	
De Stieglitz, P.	URS	100m	1	13	4		
Devan, I.	HUN	200m	1	15	2		
		400m	1	5	3		
		4×400m relay	1	3	3	3-29.4	
Donahue, J.J.	USA	Pentathlon	F		2	24	S
		Decathlon	F		4	7083.45	
Dorizas, M.	GRE	Discus throw	F		13	39,28	
		Shot put	F		11	12,05	
Drew, H.P.	USA	100m	1	15	1	11.0	
			2	1	1	11.0	
			F		DNS		
Drubina, I.	HUN	10k walk	1	2	DIS		
Duffy, J.	CAN	Marathon	F		5	2:42-18.8	
Dukes, G.B.	USA	Pole vault	F		=8	3,65	
Dumbill, T.H.	GBR	10k walk	1	2	3	50-57.6	
			F		DIS		
Duncan, J.H.	USA	Discus throw	F		3	42,28	B
		Discus throw both hands	F		5	71,13	
Duncan, R.C.	GBR	100m	1	9	3		
		200m	1	12	2		
			2	6	4		
Edmundson, C.S.	USA	400m	1	11	1	50.2	
			2	1	2		
		800m	1	4	1	1-56.5	
			2	2	2	1-55.8	
			F		7		
Ehrnreich, P.	AUT	Long jump	F		22	6,14	
Eitel, P.	CHI	100m	1	3	6		
		200m	1	11	5		
		110m hurdles	1	5	1	17.1	
			2	1	4		
Ekberg, O.R.	SWE	100m	1	17	3		
Ekberg, R.	SWE	Standing long jump	F		13	3,03	
Eke, J.	SWE	10000m	1	1	4	34-55.8	
		Cross country	F		3	46-37.6	B
Ekman, L.	SWE	Standing high jump	Q		DNQ	1,45	
Eller, J.J.	USA	110m hurdles	1	2	1	16.0	
			2	1	2	15.7	
		Pentathlon	F		DNF		
Enight, H.B.	USA	High jump	Q		DNQ	1,80	
Erickson, E.R.	USA	High jump	F		4	1,87	
Ericksson, H.	SWE	Pentathlon	F		DNF		
Erxleben, J.	USA	Marathon	F		8	2:45-47.2	
Eskola, J.	FIN	Cross country	F		4	46-54.8	
Fabre, E.	CAN	Marathon	F		11	2:50-36.2	
Failliot, P.	FRA	100m	1	3	4		
		200m	1	11	3		
		Pentathlon	F		DNF		
		Decathlon	F		DNF		
		4×100m relay	1	6	2	43.8	
		4×400m relay	1	3	1	3-22.5	
			F		2	3-20.7	S
Falk, E.	SWE	Javelin throw	F		NP	0	
Farrell, E.L.	USA	Long jump	F		=12	6,71	
		Triple jump	F		13	13,57	
Finnerud, P.	NOR	Cross country	F		20	51-16.2	
Fitzgerald, E.J.	USA	5000m	1	2	7		
Fixdal, N.	NOR	Long jump	F		=12	6,71	
		Triple jump	F		8	13,96	
Fjastad, N.	SWE	Pentathlon	F		DNF		
Fleetwood, F.	SWE	Discus throw	F		28	35,06	
		Discus throw both hands	F		7	68,22	
Fleischer, F.	AUT	100m	1	17	4		
		200m	1	13	3		
		4×100m relay	1	5	2	44.8	
Fletcher, F.	USA	Standing high jump	Q		DNQ	1,45	
		Standing long jump	F		9	3,11	
Fock, B.	SWE	10000m	1	2	6		
		Cross country	F		17	50-15.8	
		3000m team race	1	2	1	9	
			F		2	13	S
Fonbaek, O.	NOR	Marathon	F		DNF		
Forgacs, F.	HUN	800m	1	6	4		
		1500m	1	3	5		
Forshaw, J.	USA	Marathon	F		1	2:49-49.4	
Forsyth, W.C.	CAN	Marathon	F		15	2:52-23.0	
Fothi, S.	HUN	Discus throw	F		25	36,37	
Francom, S.	GBR	Marathon	F		DNF		
Franzl, V.	AUT	Long jump	F		17	6,57	
		Pole vault	Q		DNQ	3,00	
Frisell, E.	SWE	800m	1	9	3		
Fritz, W.H.	USA	Pole vault	F		=8	3,65	
Frykberg, N.	SWE	1500m	1	6	4		
		3000m team race	1	2	1	9	
			F		2	13	S
Gayevsky, P.	URS	400m	1	11	4		
		800m	1	1	6		
Gallagher, J.J.	USA	Marathon	F		7	2:44-19.4	
Gallon, T.H.	CAN	400m	1	12	3		
		4×400m relay	1	1	2	3-22.2	
Gerhardt, P.C.	USA	100m	1	12	1	11.1	
			2	1	3	10.9	
		200m	1	10	1	22.9	
			2	5	2		
Gille, K.	SWE	Pole vault	Q		DNQ	3,60	
Gillis, D.	CAN	Discus throw	F		14	39,01	
		Hammer throw	F		2	48,39	S
Giongo, F.	ITA	100m	1	9	2		
			2	4	2		
		200m	1	8	2		
			2	5	6		
		400m	1	10	3		
Gitsham, C.W.	SAF	Marathon	F		2	2:37-52.0	S

COMPETITOR	COUNTRY CODE	EVENT	ROUND	HEAT	PLACE	TIME & DISTANCE	MEDAL
Glover, E.	GBR	5000m	1	3	2	16-09-1	
			F		DNF		
		Cross country	F		16	49-53 7	
		10000m	1	1	5	35-12 8	
Goehring, L.	USA	Standing high jump	F		=4	1,50	
		Standing long jump	F		6	3,14	
Gonder, F.	FRA	Pole vault	Q		DNQ	3,50	
Goulding, G.H.	CAN	10k walk	1	1	1	47-14-5*	
			F		1	46-28-4*	G
Grandell, E.	SWE	200m	1	4	5		
Green, H.	GBR	Marathon	F		14	2:52-11-4	
Grijseels, J.	HOL	100m	1	7	4		
		200m	1	4	2		
			2	4	6		
Grumpelt, H.J.	USA	High jump	F		=5	1,85	
Gruener, W.	SWE	Marathon	F		DNF		
Gutterson, A.L.	USA	Long jump	F		1	7,60*	G
Guttman, D.	SWE	Marathon	F		DNF		
Gylche, W.E.	DEN	10k walk	1	2	4	51-13-8	
			F		DNF		
Hack, K.	AUT	Marathon	F		DNF		
Hackberg, W.	SWE	Hammer throw	F		13	38,44	
		Decathlon	F		DNF		
Haff, C.B.	USA	400m	1	7	1	50-4	
			2	4	1	49-7	
			F		5	49-5	
Hagander, S.	SWE	Javelin throw both hands	F		11	86,80	
Haglund, K.	SWE	800m	1	6	6		
Hahne, H.	URS	200m	1	3	5		
Haldorsson, J.	ISL	100m	1	8	4		
Haley, E.W.	GBR	200m	1	11	4		
		400m	1	2	1	1-06-6	
			2	4	4		
Hallberg, G.	SWE	High jump	Q		DNQ	1,75	
Halme, J.	FIN	Triple jump	F		11	13,79	
		Javelin throw	F		4	54,65	
		Javelin throw both hands	F		9	88,54	
Halpin, T.J.	USA	800m	1	9	4		
		Decathlon	F		DNF		
Halse, A.	NOR	Javelin throw	F		7	51,98	
		Javelin throw both hands	F		5	96,92	
Halt, K.	GER	Javelin throw	F		22	41,99	
		Shot put	F		14	11,16	
		Pentathlon	F		DNF		
		Decathlon	F		8	6682-445	
Hammersley, R.	CHI	Standing high jump	Q		DNQ	1,40	
Happeny, W.	CAN	Pole vault	F		=4	3,80	B
Hare, A.	GBR	1500m	1	1	3	4-39-4	
Harju, E.	FIN	1500m	1	7	4		
		Cross country	F		DNF		
		3000m team race	1	1	2	12	
Harleman, C.	SWE	Pole vault	Q		DNQ	3,60	
Hawkins, M.W.	USA	110m hurdles	1	3	1	16-1	
			2	2	1	15-7	
			F		3	15-3	B
Hedlund, F.	USA	1500m	1	6	2	4-10-8	
			F		10	4-04-1	
Heikkila, W.	FIN	Cross country	F		25	54-08-0	
Heiland, A.W.	USA	100m	1	13	3		
		200m	1	5	2		
			2	2	5		
Hellawell, H.H.	USA	10000m	1	1	12		
		Cross country	F		12	48-12-0	
Hellgren, E.	SWE	Cross country	F		DNF		
Henderson, W.E.B.	GBR	Discus throw	F		32	33,61	
Henley, E.J.	GBR	400m	1	11	2		
			2	3	6		
		800m	1	9	1	1-57-6	
			2	2	7		
		4×400m relay	1	1	1	3-19-0*	
			F		3	3-23-2	B
Hermann, M.	GER	100m	1	16	3		
		200m	1	15	1	22-9	
			2	3	4		
		400m	1	7	3		
		4×100m relay	1	5	1	43-6	
			2	3	1	42-3*	
			F		DIS		
Heuet, G.	FRA	5000m	1	5	6		
		10000m	1	1	3	34-50-0	
Hibbins, F.N.	GBR	5000m	1	4	3	15-27-6	
			F		10		
		10000m	1	2	10		
		Cross country	F		15	49-18-2	
Hill, G.N.	USA	5000m	1	1	4	15-56-8	
		10000m	1	3	7		

COMPETITOR	COUNTRY CODE	EVENT	ROUND	HEAT	PLACE	TIME & DISTANCE	MEDAL
Holden, H.W.	USA	800m	1	6	1	1-58-1	
			2	2	6		
Holmberg, C.A.	DEN	Cross country	F		26	54-24-9	
Holmer, G.	SWE	Pentathlon	F		DNF		
		Decathlon	F		3	7347-855	B
Honzatko, B.	BOH	Marathon	F		DNF		
Horine, G.L.	USA	High jump	F		3	1,89	B
Hovdenak, O.	NOR	Cross country	F		19	50-40-8	
Howard, J.A.	CAN	100m	1	13	1	11-0	
			2	5	5		
		200m	1	8	1	25-0	
			2	4	3		
		4×100m relay	1	1	1	46-2	
			2	3	2	43-5	
		4×400m relay	1	1	2	3-22-2	
Hulford, F.H.	GBR	800m	1	5	2		
			2	1	7		
		1500m	1	6	6		
Humphreys, F.	GER	10000m	1	2	9		
		Cross country	F		18	50-28-0	
Hutson, G.W.	GER	5000m	1	2	3	15-29-0	
			F		3	15-07-6	B
		3000m team race	F		3	23	B
Indricson, A.	URS	1500m	1	4	6		
Irons, F.	USA	Long jump	F		8	6,80	
Jackson, A.N.S.	GBR	1500m	1	4	1	4-10-8	
			F		1	3-56-8*	G
Jacobs, D.H.	GBR	100m	1	10	1	10-8	
			2	3	2		
		200m	1	17	1	23-2	
			2	1	2		
		4×100m relay	1	3	1	45-0	
			2	1	1	43-0*	
			F		1	42-4	G
Jacobsson, Sigfrid	SWE	Marathon	F		6	2:43-24-9	
Jacobsson, Skotte	SWE	100m	1	14	4		
		200m	1	17	2		
			2	2	6		
		Triple jump	F		17	13,33	
		Decathlon	F		DNF		
Jahn, W.	GER	800m	1	4	4	2-02-0	
Jahnzon, C.	SWE	Hammer throw	F		8	42,58	
Janda, F.	BOH	Discus throw	F		17	38,31	
		Shot put	F		15	11,15	
Jankovich, I.	HUN	100m	1	3	2		
			2	4	3		
		4×100m relay	1	6	1	43-7	
			2	2	2	42-9	
Jaerviner, W.	FIN	Discus throw	F		15	38,60	
		Discus throw both hands	F		12	66,69	
Jensen, C.J.	DEN	Cross country	F		DNF		
Jiranek, L.	BOH	100m	1	3	5		
Jirsak, J.	BOH	Pole vault	Q		DNQ	3,00	
Johansen, D.	NOR	Javelin throw both hands	F		7	98,82	
		Javelin throw	F		12	47,61	
Johansson, F.W.	FIN	5000m	1	5	3	15-31-4	
			F		DNF		
		Cross country	F		11	48-03-0	
		3000m team race	F		1	12	
Johnsson, G.	SWE	Hammer throw	F		11	39,92	
Johnstone, J.O.	USA	High jump	F		=5	1,85	
Jones, J.P.	USA	800m	1	3	1	2-01-8	
			2	1	DNS		
		1500m	1	4	2	4-12-4	
			F		4	3-57-2	
		Cross country	F		DNF		
			1	3	1	2-01-8	
Kaiser, F.H.	USA	10k walk	1	2	5	51-31-8	
			F		DNF		
Kallberg, A.	FIN	Marathon	F		DNF		
Kanakuri, S.	JPN	Marathon	F		DNF		
Kapmal, A.	URS	Marathon	F		DNF		
Karlsson, M.	SWE	5000m	1	3	1	15-34-6	
			F		6	15-18-6	
		10000m	1	2	3	33-06-2	
			F		DNF		
Karpati, O.	HUN	Marathon	F		31	3:25-21-6	
Keeper, J.	CAN	5000m	1	2	2	15-28-9	
			F		9		
		10000m	1	1	2	33-58-8	
			F		4	32-36-2	
Kellaway, H.G.	GBR	Marathon	F		DNF		
Kelly, F.W.	USA	110m hurdles	1	9	1	16-4	
			2	5	1	15-6	
			F		1	15-1	G

COMPETITOR	COUNTRY CODE	EVENT	ROUND	HEAT	PLACE	TIME & DISTANCE	MEDAL
Kern, E.	GER	100m	1	15	2		
			2	1	5		
		4×100m relay	1	5	1	43·6	
			2	3	1	42·3*	
			F		DIS		
Ketterer, E.	GER	100m	1	13	DNF		
Kingsford, P.C.	GBR	Long jump	F		14	6,65	
		Standing long jump	F		19	2,75	
Kiviat, A.R.	USA	1500m	1	3	1	4-04·4	
			F		2	3-56·9	S
		3000m team race	1	1	1	9	
			F		1	9	G
Klintberg, J.	SWE	Cross country	F		DNF		
Kobulszky, K.	HUN	Discus throw	F		19	38,15	
		Discus throw both hands	F		18	59,48	
Koczan, M.	HUN	Discus throw	F		33	33,30	
		Javelin throw	F		3	55,50	B
		Javelin throw both hands	F		12	86,39	
Kolehmainen, H.	FIN	5000m	1	4	1	15-38·9	
			F		1	14-36·6*	G
		10000m	1	1	1	33-49·0*	
			F		1	31-20·8*	G
		Cross country	F		1	45-11·6	G
		3000m team race	1	1	2	12	
Kolehmainen, T.	FIN	10000m	1	3	1	32-47·8	
			F		DNF		
		Marathon	F		DNF		
Kovacs, G.	HUN	Long jump	F		25	5,96	
Kramer, W.J.	USA	10000m	1	1	10		
		Cross country	F		DNF		
Krigsman, W.	SWE	Javelin throw	F		14	46,71	
		Javelin throw both hands	F		13	85,80	
Kroejer, G.	AUT	Triple jump	F		16	13,33	
		Javelin throw	F		NP	0	
		Pentathlon	F		DNF		
		4×100m relay	1	5	2	44·8	
Kruklin, A.	URS	1500m	1	6	5		
		Marathon	F		DNF		
Kugelberg, E.	SWE	Pentathlon	F		DNF		
		Decathlon	F		7	6758·78	
Kukkola, E.	FIN	Long jump	F		23	6,11	
		Javelin throw	F		18	44,66	
		Pentathlon	F		DNF		
Kullerstrand, K.	SWE	High jump	F		7	1,83	
Kwieton, F.	AUT	Marathon	F		20	3:00-48·0	
Kyroenen, J.	FIN	Cross country	F		7	47-32·0	
Labat, J.R.	FRA	High jump	Q		DNQ	1,75	
Labik, V.	BOH	100m	1	10	5		
		200m	2	1	4		
		400m	1	9	4		
Lagarde, C.	FRA	Discus throw	F		36	32,35	
		Shot put	F		22	9,41	
Laine, A.	FIN	High jump	Q		DNQ	1,75	
Langkjaer, S.	DEN	Pentathlon	F		DNF		
		Decathlon	F		DNF		
Larsen, O.	NOR	800m	1	3	3		
		1500m	1	4	5		
Larsen, E.	NOR	Triple jump	F		6	14,06	
Larsson, A.	SWE	Javelin throw	F		21	43,18	
Larsson, B.	SWE	10000m	1	2	7		
		Cross country	F		9	47-37·4	
Lazaro, F.	POR	Marathon	F		DNF		
Lee, G.	GBR	5000m	1	4	4		
		10000m	1	1	7		
Legat, M.	ITA	Long jump	F		28	5,50	
		Pole vault	Q		DNQ	3,00	
		Decathlon	F		DNF		
Lehmann, E.	GER	400m	1	12	4		
		800m	1	7	3		
		4×400m relay	1	2	2	3-28·5	
Lelong, C.L.	FRA	100m	1	7	3		
		200m	1	9	3		
		400m	1	5	1	50·2	
			2	2	3		
		4×100m relay	1	6	2	43·8	
		4×400m relay	1	3	1	3-22·5	
			F		2	3-20·7	S
Lemming, E.	SWE	Javelin throw	F		1	60,64*	G
		Javelin throw both hands	F		4	98,59	
		Discus throw both hands	F		11	67,08	

COMPETITOR	COUNTRY CODE	EVENT	ROUND	HEAT	PLACE	TIME & DISTANCE	MEDAL
Lemming, O.	SWE	Pentathlon	F		DNF		
		Shot put	Q		DNQ	11,57	
		Discus throw	Q		DNQ	38,19	
Lenzi, A.	ITA	Shot put	F		12	11,57	
		Discus throw	F		18	38,19	
Liesche, H.	GER	High jump	F		2	1,91	S
Lilley, T.H.	USA	Marathon	F		18	2:59-35·4	
Lind, C.J.	SWE	Discus throw	F		27	36,07	
		Discus throw both hands	F		8	68,02	
		Hammer throw	F		5	45,61	
Lindahl, A.	SWE	Cross country	F		DNF		
Lindberg, E.F.J.	USA	400m	1	10	1	50·6	
			2	2	1	48·9	
			F		3	48·4	B
		4×400m relay	1	2	1	3-23·3	
			F		1	3-16·6*	G
Lindberg, K.	SWE	100m	1	8	1	11·6	
			2	2	2		
		200m	1	9	1	23·1	
			2	6	3		
		4×100m relay	1	4	1	43·6	
			2	2	1	42·5*	
			F		2	42·6	S
Lindblom, G.	SWE	Triple jump	F		1	14,76	G
Lindblom, K.	SWE	200m	1	2	4		
Linde, N.	SWE	Discus throw both hands	F		9	67,10	
		Hammer throw	F		7	43,32	
Lindholm, A.	FIN	5000m	1	3	6		
		Cross country	F		DNF		
		3000m team race	1	1	2	12	
Lindholm, E.	SWE	400m	1	9	1	51·4	
			2	2	2	50·2	
		800m	1	1	3		
		4×400m relay	1	3	2	3-25·0	
Lindholm, I.	SWE	Triple jump	F		12	13,74	
Lindholm, J.	SWE	Pentathlon	F		DNF		
Lippincott, D.F.	USA	100m	1	16	1	10·6*	
			2	5	1	10·7	
			F		3	10·9	B
		200m	1	11	1	22·8	
			2	4	1	21·8	
			F		2	21·8	S
Ljunggren, G.	SWE	Standing long jump	F		11	3,09	
Lloyd, E.W.	GBR	Marathon	F		25	3:09-25·0	
Lodal, O.	DEN	Marathon	F		30	3:21-57·6	
Lomberg, C.	SWE	Long jump	F		16	6,62	
		Pentathlon	F		DNF		
		Decathlon	F		2	7413·51	S
Loenberg, I.	SWE	Marathon	F		DNF		
Lord, F.	GBR	Marathon	F		21	3:01-39·2	
Loewenstein, L.	URS	100m	1	6	6		
Lukeman, F.L.	CAN	100m	1	12	6		
			2	3	3		
		Pentathlon	F		3	24	B
		Decathlon	F		DNF		
		4×100m relay	1	1	1	46·2	
			2	3	2	43·5	
Lukk, K.	URS	10k walk	1	1	DNF		
Lundberg, I.	SWE	Marathon	F		28	3:16-35·2	
Lundstroem, K.	SWE	50000m	1	1	5		
		Cross country	F		13	48-45·4	
Lunghi, E.	ITA	400m	1	7	2	50·5	
			2	4	2		
		800m	1	1	2		
			2	2	5		
Lunzer, G.	HUN	Discus throw	F		21	37,88	
		Discus throw both hands	F		NP	0	
Luther, C.	SWE	100m	1	1	1	12·8	
			2	1	4		
		200m	1	4	1	23·6	
			2	5	3		
		4×100m relay	1	4	1	43·6	
			2	2	1	42·5*	
			F		2	42·6	S
McArthur, K.K.	SAF	Marathon	F		1	2:36-54·8	G
McClure, W.	USA	800m	1	1	4		
		1500m	1	7	2	4-07·3	
			F		12		
McConnell, F.D.	CAN	100m	1	14	3		
		200m	1	14	3		
		4×100m relay	1	1	1	46·2	
			2	3	2	43·5	
McCurdy, W.M.	USA	5000m	1	5	8		

COMPETITOR	COUNTRY CODE	EVENT	ROUND	HEAT	PLACE	TIME & DISTANCE	MEDAL
McDonald, P.J.	USA	Shot put	F		1	15,34*	G
		Shot put both hands	F		2	27,53	S
McGrath, M.J.	USA	Hammer throw	F		1	54,74*	G
MacIntosh, H.M.	GBR	100m	1	11	3		
		200m	1	16	2		
			2	3	DNS		
		4×100m relay	1	3	1	45·0	
			2	1	1	43·0*	
			F		1	42·4	G
Macmillan, D.	GBR	200m	1	3	2		
			2	4	5		
Madeira, L.C.	USA	1500m	1	1	2	4-27·9	
			F		13	4-06·0	
Magherian, M.	TUR	Discus throw	F		34	32,98	
		Shot put	F		19	10,63	
		Shot put both hands	F		7	19,78	
		Pentathlon	F		DNF		
		Decathlon	F		DNF		
Magnusson, E.	SWE	Discus throw	F		8	39,91	
		Discus throw both hands	F		3	77,37	B
Maguire, H.F.	USA	10000m	1	3	5	34-32·2	
			F		DNF		
Malfait, C.O.	FRA	200m	1	7	4		
		400m	1	8	3		
Malmsten, G.	SWE	Standing long jump	F		4	3,20	
Mann, P.E.	GBR	800m	1	2	1	1-56·0	
			2	1	6		
Maranda, A.	CAN	Long jump	F		27	5,37	
		Standing long jump	F		17	2,98	
		Triple jump	F		20	12,53	
Matsson, R.	SWE	High jump	Q		DNQ	1,70	
Melin, D.	SWE	Standing long jump	F		=14	3,02	
Menaul, J.A.	USA	Pentathlon	F		4	25	
Mercer, E.L.R.	USA	Long jump	F		5	6,97	
		Decathlon	F		5	7074·995	
Meredith, J.E.	USA	400m	1	3	2		
			2	3	1	48·3	
			F		4	49·2	
		800m	1	8	2		
			2	1	1	1-54·4	
			F		1	1-51·9*	G
		4×400m relay	1	2	1	3-23·3	
			F		1	3-16·6*	G
Mestecky, Z.	BOH	800m	1	5	DNF		
Meyer, A.I.	USA	100m	1	9	1	11·3	
			2	3	1	10·7	
			F		2	10·9	S
		200m	1	12	1	24·1	
			2	4	2		
Mezei, F.	HUN	200m	1	9	2		
			2	1	5		
		400m	1	8	1	50·8	
			2	1	4		
		4×400m relay	1	3	3	3-29·4	
Mickler, G.	GER	1500m	1	5	5		
		3000m team race	-	2	3	12	
Milosevic, D.	SER	100m	1	8	3		
Mishima, Y.	JPN	100m	1	16	5		
		200m	1	13	5		
		400m	1	4	2		
Modig, B.	SWE	5000m	1	2	4	16-07·1	
Moeller, E.	SWE	Standing high jump	F		=4	1,50	
		Standing long jump	F		=5	3,14	
Moeller, G.	SWE	200m	1	10	3		
		400m	1	5	4		
Moeller, H.	SWE	Discus throw	F		37	32,23	
Moller, I.	SWE	100m	1	2	1	11·5	
			2	6	4		
		200m	1	11	2		
			2	4	4		
		4×100m relay	1	4	1	43·6	
			2	2	1	42·5*	
			F		2	42·6	S
Monokanov, B.	URS	Discus throw both hands	F		19	47,37	
Monsen, O.	NOR	High jump	Q		DNQ	1,75	
Moore, W.C.	GBR	1500m	1	6	3		
		3000m team race	F		3	23	B
Motte, A.	FRA	Standing long jump	F		10	3,10	
Mourlon, R.	FRA	100m	1	11	2		
			2	4	5		
		4×100m relay	1	6	2	43·8	
Mucks, A.M.	USA	Discus throw	F		6	40,93	
		Discus throw both hands	F		15	63,83	
Mudin, I.	HUN	Shot put	F		6	12,81	

COMPETITOR	COUNTRY CODE	EVENT	ROUND	HEAT	PLACE	TIME & DISTANCE	MEDAL
Muller, E.J.	USA	Discus throw	F		12	39,35	
		Discus throw both hands	F		6	69,56	
Mueller, F.A.	CHI	800m	1	6	5		
Murphy, F.D.	USA	Pole vault	F		=4	3,80	B
Murray, W.	AUS	10k walk	1	2	DIS		
Myyrav, J.	FIN	Javelin throw	F		8	51,33	
Nazarov, D.	URS	800m	1	5	5		
		1500m	1	2	6		
Neklepayer, N.	URS	Javelin throw	F		17	44,98	
		Discus throw	F		35	32,59	
Nelson, F.T.	USA	Pole vault	F		=2	3,85	S
Nicholson, J.P.	USA	110m hurdles	1	8	1	15·5	
			2	3	1	15·4	
			F		DNF		
Nicol, G.	GBR	400m	1	12	1	50·0	
			2	1	3		
		4×400m relay	1	1	1	3-19·0*	
			F		3	3-23·2	B
Nikolsky, M.	URS	5000m	1	3	4	17-21·7	
		10000m	1	1	11		
Nixlander, E.	FIN	Discus throw	F		4	42,09	
		Discus throw both hands	F		2	77,96	S
		Shot put	F		4	13,65	
		Shot put both hands	F		3	27,14	B
Nilsson, C.	SWE	Marathon	F		32	3:26-56·4	
Nilsson, E.	SWE	Discus throw	F		10	39,69	
		Discus throw both hands	F		4	71,40	
		Shot put	F		7	12,62	
		Shot put both hands	F		5	23,37	
		Pentathlon	F		DNF		
		Decathlon	F		DNF		
Nilsson, G.	SWE	Discus throw	F		23	37,44	
		Discus throw both hands	F		10	67,09	
Nilsson, M.	SWE	Pole vault	Q		DNQ	3,20	
Nilsson, O.	SWE	Javelin throw	F		10	49,18	
		Javelin throw both hands	F		8	88,90	
		Discus throw	F		40	31,07	
Norden, G.	SWE	Triple jump	F		10	13,81	
Nordstroem, H.	SWE	5000m	1	4	2	15-49·1	
			F		DNF		
		Cross country	F		DNF		
Norman A.C.C.St.	SAF	Marathon	F		DNF		
		10k walk	1	2	2	50-17·9	
			F		DIS		
Oeberg, A.	SWE	10000m	1	1	6	35-45·0	
Ohlsson, B.	SWE	Javelin throw	F		13	46,94	
Ohlsson, H.	SWE	Triple jump	F		7	14,01	
Ohlsson, P	SWE	Long jump	F		19	6,28	
		Triple jump	F		15	13,45	
Ohlsson, T.	SWE	5000m	5	5	2	15-25·2	
		3000m team race	1	2	1	9	
			F		2	13	S
Ohrling, A.	SWE	Javelin throw	F		16	45,32	
		Javelin throw both hands	F		10	87,17	
Ohsol-Arme, A.	URS	Shot put	F		21	10,33	
Oler, W.M.	USA	High jump	Q		DNQ	1,75	
Olsen, G.	NOR	High jump	Q		DNQ	1,75	
Olsson, C.R.	SWE	Hammer throw	F		4	46,50	
Orlando, A.	ITA	5000m	1	5	7		
		10000m	1	2	5	33-44·4	
			F		5	33-31·2	
Osen, O.	NOR	Marathon	F		34	3:36-35·2	
Owen, E.	GDR	1500m	1	3	DNF		
		3000m team race	F		3	23	B
Pagani, A.	ITA	110m hurdles	1	6	3		
		High jump	Q		DNQ	1,60	
		Long jump	F		26	5,95	
		Pentathlon	F		DNF		
		Decathlon	F		DNF		
Palmas, L.E.	CHI	200m	1	15	4		
		800m	1	2	4		
Palmer, W.J.	GBR	10k walk	1	1	5	51-21·0	
			F		DNF		
Paoli, R.	FRA	Shot put	F		16	11,11	
Papazian, V.	TUR	800m	1	6	DNF		
		1500m	1	7	6		
Pasemann, R.	GER	Long jump	F		7	6,82	
		Pole vault	F		=1	3,40	

COMPETITOR	COUNTRY CODE	EVENT	ROUND	HEAT	PLACE	TIME & DISTANCE	MEDAL
Patching, G.H.	SAF	100m	1	13	2		
			2	2	1	10·9	
			F		4	11·0	
		200m	1	14	1	22·3	
			2	3	DNF		
		400m	1	15	1	51·1	
			2	3	3		
Patterson, A.	GBR	400m	1	15	4		
		800m	1	8	4		
Patterson, J.N.	USA	1500m	1	3	3	4-05·5	
Pautex, L.	FRA	Marathon	F		DNF		
Pedersen, A.	NOR	100m	1	12	4		
		400m	1	14	DIS		
Pedersen, J.	NOR	400m	1	9	2	51·6	
			2	3	5		
		800m	1	2	3		
		1500m	1	3	7		
Pedersen, N.	DEN	10k walk	1	2	DIS		
Pedersen, V.	DEN	Cross country	F		23	53-00·8	
Pelletier, M.	LUX	Discus throw	F		31	33,73	
		Shot put	F		17	11,04	
Peltonen, U.	FIN	Javelin throw	F		9	49,20	
		Javelin throw both hands	F		3	100,24	B
Penc, V.	BOH	10000m	1	1	9		
		Marathon	F		DNF		
Person, J.	GER	400m	1	13	1	55·4	
		800m	1	5	4		
		4×400m relay	1	2	2	3-28·5	
Persson, M.	SWE	5000m	1	2	5		
		10000m	1	3	4	34-18·6	
Persson, T.	SWE	100m	1	6	3		
		200m	1	18	1	23·2	
			2	1	4		
		4×100m relay	1	4	1	43·6	
			2	2	1	42·5*	
			F		2	42·6	S
Petroff, E.	URS	1500m	1	7	5		
Philbrook, G.W.	USA	Discus throw	F		7	40,92	
		Shot put	F		5	13,13	
		Decathlon	F		DNF		
Piggott, R.F.	USA	Marathon	F		9	2:46-40·7	
Pihkala, L.	FIN	800m	1	9	6		
Ponurski, W.	AUT	400m	1	1	3		
Porter, C.H.A.	GBR	5000m	1	3	3	16-23·4	
			F		11		
		3000m team race	F		3	23	B
Poulenard, C.A.C.	FRA	200m	1	2	3		
		400m	1	1	2	50·7	
			2	1	5		
		800m	1	4	3		
		4×400m relay	1	3	1	3-22·5	
			F		2	3-20·7	S
Poulter, S.H.	AUS	Marathon	F		DNF		
Povey, R.	SAF	100m	1	5	2		
			2	6	2		
		200m	1	7	2		
			2	5	5		
Powell, K.	GBR	110m hurdles	1	11	1	15·6	
			2	1	1	15·6	
			F		5	15·5	
Pritchard, E.M.	USA	110m hurdles	1	7	1	16·4	
			2	6	2	15·5	
Putnam, H.M.	USA	800m	1	2	2		
			2	1	4	1-55·0	
			F		8		
		1500m	1	5	3	4-07·6	
Quinn, P.	GBR	Shot put	F		8	12,53	
Racz, V.	HUN	100m	1	6	2		
			2	1	6		
		4×100m relay	1	6	1	43·7	
			2	2	2	42·9	
Radoczy, C.	HUN	800m	1	9	5		
Rasmussen, A.	DEN	10k walk	1	1	3	48-15·8	
			F		4	48-00·0	
Rasmussen, S.	DEN	Cross country	F		28	55-27·0	
Rasso, N.	URS	Marathon	F		DNF		
Rath, E.	AUT	Cross country	F		DNF		
		Marathon	F		33	3:27-03·8	
Rau, R.	GER	100m	1	6	1	11·5	
			2	4	2	10·9	
		200m	1	6	1	22·5	
			2	5	1	22·1	
			F		4	22·2	
		4×100m relay	1	5	1	43·6	
			2	3	1	42·3*	
			F		DIS		

COMPETITOR	COUNTRY CODE	EVENT	ROUND	HEAT	PLACE	TIME & DISTANCE	MEDAL
Rauch, R.	AUT	100m	1	2	3		
		200m	1	7	3		
		4×100m relay	1	5	2	44·8	
Reidpath, C.D.	USA	200m	1	1	1	22·6	
			2	6	1	22·1	
			F		5	22·3	
		400m	1	15	2	51·2	
			2	1	1	48·7	
			F		1	48·2*	G
		4×400m relay	1	2	1	3-23·3	
			F		1	3-16·6*	G
Reimann, E.	URS	Marathon	F		DNF		
Renz, E.	USA	10k walk	1	1	7	53-30·8	
Reynolds, J.J.	USA	Marathon	F		DNF		
Rice, R.C.	GBR	100m	1	4	1	11·4	
			2	2	3		
		200m	1	2	2		
			2	5	4		
Richards, A.W.	USA	High jump	F		1	1,93*	G
Richardson, L.	SAF	10000m	1	2	1	32-30·8*	
			F		DNF		
		Cross country	F		8	47-33·5	
Richter, R.	BOH	10k walk	1	1	DNF		
Ripzam, H.	HUN	Marathon	F		DNF		
		10k walk	1	2	8	55-20·6	
Roehr, O.	GER	High jump	Q		DNQ	1,75	
		Decathlon	F		DNF		
		4×100m relay	1	5	1	43·6	
			2	3	1	42·3*	
			F		DIS		
Rolot, G.J.B.	FRA	100m	1	9	4		
		200m	2	1	2		
			2	3	3		
		400m	1	12	5		
		4×100m relay	1	6	2	43·8	
Roenstroem, G.	SWE	Decathlon	F		DNF		
Rose, R.W.	USA	Discus throw	F		11	39,65	
		Shot put	F		2	15,25	S
		Shot put both hands	F		1	27,70*	G
		Hammer throw	F		9	42,58	
Rosenberger, J.M.	USA	400m	1	1	1	50·6	
			2	4	DNF		
Ross, C.M.	AUS	400m	1	1	4		
Rucks, A.	URS	1500m	1	4	7		
Ruffell, C.H.	GBR	1500m	1	5	8		
		5000m	1	2	6		
		10000m	1	1	8		
		Cross country	F		DNF		
Ruggero, E.	ITA	Marathon	F		DNF		
Ryan, M.J.	USA	Marathon	F		DNF		
Saaristo, J.	FIN	Javelin throw	F		2	58,66	S
		Javelin throw both hands	F		1	109,42*	G
Sakelloropoulos, H.P.	GRE	Marathon	F		26	3:11-37·0	
Salinas, R.	CHI	10k walk	1	2	7	55-02·0	
Sanchez, A.	CHI	5000m	1	5	5		
		10000m	1	2	8		
Santesson, S.	SWE	Pole vault	Q		DNQ	3,20	
Savniki, T.	HUN	800m	1	3	4		
		1500m	1	2	4		
Schaeffer, J.	AUT	Discus throw	F		29	34,87	
		Discus throw both hands	F		16	63,50	
		Shot put	F		13	11,44	
		Decathlon	F		9	6568·585	
Schurrer, R.	FRA	100m	1	6	4		
		200m	1	18	2		
			2	6	5		
		400m	1	15	5		
		4×400m relay	1	3	1	3-22·5	
			F		2	3-20·7	S
Schwartz, S.	USA	10k walk	1	1	6	53-30·8	
Schwarz, A.	URS	Standing high jump	Q		DNQ	1,40	
Schwarz, H.	URS	100m	1	7	5		
Schwedrewitz, N.	URS	Javelin throw	F		20	43,21	
Scott, H.L.	USA	5000m	1	2	1	15-23·5	
			F		7		
		10000m	1	3	3	34-14·2	
			F		DNF		
		Cross country	F		24	53-51·4	
		3000m team race	1	1	1	9	
			F		1	9	G
Scott, W.	GBR	10000m	1	3	2	32-55·2	
			F		DNF		

COMPETITOR	COUNTRY CODE	EVENT	ROUND	HEAT	PLACE	TIME & DISTANCE	MEDAL
Seedhouse, C.N.	GBR	200m	1	13	2		
			2	2	4		
		4×400m relay	1	1	1	3-19-0*	
			F		3	3-23-2	B
		400m	1	14	1	51-5	
			2	2	4		
Sheppard, M.W.	USA	400m	1	2	2	66-6	
			2	3	2	48-9	
		800m	1	7	2		
			2	1	3	1-54-8	
			F		2	1-52-0	S
		1500m	1	1	1	4-27-6	
			F		8	4-02-0	
		4×400m relay	1	2	1	3-23-3	
			F		1	3-16-6*	G
Sherman, B.F.	USA	Hammer throw	F		12	38,77	
Siikaniemi, V.	FIN	Javelin throw	F		5	52,43	
		Javelin throw both hands	F		2	101,13	S
Simonsen, A.G.	NOR	Marathon	F		23	3:04-59-4	
Sjoberg, R.	SWE	High jump	Q		DNQ	1,75	
		Pole vault	Q		DNQ	3 60	
Slavik, F.	BOH	Marathon	F		DNF		
Smedmark, R.	SWE	100m	1	4	2		
			2	3	5		
		Standing high jump	Q		DNQ	1,45	
Smith, H.	USA	Marathon	F		17	2:52-53-8	
Sockalexis, A.	USA	Marathon	F		4	2:42-07-9	
Solymar, K.	HUN	110m hurdles	1	1	2	16-6	
			2	2	4		
Sonne, H.	SWE	Javelin throw	F		11	47,33	
		Javelin throw both hands	F		14	84,96	
Sotaaen, H.	NOR	100m	1	10	4		
		200m	1	15	3		
Soutter, J.T.	GBR	400m	1	10	2		
			2	5	3		
		800m	1	7	1	2-00-4	
		4×400m relay	1	1	1	3-19-0*	
			F		3	3-23-2	E
Speroni, C.	ITA	Marathon	F		DNF		
Stenborg, K.	SWE	200m	2	1	3		
		400m	1	6	1	1-01-6	
			2	3	4		
		4×400m relay	1	3	2	3-25-0	
Stenroos, A.	FIN	10000m	1	2	4	33-28-4	
			F		3	32-21-8	B
		Cross country	F		6	47-23-4	
		3000m team race	1	1	2	12	
Stewart, W.A.	AUS	100m	1	7	1	11-0	
			2	4	4		
		200m	1	16	1	26-0	
			2	2	3		
Strobino, G.	USA	Marathon	F		3	2:38-42-4	B
Stromp, A.	POR	100m	1	5	3		
		200m	1	18	3		
Sundkvist, J.	SWE	Cross country	F		10	47-40-0	
Sustera, M.	BOH	Discus throw	F		38	31,38	
Svensson, H.	SWE	Pole vault	Q		DNQ	3,20	
Szalai, P.	HUN	100m	1	2	2		
			2	3	4		
		Long jump	F		24	5,98	
		4×100m relay	1	6	1	43-7	
			2	2	2	42-9	
Szerelemhegyi, E.	HUN	100m	1	16	4		
		400m	1	14	2		
			2	4	3		
		4×400m relay	1	3	3	3-29-4	
Szobota, F.	HUN	100m	1	17	2		
			2	4	6		
		4×100m relay	1	6	1	43-7	
			2	2	2	42-9	
Taber, N.S.	USA	1500m	1	2	1	4-25-5	
			F		3	3-56-9	B
		3000m team race	1	1	1	9	
			F		1	9	G
Taipale, A.R.	FIN	Discus throw	F		1	45,21*	G
		Discus throw both hands	F		1	82,86*	G
Tait, J.L.	CAN	800m	1	4	2		
			2	1	5		
		1500m	1	3	4		
		4×400m relay	1	1	2	3-22-2	
Ternstroem, J.	SWE	Cross country	F		5	47-07-1	
Tewanima, L.	USA	10000m	1	2	2	32-31-4	
			F		2	32-06-6	S
		Marathon	F		16	2:52-41-4	

COMPETITOR	COUNTRY CODE	EVENT	ROUND	HEAT	PLACE	TIME & DISTANCE	MEDAL
Thomas, R.B.	USA	100m	1	14	2		
			2	6	3		
Thorpe, J.	USA	High jump	F		5	1,87	
		Long jump	F		7	6,89	
		Pentathlon	F		1	5	
		Decathlon	F		1	8412·955	
Tison, A.	FRA	Discus throw	F		30	34,73	
		Shot put	F		9	12,41	
Tomaschevitsch, D.	SER	Marathon	F		DNF		
Tonini, A.	ITA	Long jump	F		18	6,44	
Toernros, G.	SWE	Marathon	F		DNF		
Townsend, A.	GBR	Marathon	F		19	3:00-05-0	
Trebe, A.L.	GBR	5000m	1	5	4		
Triantaphillacos, C.	GRE	100m	1	6	5		
Troaner, H.	AUT	Discus throw	F		5	41,24	
		Discus throw both hands	F		13	66,66	
Tsiclitiras, C.	GRE	Standing high jump	F		3	1,55	B
		Standing long jump	F		1	3,37	G
Uggla, B.	SWE	Pole vault	F		=4	3,80	B
Uhr, P.A.	SWE	High jump	Q		DNQ	1,75	
Ujlaky, R.	HUN	Discus throw	F		9	39,82	
		Discus throw both hands	F		14	66,18	
Upmal, A.	URS	Marathon	F		DNF		
Victor, J.A.	SAF	800m	1	8	3		
		1500m	1	4	3	4-12-7	
Vietz, G.	GER	5000m	1	4	5		
		10000m	1	2	11		
		Cross country	F		27	54-40-6	
		3000m team race	1	2	2	12	
Vinne, E.	NOR	Triple jump	F		4	14,14	
Voellmeke, A.	USA	10k walk	1	2	6	52-29-2	
Von Bonninghausen, H.	GER	110m hurdles	1	10	2	17-0	
			2	3	3	16-0	
Von Sige, E.	GER	1500m	1	6	1	4-09-3	
			F		11	4-05-3	
		3000m team race	1	2	2	12	
Vygoda, B.	BOH	100m	1	8	2		
			2	5	6		
Wagner, J.	SUI	Pentathlon	F		DNF		
Waitzer, J.	GER	Javelin throw	F		19	43,71	
		Discus throw	F		16	38,44	
		Pentathlon	F		DNF		
Wallach, G.C.L.	GBR	10000m	1	3	6		
		Cross country	F		DNF		
Wannag, E.	URS	Shot put	F		20	10,44	
		Discus throw	F		39	31,34	
Wardener, J.	HUN	High jump	F		=18	1,80	
Webb, E.J.	GBR	10k walk	1	1	2	47-25-4	
			F		2	46-50-4	S
Weinzinger, F.	AUT	100m	1	12	3		
		4×100m relay	1	5	2	44-8	
Wells, J.A.	GBR	200m	1	7	5		
		400m	1	13	2		
Welz, E.	GER	Discus throw	F		24	37,24	
Wendell, J.	USA	110m hurdles	1	11	2	15-7	
			2	4	1	15-5	
			F		2	15-2	S
Wenseler, H.	GER	200m	1	13	4		
		400m	1	15	3		
Westberg, J.	SWE	Marathon	F		22	3:02-05-2	
Whitney, L.A.	USA	Discus throw	F		20	37,91	
		Shot put	F		3	13,93	B
		Shot put both hands	F		4	24,09	
Wickholm, W.	FIN	110m hurdles	1	5	2	16-6	
			2	5	2	16-6	
		Decathlon	F		6	7058·795	
Wide, E.	SWE	1500m	1	7	1	4-06-0	
			F		5	3-57-6	
		3000m team race	1	2	1	9	
			F		2	13	S
Wieslander, H.	SWE	Pentathlon	F		6	28	
		Decathlon	F		1	7724·495*	G
Wihtol, R.	URS	1500m	1	2	DNF		
Wikke, F.B.	DEN	Pole vault	Q		DNQ	3,40	
Wikoff, G.M	USA	5000m	1	3	5		
Wilhelmsohn, L.	URS	800m	1	7	4		
Willfuhr, P.	GER	Javelin throw	F		23	41,05	
		Shot put	F		18	10,90	

COMPETITOR	COUNTRY CODE	EVENT	ROUND	HEAT	PLACE	TIME & DISTANCE	MEDAL
Wilson, C.P.	USA	100m	1	10	2		
			2	5	2		
		200m	1	14	2		
			2	2	2		
		4×100m relay	1	2	1	43·7	
			2	1	DIS		
Withols, R.	URS	1500m	1	2	5		
Worthington, H.T.	USA	Long jump	F		4	7,03	
Wright, M.S.	USA	Pole vault	F		=2	3,85	S
Yates, W.G.	GBR	10k walk	1	2	1	49-43·6	
			F		DIS		
Yelizarov, A.	URS	800m	1	6	7		
		1500m	1	5	6		
		4 × 400m relay	1	3	2	3-25·0	

COMPETITOR	COUNTRY CODE	EVENT	ROUND	HEAT	PLACE	TIME & DISTANCE	MEDAL
Yorke, R.F.C.	GBR	800m	1	6	3		
		1500m	1	5	4		
Young, D.B.	USA	200m	1	13	1	22·8	
			2	3	1	21·9	
			F		6	22·3	
		400m	1	5	2	50·4	
			2	5	DIS		
Zander, J.	SWE	1500m	1	5	1	4-05·5	
			F		7	4-02·0	
		3000m team race	1	2	1	9	
			F		2	13	S
Zerling, P.G.	SWE	400m	1	4	1	55·4	
			2	5	4		
		4×400m relay	1	3	2	3-25·0	

In a very close 800 metres, Ted Meredith of the USA timed his finishing sport to perfection.

All-Sport Photographic Ltd.

1920

War Heroes Compete in an Austere Antwerp

After the Second World War, it was thought appropriate to give the Games to Antwerp, partly as a consolation to Belgium, which had been ravaged by the battles that had been fought within her borders. With only 18 months to prepare, the Belgians found the task very difficult, and the stadium and pool were hardly finished. Facilities were very poor, but to the ex-servicemen who attended a pre-Games service in memory of those who died in the war, anything was an improvement on what they had become used to recently.

One of the stars of the Games was Charlie Paddock, an American sprinter dubbed the "world's fastest man", whose habit, instead of breasting the tape, was to almost high jump it with his arms flung wide in celebration.

Men's Track Events

The track was wet and soft for the **100 metres**, and the times were not expected to be very fast. In the preliminaries six sprinters clocked 10·8 sec, so the final was likely to be a close thing. When the athletes were down on their marks for the final, the Clerk of the Course asked Charlie Paddock of the USA to withdraw his fingers to behind the starting line. Loren Murchison stood up thinking the others would be ordered to do likewise; instead the starter fired his gun. Jackson Scholz of the USA was quickest into his running and led at 50 metres from Harry Edward of Britain, but the other two Americans Morris Kirksey and Paddock were also near at hand. It was a close finish with Paddock being given the nod in 10·8, with Kirksey placed next in 10·8 and Edward third in an ungenerous 11·0.

Charlie Paddock was the favourite to win the **200 metres** on the strength of his running 21·4 sec in the US trials. Harry Edward of Britain was fastest in the preliminaries with 22·0, but he unfortunately strained his thigh muscle in the semi. In the final, Paddock was away quickest and entered the straight with countryman Allen Woodring on his shoulder. At the tape he attempted his jump finish, but the under-rated Woodring breasted first in 22·0. Paddock was second in 22·1 and a fast finishing Edward third in 22·2.

One of the competitors in the **400 metres** was James Meredith of the USA, the current holder of the 440 yards world record at 47·4 sec, set in 1916. However, he was off the boil in 1920, and the most likely candidate for the gold medal was Nils Engdahl of Sweden. In the final, Engdahl ran a furious first 150 metres, drawing Frank Shea of the USA along with him, but coming off the bend into the final straight, he was headed by the American and Bevil Rudd of South Africa. Rudd's momentum carried him to a win in 49·6 and Guy Butler of Britain made a late surge to collect second place in 49·9, just beating Engdahl, who was given the same time.

Bevil Rudd of South Africa was expected to win the **800 metres** also, following his heat time of 1-55·0. When the final got under way, Thomas Campbell of the USA set the pace for the first lap until Edgar Mountain of Britain took over. Around the final bend, Rudd put in his effort and led into the straight. However, his effort had come too soon and both Albert Hill of Britain and Earl Eby of the USA sprinted past him. Hill won in 1-53·4 from Eby in 1-53·6 with Rudd collapsing across the line in 1-54·0.

In the **1,500 metres**, world record holder John Zander of Sweden was competing and he qualified for the final with 11 others. Joie Ray of the USA set the pace, before the two Britons, Philip Baker and Albert Hill, took over to lead the pack. Hill's sprint for the tape was stronger and he won in 4-01·8 from Baker in 4-02·4. Lawrence Shields of the USA followed the leaders home for third place in 4-03·1.

The arrangement of the heats was noticeably poor for the **3,000 metres team race**. Four countries competed in the first heat, with Britain and Sweden qualifying, but in the second, America and France had a walk-over, and to save their runners for the final France ran the minimum number of three instead of five. In the final Erik Backman of Sweden led most of the way with the pack in close contention, but was pipped by Hallock Brown of America who came in first in 8-45·4, Backman recorded 8-45·6 and Arlie Schardt of the USA was third in 8-46·2. The USA took the gold medal for the event with ten points from Britain's 20 and France's 30.

There were 16 qualifiers for the final of the **5,000 metres**, from four heats. After two laps, Paavo Nurmi of Finland took the lead followed by the diminutive Joseph Guillemot of France, who had been gassed during the war, and they soon opened a gap of 20 metres on the rest of the field. Guillemot appeared to catch Nurmi by surprise when he sprinted away with 180 metres to go, and he won in 14-55·6 with the Finn some 20 metres adrift in 15-00·0. Erik Backman of Sweden headed the rest of the field for third spot in 15-13·0. Guillemot, examined by doctors after the race, was found to have his heart on the right side of his chest!

Of the 16 qualifiers 15 competed in the final of the **10,000 metres**, where right from the start Paavo Nurmi took up the running closely followed by Joseph Guillemot of France and James Wilson of Britain. Wilson and Guillemot then forged ahead leaving Nurmi 20 metres back with the pack. But the leaders eventually came back to the field until with five laps to go Guillemot hotted up the pace again and took Nurmi and Wilson with him. The Finn was determined not to be caught out as he had been in the 5,000 and took the lead at the bell, fully stretching the other two runners. Once in the home straight Nurmi sprinted for the tape and won in 31-45·8 from Guillemot in 31-47·2 and Wilson in 31-50·8.

The **marathon** had been in danger of being axed from

the Olympic programme as being unnecessarily long and dangerous to health. The course was the longest in Olympic history at 42·750km and consisted of an out and back route using the same roadway. Forty-five competitors started in pouring rain and were led out of the stadium by the home favourite, Auguste Broos of Belgium. At 5km Chris Gitsham of South Africa was heading Hannes Kolehmainen of Finland with Broos third and at 15km the field was spread over nearly two kilometres from first to last. Gitsham was still in the lead at the half-way stage in 1:13-10, but at 28km his feet were in a poor state and he dropped back rapidly. Kolehmainen then took up the pace from Ettore Blasi of Italy with Juri Lossman of Estonia third and Broos fourth. Over the last 5km Lossman was catching Kolehmainen, who had to give it all he had to win in a fast 2:32-35·8, a new Olympic record. Lossman was not far behind in 2:32-48·6 and Valerio Arri, the Italian long distance champion, finished in 2:36-32·8 for third place.

A big 6ft 2in, 200lb Canadian, Earl Thomson, was the firm favourite for the **110 metres hurdles** as he had recently run 14·4 sec for 120 yards hurdles. Thomson's greatest danger in the final was Harold Barron of the USA, who had won the first semi-final while he had taken the other. For 50 metres it was Barron and Thomson neck and neck, then the strength of Thomson told and he eased away to win in 14·8 for the Olympic record on a wet, soft track. Barron was second in 15·0, being pushed at the end by Fred Murray of the USA in 15·2.

The **400 metres hurdles** was wide open with any of the six qualifying finalists capable of winning the gold. John Norton of the USA went off at a tremendous pace closely followed by the Frenchman George Andre, but at 300 metres Joe Loomis of the USA made his effort to win in a new world and Olympic record of 54·0 sec. Meanwhile, there was a fierce struggle going on behind between Norton, Andre and August Desch of the USA. Andre looked set for the silver, but tripped over the ninth hurdle, letting through Norton for second in 54·6 and Desch for third in 54·7.

Twelve starters lined up for the final of the **3,000 metres steeplechase**. Ernesto Ambrosini of Italy set the pace over the first lap, but in the second the British steeplechase specialist, Percy Hodge, took the lead which was never wrested from him. Hodge had developed a most efficient way of clearing the barriers and was soon 100 metres in the lead. In the latter stages Pat Flynn of the USA made efforts to catch him, but at the finish Hodge won in 10-00·4 with the American second in 10-18·0 and Ambrosini third in 10-27·0.

Ugo Frigerio of Italy was a small but sturdy walker with a reputation of a fast but fair style so he was favoured to do well in the **3 kilometres walk**. There were 12 competitors contesting the final with Frigerio and George Parker of Australia taking it in turns to lead. Frigerio eventually drew away to win in 13-14·2 from Parker in 13-20·6 with the 37-year-old Dick Remer of the USA third in 13-23·6.

In the final of the **10 kilometres walk**, Joe Pearman of the USA, who had a peculiar leg action, led the other 11 walkers for half the distance. At that point Ugo Frigerio injected some pace and strolled away to win in a fine 48-06·2. Behind the winner, Pearman was having a terrific race with Charles Gunn of Britain. Pearman won to take the silver with 49-40·8, while Gunn had to make do with the bronze.

The 10,000 metres **cross country** race was, in fact, held over a course of little more than 8,000 metres. There were 48 runners who contested the race from nine countries, and Paavo Nurmi of Finland outsprinted Erik Backman of Sweden to win in 27-15·0 to 27-17·6. Third was the Finn, Heikki Liimatainen, in 27-37·4. With three to score, Finland won the team event with ten points, Britain was second with 21 and Sweden third with 23.

Both the USA and France broke the existing Olympic record in the preliminaries for the **4 × 100 metres relay**, each recording 43·0. The USA led all the way in the final with good baton changing and set a new world and Olympic record of 42·2. Their team was Charlie Paddock, Jackson Scholz, Loren Murchison and Morris Kirksey. France was a respectable second in 42·6 and Sweden third in 42·9.

Britain had it all their own way in the **4 × 400 metres relay**, and their team comprising Cecil Griffiths, Bob Lindsay, John Ainsworth-Davis and Guy Butler extended their lead on each leg to win in 3-22·2. South Africa, France and the USA had a titanic fight for the lesser medals, with South Africa taking the silver in 3-24·2 and France the bronze in 3-24·8.

All-Sport Photographic Ltd.

Patrick Ryan

Born in Pallasgreen, County Limerick, on 4 January 1889, Ryan was another of the hefty Irish hammer throwers who became world record breakers after emigrating to the United States. He was self taught until he arrived in New York in 1910. Two years later he won the first of his eight US national titles.

Ryan was a particularly powerful figure, standing 6ft 4in (1,93m) and weighing nearly 20 stone (127kg), and in 1913 he heaved the hammer 189ft 6in (57,76m), a world record distance that stood for 25 years.

Going to France with the American Armed Forces in 1918 interrupted his hammer throwing for a spell, but by 1920 he was back in fine shape, and he won the Olympic title in Antwerp with 173ft 5½in (52,87m).

His success meant that for five successive Games, Irish-born Americans had won the hammer throwing title for the USA: John Flanagan in Paris 1900, St Louis 1904 and London 1908 and Matthew McGrath in Stockholm 1912, had preceded him.

Ryan eventually returned to Ireland to become a farmer in Country Limerick, where he died in 1965.

Men's Field Events

Eight competitors qualified for the **high jump** finals by leaping 1,80 metres. In the final round, six jumpers cleared 1,85, but at the next height of 1,90 only three competitors made it. Harold Muller of the USA went over on his first attempt, but both his countryman Dick Landon and Bo Ekelund of Sweden needed two tries. At 1,94, the 6ft 2in Richard Landon went clear to win the gold and Muller won the jump-off for the silver with Ekelund taking the bronze.

The **pole vault** saw 13 competitors clear 3,60 metres to qualify for the final pool, in which seven of them again vaulted 3,60. At 3,70 only Frank Foss of the USA, the world record holder, and Henry Petersen of Denmark succeeded. Foss, the winner, then requested that the bar be raised to 4,00, which he failed on his first try. Although the weather was damp with drizzle, he asked to take his next two attempts at a world record height of 4,10. This he promptly cleared, but on remeasurement the bar was found to be 4,09, but still a record. With Petersen taking the silver position, there was a five-way

All-Sport Photographic Ltd.

Bevil Rudd

Having been born in Britain in 1894, Rudd had the option of competing for Britain or South Africa, where he was educated. He chose South Africa and did them proud by winning a gold, silver and bronze at the 1920 Antwerp Games.

Action with the Royal Tank Corps in the First World War interrupted his athletics career just as he was becoming a successful track runner at Oxford University. But once back at the University after winning the Military Cross he was soon winning British titles for 440 and 880 yards.

At the Antwerp Olympics he was strongly fancied to win the 800m final after producing the fastest qualifying heat of 1-55·0, but although in the lead coming off the last bend, he was forced to take the bronze behind Britain's Albert Hill and the American Earl Eby.

Rudd was not quite so venturesome in the 400m final and his tactics of biding his time to strike paid off with a title-winning 49·6 sec, well ahead of his Cambridge University rival Guy Butler, representing Britain.

His silver was won as a member of the South African 4 × 400 metres with 3-24·2. He died in 1928, when only 34.

Albert George Hill

Albert Hill is one of only six athletes to win both the 800m and 1,500m at the same Olympics. This he achieved in Antwerp in 1920 by running five races in four days at the age of 31. He also won a silver in the 3,000m team event. His victories shocked the Americans, who were looking to their champions, Earl Eby and Joie Ray, to bring home the respective top honours. Hill's 800m time of 1-53·4 was a world record.

Born in Tooting, London, on 24 March 1889, he won his first British championship over four miles as early as 1910. Four years later he gave proof of his versatility by running second to the American champion Homer Baker over 880 yards at the UK national meet.

Hill celebrated his return to the track in 1919, after serving in the First World War, by winning the national titles for 880 yards and the mile. Two summers later, he cut three seconds off the British mile record and shortly afterwards became a professional and an outstanding coach. The most successful of those he coached was Sydney Wooderson, who became the world record-holder for 880 yards, 800 metres and the mile, but had the misfortune to damage an ankle on the eve of the Berlin Games and missed what was considered a certain Olympic medal. Hill died on 8 January 1969.

Bevil Rudd (extreme right) forges ahead to win the 400 metres for South Africa.   Dave Terry

jump-off between Edwin Myers, Ed Knourek and Eldon Jenne all from the USA, Ernfrid Rydberg of Sweden and Lauits Jorgensen of Denmark, for third. Myers emerged as the bronze medalist after a long drawn out session.

Sol Butler was rated the top man in the **long jump** at Antwerp on the basis that he had leapt 7,52 metres at the American trials, but he unfortunately pulled a muscle in the early stages. After three jumps in the final, William Petersson of Sweden led with 6,94 followed by fellow Swede Eric Abrahamsson on 6,86 and Carl Johnson of the USA with 6,82. All three improved in their last three jumps despite the sticky run-up, but ultimately it was Petersson who took the gold with 7,15, Johnson the silver at 7,09 and Abrahamsson the bronze.

Dan Ahearn of the USA was the world record holder for the **triple jump**, but was overweight and past his peak, and could only finish sixth overall. Vilho Tuulos of Finland won the competition on his very first jump of 14,50 metres in the qualifying rounds and behind him came three Swedes. Folke Jansson was unfortunate in falling back into the sand on his best attempt of 14,48, which would certainly have been a winning jump had he been able to hold his balance. He had to be satisfied with second, while Erik Almloef achieved 14,27 for third place.

Pat McDonald of the United States was expected to do well in the **shot put**, but had strained his hand in practice and managed only 14,08 metres for fourth spot. The winner was Ville Poerhoelae of Finland who had also been throwing poorly in the preliminary round with a best of 14,035, but he improved greatly to 14,81 for the gold medal. His fellow Finn, Elmer Niklander, was placed second with 14,15 and Harry Liversedge, of the USA, took the bronze.

The world record for throwing the **56-lb weight** was 12,36 metres held by Matt McGrath, but he had injured his knee in the hammer and was unable to compete. The Americans, Pat McDonald and Pat Ryan, took the top two medals with throws of 11,26 and 10,96 respectively while Carl Lindh of Sweden was the best of the Europeans and achieved 10,25 for third place.

Armas Taipale of Finland, the reigning Olympic champion, who had set the world record in the **discus throw**, seven years previously, was in contention once again. All the top throws came in the preliminary three rounds which saw the Finn dethroned in a tight contest by his compatriot and arch-rival Elmer Niklander, who attained a distance of 44,68 metres. Taipale threw 44,19 for second place while Augustus Pope of the USA recorded 42,13 for third.

It was all set to be an epic duel between Pat Ryan, the world record holder for the **hammer throw**, and Matt McGrath, the defending Olympic champion. But it was not to be, as McGrath twisted his knee in the second round and was relegated to the sidelines. Ryan achieved the winning distance of 52,87 metres in the morning preliminary rounds with Basil Bennett of the USA lying second on 48,25 and Carl Lindh of Sweden third at 48,00. Lindh later improved to 48,43 to take the silver medal and shunt Bennett into third spot. Interestingly, Tom Nicholson of Britain who had missed competing in the preliminary morning rounds was strangely allowed to throw in the finals, where he came sixth.

Finland dominated the **javelin throw**, placing first to fourth. Urko Peltonen led the qualifiers with an Olympic record of 63,60 metres followed closely by Pekka Johansson on 63,09 and world record holder Jonni Myyrae. Myyrae had been hit by a javelin in his non-throwing arm during the preliminaries and fired by the indignity of being only third, he then unleashed a mighty throw of 65,78 in the fourth round. This fell just short of his own world mark, but was more than good enough to capture the Olympic title. Peltonen and Johansson finished second and third respectively, while the fourth Finn, Juho Saaristo, with 62,39 and Alex Klumberg of Estonia with 62,39 also exceeded the old Olympic record.

The contest for the **pentathlon** was between the USA and Finland and Eero Lehtonen came out a comfortable winner with 18 points from Everett Bradley of the USA with 25 points. There was a tie for third spot between Hugo Lahtinen of Finland and Bob Le Gendre of the USA both having scored 26 points, but the Finn scored higher on the decathlon tables so was awarded the bronze medal. The best individual mark was Alex Klumberg's javelin throw of 60,76.

A soft track and wet conditions prevented outstanding performances and high scores in the **decathlon**, but it did not prevent a close competition. On the first day, Brutus Hamilton of the USA led with 3,406 points from Woldemar Wickholm of Finland, 3,375, and Bertil Ohlson of Sweden, but on the second day, Helge Loveland of Norway improved from fourth position to first to take the gold medal with 6,804·35 points. Hamilton was second with 6,770·086 with Ohlson placed third.

Percy Hodge of Britain, utilises superior barrier clearance to win the 3,000 metres steeplechase.   Dave Terry

All-Sport Photographic Ltd.

Johannes Petteri Kolehmainen

Born in Kuipio, Finland, on 9 December 1889, Hannes Kolehmainen was the first of a line of great Finnish distance runners. One of his most memorable races was winning the 5,000m in Stockholm in a world record 14-36·6, which stood for ten years.

These Games also saw him win the 10,000m and the cross country, and also set a world record of 8-36·8 in the heats of the 3,000m team event.

The following year Kolehmainen gave further proof of his immense staying power by lowering the world record for 20,000m. It was not surprising then, that when the Antwerp Games came round in 1920, the "Flying Finn", now 29, was lining up for the start of the marathon. He won his fourth Olympic gold medal in that race, again in a tight finish, this time from Jari Lossman, of Estonia, in 2:32-35·8.

Soon after these Games Kolehmainen improved the world record for 25,000m and lowered it yet again in 1922 when he also recorded new world figures for 30,000m.

Along with Paavo Nurmi, he was honoured by the Finns at the 1952 Games in Helsinki by being chosen to take over the torch with which Nurmi had lit the Olympic flame. Kolehmainen died on 11 November 1966.

Dave Terry

Charles Paddock

Charlie Paddock, who was born in Gainsville, Texas, on 11 August 1900, was probably the most spectacular sprinter of his day. He became famed for his flying leaps at the tape, never more evident than at the finish of the 200m in the Antwerp Games. He was a tremendously popular showman. Try as he would for victory with his explosive thrust approaching the tape he was pipped for the 200m gold by a tenth of a second, both in Antwerp in 1920 and in Paris in 1924 by a fellow countryman.

The 100m in Antwerp, however, saw him gain his just deserts, with a victory in 10·8 sec, by an even narrower margin from Morris Kirksey, also of the United States, who was given the same time. Both were in the team that won the 4 × 100m relay for the USA in a world record 42·2 sec, Paddock running the first leg and Kirksey the last.

His best season in 1921 saw him join the individual world record holders, four times equalling the mark of 9·6 sec for 100 yards and setting new figures of 10·4 sec for 100 metres. That same year he set a world record of 20·8 sec for 220 yards and 21·0 sec for 200 metres.

He became a Captain in the American Marines during the Second World War but sadly lost his life in an air crash in 1945.

Off to a flying start in the 100 metres is the American Charlie Paddock (fourth from left), who went on to win.

Dave Terry

MALES

COMPETITOR	COUNTRY CODE	EVENT	ROUND	HEAT	PLACE	TIME & DISTANCE	MEDAL
Aastad, E.	NOR	Long jump	F		5	6,88	
Abrahams, H.M.	GBR	100m	1	10	1	11·0	
			2	3	4		
		200m	1	5	2		
			2	4	3		
		4×100m relay	1	2	2		
			F		6		
		Long jump	F		20	6,05	
Abrahamsson, E.	SWE	Long jump	F		3	7,08	B
Ahearn, D.F.	USA	Triple jump	F		6	14,08	
Ainsworth-Davis, E.J.	GBR	400m	1	2	2		
			2	1	2		
			SF	1	3		
			F		5	50·0	
		4×400m relay	1	1	2		
			F		1	3-22·2	G
Ali-Khan, E.	FRA	100m	1	9	1	11·0	
			2	3	2		
			SF	2	2		
			F		5	11·1	
		4×100m relay	1	2	1	43·0	
			F		2	42·6	S
Almloef, E.	SWE	Triple jump	F		3	14,27	B
Ambrosini, E.	ITA	800m	1	4	4		
			SF	1	4		
		3000m team race	1	1	3	25	
			F		5	34	
		3000m steeplechase	1	1	3		
			F		3	10-27·0	B
Andersen, A.	DEN	10000m	1	2	3		
			F		DNS		
		8000m cross country	F		20		
Andersen, F.	DEN	4×100m relay	1	3	2		
			F		4		
Andersen, P.	DEN	4×100m relay	1	3	2		
			F		4		
Andre, G.	FRA	400m	1	4	2		
			2	4	3		
			SF	2	5		
		400m hurdles	1	5	2		
			SF	1	2		
			F		4	54·8	
		4×400m relay	1	1	3		
			F		3	3-24·8	B
Angier, M.S.	USA	Javelin throw	F		7	59,27	
Anselmetti, S.	SUI	3k walk	1	2	DIS		
		10k walk	1	2	DNF		
Antognini, L.	SUI	Shot put	F		19	10,32	
Argouarch, K.	FRA	800m	1	5	4		
			SF	2	6		
Arri, V.	ITA	Marathon	F		3	2:36-32·8	B
Audinet, A.	FRA	1500m	1	1	3		
			F		6		
Bache, K.	NOR	Triple jump	F		9	13,64	
Backman, E.	SWE	5000m	1	4	2		
			F		3	15-13·0	B
		10000m	1	2	2		
			F		10		
		3000m team race	1	1	1	12	
			F		4	24	
		8000m cross country	F		2	27-17·6	S
Baekkedahl, A.	NOR	4×100m relay	1	1	DIS		
Baker, B.H.	GBR	High jump	F		6	1,85	
		Triple jump	F		8	13,67	
Baker, P.J.N.	GBR	800m	1	3	1	1-56·0	
		1500m	1	4	2		
			F		2	4-02·4	S
Banerji P.	IND	400m	1	8	4		
Bangels,	BEL	3000m team race	1	1	4		
			F		6		
Barron, H.E.	USA	110m hurdles	1	2	1	15·2	
			SF	1	1	15·0*	
			F		2	15·0	S
Bartlett, W.	USA	Discus throw	F		5	40,87	
Bascunam, J.	CHI	Marathon	F		33	3:07-47·0	
Bauduin, F.	FRA	800m	1	1	3		
			SF	3	5		
Bayon, E.	FRA	400m	1	10	3		
Bennett, B.	USA	Hammer throw	F		3	48,25	B
Bergstroem, N.	SWE	5000m	1	2	4		
			F		10		
		10000m	1	3	6		
Bernard, H.	FRA	110m hurdles	1	3	5		
Bernard, J.	FRA	8000m cross country	F		32		
Bihlman, G.	USA	Shot put	F		7	13,57	
Bladin, J.	SWE	400m hurdles	1	2	2		
			SF	1	4		
		Long jump	F		9	6,57	
Blasi, E.	ITA	Marathon	F		DNF		
Blansaer, O.	BEL	Marathon	F		34	3:20-00·0	
Blewitt, C.E.	GBR	5000m	1	2	1	15-19·8	
			F		5		
		3000m team race	1	1	2		
			F		2	5	
Blomqvist, E.	SWE	Shot put	F		16	11,93	
		Javelin throw	F		8	58,18	
Boland, M.	USA	8000m cross country	F		16		
Bolin, A.	SWE	400m	1	1	3		
		800m	1	3	3		
			SF	3	4		
Bonardoni, G.	ITA	400m	1	4	3		
Bonini, G.	ITA	800m	1	1	2		
			SF	2	5		
		1500m	1	2	7		
Botin, C.	ESP	100m	1	8	3		
Bradley, E.	USA	Pentathlon	F		2	25	S
Brochart, P.	BEL	100m	1	7	1	11·4	
			2	5	2		
			SF	2	4		
		200m	1	4	1	23·2	
			2	5	2		
			SF	1	DNS		
		4×100m relay	1	2	4		
Broos, A.	BEL	Marathon	F		4	2:39-25·8	
Brossard, E.	FRA	3000m team race	1	2	1	7	S
			F		3	30	
		8000m cross country	F		31		
		3000m steeplechase	1	1	4		
Brown, H.H.	USA	5000m	1	2	3		
			F		DNF		
		3000m team race	1	2	2	14	
			F		1	10	G
Bucher, N.	SUI	Decathlon	F		10	5274	
Bukes, J.W.	SAF	100m	1	3	2		
			2	2	3		
		200m	1	5	3		
		4×100m relay	1	3	3		
Burtin, A.	FRA	1500m	1	2	4		
		3000m team race	1	2	1	7	
			F		3	30	B
Butler, G.M.	GBR	400m	1	6	2		
			2	2	2		
			SF	2	2		
			F		2	49·8	S
		4×400m relay	1	1	2		
			F		1	3-22·2	G
Butler, S.	USA	Long jump	F		7	6,60	
Cameron, J.	CAN	Hammer throw	Q		DNQ	0	
Campbell, T.	USA	800m	1	4	2		
			SF	2	2		
			F		DNF		
Camps, J.	ESP	4×100m relay	1	1	3		
Cann, H.D.	USA	Shot put	F		8	13,52	
Carroll, T.J.	GBR	High jump	F		=9	1,75	
Caste, R.	FRA	200m	1	5	1	23·0	
			2	2	3		
Changule, P.R.	IND	10000m	1	1	10		
		Marathon	F		19	2:50-45·4	
Chilo, A.	FRA	Triple jump	F		17	12,65	
Christiernsson, C.	SWE	110m hurdles	1	6	2		
			SF	2	3		
			F		6	15·9	
		400m hurdles	1	4	1	56·4	
			SF	2	2		
			F		5	55·6	
Christopher,	GBR	8000m cross country	F		19		
Clibbon, C.T.	GBR	10000m	1	3	2		
			F		14		
Coaffee, C.	CAN	100m	1	12	3		
Colbacchini, D.	ITA	110m hurdles	1	1	1	15·6	
			SF	1	4		
Colbach, J.	LUX	4×100m relay	1	1	2		
			F		5		
Connolly, J.	USA	1500m	1	3	3		
			F		10		
Cornetta, G.	USA	10000m	1	3	9		
Corteyn, O.	BEL	400m	1	9	1	52·2	
			2	2	5		
		4×400m relay	1	1	1	3-38·8	
			F		6		
Coulon, P.	FRA	Long jump	F		13	6,50	

COMPETITOR	COUNTRY CODE	EVENT	ROUND	HEAT	PLACE	TIME & DISTANCE	MEDAL
Courtin, C.	FRA	Long jump	F		18	6,23	
Crawford, R.	USA	8000m cross country	F		40		
Croci, G.	ITA	100m	1	10	3		
		4×100m relay	1	1	DIS		
Cummings, P.	GBR	8000m cross country	F		16		
Daggs, C.I.D.	USA	400m hurdles	1	4	2		
			SF	2	3		
			F		6	56·4	
D'Arcy, V.H.A.	GBR	100m	1	9	3		
			2	5	3		
		200m	1	6	3		
		4×100m relay	1	2	2		
			F		6		
Davel, H.	SAF	400m	1	3	2		
			2	3	1	51·0	
			SF	2	3		
			F		6	50·1	
		800m	1	4	3		
			SF	3	6		
		4×100m relay	1	3	3		
		4×400m relay	1	3	2	3-38·7	
			F		2	3-24·2	S
Davidson, G.	NZL	100m	1	11	2		
			2	3	3		
		200m	1	2	1	22·6	
			2	3	1	22·8	
			SF	1	3		
			F		5	22·3	
Dawson, C.	GBR	3k walk	1	1	4		
			F		6	13-30·0	
		10k walk	1	2	DNF		
De Bruyne, H.	BEL	Long jump	F		19	6,20	
De Conninck, M.	FRA	1500m	1	3	4		
Dellow, J.	CAN	Marathon	F		13	2:46-47·0	
Delvart, M.	FRA	400m	1	7	3		
		4×400m relay	1	1	3		
			F		3	3-24·8	B
Demitriades, T.	GRE	110m hurdles	1	3	5		
Desch, A.G.	USA	400m hurdles	1	1	1	57 6	
			SF	1	1	55·4	
			F		3	54·7	B
Devaney, M.	USA	3000m team race	1	2	2	14	
			F		1	10	G
		3000m steeplechase	1	1	1	10-23·0	
			F		5	10-29·0	
Devaux, A.	BEL	10000m	1	1	8		
Devaux, J.-M.	FRA	4×400m relay	1	1	3		
			F		3	3-24·8	B
De Vries, J.	HOL	100m	1	1	4		
		4×100m relay	1	2	3		
Dixon, M.	SAF	100m	1	5	3		
Doig, J.	SAF	800m	1	1	4		
			SF		7		
Dominguez,	ESP	4×100m relay	1	1	3		
Dominguez, J.	ESP	8000m cross country	F		25		
Downs,	CAN	8000m cross country	F		29		
Doyen, A.	BEL	10k walk	1	2	6		
			F		8		
Dozolme, H.	FRA	Shot put	F		15	11,96	
Dresser, I.	USA	5000m	1	4	3		
			F		DNF		
		3000m team race	1	2	2	14	
			F		1	10	G
Droux,	FRA	Triple jump	F		16	12,92	
Dunbar, E.	GBR	110m hurdles	1	6	4		
Dunne, R.J.	USA	Pentathlon	F		DNF		
Duquesne, L.	FRA	5000m	1	2	5		
		10000m	1	1	7		
		3000m team race	1	2	1	7	
			1		3	30	B
Ebert, J.	DEN	10000m	1	1	11		
		8000m cross country	F		35		
Eby, E.	USA	800m	1	2	3		
			SF	3	2		
			F		2	1-53·6	S
		4×400m relay	1	2	2		
			F		4	3-25·2	
Edward, H.F.V.	GBR	100m	1	8	2		
			2	1	1	10·8	
			SF	1	1	10·8	
			F		3	11·0	B
		200m	1	10	1	22·8	
			2	2	1	22·0	
			SF	1	2		
			F		3	22·2	B
		4×100m relay	1	2	2		
			F		6		
Ekelund, B.	SWE	High jump	F		3	1,90	B
Ekman, H.	SWE	8000m cross country	F		11	28-17·0	
Ellis, E.	USA	Decathlon	F		DNF		
Emory, R.S.	USA	400m	1	6	1	52·6	
			2	1	3		
			SF	1	4		
		4×400m relay	1	2	2		
			F		4	3-25·2	
Engdahl, N.	SWE	400m	1	7	2		
			2	1	1	50·4	
			SF	1	1	49·4	
			F		3	49·9	B
		800m	1	4	5		
		4×400m relay	1	2	3		
			F		5		
Eriksson, A.	SWE	Discus throw	F		6	39,41	
Esparjes, J.-P.	FRA	800m	1	2	4		
			SF	3	3		
			F		8	1-58·0	
Falk, R.	SWE	5000m	1	1	1	15-17·8	
			F		11		
		3000m team race	1	1	1	12	
			F		4	24	
Faller, F.W.	USA	10000m	1	2	4		
			F		8	32-38·0	
		8000m cross country	F		15		
Fallgreen, U.	FIN	Marathon	F		9	2:42-40·0	
Ferry, G.	FRA	400m	1	2	1	51·2	
			2	2	1	50·0	
			SF	2	6		
		4×400m relay	1	1	3		
			F		3	3-24·8	B
Flynn, P.J.	USA	3000m cross country	F		9	28-12·0	
		3000m steeplechase	1	2	1	10-36·0	
			F		2	10-18·0	S
Foss, F.K.	USA	Pole vault	F		1	4,09*	G
Fourneau, L.	BEL	1500m	1	4	3		
			F		11		
Frankenstein, K.	TCH	400m	1	2	3		
Franksson, R.	SWE	Long jump	F		6	6,73	
Franquenelle, A.	FRA	Pole vault	F		=8	3,50	
Freeman, E.	CAN	10k walk	1	2	DIS		
Freeman, W.	GBR	8000m cross country	F		22		
Frigerio, U.	ITA	3k walk	1	2	1	13-40·2	
			F		1	13-14·2*	G
		10k walk	1	1	1	47-06·4	
			F		1	48-06·2	G
Furnas, C.	USA	5000m	1	1	4		
			F		DNF		
Gajan, R.	FRA	Pole vault	F		14	3,50	
Garcia, M.	ESP	400m	1	10	2		
			2	3	4		
		800m	1	5	3		
			SF	1	6		
Garin, D.	SUI	10000m	1	2	5		
			F		9		
Gaschen, A.	SUI	5000m	1	1	5		
		10000m	1	1	5		
			F		10		
Geist, K.	USA	Triple jump	F		12	13,52	
Genzabula, N.	JPN	Decathlon	F		DNF		
Gerspach, E.	SUI	Decathlon	F		9	5948	
Geyer, R	FRA	3000m steeplechase	1	2	4		
Gitsham, C.	SAF	Marathon	F		DNF		
Goeutz, N.	USA	Decathlon	F		DNF		
Gouilleaux, R.	FRA	800m	1	4	1	1-58·8	
			SF	1	5		
Grany, P	FRA	Javelin throw	F		15	46,90	
Gray, G.	GBR	110m hurdles	1	3	2		
			SF	1	5		
		400m hurdles	1	1	3		
		4×400m relay	1	1	12		
			F		1	3-22·2	G
Gruner, W	SWE	Marathon	F		28	3:11-48·0	
Gubbels, C.	HOL	3k walk	1	1	9		
Guezille, C.	FRA	Long jump	F		28	5,45	
Guillemot, J.	FRA	5000m	1	4	1	15-33·0	
			F		1	14-55·6	G
		10000m	1	2	1	32-41·4	
			F		2	31-47·2	S
Grillon, G.	FRA	3000m steeplechase	1	3	6		
Guldager, B.	NOR	100m	1	4	4		
		200m	1	1	5		
		4×100m relay	1	1	DIS		

COMPETITOR	COUNTRY CODE	EVENT	ROUND	HEAT	PLACE	TIME & DISTANCE	MEDAL
Gunn, C.E.J.	GBR	3k walk	1	2	6		
			F		10		
		10k walk	1	1	5	48-22·0	
			F		3	49-44·4	B
Gustin, M.	BEL	100m	1	1	3		
		200m	1	3	3		
Gyllenstolpe, A.-E.	SWE	Decathlon	F		8	6332	
		Pentathlon	F		DNF		
Hamilton, B.	USA	Decathlon	F		2	6770·86	S
		Pentathlon	F		6	27	
Hammer, P.	LUX	200m	1	4	4		
		4×100m relay	1	1	2		
			F		5		
		Long jump	F		29	5,45	
Hansen, R.	DEN	Marathon	F		8	2:41-39·4	
Hasumi, S.	JPN	1500m	1	4	6		
Hatton, J.	GBR	10000m	1	3	5		
			F		5	32-14·0	
		3000m team race	1	1	2	11	
			F		2	20	S
Hedvall, L.	SWE	8000m cross country	F		24		
		3000m steeplechase	1	2	2		
			F		7	10-36·0	
Heggarty, W.A.	GBR	8000m cross country	F		5	27-57·0	
Hehir, W.	GBR	3k walk	1	2	5		
			F		7		
		10k walk	1	2	1	51-33·8	
			F		5	50-13·0	
Herman, E.	EST	3k walk	1	1	10		
		10k walk	1	1	DIS		
Heuet, G.	FRA	10000m	1	3	3		
			F		DNF		
		3000m team race	1	2	1	30	
			F		3		B
		8000m cross country	F		7	28-00·0	
Hewitt, T.	AUS	10000m	1	2	10		
		Marathon	F		30	3:13-27·0	
Heynneman, A.	HOL	100m	1	3	3		
		200m	1	11	2		
			2	4	5		
		4×100m relay	1	2	3		
Hill, A.G.	GBR	800m	1	2	2		
			SF	3	1	1-56·4	
			F		1	1-53·4	G
		1500m	1	1	2		
			F		1	4-01·8	G
Hill, W.A.	GBR	100m	1	1	1	11·0	
			2	2	1	11·0	
			SF	2	5		
		200m	1	3	2		
			2	5	3		
		4×100m relay	1	2	2		
			F		6		
Hodge, P.	GBR	3000m team race	1	1	2	11	
			F		2	20	S
		3000m steeplechase	1	3	1	10-17·4*	
			F		1	10-00·4*	G
Hogstroem,	SWE	8000m cross country	F		30		
Hogstroem, P.	SWE	Pole vault	F		=8	3,50	
Holmer, G.	SWE	110m hurdles	1	2	3		
		Decathlon	F		4	6533·15	
Holmstroem, A.	SWE	100m	1	11	3		
		200m	1	1	2		
			2	1	4		
		4×100m relay	1	3	1	43·4	
			F		3	42·9	B
Holsner, J.	SWE	3000m team race	1	1	1	12	
			F		4	24	
		3000m steeplechase	1	2	5		
Houben, M.	BEL	200m	1	7	2		
			2	1	5		
		4×100m relay	1	2	4		
Houslen, L.	GBR	Marathon	F		31	3:14-07·0	
Hughes, W.	AUS	110m hurdles	1	1	4		
Hulsebosch, A.	USA	3000m steeplechase	1	3	3		
			F		6	10-32·0	
Hultin, G.	SWE	110m hurdles	1	5	2		
			SF	2	6		
Hunt, W.W.	AUS	100m	1	4	1	11·0	
			2	1	4		
		200m	1	4	2		
			2	4	4		
Hunter, C.	USA	5000m	1	3	7		
Hunter, W.L.	GBR	110m hurdles	1	4	2		
			SF	2	4		
		Long jump	F		14	6,42	
Ichard, L.	FRA	Marathon	F		DNF		
Ichiro, K.	JPN	200m	1	9	4		

COMPETITOR	COUNTRY CODE	EVENT	ROUND	HEAT	PLACE	TIME & DISTANCE	MEDAL
Imbach, J.	SUI	100m	1	6	2		
			2	4	3		
		200m	1	12	2		
			2	1	2		
			SF	2	5		
		4×100m relay	1	3	4		
Ingen,	SWE	800m	1	1	5		
Irvine, F.	SAF	100m	1	4	3		
		200m	1	9	3		
		400m	1	2	4		
		4×100m relay	1	3	3		
Irwin, H.C.	GBR	5000m	1	1	2		
			F		12		
Izaguirre, I.	ESP	Shot put	F		17	11,23	
Jagenburg, H.	SWE	High jump	F		=9	1,75	
Jansson, B.	SWE	Shot put	F		9	13,27	
Jansson, F.	SWE	Triple jump	F		2	14,48	S
Jaquith, C.	USA	Triple jump	F		15	13,04	
Jarrety, M.	FRA	400m hurdles	1	2	3		
Jenne, E.	USA	Pole vault	F		7	3,60	
Jensen, A.	DEN	5000m	1	4	5		
		8000m cross country	F		28		
		Marathon	F				
Jensen, W.	DEN	Discus throw	F		7	38,23	
Jeppe, M.	SAF	110m hurdles	1	5	3		
Joannes-Powell, R.	BEL	110m hurdles	1	3	4		
		Pole vault	F		=8	3,50	
		Decathlon	F		11	5091	
Johanssen, E.	FIN	800m	1	2	5		
Johannessen, J.	NOR	Long jump	F		10	6.56	
Johansson, P.	FIN	Javelin throw	F		3	63,09	B
Johnson, C.	USA	Long jump	F		2	7,09	S
Johnson, E.	USA	10000m	1	3	8		
Jonssen, J.	NOR	100m	1	6	4		
		4×100m relay	1	1	DIS		
Jonsson, J.	DEN	5000m	1	4	5		
Jorgensen, L.	DEN	Pole vault	F		6	3,60	
Juul, E.	NOR	Triple jump	F		11	13,59	
Kaga, I.	JAP	200m	1	9	4		
Kanakuri, S.	JPN	Marathon	F		16	2:48-45·4	
Kanive, N.	LUX	Long jump	F		30	5,41	
Kanso, Y.	JPN	Marathon	F		21	2:57-03·0	
Karabamtis, D.	GRE	200m	1	7	3		
Khairy, A.	EGY	200m	1	6	4		
		400m	1	10	4		
Kindler, H.	SUI	Long jump	F		15	6,34	
Kinn, G.	SWE	Marathon	F		17	2:49-08·0	
Kioelling, F.	SWE	1500m	1	4	4		
Kirksey, M.M.	USA	100m	1	6	1	11·0	
			2	5	1	11·0	
			SF	1	3		
			F		2	10·8	S
		200m	1	12	1	23·4	
			2	4	1	22·6	
			SF	1	4		
		4×100m relay	1	1	1	43·0	
			F		1	42·2*	G
Klumberg, A.	EST	Javelin throw	F		5	62,39	
		Pentathlon	F		DNF		
Knosuke, S.	JPN	200m	1	2	6		
		10000m	1	2	9		
Knourek, E.	USA	Pole vault	F		4	3,60	
Kolehmainen, H.	FIN	Marathon	F		1	2:32-35·8*	G
Kolehmainen, T.	FIN	Marathon	F		10	2:44-03·2	
Koskenniemi, T.	FIN	5000m	1	1	3		
			F		4	15-17·0	
		8000m cross country	F		6	27-57·2	
Kranis, A.	GRE	5000m	1	3	5		
		10000m	1	3	7		
		8000m cross country	F		38		
Krokstroem, S.	SWE	200m	1	7	1	23·8	
			2	3	4		
		400m	1	3	3		
		4×400m relay	1	2	3		
			F		5		
Labat, R.	FRA	High jump	F		=9	1,80	
Lagarde, C.	FRA	Pole vault	F		=8	3,50	
Lahtinen, H.	FIN	Long jump	F		17	6,19	
		Pentathlon	F		3	26	B
Landers, S.G.	USA	Triple jump	F		5	14,17	
Landon, R.	USA	High jump	F		1	1,94*	G
Langrenay, F.	FRA	3000m steeplechase	1	1	5		
Lauvaux, H.	FRA	8000m cross country	F		17		
Lawrence, E.	CAN	1500m	1	2	5		
		10000m	1	2	6		
Lefevre, J.	BEL	Long jump	F		24	5,79	
Le Gendre, R.	USA	Pentathlon	F		4	26	

COMPETITOR	COUNTRY CODE	EVENT	ROUND	HEAT	PLACE	TIME & DISTANCE	MEDAL
Lehtonen, E.	FIN	Long jump	F		17	6,28	
		Pentathlon	F		1	18	G
Leibundeut, W.	SUI	4×100m relay	1	3	4		
Lehouck, J.	BEL	4×100m relay	1	2	4		
		Long jump	F		26	5,76	
Lenzi, A.	ITA	Shot put	F		26	12,32	
Leroy, R.	FRA	1500m	1	4	5		
Levine. F.	SAF	400m	1	4	4		
Lewden, P.	FRA	High jump	F		=7	1,80	
Liimatainen, H.	FIN	10000m	1	3	1	32-08-2	
			F		7	32-23-0	
		8000m cross country	F		3	27-37-4	B
Lillier, H.	SWE	Javelin throw	F		10	56,44	
Lincoln, J.	USA	Javelin throw	F		9	57,86	
Linder, C.	USA	Marathon	F		11	2 44-21-2	
Lindh, C.	SWE	Hammer throw	F		2	48,43	S
		56-pound weight	F		3	10,25	B
Lindh, N.	SWE	Hammer throw	F		7	44,88	
Lindsay, R.A.	GBR	400m	1	1	1	52-0	
			2	3	5		
		4×400m relay	1	1	2		
			F		1	3-22-2	G
Lindstroem, Georg	SWE	110m hurdles	1	1	3		
		400m hurdles	1	3	3		
Lindstroem, Gunnar	SWE	Javelin throw	F		6	60,52	
Lindvall, E.	SWE	100m	1	2	3		
Lively, C.	GBR	Triple jump	F		13	13,15	
		Long jump	F		22	5,87	
Liversedge, H.	USA	Shot put	F		3	14,15	B
Loomis, F.J.	USA	400m hurdles	1	5	1	54-8	
			SF	2	1	55-4	
			F		1	54-0*	G
Lorencana, J.	ESP	400m	1	9	4		
Lorrain, R.	FRA	100m	1	6	3		
		200m	1	11	1	25-0	
			2	3	3		
		4×100m relay	1	2	1	43-0	
			F		2	42-6	S
Lossman, J.	EST	5000m	1	3	10		
		10000m	1	1	9		
		Marathon	F		2	2:32-48-6	S
Lovland, H.	NOR	Decathlon	F		1	6804-35	G
		Pentathlon	F		5	27	
Lundgren, S.	SWE	800m	1	5	1	2-00-6	
			SF	2	4		
		1500m	1	2	1	4-07-0	
			F		5		
		3000m team race	1	1	12		
			F		4	24	
Lundstroem, E.	SWE	5000m	1	3	4		
			F		13		
Lussana, C.	ITA	10000m	1	3	10		
McDermaid, A.	CAN	Hammer throw	F		9	44,66	
		56-pound weight	D		4	10,12	
McDonald, P.J.	USA	Shot put	F		4	14,08	
		56-pound weight	F		1	11,26*	G
McEachern, J.	USA	Hammer throw	F		8	44,70	
McGrath, M.J.	USA	Hammer throw	F		5	46,67	
McMaster, C.C.	SAF	3k walk	1	2	2		
			F		4	13-25-2	
		10k walk	1	2	2	51-39-0	
			F		4		
McPhee, D.	GBR	1500m	1	2	2		
			F		9		
		3000m team race	1	1	2	11	
			F		2	20	S
Maccario, F.	ITA	5000m	1		DNF		
		10000m	1	1	3		
			F		4	32-02-0	
		3000m team race	1	1	3	25	
			F		5	34	
Maghoub, A.	EGY	5000m	1	3	9		
Magnusson, W.	SWE	10000m	1	1	6		
		8000m cross country	F		13		
Maguerza, J.	ESP	5000m	1	2	7		
Mahan, J.	USA	Javelin throw	F		12		
Malm, S.	SWE	100m	1	9	2		
		200m	1	10	3		
		4×100m relay	1	3	1	43-4	
			F		3	42-9	B
		4×400m relay	1	2	3		
			F		5		
Mangset, E.	NOR	400m	1	1	4		
Manhes, J.	FRA	5000m	1	1	7		
		10000m	1	1	4		
			F		6	32-26-0	
Maroney, T.A.	USA	3k walk	1	1	3		
			F		5	13-26-8	
		10k walk	1	2	3		
			F		6	50-20-6	
Martinenghi, C.	ITA	1500m	1	1	6		
		5000m	1	2	9		
		3000m team race	1	1	3	25	
			F		5	34	
		3000m steeplechase	1	3	5		
Mattsson, G.	SWE	8000m cross country	F		10	28-16-0	
		3000m steeplechase	1	3	2		
			F		4	10-27-0	
Mattsson, J.	SWE	Pole vault	F		=8	3,50	
Medecin, E.	MON	200m	1	9	5		
		Long jump	F		22	6,03	
Melendez, L.	ESP	10k walk	1	2	5		
			F		DNF		
Melis, C.	BEL	Marathon	F		27	3:10-51-0	
Mellor, C.	USA	Marathon	F		12	2:45-30-0	
Mendizabal, F.	ESP	100m	1	4	2		
			1	2	2		
			SF	1	5		
		200m	1	2	3		
		4×100m relay	1	1	3		
Merchant, J.W.	USA	Long jump	F		12	6,50	
Meredith, J.E.	USA	400m	1	4	1	51-6	
			2	2	3		
			SF	2	4		
		4×400m relay	1	2	2		
			F		4	3-25-2	
Meyers, E.	USA	Pole vault	F		3	3,60	B
Mietanen,	FIN	8000m cross country	F		23		
Migeot, J.	BEL	400m	1	6	4		
		4×400m relay	1	1	1	3-38-8	
			F		6		
Mills, A.	GBR	Marathon	F		14	2:48-05-0	
Miura, Y.	JPN	Marathon	F		24	2:59-37-0	
Moche, A.	FRA	Marathon	F		18	2:50-00-2	
Mogi. Z.	JPN	10000m	1	3	12		
Monolas, P.	GRE	Triple jump	F		18	12,60	
Morren, F.	BEL	400m	1	10	1	51-6	
			2	1	4		
		4×400m relay	1	1	1	3-38-8	
			F		6		
Mountain, E.D.	GBR	800m	1	1	1	1-57-6	
			SF	1	2		
			F		4	1-54-6	
Mourlon, R.	FRA	100m	1	2	1	11-2	
			2	1	3		
		4×100m relay	1	2	1	43-0	
			F		2	42-6	S
Muguerza, J.	ESP	5000m	1	2	7		
Muller, H.	USA	High jump	F		2	1,90	S
Murchison, L.C.	USA	100m	1	3	1	10-8	
			2	1	2		
			SF	2	3		
			F		6	11-2	
		200m	1	8	1	23-2	
			2	1	1	22-8	
			SF	1	1	22-4	
			F		4	22-2	
		4×100m relay	1	1	1	43-0	
			F		1	42-2*	G
Murphy, J.	USA	High jump	F		5	1,85	
Murray, F.S.	USA	110m hurdles	1	3	1	15-8	
			SF	2	2		
			F		3	15-2	B
Myers, E.E.	USA	Pole vault	F		3	3,75	B
Myyrae, J.	FIN	Javelin throw	F		1	65,78*	G
Nichols, A.H.	GBR	5000m	1	4	4		
			F		8		
		8000m cross country	F		12	28-20-0	
Nicholson, T.	GBR	Hammer throw	F		6	45,70	
Nielsen, A.	DEN	5000m	1	2	10		
Niklander, E.	FIN	Discus throw	F		1	44,68	G
		Shot put	F		2	14,15	S
Nilsson, E.	SWE	Shot put	F		5	13,87	
		Decathlon	F		5	6484-34	
		Pentathlon	F		DNF		
Noizieres, M.	SUI	4×100m relay	1	3	4		
Norling, T.	SWE	110m hurdles	1	2	3		
Norman, G.	CAN	Marathon	F		22	2:58-01-0	
Norman-Larsen, O.	NOR	800m	1	2	6		
Norton, J.K.	USA	400m hurdles	1	3	1	57-6	
			SF	1	3		
			F		2	54-6	S
Nugeat, J.	BEL	400m	1	3	4		

COMPETITOR	COUNTRY CODE	EVENT	ROUND	HEAT	PLACE	TIME & DISTANCE	MEDAL
Nurmi, P.	FIN	5000m	1	3	2		
			F		2	15-00-0	S
		10000m	1	1	2		
			F		1	31-45-8	G
		8000m cross country	F		1	27-15-0	G
Nylund, O.	FIN	Triple jump	F		7	13,74	
		Pentathlon	F		DNF		
Ohlsøn, B.	SWE	Decathlon	F		3	6579-80	B
		Pentathlon	F		7	30	
Oldfield, C.	SAF	400m	1	1	2		
			2	3	5		
		4×400m relay	1	2	1	3-38-7	
			F		2	3-24-2	S
Oleffe, L.	BEL	1500m	1	3	5		
Olsson, C.	SWE	Hammer throw	F		10	44,19	
Oosterlaak, J.	SAF	100m	1	11	1	11-0	
			2	4	2		
			SF	1	4		
		200m	1	10	1		
			2	5	1	23-0	
			SF	2	3		
			F		6	22-4	
		4×100m relay	1	3	3		
		4×400m relay	1	2	1	3-38-7	
			F		2	3-24-2	S
Ordonez, D.	ESP	100m	1	7	3		
		200m	1	1	3		
Orfidan, M.	FRA	110m hurdles	1	1	5		
		Long jump	F		15	6,39	
Organ, J.L.	USA	Marathon	F		7	2:41-30-0	
Orlandi, G.	ITA	200m	1	4	3		
		4×100m relay	1	1	DIS		
Otterbeen,	BEL	3000m team race	1	1	4		
			F		6		
Oura, T.	JAP	5000m	1	4	7		
Pacak, K.	TCH	5000m	1	3	6		
		1000m	1	3	11		
Paddock, C.W.	USA	100m	1	8	1	10-8	
			2	3	1	10-8	
			SF	2	1	10-8	
			F		1	10-8	G
		200m	1	6	1	23-2	
			2	3	2		
			SF	2	2		
			F		2	22-1	S
		4×100m relay	1	1	1	43-0	
			F		1	42-2*	G
Pajaron, C.	ESP	200m	1	8	3		
Panayotis, T.	GRE	Marathon	F		DNF		
Pantajotis, R.	GRE	5000m	1	1	9		
		8000m cross country	F		39		
Paoli, R.	FRA	Shot put	F		12	12,48	
Parker, G.L.	AUS	3k walk	1	1	2		
			F		2	13-20-6	S
		10k walk	1	1	3	47-31-0	
			F		DNF		
Patasoni, A.	USA	10000m	1	1	12		
Paulen, A.	HOL	800m	1	3	4		
			SF	2	3		
			F		7	1-56-4	
Pavesi, D.	ITA	3k walk	1	1	1	13-46-8	
			F		DIS		
		10k walk	1	1	4	48-12-0	
			F		9		
Pearman, J.B.	USA	3k walk	1	1	11		
		10k walk	1	1	2	47-30-0	
			F		2	49-40-8	S
Pedersen, N.	DEN	3k walk	1	1	5		
			F		11	13-44-0	
		10k walk	1	2	DIS		
Peltonen, U.	FIN	Javelin throw	F		2	63,50	S
Penton, A.	CAN	100m	1	10	2		
			2	4	5		
		200m	1	2	2		
			2	4	2		
			SF	2	4		
Persico, A.	ITA	Marathon	F		DNF		
Petersen, H.	DEN	Pole vault	F		2	3,75	S
Peterson, F.	DEN	Shot put	F		11	12,52	
Petersson, J.	FIN	Hammer throw	F		11	41,76	
		56-pound weight	F		6	9,37	
Petersson, W.	SWE	4×100m relay	1	3	1	43-4	
			F		3	42-9	B
		Long jump	F		1	7,15	G
Phillips, H.	CAN	400m	1	8	2		
Picard, A.	FRA	Javelin throw	F		13	47,09	
Pierre, D.	FRA	Discus throw	F		11	35,53	

COMPETITOR	COUNTRY CODE	EVENT	ROUND	HEAT	PLACE	TIME & DISTANCE	MEDAL
Piper, G.	GBR	Marathon	F		29	3:12-10-0	
Plant, W.	USA	10k walk	1	2	4		
			F		DNS		
Pleger, H.	LUX	High jump	F		13	1,70	
		Long jump	F		24	5,81	
Plzak, V.	TCH	200m	1	3	1	23-4	
			2	2	4		
Poerhoelae, V.	FIN	Shot put	F		1	14,81	G
		Discus throw	F		8	38,10	
Pons, D.	ESP	5000m	1	2	8		
		10000m	1	2	8		
Pope, A.	USA	Discus throw	F		3	42,13	B
Porro, A.	ITA	1500m	1	3	2		
			F		7		
Pottier, L.	BEL	Shot put	F		20	10,10	
Pribyt, K.	TCH	400m	1	6	3		
Prino,	ITA	3000m team race	1	1	3	25	
			F		5	34	
Proess, J.	LUX	400m	1	9	3		
		4×100m relay	1	1	2		
			F		5		
Proot, A.	BEL	10000m	1	2	7		
		8000m cross country	F		36		
Raeder, E.	NOR	Long jump	F		8	6,58	
Rasmussen, E.	NOR	1500m	1	2	5		
Rasmussen, G.	DEN	3k walk	1	2	DIS		
		10k walk	1	2	DIS		
Rastas, E.	FIN	8000m cross country	F		18		
Ray, J.	USA	1500m	1	4	1	4-13-4	
			F		8		
Reich, A.	TCH	110m hurdles	1	5	4		
Reidstad, O.	NOR	Pentathlon	F		DNF		
Remer, R.F.	USA	3k walk	1	2	3		
			F		3	13-23-6	B
Remouet, G.	FRA	Triple jump	F		19	12,47	
Reparez, F.	ESP	200m	1	2	5		
		4×100m relay	1	1	3		
Riccoboni, M.	ITA	100m	1	1	2		
			2	1	5		
		200m	1	10	4		
		4×100m relay	1	1	DIS		
Rissanen, O.	FIN	3000m steeplechase	1	1	3		
			F		9		
Rivez, A.	BEL	8000m cross country	F		42		
Robertson, E.	CAN	Marathon	F		35	3:55-00-0	
Roeckaert, T.	BEL	1500m	1	2	7		
Roelker, W.T.	USA	3k walk	1	2	4		
			F		8		
		10k walk	1	1	7		
			F		6		
Rose, S.	DEN	Marathon	F		6	2:41-18-0	
Roth, A.	USA	Marathon	F		DNF		
Rudd, B.G.D.	SAF	400m	1	5	1	50-6	
			2	4	1		
			SF	1	2		
			F		1	49-6	G
		800m	1	2	1	1-55-0	
			SF	2	1	1-57-0	
			F		3	1-54-0	B
		4×400m relay	1	2	1	3-38-7	
			F		2	3-24-2	S
Runstroem, S.	SWE	Triple jump	F		10	13,63	
Ruoho, J.	FIN	Pole vault	F		=8	3,50	
Ryan, P.	USA	Hammer throw	F		1	52,87	G
		56-pound weight	F		2	10,96	S
Rydberg, E.	SWE	Pole vault	F		5	3,60	
Saaristo, J.	FIN	Javelin throw	F		4	62,39	
Sahlin, I.	SWE	Triple jump	F		4	14,17	
Sakerepoulos, M.	GRE	Marathon	F		32	3:14-25-0	
Sandstroem, N.	SWE	100m	1	4	5		
		200m	1	8	5		
			2	2	5		
		4×100m relay	1	3	1	43-4	
			F		3	42-9	B
Sano, K.	JAP	5000m	1	2	6		
		10000m	1	2	9		
Saulman, R.	EST	200m	1	10	5		
		400m	1	5	3		
Schardt, A.A.	USA	3000m team race	1	2	2	14	
			F		1	10	G
Schiller, G.S.	USA	400m	1	7	1	50-4	
			2	3	2		
			SF	1	5		
Scholes, A.	CAN	Marathon	F		15	2:48-30-0	

COMPETITOR	COUNTRY CODE	EVENT	ROUND	HEAT	PLACE	TIME & DISTANCE	MEDAL
Scholz, J.V.	USA	100m	1	12	1	10·8	
			2	4	1	10·8	
			SF	1	2		
			F		4	11·0	
		4×100m relay	1	1	1	43·0	
			F		1	42·2*	G
Schotte, A.	HOL	3k walk	1	2	7		
Schuster, H.	SWE	Marathon	F		DNF		
Scott, D.M.	USA	800m	1	3	2		
			SF	1	-	1-57·2	
			F		5	1-56·0	
Seagrove, W.R.	GBR	5000m	1	3	3		
			F		6		
		3000m team race	1	1	2	11	
			F		2	20	
Seghers, J.	BEL	3k walk	1	1	6		
			F		9		
		10k walk	1	1	6	48-29·0	
			F		7		
Selvart, M.	FRA	400m	1	7	3		
Servais, A.	LUX	4×100m relay	1	1	2		
			F		5		
Servella, J.	FRA	8000m cross country	F		21		
Seurin, J.-R.	FRA	200m	1	12	3		
Shea, F.J.	USA	400m	1	3	1	50·8	
			2	4	1	51·0	
			SF	2	1	50·0	
			F		4	49·9	
		4×400m relay	1	2	2		
			F		4	3-25·2	
Shields, M.L.	USA	1500m	1	2	3		
			F		3	4-03·1	B
		3000m team race	1	2	2	14	
			F		1	10	G
Simon, M.	FRA	10k walk	1	2	8		
Simonazzi, A.	ITA	400m	1	8	3		
Slehofer, J.	TCH	3k walk	1	1	7		
		10k walk	1	1	DNF		
Smet, O.	BEL	4×100m relay	1	2	4		
		4×400m relay	1	1	1	3-39·8	
			F		6		
Smets, H.	BEL	5000m	1	4	9		
		3000m team race	1	1	4		
			F		6		
		8000m cross country	F		33		
Smith, W.	USA	110m hurdles	1	6	1	15·8	
			SF	1	2		
			F		5	15·6	
Smoke, A.	CAN	Marathon	F				
Sorensen, A.	DEN	100m	1	2	2		
			2	2	4		
		200m	1	6	2		
			2	5	4		
		4×100m relay	1	3	2		
			F		4		
Sorensen, H.	DEN	8000m cross country	F		27		
Sorensen, M.	DEN	100m	1	12	2		
			2	5	4		
		4×100m relay	1	3	2		
			F		4		
Sourin, J.	ITA	200m	1	12	3		
Speroni, C.	ITA	5000m	1	3	1	15-27·6	
			F		7		
		10000m	1	3	4		
		3000m team race	1	1	3	25	
			F		5	34	
Sprott, A.	USA	800m	1	5	2		
			SF	1	3		
			F		6	1-56·4	
Srettr, F.	TCH	Long jump	F		27	5,55	
Stenersen, R.	NOR	100m	1	9	3		
		200m	1	5	4		
		4×100m relay	1	1	DIS		
Sundblad, E.	SWE	400m	1	8	1	52·0	
			2	3	3		
			SF	2	6		
		4×400m relay	1	2	3		
			F		5		
Svahn, K.	SWE	High jump	F		=9	1,75	
Svensson, M.	SWE	Hammer throw	F		4	47,29	
		56-pound weight	F		5	9,45	
		Pentathlon	F		DNF		
Taipale, A.	FIN	Discus throw	F		2	44,19	S
		Shot put	F		10	12,94	
Tallgren, U.	FIN	Marathon	F		9	2:42-40·0	
Tammer, H.	EST	Shot put	F		6	13,60	
Templeton, R.L.	USA	Long jump	F		4	6,95	

COMPETITOR	COUNTRY CODE	EVENT	ROUND	HEAT	PLACE	TIME & DISTANCE	MEDAL
Teyssedou, H.	FRA	Marathon	F		25	3:04-00·0	
Thomson, E.	CAN	110m hurdles	1	2	1	15·2	
			SF	2	1	15·0*	
			F		1	14·8*	G
Thorsen, H.	DEN	110m hurdles	1	4	1	16·8	
			SF	1	6		
Thulin, J.	SWE	Marathon	F		23	2:59-23·0	
Thulin, E.	SWE	High jump	F		=7	1,80	
Tirard, R.	FRA	100m	1	7	2		
			2	4	4		
		200m	1	1	1	23·2	
			2	1	3		
		4×100m relay	1	2	1	43·0	
			F		2	42·6	S
Tison, A.	FRA	Discus throw	F		9	37,35	
Tomeicho, O.	JPN	5000m	1	4	6		
Tosi, G.	ITA	400m	1	5	4		
Town, T.	CAN	1500m	1	2	6		
		5000m	1	1	8		
Trichard, A.	FRA	Marathon	F		DNF		
Trullemans, P.	BEL	5000m	1	1	10		
		3000m team race	1	1	4		
			F		6		
		8000m cross country	F		41		
Tuck, A.	USA	Javelin throw	F		11		
Tugnoli, G.	ITA	Shot put	F		14	12,07	
Tuomikoski, J.	FIN	Marathon	F		5	2:40-10·8	
Tuulos, V.	FIN	Triple jump	F		1	14,50	G
Van Campenhout, J.	BEL	5000m	1	2	2		
			F		9		
		3000m team race	1	1	4		
			F		6		
		8000m cross country	F		8	28-10·0	
Van Der Wel, G.J.	HOL	5000m	1	4	9		
Van Heerden, A.G.	SAF	400m hurdles	1	2	1	57·2	
			SF	1	5		
Van Rappard, H.	HOL	200m	1	2	4		
		110m hurdles	1	6	3		
		4×100m relay	1	2	3		
Verlaecht, P.	BEL	3k walk	1	1	8		
		10k walk	1	1	DIS		
Vesamaa, I.	FIN	5000m	1	4	8		
		8000m cross country	F		14		
		3000m steeplechase	1	3	4		
Vidal, G	USA	Decathlon	F		7	6359·00	
Vignaud,	FRA	3000m team race	1	2	1		
			F		3	30	B
Vilen, E.	FIN	400m	1	5	2		
			2	2	4		
		400m hurdles	1	2	2		
			SF	2	5		
Villemson, J.	EST	1500m	1	4	DIS		
Vinne, E.	NOR	Triple jump	F		13	13,34	
Vohralik, V.	TCH	1500m	1	1	1	4-02·4	
			F		4		
Vyncke, F	BEL	5000m	1	3	8		
		8000m cross country	F		37		
Wahlin, R.	SWE	Marathon	F		23	2:59-23·0	
Waibel, A.	SUI	4×100m relay	1	3	4		
Watson, R.	USA	8000m cross country	F		34		
		3000m steeplechase	1	2	3		
			F		8	10-42·0	
Wessel, H.	HOL	Marathon	F		26	3:10-17·0	
Wezepoel, C.	HOL	100m	1	5	2		
			2	3	5		
		200m	1	9	2		
			2	3	5		
		4×100m relay	1	2	3		
Whalen, W.L.	USA	High jump	F		4	1,85	
Wheller, E.W.	GBR	400m hurdles	1	3	2		
			SF	2	4		
Wickholm, W.	FIN	Decathlon	F		6	6406·46	
Wide, E.	SWE	1500m	1	1	4		
Wiggers, C.	BEL	3k walk	1	2	8		
		10k walk	1	1	DNF		
Wilson, H.	NZL	110m hurdles	1	1	2		
			SF	1	3		
			F		4		
Wilson, J.	GBR	10000m	1	1	1	33-40·2	
			F		3	31-50·8	B
		8000m cross country	F		4	27-45·2	
Woodring, A.	USA	200m	1	9	1	22·8	
			2	2	2		
			SF	2	1	22·4	
			F		1	22·0	G
Worthington H.E.	GBR	400m	1	9	2		
			2	4	5		

COMPETITOR	COUNTRY CODE	EVENT	ROUND	HEAT	PLACE	TIME & DISTANCE	MEDAL
Wuyts, G.	BEL	Shot put	F		18	11,04	
Yamaoka, S.	JPN	200m	1	1	4		
Yount, W.	USA	110m hurdles	1	5	5	15·6	
			SF	2	5		
Zallhagen, E.	SWE	Discus throw	F		4	41,07	

COMPETITOR	COUNTRY CODE	EVENT	ROUND	HEAT	PLACE	TIME & DISTANCE	MEDAL
Zander, J.	SWE	1500m	1	3	1	4-08·1	
			F		DNF		
		3000m team race	1	1	1	12	
			F		4	24	
Zanella, R.	ITA	Marathon	F		20	2:51-09·4	
Zucca, W.	ITA	100m	1	5	1	11·4	
			2	2	5		
		4 × 100m relay	1	1	DIS		

Despite a constant drizzle, Frank Foss of America, broke the world record when winning the pole vault.

N.S. Barrett

1924

Paavo Nurmi and the Flying Finns

Paris was the first city to host the Games twice (apart from Athens in 1906). Baron de Coubertin approached retirement, and particularly wanted to wipe out the memory of the poor Games of 1900. There were huts for competitors, foreshadowing the Olympic villages of later years.

The star of the Games was the great Finnish runner Paavo Nurmi, who brought new standards to distance running. Some 60 years afterwards, however, two British runners, Harold Abrahams and Eric Liddell, became world famous when their stories were told by the film *Chariots of Fire*.

Men's Track Events

The Americans had a clutch of fast sprinters in the **100 metres**, headed by Charlie Paddock, the reigning champion. The first round gave no indication of the eventual winner, although in the second Harold Abrahams of Britain equalled the Olympic record of 10·6 sec. Abrahams was badly left at the start in his semi-final, but with long strides, he made up the deficit, and won by inches over Paddock in 10·6. In the final, the sprinters were together at 25 metres, until Abrahams appeared to change gear and drew ahead to win in yet another 10·6 (10·52 by the hundredth watch). The US runner Jackson Scholz hung on for second place in 10·8 and Arthur Porritt of New Zealand finished well to take the bronze.

Harold Abrahams was expected to shine in the **200 metres**, following his win in the 100, but the Americans Jackson Scholz and Charlie Paddock won the semi-finals. In the final, running in roped lanes, the athletes got off well together but as they emerged into the straight, it could be seen that Abrahams was lagging behind and Paddock and Scholz were leading. Scholz hit the tape first in 21·6 sec to equal the Olympic record on a heavy track with Paddock only inches back in 21·7. Meanwhile Eric Liddell of Britain was coming through for third spot in 21·9.

In the second round of the **400 metres**, Joseph Imbach of Switzerland equalled the Olympic record of 48·0 which was improved by Horatio Fitch of the USA in the semi-finals to 47·8. Like the two sprints, the lanes were staked and roped to ensure the runners did not encroach on each other. In the final, Eric Liddell of Britain drew lane six and was thus running blind so he gave it all he had, passing the 200 metres in a fast 22·2 with Fitch and Guy Butler of Britain in contention. It was here that Imbach caught his toe in the lane rope and fell headlong. In the back straight Liddell led by two metres from Fitch and drew further in front, to win in a new Olympic record of 47·6, to the Americans 48·4. Butler finished third in 48·6, while Coard Taylor of the USA, who was on his shoulder, touched the lane rope and stumbled

eight metres from the finish. In subsequent Games roped lanes were banned.

Henry Stallard of Britain was tipped as the likely winner of the **800 metres**, but unknown to many he had an injured foot. Surprisingly, in the final he set off at a furious pace followed by countryman Harry Houghton, but at 600 metres Schuyler Enck of the USA and Paul Martin of Switzerland, shadowed by Douglas Lowe of Britain, moved onto his shoulder. Suddenly, Lowe kicked and sprinted for home and the gold medal in 1-52·4. Martin got the silver in 1-52·5, while Enck just edged out Stallard for the bronze.

To race and win both the **1,500 metres** and **5,000 metres** Olympic finals within 90 minutes of each other is a stupendous feat. No wonder Paavo Nurmi was called "The Great", and even today he is a legend, remembered for his feats at three Olympic Games. After six heats, 12 qualifying runners responded to the gun in the final and Nurmi immediately took up the running with the others strung out behind him. At the end of each lap, he looked down at the watch he held in his right hand to check his progress; lap one 1-13·2 for 500 metres, lap two 2-32·0 and finally his winning time of 3-53·6 for a new Olympic record. Behind Nurmi, with 200 metres to go, Henry Stallard and Douglas Lowe, the two Britons, were fast catching Willy Schaerer of Switzerland. On the tape however, Schaerer hung on to finish second in 3-55·0 with Stallard third.

The **3,000 metres team race** saw four teams qualify for the final and there was no uncertainty about who would win, with Paavo Nurmi and Ville Ritola of Finland running. Three runners from each country scored with Finland gaining eights points from Nurmi first, Ritola second and Elias Katz fifth. Britain was second with 14 points, the USA third and France fourth.

In the **5,000 metres** final, Nurmi took up the running, and soon he and fellow Finn Ville Ritola, with Edvin Wide of Sweden, had broken away from the pack. Taking it in turns to lead, they passed 1,500 metres in 4-14·6, and 3,000 in 8-42·6, before Wide dropped off the pace after the tenth lap, leaving the two Finns to fight it out between them. Nurmi won in a new Olympic best of 14-31·2, with Ritola just behind in 14-31·4. Wide recorded 15-01·8 for third.

Nurmi did not contest the **10,000 metres**, where it was left to Ritola of Finland and Wide of Sweden to provide the entertainment. Forty-three competitors lined up for a straight final, but after 11 laps, the heart-breaking pace set by Ritola and Wide had strung out the field. Ritola, known as the "Iron Man", increased his pace and dropping Wide, went on to win in a world and Olympic record of 30-23·2. His second 5,000 metres took a mere 14-58·2. Wide finished second in 30-55·2 and the Finn Eero Berg was third in 31-43·0.

It was a hot but breezy day for the **marathon** and the

starting time was put back to 5.30 pm. The course was out and back over country roads which were hilly in parts and on the day 58 athletes assembled at the start, representing 19 countries. A little Japanese runner led around the track and various others followed suit in the early stages, but by the turning point, Albin Stenroos of Finland had taken up the pace. The 35-year-old runner had actually retired from serious athletics due to an injury and had made a come-back for this race. A bugle call announced the arrival of Stenroos at the stadium and he won in the moderate time of 2:41-22·6. After a six-minute interval, Romeo Bertini of Italy appeared, to take second place in 2:47-19·6 and the third man home was one of the favourites, Clarence De Mar of the USA, in 2:48-14·0.

Following the semi-finals of the **110 metres hurdles**, George Guthrie of the USA looked set to take the title. In the final, however, Sydney Atkinson of South Africa and Dan Kinsey of the USA got off to a snappy start and ran abreast until the eighth flight, when the South African started to inch ahead. But at the last hurdle Atkinson caught his trailing foot on the obstacle and it was enough for Kinsey to win the gold, with both clocking 15·0 sec. Crashing through the barriers behind the leaders was Guthrie. who finished in third position but was disqualified for timber topping. Sten Petterson of Sweden was awarded the bronze with a time of 15·4.

The heats of the **400 metres hurdles** passed uneventfully, but the final was a humdinger. Over the first part of the race, Charles Brookins and Morgan Taylor of the USA with Geo Andre of France set off at an unprecedented pace and left the rest behind. Andre blew up at 300 metres while Taylor fought off Brookins to win in a world and Olympic best of 52·6 sec. But he had knocked over the last hurdle and the records were disallowed and Brookins, who finished in 52·8, was disqualified for trailing a foot around his hurdle. Erik Vilen of Finland had run strongly over the latter portion of the course and was awarded the silver medal and Olympic record for his time of 53·8, while Ivan Riley of the USA came next with 54·1.

Elias Katz of Finland set a new Olympic record for the **3,000 metres steeplechase** in the heats. The final, however, was a one-horse race with Ville Ritola of Finland leading practically from gun to tape to win by 75 metres from his compatriot Katz in the record time of 9-33·6. Katz clocked 9-44·0 after a close duel with Paul Bontemps of France, who came home in 9-45·2.

There was a serious misunderstanding in the first heat of the **10 kilometres walk** when Rudolf Kuhnel, the Austrian champion, was cautioned during the race in English. Not understanding the language, he promptly stopped. A row broke out among the judges and the second heat was postponed for two days! Kuhnel was allowed to compete again, but ironically was disqualified. The final was a "walk-away" win for Ugo Frigerio of Italy who finished some 200 metres ahead in 47-49·0. In second place was George Goodwin of Britain, who clocked 48-37·0 employing an awkward style, while Cecil McMaster of South Africa was third in 49-08·0.

The most horrific race in Olympic history must surely be the 10,000 metres **cross country** race of 1924. The race was for both individual and team awards and took place on an extremely hot day. There were 39 hardy foot runners who set out from the stadium at 4.30 pm, but only 15 of them were to return. Edvin Wide of Sweden led for the first 12 minutes of the race until Paavo Nurmi of Finland sped away from his countryman Ville Ritola and the Swede. All appeared well when Nurmi entered the stadium, completed his half lap and trotted off to the dressing rooms. His time was 32-54·8. Ritola arrived somewhat tired in 34-19·4 for second place, while next to finish was the black American runner, Earl Johnson, in 35-21·0. In fourth place came Ernest Harper of Britain who plodded to the line and promptly keeled over only to be followed by two Frenchmen, H. Lauvaux encouraging L. Dolques. The latter promptly fell several times and finally collapsed with 20 metres left. Then came runners who bumped into each other or went two steps forward to one back, and out on the course it was even worse, with bodies lying about all over the place. One stalwart was repeatedly trying to run up a small hill — he never did make it. The team race was won by Finland with 11 points from America with 14 and France with 20.

The **4 × 100 metres relay** heats saw the existing world record beaten by both Great Britain and Holland in 42·0 sec before the United States responded in theirs with an outstanding 41·2. The final was nip and tuck between the

Eric Liddell

Eric Liddell was born on 16 January 1902 in Tientsin, when his father was a missionary in China. He was taken to live in Scotland at the age of five, and enjoyed all sports, particularly rugby, at which he excelled as a swift wing three-quarter. Because of his speed, he chose to concentrate more on track athletics and at the age of 21 he won both the 100 and 220 yards at the British championships.

It was not surprising thereafter that Liddell was invited to compete in the 100m, 200m, and 400m at the 1924 Paris Olympic Games. But the Scot, like his father a devout Christian, declined to run in the 100m because the heats were to be run on a Sunday. Instead that day he gave a sermon at the Scottish church in the French capital. However, he was down on his mark later in the week for the 200m and the 400m, winning the bronze over the shorter course and the gold in the 400m with an Olympic record 47·6 sec.

The following year he rejoined his father as a missionary in China. His death in a Japanese internment camp on 21 February 1945 during the Second World War came as a lasting shock to all aware of his strong Christian beliefs. He was one of the two runners whose stories were told in the award-winning film, *Chariots of Fire*.

In a close finish, Jackson Scholz (second left), the winner, vies with his great rival Charlie Paddock, matching flamboyant styles in the battle for gold and silver.

All-Sport Photographic Ltd.

USA and Britain for two legs, but in the end bad exchanges let Britain down. The USA won in a new record time of 41·0, being represented by Frank Hussey, Louis Clarke, Loren Murchison and Al Lecorey. Britain's team of Harold Abrahams, Walter Rangeey, Lance Royle and Bill Nichol were placed second with 41·2 and third was Holland in 41·8.

In the final of the **4 × 400 metres relay**, it was a three-way battle between the USA, Sweden and Britain. On the first leg Eddie Toms of Britain took a two-metre lead over Con Cochrane of America, but at the next exchange Britain's George Renwick was five metres down on America's Alan Helffrich and one on Sweden's Erik Bylehn. During the final two laps the gap widened and the USA came home the winners in a new world and Olympic time of 3-16·0 from Sweden in 3-17·0 and Britain in 3-17·4.

Men's Field Events

Tipped for the **high jump** was the new world record holder, Harold Osborn, who had started athletics as a miler. The preliminaries were held in four pools where nine jumpers qualified out of 41. The bar then advanced at three-centimetre increments until 1,88 metres. At 1,90 only Osborn, Leroy Brown of America and Pierre Lewden of France were left in. At 1,95 Lewden failed and collected the bronze medal, while at 1,98 Brown also capitulated and took the silver. Osborn then attempted 2,02, and with the second jump was very close, but ultimately had to settle for a gold and new Olympic record at 1,98.

Seven competitors in the **pole vault** qualified from two pools by vaulting 3,66 metres, where Ralph Spearow, the flying parson, was expected to win, as the world record holder, Charles Hoff, had been injured. Spearow had not given much thought about the opposition, which included an inexperienced 17-year-old American schoolboy named Lee Barnes, and was surprisingly eliminated at 3,80. At 3,90, four vaulters went clear,

Barnes, Glenn Graham and James Brooker, all from the USA, and Henry Petersen of Denmark. At 3,95 Barnes and Graham sailed over the bar and it became a jump-off situation. Repeatedly the bar had to be lowered until Barnes succeeded and won the gold medal, with Graham collecting the silver. Brooker won the jump-off over Petersen for the third spot.

William Hubbard of the USA was lying third after the preliminary three rounds of the **long jump** with 7,19 metres. Second in the competition was his countryman, Ed Gourdin, with 7,22, but leading was Sverre Hansen of Norway on 7,26. In the final three rounds Gourdin improved to 7,27, which fired Hubbard to go for the big one. It was an enormous leap well over the recent world record of 7,76, but although he sat down in the sand for 7,44, it was still enough to win the gold medal. Gourdin took the silver with 7,27 and Hansen the bronze with his 7,26.

In the **triple jump** there were fireworks in the preliminaries when Luis Brunetto of Argentina improved his personal best out of all recognition to a new Olympic record of 15,42 metres. He had even jumped a foul that measured 15,70! In the fourth round Vilho Tuulos of Finland slipped in to second spot with 15,37, but in the very last round Tony Winter, the Australian, snatched the gold medal with a world and Olympic record of 15,52. Brunetto had to be content with the silver and Tuulos the bronze.

Although there were 28 athletes competing in the **shot put** in three pools, Bud Houser of America established his winning throw of 14,99 metres in the preliminary rounds. In the final three throws, Glenn Hartranft moved up to 14,89 for the silver medal while Ralph Hills improved to 14,64 to make it one, two, three for America.

Bud Houser of the USA was in action again in the **discus throw**, where he won handily with a new Olympic record of 46,15, to achieve a shot and discus double. All the other medal-winning throws were also made in the first three rounds, resulting in Vilho Niitymaa of Finland

82

Paris, 1924

Dave Terry

Harold Osborn

Osborn, who was born at Butler, Illinois, on 13 April 1899, is the only athlete to win an individual event and the decathlon at one Olympics. This he achieved in Paris in 1924 by leaping a Games record of 1,98m (6ft 6in) in the high jump and recording the best score of 7,710 points in the decathlon.

An extremely agile competitor, he is said to have developed a jumping technique of easing the bar against the uprights as he went over. Be that as it may, high jumping rules were changed later to ensure that the pegs on which the bar rested pointed inwards towards each other, instead of being wedged into the facing side of the uprights.

Before the change of rule Osborn had set a world high jump record of 2,04m (6ft 8¾in) prior to going to the Olympics in Paris.

With international competition far more limited than it is today, his prowess was mostly confined to the United States. There he had an exceptional string of successes while establishing himself the world's outstanding high jumper of the 1920s. He not only won US indoor and outdoor high jump championships, but also the national decathlon title three times, as well as collecting a bronze medal in the triple jump in 1922. He died on 5 April 1975.

coming second with 44,95 and Tom Lieb of the USA third with 44,83.

Fred Tootell of the USA took charge of the **hammer throw**ing competition from his very first attempt of 50,60 and after three rounds was leading from Malcolm Noakes of Britain and Erik Eriksson of Finland. Tootell improved his mark to a gold medal winning 53,29 in the final rounds while Matt McGrath, winner of the event 12 years earlier and now a 45-year-old veteran, showed some of his old sparkle with a 50,84 throw for silver position. Noakes, who fouled four of his six attempts, did not improve on his earlier 48,87 and took the bronze.

The **javelin throw**ing competition was a duel between Jonni Myyrae of Finland, the defending champion and world record holder, and the up-and-coming Swede, Gunnar Lindstroem. Lindstroem took a lead in the preliminary three rounds with 60,81 to Myyrae's 59,30, but in the final three attempts the tables were turned. Myyrae launched a throw of 62,96 to retain his title with Lindstroem's 60,92 good enough for the silver medal. Eugene Oberst of the USA took the bronze with 58,35.

This was the last time that the men's **pentathlon** was contested on the Olympic calendar and in the very first event, the long jump, there was a sensation when Robert Le Gendre of the USA jumped a world best of 7,765 metres. Le Gendre, however, did not win the Pentathlon and was shunted into third place with 18 points. Second was Elemer Somfay of Hungary with 16, but the winner was Eero Lehtonen of Finland on 14 points. He had won the discus and been equal first in the 200 metres.

The **decathlon** winner was the high jumper Harold Osborn of the USA, who with the aid of a superb high jump of 1,97 metres was in second place at the end of the first day with Emerson Norton, also of the USA, leading. On the second day however, Osborn clocked a 16·0 hurdles and ran a useful 1,500 metres to win the event and establish a world and Olympic record of 7,710·755 points. Norton vaulted an outstanding 3,80 and took second place with 7,350·895, while Alex Klumberg of Estonia threw the javelin for a fine 57,20 and totalled 7,329·36 points in third spot.

Dave Terry

Harold Abrahams

For 36 years Harold Abrahams was the only European to win the Olympic 100m gold. A record 10·6 sec brought him his victory in a final that saw the American world record-holder Charlie Paddock among those he defeated.

Born in Bedford on 15 December 1899, Abrahams was a dominant figure both in sprinting and long jumping while at Cambridge University. He gained his first Olympic colours in the 1920 Antwerp Games, where he contested both sprints, the sprint relay and the long jump without success.

But in Paris he won the 100 metres gold when finishing a stride ahead of Jackson Scholz, of the USA, and his Oxford University rival Arthur Porritt, representing New Zealand. Abrahams also helped Britain to win the silver medals in the sprint relay.

His speed was used to good effect in his long jump, and just prior to the Paris Games he set a British record of 24ft 2½in (7,38m) which stood for 33 years. He did not contest this event in Paris, and the following year damaged a leg so badly while making a jump that he was forced to retire from competitive athletics. Instead he became one of Britain's most prominent officials in the sport and an outstanding BBC commentator of athletics. He died on 14 January 1978.

COMPETITOR	COUNTRY CODE	EVENT	ROUND	HEAT	PLACE	TIME & DISTANCE	MEDAL
MALES							
Aastad, E.	NOR	Long jump	F		13	6,72	
Abrahams, H.M.	GBR	100m	1	14	1	11·0	
			2	4	1	10·6*	
			SF	2	1	10·6*	
			F		1	10·6*	G
		200m	1	10	1	22·2	
			2	4	1	22·0	
			SF	1	3	21·9	
			F		6	22·3	
		4×100m relay	1	1	1	42·0*	
			SF	2	-	41·8	
			F		2	41·2	S
Adamczak, S.	POL	Pole vault	F		=15	3,20	
Aguilar, M.I.	MEX	100m	1	1	4		
		200m	1	13	5		
Aguirre, H.	MEX	Shot put	F		27	9,47	
Ahumada, H.	MEX	100m	1	11	6		
		200m	1	3	4		
Alavoine, M.	BEL	Marathon	F		15	3 03-20·0	
Albinet, L.	FRA	Long jump	F		20	6,55	
Alciati, E.	ITA	Marathon	F		DNF		
Allart, G.	FRA	110m hurdles	1	6	2		
			SF	1	5		
Ambrosini, E.	ITA	3000m steeplechase	1	2	4		
		3000m team race	1	1	4	31	
Amparan, G.	MEX	400m	1	3	4		
		800m	1	8	5		
Andersen, N.	NOR	3000m team race	1	1	3	27	
Anderson, K.W.	USA	110m hurdles	1	8	2		
			SF	2	2	15·4	
			F		5	15·8	
Anderson, N.	USA	Shot put	F		5	14,29	
Anderson, O.	USA	Decathlon	F		DNF		
Andia, T.	ESP	Cross country	F		DNF		
		3000m team race	1	2	4	30	
Andre, G.	FRA	400m hurdles	1	3	1	56·0	
			SF	2	2		
			F		4	56·1	
Antson, A.	EST	1500m	1	3	5		
Argue, J.C.	USA	Pentathlon	F		DNF		
Armand, E.B.	HAI	400m	1	4	4		
		Decathlon	F		23	5207·89	
Armstrong, L.S.	CAN	100m	1	10	3		
		200m	1	4	2		
			2	4	5		
		4×100m relay	1	2	2		
			SF	1	3	43·3	
Arnaudin, P.	FRA	400m hurdles	1	2	4		
Askildt, K.	NOR	Discus throw	F		5	43,40	
		Shot put	F		15	13,09	
Astroem, E.J.	FIN	400m	1	15	2	52·1	
			2	2	DNS		
		4×400m relay	1	2	3		
Athanassiades, B.	GRE	10000m	F				
		Marathon	F		DNF		
Atkinson, S.	SAF	110m hurdles	1	8	1	15·2	
			SF	3	2	15·2	
			F		2	15·0	S
Austen, E.E.	AUS	10k walk	1	1	DIS		
Aylwin, H.G.	CAN	400m	1	1	1	54·0	
			2	1	DNS		
		4×400m relay	1	3	2		
Badendcyck, J.	NOR	3000m team race	1	1	3	27	
Baraton, G.L.	FRA	800m	1	8	2		
			SF	1	7		
Barbaud, C.	FRA	3000m team race	1	2	2	18	
Barbazon, E.	FRA	High jump	F		10	1,80	
Barnes, L.S.	USA	Pole vault	F		1	3,95	G
Barnes, W.R.	CAN	1500m	1	5	3		
Becerril, E.	ESP	4×100m relay	1	2	3		
Beckwith, C.E.	GBR	Shot put	F		20	12,48	
Bedo, P.	HUN	Shot put	F		18	12,66	
Benardis, S.	GRE	Pentathlon	F		DNF		
		Decathlon	F		24	5139·40	
Benham, J.	GBR	Cross country	F		DNF		
Beranger, P.	FRA	Discus throw	F		14	38,93	
Berg, E.E.	FIN	10000m	F		3	31-43·0	B
		Cross country	F		DNF		
Bergstrom, G.	SWE	Cross country	F		DNF		
Bermingham, P.J.	IRL	Discus throw	F		11	40,42	
Bernard, H.	FRA	110m hurdles	1	4	3		
Bertini, R.	ITA	Marathon	F		2	2:47-19·6	S
Bessim, A.	TUR	1500m	1	6	8		

COMPETITOR	COUNTRY CODE	EVENT	ROUND	HEAT	PLACE	TIME & DISTANCE	MEDAL
Eetts, L.	SAF	400m	1	8	1	49·8	
			2	2	1	49·0	
			SF	1	6		
		4×100m relay	1	2	1	42·8	
			SF	3	4		
Biscuola, T.	ITA	Marathon	F		22	3:19-05·0	
Brackett, F.J.	GBR	400m hurdles	1	5	2		
			SF	2	3		
			F		DIS		
Biasi, E.	ITA	Marathon	F		DNF		
Blomqvist, E.	SWE	Javelin throw	F		6	56,85	
Bolten, W.V.	HOL	400m	1	7	3	53·0	
Benacina, E.	ITA	100m	1	2	2		
			2	4	5		
		4×100m relay	1	4	2		
			SF	2	3	42·9	
Bonini, G.	ITA	800m	1	2	5		
Bontemps, P.	FRA	3000m steeplechase	1	1	2		
			F		3	9-45·2	B
		3000m team race	1	2	2	18	
			F		4	31	
Boot, J.	HOL	Long jump	F		8	6,86	
		4×100m relay	1	3	1	42·0*	
			SF	3	1	42·2	
			F		3	41·8	B
Booth, V.	USA	10000m	F				
		Cross country	F		DNF		
Borner, K.	SUI	100m	1	12	3		
		200m	1	4	3		
		4×100m relay	1	5	1	42·2	
			SF	1	2	42·2	
			F		DIS		
Bosatra, L.	ITA	10k walk	1	1	4		
			F		8		
Bousselaire, M.	FRA	Shot put	F		22	12,26	
Bowman, C.	USA	100m	1	11	1	11·0	
			2	2	1	10·8	
			SF	2	3	10·7	
			F		4	10·9	
Boyd, M.V.	ALT	800m	1	3	4		
		1500m	1	6	5		
		5000m	1	3	9		
Branfing, C.	SWE	4×100m relay	1	5	1	43·8	
			SF	3	3	43·0	
Brewster, F.	ARG	400m	1	13	2	51·8	
			2	3	6		
Britton, H.	GBR	10000m	F		6	32-06·0	
Brochart, P.	BEL	100m	1	10	2		
			2	6	5		
		200m	1	11	1	23·0	
			2	6	3		
Brocker, J.K.	USA	Pole vault	F		3	3,90	B
Brookins, C.R.	USA	400m hurdles	1	1	1	54·8	
			SF	1	1	54·6	
			F		DIS		
Broos, A	BEL	Marathon	F		20	3:14-03·0	
Broos, H.A.	HOL	100m	1	6	1	11·0	
			2	1	3		
		200m	1	5	1	22·6	
			2	6	5		
		4×100m relay	1	3	1	42·0*	
			SF	3	1	42·2	
			F		3	41·8	B
Brouwer, C.L.	HOL	Marathon	F		DNF		
Brown, L.T.	USA	High jump	F		2	1,95	S
Bruni, F.	ITA	800m	1	5	4		
		1500m	1	3	6		
		3000m team race	1	1	4	31	
Brunetta, L.	ARG	Triple jump	F		2	15,42	S
Bucher, C.	SUI	Decathlon	F		15	5961·59	
		Pentathlon	F		DNF		
Buker, R.B.	USA	1500m	1	5	2		
			F		5	3-58·5	
Burghley, D.G.B.C.	GBR	110m hurdles	1	8	3		
Burtin, F.	FRA	3000m team race	1	2	2	18	
			F		4	31	
Butler, G.M.	GBR	400m	1	16	1	50·2	
			2	3	1	49·8	
			SF	1	2	47·9	
			F		3	48·6	B
		4×400m relay	1	2	1	3-22·0	
			F		3	3-17·4	B
Bylehn, E.	SWE	400m	1	14	3		
		800m	1	7	5		
		4×400m relay	1	1	2		
			F		2	3-17·0	S
Campbell, J.H.	GBR	Pole vault	F		=15	3,20	

COMPETITOR	COUNTRY CODE	EVENT	ROUND	HEAT	PLACE	TIME & DISTANCE	MEDAL
Carabatis, D.	GRE	Discus throw	Q		DNQ	0	
		Shot put	F		26	10,95	
Carayannis, A.	GRE	Pole vault	Q		DNQ	0	
Cariofyllis, A.	GRE	High jump	Q		DNQ	1,70	
Carlson, W.	SWE	Marathon	F		21	3:14-21·4	
Carr, E.W.	AUS	100m	1	14	2		
			2	6	2	10·9	
			SF	2	4		
		200m	1	7	1	22·6	
			2	2	1	21·8	
			SF	1	4		
Carreras, D.	ESP	Marathon	F		9	2:57-18·4	
Casasnovas, E.E.	ARG	400m	1	10	4		
Cator, S.M.	HAI	High jump	Q		DNQ	1,75	
		Long jump	F		12	6,81	
Cavallero, P.	ITA	Marathon	F		DNF		
Cejzik, A.	POL	Javelin throw	F		9	54,86	
		Decathlon	F		12	6319,45	
Chekib, L.E.	TUR	100m	1	14	6		
Christie, A.T.	CAN	400m	1	12	2	50·5	
			2	1	3		
		4×400m relay	1	3	2		
			F		4	3-22·8	
Christiernsson, C.-A.	SWE	110m hurdles	1	6	1	15·6	
			SF	2	1	15·4	
			F		4	15·5	
Churchill, W.J.	USA	Marathon	F		23	3:19-18·0	
Cimmermans, V.	LAT	5000m	1	1	12		
		10000m	F				
Clark, A.	GBR	3000m team race	1	1	2	15	
Clarke, F.E.	GBR	10k walk	1	2	4		
			F		6	49-59·2	
Clarke, J.P.	IRL	10000m	F				
Clarke, L.	USA	4×100m relay	1	6	1	41·2*	
			SF	1	1	41·0*	
			F		1	41·0*	G
Clayeux, A.	FRA	Triple jump	Q		DNQ	0	
Clemente, C.	ITA	Javelin throw	F		14	52,75	
Clermont, H.	FRA	10k walk	1	1	5		
			F		10		
Clibbon, C.T.	GBR	5000m	1	3	4		
			F		6	15-29·0	
Coaffee, C.H.	CAN	100m	1	2	1	11·0	
			2	3	1	10·8	
			SF	2	5		
		200m	1	2	2		
			2	3	2		
			SF	2	6		
		4×100m relay	1	2	2		
			SF	1	3	43·3	
Cochrane, C.	USA	4×400m relay	1	3	1	3-27·0	
			F		1	3-16·0*	G
Cominotto, G.	ITA	4×400m relay	1	2	2		
			F		6	3-28·0	
Comins, W.A.	USA	Long jump	Q		DNQ	0	
Connolly, J.	USA	3000m team race	1	2	1	9	
Contoli, A.	ITA	Pentathlon	F		DNF		
		Decathlon	F		11	6406·88	
Contreras, F.J.	MEX	110m hurdles	1	8	5		
		Long jump	F		28	5,73	
Costa, N.V.	BRA	400m	1	16	3		
		800m	1	4	6		
Cottin, R.	FRA	1500m	1	6	4		
Coulter, C.F.	USA	400m hurdles	1	2	1	55·0	
			SF	2	4		
Courtejaire, L.	FRA	Pentathlon	F		DNF		
Cox, W.	USA	3000m team race	1	2	1	9	
			F		3	25	B
Cummings, P.	GBR	3000m steeplechase	1	2	5		
Curiel, P.	MEX	5000m	1	3	12		
		1000Cm	F				
Cushing, J.T.	GBR	3000m steeplechase	1	2	8		
Cuthbert, J.J.	CAN	10000m	F				
		Marathon	F		13	3:00-44·6	
Dalrymple, J.	GBR	Javelin throw	F		24	46,92	
Da Silva, A.	POR	Discus throw	F		24	32,40	
Dauban, H.	GBR	Javelin throw	Q		DNQ	44,70	
Davis, C.E.	SAF	800m	1	1	4		
		1500m	1	2	5		
Davoli, A.	ITA	1500m	1	5	6		
		3000m team race	1	1	4	31	
De Boer, H.	HOL	Long jump	Q		DNQ	0	
De Coninck, M.	FRA	3000m steeplechase	1	3	4		
Decrombecque, F.	FRA	10k walk	1	2	7		
De Freitas, E.	BRA	Pole vault	F		=11	3,40	
Degland, E.	FRA	Javelin throw	F		21	48,57	

COMPETITOR	COUNTRY CODE	EVENT	ROUND	HEAT	PLACE	TIME & DISTANCE	MEDAL
Degrelle, M.	FRA	100m	1	4	1	11·0	
			2	5	2	11·0	
			SF	1	5		
		200m	1	15	1	22·6	
			2	4	3		
		4×100m relay	1	6	2		
			SF	3	2	42·5	
			F		5	42·2	
De Keizer, H.	HOL	Pole vault	F		=11	3,40	
		Pentathlon	F		DNF		
		Decathlon	F		10	6509·61	
De Mar, C.H.	USA	Marathon	F		3	2:48-14·0	B
Devaney, M.A.	USA	3000m steeplechase	1	2	2		
			F		7	10-01·0	
De Vries, J.C.	HOL	200m	1	7	3		
		4×100m relay	1	3	1	42·0*	
			SF	3	1	42·2	
			F		3	41·8	B
Dickinson, R.J.	GBR	High jump	F		15	1,75	
Dieguez, J.	ESP	10000m	F				
		Cross country	F		DNF		
		3000m team race	1	2	4	30	
Diesch, O.	ARG	4×100m relay	1	4	3		
Dobrowlski, W.	POL	100m	1	4	5		
Dodge, R.E.	USA	800m	1	6	3		
			SF	3	1	1-57·4	
			F		6	1-54·2	
Dolques, L.L.	FRA	5000m	1	2	2		
			F		7	15-33·0	
		Cross country	F		DNF		
Doolittle, R.E.	USA	5000m	1	1	7		
Dos Santos, G.J.	POR	200m	1	10	3		
Dova, F.	ARG	400m	1	11	3	51·0	
Drisin, H.	FIN	4×400m relay	1	2	3		
Dufauret, P.	FRA	Pole vault	F		=8	3,55	
Duigan, D.V.	AUS	Pentathlon	F		DNF		
		Decathlon	F		DNF		
Dupire, C.	FRA	High jump	Q		DNQ	0	
Duquesne, L.	FRA	5000m	1	3	5		
		3000m team race	1	2	2	18	
Dustan, G.	SAF	100m	1	6	2		
			2	5	4		
		200m	1	5	2		
			2	1	3		
		4×100m relay	1	2	1	42·8	
			SF	3	4		
Duthil, R.	FRA	Pole vault	F		=11	3,40	
Ebb, K.	FIN	3000m steeplechase	1	2	3		
			F		5	9-57·6	
Ebeling, S.	SWE	Cross country	F		DNF		
Eberle, J.	TCH	Marathon	F		DNF		
Ekqvist, Y.R.	FIN	Javelin throw	F		4	57,56	
Ellis, C.	GBR	1500m	1	6	3		
El Quafi, M.B.	FRA	Marathon	F		7	2:54-19·6	
Enck, S.	USA	800m	1	2	3		
			SF	3	2		
			F		3	1-52·9	B
Engdahl, N.	SWE	400m	1	11	1	49·2	
			2	6	2	48·2	
			SF	1	5		
		4×100m relay	1	5	1	43·8	
			SF	3	3	43·0	
		4×400m relay	1	1	2		
			F		2	3-17·0	S
Enrico, M.A.	ARG	100m	1	8	6		
Eriksson, A.	SWE	5000m	1	1	3		
			F		8	15-38·0	
		3000m team race	1	2	3	21	
Eriksson, E.	FIN	Hammer throw	F		4	48,74	
Escobar, E.A.	ARG	100m	1	11	5		
		200m	1	14	2		
			2	4	6		
		400m	1	12	3	51·4	
		4×100m relay	1	4	3		
Escutia, J.	MEX	400m	1	9	5		
Eskola, V.	FIN	100m	1	17	3		
		4×100m relay	1	3	3		
Eslava, D.	MEX	10k walk	1	1	10		
Eslava, J.M.	MEX	5000m	1	1	13		
		1500m	1	3	7		
Ever, V.	EST	Long jump	F		19	6,58	
		Pole vault	F		=15	3,20	
		Decathlon	F		DNF		

COMPETITOR	COUNTRY CODE	EVENT	ROUND	HEAT	PLACE	TIME & DISTANCE	MEDAL
Facelli, L.	ITA	400m	1	13	1	51·0	
			2	4	5		
		400m hurdles	1	6	2		
			SF	1	2		
		4×400m relay	1	2	2		
			F		6	3-28·0	
Fager, A.	USA	Cross country	F		8	37-40 2	
Farrimond, A.	GBR	Marathon	F		17	3:05-15·0	
Fasten, B.	SWE	Decathlon	F		DNF		
Favodon, B.	FRA	400m	1	17	1	51·2	
			2	3	3		
		4×400m relay	1	1	1	3-30·0	
			F		5	3-23·4	
Fekete, M.	HUN	10k walk	1	2	DIS		
Ferkovic, P.	YUG	Decathlon	F		18	5517·92	
Ferrario, D.	ITA	1500m	1	4	3		
Ferris, S.	GBR	Marathon	F		5	2:52-26·0	
Fery, G.	FRA	400m	1	16	2	51·1	
			2	2	4		
		4×400m relay	1	1	1	3-30·0	
			F		5	3-23·4	
Fitch, H.M.	USA	400m	1	15	1	52·0	
			2	1	1	49·0	
			SF	1	1	47·8*	
			F		2	48·4	S
Foster, C.H.	USA	10k walk	1	2	9		
Fourneau, L.M.	BEL	1500m	1	2	4		
Foussard, A.	FRA	400m hurdles	1	5	5		
Francis, I.E.	CAN	Pole vault	F		=8	3,55	
Frangipane, G.	ITA	100m	1	7	2		
			2	1	2	11·0	
			SF	2	6		
		4×100m relay	1	4	2		
			SF	2	3	42·9	
Freeman, E.	CAN	10k walk	1	1	7		
Friebe, F.	AUT	1500m	1	1	3		
Frieda, H.	USA	Decathlon	F		8	6613·30	
Frigerio, U.	ITA	10k walk	1	2	1	49-16·6	
			F		1	47-49·0	G
Fritz, R.E.	FRA	400m	1	9	2	51·0	
			2	4	4		
		4×400m relay	1	1	1	3-30·0	
			F		5	3-23·4	
Fruelsen, M.	DEN	100m	1	2	4		
		200m	1	5	4		
Fuhrherr, F.	TCH	Pole vault	F		=15	3,20	
Fuller, J.W.	CAN	400m	1	4	3	51·5	
Gaby, F.R.	GBR	110m hurdles	1	3	1	15·8	
			SF	2	3	15·7	
Galimberti, J.	BRA	Discus throw	F		20	36,52	
		Shot put	F		25	11,30	
Galtier, F.	FRA	4×400m relay	1	1	1	3-30·0	
			F		5	3-23·4	
Garaventa, G.	ITA	1500m	1	6	6		
		3000m team race	1	1	4	31	
Garces, C.A.	MEX	200m	1	2	3		
		400m	1	10	3		
Gargiullo, A.	ITA	400m	1	14	2		
			2	5	6		
		4×400m relay	1	2	2		
			F		6	3-28·0	
Garnus, O.	SUI	Discus throw	F		26	35,16	
		Shot put	F		23	12,12	
Gaspar, D.	YUG	Decathlon	F		DNF		
Gaspar, E.	HUN	High jump	F		5	1,88	
Gedvillo, A.	LAT	100m	1	16	5		
Gero, F.	HUN	100m	1	17	1	11·0	
			2	4	3		
		200m	1	9	2		
			2	4	4		
		4×100m relay	1	3	2		
			SF	2	2	42·4	
			F		4	42·0	
Gerspach, E.	SUI	Decathlon	F		6	6743·53	
Ghermati Dit Kader, M.	FRA	Marathon	F		24	3:20-27·0	
Gomes, A.	BRA	5000m	1	1	9		
		Cross country	F		DNF		
Goodwin, G.R.	GBR	10k walk	1	1	1	49-00·8	
			F		2	43-37·0	S
Gouillard, P.	FRA	Long jump	Q		DNQ	6,22	
Gourdin, E.O.	USA	Long jump	F		2	7,27	S
Graham, G.	USA	Pole vault	F		2	3,95	S
Graham, M.B.	USA	Triple jump	F		9	14,00	
Granville, P.	CAN	10k walk	1	2	6		
Gray, J.	USA	Cross country	F		DNF		
Grosclaude, M.C.	FRA	800m	1	2	4		
Gross, E.	HUN	1500m	1	1	5		
Guillouet, M.	FRA	Long jump	F		16	6,62	
Guilloux, P.	FRA	High jump	F		7	1,85	
Gundhus, H.	NOR	3000m team race	-	1	3	27	
Guthrie, G.P.	USA	110m hurdles	-	1	1	15·8	
			SF	3	1	15·2	
			F		DIS		
Hahn, L.	USA	1500m	1	6	1	4-10·8	
			F		6	3-59·0	
Hall, J.S.	IND	100m	1	11	4		
		200m	1	1	3		
Halme, R.E.	FIN	100m	1	4	2		
			2	1	5		
		4×100m relay	1	3	3		
Halonen, L.A.	FIN	Marathon	F		4	2:49-47·4	
Hamilton, B.	USA	Pentathlon	F		DNF		
Hammer, P.	LUX	100m	1	13	2		
			2	1	4		
		200m	1	5	3		
		400m	1	17	3		
		Long jump	F		23	6,24	
Hansen, S.	NOR	Long jump	F		3	7,26	B
Haro, L.J.	FIN	100m	1	9	3		
		200m	1	4	4		
		4×100m relay	1	3	3		
Harper, E.	GBR	10000m	F		5	31-58·0	
		Cross country	F		4	35-35·8	
Harris, F.J.	CAN	800m	1	3	3		
			SF	3	6		
Harrison, E.G.	GBR	110m hurdles	1	2	2		
			SF	3	4		
Hartranft, G.	USA	Discus throw	F		6	42,49	
		Shot put	F		2	14,89	S
Hasten, B.	SWE	Pentathlon	F		DNF		
Heise, A.	FRA	100m	1	9	1	11·2	
			2	4	4		
		4×100m relay	1	6	2		
			SF	3	2	42·5	
			F		5	42·2	
Helarder, Y.	FIN	Pole vault	F		=15	3,20	
Helgesen, S.	NOR	High jump	F		=8	1,83	
Helfrich, A.	USA	4×400m relay	1	3	1	3-27·0	
			F		1	3-16·0*	G
Hemmi, H.	SUI	4×100m relay	1	4	1	42·2	
			SF	1	2	42·2	
			F		DIS		
Henault, J.	BEL	High jump	F		10	1,80	
Henigan, J.	USA	Cross country	F		11	38-00·0	
Henrijean, M.	BEL	Pole vault	F		7	3,66	
Hester, G.B.	CAN	100m	1	12	1	11·2	
			2	4	2	10·7	
			SF	1	6		
		200m	1	6	1		
			2	6	4		
		4×100m relay	1	2	2		
			SF	1	3	43·3	
Heuet, G.	FRA	10000m	F		12	32-52·0	
		Cross country	F		10	37-52·0	
Hietekari, V.H.	FIN	Marathon	F		DNF		
Higginson, J.	GBR	Triple jump	F		13	13,34	
Hilger, J.	LUX	100m	1	15	3		
		200m	1	3	3		
		Long jump	F		29	5,68	
Hill, G.L.	USA	200m	1	13	1	22·0	
			2	6	1	21·8	
			SF	1	2	21·8	
			F		4	22·0	
Hills, R.G.	USA	Shot put	F		3	14,64	B
Hinge, N.F.	IND	10000m	F				
		Marathon	F		29	3:37-36·0	
Hinkel, H.R.	USA	10k walk	1	1	3		
			F		9		
Hoff, C.	NOR	400m	1	6	2	53·0	
			2	2	2		
			SF	2	5	49·0	
		800m	1	8	3		
			SF	3	3		
			F		8	1-56·7	
Honner, F.J	AUS	400m	1	3	3	53·1	
		400m hurdles	1	5	4		
		Long jump	F		14	6,63	
Houghton, H.	GBR	800m	1	2	2		
			SF	2	2		
			F		9	1-58·0	
Houser, C.	USA	Discus throw	F		1	46,15*	G
		Shot put	F		1	14,99	G
Hubbard, W.deH.	USA	Long jump	F		1	7,44	G

COMPETITOR	COUNTRY CODE	EVENT	ROUND	HEAT	PLACE	TIME & DISTANCE	MEDAL
Husgafvel, A.	FIN	100m	1	14	5		
		4×100m relay	1	3	3		
Hussey, F.	USA	4×100m relay	1	6	1	41·2*	
			SF	1	1	41·0*	
			F		1	41·0*	G
Huusari, A.	FIN	Decathlon	F		4	7005·175	
Imbach, J.	SUI	400m	1	5	1	51·8	
			2	6	1	48·0*	
			SF	2	2	48·3	
			F		DNF		
		4×100m relay	1	4	1	42·2	
			SF	1	2	42·4	
			F		DIS		
Isola, A.	FRA	3000m steeplechase	1	2	1	9-57·8	
			F		8	10-14·8	
Jackson, J.J.	FRA	200m	1	14	1	22·8	
			2	2	3		
Jamois, R.	FRA	400m	1	12	4		
Janda-Suk, F.	TCH	Discus throw	F		29	34,08	
Jandera, O.	TCH	110m hurdles	1	1	2		
			SF	2	4		
Jansen, H.	NOR	3000m team race	1	1	3	27	
Jansson, B.	SWE	Shot put	F		8	13,76	
Jansson, F.	SWE	Triple jump	F		5	14,97	
Jansson, G.	FIN	800m	1	1	3		
			SF	3	7		
Jansson, H.	SWE	High jump	F		6	1,85	
		Decathlon	F		7	6656·16	
Jarrin, A.	ECU	10000m	F				
Jarvela, N.	FIN	3000m steeplechase	1	1	4		
Jaworski, J.	POL	1500m	1	3	8		
Jekals, G.	LAT	100m	1	10	5		
		200m	1	12	3		
		Decathlon	F		14	5981·67	
Jensen, A.	DEN	Marathon	F		11	2:58-44·8	
Jensen, C.	DEN	Discus throw	F		13	39,78	
		Hammer throw	F		11	36,26	
Jensen, K.	DEN	400m	1	2	2	50·9	
			2	3	5		
		800m	1	6	1	1-58·4	
			SF	1	5		
		4×100m relay	1	5	2		
			SF	2	4		
Johansson, P.	FIN	Javelin throw	F		8	55,10	
Johansson, R.	SWE	800m	1	5	1	1-57·6	
			SF	1	4		
Johnson, D.M.	CAN	400m	1	6	1	51·8	
			2	5	2		
			SF	1	3	48·0	
			F		4	48·8	
		4×400m relay	1	3	2		
			F		4	3-22·8	
Johnson, F.P.	USA	110m hurdles	1	7	1	16·6	
			SF	1	3	15·8	
Johnson, R.E.	USA	10000m	F		8	32-17·0	
		Cross country	F		3	35-21·0	B
Johnson, W.	USA	10000m	F				
Johnson, H.A.	GBR	3000m team race	1	1	2	15	
			F		2	14	S
Johnstone, C.H.	GBR	5000m	1	1	5		
Jubeau, R.	FRA	1500m	1	3	4		
Jukola, M.	FIN	400m hurdles	1	4	2		
			SF	2	5		
Junqueras, J.	ESP	100m	1	7	4		
		200m	1	16	2		
			2	2	5		
		4×100m relay	1	2	3		
Jurando, A.	ECU	100m	1	1	5		
		Long jump	F		29	5,68	
Kaer, M.	USA	Pentathlon	F		5		
Kalkun, G.	EST	Discus throw	F		15	38,46	
Kalmins, A.	LAT	10k walk	1	2	8		
Kalous, J.	TCH	Marathon	F		DNF		
Kamerbeek, H.	HOL	Hammer throw	Q		DNQ	0	
Kanakuri, S.	JPN	Marathon	F		DNF		
Kantor, K.	AUT	5000m	1	3	10		
Karasstoyanoff, L.	BUL	1500m	1	5	5		
Karayannis, A.	GRE	4×100m relay	1	1	2		
			SF	1	4		
Kat, W.H.	HOL	400m	1	8	3	51·8	
Katz, E.	FIN	3000m steeplechase	1	1	1	9-43·8*	
			F		2	9-44·0	S
		3000m team race	1	1	1	6	
			F		1	8	G
Keemink, H.	HOL	10k walk	1	1	6		
Keller, J.	FRA	3000m team race	1	2	2	18	
Kelly, J.	IRL	3000m steeplechase	1	2	7		

COMPETITOR	COUNTRY CODE	EVENT	ROUND	HEAT	PLACE	TIME & DISTANCE	MEDAL
Keskull, R.	EST	100m	1	13	5		
		200m	1	16	3		
		400m	1	2	4		
Kibilds, A.	LAT	10k walk	1	1	8		
		Javelin throw	F		16	50,15	
		Discus throw	F		22	35,79	
		Shot put	F		19	12,53	
Kinn, G.	SWE	Marathon	F		8	2:54-33·4	
Kinsey, D.C.	USA	110m hurdles	1	5	1	15·4	
			SF	1	1	15·4	
			F		1	15·0	G
Kinsman, H.	SAF	200m	1	1	1	21·8	
			2	6	2		
			SF	2	5		
		4×100m relay	1	2	1	42·8	
			SF	3	4		
Kiraly, P.	HUN	10000m	F				
		Marathon	F		DNF		
Kirby, E.	USA	3000m team race	1	2	1	9	
			F		3	25	B
Klumberg, A.	EST	Javelin throw	Q		DNQ	49,61	
		Decathlon	F		3	7329·36	B
Koczan, M.	TCH	Javelin throw	F		23	48,39	
Kolehmainen, H.	FIN	Marathon	F		DNF		
Kostrzewski, S.	POL	800m	1	6	4		
		1500m	1	4	7		
Kranis, A.	GRE	5000m	1	3	6		
		10000m	F				
		Marathon	F		DNF		
Kuhnet, R.	AUT	10k walk	1	2	DIS		
Kulcsar, E.	HUN	5000m	1	2	8		
Kurunczy, L.	HUN	100m	1	5	1	11·4	
			2	2	4		
		200m	1	12	1	22·6	
			2	5	3		
		400m	1	3	2	52·6	
		4×100m relay	1	3	2		
			SF	2	2	42·4	
			F		4	42·0	
Kyronen, V.	FIN	Marathon	F		DNF		
Lahtinen, H.	FIN	Pentathlon	F		6		
Lakshmanan, C.K.	IND	110m hurdles	1	5	5		
Lamp, F.L.	HOL	100m	1	4	3		
Lane, C.	AUS	400m	1	9	3	51·4	
Langley, A.	GBR	Triple jump	F		15	12,74	
Lara, H.	CHI	400m hurdles	1	1	2		
			SF	2	6		
Larrabeite, C.	ESP	100m	1	6	5		
		200m	1	1	5		
Larrivee, L.	USA	3000m team race	1	2	1	9	
Larsen, A.	DEN	800m	1	7	3		
			SF	2	8		
		1500m	1	3	3		
Larssen, G.	NOR	110m hurdles	1	4	1	16·0	
			SF	3	3		
Lauseig, A.	FRA	Cross country	F		DNF		
Lauvaux, H.	FRA	10000m	F		11	32-48·0	
		Cross country	F		5	36-44·8	
Lavan, J.	IRL	200m	1	16	1	23·2	
			2	4	4		
		400m	1	8	2	51·2	
			2	6	4		
Leclercq, G.	BEL	Marathon	F		26	3:27-54·0	
		3000m steeplechase	1	1	6		
Leconey, J.A.	USA	4×100m relay	1	6	1	41·2*	
			SF	1	1	41·0*	
			F		1	41·0*	G
Le Gendre, R.L.	USA	Pentathlon	F		3	18	B
Lehtonen, E.R.	FIN	Pentathlon	F		1	14	G
Leiho, L.A.	FIN	Pentathlon	F		4		
Lermond, G.W.	USA	5000m	1	3	7		
Letherland, E.E.	GBR	Marathon	F		DNF		
Lethonen, R.	FIN	4×400m relay	1	2	3		
Lewden, P.	FRA	High jump	F		3	1,92	B
Liddell, E.H.	GBR	200m	1	3	1	22·2	
			2	2	2		
			SF	2	2	21·8	
			F		3	21·9	B
		400m	1	14	1	50·2	
			2	4	2	50·2	
			SF	2	1	48·2	
			F		1	47·6*	G
Lieb, T.J.	USA	Discus throw	F		3	44,83	B
Liewendhal, F.	FIN	1500m	1	6	2		
			F		8	4-00·3	
		3000m team race	1	1	1	6	
Liimatainen, H.	FIN	Cross country	F		12	38-12·0	

COMPETITOR	COUNTRY CODE	EVENT	ROUND	HEAT	PLACE	TIME & DISTANCE	MEDAL
Lillier, H.	SWE	Javelin throw	F		13	52,95	
Lind, C.J.	SWE	Hammer throw	F		7	44,78	
Lindstroem, G.	SWE	Javelin throw	F		2	60,92	S
Linka, A.	TCH	100m	1	2	5		
			1	8	4		
Lizarza, G.	ESP	Discus throw	F		28	34,20	
Lossman, J.	EST	Marathon	F		10	2:57-54·6	
Lovas, A.	HUN	Marathon	F		28	3:35-24·0	
Lowe, D.G.	GBR	800m	1	8	1	1-58·0	
			SF	2	1	1-56·8	
			F		1	1-52·4	G
		1500m	1	2	2		
			F		4	3-57·0	
Lowe, W.J.	IRL	100m	1	12	4		
		200m	1	7	2		
			2	5	6		
Lukaszewicz, J.	POL	3000m team race	1	1	5	41	
Lundgreen, L.	DEN	110m hurdles	1	6	3		
		400m hurdles	1	2	3		
Lundgren, S.	SWE	800m	1	2	2		
			SF	2	4		
		3000m team race	1	2	3	21	
Luoma, J.	FIN	1500m	1	1	2		
			F		12	4-03·9	
McAuley, V.	CAN	Marathon	F		14	3:02-05·4	
MacDonald, B.	GBR	3000m team race	1	1	2	15	
			F		2	14	S
MacDonald, J.O.	USA	4×400m relay	1	3	1	3-27·0	
			F		1	3-16·0*	G
McDonald, P.	CAN	400m hurdles	1	1	3		
		Triple jump	F		14	13,33	
MacEachern, J.M.	USA	Hammer throw	F		6	45,22	
MacEachern, N.H.	IRL	800m	1	6	2		
			SF	2	5		
MacGill, D.E.	CAN	5000m	1	2	7		
McGrath, D.E.	CAN	Hammer throw	F		2	50,84	S
MacIntosh, C.E.	GBR	Long jump	F		6	6 92	
Mackay, T.	CAN	800m	1	4	3		
			SF	1	8		
Mackechenneay, J.M.	CAN	200m	1	8	1	23·2	
			2	2	5		
MacKenna, J.	GBR	Marathon	F		27	3:30-40·0	
McMaster, C.C.	SAF	10k walk	1	2	2		
			F		3	49-08·0	B
Machan, J.	TCH	High jump	F		19	1,75	
		Long jump	Q		DNQ	6,09	
Maffiolini, E.	ITA	400m	1	16	4		
		4×400m relay	1	2	2		
			F		6	3-28·0	
Malmivirta, H.	FIN	Discus throw	F		8	41,16	
Malvicini, A.	ITA	Marathon	F		DNF		
Mangascia, M.	ITA	10000m	F				
Manhes, J.B.	FRA	Marathon	F		12	3:00-34·0	
Marchal, R.	FRA	10000m	F		9	32-33·0	
		Cross country	F		DNF		
Marthie, W.	SUI	5000m	1	2	11		
Martin, P.	SUI	800m	1	3	1	2-00 2	
			SF	1	3		
			F		2	1-52·5	S
Martinenghi, C.	ITA	10000m	F		7		
		Cross country	F		7	37-01·0	
Martinez, J.N.	MEX	200m	1	9	3		
		400m	1	11	4		
Marvalits, C.	HUN	Discus throw	F		10	40,82	
Mascaux, L.	FRA	5000m	1	1	4		
			F		9	15-39·0	
		3000m team race	1	2	2	18	
			F		4	31	
Matthewman, T.	GBR	200m	1	13	4		
			2	5	4		
Maynes, W.J.	CAN	4×400m relay	1	3	2		
			F		4	3-22·8	
Medecin, G.	MON	Long jump	F		22	6,51	
Medecin, G.E.	MON	Pentathlon	F		DNF		
		Decathlon	F		20	5347·5~	
Meier, A.	SUI	Long jump	F		17	6,61	
		Decathlon	F		DNF		
Mellor, C.L.	USA	Marathon	F		25	3:24-07·0	
Mendizabal, F.	ESP	100m	1	16	1	11·4	
			2	4	6		
		200m	1	2	4		
		4×100m relay	1	2	3		
Menso, J.	HOL	400m	1	9	4		
Menso, K.	HOL	800m	1	6	5		
Merchant, J.	USA	Hammer throw	F		9	41,45	

COMPETITOR	COUNTRY CODE	EVENT	ROUND	HEAT	PLACE	TIME & DISTANCE	MEDAL
Migeot, J.F.	BEL	400m	-	2	3	51·6	
		400m hurdles	-	6	3		
Miguel, J.	ESP	5000m	-	1	11		
		3000m team race	1	2	4	30	
Miller, A.J.	CAN	High jump	F		20	1,65	
Mills, A.R.	GER	Marathon	F		DNF		
Mirgain, C.	LUX	400m	1	2	5		
		800m	1	6	6		
Miura, Y.	JPN	Marathon	F		DNF		
Mobster, M.	NOR	Pentathlon	F		DNF		
Moedbeck, E.	BEL	100m	1	12	6		
Montabone, W.J.	CAN	110m hurdles	1	3	4		
		400m hurdles	1	6	4		
Montague, E.A.	GBR	3000m steeplechase	1	1	3		
			F		6	9-58·0	
Montzatko, B.	TCH	Marathon	F		DNF		
Moriaud, V.	SUI	100m	1	8	4		
		110m hurdles	1	3	3		
		4×100m relay	1	4	1	42·2	
			SF	1	2	42·2	
			F		DIS		
Morren, F.	BEL	800m	1	5	2		
			SF	2	6		
Moser, W.	SUI	110m hurdles	1	4	2		
			SF	2	5		
		Javelin throw	F		25	46,80	
Motmillers, A.	LAT	5000m	1	3	13		
		10000m	F		10	32-44·0	
Mountain, E.D.	GBR	800m	1	5	3		
			SF	3	5		
Mourlon, A.	FRA	100m	1	15	1	11·0	
			2	3	3		
		200m	1	1	2		
			2	5	2		
			SF	2	4		
		4×100m relay	1	6	2		
			SF	3	2	42·5	
			F		5	42·2	
Mourlon, R.	FRA	100m	1	17	2		
			2	2	3		
		4×100m relay	1	6	2		
			SF	3	2	42·5	
			F		5	42·2	
Murchison, L.	USA	100m	1	1	1	10·8	
			2	1	1	10·8	
			SF	1	3	11·2	
			F		6	11·0	
		4×100m relay	1	6	1	41·2*	
			SF	1	1	41·0*	
			F		1	41·0*	G
Murdoch, J.	CAN	Hammer throw	F		8	42,48	
Musket, L.	HUN	100m	1	12	5		
		110m hurdles	1	8	4		
		4×100m relay	1	3	2		
			SF	2	2	42·4	
			F		4	42·0	
Muzard, M.	FRA	Pole vault	F		=11	3,40	
Myyra, J.	FIN	Javelin throw	F		1	62,96	G
Narancic, V.	YUG	Discus throw	Q		DNQ	37,35	
		Shot put	F		13	13,21	
Nedobity, J.	TCH	5000m	1	2	12		
Negri, A.	ITA	3000m steeplechase	1	1	7		
Nepomuceno, D.	PHI	100m	1	6	6		
		200m	1	15	3		
Neufeld, W.	USA	Javelin throw	F		5	56,96	
Neumann, E.	EST	Decathlon	F		16	5899·10	
Newbery, G.	ARG	4×100m relay	1	4	3		
Newey, S.A.	GBR	3000m steeplechase	1	3	3		
			F		9		
Newman, J.H.	AUS	1500m	1	3	5		
Nichol, W.P.	GBR	100m	1	10	1	11·0	
			2	3	2	11·0	
			SF	1	4		
		200m	1	9	1	22·6	
			2	1	1	22·6	
			SF	1	6		
		4×100m relay	1	1	1	42·0*	
			SF	2	1	41·8	
			F		2	41·2	S
Niitymaa V.A.	FIN	Discus throw	F		2	44,95	S
Niklance, K.E.	FIN	Discus throw	F		7	42,09	
		Shot put	F		6	14,26	
Nilsson, E.	SWE	Pentathlon	F		DNF		
		Decathlon	F		DNF		
Noakes, M.C.	GBR	Hammer throw	F		3	48,87	B
Norland, M.	FRA	5000m	1	2	5		
		Cross country	F		15	41-38·6	

COMPETITOR	COUNTRY CODE	EVENT	ROUND	HEAT	PLACE	TIME & DISTANCE	MEDAL
Norman, R.	AUS	200m	1	8	2		
			2	3	4		
		400m	1	4	2	50·6	
			2	5	4		
		800m	1	4	5		
Norton, B.M.	USA	200m	1	2	1	21·8	
			2	4	2		
			SF	2	3	22·1	
			F		5	22·0	
Norton, E.C.	USA	Decathlon	F		2	7330·895	S
Noto, T.	JPN	400m	1	7	2	51·7	
			2	6	5		
		800m	1	7	4		
		Decathlon	F		22	5248·33	
Nuesch, W.	SUI	Discus throw	F		16	38,20	
		Shot put	F		21	12,45	
Nurmi, P.	FIN	1500m	1	4	1	4-07·6	
			F		1	3-53·6*	G
		5000m	1	2	1	15-28·6	
			F		1	14-31·2*	G
		Cross country	F		1	32-54·8	G
		3000m team race	1	1	1	6	
			F		1	8	G
Oberst, E.G.	USA	Javelin throw	F		3	58,35	B
O'Connor, J.	IRL	Triple jump	F		10	13,99	
Oda, M.	JPN	High jump	F		=10	1,80	
		Long jump	F		=10	6,83	
		Triple jump	F		6	14,35	
Odde, J.	GBR	Triple jump	F		12	13,40	
O'Grady, J.	IRL	Shot put	F		17	12,75	
Oja, J.	LAT	100m	1	5	2		
			2	3	5		
		200m	1	17	2		
			2	1	4		
Okazaki, K.	JPN	5000m	1	1	2		
			F		12		
Oldak, S.	POL	400m	1	13	3		
		800m	1	5	6		
Oldfield, C.W.	SAF	400m	1	10	1	49·6	
			2	5	1	49·0	
			SF	2	4	48·6	
		800m	1	2	1	1-58·0*	
			SF	1	6		
Ordonez, D.	ESP	100m	1	8	3		
		4×100m relay	1	2	3		
Osborn, H.M.	USA	High jump	F		1	1,98*	G
		Decathlon	F		1	7710·775	G
Osterdahl, T.	SWE	100m	1	11	3		
		4×100m relay	1	5	1	43·8	
			SF	3	3	43·0	
Paddock, C.W.	USA	100m	1	3	1	11·2	
			2	5	1	10·8	
			SF	2	2	10·7	
			F		5	10·9	
		200m	1	10	2		
			2	1	1	22·2	
			SF	2	1	21·8	
			F		2	21·7	S
Palau, M.	ESP	5000m	1	3	11		
Palauclaveras, M.	MEX	Cross country	F		DNF		
Palma, A.	ESP	Cross country	F		DNF		
Palmieri, G.	ITA	High jump	Q		DNQ	1,70	
Pandelidis, C.	GRE	100m	1	10	4		
		200m	1	11	2		
			2	3	5		
		Long jump	Q		DNQ	5,94	
		4×100m relay	1	1	2		
			SF	1	4		
Paoli, R.	FRA	Shot put	F		9	13,53	
Papafingos, A.	GRE	100m	1	9	5		
		200m	1	8	3		
		4×100m relay	1	1	2		
			SF	1	4		
Parrain, S.	FRA	200m	1	6	4		
Partridge, L.F.	GBR	110m hurdles	1	1	3		
Pastorino, P.	ITA	200m	1	1	4		
		4×100m relay	1	4	2		
			SF	2	3	42·9	
Paulen, A.	HOL	400m	1	17	2	52·0	
			2	4	1	49·0	
			SF	1	4	48·2	
		800m	1	4	1	1-59·2	
			SF	3	4	1-59·0	
Pavesi, D.	ITA	10k walk	1	1	2	49-09·0	
			F		4	49-17·0	
Payne, C.R.	USA	3000m steeplechase	1	1	5		
Peltonen, P.	FIN	Javelin throw	F		7	55,67	

COMPETITOR	COUNTRY CODE	EVENT	ROUND	HEAT	PLACE	TIME & DISTANCE	MEDAL
Pena, M.	ESP	Cross country	F		14	41-34·0	
		3000m team race	1	2	4	30	
Perpar, S.	TCH	200m	1	11	3		
Peters, W.	HOL	Triple jump	F		11	13,86	
Petersen, H.	DEN	Pole vault	F		4	3,90	
Petronnoff, K.	BUL	400m	1	3	4		
Petrounoff, K.	BUL	Long jump	F		26	6,00	
		Triple jump	F		18	12,01	
Petterson, S.	SWE	110m hurdles	1	2	1	15·6	
			SF	1	2	15·4	
			F		3	15·4	B
Peussa, A.	FIN	1500m	1	4	1	4-17·4	
			F		9	4-00·6	
Phelps, H.R.	USA	5000m	1	2	6		
Phillips, H.	CAN	800m	1	5	5		
Phillips, H.	SAF	Marathon	F		19	3:07-13·0	
Phillips, L.	FRA	800m	1	7	2		
			SF	3	8		
		1500m	1	5	4		
Pickard, V.W.	CAN	Pole vault	F		5	3,80	
		Javelin throw	Q		DNQ	44,69	
Pierre, D.	FRA	Discus throw	F		19	37,01	
		Shot put	F		16	13,07	
Pierce, S.D.	CAN	110m hurdles	1	5	3		
Pighi, A.	ITA	Discus throw	F		27	34,98	
		Pentathlon	F		DNF		
Pitt, T.K.	IND	100m	1	13	3		
		200m	1	6	3		
		400m	1	12	1	49·8	
			2	3	4		
Plaza, M.	CHI	Marathon	F		6	2:52-54·0	
Poggioli, A.	ITA	Discus throw	F		25	35,29	
Poor, T.W.	USA	High jump	F		4	1,88	
Pope, R.	USA	Discus throw	F		4	44,42	
Poerhoelae, V.	FIN	Shot put	F		7	14,10	
Porritt, A.E.	NZL	100m	1	1	2		
			2	2	2	10·9	
			SF	1	2	11·1	
			F		3	10·9	B
		200m	1	4	1	22·4	
			2	5	1	22·0	
			SF	1	5		
Porter, C.H.	GBR	3000m team race	1	1	2	15	
			F		2	14	
Pott, K.	POR	100m	1	8	5		
Pribyl, K.	TCH	400m	1	12	5		
		800m	1	8	4		
Priester, L.B.	USA	Javelin throw	F		11	54,51	
Pucci, P.	ITA	800m	1	4	4		
Puspoki, T.	HUN	110m hurdles	1	1	4		
Rahn, E.	EST	Decathlon	F		21	5292·76	
Rainio, V.J.	FIN	Long jump	F		21	6,54	
		Triple jump	F		4	15,01	
Rangeley, W.	GBR	100m	1	8	1	11·0	
			2	2	5		
		4×100m relay	11	1	1	42·0*	
			SF	2	1	41·8	
			F		2	41·2	S
Raouf, M.	TUR	100m	1	4	6		
Rastas, E.	FIN	5000m	1	1	1	15-22·2	
			F		11		
		Cross country	F		DNF		
Rauch, R.	AUT	200m	1	3	2		
			2	1	5		
Ray, J.	USA	3000m team race	1	2	1	9	
Reimann, E.	EST	Marathon	F		30	3:40-52·0	
Renwick, G.R.	GBR	400m	1	11	2	50·3	
			2	5	5		
		4×400m relay	1	2	1	3-22·0	
			F		3	3-17·4	B
Ribeiro, A.	BRA	100m	1	14	4		
		200m	1	13	3		
Richardson, L.	SAF	3000m steeplechase	1	2	6		
		Cross country	F		9	37-43·0	
Richardson, W.H.	USA	800m	1	1	2		
			SF	1	2		
			F		5	1-53·7	
Rick, E.M.	USA	3000m steeplechase	1	3	2		
			F		4	9-56·4	
Riley, I.	USA	400m hurdles	1	6	1	55·4	
			SF	2	1	56·6	
			F		3	54·1	B
Ripley, R.N.	GBR	4×400m relay	1	2	1	3-22·0	
			F		3	3-17·4	B

COMPETITOR	COUNTRY CODE	EVENT	ROUND	HEAT	PLACE	TIME & DISTANCE	MEDAL
Ritola, V.	FIN	5000m	1	3	3		
			F		2	14-31-4	S
		10000m	F		1	30-23-2	G
		3000m steeplechase	1	3	1	9-59-0	
			F		1	9-33-6*	G
		Cross country	F		2	34-19-4	S
		3000m team race	1	-	1	6	
			F		1	8	G
Rivas, C.	ARG	100m	1	1	3		
		4×100m relay	1	4	3		
Roberts, L.	SAF	High jump	F		=8	1,83	
Robertson, R.A.	USA	400m	1	2	1	50-2	
			2	4	3		
Romig, J.L.	USA	5000m	1	3	1	15-14-6	
			F		4	15-12-4	
Rose, A.C.	USA	Long jump	F		9	6,85	
Royle, L.C.	GBR	100m	1	7	1	11-0	
			2	6	3		
		4×100m relay	1	1	1	42-0*	
			SF	2	1	41-8	
			F		2	41-2	S
Rozsahegyl, G.	HUN	100m	1	9	2		
			2	5	5		
		4×100m relay	1	3	2		
			SF	2	2	42-4	
			F		4	42-0	
Ruks, A.	LAT	10k walk	1	1	9		
Ruotsalainen, G.	FIN	Marathon	F		DNF		
Russel, K.	SWE	100m	1	13	4		
Ruth, J.	BEL	Pentathlon	F		DNF		
		Decathlon	F		17	5866-67	
Ryan, J.J.	IRL	10000m	F				
		Cross country	F		DNF		
Sahlin, I.	SWE	High jump	F		=10	1,80	
		Triple jump	F		8	14,15	
Sainte Pe, R.	FRA	Hammer throw	F		10	36,27	
Sakelaropoulos, H.	GRE	Marathon	F		DNF		
Samba, C.	FRA	Javelin throw	F		20	48,65	
Sandstrom, P.J.	FIN	Long jump	F		10	6,83	
Saunders, F.C.	GBR	5000m	1	2	4		
			F		10	15-54-0	
Sayed, M.	EGY	1500m	1	1	4		
		5000m	1	1	10		
Schaerer, W.	SUI	1500m	1	2	1	4-06-6	
			F		2	3-55-0	S
Schedt, F.	AUT	100m	1	4	4		
Schiang, P.	DEN	100m	1	6	4		
		4×100m relay	1	5	2		
			SF	2	4		
Scholz, J.V.	USA	100m	1	13	1	10-8	
			2	6	1	10-8	
			SF	1	1	10-8	
			F		2	10-8	S
		200m	1	6	-	22-4	
			2	3	1	21-8	
			SF	1	1	21-8	
			F		1	21-6*	G
Schwab, A.	SUI	10k walk	1	2	3		
			F		5	49-50-0	
Seagrove, W.R.	GBR	3000m team race	1	1	2	15	
Seeward, W.R.	BRA	Javelin throw	Q		DNQ	49,39	
Sempe, G.	FRA	110m hurdles	1	5	2		
			SF	3	3	15-6	
		Decathlon	F		DNF		
Seppaelae, E.	FIN	5000m	1	2	3		
			F		5	15-18-4	
		3000m team race	1	1	1	6	
Sevisko, O.	LAT	100m	1	3	2		
			2	6	4		
		200m	1	5	5		
Sewell, A.N.	GBR	Cross country	F		DNF		
Shanahan, W.	IRL	Decathlon	F		19	5425-68	
Sheppard, R.S.	CAN	Triple jump	F		16	12.72	
Simmen, C.	SUI	400m	1	16	5		
Sindler, V.	TCH	1500m	1	6	7		
Singh, P.	IND	1500m	1	2	6		
		5000m	1	2	9		
		10000m	F				
Singh, D.	IND	Long jump	F		14	6,63	
Sipila, V.J.	FIN	10000m	F		4	31-50-2	
		Cross country	F		DNF		
Skioeld, O.	SWE	Hammer throw	F		5	45,28	
Slack, D.G.	GBR	Decathlon	F		25	5148-40	
Slack, G.D.	GBR	Pentathlon	F		DNF		
Sobotka, A.	TCH	Long jump	F		18	6,59	
Somfay, E.	HUN	Pentathlon	F		2	16	S
		Decathlon	F		DNF		
Sosnicki, S.	POL	100m	1	16	4		
		Long jump	F		31	5,67	
Spahic, A.	YUG	Pentathlon	F		DNF		
Spark, A.P.	GBR	Pentathlon	F		DNF		
		Decathlon	F		DNF		
Spearow, A.R.	USA	Pole vault	F		6	3,70	
Spe, L.	HOL	110m hurdles	1	1	3		
Spencer, S.A.	GBR	1500m	1	3	2		
			F		11	4-03-7	
Spencer, W.O.	USA	1500m	1	2	3		
Speroni, C.	ITA	10000m	F				
		Cross country	F		DNF		
Sprong, T.	HOL	Marathon	F		DNF		
Stallard, G.H.	GER	800m	1	7	1	1-57-6	
			SF	1	1	1-54-2	
			F		4	1-53-0	
		1500m	1	5	1	4-11-8	
			F		3	3-55-6	B
Stanley, L.	IRL	High jump	F		=10	1,80	
Starr, R.S.	GBR	5000m	1	1	6		
Stenroos, A.	FIN	Marathon	F		1	2:41-22-6	G
Stevenson, W.	USA	4×400m relay	1	3	1	3-27-0	
			F		1	3-16-0*	G
Steurs, G.	BEL	Marathon	F		DNF		
Steyn, C.L.	SAF	4×100m relay	1	2	1	42-8	
			SF	3	4		
Stoopen, A.	MEX	Long jump	Q		DNQ	5,48	
Strebi, W.	SUI	100m	1	11	2		
			2	3	DNS		
Studenroth, A.	USA	Cross country	F		6	36-45-4	
Sukatnieks, T.	LAT	Discus throw	F		21	35,98	
Sundstrom, S.	SWE	Shot put	F		10	13,53	
Sutherland, E.G.	SAF	Decathlon	F		5	6794-145	
Svensson, A.	SWE	400m	1	9	1	50-0	
			2	1	2		
			SF	2	6	49-3	
		4×400m relay	1	1	2		
			F		2	3-17-0	S
Svetanoff, A.	BUL	10000m	F				
Svoboda, A.	TCH	100m	1	6	3		
Svoboda, J.	TCH	Javelin throw	Q		DNQ	0	
		Pentathlon	F		DNF		
Swietochowski, S.	POL	400m	1	14	4		
Szelestowski, S.	POL	5000m	1	2	10		
		3000m team race	1	1	5	41	
Szenajch, A.	POL	100m	1	17	4		
		200m	1	13	4		
Szydlowski, Z.	POL	Javelin throw	F		26	46,00	
		Discus throw	F		24	35,71	
Taka-Gangue	FRA	Javelin throw	F		10	54,65	
Taipale, A.R.	FIN	Discus throw	F		12	40,21	
Takala, A.	FIN	Shot put	F		11	13,31	
Taki-N'dio,	FRA	Javelin throw				48,92	
Tala, S.	FIN	3000m team race	1	1	1	6	
Tallianos, J.	GRE	110m hurdles	1	5	3		
		400m hurdles	1	3	3		
		4×100m relay	1	1	2		
			SF	1	4		
Tammer, E.	EST	Shot put	F		12	13,28	
Tani, S.	JPN	100m	1	14	2		
		200m	1	12	2		
			2	3	3		
Tashiro, K.	JPN	Marathon	F		DNF		
Tatham, W	GBR	400m hurdles	1	4	3		
Taylor, F.M.	USA	400m hurdles	1	5	1	55-8	
			SF	1	2		
			F		1	52-6	G
Taylor, J.C.	USA	400m	1	7	1	50-8	
			2	3	2		
			SF	2	3	48-4	
			F		5	56-0	
Tell, G.	FRA	10000m	F		7	32-12-0	
Theard, V.A.	HAI	100m	1	7	3		
		200m	1	17	1	23-6	
			2	3	6		
Thompson, E.R.	ARG	400m hurdles	1	5	3		
		Decathlon	F		13	6310-52	
Thorsen, H.	DEN	400m hurdles	1	3	2		
			SF	1	6		
		4×100m relay	1	5	2		
			SF	2	4		
Thuresson, S.	SWE	10000m	F				
		3000m team race	1	2	3	21	
		Cross country	F		DNF		

COMPETITOR	COUNTRY CODE	EVENT	ROUND	HEAT	PLACE	TIME & DISTANCE	MEDAL
Tibbetts, W.	USA	3000m team race	1	2	1	9	
			F		3	25	B
Toldy, A.	HUN	Discus throw	F		9	41,09	
Tommasi, V.	ITA	Long jump	F		7	6,89	
Toms, E.J.	GBR	400m	1	10	2		
			2	1	4		
		4×400m relay	1	2	1	3-22·0	
			F		3	3-17·4	B
Tootell, F.D.	USA	Hammer throw	F		1	53,29	G
Torpo, K.J.	FIN	Shot put	F		4	14,45	
Torre, E.	ITA	100m	1	15	2		
			2	2	6		
		4×100m relay	1	4	2		
			SF	2	3	42·9	
Truelsen, M.	DEN	4×100m relay	1	5	2		
			SF	2	4		
Tuulos, V.	FIN	Long jump	F		4	7,07	
		Triple jump	F		3	15,37	B
Ugarte, A.	CHI	110m hurdles	1	2	3		
Unger, G.	SWE	Pentathlon	F		DNF		
Uyeda, S.	JPN	Pentathlon	F		DNF		
Valente, A.	ITA	10k walk	1	2	4		
			F		7		
Van Den Berge, M.	HOL	100m	1	8	2		
			2	3	4		
		200m	1	15	2		
			2	5	5		
		4×100m relay	1	3	1	42·0*	
			SF	3	1	42·2	
			F		3	41·8	B
Van De Putte, F.	BEL	Marathon	F		DNF		
Vandervelde, C.	BEL	5000m	1	1	8		
		10000m	F		DNF		
Van Der Wee, J.	BEL	1500m	1	4	6		
Van Kampen, J.H.	HOL	100m	1	12	2		
			2	5	3		
		200m	1	10	4		
Van Rappard, O.	HOL	110m hurdles	1	3	2		
			SF	1	4		
		400m hurdles	1	6	5		
Vautier, M.	FRA	Pole vault	F		=8	3,55	
Velasco, F.	ESP	Cross country	F		13	39-07·3	
		3000m team race	1	2	4	30	
Venkoff, V.	BUL	10000m	F				
Verger, G.	FRA	Marathon	F		DNF		
Viel, R.	FRA	400m hurdles	1	4	1	57·2	
			SF	1	5		
		Pentathlon	F		DNF		
Vilen, E.V.	FIN	400m	1	1	2	54·8	
			2	5	3		
		400m hurdles	1	2	2		
			SF	1	3		
			F		2	53·8*	S
		4×400m relay	1	2	3		
Villacis, B.	ECU	Marathon	F		DNF		
Vince, A.J.	CAN	100m	1	16	2		
			2	1	6		
		4×100m relay	1	2	2		
			SF	1	3	43·3	
Vrettos, C.	GRE	Shot put	F		14	13,25	
Watson, R.B.	USA	1500m	1	4	2		
			F		7	3-59·9	
Watters, J.N.	USA	800m	1	4	2		
			SF	2	3		
			F		7	1-54·8	
Watts, G.H.	GBR	10k walk	1	2	DIS		
Webber, C.J.	GBR	3000m team race	1	1	2	15	
			F		2	14	S
Webster, J.E.	GBR	10000m	F				
		Cross country	F		DNF		
Weiss, Z.	POL	1500m	1	7	5		
		200m	1	14	3		
Wejnarth, G.	SWE	400m	1	3	1	50·2	
			2	2	3		
		4×100m relay	1	5	1	43·8	
			SF	3	3	43·0	
		4×400m relay	1	1	2		
			F		2	3-17·0	S
Welchel, J.	USA	Javelin throw	F		12	52,98	
Wendling, F.E.	USA	Marathon	F		16	3:05-09·8	
Wiberg, C.	SWE	100m	1	9	4		
Wide, E.	USA	5000m	1	3	2		
			F		3	15-01·8	B
		10000m	F		2	30-55·2	S
		Cross country	F		DNF		
		3000m team race	1	2	3	21	
Wilhelme, L.	FRA	Long jump	F		5	6,99	
		Triple jump	F		17	12,66	
Williams, B.A.	USA	Marathon	F		DNF		
Williams, J.E.	GBR	Cross country	F		DNF		
Wilson, E.C.	USA	400m	1	4	1	49·6	
			2	6	3		
Wilson, R.E.	USA	Triple jump	F		7	14,23	
Winter, A.W.	AUS	Triple jump	F		1	15,52*	G
Wipf, H.	SUI	Javelin throw	Q		DNQ	48,57	
Wiriath, R.	FRA	800m	1	1	1	1-59·0	
			SF	2	7		
		1500m	1	1	1	4-13·8	
			F		10	4-02·8	
Woods, R.S.	GBR	Shot put	F		24	11,77	
Wright, D.M.	GBR	Marathon	F		DNF		
Yrjoelae, I.	FIN	Pentathlon	F		DNF		
		Decathlon	F		DNF		
Yrjoelae, P.	FIN	Decathlon	F		9	6548.525	
Zaharopoulos, G.	GRE	Javelin throw	F		15	51,17	
		Discus throw	F		30	34,02	
		Pentathlon	F		DNF		
Zaidin, P.	FRA	Hammer throw	F		12	36,15	
Zani, O.	BRA	Discus throw	F		23	35,72	
		Shot put	F		NP	0	
		Hammer throw	F		14	33,89	
Zeegers, J.	HOL	1500m	1	4	4		
		5000m	1	3	6		
Zemi, C.	ITA	Discus throw	F		17	37,46	
		Hammer throw	F		13	35,00	
Ziffer, S.	POL	5000m	1	1	14		
		3000m steeplechase	1	3	5		
		3000m team race	1	1	5	41	
Zinner, F.	BEL	Pentathlon	F		DNF		
Zucca, V.	ITA	100m	1	16	3		
Zuna, F.T.	USA	Marathon	F		18	3:05-52·2	

1928

The First Women Track and Field Competitors

In Amsterdam, women athletes appeared in track and field events for the first time and the Germans came back into the fold, but the USSR, who still had not taken part in the Olympics, decided to hold its own Games. The French government too, were reluctant to participate but were shamed into sending a team when Francois Coty of the cosmetics company offered to finance it himself.

Paavo Nurmi added to his laurels and his reputation in his last Olympic Games, but the surprise was the eclipse of the United States athletes on the track, particularly in the sprints and hurdles races, where they usually shone. A 19-year-old Canadian, Percy Williams, was the hero of the sprints, and an aristocratic Englishman, Lord Burghley, took the 400 metres hurdles.

Men's Track Events

Three times the Olympic **100 metres** record of 10·6 sec was equalled in the preliminaries, first by Percy Williams of Canada in the second round, then by Jack London of Britain and finally by Bob McAllister of the USA. There was a tense silence as Franz Miller, the German starter, sent the men to their marks for the final. After two false starts made by Legg of South Africa and Wykoff of the USA, Williams immediately showed in front and was never headed to win in 10·8 on a slow wet track. A metre covered the other five finalists at 80 metres, before London forced himself into the silver position with Lammers of Germany taking bronze, both recording 10·9.

Two of the favourites in the **200 metres**, Helmut Koernig of Germany and Charles Borah, the US champion, contested the last heat of the second round with the young Canadian 100 metres winner, Percy Williams. With only two to qualify, Borah was squeezed into third place as Koernig equalled the Olympic record of 21·6 sec. The track was sodden for the final, but it did not hinder the start and Koernig entered the finishing straight a trifle ahead of Jackson Scholz of the USA. Then with 50 metres left, Williams and Walter Rangeley of Britain eased past Koernig. Williams won with his stronger finish in 21·8 from Rangeley in 21·9 and a tie was announced between Koernig and Scholz for third place. The next day the judges advised the two third placers that there would be a run-off during that very morning. Scholz, who had been out on the binge the night before, declined to race and Koernig was given the bronze medal.

In the final of the **400 metres**, Ray Barbuti of the USA set the pace and led through 200 in 22·7 sec with Joachim Buechner of Germany and Herman Phillips in contention. Entering the home straight Barbuti had a four-metre lead, but 50 metres from home, James Ball of Canada came up fast. Barbuti's lunge at the tape sent him sprawling onto the track, but it got him the gold from Ball, with times of 47·8 to 48·0, which did not reflect the closeness of the finish. Buechner took the bronze also in a tight finish from John Rinkel of Britain in 48·2.

Loyd Hahn of the USA had high expectations of winning the **800 metres** following a fast semi-final of 1-52·6 when he beat two other fancied runners, Phil Edwards of Canada and Sera Martin of France. Douglas Lowe of Britain, the defending champion, led at the start having the advantage of the inside position, but Hahn soon took command with Edwards and the Briton tucked in behind him. With 100 metres to go Lowe took off and won in the Olympic record time of 1-51·8, followed by Hermann Engelhard of Germany and Erik Bylehn of Sweden, who were coming along fast. Bylehn took the silver in 1-52·8 from Engelhard in 1-53·2.

Jules Ladoumegue, of France, had run the **1,500 metres** in 3-52·6 at the French championships and was rated favourite for the gold medal. In the final, however, the two Finns Harri Larva and Eino Purje controlled the race with laps of 61·0, 63·4 and 65·4 before Ladoumegue made a strike for home from 250 metres out. Larva was drawn along, and upon entering the home straight he passed the Frenchman 20 metres from the finish to win in 3-53·2, shaving Nurmi's Olympic record. Ladoumegue clocked 3-53·8 while Purje just held on to the last medal position from a fast closing Hans Wichmann of Germany in 3-56·4.

It was a foregone conclusion that one of Paavo Nurmi or Ville Ritola, the Finnish duo, would win the **5,000 metres**. Brian Oddie of Britain led from the gun in the final, but after two laps Nurmi took up the running, although he was still suffering from aches and pains sustained in the steeplechase heats and appeared uncomfortable. He was followed by Ritola, Leo Lermond of the USA and Edvin Wide of Sweden. On the penultimate lap, Nurmi made a long drive for home, but coming off the final bend appeared to allow Ritola to pass him on the inside. Ritola sprinted away to win in 14-38·0 to Nurmi's 14-40·0. Nurmi constantly glanced over his shoulder to make sure he was safe, leaving Wide to finish third in 14-41·2.

As in the 5,000 metres, the **10,000 metres** was a straight final with the same three actors, Paavo Nurmi and Ville Ritola of Finland and Edvin Wide of Sweden. Walter Beavers of Britain led the first circuit in 62·2, Joie Ray of the USA then went to the front, before Ritola took up the running in the fifth. Beavers briefly took the lead again when the pace slackened, but in the tenth lap the trio of Ritola, Nurmi and Wide ran away from the rest of the field. Wide was eventually dropped and Nurmi spurted over the last 20 metres to beat Ritola in the new Olympic record of 30-18·8 to 30-19·4, with the Swede finishing third in 31-00·8.

The **marathon** was on a flat out and back course over roadway and cobbles with the weather cool and a strong breeze blowing. A huge field of 75 surged away with South Africa's one-armed runner M.J. Steytler, waving his one arm, in the lead. Joie Ray of the USA, one of the fancied runners, took over before passing through the marathon gate and Seilchiro Tsuda of Japan, J. Linsen of Belgium, Martti Marttelin and Eino Rastas of Finland all took turns in leading over the first half of the race. At 35km, Kanamatsu Yamada of Japan headed the pack and at 37km, Miguel Plaza of Chile took over. However, lurking in the pack was the novice marathon runner, Mohammed El Ouafi, an Algerian Arab running for France. He hit the front in the 40th kilometre and drew away with Plaza trailing him, to win in 2:32-57. The embarrassed El Ouafi was immediately embraced and kissed by a French time-keeper. Plaza was placed second in 2:33-23 and Martti Marttelin third in 2:35-02.

In the **110 metres hurdles**, George Weightman-Smith of South Africa beat the listed world record in the semi-finals with 14·6 sec and was favourite to take the Olympic title. John Collier, Leighton Dye and Steve Anderson, all of the USA forged away at the gun with Sydney Atkinson of South Africa just behind. Unfortunately, Weightman-Smith, running in the chewed-up inside lane, hit a hurdle and was out of contention. Atkinson got home inches ahead of Anderson in the same time of 14·8. Collier was placed third in 14·9.

Morgan Taylor of the USA was world record holder for the **400 metres hurdles**, while his fellow countryman, Johnny Gibson, held the 440-yards hurdles record. Surprisingly, Gibson was eliminated in his semi-final, while Taylor beat the Olympic record with 53·4 sec. In the final Lord David George Brownlow Cecil Burghley of Britain, an ungainly hurdler, known as "Davy" to his friends, went off like a rocket. Running in lane five, Burghley caught up with his fellow countryman, George Livingstone-Learmonth, in lane six, by the third hurdle and when Frank Cuhel and Morgan Taylor, both of America, came abreast of him when coming off the final turn, he fought off the challenge and won his gold in 53·4 to equal the Olympic record. Cuhel took silver and Taylor bronze, both being credited with 53·6.

Paavo Nurmi of Finland competed in the **3,000 metres**

steeplechase and although a great runner, he was a poor hurdler. In his heat, he hesitated at the first water jump, attempted to climb on top of the barrier and fell on his back into the water. After this he was a little more respectful of the obstacle and qualified with the aid of superior running. In the final, Toivo Loukola and Ove Andersen, both of Finland, set the pace. On the fifth lap, Loukola forged ahead and in the sixth established a 13-second lead, before going on to finish in a new Olympic record of 9-21·8. Behind him, Nurmi had cut back his lead on the last lap to record 9-31·2 for the silver medal, while Andersen was in third in 9-35·6.

The American team for the **4 × 100 metres relay** consisted of Frank Wykoff, James Quinn, Charles Borah and Henry Russell and they clocked 41·2 sec in the heats, just a shade outside the world record. Their main rivals in the final were the German team of George Lammers, Richard Corts, Hubert Houben and Helmut Koernig, who were on level pegging until the last baton exchange, where they lost a metre which they never regained. The US team equalled the world record and set a new Olympic record in 41·0, with Germany recording 41·2 and Great Britain 41·8 for silver and bronze respectively.

Once again the USA and Germany were the strongest contenders for a relay, this time the **4 × 400 metres relay**. The line-up for America was George Baird, Emerson Spencer, Fred Alderman and Ray Barbuti and for Germany the team was Otto Neumann, Richard Krebs, Hary Storz and Hermann Engelhard. At the first change America was a metre ahead, which Spencer extended to five at the half-way stage. Germany closed a little on the third leg, but Barbuti played with Engelhard and allowed him to catch up before surging away to give the USA a 3-14·2 world and Olympic record. Germany clocked 3-14·8 and Canada 3-15·4.

Men's Field Events

Harold Osborn of the USA, the defending Olympic **high jump** champion, was not up to his 1924 standard and finished fifth, but jumpers were now inhibited by the no-diving-rule and the take-off at Amsterdam was soft. Despite these limitations, five aspiring athletes cleared

All-Sport Photographic Ltd.

Ville Ritola

One of the famed "Flying Finns", Ville Ritola often had to play a supporting role to his countryman, Paavo Nurmi. He was born in 1896 but emigrated to the United States in 1920, and there won national titles before returning to Finland in 1924.

Having beaten Nurmi's world record for the 10,000m earlier that year the Finnish selectors chose him in preference to Nurmi for the Olympic race. Ritola duly showed appreciation by reducing his world record by 12 sec to 30-23·2, in winning the gold medal for the event.

In the 5,000m Ritola had to be satisfied with the silver behind Nurmi, but within 48 hours he was setting more world best figures when securing the gold in the 3,000m steeplechase with a time of 9-33·6. And he received two additional medals. One for being a member of Finland's winning 3,000m team (gold) and the other for the cross country event (silver).

Along with Nurmi, he was chosen for Olympic action again at the Amsterdam Games of 1928. Nurmi narrowly beat him in the 10,000m, but Ritola took his revenge with an equally narrow victory over his illustrious colleague in the 5,000m.

Ritola collected eight medals, from two Olympics, compared to Nurmi's 12 from three Games.

Into the stadium comes Mohammed El Ouafi of Algeria, and France, to win the Amsterdam marathon.

Dave Terry

On the final lap, the two Finns, Toivo Loukola (790) and Ove Andersen (759) match strides, before the former goes on to win.

Dave Terry

1,91 metres and only Bob King of the USA managed the next height of 1,94 to win the gold. The four tieing competitors were now given a further jump at 1,94 and all failed again. The bar was then lowered and raised a total of five times to determine places two to five. The silver went to Ben Hedges of the USA and the bronze to Claude Menard of France.

The firm favourite for the **pole vault** was Lee Barnes of the USA, who had earlier in the year set a world record of 4,30 metres. The bar was set at 3,95 and five vaulters cleared at their first attempt: Sabin Carr, Bill Droegemueller, Charles McGinnis and Barnes of the USA, and Victor Pickard of Canada, who happened to be currently at an American college. At 4,00 only Carr and Droegemueller succeeded. They then elected to jump at 4,10 and once again they soared over the bar but at 4,20 only Carr had the elevation to tuck over for first place and an Olympic record. He then had the bar raised to a new world record height of 4,31, but could not make it. McGinnis gained the bronze in a jump-off with Pickard and Barnes, giving America a one-two-three.

Three highly talented athletes lined up in the **long jump**, Ed Hamm, the new world record holder, Will DeHart Hubbard, the former record holder and reigning Olympic champion, both of the USA and Silvio Cator from tiny Haiti. The last-named was to improve the world mark to 7,93 metres five weeks later. Four runways were in use for the first three jumps, in which all the best marks were recorded and the top six were then conducted to another runway and had to prepare all over again for their three final jumps. Not surprisingly, none of them improved. Hamm took the gold medal with 7,73, Cator the silver with 7,58 and Al Bates of the USA the bronze at 7,40. Hubbard's injured ankle unfortunately precluded him from the medals and he managed only 7,11.

Tony Winter of Australia, the defending champion in the **triple jump**, failed to qualify, while Wim Peters of Holland, another man who might have expected to gain a medal, finished only in seventh place. The first three jumps were conducted on two runways and it was at this stage that Mikio Oda of Japan achieved 15,21 for Japan's first-ever gold medal. The move to a third runway enabled Lev Casey of the USA to improve to 15,17 for the silver medal and Vilho Tuulos of Finland to get the

bronze with 15,11. This was Tuulos's third medal in three Games. His other two were a bronze in 1924 and a gold in 1920, both in the triple jump.

Emil Hirschfeld of Germany was tipped for the **shot put** title, on the strength of his recent world record of 15,79 metres. The preliminary three puts were contested in two pools, after which Hirschfeld found he was in second place with 15,72, just behind Herman Brix of the USA on 15,75. Another American, John Kuck, was lying third with 15,43, but he had a trick up his sleeve, for he unleashed a mighty 15,87 for the gold in the final rounds. Neither Brix in the silver medal position nor Hirschfeld in the bronze had an answer to this.

Most of the informed judges considered the competition in the **discus throw** to be a struggle between the defending champion Bud Houser of the USA and the new world record holder Hans Hoffmesiter of Germany. When the competition got under way, the first three throws took place in four pools, where first, James Corson of the USA broke the Olympic record with 47,10, then Bud Houser responded with 47,32. In the final three throws Antero Kivi of Finland improved to 47,23 and also exceeded the old record. The result, first Houser, second Kivi and third Corson, with Hoffmeister throwing only 39,17.

The preliminary round for the **hammer throw** saw Ossian Skioeld of Sweden throwing 51,29 metres to lead from Edmund Black of the USA with 49,03 and the novice, Pat O'Callaghan of Ireland with 47,07. Skioeld and Black did not improve, but O'Callaghan did. On his penultimate attempt he launched a gold winning 51,39 to leave the Swede with the silver and the American with the bronze medal.

Eino Penttilaa of Finland was the current world record holder in the **javelin throw**, but he had injured his foot and was below his best. All the top throws came in the preliminary first three rounds, where on his very first throw, Erik Lundkvist of Sweden lofted his wooden spear a distance of 66,60 metres for a new Olympic record and premier position. Bela Szepes of Hungary laid claim to the silver position with 65,26 while Olav Sunde of Norway produced a 63,97 throw to shut out the more favoured Finns.

Paavo Yrjoelae from Finland, twice a world record holder in the **decathlon**, was the firm favourite for this

All-Sport Photographic Ltd.

Lord Burghley, Marquis of Exeter

David Cecil Brownlow, Lord Burghley, distinguished himself both as a great athlete and a forthright member of the International Olympic Committee, as President of the Amateur Athletic Association of England and also the International Amateur Athletic Federation.

Born on 5 February 1905 and educated at Eton and Cambridge University, Lord Burghley broke a 28-year unbeaten run by Americans when he won the 400m hurdles final for Britain at the 1928 Amsterdam Olympic Games. In Los Angeles four years later he finished fourth in the 400m hurdles final and helped Britain take the silver medals in the 4 × 400m relay.

The following year he became a member of the International Olympics Committee and in 1948 was responsible for organising the Games in London.

Extremely popular both on and off the track, Lord Burghley, while at Cambridge, was an unmistakable force in the University's successful track and field side and the inspiration behind the development of so many outstanding hurdlers.

An official report said of Lord Burghley: "He was a man who reinforced his nobility with the virtue of complete honesty." He died on 21 October 1981.

event, and justified the position, but the lesser medals were up for grabs. Leading after the first day was Helge Jansson of Sweden with 4,178 points, closely followed by Achilles Jaervinen of Finland on 4,136 and Jim Stewart of the USA with 4,127. Lurking, ready to strike on 4,103 was Yrjoelae, who had scored well in the shot, and high jump. He clinched the gold medal with an excellent 42,09 discus throw and a useful 4-44·0 1,500 metres to score 8,053·29 points, for a new world and Olympic record. Runner-up was Jaervinen with 7,931·50 and Ken Doherty, later on a famous American coach, improved throughout the competition to gain the bronze with 7,706·65.

Women's Events

There were several likely candidates for top honours following the heats and semi-finals of the **100 metres**. Among them was Miss Myrtle Cook of Canada, who had recently equalled the world record held by Elizabeth Robinson, of the USA, in 12·0 sec. Under starter's orders, she made the fatal blunder of making two false starts and promptly broke down in tears by the side of starter. A similar fate befell Fraulein Leni Schmidt, a blonde German girl, but she was made of sterner stuff and waved her fist at the starter who wisely backed off. The four remaining sprinters eventually got away and fought a close battle right to the tape. Robinson was awarded first place in 12·2, with Fanny Rosenfeld of Canada given 12·3, but not without a protest from the Canadian team manager. Third was Ethel Smith, also of Canada, in 12·3.

The **800 metres** turned out to be a controversial event due to the pundits debating whether or not such a long race was suitable for young ladies. Inga Gentzel of Sweden was tipped to win, as she had recently run a new

world record time of 2-20·0, and following the heats she was one of nine girls lined up for the final. Kinue Hitomi, the talented Japanese girl, set the pace chased by Lina Radke and Marie Dollinger, both of Germany. With 300 metres to go Radke made her bid for glory, drawing along Gentzel, with Hitomi trailing along third. Radke went on to win in 2-16·8 for a new world record with Hitomi spurting into second place, recording 2-17·6 and Gentzel coming third, improving her time to 2-18·8. Six of the nine runners collapsed onto the ground where a couple had to be stretchered off and it was not until 1960 that the event reappeared in the Olympic Games.

Prior to the Games, the listed world record in the **4 × 100 metres relay** was 49·8 sec, but in the first heat Canada clocked 49·3 and in the second the USA clocked 49·3. The final was a close fought duel between the two with Canada winning by a long metre in the new record time of 48·4. The winning team was Ethel Smith, Fanny Rosenfeld, Florence Bell and Myrtle Cook. The USA took the silver in 48·6 and Germany the bronze in 49·0.

In the **high jump** Carolina Gisolf as the world record holder was expected to win, but was completely upstaged by the most photographed girl of the Amsterdam Games, Ethel Catherwood of Canada. Ten ladies cleared the bar at 1,48 metres, but only Catherwood, Gisolf and Mildred Wiley of the USA jumped the next height. At 1,59 only Catherwood jumped clear for the gold, while Gisolf won the jump-off for silver over Wiley who took the bronze.

Halina Konopacka of Poland came to the Games as the world record holder for the **discus throw** and improved her mark to 39,62 metres in winning the coveted Olympic title. The American girl Lillian Copeland claimed the silver by throwing 37,08 and Ruth Svedberg of Sweden narrowly won the bronze with 35,92.

All-Sport Photographic Ltd.

Percy Williams

Percy Williams is the only Canadian to win an Olympic 100m sprint title. He was the big surprise of the 1928 Amsterdam Games and not only did he receive the gold for the short sprint, but he completed a great "double" by becoming champion at 200m also. And he was only 20, having been born on 19 May 1908 in Vancouver.

It was not until the final Williams equalled the Olympic 100m record of 10·6 sec in the second round that the experts really sat up and took notice of him. However, two more powerful looking athletes, Bob McAllister (USA) and Jack London (Great Britain) repeated the time in winning the semi-finals, so he was by no means the favourite for the final. But after two false starts by opponents, the young Canadian was first into the lead and was never caught.

With Williams winning a second gold in the 200m it was not surprising that he became a national hero back home. It is reported that he travelled across Canada by train on his return, accompanied by his mother. At various stops along the way — Montreal, Hamilton and Winnipeg — he was said to have been presented with a wide variety of gifts. Thousands cheered his arrival in Vancouver, where appreciation for his unexpected Olympic "double" was overwhelming.

Dave Terry

Douglas Lowe

Douglas Lowe was the first of three runners to successfully defend his Olympic 800m title (1924 and 1928), the other two being Mal Whitfield of the USA (1948 and 1952) and Peter Snell of New Zealand (1960 and 1964). Lowe, who was born in Manchester on 7 August 1902, blossomed as a middle distance runner of outstanding ability while studying law at Cambridge University. In addition to improving his speed, he developed a canny tactical sense, and this played a notable part in gaining his first Olympic success in Paris where he beat Paul Martin, of Switzerland, by a mere 0·1 sec.

Two summers later he was involved in another memorable thriller when racing Dr Otto Peltzer, of Germany, over 880 yards at the Stamford Bridge track in London.

By the time the Amsterdam Olympics came round Lloyd Hahn, the American champion, and the Frenchman Seraphin Martin, had been producing the fastest 800m runs, Martin in fact having reduced the world record to 1-50·6. The strong-minded Lowe was undeterred and romped home the winner again in an Olympic record of 1-51·8.

On his retirement, he became secretary of the Amateur Athletic Association for a spell, before concentrating on his legal responsibilities and becoming a QC.

All-Sport Photographic Ltd.

Paavo Nurmi

Born in Turku, Finland, on 13 June 1897, Paavo Nurmi became one of the all-time great athletes. Famed for his running with a stopwatch in his hand, he revelled in racing over any distance from 1,500 metres to 20,000 metres. And he had the distinction of breaking 29 world records in 16 different events and winning nine Olympic gold medals and three silvers.

His exciting career was terminated internationally in 1932, following allegations that he had infringed his amateur status — a charge he always hotly denied. The Finnish Association allowed him to compete again in domestic events and he finally retired in 1933 after winning his national 1,500m championship as a "national amateur".

The first of Nurmi's Olympic successes were achieved at the 1920 Antwerp Games where he won the 10,000m and the cross country. In Paris four years later, in addition to a repeat of the cross country "double", he won the 1,500m, 5,000m and was in Finland's winning 3,000m team. In 1928 he took the title again for the 10,000m.

In recognition of his greatness as a runner a bronze statue of him graces the entrance to the Helsinki Olympic stadium. He died on 2 October 1973.

Dave Terry

Clarence Houser

Clarence Houser, who was born on 25 September 1901, was the man responsible for introducing speed rotation in the circle before releasing the disc in discus throwing. He became so proficient in the art that in 1926 he broke the world record with a heave of 158ft 1¾in (48,20m), a particularly exceptional achievement because though 6ft (1·83 m) tall, he weighed no more than 13 stone (82·6kg).

The world record was not the only outstanding achievement of his athletics career — he also won three Olympic gold medals. Oddly enough the first of them came in the shot, at Paris in 1924. The second followed five days later in the discus, with an Olympic record 151ft 5in (46,15m).

Only once before had this Olympic "double" been achieved, by Robert Garrett of the United States at the inaugural 1896 Games in Athens, and it has never been achieved since. In Amsterdam four years later he retained his discus crown with an improved Olympic record throw of 155ft 2½in (47,32m).

By this time he had become a qualified dentist and soon after he gave up his international sporting activities to concentrate on his dental practice.

Houser's intellectual approach to discus throwing enabled him to evolve a technical skill superior to his opponents.

MALES

COMPETITOR	COUNTRY CODE	EVENT	ROUND	HEAT	PLACE	TIME & DISTANCE	MEDAL
Aastad, E.	NOR	Long jump	F		14	7,07	
Abbott, D.	USA	5000m	1	2	11		
Adams, R.A.	CAN	100m	1	6	2		
			2	6	4		
		200m	1	6	2		
			2	1	3		
		4×100m relay	1	1	1	42·2	
			F		DIS		
Adelheim, A.	FRA	400m hurdles	1	1	4		
Adolfsson, H.	SWE	High jump	F		=11	1,84	
Agee, W.	USA	Marathon	F		44	2·58-50	
Aguire, J.	MEX	Discus throw	Q		DNQ	33,21	
		Shot put	Q		DNC	11,33	
Aizawa, I.	JPN	100m	1	6	4		
		200m	1	6	3		
		4×100m relay	1	3	3		
Akelaitis, A.	LIT	High jump	Q		DNQ	1,60	
Albe, E.L.	ARG	100m	1	4	6		
Albrich, L.	RUM	110m hurdles	1	1	4		
Alderman, F.P.	USA	4×400m relay	1	1	1	3-21·6	
			F		1	3-14·2*	G
Ali, T.M.	TUR	100m	1	5	5		
		4×100m relay	1	3	4		
Alvarado, O.	CHI	100m	1	11	4		
		Long jump	Q		DNQ	6·51	
Alzieu, C.	FRA	Long jump	Q		DNQ	6,70	
Andersen, O.	FIN	3000m steeplechase	1	3	2		
			F		3	9-35·6	B
Anderson, J.F.	USA	Discus throw	F		5	44·87	
Anderson, S.E.	USA	110m hurdles	1	4	1	15·0	
			SF	2	1	14·8*	
			F		2	14·8	S
Andersson, A.	SWE	110m hurdles	1	3	3		
		Decathlon	F		8	7109·635	
Anglim, P.	IRL	Long jump	Q		DNQ	6,81	
Ashby, S.T.	GBR	1500m	1	3	3		
Askildt, K.	NOR	Discus throw	F		13	42,57	
Atkinson, S.J.M.	SAF	100m	1	2	1	11·2	
			2	3	5		
		110m hurdles	1	3	2	15·0	
			SF	2	2		
			F		1	14·8	G
		Long jump	Q		DNQ	0	
Auvergne, G.	FRA	100m	1	14	2		
			2	3	3		
		4×100m relay	1	2	1	41·8	
			F		4	42·0	
Bach, G.	DEN	Marathon	F		51	3:09-30	
Baird, G.H.	USA	4×400m relay	1	1	1	3-21·6	
			F		1	3-14·2*	G
Ball, J.A.	CAN	400m	1	8	1	55·8	
			2	2	1	49·2	
			SF	1	1	48·6	
			F		2	48·0	S
		4×400m relay	1	1	2		
			F		3	3-15·4	B
Balogh, L.	HUN	Long jump	Q		DNQ	6,79	
Baran, J.	POL	Discus throw	Q		DNQ	41,77	
Baraton, G.	FRA	800m	1	4	1	2-03·4	
			SF	2	DNS		
Barbuti, R.J.	USA	400m	1	6	1	49·8	
			2	3	1	48·8	
			SF	1	2	48·8	
			F		1	47·8	G
		4×400m relay	1	1	1	3-21·6	
			F		1	3-14·2*	G
Barnes, L.	USA	Pole vault	F		5	3,95	
Barrientos, J.E.	CUB	100m	1	13	1	11·0	
			2	4	5		
Barsy, L.	HUN	400m	1	10	1	55·6	
			2	6	2		
			SF	1	4	49·2	
		800m	1	7	2	1-59·0	
			SF	1	4	1-56·2	
		4×400m relay	1	1	2		
Barth, H.	GER	Decathlon	F		11	6850·305	
Bartl, J.	TCH	100m	1	10	3		
		200m	1	8	5		
		400m	1	4	2		
			2	5	3		
		4×400m relay	1	2	5		
Bartlett, L.M.	USA	Javelin throw	Q		DNQ	57,57	
Bartolini, N.	ITA	3000m steeplechase	1	1	6		
Barucco, A.	ARG	100m	1	11	3		
		200m	1	9	2		
			2	5	3		

COMPETITOR	COUNTRY CODE	EVENT	ROUND	HEAT	PLACE	TIME & DISTANCE	MEDAL
Bates, A.H.	USA	Long jump	F		3	7,40	B
Bayer, R.	CHI	Hammer throw	F		8	46,34	
Beavers, W.	GBR	5000m	1	1	5		
		10000m	F		9	31-48·0	
Beccali, L.	ITA	1500m	1	1	4		
Beddari, S.	FRA	5000m	1	1	9		
		10000m	F		16		
Bell, R.D.	GBR	1500m	1	5	6		
Benares, H.	CHI	Discus throw	Q		DNQ	38,18	
Benz, A.F.M.	HOL	100m	1	8	4		
Bedinger, B.E.	USA	Decathlon	F		17	6619·375	
Bernardis, S.	GRE	Pole vault	Q		DNQ	3,30	
		Decathlon	F		20	6149·91	
		4×400m relay	1	2	6		
Bertheloot, G.	BEL	800m	1	1	5		
Berrini, R.	ITA	Marathon	F		DNF		
Bessim, A.	TUR	800m	1	6	4		
Bidduloh, N.S.	GBR	3000m steeplechase	1	2	4		
Bignall, H.J.	GBR	Marathon	F		21	2:45-44	
Biniakowski, K.	POL	400m	1	11	3		
		4×400m relay	1	1	4		
Black, E.F.	USA	Hammer throw	F		3	49,03	B
Blankers, J.	HOL	Triple jump	F		=9	14,35	
Blewitt, C.E.	GER	3000m steeplechase	1	3	6		
Boecher, H.	GER	1500m	1	2	1	3-59·6	
			F		DNF		
Boltze, W.	GER	5000m	1	2	7		
Bond, L.T.	GBR	Pole vault	Q		DNQ	3,50	
Boneder, W.	GER	High jump	F		16	1,80	
Bourgeois, L.H.	USA	Triple jump	F		11	14,28	
Boot, J.	HOL	100m	1	3	3		
Borah, C.E.	USA	200m	1	7	2		
			2	6	3		
		4×100m relay	1	3	1	41·2	
			F		1	41·0*	G
Bowman, S.	USA	Triple jump	F		=9	14,35	
Bracey, C.O.	USA	100m	1	14	1	11·0	
			2	6	1	10·8	
			SF	1	5	10·8	
Bricker, C.	CAN	Marathon	F		10	2:39-24	
Britstra, J.G.	HOL	110m hurdles	1	7	4		
Brix, H.H.	USA	Shot put	F		2	15,75	S
Brochart, P.	BEL	100m	1	3	2		
			2	6	5		
		200m	1	8	2		
			2	4	3		
		4×100m relay	1	2	3		
Broers, L.P.	BEL	Marathon	F		18	2:44-37	
Broos, H.A.	HOL	200m	1	13	2		
			2	3	5		
		400m	1	7	2		
			2	5	2		
			SF	1	5		
		4×400m relay	1	2	4		
Brugmann, H.	DEN	Long jump	Q		DNQ		
		Triple jump	Q		DNQ	13,82	
Buechner, J.	GER	400m	1	5	1	50·6	
			2	6	1	48·6	
			SF	2	1	48·6	
			F		3	48·2	B
Buhrmann, F.C.	HOL	High jump	Q		DNQ	1,70	
Burghley, D.G.B.C.	GBR	110m hurdles	1	9	2		
			SF	2	3		
		400m hurdles	1	1	1	57·0	
			SF	1	3	54·0	
			F		1	53·4*	G
Burns, R.	IND	100m	1	11	6		
		200m	1	3	4		
Burton-Durham, A.S.	SAF	100m	1	3	2		
			2	2	5		
		200m	1	12	3		
Butler, G.M.	GBR	200m	1	11	1	22·8	
			2	3	4		
Bylehn, E.	SWE	800m	1	1	2	1-59·2	
			SF	2	1	1-55·6	
			F		2	1-52·8	S
		4×400m relay	1	2	2		
			F		4	3-15·8	
Callard, V.S.	CAN	5000m	1	3	8		
Carabatis, D.	GRE	Discus throw	Q		DNQ	31,87	
		Shot put	Q		DNQ	12,98	
Carayannis, A.	GRE	Pole vault	Q		DNQ		
Cariofilis, A.	GRE	High jump	Q		DNQ	1,77	
Cariofilis, J.	GRE	High jump	Q		DNQ	1,77	
Carlini, G.	ITA	110m hurdles	1	7	3		
		4×400m relay	1	2	3		

COMPETITOR	COUNTRY CODE	EVENT	ROUND	HEAT	PLACE	TIME & DISTANCE	MEDAL
Carlton, J.A.	AUS	100m	1	11	2		
			2	5	5		
		200m	1	3	2		
			2	6	4		
Carr, S.W.	USA	Pole vault	F		1	4,20*	G
Carter, E.N.	USA	1500m	1	6	3		
Casey, L.B.	USA	Triple jump	F		2	15,17	S
Caskey, K.H.	USA	Hammer throw	F		12	44,80	
Castelli, G.	ITA	200m	1	12	2		
			2	6	5		
		4×100m relay	1	1	3		
Cator, S.	HAI	Long jump	F		2	7,58	S
Cejzik, A.	POL	Decathlon	F		18	6356·80	
Cerbonney, A.	FRA	100m	1	13	2		
			2	2	6		
		200m	1	8	1	22·2	
			2	3	3		
		4×100m relay	1	2	1	41·8	
			F		4	42·0	
Chauncy, F.C.L.	GBR	400m hurdles	1	2	2		
			SF	1	6		
Chavarri, E.	ESP	100m	1	16	3		
		4×100m relay	1	1	5		
Cherrier, A.	FRA	High jump	F		=7	1,88	
Chinassi, R.	TUR	100m	1	10	4		
		4×100m relay	1	3	4		
Churchill, T.	USA	Decathlon	F		5	7417·115	
Cimmermans, V.	LAT	Marathon	F		DNF		
Clark, A.F.	IRL	110m hurdles	1	4	3		
Coenjaerts, P.	BEL	800m	1	4	5		
		4×400m relay	1	1	5		
Cohen, H.J.	GBR	Long jump	Q		DNQ	6,39	
Collier, J.S.	USA	110m hurdles	1	7	1	15·0	
			SF	3	2		
			F		3	14·9	B
Cominotto, G.	ITA	800m	1	6	3	2-02·4	
			SF	2	6		
		4×400m relay	1	2	3		
Conger, R.	USA	1500m	1	5	1	4-02·6	
			F		10		
Conner, F.N.	USA	Hammer throw	F		6	46,75	
Constable, G.C.	GBR	10000m	F		12		
Conton, A.	ITA	Marathon	F		DNF		
Conturbia, A.	SUI	Discus throw	Q		DNQ	41,90	
Corson, J.H.	USA	Discus throw	F		3	47,10	B
Corts, R.	GER	100m	1	1	2		
			2	2	2		
			SF	2	5	10·8	
		4×100m relay	1	2	2		
			F		2	41·2	S
Costas, F.	MEX	100m	1	5	4		
		200m	1	8	6		
Coughlan, G.N.	IRL	800m	1	7	6		
		3000m steeplechase	1	2	DNF		
Craner, W.W.	GBR	4×400m relay	1	3	1	3-20·6	
			F		5	3-16·4	
Cristescu, V.	RUM	Marathon	F		DNF		
Csegezy, G.	RUM	Decathlon	F		26	5081·60	
Cuhel, F.J.	USA	400m hurdles	1	6	1	54·6	
			SF	1	2	53·8	
			F		2	53·6	S
Culi, J.	ESP	Pole vault	Q		DNQ	3,50	
Cullen, L.D.E.	IRL	200m	1	2	3		
Cummings, H.	USA	200m	1	2	1	22·4	
			2	1	2		
			SF	2	4	22·1	
Cussen, D.J.	IRL	100m	1	15	2		
			2	1	5		
Da Costa, J.P.	POR	110m hurdles	1	9	5		
Dalton, M.J.	USA	3000m steeplechase	1	1	2		
			F		7		
Danogany, E.	HUN	Discus throw	Q		DNQ	41,78	
Daranyi, J.	HUN	Shot put	F		8	14,35	
Dartigues, H.	FRA	3000m steeplechase	1	3	3		
			F		5	9-40·0	
David, J.	RUM	Discus throw	Q		DNQ	37,49	
		Shot put	Q		DNQ	12,82	
De Boer, H.	HOL	Long jump	F		6	7,32	
Degland, E.	FRA	Javelin throw	Q		DNQ	52,82	
De Gortari, A.	MEX	Long jump	Q		DNQ	6,97	
Degrelle, M.	FRA	200m	1	2	2		
			2	4	4		
De Lima, J.A.P.R.	POR	100m	1	12	4		
		200m	1	13	4		
De Mar, C.H.	USA	Marathon	F		27	2:50-42	

COMPETITOR	COUNTRY CODE	EVENT	ROUND	HEAT	PLACE	TIME & DISTANCE	MEDAL
Dengra, S.	ARG	800m	1	6	1	2-01·2	
			SF	2	7		
		1500m	1	3	5		
Denis, M.	FRA	Marathon	F		28	2:51-15	
Dobermann, R.	GER	Long jump	Q		DNQ	6,91	
Docherty, A.	CAN	1500m	1	5	5		
Doherty, J.K.	USA	Decathlon	F		3	7706·65	B
Douda, F.	TCH	Discus throw	Q		DNQ	41,19	
		Shot put	Q		DNQ	13,12	
Droegemueller, W.H.	USA	Pole vault	F		2	4,10	S
Dufau, A.	FRA	100m	1	12	3		
		4×100m relay	1	2	1	41·8	
			F		4	42·0	
Duhour, E.	FRA	Shot put	F		11	13,72	
Dujardin, J.	BEL	100m	1	1	3		
		200m	1	13	3		
		4×100m relay	1	2	3		
Dupont, G.	FRA	400m	1	1	2		
			2	3	4		
		4×400m relay	1	3	2		
			F		6	3-19·4	
Duquesne, L.	FRA	5000m	1	1	8		
		3000m steeplechase	1	2	2		
			F		6	9-40·6	
Dye, L.	USA	110m hurdles	1	5	1	15·0	
			SF	1	1	14·8*	
			F		4	14·9	
Edwards, P.	CAN	400m	1	3	1	49·8	
			2	5	1	49·2	
			SF	2	6	50·2	
		800m	1	8	1	1-59·4	
			SF	3	2	1-52·8	
			F		4	1-54·0	
		4×400m relay	1	1	2		
			F		3	3-15·4	B
Effern, W.F.	HOL	1500m	1	6	7		
Egri, K.	HUN	Discus throw	Q		DNQ	41,89	
Eijsker, G.	HOL	Discus throw	Q		DNQ	39,80	
Ekloef, N.E.	SWE	5000m	1	2	1	15-07·4	
			F		DNF		
		3000m steeplechase	1	1	3		
			F		4	9-38·0	
Ellis, C.	GBR	1500m	1	6	1	4-01·8	
			F		5	3-57·6	
Elofs, A.A.B.	SWE	Marathon	F		DNF		
El Ouafi, A.B.	FRA	Marathon	F		1	2:32-57	G
Engelhard, H.	GER	800m	1	5	2	1-57·0	
			SF	2	3	1-56·8	
			F		3	1-53·2	B
		4×400m relay	1	2	1	3-20·8	
			F		2	3-14·8	S
Enis, H.	TUR	100m	1	16	5		
		4×100m relay	1	3	4		
Eriksson, E.G.	FIN	Hammer throw	F		9	46,22	
Etienne, G.	BEL	Javelin throw	Q		DNQ	54,34	
		Decathlon	F		23	5256·62	
Eyschen, F.	LUX	100m	1	16	4		
		400m	1	13	5		
Facelli, L.	ITA	400m hurdles	1	6	2		
			SF	2	2		
			F		6	55·8	
		4×400m relay	1	2	3		
Farkas, M.	HUN	Decathlon	F	21	5	6015·635	
Feger, R.	FRA	400m	1	12	1	51·4	
			2	2	2		
			SF	2	5	49·6	
		4×400m relay	1	3	2		
			F		6	3-19·4	
		800m	1	5	4		
Fekete, E.	HUN	Long jump	Q		DNQ	6,77	
		Triple jump	Q		DNQ	14,07	
Feldmann, F.	EST	Shot put	F		12	13,54	
Ferrer, E.	ESP	Marathon	F		52	3:11-05	
Ferrera, G.	ITA	Marathon	F		34	2:53-10	
Ferris, S.	GBR	Marathon	F		8	2:37-41	
Fitzpatrick, J.R.	CAN	100m	1	1	1	11·0	
			2	1	2		
			SF	2	6	10·9	
		200m	1	3	1	22·8	
			2	5	1	22·0	
			SF	2	3	22·1	
			F		5	22·1	
		4×100m relay	1	1	1	42·2	
			F		DIS		
Flouret, J.	FRA	Long jump	Q		DNQ	6,64	
Ford, H.	GBR	Decathlon	F		DNF		

COMPETITOR	COUNTRY CODE	EVENT	ROUND	HEAT	PLACE	TIME & DISTANCE	MEDAL
Forys, C.	POL	1500m	1	6	6		
Frangoudis, R.	GRE	100m	1	9	6		
		200m	1	2	4		
		4×100m relay	1	1	4		
		4×400m relay	1	2	6		
Frederiksen, G.	NOR	Triple jump	Q		DNQ	13,39	
		Decathlon	F		DNF		
Frick, H.	USA	Marathon	F		41	2:57-24	
Fritz, A.	RUM	Shot put	Q		DNQ	12,55	
Fuller, E.A.	USA	800m	1	4	2	2-03.8	
			SF	1	1	1-55.6	
			F		7	1-55.0	
Furuyama, I.	JPN	Discus throw	Q		DNQ	37,89	
Gaby, F.R.	GBR	110m hurdles	1	8	1	15.2	
			SF	1	2	14.9	
			F		6	15.2	
Galambos, J.	HUN	Marathon	F		49	3:05-58	
Garcia, A.	MEX	400m	1	15	4		
		800m	1	3	5		
		4×400m relay	1	3	3		
Gegan, W.T.	USA	3000m steeplechase	1	1	4		
Geissler, H.	AUT	100m	1	14	3		
		200m	1	12	1	22.6	
			2	1	4		
		400m	1	13	1	50.2	
			2	2	5		
Gerault, J.	FRA	Marathon	F		23	2:46-08	
Gerhardt, P.	GER	Marathon	F		50	3:09-30	
Gero, F.	HUN	100m	1	4	1	10.8	
			2	1	3		
		200m	1	8	3		
		4×100m relay	1	3	DIS		
Gero, M.	HUN	400m	1	14	3		
		4×400m relay	1	1	3		
Gibson, J.A.	USA	400m hurdles	1	2	1	57.0	
			SF	2	4	54.4	
Gill, C.W.	GER	100m	1	7	2		
			2	2	3		
		200m	1	15	1	22.2	
			2	2	2		
			SF	2	5	22.4	
		4×100m relay	1	1	2		
			F		3	41.8	B
Glover, S.B.	CAN	4×400m relay	1	1	2		
			F		3	3-15.4	B
Goldsmith, E.	SUI	100m	1	14	5		
		4×100m relay	1	3	2		
			F		5	42.6	
Gomez, M.	MEX	100m	1	3	4		
		200m	1	5	2		
			2	5	2		
			SF	1	5		
Gonzaga, A.	PHI	100m	1	16	2		
			2	5	4		
		200m	1	5	3		
Gordon, C.E.S.	GBR	High jump	F		=17	1,70	
Gordon, E.L.	USA	Long jump	F		7	7,32	
Green, A.W.	GBR	400m	1	12	2		
			2	1	3		
Griffin, D.	CAN	1500m	1	4	4		
Groeneweg, C.	HOL	Marathon	F		DNF		
Groscol, A.	BEL	100m	1	15	4		
		200m	1	5	4		
		4×100m relay	1	2	3		
Gwinn, D.S.	USA	Hammer throw	F		5	47,15	
Haenchen, H.	GER	Discus throw	F		14	42,08	
Hagen, G.	NOR	Decathlon	F		DNF		
Hahn, L.	USA	800m	1	5	1	1-56.8	
			SF	3	1	1-52.6	
			F		5	1-54.2	
		1500m	-	2	DNF		
Haidar, S.	TUR	High jump	Q		DNQ	1,70	
Hajdu, A.	HUN	4×100m relay	1	3	DIS		
Hall, J.S.	IND	200m	1	8	4		
		400m	1	9	2		
			2	1	5		
Hallberg, O.H.	SWE	Long jump	F		10	7,18	
Hambidge, J.H.	GBR	200m	1	14	2		
			2	1	5		
Hamid, A.	IND	110m hurdles	1	9	4		
		400m hurdles	1	6	6		
Hamm, E.B.	USA	Long jump	F		1	7,73*	G
Hanlon, J.A.T.	GBR	400m	1	15	3		
Hannig, A.	CHI	200m	1	3	5		
		400m	1	6	5		
Harlow, C.V.	USA	Javelin throw	Q		DNQ	55,35	
Harper, E.	GBR	Marathon	F		22	2:45-44	

COMPETITOR	COUNTRY CODE	EVENT	ROUND	HEAT	PLACE	TIME & DISTANCE	MEDAL
Haworth, C.	USA	5000m	1	1			
Haydu, J.	RUM	Decathlon	F		DNF		
Heap, J.C.	GBR	100m	1	4	5		
Hedges, M.B.	USA	High jump	F		2	1,91	S
Helgas, L.H.	FIN	1500m	-	6	4	4-06.0	
Hempel, P.	GER	Marathon	F		31	2:52-01	
Henigan, J.	USA	Marathon	F		39	2:56-50	
Hennings, W.M.	HOL	100m	1	1	4		
Henrijean, M.	BEL	Pole vault	Q		DNQ	3,50	
Herremans, J.	BEL	Javelin throw	Q		DNQ	56,33	
Hester, G.B.	CAN	100m	1	5	2		
			2	3	4		
		200m	1	9	DIS		
		4×100m relay	1	1	1	42.2	
			F		DIS		
Hines, C.B.	USA	Javelin throw	Q		DNQ	57,17	
Hirschfeld, E.	GER	Shot put	F		3	15,72	B
Hoerger, G.	GER	Marathon	F		46	2:59-01	
Hoffmeister, H.	GER	Discus throw	Q		DNQ	39,17	
Hoogerwerf, A.	HOL	400m	1	5	2		
			2	2	4		
		800m	1	3	6		
		4×400m relay	1	2	4		
Houben, H.	GER	100m	1	8	1	11.0	
			2	3	2		
			SF	1	4	10.7	
		4×100m relay	1	2	2		
			F		2	41.2	S
Houghton, H.	GBR	800m	1	4	6		
Houser, L.C.	USA	Discus throw	F		1	47,32*	G
Howland, R.L.	GER	Shot put	Q		DNQ	12,52	
Hubbard, W.deH.	USA	Long jump	F		=11	7,11	
Huber, E.	GER	Decathlon	F		15	6702-82	
Hughes, F.	CAN	Marathon	F		43	2:58-12	
Huhr, F.	GER	High jump	F		=17	1,70	
Hyde, G.R.	ALS	1500m	1	1			
		500m	1	1			
Iturbe, L.	MEX	400m	1	10	2		
			2	4	5		
		800m	1	8	5		
		4×400m relay	1	3	3		
Jackson, J.	FRA	400m	1	15	2		
			2	4	3		
		4×400m relay	1	3	2		
			F		6	3-19.4	
Jacobs, D.R.	SAF	1500m	1	6	5		
		10000m	F		20		
Jaervinen, A.E.J.	FIN	Decathlon	F		2	7931-50	S
Jaervinen, E.V.	FIN	Triple jump	F		6	14,65	
Jandera, O.	TCH	110m hurdles	1	1	2		
			SF	2	6		
Janssen, H.	SWE	Decathlon	F		6	7286-28	
Jaworski, J.	POL	1500m	1	1			
Joannes-Powell, R.	BEL	110m hurdles	1	5	4		
		Pole vault	Q		DNQ		
		Decathlon	F		25	5190-65	
Johnston, H.A.	GBR	5000m	1	3	3	15-08.3	
			F		8		
Jordans, ...	LAT	Discus throw	F		12	42,78	
Jorgensen, L.	DEN	100m	1	9	4		
Kaan, A.J.	HOL	110m hurdles	1	2	4		
Kalaugher, W.G.	NZL	110m hurdles	1	3	4		
		Triple jump	Q		DNQ	12,94	
Kalkun, G.	EST	Discus throw	F		10	43,09	
Kallay, B.	YUG	Decathlon	F		24	5210-65	
Kamerbeek, H.	HOL	Hammer throw	F		10	46,02	
Kamstra, J.H.	HOL	High jump	Q		DNQ	1,70	
Karlovits, J.	HUN	Pole vault	F		8	3,80	
Keay, A.H.	CAN	3000m steeplechase	1	1	8		
Keller, P.	FRA	800m	1	3	1	1-59.0	
			SF	1	3	1-56.0	
			F		8	1-57.0	
		1500m	1	5	2		
			F		11		
Kelley, R.M.	USA	Triple jump	Q		DNQ	13,64	
Kentta, E.	FIN	Discus throw	F		6	44,17	
Kesmarki, C.	HUN	High jump	F		=11	1,84	
Kibblewhite, W.E.	CAN	5000m	1	1			
Kimura, K.	JPN	High jump	F		6	1,88	
King, R.W.	USA	High jump	F		1	1,94	G
Kinn, G.	SWE	Marathon	F		25	2:47-35	
Kinnunen, A.	FIN	1500m	1	2	3	4-01.5	
		5000m	1	2	2	15-10.8	
			F		6	15-02.0	
Kinsman, H.P.	SAF	200m	1	15	2		
			2	5	DNF		

COMPETITOR	COUNTRY CODE	EVENT	ROUND	HEAT	PLACE	TIME & DISTANCE	MEDAL
Kittel, A.	TCH	800m	1	7	4		
		1500m	1	1	2		
			F		8	4-00.4	
Kivi, A.L.	FIN	Discus throw	F		2	47,23	S
Kjellstroem, E.T.H.	SWE	110m hurdles	1	5	3		
		400m hurdles	1	4	3		
Klaasse, A.	HOL	5000m	1	3	6		
Kleger, F.	ARG	Hammer throw	F		7	46,61	
Knenicky, K.	TCH	100m	1	8	3		
		200m	1	10	2		
			2	4	5		
		4×400m relay	1	2	5		
Knol, J.	HOL	Javelin throw	Q		DNQ	52,68	
Koechermann, E.	GER	Long jump	F		5	7,35	
Koepke, F.	GER	High jump	F		=11	1,84	
Koernig, H.	GER	200m	1	10	1	22.8	
			2	6	1	21.6*	
			SF	2	1	21.8	
			F		3	21.9	B
		4×100m relay	1	2	2		
			F		2	41.2	S
Kohn, O.	GER	5000m	1	3	5		
Korholin-Kosi, K.Y.	FIN	Marathon	F		7	2:36-37.0	
Korpela, M.K.	FIN	800m	1	5	7		
Koscak, J.	TCH	5000m	1	2	8		
Kostrzewski, S.	POL	400m	1	3	4		
		400m hurdles	1	5	2		
			SF	1	5		
		4×400m relay	1	1	4		
Krause, H.H.	GER	1500m	1	6	2		
			F		7	3-59.0	
Krebs, R.	GER	4×400m relay	1	2	1	3-20.8	
			F		2	3-14.8	S
Krenz, E.C.W.	USA	Shot put	F		4	14,99	
Krof, A.	TCH	Marathon	F		16	2:43-18	
Krotoff, G.R.	FRA	400m	1	3	2		
			2	1	2		
			SF	1	6		
		4×400m relay	1	3	2		
			F		6	3-19.4	
Kuck, J.H.	USA	Shot put	F		1	15,87*	G
Kugelberg, B.F.A.	SWE	200m	1	2	1	22.4	
			2	3	2		
			SF	2	6	22.6	
		4×400m relay	1	2	2		
			F		4	3-15.8	
Kuokko, I.	FIN	Marathon	F		24	2:46-34	
Laaksonen, V.	FIN	Marathon	F		12	2:41-35	
Laas, K.	EST	Marathon	F		DNF		
Labourdette, F.	ESP	Long jump	Q		DNQ	6,16	
Ladewig, W.	GER	Decathlon	F		10	6881.52	
Ladoumegue, J.	FRA	1500m	1	3	2		
			F		2	3-53.8	S
Lammers, G.	GER	100m	1	9	1	10.8	
			2	6	2		
			SF	2	2	10.7	
			F		3	10.9	B
		4×100m relay	1	2	2		
			F		2	41.2	S
Lamoree, G.	HOL	Long jump	Q		DNQ	6,87	
		Triple jump	Q		DNQ	14,08	
Lamppu, A.	FIN	Javelin throw	F		9	61,45	
Lamprou, A.A.	GRE	100m	1	1	5		
		200m	1	12	4		
		4×100m relay	1	1	4		
Landheer, H.H.	HOL	Marathon	F		30	2:51-59	
Langenus, J.	BEL	3000m steeplechase	1	1	7		
Langenraedt, E.	BEL	400m	1	4	3		
		4×400m relay	1	1	5		
Larsen, A.	DEN	800m	1	2	6		
		1500m	1	2	5		
Larsen, H.	DEN	400m hurdles	1	1	5		
Larva, H.E.	FIN	1500m	1	4	2	4-02.0	
			F		1	3-53.2*	G
Lauvaux, H.	FRA	10000m	F		DNF		
Lavan, S.	IRL	200m	1	6	4		
		400m	1	6	2		
			2	5	5		
Lay, S.A.	NZL	Javelin throw	F		7	62,89	
Ledesma, I.	ARG	800m	1	8	4		
		1500m	1	4	5		

COMPETITOR	COUNTRY CODE	EVENT	ROUND	HEAT	PLACE	TIME & DISTANCE	MEDAL
Legg, W.B.	SAF	100m	1	7	1	11.0	
			2	1	1	10.8	
			SF	1	3	10.6	
			F		5	11.0	
		200m	1	9	1	22.4	
			2	2	1	21.8	
			SF	1	DNF		
Leigh-Wood, R.	GBR	400m	1	8	2		
			2	6	3		
		4×400m relay	1	3	1	3-20.6	
			F		5	3-16.4	
Lemperle, H.	GER	Decathlon	F		19	6293.75	
Lenth, A.	NOR	Long jump	Q		DNQ	6,60	
Lepaffe, A.	BEL	110m hurdles	1	1	3		
Lermond, L.	USA	5000m	1	1	1	15-02.6	
			F		4	14-50.0	
Lewden, P.	FRA	High jump	F		=7	1,88	
Liettu, P.	FIN	Javelin throw	F		4	63,86	
Light, F.	GBR	5000m	1	1	7		
Lind, C.J.	SWE	Hammer throw	Q		DNQ	44,46	
Lindblad, H.	SWE	Pole vault	F		7	3,90	
		Decathlon	F		9	7071.425	
Lindgren, J.G.	SWE	10000m	F		4	31-26.0	
		3000m steeplechase	1	3	4		
Lindstrom, G.	SWE	Javelin throw	Q		DNQ	58,69	
Linsen, J.	BEL	Marathon	F		42	2:58-08	
Little, G.B.	CAN	800m	1	2	2	1-57.8	
			SF	2	4	1-57.6	
Livingstone-Learmonth, T.C.	GBR	400m hurdles	1	3	1	56.2	
			SF	2	1	54.0	
			F		5	54.2	
London, J.E.	GBR	100m	1	5	1	10.8	
			2	4	2		
			SF	2	1	10.6*	
			F		2	10.9	S
		4×100m relay	1	1	2		
			F		3	41.8	B
Loukola, T.A.	FIN	10000m	F		7	31-39.0	
		3000m steeplechase	1	3	1	9-37.6	
			F		1	9-21.8*	G
Lowe, D.G.A.	GBR	800m	1	6	2	2-02.2	
			SF	1	2	1-55.8	
			F		1	1-51.8*	G
		4×400m relay	1	3	1	3-20.6	
			F		5	3-16.4	
Lucas, B.	GBR	110m hurdles	1	6	1	15.2	
			SF	3	6		
Lundgreen, L.	DEN	400m	1	6	3		
		110m hurdles	1	8	5		
		400m hurdles	1	6	3		
Lundgren, S.	SWE	Decathlon	F		14	6727.045	
Lundkvist, E.H.	SWE	Javelin throw	F		1	66,60*	G
McAllister, R.F.	USA	100m	1	16	1	10.8	
			2	2	1	10.8	
			SF	1	1	10.6*	
			F		6	11.0	
Macbeth, F.W.	CAN	400m	1	14	2		
			2	6	5		
McEachern, N.J.	IRL	800m	1	8	3	1-59.8	
			SF	1	DNF		
McGinnis, C.E.	USA	High jump	F		=7	1,88	
		Pole vault	F		3	4,10	B
McLellan, S.	CAN	Marathon	F		26	2:49-33	
Madsen, A.	DEN	Marathon	F		DNF		
Magdics, L.	HUN	400m	1	13	3		
		4×400m relay	1	1	3		
Magnusson, K.R.	SWE	5000m	1	1	4	15-03.8	
			F		5	14-59.6	
		10000m	F		6	31-37.2	
Malanowski, F.	POL	800m	1	7	5		
Mangos, A.	GRE	800m	1	3	7		
Mannaert, J.	FRA	200m	1	11	2		
			2	5	4		
Marchal, R.	FRA	10000m	F		11		
Marchand, R.	FRA	110m hurdles	1	3	2		
			SF	2	5		
Marien, J.	BEL	Marathon	F		56	3:16-13	
Martin, P.	SUI	800m	1	3	2	1-59.4	
			SF	3	4	1-53.6	
		1500m	1	4	1	4-00.8	
			F		6	3-58.4	
Martin, S.	FRA	800m	1	7	1	1-58.8	
			SF	3	3	1-53.0	
			F		6	1-54.6	
		1500m	1	1	DNF		
Marton, J.	HUN	1500m	1	1	3		

COMPETITOR	COUNTRY CODE	EVENT	ROUND	HEAT	PLACE	TIME & DISTANCE	MEDAL
Marttelin, M.B.	FIN	Marathon	F		3	2:35-02	B
Marvalits, C.	HUN	Discus throw	Q		DNQ	41,17	
Matilainen, J.	FIN	400m hurdles	1	3	4		
Matilainen, K.	FIN	10000m	F		8	31-45·0	
Mattila, R.	FIN	100m	1	14	6		
Max-Robert, E.	FRA	400m hurdles	1	6	5		
Maxwell, R.	USA	400m hurdles	1	1	2		
			SF	2	5		
Medecin, G.	MON	Long jump	Q		DNQ	6,51	
		Decathlon	F		DNF		
Meier, A.	SUI	Long jump	Q		DNQ	6,80	
		Decathlon	F		DNF		
Meier, W.	GER	Long jump	F		4	7,39	
Meimer, J.	EST	Decathlon	F		13	6733·15	
		Javelin throw	F		8	61.46	
Menard, C.	FRA	High jump	F		3	1,91	B
Messner, V.	YUG	Javelin throw	Q		DNQ	53,70	
Michelsen, A.	USA	Marathon	F		9	2:38-56	
Miki, Y.	JPN	110m hurdles	1	9	1	15·4	
			SF	1	6		
Miles, J.C.	CAN	Marathon	F		17	2:43-32·0	
Miquel, J.	ESP	400m	1	7	3		
		800m	1	8	6		
Miropoulos, E.	GRE	110m hurdles	1	8	4		
		400m hurdles	1	1	3		
		4×100m relay	1	1	4		
		4×400m relay	1	2	6		
Molnar, F.	HUN	Triple jump	Q		DNQ	13,36	
Montabone, W.J.	CAN	400m hurdles	1	6	4		
Montgomery, J.L.	USA	3000m steeplechase	1	3			
Moraila, J.	MEX	100m	1	2	3		
		400m	1	9	1	60·0	
			2	3	5		
		4×400m relay	1	3	3		
Morgan, V.E.	GBR	3000m steeplechase	1	3	5		
Mottmillers, A.	LAT	Marathon	F		38	2:56-45	
Moulin, J.	LUX	100m	1	9	5		
		200m	1	10	3		
Mourlon, A.	FRA	100m	1	1	2		
			2	4	4		
		200m	1	1	2		
			2	2	5		
		4×100m relay	1	2	1	41·8	
			F		4	42·0	
Mueller, F.	GER	800m	1	7	3	1-59·4	
			SF	3	6	1-53·9	
Mueller, J.	GER	Pole vault	F		9	3,65	
Muggeridge, A.J.	GBR	10000m	F		5	31-31·8	
Munagorri, F.	ESP	100m	1	3	6		
		4×100m relay	1	1	5		
Munroe, A.W.	CAN	High jump	Q		DNQ	1,77	
		Triple jump	Q		DNQ	13,87	
Murphy, J.	IND	800m	1	7	7		
Mydtlyng, O.	NOR	High jump	Q		DNQ	1,77	
Nagatani, J.	JPN	10000m	F		19		
		Marathon	F		48	3:03-34	
Nakazawa, Y.	JPN	Pole vault	F		6	3,90	
		Decathlon	F		22	5672·17	
Nambu, C.	JPN	Long jump	F		9	7,25	
		Triple jump	F		4	15,01	
		4×100m relay	1	3	3		
Natale, S.	ITA	Marathon	F		DNF		
Neame, D.M.L.	GBR	110m hurdles	1	4	4		
Nedobity, K.	TCH	10000m	F		17		
Neumann, O.	GER	400m	1	14	1	50·6	
			2	3	3		
		4×400m relay	1	2	1	3-20·8	
			F			3-14·8	S
Nicolaisen, A.	DEN	Pole vault	Q		DNQ	3.50	
Niggl, H.	SUI	200m	1	4	4		
		4×100m relay	1	3	2		
			F		5	42·6	
Noel, G.	BEL	Pole vault	Q		DNQ	3,30	
		Decathlon	F		27	4606·74	
Noel, J.	FRA	Discus throw	Q		DNQ	40,23	
Nokes, M.C.	GBR	Hammer throw	F		11	45,37	
Nowak, Z.	POL	Long jump	Q		DNQ	6,57	
Nuesch, W.	SUI	Shot put	F		10	13,77	
Nurmi, P.J.	FIN	5000m	1	3	4		
			F		2	14-40·0	S
		10000m	F		1	30-18·8*	G
		3000m steeplechase	1	2	1	9-58·8	
			F		2	9-31·2	S
O'Callaghan, C.	IRL	Decathlon	F		DNF		
O'Callaghan, P.	IRL	Hammer throw	F		1	51,39	G

COMPETITOR	COUNTRY CODE	EVENT	ROUND	HEAT	PLACE	TIME & DISTANCE	MEDAL
Oda, M.	JPN	High jump	F		=7	1,88	
		Triple jump	F		1	15,21	G
		Long jump	F		=11	7,11	
		4×100m relay	1	3	3		
Oddie, B.C.V.	GBR	5000m	1	2	4	15-16·0	
			F		9		
Okita, Y.	JPN	Discus throw	Q		DNQ	36,38	
		Hammer throw	Q		DNQ	44,41	
Oliver, E.H.	GBR	3000m steeplechase	1	1	5		
Olsen, H.O.E.	DEN	Marathon	F		DNF		
Orban, F.	HUN	High jump	Q		DNQ	1,77	
Ordonez, D.	ESP	100m	1	4	4		
		200m	1	1	5		
		4×100m relay	1	1	5		
Osborn, H.N.	USA	High jump	F		5	1,91	
Oyarbide, J.	ESP	5000m	1	2	5		
Paddock, C.W.	USA	200m	1	5	1	22·2	
			2	3	1	21·8	
			SF	1	4		
Paizsa, J.	HUN	100m	1	9	3		
		4×100m relay	1	3	DIS		
Pacli, R.	FRA	Discus throw	Q		DNQ	36,82	
		Shot put	Q		DNQ	12,68	
Paouris, A.	GRE	5000m	1	2	9		
Paulen, A.	HOL	400m	1	13	2		
			2	6	4		
		800m	1	2	4		
		4×400m relay	1	2	4		
Paulus, E.	GER	Discus throw	F		7	44,15	
Payne, H.W.	GBR	Marathon	F		13	2:42-29	
Pele, R.	FFA	5000m	1	2	6		
Peltzer, O.	GER	800m	1	2	1	1-57·4	
			SF	1	5		
		1500m	1	5	4		
			1	3	7		
Pena, A.	ESP	5000m	1	3	7		
		10000m	F		13		
Penttilaa, E.	FIN	Javelin throw	F		6	63,20	
Percival, L.R.	GBR	400m hurdles	1	5	3		
Peter L.	RUM	100m	1	5	3		
		200m	1	1	6		
Peters, W.	HOL	Triple jump	F		7	14,55	
Petersen, A.	DEN	5000m	1	1	6		
Petkerics, S.	LAT	5000m	1	1	2	15-03·0	
			F		7		
		10000m	F		15		
Petrailis, J.	LIT	5000m	1	2	10		
Petrides, C.	GRE	100m	1	3	5		
		Long jump	Q		DNQ	6,63	
		Triple jump	Q		DNQ	13,83	
		4×100m relay	1	1	4		
		4×400m relay	1	2	6		
Pettersson, S.C.L.	SWE	110m hurdles	1	8	2		
			SF	3	3		
		400m hurdles	1	5	1	55·8	
			SF	2	3		
			F		4	53·8	
		4×400m relay	1	2	2		
			F		4	3-15·8	
Phelan, T.D.	IRL	Triple jump	Q		DNQ	13,73	
Phillips, H.	USA	400m	1	1	1	49·4	
			2	1	1	49·6	
			SF	2	2	49·1	
			F		6	49·0	
Pickard, V.W.	CAN	Pole vault	F		4	3,95	
Pighi, A.	ITA	Discus throw	Q		DNQ	41,42	
Pilling, D.W.	CAN	Javelin throw	F		12	59,16	
Pina, J.E.	ARG	100m	1	6	1	11·0	
			2	5	2		
			SF	1	6	11·0	
		200m	1	11	3		
Plaza, M.J.	CHI	Marathon	F		2	2:33-23	S
Poggioli, A.	ITA	Hammer throw	F		4	48,37	
Postma, G.	HOL	Discus throw	Q		DNQ	35,94	
Predanic, F.	YUG	1500m	1	3	6		
Prinsen, F.	BEL	200m	1	4	3		
		400m	1	2	2		
			2	4	4		
		4×400m relay	1	1	5		
Purje, E.A	FIN	1500m	1	3	1	4-00·8	
			F		3	3-56·4	B
		5000m	1	1	3	15-03·6	
			F		DNS		
Puspoki, T.	HUN	Long jump	Q		DNQ	6,45	
Quinn, J.F.	USA	4×100m relay	1	3	1	41·2	
			F		1	41·0*	G

COMPETITOR	COUNTRY CODE	EVENT	ROUND	HEAT	PLACE	TIME & DISTANCE	MEDAL
Raggambi, S.	HUN	100m	1	11	1	11·0	
			2	2	4		
		4×100m relay	1	3	DIS		
Rainio, V.J.	FIN	Triple jump	F		8	14,41	
Ramadier, P.	FRA	Pole vault	Q		DNQ		
Rangeley, W.	GBR	100m	1	10	1	11·0	
			2	6	3		
		200m	1	13	1	22·0	
			2	4	2		
			SF	1	2		
			F		2	21·9	S
		4×100m relay	1	1	2		
			F		3	41·8	B
Rastas, E.	FIN	Marathon	F		14	2:43-08	
Ray, J.W.	USA	10000m	F		14		
		Marathon	F		5	2:36-04	
Razaitis, V.	LIT	Javelin throw	Q		DNQ	51,16	
Reiser, F.	ITA	100m	1	2	4		
		4×100m relay	1	1	3		
Revans, R.W.	GBR	Long jump	Q		DNQ	6,58	
Ring, C.E.	USA	110m hurdles	1	2	1	15·0	
			SF	3	4		
Rinkel, J.W.J.	GBR	400m	1	4	1	50·2	
			2	4	2		
			SF	2	3	49·1	
			F		4	48·4	
		4×400m relay	1	3	1	3-20·6	
			F		5	3-16·4	
Rinne, V.	FIN	Javelin throw	Q		DNQ	58,04	
Ritola, V.	FIN	5000m	1	2	2	15-10·8	
			F		1	14-38·0	G
		10000m	F		2	30-19·4	S
		3000m steeplechase	1	1	1	9-46·6	
			F		DNF		
Robinson, S.	USA	1500m	1	4	DNF		
Romig, J.L.	USA	10000m	F		DNF		
Rothert, H.P.	USA	Shot put	F		7	14,68	
Rottman, O.	RUM	Javelin throw	Q		DNQ	50,93	
Russell, H.A.	USA	100m	1	15	1	11·0	
			2	3	1	10·8	
			SF	2	4	10·8	
		4×100m relay	1	3	1	41·2	
			F		1	41·0*	G
Russu, T.	RUM	High jump	Q		DNQ	1,70	
Sager, A.W.	USA	Javelin throw	F		10	60,46	
Salinas, V.	CHI	400m	1	12	3		
Santos, H.	POR	3000m steeplechase	1	2	6		
Schindler, W.	TCH	800m	1	5	3	1-57·0	
			SF	1	7		
		1500m	1	3	4		
		4×400m relay	1	2	5		
Schlokat, B.	GER	Javelin throw	F		5	63,40	
Schloeske, Helmut	GER	Long jump	Q		DNQ	6,99	
Schloeske, Hermann	GER	200m	1	7	1	25·0	
			2	2	3		
Schmit, G.	LUX	100m	1	14	4		
Schmit, L.	LUX	800m	1	1	7		
Schmidt, R.	GER	400m	1	15	1	50·0	
			2	1	4		
Schneider, K.	GER	Marathon	F		47	2:59-36	
Scholz, J.	USA	200m	1	6	1	22·2	
			2	4	1	21·8	
			SF	2	2	22·0	
			F		4	21·9	
Schopp, O.	RUM	110m hurdles	1	2	5		
		High jump	Q		DNQ	1,70	
Schueller, J.	GER	200m	1	4	1	22·0	
			2	1	1	22·0	
			SF	1	3		
			F		6	22·2	
Schwemminas, H.	LIT	100m	1	12	5		
		200m	1	9	3		
Semih, S.	TUR	100m	1	6	5		
		4×100m relay	1	3	4		
Sempe, G.	FRA	110m hurdles	1	1	1	15·0	
			SF	3	5		
Serrahima, J.	ESP	100m	1	11	5		
		200m	1	3	3		
		4×100m relay	1	1	5		
Serwy, J.	BEL	10000m	F		18		
Simmons, H.A.	GBR	High jump	F		=11	1,84	
Singh, C.	IND	10000m	F		DNF		
Singh, D.	IND	Long jump	Q		DNQ	6,45	
Singh, G.	IND	10000m	F		DNF		
Sipilae, V.	FIN	Marathon	F		14	2:43-08	
Sittig, J.F.	USA	800m	1	1	3	2-00·6	
			SF	3	5		

COMPETITOR	COUNTRY CODE	EVENT	ROUND	HEAT	PLACE	TIME & DISTANCE	MEDAL
Sjoestedt, B.	FIN	110m hurdles	1	7	2		
			SF	2	4		
Skioeld, O.E.	SWE	Hammer throw	F		2	51,29	S
Smith, J.M.L.	USA	5000m	1	3	1	15-04·0	
			F		10		
		10000m	F		DNF		
Smith, J.S.	GBR	10000m	F		10	31-50·0	
Smouha, E.R.	GBR	4×100m relay	1	1	2		
			F		3	41·8	B
Snider, E.	USA	400m	1	2	1	50·4	
			2	2	3		
Spel, L.	HOL	110m hurdles	1	9	3		
Spencer, E.L.	USA	4×400m relay	1	1	1	3-21·6	
			F		1	3-14·2*	G
Spencer, W.O.	USA	3000m steeplechase	1	2	3		
			F		8		
Sprong, T.	HOL	Marathon	F		DNF		
Starr, R.S.	GBR	300m	1	8	2	1-59·8	
			SF	2	5		
Stavrinos, B.	GRE	400m	1	13	4		
		800m	1	1	6		
Stefanovitch, D.	YUG	Marathon	F		53	3:11-35	
Steinhardt, H.	GER	110m hurdles	1	6	2		
			SF	1	4		
Stelges, H.	GER	Marathon	F		19	2:45-27	
Stenerud, H.	NOR	Discus throw	F		4	45,80	
		Hammer throw	Q		DNQ	41,06	
Steurs, G.	BEL	Marathon	F		37	2:54-48	
Stewart, J.D.	USA	Decathlon	F		4	7624·135	
Steytler, M.J.	SAF	Marathon	F		40	2:57-21	
Stoa, J.	NOR	Marathon	F		36	2:54-15	
Storz, H.	GER	400m	1	7	1	50·6	
			2	4	1	49·4	
			SF	1	3	49·0	
			F		5	48·8	
		4×400m relay	1	2	1	3-20·8	
			F		2	3-14·8	S
Stoschek, E.	GER	Javelin throw	F		11	59,86	
Strand, O.	NOR	800m	1	4	3	2-03·8	
			SF	3	8		
Stuart, C.S.	AUS	400m	1	14	4		
		800m	1	5	6		
Sumiyoshi, K.	JPN	Javelin throw	Q		DNQ	59,05	
Sunde, O.	NOR	Javelin throw	F		3	63,97	B
Sutter, A.	SUI	Long jump	Q		DNQ	6,23	
Svensson, E.	SWE	Long jump	F		8	7,29	
Swinnen, M.	BEL	400m hurdles	1	2	3		
Szalay, E.	HUN	400m	1	6	4		
		4×400m relay	1	1	3		
Szepes, B.	HUN	Javelin throw	F		2	65,26	S
Tarnogrocki, W.	GER	800m	1	3	4		
Taskinen, K.H.	FIN	Discus throw	F		11	43,00	
Tatham, W.G.	GBR	800m	1	2	3	1-58·2	
			SF	3	7		
Tavernari, E.	ITA	800m	1	4	4		
		4×400m relay	1	2	3		
Taylor, F.M.	USA	400m hurdles	1	1	1	55·2	
			SF	1	1	53·4*	
			F		3	53·6	B
Tell, G.	FRA	Marathon	F		29	2:51-18	
Terrazas, A.	MEX	Marathon	F		32	2:52-22	
Theard, V.A.	HAI	100m	1	9	2		
			2	4	3		
		200m	1	1	3		
Thesingh, H.N.	HOL	High jump	Q		DNQ	1,77	
Thomas, R.H.	GBR	1500m	1	4	3		
Tierney, J.P.	USA	400m	1	11	1	49·8	
			2	5	4		
Toetti, E.	ITA	100m	1	6	3		
		200m	1	15	3		
		4×100m relay	1	1	3		
Toki, T.	JPN	Decathlon	F		12	6757·605	
		4×100m relay	1	3	3		
Tommasi, V.	ITA	Long jump	Q		DNQ	6,76	
Tommelstad, E.	NOR	High jump	F		=11	1,84	
Topelius, M.L.	FIN	Decathlon	F		16	6642·115	
Toribio, S.	PHI	High jump	F		4	1,91	
Torre, E.	ITA	Long jump	Q		DNQ	6,76	
		4×100m relay	1	1	3		
Torres, J.	MEX	Marathon	F		40	2:54-00	
Trandem, J.	NOR	Discus throw	F		8	43,97	
		Shot put	Q		DNQ	13,40	
Trojanowski, W.	POL	110m hurdles	1	8	6		
Tschopp, W.	SUI	100m	1	15	3		
		4×100m relay	1	3	2		
			F		5	42·6	
Tsuda, S.	JPN	Marathon	F		6	2:36-20	

COMPETITOR	COUNTRY CODE	EVENT	ROUND	HEAT	PLACE	TIME & DISTANCE	MEDAL
Tulikoura, T.	FIN	Long jump	Q		DNQ	6,88	
		Triple jump	F		5	14,70	
Turner, G.	GBR	High jump	Q		DNQ	1,77	
Tuulos, V.	FIN	Long jump	F		=11	7,11	
		Triple jump	F		3	15,11	B
Uebler, W.	GER	Shot put	F		6	14,89	
Ugarte, A.	CHI	110m hurdles	1	6	3		
Vallania, V.	ARG	110m hurdles	1	1	D S		
		High jump	Q		DNQ	1,77	
Van Den Berge, M.	HOL	100m	1	10	2		
			2	1	2		
		200m	1	4	2		
			2	2	4		
		400m	1	1	4		
		4×400m relay	1	2	4		
Van Der Ley, J.H.	HOL	Javelin throw	Q		DNQ	47,73	
Van Der Steen, W.	HOL	Marathon	F		57	3:19-53	
Van Der Zee, A.	HOL	Pole vault	Q		DNQ	3,30	
Van Geyzel, C.T.	GBR	High jump	Q		DNQ	1,77	
Van Leenen, P.	HOL	Marathon	F		55	3:14-37	
Van Leeuwen, A.	HOL	110m hurdles	1	5	4		
Van Musscher, S.	HOL	Triple jump	Q		DNQ	13 93	
Van Welsenes, A.	HOL	Long jump	Q		DNQ	6,96	
Verken, E.	BEL	4×400m relay	1	1	5		
Vermeulen, J.	HOL	Marathon	F		54	3:13-47	
Vesely, L.	AUT	110m hurdles	1	2	3		
		Decathlon	F		7	7274.85	
Viel, R.	FRA	400m hurdles	1	3	2	56.2	
			SF	1	4		
Viljoen, J.H.	SAF	100m	1	8	2		
			2	5	3		
		110m hurdles	1	2	2		
			SF	1	5		
		Long jump	Q		DNQ	6,44	
		Triple jump	Q		DNQ	12,49	
		Decathlon	F		DNF		
Villasenor, V.M.	MEX	400m	1	1	5		
		4×400m relay	1	3	3		
Vintousky, R.	FRA	Pole vault	Q		DNQ		
Virgile, I.	RUM	Decathlon	F		DNF		
Viseur, E.	BEL	3000m steeplechase	1	2	5		
Von Wachenfeldt, B.	SWE	4×400m relay	1	2	2		
			F		4	3-15-8	
Vos, A.	BEL	Shot put	Q		DNQ	12,52	
Vykoupil, J.	TCH	100m	1	12	2		
			2	1	6		
		200m	1	14	3		
		400m	1	3	3		
		4×400m relay	1	2	5		
Wagner, R.	CHI	100m	1	7	3		
Wahlstedt, A.I.	FIN	Shot put	F		5	14,69	
		Decathlon	F		DNF		
Wahlstedt, A.S.	FIN	High jump	Q		DNQ		
Walter, J.S.	CAN	1500m	1	2			
Walters, A.G.	CAN	800m	1	5	5		
		1500m	1	2	4		
Wanderer, F.	GER	Marathon	F		DNF		
Watson, A.J.	AUS	110m hurdles	1	8	3		
		400m hurdles	1	3	3		
Watson, R.B.	USA	800m	1	3	3	1-59-6	
			SF	2	2	1-56-8	
			F		9	2-03 0	
Weibel, W.	SUI	100m	1	4	3		
		4×100m relay	1	3	2		
			F		5	42·6	
		200m	1	1	4		
Weicker, F.E.	USA	Discus throw	F		9	43,81	
Weightman-Smith, G.C.	SAF	110m hurdles	1	2	1	14.8*	
			SF	3	1	14.6*	
			F		5	15·0	
		Javelin throw	Q		DNQ	54,37	
		Decathlon	F		DNF		
Weiss, Z.	POL	400m	1	1	3		
		4×400m relay	1	1	4		
Wennstroem, E.V.	SWE	110m hurdles	1	4	2		
			SF	1	3	14·9	
Whyte, W.M.	AUS	800m	1	2	5		
		1500m	1	2	2		
			F		9		
Wichmann, H.G.	GER	1500m	1	1	1	4-03-0	
			F		4	3-56-8	
Wide, E.	SWE	1500m	1	5	3		
		5000m	1	3	2	15-05-0	
			F		3	14-41-2	B
		10000m	F		3	31-00-8	B
Wilen, E.V.	FIN	400m hurdles	1	4	2	56·5	
			SF	2	6		
Williams, P.	CAN	100m	1	12	1	11·0	
			2	4	1	10·6*	
			SF	1	2	10·6	
			F		1	10·8	G
		200m	1	14	1	22·6	
			2	6	2	21·8	
			SF	1	1	22·0	
			F		1	21·8	G
		4×100m relay	1	1	1	42·2	
			F		DIS		
Wilson, A.S.	CAN	400m	1	11	2		
			2	3	2		
			SF	2	4	49·2	
		800m	1	1	1	1-59-2	
			SF	1	6		
		4×400m relay	1	1	2		
			F		3	3-15-4	B
Winter, A.W.	AUS	Long jump	Q		DNQ		
		Triple jump	F		12	14,15	
Wood, H.	GBR	Marathon	F		11	2:41-15	
Woods, R.S.	GBR	Shot put	Q		DNQ	12,70	
Wright, D. McL.	GBR	Marathon	F		20	2:45-30	
Wyer, P.	CAN	Marathon	F		45	2:58-52	
Wykoff, F.C.	USA	100m	1	3	1	11·0	
			2	5	1	10·8	
			SF	2	3	10·7	
			F		4	11·0	
		4×100m relay	1	3	1	41·2	
			F		1	41·0*	G
Yamada, K.	JPN	Marathon	F		4	2:35-29	
Yrjoelae, P.I.	FIN	High jump	Q		DNQ	1,77	
		Decathlon	F		1	8053·29*	G
		Shot put	F		9	14,01	
Zacharopoulos, G.	GRE	Javelin throw	Q		DNQ	55,50	
Zeegers, A.	HOL	800m	1	1	4		
		1500m	1	1	5		
Zerni, C.	ITA	Discus throw	Q		DNQ	39,95	
		Hammer throw	Q		DNQ	44,47	
Zinner, F.	BEL	100m	1	13	3		
		Discus throw	Q		DNQ	34,35	
		4×100m relay	1	2	3		
Zuber, F.	PCL	400m	1	4	4		
		4×400m relay	1	1	4		
Zyka, F.	TCH	Marathon	F		33	2:52-42	

FEMALES

COMPETITOR	COUNTRY CODE	EVENT	ROUND	HEAT	PLACE	TIME & DISTANCE	MEDAL
Adams-Ray, B.A.	SWE	High jump	F		13	1,45	
Aengenendt, E.	HOL	100m	1	7	3		
		4×100m relay	1	1	2		
			F		5	49·8	
Ahlstrand, A.M.	SWE	High jump	F		15	1,40	
Bell, F.L.	CAN	100m	1	3	2	13·0	
			SF	3	3		
		4×100m relay	1	1	1	49·3*	
			F		1	48·4*	G
Boeckman, D.H.	USA	800m	1	1	6		
Bonetsmeller, E.	GER	High jump	F		18	1,40	
Bonfanti, L.	ITA	100m	1	5	3		
		4×100m relay	1	2	3		
			F		6	53·6	
Bons, H.	FRA	High jump	F		11	1,45	
Borsan, P.	ITA	Discus throw	F		13	30,67	
Braumueller, I.	GER	High jump	F		7	1,48	
Brieier, N.	HOL	100m	1	6	3	13·1	
		4×100m relay	1	1	2		
			F		5	49·8	
Buisma Y.	HOL	High jump	F		NP	0	
Cartwright, E.	USA	100m	1	4	2		
			SF	3	4		
Catherwood, E.	CAN	High jump	F		1	1,59*	G
Clark, M.R.	SAF	100m	1	6	2	13·0	
			SF	1	6		
		High jump	F		5	1,48	
Cloupet, E.	FRA	High jump	F		14	1,40	
Cook, M.A.	CAN	100m	1	6	1	12·8	
			SF	2	2		
			F		DIS		
		4×100m relay	1	1	1	49·3*	
			F		1	48·4*	G
Copeland, L.	USA	Discus throw	F		2	37,08	S
Cross, J.	USA	4×100m relay	1	2	1	49·8	
			F		2	48·6	S
Degrande, I.	BEL	800m	1	3	5		
Dekens, B.J.	HOL	Discus throw	F		17	29,36	

COMPETITOR	COUNTRY CODE	EVENT	ROUND	HEAT	PLACE	TIME & DISTANCE	MEDAL
Dollinger, M.	GER	800m	1	1	1	2-22·4*	
			F		7	2-23·0	
Duchateau, W.M.	HOL	800m	1	3	4		
Gagneux, G.	FRA	100m	1	5	1	13·0	
			SF	1	3		
		4×100m relay	1	1	3		
			F		4	49·6	
Gentzel,°I.K.	SWE	800m	1	1	2		
			F		3	2-18·8	B
		4×100m relay	1	1	4		
Gisolf, C.A.	HOL	High jump	F		2	1,56	S
Grooss, J.H.	HOL	100m	1	2	3		
		4×100m relay	1	1	2		
			F		5	49·8	
Guyot, S.	FRA	800m	1	2	7		
Heublein, G.	GER	Discus throw	F		5	35,56	
Hitomi, K.	JPN	100m	1	3	1	12·8*	
			SF	2	4		
		800m	1	2	2		
			F		2	2-17·6	S
Holdmann, A.	GER	100m	1	1	1	13·0*	
			SF	1	4		
		4×100m relay	1	2	2		
			F		3	49·0	B
Holley, M.	USA	High jump	F		9	1,48	
Jenkins, M.H.	USA	Discus throw	F		19	27,07	
Jikeli, B.	RUM	Discus throw	F		18	28,19	
Junker, H.	GER	100m	1	4	1	12·8*	
			SF	2	5		
		4×100m relay	1	2	2		
			F		3	49·0	B
Karlsons, E.	LAT	Discus throw	F		14	30,60	
Kellner, R.	GER	4×100m relay	1	2	2		
			F		3	49·0	B
Kilosowna, G.	POL	800m	1	2	3		
			F		8		
Kobielska, G.	POL	Discus throw	F		8	32,72	
Konopacka, H.	POL	Discus throw	F		1	39,62*	G
Laudre, L.	FRA	High jump	F		12	1,45	
Lauterbach, J.	AUT	800m	1	3	8		
Liepinsch, S.	LAT	100m	1	9	3		
MacDonald, F.	USA	800m	1	3	2		
			F		6	2-22·6	
MacDonald, R.	USA	Discus throw	F		15	30,25	
McNeil, L.T.	USA	4×100m relay	1	2	1	49·8	
			F		2	48·6	S
Maeder, C.	GER	Discus throw	F		9	32,22	
Maguire, C.	USA	High jump	F		8	1,48	
Mallon, A.J.	HOL	800m	1	1	4		
Marchini, G.	ITA	800m	1	2	9		
		4×100m relay	1	2	3		
			F		6	53·6	
Michaelis, H.C.	HOL	Discus throw	F		11	31,04	
Mollenhauer, P.	GER	Discus throw	F		12	30,94	
Moraschi, M.	ITA	100m	1	3	4		
Neveu, M.	FRA	800m	1	3	6		
Notte, H.	GER	High jump	F		6	1,48	
Oestreich, E.	GER	800m	1	1	5		
Orendi, I.	RUM	High jump	F		19	1,35	
Perkaus, E.	ALT	Discus throw	F		6	33,54	
Petit-Diagre, L.G.	BEL	Discus throw	F		20	25,28	
Petterson, E.C.	SWE	800m	1	2	8		
		4×100m relay	1	1	4		
Plancke, Y.	FRA	100m	1	4	3		
		4×100m relay	1	1	3		
			F		4	49·6	
Pollazzo, D.	ITA	100m	1	1	3		
		4×100m relay	1	2	3		
			F		6	53·6	
Radideau, M.	FRA	100m	1	9	2		
			SF	3	6		
		4×100m relay	1	1	3		
			F		4	49·6	
Radke, L.	GER	800m	1	2	1	2-26·0	
			F		1	2-16·8*	G

COMPETITOR	COUNTRY CODE	EVENT	ROUND	HEAT	PLACE	TIME & DISTANCE	MEDAL
Radziulyte, P.	LIT	800m	1	3	9		
Reichardt, M.B.	USA	Discus throw	F		7	33,52	
Reuter, M.	GER	Discus throw	F		4	35,86	
Robinson, Edith F.	AUS	100m	1	1	2		
			SF	2	3		
Robinson, Ethel	AUS	800m	1	2	5		
Robinson, E.M.	USA	100m	1	7	2		
			SF	2	1	12·4*	
			F		1	12·2*	G
		4×100m relay	1	2	1	49·8	
			F		2	48·6	S
Rosenfeld, F.	CAN	100m	1	7	1	12·6*	
			SF	1	1	12·4*	
			F		2	12·3	
		4×100m relay	1	1	1	49·3*	
			F		1	48·4*	G
		800m	1	1	3		
			F		5	2-22·4	
Ruda, E.	HUN	Discus throw	F		16	29,65	
Schmidt, L.	GER	100m	1	6	1	12·8*	
			SF	3	1	12·8	
			F		DIS		
		4×100m relay	1	2	2		
			F		3	49·0	B
Segers, J.	BEL	800m	1	2	6		
		4×100m relay	1	2	4		
Shiley, J.	USA	High jump	F		4	1,51	
Smith, E.M.	CAN	100m	1	9	1	12·6*	
			SF	1	2		
			F		3	12·3	B
		4×100m relay	1	1	1	49·3*	
			F		1	48·4*	G
Steinberg, E.	GER	100m	1	2	1	12·8*	
			SF	3	2		
			F		4	12·4	
Stevens, L.	BEL	High jump	F		10	1,48	
		4×100m relay	1	2	4		
Sundberg, M.E.	SWE	100m	1	5	2		
			SF	2	6		
		4×100m relay	1	1	4		
Svedberg, R.A.	SWE	100m	1	2	4		
		Discus throw	F		3	35,92	B
		4×100m relay	1	1	4		
Tabacka, O.	POL	800m	1	3	7		
Ter Horst, E.	HOL	100m	1	8	3		
		4×100m relay	1	1	2		
			F		5	49·8	
Thompson, J.	CAN	800m	1	3	1	2-23·2	
			F		4	2-21·4	
Toitgens, J.	BEL	Discus throw	F		21	24,40	
Van Crombrugge, R.	BEL	4×100m relay	1	2	4		
Van Noort, A.	HOL	800m	1	2	4		
Van Truyen, E.	BEL	High jump	F		17	1,40	
		4×100m relay	1	2	4		
Vellu, L.	FRA	100m	1	6	4		
		Discus throw	F		10	31,29	
		4×100m relay	1	1	3		
			F		4	49·6	
Verschueren, S.	BEL	100m	1	9	4		
		High jump	F		16	1,40	
Vivenza, V.	ITA	4×100m relay	1	2	3		
			F		6	53·6	
Vrana, A.M.	USA	100m	1	3	3		
Washburn, M.T.	USA	100m	1	2	2		
			SF	1	5		
		4×100m relay	1	2	1	49·8	
			F		2	48·6	S
Wever, E.	GER	800m	1	3	3		
			F		9		
Wiley, M.O.	USA	High jump	F		3	1,56	B
Wilson, N.	NZL	100m	1	8	2		
			SF	3	5		
Wilson, R.B.	USA	800m	1	2	10		

1932

Babe Didrikson's All-Round Performance

Despite the farce of the previous Games in America, when few Europeans had bothered to go, and the Wall Street crash of 1929, the Los Angeles Games of 1932 were extremely successful. Good organisation and transport arrangements got over many problems, and there was the first Olympic village (for men — women competitors were accommodated in a large hotel.)

Because of the excellent track, made of crushed peat, many world records were broken. Paavo Nurmi could not take part because of allegations of professionalism. He watched, as did Jim Thorpe, who had difficulty in getting into the stadium at all.

Of all the outstanding athletes, the one who will be remembered longest is Mildred "Babe" Didrikson. An outstanding all-round performer in many sports, she was restricted to three events, as were all women athletes, and won two gold medals and a silver, which could also easily have been a gold.

Men's Track Events

The **100 metres** was an outstanding event at Los Angeles as sprint standards moved up a notch with the old Olympic record being equalled or beaten 13 times. From 10·6 sec it was reduced to 10·4 in the heats by Eddie Tolan of the USA and the final was expected to be a brilliant race. From the gun, the diminutive Japanese sprinter, Takayoshi Yoshioka, grabbed half-a-metre on the rest of the sprinters, but at 40 metres Tolan shot past, with his fellow countryman, Ralf Metcalfe a metre back. At the finish, the effort of the athletes was evident as they lunged for the tape, with Tolan and Metcalfe locked together in 10·3, with the former getting the nod. Arthur Jonath of Germany took the bronze in similar fashion from George Simpson of the USA, both recording 10·4 and Dan Joubert of South Africa was not far away in 10·5. (Automatic timings: Tolan 10·38, Metcalfe 10·38, Jonath 10·50, Simpson 10·53 and Joubert 10·60).

As in the short sprint the **200 metres** drew on the same men and again the Olympic record of 21·6 sec was beaten or equalled, this time on 15 occasions. Both Carlos Bianchi Luti of Argentina and Arthur Jonath of Germany were timed at 21·4 in the second round and were expected to perform well. Luti of Argentina got away first at the second time of asking in the final, but coming out of the curve George Simpson of the USA was just up on him. Sixty metres from the line the little American, Eddie Tolan, made his move and powered past the rest to win in 21·2 (21·12 on the automatic timer), with Simpson a good two metres back in 21·4. Ralf Metcalfe of the USA, a slow starter, just pipped Jonath for third, both recording 21·5.

Bill Carr and Ben Eastman, both Americans, were in a league of their own over the **400 metres**. Eastman had earlier in the year sliced the 440 yards record down by one whole second to 46·4 sec, while Carr had run 47·0. Carr kept up the momentum, producing a new Olympic record of 47·25 in the semi-finals and the scene was set for a great final. Eastman got off at a cracking pace, covering the 100 in 10·8 and 200 in 21·7. Carr passed the latter mark in 22·1 and then put in a strong bend to come within reaching distance of Eastman at 300 metres. With 80 metres to go he drew level and went on to win in 46·1 to 46·4, with Alex Wilson of Canada one second adrift in third place. (Automatic timings: Carr 46·28, Eastman 46·50).

The studious, bespectacled Tommy Hampson, of Great Britain, was an unlikely candidate to win the **800 metres**. He was, however, a man of conviction with a racing brain in his head. The preliminary heats were uneventful and eight nervous runners, including Hampson, in his Panama hat, waited to come under starter's orders in the final. After two false starts they were away, and Phil Edwards of Canada raced through the 200 mark in 24·4 and 400 in 52·8, with Eddie Genung of the USA eight yards further back. The chasing group then piled on the pace, with Wilson leading Hampson past Genung and Edwards. With 50 metres remaining Hampson produced a tremendous effort and won by a metre at the tape in a new world and Olympic record of 1-49·8 (actually 1-49·70 on the automatic timer). Wilson recorded 1-49·9 and Edwards 1-51·5.

Jules Ladoumegue, the French world record holder at **1,500 metres**, had been declared a professional, and Finland's Harri Larva, the reigning champion, had gone off the boil. The new champion would surely come from one of the rising stars and after the three heats, 11 hopefuls lined up for the final. There was a rapid scramble for position at the start with Phil Edwards of Canada spurting into the lead followed by Jack Lovelock of New Zealand, Luigi Beccali of Italy and three Americans. Then came Erik Ny of Sweden, Eino Purje of Finland and the holder, Larva. With two laps to go, Glenn Cunningham of the USA was striding out hard in front followed by Edwards, Lovelock, Beccali and the Englishman Jerry Cornes. Over the next lap or so there was a lot of jockeying for position but off the final bend, Beccali swept past the leader, Edwards, and stormed to the finish in 3-51·20, a new Olympic record. Meanwhile, Cornes was fast overtaking Cunningham, and just managed to pip Edwards at the tape in 3-52·6, for the silver, with Edwards recording 3-52·8 for the bronze.

Lauri Lehtinen of Finland had recently set a new world record of 14-17·0 at **5,000 metres** and was expected to run away with the event. Two heats weeded out the lesser lights and the final commenced with Ralph Hill of the USA dashing into the lead. But following the completion of the first circuit, Lehtinen had taken charge, and five laps further on the battle lay between him, Hill and Lauri Virtanen, also of Finland, John

Savidan of New Zealand and Gunnar Lindgren of Sweden. With three laps remaining, Lehtinen stepped up the pace taking Hill and Virtanen with him, but the latter soon dropped away. Hill hung to Lehtinen like a limpet and 50 metres from the finish attempted to pass on the outside whereupon the Finn moved into the second lane and blocked him. Hill next tried passing on the inside, but was blocked again, and Lehtinen won with the American on his shoulder. Both were given the same time of 14-30·0 (Lehtinen recorded 14-29·91 on the automatic timer) with Virtanen third in 14-44·0. The crowd objected violently to Lehtinen's tactics, but there was no official protest.

The **10,000 metres** was a straight final and on pre-Games form Janusz Kusocinski of Poland and Lauri Virtanen were the favourites. The Pole went into the lead from the gun, and at 1,500 metres, passed in 4-17, followed by Volmari Iso-Hollo of Finland, Virtanen, Max Syring of Germany, Gunnar Lindgren of Sweden and John Savidan of New Zealand. At the half-way stage, Syring and Lindgren had been dropped. Savidan was the next to go, while Virtanen struggled to stay with the two leaders. In the last lap Kusocinski drew away from Iso-Hollo and won by 12 metres in 30-11·4 (30-11·42 on the automatic timer), a new Olympic record. Iso-Hollo clocked 30-12·6 and Virtanen 30-35·0.

In 1932 the great Paavo Nurmi of Finland had **marathon** ambitions, having run a super-fast short course marathon race of 40·2km in 2:22-03·8, worth something under 2:30-00, and in spikes. But he was accused of professionalism and the International Amateur Athletic Federation temporarily suspended him. With Nurmi in the stands, unfortunately only an onlooker, Juan Carlos Zabala, a novice marathon runner from Argentina, led the runners out of the stadium. Pomposo of Mexico, Lauri Virtanen of Finland and Duncan McLeod Wright of Britain came next and were in contention over a long period. However, Virtanen drank a glass of milk on completing 19 miles and shortly afterwards retired. At 22 miles Zabala headed Wright, Armas Toivonen of Finland and Sam Ferris of Britain, 20 seconds covering the lot, but on reaching the tape the Argentinian had a handy 100 metres lead, finishing in 2:31-36. Ferris arrived in 2:31-55 and Toivonen in 2:32-12, all beating the previous Olympic record.

All three of the Americans competing in the **110 metres hurdles** had either beaten or equalled the listed world record of 14·4 sec that year and in the semi-finals two of them, George Saling and Percy Beard, clocked 14·4. After one false start in the final, Keller of the USA led for three flights with Beard, a stylish hurdler, closing on him. Keller then hit his fifth flight and Beard the sixth. Meanwhile, Saling had overtaken them both, and although he tripped on the final hurdle, he stumbled on to the finish to win in 14·6. Beard hung on to second place in 14·7 while confusion reigned over the third placing. Keller was at first given the bronze, but the photo-finish picture showed that Donald Finlay of Great Britain had caught him in a desperate drive for the finish. (Automatic timings: Saling 14·57, Beard 14·69 and Finlay 14·74).

Ireland's Bob Tisdall was an all-rounder and Glenn Hardin of the USA was a high hurdler. But both were novices at the **400 metres hurdles**, compared with Morgan Taylor of America, the world record holder, and David Burghley the reigning Olympic champion. These hurdlers clashed in the final with Tisdall in lane three, Taylor four, Burghley five and Hardin in the unfavourable outside. Johan Areskoug of Sweden went off much too fast and blew up at 300 metres. Tisdall swept by him and held a four-metre lead into the final straight, and despite hitting the last hurdle won in 51·8 sec. Behind him there was a titanic struggle, with Hardin beating Taylor in 52·0, with Burghley barely a metre further back. Although Tisdall got the gold medal, Hardin carried off both world and Olympic records, as the Irishman had knocked down a hurdle. (Automatic timings: Tisdall 51·67, Hardin 51·85 and Taylor 51·96).

Olympic records were set in both heats of the **3,000 metres steeplechase** where Thomas Evenson of Britain did 9-18·8, then Volmari Iso-Hollo of Finland showed 9-14·6. In the final, Iso-Hollo took command at the end of the second lap, followed by Evenson, Glen Dawson and Joe McCluskey, both of the USA. Lap by lap Iso-Hollo extended his lead and sprinted to finish 40 metres ahead. Beyond belief, he was urged to run another 450-metre lap which he did with some puzzlement — the replacement lap recorder had got it wrong. His time was 10-33·4, but really 9-08·4. Behind

Dave Terry

Matti Jaervinen

Matti Jaervinen was a truly remarkable thrower. Born in 1909, he had been given every encouragement as a youngster by his father, Werner, who himself was a discus thrower for Finland in the 1908 and 1912 Games.

At 18 years of age Matti's progress was hindered because of a tennis elbow but by the time he was 20 he had begun a run of eight successive title wins in the Finnish championships and 1930 saw him break the first of his world records, a feat he had repeated ten times by 1936.

His first was 234ft 9½in (71,57m), following which he improved his marks three times in the space of a month to 239ft 3½in (72,94m), which not surprisingly made him a hot favourite to win the Olympic title in Los Angeles in 1932. And just before those Games he lifted the world's best figures to 242ft 10in (74,02m). He did not disappoint his national followers and proved so superior that he won the gold with 9½ft (2.80m) to spare.

By 1936 he had taken the world mark to 253ft 4½in (77,23m) but developed a back injury just before the Berlin Games to wreck his chances of keeping his Olympic title, though he did reach 227ft (69,18m) for fifth place.

him McCluskey was second at the proper finish, but Evenson was stronger over the longer race and got the silver to McClusky's bronze.

For the first time a **50 kilometres walk** was contested at the Games, the previous shorter and faster competitions having come in for much criticism, due to walkers running and not walking. Janis Dalinsh of Latvia and Ugo Frigerio of Italy were the two men with reputations, but Tommy Green of Britain had been around a long time — 39 years to be exact. In the earlier stages, Francesco Pretti of Italy held the lead, before Dalinsh took over at 10km and passed 25km in 2:23-11, leading Green, Frigerio and fellow Italian Ettore Rivolta. Dalinsh and Green then forged ahead until 2km from home where the Latvian suffered leg cramps which allowed Green to pile up a long lead to win in 4:50-10. Meanwhile, Dalinsh was having his work cut-out to hold off Frigerio, which he did in 4:57-20 to 4:59-06.

With such a wealth of sprinters at the Games, it was inevitable that the world record for the **4 × 100 metres relay** should go and in the preliminaries the US team of Bob Kiesel, Emmett Toppino, Hec Dyer and Frank Wykoff knocked two tenths off it with 40·6 sec. In the final, America's nearest rival was Germany, who were drawn three lanes outside them. At the end of the first leg Kiesel was two metres up and Toppino was five at the end of the next. Dyer increased this to seven, before Wykoff raced away to a 40·0 win (40·10 on the automatic timer) and a new world record. Germany were second in 40·9 while Italy had a close tussle with Canada, just beating them for the bronze.

Both Britain and Canada had excellent **4 × 400 metres relay** teams, but they could not hold a candle to the USA, who beat the world record with 3-11·8 in the heats. Ivan Fuqua was America's first leg runner in the final and his 47·1 left Johan Buechner of Germany three metres down. Taking over for the USA was Edgar Ablowich, whose 47·6 gave him a nine-metre advantage

over Tommy Hampson of Britain. Then came Karl Warner with 47·3, to lead by 14 metres from Britain's Lord Burghley. The final leg was run by Bill Carr in 46·2 for a total time of 3-08·2 (3-08·14 on the automatic timer), another world record, against Britain's 3-11·2 and Canada's 3-12·8.

Men's Field Events

George Spitz of the USA was the hot tip to win the **high jump**, but he competed with an injured foot and eventually slipped to ninth place. Four jumpers cleared at 1,97 metres: Duncan McNaughton of Canada, Bob van Osdel and Cornelius Johnson, both of the USA, and Simeon Toribio of the Philippines. The height was next raised to 2,00 and all failed their three attempts, plus the fourth jump allowed under the tie rule. This resulted in the bar being lowered to 1,97, at which height McNaughton succeeded again and won the gold. Van Osdel then cleared for the silver, leaving Toribio with the bronze.

In the **pole vault**, Bill Miller and Bill Graber, both of the USA, and Shuhei Nishida of Japan, vaulted 4,15 metres with their bamboo poles. At 4,20 George Jefferson, who had elected to miss out at 4,15, cleared, as did Miller and Nishida, with Graber, the world record holder, passing. But at 4,25 Jefferson and Graber failed their three attempts, which meant that the former collected the bronze medal. Both Miller and Nishida cleared 4,30, and Miller cleared 4,31 on his last vault to take the gold and a new Olympic record, leaving the gallant Japanese, who had pleased the crowd with his determination, to take silver.

Ed Gordon of the USA won the **long jump** with 7,64 metres, his very first leap, while fellow American Charles Redd needed only two jumps to achieve his best of 7,60 to earn the silver. The world record holder, Chuhei Nambu of Japan, took the bronze with 7,45 in

An unusual rear view of the 200 metres finish, with Eddie Tolan, "the Midnight Express" from America, breaking the tape.

Dave Terry

the first round, although well down on his personal best of 7,98.

If Chuhei Nambu was disappointing in the long jump, he was far from that in the **triple jump** and went straight into the lead in the first round with 15,07 metres to equal his personal best. However, in the next round he was shunted into second spot when Eric Svensson of Sweden jumped 15,32. This fired Nambu to try harder and on his third effort he improved to 15,22, but was still 11 centimetres short of the leader. Such was his determination that on his fifth try he hopped the prodigious distance of 6,40 then stepped and jumped to a world and Olympic record of 15,72. Behind Svensson in third position was Kenkichi Oshima of Japan with 15,12. Unhappily the previous Olympic champion and world record holder, Mikio Oda, was injured and only made 12th place.

Frantisek Douda, the Czech world record holder in the **shot put** was rated favourite to win, but he had to bow to two Americans on the day. Both Douda at 15,61, and Harlow Rothert of the USA at 15,67, set their best marks in the first round for bronze and silver respectively, but Leo Sexton of the USA started off with 15,60, and improved to 15,72 in the third and 15,94 in the fourth round. Still not satisfied he heaved 16,00 with his final throw for the gold and Olympic record.

The **discus throw** competition was full of excitement, with the Olympic record constantly being broken. First Jules Noel of France threw 47,74 metres to exceed the old mark, then minutes later Henri Laborde of the USA improved it further with 48,23. However, in the second round the American, John Anderson, launched the discus to 48,86, in the third to 49,39 and in the fifth to 49,49 to take the record and the gold. Laborde improved to 48,47 for silver while Paul Winter of France moved up to third with 47,85.

Twelve years before, Ville Poerhoelae of Finland had won the shot put but now, at the age of 34, he was co-favourite for the **hammer throw**. Even older at 43 was Ossian Skioeld of Sweden, the silver medalist from 1928. Pat O'Callaghan, the reigning champion and other co-favourite, threw 52,21 metres in the second round against Poerhoelae's 52,27 and there it rested until the final round when the Irishman unleashed a mighty 53,92 for top honours. Peter Zaremba of the USA filled the third place with a useful 50,33.

Matti Jaervinen of Finland was the world record holder in the **javelin throw**, having raised the event to new heights. Every one of his six attempts went beyond the 66,60 metres flag marking the Olympic record, and each drew gasps from the crowd. In the first round Gottfried Weimann of Germany threw a new record of 68,18, but only minutes later Jaervinen started his onslaught: 71,25; 70,42; 72,71; 71,31; 72,56 and lastly 67,91. In second place, compatriot Martti Sippala threw 68,14 and then 69,80, while the third Finn, Eino Penttilaa, a former world record holder, took third place.

For the **decathlon**, the leading favourites were the world record holder Achilles Jaervinen, brother of the javelin thrower, and the former record holder Paavo Yrjoelae, both from Finland. The first day saw Indian-American Wilson Charles perform a 7,24 long jump, while Jim Bausch, the 200lb American had an outstanding shot put of 15,32. Leading at the end of the day with 4,266·2 points was Charles, followed by Hans Sievert of Germany and Jaervinen. The second day belonged to America's Jim Bausch. Three superb

performances raised him from fourth to the gold medal position: a discus of 44,58, a vault of 4,00 and a javelin of 61,91 for a total of 8,462·23 points, a new world and Olympic record. Jaervinen was second with 8,292·48 and Wolfrad Eberle of Germany third.

Women's Events

Stanislawa Walasiewicz of Poland was the star of the **100 metres**, equalling the world record of 11·9 in heat, semi-final and final. In the final Hilda Strike of Canada was nearly a metre up at the start, but Walasiewicz drew level at 50 metres and after they had raced abreast for 30 metres, the Polish girl drove hard for the line and won narrowly, both being given 11·9. Behind the two leaders, there was another battle going on in which Wilhelmina von Bremen of the USA clinched the bronze medal in 12·0. Later the winner adopted American citizenship under the name of Stella Walsh. In 1980 she was shot dead by raiders attempting to rob a store, and an autopsy showed her to have a female chromosome deficiency.

In the **80 metres hurdles** was the female star of the whole Games, Mildred Didrikson, who was to collect two golds and one silver at Los Angeles. In the heats she equalled the world record of 11·8 sec, but in the final she was up against fellow American Evelyne Hall, who was fast. Violet Webb of Britain was quickest away, and led over the first hurdle but by the next flight the two Americans were locked together in front, and Didrikson had only inches to spare at the tape, both being given the record time of 11·7. There was a four-way tussle for the bronze with Marjorie Clark of South Africa taking it in 11.8.

The **4 × 100 metres relay** was a ding-dong scrap between the USA and Canada. At the first exchange the USA was just ahead, but at the next Canada had inched to the front. The last changeover was fatal for Canada, who lost two metres, which allowed the USA to storm through the tape in 47·0 sec for a new Olympic and world record. Canada finished less than a metre down in the silver medal position and South Africa were third, a similar distance behind. Actually the race was automatically timed at 46·86, and this was the time that was accepted as a world record.

Mildred Didrikson the wonder girl featured in the **high jump** along with her American colleague, Jean Shiley and four girls in the competition cleared 1,575 metres. At 1,60 Carolina Gisolf of Holland was eliminated. The bar then went up to 1,625, at which Eva Dawes of Canada failed but collected a bronze medal. At 1,67 Shiley and Didrikson failed, so the bar was put down to 1,65 and they both went clear. Didrikson's jump, however, was ruled as illegal, so she got the silver with Shiley the gold and a new world record.

In the **discus throw**, both the world record holder, Greta Heublein of Germany, and the former holder, Jadwiga Wajsowna of Poland, were competing. Two American girls took the top honours, however. Lilian Copeland threw a new Olympic record of 40,58 metres to win, and Ruth Osburn, a comparative novice, threw 40,12 for second place. Wajsowna managed to salvage third place with 38,74.

World record holder Ellen Braumueller of Germany was expected to win the **javelin throw**, but against her was the 19-year-old Mildred Didrikson of the USA. It was a close competition, with Didrikson taking gold with a record 43,68 metres to Braumueller's 43,49. Tilly Fleischer of Germany was not far behind with 43,15.

A preliminary round of the 800 metres shows Phil Edwards, the coloured Canadian athlete, tracking Eddie Genung of America to qualify for the final, where he won the bronze medal.   All-Sport Photographic Ltd.

Bill Carr, the American, who tragically lost his life the following year, is seen winning his 400 metres semi-final heat.   Dave Terry

Dave Terry

Pat O'Callaghan

Pat O'Callaghan was born at Kanturk, Co. Cork, on 28 January 1905, and became one of the heroes of Irish athletics history. Only a year after starting seriously to learn hammer throwing, he became Olympic champion for the event in Amsterdam in 1928, his country's first ever winner of a Games gold. His victory came with a personal best of 51,39m (168ft 7in).

He defended the title in Los Angeles in 1932, when with one throw remaining he was trailing the Finn, Ville Poerhoelae. But O'Callaghan was in no mood to surrender his crown and with his final effort he swirled the hammer to 53,92m (176ft 11in) for a dramatic win.

O'Callaghan not only excelled with the hammer, but he was also an outstanding performer with the discus and the 56-lb shot.

The politcal situation prevented his going to Berlin for the 1936 Games, but his skill with the hammer was forcibly demonstrated once more the following year. From a circle six inches too small and with a hammer six ounces overweight he reached 59,56m (195ft 5in), well beyond the world record which had stood for 24 years. But, because of the size of the circle, the performance was never officially accepted.

All-Sport Photographic Ltd.

Mildred Didrikson

Born at Port Arthur, Texas, on 26 June 1914, "Babe" Didrikson became one of the world's greatest sportswomen of all time. At the US trials for the 1932 Olympics in Los Angeles she won six of the eight events in which she took part, in the space of three hours, setting world records for the 80m hurdles, javelin and high jump.

As she was not permitted to contest more than three events at the Olympics, not surprisingly, she chose the three for which she had set the world marks. At the Games she won the javelin with 143ft 4in (43,68m), an Olympic record; the 80m hurdles with a world record 11·7 sec and tied with the winner of the high jump, her compatriot Jean Shiley, with a world record 5ft 5in (1,65m). In this event she was placed second for jumping with an illegal diving style.

Within a year Didrikson was deprived of her amateur status because her picture and name were being used for advertising.

She later married George Zaharias, a well-known wrestler and chose to concentrate on golf for her sport. Here again she became a leading player, winning many major tournaments in the States including the US Women's Open championship by 12 strokes. She died of cancer on 27 September 1956.

Dave Terry

Robert Tisdall

Bob Tisdall was born in Ceylon in 1907, and not until he attended Cambridge University did he give any indication of the athletics prowess that won him the Olympic 400m hurdles title in Los Angeles in 1932. The previous year he had won four events, the 120 yards hurdles, 440 yards, long jump and shot, for Cambridge in the annual inter-Varsity match.

In the early summer of 1932 Tisdall asked the Irish athletics selectors to consider him for their Olympic team, but it was not until he won the 440 yards hurdles in the Irish national championships that it was decided to include him. Even so, the officials did consider him a little raw for the event.

For three months of that year Tisdall lived in a converted railway carriage in a Sussex orchard to concentrate on training. On arrival in Los Angeles after a two weeks journey he felt so tired he rested in bed for 15 hours a day right up to the time to contest his heat. Winning through to the semi-final he tied the Olympic record of 52·8 sec to qualify for the final. Then followed the race of his life — a world record 51·7 sec to win the gold medal. But because he knocked down the last hurdle, rules existing then would not allow his time to be officially ratified, so the second placed Glenn Hardin, of the USA, with 51·9 sec, was accepted instead as the all-time world's fastest.

The 39-year-old Briton, Tommy Green, the oldest winner at Los Angeles, strolls home in the 50 kilometres walk.   Dave Terry

Dave Terry

Tommy Hampson

Winning the 800m at Los Angeles in the 1932 Games gave Britain a remarkable four-in-a-row series of Olympic victories for the event, but none of these successes came as a bigger surprise than Hampson's.

Born in 1907, he had been no faster than 1·56 three years before. A season later, he won the British Empire Games 880 yards in Hamilton, Canada, to show he was thriving on the good coaching he was receiving at Oxford University. And by the time the Olympic selection was made, he had won the British half-mile championship for three successive summers.

However, so powerful was the line-up against him in Los Angeles that few even considered him for a medal, with the French world record-holder, Seraphin Martin, and the much fancied Canadians, Alex Wilson and Phil Edwards, seeking honours. But content to track the leaders for most of the way, Hampson, on entering the final straight, gave the race everything he had, got the lead and hung onto it right to the tape to become the world's first to break the 1·50·0 barrier with 1·49·7. Wilson finished so close that he, too, dipped inside 1·50·0 with 1·49·9, leaving Edwards to finish third.

Hampson, who became a schoolmaster, died in 1965.

All-Sport Photographic Ltd.

Stanislawa Walasiewicz

Although born as Stanislawa Walasiewicz in Wierzchownia, Poland, on 11 April 1911, this outstanding athlete was known as Stella Walsh after being taken to live in the United States when two years of age. Stella became a leading figure in women's athletics from the age of 19 until she was 43! Her successes included 31 United States outdoor titles and 16 Polish championships, gained not only as a great sprinter but for long jumping, discus throwing and pentathlon.

Her initial major international achievement was becoming the first woman to break through the 11·0 sec barrier for 100yds in 1930. With the approach of the 1932 Los Angeles Games, Americans were seeing her as a potential gold medal winner for them.

But while she was considering becoming a naturalised American, Stella's job with the New York Central Railroad was terminated. Then the day before she was scheduled to take out US naturalisation papers she was offered an appointment with the Polish consulate in New York. She accepted and chose to run for Poland at the Olympics, where she won the 100m final for the country of her birth in a world record 11·9 sec.

On 4 December 1980 she was shopping in Cleveland and was shot and killed when caught in the middle of a robbery.

Dave Terry

Eddie Tolan

Born in Denver, Colorado, on 29 September 1908, he made major international sporting headlines when in May 1929 he became the first man to record 9.5 sec for 100 yards. During the same year he twice equalled the world record of 10·4 sec for 100 metres.

Not surprisingly, he had a keen eye on the Olympics scheduled for Los Angeles in 1932. All seemed to be going well for his gold medal prospects until in the American team trials, Ralph Metcalfe, another black sprinter, beat him to the line in both the sprint finals.

Two weeks later, with Olympic honours at stake, the stocky Tolan was in no mood to be eclipsed again, by anyone. He wasn't, though it took a world record-equalling 10·3 sec for him to snatch victory by an inch from Metcalfe.

Tolan's confidence was riding high now and in the 200m final he was a clear winner of a second gold with 21·2 sec, the fastest ever run at an Olympics.

Had Tolan been included in the 4 × 100m relay quartet, he could have become the first man to win three golds from the sprinting events. He died in Detroit on 31 January 1967.

COMPETITOR	COUNTRY CODE	EVENT	ROUND	HEAT	PLACE	TIME & DISTANCE	MEDAL
MALES							
Ablowich, E.	USA	4×400m relay	1	1	1	3-11·8*	
			F		1	3-8·14*	G
Adelheim, A.	FRA	400m hurdles	1	3	4	54·3	
			SF	2	5	53·2	
Alanis, S.	MEX	Triple jump	F		15	13,28	
Alvarez, M.	MEX	400m	1	4	6	49·9	
		4×400m relay	1	2	4	3-23·4	
Anderson, J.F.	USA	Discus throw	F		1	49,49*	G
Anno, I.	JPN	100m	1	3	3	10·9	
			2	4	5	10·9	
		4×100m relay	1	1	2	41·8	
			F		5	41·3	
Areskoug, J.K.	SWE	400m	1	1	4	50·7	
		400m hurdles	1	3	3	54·5	
			SF	2	2	53·2	
			F		6	54·5	
Arguello, R.	MEX	400m	1	6	4	50·9	
		4×400m relay	1	2	4	3-23·4	
Bacsalmasi, P.	HUN	Triple jump	F		9	14,33	
		Decathlon	F		10	7001·73	
Bailey, G.W.	GBR	3000m steeplechase	1	2	4	9-16·0	
			F		5	10-53·2	
		5000m	1	1	8		
Ball, J.	CAN	400m	1	3	2	50·0	
			2	2	4	49·3	
			SF	2	6		
		4×400m relay	1	2	3	3-21·3	
			F		3	3-12·3	B
Barber, R.	USA	Long jump	F		5	7,39	
Bartlett, L.	USA	Javelin throw	F		5	64,46	
Bartolini, N.	ITA	3000m steeplechase	1	1	5		
			F		10	11-29·0	
Barwick, E.W.	AUS	1500m	1	2	7		
Bausch, J.A.S.	USA	Decathlon	F		1	8462·23*	G
Beard, P.	USA	110m hurdles	1	1	1	14·80	
			SF	2	2	14·6	
			F		2	14·69	S
Beccali, L.	ITA	1500m	1	3	1	3-59·6	
			F		1	3-51·20*	G
Begeot, F.	FRA	Marathon	F		16	2:53-34	
Berger, C.D.	HOL	100m	1	7	2	11·1	
			2	1	4	10·7	
		200m	1	5	2	25·5	
			2	1	5	22·0	
Berra, H.	ARG	100m	1	7	3	11·2	
		Decathlon	F		DNF		
		Long jump	F		7	6,66	
Black, S.A.	NZL	200m	1	3	3	23·1	
			2	3	5	22·0	
		400m	1	5	4	49·9	
Borchmeyer, E.	GER	200m	1	1	1	22·1	
			2	1	3	21·3	
			SF	1	5	21·8	
		4×100m relay	1	1	1	41·22*	
			F		2	40·9	S
Bowman, S.	USA	Triple jump	F		7	14,87	
Bricker, C.	CAN	10000m	F		8		
		Marathon	F		12	2:47-58	
Brown, J.	CAN	4×100m relay	1	2	3	45·0	
			F		4	41·3	
Buechner, J.	GER	400m	1	2	2	49·3	
			2	2	3	48·9	
			SF	1	6	49·2	
		4×400m relay	1	1	3	3-25·4	
			F		4	3-14·4	
Burghley, D.G.B.C.	GBR	110m hurdles	1	4	3	15·1	
			SF	1	2	14·6	
			F		5	14·83	
		400m hurdles	1	4	2	55·1	
			SF	1	3	53·0	
			F		4	52·01	
		4×400m relay	1	2	2	3-21·8	
			F		2	3-11·2	S
Burns, J.A.	GBR	5000m	1	2	1	15-25·8	
			F		7	15-04·0	
Camberos, M.	MEX	Javelin throw	F		13	41,71	
Cardoso, A.	BRA	10000m	F		13		
Carlini, G.	ITA	4×400m relay	1	1	2	3-22·8	
			F		6	3-17·8	
Carr, R.J.	IND	4×100m relay	1	1	5		
Carr, W.A.	USA	400m	1	4	1	48·70	
			2	1	1	48·31	
			SF	1	1	47·25*	
			F		1	46·28*	G
		4×400m relay	1	1	1	3-11·3*	
			F		1	3-08·14*	G
Castelli, G.	ITA	4×100m relay	1	2	2	42·8	
			F		3	41·2	B
Cator, S.	HAI	Long jump	F		9	5,93	
Chacarelli, F.	ARG	10000m	F		12		
		Marathon	F		17	2:55-49	
Charles, W.D.	USA	Decathlon	F		4	7985·00	
Chisholm, W.H.	USA	50k walk	F		9	5:51-00	
Chlentzos, P.	GRE	Pole vault	F		7	3,75	
Cho, S.	JPN	400m	1	5	5	50·0	
		400m hurdles	1	1	4	56·5	
Churchill, K.	USA	Javelin throw	F		6	63,24	
Cieman, H.	CAN	50k walk	F		DNF		
Clouthier, A.	MEX	Javelin throw	F		12	46,38	
Coffman, C.C.	USA	Decathlon	F		7	7534·41	
Connor, F.N.	USA	Hammer throw	Q		DNQ		
Cornes, J.F.	GBR	1500m	1	1	2	4-01·0	
			F		2	3-52·6	S
Coulter, T.	CAN	400m hurdles	1	2	DIS		
Crespo, E.	MEX	Long jump	F		10	5,83	
Crosbie, E.	USA	50k walk	F		8	5:28-02	
Crowley, F.	USA	1500m	1	3	4	4-00·0	
			F		8	3-56·6	
Cudworth, E.	CAN	Marathon	F		18	2:58-35	
Cunningham, G.	USA	1500m	1	1	1	3-55·8	
			F		4	3-53·4	
Dalinsh, J.	LAT	50k walk	F		2	4:57-20	S
Danz, M.	GER	800m	1	3	5	1-55·0	
Daranyi, J.	HUN	Shot put	F		7	14,67	
Davila, F.D.R.	MEX	Hammer throw	F		11	41,61	
Dawson, G.W.	USA	3000m steeplechase	1	2	3	9-15·0	
			F		6	10-58·0	
De Almeida, J.X.	BRA	100m	1	2	2	11·0	
			2	4	4	10·8	
Dean, D.E.	USA	5000m	1	1	7		
			F		8	15-08·5	
De Anda, C.	MEX	400m	1	2	4	49·8	
		4×400m relay	1	2	4	3-23·4	
De Araujo, H.	BRA	100m	1	7	5	11·5	
De Bruyn, P.	GER	Marathon	F		15	2:52-39	
De Castro, L.A.P.	BRA	Pole vault	F		6	3,90	
De Figueiredo, C.	BRA	Long jump	F		8	6,43	
De Magalhaes, S.	BRA	110m hurdles	1	1	4	15·4	
		400m hurdles	1	2	4	55·1	
De Negri, M.	ITA	4×400m relay	1	1	2	3-22·8	
			F		6	3-17·8	
De Rosso, H.	ARG	800m	1	2	5	1-54·9	
		1500m	1	1	5	4-06·0	
Dhawan, M.C.	IND	Triple jump	F		14	13,66	
		4×100m relay	1	1	5		
Dimsa, J.	LAT	Decathlon	F		DNF		
Donogan, I.	HUN	Discus throw	F		5	47,07	
Dos Reis, C.A.	BRA	400m hurdles	1	4	4	55·8	
Douda, F.	TCH	Discus throw	F		15	42,39	
		Shot put	F		3	15,61	B
Duhour, C.	FRA	Discus throw	F		16	40,22	
		Shot put	F		11	13,96	
Dyer, H.M.	USA	4×100m relay	1	2	1	40·61*	
			F		1	40·10*	G
Eastman, B.	USA	400m	1	2	1	49·02	
			2	3	1	48·90	
			SF	2	1	47·60	
			F		2	46·50	S
Eberle, W.	GER	Decathlon	F		3	8030·80	B
Edwards, P.	CAN	800m	1	1	2	1-55·1	
			F		3	1-51·5	B
		1500m	1	1	4	4-03·5	
			F		3	3-52·8	B
		4×400m relay	1	2	3	3-21·8	
			F		3	3-12·8	B
Elliot, A.J.	NZL	100m	1	3	2	10·8	
			2	3	3	10·9	
			SF	1	5	10·99	
		200m	1	6	3	22·2	
			2	4	3	21·8	
			SF	2	5	21·9	
Elsa, P.	ARG	Discus throw	F		18	34,36	
		Shot put	F		14	11,21	
Engl, A.	TCH	100m	1	2	3	11·2	
			2	2	4	11·1	
		200m	1	6	4	22·3	
Englehart, S.E.	GBR	200m	1	1	3	23·8	
			2	4	4	21·8	
		4×100m relay	1	1	3	42·0	
			F		6	41·8	
Evans, C.V.	NZL	800m	1	1	4	1-56·6	
Evenson, T.	GBR	3000m steeplechase	1	1	1	9-18·8*	
			F		2	10-46·0	S

COMPETITOR	COUNTRY CODE	EVENT	ROUND	HEAT	PLACE	TIME & DISTANCE	MEDAL
Facelli, L.	ITA	400m hurdles	1	4	1	55·07	
			SF	2	3	53·1	
			F		5	53·0	
		4×100m relay	1	2	2	42·8	
			F		3	41·2	B
		4×400m relay	1	1	2	3-22·8	
			F		6	3-17·8	
Fanelli, M.	ITA	Marathon	F		13	2:49-09	
Ferris, S.	GBR	Marathon	F		2	2:31-55	S
Finlay, D.O.	GBR	110m hurdles	1	2	1	14·84	
			SF	1	3	14·6	
			F		3	14·74	B
		4×100m relay	1	1	3	42·0	
			F		6	41·8	
Fitzgerald, E.	IRL	Triple jump	F		4	15,01	
Frangoudis, R.	GRE	4×100m relay	1	1	4		
Frigerio, U.	ITA	50k walk	F		3	4:59-06	B
Fujita, T.	JPN	110m hurdles	1	2	3	15·1	
			2	2	4	14·8	
Fuller, S.C.	GBR	100m	1	7	4	11·3	
		200m	1	2	3	22·4	
			2	2	5	22·1	
		4×100m relay	1	1	3	42·0	
			F		6	41·8	
Fuqua, I.	USA	4×400m relay	1	1	1	3-11·8*	
			F		1	3-08·14*	G
Furia, A.	ITA	3000m steep echase	1	2	6		
Furth, S.H.	USA	Triple jump	F		6	14,88	
Gallop, H.	CAN	3000m steeplechase	1	2	7		
Gamboa, A.	MEX	110m hurdles	1	3	6	15·4	
Geerling, E.	GER	100m	1	6	3	11·3	
			2	3	5	11·1	
Genta, R.	ARG	200m	1	5	1	25·3	
			2	2	3	21·8	
			SF	2	6	22·0	
Genung, E.	USA	800m	1	1	1	1-54·73	
			F		4	1-51·7	
Giacosa, S.A.	ARG	100m	1	3	5	11·1	
Giorgiu, C.	BRA	Hammer throw	F		13	36,45	
Giogu, G.	BRA	10000m	F		13		
Giusfredi, A.	BRA	110m hurdles	1	3	5	15·3	
Golding, G.A.	AUS	400m	1	4	2	49·0	
			2	1	3	48·6	
			SF	1	3	48·0	
			F		6	48·8	
		400m hurdles	1	4	3	55·2	
			SF	1	4	53·1	
Gomes, N.	BRA	800m	1	1	6		
Gon, T.	JPN	Marathon	F		9	2:42-52	
Gonzalez, A.	MEX	400m hurdles	1	1	5	56·7	
Gonzalez, V.	MEX	5000m	1	2	8	16-00·0	
Gordon, E.L.	USA	Long jump	F		1	7,64	G
Gordon, J.A.	USA	400m	1	6	1	50·6	
			2	2	1	48·66	
			SF	2	3	48·2	
			F		5	48·2	
Graber, W.	USA	Pole vault	F		4	4,15	
Gray, N.	USA	Shot put	F		5	15,46	
Green, T.W.	GBR	50k walk	F		1	4:50-10*	G
Gregory, L.P.	USA	10000m	F		DNF		
Guimaraes, R.V.	BRA	110m	1	6	4	11·4	
Haehnel, K.	GER	50k walk	F		4	5:06-06	
Hallowell, N.P.	USA	1500m	1	2	2	3-58·1	
			F		6	3-55·0	
Hampson, T.	GBR	800m	1	3	1	1-53·0	
			F		1	1-49·70*	G
		4×400m relay	1	2	2	3-21·8	
			F		2	3-11·2	S
Hardin, G.	USA	400m hurdles	1	2	3	55·0	
			SF	1	1	52·79*	
			F		2	51·85*	S
Harper, R.St G.T.	GBR	110m hurdles	1	1	2	14·9	
			SF	2	5	14·9	
Hart, H.B.	SAF	Discus throw	F		12	43,33	
		Decathlon	F		11	6799·25	
		Shot put	F		10	14,22	
Hartington-Andersen, A.	DEN	Marathon	F		10	2:44-38	
Haug, B.	NOR	High jump	F		=9	1,85	
Healey, J.F.	USA	400m hurdles	1	3	1	54·06	
			SF	2	4	53·2	
Heks, O.	TCH	Marathon	F		8	2:41-35	
Heljasz, Z.	POL	Discus throw	F		13	42,59	
		Shot put	F		9	14,49	

COMPETITOR	COUNTRY CODE	EVENT	ROUND	HEAT	PLACE	TIME & DISTANCE	MEDAL
Hendrix, F.	GER	200m	1	4	2	22·3	
			2	2	4	21·9	
		4×100m relay	1	1	1	41·22*	
			F		2	40·9	S
Henigan, J.P.	USA	Marathon	F		DNF		
Hernandez, S.	MEX	Marathon	F		DNF		
Hill, R.	USA	5000m	1	1	1	14-59·76	
			F		2	14-30·0	S
Hillhouse, J.A.	AUS	5000m	1	1	6	15-14·0	
			F		9	15-15·0	
Hinkel, H.R.	USA	50k walk	F		DNF		
Hirschfeld, E.	GER	Discus throw	F		14	42,42	
		Shot put	F		4	15,56	
Hornbostel, C.C.	USA	800m	1	2	1	1-52·4	
			F		6	1-52·7	
Hutton, L.	CAN	Long jump	F		NP	0	
Iso-Hollo, V.	FIN	3000m steeplechase	1	2	1	9-14·6*	
			F		1	10-33·4	G
		10000m	F		2	30-12·6	S
Iturbe, I.	MEX	800m	1	2	7	1-55·6	
Janausch, E.	AUT	Discus throw	F		10	44,82	
Jansson, G.	SWE	Hammer throw	F		7	47,79	
Jaervinen, A.	FIN	Decathlon	F		2	8292·48	S
Jaervinen, K.V.	FIN	Shot put	F		12	13,91	
Jaervinen, M.H.	FIN	Javelin throw	F		1	72,71*	G
Jefferson, G.G.	USA	Pole vault	F		3	4,20	B
Jessup, P.B.	USA	Discus throw	F		8	45,25	
Johannesen, H.	NOR	400m	1	2	3	49·5	
			2	2	5	49·4	
		800m	1	2	4	1-54·3	
Johnson, C.C.	USA	High jump	F		4	1,97	
Jonath, A.	GER	100m	1	3	1	10·67*	
			2	4	1	10·68	
			SF	2	3	10·7	
			F		3	10·50	B
		200m	1	6	1	21·9	
			2	4	1	21·48	
			SF		1	21·5	
			F		4	21·5	
		4×100m relay	1	1	1	41·22*	
			F		2	40·9	S
Joubert, D.J.	SAF	100m	1	6	1	11·0	
			2	4	2	10·6	
			SF	1	2	10·8	
			F		5	10·60	
		200m	1	7	2	22·3	
			2	3	3	21·7	
			SF	1	4	21·7	
Keller, J.	USA	110m hurdles	1	4	1	15·01	
			SF	1	1	14·63*	
			F		4	14·8	
Keller, P.-J.	FRA	800m	1	1	DNF		
Kiesel, R.A.	USA	4×100m relay	1	2	1	40·61*	
			F		1	40·10*	G
Kimura, K.	JPN	High jump	F		6	1,94	
Kin, O.	JPN	Marathon	F		6	2:37-28	
King, E.	CAN	800m	1	3	4	1-54·4	
		1500m	1	2	3	3-58·6	
			F		DNS		
Kitamoto, M.	JPN	5000m	1	1	9		
		10000m	F		9		
Kleger, F.	ARG	Hammer throw	F		6	48,33	
Koechermann, E.	GER	Long jump	F		11	5,72	
Koernig, H.	GER	100m	1	4	2	11·0	
			2	2	3	11·0	
			SF	1	6	11·2	
		4×100m relay	1	1	1	41·22*	
			F		2	40·9	S
Kotkas, K.	FIN	Discus throw	F		7	45,87	
Kusocinski, J.	POL	10000m	F		1	30-11·42*	G
Kyronen, V.	FIN	Marathon	F		DNF		
Laborde, H.J.	USA	Discus throw	F		2	48,47	S
Lambrou, A.	GRE	100m	1	5	3	11·3	
		4×100m relay	1	1	4	41·6	
Larva, H.	FIN	1500m	1	2	4	3-58·8	
			F		9	3-57·0	
Lehtinen, L.A.	FIN	5000m	1	1	2	15-05·5	
			F		1	14-29·91*	G
Lewis, R.	CAN	400m	1	6	2	50·7	
			2	3	5	49·1	
		4×400m relay	1	2	3	3-21·8	
			F		3	3-12·8	B
Lindgren, G.	SWE	5000m	1	1	3	15-06·0	
			F		5	14-54·7	
		10000m	F		6	31-37·0	
Lippi, G.	ITA	3000m steeplechase	1	1	4		
			F		7	11-04·0	

COMPETITOR	COUNTRY CODE	EVENT	ROUND	HEAT	PLACE	TIME & DISTANCE	MEDAL
Liu, Chang-Chun	CHN	100m	1	2	5	11·5	
		200m	1	3	4	22·4	
Lovelock, J.E.	NZL	1500m	1	2	1	3-58·0	
			F		7	3-55·6	
Luomanen, M.	FIN	1500m	1	1	3	4-01·5	
			F		10	3-57·8	
Luti, C.B.	ARG	100m	1	4	1	10·8	
			2	1	2	10·5	
			SF	2	4	10 73	
		200m	1	6	3	22·2	
			2	1	·	21·46*	
			SF	1	3	21·6	
			F		5	21·6	
McCluskey, J.P.	USA	3000m steeplechase	1	2	2	9-11·8	
			F		3	10-46·2	B
McDougall, G.	USA	Hammer throw	F		5	49,12	
McNaughton, D.	CAN	High jump	F		1	1,97	G
Madarasz, A.	HUN	Discus throw	F		6	46,52	
Mantikas, C.	GRE	400m	1	4	5	49 6	
		110m hurdles	1	4	2	15 1	
			SF	2	6	15 0	
		400m hurdles	1	1	3	56 4	
			SF	2	6	53 4	
		4×100m relay	1	1	4		
Marcondes, M.	BRA	Marathon	F		DNF		
Maregatti, R.	ITA	4×100m relay	1	2	2	42·8	
			F		3	41·2	B
Markersen, C.	DEN	1500m	1	1	6	4-06·5	
Martin, P.	SUI	800m	1	1	5	1-58·4	
		1500m	1	2	5	3-59·1	
Martin, S.	FRA	800m	1	3	2	1-53·2	
			F		8	1-53·6	
Maasik, A.	EST	50k walk	F		10	6:19-00	
Masuda, I.	JPN	400m	1	3	3	50·1	
		4×400m relay	1	2	1	3-16 8	
			F		5	3-14 6	
Matilainen, M.	FIN	3000m steeplechase	1	2	5	9-43 0	
			F		4	10-52·4	
Medina, H.	BRA	Javelin throw	F		11	58,00	
Menard, C.	FRA	High jump	F		=9	1,85	
Metcalf, M.W.	USA	Javelin throw	F		7	61,89	
Metcalfe, R.	USA	100m	1	5	1	11·0	
			2	3	1	10·7	
			SF	2	1	10·65	
			F		2	10·38*	S
		200m	1	3	2	22·5	
			2	1	1	21·59*	
			SF	1	1	21·52	
			F		3	21·5	B
Metzner, A.	GER	400m	1	1	1	50·4	
			2	3	6	49·2	
		4×400m relay	1	1	3	3-22·4	
			F		4	3-14·4	
Michelsen, A.R.	USA	Marathon	F		7	2:39-38	
Miles, J.	CAN	Marathon	F		14	2:50-32	
Miller, W.W.	USA	Pole vault	F		1	4,31*	G
Miropoulos, E.	GRE	400m hurdles	1	3	4	55·2	
		4×100m relay	1	1	4		
Mochizuki, S.	JPN	Pole vault	F		5	4,00	
Moraila, J.	MEX	100m	1	4	4	11·2	
		4×400m relay	1	2	4	3-23·4	
Morales, J.	MEX	10000m	F		7	32-03·8	
Moralis, J.	GRE	50k walk	F		DNF		
Morel, R.	FRA	800m	1	2	6	1-55·2	
Murphy, M.	IRL	3000m steeplechase	1	2	DNF		
Musquiz, E.	MEX	200m	1	6	5	22·4	
Nagao, S.	JPN	Javelin throw	F		10	59,83	
Nagao, Y.	JPN	Hammer throw	F		10	43,41	
Nakajima, I.	JPN	200m	1	4	1	22·2	
			2	4	4	21·9	
		4×100m relay	1	·	2	41·8	
			F		5	41·3	
		4×400m relay	1	2	1	3-16·8	
			F		5	3-14·6	
Nambu, C.	JPN	Long jump	F		3	7,45	B
		Triple jump	F		·	15,72*	G
		4×100m relay	1	1	2	41·8	
Narancic, Y.	YUG	Shot put	F		12	14,14	
		Discus throw	F		17	36,51	
Nehb, W.	GER	400m	1	4	5	49·4	
		4×400m relay	1	1	3	3-25·4	
			F		4	3-14·4	
Nelli, C.J.	BRA	Pole vault	F		NP	0	

COMPETITOR	COUNTRY CODE	EVENT	ROUND	HEAT	PLACE	TIME & DISTANCE	MEDAL
Nishi, T.	JPN	200m	1	7	3	22·4	
			2	4	5	21·9	
		4×400m relay	1	2	1	3-16·8	
			F		5	3-14·6	
Nishida, S.	JPN	Pole vault	F		2	4,30	S
Noel, J.	FRA	Discus throw	F		4	47,74	
		Shot put	F		8	14,53	
Nottbrock, F.	GER	400m hurdles	1	2	2	55·0	
			SF	1	6	53·7	
Ny, E.	SWE	1500m	1	3	3	3-59·9	
			F		5	3-54·6	
O'Callaghan, P.	IRL	Hammer throw	F		1	53,92	G
Ochiai, M.	JPN	Hammer throw	F		12	41,00	
Oda, M.	JPN	Triple jump	F		12	13,97	
Oki, S.	JPN	400m	1	1	2	50·5	
			2	2	6		
		4×400m relay	1	2	1	3-16·8	
			F		5	3-14·6	
Oldag, H.	USA	Marathon	F		11	2:47-26	
Oliva, L.	ARG	3000m steeplechase	1	1	DNF		
Ono, M.	JPN	High jump	F		=7	1,90	
Ortiz, F.A.	MEX	100m	1	1	3	11·2	
			2	1	5	10·7	
Ortiz, P.	MEX	1500m	1	3	6	4-18·0	
Oshima, K.	JPN	Triple jump	F		3	15,12	B
Ottey, T.C.	USA	10000m	F		DNF		
Page, E.L.	GBR	100m	1	2	2	11·1	
			2	3	4	10·9	
		4×100m relay	1	1	3	42·0	
			F		6	41·8	
Papanikolaou, N.	GRE	Triple jump	F		13	13,92	
Pearson, B.	CAN	100m	1	5	2	11·1	
			2	4	3	10·7	
			SF	2	5	10·95	
		200m	1	7	1	22·3	
			2	2	2	21·8	
			SF	1	6	21·9	
		4×100m relay	1	2	3	45·0	
			F		5	41·3	
Peltzer, O.	GER	800m	1	2	3	1-53·6	
			F		9		
		1500m	1	3	DNF		
		4×400m relay	1	1	3	3-25·4	
			F		4	3-14·4	
Pentti, E.	USA	10000m	F		DNF		
Penttilaa, E.	FIN	Javelin throw	F		3	68,70	B
Pereira, A.	BRA	Shot put	Q		DNQ		
Perry, G.	COL	Marathon	F		DNF		
Peters, W.	HOL	Triple jump	F		5	14,93	
Pettersson, E.	SWE	5000m	1	2	3	15-36·4	
			F		DNF		
Pettersson, S.	SWE	400m	1	3	4	50·2	
		400m hurdles	1	1	2	56·1	
			SF	1	5	53·2	
Plawczyk, J.	POL	High jump	F		=7	1,90	
Poggioli, A.	ITA	Hammer throw	F		8	46,90	
Pomposo, M.	MEX	Marathon	F		20	3:10-51	
Poernoelae, V.	FIN	Hammer throw	F		2	52,27	S
Portland, J.	CAN	High jump	F		=9	1,85	
		Triple jump	F		16	13,27	
Powell, J.V.	GBR	800m	1	1	3	1-55·6	
			F		7	1-53·1	
Pretti, F.	ITA	50k walk	F		DNF		
Pritchard, W.H.	USA	3000m steeplechase	1	1	2	9-19·2	
			F		8	11-04·5	
Puglisi, D.	BRA	400m	1	6	3	50·8	
			2	1	5	50·1	
		800m	1	3	6		
Purje, E.A.	FIN	1500m	1	3	2	3-59·7	
			F		DNF		
Quintric, H.	FRA	50k walk	F		7	5:27-25	
Rajasaari, O.R.	FIN	Triple jump	F		11	14,20	
Rampling, G.L.	GBR	400m	1	5	2	49·5	
			2	2	2	48·8	
			SF	1	4	48·0	
		4×400m relay	1	2	2	3-21·8	
			F		2	3-11·2	S
Rankine, R.	CAN	5000m	1	2	3	15-39·6	
			F		10	15-24·0	
Ravensdale, A.	CAN	110m hurdles	1	3	4	15·2	
Reid, C.L.	USA	Long jump	F		2	7,60	S
Reid, F.P.	GBR	100m	1	1	DNF		
Reinikka, I.J.	FIN	High jump	F		5	1,94	
Rekers, P.E.	USA	5000m	1	1	2	15-34·6	
			F		DNF		
Remecz, J.	HUN	Discus throw	F		9	45,02	
Remirez, F.	MEX	100m	1	5	4	11·4	

COMPETITOR	COUNTRY CODE	EVENT	ROUND	HEAT	PLACE	TIME & DISTANCE	MEDAL
Ribas, J.	ARG	10000m	F		11		
		Marathon	F		DNF		
Riesen, P.	SUI	High jump	F		14	1,80	
Rinner, F.	AUT	400m	1	5	1	49.2	
			2	3	2	48.9	
			SF	1	5	48.8	
Rivolta, E.	ITA	50k walk	F		5	5:07-39	
Roccati, F.	ITA	Marathon	F		DNF		
Rochard, R.	FRA	5000m	1	2	4	15-37.8	
			F		DNF		
Rodriguez, A.	POR	100m	1	1	5	11.5	
Rodriguez, J.M.	MEX	5000m	1	1	10		
		10000m	F		12		
Rodriguez, A.	MEX	1500m	1	1	7		
Romero, R.L.	USA	Triple jump	F		8	14,85	
Rothert, H.P.	USA	Shot put	F		2	15,67	S
Saling, G.J.	USA	110m hurdles	1	2	2	15.0	
			SF	2	1	14.55*	
			F		1	14.57	G
Sanchez, E.	MEX	200m	1	2	4	22.8	
Sanchez, R.	MEX	110m hurdles	1	4	4		
Savidan, J.W.	NZL	5000m	1	1	5	15-08.2	
			F		4	14-49.6	
		10000m	F		4	31-09.0	
Schwab, A.T.	SUI	50k walk	F		DNF		
Sexton, L.	USA	Shot put	F		1	16,00*	G
Siedlecki, Z.	POL	Decathlon	F		DNF		
Sievert, H.-H.	GER	Discus throw	F		11	44,51	
		Shot put	F		6	15,07	
		Decathlon	F		5	7941·07	
Sievert, P.	GER	50k walk	F		6	5:16-41	
Silva, J.C.	BRA	Marathon	F		19	3:02-06	
Simpson, G.L.	USA	100m	1	2	1	10.9	
			2	2	1	10.74	
			SF	2	2	10.7	
			F		4	10.53	
		200m	1	5	3	26.5	
			2	3	2	21.6	
			SF	1	2	21.54	
			F		2	21.4	S
Sippala, M.K.	FIN	Javelin throw	F		2	69,80	S
Sjoestedt, B.	FIN	110m hurdles	1	3	2	14.9	
			SF	1	5	15.0	
Skioeld, O.	SWE	Hammer throw	F		4	49,25	
Skoog, F.	SWE	1500m	1	2	6	3-59.6	
Spitz, G.B.	USA	High jump	F		=9	1,85	
Stoneley, C.H.	GBR	400m	1	4	3	49.3	
			2	3	4	49.2	
			SF	2	5		
		4×400m relay	1	2	2	3-21.8	
			F		2	3-11.2	S
Strandvall, B.J.	FIN	400m	1	3	1	49.8	
			2	3	3	49.0	
			SF	2	4	48.6	
Sumiyoshi, K.	JPN	Javelin throw	F		8	61,14	
Sunde, O.	NOR	Javelin throw	F		9	60,81	
Sutton, M.	IND	100m	1	2	4	11.4	
		110m hurdles	1	3	3	15.1	
			SF	1	4	14.9	
		4×100m relay	1	1	5		
Svensson, E.	SWE	Long jump	F		4	7,41	
		Triple jump	F		2	15,32	S
Syring, M.	GER	5000m	1	2	6	15-48.5	
			F		6	14-59.0	
		10000m	F		5	31-35.0	
Tabai, F.	ITA	Triple jump	F		10	14,29	
Tajima, N.	JPN	Long jump	F		6	7,15	
Takenaka, S.	JPN	5000m	1	2	7	15-56.0	
			F		11	17-20.0	
		10000m	F		10		
Taylor, F.M.	USA	400m hurdles	1	1	1	55.65*	
			SF	1	2	52.9	
			F		3	51.96	B
Theard, A.	HAI	100m	1	1	4	11.4	
Tisdall, R.M.N.	IRL	400m hurdles	1	2	1	54.63*	
			SF	2	1	52.60*	
			F		1	51.67	G
		Decathlon	F		8	7327·17	
Toetti, E.	ITA	4×100m relay	1	2	2	42.8	
			F		3	41.2	B
Toivonen, A.A.	FIN	Marathon	F		3	2:32-12	B
Toivonen, V.	FIN	3000m steeplechase	1	1	3	9-41.0	
			F		9	11-10.2	

COMPETITOR	COUNTRY CODE	EVENT	ROUND	HEAT	PLACE	TIME & DISTANCE	MEDAL
Tolan, E.	USA	100m	1	1	1	10.9	
			2	1	1	10.53*	
			SF	1	1	10.81	
			F		1	10.38*	G
		200m	1	2	2	22.0	
			2	1	1	21.56*	
			SF	2	3	21.7	
			F		1	21.12*	G
Tommasi, A.	ITA	High jump	F		=9	1,85	
Toppino, E.	USA	4×100m relay	1	2	1	40.61*	
			F		1	40.10*	G
Toribio, S.G.	PHI	High jump	F		3	1,97	B
Tsuda, S.	JPN	Marathon	F		5	2:35-42	
Turba, G.	ITA	4×400m relay	1	2	2	3-22.8	
			F		6	3-17.8	
Turner, E.T.	USA	800m	1	3	3	1-54.0	
			F		5	1-52.5	
Vandelli, F.	ITA	Hammer throw	F		9	45,16	
Van Osdel, R.	USA	High jump	F		2	1,97	S
Vasconcelos, M.	MEX	800m	1	1	7	2-00.0	
Vermeux, R.A.	IND	100m	1	3	4	11.0	
		200m	1	7	4	22.5	
		4×100m relay	1	1	5		
Vigneron, R.	FRA	3000m steeplechase	1	1	6	9-57.0	
Virtanen, L.J.	FIN	5000m	1	1	4	15-06.4	
			F		3	14-44.0	B
		10000m	F		3	30-35.0	B
		Marathon	F		DNF		
Wade, L.	CAN	1500m	1	3	5	4-00.5	
Walters, W.J.	SAF	200m	1	2	1	21.83	
			2	1	2	21.6	
			SF	2	2	21.7	
			F		6	21.9	
		400m	1	5	3	49.8	
			2	1	2	48.5	
			SF	2	2	48.2	
			F		4	48.2	
Warner, K.D.	USA	4×400m relay	1	1	1	3-11.8*	
			F		1	3-08.14*	G
Wegner, E.	GER	110m hurdles	1	1	3	15.1	
			SF	1	DNF		
		Decathlon	F		9	7179·93	
Weimann, G.	GER	Javelin throw	F		4	68,18	
Welscher, W.	GER	110m hurdles	1	3	1	15.02	
			SF	2	3	14.8	
			F		DIS		
Williams, P.	CAN	100m	1	4	3	11.1	
			2	1	3	10.6	
			SF	1	4	10.91	
		200m	1	4	3		
		4×100m relay	1	2	3	45.0	
			F		4	41.3	
Wilson, A.	CAN	400m	1	1	3	50.5	
			2	1	4	49.6	
			SF	1	2	47.8	
			F		3	47.4	B
		800m	1	2	2	1-52.5	
			F		2	1-49.9	S
		4×400m relay	1	2	3	3-21.8	
			F		3	3-12.8	B
Winter, P.	FRA	Discus throw	F		3	47,85	B
		Shot put	F		13	13,14	
Wright, H.	CAN	100m	1	6	2	11.2	
			2	2	2	10.9	
			SF	2	6	11.1	
		200m	1	3	1	22.8	
			2	4	2	21.7	
			SF	2	4	21.8	
		4×100m relay	1	2	3	45.0	
			F		4	41.3	
Wright, D.McL.	GBR	Marathon	F		4	2:32-41	
Wykoff, F.C.	USA	4×100m relay	1	2	1	40.61*	
			F		1	40.10*	G
Yoshioka, T.	JPN	100m	1	7	1	10.9	
			2	3	2	10.8	
			SF	1	3	10.83	
			F		6	10.7	
		200m	1	1	2	22.3	
			2	3	4	21.8	
		4×100m relay	1	1	2	41.8	
			F		5	41.3	
Yrjoelae, P.	FIN	Decathlon	F		6	7688·09	
Zabala, J.C.	ARG	Marathon	F		1	2:31-36*	G
Zaremba, P.	USA	Hammer throw	F		3	50,33	B

COMPETITOR	COUNTRY CODE	EVENT	ROUND	HEAT	PLACE	TIME & DISTANCE	MEDAL
FEMALES							
Aalten, C.	HOL	100m	1	4	2	12·6	
			SF	2	6	12·4	
		4×100m relay	F		4	48·0	
Braumueller, E.	GER	4×100m relay	F		6		
		High jump	F		10	1,41	
		Discus throw	F		8	33,15	
		Javelin throw	F		2	43,49	S
Carew, M.L.	USA	4×100m relay	F		1	46·86*	G
Clark, M.	SAF	100m	1	1	5	12·5	
		80m hurdles	1	1	3	11·9	
			F		3	11·8	B
		High jump	F		5	1,58	
Copeland, L.	USA	Discus throw	F		1	40,58*	G
Dalmolen, J.	HOL	4×100m relay	F		4	48·0	
Dawes, E.	CAN	High jump	F		3	1,60	B
Didrikson, M.	USA	80m hurdles	1	1	1	11·8*	
			F		1	11·7*	G
		High jump	F		2	1,65	S
		Javelin throw	F		1	43,68*	G
Dogura, A.	JPN	100m	1	4	4	12·9	
		4×100m relay	F		5	48·9	
Dollinger, M.	GER	100m	1	1	1	12·2*	
			SF	1	2	12·4	
			F		4	12·2	
		4×100m relay	F		6		
Du Mee, E.	HOL	100m	1	2	4	12·3	
		4×100m relay	F		4	48·0	
Fleisher, T.	GER	4×100m relay	F		6		
		Discus throw	F		4	36,12	
		Javelin throw	F		3	43,15	B
Frizzell, Mary	CAN	100m	1	1	2	12·1	
			SF	2	5	12·3	
		4×100m relay	F		2	47·0	S
Frizzell, Mildred	CAN	4×100m relay	F		2	47·0	S
Furtsch, E.	USA	4×100m relay	F		1	46·86*	G
Gindele, N.	USA	Javelin throw	F		5	37,95	
Gisolf, C.A.	HOL	High jump	F		4	1,58	
Hall, E.	USA	80m hurdles	1	2	1	12·0	
			F		2	11·7	S
Halstead, N.	GBR	4×100m relay	F		3	47·6	B
Harrington, E.	USA	100m	1	3	5	12·6	
Heublein, G.	GER	4×100m relay	F		6		
		Discus throw	F		5	34,66	
Hirohashi, Y.	JPN	High jump	F		8	1,49	
Hiscock, E.M.	GBR	100m	1	3	3	12·3	
			SF	2	3	12·0	
			F		5	12·3	
		4×100m relay	F		3	47·6	B
Ishizu, M.	JPN	Discus throw	F		7	33,52	
		Javelin throw	F		8	30,81	
Jenkins, M.	USA	Discus throw	F		9	30,22	
Johnson, E.	GBR	100m	1	4	5	13·9	
Kench, T.	NZL	100m	1	4	3	12·7	
			SF	1	6		
Muraoka, M.	JPN	4×100m relay	F		5	48·9	
Nakanishi, M.	JPN	80m hurdles	1	1	DNF		
		4×100m relay	F		5	48·9	
Notte, H.	GER	High jump	F		7	1,55	
Osburn, R.	USA	Discus throw	F		2	40,12	S
Palmer, L.	CAN	4×100m relay	F		2	47·0	S
Porter, G.A.	GBR	100m	1	1	4	12·4	
		4×100m relay	F		3	47·6	B
Rogers, A.J.	USA	4×100m relay	F		1	46·86*	G
		High jump	F		6	1,58	
Russell, G.	USA	Javelin throw	F		6	36,73	
Sagara, Y.	JPN	High jump	F		9	1,46	
Schabinska, F.	POL	80m hurdles	1	2	4	12·3	
Schaller, S.	USA	80m hurdles	1	1	2	11·8	
			F		4	11·9	
Schuurman, T.W.	HOL	100m	1	3	1	12·2	
			SF	1	4	12·4	
		4×100m relay	F		4	48·0	
Shibata, T.	JPN	100m	1	3	6	12·7	
Shiley, J.	USA	High jump	F		1	1,65*	G
Shimpo, M.	JPN	Javelin throw	F		4	39,07	
Strike, H.	CAN	100m	1	1	3	12·3	
			SF	1	1	12·4	
			F		2	11·9*	S
		4×100m relay	F		2	47·0	S
Taylor, B.	CAN	80m hurdles	1	1	4	12·0	
Uribe, M.	MEX	Javelin throw	F		7	33,66	
Vandervleit, M.	CAN	100m	1	3	2	12·3	
			SF	2	4		
Von Bremen, W.	USA	100m	1	1	2	12·3	
			SF	2	2	12·0	
			F		3	12·0	B
		4×100m relay	F		1	46·86*	G
Wajsowna, J.	POL	Discus throw	F		3	38,74	B
Walasiewicz, S.	POL	100m	1	2	1	11·9*	
			SF	2	1	11·9*	
			F		1	11·9*	G
		Discus throw	F		6	33,60	
Watanabe, S.	JPN	100m	1	2	3	12·2	
			SF	1	5		
		4×100m relay	F		5	48·9	
Wearne, A.E.	AUS	100m	1	3	4	12·5	
Webb, V.	GBR	80m hurdles	1	2	2	12·1	
			F		5	11·9	
		4×100m relay	F		3	47·6	B
Wilde, E.	USA	100m	1	4	1	12·4	
			SF	1	3	12·4	
			F		6	12·3	
Wilson, A.	CAN	80m hurdles	1	2	3	12·1	
			F		6	12·0	

Juan Carlos Zabala, the novice ruaner from the Argentine, ran himself to a standstill when winning the marathon.

All-Sport Photographic Ltd.

1936

Jesse Owens Mocks the Nazi Propaganda Machine

Unfortunately, the Berlin Olympic Games of 1936 have gone down in history more for the politics than the athletics. The world was preparing for the Second World War. The Spanish Civil War was beginning, and Adolf Hitler and his Nazi party had risen to power in Germany. Hitler used the Games as an opportunity to show the world the superiority of the Aryan race. Swastikas, the symbol of the Nazi party, were everywhere. There was martial music and the airship *Hindenburg* hovered over the stadium.

The Germans were to be, in fact, the most successful nation in the Games, but the whole plan misfired principally because of one man: the black American athlete Jesse Owens. Owens won the four gold medals and Hitler, it appeared, refused to shake his hand. For all the planning and expense of the Games the lasting memory is of this petty gesture to one poor black man, Owens, who defied the nation and the men who thought they were the most powerful in the world.

Men's Track Events

Traditionally, the **100 metres** commenced on the first day, where Jesse Owens won the last of the heats in an Olympic record equalling 10·3 sec. In the second round, he swept past Takayoshi Yoshioka of Japan to cut the tape in 10·2, a world best, which was later labelled as being wind-assisted. The next day the semi-finals were run. Owens took the first race from Frank Wykoff of the USA and Lennart Strancberg of Sweden in a moderate 10·4, and Ralph Metcalfe of the USA the second from Martinus Osendarp of Holland and Eric Borchmeyer of Germany in 10·5. An hour and a quarter later all was set for the final. Owens was off the blocks like a catapult, while Metcalfe had one of his worst starts, and was soon a couple of metres down on the leader. Slowly, he hauled back the field but was a stride short of Owens at the tape, with Osendarp just edging out Wykoff for the bronze medal. The time was an impressive 10·3.

The day after the short sprint final, the **200 metres** commenced with Jesse Owens breaking the Olympic record in the first round with 21·1 sec, a feat he also produced in the next round. In the first semi-final Mack Robinson, the US second string, equalled this, while Owens took it easy in the other semi-final, clocking 21·3 Osendarp and Paul Haenni of Switzerland behind him With the final underway, Owens glided around the turn and headed the field by two metres into the straight. With silk-like strides he raced to the tape, as behind him Robinson was getting the better of Osendarp, with the other three well back. Owens' time of 20·7 was an amazing one in such conditions, and it left the runner-up four metres adrift.

A novice, Archie Williams, a second year student at the University of California, was the fastest runner in the first round of the **400 metres**. In 1935 he had barely beaten 50·0 sec, but had set a world record of 46·1 in June 1936 and won his heat in 47·8. James Lu Valle of the USA was the fastest winner with 47·6 in the second round but Williams was quickest in the semi-finals, coming home from Bill Roberts of Britain and John Loaring of Canada in 47·2. Just over two hours later the runners were required to line-up for the final. Godfrey Brown of Britain, a class 100 yards sprinter, set off in the outside lane at an alarming rate, drawing Williams with him. He then eased a little which allowed Williams to pass him and Lu Valle to catch up. Realising his mistake, Brown made a tremendous effort along the finishing straight and had reduced a three-yard lead to a couple of feet at the tape. Williams was given a time of 46·5 and Brown an ungenerous 46·7, with Lu Valle pipping Roberts for the bronze. (Automatic timings: Williams 46·66, Brown 46·68 and Lu Valle 46·84).

For the final of the **800 metres**, John Woodruff's instructions were to take the lead and keep out of trouble. However, Phil Edwards of Canada led off in his usual way, and Woodruff, a superb black runner from the USA, was boxed-in, and allowed himself to drop back until he was last. Going into the back-straight of the final lap Edwards led, with Mario Lanzi of Italy on his shoulder, and Kazimiez Kucharski of Poland hanging on grimly. Woodruff, however, had plenty left and with a withering drive off the final bend he left the others in his wake in 1-52·9. Meanwhile, Lanzi helped by the shouts from Crown Prince Umberto, sitting beside Hitler, was just two yards short of an exhausted Woodruff at the tape, with Edwards holding off Kucharski for the bronze medal.

One of the classic races of the track, the **1,500 metres** turned out to be the race of the Games. Jack Lovelock of New Zealand, who had won the "dream mile" at Princeton in 1933, in a then world record, was up against a phalanx of stars: Glenn Cunningham of the USA, who held the mile record; Sydney Wooderson of Britain, who was to take the record the following year, Luigi Beccali of Italy, the holder of the Olympic title and former record holder at 1,500 metres, and two aspiring Americans in Archie San Romani and Gene Venzke. Sydney Wooderson was the only casualty in the heats among the favoured; he limped home with a broken bone in his foot. Twelve toed the line for the final and on the gun John Cornes of Britain, the silver medallist from four years earlier, broke away to stretch the field out over the first 300 metres. The German hope, Friedrich Schaumburg, then took over from Cornes, but by 700 metres Cunningham had gone to the front, to lead from Eric Ny of Sweden, Schaumburg, Lovelock and Beccali. At 900, Ny overtook Cunningham with San Romani moving up to fifth, but with the sound of the bell in his ears, Lovelock also whipped past Cunningham onto the shoulder of Ny. Coming off the turn into the final back straight, Lovelock made his great effort, to which Cunningham responded, but the New Zealander was now in top gear, and won by six metres in 3-47·8, a new world record. Cunningham was also under the old mark with 3-48·4, Beccali was third in 3-49·2, with San Romani at 3-50·0 and Edwards at 3-50·4 also bettered the previous Olympic record.

In the early stages of the **5,000 metres** final the lead was shared by Don Lash of the USA, Kohei Murakoso of Japan and the three Finnish runners, Gunnar Hoeckert, Lauri Lehtinen, the winner from Los Angeles, and Ilmari Salminen. Lash had burnt himself out by 3,000 metres and gradually dropped back, but the procession continued until two laps from home where Hoeckert went ahead and forced the pace. As he did so, Salminen tripped and fell, picked himself up, but had lost 50 metres. At the bell Hoeckert led Lehtinen by two metres, with Murakoso and John Jonsson of Sweden following and he continued to extend his lead throughout the last lap to win in 14-22·2, a new Olympic record. The previous holder, Lehtinen was timed in 14-25·8 and Jonsson out-kicked Murakoso for the bronze medal.

The **10,000 metres** was a straight final run on the first day of the athletic competitions, with 29 contenders. At the half-way stage, Kohei Murakoso of Japan led the three Finns, Ilmari Salminen, Arvo Askola and Volmari Iso-Hollo. On the 13th lap Askola took up the running and the Finns began taking it in turns to lead. At the bell Salminen went into overdrive and pulled Askola with him, but even he could not sustain the pace as Salminen's long legs took him to the finishing line in 30-15·4. Askola took the silver in 30-15·6 while Iso-Hollo out-paced Murakoso for the bronze in 30-20·2.

Japan had stamped a mark on **marathon** running some eight years before, although two of their three competitors were actually born in Korea, then part of the Japanese Empire. The reigning champion, Juan Carlos Zabala of Argentina, led the 56 runners on the track before they pounded the mostly flat macadam roads. For 28 of the 42 kilometres Zabala led a following group of Manoel Dias of Portugal, Kitei Son of Japan and Ernest Harper of Britain, with the eventual bronze medallist, Shoryu Nan of Japan, well back in the middle

of the field. Dias was the first to crack of the leading group, and when Zabala fell back at 19km, Son took up the lead with Harper trailing him. Son gradually drew away from Harper at 32km, with Nan only three minutes behind the Briton in third place. So it continued, with Son drawing away and Nan catching Harper. Son entered the stadium and finished like a sprinter in 2:29-19·2, a new Olympic record, while Harper, a very tired man, came home in 2:31-23·2, also under the Olympic record. Nan was not far behind in 2:31-42·0 with the two Finns Erkki Tamila and Vaino Muinonen fourth and fifth.

Forrest Towns of the USA was the clear favourite for the **110 metres hurdles** following his 14·1 sec world record in America, and he equalled his world record in the semi-final. In the final, Fred Pollard of the USA made a blitz start and led the notoriously slow starter Towns by half-a-metre, but Towns caught his fellow American at the third hurdle and went on to win in 14·2. Meanwhile, Pollard was heading Don Finlay of Britain until he clipped the last barrier and Finlay slipped ahead for the silver. Both were timed at 14·4, together with Hakan Lidman of Sweden who was fourth. Incidentally, the L-shaped tilt hurdle was used for the very first time during this event.

Miguel White of the Philippines was the fastest qualifier of the six heats of the **400 metres hurdles** in 53·4 sec. Next day, in the semi-finals, Glenn Hardin, of the USA, the world record holder, won the first in 53·2 from White 53·4 and Christos Mantikas of Greece 53·5. But that was not as quick as Joe Patterson of the USA's nippy 52·8 in the second semi to beat off the Canadian, John Loaring, who recorded 53·1. In the final, Hardin drew the outside lane, while Patterson was on the inside and at the half way stage he was actually down on Patterson, despite the difference in stagger. Patterson, however, paid for his pace over the third 100 metres. It was here that Hardin put in a strong surge and entered the straight one metre up on Loaring, Patterson and White who were practically level. From now on it was down to the strongest, and Hardin won in 52·4, 1·8 sec outside his world record. Second was Loaring in 52·7 and the bronze went to White in 52·8, while Patterson staggered home fourth in 53·0.

The final of the **3,000 metres steeplechase** saw Willy

All-Sport Photographic Ltd.

Jesse Owens

Jesse Owens ranks among the world's all-time great athletes.

He was born in Danville, Alabama, on 12 September 1913, one of eleven children of poor parents.

As he developed as an athlete, University coaches showered him with offers of sport scholarships. Asked his name, he said "JC", which sounded like "Jesse", by which he became famous. He chose Ohio State, and competing in a major meet at Ann Arbor, Michigan, in 1935 he bettered five world records and tied another, all in less than an hour. His new world marks were for 220 yards, 200 metres, 220 yards hurdles, 200 metres hurdles and the long jump. His long jump of 8,13m (26ft 8¼in) stood unbeaten for 25 years.

Jesse's fame soared even higher when at the Berlin Olympics the following year he ignored the German jibes against black competitors and won gold medals for the 100 metres, 200 metres, long jump and 4 × 100 metres relay.

Turning professional after the Games, he became heavily in debt through business failures. Years later he was appointed an official international representative for his country in affairs associated with sport and became a much admired "ambassador" for the USA. He married when 18 and had three daughters by his wife Ruth. He died on 31 March 1980.

Heyn of Germany go in to an early lead over the 12-strong field, but by 300 metres, Volmari Iso-Hollo, of Finland, the defending champion, had taken command and set a hot pace. Only Martti Matilainen tried to go with him, but in the fourth lap he cracked. Iso-Hollo built up a lead of 30 metres and won without troubling himself in 9-03·8, a new Olympic record. The chasing group of Kaarlo Tuominen, Matilainen, both of Finland, Alfred Dompert of Germany and Harold Manning of the USA gave it their all for the minor places. Tuominen won the battle for the silver in 9-06·8, closing up on the winner and Dompert passed Matilainen 200 metres from the finish to secure the bronze medal in 9-07·2. Matilainen and Manning, with 9-09·0 and 9-11·2 respectively, were also both inside the previous Olympic record.

Thirty-one competitors set out for the **50 kilometres walk** on an out and back course through the Grunewald Forest. Harold Whitlock of Britain was one of the last to leave the stadium, although he was back in the pack at 10km. At this stage, Friedrich Prehn of Germany was in the lead, but at 20km it was the turn of Czechoslovakian Jaroslav Stork to spearhead the walkers. Whitlock was now in ninth position, moving up all the time, and at 30km he was only a minute behind the leader, Janis Dalinsh of Latvia. When Dalinsh dropped out at 33km, the Briton could not be stopped and won in a new Olympic record of 4:30-41·4. Tell Schwab of Switzerland worked his way through for a silver medal in 4:32-09·2 and Adalberta Bubenko of Latvia claimed the bronze with 4:32-42·2.

With the strength of America's sprinters, it was a foregone conclusion that they would win the **4 × 100 metres relay**. The US team earmarked were Foy Draper, Frank Wykoff, Sam Stoller and Marty Glickman, the latter two being Jewish. America's head coach, Lawson Robinson, got wind that both the Dutch and German teams had run trials in 40·5 and rescheduled the team to exclude the two Jewish members and include Jesse Owens and Ralph Metcalfe. He was accused of being anti-Jewish on the grounds that both Stoller and Glickman had recently beaten Draper in trials. The American team went on to clock 40·0 sec in the heats to equal the world and Olympic record, and they improved to 39·8 in the final to take the premier position and gold medals. Italy surprised everyone with their slick baton changing to take second place, despite four moderate sprinters, while Germany was third, and the other medal favourites, Holland, were disqualified.

Whilst coach Lawson was probably right in picking a strong 4 × 100 metres squad, he did not pay the same attention to his **4 × 400 metres relay** team. He left out his two fastest men, Archie Williams and James Lu Valle and the inevitable happened. Great Britain produced four runners as good as the best Americans: Fred Wolff, Godfrey Rampling, Bill Roberts and Godfrey Brown They ran 3-09·0, the second fastest time ever, to take the gold medals. Their splits were respectively 49·2; 46·7 46·4, 46·7. The Americans clocked 3-11·0 and Germany just beat Canada for third place, both being given 3-11·8.

Men's Field Events

There was a quiet revolution taking placing in the world of the **high jump**, where the new technique of straddling the bar had taken hold. When the bar reached 1,97 metres there were three Americans, three Japanese, two Finns and a German left in the competition. The three

Glenn Cunningham of the USA, overcame childhood disability to place second against Jack Lovelock in the 1,500 metres. All-Sport Photographic Ltd.

A view of the 400 metres hurdles field at the second flight. Glenn Hardin (nearest camera) won the race in 52·4 sec for the States. Dave Terry

On the line, the coloured American Archie Williams, pips Godfrey Brown of Britain in the 400 metres final.

Dave Terry

Dave Terry

Volmari Iso-Hollo

Born on 1 May 1907 at Ylojarvi, Finland, Volmari Iso-Hollo became one of the famed "Flying Finns" of the 1930s and the only man to successfully defend his Olympic 3,000m steeplechase title. The first of his Olympic successes was achieved at the 1932 Games in Los Angeles, where after finishing second in the 10,000m, he set an Olympic record of 9-14·6 in the 3,000m steeplechase heats the next day. Consequently surprise was expressed when subsequently he won the final and his time had slowed to 10-33·4. An immediate inquiry revealed that the scorer had missed a lap, which led to the finalists running an extra 460 metres.

There were no such upsets at Berlin four years later, where Iso-Hollo improved the Olympic record to 9-03·8. And he was also third in a clean sweep by the Finns in the 10,000 metres.

He was often regarded as "the grandmaster without a world record". This was due to steeplechase times in those days not being recognised. On the one occasion he did break a world record, over 5,000m in 1932, he had to be content with second place behind his countryman, Lauri Lehtinen.

Iso-Hollo was never quite as enthusiastic about training, which many considered was the reason he did not reach his full potential. He died on 23 June 1969.

Dave Terry

Forest Towns

Forest Towns, born in 1914, was the first man to break the 14 sec barrier for the 110m hurdles. His time of 13·7 sec at the Bislett Stadium, Oslo, in 1936 was four-tenths of a second inside the previous best. Because of this exceptional margin, International Amateur Athletic Association officials became dubious of its authenticity — so dubious that it took two years to be officially ratified. It stood as the record for 14 years.

Earlier that same season the 6ft 2in (1.88m) American from Georgia, showed what a gifted hurdler he was by breaking the world record for the first time, with 14·1 sec in the US national collegiate championships, a performance that made him a hot favourite for the Olympic title in Berlin. There he maintained his exceptional form by repeating the 14·1 sec in his semi-final and winning the final by three metres from the British champion, Donald Finlay, in 14·2 sec.

The progress of the world record from Town's 13·7 sec to the present day world best of 12·93 sec, serves to convince many who have studied film of the American's run that, because his superb hurdling technique and speed between his take-offs were so exceptional for those years, there really wasn't anything phoney about his time.

The last lap of the 800 metres final sees Phil Edwards of Canada, leading the eventual winner, John Woodruff of America. Dave Terry

Americans cleared this height, as did Kotkas of Finland and Kimio Yata of Japan, but at 2,00, the Japanese jumper was eliminated. The bar was then raised to 2,03 and only Cornelius Johnson succeeded, to take the gold and Olympic record. He next tried for the world record height of 2,08, but it eluded him. A jump-off decided the silver for Dave Albritton and bronze for Delos Thurber, both of the USA.

One man who was not in Berlin for the **pole vault** was the world record holder George Varoff, who had only come fourth in the American trials at 4,27 metres. The vault was a two-way fight for the medals between the USA and Japan. Four jumpers managed to lever themselves over 4·25, but only Earle Meadows of the USA went higher to 4,35 for the gold and Olympic record. The bar was then lowered to 4,25 under the jump-off rules and William Sefton of the USA failed, which left Shuhei Nishida and Sueo Oe, both of Japan, to jump again. The Japanese team manager would not allow this, nominating Nishida for the silver and Oe for the bronze. Back in Japan, the two medals were cut in half and brazed together again — half silver, half bronze.

The **long jump** is still one of the most talked about events in athletic history and Jesse Owens nearly did not make it, when a run-through and one foul, left one jump between him and the final. Advised by fellow competitor Lutz Long of Germany to play safe and jump well before the board, Jesse made it on his third attempt. With his first jump of the final, Owens set a new Olympic record

of 7,74 metres. In the second round, Long equalled this jump, but Jesse responded with 7,87. Again, in the fifth round Long matched Owens' 7,87 and Jesse improved once more to 7,94. In the last round he extended his lead to 8,06, 33 centimetres better than the previous Olympic record. Lutz Long took the silver with 7,87 and the bronze medal went to Naota Tajima of Japan.

For more than ten years Japan had been producing world class performers in the **triple jump** and 1936 was no exception. In the first round of the finals Naoto Tajima leapt 15,76 metres, within two centimetres of the world record. Three rounds later he extended his mark to the magic 16,00 barrier, a performance he achieved on a diet of early morning knee-bends. The Japanese second string, Masao Harada, waited for the final round to seize the silver medal with a 15,66 jump and Jack Metcalfe of Australia took third position with his opening jump of 15,50.

Jack Torrance, the 280lb American world record holder for the **shot put** at 17,40 metres was, with Hans Woellke of Germany the joint favourite to take the title, but Jack was sadly off form and could only finish fifth. Woellke started with a 15,96 heave, but was overtaken in the second round by Sulo Barlund of Finland with 16,03. Barlund improved to 16,12 in the fifth round, but Woellke, using all his aggression, exceeded the Finns put with 16,20 to take the gold record. Gerhard Stock of Germany was placed third with 15,66. Woellke's reward came when General Goering raised him from a police sergeant to a lieutenant.

Willy Schroeder of Germany was the world record holder in the **discus throw** at 53,10 metres, but Ken Carpenter of the USA was nearly as good. Carpenter took time to get into his throwing and after three rounds he was lying third with 48,98, behind Gordon "Slinger" Dunn, the US number two, who was on 49,36 and the Italian Giorgio Oberweger on 49,23. However, in the fifth round Carpenter flipped the platter to a new Olympic record of 50,48, while the other two failed to improve and had to settle for silver and bronze. Schroeder, who threw 47,93 for fifth spot, was unable to lift himself despite the German crowd chanting: "Take your discus in you hand and throw it for the fatherland".

By 1936 the mastery of **hammer throw**ing had fallen to the Europeans. The only notable absentee was Jaroslav Knotek, the 55 metre Czech thrower, leaving three men with a gold medal chance: Karl Hein and Erwin Blask of Germany and Fred Warngard of Sweden. Their first round throws were all very close, at just over the 52 metre line. However, in the second round Blask blasted off a 55,04 effort. Warngard responded with 54,03 in the third and in the next round he moved closer to Blask with 54,83, while Hein produced his first decent throw with 54,70. With perfect timing, Hein rotated and launched his final throw — 56,49 and the gold was his. Both Blask in second and Warngard in third exceeded the old Olympic record.

Matti Jaervinen, known to his fellow throwers as "Mr Javelin" was both world record holder and the reigning Olympic champion for the **javelin throw**. Matti started well, leading the field in the first round with 68,30 metres, but the next round saw the rising Finnish star Yrjo Nikkanen take the lead with 70,77. The fifth round settled where the medals were going. Adolf Hitler had shortly taken his seat in his box and Gerhard Stock of Germany took the opportunity to show what he could do: 71,84, good enough for the gold medal. Kalervo Toivonen of Finland next showed what he could do with a 70,72 launch for the bronze behind Nikkanen's silver effort. Jarvinen could only manage fifth place, 7,48 down on his world record.

Glenn Morris came to the **decathlon** in 1936 and left it in 1936. In two competitions he broke the world record twice. The first occasion was to qualify for the Olympics and the second was to win an Olympic medal. Then he was off to Hollywood to star in films. Morris's principal competition came from his team-mates Bob Clark, who finished second, and Jack Parker, who was third. Clark took an early lead due to an excellent long jump of 7,62 metres. Morris was tops in the 100 metres with 10.9, in the shot with 14,40 and in the 400 with 49·4, where he finally overtook Clark. The second day of the event saw Morris stretching his lead all the way: hurdles 14.9, discus 43,02, pole vault 3,80 and javelin 54,52. With only the 1,500 to go he was within striking distance of his recent record of 7,884 points, but he needed to run the race 15 seconds faster than he had ever done before. With the help of fellow competitor Maurice Boulanger, Glenn Morris achieved his target with 7,900 points — a new Olympic and world record. Clark scored 7,601 and Parker 7,275.

Women's Events

Asked how come she was so speedy, Helen Stephens replied: "I guess it came from chasing jack rabbits on dad's farm". In the **100 metres** heats, Stephens, of the USA, ran 11·4, two metres faster than the listed world record, with the next competitor 10 metres back. An 11·5 semi-final and Helen was ready to show those other girls how to really sprint. The three German girls in the final got away first, but from 20 metres it was Stephens all the way in 11·5 over her main rival Stella Walasiewicz of Poland, in 11·7, with Kath Krauss at 11·9, proving the best of the German girls. Unfortunately, all three winning times were wind assisted and could not be accepted as Olympic records.

Trebisonda Valla of Italy quickly made her mark by recording a wind-assisted 11·6 sec in the semi-finals of the **80 metres hurdles**, equal to the world record. But in the final, five of the six girls crossed the last flight of hurdles in a line and it took half an hour to sort out the placings as the photo-finish timer had to be consulted. The confirmed times were Valla 11·75, Anny Steur of Germany 11·81 and Elizabeth Taylor of Canada 11·81.

Undoubtedly the fastest team in the **4 × 100 metres relay** was Germany who had clocked a new world record of 46·4 sec in the preliminaries and were looking to reduce this time in the finals. As predicted, they ran away from the USA, Britain, Canada, Italy and Holland, for whom Fanny Blankers-Koen was running. They were ten metres in the lead at the last change-over, when Ilse Doerffeldt dropped the baton. The USA went on to win in 46·9, from Britain in 47·6 and Canada in 47·8. Ilse broke down in tears, to be comforted by the Fuhrer later on.

Fraulein Margarete Bergmann was a Jewess and lived in Stuttgart in Fascist-occupied Germany. She was also the best female **high jump**er that Germany had in 1936, having cleared 1,60 metres in her home town five weeks before the Games. But Bergmann was not allowed to compete in the German championships, nor the Olympics. With the competition well into the latter stages, five girls cleared 1,58 and the bar was raised to 1,60. At this height, both Dora Ratjen of Germany and Marguerite Nicolas of France failed and the bar was raised to 1,62, where the three remaining jumpers also failed. They were each given to a fourth chance under the jump-off process and Ibolya Csak of Hungary cleared to claim the gold medal, although her winning height was officially shown as 1,60. The bar was lowered to 1,60, and Dorothy Odam of Britain succeeded and took the silver, leaving Elfriede Kaun of Germany with the bronze. Later, it was discovered that Ratjen was a hermaphrodite and her name was struck off the list of competitors.

Gisela Mauermayer of Germany was the current world record holder for the **discus throw**, while Jadwiga Wajsowna of Poland was the previous holder. The competition was decided in the first round when Mauermayer threw an Olympic record of 47,63, to Wajsowna's 44,69. Although the Polish girl improved to 46,22, it was not enough and she had to settle for second place. Some way behind, with 39,80, Paula Mollenhauer of Germany claimed the third place.

Poland's Maria Kwasniewska's first round leading toss of 41,80 metres in the **javelin throw** was short lived when Tilly Fleischer of Germany soared one out to 44,69 in the second round and improved to 45,18 in the fifth. Meanwhile, fellow German Luise Kreuger threw 43,29 in the third round to take the silver, thus leaving Kwasniewska with the bronze. Immediately after the medal ceremony, the girls were conducted to Hitler's box where handshaking and backslapping took place.

Kitei Son, the Korean athlete running for Japan, leads the marathon field from the stadium.

All-Sport Photographic Ltd.

All-Sport Photographic Ltd.

Harold Whitlock

Britain for many years has been a country possessing outstanding long distance walkers, so it was pleasing for them to see a 50km walk introduced to the Olympic programme in 1932. Tommy Green, a 39-year-old railway worker from England, became the first to win the title — and by as much as seven minutes. By this time, Harold Whitlock, a London automobile mechanic, was beginning to figure prominently on the distance walking scene. He captured his first major title when in 1933, aged 29, he won the English 50km championship.

Securing the national title again in 1935 and 1936, Whitlock became an obvious choice for the Olympics in Berlin. There he repeated his splendid form by winning the gold medal in 4:30-41·1, almost 20 minutes faster than Green's 1932 win.

Whitlock was not without his problems in that race. After moving into the lead at 33km he became ill and was sick for a stretch of more than 5km. Still he kept walking and recovered to win by a wide margin, becoming Britain's only individual title winner at the Berlin Games.

He won the English title for another three years and even after the Second World War he was back in racing action. Whitlock was still representing Britain at the Helsinki Olympics in 1952 at the age of 48.

COMPETITOR	COUNTRY CODE	EVENT	ROUND	HEAT	PLACE	TIME & DISTANCE	MEDAL
Csanyi, Z.	HUN	Decathlon	F		DNF		
Cuba, A.	PER	100m	1	4	5		
Cunningham, G.	USA	1500m	1	1	2	3-54.8	
			F		2	3-48.4	S
Cuzol, R.	FRA	3000m steeplechase	1	1	9		
Daellenbach, F.	SUI	Decathlon	F		13	6311	
Dahlgren, L.E.	SWE	Decathlon	F		DNF		
Dalins, J.	LAT	50k walk	F		DNF		
Danielsson, O.G.A.	SWE	400m	1	1	2	48.6	
			2	3	4	49.6	
		4×400m relay	1	2	2	3-14.6	
			F		5	3-13.0	
Dannaher, P.	SAF	100m	1	2	2	11.0	
			2	4	6		
		200m	1	5	5		
		4×100m relay	1	1	3	41.7	
Daranyi, J.	HUN	Shot put	F		12	14,63	
Dawson, G.W.	USA	3000m steeplechase	1	1	4	9-29.2	
			F		8	9-21.2	
De Bruyn, P.	GER	Marathon	F		DNF		
De Castro Mello, I.	BRA	High jump	Q		DNQ	1,80	
Deckard, T.M.	USA	5000m	1	2	9		
De Guzman, N.	PHI	100m	1	7	3	11.1	
		200m	1	3	5		
De La Guerra, C.	PER	Long jump	Q		DNQ		
Del Vecchio, P.	COL	Triple jump	Q		DNQ		
Demetropoulos, C.	GRE	Hammer throw	Q		DNQ		
De Oliveira, M.C.	BRA	Long jump	F		15	7,05	
Desroches, R.	FRA	3000m steeplechase	1	2	7		
Dessecker, W.	GER	800m	1	6	3	1-56.0	
			2	1	5	1-55.3	
Devrint, D.	BEL	100m	1	12	4		
		200m	1	8	4		
Dias, M.	POR	Marathon	F		17	2:49-00.0	
Dickinson, B.C.	AUS	Triple jump	F		16	14,48	
Dill, H.	GER	50k walk	F		16	4:51-26.0	
Dimsa, J.	LAT	Decathlon	F		DNF		
Doitschev, L.	BUL	Decathlon	F		14	6307	
Dominos, X.	BRA	100m	1	9	5		
Dompert, A.	GER	3000m steeplechase	1	1	1	9-27.2	
			F		3	9-07.2	B
Dondelinger, F.	FRA	200m	1	2	5		
		4×100m relay	1	2	4	42.6	
Douda, F.	TCH	Shot put	F		7	15,28	
Drake, N.H.	GBR	Hammer throw	Q		DNQ		
Draper, F.	USA	4×100m relay	1	1	1	40.0*	
			F		1	39.8*	G
Dreyer, H.F.	USA	Hammer throw	F		9	50,42	
Dunn, G.G.	USA	Discus throw	F		2	49,36	S
Du Plessis, A.S.	SAF	Pole vault	F		=17	3,80	
Duval, F.	FRA	Marathon	F		16	2:48-39.8	
Eaton, W.E.	GBR	10000m	F				
Ebeid, M.E.	EGY	400m	1	3	4	50.5	
Edfeldt, P.O.	SWE	4×400m relay	1	2	2	3-14.6	
			F		5	3-13.0	
Edwards, P.A.	CAN	800m	1	1	1	1-53.7	
			2	2	3	1-53.2	
			F		3	1-53.6	B
		1500m	1	3	3	3-56.2	
			F		5	3-50.4	
		4×400m relay	1	3	2	3-15.0	
			F		4	3-11.8	
Eggenberg, R.	SUI	High jump	F		=12	1,85	
Eha, F.	SUI	Marathon	F		39	3:18-17.0	
Eichberger, F.	AUT	800m	1	5	3	1-56.3	
			2	1	6	1-56.2	
		1500m	1	4	6	3-59.2	
Ekholdt, R.	NOR	1500m	1	4	7		
Ekman, J.H.	SWE	3000m steeplechase	1	1	6	9-43.2	
Elias, J.	TCH	Hammer throw	Q		DNQ		
El Sayed, I.K.O.	EGY	Javelin throw	Q		DNQ		
Enochsson, T.S.	SWE	Marathon	F		10	2:43-12.0	
Evenson, T.	GBR	3000m steeplechase	1	1	5	9-41.2	
Facelli, L.	ITA	400m hurdles	1	2	3	55.1	
Fahoum, G.	EGY	100m	1	5	4		
		200m	1	6	4		
Farias, R.J.	PER	Marathon	F		42	3:33-24.0	
Favor, D.E.	USA	Hammer throw	F		6	51,01	
Ferrario, A.	ITA	4×400m relay	1	3	4	3-16.6	
Fialka, K.	POL	Marathon	F		DNF		
Finlay, D.O.	GBR	110m hurdles	1	3	1	14.7	
			SF	2	1	14.5	
			F		2	14.4	S
		4×100m relay	1	2	4	42.4	
Firea, V.	RUM	50k walk	F		20	5:09-39.0	
Fischer, F.	AUT	5000m	1	1	11		
Fitch, A.L.	USA	4×400m relay	1	1	1	3-13.0	
			F		2	3-11.0	S
Flachberger, F.	AUT	High jump	Q		DNQ	1,80	
Fondevila, A.E.	ARG	100m	1	9	3	11.0	
		200m	1	6	6		
Francis, S.H.	USA	Shot put	F		4	15,45	
Frangoudis, R.	GRE	100m	1	11	3	10.8	
		200m	1	5	2	22.1	
			2	2	4		
Frick, X.	LIE	100m	1	9	6		
		200m	1	2	6		
Fritsch, H.	GER	Discus throw	F		11	45,10	
Fritsch, W.	CHI	400m hurdles	1	5	6	58.3	
Fritz, W.D.	CAN	400m	1	7	2	49.0	
			2	2	3	48.4	
			SF	2	3	47.4	
			F		5	47.8	
		4×400m relay	1	3	2	3-15.0	
			F		4	3-11.8	
Fu, B.L.	CHN	Pole vault	F		=17	3,80	
Fukuda, T.	JPN	400m hurdles	1	1	4	56.8	
Gaillard, L.	FRA	400m hurdles	1	2	5	56.4	
Gall, L.	RUM	Marathon	F		23	2:55-02.0	
Gancarz, B.	POL	Marathon	F		33	3:03-11.0	
Gebhardt, M.	GER	10000m	F		7	31-29.6	
Geeraert, R.	BEL	1500m	1	1	7		
Gehmert, G.	GER	High jump	F		=10	1,90	
Genghini, A.	ITA	Marathon	F		DNF		
Georgaco-poulos, G.	GRE	800m	1	5	6	1-57.3	
		1500m	1	1	6	4-01.4	
Gerdes, F.	GER	Javelin throw	F		=17	55,93	
Gero, G.	HUN	100m	1	8	3	11.3	
Gibson, H.A.	SAF	Marathon	F		8	2:38-04.0	
Gillmeister, E.	GER	4×100m relay	1	3	1	41.4	
			F		3	41.2	B
Ginty, J.	GBR	3000m steeplecahse	1	3	5	9-56.6	
Glatigny, A.	FRA	1500m	1	3	6	3-59.6	
Gobbato, G.	ITA	50k walk	F		14	4:49-51.0	
Goic, P.	YUG	Hammer throw	Q		DNQ		
Goix, R.	FRA	1500m	1	4	1	3-54.0	
			F		8	3-53.8	
Gonnelli, T.	ITA	4×100m relay	1	1	2	41.1	
			F		2	41.1	S
Gonzales, V.	MEX	5000m	1	2	13		
Gorsek, E.	YUG	800m	1	2	5	1-59.5	
		1500m	1	2	8		
Graber, W.N.	USA	Pole vault	F		5	4,15	
Graham, R.	GBR	1500m	1	3	4	3-56.6	
Grandin, G.	SWE	50k walk	F		DIS		
Greulich, B.	GER	Hammer throw	F		7	50,61	
Grimbeek, E.	SAF	100m	1	3	2	10.9	
			2	2	5		
		200m	1	7	2	21.8	
			2	3	3	21.94	
			SF	1	6		
		4×100m relay	1	1	3	41.7	
Gudenus, J.B.	AUT	400m	1	2	5	52.9	
Guhl, A.	SUI	Decathlon	F		6	7033	
Guillez, G.	FRA	4×400m relay	1	3	3	3-15.2	
Gutierrez, C.E.	COL	100m	1	4	6		
		Javelin throw	Q		DNQ		
Gutierrez, P.	MEX	Long jump	Q		DNQ		
Gyenes, G.	HUN	100m	1	4	1	10.7	
			2	1	5		
		200m	1	4	2	22.1	
			2	4	4		
		4×100m relay	1	2	3	42.0	
Haenni, P.	SUI	100m	1	11	1	10.7	
			2	2	2	10.6	
			SF	1	4	10.7	
		200m	1	5	1	21.9	
			2	1	2	21.39	
			SF	2	3	21.6	
			F		4	21.6	
		4×100m relay	1	3	4	42.2	
Haley, J.	CAN	High jump	F		=12	1,85	
Hamann, H,	GER	4×400m relay	1	3	1	3-15.0	
			F		3	3-11.8	S
Handley, F.R.	GBR	800m	1	4	4	1-58.9	
			2	1	8		
Hansen, R.	NOR	5000m	1	2	5	15-12.6	
			F		9	14-48.0	
Harada, M.	JPN	Long jump	Q		DNQ		
		Triple jump	F		2	15,66	S
Haralambieff, B.	BUL	Marathon	F		36	3:08-53.8	

COMPETITOR	COUNTRY CODE	EVENT	ROUND	HEAT	PLACE	TIME & DISTANCE	MEDAL
Harbig, R.	GER	800m	1	1	6	1-56.3	
		4×400m relay	1	3	1	3-15.0	
			F		3	3-11.3	B
Hardin, G.F.	USA	400m hurdles	1	6	1	53.5	
			SF	1	1	53.15	
			F		1	52.4	G
Harper, E.	GBR	Marathon	F		2	2:31-23.2	S
Hartikka, N.	FIN	1500m	1	4	5	3-59.0	
Haugland, E.	NOR	Triple jump	F		14	14,56	
Haunzwickel, J.	AUT	Pole vault	F		=6	4,00	
Havalet, P.	RUM	Discus throw	Q		DNQ		
Hedvall, A.	SWE	Discus throw	F		8	46,20	
Heim, C.	FRA	Long jump	Q		DNQ		
Hein, K.	GER	Hammer throw	F		1	56,49*	G
Heino, S.	FIN	Hammer throw	F		10	49,93	
Hellstroem, B.J.	SWE	5000m	1	2	4	15-12.0	
			F		14		
Hemmer, P.	LUX	800m	1	1	5	1-56.3	
		1500m	1	1	10		
Henry, G.	FRA	400m	1	2	1	49.2	
			2	2	5	49.4	
		4×400m relay	1	3	4	3-15.2	
Heyn, W.	GER	3000m steeplechase	1	2	3	9-41.2	
			F		9	9-26.4	
Hillbrecht, G.	GER	Discus throw	Q		DNQ		
Hoeckert, G.	FIN	5000m	1	2	1	15-10.2	
			F		1	14-22.2*	G
Hoffmann, J.	TCH	Long jump	Q		DNQ		
Hofman, K.	POL	High jump	Q		DNQ	1,70	
		Triple jump	Q		DNQ		
Hofmeister, C.	ARG	200m	1	8	3	22.3	
			2	2	6		
		4×100m relay	1	2	2	41.3	
			F		4	42.2	
Holmes, C.B.	GBR	100m	1	11	2	10.8	
			2	1	6		
Holmqvist, H.E.	SWE	3000m steeplechase	1	2	4	9-44.4	
			F		DNF		
Hopkins, J.	GBR	50k walk	F		DNF		
Hoplicek, K.	TCH	Shot put	F		15	14,12	
Hornberger, G.	GER	100m	1	6	2	10.7	
			2	1	4	10.7	
		4×100m relay	1	3	1	41.4	
			F		3	41.2	B
Hornbostel, C.C.	USA	800m	1	1	2	1-53.7	
			2	3	1	1-53.2	
			F		5	1-54.2	
Horvath, I.	HUN	Shot put	F		14	14,32	
Hosek, B.	TCH	1500m	1	3	5	3-59.4	
		3000m steeplechase	1	1	7		
Hosek, V.	TCH	3000m steeplechase	1	2	8		
Houtzager, J.M.F.	HOL	Hammer throw	Q		DNQ		
Huber, E.	GER	Decathlon	F		4	7087	
Huebscher, E.	AUT	800m	1	2	4	1-57.3	
			2	2	7		
		1500m	1	2	9		
Humber, A.B.	CAN	100m	1	8	2	10.8	
			2	3	5		
		200m	1	4	1	22.1	
			2	2	3	22.1	
			SF	2	5	22.0	
		4×100m relay	1	3	2	41.5	
			F		5	42.7	
Huruta, Y.	JPN	110m hurdles	1	1	6		
Husek J.	TCH	3000m steeplechase	1	3	8		
Ichihara, M.	JPN	400m hurdles	1	3	4	54.7	
		4×400m relay	1	1	4	3-13.4	
Igloi, M.	HUN	1500m	1	1	5	3-55.0	
Imai, K.	JPN	400m	1	5	5	51.0	
		3000m steeplechase	1	2	9		
Ingvarsson, S.	ISL	100m	1	6	5		
Innocenti, P.	ITA	Pole vault	F		=6	4,00	
Ionescu, C.	RUM	Long jump	Q		DNQ		
Iso-Hollo, V.	FIN	10000m	F		3	30-20.2	B
		3000m steeplechase	1	2	1	9-34.0	
			F		1	9-03.8*	G
Ivanovic, I.S.	YUG	110m hurdles	1	6	2	15.1	
			SF	2	4	15.2	
		400m hurdles	1	5	3	54.7	
Ja, K.	CHN	Discus throw			DNQ		
Jaervinen, A.	FIN	Decathlon	F		DNF		
Janausch, E.	AUT	Discus throw	Q		DNQ		
		Hammer throw	Q		DNQ		
Jansson, A.G.	SWE	5000m	1	1	6	15-10.4	
Jansson, J.-G.	SWE	Hammer throw	F		12	49,28	
Jarvinen, M.	FIN	Javelin throw	F		5	69,18	
Joch, E.	GER	Triple jump	F		7	14,88	
Johannesen, H.	NOR	800m	1	3	3	1-54.9	
			2	3	6	1-56.0	
Johnson, C.C.	USA	High jump	F		1	2,03*	G
Johnson, T.L.	GBR	50k walk	F		17	4:54-56.0	
Jonsson, H.J.	SWE	5000m	1	3	1	14-54.6	
			F		3	14-29.0	B
Joye, P.	FRA	400m hurdles	1	1	3	54.1	
		4×400m relay	1	3	3	3-15.2	
Jud, A.	SUI	400m	1	1	4	49.4	
		4×100m relay	1	3	4	42.2	
Juergis, O.	LAT	Javelin throw	F		13	60,71	
Kalima, L.	FIN	High jump	F		=6	1,94	
Kappler, E.	RUM	400m	1	4	5	50.4	
Kelen, J.	HUN	5000m	1	2	10		
		10000m	F		12	32-01.0	
Kelley, J.A.	USA	Marathon	F		18	2:49-32.4	
Kennedy, R.K.I.	GBR	High jump	Q		DNQ	1,80	
Kersch, M.	GER	100m	1	1	3	10.8	
Khaleb, N.	FRA	Marathon	F		12	2:45-34.0	
Khan, M.M.	AFG	100m	1	3	6		
		Long jump	Q		DNQ		
Klasek, M.	TCH	Pole vault	F		=17	3,80	
Klasema, M.	HOL	Long jump	Q		DNQ		
		Triple jump	F		15	14,55	
Klein, J.	TCH	Javelin throw	Q		DNQ		
		Decathlon	F		16	5883	
Kleut, N.	YUG	Discus throw	Q		DNQ		
Klupsch, R.	GER	400m	1	8	3	49.1	
			2	4	4	48.8	
Knenicky, K.	TCH	400m	1	2	2	49.6	
			2	4	6	49.6	
		4×400m relay	1	3	5	3-22.0	
Knotek, J.	TCH	Hammer throw	Q		DNQ		
Koehler, E.	USA	50k walk	F		23	5:20-18.2	
Koenig, A.	AUT	200m	1	8	6		
		400m	1	8	4	49.4	
Koltai, H.	HUN	Long jump	Q		DNQ		
Komanek, L.	TCH	110m hurdles	1	3	5		
Korejs, J.	TCH	Pole vault	F		=6	4,00	
Kotkas, K.	FIN	High jump	F		4	2,00	
		Discus throw	Q		DNQ		
Kotratschek, K.	AUT	Triple jump	F		23	13,15	
Koutonen, A.	FIN	Hammer throw	F		4	51,90	
Kovacevic, A.	YUG	Shot put	F		11	14,74	
Kovacs, J.	HUN	400m hurdles	1	1	1	53.7	
			SF	2	5	54.0	
		4×100m relay	1	2	3	42.0	
		4×400m relay	1	1	2	3-17.0	
			F		6	3-14.8	
Kratky, B.	TCH	High jump	Q		DNQ	1,70	
		4×400m relay	1	3	5	3-22.0	
Krevs, I.	YUG	5000m	1	1	12		
Krombach, J.	LUX	400m	1	6	5	50.4	
Kruhklins, A.	LAT	50k walk	F		DIS		
Kubota, H.	JPN	400m	1	4	6	50.8	
		4×400m relay	1	1	4	3-18.4	
Kucharski, K.	POL	800m	1	6	2	1-55.7	
			2	1	2	1-54.7	
			F		4	1-53.8	
		4×400m relay	1	1	3	3-17.6	
Kuerten, W.	GER	400m hurdles	1	6	2	54.6	
			SF	1	6	54.5	
Kuntsi, R.	FIN	Shot put	F		13	14,61	
Kunz, R.	SUI	110m hurdles	1	5	4		
Kuuse, A.	EST	High jump	F		=10	1,90	
Kwong, Tse-To	CHN	Long jump	Q		DNQ		
		Triple jump	Q		DNQ		
Kyriakides, S.	GRE	Marathon	F		11	2:43-20.0	
Laisne, E.	FRA	50k walk	F		8	4:41-40.0	
Lambrakis, G.	GRE	Long jump	Q		DNQ		
		Triple jump	Q		DNQ		
Langmayr, J.	AUT	110m hurdles	1	2	3	15.1	
Lanz, M.	ITA	400m	1	3	2	49.3	
			2	1	3	48.8	
			SF	1	4	48.2	
		800m	1	5	2	1-56.1	
			2	3	2	1-54.1	
			F		3	1-53.3	S
		4×400m relay	1	3	3	3-16.6	
Larsen, B.	DEN	1500m	1	1	8		
Larsen, E.	DEN	Pole vault	F		=17	3,80	
Larsson, L.A.	SWE	3000m steeplechase	1	3	4	9-52.4	
			F		9	9-16.6	
Lash, D.R.	USA	5000m	1	1	3	15-04.4	
			F		13		
		10000m	F		8	31-39.4	

COMPETITOR	COUNTRY CODE	EVENT	ROUND	HEAT	PLACE	TIME & DISTANCE	MEDAL
Lavenas, J.A.E.	ARG	1?0m hurdles	1	4	2	15·1	
			SF	1	6		
		400m hurdles	1	4	2	54·5	
			SF	1	5	54·5	
		4×100m relay	1	2	2	41·9	
			F		4	42·2	
Lavery, T.P.	SAF	1?0m hurdles	1	1	1	15·0	
			SF	1	6	15·6	
		4×100m relay	1	1	3	41·7	
Le Curon, R.	FRA	5000m	1	2	6	15-14·2	
Lefebvre, R.	FRA	5000m	1	1	7	15-15·4	
Leheurteur, F.	FRA	Marathon	F		31	3:01-11·0	
Lehtinen, L.	FIN	5000m	1	3	4	15-00·0	
			F		2	14-25·8	S
Leichtnam, P.	FRA	1500m	1	2	4	4-01·0	
Leichum, W.	GER	Long jump	F		=4	7,73	
		4×100m relay	1	3	1	41·4	
			F		3	41·2	B
Leitner, E.	AUT	1?0m hurdles	1	5	3	15·3	
		400m hurdles	1	6	3	54·9	
Lelande, T.F.	SAF	Marathon	F		27	2:57-20·0	
Liddle, J.	CAN	800m	1	5	7		
		1500m	1	2	10		
Lidman, E.H.	SWE	110m hurdles	1	6	1	14·9	
			SF	1	2	14·5	
			F		4	14·5	
Limon, M.N.	CAN	400m	1	4	2	49·2	
			2	4	5	48·9	
		4×400m relay	1	3	2	3-15·0	
			F		4	3-11·8	
Lindeque, W.A.	SAF	800m	1	6	5	1-56·4	
		4×400m relay	1	1	4	3-17·8	
Lindgren, E.L.H.	SWE	100m	1	5	2	10·8	
			2	2	6		
		4×100m relay	1	3	3	41·5	
Ling, S.C.	CHN	110m hurdles	1	4	5		
Linne, E.O.	SWE	Hammer throw	F		14	47,61	
Lippi, G.	ITA	3000m steeplechase	1	1	8		
Liu, C.C.	CHN	100m	1	11	5		
		200m	1	6	5		
		4×100m relay	1	2	6	44·8	
Ljungberg, B.A.	SWE	Pole vault	F		=6	4,00	
		Triple jump	F		18	14,35	
Loaring, J.W.	CAN	400m	1	1	3	49·1	
			2	3	3	49·3	
			SF	1	3	48·1	
			F		6	48·2	
		400m hurdles	1	3	2	54·3	
			SF	2	2	53·1	
			F		2	52·7	S
		4×400m relay	1	3	2	3-15·0	
			F		4	3-11·8	
Loef, D.	SWE	50k walk	F		DIS		
Lokajski, E.	POL	Javelin throw	F		7	66,39	
Long, L.	GER	Long jump	F		2	7,87	S
		Triple jump	F		10	14,62	
Lonlas, A.	FRA	10000m	F		20	32-58·0	
Lorenz, H.	TCH	4×400m relay	1	3	5	3-22·0	
Lovelock, J.E.	NZL	1500m	1	2	3	4-00·6	
			F		1	3-47·8*	G
Luckhaus, E.	POL	Triple jump	F		11	14,61	
Lunak, M.	TCH	Marathon	F		19	2:50-26·0	
Lu Valle, J.E.	USA	400m	1	5	1	49·1	
			2	4	1	47·6	
			SF	2	1	47·1	
			F		3	46·84	B
McCabe, B.F.	GBR	800m	1	3	1	1-54·5	
			2	3	3	1-55·4	
			F		9		
McCluskey, J.P.	USA	3000m steeplechase	1	3	2	9-45·2	
			F		10	9-29·4	
McMahon, W.F.	USA	Marathon	F		DNF		
McPhee, H.P.	CAN	100m	1	5	1	10·8	
			2	4	3	10·6	
			SF	2	4	10·7	
		200m	1	6	2	21·8	
			2	3	2	21·90	
			SF	2	6	22·0	
		4×100m relay	1	3	2	41·5	
			F		5	42·7	
Madarasz, A.	HUN	Discus throw	Q		DNQ		
Maffei, A.	ITA	Long jump	F		=4	7,73	
Magalhaes, S.	BRA	400m hurdles	1	5	2	54·2	
			SF	2	3	53·3	
			F		5	54·0	
Mala, P.	TCH	Javelin throw	Q		DNQ		
Malasig, T.P.	PHI	400m hurdles	1	4	5	56·1	

COMPETITOR	COUNTRY CODE	EVENT	ROUND	HEAT	PLACE	TIME & DISTANCE	MEDAL
Mangan, A.J.	USA	50k walk	F		21	5:12-00·2	
Manning, H.	USA	3000m steeplechase	1	2	2	9-34·8	
			F		5	9-11·2	
Mantikas, C.	GRE	110m hurdles	1	1	3	15·2	
		400m hurdles	1	5	1	53·8	
			SF	1	3	53.51	
			F		6	54·2	
Marcenaro, C.	PER	800m	1	2	6	2-00·8	
Marchand, B.	SUI	100m	1	2	3	11·2	
		4×100m relay	1	3	4	42·2	
Mariani, O.	ITA	4×100m relay	1	1	2	41·1	
			F		2	41·1	S
Markusic, R.	YUG	Javelin throw	Q		DNQ		
Martens, H.	GER	High jump	Q		DNQ	1,70	
Martin, P.	SUI	800m	1	4	6	2-00·0	
		1500m	1	1	9		
Mastroienni, S.	ITA	5000m	1	3	6	15-02·2	
Maszewski, A.	POL	4×400m relay	1	1	3	3-17·6	
Matilainen, M.	FIN	1500m	1	2	DNF		
		3000m steeplechase	1	1	2	9-28·4	
			F		4	9-09·0	
Matsuno, E.	JPN	Hammer throw	Q		DNQ		
Matthews, C.H.	NZL	5000m	1	3	8		
Meadows, E.	USA	Pole vault	F		1	4,35*	G
Medinger, M.	LUX	5000m	1	3	13		
Mehlhose, H.	GER	1500m	1	3	8		
Mendes, A.	BRA	High jump	Q		DNQ	1,80	
Mendes, J.	POR	Marathon	F		DNF		
Mendoza, G.	PER	Marathon	F		26	2:57-17·8	
Mersch, F.	LUX	100m	1	11	4		
		Long jump	Q		DNQ		
Mertens, E.	GER	800m	1	3	4	1-55·1	
			2	2	5	1-54·9	
Meskens, F.	BEL	Marathon	F		20	2:51-19·0	
Metaxas, C.	GRE	Javelin throw	Q		DNQ		
Metcalf, M.W.	USA	Javelin throw	F		15	58,20	
Metcalfe, J.P.	AUS	Triple jump	F		3	15,50	B
		High jump	F		=12	1,85	
Metcalfe, R.H.	USA	100m	1	7	1	10·8	
			2	3	1	10·5	
			SF	2	1	10·5	
			F		2	10·4	S
		4×100m relay	1	1	1	40·0*	
			F		1	39·8*	G
Metzner, A.	GER	400m	1	3	3	50·2	
			2	3	DNS		
Meyer, G.	SUI	4×100m relay	1	3	4	42·2	
Mikic, J.	YUG	Triple jump	F		21	13,90	
Minai, M.	HUN	200m	1	8	5		
		4×100m relay	1	2	3	42·0	
Mohr, H.	YUG	High jump	Q		DNQ	1,70	
Mori, E.	ITA	400m hurdles	1	3	6	55·6	
Morris, G.E.	USA	Decathlon	F		1	7900*	G
Mostert, J.	BEL	1500m	1	4	4	3-56·6	
Motmillers, A.	LAT	Marathon	F		28	2:58-02·0	
Mueller, J.	GER	Pole vault	F		=17	3,80	
Muinonen, V.	FIN	Marathon	F		5	2:33-46·0	
Munoz, R.	CHI	400m	1	7	5	50·5	
Murakami, T.	JPN	110m hurdles	1	3	2	15·3	
			SF	1	5	15·1	
Murakoso, K.	JPN	5000m	1	3	2	14-56·0	
			F		4	14-30·0	
		10000m	F		4	30-25·0	
Naban, A.	BRA	Hammer throw	Q		DNQ		
Nakamura, K.	JPN	1500m	1	2	6	4-04·8	
Nan, S.	JPN	Marathon	F		3	2:31-42·0	B
Narancic, V.	YUG	Discus throw	Q		DNQ		
Naraoka, R.	JPN	50k walk	F		19	5:07-15·0	
Natvig, E.	NOR	High jump	Q		DNQ	1,80	
		Decathlon	F		10	6759	
Navarette, H.	COL	5000m	1	3	12		
Neckermann, K.	GER	100m	1	3	3	21·8	
			2	4	3	21·6	
			SF	1	5	21·8	
Nemes, F.	RUM	400m	1	5	4	50·9	
Neumann, J.	SUI	Javelin throw	Q		DNQ		
Neuruhrer, F.	AUT	High jump	Q		DNQ	1,70	
Nevens, R.	BEL	Marathon	F		24	2:55-51·0	
Newman, J.L.	GBR	High jump	Q		DNQ		
Nielsen, H.	DEN	5000m	1	2	7		
Nikkanen, Y.	FIN	Javelin throw	F		2	70,77	S
Nishida, S.	JPN	Pole vault	F		2	4,25	S
Noel, J.	FRA	Shot put	Q		DNQ		
		Discus throw	F		12	44,56	
Noji, J.	POL	5000m	1	2	3	15-11·2	
			F		5	14-33·4	
		10000m	F		14	32-13·0	

COMPETITOR	COUNTRY CODE	EVENT	ROUND	HEAT	PLACE	TIME & DISTANCE	MEDAL
Norris, A.J.	GBR	Marathon	F		DNF		
Nottbrock, F.	GER	400m hurdles	1	2	1	54.7	
			SF	2	6	54.8	
Ny, E.O.S.	SWE	1500m	1	1	1	3-54.8	
			F		11	3-57.6	B
Oberweger, G.	ITA	Discus throw	F		3	49,23	B
O'Brien, E.T.	USA	4×400m relay	1	1	1	3-13.0	
			F		2	3-11.0	S
O'Connor, L.G.	CAN	110m hurdles	1	1	2	15.1	
			SF	2	3	15.0	
			F		5	14.8	
Oedmark, A.	SWE	High jump	F		=12	1,85	
Oe, S.	JPN	Pole vault	F		3	4,25	3
Oliva, L.	ARG	Marathon	F		DNF		
Orr, L.P.	CAN	100m	1	10	3	10.6	
		200m	1	3	2	21.6	
			2	1	1	21.37	
			SF	1	2	21.3	
			F		5	21.6	
		4×100m relay	1	3	2	41.5	
			F		5	42.7	
Osendarp, M.B.	HOL	100m	1	10	1	10.5	
			2	1	2	10.6	
			SF	2	2	10.6	
			F		3	10.5	B
		200m	1	2	1	21.7	
			2	4	2	21.3	
			SF	2	2	21.5	
			F		3	21.3	B
		4×100m relay	1	2	1	41.3	
			F		DIS		
Oshima, M.	JPN	Triple jump	F		6	15,07	
Ospelt, O.	LIE	100m	1	6	6		
		Discus throw	Q		DNQ		
Otahal, S.	TCH	800m	1	3	7		
Otto, P.	DEN	High jump	F		=12	1,85	
Owens, J.C.	USA	100m	1	12	1	10.3*	
			2	2	1	10.2*	
			SF	1	1	10.4	
			F		1	10.3	G
		200m	1	3	1	21.1*	
			2	3	1	21.1*	
			SF	2	1	21.40	
			F		1	20.7	G
		Long jump	F		1	8,06*	G
		4×100m relay	1	1	1	40.0*	
			F		1	39.8*	G
Packard, R.R.	USA	200m	1	7	1	21.2	
			2	1	3	21.40	
			SF	1	4	21.6	
Palme, H.A.	SWE	Marathon	F		13	2:46-08.4	
Pantazis, C.	GRE	High jump	Q		DNQ	1,70	
Papageorgiou, N.	GRE	Javelin throw	Q		DNQ		
Parker, J.	USA	Decathlon	F		3	7275	B
Patterson, J.H.	USA	400m hurdles	1	4	1	54.4	
			SF	2	1	52.8	
			F		4	53.0	
Paul, R.	FRA	100m	1	5	3	11.0	
		Long jump	F		8	7,34	
		4×100m relay	1	2	5	42.6	
Pei, K.-L.	CHN	Discus throw	Q		DNQ		
Pennington, A.	GBR	100m	1	10	2	10.6	
			2	3	2	10.6	
			SF	1	6		
		200m	1	2	3	22.1	
		4×100m relay	1	2	4	42.4	
Pentti, E.I.W.	USA	10000m	F		16	32-23.0	
Peraesalo, V.	FIN	High jump	F		=12	1,85	
Pereira, A.	BRA	Shot put	Q		DNQ		
Perez, R.	MEX	Pole vault	Q		DNQ	3,50	
Petit, R.	FRA	800m	1	3	2	1-54.8	
			2	3	4	1-55.7	
Pilbrow, A.G.	GBR	110m hurdles	1	4	3	15.5	
Plawczyk, J.	POL	High jump	F		22	1,80	
		Decathlon	F		9	6871	
Poh, K.S.	CHN	100m	1	5	5		
		200m	1	5	4		
		4×100m relay	1	2	6	44.8	
Polame, R.	TCH	Long jump	Q		DNQ		
Pollard, F.D.	USA	110m hurdles	1	2	1	14.7	
			SF	2	2	14.6	
			F		3	14.4	B
Poerhoelae, V.	FIN	Hammer throw	F		11	49,89	
Potts, J.H.	GBR	10000m	F		DNF		
Powell, J.V.	GBR	800m	1	5	1	1-56.0	
			2	2	4	1-54.8	
		4×400m relay	1	2	1	3-14.4	
Prebolin, A.	FRA	Long jump	Q		DNQ		
Prenn, F.	GER	50k walk	F		DIS		
Prendergast, B.L.	GBR	Discus throw	Q		DNQ		
Proksch, A.	AUT	Pole vault	F		=6	4,00	
Raff, H.-H.	GER	3000m steeplechase	1	3	DNF		
Ragni, E.	ITA	4×100m relay	1	1	2	41.1	
			F		2	41.1	S
Rahim, A.	AFG	Shot put	Q		DNQ		
Rajasaari, O.R.	FIN	Long jump	Q		DNQ		
		Triple jump	F		13	14,59	
Ramadier, P.	FRA	Pole vault	F		=17	3,80	
Ramirez, N.T.	PHI	110m hurdles	1	3	4		
		Long jump	Q		DNQ		
Rampling, G.L.	GBR	400m	1	6	2	48.6	
			2	4	3	48.0	
			SF	2	4	47.5	
		4×400m relay	1	2	1	3-14.4	
			F		1	3-09.0	G
Rangeley, W.	GBR	4×100m relay	1	2	4	42.4	
Rankine, R.S.	CAN	5000m	1	1	10		
		10000m	F				
Rasdal, O.	NOR	10000m	F		9	31-40.4	
Rasmussen, W.	DEN	Long jump	Q		DNQ		
Reavell-Carter, L.	GBR	Discus throw	Q		DNQ		
Reccius, H.	CHI	Triple jump	Q		DNQ		
Reeve, A.V.	GBR	5000m	1	1	5	15-06.8	
			F		DNF		
Remer, E.	CHI	Decathlon	F		DNF		
Reniger, K.	SUI	50k walk	F		7	4:40-45.0	
Renikka, A.	FIN	Pole vault	Q		DNQ	3,70	
		Decathlon	F		11	6755	
Revolle, R.	FRA	3000m steeplechase	1	3	3	9-50.6	
			F		11	9-40.8	
Ribenyi, T.	HUN	400m	1	1	5	50.1	
		4×400m relay	1	1	2	3-17.0	
			F		6	3-14.8	
Richardson, S.	CAN	Long jump	F		14	7,13	
		Triple jump	F		20	14,21	
		4×100m relay	1	3	2	41.5	
			F		5	42.7	
Ridi, U.	ITA	400m hurdles	1	4	4	55.5	
Rinner, F.	AUT	200m	1	4	3	22.4	
			2	3	5		
Rivolta, E.	ITA	50k walk	F		12	4:48-47.0	
Roberts, W.	GBR	400m	1	1	1	48.1	
			2	1	1	47.7	
			SF	1	2	48.0	
			F		4	46.87	
		4×400m relay	F		1	3-09.0	G
Robertson, D. McN.	GBR	Marathon	F		7	2:37-06.2	
Robinson, M.M.	USA	200m	1	8	1	21.6	
			2	4	1	21.2	
			SF	1	1	21.1*	
			F		2	21.1	S
Rochard, R.	FRA	5000m	1	3	7	15-12.2	
Romero, R.L.	USA	Triple jump	F		5	15,08	
Rosicky, E.	TCH	800m	1	4	5	1-59.5	
		4×400m relay	1	3	5	3-22.0	
Rossi, M.	ITA	4×400m relay	1	3	3	3-16.6	
Rothmayer, W.	AUT	Marathon	F		32	3:02-32.0	
Rowe, W.J.A.	USA	Hammer throw	F		5	51,66	
Rushton, F.M.	SAF	400m hurdles	1	5	4	55.2	
		4×400m relay	1	3	4	3-17.8	
Sakellariou, A.	GRE	100m	1	1	5		
		200m	1	1	6		
Salcedo, M.	PHI	100m	1	3	4		
		200m	1	1	4		
Salminen, I.	FIN	5000m	1	1	4	15-06.0	
			F		6	14-39.8	
		10000m	F		1	30-15.4	G
Sanchez, J.D.	COL	100m	1	3	5		
Sandstroem, K.O.	SWE	4×100m relay	1	3	3	41.5	
Sande, A.	ARG	100m	1	2	4		
		4×100m relay	1	2	2	41.9	
			F		4	42.2	
San Romani, A.J.	USA	1500m	1	4	2	3-55.0	
			F		4	3-50.0	
Sariola, T.	FIN	100m	1	6	4		
		4×100m relay	1	1	4	42.0	
Sasaki, K.	JPN	100m	1	12	2	11.0	
			2	3	6		
Schaumburg, F.	GER	1500m	1	4	3	3-55.2	
			F		10	3-56.2	
Schein, E.	GER	200m	1	2	2	22.0	
			2	1	5	21.67	
Scheele, H.	GER	400m hurdles	1	4	3	54.6	
Schlegel, A.	CHI	Pole vault	F		24	3,60	
Schoenrock, W.	GER	10000m	F		21	32-59.0	

COMPETITOR	COUNTRY CODE	EVENT	ROUND	HEAT	PLACE	TIME & DISTANCE	MEDAL
Schofield, M.D.	USA	400m hurdles	1	2	2	54·8	
			SF	1	4	53·55	
Scholtz, C.B.	SAF	800m	1	3	5	1-57·6	
		1500m	1	2	5	4-02·0	
Schonheyder, R.	NOR	400m	1	4	4	49·4	
Schroeder, W.	GER	Discus throw	F		5	47,93	
Schuban R.	EST	1500m	1	3	9		
Schulz, S.	GER	Pole vault	F		=17	3,80	
Schwab, A.T.	SUI	50k walk	F		2	4:32-09·2	S
Seeger, F.	SUI	100m	1	7	4		
Sefton, W.H.	USA	Pole vault	F		4	4,25	
Segerstroem, E.	SWE	50k walk	F		11	4:43-30·4	
Sheffield, J.	GBR	400m hurdles	1	6	5	58·1	
Shimizu, K.	JPN	110m hurdles	1	5	5		
Shiwaku, T.	JPN	Marathon	F		DNF		
Shore, D.V.	SAF	400m	1	2	3	49·9	
			2	1	5	49·6	
		4×400m relay	1	3	4	3-17·8	
Sicard, A.	FRA	10000m	F		19	32-25·0	
Siefert, H.	DEN	5000m	1	1	2	15-02·8	
			F		10	14-48·4	
		10000m	F		10	31-52·6	
Siegers, J.	GER	10000m	F		22		
Sievert, H.-H.	GER	Shot put	F		10	14,79	
Sigurdsson, S.	ISL	High jump	Q		DNQ	1,80	
		Triple jump	F		22	13,58	
Simacek, L.	AUT	3000m steeplechase	1	3	9		
Simon, I.	HUN	5000m	1	1	9		
Singh, G.I.L.	IND	5000m	1	1	15		
		10000m	F		DNF		
Sir, J.	HUN	100m	1	7	2	10·8	
			2	2	3	10·7	
			SF	2	6	10·9	
		200m	1	5	3	22·2	
			2	1	4	21·65	
		4×100m relay	1	2	3	42·0	
Sivertsen, H.	NOR	Discus throw	F		10	45,89	
Skawinski, P.	FRA	400m	1	8	1	48·9	
			2	4	2	48·0	
			SF	1	5	52·0	
Skiadas, J.	GRE	110m hurdles	1	4	4		
		400m hurdles	1	3	5	55·3	
Sliwak, T.	POL	4×400m relay	1	1	3	3-17·6	
Smallwood, R.H.	USA	400m	1	4	1	49·0	
			2	1	2	48·6	
			SF	1		DNS	
Sobotka, Z.	TCH	High jump	Q		DNQ	1,70	
Somlo, L.	HUN	Triple jump	F		12	14,60	
Son, K.	JPN	Marathon	F		1	2:29-19·2*	G
Sorlie, R.	NOR	Discus throw	F		4	48,77	
Soulier, R.	FRA	800m	1	6	4	1-56·1	
			2	2	6	1-56·8	
Spampani, O.	ITA	4×400m relay	1	3	3	3-16·6	
Sporn, S.	YUG	Marathon	F		41	3:30-47·0	
Stadler, E.	GER	5000m	1	1	8		
Staley, R.M.	USA	110m hurdles	1	4	1	15·0	
			SF	1	4	14·8	
Stein, C.	LUX	800m	1	4	7		
		1500m	1	4	9		
Steinmetz, A.	GER	200m	1	7	3	21·9	
			2	3	DIS		
Stenqvist, A.W.	SWE	Long jump	F		=10	7,30	
		4×100m relay	1	3	3	41·5	
Stepisnik, M.	YUG	Hammer throw	Q		DNQ		
Sterzl, F.	AUT	Decathlon	F		DNF		
Stoeck, G.	GER	Shot put	F		3	15,66	B
		Javelin throw	F		1	71,84	G
Stork, J.	TCH	50k walk	F		4	4:34-00·2	
Strandberg, H.L.	SWE	100m	1	1	1	10·7	
			2	1	1	10·5	
			SF	1	3	10·5	
			F		6	10·9	
Strandvall, B.	FIN	200m	1	6	3	22·6	
			2	4	5		
		400m	1	6	3	49·3	
			2	2	6	49·9	
		4×100m relay	1	1	4	42·0	
Stroemberg, S.E.	SWE	400m	1	2	4	50·0	
		4×400m relay	1	2	2	3-14·6	
			F		5	3-13·0	
Struckl, R.	AUT	100m	1	10	4		
Studer, J.	SUI	Long jump	Q		DNQ		
Suarez, G.	PER	Marathon	F		35	3:08-18·0	
Sulc, J.	TCH	Marathon	F		38	3:11-47·4	
Sule, G.	EST	Javelin throw	F		11	63,26	
Sundesson, H.L.	SWE	10000m	F		13	32-11·8	
Suomela, O.	FIN	Triple jump	F		9	14,72	

COMPETITOR	COUNTRY CODE	EVENT	ROUND	HEAT	PLACE	TIME & DISTANCE	MEDAL
Suzuki, B.	JPN	100m	1	4	2	10·7	
			2	4	4		
		4×100m relay	1	1	DIS		
Suzuki, F.	JPN	10000m	F				
Swami, C.S.	IND	Marathon	F		37	3:10-44·0	
Sweeney, A.W.	GBR	100m	1	9	2	10·7	
			2	2	2	10·6	
			SF	2	5	10·7	
		200m	1	3	4		
Syllas, N.	GRE	Discus throw	F		6	47,75	
Syring, M.	GER	5000m	1	3	10		
Szabo, M.	HUN	800m	1	4	2	1-57·8	
			2	1	4	1-55·1	
		1500m	1	3	2	3-55·6	
			F		7	3-53·0	
Szilagyi, J.	HUN	5000m	1	3	9		
		3000m steeplechase	1	2	5	9-53·4	
Sznajder, W.	POL	Pole vault	F		=6	4,00	
Tajima, N.	JPN	Long jump	F		3	7,74	B
		Triple jump	F		1	16,00*	G
Takac, J.	TCH	Marathon	F		21	2:51-20·0	
Takata, S.	JPN	Shot put	Q		DNQ		
Tamila, E.	FIN	Marathon	F		4	2:32-45·0	
Tammisto, A.	FIN	200m	1	8	2	22·2	
			2	3	4	22·07	
		4×100m relay	1	1	4	42·0	
Tanaka, Hideo	JPN	5000m	1	2	11		
		3000m steeplechase	1	3	6	10-00·4	
Tanaka, Hiroshi	JPN	High jump	F		=6	1,94	
Taniguchi, M.	JPN	200m	1	1	3	22·2	
			2	2	5		
		4×100m relay	1	1	DIS		
Tarkiainen, M.	FIN	Marathon	F		9	2:39-33·0	
Tay, L.L.	CHN	400m	1	3	6	52·4	
Teileri, O.	FIN	1500m	1	1	4	3-55·6	
Temesvari, F.	HUN	800m	1	1	4	1-55·0	
			2	3	7		
Ternstroem, L.I.W.	SWE	4×100m relay	1	3	3	41·5	
Terry, A.	USA	Javelin throw	F		6	67,15	
Thacker, E.T.	SAF	High jump	F		=12	1,85	
Theunissen, M.W.	SAF	100m	1	6	1	10·7	
			2	3	4		
		200m	1	6	1	21·7	
			2	2	2	21·9	
			SF	2	4	21·8	
		4×100m relay	1	1	3	41·7	
Thompson, H.	CAN	1500m	1	4	8		
Thomsen, S.A.	DEN	110m hurdles	1	1	4		
		High jump	Q		DNQ	1,80	
Thornton, J.	GBR	110m hurdles	1	2	2	15·0	
			SF	1	3	14·7	
			F		5	14·7	
Thurber, D.P.	USA	High jump	F		3	2,00	B
Togami, K.	JPN	Long jump	F		16	6,18	
Toivonen, K.	FIN	Javelin throw	F		3	70,72	B
Tolamo, M.	FIN	Javelin throw	Q		DNQ		
		Decathlon	F		DNF		
Tomie, T.	JPN	800m	1	3	6	1-59·9	
Toomsalu, R.	EST	100m	1	3	3	11·0	
		Long jump	Q		DNQ		
Toribio, S.G.	PHI	High jump	F		=12	1,85	
Torrance, J.	USA	Discus throw	F		5	15,38	
Torreggiani, A.C.	MLT	100m	1	12	5		
Torres, E.	COL	1500m	1	3	11		
Toscani, A.F.C.	HOL	50k walk	F		10	4:42-59·4	
Tostain, L.	FRA	10000m	F		18	32-24·2	
Towns, F.G.	USA	110m hurdles	1	5	1	14·5	
			SF	1	1	14·1*	
			F		1	14·2	G
Traynor, G.T.	GBR	Long jump	Q		DNQ		
Tuominen, K.	FIN	3000m steeplechase	1	3	1	9-40·4	
			F		2	9-06·8	S
Turczyk, W.	POL	Javelin throw	F		10	63,36	
Tuschek, F.	AUT	Marathon	F		14	2:46-29·0	
Ueno, N.	JPN	Javelin throw	Q		DNQ		
Utiger, G.	SUI	5000m	1	1	14		
Vadas, J.	HUN	400m	1	4	3	49·2	
			2	3	DNS		
		800m	1	5	4	1-56·5	
			2	2	8		
		4×400m relay	1	1	2	3-17·0	
			F		6	3-14·8	
Valdez, P.	PER	800m	1	1	7		
		1500m	1	4	DNF		

COMPETITOR	COUNTRY CODE	EVENT	ROUND	HEAT	PLACE	TIME & DISTANCE	MEDAL
Van Beveren, W.	HOL	100m	1	3	1	10 8	
			2	3	3	10 7	
			SF	1	5	10 8	
		200m	1	1	1	21 4	
			2	2	1	21 7	
			SF	1	3	21 5	
			F		6	21 9	
		4×100m relay	1	2	1	41 3	
			F		DIS		
Van Der Poll, J.F.	HOL	Javelin throw	F		16	56,25	
Van Rumst, O.	BEL	5000m	1	2	12		
		3000m steeplechase	1	2	6	10-05-0	
Varszegi, J.	HUN	Javelin throw	F		8	65,30	
Vattnes, K.	ISL	Javelin throw	Q		DNQ		
Velcopoulos, S.	GRE	800m	1	1	8		
Venzke, G.C.	USA	1500m	1	2	1	4-00-4	
			F		9	3-55-0	
Verhaert, J.	BEL	400m	1	3	5	50-7	
		800m	1	1	3	1-54-3	
			2	3	8		
Viiding, A.	EST	Shot put	F		8	15,23	
Vilmundarson, K.	ISL	Decathlon	F		DNF		
Virtanen, P.	FIN	100m	1	4	3	10-9	
		4×100m relay	1	1	4	42-0	
Vitek, J.	TCH	Shot put	Q		DNQ		
Vitek, M.	TCH	Discus throw	Q		DNQ		
		Shot put	Q		DNQ		
Voigt, H.C.	GER	4×400m relay	1	3	1	3-16-0	
			F		3	3-11-8	B
Von Stuelpnagel, F.	GER	4×400m relay	1	3	1	3-16-0	
			F		3	3-11-8	B
Von Wachenfeldt, K.J.B.	SWE	400m	1	8	2	49 0	
			2	2	4	48-5	
		4×400m relay	1	2	2	3-14-6	
			F		5	3-13-0	
Vosolsbe, J.	TCH	Long jump	F		13	7 18	
Wagner, J.	LUX	Shot put	Q		DNQ		
		Discus throw	Q		DNQ		
Wallace M.	CAN	5000m	1	3	11		
		10000m	F				
Wang, S.L.	CHN	Triple jump	Q		DNQ		
Wang, T.-L.	CHN	Marathon	F		40	3:25-36-4	
Ward, P.D.	GBR	5000m	1	3	3	14-59-0	
			F		11		
Warngard, O.A.F.	SWE	Hammer throw	F		3	54,33	B
Watson, A.J.	AUS	110m hurdles	1	6	4		
		400m hurdles	1	3	3	54 5	
Webster, F.R.	GBR	Pole vault	F		=6	4,00	
Webster, H.	CAN	Marathon	F		DNF		
Wegner, E.	GER	110m hurdles	1	5	2	15 1	
			SF	2	5		
Weimann, G.	GER	Javelin throw	F		9	65,38	
Weinkoetz, G.	GER	High jump	F		=6	1,94	
Welscher, W.	GER	110m hurdles	1	2	4		
Wennberg, E.Y.	SWE	800m	1	1	9		
Wenzel, O.	CHI	Decathlon	F		15	6058	
West, S.R.	GBR	High jump	Q		DNQ	1,70	
White, M.S.	PHI	110m hurdles	1	6	5		
		400m hurdles	1	3	1	53 4	
			SF	1	2	53-12	
			F		3	52 8	B
Whiteside, E.C.	IND	100m	1	10	5		
		200m	1	7	4		
Whitlock, H.H.	GBR	50k walk	F		1	4:30-41-4*	G
Wiard, C.A.	GBR	4×100m relay	1	2	4	42 4	
Wihtols, W.	LAT	3000m steeplechase	1	1	3	9-28-8	
			F		7	9-18-8	
Wilkins, D.G.	USA	Triple jump	F		8	14,33	
Williams, A.F.	USA	400m	1	7	1	47 8	
			2	3	1	48 0	
			SF	1	1	47 2	
			F		1	46-66	G
Williamson, H.W.	USA	800m	1	2	1	1-56-2	
			2	2	1	1-53-1	
			F		6	1-55-8	
Winter, P.	FRA	Discus throw	Q		DNQ		
Wirtz, J.	FRA	Hammer throw	F		16	45,39	
Woeber, R.	AUT	10000m	F		15	32-22-0	
		Marathon	F		22	2:51-38-0	
Woellke, H.	GER	Shot put	F		1	16,20*	G
Woellner, H.	GER	Triple jump	F		4	15,27	
Wolff, F.F.	GBR	4×400m relay	1	2	1	3-14-4	
			F		1	3-09-0	G
Wong, Y.K.	CHN	110m hurdles	1	2	5		
		4×100m relay	1	2	6	44-8	
Wood, W.D.	USA	Discus throw	F		13	43,83	
Wooderson, S.C.	GBR	1500m	1	4	DNF		

COMPETITOR	COUNTRY CODE	EVENT	ROUND	HEAT	PLACE	TIME & DISTANCE	MEDAL
Woodruff, J.	USA	800m	1	4	3	1-58-7	
			2	1	1	1-52-7	
			F		1	1-52-9	G
Worrall, J.	CAN	110m hurdles	1	3	3	15-6	
		400m hurdles	1	2	4	55-5	
Wotapek, J.	AUT	Discus throw	F		9	46,05	
Wu, P.-H.	CHN	High jump	Q		DNQ	1,70	
Wudyka, S.J.	USA	10000m	F				
Wyer, P.	CAN	Marathon	F		30	3:00-11-0	
Wykoff, F.C.	USA	100m	1	9	1	10-6	
			2	1	3	10-6	
			SF	1	2	10-5	
			F		4	10-6	
		4×100m relay	1	1	1	40-0*	
			F		1	39-8*	G
Xavier, J.	BRA	100m	1	12	3	11-1	
		200m	1	1	5		
Yata, K.	JPN	High jump	F		5	1,97	
Yazawa, M.	JPN	200m	1	2	4		
		4×100m relay	1	1	DIS		
Yoshioka, T.	JPN	100m	1	1	2	10-8	
			2	2	4		
		4×100m relay	1	1	DIS		
Young, R.C.	USA	4×400m relay	1	1	1	3-13-0	
			F		2	3-11-0	S
Zatz, D.N.	USA	Shot put	F		6	15,32	
Zabala, J.C.	ARG	10000m	F		6	31-22-0	
		Marathon	F		DNF		
Zamperini, L.	USA	5000m	1	3	4	15-02-2	
			F		8	14-46-8	
Zsitvai, Z.	HUN	400m	1	5	3	49-8	
			2	1	4	49-4	
		4×400m relay	1	1	2	3-17-0	
			F		6	3-14-8	
Zsuffka, V.	HUN	Pole vault	F		=6	4,00.	
FEMALES							
Albus, E.	GER	100m	1	1	1	12-4	
			SF	1	3	12-2	
			F		6	12-3	
		4×100m relay	1	2	1	46-4*	
			F		DIS		
Arden, A.J.	USA	High jump	F		=8	1,50	
Atkins, R.	CAN	80m hurdles	1	4	4		
Bauma, H.	AUT	Javelin throw	F		4	41,66	
Bell, M.M.	CAN	High jump	F		=8	1,50	
Bland, H.C.	USA	100m	1	1	4		
		4×100m relay	1	1	1	47-1	
			F		1	46-9	G
Blankers-Koen, F.E.	HOL	High jump	F		=5	1,55	
		4×100m relay	1	1	3	48-4	
			F		5	48-8	
Bongiovanni, L.	ITA	4×100m relay	1	3	3	48-6	
			F		4	48-7	
Brookshaw, E.	CAN	4×100m relay	1	1	2	48-0	
			F		3	47-8	B
Brown, A.K.	GBR	100m	1	5	3	12-6	
		4×100m relay	1	2	2	47-5	
			F		2	47-6	S
Bullano, F.	ITA	4×100m relay	1	3	3	48-6	
			F		4	48-7	
Burch, B.L.	USA	Javelin throw	F		13	28,84	
Burke, B.A.	GBR	100m	1	6	2	12-4	
			SF	2	4		
		4×100m relay	1	2	2	47-5	
			F		2	47-6	S
Cameron, H.M.	CAN	100m	1	1	3	12-7	
		4×100m relay	1	1	2	48-0	
			F		3	47-8	B
Carrington, N.	GBR	High jump	F		=8	1,50	
Carter, D.J.	AUS	High jump	F		=5	1,55	
Connal, K.	GBR	Javelin throw	F		14	27,80	
Csak, I.	HUN	High jump	F		1	1,60	G
De Kock, C.	HOL	Javelin throw	F		8	36,93	
De Vries, A.E.C.	HOL	100m	1	4	3	13-0	
		4×100m relay	1	1	3	48-4	
			F		5	48-8	
Doerffeldt, I.	GER	4×100m relay	1	2	1	46-4*	
			F		DIS		
Dollinger, M.	GER	100m	1	6	1	12-0	
			SF	2	1	12-0	
			F		4	12-0	
		4×100m relay	1	2	1	46-4*	
			F		DIS		

COMPETITOR	COUNTRY CODE	EVENT	ROUND	HEAT	PLACE	TIME & DISTANCE	MEDAL
Dolson, M.J.	CAN	100m	1	2	2	12.3	
			SF	2	5		
		4×100m relay	1	1	2	48.0	
			F		3	47.8	B
Doorgeest, A.M.	HOL	80m hurdles	1	3	5		
Eberhardt, L.	GER	Javelin throw	F		6	41,37	
Eckert, D.	GER	80m hurdles	1	2	2	12.0	
			SF	2	2	11.8	
			F		6	12.0	
Essman, R.	FIN	100m	1	3	2	12.8	
			SF	2	6		
		4×100m relay	1	2	4	49.5	
Ferrera, E.C.	USA	Discus throw	F		18	32,52	
Fleischer, T.	GER	Javelin throw	F		1	45,18*	G
From, E.	FIN	100m	1	2	4		
		4×100m relay	1	2	4	49,5	
Gabric, L.	ITA	Discus throw	F		10	34,31	
Hagemann, A.	GER	Discus throw	F		19	28,48	
Halttu, R.	FIN	100m	1	1	5		
		4×100m relay	1	2	4	49.5	
Held, M.	AUT	Discus throw	F		11	34,05	
Hiscock, E.	GBR	100m	1	4	1	12.6	
			SF	1	4		
		4×100m relay	1	2	2	47.5	
			F		2	47.6	S
Hofman, F.	YUG	100m	1	2	5		
Kaun, E.	GER	High jump	F		3	1,60	B
Kelly, K.	USA	High jump	F		=8	1,50	
Kojima, F.	JPN	Discus throw	F		15	33,66	
Kolbach, V.	AUT	80m hurdles	1	2	5		
		Discus throw	F		13	34,00	
		4×100m relay	1	1	4	49.9	
Komiya, E.	JPN	100m	1	2	4		
Koning, E.G.	HOL	100m	1	3	3	12.9	
		4×100m relay	1	1	3	48.4	
			F		5	48.8	
Koopmans, J.M.	HOL	High jump	F		=13	1,40	
		Discus throw	F		16	33,50	
Krauss, K.	GER	100m	1	5	1	12.1	
			SF	1	2	11.9	
			F		3	11.9	B
		4×100m relay	1	2	1	46.4*	
			F		DIS		
Krueger, L.	GER	Javelin throw	F		2	43,29	S
Kwasniewska, M.	POL	Javelin throw	F		3	41,80	B
Lanitis, D.	GRE	100m	1	6	3	12.8	
		80m hurdles	1	1	3	12.6	
			SF	1	6		
Lee, Shen	CHN	100m	1	3	5		
Le Viseur, H.	GER	80m hurdles	1	4	5		
Lipasti, I.	FIN	High jump	F		16	1,30	
		Javelin throw	F		10	33,69	
		4×100m relay	1	2	4	49.5	
Lundstrom, B.E.	SWE	Discus throw	F		6	35,92	
Mabille, Y.	FRA	100m	1	6	4		
		80m hurdles	1	1	5		
Machmer, C.	AUT	100m	1	4	4		
		80m hurdles	1	3	6		
		4×100m relay	1	1	4	49.9	
Martinez, R.	CHI	100m	1	6	5		
Mauermayer, G.	GER	Discus throw	F		1	47,63*	G
Meagher, A.A.	CAN	100m	1	5	2	12.4	
			SF	1	5		
		4×100m relay	1	1	2	48.0	
			F		3	47.8	B
Mineshima, H.	JPN	Discus throw	F		5	37,35	
Mitsui, M.	JPN	80m hurdles	1	2	4		
Mollenhauer, P.	GER	Discus throw	F		3	39,80	B
Nakamura, K.	JPN	Discus throw	F		4	38,24	
Neferovic, V.	YUG	Discus throw	F		17	33,02	
Neumann, M.	AUT	100m	1	2	3	12.9	
		4×100m relay	1	1	4	49.9	
Nicolas, M.	FRA	High jump	F		4	1,58	
Niesink, A.E.	HOL	Discus throw	SF		7	35,21	
Nishida, J.	JPN	High jump	F		=13	1,40	
Nowak, W.	AUT	High jump	F		=8	1,50	
O'Brien, A.V.	USA	80m hurdles	1	3	2	12.0	
			SF	1	4	11.8	
Odam, D.	GBR	High jump	F		2	1,60	S
Olney, V.	GBR	4×100m relay	1	2	2	47.5	
			F		2	47.6	S
Perrou, M.	FRA	100m	1	3	4		
Pickett, T.A.	USA	80m hurdles	1	2	3	12.4	
			SF	2	6		
Puchberger, M.	AUT	80m hurdles	1	1	4		
Robinson, E.	USA	4×100m relay	1	1	1	47.1	
			F		1	46.9	G
Rogers, A.	USA	100m	1	4	2	12.8	
			SF	2	3	12.1	
			F		5	12.2	
		High jump	F		=5	1,55	
		4×100m relay	1	1	1	47.1	
			F		1	46.9	G
Romanic, V.	YUG	100m	1	5	4		
Schaller, S.	USA	80m hurdles	1	4	1	11.8	
			SF	2	4		
Schieferova, M.	TCH	Discus throw	F		12	34,03	
Stanojevic, J.	YUG	Javelin throw	F		12	29,88	
Stafanini, Z.	YUG	80m hurdles	1	4	6		
Stephens, H.H.	USA	100m	1	2	1	11.4	
			SF	1	1	11.5	
			F		1	11.5	G
		Discus throw	F		9	34,33	
		4×100m relay	1	1	1	47.1	
			F		1	46.9	G
Steuer, A.	GER	80m hurdles	1	3	3	12.1	
			SF	1	3	11.7	
			F		2	11.81	S
Stevens, C.	BEL	High jump	F		=13	1,40	
Taylor, E.G.	CAN	80m hurdles	1	3	1	12.0	
			SF	1	2	11.7	
			F		3	11.81	B
Ter Braake, C.	HOL	80m hurdles	1	4	3	12.0	
			SF	2	1	11.8	
			F		5	11.8	
		4×100m relay	1	1	3	48.4	
			F		5	48.8	
Testoni, C.	ITA	100m	1	5	5		
		80m hurdles	1	1	1	12.0	
			SF	2	3	11.8	
			F		4	11.82	
		4×100m relay	1	2	3	48.6	
			F		4	48.7	
Tiffen, K.	GBR	80m hurdles	1	1	2	12.2	
			SF	2	5		
Valla, T.	ITA	80m hurdles	1	4	2	11.9	
			SF	1	1	11.6	
			F		1	11.75	G
		4×100m relay	1	2	3	48.6	
			F		4	48.7	
Vancura, J.	AUT	100m	1	1	2	12.5	
			SF	1	6		
		4×100m relay	1	1	4	49.9	
Van Kesteren, J.	BEL	Javelin throw	F		11	33,13	
Vellu, L.	FRA	Discus throw	F		14	33,95	
Wajsowna, J.	POL	Discus throw	F		2	46,22	S
Walasiewicz, S.	POL	100m	1	3	2	12.5	
			SF	2	2	12.0	
			F		2	11.7	S
Webb, V.	GBR	80m hurdles	1	2	1	11.8	
			SF	1	5	11.8	
Whitehead, G.	GBR	80m hurdles	1	3	4		
Wilhelmsen, G.	USA	Javelin throw	F		7	37,35	
		Discus throw	F		8	34,43	
Worst, M.V.	USA	Javelin throw	F		9	36,69	
Yamamoto, S.V.	JPN	Javelin throw	F		5	41,45	

1948

Fanny Blankers-Koen, a Popular Heroine

The Games were awarded to London in 1948, and despite the shortages associated with the war (Britain was experiencing food and clothes rationing) and grey, wet weather, the Games were a success. There were outstanding performances, including the Olympic debut of Emil Zatopek, but the athlete who took over the headlines and the affection of the spectators was a 30-year-old mother from Holland, Francina Blankers-Koen, who broke the tape 11 times in heats and finals. Popularly known as "Fanny", she won four gold medals.

Men's Track Events

Melvin Patton, known as "Pell Mel" among his sprinting friends, was the firm favourite for the **100 metres**. He had earlier in the year run a world record 9·3 sec for the 100 yards, beating the man who appeared his most dangerous rival, Lloyd LaBeach of Panama, by a narrow margin. In the American trials, Harrison Dillard had attempted four races in one hour and had failed in the hurdles, where he was world record holder. Luckily, he had qualified as America's third string for the 100 metres, but was little fancied. On the second start in the final, Dillard was away perfectly and was soon leading fellow-American Barney Ewell. Both Patton and McDonald Bailey of Britain had poor starts. Dillard held his lead all the way and won in 10·3 sec with Ewell placed second in 10·4. There was a close battle for third place between LaBeach and Alistair McCorquodale of Britain, which was won narrowly by the former, with both men being given a time of 10·4 sec.

The favourite for the **200 metres** was "Hustling" Herb McKenley of Jamaica, but Lloyd LaBeach of Panama had recently run 20·3 for 220 yards on a straight track. In the final, Barney Ewell started fast and was a couple of metres up on the field at the crown of the bend. However, coming off the bend Mel Patton of the States reached Ewell's shoulder and went slightly ahead in the straight. Patton reached the tape first in 21·1 sec on a wet and yielding track, while Ewell came home second and was also given 21·1. Third was LaBeach in 21·2 after a dour struggle with McKenley.

The **400 metres** saw two Jamaicans, Arthur Wint and Herb McKenley vying for honours. They had grown up together and whenever they had raced each other in their home country, Wint had always won. Wint had then gone to Britain and McKenley to America, where he dominated 400 metres racing and set a world record of 45·9 sec. In the semi-finals Wint had surprised with a scintillating 46·3 so a good race was in prospect. In the final, McKenley was on the inside lane with Wint immediately outside him. At the gun McKenley shot straight into the lead and reached the 200 in a fast 21·4, with his great rival following in 22·2. Around the turn

the 6ft 4½in Wint ate up the deficiency with his enormous nine-foot strides and 15 metres from the tape he swept by and won in an Olympic record-equalling 46·2. McKenley was timed at 46·4 for second place, with the fast finishing Mal Whitfield of America taking third position in 46·6.

Marcel Hansenne of France had run the fastest **800 metres** time in 1948 and was expected to win the final following his 1-50·5 victory in the semi-finals. Nine runners lined up and Robert Chef d'Hotel of France jumped into the lead, closely followed by Hansenne with the other athletes bumping each other as they raced around the first bend. At the bell in 54·2, Mal Whitfield took the lead and stretched the field in the backstraight, followed by Hansenne. Arthur Wint of Jamaica made a determined effort around the final bend and came into contention in the home straight, but Whitfield held on to his lead and won in a new Olympic record of 1-49·2. Wint's strong finish obtained second position in 1-49·5, with Hansenne third in 1-49·8.

The **1,500 metres** was a race in which the co-holder of the world record, Lennart Strand of Sweden, was considered to be unbeatable. Three of the four heats were won by Swedes, with the fourth going to Willie Slijkhuis of Holland. At the start of the final, Marcel Hansenne of France took the lead and passed 400 metres in 58·3 and 800 in 2-02·6. He continued to lead for another 200 metres with Strand following. At this point Henry Eriksson of Sweden dashed to the front with everybody trying to hang on to him. Only Strand succeeded, and the two forged ahead. With 50 metres to go, Strand appeared to give up and Eriksson won in 3-49·8, Strand only just holding off the fast-finishing Slijkhuis for second place, both being timed at 3-50·4.

Heat two of the **5,000 metres** saw Emil Zatopek of Czechoslovakia and Erik Ahlden of Sweden engage in an unnecessarily fast duel, which was won by the latter in 14-34·2. In the final, these same two runners set a strong pace over the first couple of laps, then shared the lead with Bertil Albertsson of Sweden as the 3,000 metres mark was passed in 8-33·0. In the ninth lap, Gaston Reiff of Belgium injected some pace, at first taking Willie Slijkhuis of Holland and Zatopek with him, but then he took command and established a 30-metre lead over the two following runners. With 300 metres left, Zatopek sprinted after Reiff and in an exciting finish just failed to catch him, as the Belgian won in a new Olympic record of 14-17·6. Zatopek recorded 14-17·8 for second place and Slijkhuis 14-26·8 for third.

The **10,000 metres** was run as a straight final. Among the competitors expected to produce the fireworks were the world record holder Viljo Heino of Finland, and Emil Zatopek, who had run close to the Finn's record. Heino took up the running during the first lap, followed by Evert Heinstrom and Salomon Kononen, both of

Arthur Wint

Arthur Wint was a superb athlete with a giant stride to match his 6ft 4½in height. Born in Manchester, Jamaica, on 25 May 1920, the son of a minister and a Scottish mother, he arrived in England during the Second World War to become an RAF fighter pilot.

Staying in England after the war to study medicine, he soon showed an unusual turn of speed on the running track and while he was picked to compete for Britain in international matches, it was Jamaica who had first call for the Olympics. In the 1948 400m final at the London Games he won a thrilling duel with his countryman, Herb McKenley, to take the gold in 46·2 sec, which equalled the Olympic record. This success compensated handsomely for his narrow defeat by Mal Whitfield, of the USA, in the 800m final.

The immensely popular Wint again contested the Games in Helsinki 1952 but here it was only silver medals for him, again behind Whitfield in both the 400m and 800m. There was a golden reward for him, however, before the Games were over — in the 4 × 400m relay. Along with Les Laing, McKenley and George Rhoden, his Jamaican team shattered the American's world record by a huge five seconds.

Wint later became Jamaica's High Commissioner in London.

Finland. In the ninth lap Zatopek made his move to the front and Heino took up the challenge. For seven more laps Heino was stride for stride with his adversary, then Zatopek put in a devastating sprint and opened up a gap of 30 metres, whereupon Heino left the track. The trailing group now consisted of Heinstrom, Bertil Albertsson of Sweden and the Algerian Alain Mimoun, representing France. Zatopek continued to increase his lead and won in a new Olympic record of 29-59·6. Mimoun captured the race for second place in 30-47·4 from Albertsson, who was third with 30-53·6.

The man tipped to win the **marathon** was Yun-Bok Suh of Korea, who had won the Boston Marathon the year before in a very fast time. Eusebio Guinez of Argentina was the early leader, but at 10km Etienne Gailly of Belgium led a string of runners. Gailly kept his lead until 33km when he went through a bad patch and was joined by Yun-Chil Choi of Korea, Delfo Cabrera and Guinez, both of Argentina, and Tom Richards of Britain. With 2,500 metres to go Bailly had recovered and was winging his way back to the stadium with Cabrera in hot pursuit and Tom Richards a further 50 metres behind. When Gailly appeared in the stadium he was in a groggy state and Cabrera swept past him to win in 2:34-51·6. Not far behind, Richards secured second place in 2:35-07·6 and the Belgian eventually tottered across the line for third place in 2:35-33·6.

America's best **110 metres hurdles** exponent, Harrison Dillard, did not qualify for his country's team, but that did not make much difference to the USA, who made a clean sweep in this event. In the semi-finals, Bill Porter equalled the Olympic record of 14·1 and his two colleagues both recorded 14·2. In the final, Clyde Scott of America was out of his blocks first but the other Americans Porter and Craig Dixon caught up at the third flight. Porter clipped the hurdle and Dixon went away in front. Dixon then misjudged the eighth flight and Porter broke the Olympic record to win in 13·9 sec. Scott also overtook Dixon and held on to take second place in 14·1, with both men being given the same time.

Both Rune Larsson of Sweden and Roy Cochran of the USA ran 51·9 sec in the **400 metres hurdles** semi-finals to beat the listed world record. In the final, Cochran and the unknown Duncan White of Ceylon set off at a very sharp pace. Cochran opened up a six-metre lead around the bend, and strode down the home straight. Despite fumbling at the last hurdle, he won in the new record time of 51·1 sec, while White hung on to his fast pace and came home second in 51·8. There was a battle for third place between Larsson and Dick Ault, which was resolved when the American minced his strides at the ninth flight to let through Larsson for the bronze medal in 52·2.

The **3,000 metres steeplechase** was a specialist event of the Swedes and the only runner outside Sweden that was given a chance was Rafael Pujazon of France. In the final, the lead alternated until Erik Elmsaeter of Sweden started forcing the pace half-way through the race. Tore Sjoestrand of Sweden shared some pacemaking with his fellow Swede and on the last lap put in a powerful piece of running to win by 30 metres in 9-04·6. His compatriot, Elmsaeter, was a comfortable second in 9-08·2 while the third Swede, Hagstroem, got home for the bronze medal in 9-11·8, when Pujazon dropped out of the race.

Heat one of the **10 kilometres walk** was extremely fast, with John Mikaelsson of Sweden stepping it out with Charles Morris of Britain. The former won in 45-03·0 for a new Olympic record and Morris was timed at 45-10·4. The final saw a repeat performance by Mikaelsson, but the track was now wet, heavier and therefore slower and Mikaelsson was a very tired man at the finish. Ingemar Johansson of Sweden came in second in 45-43·8, while Fritz Schwab of Switzerland had a great tussle with Morris and Harry Churcher, both of Britain, before winning third place in 46-00·2.

John Ljunggren of Sweden was in a class by himself in the **50 kilometres walk** over a hilly and gruelling course. He led from the start and was 40 seconds in front of Edgar Bruun of Norway at 5km. At the half-way stage Ljunggren was timed at 1:19-58 with Rex Whitlock, brother of the 1936 winner, in second position some six minutes behind. The Swede won by 1·3km in 4:41-52. Gaston Godel of Switzerland, the second walker to enter the stadium, did not realise that there was anyone ahead of him and joyously waved his arms about believing that the gold medal was in the bag. His time was 4:48-17, and only 14 seconds behind Godel came Tebbs Lloyd Johnson of Britain, to claim the bronze.

The **4 × 100 metres relay** was a dead certainty for the USA squad, even though it included Lorenzo Wright,

In a clean sweep, the three Americans take all the medals for the 110 metres hurdles. The winner Bill Porter, is flanked by Clyde Scott (left) and Craig Dixon (right).

the reserve. At the gun Barney Ewell led off for them and passed to Wright. The third American runner was Harrison Dillard, who opened a two-metre lead, then Mel Patton grabbed the baton and stormed to a five-metre win in 40·6 sec. Second was Great Britain in 41·3 and third Italy in 41·5.

The two favourites for the **4 × 400 metres relay** were the USA and Jamaica. The first leg of the final was run by Art Harnden for the US and he fought George Rhoden of Jamaica all the way to hold a marginal lead in 48·0 sec. Then Cliff Bourland took over from Harnden and swept around the track in 47·3 to establish a 14-metre advantage over Les Laing of Jamaica. Was Jamaica worried? No, they had the world's two greatest 400 metres runners in Arthur Wint and Herb McKenley waiting to run. Roy Cochran was away for America on the third leg and Wint went after him like the wind. So fast did Wint go that he got cramp along the backstraight and had to hop off the track, leaving Cochran to complete his lap in 47·8 before handing to Mal Whitfield, who clocked 47·3 to record a win for the US in 3-10·4. France was a modest second in 3-14·8 while Sweden came third in 3-16·0.

Men's Field Events

America came to London for the **high jump** with a clutch of jumpers capable of 2,02 metres, but at 1,90 their trials winner, Verne McGrew, failed three times. At 1,95 five jumpers cleared and one of them, John Winter of Australia, strained his back. The Australian knew he had only one good jump left in him, so at the next height of 1,98 he gave it all he got. He succeeded, nobody else

Gaston Reiff

Reiff had the distinction of beating the great Emil Zatopek in the 5,000m Olympic final in London in 1948, although some said it was probably because the famous Czech had not fully recovered from winning the 10,000m earlier in the Games. Be that as it may, Zatopek, some 50 metres or so down at the bell, chased the leading Reiff with a remarkable burst over the last 300 and was catching the Belgian so rapidly that the roar of the crowd increased with his every stride. Reiff thought the applause was for him until he looked round and saw Zatopek almost on his heels. The Belgian managed an extra spurt to gain the verdict by a metre.

Reiff, born at Braine L'Allena in 1921, was a quiet and unassuming man who had developed an intense love for athletics following junior successes in cross country running. He twice won the Belgian junior title before becoming the national senior champion at cross country. Following his London Olympic success he ran a world record for 2,000m (5-7·0) and in 1949 set a world mark for 3,000m (7-58·8).

In 1952 Reiff proved by running a world record for two miles (8-40·4), that he was competing as well as ever, but tension seemed to grip him when he went to the line to defend the Olympic title in Helsinki in 1952 and he dropped out.

Following in the footsteps of Zabala, the 1932 winner of the marathon, Delfo Cabrera of the Argentine, overtakes a very tired Etienne Gailly, with the finish in sight.

Henry Eriksson beats his more favoured Swedish compatriot, Lennart Strand (195), in the 1,500 metres final.

did so and the gold medal was his. The new count-back rule decided that Bjorn Paulsen of Norway was second and George Stanich of America was third. The unluckiest man was American Dwight Edleman, who only just tipped the bar off at 1,98 and finished fourth.

Boo Morcom of the USA was favourite to win the **pole vault**, but had strained his knee and was anxious to make every jump count. Having cleared 3,95 metres without difficulty, he elected to leave his next attempt to 4,20 and failed three times Three vaulters then went clear, Guinn Smith and Bob Richards, both of the USA, and Erikki Kataja of Finland. By this time the rain was coming down and the jumpers were wet and miserable. The bar was raised to 4,30 and Smith levered himself over on his third attempt to take the gold medal. He had one shot at 4,40 for the Olympic record, before he called it a day. Kataja took the silver position on the count-back rule, with Richards securing the bronze.

Willie Steele of the USA was the best **long jump** exponent since Jesse Owens. In the qualifying rounds he had jumped 7,78 metres and fellow-American Lorenzo Wright 7,53, but preliminary marks no longer counted towards the medals. On his very first jump in the finals, Steele strained a tendon in his jumping leg while leaping 7,825, and was confined to watching from then on. Was it enough? He need not have worried, as Thomas Bruce of Australia could manage only 7,55 for second place,

with Herb Douglas of America third at one centimetre less.

The **triple jump** lacked lustre without the Japanese jumpers competing. In their absence, George Avery of Australia was rated the best of the field; he was certainly the best technician. He led the qualifiers with 15,335 metres and began the final with a jump of 15,365. Arne Ahman of Sweden immediately responded with 15,40, which was the gold medal jump. Avery could not improve and was placed second, with Ruhi Sarialp of Turkey, a surprise bronze medallist with 15,02.

Chuck Fonville, the world's greatest **shot put** exponent, failed the American trials and did not even make the team. The three who did, however, were a match for anyone in the world. "Moose" Thompson was the one on form and with each and every one of his valid puts he exceeded the old Olympic record. He won the competition with 17,12 metres and his one foul throw went even further. Jim Delaney threw 16,68 for second place and the slightly built Jim Fuchs, managed 16,42 for third. Both exceeded the previous record in a clean sweep for the USA.

The Italians had a strong hand in the **discus throw** with Adolfo Consolini and Giuseppe Tosi, the top two throwers in Europe being pitted against America's best, Fortune Gordien. In the preliminaries Consolini and Tosi both bettered the Olympic record with 51,08 and

All-Sport Photographic Ltd.

Fanny Blankers-Koen

Certainly the most remarkable woman track and field athlete to be produced by Holland, Fanny Blankers-Koen received justifiable world acclaim for winning four gold medals — 100m, 200m, 80m hurdles and 4 × 100m relay — at the 1948 Olympics in London. The achievement was all the more enhanced because by this time she was a 30-year-old mother. The Second World War had intervened since she had tied for sixth place in the high jump at the Berlin Games in 1936. But she had given plenty of warning of what her opponents could expect in London by setting world records for the women's 100m and 80m hurdles during her build-up for the Olympics.

Born as Francina Koen in Amsterdam on 26 April 1918, Fanny married her coach, the late Jan Blankers, a former Dutch triple jump champion, and gave him full credit for the long list of successes gained under his guidance.

So versatile was she as an athlete that between 1938 and 1951 she set seven world records in seven different events: 100 yards, 100m, 220 yards, 80m hurdles, high jump, long jump and pentathlon. There is no knowing how many more she would have recorded had the war not intervened.

She also collected eight gold medals from her endeavours in the European Championships of 1938, 1946 and 1950.

50,56 metres respectively. Tosi led in the first round of the finals with 51,78, but Consolini responded in the second with 52,78 to win the competition with a new Olympic record. Tosi won the silver with his first-round effort and Gordien the bronze with a third-round throw of 50,77.

Germany was not allowed to compete in 1948, so their three world-rated **hammer throw**ers were not in London. Imre Nemeth of Hungary, the new world record-holder, dominated the competition from the start. On his first throw he reached 53,59 metres, on his second 55,44 and on his last a winning 56,07. Ivan Gubijan of Yugoslavia was a surprise second with 54,27, beating the best of the Americans, Bob Bennett who achieved 53,73. Bo Ericson of Sweden, the current European champion, was sixth.

It was unfortunate that both Martin Biles of America and Arne Berglund of Sweden had their best performances in the qualifying round of the **javelin throw** and were not allowed to carry them forward. Biles recorded 67,68 and Berglund 67,02 metres. In the final, Tapio Rautavaara of Finland secured the gold medal with his very first throw of 69,77. Steve Seymour, the highly rated American, achieved 67,56 on his third attempt for the silver, while Jozef Varszegi of Hungary threw 67,03 for bronze.

In the **decathlon**, Ignace Heinrich of France was strongly tipped to win, although conditions for the two-day event were abysmal with rain and an overcast sky. The competition was very close on the first day with Enrique Kistenmacher of Argentina leading with 3,897 points, from Heinrich on 3,880 and the 17-year-old American Bob Mathias on 3,848. The fourth and fifth men were right behind, the Americans Floyd Simmons and Irving Mondschein recording 3,843 and 3,811 respectively. There was little change in the positions on the second day, until Mathias produced a fine pole vault of 3,50 metres under the floodlights and a javelin throw of 50,32 metres to take command. The final event, the 1,500 metres was run at 10.30 pm at night, twelve hours after he had run the hurdles that morning! Young Mathias won with a score of 7,139 from Heinrich, 6,974, and Simmons, 6,950.

Mel Patton

Mel Patton, born in 1924, had proved himself a High School sprinter well above average before going off to join the United States Navy. When he became a freshman in 1946 at the University of California, a superb edge was put on his speed by the leading American coach of the day, Dean Cornwell, and within a year Patton had equalled the world record for 100 yards with 9·4 sec.

The following season he was in greater shape and in the May of that year improved the world record to 9·3 sec. Who else, then, could be favourite for the Olympic 100m title in London two months later? But the gold medallion for this event was not for Patton. Tension gripped him and he finished fifth.

But he was not going to allow nerves to get the better of him in the 200m, and this he won in 21·2 sec. He then added another gold to his collection by anchoring the Americans' winning 4 × 100m relay team.

A year later he set a world record for 200m and 220 yards on a straight course of 20·2 sec, and twice helped his University team to better the world record for 4 × 200m and 4 × 220 yards relays. A strong following wind prevented his best 100 yards run of 9·1 sec that year being accepted as a world record.

He later became a professional athlete.

Making up for his disappointment in the high hurdles. Harrison Dillard (extreme left) wins the 100 metres final from fellow American, Barney Ewell (70).

Adolfo Consolini

A discus thrower of exceptional consistency, Adolfo Consolini competed in four Olympic Games but only once landed the gold medal, at his first attempt in 1948. There his toughest challenge came from his countryman Giuseppe Tosi, who like Consolini, was a world class athlete.

Consolini made an encouraging start at Wembley by exceeding the Olympic record with his first throw. Tosi replied by sending the discus 15 inches further. Back came Consolini with all the speed and crispness he could command to reach 173ft 1½in (52,78m) and become the champion.

He was in the hunt again in Helsinki four years later, but although he improved on his London distance he found his master in Sim Iness, the new American world record-holder.

Consolini tried yet again in Melbourne in 1956 but his best this time left him in sixth place to another master of the discus throwing art, Al Oerter. By 1960 in Rome, while still throwing well, he found the standard of world competition was rising fast, and he was left to fill 17th place.

Consolini, who was born in 1917, improved the world record three times between 1941 and 1948. His other successes included winning the European championships on three occasions. He died in 1969.

Seen clearing the final flight of the 400 metres hurdles is the America, Roy Cochran, who won with ease.

Women's Events

In the **100 metres** was Fanny Blankers-Koen of Holland, who during the war years had made a big reputation for herself as a sprinter, hurdler and jumper. Earlier in the year she had equalled the world record of 11·5 sec and was everyone's favourite to take the Olympic title. Her nearest rival seemed to be Dorothy Manley of Britain, who had clocked 12·1 in the heats. In the final, Blankers-Koen was never headed after the first 20 metres and won in 11·9. The race for second place was very close between Manley, Shirley Strickland of Australia and Viola Myers of Canada and a photo-finish picture was called for. Manley was given silver position and Strickland the bronze. All three girls recorded 12·2.

For the first time, an Olympic **200 metres** for women was run, and also for the first time seven lanes were used for a sprint race. This was to allow two athletes from each of seven heats to progress to the two semi-finals. In the first semi-final, Fanny Blankers-Koen was an easy winner in a fast 24·3 sec, while the second race saw a dead-heat between Shirley Strickland and Audrey Williamson of Britain. Fanny drew the outside lane in the final and she simply swept around the turn and into the straight without seeing another competitor. Her winning time on a wet track was 24·4. Behind her, there was a close battle for the lesser places with Williamson winning the silver in 25·1 and Audrey Patterson of the USA taking the bronze. Many years later the photo-finish picture for this race was closely examined by an expert, who pronounced Strickland to have been the winner of the bronze medal.

Fanny Blankers-Koen's third race was the **80 metres hurdles**, at which she had set a world record of 11·0 sec. Blankers-Koen duly broke the Olympic record in her heat in 11·3, while Maureen Gardner, of Britain, another strong contender for the medals, was nearly eliminated in the semi-finals when she crashed through three hurdles. In the final it was Gardner who was quickest off the mark and she led most of the way with Blankers-Koen and Shirley Strickland just behind. Blankers-Koen's superior stamina took her to the tape first in 11·2 with Gardner second in the same time, a new Olympic record. Strickland was just behind and was given 11·4.

The heats of the **4 × 100 metres relay** indicated that the final was going to be closely fought. The first two legs saw Denmark ahead with Australia, Britain and Canada in close attendance. Shirley Strickland for Australia took her team into the lead on the third leg, with Holland and Canada next. However, Fanny Blankers-Koen took over for the anchor leg one metre down and led Holland to victory in 47·5 sec. It was her fourth gold medal of the games. Australia was second in 47·6 and Canada third with 47·8.

Although Fanny Blankers-Koen was the world record-holder in the **high jump**, she did not contest this event. Six competitors cleared 1,58 metres, but at 1,61 only Alice Coachman of the USA, Dorothy Tyler of Britain, the silver medallist from Berlin eight years previously, and Micheline Ostermeyer of France were left in. At 1,64 Ostermeyer failed and took third place. The bar was then raised to 1,66 and both Coachman and Tyler succeeded. At 1,68 Coachman cleared first time and was rewarded with first place. Tyler cleared on her second attempt and was second. Both girls later failed at 1,70.

The standard in the **long jump** was lower than expected. Olga Gyarmati of Hungary had jumped 5,99 metres earlier in the year, but her winning jump in the Olympic competition was only 5,695. Naomi de Portela of Argentina was second with 5,60 and Ana-Britt Leyman of Sweden was third at 5,575.

The **shot put** contest was won by Micheline Ostermeyer of France who threw 13,75 metres. She was a talented pianist who had recently graduated from the Paris Conservatory of music. Second was Amelia Piccinini of Italy with 13,09, just beating Ine Schaeffer of Austria into third place by one centimetre.

Micheline Ostermeyer won the **discus throw** as well as the shot. Her winning distance was 41,92 metres with Edera Cordiale-Gentile not far behind in second place with 41,17. Third came Jacqueline Mazeas of France, who threw 40,47.

Herma Bauma of Austria was a well-known **javelin thrower** of the 1930s and 1940s. She obtained a well deserved victory, with an Olympic record of 45,57 metres. Second was Kaisa Parviainen of Finland, the home of javelin throwing, with 43,79, and third, Lily Carlstedt of Denmark, with 42,08.

Imre Nemeth of Hungary swings to victory in the hammer event. His son Miklos won the javelin throw in 1976.

All-Sport Photographic Ltd.

COMPETITOR	COUNTRY CODE	EVENT	ROUND	HEAT	PLACE	TIME & DISTANCE	MEDAL
MALES							
Abdullah, B.	FRA	10000m	F		6	31-7·8	
Acarbay, E.	TUR	400m	1	9	5	53·0	
		4×400m relay	1	2	5	3-35·0	
Adamczyk, E.	POL	Long jump	F		11	6,73	
		Decathlon	F		9	6712	
Adarraga, J.	ESP	800m	1	3	7		
		1500m	1	2	8		
Adedoyin, A.	GBR	Long jump	F		5	7,27	
		High jump	F		12	1,90	
Aguirre, J.	MEX	Long jump	Q		DNQ		
		Triple jump	Q		DNQ		
Ahlden, E.	SWE	5000m	1	2	1	14-34·2	
			F		4	14-28·6	
Ahman, A.	SWE	Triple jump	F		1	15,40	G
Aksur, K.	TUR	100m	1	12	5		
		200m	1	7	4		
		4×100m relay	1	1	4		
Alcarcon, E.	MEX	5000m	1	3	8		
Albans, W.	USA	Triple jump	F		10	14,33	
Alberti, H.	ARG	400m hurdles	1	1	3	54·6	
		4×400m relay	1	3	3	3-21·2	
Albertsson, B.	SWE	5000m	1	3	3	15-07·8	
			F		5	14-39·0	
		10000m	F		3	30-53·6	B
Alnevik, F.	SWE	400m	1	5	2	50·2	
			2	1	6	50·6	
		4×400m relay	1	3	2	3-21·0	
			F		3	3-16·0	B
Alzamora, H.	PER	110m hurdles	1	6	4		
Anchante, M.R.	PER	100m	1	4	4		
Andersson, E.P.	SWE	Decathlon	F		5	6877	
Andre, J.	FRA	400m hurdles	1	1	2	54·5	
			SF	1	6	56·3	
Anguita, C.S.	CHI	100m	1	6	4		
Aparicio, J.	COL	400m	1	2	4	50·8	
		400m hurdles	1	1	4	55·1	
Appellaniz, P.	ESP	Javelin throw	Q		DNQ		
Archer, J.	GBR	4×100m relay	1	2	1	41·4	
			F		2	41·3	S
Arifon, J.	FRA	400m hurdles	1	2	2	56·9	
			SF	1	4	52·2	
Arvidsson, G.	SWE	Shot put	F		5	15,37	
Ascune, H.	URU	High jump	F		=14	1,87	
		Decathlon	F		20	6026	
		4×100m relay	1	2	5	42·8	
Askew, H.	GBR	Long jump	F		9	6,93	
Ault, R.	USA	400m hurdles	1	5	1	54·7	
			SF	1	2	52·1	
			F		4	52·4	
Avalos, A.	ARG	800m	1	5	5	1-56·6	
		4×400m relay	1	3	3	3-21·2	
Avery, G.	AUS	Triple jump	F		2	15,36	S
Baarnaas, P.	NOR	50k walk	F		DNF		
Bailey, E.McD.	GBR	100m	1	6	1	10·5	
			2	2	2	10·6	
			SF	2	3	10·6	
			F		6	10·6	
Balafas, T.	GRE	Pole vault	Q		DNQ		
Bally, E.	FRA	100m	1	12	DNF		
		200m	1	10	4		
Banhalmi, F.	HUN	400m	1	2	3	49·6	
Barbosa, J.	PUR	Pole vault	F		=9	3,95	
Barkway, R.	GBR	110m hurdles	1	1	4		
Barry, J.	IRL	1500m	1	1	8		
		5000m	1	1	DNF		
Barten, H.	USA	800m	1	2	1	1-55·6	
			SF	3	1	1-51·7	
			F		4	1-50·1	
Bartha, L.	HUN	100m	1	12	3	11·1	
		4×100m relay	1	2	2	41·4	
			F		4	41·6	
Barthel, J.	LUX	800m	1	4	3	1-54·8	
			SF	1	6	1-54·6	
		1500m	1	3	3	3-56·4	
			F		9		
Bartram, J.	AUS	100m	1	8	2	10·8	
			2	3	3	10·6	
			SF	1	4		
		400m	1	6	2	50·8	
			2	3	4	49·9	
		4×100m relay	1	2	3	41·5	
Beckus, R.	USA	Triple jump	Q		DNQ	14,03	
Bernard, C.	FRA	High jump	Q		DNQ		
Bengtsson, I.	SWE	800m	1	6	2	1-52·9	
			SF	2	1	1-51·2	
			F		5	1-50·5	

COMPETITOR	COUNTRY CODE	EVENT	ROUND	HEAT	PLACE	TIME & DISTANCE	MEDAL
Bennett, R.	USA	Hammer throw	F		3	53,73	B
Bergkvist, G.	SWE	1500m	1	4	1	3-51·8	
			F		5	3-52·2	
Berglund, A.	SWE	Javelin throw	F		10	62,62	
Berkay, E.	TUR	110m hurdles	1	1	5		
		4×100m relay	1	1	4		
Bernard, O.	SUI	110m hurdles	1	5	2	14·9	
			SF	1	5		
Bertolini, V.	ITA	50k walk	F		DNF		
Biedermann, A.	ARG	200m	1	3	4		
		4×100m relay	1	3	3	42·4	
Biles, M.	USA	Javelin throw	F		6	65,17	
Birrell, J.	GBR	110m hurdles	1	1	4		
Bjarnasson, A.	ISL	4×100m relay	1	3	4	42·9	
Bjurstroem, R.	SWE	50k walk	F		6	4:56-43	
Bloch, P.	NOR	100m	1	5	3	11·1	
		200m	1	8	5		
Bobin, R.	FRA	Triple jump	Q		DNQ		
Bolen, D.	USA	400m	1	6	1	50·1	
			2	4	1	48·0	
			SF	2	2	47·9	
			F		4	47·2	
Bonnhoff, G.	ARG	100m	1	9	2	10·8	
			2	4	5		
		200m	1	7	1	22·2	
			2	2	4		
		4×100m relay	1	3	3	42·4	
Bourgaux, F.	BEL	200m	1	10	3	22·9	
		4×100m relay	1	2	4		
Bourland, C.	USA	200m	1	8	1	21·3	
			2	2	1	21·3	
			SF	2	1	21·5	
			F		5	21·3	
		4×400m relay	1	1	1	3-12·6	
			F		1	3-10·4	G
Bouvet, C.	FRA	Pole vault	Q		DNQ		
Braekman, P.	BEL	100m	1	5	4		
		110m hurdles	1	1	2	15·2	
			SF	1	4		
		4×100m relay	1	2	4		
Bralo, R.	ARG	10000m	F				
Braughton, J.	GBR	5000m	1	1	10		
Breitman, G.	FRA	Pole vault	Q		DNQ		
Brewer, E.	GBR	Discus throw	Q		DNQ		
Bruce, T.	AUS	Long jump	F		2	7,55	S
		4×100m relay	1	2	3	41·5	
Bruun, E.	NOR	50k walk	F		4	4:53-18	
Bryngeirsson, T.	ISL	Pole vault	Q		DNQ		
Brys, J.	BEL	800m	1	3	4	1-55·9	
			SF	1	5	1-53·2	
Buchel, G.	LIE	Decathlon	F		DNF		
Bulic, J.	YUG	4×400m relay	1	3	4	3-25·4	
Burton, W.	USA	Discus throw	Q		DNQ	43,78	
Butt, M.S.	PAK	100m	1	11	4		
		200m	1	9	2	22·8	
			2	4	6		
Cabrera, D.	ARG	Marathon	F		1	2:34-51·6	G
Caron, H.	FRA	50k walk	F		11	5:08-15	
Carvajal, J.	ESP	Discus throw	Q		DNQ		
Casado, B.	PUR	High jump	Q		DNQ		
Cascino, S.	ITA	50k walk	F		14	5:20-03	
Cederquist, P.	DEN	Hammer throw	Q		DNQ		
Cevona, V.	TCH	1500m	1	2	2	3-53·2	
			F		4	3-51·2	
Chambers, R.	USA	800m	1	3	3	1-54·3	
			SF	2	3	1-52·9	
			F		6	1-52·1	
Chefd'hotel, R.	FRA	800m	1	4	2	1-56·2	
			SF	3	2	1-52·0	
			F		7	1-53·0	
		4×400m relay	1	2	2	3-17·0	
			F		2	3-14·8	S
Chen, Y.-L.	CHN	400m	1	1	3	50·9	
Chesneau, M.	FRA	3000m steeplechase	1	3	4	9-27·6	
			F		11	9-30·2	
Chevalier, L.	FRA	10k walk	1	2	DIS		
Choi, Y.-C.	KOR	Marathon	F		DNF		
Chote, M.	GBR	Javelin throw	Q		DNQ		
Christen, W.	SUI	400m hurdles	1	5	3	56·7	
Christensen, H.	DEN	800m	1	2	DNF		
Churcher, H.	GBR	10k walk	1	2	1	46-26·4	
			F		5	46-28·0	
Clancy, C.	IRL	Discus throw	Q		DNQ		
Clark, D.	GBR	Hammer throw	F		11	48,35	

COMPETITOR	COUNTRY CODE	EVENT	ROUND	HEAT	PLACE	TIME & DISTANCE	MEDAL
Clausen, H.	ISL	100m	1	6	2	11·0	
			2	2	6		
		200m	1	1	3	22·2	
		4×100m relay	1	3	4	42·9	
		4×400m relay	1	2	6		
Clausen, O.	ISL	100m	1	9	4		
		Decathlon	F		12	6444	
Cochran, R.	USA	400m hurdles	1	1	1	53·9	
			SF	2	1	51·9*	
			F		1	51·1*	G
		4×400m relay	1	1	1	3-12·6	
			F		1	3-10·4	G
Coleman, J.	SAF	Marathon	F		4	2:36-06·0	
Consiglieri, M.	PER	Discus throw	Q		DNQ		
Consolini, A.	ITA	Discus throw	F		1	52,78*	G
Corsaro, G.	ITA	10k walk	1	2	4	47-26·8	
			F		9		
Cosic, A.	YUG	4×400m relay	1	3	4	3-25·4	
Costa, R.	BRA	200m	1	5	2	22·2	
			2	1	6		
		400m	1	10	2	49·2	
			2	1	3	48·7	
			SF	2	5	49·1	
		4×100m relay	1	1	3	42·4	
Costantino, S.	ITA	Marathon	F		DNF		
Cote, G.	CAN	Marathon	F		17	2:48-31·0	
Courron, L.	FRA	10k walk	1	2	5	48-13·0	
Cousin, P.	FRA	Marathon	F		DNF		
Cox, S.	GBR	10000m	F		7	31-08·0	
Coy, E.	CAN	Shot put	Q		DNQ		
		Discus throw	Q		DNQ		
Coyle, D.	IRL	Hammer throw	Q		DNQ		
Crapet, R.	FRA	400m	1	10	3	49·4	
Cretaine, J.	FRA	Decathlon	F		22	5829	
Cros, Y.	FRA	400m hurdles	1	5	2	55·7	
			SF	2	2	52·5	
			F		5	53·3	
Crosbie, E.	USA	50k walk	F		12	5:15-16	
Cross, S.	GBR	Triple jump	Q		DNQ		
Csanyi, G.	HUN	100m	1	7	3	11·1	
		4×100m relay	1	2	2	41·4	
			F		4	41·6	
Curotta, M.	AUS	100m	1	9	1	10·7	
			2	2	3	10·8	
			SF	1	6		
		400m	1	10	1	49·1	
			2	2	2	48·4	
			SF	1	2	47·2	
			F		5	47·9	
		4×100m relay	1	2	3	41·5	
Curry, T.	GBR	3000m steeplechase	1	1	7		
Dalrymple, M.	GBR	Javelin throw	Q		DNQ		
Damitio, G.	FRA	High jump	F		5	1,95	
		Long jump	F		6	7,07	
Da Silva, A.F.	BRA	Triple jump	F		11	14,31	
Da Silva, A.P.	BRA	100m	1	5	2	10·6	
			2	4	4		
		200m	1	8	2	21·9	
			2	2	3	22·0	
			SF	1	4		
		4×100m relay	1	1	3	42·4	
Da Silva, H.C.	BRA	100m	1	8	4		
		Triple jump	F		8	14,49	
		4×100m relay	1	1	3	42·4	
Dayer, A.	BEL	Decathlon	F		26	5586	
De Bruyn, A.D.	HOL	Discus throw	Q		DNQ		
Delaney, F.	USA	Shot put	F		2	16·68	S
De Morais, J.R.	POR	100m	1	11	2	10·9	
			2	1	6		
		200m	1	3	3	22·6	
		Triple jump	Q		DNQ		
Deni, J.	USA	50k walk	F		15	5:28-33	
Dennolf, S.	SWE	10000m	F		5	31-05;0	
Denroche, C.	IRL	4×400m relay	1	1	DIS		
De Nunes, L.	POR	Triple jump	Q		DNQ		
De Oliveira, G.	BRA	Triple jump	F		5	14,82	
De Ruyter, F.	HOL	800m	1	5	2	1-54·4	
			SF	3	6	1-54·6	
		1500m	1	1	4	3-55·2	
De Saram, J.	CEY	200m	1	2	2	23·1	
			2	2	6		
		400m	1	9	3	51·2	
Dill, H.	BER	100m	1	4	5		
		200m	1	4	5		
		400m	1	6	3	53·0	
		4×100m relay	1	2	6	45·4	

COMPETITOR	COUNTRY CODE	EVENT	ROUND	HEAT	PLACE	TIME & DISTANCE	MEDAL
Dillard, H.	USA	100m	1	5	1	10·4	
			2	1	1	10·4	
			SF	1	1	10·5	
			F		1	10·3*	G
		4×100m relay	1	1	1	41·1	
			F		1	40·6	G
Dinctourk, S.	TUR	800m	1	4	7		
		4×400m relay	1	2	5	3-35·0	
Dixon, C.	USA	110m hurdles	1	6	1	14·2	
			SF	1	1	14·2	
			F		3	14·1	B
Dolan, P.	IRL	4×400m relay	1	1	DIS		
Doms, J.	BEL	3000m steeplechase	1	1	6	9-41·8	
Dordoni, G.	ITA	10k walk	1	1	4	46-25·8	
			F		8		
Douglas, E.	GBR	Hammer throw	Q		DNQ		
Douglas, H.	USA	Long jump	F		3	7,54	B
Drake, N.	GBR	Hammer throw	Q		DNQ		
Dreyer, H.	USA	Hammer throw	F		9	51,37	
Edleman, T.	USA	High jump	F		4	1,95	
Ehlers, G.	CHI	400m	1	11	3	49·5	
		4×400m relay	1	2	4	3-23·8	
Elschen, C.	USA	1500m	1	2	6	4-00·2	
Elmsaeter, E.	SWE	3000m steeplechase	1	1	1	9-15·0	
			F		2	9-08·2	S
Epalle, C.	FRA	Triple jump	Q		DNQ		
Eranzquin, F.	ESP	Discus throw	Q		DNQ		
Ericson, B.	SWE	Hammer throw	F		6	52,98	
Eriksson, H.	SWE	1500m	1	3	1	3-53·8	
			F		1	3-49·8	G
Eriksson, P.	SWE	Decathlon	F		7	6731	
Evans, G.	ARG	400m	1	2	5	51·8	
		4×400m relay	1	3	3	3-21·2	
Evans, L.	CAN	Marathon	F		16	2:48-07·0	
Everaert, R.	BEL	10000m	F		DNF		
		3000m steeplechase	1	3	3	9-26·4	
			F		9	9-28·2	
Ewell, H.	USA	100m	1	1	1	10·5	
			2	2	1	10·5	
			SF	1	2	10·5	
			F		2	10·4	S
		200m	1	4	1	21·6	
			2	1	2	21·8	
			SF	1	3	21·8	
			F		2	21·1	S
		4×100m relay	1	1	1	41·1	
			F		1	40·6	G
Eyjolfsson, T.	ISL	4×100m relay	1	3	4	42·9	
Fahy, P.	IRL	10000m	F				
Fairgrieve, J.	GBR	200m	1	7	2	22·2	
			2	3	4		
Fayos, M.	URU	100m	1	12	1	11·0	
			2	3	5		
		200m	1	12	4		
		4×100m relay	1	2	5	42·8	
Felton, S.	USA	Hammer throw	F		4	53,66	
Ferrando, S.	PER	100m	1	10	5		
		200m	1	10	2	22·5	
			2	3	5		
Figueroa, H.	CHI	Decathlon	F		20	6026	
Fikejz, J.	TCH	Long jump	Q		DNQ		
Finlay, D.	GBR	110m hurdles	1	5	4		
Fortun, R.	CUB	100m	1	8	1	10·7	
			2	4	3	10·6	
			SF	2	5	10·7	
		200m	1	3	1	21·9	
			2	4	3	22·0	
			SF	2	6		
Foster, S.	JAM	110m hurdles	1	5	3	15·1	
Fournier, L.	CAN	Decathlon	F		25	5590	
Frank, V.	USA	Discus throw	Q		DNQ	42,00	
Fransson, U.	SWE	Discus throw	F		10	45,25	
Frayer, H.	FRA	110m hurdles	1	1	2	15·5	
			SF	2	6		
Frederick, W.A.	CAN	Marathon	F		23	2:52-12·0	
Frederiksen, S.	DEN	Hammer throw	F		10	50,07	
Frieden, P.	LUX	3000m steeplechase	1	3	8		
Frischknecht, H.	SUI	Marathon	F		DNF		
Fuchs, J.	USA	Shot put	F		3	16,42	B
Fuse, J.	ARG	Hammer throw	Q		DNQ		
Gailly, E.	BEL	Marathon	F		3	2:35-33·6	B
Garoza, L.	PER	Pole vault	Q		DNQ		
Garay, S.	HUN	1500m	1	4	3	3-53·0	
			F		7	3-52·8	
Garcia, A.	CUB	100m	1	1	4		
		200m	1	4	3	22·2	
		400m	1	4	4	50·2	

COMPETITOR	COUNTRY CODE	EVENT	ROUND	HEAT	PLACE	TIME & DISTANCE	MEDAL
Gardner, P.	AUS	110m hurdles	1	3	2	14·6	
			SF	1	2	14·5	
			F		5	14·7	
Geary, G.	ARG	200m	1	6	3	23·0	
Gehrmann, D.	USA	1500m	1	1	3	3-54·8	
			F		10		
Gerber, O.	SUI	Decathlon	F		27	5558	
Gierutto, W.	POL	Shot put	F		10	14,37	
		Decathlon	F		19	6106	
Giles, J.A.	GBR	Shot put	F		11	13,73	
Godel, G.	SUI	50k walk	F		2	4:48-17	S
Goellors, H.	SWE	Pole vault	F		=7	3,95	
Goffberg, H.	USA	10000m	F		DNF		
Goldoanyi, B.	HUN	100m	1	3	2	11·0	
			2	2	5		
		4×100m relay	1	2	2	41·4	
			F		4	41·6	
Gonzalez, F.	MEX	Hammer throw	Q		DNQ		
Gordien, F.	USA	Discus throw	F		3	50,77	B
Gossett, H.	BEL	100m	1	2	5		
Green, C.	AUS	110m hurdles	1	4	5		
Gregory, J.	GBR	4×100m relay	1	2	1	41·4	
			F		2	41·3	S
Gubijan, I.	YUG	Hammer throw	F		2	54,27	S
Guenther, E.	SUI	5000m	1	3	9		
Guida, G.	USA	400m	1	11	1	49·0	
			2	3	2	48·0	
			SF	2	3	48·3	
			F		6	50·2	
Guiney, D.	IRL	Shot put	Q		DNQ		
Guinez, E.	ARG	10000m	F				
		Marathon	F		5	2:36-36·0	
Gundersen, B.	NOR	High jump	F		=14	1,87	
Guyodo, A.	FRA	3000m steeplechase	1	1	2	9-17·2	
			F		4	9-13·6	
Guzman, J.	CHI	400m hurdles	1	4	4	55·9	
		4×400m relay	1	2	4	3-23·8	
Haggis, E.	CAN	100m	1	10	2	10·9	
			2	1	5		
		200m	1	1	2	22·2	
			2	4	5		
		4×100m relay	1	3	2	42·3	
			F		5	41·9	
Hagstroem, G.	SWE	3000m steeplechase	1	2	2	9-22·6	
			F		3	9-11·8	B
Hakansson, S.	SWE	Marathon	F		28	3:00-09·0	
Halldorsson, P.	ISL	4×400m relay	1	2	6		
Hallgren, A.	SWE	Triple jump	F		9	14,48	
Hammer, K.	NOR	10k walk	1	1	7		
Hansenne, M.	FRA	800m	1	1	1	1-54·6	
			SF	1	1	1-50·5	
			F		3	1-49·8	B
		1500m	1	4	2	3-52·8	
			F		11		
Hardmeier, O.	SUI	400m	1	4	3	49·2	
		4×400m relay	1	1	4	3-23·0	
Hardmo, G.	SWE	10K walk	1	2	5	47-34·8	
			F		DIS		
Harnden, A.	USA	4×400m relay	1	1	1	3-12·6	
			F		1	3-10·4	G
Harris, D.	NZL	800m	1	2	2	1-56·6	
			SF	2	DNF		
Hasso, L.	IRQ	400m	1	3	5	56·8	
Hausen, I.Z.	BRA	100m	1	2	2	10·9	
			2	1	4		
		200m	1	11	2	22·2	
			2	4	4		
		4×100m relay	1	1	3	42·4	
Hawkey, R.	GBR	Triple jump	Q		DNQ		
Heber, R.	ARG	Javelin throw	Q		DNQ		
Heino, V.	FIN	10000m	F		DNF		
		Marathon	F		11	2:41-32·0	
Heinrich, I.	FRA	Discus throw	Q		DNQ		
		Decathlon	F		2	6974	S
Heinstrom, E.	FIN	10000m	F		DNF		
Henniger, E.	CAN	800m	1	4	5	1-55·4	
Hietanen, M.	FIN	Marathon	F		DNF		
Hitelman, J.	CHI	400m	1	12	4	51·5	
		4×400m relay	1	2	4	3-23·8	
Holden, J.	GBR	Marathon	F		DNF		
Holland, J.	NZL	400m hurdles	1	3	1	54·6	
			SF	2	6	53·9	
Holmberg, R.	FIN	400m	1	7	5	50·6	
		4×400m relay	1	3	1	3-20·6	
			F		4	3-24·8	
Holmvang, G.	NOR	Decathlon	F		10	6663	

COMPETITOR	COUNTRY CODE	EVENT	ROUND	HEAT	PLACE	TIME & DISTANCE	MEDAL
Holst-Soerensen, N.	DEN	800m	1	3	1	1-54·2	
			SF	3	3	1-52·4	
			F		8	1-53·4	
Honkonen, U.	FIN	High jump	F		=14	1,87	
Horulu, K.	TUR	400m	1	10	4	51·5	
		400m hurdles	1	3	3	55·1	
		4×400m relay	1	2	5	3-35·0	
Houtzager, J.	HOL	Hammer throw	F		12	45,69	
Howell, R.	GBR	3000m steeplechase	1	3	7		
Hubert, C.	FRA	50k walk	F		8	5:03-12	
Hubler, H.	SUI	1500m	1	4	8		
Hutchins, J.	CAN	800m	1	6	3	1-55·5	
			SF	1	4	1-52·6	
		1500m	1	2	4	3-54·4	
Huutoniemi, A.	FIN	Discus throw	F		9	45,28	
Ibanez, S.	ARG	50k walk	F		DNF		
Imostroza, A.	CHI	Marathon	F		15	2:47-48·0	
Isaack, G.	ARG	100m	1	7	4		
		4×100m relay	1	3	3	42·4	
Ishman, R.	TUR	800m	1	5	6	2-01·1	
		1500m	1	3	7		
		4×400m relay	1	2	5	3-35·0	
Jackes, A.	CAN	High jump	F		6	1,90	
Jacona, N.	MLT	100m	1	1	5		
Jadresic, A.	CHI	High jump	F		=9	1,90	
Joensson, T.	SWE	50k walk	F		10	5:05-08	
Johansson, I.	SWE	10k walk	1	1	5	46-44·2	
			F		2	45-43·8	S
Johansson, D.	FIN	1500m	1	2	3	3-54·0	
			F		12		
Johnson, P.	BER	100m	1	9	6		
		200m	1	9	4		
		4×100m relay	1	2	6	45·4	
Johnsen, S.	NOR	Discus throw	F		8	46,54	
Johnson, T.	GBR	50k walk	F		3	4:48-31	B
Jones, K.	GBR	100m	1	4	2	10·6	
			2	1	3	10·7	
			SF	2	6	10·9	
		4×100m relay	1	2	1	41·4	
			F		2	41·3	S
Jones, S.	GBR	Marathon	F		30	3:09-16·0	
Jonsson, M.	ISL	4×400m relay	1	2	6		
Jonsson, O.	ISL	800m	1	3	5	1-55·4	
		1500m	1	3	6	4-03·2	
Jorgensen, E.	DEN	1500m	1	1	2	3-54·2	
			F		8	3-52·8	
Josset, R.	FRA	Marathon	F		DNF		
Jouppila, P.	FIN	Shot put	F		7	14,59	
Julve, E.	PER	Decathlon	F		DNF		
		Discus throw	F		12	44,05	
Jutz, J.	SUI	Marathon	F		29	3:03-55·0	
Kaas, E.	NOR	Pole vault	Q		4	4,10	
Kahnert, J.	ARG	Shot put	Q		DNQ		
Kainlauri, A.	FIN	3000m steeplechase	1	3	2	9-25·8	
			F		10	9-29·0	
Kalina, C.	TCH	Shot put	F		8	14,55	
Karageorgos, G.	GRE	400m	1	1	4	54·5	
		800m	1	5	7		
Kataja, E.	FIN	Pole vault	F		2	4,20	S
Keller, W.	SUI	400m	1	7	4	50·3	
		4×400m relay	1	1	4	3-23·0	
Kelley, J.A.	USA	Marathon	F		21	2:51-56·0	
Kerebel, J.	FRA	4×400m relay	1	2	1	3-17·0	
			F		2	3-14·8	S
Khan, A.	PAK	Shot put	Q		DNQ		
		Discus throw	Q		DNQ		
Khan, M-u-H.	PAK	110m hurdles	1	6	5		
		400m hurdles	1	2	4	59·5	
Khang, W.-I.	KOR	Discus throw	Q		DNQ		
		Hammer throw	F		13	43,93	
Khedr, R.	EGY	800m	1	1	7		
Kiesewetter, L.	TCH	Javelin throw	F		11	60,25	
Kim, W.-K.	KOR	Long jump	Q		DNQ		
		Triple jump	F		12	14,25	
Kirk, J.	USA	400m hurdles	1	6	2	54·3	
			SF	1	5	52·5	
Kirstetter, R.	FRA	Discus throw	Q		DNQ		
Kiss, J.	HUN	Marathon	F		19	2:50-20·0	
Kistenmacher, E.	ARG	Long jump	F		10	6,80	
		Decathlon	F		4	6929	
Kjersem, J.	NOR	10000m	F				
Klein, H.	FRA	1500m	1	1	6	3-59·8	
Kleyn, J.	HOL	100m	1	12	4		
Klics, F.	HUN	Discus throw	F		5	48,21	
Knotek, O.	TCH	Hammer throw	Q		DNQ		
Knott, G.	AUS	10k walk	1	1	6		

COMPETITOR	COUNTRY CODE	EVENT	ROUND	HEAT	PLACE	TIME & DISTANCE	MEDAL
Koenoenen, S.	FIN	10000m	F		9		
Koru, S.	TUR	Marathon	F		20	2:51-07·0	
Koskela, V.	FIN	5000m	1	1	2	14-58·4	
			F		7	14-47·0	
Koutonen, E.	USA	Triple jump	Q		DNQ	14,57	
Kremer, R.	LUX	Decathlon	F		DNF		
Kuivamaeki, R.	FIN	Hammer throw	Q		DNQ		
Kunnen, H.	BEL	400m	1	12	1	50·4	
			2	2	DNS		
Kuong, C.-O.	KOR	Marathon	F		25	2:56-54·0	
Kurikkala, J.	FIN	Marathon	F		13	2:42-48·0	
Kuzmicki, W.	POL	Decathlon	F		16	6153	
Kyriakides, S.	GRE	Marathon	F		18	2:49-00·0	
LaBeach, L.	PAN	100m	1	3	1	10·5	
			2	4	1	10·5	
			SF	2	2	10·-	
			F		3	10·-	3
		200m	1	12	1	21·-	
			2	3	1	21·7	
			SF	2	2	21·3	
			F		3	21·3	3
Labarthe, A.	CHI	100m	1	11	3	11·4	
Lacaze, P.	FRA	High jump	F		=9	1,90	
Laing, L.	JAM	100m	1	1	3	11·4	
		200m	1	6	2	21·5	
			2	3	2	21·5	
			SF	2	3	21·6	
			F		6	21·6	
		4×400m relay	1	2	1	3-14·0	
			F		DNF		
Lambrou, J.	GRE	high jump	Q		DNQ		
Lammers, J.	HOL	200m	1	12	2	22·0	
			2	1	4		
		4×100m relay	1	3	1	41·7	
			F		6	41·5	
Lapuente, F.	ARG	100m	1	2	4		
		4×100m relay	1	3	3	42·4	
Larochelle, W.	CAN	400m hurdles	1	6	4	54·9	
		4×400m relay	1	2	3	3-19·0	
Larsen, H.K.	DEN	Marathon	f		10	2:41-22·0	
Larsen, P.	DEN	Triple jump	F		4	14,88	
Larsson, R.	SWE	400m	1	2	2	49·2	
			2	3	3	48·8	
			SF	1	DNS		
		400m hurdles	1	4	2	54·5	
			SF	1	1	51·9*	
			F		3	52·2	B
		4×400m relay	1	3	2	3-21·0	
			F		3	3-16·0	B
Laskau, H.	USA	10k walk	1	2	DS		
Laszlo, S.	HUN	50k walk	F		13	5:16-50	
Lataster, J.	HOL	5000m	1	1	8		
		10000m	F				
Le Bas, J.	FRA	200m	1	5	-	22·0	
			2	1	5		
		4×100m relay	1	3	5		
Lee, Y.-S.	KOR	800m	1	1	6	2-01·4	
		1500m	1	4	9		
Legrain, P.	FRA	Hammer throw	Q		DNQ		
Lehtila, Y.	FIN	Shot put	F		6	15,05	
Leirud, B.	NOR	High jump	F		13	1,90	
Lewis, G.	TRI	100m	1	10	1	10·8	
			2	2	4		
		200m	1	8	3	22·4	
Lewis, L.	GBR	400m	1	7	1	48·9	
			2	1	5	49·5	
		4×400m relay	1	1	3	3-14·2	
Lidman, H.	SWE	110m hurdles	1	4	2	14·7	
			SF	1	3	14·6	
			F		6	14·9	
Likens, R.	USA	Javelin throw	F		8	64,57	
Lindberg, A.	SWE	Pole vault	F		=9	3,80	
Lindsay, A.	GBR	Triple jump	Q		DNQ		
Lines, S.	BER	100m	1	6	6		
		200m	1	1	4		
		4×100m relay	1	2	6	45·4	
Linssen, F.	BEL	200m	1	4	4		
		4×100m relay	1	2	4		
Lipski, B.	POL	100m	1	1	6		
		200m	1	1	5		
Listur, P.	URU	High jump	Q		DNQ		
Litaudon, N.	FRA	4×100m relay	1	3	5		
Ljunggren, J.	SWE	50k walk	F		1	4:41-52	G
Ljunggren, O.	SWE	800m	1	5	1	1-56·-	
			SF	3	4	1-52·3	
Lomowski, M.	POL	Shot put	F		4	15,43	
		Discus throw	Q		DNQ		
Lopez, H.	URU	100m	1	4	1	10·5	
			2	1	2	10·6	
			SF	1	5		
		200m	1	11	1	22·1	
			2	3	6		
		4×100m relay	1	2	5	42·8	
Lou, W.-N.	CHN	5000m	1	2	8		
		10000m	F				
		Marathon	F		DNF		
Lovna, B.	PHI	100m	1	6	5		
		200m	1	2	3	23·2	
Lucas, W.	GBR	5000m	1	2	7		
Lundberg, R.	SWE	Pole vault	F		5	4,10	
Lundqvist, K.	SWE	400m	1	3	2	50·0	
			2	4	5	48·8	
		4×400m relay	1	3	2	3-21·0	
			F		3	3-16·0	B
Lunis, J.	FRA	400m	1	5	1	49·3	
			2	4	4	48·4	
		4×400m relay	1	2	2	3-17·0	
			F		2	3-14·8	S
Luoto, T.	FIN	1500m	1	1	5	3-58·0	
Lutkeveld, N.	HOL	Javelin throw	Q		DNQ		
Luyt, S.	SAF	Marathon	F		6	2:38-11·0	
McCooke, S.	GBR	10000m	F				
McCorquodale, A.	GBR	100m	1	1	2	10·5	
			2	3	2	10·5	
			SF	1	3	10·7	
			F		4	10·4	
		200m	1	10	1	22·3	
			2	4	2	21·8	
			SF	2	5		
		4×100m relay	1	2	1	41·4	
			F		2	41·3	S
McCullough, E.	CAN	400m	1	7	3	49·9	
		4×400m relay	1	2	3	3-19·0	
McFarlane, D.	CAN	400m	1	8	3	49·5	
		4×100m relay	1	3	2	42·3	
			F		5	41·9	
		4×400m relay	1	2	3	3-19·0	
McFarlane, R.	CAN	400m	1	12	2	50·6	
			2	4	3	48·4	
			SF	2	6	51·7	
		4×400m relay	1	2	3	3-19·0	
McGrew, V.	USA	High jump	F		=14	1,87	
McKeand, L.	AUS	Triple jump	F		7	14,53	
McKenley, H.	JAM	200m	1	1	1	21·3	
			2	1	1	21·3	
			SF	1	1	21·4	
			F		4	21·2	
		400m	1	2	1	48·4	
			2	3	1	48·0	
			SF	2	1	47·3	
			F		2	46·4	S
		4×400m relay	1	2	1	3-14·0	
			F		DNF		
McKenzie, B.	JAM	100m	1	8	2	10·8	
		200m	1	5	3	22·4	
McMillen, R.	USA	3000m steeplechase	1	1	8		
Maehlum, O.	NOR	Javelin throw	F		5	65,32	
Maekelae, V.	FIN	5000m	1	2	3	14-45·8	
			F		8	14-43·0	
Maekelae, Y.	FIN	Decathlon	F		13	6421	
Maggi, E.	FRA	10k walk	1	1	3	45-44·2	
			F		6	47-02·8	
Mahoney, F.	BER	100m	1	3	3	11·8	
		4×100m relay	1	2	6	45·4	
Malchiodi, E.	ARG	Shot put	Q		DNQ		
		Discus throw	Q		DNQ		
Malik, N.	PAK	Shot put	Q		DNQ		
		Discus throw	Q		DNQ		
Manninen, A.	USA	Marathon	F		24	2:56-49·0	
Marcelja, D.	YUG	Decathlon	F		18	6141	
Marie, A.	FRA	110m hurdles	-	5	1	14·9	
			SF	1	DNF		
Marnis, C.	GRE	100m	-	4	6		
		Long jump	Q		DNQ		
Marineau, H.A.	GBR	50k walk	F		5	4:53-58	
Mathias, R.	USA	Decathlon	F		1	7139	G
Maung, S.	BUR	100m	-	12	6		
		200m	-	11	4		
Mavrapostolos, B.	GRE	5000m	-	2	9		
		3000m steeplechase	-	1	9		
Mavroidis, B.	GRE	800m	-	2	5	1-57·4	
		1500m	1	2	7		
		4×400m relay	1	3	5	3-33·0	

COMPETITOR	COUNTRY CODE	EVENT	ROUND	HEAT	PLACE	TIME & DISTANCE	MEDAL
Mayordome, G.	FRA	800m	1	6	4	1-55·7	
			SF	2	4	1-54·3	
Mazille, P.	FRA	50k walk	F		7	5:01-40	
Melin, A.	SWE	Marathon	F		12	2:42-20·0	
Meyer, J.	HOL	100m	1	4	3	11·0	
		4×100m relay	1	3	1	41·7	
			F		6	41·9	
Mikaelsson, J.	SWE	10k walk	1	1	1	45-03·0*	
			F		1	45-13·2	G
Mimoun, A.	FRA	5000m	1	3	6	15-11·2	
		10000m	F		2	30-47·4	S
Miranda, C.	ESP	10000m	F				
		3000m steeplechase	1	1	4	9-24·2	
			F		8	9-25·0	
Missoni, O.	ITA	400m hurdles	1	4	1	53·9	
			SF	2	3	53·4	
			F		6	54·0	
		4×400m relay	1	1	2	3-14·0	
			F		DNF		
Moberg, L.	SWE	Triple jump	F		13	14,21	
Mondschein, I.	USA	Decathlon	F		8	6715	
Monges, C.	MEX	400m	1	5	3	50·9	
Mongrut, A.	PER	800m	1	2	6	1-58·7	
		1500m	1	1	10		
Monti, C.	ITA	4×100m relay	1	1	2	41·3	
			F		3	41·5	B
Moody, H.	GBR	Shot put	Q		DNQ		
Morcom, A.	USA	Pole vault	F		6	3,95	
Morris, C.	GBR	10k walk	1	1	2	45-10·4	
			F		4	46-04·0	
Morris, R.A.	GBR	1500m	1	4	6	3-55·8	
Mukhtar, A.	EGY	Decathlon	F		28	5031	
Mukhtar, F.D.	EGY	100m	1	7	5		
Mullins, P.	AUS	Decathlon	F		6	6739	
Mulvihill, F.	IRL	Marathon	F		26	2:57-35·0	
Myles, R.	IRL	4×400m relay	1	1	DIS		
Nankeville, G.	GBR	1500m	1	3	2	3-55·8	
			F		6	3-52·6	
Nelson, W.	NZL	5000m	1	1	6	15-34·4	
		10000m	F				
Nemeth, I.	HUN	Hammer throw	F		1	56,07	G
Nesbitt, J.	GBR	Discus throw	Q		DNQ		
Ng, L.-C.	CHN	400m hurdles	1	5	4	57·7	
Nicklen, N.	FIN	High jump	F		=14	1,87	
Nielsen, I.B.B.	DEN	1500m	1	4	7		
Nikkinen, S.	FIN	Javelin throw	F		12	58,05	
Nilsson, R.	SWE	Shot put	Q		DNQ		
Nussbaum, F.	SUI	Decathlon	F		23	5808	
Nyberg, E.	SWE	5000m	1	1	1	14-58·2	
			F		DNF		
Nvqvist, K.	FIN	Discus throw	F		6	47,33	
Oberweger, G.	ITA	Discus throw	Q		DNQ		
O'Brien, J.	CAN	100m	1	2	3	10·9	
		4×100m relay	1	3	2	42·3	
			F		5	41·9	
Oestling, G.	SWE	Marathon	F		7	2:38-40·6	
Olenius, V.	FIN	Pole vault	F		=7	3,95	
Olesen, A.	DEN	3000m steeplechase	1	2	5	9-33·6	
Olney, H.	GBR	5000m	1	3	7		
Omiros-Crosfield, P.	GRE	110m hurdles	1	3	5		
Omnes, G.	FRA	110m hurdles	1	6	3	15·2	
Onel. C.	TUR	800m	1	2	7		
		1500m	1	1	7		
		3000m steeplechase	1	3	5	9-28·4	
Ostas, R.	TUR	100m	1	9	5		
		200m	1	9	3	23·0	
		4×100m relay	1	1	4		
O'Toole, E.	USA	10000m	F		10		
Overton, W.	USA	3000m steeplechase	1	3	6	10-14·4	
Ozcan, M.	TUR	5000m	1	2	11		
		3000m steeplechase	1	2	7		
Palmeiro, M.	ARG	1500m	1	3	5	4-01·6	
Paris, A.	FRA	10000m	F				
Parlett, H.	GBR	800m	1	1	2	1-55·0	
			SF	1	3	1-50·9	
			F		9	1-54·0	
Parnell, C.	CAN	800m	1	3	6	1-55·4	
		1500m	1	3	DNF		
Parry, J.C.	CAN	100m	1	7	DNF		
Paterlini, L.	ITA	4×400m relay	1	1	2	3-14·0	
			F		DNF		
Paterson, A.	GBR	High jump	F		=7	1,90	
Patine, P.	PER	Shot put	Q		DNQ		

COMPETITOR	COUNTRY CODE	EVENT	ROUND	HEAT	PLACE	TIME & DISTANCE	MEDAL
Patton, M.	USA	100m	1	2	1	10·6	
			2	3	1	10·4	
			SF	2	1	10·4	
			F		5	10·5	
		200m	1	6	1	21·6	
			2	4	1	21·4	
			SF	1	2	21·6	
			F		1	21·1	G
		4×100m relay	1	1	1	41·1	
			F		1	40·6	G
Paulsen, B.	NOR	High jump	F		2	1,95	S
Pavitt, R.	GBR	High jump	Q		DNQ		
Peiris, G.	CEY	Long jump	Q		DNQ		
		Triple jump	Q		DNQ		
Peraelae, H.	FIN	5000m	1	3	4	15-07·8	
			F		11		
Pereira, A.	POR	Long jump	Q		DNQ		
Pereira, A.	BRA	Triple jump	F		8	14,49	
Perez, W.	URU	100m	1	10	3	11·0	
		200m	1	8	4		
		4×100m relay	1	2	5	42·8	
Perucconi, E.	ITA	4×100m relay	1	1	2	41·3	
			F		3	41·5	B
Peters, J.	GBR	10000m	F		8	31-16·0	
Petrakis, S.	GRE	100m	1	10	6		
		200m	1	2	4		
		400m	1	11	4	54·5	
		4×400m relay	1	3	5	3-33·0	
Petropoulakis, L.	GRE	110m hurdles	1	2	4		
		400m hurdles	1	2	3	57·9	
		4×400m relay	1	3	5	3-33·0	
Pettersson, G.	SWE	Javelin throw	F		9	62,80	
Pettie, D.	CAN	200m	1	12	3	22·0	
		4×100m relay	1	3	2	42·3	
			F		5	41·9	
Phillips, E.	IND	100m	1	12	2	11·0	
			2	4	6		
		200m	1	3	5		
Piesset, A.	FRA	Marathon	F		DNF		
Pike, M.W.	GBR	4×400m relay	1	1	3	3-14·2	
Pilhatsch, A.	AUT	High jump	Q		DNQ		
Piqueras, J.	PER	Pole vault	Q		DNQ		
Pocovi, A.	ARG	400m	1	3	3	50·7	
		4×400m relay	1	3	3	3-21·2	
Pope, M.	GBR	400m hurdles	1	3	4	55·3	
Porter, W.	USA	110m hurdles	1	1	1	14·3	
			SF	2	1	14·1*	
			F		1	13·9*	G
Porthault, A.	FRA	4×100m relay	1	3	5		
Poulsen, A.	DEN	5000m	1	1	7		
Pouzieux, M.	FRA	5000m	1	2	3	15-07·8	
Poyan, D.	ESP	1500m	1	3	DNF		
Pretti, F.	ITA	50k walk	F		DNF		
Pugh, D.	GBR	400m	1	11	2	49·3	
			2	4	6	48·9	
		4×400m relay	1	1	3	3-14·2	
Pujazon, R.	FRA	3000m steeplechase	1	2	1	9-20·8	
			F		DNF		
Racic, M.	YUG	400m	1	1	2	50·5	
			2	3	6	52·1	
		4×400m relay	1	3	4	3-25·4	
Ragazos, A.	GRE	Marathon	F		DNF		
Ramjohn, M.	TRI	5000m	1	1	11		
		10000m	F				
Ramsay, J.	AUS	400m	1	4	5	50·3	
		800m	1	1	3	1-55·0	
			SF	2	5	1-54·9	
Ramstrad, I.	NOR	Discus throw	F		4	49,21	
Rautavaara, K.	FIN	Javelin throw	F		1	69,77	G
Rautio, K.	FIN	Triple jump	F		6	14,70	
Reardon, J.	IRL	400m	1	1	1	48·4	
			2	4	2	48·3	
			SF	1	5	47·9	
		4×400m relay	1	1	DIS		
Reavell-Carter, L.	GBR	Discus throw	Q		DNQ		
Rebello, H.	IND	Triple jump	F		NP	0	
Rebula, O.	YUG	Decathlon	F		DNF		
Recordon, M.	CHI	110m hurdles	1	1	3	15·3	
		Decathlon	F		24	5730	
Reiff, G.	BEL	5000m	1	3	2	15-07·0	
			F		1	14-17·6*	G
Rendin, B.	SWE	110m hurdles	1	1	3	15·5	
Reyes, M.	PER	100m	1	4	4		
		Triple jump	Q		DNQ		
Reyneke, J.	SAF	10k walk	1	1	DIS		

COMPETITOR	COUNTRY CODE	EVENT	ROUND	HEAT	PLACE	TIME & DISTANCE	MEDAL
Rhoden, G.	JAM	400m	1	4	1	48·4	
			2	1	2	48·6	
			SF	1	4	47·7	
		4×400m relay	1	2	1	3-14·0	
			F			DNF	
Richards, R.	USA	Pole vault	F		3	4,20	B
Richards, T.	GBR	Marathon	F		2	2:35-07·6	S
Roberts, W.	GBR	400m	1	8	2	48·9	
			2	2	4	48·6	
		4×400m relay	1	1	3	3-14·2	
Robison, C.F.	USA	5000m	1	2	DNF		
Rocca, G.	ITA	4×400m relay	1	1	2	3-14·0	
			F			DNF	
Rodriguez, G.	MEX	100m	1	2	6		
		200m	1	7	5		
Roininen, L.	CAN	Javelin throw	Q		DNQ		
Rojo, G.	ESP	5000m	1	2	6	15-19·0	
		10000m	F				
Rosas, M.	COL	400m	1	3	4	51·4	
		400m hurdles	1	4	5	55·9	
Rosier, R.	BEL	800m	1	2	4	1-56·7	
			SF	3	DNF		
Ross, H.	USA	3000m steeplechase	1	2	4	9-30·4	
			F		7	9-23·2	
Sabater, J.	PUR	110m hurdles	1	4	3	15·3	
Sabolovic, Z.	YUG	400m	1	3	1	49·9	
			2	1	4	49·2	
		4×400m relay	1	3	4	3-25·4	
Said, A.ben	FRA	10000m	F		6	31-07·8	
Salman, D.	IRQ	100m	1	7	DNF		
		200m	1	4	6		
Salmond, D.	CAN	1500m	1	1	9		
		5000m	1	1	9		
Sarialp, R.	TUR	Triple jump	F		3	15,02	B
		4×100m relay	1	1	4		
Scheurer, A.	SUI	Decathlon	F		DNF		
Schewetta, F.	FRA	400m	1	9	2	48·9	
			2	3	5	49·9	
		4×400m relay	1	2	2	3-17·0	
			F		2	3-14·8	S
Schiesser, K.	SUI	Marathon	F		22	2:52-09·0	
Scholten, G.	HOL	200m	1	11	3	22·2	
		4×100m relay	1	3	1	41·7	
			F		6	41·9	
Schwab, F.	SUI	10k walk	1	2	2	46-38·0	
			F		3	46-00·2	B
Scott, C.L.	USA	110m hurdles	1	2	1	14·8	
			SF	2	2	14·2	
			F		2	14·1	S
Segedin, P.	YUG	3000m steeplechase	1	2	3	9-25·0	
			F		6	9-20·4	
Seger, J.	LIE	Decathlon	F		DNF		
Senn, W.	SUI	Shot put	Q		DNQ		
Sensini, A.	ARG	Marathon	F		9	2:39-30·0	
Seymour, S.	USA	Javelin throw	F		2	67,56	S
Sharaga, F.	USA	10k walk	1	1	DIS		
Shim, B.-S.	KOR	5000m	1	2	10		
Shore, D.	SAF	200m	1	3	2	22·1	
			2	2	5		
		400m	1	4	2	49·0	
			2	2	3	48·5	
			SF	2	4	48·8	
Siddi, A.	ITA	4×100m relay	1	1	2	41·3	
			F		3	41·5	B
		4×400m relay	1	1	2	3-14·0	
			F			DNF	
Sigurdsson, J.	ISL	Javelin throw	Q		DNQ		
Sigurdsson, R.	ISL	400m	1	12	3	51·4	
		4×400m relay	1	2	6		
Sigurdsson, S.	ISL	Shot put	F		12	13,66	
Sillon, V.	FRA	Pole vault	F		=9	3.95	
Siltaloppi, P.	FIN	3000m steeplechase	1	1	3	9-22·4	
			F		5	9-19·6	
Silva, C.	CHI	100m	1	6	4		
		4x40m relay	1	2	4	3-23·8	
Simmons, F.M.	USA	Decathlon	F		3	6950	B
Singh, B.	IND	Long jump	F		NP	0	
		Decathlon	F		DNF		
Singh, C.	IND	Marathon	F		DNF		
Singh, S.G.	IND	High jump	F		=14	1,87	
Singha, S.	IND	10k walk	1	2	DIS		
		50k walk	F		DNF		
Sink, R.	USA	1500m	1	4	5	3-53·2	
Sjoestrand, T.	SWE	3000m steeplechase	1	3	1	9-21·0	
			F		1	9-04·6	G

COMPETITOR	COUNTRY CODE	EVENT	ROUND	HEAT	PLACE	TIME & DISTANCE	MEDAL
Slijkhuis, W.	HOL	1500m	1	2	1	3-52·4	
			F		3	3-50·4	B
		5000m	1	3	1	15-06·8	
			F		3	14-26·8	B
Smith, G.	USA	Pole vault	F		1	4,30	G
Soederkvist, E.	SWE	Hammer throw	F		8	51,48	
Somnath, S.	IND	Hammer throw	Q		DNQ		
Sonck, J.	FIN	Decathlon	F		17	6142	
Sorenson, S.	ISL	Triple jump	Q		DNQ		
Sprecher, P.	FRA	Decathlon	F		14	6401	
Stanich, G.	USA	High jump	F		3	1,95	B
Stevem, P.	NOR	Decathlon	F		11	6552	
Steele, W.	USA	Long jump	F		1	7,82	G
Stefanovic, D.	YUG	3000m steeplechase	1	1	5	9-39·6	
Stephan, J.	FRA	100m	1	10	4		
		200m	1	12	5		
Stokken, M.	NOR	5000m	1	2	4	15-04·4	
			F		10		
		10000m	F		4	30-58·6	
Stone, C.	USA	5000m	1	1	3	14-58·6	
			F		6	14-39·4	
Storskrubb, A.	FIN	400m hurdles	1	3	2	54·6	
			SF	2	5	53·5	
		4×400m relay	1	3	1	3-20·6	
			F		4	3-24·8	
Strand, L.	SWE	1500m	1	1	1	3-54·2	
			F		2	3-50·4	S
Stratakos, S.	GRE	400m	1	12	5	52·8	
		800m	1	6	5	2-02·2	
		4×400m relay	1	3	5	3-33·0	
Streuli, H.	SUI	800m	1	5	3	1-56·5	
			SF	3	DNF		
Studer, J.	SUI	Long jump	Q		DNQ		
Suarez, M.	ESP	110m hurdles	1	3	3	15·9	
Suh, Y.-B.	KOR	Marathon	F		27	2:59-36·0	
Suvanto, T.	FIN	400m	1	9	4	51·5	
		4×400m relay	1	3	1	3-20·6	
			F		4	3-24·8	
Syllas, N.	GRE	Discus throw	F		7	47,25	
Systad, J.	NOR	Marathon	F		8	2:38-41·0	
Taddia, T.	ITA	Hammer throw	F		7	51,74	
Talja, O.	FIN	400m	1	8	4	50·4	
		4×400m relay	1	3	1	3-20·6	
			F		4	3-24·8	
Tamminen, L.	FIN	Hammer throw	F		5	53,08	
Tannander, K.	SWE	Decathlon	F		15	6325	
Tarraway, H.	GBR	800m	1	5	4	1-56·6	
			SF	2	DNF		
Theys, L.	BEL	3000m steeplechase	1	2	6	9-37·4	
Thompson, C.C.F.O.	GUY	100m	1	11	5		
		Long jump	Q		DNQ		
Thompson, J.	USA	5000m	1	3	5	15-08·4	
Thompson, W.	USA	Shot put	F		1	17,12*	G
Thorvaldsson, F.	ISL	100m	1	4	5		
		Long jump	Q		DNQ		
		4×100m relay	1	3	4	42·9	
Tima, F.	HUN	4×100m relay	1	2	2	41·4	
			F		4	41·6	
Tissot, R.	FRA	Javelin throw	Q		DNQ		
Tito, M.	ITA	4×100m relay	1	1	2	41·3	
			F		3	41·5	B
Toivari, P.	FIN	3000m steeplechase	1	2	8		
Torres, A.	ARG	800m	1	1	5	1-56·7	
Torres, J.L.	ESP	Discus throw	Q		DNQ		
Tosi, G.	ITA	Discus throw	F		2	51,78	S
Treloar, J.	AUS	100m	1	7	1	10·5	
			2	4	2	10·5	
			SF	2	4	10·7	
		200m	1	9	1	21·7	
			2	2	2	21·5	
			SF	2	4		
		4×100m relay	1	2	3	41·5	
Trepp, M.	SUI	400m	1	8	5	50·9	
		4×400m relay	1	1	4	3-23·0	
Triulzi, A.	ARG	110m hurdles	1	3	1	14·6	
			SF	2	3	14·6	
			F		4	14·6	
Tudor, G.	GBR	3000m steeplechase	1	2	9		
Tull, W.	TRI	800m	1	4	6	1-55·7	
			1	2	9		
Tunner, H.	AUT	Discus throw	F		11	44,43	
Ulloa, R.S.deH.	ESP	100m	1	5	5		
Unsworth, R.T.	GBR	400m hurdles	1	4	3	55·1	

COMPETITOR	COUNTRY CODE	EVENT	ROUND	HEAT	PLACE	TIME & DISTANCE	MEDAL
Vade, B.	NOR	400m	1	7	2	49·6	
			2	2	5	49·7	
		800m	1	3	2	1-54·2	
			SF	1	DNF		
Valberg, L.	SIN	High jump	F		=14	1,87	
Valle, P.	GBR	200m	1	2	1	22·3	
			2	1	3	22·1	
			SF	1	4		
Valmy, R.	FRA	100m	1	7	2	10·8	
			2	3	4		
		4×100m relay	1	3	5		
Vandewattyne, M.	BEL	5000m	1	1	4	15-14·0	
			F		9		
Vandewiele, I.	BEL	100m	1	11	1	10·8	
			2	3	6		
		4×100m relay	1	2	4		
Van Heerden, A.	SAF	100m	1	6	3	11·1	
		200m	1	4	2	21·8	
			2	3	3	21·9	
			SF	1	6		
Varszegi, J.	HUN	Javelin throw	F		3	67,03	B
Vefling, K.	NOR	1500m	1	4	4	3-53·0	
Vera, C.	CHI	Triple jump	Q		DNQ		
Verhas, R.	BEL	Shot put	Q		DNQ		
		Discus throw	Q		DNQ		
Vernier, Jean	FRA	1500m	1	3	4	3-57·6	
Vernier, Jacques	FRA	5000m	1	1	5	15-28·0	
Vesterinen, P.	FIN	Javelin throw	F		4	65,89	
Vicente, C.	PUR	Pole vault	F		=9	3,95	
Vickers, J.	IND	110m hurdles	1	4	1	14·7	
			SF	2	4	14·7	
Villaplana, E.	ESP	50k walk	F		9	5:03-31	
Vilmundarson, V.	ISL	Shot put	Q		DNQ		
Vogel, T.	USA	Marathon	F		14	2:45-27·0	
Volkmer, K.	SUI	800m	1	1	4	1-55·3	
			SF	1	DNF		
		4×400m relay	1	1	4	3-23·0	
Vujacic, D.	YUG	Javelin throw	Q		DNQ		
Vujacic, M.	YUG	Javelin throw	F		7	64,89	
Wahli, H.	SUI	High jump	F		=7	1,90	
Weber, E.	USA	10k walk	1	1	8		
Webster, F.	GBR	Pole vault	Q		DNQ		
Weinberg, R.	AUS	110m hurdles	1	6	2	15·0	
			SF	2	5		
Weinecker, A.	USA	50k walk	F		16	5:30-14	
West, R.	GBR	10k walk	1	2	3	47-11·6	
			F		7		
Westman, A.	SWE	400m hurdles	1	6	3	54·5	
White, C.	GBR	800m	1	2	3	1-56·6	
			SF	3	5	1-53·0	
White, D.	CEY	200m	1	6	4	53·6	
		400m hurdles	1	6	1	53·6	
			SF	1	3	52·1	
			F		2	51·8	S
Whitfield, M.	USA	400m	1	8	1	48·3	
			2	1	1	48·0	
			SF	1	3	47·4	
			F		3	46·6	B
		800m	1	6	1	1-52·8	
			SF	1	2	1-50·7	
			F		1	1-49·2*	G
		4×400m relay	1	1	1	3-12·6	
			F		1	3-10·4	G
Whitlock, R.	GBR	50k walk	F		DNF		
Whittle, H.	GBR	400m hurdles	1	2	1	56·9	
			SF	2	4	53·4	
		Long jump	F		7	7,03	
Widenfelt, G.	SWE	High jump	F		=9	1,90	
Wilson, D.	GBR	1500m	1	2	5	3-54·8	
Will, F.L.	USA	10000m	F		11		
Wint, A.	JAM	400m	1	9	1	47·7	
			2	2	1	47·7	
			SF	1	1	46·3	
			F		1	46·2*	G
		800m	1	4	1	1-53·9	
			SF	2	2	1-52·7	
			F		2	1-49·5	S
		4×400m relay	1	2	1	3-14·0	
			F		DNF		
Winter, J.	AUS	High jump	F		1	1,98	G
Winter, V.	TCH	800m	1	4	4	1-55·1	
			SF	2	6	1-57·7	
Winther, G.	NOR	50k walk	F		DNF		
Wolfbrandt, L.	SWE	4×400m relay	1	3	2	3-21·0	
			F		3	3-16·0	B
Wright, L.	USA	Long jump	F		4	7,45	
		4×100m relay	1	1	1	41·1	
			F		1	40·6	G

COMPETITOR	COUNTRY CODE	EVENT	ROUND	HEAT	PLACE	TIME & DISTANCE	MEDAL
Wuerth, F.	AUT	Long jump	F		8	7,00	
		Triple jump	Q		DNQ		
Yataganas, C.	GRE	Shot put	F		9	14,54	
Yung, H.-A.	KOR	Discus throw	Q		DNQ		
Zamorra, R.M.	CUB	100m	1	9	3	11·1	
		200m	1	7	3	23·0	
Zatopek, E.	TCH	5000m	1	2	2	14-34·4	
			F		2	14-17·8	S
		10000m	F		1	29-59·6*	G
Zerjal, D.	YUG	Discus throw	Q		DNQ		
Ziraman, H.	TUR	Javelin throw	Q		DNQ		
Zuniga, E.	CHI	Hammer throw	Q		DNQ		
Zwann, J.G.	HOL	100m	1	8	5		
		110m hurdles	1	4	4		
		4x100m relay	1	3	1	41·7	
			F		6	41·9	

FEMALES

COMPETITOR	COUNTRY CODE	EVENT	ROUND	HEAT	PLACE	TIME & DISTANCE	MEDAL
Aberg, M.	SWE	Discus throw	F		7	38,48	
Almqvist, I.	SWE	Javelin throw	F		10	37,26	
Arenander, G.	SWE	Discus throw	F		12	36,25	
Batter, D.	GBR	100m	1	5	1	12·6	
			SF	1	4		
Bauma, H.	AUT	Javelin throw	F		1	45,57*	G
Beckett, V.	JAM	80m hurdles	1	4	6		
		High jump	F		4	1,58	
		Long jump	F		11	5,14	
Bergendorff, B.	DEN	100m	1	7	2	12·6	
			SF	2	4		
		4x100m relay	1	3	2	48·1	
			F		5	48·2	
Birtwistle, M.	GBR	Shot put	Q		DNQ		
		Discus throw	F		19	33,02	
Blankers-Koen, F.	HOL	100m	1	1	1	12·0	
			SF	1	1	12·0	
			F		1	11·9	G
		200m	1	1	1	25·7*	
			SF	1	1	24·3*	
			F		1	24·4	G
		80m hurdles	1	1	1	11·3*	
			SF	1	1	11·4	
			F		1	11·2*	G
		4x100m relay	1	3	1	47·6	
			F		1	47·5	G
Bourkel, C.	LUX	High jump	F		=14	1,40	
Bruk, A.	TCH	Shot put	F		6	12,50	
Butia, A.	YUG	100m	1	8	5		
		200m	1	4	5		
Canty, J.	AUS	Long jump	F		7	5,38	
Caurla, L.	FRA	100m	1	1	5		
Cardosa, H.	BRA	100m	1	7	3	13·2	
		200m	1	2	4		
Carlstedt, L.	DEN	Javelin throw	F		3	42,08	B
Cheater, M.	CAN	100m	1	4	4		
		200m	1	7	3	26·4	
Cheeseman, S.	GBR	200m	1	2	2	25·7	
			SF	2	4		
Clara, E.	BRA	100m	1	5	4		
		High jump	F		=17	1,40	
		Shot put	Q		DNQ		
Clarke, G.	GBR	Javelin throw	F		15	29,59	
Coachman, A.	USA	High jump	F		1	1,68*	G
Colchen, A.	FRA	High jump	F		=14	1,40	
Cordiale-Gentile, E.	ITA	Discus throw	F		2	41,17	S
Crowther, B.	GBR	80m hurdles	1	3	5		
		High jump	F		6	1,58	
Curtot-Chabot, Y.	FRA	Long jump	F		8	5,34	
Dammers, E.	HOL	Javelin throw	F		8	38,23	
Decker, M.	LUX	100m	1	2	5		
		200m	1	5	5		
De Jongh, G.	HOL	100m	1	9	2	12·9	
			SF	3	6		
		200m	1	6	3	26·2	
De Portela, N.S.	ARG	100m	1	2	3	13·1	
		80m hurdles	1	2	3	11·8	
			SF	2	4		
		Long jump	F		2	5,60	S
Dodson, D.	USA	Shot put	Q		DNQ		
		Discus throw	F		16	34,69	
		Javelin throw	F		4	41,96	
Dredge, D.	CAN	High jump	F		5	1,58	
Edness, P.	BER	100m	1	8	3	13·6	
		200m	1	1	5		
Erskine, M.	GBR	Long jump	Q		DNQ		
Faggs, M.	USA	200m	1	1	3	26·0	

COMPETITOR	COUNTRY CODE	EVENT	ROUND	HEAT	PLACE	TIME & DISTANCE	MEDAL
Faugouin, R.	FRA	200m	1	6	2	25·9	
			SF	1	5		
		4x100m relay	1	1	3	48·1	
Foster, D.	CAN	200m	1	2	3	26·1	
		4x100m relay	1	1	1	47·9	
			F		3	47·8	B
Gabric-Calvesi, L.	ITA	Discus throw	F		17	34,11	
Gardner, D.	GBR	High jump	F		3	1,55	
Gardner, M.	GBR	80m hurdles	1	2	1	11·6	
			SF	2	3	11·8	
			F		2	11·2	S
		4x100m relay	1	2	1	48·4	
			F		4	48·0	
Gilmore, D.	CAN	200m	1	4	4		
Gordon, S.	CAN	High jump	F		=11	1,50	
Gyarmati, O.	HUN	High jump	F		=17	1,40	
		Long jump	F		1	5,69*	G
Haidegger, L.	AUT	Discus throw	F		5	38,81	
Huber, M.	CHI	80m hurdles	1	1	5		
		4x100m relay	1	2	3	51·5	
Ingrova, D.	TCH	Javelin throw	F		7	39,64	
Iverson, A.	DEN	High jump	F		=9	1,50	
Jackson, N.	USA	200m	1	4	3	25·8	
		4x100m relay	1	3	3	48·3	
James, M.	FIN	80m hurdles	1	1	4		
Jenny, G.	AUT	4x100m relay	1	2	2	50·0	
			F		6	49·2	
Jones, P.	CAN	100m	1	9	1	12·7	
			SF	2	2	12·6	
			F		5	12·3	
		4x100m relay	1	1	1	47·9	
			F		3	47·8	B
Jordan, W.S.	GBR	100m	1	3	2	12·7	
			SF	3	5		
Karelse, N.	HOL	200m	1	7	2	26·0	
			SF	2	5		
		Long jump	F		5	5,54	
Kaszubski, F.	USA	Shot put	Q		DNQ		
		Discus throw	F		11	36,50	
Kavounidou, D.	GRE	80m hurdles	1	2	5		
King, J.	AUS	100m	1	3	4		
		200m	1	3	1	25·9	
			SF	1	6		
		4x100m relay	1	1	2	48·0	
			F		2	47·6	S
Komarkova, J.	TCH	Shot put	F		5	12,92	
Koning, j.	HOL	Javelin throw	F		6	40,33	
Kretschmer, B.	CHI	100m	1	3	5		
		200m	1	5	6		
		4x100m relay	1	2	3	51·5	
Laurent, S.	FRA	Shot put	F		10	12,03	
Lee, L.	GBR	Long jump	Q		DNQ		
Leyman, A.	SWE	200m	1	5	4		
		Long jump	F		3	5,57	B
Lightbourn, P.	BER	100m	1	6	2	13·0	
			SF	1	6		
		200m	1	3	2	27·0	
			SF	1	7		
		Long jump	Q		DNQ		
Lomska, L.	TCH	80m hurdles	1	2	2	11·8	
			SF	1	3	12·0	
			F		5	11·9	
Long, M.	GBR	Javlin throw	F		14	30,29	
Lovso-Nielsen, G.	DEN	100m	1	3	1	12·6	
			SF	1	3	12·7	
		4x100m relay	1	3	2	48·1	
			F		5	48·2	
Ludwig, M.	LUX	Long jump	Q		DNQ		
Luz, M.	BRA	200m	1	1	4		
		4x100m relay	1	1	4	49·0	
MacKay, N.	CAN	4x100m relay	1	1	1	47·9	
			F		3	47·8	B
McKinnon, B.	AUS	100m	1	1	3	12·7	
		200m	1	6	1	25·9	
			SF	2	DNF		
		4x100m relay	1	1	2	48·0	
			F		2	47·6	S
Magnin-Lamouche, J.	FRA	80m hurdles	1	2	4		
Manley, D.	GBR	100m	1	6	1	12·1	
			SF	2	1	12·4	
			F		2	12·2	S
		4x100m relay	1	2	1	48·4	
			F		4	48·0	
Manuel, T.	USA	80m hurdles	1	1	5		
		Javelin throw	F		12	33,82	
		4x100m relay	1	3	3	48·3	
Martel, Y.	FRA	Long jump	Q		DNQ		
Maston, J.	AUS	Long jump	Q		DNQ		
		4x100m relay	1	1	2	48·0	
			F		2	47·6	S
Matej, J.	YUG	Discus throw	F		21	30,25	
Mazeas, J.	FRA	Discus throw	F		3	40,47	B
Mello, I.	ARG	Shot put	F		9	12,08	
		Discus throw	F		8	38,44	
Mertin, J.	HUN	100m	1	1	5		
Millard, A.	CHI	4x100m relay	1	2	3	51·5	
		200m	1	6	5		
Monginou, Y.	FRA	80m hurdles	1	3	1	11·7	
			SF	2		11·8	
			F		4	11·8	
Morg, G.	BRA	Long jump	Q		DNQ		
		4x100m relay	1	1	4	49·0	
Moussier, J.	FRA	100m	1	9	3		
		4x100m relay	1	1	3	48·1	
Myers, V.	CAN	100m	1	1	2	12·5	
			SF	3	1	12·4	
			F		4	12·3	
		4x100m relay	1	1	1	47·9	
			F		3	47·8	B
Naukkarinen, K.	FIN	80m hurdles	1	4	4		
Nielsen, B.	DEN	100m	1	2	2	12·9	
			SF	1	3	12·7	
		4x100m relay	1	3	2	48·1	
			F		5	48·2	
Nissen, H.	DEN	4x100m relay	1	3	2	48·1	
			F		5	48·2	
Nowakowa, H.	POL	Long jump	Q		DNQ		
Oberbreyer, M.	AUT	100m	1	1	4		
		80m hurdles	1	3	3	11·9	
			SF	1	2	11·9	
			F		5	11·9	
		Long jump	F		9	5,24	
		4x100m relay	1	2	2	50·0	
			F		6	49·2	
Olsson, E.	SWE	Shot put	F		11	11,84	
Ostermeyer, M.	FRA	High jump	F		3	1,61	B
		Shot put	F		1	13,75*	G
		Discus throw	F		1	41,92	G
Pak, P.-S.	KOR	Discus throw	F		18	33,80	
Parhorst-Niesink, A.	HOL	Discus throw	F		6	38,74	
		Shot put	Q		DNQ		
Parviainen, K.	FIN	Long jump	Q		DNQ		
		Javelin throw	F		2	43,79	S
Patterson, A.	USA	100m	1	3	3	12·8	
		200m	1	5	1	25·5	
			SF	1	2	25·0	
			F		3	25·2	B
		4x100m relay	1	3	3	48·3	
Paulsen, L.	NOR	100m	1	9	4		
		Shot put	Q		DNQ		
Pavlousek, G.	AUT	100m	1	8	4		
		200m	1	6	4		
		4x100m relay	1	2	2	50·0	
			F		6	49·2	
Phipps, C.	JAM	200m	1	6	6		
		High jump	F		=11	1,50	
Piccinini, A.	ITA	Shot put	F		2	13,09	S
Pircucci, S.	ITA	Long jump	Q		DNQ		
Pini, L.	BRA	200m	1	3	3	27·6	
		4x100m relay	1	1	4	49·0	
Pletts, M.	GBR	4x100m relay	1	2	1	48·4	
			F		4	48·0	
Radosavljevic, M.	YUG	Shot put	F		7	12,35	
Reed, E.	USA	High jump	F		=14	1,40	
		Long jump	F		12	4,83	
Reid, B.	GBR	Shot put	F		8	12,17	
		Discus throw	F		14	35,84	
Renard, M.	BEL	100m	1	6	3	13·6	
		200m	1	3	4		
Robb, D.	SAF	100m	1	4	2	12·4	
			SF	2	3	12·7	
		200m	1	4	1	25·3*	
			SF	2	3	25·1	
			F		6	25·5	
Robinson, C.	USA	80m hurdles	1	3	4		
		High jump	F		=11	1,50	
Roos-Lodder, P.	HOL	Discus throw	F		13	36,15	
Ruas, S.	FRA	High jump	F		=9	1,50	
Russell, K.	JAM	100m	1	5	2	12·9	
			SF	2	6		
		200m	1	5	3	26·3	
		Long jump	F		6	5,49	

COMPETITOR	COUNTRY CODE	EVENT	ROUND	HEAT	PLACE	TIME & DISTANCE	MEDAL
Saeys, N.	BEL	Javelin throw	F		13	31,77	
Schaeffer, P.	AUT	Shot put	F		3	13,08	B
Schilling, G.	AUT	Javelin throw	F		9	38,01	
Schlaeger, M.	AUT	Shot put	F		12	11,77	
		Discus throw	F		15	34,79	
Shepherd, J.	GBR	Long jump	Q		DNQ		
Sicnerova, O.	TCH	100m	1	7	1	12·4	
			SF	3	3	12·5	
		200m	1	3	DNF		
Silburn, K.	CAN	High jump	F		19	1,40	
		Long jump	Q		DNQ		
Sinoracka, M.	POL	Javelin throw	F		11	35,74	
Souza, B.	BRA	100m	1	2	4		
		4x100m relay	1	1	4	49·0	
Sprecher, L.	FRA	100m	1	7	5		
		200m	1	1	2	26·0	
			SF	2	6		
		4x100m relay	1	1	3	48·1	
Stad-de Jong, X.	HOL	100m	1	8	2	12·9	
			SF	2	5		
		4x100m relay	1	3	1	47·6	
			F		1	47·5	G
Steinegger, I.	AUT	High jump	F		7	1,55	
		Long jump	F		9	5,19	
Steurer, E.	AUT	80m hurdles	1	4	1	12·2	
			SF	2	6		
		4x100m relay	1	2	2	50·0	
			F		6	49·2	
Strickland, S.	AUS	100m	1	2	1	12·4	
			SF	1	2	12·4	
			F		3	12·2	B
		200m	1	4	2	25·8	
			SF	2	1	24·9	
			F		4	25·2	
		80m hurdles	1	3	2	11·9	
			SF	2	1	11·7	
			F		3	11·3	B
		4x100m relay	1	1	2	48·0	
			F		2	47·6	S
Tagliaferi, L.	ITA	100m	1	8	1	12·8	
			SF	1	5		
Teoman, Y.	TUR	100m	1	7	4		
Teunissem-Waalboer, J.	HOL	Javelin throw	F		5	40,92	

COMPETITOR	COUNTRY CODE	EVENT	ROUND	HEAT	PLACE	TIME & DISTANCE	MEDAL
Thompson, C.A.	JAM	100m	1	4	1	12·4	
			SF	3	2	12·5	
			F		6	12·4	
		200m	1	2	1	25·6*	
			SF	1	4		
Tiltsch, F.	AUT	Discus throw	F		9	37,19	
Toulouse, J.	FRA	80m hurdles	1	1	3	12·0	
			SF	1	5		
		4x100m relay	1	1	3	48·1	
Tyler, D.	GBR	High jump	F		2	1,68*	S
Upton, J.	GBR	80m hurdles	1	1	2	11·8	
			SF	1	4		
Van der Kade-Koudijs, G.	HOL	80m hurdles	1	4	2	12·2	
			SF	2	5		
		Long jump	F		4	5,57	
		4x100m relay	1	3	1	47·6	
			F		1	47·5	G
Veste, P.	FRA	Shot put	F		4	12,98	
		Discus throw	F		10	36,84	
Wajs-Marcinkiewicz, J.	POL	Discus throw	F		4	39,30	
Walker, M.	GBR	200m	1	5	2	25·8	
			SF	1	3	25·3	
			F		5	25·4	
		4x100m relay	1	2	1	48·4	
			F		4	48·0	
Walker, M.E.	USA	100m	1	4	3	12·8	
		4x100m relay	1	3	3	48·3	
Walraven, J.	USA	80m hurdles	1	4	3	12·6	
			SF	1	6		
		Long jump	Q		DNQ		
Weller, A.	CHI	200m	1	7	DIS		
		4x100m relay	1	2	3	51·5	
Whyte, E.	GBR	Shot put	Q		DNQ		
		Discus throw	F		20	32,46	
Williamson, A.	GBR	200m	1	7	1	25·4	
			SF	2	1	24·9	
			F		2	25·1	S
Witziers-Timmer, J.	HOL	4x100m relay	1	3	1	47·6	
			F		1	47·5	G
Young, L.	USA	100m	1	5	3	13·0	
		Long jump	Q		DNQ		

Tapio Rautavaara of Finland, crowns his long career with a javelin win in London.

Zatopek's 38 Miles and Three Gold Medals

Helsinki was given the Games in 1952, and it was generally agreed that these were the friendliest Games yet. There was controversy over the Soviets not wanting their athletes to stay in the Olympic village, and eventually a separate village was built for the Communist countries, but the two groups of athletes were much readier to meet and chat than their political masters. There was also plenty of discussion over the photo-finish of the 100 metres, and there are still some who think that a dead-heat would have been a fairer result.

There was no doubt about the star of the games, however. The great Czech runner Emil Zatopek won the 10,000 metres and 5,000 metres as expected, but then ran in his first marathon, bringing his "mileage" for the games up to 62·2km, or over 38½ miles. He won very easily and established himself as an Olympic legend.

Men's Track Events

There were two popular favourites for the **100 metres** title, Art Bragg of the USA and McDonald Bailey of Britain. Bragg pulled a muscle in the semi-finals, but Herb McKenley of Jamaica and Lindy Remigino of the USA were running just as fast as Bailey in the preliminary heats. Remigino and Dean Smith of the USA had the best of the starts in the final, while Bailey and McKenley had the poorest. At 50 metres, Remigino was just in front of Bailey and Smith, but McKenley was finishing like a train. They all seemed to breast the tape together and while Remigino was congratulating McKenley as the winner, the photo-finish picture was called for. Remigino was declared the victor with McKenley second, Bailey third and Smith fourth. All were given the time of 10·4 sec in the closest finish in Olympic history. (Automatic timings: Remigino 10·79, McKenley 10·80, Bailey 10·83 and Smith 10·84).

The semi-final winners in the **200 metres** were Andy Stanfield of the USA and McDonald Bailey of Britain and many people thought the winner would be one of these two. In the final, Stanfield was in lane three, Bailey four, Jim Gathers in six and his fellow American Thane Baker in seven. The Briton had a beautiful start and was in the lead around the bend, but entering the straight he was overtaken by Stanfield and Baker, and the former raced away for a win in 20·7 sec to equal the world and Olympic record. Baker held on to take the silver, while Gathers finished fast for the bronze, both recording 20·8. Bailey tied-up and was fourth (Automatic timings: Stanfield 20·81, Baker 20·97 and Gathers 21·08).

The semi-finals of the **400 metres** were fiercely contested, with eight runners going under 47·0 sec. It looked to be a repeat of 1948, when Arthur Wint won one in 46·3 and Herb McKenley the other in 46·4. The draw for positions in the final saw Mal Whitfield of the USA on the inside, then Wint, Carl Haas of Germany, McKenley, Ollie Matson of the USA and George Rhoden of Jamaica. Wint was off like a rocket and passed the 200 in 21·7, with Rhoden well back followed by McKenley. Rhoden then powered round the turn to lead into the home straight, chased hard by McKenley and Wint fading badly. He just held on to be first, with McKenley second, both in a new Olympic record of 45·9. Matson won the contest for the bronze in 46·8. (Automatic timings: Rhoden 46·09, McKenley 46·20 and Matson 46·94).

The **800 metres** was also set for a repeat duel — between Mal Whitfield and Arthur Wint of Jamaica, the first two, four years earlier. Gunnar Nielsen of Denmark shot off into the lead in the final, but Wint soon took command of the race and moved through the 400 in 54·0 sec, with Whitfield just behind. Whitfield overtook Wint and entered the finishing straight with five of the contenders challenging. The American did not fade and led a string of runners past the finish in 1-49·2 to equal his own Olympic record. Wint finished second in 1-49·4 and Heinz Ulzheimer of Germany third in 1-49·7, just edging out Nielsen. (Automatic timings: Whitfield 1-49·34, Wint 1-49·63 and Ulzheimer 1-49·78).

The standard of **1,500 metres** running had reached an all-time high and the universal favourite to win at Helsinki was Werner Lueg of Germany, who had recently equalled the world record. Also tipped were Wim Slijkhuis of Holland, the European champion, and the rising British star Roger Bannister. The final saw Rolf Lamers of Germany tow the field round the first lap in a nippy 57·8 sec, which then slowed to 2-01·4 for the second. At the end of this lap, Lueg went into the lead passing the marker in 3-03·0 with Olle Aberg of Sweden, Patrick El Mabrouk of France and Bannister bunched behind him. In the back straight Lueg took off with 200 metres to go, followed by Josey Barthel of Luxemburg, Robert MacMillen of the USA, Bannister and El Mabrouk, in hot pursuit. Down the home straight everyone was sprinting with Barthel and MacMillen catching the leader. Barthel, the outsider, got to the tape first, just ahead of MacMillen in second place, both being timed in a new Olympic record of 3-45·2. Lueg was third in 3-45·4 with Bannister and El Mabrouk finishing next. (Automatic timings: Barthel 3-45·28, MacMillen 3-45·39 and Lueg 3-45·67).

Major Emil Zatopek of Czechoslovakia was a man to be feared, not for his military aggression, but for his devastating running on the track. For the **5,000 metres** he was joint favourite with Herbert Schade of Germany and the reigning Olympic champion Gaston Reiff of Belgium. Schade took the heats seriously and won his in a new Olympic record of 14-15·4 (14-15·44), while Zatopek was chatting away to his rivals in the next heat. The final saw Chris Chataway of Britain take up the lead for a swift 65·8 sec opening lap. He handed over to Schade, who held it until the sixth, when Zatopek alternated the lead with him. Gordon Pirie of Britain briefly stomped to the front and the pace hotted up as Reiff dropped out with the order of running becoming Schade, Zatopek, Chataway, Pirie and Alan Mimoun of France. At the bell, Zatopek led, but down the back straight Chataway shot to the front with Schade and Mimoun behind him. Zatopek then took charge around the final bend and kicked for home, with Schade and Mimoun in pursuit, at which point Chataway tripped on the kerb and fell. Zatopek won in 14-06·6, with Mimoun second in 14-07·4 and Schade third in 14-08·6. (Automatic timings: Zatopek 14-06·72, Mimoun 14-07·58 and Schade 14-08·80).

The **10,000 metres** saw a field of 32 begin the final at a moderate pace. By the sixth lap Emil Zatopek had seen enough and went to the front, hotting up the pace so that only Alain Mimoun of France and Gordon Pirie of Britain attempted to go with him, while the Russian, Alex Anufriev, led the rest of the field. For ten laps the three leaders stuck together, then Pirie was dropped, and three circuits later, Mimoun suffered the same fate. The Czech went on to win in an Olympic record of 29-17·0, from Mimoun in 29-32·8 and Anufriev in 29-48·2.

The **marathon** course at Helsinki was predominantly flat over macadam roads and the weather was warm but breezy. Jim Peters of Britain was the pre-race favourite on account of his recent world best of 2:20-42·2, but the man they were all wary of was Emil Zatopek of Czechoslovakia, who had never run a marathon in his life. Peters set the 66 competitors a hot pace, but at 15km he had been joined by Gustaf Jansson of Sweden and Zatopek. The Englishman was feeling the pace at 20km, and slipped behind by over a minute in the next ten kilometres as Zatopek led in 1:38-42, followed 24 seconds later by Jansson. At 32km Peters had severe cramp and had to sit down on the roadside. Eventually he gave up, while Zatopek kept increasing his lead and finished relatively fresh in the new Olympic time of 2:23-03·2. Peters said of him: "He can run 2:15-00". Meanwhile the little-known Reinaldo Gorno of Argentina was rapidly overhauling Jansson and finished second in 2:25-35·0.

In the very first heat of the **110 metres hurdles**, Harrison Dillard equalled the Olympic record and set about seeking compensation for four years earlier. In the final, his greatest threat was the 6ft 3in Jack Davis of the USA, who was normally a slow starter. He chose the final to make one of the quickest starts of his life, but Dillard was even faster and led at the third hurdle. Davis was one of the hottest finishers ever and despite hitting three flights he came within inches of winning, Dillard just holding on to take the gold, with both men being timed in 13·7 sec. Art Barnard completed a clean sweep for America by taking the bronze in 14·1. (Automatic timings: Dillard 13·91, Davis 14·00 and Barnard 14·40).

Charlie Moore of the USA had set a new Olympic record, easing up, in the second heat of the **400 metres hurdles**, but for the final the track was wet and heavy, with little prospect of record breaking performances. With Moore in the outside lane, his leading antagonist Yuriy Lituyev of Russia on the inside track had him within his sights and for five flights there was little to chose between them, until the American drew away. Lituyev then put in some hard work off the bend and drew level at the eighth hurdle, but Moore was too

America's Horace Ashenfelter made a great breakthrough in 1952 when he beat the more fancied Russian, Vladimir Kazantsev, in the 3,000 metres steeplechase final.

strong on the run-in and won in 50·8 sec to equal his record. Lituyev recorded 51·3 and John Holland of New Zealand 52·2. (Automatic timings: Moore 51·06, Lituyev 51·51 and Holland 52·26).

There was a remarkable improvement in **3,000 metres steeplechase** standards in 1952, as eight athletes bettered the old Olympic record. In the first heat, Vladimir Kazantsev of Russia set a new record with 8-58·0 before Horace Ashenfelter of America reduced this to 8-51·0. At the start of the final Olavi Rinteenpaa of Finland went to the front. But then Mikhail Saltykov took over, until Ashenfelter decided to hot up the pace in the third lap and took Kazantsev along with him, with the field stringing out. At the end of the sixth lap, John Disley of Britain moved up to third and with 250 metres to go Kazantsev began to sprint. Ashenfelter waited until he had negotiated the water jump 150 metres from home to counter the Russian, and ran away to win in the world record time of 8-45·4. Kazantsev finished in 8-51·6 and was nearly caught by the bronze medallist Disley on 8-51·8. (Automatic timings: Ashenfelter 8-45·68, Kazantsev 8-51·52 and Disley 8-51·94).

The **10 kilometres walk** was marred by large numbers of cautions and disqualifications, which resulted in the removal of track walking from the Olympic Games. John Mikaelsson of Sweden was the defending champion and Fritz Schwab of Switzerland, the bronze medallist from the London Games, was also competing. In the final, George Coleman of Britain led for the first 2·5km, when Mikaelsson strode past and went on to win in 45-02·8, beating his own Olympic record. There was a terrific duel between Schwab and Bruno Junk of Russia, which reached such a pitch that in the last 50 metres both men ran! Schwab got the silver and Junk the bronze, and amazingly the "runners" were not disqualified. (Automatic timings: Mikaelsson 45-02·85. Schwab 45-41·03 and Junk 45-41·05).

Thirty-one competed in the **50 kilometres walk** on a far from easy course and Sandor Laszlo of Hungary set the early pace followed by the defending champion, John Ljunggren of Sweden and Giuseppe Dordoni of Italy. At 15km, Ljunggren had a 20-second lead over Dordoni with Laszlo fading, but a little after 35km he cracked. Dordoni won in 4:28-07·8, looking quite fresh, Dolezal was second in 4:30-17·8 and Antal Roka of Hungary improved to finish third in 4:31-27·2. Harold Whitlock of Britain, the 1936 victor, came 11th.

The **4 × 100 metres relay** resolved itself into a battle between the USA, Russia, Hungary and Britain. Russia gave the United States a fright over the first two legs by getting a lead of two metres with their slick baton changing, but had a poor last exchange which allowed America to win in 40·1 sec, with the Soviets being timed at 40·3. The USA was represented by Dean Smith, Harrison Dillard, Lindy Remigino and Andy Stanfield. The race for the bronze was only decided in the last leg, when the Hungarian anchor runner, Bela Goldovanyi, shot past Brian Shenton to take third position in 40·5. (Automatic timings: USA 40·26, USSR 40·58 and Hungary 40·83).

Jamaica had been smarting for four years over their failure in London in the **4 × 400 metres relay**, and now they had an even faster team. On the first leg of the final Ollie Matson of the USA just held off Arthur Wint of Jamaica with 46·7 to 46·8 and on the second, Eugene Cole of the States stacked up a sizeable lead over Les Laing with 45·5 to 47·0. The race really exploded into life during the third section, when Herb McKenley of Jamaica ran a storming leg of 44·6 to overtake Charlie Moore, 46·3, and gave George Rhoden a half-a-metre advantage over Mal Whitfield. And that's the margin Jamaica won by in 3-03·9, for a new world and Olympic record. The USA recorded 3-04·4, while Germany were third in 3-06·6. (Automatic timings: Jamaica 3-04·4, USA 3-04·21 and Germany 3-06·78).

All-Sport Photographic Ltd.

Bob Mathias

Winning the decathlon at the 1948 Games in London at the age of 17 made Bob Mathias the youngest athlete to become an Olympic champion. His success was all the more remarkable because it was only his third attempt at this gruelling ten-event competition.

Mathias was born at Tulare on 17 November 1930, and in his first decathlon after leaving High School he surprised himself by scoring 7,094 points. This encouraged him to contest the US national title which he won with 7,224 points to earn the trip to the Olympics, where he scored 7,139 points. Two years later he raised the world record to 7,453 points, and at Helsinki in 1952 improved his world mark to 7,887 in becoming the first to win the Olympic title twice.

His successful career — ten major competitions without defeat, including five US national championships — was unfortunately halted internationally in 1953 because he was being deprived of his amateur status for appearing in a film about his sporting life. He was, however, allowed to continue in service competitions.

In 1966 the 6ft 3in. 15½ stone Mathias was elected to the American House of Representatives as a Republican Congressman.

The two Jamaicans, George Rhoden (296) and Herb McKenley (295), hit the tape in a blanket finish for the 400 metres title. Rhoden got the nod from the judges.

Men's Field Events

Walt Davis was America's hope for the **high jump**. At eight he had been a polio victim and at 11 he could barely walk, but at 21 he could jump 2,10 metres. Seven men cleared 1,95 and four of them 1,98: Davis and Ken Wiesner of America, Jose da Conceicao of Brazil and Gosta Svensson of Sweden. When the bar was raised to 2,01, Davis and Wiesner succeeded, but the other two failed and Da Conceicao took the bronze under the count-back rule. Then the bar was elevated to a new Olympic record height of 2,04. Wiesner failed and took the silver, while Davis cleared for the gold on his second attempt.

The two Americans, Don Laz and the Reverend Bob Richards, were both tipped for the top medals of a **pole vault** competition, where 19 of the 25 starters qualified for the final and Swedish steel poles were now all the rage, being more reliable than the old bamboo ones. The bar was initially set at 3,60 metres and it took five hours before it reached its ceiling of 4,60. Nine competitors cleared 4,20, but only five managed ten centimetres more: Richards, Laz, Ragnar Lundberg of Sweden, the reigning European champion, Pyotr Denisenko of Russia, the European record holder, and Valto Olenius of Finland. At 4,40 the Finn failed and the bar moved to 4,50, where only Laz and Richards got over, on their second attempts. Lundberg took the bronze medal with 4,40, due to fewer jumps in the competition. At 4,55 it looked as if the competition was all but finished, until Richards squeezed over on his last try for the gold and an Olympic record. Laz was second with 4,50.

George Brown of the USA was a firm favourite for the **long jump** gold where only seven jumpers reached the qualifying standard of 7,20 metres and five lesser men made up the required 12 for the final. Brown fouled the board twice in the final, moved his check mark back and blasted down the runway once more to launch himself to 7,90. Up went the red flag and he was out of the competition. Jerome Biffle of the USA won the event at 7,57, and he had only two out of six valid jumps. His team-mate, Meredith Gourdine came second with 7,53, while Odon Foldessi of Hungary was third with a disappointing 7,30.

The **triple jump** was a contest between the "rubber ball" of Brazil, Adhemar da Silva, the world record-holder, and the muscular strong man of Russia; Leonid Scherbakov, European champion and record holder. Da Silva stated off the finals with a near world record jump of 15,95 metres. His second jump of 16,12, broke the record and his fourth hopped 6,02, stepped 4,22 and jumped 5,98 for a fantastic 16,22. In all, he had four jumps beyond his previous world best. Drawn into the euphoria was Scherbakov, who launched himself to 15,98 for a new European record, and Arnoldo Devonish, of Venezuela, who improved his best from 15,04 to 15,52 for the bronze medal.

Jim Fuchs of the USA, the current world record-holder, was expected to outshine everyone else in the **shot put**, but he was nursing a very painful finger on his throwing hand and did well to come third. The struggle for gold was between his two 20-year-old team-mates, Darrow Hooper and Parry O'Brien. On his very first put

Lindy Remigino

Lindy Remigino was the surprise packet of the 1952 Games. He had never won a major championship in his own country and only narrowly qualified for the US team, yet in Helsinki he took the gold medal for the 100 metres.

It was a thrilling final every stride of the way. Remigino was fastest from the blocks and had a clear lead at half-way with Herb McKenley, of Jamaica, in hot pursuit. But the slightly built American held on to take the title in 10·4 sec, a time given also to McKenley, placed second, Emmanuel McDonald Bailey, of Great Britain, third, and Dean Smith, USA, fourth. McKenley came storming through at the finish and the general belief was that he had won. But a lengthy study of the photo-finish by judges using a set-square convinced them that Remigino had earned the verdict by having his right shoulder fractionally ahead of McKenley's chest. Remigino collected a second gold when the USA won the 4 × 100m relay.

As if to prove there had been no fluke about his Olympic 100m win, soon after Helsinki, Remigino twice beat McDonald Bailey over the distance, and in Oslo he tied the world record of 10·2 sec, of which McDonald Bailey was a co-holder. The American however could not have his run ratified because of the strength of the following wind.

All-Sport Photographic Ltd.

Emil Zatopek

Emil Zatopek must rank with Paavo Nurmi and Jesse Owens as one of the world's three finest athletes of all time. He revolutionised distance running, and in doing so broke all world records from 5,000m to 30,000m. He favoured training in army boots and by this means developed exceptional stamina when racing in lighter shoes.

He was born in Koprivnice, Moravia, on 22 September 1922 and won his first Olympic title at the 1948 Games in London with a thrilling victory over the famed French champion Alain Mimoun. But it was in Helsinki four years later that he showed his real world-beating qualities. He retained his 10,000m title in a time 42 seconds faster than his London win, and went on to take the 5,000m in Olympic record time. Not content with these successes he later chose to contest the marathon, an event he had never previously attempted.

Around the 20-mile mark, when running level with Britain's Jim Peters, the favourite, he calmly asked if he (Zatopek) was going too fast to last. Peters, experiencing extreme pressure to maintain the pace, had difficulty in replying and shortly afterwards dropped out, exhausted. Zatopek merrily went on his way to a third gold medal and won by a large margin.

His wife Dana won the javelin at the same Olympics.

Mal Whitfield

In spite of the brilliance of Jamaican runners throughout his career, Mal Whitfield always had the edge when it came to major 800m events, particularly at the Olympic Games. An athlete with a beautifully smooth action, he brought off a brilliant victory over Jamaica's tall Arthur Wint with a devastating late burst in the 1948 800m final, to set an Olympic record of 1:49·2, just 0·3 sec ahead of Wint.

Whitfield, who was born in Bay City, Texas, on 11 October 1924, had to shelve his track running for a spell while he went off to serve as a rear-gunner with the American Air Force in Korea. But by 1952 he was back in racing shape and representing the US in the 800m at Helsinki.

Again it was Jamaica's Wint stalking him for the title, and a titanic battle between them had the packed stadium on the edge of their seats.

Once more it was Whitfield who snatched the verdict, extraodianrily enough in the identical time with which he had won his previous Olympic gold.

Whitfield, who between 1948 and 1954 won 66 of 69 half-mile races and set world records for the 880 yards (1-48·6) and 1,000m (2-20.8), decided to retire after failing to qualify for the Melbourne Games.

Joseph Csermak of Hungary, the protege of the reigning champion, Imre Nemeth, exceeded all expectations when he usurped his master to win the hammer competition.

Harrison Dillard

Few personal Olympic stories match the experience of hurdler Harrison Dillard. From May 1947 to June 1948 he was undefeated in 82 races. Yet when it came to the American trials for the Olympic Games in London, he fell in the high hurdles and failed to qualify, as only the first three in the trials were automatically selected for the Games.

Dillard's only chance was to try and prove himself fast enough for the American sprint relay team. He succeeded not just as the fourth fastest qualifier, but as the third best which also entitled him to contest the individual 100m sprint. And, dream of dreams, Dillard went out and won that Olympic final in 10·3 sec, equalling the record of his home town hero, Jesse Owens.

After this, the immaculate Dillard continued his domination of the world's best high hurdlers and at the 1952 Games in Helsinki he achieved his cherished wish of becoming the 110m hurdles Olympics champion. It was his fourth Olympic gold, as he also ran in the American winning sprint relay teams of 1948 and 1952.

Dillard was born in Cleveland, Ohio, on 8 July 1923, and an early joy in his athletics career was having Jesse Owens make a present to him of the racing shoes in which the great man won his Olympic races.

of 17,41, O'Brien won the competition, although Hooper came very close, with a last throw of 17,39. The injured Fuchs made only two throws, the better being 17,06, while Jiri Skobla, the top European, disappointed in ninth place.

On paper, the **discus throw** appeared to be a duel between the defending Olympic champion, Adolfo Consolini of Italy, and the American, Fortune Gordien, the world record-holder. However, the man on form was Sim Iness, of the USA, who was brilliantly consistent, with all of his six attempts being over 52,78 metres, the previous Olympic record. He won with a throw of 55,03, with Consolini second with 53,78 and Jim Dillon of America third with 53,28. Gordien could manage only fourth with 52,66.

Karl Wolf and Karl Storch, both of Germany, Sverre Strandli, of Norway, and the defending champion and world record-holder, Imre Nemeth of Hungary, were favourites for the **hammer throw**. Strandli was eliminated at 56,36 metres, which would have won the previous Olympics, and Wolf barely scraped into the final six. A newcomer, Jozsef Csermak of Hungary, a protege of Nemeth, immediately went into the lead with 58,48 and on his third throw shattered the world record with 60,34 to win the competition. The battle for the silver between Storch and Nemeth was won by the consistent Storch at 58,86, while Nemeth gained the bronze with 57,74.

It had usually been a Finn who had won the **javelin throw**, and records proved that the title had never gone outside Europe, but on this occasion the USA could now boast of two world-class throwers in Cy Young and Bill Miller, while Bud Held had topped the rankings in 1951. In the finals, Miller went straight into the lead with 72,46 metres in the first round, to which Young responded with 73,78, a new Olympic record, to take the gold in the next. The bronze position went to the top Finn, Toivo Hyytiainen, at 71,89, while Held was troubled with his back and could only finish ninth.

The three medallists from the 1948 **decathlon** were all competing again and the defending champion, Bob Mathias of the USA, had in the meantime raised the world record twice. There was no holding Mathias on the

first day, and he scored 4,367 points, according to the new tables in use. An 18-year-old American, Milt Campbell, scored 4,111 and another American, Floyd Simmons, 3,924, while the European champion, Ignace Heinrich of France, injured his foot in the high jump and retired. On the second day, Mathias continued at a high level and established a new world and Olympic record of 7,887 points. Under the old tables, the total would have been 8,450, which meant that in three increments he had improved the record an unprecedented 550 points.

Women's Events

Marjorie Jackson of Australia, who twice ran 11·6 and twice 11·5 sec, was the outstanding sprinter in the **100 metres**. Unfortunately, the defending champion, Fanny Blankers-Koen of Holland, qualified for the first semi-final, but later withdrew suffering from a virus. In the final, Jackson was never headed and won in 11·5 to equal the world and Olympic record. Second, was Daphne Hasenjager of South Africa, back in 11·8, but clear of Shirley Strickland of Australia in 11·9, who just nosed out fellow Australian Winsome Cripps, also given 11·9. (Automatic timings: Jackson 11·67, Hasenjager 12·05, Strickland 12·12 and Cripps 12·16).

In the heats of the **200 metres**, Marjorie Jackson equalled the world record with a time of 23·6 sec and in the semi-finals she went even faster, clocking 23·4, with Nadeshda Khnykina of Russia recording the next best time of 24·1. Jackson, known as the "blue flash", was in the inside lane for the final and quickly into her running, winning comfortably in 23·7. There was a terrific race for second place, with Bertha Brouwer of Holland taking the silver medal from Khnykina, third and Winsome Cripps, fourth, all in 24·2. (Automatic timings: Jackson 23·59, Brouwer 24·25, Khnykina 24·37 and Cripps 24·40).

The **80 metres hurdles** saw Shirley Strickland of Australia equal the world record of 10·8 sec in the heats. She did this again in the semi-finals, when beating Maria Sander of Germany and Jean Desforges of Britain, both being timed at 10·9, but it was ruled wind-assisted. Strickland was away smartly in the final with Blankers-Koen pulling up at the third barrier, which caused Desforges to hesitate and lose ground. The Australian won comfortably in 10·9, a new world record, while Maria Golubnicharya of Russia just held off Sander for second place, both being given 11·1. (Automatic timings: Strickland 11·01, Golubnicharya 11·24 and Sander 11·30).

Australia set a new world record of 46·1 sec in the very first heat of the **4 × 100 metres relay** and in the third heat Germany also dipped under the old record with 46·3. The final was a very close race between the USA, Germany, Britain, Russia and Australia. However, the baton exchange between Winsome Cripps and Marjorie Jackson, on the last leg, was fatal. Cripps passed the stick, but immediately knocked it out of Jackson's hand with her knee, and gone were Australia's chances. The USA were having a tremendous tussle with Germany and got home by inches in a world record breaking 45·9, a similar time being clocked for the silver medallists. Britain won the contest with Russia for third place in 46·2. (Automatic timings: USA 46·14, Germany 46·18 and GBR 46·14).

Seven of the 17 **high jump** contestants cleared 1,58 metres, among them Dorothy Tyler, the silver medallist from both Berlin and London. At 1,63 only three succeeded; Esther Brand of South Africa, Sheila Lerwill of Britain, the world record-holder, and Aleksandra Chudina of Russia. Chudina was eliminated at 1,65 and took the bronze and when the bar was raised to 1,67, only Brand cleared it with her scissors style, to win the gold from Lerwill.

Nine competitors in the **long jump** exceeded the previous Olympic record of 5,69 metres, with Yvette Williams jumping 6,16 in the qualifying rounds. The final saw Shirley Cawley of Britain jumping 5,92 in the first round, but several jumps later Aleksandra Chudina of Russia sailed to 5,99. Chudina improved to 6,14 in the next round, but Williams, of New Zealand, saved her big effort for her fourth jump, clearing 6.24 to win the competition in a new Olympic record. Chudina was second and Cawley third.

Galina Zybina of Russia had recently broken the world **shot put** record and was the clear favourite for the gold, but the preliminary rounds saw Claudia Tochenova, also of Russia, break the Olympic record with 13,88 metres. However, in the final Zybina

powered the missile to 15,28 for a new world record and gold medal. Marianne Werner of Germany responded with 14,57 to take the silver, leaving Tochenova in third place.

Although Nina Dumbadze of Russia was the world record-holder in the **discus throw**, her compatriot Nina Romaschkova was nearly as good. The on-form Romaschkova first flipped the discus to 50,84 and then to 51,42 for the gold medal and a new Olympic record. Behind her came another Russian, Elizaveta Bagryantseva, who threw 47,08, and then a below-form Dumbadze with 46,29.

The Olympic record went in the qualifying rounds of the **javelin throw** when Aleksandra Chudina of Russia threw 46,17. But in the very first round of the final, Dana Zatopekova of Czechoslovakia, wife of Emil Zatopek, hurled her javelin 50,47 metres for the family's fourth gold medal of the Games. The unfortunate Chudina had a final fling of 50,01 that came very close to the winning throw, but ultimately had to settle for second, while Elena Gorchakova of Russia obtained third place with 49,76.

In the closest finish in Olympic history, the first four men home in the 100 metres were given the same time. The winner was Lindy Remigino of America (98).

MALES

COMPETITOR	COUNTRY CODE	EVENT	ROUND	HEAT	PLACE	TIME & DISTANCE	MEDAL
Abdallah, B.	FRA	10000m	F		17	30-53·0	
Abdelkrim, B.	FRA	5000m	1	2	12	15-10·2	
Aberg, O.	SWE	1500m	1	3	1	3-51·14	
			SF	2	2	3-50·71	
			F		7	3-47·20	
Acarbay, P.	TUR	400m	1	4	5	50·83	
		400m hurdles	1	7	5	1-02·8	
Acosta, M.	ARG	100m	1	7	6	11·58	
		4×100m relay	1	3	3	41·56	
			SF	1	4	41·61	
Acquaah, G.	GHA	100m	1	7	5	11·47	
		4×100m relay	1	2	4	42·27	
Adamczyk, E.	POL	Pole vault	Q		DNQ		
Adamik, Z.	HUN	400m	1	1	4	48·70	
		4×400m relay	1	2	3	3-13·96	
Adams, R.	CAN	Decathlon	F		19	5530	
Aguilera, N.	MEX	Pole vault	Q		DNQ		
Ahman, A.	SWE	Triple jump	F		15	14,05	
Ajado, E.	NGR	100m	1	9	4	11·25	
		200m	1	4	4	22·92	
Albertsson, B.	SWE	5000m	1	3	2	14-25·80	
			F		9	14-27·8	
		10000m	F		12	30-34·6	
Alho, O.	FIN	110m hurdles	1	1	6	15·63	
Allday, P.	GBR	Hammer throw	F		21	49,70	
Allen, L.	GBR	10k walk	1	2	DIS		
Altiok, A.	TUR	Triple jump	Q		DNQ	13,62	
Amatayakul, P.	THA	400m	1	2	6	53·23	
		4×100m relay	1	2	6	44·81	
Anderson, T.	GBR	Pole vault	Q		DNQ		
Anderson, B.	CUB	110m hurdles	1	3	4	15·24	
		4×100m relay	1	2	3	42·14	
			SF	2	4	41·67	
Andersson, A.	SWE	5000m	1	1	4	14-25·09	
			F		8	14-26·0	
Anderton, J.	SAF	400m	1	2	5	50·35	
		4×400m relay	1	3	4	3-15·09	
Andrushenko, N.	URS	Long jump	Q		DNQ	6,74	
Annexy, J.	PUR	Hammer throw	Q		DNQ	0	
Anufriyev, A.	URS	5000m	1	3	1	14-23·83	
			F		10	14-31·4	
		10000m	F		3	29-48·2	B
Apro, J.	HUN	3000m steeplechase	1	2	3	9-00·60	
			F		9	9-04·30	
Argcangeli, T.	ITA	10k walk	1	2	7	48-00·2	
Arogundade, M.	NGR	200m	1	12	5	22·71	
		4×100m relay	1	4	2	42·63	
			SF	2	5	42·01	
Ascune, H.	URU	High jump	Q		DNQ	1,80	
Ashbaugh, W.	USA	Triple jump	F		4	15,39	
Ashenfelter, H.	USA	3000m steeplechase	1	3	1	8-51·17*	
			F		1	8-45·68*	G
Aslam, H.	PAK	Marathon	F		38	2:43-38·2	
Aslam, J.	PAK	100m	1	9	2	11·18	
			2	1	4	11·02	
		200m	1	9	3	22·14	
		4×100m relay	1	4	3	42·91	
			SF	1	6	42·15	
Aytar, A.	TUR	Marathon	F		DNF		
Aziz, A.	PAK	100m	1	11	5	11·48	
		200m	1	8	5	23·02	
		4×100m relay	1	4	3	42·91	
			SF	1	6	42·15	
Baboie, I.	RUM	50k walk	F		8	4:41-52·8	
Back, R.	FIN	400m	1	2	2	48·58	
			2	2	5	51·53	
		4×400m relay	1	1	6	3-16·67	
Backus, R.	USA	Hammer throw	F		13	52,11	
Baghanbachi, A.	IRN	5000m	1	2	11	15-03·0	
		3000m steeplechase	1	2	6	9-13·43	
Bailey, E. McD.	GBR	100m	1	3	1	10·65	
			2	1	1	10·73	
			SF	1	1	10·74	
			F		3	10·83	
		200m	1	13	1	21·66	
			2	3	1	21·27	
			SF	2	1	21·46	
			F		4	21·14	
		4×100m relay	1	2	1	41·43	
			SF	1	3	41·24	
			F		4	40·85	
Baker, T.	USA	200m	1	2	1	21·62	
			2	2	1	21·64	
			SF	2	2	21·50	
			F		2	20·97	S
Bakos, J.	HUN	800m	1	3	3	1-54·5	
			SF	3	7	1-55·70	
Balafas, T.	GRE	Pole vault	F		17	3,80	
Bally, E.	FRA	100m	1	2	1	10·97	
			2	2	4	10·98	
		200m	1	1	2	22·03	
			2	5	3	22·02	
		4×100m relay	1	1	2	40·98	
			SF	2	2	41·02	
			F		5	41·10	
Banhalmi, F.	HUN	400m	1	5	4	49·55	
		4×400m relay	1	2	3	3-13·96	
Bannister, R.	GBR	1500m	1	4	3	3-56·13	
			SF	2	5	3-50·92	
			F		4	3-46·30	
Baran, I.	FIN	100m	1	8	4	11·32	
		4×100m relay	1	1	4	42·20	
Barias, J.	GUA	100m	1	1	7	11·56	
		200m	1	15	5	22·88	
Barkay, E.	TUR	110m hurdles	1	1	4	15·34	
Barnard, A.	USA	110m hurdles	1	6	1	14·61	
			SF	1	2	14·44	
			F		3	14·40	B
Barnes, J.	USA	800m	1	3	2	1-54·5	
			SF	2	4	1-53·54	
Bart, R.	FRA	400m hurdles	1	4	3	54·64	
			2	1	4	53·33	
		4×400m relay	1	1	2	3-12·72	
			F		6	3-10·33	
Barthel, J.	LUX	1500m	1	1	1	3-51·75	
			SF	2	1	3-50·51	
			F		1	3-45·28*	G
Batun, A.	ISR	High jump	Q		DNQ	1,70	
Baumgartner, J.	SUI	800m	1	1	5	1-57·1	
Beckles, E.	ARG	200m	1	7	3	22·73	
		4×100m relay	1	3	3	41·56	
			SF	1	4	41·61	
Bell, D.	VEN	110m hurdles	1	3	5	15·96	
Bell, T.	AUS	High jump	F		=24	1,80	
Belokurov, N.	URS	1500m	1	5	4	3-56·47	
			SF	2	11	3-55·49	
Benaras, M.	PAK	Marathon	F		DNF		
Benard, C.	FRA	High jump	F		=18	1,90	
Bengtsson, O.	SWE	Javelin throw	F		11	65,50	
Berglund, P.	SWE	Javelin throw	F		10	67,47	
Beres, E.	HUN	5000m	1	2	3	14-19·66	
			F		7	14-24·8	
Bernard, O.	SUI	110m hurdles	1	1	3	15·29	
Berti, A.	ITA	Marathon	F		53	2:58-36·2	
Betton, A.	USA	High jump	F		7	1,95	
Biffle, J.	USA	Long jump	F		1	7,57	G
Billas, L.	FRA	Marathon	F		DNF		
Bjarnason, A.	ISL	4×100m relay	1	4	DIS		
		100m	1	1	5	11·40	
		200m	1	11	4	22·51	
Blackman, R.	USA	400m hurdles	1	3	3	54·8	
			2	4	2	52·88	
			SF	1	5	52·86	
Bloech, R.	AUT	400m	1	2	3	49·82	
Boennhoff, G.	ARG	200m	1	1	1	21·72	
			2	4	1	21·67	
			SF	2	3	21·75	
			F		6	21·59	
		4×100m relay	1	3	3	41·56	
			SF	1	4	41·61	
Bonino, R.	FRA	100m	1	11	3	11·00	
		4×100m relay	1	1	2	40·98	
			SF	2	2	41·02	
			F		5	41·10	
Booysen, S.	SAF	200m	1	11	1	22·03	
			2	3	4	22·09	
		400m	1	12	4	49·17	
Boerjesson, A.	SWE	10k walk	1	1	7	47-32·4	
Boulanger, J.	FRA	Triple jump	Q		DNQ	14,49	
Boysen, A.	NOR	800m	1	7	1	1-53·2	
			SF	1	4	1-50·57	
		1500m	1	6	3	3-55·15	
			SF	1	6	3-51·33	
			F		11	3-51·75	
Bragg, A.	USA	100m	1	10	1	10·73	
			2	4	2	10·75	
			SF	1	6	11·43	
Braennstroem, G.	SWE	400m	1	6	4	50·32	
		4×400m relay	1	1	3	3-13·55	
Brasher, C.	GBR	3000m steeplechase	1	3	4	9-03·18	
			F		11	9-14·0	
Brault, H.	FRA	200m	1	12	3	22·48	

COMPETITOR	COUNTRY CODE	EVENT	ROUND	HEAT	PLACE	TIME & DISTANCE	MEDAL
Brazhnik, V.	URS	Pole vault	F		7	4,20	
Breder, T.	SAA	Long jump	Q		DNQ	6,88	
Breitman, G.	FRA	Pole vault	Q		DNC		
		Decathlon	F		DNF		
Brown, G.	USA	Long jump	F		NP	0	
Broz, F.	TCH	100m	1	11	4	11·32	
		200m	1	15	3	22·35	
		4×100m relay	1	3	2	41·49	
			SF	2	3	41·46	
			F		6	41·41	
Bruun, E.	NOR	50k walk	F		17	4:52-48-4	
Bryngeirsson, T.	ISL	Pole vault	F		=14	3,95	
Buch Silva, H.	BRA	Pole vault	Q		DNQ	3,60	
Budzynski, R.	POL	200m	1	3	2	23·37	
			2	4	6	22·51	
Buhl, Z.	POL	4×100m relay	1	1	3	42·00	
			SF	1	5	41·91	
Bulanchik, E.	URS	110m hurdles	1	2	1	14·65	
			SF	2	2	14·70	
			F		4	14·73	
Burgard, W.	SAA	Triple jump	Q		DNQ	13,86	
Bussotti, A.	ITA	Marathon	F		46	2:52-55-0	
Butenko, B.	URS	Discus throw	F		11	48,15	
Butt, M.	PAK	100m	1	7	3	11·17	
		200m	1	11	3	22·34	
		4×100m relay	1	4	3	42·91	
			SF	1	6	42·15	
Cabrera, D.	ARG	Marathon	F		6	2:26-42-4	
Camacho, F.	VEN	800m	1	7	5	2-00-0	
		1500m	1	1	7	4-18-0	
Campbell, M.	USA	Decathlon	F		2	6975	S
Camus, Y.	FRA	400m	1	8	2	48·06	
			2	4	4	48·43	
		4×100m relay	1	1	2	40·98	
			SF	2	2	41·02	
			F		5	41·10	
Capozzoli, C.	USA	5000m	1	1	7	14-39-0	
Carr, E.	AUS	200m	1	17	1	22·19	
			2	3	3	21·98	
		400m	1	1	3	48·23	
		4×100m relay	1	2	5	42·38	
		4×400m relay	1	3	5	3-16-00	
Carroll, J.	CAN	400m	1	3	2	48·05	
			2	3	3	47·82	
			SF	2	5	47·61	
		4×400m relay	1	3	2	3-11·49	
			F		4	3-09·37	
Cascino, S.	ITA	50k walk	F		19	4:56-46-0	
Casimiro, F.	POR	200m	1	15	4	22·72	
		400m	1	6	7	52·33	
		4×100m relay	1	1	6	43·01	
Castro, F.	PUR	Triple jump	Q		DNQ	13,37	
Cederquist, P.	DEN	Hammer throw	F		16	51,60	
Celedon, L.	CHI	Marathon	F		14	2:33-45-8	
Ceraj, Z.	YUG	5000m	1	2	14	15-17-8	
Cevona, V.	TCH	1500m	1	6	2	3-53-45	
			SF	1	7	3-51-37	
Chaaban, F.	EGY	100m	1	9	6	11·51	
		200m	1	5	4	22·90	
		Triple jump	Q		DNQ	13,45	
		4×100m relay	1	1	7	43·02	
Charriere, R.	SUI	50k walk	F		26	5:08-59-0	
Chataway, C.	GBR	5000m	1	3	5	14-27-35	
			F		5	14-18-38	
Chevalier, L.	FRA	10k walk	1	1	3	45-58-0	
			F		4	45-50-28	
Chevgun, P.	URS	800m	1	4	2	1-51-3	
			SF	1	7	1-53-25	
Chivell, W.	SAF	4×400m relay	1	3	4	3-15-09	
Choi, C.S.	KOR	Marathon	F		33	2:41-23-0	
Choi, Y.	KOR	Triple jump	Q		DNQ	14,44	
Choi, Y.C.	KOR	Marathon	F		4	2:26-36-0	
Clark, D.	GBR	Hammer throw	F		18	51,07	
Clement, D.	CAN	400m	1	10	5	50·19	
		4×400m relay	1	3	2	3-11·49	
			F		4	3-09·37	
Cleve, U.	GER	800m	1	7	5	1-53-4	
			SF	1	5	1-51-77	
Cole, E.	USA	400m	1	9	1	48·44	
			2	4	2	47·88	
			SF	1	4	46·94	
		4×400m relay	1	2	1	3-11·67	
			F		2	3-04·21	S
Coleman, G.	GBR	10k walk	1	2	1	46-12-4	
			F		5	46-06-69	
Collins, P.	CAN	Marathon	F		40	2:45-58-0	
Colon, T.	PUR	110m hurdles	1	4	4	15·48	
Consolini, A.	ITA	Discus throw	F		2	53,78	S
Constantin, R.	RUM	Marathon	F		DNF		
Corbitt, T.	USA	Marathon	F		44	2:51-09-0	
Coskul, O.	TUR	5000m	1	2	8	14-36-2	
		10000m	F		15	30-42-4	
Cosmas, P.	GRE	400m hurdles	1	3	2	53·9	
			2	2	2	55·50	
		Decathlon	F		DNF		
Cox, S.	GBR	Marathon	F		DNF		
Crosby, G.	CAN	110m hurdles	1	4	3	15·11	
		4×100m relay	1	1	5	42·73	
Csanyi, G.	HUN	100m	1	5	2	11·09	
			2	4	5	11·07	
		4×100m relay	1	3	1	41·15	
			SF	2	1	40·99	
			F		3	40·83	B
Csermak, J.	HUN	Hammer throw	F		1	60,34*	G
Curotta, M.	AUS	400m	1	7	2	48·87	
			2	2	4	48·86	
		4×100m relay	1	2	5	42·38	
		4×400m relay	1	3	5	3-16-00	
Da Conceicao, J.T.	BRA	High jump	F		3	1,98	B
		Triple jump	Q		DNQ	14,46	
Dacak, J.	TCH	Hammer throw	F		4	56,81	
Dagmroff, N.	BUL	Triple jump	Q		DNQ		
Damitio, G.	FRA	High jump	F		=13	1,90	
Danubic, B.	YUG	Javelin throw	F		5	70,55	
Da Silva, A.F.	BRA	Triple jump	F		1	16,22*	G
David, J.	TCH	400m	1	12	5	49·23	
		4×100m relay	1	3	2	41·49	
			SF	2	3	41·46	
			F		6	41·41	
Davis, J.	USA	110m hurdles	1	3	1	14·23	
			SF	2	1	14·62	
			F		2	14·00	S
Davis, W.	USA	High jump	F		1	2,04*	G
Degats, J.	FRA	400m	1	7	1	48·60	
			2	3	5	48·90	
		4×400m relay	1	1	2	3-12·72	
			F		6	3-10·33	
Delelienne, J.	BEL	High jump	F		=9	1,90	
Dermynck, L.	BEL	800m	1	6	6	1-57-4	
Deri, J.	USA	50k walk	F		DNF		
Denizenko, P.	URS	Pole vault	F		4	4,40	
Denley, M.	GBR	Javelin throw	Q		DNQ	61,58	
De Oliveira, G.	BRA	Long jump	Q		DNQ	6,71	
		Triple jump	F		7	14,95	
De Sa, A.F.	BRA	Long jump	F		4	7,23	
Destet, L.	BEL	800m	1	4	4	1-52-9	
Devonish, A.	VEN	Triple jump	F		3	15,52	B
Dewachtere, C.	BEL	Marathon	F		18	2:34-32-0	
Dhanda, S.	IND	800m	1	6	2	1-52-0	
			SF	3	6	1-54-84	
Dick, A.	GBR	400m	1	9	6	48·84	
			2	3	6	49·20	
		4×400m relay	1	2	2	3-12·67	
			F		5	3-10·23	
Dillard, H.	USA	110m hurdles	1	1	1	14·03*	
			SF	1	1	14·15	
			F		1	13·91*	G
		4×100m relay	1	1	1	40·34	
			SF	1	1	40·51	
			F		1	40·26	G
Dillion, J.	USA	Discus throw	F		3	53,28	B
Dimitrievic, M.	YUG	High jump	F		=20	1,80	
Dinu, C.	RUM	Marathon	F		31	2:39-42-2	
Disley, J.	GBR	3000m steeplechase	1	2	1	8-59-59	
			F		3	8-51-94	B
Ditta, F.	PAK	10k walk	1	1	DIS		
Djian, R.	FRA	800m	1	4	5	1-54-3	
Djuraskovic, B.	YUG	3000m steeplechase	1	2	10	9-23-2	
Dlugoberski, M.	POL	1500m	1	1	6	3-57-70	
Dobromi, J.	HUN	Marathon	F		7	2:28-04-8	
Doher, J.	FRA	110m hurdles	1	6		16-02	
Dohrow, G.	GER	1500m	1	1	2	3-51-90	
			SF	2	10	3-55-27	
Dolan, P.	IRL	100m	1	2	3	11·12	
		200m	1	15	2	22·04	
			2	2	3	22·15	
		400m	1	10	3	48·81	
Dolezal, J.	TCH	10k walk	1	2	5	47-06-2	
			F		DNS		
		50k walk	F		2	4:30-17-8	S
Dordoni, G.	ITA	50k walk	F		1	4:28-07-8*	G

COMPETITOR	COUNTRY CODE	EVENT	ROUND	HEAT	PLACE	TIME & DISTANCE	MEDAL
Doubleday, K.	AUS	110m hurdles	1	4	1	14·65	
			SF	1	3	14·74	
			F		5	14·82	
		400m hurdles	1	2	3	55·4	
			2	3	6	1·00·2	
		4×100m relay	1	2	5	42·38	
		4×400m relay	1	3	6	3·16·00	
Douglas, E.	GBR	Hammer throw	Q		DNQ	48,25	
Doybak, E.	TUR	400m	1	6	6	51·34	
		400m hurdles	1	2	6	56·5	
Dragomir, Z.	RUM	Pole vault	F		=18	3,80	
Druetzler, W.	USA	1500m	1	2	1	3·51·66	
			SF	1	4	3·51·16	
			F		12	3·56·0	
Dumitru, C.	RUM	Hammer throw	F		12	52,77	
Dybenko, G.	URS	Hammer throw	F		8	55,03	
Dyrgall, V.	USA	Marathon	F		13	2:32-52·4	
Efstathiadis, R.	GRE	Pole vault	F		=14	3,95	
Eichenberger, W.	SUI	200m	1	2	4	22·98	
		4×100m relay	1	3	5	41·81	
Ekfeldt, T.	SWE	4×400m relay	1	1	3	3·13·55	
Eleuterio, E.	POR	200m	1	5	5	23·37	
		4×100m relay	1	1	6	43·01	
El Fattah, A.A.	EGY	Marathon	F		51	2:56-56·0	
Elliott, G.	GBR	Pole vault	Q		DNQ	3,80	
		Decathlon	F		9	6044	
El Mabrouk, P.	FRA	800m	1	8	1	1·52·0	
			SF	2	DNS		
		1500m	1	4	1	3·55·71	
			SF	1	5	3·51·25	
			F		5	3·46·35	
El Sherbiny, G.	EGY	Pole vault	Q		DNQ		
Engel, M.	USA	Hammer throw	F		24	0	
Engelhardt, D.	GER	Marathon	F		30	2:39-37·2	
Ericsson, I.	SWE	1500m	1	1	3	3·52·14	
			SF	2	3	3·50·77	
			F		8	3·47·70	
Ericzon, R.	SWE	Javelin throw	F		7	69,04	
Eriksson, S.	SWE	400m hurdles	1	6	2	54·3	
			2	1	5	53·96	
Erinle, T.	NGR	100m	1	10	3	11·12	
		4×100m relay	1	4	2	42·63	
			SF	2	5	42·01	
Esztergomi, M.	HUN	Marathon	F		21	2:35-10·0	
Ethirveerasing-ham, N.	CEY	High jump	Q		DNQ	1,80	
Evans, F.	GBR	800m	1	7	3	1·53·8	
			SF	3	8	1·56·99	
Eyre, L.	GBR	1500m	1	2	8	3·53·34	
Fahmy, W.	EGY	1500m	1	6	9	4·11·2	
Fait, B.	ITA	10k walk	1	2	6	47·23·4	
			F		8	46·25·6	
Faucher, P.	FRA	Long jump	F		8	7,02	
Fazil, M.	PAK	4×100m relay	1	4	3	42·91	
			SF	1	6	42·15	
Fedorov, G.	URS	Shot put	F		7	16,06	
Felton, S.	USA	Hammer throw	F		11	53,32	
Fernandes, F.	POR	400m hurdles	1	7	4	56·8	
		Decathlon	F		16	5604	
Fernandez, C.	ARG	Marathon	F		DNF		
Ferrer, P.	VEN	400m hurdles	1	4	5	1·02·1	
Figueroa, H.	CHI	Decathlon	F		17	5592	
Filippov, V.	URS	Triple jump	Q		DNQ	0	
Filiput, A.	ITA	400m hurdles	1	8	1	53·8	
			2	1	3	53·00	
			SF	2	=2	52·98	
			F		6	54·49	
		4×400m relay	1	2	4	3·15·23	
Filo, M.	TCH	400m	1	8	3	48·91	
Firea, V.	RUM	3000m steeplechase	1	1	9	9·29·2	
Flores, D.	GUA	Marathon	F		22	2:35-40·0	
Foldessi, O.	HUN	Long jump	F		3	7,30	B
Fonck, J.	LUX	110m hurdles	1	6	6	16·35	
		400m hurdles	1	1	5	57·93	
Fortun, R.	CUB	100m	1	8	1	10·93	
			2	3	2	10·90	
			SF	2	4	10·92	
		200m	1	4	1	21·98	
			2	2	2	21·98	
			SF	2	4	21·93	
		4×100m relay	1	2	3	42·14	
			SF	2	4	41·67	
Francis, A.	PUR	400m hurdles	1	8	4	54·0	
Franco, A.	PHI	High jump	Q		DNQ		
Frayer, H.	FRA	Decathlon	F		11	5772	
Frieden, P.	LUX	5000m	1	3	13	15·23·2	
Frischknecht, H.	SUI	10000m	F		31	35·34·0	
Fritz, F.	AUT	Pole vault	Q		DNQ		
Fuchs, E.	GER	100m	1	12	3	11·19	
Fuchs, J.	USA	Shot put	F		3	17,06	B
Galan, R.	ARG	100m	1	4	2	11·11	
			2	3	5	11·08	
		4×100m relay	1	3	3	41·56	
			SF	1	4	41·61	
Galin, R.	YUG	Hammer throw	F		17	51,37	
Gallin, O.	ISR	Discus throw	Q		DNQ	40,76	
Garai, S.	HUN	1500m	1	6	7	4·01·53	
Garcia, A.	CUB	200m	1	8	2	22·14	
			2	4	4	22·11	
		400m	1	9	4	49·34	
		4×100m relay	1	2	3	42·14	
			SF	2	4	41·67	
Gathers, J.	USA	200m	1	12	1	21·42	
			2	1	1	21·64	
			SF	1	2	21·58	
			F		3	21·08	B
Geister, H.	GER	400m	1	8	1	47·99	
			2	3	2	47·81	
			SF	2	4	47·00	
		4×400m relay	1	3	1	3·10·57	
			F		3	3·06·78	B
Gerdil, M.	FRA	200m	1	6	2	22·71	
			2	3	5	22·37	
Gerhardt, J.	USA	Triple jump	F		11	14,69	
Gevert, J.	CHI	110m hurdles	1	5	3	15·44	
		400m hurdles	1	3	5	56·1	
Giles, J.A.	GBR	Shot put	Q		DNQ	13,73	
Gill, A.	ISR	400m	1	5	5	50·27	
		800m	1	7	4	2·00·9	
Gillet, D.	FRA	1500m	1	1	8	4·26·6	
Goker, T.	TUR	800m	1	2	5	1·55·9	
		1500m	1	2	8	4·01·02	
Goldovanyi, B.	HUN	4×100m relay	1	3	1	41·15	
			SF	2	1	40·99	
			F		3	40·83	B
Gomes, W.	BRA	400m hurdles	1	7	2	56·0	
			2	2	6	59·4	
Gordien, F.	USA	Discus throw	F		4	52,66	
Gorno, R.	ARG	Marathon	F		2	2:25-35·0	S
Goudeau, J.-P.	FRA	400m	1	10	4	48·94	
		4×400m relay	1	1	2	3·12·72	
			F		6	3·10·33	
Gourdine, M.	USA	Long jump	F		2	7,53	S
Grabowski, H.	POL	Long jump	Q		DNQ	6,77	
Gracie, D.	GBR	400m hurdles	1	7	1	54·2	
			2	2	3	53·94	
			SF	1	4	52·65	
Graeffe, E.	FIN	400m hurdles	1	3	4	55·0	
		4×400m relay	1	1	6	3·16·67	
Graj, A.	POL	5000m	1	2	7	14·30·0	
Gregory, J.	GBR	4×100m relay	1	2	1	41·43	
			SF	1	3	41·24	
			F		4	40·85	
Griesser, F.	SUI	100m	1	8	5	11·54	
Grigalka, O.	URS	Discus throw	F		6	50,71	
		Shot put	F		4	16,78	
Grigorjev, L.	URS	Long jump	F		6	7,14	
Grossi, L.	ITA	200m	1	12	4	22·49	
		4×400m relay	1	2	4	3·15·23	
Gruber, A.	AUT	Marathon	F		39	2:45-02·0	
Gubijan, J.	YUG	Hammer throw	F		9	54,54	
Gude, H.	GER	3000m steeplechase	1	2	4	9·04·74	
			F		8	9·01·36	
Gudmundsson, F.	ISL	Discus throw	Q		DNQ	45,00	
Guillier, L.	FRA	Discus throw	Q		DNQ	43,88	
		Shot put	F		11	14,84	
Gundersen, B.	NOR	High jump	F		8	1,90	
Guobadia, B.	NGR	High jump	F		=20	1,80	
Gutierrez, G.	VEN	100m	1	4	5	11·42	
		400m	1	6	2	48·82	
			2	1	4	48·75	
Haas, K.-F.	GER	400m	1	1	1	47·58	
			2	2	3	47·66	
			SF	1	2	46·56	
			F		4	47·22	
		4×400m relay	1	3	1	3·10·57	
			F		3	3·06·78	B
Haddad, H.	CHI	Discus throw	Q		DNQ	42,89	
Haefliger, O.	SUI	Discus throw	Q		DNQ	42,73	
Haest, H.	BEL	Hammer throw	F		22	48,78	
Haidegger, R.	AUT	400m	1	7	4	50·01	
		400m hurdles	1	1	4	54·87	
Halme, P.	FIN	High jump	F		=11	1,90	
Halmetoja, O.	FIN	Hammer throw	F		19	50,82	

COMPETITOR	COUNTRY CODE	EVENT	ROUND	HEAT	PLACE	TIME & DISTANCE	MEDAL
Hamilius, J.	LUX	400m	1	9	6	50.75	
		4×400m relay	1	1	5	3-16.33	
Hammer, F.	LUX	200m	1	9	4	22.63	
		400m	1	12	6	49.90	
		4×400m relay	1	1	5	3-16.33	
Hammer, K.	NOR	10k walk	1	1	8	49-03.4	
Hapernagel, F.	GER	4×100m relay	1	3	4	41.63	
Haraldsson, H.	ISL	100m	1	3	5	11.32	
		200m	1	1	4	22.56	
		4×100m relay	1	4	DIS		
Hardy, R.	GBR	10k walk	1	1	DIS		
Harting, H.	GUA	1500m	1	1	DNF		
Hasegawa, K.	JPN	Triple jump	Q		DNQ	14.39	
Hautamaeki, E.	FIN	Decathlon	F		DNF		
Hayward, F.	CAN	50k walk	F		25	5:04-40.4	
Hayward, W.	SAF	Marathon	F		10	2:31-50.2	
Heber, R.	ARG	Javelin throw	F		15	62,82	
Heinen, J.	GER	4×100m relay	1	3	4	41.63	
Heinrich, I.	FRA	Decathlon	F		DNF		
Held, F.	USA	Javelin throw	F		9	68,42	
Hellsten, V.	FIN	4×100m relay	1	-	4	42-20	
		100m	1	7	4	11.36	
		200m	1	10	2	22.41	
			2	2	5	22.61	
Herman, F.	BEL	1500m	1	5	2	3-56.37	
			SF	2	9	3-54.04	
Herssens, W.	BEL	High jump	Q		DNQ		
		Triple jump	Q		DNQ	13,52	
Hesselmann, G.	GER	3000m steeplechase	1	1	2	9-04.93	
			F		6	8-55.98	
Hietanen, M.	FIN	Marathon	F		17	2:34-01.0	
Higgins, T.	GBR	400m	1	4	2	48.77	
			2	4	5	49.22	
		4×400m relay	1	2	2	3-12.67	
			F		5	3-10.23	
Hildreth, P.	GBR	110m hurdles	1	6	2	14.94	
			SF	1	6	15.15	
Hilli, A.	FIN	400m hurdles	1	5	2	54.6	
			2	2	4	54.28	
Hiltunen, R.	FIN	Triple jump	F		9	14,85	
Hindmar, L.	SWE	10k walk	1	2	3	47-06.0	
			F		DIS		
Hipp, S.	GER	Decathlon	F		5	6449	
		Discus throw	Q		DNQ	43,38	
Hofstetter, W.	SUI	Pole vault	Q		DNQ	3.90	
Holland, J.	NZL	400m hurdles	1	6	1	53.3	
			2	2	1	52.24	
			SF	1	2	52.22	
			F		3	52.26	B
Homonnai, T.	HUN	Pole vault	F		=11	4,10	
Hong, C.O.	KOR	Marathon	F		DNF		
Hooper, C.D.	USA	Shot put	F		2	17,39	S
Horcic, M.	TCH	100m	1	1	4	11.23	
		200m	1	13	2	22.52	
			2	1	5	22.44	
		4×100m relay	1	3	2	41.49	
			SF	2	3	41.46	
			F		6	41.41	
Horulu, K.	TUR	400m hurdles	1	6	4	55.2	
Hoskins, G.	NZL	1500m	1	5	1	3-56.33	
			SF	1	11	3-52.72	
Hosoda, T.	JPN	100m	1	6	2	11.14	
			2	4	4	11.03	
		200m	1	12	2	22.36	
			2	6	6	22.49	
Hubert, C.	FRA	50k walk	F		18	4:55-28.2	
Hussain, F.	PAK	Hammer throw	Q		DNQ	48,36	
Hutchins, J.	CAN	800m	1	3	1	1-54.5	
			SF	3	4	1-52.81	
		4×400m relay	1	3	2	3-11.49	
			F		4	3-09.37	
Hutchison, R.	CAN	100m	1	2	5	11.26	
		200m	1	16	2	22.66	
			2	3	6	22.55	
		4×100m relay	1	1	5	42.73	
Huutoniemi, A.	FIN	Discus throw	Q		DNQ	42,79	
Hyytiainen, T.	FIN	Javelin throw	F		3	71,89	B
Iden, G.	GBR	Marathon	F		9	2:30-42.0	
Ignatev, A.	URS	400m	1	2	1	48.22	
			2	4	3	48.25	
			SF	1	5	47.49	
		4×400m relay	1	3	3	3-12.65	
Iharos, S.	HUN	1500m	1	1	5	3-56.35	
Iimuro, Y.	JPN	Triple jump	F		6	14,99	
Ilic, V.	YUG	5000m	1	3	12	14-51.6	
Iljasov, J.	URS	High jump	F		=13	1,90	
Iness, S.	USA	Discus throw	F		1	55,03*	G

COMPETITOR	COUNTRY CODE	EVENT	ROUND	HEAT	PLACE	TIME & DISTANCE	MEDAL
Inostroza, R.	CHI	10000m	F		23	31-28.6	
		Marathon	F		DNF		
Inoue, O.	JPN	5000m	1	1	12	14-59.0	
Iqbal, M.	PAK	Hammer throw	Q		DNQ	47,15	
Iriarte, B.	VEN	Long jump	Q		DNQ	6,82	
		Javelin throw	Q		DNQ	52,13	
		Decathlon	F		12	5770	
Israelsson, K.	SWE	Long jump	F		7	7,10	
Ivakin, G.	URS	800m	1	5	5	1-56.4	
Jack, W.	GBR	100m	1	4	1	11.05	
			2	3	3	10.94	
			SF	2	5	11.01	
		4×100m relay	1	2	1	41.43	
			SF	1	3	41.24	
			F		4	40.85	
Jacob, I.	IND	400m	1	4	6	51.48	
Janacek, V.	TCH	200m	1	9	1	21.99	
			2	3	2	21.93	
			SF	1	6	22.12	
Janssens, D.	BEL	1500m	1	3	7	3-55.98	
Jansson, G.	SWE	Marathon	F		3	2:26-07.0	B
Jennings, A.	SAF	1500m	1	3	6	3-55.69	
Jeszenski, L.	HUN	3000m steeplechase	1	3	6	9-11.10	
Johansen, K.	NOR	Discus throw	Q		DNQ		
Johanson, K.	ISL	5000m	1	3	14	15-23.8	
		10000m	F		26	32-00.0	
Johansson, D.	FIN	1500m	1	3	2	3-51.22	
			SF	1	1	3-49.60	
			F		10	3-50.24	
Johnsen, S.	NOR	Discus throw	Q		DNQ	45,12	
Johnson, K.	GBR	3000m steeplechase	1	1	7	9-27.0	
Jones, T.	USA	Marathon	F		36	2:42-50.0	
Juhasz, B.	HUN	10000m	F		14	30-39.6	
Julin, U.	FIN	3000m steeplechase	1	3	5	9-09.54	
Jungwirth, S.	TCH	1500m	1	2	3	3-52.58	
			SF	2	7	3-51.72	
Junk, B.	URS	10k walk	1	1	1	45-05.8	
			F		3	45-41.05	B
Kaas, E.	NOR	Pole vault	F		16	3,80	
Kalyaev, L.	URS	4×100m relay	1	4	1	41.45	
			SF	1	2	40.01	
			F		2	40.58	S
Karadi, P.	HUN	200m	1	18	3	22.24	
Karlsson, B.	SWE	5000m	1	2	9	14-45.8	
		10000m	F		13	30-35.8	
Karlsson, G.	SWE	3000m steeplechase	1	1	3	9-05.59	
			F		12	10-26.4	
Karvonen, V.	FIN	Marathon	F		5	2:26-41.8	
Kataja, E.	FIN	Pole vault	F		10	4,10	
Kazantsev, M.	USR	100m	1	3	3	11.16	
Kazantsev, P.	URS	50k walk	F		23	5:02-37.8	
Kazantsev, V.	URS	3000m steeplechase	1	1	1	8-58.17*	
			F		2	8-51.52	S
Keane, D.	AUS	10k walk	1	1	5	46-55.2	
			F		10	47-37.0	
Keith, W.	SAF	10000m	F		28	32-32.4	
		Marathon	F		19	2:34-38.0	
Khan, J.	PAK	Javelin throw	Q		DNQ	55,56	
Khan, M.	PAK	400m hurdles	1	5	4	56.3	
		4×400m relay	1	2	6	3-23.2	
Kielas, J.	POL	3000m steeplechase	1	2	7	9-15.62	
Kinami, M.	JPN	110m hurdles	1	6	3	15.31	
King, S.	USA	10k walk	1	2	9	51-08.6	
Kintziger, R.	BEL	Discus throw	Q		DNQ	41,46	
Kiszka, E.	POL	100m	1	5	3	11.13	
		4×100m relay	1	1	3	42.00	
			SF	1	5	41.91	
Kjersem, J.	NOR	Marathon	F		24	2:36-14.0	
Klics, H.	HUN	Discus throw	F		5	51,13	
Knjazev, V.	URS	Pole vault	F		8	4,20	
Kocak, E.	TUR	800m	1	7	4	1-54.5	
		1500m	1	6	8	4-01.77	
Kocourek, E.	ARG	110m hurdles	1	2	3	15.20	
Kolev, A.	BUL	100m	1	2	2	11.01	
		200m	1	17	2	22.24	
			2	4	3	22.07	
Korbar, R.	POL	800m	1	3	4	1-54.7	
Koschel, H.	GER	Javelin throw	F		12	64,54	
Koskela, V.	FIN	5000m	1	3	11	14-50.8	
		10000m	F		16	30-43.0	
Koskinen, A.	FIN	High jump	F		=24	1,80	
Kovacs, J.	HUN	5000m	1		14	17-09.2	
Kowal, S.	POL	Triple jump	Q		DNQ		
Kozhevnikov, P.	URS	Decathlon	F		DNF		
Krajcar, F.	YUG	Marathon	F		DNF		

COMPETITOR	COUNTRY CODE	EVENT	ROUND	HEAT	PLACE	TIME & DISTANCE	MEDAL
Kraus, P.	GER	200m	1	9	2	22·06	
			2	2	4	22·19	
		4×100m relay	1	3	4	41·63	
Kressevich, G.	ITA	50k walk	F		10	4:44-30·2	
Kristensen, H.	DEN	50k walk	F		20	4:57-35·8	
Krivonosov, M.	URS	Hammer throw	F		24	0	
Krzyzanowski, T.	POL	Shot put	F		10	15,08	
Kuchurin, N.	URS	1500m	1	4	8	4-01·80	
Kuivamaeki, R.	FIN	Hammer throw	F		14	51,85	
Kuznyetsov, V.	URS	Javelin throw	F		6	70,37	
Kuznyetsov, S.	URS	Decathlon	F		10	5937	
Kwancharoen, B.	THA	800m	1	6	7	2-12·6	
LaBeach, B.	JAM	100m	1	8	2	11·09	
			2	1	5	11·05	
Labidi, B.	FRA	10000m	F		25	31-52·2	
Lagos, E.	CHI	High jump	Q		DNQ	1,80	
Laing, L.	JAM	200m	1	15	1	21·97	
			2	5	2	21·74	
			SF	1	3	21·80	
			F		5	21·45	
		4×400m relay	1	1	1	3-12·13	
			F		1	3-04·04*	G
Laing, W.	GHA	Triple jump	Q		DNQ	14,09	
Lamers, R.	GER	1500m	1	3	3	3-52·72	
			SF	2	6	3-51·30	
			F		6	3-47·18	
Landqvist, S.	SWE	1500m	1	2	2	3-52·31	
			SF	1	8	3-51·45	
Landstroem, E.	FIN	Decathlon	F		14	5694	
Landy, J.	AUS	5000m	1	1	10	14-56·4	
		1500m	1	4	5	3-57·14	
Larsen, P.	DEN	Triple jump	F		13	14,62	
Larsson, R.	SWE	4×400m relay	1	1	3	3-13·55	
		400m hurdles	1	5	3	55·9	
			2	4	3	53·35	
			SF	1	6	54·06	
Larusson, G.	ISL	400m	1	8	4	49·81	
		800m	1	8	7	1-56·5	
Laryea, G.	GHA	100m	1	1	3	11·18	
		4×100m relay	1	2	4	42·27	
Laskau, H.	USA	10k walk	1	1	DIS		
Laszlo, S.	HUN	50k walk	F		12	4:45-55·8	
Lavery, J.	CAN	400m	1	11	1	48·47	
			2	1	2	47·67	
			SF	1	6	47·83	
		4×400m relay	1	3	2	3-11·49	
			F		4	3-09·37	
Lawson, A.	GHA	4×100m relay	1	2	4	42·27	
Laz, D.	USA	Pole vault	F		2	4,50	S
Leane, P.	AUS	High jump	F		=24	1,80	
		Long jump	Q		DNQ	6,40	
		Decathlon	F		DNF		
Leangtanom, S.	THA	1500m	1	6	10	4-32·6	
Leblond, J.	BEL	Marathon	F		32	2:40-37·0	
Lebron, J.	PUR	110m hurdles	1	2	5	15·71	
Lebrun, A.	FRA	3000m steeplechase	1	2	8	9-17·8	
Leccese, F.	ITA	100m	1	8	3	11·18	
		4×100m relay	1	2	2	41·73	
			SF	2	DNS		
Legrain, P.	FRA	Hammer throw	F		23	46,38	
Leirud, B.	NOR	High jump	F		17	1,90	
Leiva, J.	VEN	100m	1	6	5	11·31	
		200m	1	5	3	22·38	
Leppaenen, E.	FIN	Javelin throw	F		16	62,61	
Lesage, R.	FRA	50k walk	F		16	4:52-37·8	
Lewandowski, S.	POL	1500m	1	5	7	4-00·87	
Lewis, L.	GBR	400m	1	1	2	47·95	
			2	1	5	49·09	
		4×400m relay	1	2	2	3-12·67	
			F		5	3-10·23	
Lillington, A.	GBR	100m	1	1	2	11·06	
			2	2	6	11·26	
Lind, L.	SWE	Pole vault	F		=11	4,10	
Linssen, F.	BEL	200m	1	4	3	22·37	
		4×400m relay	1	1	4	3-16·05	
Lippai, A.	HUN	400m hurdles	1	8	3	54·0	
			2	3	2	52·93	
			SF	2	3	53·10	
Liska, L.	TCH	800m	1	6	3	1-52·3	
			SF	2	6	1-55·04	
Lituyev, J.	URS	4×400m relay	1	3	3	3-12·65	
		400m	1	11	1	49·01	
		400m hurdles	1	4	1	53·56	
			2	3	1	52·37	
			SF	1	1	51·90	
			F		2	51·51	S
Ljunggren, J.	SWE	50k walk	F		9	4:43-45·2	

COMPETITOR	COUNTRY CODE	EVENT	ROUND	HEAT	PLACE	TIME & DISTANCE	MEDAL
Ljungqvist, A.	SWE	High jump	F		15	1,90	
Lobastov, S.	URS	50k walk	F		5	4:32-34·2	
Loeve, T.	ISL	Discus throw	Q		DNQ	44,28	
Lombardo, V.	ITA	400m	1	7	3	49·53	
Lopes, E.	POR	Triple jump	Q		DNQ		
Lorger, S.	YUG	110m hurdles	1	3	2	15·08	
			SF	2	4	15·09	
Lowagie, A.	BEL	400m	1	7	5	50·26	
		4×400m relay	1	1	4	3-16·05	
Lucioli, A.	ITA	Hammer throw	Q		DNQ	48,74	
Lueg, W.	GER	1500m	1	6	1	3-52·31	
			SF	1	2	3-50·06	
			F		3	3-45·67	B
Luethy, F.	SUI	800m	1	8	5	1-55·0	
		1500m	1	2	7	3-56·52	
Lundberg, R.	SWE	Pole vault	F		3	4,40	B
Lunyov, T.	URS	400m hurdles	1	2	1	54·3	
			2	4	1	52·87	
			SF	2	6	53·30	
Lusenius, K.	FIN	3000m steeplechase	1	1	6	9-26·8	
Luettge, R.	GER	50k walk	F		13	4:47-28·6	
Luyt, S.	SAF	Marathon	F		11	2:32-41·0	
McFarlane, D.	CAN	100m	1	9	5	11·25	
		200m	1	3	1	22·94	
			2	5	5	22·33	
		4×100m relay	1	1	5	42·73	
McKenley, H.	JAM	100m	1	5	1	10·88	
			2	4	1	10·72	
			SF	2	1	10·74	
			F		2	10·80	S
		400m	1	5	1	48·09	
			2	4	1	47·56	
			SF	2	1	46·53	
			F		2	46·20*	S
		4×400m relay	1	1	1	3-12·13	
			F		1	3-04·04*	G
MacMillan, D.	AUS	800m	1	5	3	1-55·0	
			SF	1	8	1-58·4	
		1500m	1	1	4	3-52·30	
			SF	1	3	3-50·81	
			F		9	3-49·77	
McMillen, R.	USA	1500m	1	4	2	3-55·82	
			SF	2	4	3-50·84	
			F		2	3-45·39	S
Maca, M.	TCH	Hammer throw	F		15	51,78	
Mach, G.	POL	200m	1	11	2	22·16	
			2	6	4	22·12	
		400m	1	10	2	48·64	
Maggi, E.	FRA	10k walk	1	2	2	46-47·8	
			F		7	46-08·16	
Maia, R.	POR	100m	1	11	6	11·79	
		4×100m relay	1	1	6	43·01	
Maissant, J.	FRA	Discus throw	F		17	43,40	
Majekodunmi, J.	NGR	High jump	F		=9	1,90	
Mamonov, O.	URS	High jump	Q		DNQ	0	
Mann, G.	IND	3000m steeplechase	1	1	12	9-48·6	
Marquis, G.	SUI	50k walk	F		24	5:02-56·2	
Marshall, M.	NZL	800m	1	1	4	1-56·2	
		1500m	1	4	7	4-01·03	
Martin Du Gard, J.P.	FRA	4×400m relay	1	1	2	3-12·72	
			F		6	3-10·33	
Martufi, E.	ITA	Marathon	F		DNF		
Marulin, F.	URS	3000m steeplechase	1	2	5	9-08·73	
Mateev, B.	URS	Discus throw	F		10	48,70	
Mathias, R.	USA	Decathlon	F		1	7887*	G
Mathur, S.	IND	Marathon	F		52	2:58-09·2	
Matoba, J.	JPN	400m	1	4	3	49·57	
		4×100m relay	1	1	3	3-20·55	
Matson, O.	USA	400m	1	12	1	48·17	
			2	2	2	47·53	
			SF	2	3	46·99	
			F		3	46·94	B
		4×400m relay	1	2	1	3-11·67	
			F		2	3-04·21	S
Matteucci, A.	ITA	Javelin throw	F		17	61,67	
Mattos, G.	USA	Pole vault	F		9	4,20	
Mavroidis, B.	GRE	800m	1	3	6	1-58·7	
		1500m	1	4	9	4-07·8	
Mazorra, R.	CUB	100m	1	2	4	11·19	
		200m	1	16	6	22·52	
			2	1	6	31·0	
M'Baye, M.	FRA	Triple jump	Q		DNQ	14,39	
Melcher, A.	CHI	Hammer throw	Q		DNQ	45,55	
Merdyanov, A.	BUL	100m	1	6	4	11·29	
Mihail, M.	GRE	Triple jump	Q		DNQ	0	
Mihalic, F.	YUG	10000m	F		18	30-53·2	

COMPETITOR	COUNTRY CODE	EVENT	ROUND	HEAT	PLACE	TIME & DISTANCE	MEDAL
Mikaelsson, J,	SWE	10k walk	1	1	2	45-10·0	
			F		1	45-02·85*	G
Milakov, M.	YUG	Pole vault	F		13	4,10	
Mildh, S.	FIN	400m	1	12	7	50·36	
		4×400m relay	1	1	6	3-16·67	
Miller, R.	CAN	Pole vault	Q		DNQ	3,90	
Miller, R.D.W.	GBR	Javelin throw	F		14	63,75	
Miller, W.	USA	Javelin throw	F		2	72,46	S
Mimoun, A.	FRA	5000m	1	1	1	14-19·15	
			F		2	14-07·58	S
		10000m	F		2	29-32·8	S
Modoy, G.	URS	800m	1	1	3	1-55·8	
			SF	2	7	1-56·12	
Moens, R.	BEL	400m	1	5	3	48·71	
		4×400m relay	1	1	4	3-16·05	
Montanari, W.	ITA	100m	1	7	7	12·25	
Montez, J.	USA	1500m	1	5	6	3-58·10	
Moore, C.	USA	400m hurdles	1	1	1	51·92	
			2	1	1	50·98*	
			SF	2	1	52·09	
			F		1	51·06	G
		4×400m relay	1	2	1	3-11·67	
			F		2	3-04·21	S
Morgenthaler, R.	SUI	Marathon	F		50	2:56-33·0	
Moskatchenkov, J.	URS	Marathon	F		20	2:34-43·8	
Muhlethaler, E.	SUI	200m	1	13	4	23·26	
		4×100m relay	1	3	5	41·81	
Muroya, Y.	JPN	800m	1	3	4	1-54·0	
		4×400m relay	1	1	7	3-20·55	
Nankeville, W.	GBR	1500m	1	5	3	3-56·48	
			SF	1	9	3-51·93	
Nemeth, I.	HUN	Hammer throw	F		3	57,74	3
Nielsen, G.	DEN	800m	1	8	2	1-53·0	
			SF	·	1	1-50·02	
			F		4	1-49·84*	
Nikkinen, S.	FIN	Javelin throw	F		8	68,30	
Nilsen, R.	NOR	Triple jump	F		5	15,13	
Nilsson, E.	SWE	3000m steeplechase	1	2	11	9-25·0	
Nilsson, R.F.	SWE	Discus throw	F		7	50,06	
		Shot put	F		5	16,55	
Nishida, K.	JPN	Marathon	F		25	2:35-19·0	
Niskanen, H.	FIN	10000m	F		19	30-59·6	
Norman, R.	SWE	Triple jump	F		8	14,89	
Norris, F.	GBR	10000m	F		8	30-09·8	
Norrstroem, H.	SWE	Marathon	F		29	2:38-57·4	
Nyqvist, K.	FIN	Discus throw	F		12	47,72	
Nystroem, V.	SWE	10000m	F		6	29-54·8	
O'Brien, W.P.	USA	Shot put	F		1	17,41*	G
Ohaco, E.	CHI	110m hurdles	1	1	5	15·61	
Okano, E.	JPN	400m hurdles	1	1	3	54·42	
			2	4	6	54·42	
		4×400m relay	1	1	7	3-20·55	
Olenius, V.	FIN	Pole vault	F		5	4·30	
Oliver, R.	PUR	Javelin throw	Q		DNQ	52,40	
		Decathlon	F		21	5228	
Olowa, R.	NGR	200m	1	14	1	22·89	
			2	2	6	22·69	
		4×100m relay	1	4	2	42·63	
			SF	2	5	42·01	
Olowu, K.	NGR	100m	1	12	4	11·27	
		Long jump	Q		DNQ		
		4×100m relay	1	4	2	42·63	
			SF	2	5	42·01	
Olsen, R.	NOR	10k walk	1	2	8	49-03·8	
Olsen, V.	NOR	Marathon	F		16	2:33-58·4	
Omar-Aly, Y.	EGY	100m	1	1	6	11·53	
		200m	1	7	4	23·26	
		4×100m relay	1	1	7	43·02	
Onel, C.	TUR	1500m	1	3	8	3-58·42	
		3000m steeplechase	1	1	4	9-06·02	
			F		10	9-04·73	
Osagie, N.	NGR	High jump	F		=18	1,90	
Osinski, W.	POL	Marathon	F		47	2:54-38·2	
Osterberger, A.	FRA	Hammer throw	Q		DNQ	47,87	
Ostling, G.	SWE	Marathon	F		12	2:32-48·4	
Otenhajmer, A.	YUG	1500m	1	4	6	3-58·20	
Owoo, J.	GHA	High jump	F		=20	1,80	
Owusu, J.	GHA	4×100m relay	1	2	4	42·27	
Page, P.	SUI	100m	1	2	10	14-57·0	
Pakpuang, B.	THA	100m	1	4	6	11·85	
		200m	1	14	2	24·15	
		4×100m relay	1	2	6	44·81	
Paquete, T.	POR	4×100m relay	1	1	6	43·01	
		100m	1	5	=5	11·45	
Paraschivescu, D.	RUM	50k walk	F		7	4:41-05·2	
Paris, A.	FRA	3000m steeplechase	1	3	7	9-30·0	
Parker, A.	GBR	5000m	1	2	2	14-18·47	
			F		11	14-37·0	
Parker, F.	GBR	110m hurdles	1	4	2	15·08	
			SF	2	=5	15·31	
Parnell, C.	CAN	800m	1	8	3	1-53·1	
			SF	1	6	1-52·92	
		1500m	1	3	4	3-53·75	
			SF	1	12	3-52·91	
Partanen, H.	FIN	Discus throw	Q		DNQ	45,71	
Paterson, A.	GBR	High jump	F		=24	1,80	
Pavitt, R.	GBR	High jump	F		5	1,95	
Pavlovic, S.	YUG	5000m	1	1	13	14-59·2	
Pearman, R.	USA	800m	1	4	1	1-51·6	
			SF	3	3	1-52·70	
			F		7	1-52·31	
Pelkonen, R.	FIN	400m hurdles	1	4	2	54·32	
			2	4	5	54·06	
Pella, R.	CAN	Discus throw	F		14	46,63	
Perko, A.K.	FIN	Shot put	Q		DNQ	14,50	
Perry, L.	AUS	5000m	1	3	4	14-27·18	
			F		6	14-23·16	
Perz, H.	AUT	5000m	1	1	11	14-57·2	
		10000m	F		27	32-13·2	
Peters, J.	GBR	Marathon	F		DNF		
Petrakis, S.	GRE	100m	1	3	6	11·33	
		200m	1	2	3	22·64	
Pharaoh, M.	GBR	Discus throw	Q		DNQ	45,24	
Piags, E.	URS	400m	1	9	3	49·29	
		4×400m relay	1	3	3	3-12·65	
Pinto, L.	IND	100m	1	11	2	11·00	
			2	2	3	10·98	
			SF	1	4	10·94	
		200m	1	18	2	21·83	
			2	1	2	21·80	
			SF	2	5	22·01	
Pirie, D.A.G.	GBR	5000m	1	1	5	14-26·47	
			F		4	14-18·31	
		10000m	F		7	30-09·5	
Planas, E.	CUB	400m	1	1	5	49·44	
		800m	1	2	6	1-57·6	
		4×100m relay	1	2	3	42·14	
			SF	2	4	41·67	
Planck, I.	DEN	5000m	1	3	6	14-31·66	
Plum, J.	DEN	Discus throw	F		13	47,26	
Popov, N.	URS	5000m	1	1	6	14-28·84	
		10000m	F		11	30-24·2	
Popov, S.	URS	110m hurdles	1	1	2	14·99	
			SF	1	4	15·04	
Porhault, A.	FRA	100m	1	12	2	11·04	
			2	1	3	10·99	
			SF	1	5	11·04	
		4×100m relay	1	1	2	40·98	
			SF	2	2	41·02	
			F		5	41·10	
Porto, B.	ITA	4×400m relay	1	2	4	3-15·23	
Pospisil, Z.	TCH	100m	1	9	3	11·25	
		4×100m relay	1	3	2	41·49	
			SF	2	3	41·46	
			F		6	41·41	
Posti, H.	FIN	10000m	F		4	29-51·4	
Potrzebowski, E.	POL	800m	1	2	2	1-52·6	
			2	3	5	1-54·03	
		1500m	1	5	6	3-56·91	
Pozhidaev, I.	URS	10000m	F		9	30-13·4	
Prat, P.	FRA	3000m steeplechase	1	1	11	9-32·8	
Prentice, R.	AUS	Marathon	F		37	2:43-13·4	
Price, N.	SAF	Long jump	F		11	6,40	
		Triple jump	Q		DNQ	0	
Profeti, A.	ITA	Shot put	F		12	14,74	
Prossinag, F.	AUT	1500m	1	3	5	3-54·76	
Puolakka, E.	FIN	Marathon	F		8	2:29-35·0	
Pueronen, J.	FIN	Pole vault	F		=18	3,80	
Pystynen, A.	FIN	1500m	1	2	5	3-53·33	
Radovanovic, R.	YUG	Triple jump	Q		DNQ	14,13	
Radziwonowicz, Z.	POL	Javelin throw	Q		DNQ	61,50	
Rahman, A.	PAK	400m	1	1	6	51·47	
		4×400m relay	1	2	6	3-23·2	
			F		DNF		
Ramos, R.	POR	Triple jump	F		12	14,69	
Rashid, A.	PAK	10000m	F		30	33-50·4	
Rask, K.P.	FIN	Shot put	Q		DNQ	14,08	
Rasquin, G.	LUX	400m	1	2	4	50·12	
		4×400m relay	1	1	5	3-16·38	
Rautio, K.	FIN	Triple jump	Q		DNQ	14,14	
Rebula, O.	YUG	Decathlon	F		15	5648	
Redykin, N.	URS	Hammer throw	F		5	56,55	
Reed, I.	AUS	Discus throw	Q		DNQ	45,12	
Reiff, G.	BEL	5000m	1	1	3	14-23·98	
			F		DNF		

COMPETITOR	COUNTRY CODE	EVENT	ROUND	HEAT	PLACE	TIME & DISTANCE	MEDAL
Reikko, O.	FIN	Decathlon	F		13	5725	
Remigino, L.	USA	100m	1	11	1	10·73	
			2	2	1	10·68	
			SF	2	2	10·74	
			F		1	10·79	G
		4×100m relay	1	1	1	40·34	
			SF	1	1	40·51	
			F		1	40·26	G
Reymond, G.	SUI	10k walk	1	1	4	46-35·2	
			F		9	46-38·6	
Rhoden, G.	JAM	400m	1	10	1	48·28	
			2	2	1	47·24	
			SF	2	2	46·61	
			F		1	46·09*	G
		4×400m relay	1	1	1	3-12·13	
			F		1	3-04·04*	G
Richards, R.	USA	Pole vault	F		1	4,55*	G
Ring, H.	SWE	800m	1	5	1	1-53·6	
			SF	2	3	1-53·27	
			F		9	1-54·23	
Rinteenpaeae, O.	FIN	3000m steeplechase	1	2	2	8-59·71	
			F		4	8-55·60	
Rivera, F.	PUR	400m	1	11	3	49·48	
		800m	1	5	6	1-57·6	
Rocca, G.	ITA	400m	1	6	3	49·51	
		4×400m relay	1	2	4	3-15·23	
Roennholm, R.	FIN	800m	1	8	6	1-55·7	
Roetzer, K.	AUT	5000m	1	3	10	14-49·4	
Roka, A.	HUN	50k walk	F		3	4:31-27·2	B
Roman, H.	PUR	Decathlon	F		20	5264	
		Triple jump	Q		DNQ		
Roque, A.	BRA	400m	1	12	3	49·05	
		800m	1	6	5	1-54·1	
Rosario, R.	PUR	Shot put	Q		DNQ	14,21	
Ross, H.	USA	3000m steeplechase	1	2	12	9-44·0	
Ross, J.	CAN	800m	1	6	4	1-52·5	
		1500m	1	6	4	3-55·60	
			SF	2	12	4-00·6	
Roubanis, G.	GRE	Pole vault	Q		DNQ		
Roubanis, A.	GRE	Javelin throw	Q		DNQ	60,55	
Roudnitska, E.	FRA	110m hurdles	1	2	2	15·11	
			SF	1	5	15·15	
Roudny, J.	TCH	3000m steeplechase	1	1	5	9-06·92	
Saat, T.	HOL	100m	1	7	2	11·02	
			2	2	2	10·93	
			SF	2	6	11·12	
		200m	1	5	1	22·17	
			2	1	3	21·87	
Sakellarkis, B.	GRE	Triple jump	Q		DNQ	14,05	
Saksvik, O.	NOR	5000m	1	1	9	14-55·4	
Saltykov, M.	URS	3000m steeplechase	1	3	2	8-56·02	
			F		7	8-56·47	
Sanadze, L.	URS	100m	1	4	3	11·13	
		200m	1	2	2	22·26	
			2	5	4	22·26	
		4×100m relay	1	4	1	41·45	
			SF	1	2	41·01	
			F		2	40·58	S
Sando, F.	GBR	10000m	F		5	29-51·8	
Sangermano, L.	ITA	200m	1	18	4	22·38	
Sankosik, A.	THA	4×100m relay	1	2	6	44·81	
		100m	1	10	6	11·76	
		200m	1	16	4	23·64	
Sanni-Thomas, M.	GHA	800m	1	1	6	2-05·8	
Santee, W.	USA	5000m	1	2	13	15-10·4	
Savidge, J.A.	GBR	Shot put	F		6	16,19	
Sawada, B.	JPN	Pole vault	F		6	4,20	
Scerbakov, J.	URS	Javelin throw	F		13	64,52	
Schade, H.	GER	5000m	1	2	1	14-15·44	
			F		3	14-08·80	B
Schaeffer, R.	LUX	200m	1	10	3	22·76	
		4×400m relay	1	1	5	3-16·38	
Scherbakov, L.	URS	Triple jump	F		2	15,98	S
Schirmer, F.	GER	Decathlon	F		8	6118	
Schlegel, J.	FRA	5000m	1	3	9	14-45·6	
Schmid, K.	SUI	400m hurdles	1	6	5	57·5	
Schneider, E.	SUI	400m	1	12	2	48·86	
			2	1	6	49·32	
		4×400m relay	1	2	5	3-15·36	
Schneider, W.	SUI	100m	1	6	3	11·22	
		4×100m relay	1	3	5	41·81	
Schoonjans, R.	BEL	3000m steeplechase	1	3	8	9-30·6	
Schwab, F.	SUI	10k walk	1	2	4	47-06·0	
			F		2	45-41·03	S
Schwabi, A.	AUT	Shot put	F		13	14,45	
Schwarz, H.	SUI	400m hurdles	1	7	3	56·3	
			2	1	6	54·09	

COMPETITOR	COUNTRY CODE	EVENT	ROUND	HEAT	PLACE	TIME & DISTANCE	MEDAL
Scott, A.	GBR	400m hurdles	1	6	3	54·9	
			2	4	4	53·69	
Segedin, P.	YUG	3000m steeplechase	1	3	9	9-40·2	
Semenov, I.	URS	5000m	1	2	6	14-28·8	
Shafei, E.	EGY	100m	1	4	4	11·40	
		200m	1	16	3	22·75	
		4×100m relay	1	1	7	43·02	
Shafi, M.	PAK	4×400m relay	1	2	6	3-23·2	
		400m hurdles	1	2	4	56·1	
Shaw, G.	USA	Triple jump	Q		DNQ	14,39	
Shenton, B.	GBR	200m	1	10	1	22·12	
			2	6	5	22·24	
		4×100m relay	1	2	1	41·43	
			SF	1	3	41·24	
			F		4	40·85	
Siddi, A.	ITA	400m	1	11	4	51·03	
		4×100m relay	1	2	2	41·73	
			SF	2	DNS		
Sidlo, J.	POL	Javelin throw	Q		DNQ	62,16	
Sigurdsson, P.	ISL	100m	1	10	5	11·55	
		4×100m relay	1	4	DIS		
Simmons, F.	USA	Decathlon	F		3	6788	B
Simon, O.	ESP	Triple jump	Q		DNQ	0	
Simonet, J.	BEL	Marathon	F		23	2:35-43·0	
Simonsen, E.	DEN	Marathon	F		42	2:46-41·4	
Sjogren, L.	USA	50k walk	F		DNF		
Skobla, J.	TCH	Shot put	F		9	15,92	
Slepnev, G.	URS	4×400m relay	1	3	3	3-12·65	
Slijkhuis, W.	HOL	1500m	1	3	DNF		
Smeal, C.	AUS	Marathon	F		45	2:52-23·0	
Smith, D.	USA	100m	1	12	1	10·90	
			2	3	1	10·69	
			SF	1	2	10·78	
			F		4	10·84	
		4×100m relay	1	1	1	40·34	
			SF	1	1	40·51	
			F		1	40·26	G
Snellman, P.	FIN	Long jump	F		9	7,02	
Snidvongs, K.	THA	High jump	Q		DNQ		
		Long jump	Q		DNQ	5,31	
		Triple jump	Q		DNQ	0	
Sobrero, G.	ITA	200m	1	13	3	22·66	
		4×100m relay	1	2	2	41·73	
			SF	2	DNS		
Soederlund, A.	SWE	50k walk	F		28	5:30-56·6	
Soederberg, C.	SWE	3000m steeplechase	1	3	3	9-02·30	
			F		5	8-55·87	
Soedarmodjo, M.	INA	High jump	F		=20	1,80	
Soeter, I.	RUM	High jump	F		6	1,95	
Soetewey, O.	BEL	800m	1	5	4	1-55·4	
Sola, G.	CHI	3000m steeplechase	1	1	10	9-32·2	
Solares, V.	GUA	800m	1	5	7	2-01·4	
Solymosi, E.	HUN	400m	1	3	3	49·32	
		4×400m relay	1	2	3	3-13·96	
Sorensen, S.	DEN	Marathon	F		48	2:55-21·0	
Sourek, J.	TCH	Marathon	F		35	2:41-40·4	
Sousa, J.	MEX	100m	1	3	4	11·31	
		400m	1	6	5	50·47	
Stacey, N.	GBR	200m	1	4	2	22·07	
			2	4	2	21·79	
			SF	1	5	21·95	
		4×400m relay	1	2	2	3-12·67	
			F		5	3-10·23	
Stalder, P.	SUI	4×400m relay	1	2	5	3-15·36	
Stanfield, A.	USA	200m	1	7	1	22·00	
			2	5	1	21·21	
			SF	1	1	21·23	
			F		1	20·81*	G
		4×100m relay	1	1	1	40·34	
			SF	1	1	40·51	
			F		1	40·26	G
Stavem, P.	NOR	Discus throw	F		16	46,00	
		Shot put	F		8	16,02	
Stawczyk, Z.	POL	200m	1	7	2	22·22	
			2	1	4	22·12	
		4×100m relay	1	1	3	42·00	
			SF	1	4	41·91	
Steger, J.	SUI	400m	1	3	4	49·35	
		4×400m relay	1	2	5	3-15·36	
Steines, G.	GER	800m	1	8	3	1-52·7	
			SF	2	4	1-52·99	
			F		6	1-50·81	
		4×400m relay	1	3	1	3-10·57	
			F		3	3-06·78	B
Stokes, J.	GUA	400m	1	8	6	53·81	
Stokken, M.	NOR	5000m	1	3	7	14-39·0	
		10000m	F		10	30-22·2	

COMPETITOR	COUNTRY CODE	EVENT	ROUND	HEAT	PLACE	TIME & DISTANCE	MEDAL
Stone, C.	USA	5000m	1	3	8	14-42·8	
		10000m	F		20	31-02·5	
Storch, K.	GER	Hammer throw	F		2	58,86	S
Strandli, S.	NOR	Hammer throw	F		7	56,36	
Stritoff, D.	YUG	3000m steeplechase	1	1	8	9-28·0	
Strunc, J.	FRA	50k walk	F		21	4:59-03·2	
Suchenski, D.	POL	4×100m relay	1	1	3	42·00	
			SF	1	5	41·91	
Suchkov, G.	URS	Marathon	F		28	2:38-28·8	
Suikkari, J.	FIN	400m	1	3	5	50·92	
Sukharev, V.	URS	100m	1	7	1	10·93	
			2	4	3	10·92	
			SF	1	3	10·86	
			F		5	10·38	
		200m	1	3	1	22·08	
			2	6	3	21·88	
		4×100m relay	1	4	1	41·45	
			SF	1	2	41·01	
			F		2	40·58	S
Sutter, A.	SUI	5000m	1	1	3	14-45·2	
Sutton, W.	CAN	100m	1	5	=5	11·45	
		200m	1	11	5	22·53	
		4×100m relay	1	1	5	42·73	
Suvivuo, V.	FIN	110m hurdles	1	5	2	15·21	
			SF	2	=5	15·31	
Svadanandana, S.	THA	400m	1	8	5	53·63	
Svensson, G.	SWE	High jump	F		2	1,98	
Syllas, N.	GRE	Discus throw	F		9	48,99	
Syllis, B.	GRE	200m	1	10	2	22·88	
		400m	1	4	2	49·79	
Syrjaenen, R.	FIN	110m hurdles	1	2	4	15·63	
Systad, J.	NOR	Marathon	F		34	2:41-29·8	
Szentgali, L.	HUN	4×400m relay	1	2	3	3-13·96	
Tabak, D.	ISR	100m	1	6	1	11·12	
			2	3	6	11·10	
		200m	1	6	1	22·60	
			2	4	5	22·34	
Taddia, T.	ITA	Hammer throw	F		10	54,27	
Taipale, I.	FIN	5000m	1	1	2	14-22·83	
			F		12	14-40·0	
Tajima, M.	JPN	100m	1	2	6	11·29	
		Long jump	F		10	7.00	
Takahashi, S.	JPN	3000m steeplechase	1	2	9	9-21·6	
Talja, O.	FIN	800m	1	2	4	1-52·9	
Tamminen, L.	FIN	Hammer throw	F		10	50,05	
Tannander, K.	SWE	Decathlon	F		7	6308	
Tavisalo, P.	FIN	100m	1	5	4	11·30	
		200m	1	8	4	22·45	
		4×100m relay	1	1	4	42·20	
		4×400m relay	1	1	6	3-16·67	
Telen, T.A.	FIN	Shot put	Q		DNC	14,30	
Teodosiu, V.	RUM	Marathon	F		41	2:46-00·8	
Theys, L.	BEL	5000m	1	2	4	14-21·62	
			F		14	14-59·0	
Thogersen, T.	DEN	10000m	F		24	31-47·8	
Thorsteinsson, I.	ISL	110m hurdles	1	6	4	15·76	
		400m hurdles	1	2	5	56·5	
		4×100m relay	1	4	DIS		
Thunestvedt, R.	DEN	10k walk	F		9	50-42·8	
Thureau, J.	FRA	400m hurdles	1	8	5	56·7	
Tokarev, L.	URS	4×100m relay	1	4	1	41·45	
			SF	1	2	41·01	
			F		2	40·58	S
Tolgyesi, V.	HUN	1500m	1	4	4	3-56·20	
			SF	2	8	3-53·56	
Tosi, G.	ITA	Discus throw	F		8	49,03	
Tran, L.-V.	VNM	10000m	F		32	37-33·0	
Treloar, J.	AUS	100m	1	1	1	10·92	
			2	1	2	10·84	
			SF	2	3	10·76	
			F		6	10·91	
		200m	1	18	1	21·75	
			2	6	1	21·86	
			SF	2	DNF		
Trossbach, W.	GER	110m hurdles	1	3	3	15·24	
Tsibulenko, V.	URS	Javelin throw	F		4	71,72	
Tunbridge, D.	GBR	50k walk	F		15	4:50-40·4	
Tuomaala, E.	FIN	5000m	1	2	5	14-26·8	
			F		13	14-54·2	
Turakainen, A.	FIN	4×100m relay	1	1	4	42·20	
		200m	1	1	3	22·55	
Turan, N.	TUR	Discus throw	Q		DNQ	41,45	
		Shot put	Q		DNQ	13,00	
Uchikawa, Y.	JPN	Marathon	F		DNF		
Ukhov, V.	URS	50k walk	F		6	4:32-51·6	

COMPETITOR	COUNTRY CODE	EVENT	ROUND	HEAT	PLACE	TIME & DISTANCE	MEDAL
Uzheimer, H.	GER	800m	1	6	1	1-51·4	
			SF	3	1	1-52·07	
			F		3	1-49·78	B
		4×400m relay	1	3	1	3-10·57	
			F		3	3-06·78	B
Urr, P.	KOR	200m	1	13	5	23·41	
Uusihauta, P.	FIN	Triple jump	Q		DNQ	14,38	
Uytterhoeven, A.	BEL	400m	1	9	5	50·21	
		4×400m relay	1	1	4	3-16·05	
Vaehaeranta, U.	FIN	1500m	1	5	5	3-56·85	
Valkama, J.	FIN	Long jump	Q		DNQ	6,97	
Valtonen, J.	FIN	Long jump	F		5	7,16	
Van Biljon, L.	SAF	400m	1	5	2	48·31	
			2	3	4	48·63	
		4×400m relay	1	3	4	3-15·09	
Van De Wattyne, M	BEL	10000m	F		22	31-15·8	
Van De Zande, A.	HOL	Marathon	F		15	2:33-50·0	
Van Den Rydt, A.	BEL	5000m	1	3	15	15-51·2	
		10000m	F		29	33-13·4	
Vanaslit, A.	THA	100m	1	2	7	11·61	
		200m	1	7	5	23·50	
		4×100m relay	1	2	6	44·81	
Vanin, F.	URS	Marathon	F		27	2:38-22·0	
Vansovich, E.	URS	High jump	F		28	1,80	
Varasdi, G.	HUN	4×100m relay	1	3	1	41·15	
			SF	2	1	40·99	
			F		3	40·83	B
Varszegi, J.	HUN	Javelin throw	Q		DNQ	56,82	
Veeser, R.	SUI	Hammer throw	Q		DNQ	48,50	
Velasques, L.	GUA	Marathon	F		DNF		
Velsvebel, M.	URS	1500m	1	2	4	3-52·72	
			SF	1	10	3-52·58	
Vera, C.	CHI	Decathlon	Q		DNF		
		Long jump	Q		DNQ	7,07	
Vernier, Jean	FRA	1500m	1	6	5	3-56·61	
Vicente, J.	PUR	Pole vault	Q		DNQ		
Viljanen, P.	FIN	50k walk	F		14	4:49-16·4	
Visser, H.	HOL	Long jump	F		NP	0	
Vittorio, C.	ITA	100m	1	3	2	10·98	
			2	4	6	11·19	
		4×100m relay	1	2	2	41·73	
			SF	2	DNS		
Volkov, V.	URS	Decathlon	F		4	6674	
Von Gunten, E.	SUI	400m	1	5	6	50·88	
		4×400m relay	1	2	5	3-15·36	
Wahli, H.	SUI	High jump	F		16	1,90	
Warnemuende, L.	GER	Marathon	F		43	2:50-00·0	
Wazny, A.	POL	Pole vault	Q		DNQ	3,80	
Webster, A.	GBR	800m	1	1	2	1-55·5	
			SF	1	3	1-50·26	
			F		5	1-50·47	
Wehli, H.	SUI	100m	1	10	2	11·00	
			2	2	5	11·05	
		200m	1	8	3	22·35	
		4×100m relay	1	3	5	41·81	
Wehrli, M.	SUI	Decathlon	F		18	5561	
Weinacker, A.	USA	50k walk	F		22	5:01-00·4	
Weinberg, R.	AUS	110m hurdles	1	5	1	14·62	
			SF	2	3	14·99	
			F		6	15·15	
		4×100m relay	1	2	5	42·38	
		4×400m relay	1	3	5	3-16·00	
Weinberg, Z.	POL	Triple jump	F		10	14,76	
Weller, G.	ARG	50k walk	F		DNF		
Wells, P.	GBR	High jump	F		=11	1,90	
West, J.	IRL	Marathon	F		49	2:56-22·8	
White, T.	GBR	800m	1	2	3	1-52·7	
			SF	2	5	1-53·79	
Whitlock, H.	GBR	50k walk	F		11	4:45-12·6	
Whitlock, R.	GBR	50k walk	F		4	4:32-21·0	
Whitfield, M.	USA	400m	1	6	1	48·68	
			2	3	1	47·74	
			SF	1	3	46·64	
			F		6	47·30	
		800m	1	2	1	1-52·5	
			SF	1	2	1-50·15	
			F		1	1-49·34*	G
		4×400m relay	1	2	1	3-11·67	
			F		2	3-04·21	S
Whitle, H.	GBR	400m hurdles	1	8	2	53·9	
			2	3	3	52·94	
			SF	2	=2	52·98	
			F		5	53·36	
Widenfelt, G.	SWE	Decathlon	F		6	6388	
Wiesner, K.	USA	High jump	F		2	2,01	S
Wilke, P.	SAF	400m hurdles	1	8	1	54·5	
			2	3	5	54·76	

COMPETITOR	COUNTRY CODE	EVENT	ROUND	HEAT	PLACE	TIME & DISTANCE	MEDAL
Wilkie, R.	SAF	4×400m relay	1	3	4	3-15·09	
Williams, S.	NGR	Long jump	Q		DNQ	6,98	
Wilt, F.	USA	10000m	F		21	31-04·0	
Wint, A.	JAM	400m	1	3	1	47·42	
			2	1	1	46·98	
			SF	1	1	46·38	
			F		5	47·24	
		800m	1	5	2	1-54·2	
			SF	2	1	1-52·88	
			F		2	1-49·63	S
		4×400m relay	1	1	1	3-12·13	
			F		1	3-04·04*	G
Winther, G.	NOR	50k walk	F		27	5:11-40·2	
Wolf, K.	GER	Hammer throw	F		6	56,49	
Wolfbrandt, L.	SWE	400m	1	4	1	48·57	
			2	1	3	48·08	
		800m	1	1	1	1-55·3	
			SF	3	2	1-52·59	
			F		8	1-52·38	
		4×400m relay	1	1	3	3-13·55	
Wuerth, F.	AUT	Long jump	Q		DNQ	6,99	
		Triple jump	Q		DNQ		
Yamada, K.	JPN	Marathon	F		26	2:38-11·2	
Yamamoto, K.	JPN	4×400m relay	1	1	7	3-20·55	
Yamamoto, T.	JPN	Triple jump	F		14	14,57	
Yarmysh, I.	URS	10k walk	1	1	6	47-26·0	
			F		6	46-07·07	
Yataganas, C.	GRE	Discus throw	F		15	46,23	
		Shot put	Q		DNQ	14,05	
Yazgi, F.	EGY	110m hurdles	1	2	6	16·26	
		4×100m relay	1	1	7	43·02	
Ylander, L.	SWE	400m hurdles	1	1	2	53·90	
			2	3	4	53·29	
Yoder, L.	USA	400m hurdles	1	2	2	55·2	
			2	2	2	53·40	
			SF	2	4	53·08	
Yoma, P.	CHI	400m hurdles	1	4	4	57·03	
Young, C.	USA	Javelin throw	F		1	73,78*	G
Yulin, A.	URS	400m hurdles	1	3	1	53·6	
			2	1	2	52·64	
			SF	1	3	52·28	
			F		4	52·81	
Zandt, W.	GER	100m	1	9	1	11·03	
			2	3	4	10·98	
		200m	1	5	2	22·23	
			2	6	2	21·87	
			SF	4	4	21·92	
		4×100m relay	1	3	4	41·63	
Zarandi, L.	HUN	100m	1	10	4	11·26	
		4×100m relay	1	3	1	41·15	
			SF	2	1	40·99	
			F		3	40·83	B
Zatopek, E.	TCH	5000m	1	3	3	14-25·81	
			F		1	14-06·72*	G
		10000m	F		1	29-17·0*	G
		Marathon	F		1	2:23-03·2*	G
Zeb, A.	PAK	400m	1	3	6	51·25	
		800m	1	3	5	1-56·3	
		4×400m relay	1	2	6	3-23·2	
Zeltynysh, P.	URS	10k walk	1	2	DIS		
Ziraman, J.H.	TUR	Javelin throw	Q		DNQ	61,19	

FEMALES

COMPETITOR	COUNTRY CODE	EVENT	ROUND	HEAT	PLACE	TIME & DISTANCE	MEDAL
Alexandrova, A.	URS	80m hurdles	1	5	3	11·86	
Antes, H.	SAA	80m hurdles	1	2	4	12·31	
		4×100m relay	1	1	5	49·22	
Armitage, H,	GBR	100m	1	4	2	12·57	
			2	1	5	12·58	
		4×100m relay	1	2	2	46·84	
			F		3	46·41	B
Arndt, M.	POL	200m	1	1	6	26·29	
		4×100m relay	1	1	4	48·21	
Augustsson, A.L.	SWE	100m	1	5	2	12·67	
			2	3	5	12·66	
		4×100m relay	1	2	4	48·06	
Autio, A.	FIN	80m hurdles	1	5	6	12·31	
		4×100m relay	1	3	6	50·34	
Bagryantseva, E.	URS	Discus throw	F		2	47,08	S
Bartha, L.	HUN	100m	1	2	3	12·90	
		4×100m relay	1	2	DIS		
Bauma, H.	AUT	Javelin throw	F		9	42,54	
Bausenwein, I.	GER	Javelin throw	F		12	41,16	
Berkovska, T.	BUL	100m	1	1	2	12·43	
			2	1	6	12·60	
		200m	1	1	3	25·49	

COMPETITOR	COUNTRY CODE	EVENT	ROUND	HEAT	PLACE	TIME & DISTANCE	MEDAL
Bielansky, H.	AUT	8Cm hurdles	1	4	4	12·10	
Blankers-Koen, F.	HOL	100m	1	11	1	12·18	
			2	2	2	12·22	
			SF	1	DNS		
		80m hurdles	1	2	1	11·34	
			SF	2	2	11·42	
			F		DNF		
Bocian, L.	POL	100m	1	2	4	13·10	
Bollinger, G.	SUI	80m hurdles	1	6	6	12·56	
		Long jump	Q		DNQ	5,14	
		Shot put	Q		DNQ	11,48	
		Discus throw	F		17	36,36	
Brand, E.	SAF	High jump	F		1	1,67	G
		Discus throw	Q		DNQ	35,79	
Bregula, M.	POL	Shot put	F		10	12,93	
Brouwer, B.	HOL	100m	1	3	2	12·26	
			2	1	3	12·33	
			SF	2	4	12·32	
		200m	1	4	1	24·81	
			SF	1	2	24·41	
			F		2	24·25	S
		4×100m relay	1	1	2	47·32	
			F		6	47·16	
Buch, N,	HOL	100m	1	6	3	12·95	
		4×100m relay	1	1	2	47·32	
			F		6	47·16	
Buglia, L.	ARG	100m	1	3	33	12·62	
		4×100m relay	1	1	3	48·11	
		Long jump	Q		DNQ		
Cawley, S.	GBR	Long jump	F		3	5,92	B
Cesarini, V.	ITA	100m	1	3	3	12·78	
		4×100m relay	1	2	3	47·68	
Cheeseman, S.	GBR	200m	1	1	1	25·03	
			SF	1	4	24·97	
		4×100m relay	1	2	2	46·84	
			F		3	46·41	B
Choi, M.	KOR	Shot put	Q		DNQ		
Chudina, A.	URS	High jump	F		3	1,63	B
		Long jump	F		2	6,14	S
		Javelin throw	F		2	50,01	S
Ciach, M.	POL	Javelin throw	F		7	44,31	
Coates, D.	GBR	Javelin throw	F		15	40,17	
Cripps, W.	AUS	100m	1	1	1	12·18*	
			2	3	3	12·30	
			SF	1	2	12·16	
			F		4	12·16	
		200m	1	6	1	24·54	
			SF	2	2	24·47	
			F		4	24·40	
		4×100m relay	1	1	1	46·22*	
			F		5	46·86	
Curtet, Y.	FRA	Long jump	F		23	5,30	
Darnowski, C.	USA	80m hurdles	1	5	5	12·29	
De Campou, A.	FRA	100m	1	7	3	12·44	
		4×100m relay	1	3	4	47·79	
De Castro, D.	BRA	200m	1	2	3	25·22	
		High jump	F		12	1,50	
De Jongh, G.	HOL	200m	1	2	5	25·48	
		4×100m relay	1	1	2	47·32	
			F		6	47·16	
De Menezes, H.C.	BRA	100m	1	7	4	12·83	
		Long jump	F		24	4,98	
Desforges, J.	GBR	80m hurdles	1	4	1	11·51	
			SF	1	3	11·37	
			F		5	11·75	
		4×100m relay	1	2	2	46·84	
			F		3	46·41	B
Devine, P.	GBR	200m	1	3	3	25·25	
Dicks, J.	USA	Shot put	Q		DNQ	11,44	
Dos Santos, W.	BRA	80m hurdles	1	6	2	11·58	
			SF	2	5	11·74	
		Long jump	F		21	5,36	
D'Souza, M.	IND	100m	1	9	5	13·40	
		200m	1	3	7	26·80	
Dudal, E.	FRA	Long jump	Q		DNQ	5,21	
Dumbadze, N.	URS	Discus throw	F		3	46,29	B
Dunska, E.	POL	Long jump	F		12	5,65	
Dwyer, D.	USA	200m	1	5	DNF		
Eckel, I.	SAA	4×100m relay	1	1	5	49·22	
Elloy, C.	FRA	80m hurdles	1	1	4	12·31	
Erbetta, G.	ARG	200m	1	1	4	25·83	
		4×100m relay	1	1	3	48·11	
		Long jump	F		18	5,47	
Ericsson, S.	SWE	High jump	F		14	1,50	
Ewing, G.	GUA	100m	1	11	4	13·05	
		200m	1		5	27·02	

COMPETITOR	COUNTRY CODE	EVENT	ROUND	HEAT	PLACE	TIME & DISTANCE	MEDAL
Faggs, M.	USA	100m	1	2	1	12·44	
			2	2	3	12·22	
			SF	1	3	12·16	
			F		=5	12·27	
		200m	1	6	3	24·71	
		4×100m relay	1	2	1	46·77	
			F		1	46·14*	G
Farmer, S.	GBR	Discus throw	F		15	37,96	
Finger, U.	SAA	4×100m relay	1	1	5	49·22	
		Long jump	Q		DNC	5,27	
Flament, C.	FRA	80m hurdles	1	5	2	11·83	
			SF	2	6	11·89	
Fontan, A.	ARG	100m	1	7	5	13·33	
		4×100m relay	1		3	48·11	
Foulds, J.	GBR	100m	1	7	2	12·34	
			2	3	4	12·45	
		4×100m relay	1	2	2	46·84	
			F		3	46·41	B
Gabarrus, M.	FRA	200m	1	4	2	25·49	
			SF	2	7	25·46	
		4×100m relay	1	3	4	47·79	
Ganeker, G.	URS	High jump	F		11	1,55	
Gentile, E.	ITA	Discus throw	F		14	33,22	
Ghose, N.	IND	100m	1	1	5	13·80	
		80m hurdles	1	2	5	13·07	
Glashoerster, I.	SAA	4×100m relay	1	1	5	49·22	
Glotin, S.	FRA	Long jump	Q		DNQ	5,27	
Gokieli, E.	URS	80m hurdles	1	3	1	11·59	
			SF	1	4	11·46	
Golubnichaya, M.	URS	80m hurdles	1	6	1	11·29	
			SF	2	1	11·35	
			F		2	11·24	S
Gorchakova, E.	URS	Javelin throw	F		3	49,76	B
Greppi, M.	ITA	80m hurdles	1	1	2	11·95	
			SF	1	6	11·80	
		4×100m relay	1	2	3	47·68	
Gyarmati, O.	HUN	200m	1	3	4	25·77	
		4×100m relay	1	2	DIS		
		Long jump	F		10	5,67	
Haidegger, E.	AUT	Discus throw	F		5	43,49	
Hannerz, I.	SWE	100m	1	12	5	13·09	
		4×100m relay	1	2	4	48·06	
Hardy, C.	USA	100m	1	7	1	12·18*	
			2	4	4	12·31	
		200m	1	3	2	24·91	
			SF	2	4	24·93	
		4×100m relay	1	2	1	46·77	
			F		1	46·14*	G
Hasenjager, D.	SAF	100m	1	10	1	12·16	
			2	3	1	12·19	
			SF	2	1	12·13	
			F		2	12·05	S
		200m	1	6	2	24·58	
			SF	1	3	24·60	
			F		6	24·72	
Heikkilae, S.	FIN	High jump	F		16	1,40	
Heinz, L.	ARG	100m	1	1	3	13·01	
		200m	1	5	4	26·00	
		4×100m relay	1	1	3	48·11	
Hofknecht, L.	GER	Long jump	F		15	5,54	
Hopkins, T.	GER	High jump	F		4	1,58	
Horovitz, L.R.	ISR	80m hurdles	1	4	6	12·74	
Huber, M.	CHI	80m hurdles	1	2	DNF		
Ilwicka, M.	POL	4×100m relay	1	1	4	48·21	
		Long jump	Q		DNQ	5,09	
Jackson, M.	AUS	100m	1	8	1	11·86*	
			2	1	1	11·84*	
			SF	1	1	11·75*	
			F		1	11·67*	G
		200m	1	3	1	23·73*	
			SF	1	1	23·59*	
			F		1	23·89	G
		4×100m relay	1	1	1	46·22*	
			F		5	46·86	
Johnson, A.	GBR	200m	1	4	4	25·59	
Johnston, V.	AUS	4×100m relay	1	1	1	46·22*	
			F		5	46·86	
		Long jump	F		8	5,74	
Jones, B.	USA	4×100m relay	1	2	1	46·77	
			F		1	46·14*	G
Jones, P.	BER	100m	1	10	5	13·55	
		Long jump	Q		DNQ	4,92	
Jones, T.	BER	100m	1	8	4	12·75	
		Long jump	F		22	5,33	
Josephs, D.	CAN	High jump	F		13	1,50	
		Long jump	F		17	5,47	
Jozsane, D.	HUN	Discus throw	F		8	41,61	
Kalashnikova, V.	URS	100m	1	9	2	12·32	
			2	3	2	12·26	
			SF	2	5	12·41	
		4×100m relay	1	3	2	47·01	
			F		4	46·42	
Kazantseva, F.	URS	200m	1	1	5	25·92	
Kelsby, L.	DEN	Javelin throw	F		5	46,23	
Keskinen, S.	FIN	80m hurdle	1	4	5	12·68	
Khnykina, N.	URS	100m	1	12	1	12·25	
			2	4	3	12·29	
			SF	1	4	12·17	
		200m	1	2	1	24·47*	
			SF	2	1	24·16	
			F		3	24·37	B
		4×100m relay	1	3	2	47·01	
			F		4	46·42	
Kile, G.	GER	Shot put	F		5	13,84	
Klein, H.	GER	100m	1	4	1	12·30	
			2	4	1	12·27	
			SF	2	6	12·53	
		200m	1	2	2	24·83	
			SF	2	3	24·65	
			F		5	24·72	
		4×100m relay	1	3	1	46·42	
			F		2	46·18	S
Knab, U.	GER	200m	1	1	2	25·26	
			SF	1	7	25·76	
		4×100m relay	1	3	1	46·42	
			F		2	46·18	S
Koivuniemi, K.	FIN	Discus throw	F		11	40,33	
Konrad, E.	RUM	100m	1	9	4	13·10	
		200m	1	2	6	26·04	
Kosova, N.	URS	High jump	F		=7	1,58	
Kotlusek, N.	YUG	Shot put	F		14	11,98	
Kress, D.	GER	Shot put	F		11	12,91	
Kritkova, J.	TCH	Shot put	F		12	12,73	
Krueger, J.	GER	Javelin throw	F		8	44,30	
Krysinska, E.	POL	Shot put	Q		DNQ	11,50	
Laborie, D.	FRA	100m	1	11	3	12·88	
		4×100m relay	1	3	4	47·79	
Lancy, M.	USA	Long jump	F		7	5,75	
Laensivuori, P.	FIN	200m	1	5	5	27·66	
Larking, G.	SWE	High jump	F		9	1,55	
Larney, M.	USA	Javelin throw	F		13	40,58	
Law, L.	CAN	100m	1	8	3	12·70	
		200m	1	7	2	25·82	
			SF	1	6	25·63	
		80m hurdles	1	4	3	12·09	
		4×100m relay	1	3	3	47·47	
Leone, G.	ITA	100m	1	6	1	12·38	
			2	1	4	12·42	
		4×100m relay	1	2	3	47·68	
Lerwill, S.	GBR	High jump	F		2	1,65	S
Lituyeva, V.	URS	Long jump	F		11	5,65	
Lousteau, A.M.	FRA	200m	1	3	5	25·78	
Lust, W.	HOL	80m hurdles	1	3	3	11·69	
		4×100m relay	1	1	2	47·32	
			F		6	47·16	
		Long jump	F		5	5,81	
McKenzie, E.	CAN	100m	1	10	2	12·41	
			2	2	5	12·44	
		200m	1	5	2	25·66	
			SF	2	5	25·30	
		4×100m relay	1	3	3	47·47	
Magnusson, G.	SWE	4×100m relay	1	2	4	48·06	
		Long jump	F		20	5,43	
Manoliu, L.	RUM	Discus throw	F		6	42,65	
Martelli, V.	ITA	200m	1	3	6	26·53	
Martin, G	CHI	Javelin throw	Q		DNQ	36,94	
Maskell, E.	SAF	100m	1	12	2	12·26	
			2	2	5	12·38	
		80m hurdles	1	2	2	11·80	
			SF	1	5	11·50	
Mello, .	ARG	Shot put	Q		DNQ	10,82	
		Discus throw	F		12	39,04	
Mettal, L.	ISR	High jump	F		17	1,40	
		Long jump	Q		DNQ	5,16	
Millard, A.	CHI	200m	1	4	3	25·58	
		Long jump	F		13	5,59	
Minicka, G.	POL	200m	1	7	4	26·17	
		4×100m relay	1	1	4	48·21	
Miyashita, M.	JPN	80m hurdles	1	1	3	12·06	
Modrachova, O.	TCH	High jump	F		5	1,58	
Monginou, Y.	FRA	100m	1	8	2	12·64	
			2	2	6	12·66	
		80m hurdles	1	6	3	11·64	
		4×100m relay	1	3	4	47·79	

COMPETITOR	COUNTRY CODE	EVENT	ROUND	HEAT	PLACE	TIME & DISTANCE	MEDAL
Moreau, J.	USA	100m	1	6	2	12·68	
			2	3	6	12·67	
		4×100m relay	1	2	1	46·77	
			F		1	46·14*	G
Mueller, M.	GER	Javelin throw	F		6	44,37	
Musso, M.	ITA	80m hurdles	1	5	4	12·17	
Novakova, L.	TCH	Javelin throw	F		13	38,83	
O'Halloran, F.	CAN	200m	1	2	4	25·45	
		4×100m relay	1	3	3	47·47	
Olson, E.	SWE	Shot put	F		13	12,46	
Oesterdahl, M.	FIN	4×100m relay	1	3	5	50·34	
		Long jump	F		9	5,73	
Parviainen, K.	FIN	Javelin throw	F		16	39,82	
Petersen, M.	GER	100m	1	11	2	12·32	
			2	1	2	12·30	
			SF	1	5	12·19	
		4×100m relay	1	3	1	46·42	
			F		2	46·18	S
Pfueller, I.	ARG	Shot put	Q		DNQ	11,85	
		Discus throw	F		7	41,73	
Pokki, U.	FIN	100m	1	1	4	13·06	
		4×100m relay	1	3	5	50·34	
Poentinen, S.	FIN	80m hurdles	1	3	4	12·22	
		High jump	F		15	1,50	
Pretot, S.	SUI	100m	1	6	5	14·93	
Puente, E.	URU	Javelin throw	F		10	41,44	
Radosavljevic, M.	YUG	Shot put	F		7	13,30	
Rakhely, G.	HUN	100m	1	5	4	12·95	
		4×100m relay	1	2	DIS		
Raettyae, E.	FIN	Javelin throw	F		14	40,56	
Romaschkova, N.	URS	Discus throw	F		1	51,42*	G
Russell, K.	JAM	Long jump	Q		DNQ	5,10	
Saari, M.	FIN	Shot put	F		8	13,02	
Sander, M.	GER	100m	1	5	1	12·42	
			2	2	1	12·20	
			SF	2	3	12·24	
			F		=5	12·27	
		80m hurdles	1	5	1	11·41	
			SF	1	2	11·19	
			F		3	11·38	B
		4×100m relay	1	3	1	46·42	
			F		2	46·18	S
Schenk, F.	AUT	High jump	F		6	1,58	
Schmelzer, I.	GER	Long jump	F		4	5,90	
Seaborne, P.	GBR	80m hurdles	1	3	2	11·62	
			SF	2	4	11·71	
Sechenova, E.	URS	200m	1	7	1	25·46	
			SF	1	5	25·32	
		4×100m relay	1	3	2	47·01	
			F		4	46·42	
Seonbuchner, A.	GER	80m hurdles	1	4	2	11·55	
			SF	2	3	11·70	
			F		4	11·46	
Shivas, Q.	GBR	100m	1	9	3	12·82	
Sicoe, A.	RUM	100m	1	4	4	12·93	
		200m	1	5	3	25·82	
Sipilae, K.	FIN	100m	1	4	5	13·70	
		4×100m relay	1	3	5	50·34	
Sjoestroem, N.	SWE	100m	1	10	3	12·71	
		4×100m relay	1	2	4	48·06	

COMPETITOR	COUNTRY CODE	EVENT	ROUND	HEAT	PLACE	TIME & DISTANCE	MEDAL
Soos, K.	HUN	200m	1	7	8	26·05	
		80m hurdles	1	2	3	11·98	
Staniek G.	AUT	Javelin throw	Q		DNQ		
Steurer, E.	AUT	100m	1	12	4	12·86	
		80m hurdles	1	6	4	11·74	
Strickland, S.	AUS	100m	1	9	1	12·20	
			2	4	2	12·28	
			SF	2	2	12·17	
			F		3	12·12	B
		80m hurdles	1	1	1	11·24*	
			SF	1	1	11·16*	
			F		1	11·01*	G
		4×100m relay	1	1	1	46·22*	
			F		5	46·86	
Szwajkowska, E.	POL	200m	1	5	1	25·60	
			SF	2	6	25·45	
		4×100m relay	1	1	4	48·21	
Tagliaferri, L.	ITA	100m	1	2	2	12·86	
			2	4	6	13·14	
		4×100m relay	1	2	3	47·68	
Tangen, J.A.	NOR	100m	1	6	4	13·18	
		80m hurdles	1	1	5	12·51	
Teng, P.-W.	SIN	100m	1	3	4	14·08	
		80m hurdles	1	3	5	13·09	
Thomas, E.	CHI	Javelin throw	Q		DNQ	0	
Thorne, R.	CAN	100m	1	5	3	12·77	
		4×100m relay	1	3	3	47·47	
Threapleton, P.	GBR	80m hurdles	1	6	5	11·88	
Tilkovszki, I.	HUN	100m	1	10	4	12·75	
		4×100m relay	1	2	DIS		
Tiltsch, F.	AUT	Discus throw	F		18	27,84	
Tochenova, C.	URS	Shot put	F		3	14,50	B
Torikka, E.	FIN	Javelin throw	F		17	39,58	
Turci, A.	ITA	Javelin throw	F		11	41,20	
Turova, I.	URS	100m	1	2	2	12·25	
			2	2	4	12·28	
		4×100m relay	1	3	2	47·01	
			F		4	46·42	
Tyschkevich, T.	URS	Shot put	F		4	14,42*	
Tyler, D.	GBR	High jump	F		=7	1,58	
Tyurkina, N.	URS	Long jump	F		6	5,81	
Veste, P.	FRA	Shot put	F		9	12,96	
		Discus throw	F		16	37,64	
Von Nitzsch, E.	GER	Long jump	F		14	5,57	
Walters, H.	JAM	100m	1	12	3	12·53	
		200m	1	6	4	25·59	
Werner, M.	GER	Shot put	F		2	14,57	S
		Discus throw	F		9	41,03	
Whitty, A.	CAN	High jump	F		10	1,55	
Williams, Y.	NZL	Long jump	F		1	6,24*	G
		Shot put	F		6	13,35	
		Discus throw	F		10	40,48	
Willoughby, C.	GBR	Long jump	F		19	5,44	
Winterberg, O.	ISR	Discus throw	Q		DNQ	34,18	
Yoshikawa, A.	JPN	100m	1	5	5	13·00	
		Long jump	F		16	5,54	
Yoshino, T.	JPN	Discus throw	F		4	43,81	
Yubi, A.	MEX	Javelin throw	Q		DNQ	34,18	
Zatopekova, D.	TCH	Javelin throw	F		1	50,47*	G
Zybina, G.	URS	Shot put	F		1	15,28*	G
		Javelin throw	F		4	48,35	

1956

The Games Go to the Southern Hemisphere

For the first time, the Olympics were held in the southern hemisphere, where Melbourne was the host city. There was much pre-Games conflict, principally when the USSR invaded Hungary to quell the new spirit of liberalism there, but the British and French were also involved in a bitter dispute over the Suez Canal, between Egypt and Israel. Hungary, whose team were in transit to Melbourne at the height of the crisis, took part in the Games, and did well.

There were many outstanding track and field performances and Betty Cuthbert, Shirley Strickland, Bobby Morrow and Vladimir Kuts all sealed distinguished careers, in which they won two or more Olympic gold medals.

Men's Track Events

There were so many hot sprinters in the USA that two world **100 metres** record holders, at 10·1 sec, did not even make their team. Seventy competitors contested the preliminaries, in which Americans Bobby Morrow and Ira Murchison equalled the Olympic record of 10·3, the former twice. The final was run against an adverse wind with Hector Hogan of Australia off to the fastest start of his career. But Morrow was quickly into his running and caught Hogan at the half way stage, going away to win by nearly two metres in 10·5. Meanwhile, Murchison and Thane Baker of America were alongside Hogan at 75 metres, before Baker's superior dip got him the silver medal, also in 10·5. Hogan held on for the bronze, recording 10·6. (Automatic timings: Morrow 10·62, Baker 10·77 and Hogan 10·77).

Bobby Morrow had come to Melbourne with bigger hopes for the **200 metres** than the 100, although all three Americans had hit the world record standard of 20·6 sec during that season. The lane draw placed Morrow in three, and fellow Americans, Andy Stanfield in four and Thane Baker in six. Baker was so nervous in the final that he put his blocks in backwards and had to be told about it. At the gun, the three Americans streaked around the bend with Stanfield a fraction ahead coming into the straight. Morrow then swept past his rivals and won in 20·6, a new Olympic record, from Stanfield 20·7 and Baker at 20·9 (Automatic timings: Morrow 20·75, Stanfield 20·97 and Baker 21·05).

Lou Jones was the world record holder at 45·2 sec in the **400 metres** and Jim Lea, also of the USA, had set the world standard for the 440 yards at 45·8, so an exciting duel was in prospect. The surprise in the second round was the demise of Lea, who had been recovering from injury. The second semi-final was a tremendous race with four fighting it out to the line. Charlie Jenkins of the USA won from Voitto Hellsten of Finland, both recording 46·1, Karl Haas of Germany with 46·2 and Kevan Gosper of Australia, who was most unlucky to be

edged into fourth place with 46·2. At the gun to start the final, Jones flew the first 200 in 21·8 with Ardalion Ignatiev of Russia a metre down and the others a little off the pace. Into the final bend, the cold wind hit the runners, and Jones wilted. Jenkins passed the fading Ignatyev with 25 metres to go and won in 46·7, while Haas, finishing fastest, took the silver in 46·8. Ignatiev and Hellsten tied for third, both recording 47·0. (Automatic timings: Jenkins 46·85, Haas 47·12, Hellsten and Ignatev 47·15).

The world record-holder in the **800 metres** was Roger Moens of Belgium, but he was unfortunately not competing. Tom Courtney of the USA took the lead from the start in the final, but at 150 metres, fellow American Arnie Sowell was in front with Courtney, Auden Boysen of Norway and Derek Johnson of Britain, following him in that order. Courtney drew alongside Sowell at 600 metres, but coming into the final straight, a gap opened between the Americans and Johnson seized the opportunity to burst through to the front with amazing acceleration. Courtney, caught by surprise, slowly pulled Johnson back and won by inches on the line in 1-47·7, a new Olympic record. Johnson was timed at 1-47·8, while Boysen also overtook Sowell to be placed third in 1-48·1. (Automatic timings: Courtney 1-47·75, Johnson 1-47·88 and Boysen 1-48·25).

Among the **1,500 metres** competitors was the world record holder, Istvan Rozsavolgyi of Hungary, and the defending Olympic champion, Josef Barthel, but neither reached the final. The 12 finalists strode away at the crack of the pistol with Murray Halberg of New Zealand leading Brian Hewson of Britain, and passing 400 metres in 58·4 sec. At 600, Merv Lincoln of Australia took up the running, moving through 800 in 2-00·1, but Hewson had taken the initiative shortly before reaching 1,200 in 3-01·3. At this stage of the race, Klaus Richtzenhain of Germany and Ian Boyd of Britain were just behind with Australia's John Landy and Ireland's Ron Delany catching up. Off the final bend, the relatively unknown Delany passed Richtzenhain and Boyd and tore down the straight, overtaking a fading Hewson, to win in an Olympic record of 3-41·2. His last lap was an astonishing 53·8. Richtzenhain just reached the tape for the silver medal as Landy, with a late burst, came up to his shoulder to take the bronze, both being timed in 3-42·0. (Automatic timings: Delany 3-41·49, Richtzenhain 3-42·02 and Landy 3-42·03).

Gordon Pirie of Britain was the favourite in the **5,000 metres** due to his recent world record and victory over Russia's Vladimir Kuts. In the final, Kuts used follow-my-leader tactics and, running the first lap in a sharp 61·8 sec, forced the pace. At 3km, in 8-11·2, only the three Britons, Gordon Pirie, Derek Ibbotson and Chris Chataway, were in contention, with Albert Thomas of Australia some 40 metres back. Chataway suffered

171

All-Sport Photographic Ltd.

Vladimir Kuts

Born in Aleksino, in the Ukraine, on 7 February 1927, Kuts was 24 when he thought he would have a change from boxing, his first sport, and switch to running. Within two years he was in the world top-six rankings for 5,000m and 10,000m. By this time the stocky Russian marine had developed an urge to prove himself the world's best at both distances. And this attitude drove him to a dramatic victory in the 5,000m at the 1954 European championships in Berne, where he completely out-raced Emil Zatopek and Chris Chataway, both of whom had broken world records earlier in the year. Kuts's reward was a world record in 13-56·6.

Thereafter he virtually dominated races at these distances, breaking the world mark three more times and crowning an exciting racing career with victories in both the 5,000m and 10,000m at the 1956 Olympic Games in Melbourne. That same year he also reduced the 10,000m world record to 28-30·4.

Kuts' experimental training programme seemed to take it out of him physically once his running career had ended, as he suffered a series of heart attacks, the fourth of which he died from on 17 August 1975.

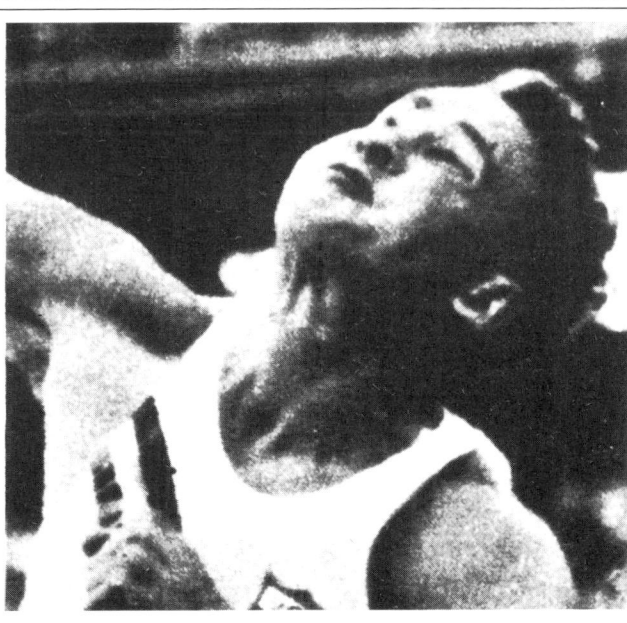

Parry O'Brien

Parry O'Brien's renown as a shot-putter is due as much to his style as to his performances. He pioneered the method by which the competitor starts with his back towards the direction of the throw, thus giving the athlete more time to exert force.

He also became the first man to break through the 60ft barrier and two years later he exceeded 61ft. And he was the first again to heave beyond 62 and 63 feet. In all, eight times winner of the American championship, he broke the world record on ten occasions, first with 18,00m (59ft 0¾in) in 1953 and finally with 19,30m (63ft 4in) in 1959.

His 1952 Olympic success in Helsinki was repeated four years later in Melbourne, but in spite of his world records prior to the Rome Games in 1960, his team colleague Bill Nieder grabbed a surprise win there, leaving O'Brien to take the silver.

O'Brien was still going strong in 1964 but although he exceeded all his previous Olympic throws in Tokyo, his performance was good enough for only fourth place, this time behind another of his compatriots, Dallas Long.

O'Brien was born in Santa Monica, California, on 28 January 1932, and his life-time best of 19,70m (64ft 7½in) came when he was 34 years of age.

Shirley Strickland

Shirley, born on 18 July 1925 at Guildford, Western Australia, surprisingly found herself in the Australian Olympic team for London in 1948 only months after she had taken to athletics seriously after graduating from the University of Western Australia.

It was a test of her character to face such experienced opposition as the famed Dutch star Fanny Blankers-Koen. But she stood the Wembley Stadium tests well and was rewarded with bronze medals from the 100m and 80m hurdles and a silver in the sprint relay.

She received the bronze again for the 100m in Helsinki four years later, but bagged her first gold there in the 80m hurdles with a world record 10·9 sec. And she became the proud recipient of two more golds, using her married name, de la Hunty, when the Games took place in Melbourne — for the 80m hurdles in which she improved the Olympic record to 10·7 sec, and the sprint relay where she ran the first leg of the Australian team's world-record breaking race.

Her father David had been a noted professional sprinter and hurdler in his younger days and that meant Shirley was never wanting for guidance or support. Shirley later became the assistant lecturer in physics and mathematics at Perth Technical College.

Easy does it! Charles Dumas of America, the first man to clear seven feet, goes clear for Olympic gold.

stomach cramps at 4km and dropped back, while Ibbotson and Pirie hung on 10 metres adrift of Kuts. The Russian then began to pull away and finished in 13-39-6 for an Olympic record, with Pirie outkicking his fellow Briton to take silver in 13-50-6 to Ibbotson's 13-54 4. (Automatic timings: Kuts 13-39-86, Pirie 13-50-78 and Ibbotson 13-54-60).

The Russian running machine, Vladimir Kuts, was everyone's tip for the **10,000 metres** when 21 runners lined up in three rows for the final. Immediately, Kuts went into the lead and cut out a devilish pace. Lap after lap he pushed the pace, with only Britain's Gordon Pirie hanging on behind him. The 5km was passed in 14-06-8, just a fraction outside the 1952 Olympic 5km record of Zatopek, and shortly after, Kuts raised the tempo even further, demoralising Pirie, who eased up and eventually finished eighth. Kuts kept on and won in the Olympic record time of 28-45-6. The chasing group behind the leaders were Allan Lawrence of Australia, Hungary's Jozsef Kovacs and Britain's Ken Norris. Norris dropped out of the hunt at 8km, while Lawrence and Kovacs steadily pulled back on Kuts. Kovacs took the silver with a last lap surge in 28-52-4 from Lawrence 28-53-6. (Automatic timings: Kuts 28-45-59, Kovacs 28-52-36 and Lawrence 28-53-59).

Veikko Karvonen of Finland was the favourite for the **marathon**, where among the starters were former track rivals Alain Mimoun and Emil Zatopek, the defending champion from Czechoslovakia, who was nursing a hernia operation. For the first time in Olympic history, there was a false start. At 10km, on a very hot day a leading group of 14 was headed by Paavo Kotila of Finland in 33-30-0, but by 20km that was down to six who clocked 68-03-0: Mimoun, Franjo Mihalic of Yugoslavia, Karvonen, Russia's Ivan Filine and Albert Ivanov and John Kelley of America. Just before the turning point, Mimoun broke away from the pack and at

30km in 1:41-47 he had a 72-second lead over Mihalic, Karvonen and Japan's Yoshiaki Kawashima, with Zatopek fifth, nearly a minute further back. At the finish, it was Mimoun in 2:25-00 from Mihalic 2:26-32 and Karvonen 2:27-47.

America's Jack Davis had barely missed winning the **110 metres hurdles** four years previously, and as the current world record holder, he was fully expected to collect a gold medal. In the final, the wind was against the hurdlers as they settled on their blocks and at the gun Lee Calhoun of America, Davis' great rival, rose first, fractionally ahead of Stanko Lorger of Yugoslavia. Half a metre behind was Davis, and Martin Lauer of Germany. At the second flight, Calhoun headed Davis but they came abreast at the fourth hurdle and, locked together, they raced towards the finish. Both men dipped low for the tape in 13-5 sec for an Olympic record, an amazing time against the wind. The photo-finish picture showed Calhoun had won the gold by three-hundredths of a second from Davis, with the USA's Joel Shankle an easy third in 14-1 to complete a clean sweep for America. (Automatic timings: Calhoun 13-70, Davis 13-73 and Shankle 14-25).

One of the principal contenders for the **400 metres hurdles** title was the USA's Eddie Southern, who set an extravagant Olympic record of 50-1 sec in his semi-final, with both Glenn Davis, the world record holder, and Josh Culbreath, of the USA, dipping under 51-0. In the final, the 18-year-old Southern set off at a terrific pace, reaching his fifth hurdle in 22-5 against Davis' 22-7. But coming off the final bend, Davis had a slight lead over Southern with Culbreath, Yuri Lituyev of the USSR and Gerd Potgieter of South Africa a pace behind, contending for the third position. Davis took the gold in 50-1 to equal the Olympic record with Southern taking the silver in 50-8. Meanwhile, approaching the last flight, Potgieter had a metre lead over Culbreath and three

Bobby Morrow

Morrow vied with Vladimir Kuts, the Russian dual gold medallist, for the distinction of being the athlete of the Games in Melbourne in 1956 with a brilliant gold medal "double" in the 100m and 200m sprints and by winning a third gold when he anchored the US team in the 4 × 100m relay. Only Jesse Owens, 20 years before him, had previously been a winner in these three events at the same Olympics.

Bobby Morrow was born in Harlingen, Texas, on 15 October 1935 and shot to the fore of major championship sprinting when, at the age of 20, he won the American national 100 yards in 9·5 sec. The following year he assured his Olympic selection with victories in both the 100m and 200m at the US trials.

At Melbourne he revelled in the tense competition and equalled the Olympic 100m record of 10·3 sec in the second round and again in his semi-final, despite a headwind.

But it was over the 200m he was at his most dominant in Melbourne. Racing away from all his opponents in the home straight he tied the world record of 20·6 sec to win the title. His relay team broke a world record which had stood for 20 years, when covering the 400m circuit in 39·5 sec.

Between 1956 and 1958 Morrow was involved in 14 world record performances.

Bob Richards

Born in Champaign, Illinois, on 20 February 1926, Richards became a Minister in the Church of the Brethren and had an exciting sporting career, pole vaulting towards the heavens.

Nicknamed "The Vaulting Vicar", he was a competitor in the days of the steel pole, when clearing 15 feet was an outstanding international achievement. This he achieved for the first time in 1951, but not before he had won the bronze medal for the event at the Olympics in London and been American champion on three occasions. Further national title wins in 1951 (tied) and 1952 put Richards in fine shape for the Helsinki Games in 1952, where he won the gold with a record clearance only ¾in short of the 15 feet (4,55m).

Melbourne, in 1956, saw him become the first pole vaulter to successfully defend his Olympic title, with a mark just ¼in higher than his clearance in Helsinki four years earlier.

In addition to another four American pole vault title wins from 1954 to 1957, Richards showed his versatility by winning the USA's decathlon title three times. These successes led to his representing the United States for this competition in Melbourne, but he withdrew after nine of the ten events involved.

Christopher Brasher

Britain had three highly competent steeplechasers lined up for the final of the 3,000m event at Melbourne in 1956: John Disley, Eric Shirley and Chris Brasher. Disley was thought to be the most likely of them to win because he was racing faster than when finishing third in Helsinki four years previously. Brasher had never so much as won a national title back home, so it came as a surprise when he romped home a decisive winner in a Games record of 8-41·2.

But sensation was to follow. An official continued to hold a red protest flag at the last water jump. Investigation revealed that the judge considered Brasher was responsible for a foul when making his jump. Then came the shock announcement that he had been disqualified.

Brasher had anxious hours of waiting. With some of the finalists in support he made his case to the Jury, won his argument and finally had the Olympic title restored to him.

Brasher was born in Georgetown, Guyana, on 21 August 1928, and was one of Roger Bannister's pace-makers in the first-ever four-minute mile in 1954. After his athletics career he became a highly successful sports journalist, television broadcaster and Organiser of the London Marathon.

over Lituyev, but fate, or rather the hurdle, hit Potgieter and he tumbled to the ground leaving Culbreath to collect the bronze in 51·6. (Automatic timings: Davis 50·29, Southern 50·94 and Culbreath 51·74).

Sandor Rozsnyoi of Hungary, the world record holder, was most people's favourite for the **3,000 metres steeplechase**. The final saw Ernst Larsen of Norway head the pack, passing the first lap in 65·7 and recording 5-51·0 at 2km, followed by Rozsnyoi, Russia's Semyon Rzhishchin, Eric Shirley and John Disley, both of Britain, Charlie Jones of the USA and Chris Brasher, Britain's third string, in that order. With 350 to go, Rozsnyoi shot into the lead, closely followed by Larsen and Brasher, but coming off the curve, Larsen moved wide of Rozsnyoi, take a hurdle and Brasher, seeing his opportunity, squeezed between them and spurted to the front. Brasher ran hard all the way to win in 8-41·2 for an Olympic record. Rozsnyoi got the upper hand of the Norwegian and finished second in 8-43·6 to Larsen's 8-44·0. Heinz Laufer of Germany was fourth in 8-44·4, while fifth and sixth placed were Rzhischen and Disley, both 8-44·6, and all within the old record. Brasher was initially disqualified for hindering Larsen and Rozsnyoi when he pushed between them, but that evening he was reinstated as the gold medal winner. (Automatic timings: Brasher 8-41·35, Rozsnyoi 8-43·68 and Larsen 8-44·05).

The **20 kilometres walk** was a new event to the Olympic programme, replacing the previous 10km track walk which had been the object of disagreement by the judges as to what was fair walking. Missing from the line-up was Russia's fastest man Mikhail Lavrov, who was concentrating on the 50km walk. Alex Oakley of Canada assumed the lead at the start, but he was soon disqualified and at 5km it was Giuseppe Dordon of Italy, the Britons Stan Vickers and George Coleman, plus the Swedes John Ljunggren and Lars Hindmar who made up the leading group. Virtually the same cluster passed 10km in 45-36·0, but five kilometres further the Russian Antannas Mikenas was in front in 68-27·0, followed at short intervals by Ljunggren and Leonard Spirin of Russia. The Russians came on strong in the latter stages, with Spirin first in 1:31-27·4 from Mikenas 1:32-03·0 and Bruno Junk third with 1:32-12·0, and the medal winners showed their pleasure by kissing each other.

In the **50 kilometres walk**, Grigoriy Klimov of the USSR was the fastest man of the year and therefore the favourite. The race started at a steady pace and after 2km, Norman Read of New Zealand was in the van. At 10km there was a leading group of nine, led by Yevgeriy Maskinskov of the USSR and by the half way point he was over two minutes in advance of his compatriot Mikhail Lavrov in 2:0-38, with Read and Abdon Pamich of Italy close at hand. However, at 40km, Read had reduced Maskinskov's lead to 47 sec, with Klimov, who later collapsed, over six minutes behind. Read went from strength to strength and won handily in 4:30-42·8 from Maskinskov in 4:32-57·0 and the 1948 champion, John Ljunggren of Sweden, in 4:35-02·0.

It was a foregone conclusion that the USA would win the **4 × 100 metres relay**, with the interest centred on whether Germany or the USSR would get the silver medals. In the final, Ira Murchison led off for the USA in the outside lane and passed to Lemon King, with Russia a good metre down. King streaked down the backstraight and fumbled the baton into Thane Baker's hand, which allowed Russia to close up. A fine turn by

In the final of the 800 metres, a good big un, Tom Courtney of the USA, beat a good little un, in Britain's Derek Johnson, but there wasn't much to spare.

After a thrilling 1,500 metres, John Landy (left) the bronze medallist and Ron Delany of Ireland who struck gold, enthuse over their performances.

Baker, but a poor pass to Bobby Morrow, saw Russia and Germany still just behind the Americans. Finally, Morrow made certain of victory with a new world record of 39·5 sec, while the USSR chased them home in 39·8. Germany, with an injured Manfred Germar running, barely held off Italy to take third in 40·3. (Automatic timings: USA 39·60, USSR 39·93 and Germany 40·34).

Australia was the surprise package of the **4 × 400 metres relay**, when they took the silver medal over the traditionally powerful teams from Britain and Germany. The final got underway when an overweight Lou Jones of the USA gained a metre lead over Australia, with Germany third. But in the second leg, Jesse Mashburn barely held off Australia's David Lean, who came up on his shoulder, while Britain moved into third place. Eventually, Charlie Jenkins of the USA put matters beyond doubt with a 45·5 third lap and Tom Courtney powered the anchor leg in 45·8 to give America victory with 3-04·8, from Australia's 3-06·2 and Britain's 3-07·2. (Automatic timings: USA 3-04·81, Australia 3-06·19 and Britain 3-07·19).

Men's Field Events

Commencing at 10.0 am in the morning, the **high jump** finished nearly ten hours later. Ten of 31 entries cleared 2,00 metres and four proceeded beyond the Olympic record of 2,06 to 2,08. Charles Dumas of the USA and Igor Kachkarov of the USSR surmounted the bar first time, while Australia's Chilla Porter needed two attempts to succeed. Sig Pettersson of Sweden failed all his trys and bowed out in fourth place. The bar now went up to 2,10 and Dumas got over at his second attempt and Porter at his third, leaving Kachkarov with the bronze medal. Up again to 2,12, and Dumas skimmed over on his third attempt to win the gold. He had one try at 2,14 but it was past 10.30 pm and he finally bowed out.

The Rev Bob Richards of the USA, the defending champion, was up against his keenest rival in the **pole vault**, compatriot Bob Gutowski. At 4,25 metres eight vaulters cleared, but half of them failed to achieve an additional ten centimetres. The four remaining were Richards, Gutowski and George Mattos, all representing USA and Georgios Roubanis of Greece. After Mattos failed at 4,40, the other three cleared 4,50, but at 4,53 Roubanis found it too much and settled for the bronze. The medal positions were resolved when Richards cleared 4,56 on his second attempt to break his own Olympic record and Gutowski, who was an inch away, settled for the silver.

Greg Bell of the USA was tipped to win the **long jump**, as his two main rivals were not competing: Ernie Shelby of the USA did not make the team and Henk Visser of Holland was absent because his country declined to compete. Conditions for the competition were bad, as strong and gusty winds blew in the face of the jumpers. In the first round of the final, John Bennett of the USA led with 7,68 metres, with Dmitriy Bondarenko of the USSR lying second at 7,44. Bell then produced a fine leap, for the conditions, of 7,83 in the next round, which ultimately proved to be the gold medal jump. Bennett's first round 7,68 took the silver, while Jorma Valkama of Finland collected the bronze with 7,48.

In the first round of the finals of the **triple jump**, Bill Sharpe of the USA took the lead with a leap of 15,88 metres, but in the next round the fireworks really started

when the muscular Vilhjalmur Einarsson of Iceland hopped, stepped and jumped 16,22 for a new Olympic record. On his third jump, Vitold Kreer of the USSR improved to 16,02, but Adhemar Ferreira da Silva of Brazil, the defending champion and world record holder, was building up to something special for his fourth trial, and when he landed at 16,35 to improve the Games' record, it was good enough for the gold. Einarsson took the silver with 16,26 and Kreer the bronze with 16,02.

Parry O'Brien of the USA was king of the **shot put** circle; he was the reigning Olympic champion and had put the world record out of reach of anyone else. O'Brien led off in the first round with a new Olympic record of 17,92 metres. In fact, every one of his six puts exceeded the old record and he improved to 18,47 and finally to 18,57, when winning the gold medal. Behind him, the USA's Bill Nieder reached 18,18 for the silver position while Jiri Skobla of Czechoslovakia, the top shot putter in Europe, threw 17,65 for the bronze.

Expectations of a tremendous battle in the **discus throw**ing competition between the world record holder, Fortune Gordien of the USA and the legendary Adolfo Consolini of Italy did not materialise, despite big practice throws of 60 and 59 metres respectively. Consolini threw below par and Gordien was usurped by one of his fellow countrymen. It all happened in the first round, when after Gordien had thrown 54,75 metres, young Al Oerter sent a beautiful throw out to 56,36 for an Olympic record and the gold. Gordien tried to respond, but could only reach 54,81 on his last throw, for the silver medal. Mark Pharoah of Britain was lying third at one stage, but Des Koch made it a clean sweep for the USA by taking the bronze.

The **hammer throw**ing world record had become a shuttlecock during 1956 between Mikhail Krivonossov of the USSR and Hal Connolly of the USA. Connolly had a withered left arm caused by fractures while engaged in football and wrestling, and he often claimed that it helped him to wrap his arm across his chest when throwing. Anatoliy Samotsvetov of the USSR led in the first round with 62,10 metres from Krivonossov at 60,59, both throws being better than the record, while their countryman Dmitriy Egorov reached 60,22. In the second round Krivonossov improved the record again to 63,00, while Al Hall of the USA slipped into third position with 61,83. Connolly finally struck gold in the fifth round, with yet another Games record of 63,19 and in the last round Samotsvetov achieved 62,56. Result: Connolly 63,19 for gold, Krivonossov 63,03 for silver and Samotsvetov 62,56 for bronze.

Two on-form former world record holders for the **javelin throw** were not at Melbourne: the USA's Bud Held, who came fourth by one inch at his national trials, and Soini Nikkinen of Finland, because the Finns were sending no javelin men to the Games. In 1953, Bud Held's brother had developed the thicker aerodynamic javelin and the new style steel Seefab implements were in use at Melbourne. In the preliminaries, the Games record was beaten by three throwers: Vladimir Kouznetsov of the USSR 73,90, Norway's Egil Danielsen at 74,04 and the USA's Cy Young with 74,76. During the competition proper, the record was constantly being improved, and in the first round Germany's Herbert Koschel threw 74,68, while Viktor Tsiboulenko of the USSR achieved 74,96 and improved to 75,84 in the next round. In round three, one of the favourites, Janusz Sidlo of Poland, sailed one out to

79,98 to take the lead, but the surprise came in the fifth round as Danielsen arced his javelin into the wind and it seemed to sail on and on, eventually coming to earth at 85,71, a new world record and the gold medal. Tsiboulenko responded to this with 79,50, which brought him the bronze behind Sidlo's silver medal throw of 79,98.

It was an injured Rafer Johnson, the USA's world record holder, who faced up to fellow American Mit Campbell, the silver medallist from Helsinki, and the European champion, Vasiliy Kouznetsov of the USSR in the **decathlon**. Campbell led throughout the competition and scored an Olympic record of 7,937 points, just 43 points shy of Johnson's world best and if his 3,40 metres pole vault had been better he would have taken that record as well. His 110 hurdles of 14·0 sec was superb and would have placed him third in the individual event. His marks were 100m in 10·8 sec; long jump 7,33 metres; shot, 14,76 metres; high jump, 1,89 metres; 400m in 48·8 sec; 110m hurdles in 14·0 sec; discus, 44,98 metres pole vault, 3,40 metres; javelin, 57,08 metres; and 1,500m in 4-50·6. Johnson strained a stomach muscle in the long jump, but still managed to hold second from start to finish and score 7,587 points to beat Kouznetsov, who was third all the way through and totalled 7,465 points.

Women's Events

There were a host of good sprinters in the **100 metres**, but it came as a surprise in the heats when 18-year-old Betty Cuthbert of Australia set a new Olympic record of 11·4 sec against the wind. Christa Stubnick of Germany won the first semi-final in 11·9 from Cuthbert, while in the second, Marlene Matthews of Australia beat Heather Armitage of Britain, both recording 11·6. In the final, the girls got away to a good start and again racing into the wind, the powerful Cuthbert won in 11·5 from Stubnick second and Matthews third, both timed at 11·7. (Automatic timings: Cuthbert 11·82, Stubnick 11·92 and Matthews 11·94).

Betty Cuthbert of Australia, the world record holder, was again a force in the **200 metres**, as she set an Olympic record of 23·5 sec in her heat, while June Paul of Britain did 23·8 in hers and Christa Stubnick of Germany ran 23·9 in the semi-finals. After one false start in the final, the sprinters were evenly matched around the bend, but coming into the straight Cuthbert drove powerfully along to win in 23·4 and break the Games record yet again. Stubnick fought off Marlene Matthews of Australia to win the silver medal in 23·7 to 23·8. (Automatic timings: Cuthbert 23·55, Stubnick 23·89 and Matthews 24·10).

Conditions in the **80 metres hurdles** were variable, with the wind sometimes blowing with and sometimes against the runners. Centa Gastl of Germany had come to the Games with a world record of 10·6 sec, but after equalling the Olympic record in her heat she was eliminated in the semi-finals. Shirley Strickland (de la Hunty) was the defending champion and twice in the preliminaries she ran 10·8 against the wind to better her Games record. In the final, the wind was blowing against the runners, but Strickland made a perfect start and was half a metre ahead at the first hurdle. She increased her lead, hurdle by hurdle, and won in 10·7 for a new Games record. Gisela Kohler of Germany hurdled well to come second in 10·9 with Norma Thrower of Australia third at 11·0 (Automatic timings: Strickland 10·96, Kohler 11·12 and Thrower 11·25).

Leading up to the Games, the USSR, Britain and Germany had each in turn improved the world record for the **4 × 100 metres relay**. In the first heat Australia inched out Germany, both being credited with a world best of 44·9, while in the second heat Britain beat the USA 45·3 to 45·4. Over the first leg of the final, Anne Pashley for Britain commanded a lead which was maintained by the next two runners, Jean Scrivens and June Paul. Heather Armitage was Britain's last runner, but with 50 metres to go Betty Cuthbert went by her at a devilish speed to win for Australia in 44·5, a new world record. The Australian team was Shirley Strickland, Norma Crocker, Fleur Mellor and Cuthbert. Britain took the silver medals in 44·7 and the USA the bronze with 44·9, while Germany muffed the baton changes to finish sixth. (Automatic timings: Australia 44·65, Britain 44;70 and USA 45·04).

In the **high jump**, Iolanda Balas of Rumania came to the Games as the 1,75 metres world record holder, but went away fifth, and without her record. The girl who

Adhemar Ferreira da Silva

Adhemar Ferreira da Silva, born at São Paulo on 29 September 1927, was the man to awaken the enthusiasm of the Brazilian public to the pleasures of international athletics. Aided by a German coach, Dietrich Gerner, he became his country's super hero when he won Brazil's first ever Olympic athletics gold medal in the triple jump at the 1952 Helsinki Games, with a world record clearance of 53ft 2½in (16,22m).

Not that Brazil expected any other result from their talented jumper. In the two years prior to Helsinki he had twice exceeded the world record and during the Games he bettered his previous best figures four times.

The greatest of all his world marks came in 1955 when he reached what was then an incredible distance of 54ft 4in (16,56m), which gave his confidence another boost as he prepared for the defence of his crown in Melbourne.

Competition there was keener than ever, yet Da Silva rose magnificently to the challenge, particularly that of Iceland's Vilhjalmur Einarsson. After the Icelander had taken a second round lead, he produced a winning mark of 53ft 7½in (16,35m) which added five inches to his previous Olympic record.

The Brazilian went in search of honours again in the 1960 Rome Games, but could only finish in 14th position.

upset the form book was Mildred McDaniel of the USA, who cleared the bar at 1,70 with the straddle technique at her second attempt to win the Olympic gold. She then requested the bar be raised to the world record height of 1,76, which she again surmounted on her second try. Not satisfied with this she asked for the bar to be raised to 1,80, but this proved a little beyond her capabilities. There were six other jumpers who had cleared the bar at 1,67 and after the judges had deliberated over the count-back rule both Thelma Hopkins of Britain and Maria Pissareva of the USSR each received a silver medal.

Elzbieta Krzesinska of Poland, the world record holder, dominated the **long jump** competition. She led the qualifers with 6,13 metres and in the finals jumped 6,20 with her first attempt. And then on her second, leapt an enormous 6,35 to equal her own world record and collect the gold. The Russian Nadyezhda Dvalishvili was in second position with 6,00 for two rounds, until Willye White of the USA cleared 6,06 to overtake her. Dvalishvili responded in the fifth round with 6,07, but White gave it all she had on her last jump and took the silver with 6,09, to leave the Russian in third place.

Galina Zybina of the USSR, the world record holder for the **shot put**, was a big strong girl, but nothing like her compatriot, Tamara Tychkevitch, who weighed nearly 17½ stone (111·5kg). Zybina opened her account in the finals with a 16,36 metres Olympic record which she subsequently extended to 16,53, while Tychkevitch left it to her last put to explode to a personal best of

16,59 and win the gold medal. Meanwhile, there was a duel going on for third place between Marianne Werner of Germany and Sianaida Doinikova of the USSR. Werner finally won the bronze with a throw of 15,61.

Nina Ponomaryeva of the USSR was the defending champion for the **discus throw**, but her compatriot and great rival, Nina Dumbadze, was not at Melbourne. Another Russian, Irina Begliakova led the competition with a new Olympic record of 51,74 metres after the first round, being closely followed by Ponomaryeva with 51,03. Later, Begliakova increased her lead to 52,54, but Olga Fikotova of Czechosolvakia moved into second place with 52,04 and then threw 52,28, followed by a mighty 53,69 to take the crown, and Olympic record. Begliakova could not do better than her 52,54 for the silver, while Ponomaryeva finished with 52,02 for the bronze.

The **javelin throw** was considered to be a contest between the defending champion, Dana Zatopkova of Czechoslovakia and the Russians. The on-form Russian was Inese Jaunzeme whose very first throw in the final settled matters with an Olympic record of 51,63 metres. This she improved to 53,40 in the fourth round and to 53,86 in the last to win the Olympic title. While this was happening, there was a fierce contest in progress for the lesser medals between the world record holder, Nadyshda Koniaeva, Zatopkova, Marlene Ahrens of Chile and Ingrid Almqvist of Sweden. Almqvist first threw 49,74 only to be overtaken by Zatopkova with 49,83, then Koniaeva with 50,28 and finally Ahrens with the silver medal winning throw of 50,38.

All-Sport Photographic Ltd.

Harold Connolly

Harold Connolly will be best remembered not only for his winning the hammer throwing title at the Melbourne Olympics in 1956 but also for winning the heart of Olga Fikotova, the Czech discus thrower who also won a gold medal there. Their romance fascinated the world, largely because of the cold war being particularly fierce at a time when they were keen to be married. In 1957, however, the Czech authorities finally relented and the wedding took place in Prague with Emil Zatopek, Czechoslovakian four-times Olympic champion, being their best man.

Connolly, born in 1931, tried his luck at hammer throwing at college when he realised he was too short to become a successful shot-putter. With help from German coaches he made rapid progress and in 1955 became the first American to land the missile beyond 200ft (60,96m). A year later he was not only winning the Olympic title with a Games record 207ft 3½in (63,19m), but making the first of his seven world record throws. He ceased competing after landing the hammer at 233ft 9½in (71,26m) in 1965, but only for a spell. Neither he, nor his wife, could resist the opportunity to come back for their fourth Olympics in Mexico City and said, that going to the Games was like having a honeymoon all over again.

Milt Campbell failed to make the American team in the high hurdles, but made amends by winning the Olympic decathlon with ease.

MALES

COMPETITOR	COUNTRY CODE	EVENT	ROUND	HEAT	PLACE	TIME & DISTANCE	MEDAL
Achurch, J.D.	AUS	Javelin throw	Q		DNQ		
Agostini, M.	TRI	100m	1	2	1	10.98	
			2	1	2	10.75	
			SF	1	2	10.79	
			F		6	10.88	
		200m	1	3	1	21.80	
			2	1	2	21.35	
			SF	2	2	21.48	
			F		4	21.35	
Ahlund, G.R.	SWE	5000m	1	1	7	15-12.0	
		10000m	F		19		
Ahmad, A.R.B.	MAL	400m	1	7	5	50.93	
Ahumada, R.	MEX	100m	1	1	5	11.26	
		200m	1	1	3	21.96	
Ajado, E.A.	NGR	100m	1	11	1	11.01	
			2	3	5	11.02	
		4×100m relay	1	4	DIS		
Akagi, K.	JPN	200m	1	6	1	22.26	
			2	2	5	21.9	
		400m	1	1	DIS		
		4×100m relay	1	4	3	42.30	
			SF	2	6	41.57	
		4×400m relay	1	2	4	3-13.75	
Alard, P.	FRA	Discus throw	Q		DNQ		
Allday, P.	GBR	Hammer throw	F		9	58,00	
Allsopp, E.	AUS	20k walk	F		10	1:35-43-0	
		50k walk	F		DIS		
Amu, A.K.O.	NGR	400m	1	3	5	49.57	
		4×100m relay	1	4	DIS		
Anentia, A.	KEN	5000m	1	1	6	14-37.30	
Anthony, D.W.J.	GBR	Hammer throw	F		12	56,72	
Aparicio, J.	COL	400m	1	2	5	49.14	
		400m hurdles	1	3	3	52.14	
		4×400m relay	1	2	6	3-27.4	
Ashenfelter, H.	USA	3000m steeplechase	1	1	6	8-51.12	
Aslam, M.	PAK	Marathon	F		22	2:44-33.0	
Asplund, K.B.	SWE	Hammer throw	Q		DNQ		
Auer, I.K.	FIN	3000m steeplechase	1	2	7	9-04.57	
Ayub, M.	PAK	Discus throw	Q		DNQ		
Aziz, A.	PAK	200m	1	9	5	22.98	
		4×100m relay	1	1	3	41.42	
			SF	2	5	40.78	
Azlam, Bna-R.	MAL	100m	1	1	6	11.41	
Baghbanbashi, A.	IRN	Marathon	F		DNF		
Bailey, J.J.	AUS	800m	1	3	1	1-51.13	
			SF	2	7	1-51.40	
Baker, W.T.	USA	100m	1	9	1	10.93	
			2	4	1	10.62	
			SF	2	2	10.61	
			F		2	10.77	S
		200m	1	7	1	21.92	
			2	3	1	21.34	
			SF	1	1	21.21	
			F		3	21.05	B
		4×100m relay	1	1	1	40.53	
			SF	1	1	40.34	
			F		1	39.60	G
Baliaev, B.	URS	Shot put	F		5	16,96	
Ballieux, A.	BEL	1500m	1	1	6	3-49.94	
Balodis, V.	AUS	Discus throw	Q		DNQ		
Bantum, K.O.	USA	Shot put	F		4	17,48	
Baraldi, G.	ITA	800m	1	4	4	1:51.90	
		1500m	1	3	6	3-52.20	
Baranowski, Z.	PCL	4×100m relay	1	4	1	40.97	
			SF	1	2	41.12	
			F		6	40.75	
Barbu, I.	RUM	20k walk	F		15	1:41-37-8	
		50k walk	F		10	5:08-33-6	
Barnard, J.H.	SAF	Marathon	F		DNF		
Baronda, C.	PHI	High jump	F		17	1,92	
Bartenev, L.	URS	100m	1	7	1	10.87	
			2	4	4	10.84	
		200m	1	12	2	21.94	
			2	1	4	21.53	
		4×100m relay	1	3	1	40.77	
			SF	2	1	40.36	
			F		2	39.93	S
Barthel, J.	LUX	1500m	1	1	9	3-50.64	
Battista, E.	FRA	Triple jump	F		16	15,15	
Beckert, L.	GER	Marathon	F		19	2:42-10-0	
Bell, G.C.	USA	Long jump	F		1	7,83	G
Bennett, J.D.	USA	Long jump	F		2	7,68	S
Bernard, J.C.	FRA	110m hurdles	1	2	3	14.88	
			SF	2	6	14.78	

COMPETITOR	COUNTRY CODE	EVENT	ROUND	HEAT	PLACE	TIME & DISTANCE	MEDAL
Bayene, A.	ETH	400m	1	8	5	51.53	
		800m	1	3	8		
		4×400m relay	1	3	5	3-29.93	
Birkay, G.	ETH	Marathon	F		32	2:58-49-0	
Blackney, R.L.	AUS	3000m steeplechase	1	2	10	9-16-0	
Boit, K.	AUS	400m	1	4	3	49.98	
			2	4	6	49.18	
		4×400m relay	1	3	4	3-17-68	
Bolotnikov, P.	URS	5000m	1	1	4	14-28.17	
			F		9	14-22.63	
		10000m	F		16		
Bonas, C.	VEN	100m	1	7	4	10.99	
		4×100m relay	1	1	4	42.10	
Bondarenko, D.	URS	Long jump	F		4	7,44	
Bonino, R.	FRA	100m	1	8	2	10.96	
			2	4	5	10.96	
		4×100m relay	1	2	2	40.99	
			SF	1	4	41.37	
Boukhantsov, K.	URS	Discus throw	F		12	48,58	
Boulatov, V.	URS	Pole vault	F		9	4,15	
Bowden, D.P.	USA	1500m	1	2	11	4-00-0	
Box, K.J.	GBR	100m	1	4	2	10.96	
			2	3	6	11.45	
		4×100m relay	1	1	2	41.30	
			SF	2	3	40.68	
			F		5	40.74	
Boyd, I.H.	GBR	1500m	1	1	3	3-47.13	
			F		8	3-42.94	
Boysen, A.	NOR	800m	1	1	1	1-52.08	
			SF	2	2	1-50.20	
			F		3	1-48.25	B
Brasher, C.W.	GBR	3000m steeplechase	1	2	4	8-54.19	
			F		1	8-41.35*	G
Bruce, I.B.	AUS	Long jump	Q		DNQ		
		Decathlon	F		11	6,025	
Bruno, A.	Ven	4×100m relay	1	1	4	42.10	
Bumroongpruck, M.	THA	200m	1	3	6	24.59	
Burger, M.D.	SAF	110m hurdles	1	3	3	14.59	
			SF	1	6	14.95	
Butchart, B.E.	AUS	800m	1	4	3	1-51.67	
			SF	1	4	1-53.81	
			F		8		
Calhoun, L.Q.	USA	110m hurdles	1	2	1	14.36	
			SF	2	1	14.18	
			F		1	13.70*	G
Cambadelis, J.	GRE	110m hurdles	1	4	5	15.28	
		400m hurdles	1	4	2	53.66	
			SF	2	6	53.93	
Campbell, M.	USA	Decathlon	F		1	7,937*	G
Camus, Y.	FRA	200m	1	12	3	22.37	
Cann, J.	AUS	Decathlon	F		10	6,278	
Carr, G.A.	GBR	Discus throw	F		10	50,72	
Carragher, C.	AUS	100m	1	7	3	10.98	
		4×100m relay	1	2	1	40.72	
			SF	2	4	40.72	
Chandra, M.H.	MAL	800m	1	2	7	1-56.27	
Chataway, C.J.	GBR	5000m	1	3	5	14-32.87	
			F		11	14-28.63	
Cherbakov, L.	URS	Triple jump	F		6	15,80	
Cherniavskiy, I.	URS	5000m	1	3	3	14-32.49	
			F		10	14-22.67	
		10000m	F		6	29-31-6	
Chiesa, G.	ITA	Pole vault	F		9	4,15	
Chigbolu, J.O.	NGR	High jump	F		9	2,00	
Chittick, J.	AUS	110m hurdles	1	2	5	15.18	
Choi, C.S.	KOR	Marathon	F		12	2:36-53-0	
Choi, Y.K.	KOR	Triple jump	F		21	14,65	
Chromik, J.	POL	5000m	1	3	7	14-51.4	
Clark, R.S.	GBR	Marathon	F		DNF		
Clement, D.B.	CAN	800m	1	2	8	1-56.92	
		4×400m relay	1	1	1	3-10.59	
			F		5	3-10.33	
Cockburn, M.	CAN	400m	1	1	2	49.07	
			2	2	6	49.74	
		4×400m relay	1	1	1	3-10.59	
			F		5	3-10.33	
Colarossi, M.	ITA	100m	1	1	4	11.14	
Coleman, G.W.	GBR	20k walk	F		7	1:34-01-8	
Coleman, P.Y.	USA	3000m steeplechase	1	2	9	9-10-0	
Conley, P.R.	USA	Javelin throw	F		10	69,74	
Connolly, H.V.	USA	Hammer throw	F		1	63,19*	G
Consolini, A.	ITA	Discus throw	F		6	52,21	
Costes, N.	USA	Marathon	F		20	2:42-20-0	

COMPETITOR	COUNTRY CODE	EVENT	ROUND	HEAT	PLACE	TIME & DISTANCE	MEDAL
Courtney, T.W.	USA	800m	1	2	1	1-52·83	
			SF	1	1	1-53·62	
			F		1	1-47·75*	G
		4×400m relay	1	1	2	3-10·80	
			F		1	3-04·81	G
Crawford, R.	AUS	20k walk	F		13	1 39-35·0	
		50k walk	F		13	5 22-35·0	
Crowe, M.F.	AUS	Hammer throw	Q		DNQ		
Cruttenden, A.R.	GBR	Long jump	F		9	7·15	
Cruz, R.	PUR	Pole vault	Q		DNQ		
Csanyi, G.	HUN	4×100m relay	1	4	2	41·45	
			SF	1	5	41·51	
Csermak, J.	HUN	Hammer throw	F		5	60 70	
Culbreath, J.	USA	400m hurdles	1	3	1	51 06	
			SF	2	1	50 97	
			F		3	51·74	B
Cullen, P.S.	GBR	Javelin throw	Q		DNQ		
Cury, G.	FRA	400m hurdles	1	3	2	51·76	
			SF	1	4	51·66	
Da Conceicao, J.T.	BRA	200m	1	1	1	21·61	
			2	2	3	21·46	
			SF	1	3	21·53	
			F		6	21·56	
		4×100m relay	1	3	3	41·70	
			SF	1	6	43·87	
Danielsen, E.	NOR	Javelin throw	F		1	85,71*	G
D'Asnach, S.	ITA	200m	1	4	2	22·35	
			2	3	6	22·82	
David, A.	FRA	100m	1	6	4	11·24	
		4×100m relay	1	2	2	40·99	
			SF	1	4	41·37	
Da Sa, A.F.	BRA	4×100m relay	1	3	3	41·70	
			SF	1	6	43·87	
		Long jump	Q		DNQ	7,15	
Da Silva, A.F.	BRA	Triple jump	F		1	16,35*	G
Davies, M.J.	SAF	Marathon	F		14	2:39-48·0	
Davis, G.A.	USA	400m hurdles	1	1	1	51·33	
			SF	1	2	50·78	
			F		1	50·29	G
Davis, I.S.	USA	Triple jump	F		11	15,40	
Davis, J.W.	USA	100m hurdles	1	1	1	14·17	
			SF	1	1	14·28	
			F		2	13·73	S
De Barros, J.M.	BRA	100m	1	2	4	11·15	
		200m	1	6	2	22·30	
			2	4	5	23·88	
		4×100m relay	1	3	3	41·70	
			SF	1	6	43·87	
Degats, J.	FRA	400m	1	2	2	48·32	
			2	2	5	48·79	
		4×400m relay	1	2	3	3-11·76	
De Jesus, O.	PUR	400m hurdles	1	1	4	54·08	
		4×400m relay	1	2	5	3-13·81	
Delany, R.M.	IRL	1500m	1	2	3	3-47·48	
			F		1	3-41·49*	G
Delecour, J.	FRA	4×100m relay	1	2	2	40 99	
			SF	1	4	41 37	
Delgado, I.	PUR	4×400m relay	1	2	5	3-13·81	
Dellinger, W.S.	USA	5000m	1	1	3	14-26·92	
			F		DNF		
Denman. E.	USA	50k walk	F		11	5 12-14·0	
Denton, P.L.	AUS	Pole vault	Q		DNQ		
Depastas, E.	GRE	800m	1	2	3	1-53·23	
			SF	2	8	1-52·19	
		1500m	1	2	7	3-51·79	
Diaz, A.	CHI	Hammer throw	Q		DNQ		
Disley, J.I.	GBR	3000 steeplechase	1	1	2	8-46·93	
			F		6	8-44·79	
Ditta, A.	PAK	Pole vault	Q		DNQ		
Djian, R.	FRA	800m	1	5	2	1-51 15	
			SF	2	6	1-50 47	
Dohrow, G.	GER	800m	1	3	6	1-53·90	
		1500m	1	2	9	3-58·0	
Dolezal, J.	TCH	20k walk	F		DIS		
		50k walk	F		DNF		
Donath, B.W.	AUS	Shot put	F		9	16,52	
Donazar, F.	URU	Long jump	F		12	6·57	
Dordoni, G.	ITA	20k walk	F		9	1:35-00·4	
dos Santos, L.	BRA	400m hurdles	1	6	4	53·99	
Doubleday, K.L.	AUS	110m hurdles	1	1	5	14·98	
Dumas, C.E.	USA	High jump	F		1	2,12*	G
Du Plessis, S.J.	SAF	Discus throw	F		13	48,49	
Egorov, D.	URS	Hammer throw	F		7	60,22	
Einarsson, V.	ISL	Triple jump	F		2	16,26	S
Engo, P.B.	NGR	Triple jump	F		17	15,03	
Ericsson, I.A.H.	SWE	1500m	1	2	5	3-49·20	

COMPETITOR	COUNTRY CODE	EVENT	ROUND	HEAT	PLACE	TIME & DISTANCE	MEDAL
Erinle, T.A.	NGR	100m	1	2	3	11·09	
		4×100m relay	1	4	DIS		
Esiri P.	NGR	Triple jump	F		DNQ		
Estick, R.C.	JAM	200m	1	12	5	25·81	
Etnirveera-singam, N.	CEY	High jump	F		21	1,86	
Etolu, P.	UGA	High jump	F		12	1,96	
Farahi, N.-R.	IRN	Decathlon	F		12	5,103	
Farrell, M.A.	GBR	800m	1	2	2	1-52·86	
			SF	1	3	1-53·78	
			F		5	1-49·29	
Farrell, T.S.	GBR	400m hurdles	1	3	4	52·88	
Fedosseev, O.	URS	Long jump	F		8	7,27	
Fereke, B.	ETH	Marathon	F		29	2:53-37·0	
Filine, I.	URS	Marathon	F		7	2:30-37·0	
Foik, M.	POL	100m	1	5	1	10·74	
			2	4	3	10·83	
			SF	2	5	10·84	
		4×100m relay	1	4	1	40·97	
			SF	1	2	41·12	
			F		6	40·75	
Foldessy, O.	HUN	Long jump	Q		DNQ		
Fontecilla, E.	CHI	800m	1	3	5	1-52·94	
		1500m	1	3	10	3-58·45	
		Marathon	F		DNF		
		3000m steeplechase	1	2	DNF		
Foreman, J.F.	CAN	200m	1	8	4	22·28	
		4×100m relay	1	3	4	41·75	
Fournier, M.	FRA	High jump	F		11	1,96	
Francis, A.	PUR	400m hurdles	1	4	3	54·38	
Futterer, H.	GER	100m	1	10	2	11·10	
			2	1	5	10·99	
		4×100m relay	1	2	3	41·00	
			SF	2	2	40·64	
			F		3	40·34	B
Gabriel, V.I.	NGR	High jump	F		19	1,92	
Gabuh, B.P.	NGR	Triple jump	Q		DNQ		
Gadsden, N.E.	AUS	Hammer throw	Q		DNQ		
Galtiati, F.	ITA	100m	1	5	3	11·00	
		4×100m relay	1	3	2	41·07	
			SF	1	3	41·14	
			F		4	40·43	
Garcia, B.B.	USA	Javelin throw	F				
Gardner, K.A. St.H.	JAM	100m	1	6	3	11·22	
		110m hurdles	1	3	5	14·65	
		4×400m relay	1	3	2	3-11·07	
			F		DIS		
Germar, M.	GER	100m	1	6	1	10·91	
			2	4	2	10·80	
			SF	1	3	10·85	
			F		5	10·86	
		200m	1	1	2	21·88	
		4×100m relay	1	2	3	41·00	
			SF	2	2	40·64	
			F		3	40·34	B
Ghiselli, G.	ITA	200m	1	7	5	22·68	
		4×100m relay	1	3	2	41·07	
			SF	1	3	41·14	
			F		4	40·43	
Gipson, G.C.	AUS	200m	1	9	3	22·06	
		400m	1	5	2	47·87	
			2	2	4	47·45	
		4×400m relay	1	2	2	3-10·57	
			F		2	3-06·19	S
Gnocchi, L.	ITA	100m	1	2	2	11·04	
			2	2	4	10·96	
		4×100m relay	1	3	2	41·07	
			SF	1	3	41·14	
			F		4	40·43	
Goddard, J.	TRI	100m	1	10	4	11·19	
		200m	1	10	5	22·23	
Goldovanyi, B.	HUN	100m	1	7	2	10·88	
			2	1	4	10·95	
		200m	1	7	2	22·08	
			2	1	5	21·64	
		4×100m relay	1	4	2	41·45	
			SF	1	5	41·51	
Goodacre, G.C.	AUS	400m hurdles	1	2	3	52·58	
Goodman, J.W.	AUS	400m	1	8	4	48·73	
Gorchkov. A.	URS	Javelin throw	F		8	70,32	
Gordien, F.E.	USA	Discus throw	F		2	54,81	S
Gosal, J.E.W.	INA	100m	1	5	5	11·09	
Gosper R.K.	AUS	400m	1	7	1	48·07	
			2	4	1	46·83	
			SF	2	4	46·45	
		4×400m relay	1	2	2	3-10·57	
			F		2	3-06·19	S

COMPETITOR	COUNTRY CODE	EVENT	ROUND	HEAT	PLACE	TIME & DISTANCE	MEDAL
Goudeau, J.-P.	FRA	200m	1	1	=4	22·13	
		4×400m relay	1	2	3	3-11·76	
Grabowski, H.	POL	Long jump	F		10	7,15	
Grant, R.J.	AUS	Javelin throw	Q		DNQ		
Gratchev, K.	URS	400m	1	1	4	49·58	
		4×400m relay	1	3	3	3-11·27	
Gray, R.	AUS	Triple jump	Q		DNQ		
Gregory, L.S.	AUS	4×400m relay	1	2	2	3-10·57	
			F		2	3-06·19	S
Grichaev, B.	URS	Marathon	F		DNF		
Grigalka, O.	URS	Discus throw	F		5	52,37	
Gruber, A.	AUT	Marathon	F		23	2:46-20·0	
Gutowski, R.	USA	Pole vault	F		2	4,53	S
Haarhoff, P.	FRA	400m	1	6	3	49·99	
			2	3	4	47·82	
		4×400m relay	1	2	3	3-11·76	
Haas, K.F.	GER	200m	1	2	1	21·56	
			2	3	3	21·68	
			SF	1	5	21·74	
		400m	1	5	1	47·29	
			2	4	2	47·37	
			SF	2	3	46·29	
			F		2	47·12	S
		4×400m relay	1	2	1	3-09·88	
			F		4	3-08·27	
Haddad, H.	CHI	Discus throw	F		16	46,00	
Haile, B.	ETH	4×100m relay	1	3	5	44·47	
Hailu, A.	ETH	100m	1	11	5	11·54	
		200m	1	7	6	23·25	
		400m	1	3	4	49·18	
		4×100m relay	1	3	5	44·47	
		4×400m relay	1	3	5	3-29·93	
Haisley, E.L.O.	JAM	High jump	F		15	1,96	
Halberg, M.G.	NZL	1500m	1	1	4	3-47·39	
			F		11	3-46·09	
Hall, A.N.	USA	Hammer throw	F		4	61,96	
Hall, E.W.	GBR	50k walk	F		9	5:03-59·0	
Hamamura, H.	JPN	Marathon	F		16	2:40-53·0	
Hammer, F.	LUX	200m	1	4	4	23·14	
		Long jump	Q		DNQ		
Hanlin, R.P.	AUS	Shot put	F		11	16,08	
Harding, R.R.	CAN	100m	1	11	3	11·20	
		4×100m relay	1	3	4	41·70	
Hardy, R.	GBR	20k walk	F		8	1:34-40·4	
Hart, R.L.	USA	10000m	F		21		
Hartung, K.	GER	Marathon	F		28	2:52-14·0	
Hellsten, V.V.	FIN	400m	1	4	1	48·52	
			2	3	1	46·85	
			SF	2	2	46·20	
			F		=3	47·15	B
		4×400m relay	1	1	4	3-11·52	
		10000m	F		14		
Herman, F.	BEL	3000m steeplechase	1	1	DNF		
Herrman, S.	GER	1500m	1	3	DNF		
Herssens, W.	BEL	Triple jump	Q		DNQ		
		Decathlon	F		DNF		
Hewson, B.S.	GBR	1500m	1	3	2	3-48·10	
			F		5	3-42·69	
Hewson, J.E.	USA	20k walk	F		17	1:46-24·8	
Hicks, H.J.	GBR	Marathon	F		15	2:39-55·0	
Higgins, F.P.	GBR	400m	1	8	1	47·98	
			2	2	3	47·43	
			SF	1	5	47·65	
		4×400m relay	1	3	1	3-08·76	
			F		3	3-07·19	B
Hildreth, P.B.	GBR	110m hurdles	1	4	4	14·68	
Hindmar, L.E.	SWE	20k walk	F		DIS		
Hiroshima, K.	JPN	Marathon	F		33	3:04-17·0	
Hogan, H.D.	AUS	100m	1	8	1	10·72	
			2	3	1	10·78	
			SF	2	3	10·62	
			F		3	10·77	B
		200m	1	8	2	21·97	
			2	3	4	21·90	
		4×100m relay	1	2	1	40·72	
			SF	2	4	40·72	
Hunter, O.S.	GUY	100m	1	10	5	11·22	
		200m	1	7	4	22·54	
Husson, G.	FRA	Hammer throw	F		13	55,02	
Ibbotson, G.D.	GBR	5000m	1	2	4	14-18·78	
			F		3	13-54·60	B
Iglesias, E.	CUB	100m	1	3	5	11·50	
		110m hurdles	1	4	2	14·52	
			SF	1	3	14·73	

COMPETITOR	COUNTRY CODE	EVENT	ROUND	HEAT	PLACE	TIME & DISTANCE	MEDAL
Ignatiev, A.	URS	400m	1	6	1	48·69	
			2	2	1	46·88	
			SF	1	1	46·93	
			F		=3	47·15	B
		4×400m relay	1	3	3	3-11·27	
Iqbal, M.	PAK	Hammer throw	F		11	56,97	
Ishikawa, Y.	JPN	High jump	F		12	1,96	
Ivanov, A.	URS	Marathon	F		DNF		
Jack, H.R.	AUS	Long jump	Q		DNQ		
Jaiswang, P.	THA	800m	1	2	9		
Jakabfy, S.	HUN	200m	1	5	5	21·78	
		4×100m relay	1	4	2	41·45	
			SF	1	5	41·51	
Jalal, K.	PAK	Javelin throw	Q		DNQ		
Janecek, V.	TCH	200m	1	2	2	21·85	
			2	4	4	22·26	
		4×400m relay	1	1	3	3-10·96	
Janiszewski, Z.	POL	Pole vault	F		12	4,15	
Janke, F.	GER	5000m	1	3	6	14-40·89	
Jarzembowski, J.	POL	100m	1	1	2	10·95	
			2	3	4	10·98	
		200m	1	10	4	21·91	
		4×100m relay	1	4	1	40·97	
			SF	1	2	41·12	
			F		6	40·75	
Jazy, M.	FRA	1500m	1	1	7	3-49·95	
Jenkins, C.L.	USA	400m	1	3	3	48·82	
			2	4	3	47·63	
			SF	2	1	46·19	
			F		1	46·85	G
		4×400m relay	1	1	2	3-10·60	
			F		1	3-04·81	G
Jeszenszki, L.	HUN	3000m steeplechase	1	2	8	9-04·99	
Jirasek, J.	TCH	4×400m relay	1	1	3	3-10·96	
Johnson, A.	GBR	50k walk	F		8	5:02-19·0	
Johnson, D.J.N.	GBR	800m	1	5	1	1-50·93	
			SF	2	3	1-50·23	
			F		2	1-47·88	S
		4×400m relay	1	3	1	3-08·76	
			F		3	3-07·19	B
Johnson, G.	LBR	400m	1	7	6	54·8	
		800m	1	4	7		
		4×100m relay	1	1	5	44·96	
Johnson, R.L.	USA	Decathlon	F		2	7587	S
Jones, C.N.	USA	3000m steeplechase	1	1	4	8-47·57	
			F		9	9-13·0	
Jones, L.W.	USA	400m	1	1	1	48·30	
			2	1	1	47·42	
			SF	1	3	47·32	
			F		5	48·35	
		4×400m relay	1	1	2	3-10·60	
			F		1	3-04·81	G
Joseph, L.S.	KEN	High jump	F		18	1,92	
Joyce, J.R.	AUS	110m hurdles	1	3	6	15·02	
Jungwirth, S.	TCH	1500m	1	1	2	3-46·79	
			F		6	3-42·80	
Junk, B.	URS	20k walk	F		3	1:32-12·0	B
Kachkarov, I.	URS	High jump	F		3	2,08	B
Kadiaikine, E.	URS	3000m steeplechase	1	1	9	9-09·6	
Kalim, K.	PAK	110m hurdles	1	2	6	16·32	
		400m hurdles	1	2	=4	55·36	
Kamamoto, F.	JPN	Hammer throw	Q		DNQ		
Kane, H.	GBR	400m hurdles	1	2	2	51·85	
			SF	2	5	52·95	
Kantorek, P.	TCH	10000m	F		11		
		Marathon	F		27	2:52-05·0	
Kanuti, A.S.	KEN	Marathon	F		31	2:58-42·0	
Karupiah, S.	MAL	100m	1	9	3	11·56	
Karvonen, V.L.	FIN	Marathon	F		3	2:27-47·0	B
Kawashima, Y.	JPN	Marathon	F		5	2:29-19·0	
Keane, D.M.	AUS	20k walk	F		6	1:33-52·0	
Kelley, J.J.	USA	Marathon	F		21	2:43-40·0	
Kerr, G.E.	JAM	400m	1	6	2	49·74	
			2	4	4	47·47	
		4×400m relay	1	3	2	3-11·07	
			F		DIS		
Kesevan, S.	SIN	100m	1	4	4	11·35	
		200m	1	8	5	23·33	
Keter, K.	KEN	800m	1	3	7	1-56·13	
		4×400m relay	1	3	4	3-17·68	

COMPETITOR	COUNTRY CODE	EVENT	ROUND	HEAT	PLACE	TIME & DISTANCE	MEDAL
Khaliq, A.	PAK	100m	1	3	2	10·97	
			2	2	2	10·78	
			SF	1	4	10·93	
		200m	1	5	1	21·32	
			2	1	1	21·34	
			SF	1	4	21·58	
		4×100m relay	1	1	3	41·42	
			SF	2	5	40·78	
Khan, A.	PAK	400m	1	1	3	49·19	
		800m	1	4	5	1-52·71	
King, L.	USA	4×100m relay	1	1	1	40·53	
			SF	1	1	40·34	
			F		1	39·60*	G
Kinsella, E.F.	IRL	110m hurdles	1	1	4	14·66	
Kivela, E.O.	FIN	200m	1	10	6	22·56	
		4×400m relay	1	1	4	3-11·52	
Kiyofuji, A.	JPN	100m	1	8	3	11·00	
		200m	1	9	4	22·56	
		4×100m relay	1	4	6	42·30	
			SF	2	6	41·57	
Klics, F.	HUN	Discus throw	F		7	51,82	
Klimov, G.	URS	50k walk	F		DNF		
Knorzer, L.	GER	4×100m relay	1	2	3	41·00	
			SF	2	2	40·64	
			F		3	40·34	B
Koch, D.D.	USA	Discus throw	F		3	54,40	B
Kogake, T.	JPN	Triple jump	F		8	15,64	
Kojima, Y.	JPN	Hammer throw	Q		DNQ		
Konovalov, Y.	URS	100m	1	12	2	10·92	
			2	2	3	10·93	
			SF	1	6	11·11	
		200m	1	3	3	22·09	
		4×100m relay	1	3	1	40·77	
			SF	2	1	40·36	
			F		2	39·93	S
Konrad, W.	GER	10000m	F		13		
Konstantinidis, D.	GRE	800m	1	1	5	1-53·03	
Kopyto, J.	POL	Javelin throw	F		5	74,23	
Koschel, H.	GER	Javelin throw	F		4	74,68	
Kotila, P.E.	FIN	Marathon	F		13	2:38-59·0	
Koutenko, I.	URS	Decathlon	F		DNF		
Kouznetsov, V.	URS	Javelin throw	F		12	67,14	
		Decathlon	F		3	7,465	B
Kovacs, J.	HUN	10000m	F		2	28-52·36	S
Krasznai, S.	HUN	Javelin throw	F		13	66,33	
Kreer, V.	URS	Triple jump	F		3	16,02	B
Krivonossov, M.	URS	Hammer throw	F		2	63,03	S
Kropidlowski, K.	POL	Long jump	F		6	7,30	
Kruse, G.	ARG	Discus throw	F		11	49,89	
Krzyszkowiak, Z.	POL	10000m	F		4	29-05·41	
		3000m steeplechase	1	1	5	8-48·29	
Kuhl, J.	GER	400m	1	3	2	48·74	
			2	1	5	48·0	
		4×400m relay	1	2	1	3-09·83	
			F		4	3-03·27	
Kushnir, D.	ISR	Long jump	Q		DNQ		
Kuts, V.	URS	5000m	1	2	2	14-15·47	
			F		1	13-39·86*	G
		10000m	F		1	28-45·59*	G
Kyle, D.H.	CAN	5000m	1	2	8	14-59·0	
		10000m	F		23		
Lambrechts, M.	BEL	400m hurdles	1	5	5	54·24	
Land, R.C.	AUS	100m	1	6	2	11·05	
			2	1	6	11·15	
		4×100m relay	1	2	1	40·72	
			SF	2	4	40·72	
Landstrom, E.E.	FIN	Pole vault	F		7	4,25	
Landy, J.M.	AUS	1500m	1	3	3	3-48·67	
			F		3	3-42·03	B
Larsen, E.	NOR	3000m steeplechase	1	1	3	8-46·96	
			F		3	8-44·05	B
Laskau, H.H.	USA	20k walk	F		12	1:38-46·8	
Lassenius, L.T.	FIN	Decathlon	F		7	6565	
Lauer, M.	GER	110m hurdles	1	4	1	14·41	
			SF	1	2	14·57	
			F		4	14·67	
		Decathlon	F		5	6853	
Laufer, H.	GER	3000m steeplechase	1	2	3	8-53·23	
			F		4	8-44·53	
Lavelli, G.F.	ITA	Marathon	F		DNF		
Lavrov, M.	URS	50k walk	F		DIS		
Lawrence, A.C.	AUS	5000m	1	2	1	14-14·67	
			F		DNS		
		10000m	F		3	28-53·59	B
Lea, J.G.	USA	400m	1	2	3	48·41	
			2	3	5	48·33	
Lean, D.F.	AUS	400m hurdles	1	1	2	51·55	
			SF	2	2	51·45	
			F		5	51·93	
		4×400m relay	1	2	2	3-10·57	
			F		2	3-06·19	S
Leane, P.F.	AUS	Decathlon	F		9	6427	
Lee, C.H.	KOR	Marathon	F		4	2:28-45·0	
Lee, K.F.	MAL	100m	1	12	5	11·84	
		200m	1	8	6	23·94	
Legesse, B.	ETH	100m	1	6	6	11·94	
		200m	1	3	5	23·63	
		400m	1	1	5	50·83	
		4×100m relay	1	3	5	44·47	
		4×400m relay	1	3	5	3-29·93	
Lehto, T.	FIN	Triple jump	F		18	14,91	
Leva, E.	BEL	800m	1	3	3	1-52·03	
			SF	2	4	1-50·44	
			F		7	1:51·75	
		1500m	1	2	12	4-06·0	
Levenson, S.A.	CAN	100m	1	10	1	10·94	
			2	3	3	10·93	
			SF	1	5	10·94	
		4×100m relay	1	3	4	41·70	
Lievore, G.	ITA	Javelin throw	F		6	72,88	
Lim, W.D.	KOR	Marathon	F		DNF		
Lincoln, M.G.	AUS	1500m	1	2	1	3-45·63	
			F		12		
Ling, T.S.	ROC	Long jump	Q		DNQ		
Lindner, D.	GER	20k walk	F		DIS		
Lisserko, C.	FRA	200m	1	11	1	22·06	
			2	2	DNF		
		4×100m relay	1	2	2	40·99	
			SF	1	4	41·37	
Lituyev, Y.	URS	400m hurdles	1	5	1	51·69	
			SF	2	3	51·78	
			F		4	51·91	
		4×400m relay	1	3	3	3-11·27	
Ljunggren, J.A.	SWE	20k walk	F		4	1:32-24·0	
		50k walk	F		3	4:35-02·0	B
Lochilov, V.	URS	Shot put	F		13	15,62	
Lombardo, V.	ITA	200m	1	3	2	21·94	
			2	2	4	21·53	
		4×100m relay	1	3	2	41·07	
			SF	1	3	41·14	
			F		4	40·43	
Lorger, S.	YUG	110m hurdles	1	2	2	14·75	
			SF	1	4	14·73	
			F		5	14·68	
Lundberg, T.R.	SWE	Pole vault	F		5	4,25	
MacDonald, B.D.	USA	20k walk	F		16	1:43-25·6	
McGlynn, E.F.	AUS	4×100m relay	1	2	1	40·72	
			SF	2	4	40·72	
McKenzie, G.E.	USA	10000m	F		18		
MacMillan, D.R.T.	AUS	800m	1	2	4	1-53·50	
Macquet, M.	FRA	Javelin throw	F		7	71,84	
Mahmud, J.	PAK	800m	1	5	6	1-59·5	
		1500m	1	2	14	4-15·0	
Maiyoro, N.	KEN	5000m	1	3	2	14-29·59	
			F		7	14-18·99	
Malcherczyk, R.	POL	Triple jump	F		10	15,54	
Mandlik, V.	TCH	200m	1	8	1	21·79	
			2	3	2	21·56	
			SF	2	5	21·74	
		4×400m relay	1	1	3	3-10·96	
Martin-Du-Gard, J.P.	FRA	400m	1	8	3	48·39	
			2	4	6	48·37	
		4×400m relay	1	2	3	3-11·76	
Martinez, R.	PUR	Javelin throw	Q		DNQ		
Martins, E.	LBR	4×100m relay	1	1	1	44·96	
		Long jump	Q		DNQ		
Mashburn, J.W.	USA	4×400m relay	1	1	2	3-10·60	
			F		1	3-04·81	G
Maskinskov, Y.	URS	50k walk	F		2	4:32-57·0	S
Mattos, G.F.	USA	Pole vault	F		4	4,35	
Matveev, B.	URS	Discus throw	F		9	51,38	
Meconi, S.	ITA	Shot put	F		10	16,28	
Mehar, R.	IND	Long jump	Q		DNQ		
Meier, W.	GER	Decathlon	F		6	6773	
Mihalic, F.	YUG	Marathon	F		2	2:26-32·0	S
Mikenas, A.	URS	20k walk	F		2	1:32-03·00	S
Mikhailov, A.	URS	110m hurdles	1	3	4	14·63	
Mildh, S.O.	FIN	400m hurdles	1	5	3	52·19	
		4×400m relay	1	1	4	3-11·52	
Mimoun, A.	FRA	10000m	F		12		
		Marathon	F		1	2:25-00·0	G
Mona, I.G.P.-O.	INA	High jump	Q		DNQ		

COMPETITOR	COUNTRY CODE	EVENT	ROUND	HEAT	PLACE	TIME & DISTANCE	MEDAL
Money, K.E.	CAN	High jump	F		5	2,03	
Moroney, M.M.	AUS	Long jump	Q		DNQ		
Morris, C.J.	AUS	Hammer throw	Q		DNQ		
Morrow, B.	USA	100m	1	12	1	10·47	
			2	1	1	10·55	
			SF	2	1	10·52	
			F		1	10·62	G
		200m	1	9	1	21·95	
			2	4	1	22·03	
			SF	1	2	21·43	
			F		1	20·75*	G
		4×100m relay	1	1	1	40·53	
			SF	1	1	40·34	
			F		1	39·60*	G
Mugosa, V.	YUG	5000m	1	1	2	14-25·71	
			F		DNF		
Munoz, A.	COL	4×400m relay	1	2	6	3-27·4	
Murchison, I.J.	USA	100m	1	1	1	10·67	
			2	2	1	10·55	
			SF	1	1	10·79	
			F		4	10·79	
		400m relay	1	1	1	40·53	
			SF	1	1	40·34	
			F		1	39·60*	G
Muroya, Y.	JPN	300m	1	1	3	1-52·40	
			SF	1	6	1-54·68	
		4×400m	1	2	4	3-13·75	
Myitung, N.	BIR	10000m	F		DNF		
		Marathon	F		26	2:49-32·0	
Nawaz, M.	PAK	Javelin throw	F		14	62,55	
Nduga, B.K.	UGA	100m	1	4	1	10·88	
			2	2	6	12·95	
		200m	1	10	7	22·89	
Nieder, W.H.	USA	Shot put	F		2	18,18	S
Nielsen, N.G.	DEN	800m	1	4	1	1-51·27	
			SF	1	DNS		
		1500m	1	3	4	3-48·80	
			F		10	3-45·58	
Nigousse, R.	ETH	100m	1	2	6	12·07	
		200m	1	4	5	23·89	
		4×100m relay	1	3	5	44·47	
Niklas, A.	POL	Hammer throw	F		10	57,70	
Nilsen, B.H.	NOR	100m	1	7	6	11·11	
		200m	1	7	3	22·33	
Nilsson, N.B.	SWE	High jump	Q		DNQ		
Nilsson, T.H.	SWE	Marathon	F		9	2:33-33·0	
Norris, F.	GBR	Marathon	F		DNF		
Norris, K.L.	GBR	10000m	F		5	29-21·6	
Nyberg, J.E.	SWE	Marathon	F		8	2:31-21·0	
Oakley, A.H.	CAN	20k walk	F		DIS		
Oberste, W.	GER	4×400m relay	1	2	1	3-09·88	
			F		4	3-08·27	
Obi, T.	NGR	100m	1	7	5	11·10	
O'Brien, W.P.	USA	Shot put	F		1	18,57*	G
Oerter, A.A.	USA	Discus throw	F		1	56,36*	G
Ogushi, K.	JPN	400m hurdles	1	1	3	53·22	
		4×400m relay	1	2	4	3-13·75	
Ogwang, L.	UGA	Long jump	Q		DNQ		
		Triple jump	F		20	14,72	
Oksanen, E.I.	FIN	Marathon	F		10	2:36-10·0	
Oliver, B.T.	AUS	Triple jump	Q		DNQ		
Ollerenshaw, K.	AUS	Marathon	F		25	2:48-12·0	
Olowu, K.A.B.	NGR	Long jump	F		5	7,36	
Oluwa, R.A.	NGR	4×100m relay	1	4	DIS		
		Long jump	Q		DNQ		
Palmer, W.B.	GBR	Shot put	F		12	15,81	
Palou, O.	URS	Decathlon	F		4	6930	
Pamich, A.	ITA	20k walk	F		11	1:36-03·6	
		50k walk	F		4	4:39-00·0	
Papavasiliou, G.	GRE	1500m	1	3	9	3-57·57	
		3000m steeplechase	1	1	8	8-55·83	
Paraschivescu, D.	RUM	20k walk	F		14	1:39-57·4	
		50k walk	F		DNF		
Parker, F.J.	GBR	110m hurdles	1	2	1	15·00	
Parker, R.	AUS	400m hurdles	1	4	1	53·51	
			SF	1	6	52·72	
Parrington, J.D.	CAN	100m	1	4	5	11·62	
		200m	1	11	5	22·61	
		4×100m relay	1	3	4	41·70	
Peever, B.	AUS	Pole vault	Q		DNQ		
Perera, K.	MAL	400m	1	2	7	51·96	
		800m	1	3	9		
Perry, L.J.	AUS	Marathon	F		DNF		
Petrov, A.	URS	Pole vault	F		11	4,15	
Pettersson, S.R.H.	SWE	High jump	F		4	2,06	
Pharaoh, M.	GBR	Discus throw	F		4	54,27	

COMPETITOR	COUNTRY CODE	EVENT	ROUND	HEAT	PLACE	TIME & DISTANCE	MEDAL
Pipine, P.I.	URS	1500m	1	1	10	3-50·86	
Pirie, D.A.G.	GBR	5000m	1	1	1	14-25·69	
			F		2	13-50·78	S
		10000m	F		8	29-49·6	
Poerschke, M.	GER	4×400m relay	1	2	1	3-09·88	
			F		4	3-08·27	
Pohl, L.	GER	200m	1	12	1	21·78	
			2	1	3	21·49	
			SF	2	4	21·64	
		4×100m relay	1	2	3	41·00	
			SF	2	2	40·64	
			F		3	40·34	B
Poliakov, V.	URS	High jump	Q		DNQ		
Porbadnik, K.	GER	10000m	F		17		
		Marathon	F		DNF		
Porrassalmi, J.W.	FIN	Long jump	Q		DNQ		
Porter, C.M.	AUS	High jump	F		2	2,10	S
Potgieter, G.C.	SAF	400m hurdles	1	5	2	52·05	
			SF	1	3	51·30	
			F		6	56·0	
Power, D.W.	AUS	10000m	F		7	29-49·2	
Preussger, M.	GER	Pole vault	F		8	4,25	
Price, N.G.	SAF	Long jump	F		7	7,28	
Putu, E.	LBR	100m	1	6	5	11·44	
		200m	1	11	7	24·33	
		4×100m relay	1	1	5	44·96	
Racik, K.	YUG	Hammer throw	F		6	60,36	
Radosevic, D.	YUG	Discus throw	F		8	51,69	
Rae, M.L.	NZL	100m	1	3	1	10·84	
			2	1	3	10·78	
			SF	2	4	10·68	
		200m	1	5	2	21·57	
			2	4	2	22·12	
			SF	1	6	21·75	
Rahkamo, K.T.	FIN	Triple jump	F		14	15,21	
Ram, S.C.	IND	110m hurdles	1	4	6	15·40	
Ramzan, A.	PAK	Long jump	Q		DNQ		
		Triple jump	Q		DNQ		
Rantala, H.K.	FIN	Triple jump	F		19	14,87	
Rashid, A.	PAK	Marathon	F		30	2:57-47·0	
Rashid, M.	PAK	Long jump	Q		DNQ		
		Triple jump	Q		DNQ		
Rasquin, G.	LUX	400m	1	7	4	50·76	
		800m	1	1	4	1-52·88	
Rawson, M.A.	GBR	800m	1	1	2	1-52·20	
			SF	2	5	1-50·45	
Raziq, G.	PAK	100m	1	10	6	11·26	
		110m hurdles	1	1	3	14·65	
			SF	2	5	14·75	
		4×100m relay	1	1	3	41·42	
			SF	2	5	40·78	
Read, N.R.	NZL	50k walk	F		1	4:30-42·8	G
Reavis, P.M.	USA	High jump	F		7	2,00	
Rehak, M.	TCH	Triple jump	F		5	15,85	
Rekola, P.J.	FIN	200m	1	11	4	22·22	
		4×400m relay	1	1	4	3-11·52	
Rich, M.W.	AUS	Triple jump	Q		DNQ		
Richards, A.W.	NZL	Marathon	F		17	2:41-34·0	
Richards, R.E.	USA	Pole vault	F		1	4,56*	G
		Decathlon	F		DNF		
Richtzenhain, K.	GER	800m	1	5	5	1-53·47	
		1500m	1	1	1	3-46·76	
			F		2	3-42·02	S
Ridgway, C.E.	AUS	High jump	F		7	2,00	
Rinteenpaa, O.O.	FIN	3000m steeplechase	1	1	11	9-10·0	
Rivera, F.	PUR	800m	1	1	6	1-56·58	
		4×400m relay	1	2	5	3-13·81	
Robbins, N.J.	AUS	3000m steeplechase	1	2	5	8-55·62	
			F		7	8-50·36	
Roberts, J.	LBR	100m	1	5	6	11·45	
		200m	1	3	DIS		
		4×100m relay	1	1	5	44·96	
Robinson, T.A.	BAH	100m	1	5	4	11·06	
		200m	1	5	4	21·76	
Rodriguez, I.	PUR	200m	1	11	2	22·06	
			2	3	5	22·16	
		400m	1	7	3	48·86	
			2	1	3	47·64	
			SF	1	6	47·86	
		4×400m relay	1	2	5	3-13·81	
Roka, A.	HUN	50k walk	F		5	4:50-09·0	
Romero, R.	VEN	100m	1	3	4	11·14	
		200m	1	10	2	21·85	
		4×100m relay	1	1	4	42·10	
Rotich, B.	KEN	400m	1	2	4	48·90	
		4×400m relay	1	3	4	3-17·68	
Roubanis, G.	GRE	Pole vault	F		3	4,50	B

COMPETITOR	COUNTRY CODE	EVENT	ROUND	HEAT	PLACE	TIME & DISTANCE	MEDAL
Roudnitska, E.	FRA	110m hurdles	1	-	2	14·49	
			SF	-	5	14·87	
Roveraro, G.	ITA	High jump	Q		DNQ		
Rozsnyoi, S.	HUN	3000m steeplechase	1	1	1	8-46·89	
			F		2	8-43·68	S
Rozsavolgyi, I.	HUN	1500m	1	1	5	3-49·54	
Russell, J.	AUS	Marathon	F		18	2:41-44·0	
Rut, T.	POL	Discus throw	Q		DNQ		
		Hammer throw	F		14	53,43	
Rzhishchin, S.	URS	3000m steeplechase	1	2	2	8:53·18	
			F		5	8:44·58	
Sakurai, K.	JPN	Triple jump	F		7	15,73	
Salisbury, J.E.	GBR	400m	1	5	3	47·95	
			2	1	2	47·60	
			SF	2	5	47·47	
		4×400m relay	1	3	1	3-08·76	
			F		3	3-07·19	B
Salsola, O.A.T.	FIN	1500m	1	2	8	3-55·0	
Samotsvetov, A.	URS	Hammer throw	F		3	62,56	B
Sando, F.	GBR	10000m	F		10	30-05·0	
Sandoval, R.	CHI	800m	1	5	4	1-52·12	
		1500m	1	2	10	3-58·0	
Sandstrom, E.R.	GBR	100m	1	11	2	11·05	
			2	4	6	11·03	
		200m	1	11	3	22·18	
		4×100m relay	1	1	2	41·30	
			SF	2	3	40·68	
			F		5	40·74	
Sang, O.S.	KOR	800m	1	4	6	1-55·56	
		1500m	1	2	13	4-09·0	
Savel, I.	RUM	400m hurdles	1	6	2	52·31	
			SF	2	4	52·06	
Schade, H.	GER	5000m	1	2	5	14-19·25	
			F		12	14-31·90	
		10000m	F		9	30-00·6	
Schmidt, E.	POL	200m	1	9	2	22·03	
			2	1	6	21·73	
		4×100m relay	1	4	1	40·97	
			SF	1	2	41·12	
			F		6	40·75	
Schmidt, P.	GER	800m	1	2	6	1-55·71	
Scott, N.I.	NZL	1500m	1	3	1	3-48·09	
			F		7	3-42·87	
Segal, D.H.	GBR	100m	1	12	3	11·02	
		200m	1	8	3	22·22	
		4×100m relay	1	1	2	41·30	
			SF	2	3	40·68	
			F		5	40·74	
Shankle, J.W.	USA	110m hurdles	1	3	1	14·20	
			SF	2	2	14·23	
			F		3	14·25	B
Sharif Butt, M.	PAK	100m	1	11	4	11·26	
		200m	1	4	3	22·38	
		4×100m relay	1	1	3	41·42	
			SF	2	5	40·78	
Sharpe, W.J.	USA	Triple jump	F		4	15,88	
Shaw, G.D.	USA	Triple jump	F		12	15,33	
Shaw, R.D.	GBR	400m hurdles	1	6	3	52·62	
Shenton, B.	GBR	200m	1	10	3	21·87	
			2	4	3	22·15	
			SF	2	6	22·08	
		4×100m relay	1	1	2	41·30	
			SF	2	3	40·68	
			F		5	40·74	
Shibata, H.	JPN	Triple jump	F		13	15,25	
Shirley, E.	GBR	3000m steeplechase	1	2	1	8-52·72	
			F		8	8-57·0	
Sidlo, J.	POL	Javelin throw	F		2	79,93	S
Sierra, C.	COL	4×400m relay	1	2	6	3-27·4	
Sillon, V.	FRA	Pole vault	Q		DNQ		
Silva, J.	CHI	Marathon	F		DNF		
Singh, A.	IND	High jump	F		14	1,96	
Singh, J.	IND	400m hurdles	1	2	=4	55·36	
Singh, Milkha	IND	200m	1	2	4	22·47	
		400m	1	5	4	49·07	
Singh, Mohinder	IND	Triple jump	F		15	15,20	
Singh, S.	IND	800m	1	3	4	1-52·57	
Sitkine, V.	URS	High jump	F		6	2,00	
Sium, B.D.	NBO	Triple jump	Q		DNQ		
Sjogren, L.A.	USA	50k walk	F		12	5:12-34·0	
Skobla, J.	TCH	Shot put	F		3	17,65	B
Skront, M.	TCH	50k walk	F		DNF		
Sloan, L.D.L.	CAN	400m	1	4	4	50·18	
		4×400m relay	1	1	1	3-10·59	
			F		5	3-10·33	
Smith, R.C.	AUS	50k walk	F		6	4:56-08·0	

COMPETITOR	COUNTRY CODE	EVENT	ROUND	HEAT	PLACE	TIME & DISTANCE	MEDAL
Sobrinho, J.	BRA	100m	1	10	3	11·14	
		200m	1	5	3	21·67	
		4×100m relay	1	3	3	41·70	
			SF	1	6	43·87	
Sokolov, E.	URS	1500m	1	2	6	3-49·27	
Solorzano, A.	VEN	200m	1	4	DIS		
		4×100m relay	1	1	4	42·10	
Somblngo, P.	PHI	400m	1	2	6	49·50	
		400m hurdles	1	1	5	54·66	
Somogyi, J.	HUN	50k walk	F		DNF		
Song, K.S.	KOR	Hammer throw	Q		DNQ		
Sonoda, Y.	JPN	Long Jump	Q		DNQ		
Southern, S.E.	USA	400m hurdles	1	2	1	51·41	
			SF	1	1	50·26*	
			F		2	50·94	S
Sowell, A.	USA	800m	1	3	2	1-51·27	
			SF	2	1	1-50·08	
			F		4	1-48·41	
Spence, Malcolm	JAM	200m	1	5	6	21·86	
		400m	1	7	2	48·31	
			2	2	2	47·42	
			SF	2	6	47·52	
		4×400m relay	1	3	2	3-11·07	
			F		DIS		
Spence, Melville	JAM	200m	1	1	=4	22·13	
		400m	1	8	2	48·00	
			2	3	3	47·38	
			SF	1	4	47·58	
		4×400m relay	1	3	2	3-11·07	
			F		DIS		
Spence, M.C.	SAF	400m	1	3	1	47·77	
			2	3	2	47·08	
			SF	1	2	47·27	
			F		6	48·40	
Spirin, L.	URS	20k walk	F		1	1:31-27·4	G
Spurrier, L.V.	USA	800m	1	4	2	1-51·52	
			SF	1	2	1-53·71	
			F		6	1-49·38	
Srinaka, M.	THA	200m	1	11	6	23·88	
		4×100m relay	1	2	4	44·37	
Srisombati, S.	THA	1500m	1	2	15	4-30·0	
Stanfield, A.W.	USA	200m	1	4	1	21·69	
			2	2	1	21·22	
			SF	2	1	21·35	
			F		2	20·97	S
Steinbach, M.	GER	100m	1	3	3	10·99	
Steines, B.	GER	110m hurdles	1	3	2	14·59	
			SF	2	4	14·70	
Stephens, D.J.	AUS	10000m	F		20		
Stoliarov, B.	URS	110m hurdles	1	4	3	14·54	
			SF	2	3	14·64	
			F		6	14·71	
Stone, C.C.	USA	5000m	1	2	7	14-52·0	
Strandli, S.	NOR	Hammer throw	F		8	59,21	
Suh, Y.-J.	KOR	Long jump	Q		DNQ		
Sukhanov, S.	URS	1500m	1	3	7	3-52·96	
Sukharev, V.	URS	4×400m relay	1	3	1	40·77	
			SF	2	1	40·36	
			F		2	39·93	
Sutinen, M.	FIN	Pole vault	F		DNQ		
Suzuki, S.	JPN	800m	1	2	5	1-54·29	
		4×400m relay	1	2	4	3-13·75	
Szabo, M.	HUN	5000m	1	3	4	14-32·83	
			F		4	14-03·38	
Szentgali, L.	HUN	800m	1	5	3	1-51·89	
			SF	1	5	1-53·94	
Syrovatsky, L.	FRA	Javelin throw	Q		DNQ		
Tabori, L.	HUN	1500m	1	2	4	3-48·21	
			F		4	3-42·55	
		5000m	1	2	3	14-18·75	
			F		6	14-09·99	
Taipale, I.R.	FIN	5000m	1	2	6	14-24·2	
		10000m	F		22		
Tajima, M.	JPN	4×100m relay	1	1	3	42·30	
			SF	2	6	41·57	
		Long jump	Q		DNQ		
Tan, E.Y.	SIN	100m	1	9	4	11·63	
		Triple jump	Q		DNQ		
Tchernobai, V.	URS	Pole vault	F		13	4,00	
Ter-Ovanesyan, I.	URS	Long jump	F		NP	0	
Thackwray, D.A.	USA	Marathon	F		DNF		
Thogersen, T.P.	DEN	5000m	1	1	5	14-29·34	
			F		8	14-21·81	
		10000m	F		15		
Thomas, A.G.	AUS	5000m	1	3	1	14-14·41	
			F		6	14-05·03	
Thomas, G.E.	AUS	3000m steeplechase	1	1	10	9-09·8	

COMPETITOR	COUNTRY CODE	EVENT	ROUND	HEAT	PLACE	TIME & DISTANCE	MEDAL
Thomas, R.	FRA	Shot put	F		14	15,31	
Thompson, D.J.	GBR	50k walk	F		DNF		
Thorbjornsson, H.	ISL	100m	1	1	3	11·12	
Tjornebo, G.	SWE	3000m steeplechase	1	2	6	9-02·13	
Tobacco, C.T.	CAN	400m	1	2	1	47·92	
			2	1	4	47·79	
		4×400m relay	1	1	1	3-10·59	
			F		5	3-10·33	
Tokarev, B.	URS	100m	1	5	2	10·90	
			2	3	2	10·87	
			SF	2	6	10·91	
		200m	1	10	1	21·62	
			2	2	2	21·42	
			SF	2	3	21·50	
			F		5	21·42	
		4×100m relay	1	3	1	40·77	
			SF	2	1	40·36	
			F		2	39·93	S
Tongaram, S.	THA	400m	1	4	5	53·61	
Trousil, J.	TCH	200m	1	3	4	22·54	
		4×400m relay	1	1	3	3-10·96	
Truex, M.E.	USA	10000m	F		DNF		
Tsai Cheng Fu	ROC	400m hurdles	1	3	6	54·84	
Tsakanikas, G.	GRE	Shot put	F		8	16,56	
Tsiboulenko, V.	URS	Javelin throw	F		3	79·50	B
Turton, E.	TRI	100m	1	9	2	11·38	
			2	2	5	11·2	
Uddebom, E.	SWE	Shot put	F		6	16,65	
		Discus throw	F		14	48,28	
Ushio, K.	JPN	100m	1	4	3	11·09	
		200m	1	2	5	22·64	
		4×100m relay	1	4	3	42·30	
			SF	2	6	41·57	
Vacharabhan, P.	THA	100m	1	12	4	11·57	
		200m	1	12	4	23·92	
		4×100m relay	1	2	4	44·37	
Valkama, J.R.	FIN	Long jump	F		3	7,48	B
Varasdi, G.	HUN	100m	1	8	4	11·00	
		4×100m relay	1	4	2	41·45	
			SF	1	5	41·51	
Van Den Driessche, A.	BEL	Marathon	F		24	2:47-18·0	
Vernon, J.B.	AUS	High jump	Q		DNQ		
Vickers, S.F.	GBR	20k walk	F		5	1:32-34·2	
Vlasenko, V.	URS	3000m steeplechase	1	1	7	8-54·99	
Voradilok, V.	THA	100m	1	2	5	11·78	
		4×100m relay	1	2	4	44·37	
Waern, D.J.R.	SWE	1500m	1	3	5	3-48·84	
Wahlander, T.E.G.O.	SWE	Long jump	Q		DNQ		
Waide, A.	SWE	Marathon	F		11	2:36-21·0	
Walters, J.D.	USA	1500m	1	3	8	3-55·60	
Wanyoke, K.E.	KEN	400m	1	6	4	50·74	
		4×400m relay	1	3	4	3-17·68	
Wazny, Z.	POL	Pole vault	F		6	4,25	
Wegmann, K.-H.	GER	Shot put	F		7	16,63	
Weinacker, A.	USA	50k walk	F		7	5:00-16·0	
Wells, P.	GBR	High jump	F		16	1,96	
Wheeler, M.K.V.	GBR	400m	1	4	2	49·37	
			2	4	5	48·05	
		4×400m relay	1	3	1	3-08·76	
			F		3	3-07·19	B
Wheeler, T.S.	USA	1500m	1	1	8	3-50·02	
Will, H.	GER	Javelin throw	F		9	69,86	
Wilmshurst, K.S.D	GBR	Long jump	F		11	7,14	
		Triple jump	F		9	15,54	
Wilson, V.T.	USA	High jump	F		10	2·00	
Winston, D.F.	AUS	200m	1	2	3	22·20	
Wirjodimedjo, M.	INA	High jump	Q		DNQ		
Wolde, M.	ETH	800m	1	1	7	1-58·0	
		1500m	1	1	11	3-51·0	
		4×100m relay	1	3	5	3-29·93	
Wongchaoom, S.	THA	100m	1	11	6	11·95	
		4×100m relay	1	2	4	44·37	
Wood, K.	GBR	1500m	1	2	2	3-46·90	
			F		9	3-44·76	
Wu, C.-T.	ROC	Triple jump	Q		DNQ		
Yang, C.K.	ROC	High jump	F		20	1,86	
		Decathlon	F		8	6,521	
Yankoff, A.	FRA	400m hurdles	1	5	4	53·30	
Yaqub, M.	PAK	400m hurdles	1	3	5	53·18	
Young, C.C.	USA	Javelin throw	F		11	68,64	
Yulin, A.	URS	400m hurdles	1	6	1	52·22	
			SF	1	5	51·79	
		4×400m relay	1	3	1	3-11·27	
Zapata, G.	COL	110m hurdles	1	2	6	15·58	
		4×400m relay	1	2	6	3-27·4	

COMPETITOR	COUNTRY CODE	EVENT	ROUND	HEAT	PLACE	TIME & DISTANCE	MEDAL
Zatopek, E.	TCH	Marathon	F		6	2:29-34·0	
Zimny, K.	POL	5000m	1	1	DNF		
FEMALES							
Ahrens, M.	CHI	Javelin throw	F		2	50,38	S
Allday, S.	GBR	Discus throw	Q		DNQ		
		Shot put	F		15	12,71	
Almqvist, I.M.	SWE	Javelin throw	F		5	49,74	
Anderson, K.L.	USA	Javelin throw	F		8	48,00	
Armitage, H.J.	GBR	100m	1	4	1	11·81	
			SF	2	2	11·87	
			F		6	12·10	
		200m	1	5	1	24·87	
			SF	2	4	24·78	
		4×100m relay	1	2	1	45·38	
			F		2	44·70	S
Avellan, I.E.	ARG	Discus throw	F		6	46,73	
Balas, I.	RUM	High jump	F		5	1,67	
Ballod, V.	URS	High jump	F		11	1,60	
Begliakova, I.	URS	Discus throw	F		2	52,54	S
Bennett, A.E.	GBR	High jump	F		16	1,55	
Bernoth, C.E.	AUS	High jump	F		14	1,60	
Bertoni, L.	ITA	200m	1	4	3	25·33	
		4×100m relay	1	1	3	45·91	
			F		5	45·90	
Besedina, N.	URS	80m hurdles	1	3	5	11·59	
Borwick, N.	AUS	Long jump	F		8	5,82	
Botchkareva, I.	URS	4×100m relay	1	2	3	46·20	
			F		4	45·81	
Branner, R.	AUT	Shot put	F		7	14,60	
Breen, M.P.	AUS	Shot put	Q		DNQ		
Brommel, A.	GER	Discus throw	Q		DNQ		
		Javelin throw	F		13	44,67	
Brown, E.	USA	Discus throw	F		4	51,35	
		Shot put	F		6	15,12	
Bystrova, G.	URS	80m hurdles	1	4	2	11·09	
			SF	2	1	11·14	
			F		4	11·25	
Capdevielle, C.	FRA	100m	1	5	2	12·10	
			SF	1	6	12·53	
		4×100m relay	1	1	4	46·39	
Chaprounova, V.	URS	Long jump	F		6	5,85	
Choong, A.	MAL	100m	1	5	4	12·73	
Cinco, M.	PHI	80m hurdles	1	3	7	12·20	
Cooke, G.J.	AUS	80m hurdles	1	3	3	11·45	
			SF	2	3	11·25	
			F		6	11·60	
Cooper, J.	AUS	High jump	F		15	1,55	
Cotton, S.V.	AUS	Discus throw	Q		DNQ		
Croker, N.W.	AUS	200m	1	3	2	25·10	
			SF	1	3	24·41	
			F		4	24·22	
		4×100m relay	1	1	1	45·00	
			F		1	44.65*	G
Cuthbert, B.	AUS	100m	1	3	1	11·72	
			SF	1	2	12·08	
			F		1	11·82	G
		200m	1	1	1	23·60	
			SF	1	1	23·75	
			F		1	23·55*	G
		4×100m relay	1	1	1	45·00*	
			F		1	44·65*	G
Daniels, I.F.	USA	100m	1	3	2	11·91	
			SF	1	3	11·94	
			F		4	11·98	
		4×100m relay	1	2	2	45·52	
			F		3	45·04	B
Darnowski, C.S.	USA	80m hurdles	1	2	4	12·02	
Deubel, P.	USA	Shot put	Q		DNQ		
Diaz, B.	CUB	80m Hurdles	1	1	2	11·51	
			SF	1	5	11·42	
Doinikova, Z.	URS	Shot put	F		4	15,54	
Donaghy, J.M.	NZL	High jump	F		7	1,67	
Dvalishvili, N.	URS	Long jump	F		3	6·07	B
Elkina, A.	URS	Discus throw	F		5	48,20	
Ellis, M.L.	USA	200m	1	3	3	26·46	
Faggs, M.	USA	100m	1	1	3	12·36	
		200m	1	1	2	24·99	
			SF	2	5	25·06	
		4×100m relay	1	2	2	45·52	
			F		3	45·04	B
Figwer, U.	POL	Discus throw	F		6	48,16	
Fikotova, O.	TCH	Discus throw	F		1	53,69*	G
Fisch, E.	GER	Long jump	F		4	5,89	
Fluchot, M.	FRA	100m	1	1	4	12·55	
		200m	1	6	4	25·12	
		4×100m relay	1	1	4	46·39	

COMPETITOR	COUNTRY CODE	EVENT	ROUND	HEAT	PLACE	TIME & DISTANCE	MEDAL
Flynn, A.M.	USA	High jump	Q		DNQ		
Fuhrmann, I.	GER	100m	1	5	3	12·31	
		200m	1	6	3	25·05	
Gastl, C.	GER	80m hurdles	1	1	1	11·18	
			SF	2	4	11·30	
George, I.M.	CAN	Javelin throw	Q		DNQ		
Geyser, H.L.	SAF	High jump	F		8	1,64	
Golubnichaya, M.	URS	80m hurdles	1	2	2	11·25	
			SF	1	3	11·12	
			F		5	11·50	
Greppi, M.	ITA	80m hurdles	1	1	5	12·66	
		4×100m relay	1	1	3	45·91	
			F		5	45·90	
Gyarmati, O.	HUN	Long jump	F		11	5,66	
Haslam, E.	CAN	100m	1	4	4	11·98	
		200m	1	5	4	25·27	
		4×100m relay	1	1	5	46·79	
Heath, J.M.	AUS	Javelin throw	Q		DNQ		
Henry, S.	FRA	200m	1	5	3	25·13	
Hoffmann, H.	GER	Long jump	F		10	5,73	
Hopkins, T.E.	GBR	High jump	F		=2	1,67	S
		Long jump	Q		DNQ		
Hoskin, S.	GBR	Long jump	Q		DNQ		
Innis, H.	AUS	Javelin throw	Q		DNQ		
Itkina, M.	URS	200m	1	2	1	24·31	
			SF	1	4	24·42	
		4×100m relay	1	2	3	46·20	
			F		4	45·81	
Jackman, L.	AUS	Discus throw	F		13	40,84	
Jaunzeme, I.	URS	Javelin throw	F		1	53,86*	G
Jesudason, J.E.	SIN	100m	1	1	5	13·41	
Johnson, M.	AUS	Long jump	Q		DNQ		
Kilian, I.	GER	High jump	F		18	1,55	
Klass, M.B.	SIN	100m	1	2	7	12·57	
		200m	1	1	4	26·37	
Knapp, R.	AUT	High jump	F		12	1,60	
Kohler, G.I.	GER	100m	1	4	2	11·85	
			SF	2	5	12·07	
		200m	1	2	2	24·53	
			SF	2	3	24·48	
			F		6	24·68	
		80m hurdles	1	3	1	11·11	
			SF	1	2	10·93	
			F		2	11·12	S
		4×100m relay	1	1	2	45·07	
			F		6	47·29	
Koniaeva, N.	URS	Javelin throw	F		3	50,28	B
Koshelova, O.	URS	200m	1	5	5	25·38	
Kotlusek, N.	YUG	Discus throw	F		12	42,16	
		Shot put	F		8	14,56	
Kozak, D.E.	CAN	4×100m relay	1	1	5	46·79	
		Long jump	Q		DNQ		
Krepkina, V.	URS	100m	1	1	2	12·08	
			SF	2	4	12·07	
		4×100m relay	1	2	3	46·20	
			F		4	45·81	
Krzesinska, E.	POL	Long jump	F		1	6,35*	G
Kurrell, P.J.	USA	Discus throw	Q		DNQ		
Kusion, M.	POL	100m	1	2	4	12·34	
		4×100m relay	1	2	4	46·58	
		Long jump	F		9	5,79	
Kyle, M.	IRL	100m	1	4	6	12·48	
		200m	1	1	5	26·57	
Lafrenz, A.-K.	GER	Discus throw	Q		DNQ		
		Shot put	F		12	13,72	
Lambert, M.	FRA	80m hurdles	1	4	3	11·13	
			SF	1	4	11·37	
		Long jump	F		5	5,88	
Larking, G.M.	SWE	High jump	F		4	1,67	
Larney, M.L.	USA	Discus throw	Q		DNQ		
		Javelin throw	F		11	45,27	
Lawrence, V.D.	AUS	Discus throw	Q		DNQ		
		Shot put	F		13	13,12	
Leone, G.	ITA	100m	1	1	1	12·00	
			SF	1	3	12·22	
			F		5	12·07	
		200m	1	3	3	25·77	
		4×100m relay	1	1	3	45·91	
			F		5	45·90	
Lerczak, B.	POL	100m	1	3	4	12·37	
		200m	1	5	2	24·99	
			SF	1	6	25·12	
		4×100m relay	1	2	4	46·58	
Luttge, J.	GER	Shot put	F		11	13,88	
McDaniel, M.L.	USA	High jump	F		1	1,76*	G
MacDonald, J.	CAN	Discus throw	Q		DNQ		
		Shot put	F		10	14,31	

COMPETITOR	COUNTRY CODE	EVENT	ROUND	HEAT	PLACE	TIME & DISTANCE	MEDAL
Manoliu, L.	RUM	Discus throw	F		9	43,90	
Masdammer, C.I.	GUI	100m	1	6	5	12·87	
		200m	1	4	4	25·73	
Mason, M.M.	AUS	High jump	F		6	1,67	
Matheson, D.E.	CAN	100m	1	3	6	12·59	
		200m	1	1	3	25·86	
		4×100m relay	1	1	5	46·79	
Mathews, M.J.	AUS	100m	1	2	1	11·81	
			SF	2	1	11·80	
			F		3	11·94	B
		200m	1	6	1	24·16	
			SF	2	2	24·42	
			F		3	24·10	B
Matthews, M.R.	USA	4×100m relay	1	2	2	45·52	
			F		3	45·04	B
		Long jump	Q		DNQ		
Mayer, B.	GER	4×100m relay	1	1	2	45·07	
			F		6	47·29	
Mellor, F.N.	AUS	4×100m relay	1	1	1	45·00*	
			F		1	44·65*	G
Mertova, S.	TCH	Discus throw	F		8	45,78	
Minicka, G.	POL	200m	1	2	4	25·19	
		4×100m relay	1	2	4	46·58	
		Long jump	F		12	5,64	
Modrachova, O.	TCH	High jump	F		10	1,64	
Mueller, B.A.	USA	80m hurdles	1	1	4	11·83	
Musso, M.	ITA	100m	1	3	5	12·40	
		4×100m relay	1	1	3	45·91	
			F		5	45·90	
Pashley, A.	GBR	100m	1	3	3	11·94	
		4×100m relay	1	2	1	45·38	
			F		2	44·70	S
Paternoster, P.	ITA	Discus throw	F		11	42,83	
		Javelin throw	Q		DNQ		
Paul, J.	GBR	100m	1	6	2	12·15	
			SF	1	4	12·24	
		200m	1	4	1	24·00	
			SF	2	1	24·36	
			F		5	24·30	
		4×100m relay	1	2	1	45·38	
			F		2	44·70	S
Peggion, F.	ITA	100m	1	2	6	12·55	
Picado, A.	FRA	80m hurdles	1	3	4	11·50	
		4×100m relay	1	1	4	46·39	
Pissareva, M.	URS	High jump	F		=2	1,67	S
Ponomaryeva, N.	URS	Discus throw	F		3	52,02	B
Popova, G.M.	URS	100m	1	5	1	11·86	
			SF	1	5	12·34	
Quinton, C.L.	GBR	80m hurdles	1	1	3	11·63	
			SF	1	6	11·61	
Rao, M.L.	IND	100m	1	1	DNF		
Raue, E.	GER	Javelin throw	F		10	45,87	
Rever, M.	CAN	100m	1	2	5	12·36	
		200m	1	6	5	26·17	
		4×100m relay	1	1	5	46·79	
Rezchikova, G.	URS	100m	1	2	2	12·11	
			SF	2	6	12·23	
		4×100m relay	1	2	3	46·20	
			F		4	45·81	
Richter, H.J.	POL	100m	1	4	5	12·38	
		4×100m relay	1	2	4	46·58	
Robertson, I.R.	USA	80m hurdles	1	3	6	12·02	
Rudolph, W.G.	USA	200m	1	2	3	24·83	
		4×100m relay	1	2	2	45·52	
			F		3	45·04	B
Sander, M.	GER	80m hurdles	1	4	4	11·22	
		4×100m relay	1	1	2	45·07	
			F		6	47·29	
Sanopal, F.	PHI	80m hurdles	1	4	5	12·15	
Scrivens, J.E.	GBR	200m	1	6	2	24·27	
			SF	1	5	24·66	
		4×100m relay	1	2	1	45·38	
			F		2	44·70	S
Shida, Y.	JPN	Javelin throw	F		12	44,96	
Sloper, V.I.	NZL	Shot put	F		5	15,34	
Strickland, S.B.	AUS	100m	1	4	3	11·86	
		80m hurdles	1	2	1	11·02	
			SF	1	1	10·89*	
			F		1	10·96	G
		4×100m relay	1	1	1	45·00*	
			F		1	44·65*	G
Stuart, M.F.	NZL	100m	1	6	3	12·38	
		80m hurdles	1	2	3	11·46	
			SF	2	6	11·51	

COMPETITOR	COUNTRY CODE	EVENT	ROUND	HEAT	PLACE	TIME & DISTANCE	MEDAL
Stubnick, C.	GER	100m	1	6	1	11·89	
			SF	1	1	12·05	
			F		2	11·92	S
		200m	1	3	1	24·58	
			SF	1	2	24·17	
			F		2	23·89	S
		4×100m relay	1	1	2	45·07	
			F		6	47·29	
Takahashi, Y.	JPN	Long jump	Q		DNQ		
Testa, L.A.	USA	Shot put	F		14	13,06	
Thrower, N.C.	AUS	80m hurdles	1	4	1	10·94	
			SF	2	2	11·20	
			F		3	11·25	B
Tychkevitch, T.	URS	Shot put	F		1	16,59*	G
Tyler, D.J.B.	GBR	High jump	F		12	1,60	
Usenik, M.	YUK	Shot put	F		9	14,49	
Vigh, E.	HUN	Javelin throw	F		7	48,07	
Voborilova, J.	TCH	High jump	F		8	1,64	
		Discus throw	F		7	45,84	

COMPETITOR	COUNTRY CODE	EVENT	ROUND	HEAT	PLACE	TIME & DISTANCE	MEDAL
Wainwright, P.	GBR	80m hurdles	1	2	5	12·06	
Weigel, B.D.E.	NZL	Long jump	F		7	5,85	
Werner, M.	GER	Discus throw	F		10	43,34	
		Shot put	F		3	15,61	B
Wershoven, A.	USA	Javelin throw	F		14	44,29	
White, W.B.	USA	Long jump	F		2	6,09	S
Whitty, A.A.	CAN	High jump	F		16	1,55	
Williams, L.	USA	100m	1	2	3	12·14	
Willis, E.M.	AUS	Long jump	Q		DNQ		
Winter, E.M.	SAF	100m	1	6	4	12·59	
		80m hurdles	1	3	2	11·28	
			SF	2	5	11·47	
Wojtaszek, A.	POL	Javelin throw	F		9	46,92	
Woodlock, M.J.	AUS	Shot put	Q		DNQ		
Wright, M.F.	AUS	Javelin throw	Q		DNQ		
Yugora, V.	URS	200m	1	4	2	25·13	
			SF	2	6	25·12	
Yoshino, T.	JPN	Discus throw	Q		DNQ		
Zatopkova, D.	TCH	Javelin throw	F		4	49,83	
Zybina, G.	URS	Shot put	F		2	16,53	S

The 20km walkers seen pounding the track shortly after the gun, with Alex Oakley of Australia in the lead from Russia's Bruno Junk and Britain's Stan Vickers.

1960

Elliott's Electric Pace and Bikila's Bare Feet

Some 1,567 years after the Emperor Theodosius the Great had ended the ancient Olympic Games, the modern Games arrived in his home city of Rome.

Some of the old Roman sites were used, and in particular the marathon began at the Capitol Hill and finished near the Arch of Constantine, less than a mile from which was the obelisk of Axum, plundered from Ethiopia by Italian troops. It was here that the surprise winner of the Games, an Ethiopian called Abebe Bikila, decided in advance to make his effort in the marathon. He drew away to win, running in bare feet, creating a new world best time.

Among other excellent performances, pride of place must go to Herb Elliott, another world record-breaker, who ran away from a powerful 1,500 metres field to win by 2·8 sec, the biggest winning margin at the time, and exceeded only by Kip Keino at altitude since.

Men's Track Events

Harry Jerome of Canada and Armin Hary of Germany had both broken the world **100 metres** record with 10·0 sec and the German had the reputation of being the fastest starter that ever was. It was claimed that his reaction time to the gun was only one tenth of a second. Hary clocked the fastest time in the preliminary heats with 10·2, while Jerome pulled a muscle when leading in the first semi-final and was out of the reckoning. In the final, both Hary and Dave Sime of the USA got away before the gun and neither were penalised, but on the second start Hary broke and was warned. Understandably, he did not have his usual "blitz" start on the third attempt, but his tremendous pick-up took him clear of the field at 30 metres, with both Sime and Peter Radford of Britain having relatively poor starts. Hary maintained his lead and won in 10·2 to equal the Olympic record. But it was a close thing as Sime, and behind him, Radford, were sprinting faster over the latter half of the race. Sime also finished in 10·2 for second place, with Radford third in 10·3. (Automatic timings: Hary 10·32, Sime 10·35 and Radford 10·42).

In the **200 metres**, Peter Radford had set a world record over the longer 220 yards, while Ray Norton of America was considered the best bend runner in the world. However, the man that shone throughout the preliminaries was Livio Berruti of Italy, who equalled the world record in the second semi-final, when beating Norton by two metres. In the final, after one false start, Berruti just motored around the bend leaving everyone in his wake and carried on up the straight to win in another record equalling 20·5 sec, before sprawling onto the ground in dramatic fashion. Norton tied up in the finishing stretch, and it was the fast finishing Les Carney of the USA who took second in 20·6, while France's Abdou Seye, who had run a slow bend, finished the

fastest to place third with 20·7. (Automatic timings: Berruti 20·62, Carney 20·69 and Seye 20·83).

The semi-finals of the **400 metres** were fast with America's third string, Otis Davis, winning the first race in 45·5 from Milkha Singh of India in 45·9, and Karl Kaufmann of Germany the second in 45·7 from Mal Spence of South Africa in 45·8. In the final it was Spence who went out fast and hit the 200 in 21·2, with Singh two metres back, followed by Kaufmann and Davis. Davis then made his effort with 150 to go, and led at 300 in 32·6, with America's Earl Young and Spence behind him and Kaufmann fourth. Slowly, Kaufmann pulled back Davis and they lunged at the tape together, both clocking 44·9 for a new world record. Davis got the nod for the gold by one-hundredth of a second. Spence fought off Singh in the closing stages and took third in 45·5 to 45·6. (Automatic timings: Davis 45·07, Kaufmann 45·08 and Spence 45·60).

Roger Moens of Belgium, the world record holder, was the strongest tip for the **800 metres**, with George Kerr of the West Indies regarded as the danger. Kerr won the first semi-final in 1-47·1 for an Olympic record from Christian Waegli of Switzerland and surprisingly, Peter Snell of New Zealand won the other from Moens, in 1-47·2. Waegli took up the running at the start of the final and passed the 400 in 51·9, followed closely by Paul Schmidt of Germany, Kerr, Moens and Snell. With his arms swinging, Moens made his bid at 600 and winged his way towards the finish. He hardly saw Snell spurt by on the inside to win in 1-46·3 for a new Olympic record. Moens finished just behind in 1-46·5, with Kerr third at 1-47·1. (Automatic timings: Snell 1-46·48, Moens 1-46·55 and Kerr 1-47·25).

Herb Elliott, the world record holder, and a strong **1,500 metres** favourite, was content to fall in behind the leaders as Michel Bernard of France took up the running in the final, followed by Dan Waern of Sweden and Zoltan Vamos of Rumania. The 400 was passed in 58·2 and the 800 in a spritely 1-57·8. Elliott then spurted to the front and hotted things up, passing the 1,200 in 2-54·0 and finishing in 3-35·6 for a new world record. His last 800 took an amazing 1-53·1. Meanwhile, Istvan Rozsavoelgyi of Hungary was lying second until Michel Jazy of France struck coming off the last curve, and won the race for second place in 3-38·4, with the Hungarian third in 3-39·2.

In the **5,000 metres**, the fancied Gordon Pirie of Britain was eliminated in the heats, finding the hot sun too much for him. The final started off quietly with Kazimierz Zimny of Poland leading for nearly nine laps and passing 3km in 8-19·3, before Dave Power of Australia went to the front and zipped up the pace. On reaching 4km, Murray Halberg of New Zealand put in a devilish lap of 61·8 and opened up a gap of 25 metres. Halberg, with a withered arm as a result of injury

189

Nearest the camera, Armin Hary, the West German, blitz started the 100 metres to win the gold medal ahead of Dave Sime, not in picture, and Peter Radford (second left).

sustained in a rugby accident, was gradually pulled back by the chasing group, but won in 13-43·4. Behind him there was some desperate sprinting with Hans Grodotzki of Germany taking the silver in 13-44·6 from the fast finishing Zimny 13-44·8. (Automatic timings: Halberg 13-43·76, Grodotzki 13-45·01 and Zimny 13-45·09).

It was a straight final in the **10,000 metres**, with a large field of 33 competing, and following his win in the 5,000 metres, Murray Halberg was tipped to win. The initial pace was very moderate, with 20 of the runners in contention at 5km, which was passed in 14-22·2. With seven laps left, Dave Power of Australia made a big surge from the front with the Russians, Pyotr Bolotnikov and Alek Desyatchikov and Hans Grodotzki of Germany, going with him. Bolotnikov bided his time but kicked hard with 700 to go and built up a big lead to win in 28-32·2 for a new Olympic record, while Grodotzki outsprinted the other two to take the silver in 28-37·0. Power secured the bronze in 28-38·2. (Automatic timings: Bolotnikov 28-32·18, Grodotzki 28-32·18 and Power 28-37·65).

For the first time ever, the **marathon** neither started nor finished at the stadium. The route was a kind of tour of ancient Rome starting at Capitol Hill in Campidoglio Square and finishing at the Arch of Constantine, at one end of the Appian Way. And it was in this setting that 69 runners came under orders late one afternoon on a very hot day. At 10km, the leading group included the two Britons Arthur Keily and Brian Kilby, the bare footed Abebe Bikila of Ethiopia and Allal Saoudi of Morocco. Rhadi of Morocco moved into the lead at 20km,

followed by Bikila, and the same two led at 30km in 1:34-29 with Barry Magee of New Zealand and Sergei Popov of Russia 1-23 behind. However, at 41km Bikila opened a gap on Rhadi and won in a new world best of 2:15-16·2. Rhadi was second at 2:15-41·6 and Magee third with 2:17-18·2.

Lee Calhoun of the USA, the champion, was tipped to win the **110 metres hurdles** again, even though four men had gone under 14·0 sec in the preliminaries. America's Calhoun and Willie May clocked 13·7, while Martin Lauer of Germany and Russia's Antatoliy Mikhailov, who was later eliminated, recorded 13·9. The wind was against the runners in the final where Calhoun was quickest away with smooth technique over the hurdles, but May, who had greater speed between the flights, caught up with him. However, at the finish, Calhoun managed to outlean May at the tape, and won by one-hundredth of a second on the photo, both being given 13·8. A second duel was simultaneously contested between America's Hayes Jones and Lauer. Lauer hit three hurdles and lost third place to Jones, with both being given 14·0. (Automatic timings: Calhoun 13·98, May 13·99 and Jones 14·17).

The **400 metres hurdles** saw another defending champion in world record holder Glenn Davis of the USA, attempting to retain his title. In the final, his fellow American Dick Howard went out from the blocks very fast and was two metres up at half-way from Helmut Janz of Germany, Davis, who was having problems chopping at each hurdle, and Cliff Cushman of the USA. But, around the final bend, Davis overtook Howard and steamed up the straight to win in 49·3, a new Olympic record. Cushman made great efforts over the latter part of the race and forced himself into second place in 49·6, with Howard third in 49·7 and Janz fourth in 49·9. (Automatic timings: Davis 49·51, Cushman 49·77 and Howard 49·90).

Chromik of Poland, the European champion, was knocked out in the **3,000 metres steeplechase** heats, from which nine qualified for the final. The final was held on a hot day and Alexey Konov of Russia went into the lead with Gaston Roelants of Belgium and fellow countryman Nikolay Sokolov on his shoulder. Sokolov went to the front, but was overtaken by Zdzislaw Krzyszkowiak, the world record holder from Poland, with 300 to go. His opponents could not respond and he won easily in 8-34·2 from Sokolov in 8-36·4 and Semyon Rzhishchin, another Russian, third in 8-42·2. (Automatic timings: Krzyszkowiak 8-34·30, Sokolov 8-36·55 and Rzhishchin 8-42·34).

The fastest time of the year for the **20 kilometres walk** had been set by Ken Matthews of Britain, while his compatriot Stan Vickers was European champion. Matthews led at 5km in 22-11·4 from Noel Freeman of Australia and Vladimir Golubnichy of the USSR, but at 10km, it was the latter who passed the check mark first in 45-13·4. Matthews eventually retired with leg troubles. At 15km Golubnichy was still in front with Gennadiy Solodov of the USSR next and Freeman third. Solodov later found the heat too much and retired, while Golubnichy went on to win in 1:34-07·2 from Freeman in 1:34-16·4 and Vickers in 1:34-56·4.

Don Thompson had prepared for the **50 kilometres walk** by simulating the hot conditions of 32°C (90°F) in his bathroom, where he exercised daily. There were three former champions in the field, Norman Read of New Zealand from 1956, Giuseppe Dordoni of Italy from 1952 and John Ljunggren of Sweden from 1948, but it was the little known Ajit Singh of India who took the lead. Between 20km and 22km, a number of the leading group flagged, while Grigoriy Klimov of Russia and Noel Freeman of Australia were disqualified, leaving Thompson alone at the front. The Briton passed the half-way stage in 2:10-30, 67 seconds up on Ljunggren and Alek Cherbina of Russia, but at 45km he was caught

Tamara Press, the 'Iron Lady' of Russian throwing, scooped two medals at Rome, the shot put gold and the discus silver.   Mark Shearman

by the Swede, with Abdon Pamich of Italy 78 seconds behind. But at 47km Thompson was moving away again and he won in 4:25-30·0 for a Games record. Ljunggren was second in 4:25-47·0 and Pamich third with 4:27-55·4.

Germany had a well-drilled team for the **4 × 100 metres relay** and did the unheard of by equalling the world record of 39·5 sec in a heat. However, the USA, the perpetual winners of the event, were undismayed and won their heat in 39·7. In the final, Bernd Cullmann for Germany ran a superb first leg to hold a slight lead over Frank Budd of America, who passed to Ray Norton, but Norton had gone off too early and the exchange was made three metres outside the box. Armin Hary of Germany and Norton ran neck and

Lee Calhoun

Lee Calhoun is the only man to win the Olympic 110m hurdles title twice and both victories were decided by the photo-finish camera. At Melbourne in 1956 he was given the verdict over his American compatriot Jack Davis both credited with 13·5 sec and in the 1960 Rome Games, Willie May, another American, tied Calhoun's winning 13·8 sec. The photo-finish film showed a difference of only 2/100th sec between them.

There were some doubts whether Calhoun would be allowed to defend his title in Rome as he had received a honeymoon trip to Paris and also a swimming pool for his home. This led to his being suspended indefinitely by the American AAU. The suspension was only lifted when Calhoun gave the pool to a boys' club.

Following his success in Rome, he reduced the world record for the high hurdles event to 13·2 sec in Berne, before returning home. This performance remained unbeaten until Rod Milburn, a subsequent winner of the Olympic title, chipped 0·1 sec off the time, 13 years later.

Rome provided a particularly memorable Games for the small town of Laurel, Mississippi, where Calhoun was born on 23 February 1933, because it was also the birthplace of Ralph Boston, who won the long jump title.

neck, but Norton's pass to Stone Johnson was poor and Germany's Walter Mahlendorf snatched a two-metre advantage to pass the stick to Martin Lauer. America's anchor runner, Dave Sime, then stormed down the track and won in 39·4 by half a metre from Germany in 39·5. The USA were of course disqualified for the irregular baton change, leaving Germany as the gold medallists. Meanwhile Britain, who had only qualified in the semi-finals when Nigeria got themselves disqualified, were battling with Russia and Italy. In a close fight, the USSR took the silver position in 40·1, Britain the bronze in 40·2 with Italy fourth in 40·2. (Automatic timings: Germany 39·66, USSR 40·24 and Britain 40·32).

The **4 × 400 metres relay** was another duel between Germany and the USA. Jack Yerman led off for the States and ran his leg in 46·2, with Mal Spence of the West Indies next in 46·5, and the German back in fourth. Manfred Kinder then ran a storming leg of 44·9 for Germany, but Glenn Davis virtually won the event for America on the third leg by running 45·4 to Johannes Kaiser's 45·9. Karl Kaufmann had a six-metres deficit against the 400 metres Olympic champion, Otis Davis. Davis, of course won in 3-02·2, a new world record, from Germany 3-02·7 with the British West Indies third in 3-04·0. (Automatic timings: USA 3-02·37, Germany 3-02·84 and West Indies 3-04·13).

Men's Field Events

In the **high jump**, John Thomas of the USA was the big find of the season and had improved the world record by an incredible six centimetres! Unfortunately for him, the competition was drawn out, spanning some ten hours and by then he was suffering from dysentry. The tension increased as Charlie Dumas of America, the defending champion, cleared 2,03 metres but went out in sixth place. Thomas and three Russians, Robert Shavlakadze, Valeriy Brumel and Victor Bolshov tackled 2,12 to equal the Olympic record and Shavlakadze and Bolshov cleared first time, while Brumel needed three goes and Thomas passed. At 2,14, Shavlakadze again went over first time, while the other three needed two attempts. The bar was now raised to 2,16 and Shavlakadze did his trick once again to win the gold medal. Under the

The superb American all-rounder, Rafer Johnson, captured the decathlon title despite injury.

Wilma Rudolph

The wonder is that Wilma Rudolph ever became a track runner, let alone a triple gold medal winner at the 1960 Games in Rome. She was born at Clarksville, Tennessee, on 23 June 1940, and illness as a four-year-old left her paralysed: not until she was seven was she able to walk normally again. But by the time she was 16 she had won a place in the American team for the Olympics in Melbourne and there she became one of the youngest ever to win an athletics medal when the US finished third in the 4 × 100m relay.

By the time the Rome Games came round in 1960 she was a world record-holder for 200m with 22·9 sec. Those who thought this to be a mere "flash in the pan" performance had a rude awakening in Rome, when in her semi-final heat of the 100m, she tied the world record with 11·3 sec. In the final she was even faster with 11 sec flat, but this time could not be officially ratified as a world best mark because of the wind.

Again in the 200m final the tall, elegant Wilma raced home a clear winner and on the closing day of the Games she was involved in another world record performance, anchoring the US team to victory in the 4 × 100m relay in 44·5 sec.

Before retiring after the following season, she had lowered the women's world mark for 100m to 11·2 sec.

Don "Tarzan" Bragg of the USA, the last of the great metal pole vaulters, broke the Olympic record by a substantial margin on his way to the gold medal.

Despite the handicap of a withered arm, New Zealander, Murray Halberg, shrugged his way to victory in the 5,000 metres.

count-back rule Brumel took the silver and Thomas the bronze.

Don "Tarzan" Bragg was the top dog in the **pole vault** and was one of the last of the steel pole jumpers. The 13 finalists had no problems until the bar reached 4,40 metres and the field was reduced to ten, but by 4,50 a further three had exceeded their limit and four more at 4,55. First time clearances at this height were achieved by Bragg, the USA's Ron Morris, and Eeles Landstroem of Finland, while Rolando Cruz of Puerto Rico succeeded on his second try. With the bar now elevated to 4,60, Bragg sailed over first time and Morris needed two attempts but the other two failed, with Landstoem taking the bronze medal. The vaulters agreed for the bar to be raised to 4,70 and Bragg did his jack-knife act over the bar to win the competition, on Morris failing. A new world record height of 4,82 was attempted and two of Bragg's three vaults were near misses.

Jesse Owens' 25-year-old **long jump** world record had been beaten before the Games by Ralph Boston of the USA but, Igor Ter-Ovanesyan of the USSR, the European champion and record holder, was the early leader in the competition. jumping 7,90 metres in the first round. In the next round, America's Bo Roberson went into the lead with 8,03, and Boston finally responded in the third with a new Olympic record of 8,12. There was a lull in the jumping until the final round when Roberson came within an ace of winning with 8,11. But it was only good enough for the silver medal, while Ter-Ovanesyan improved to 8,04 for the bronze.

There had been a great leap forward in **triple jump** standards and Jozef Schmidt of Poland had brought science to the sport. No longer was just natural spring of tree-trunk legs sufficient: blazing speed and stroking the ground was the Polish answer. Schmidt, in the qualifying rounds, immediately set a new Olympic record of 16,44 metres. And in the final he started where he had

left off, with his very first jump improving the record to 16,78, and two jumps later to 16,81, to win his first Olympic title. The competition was more about the minor places and on his fourth attempt Vladimir Goryayev of the USSR secured the silver medal with a jump of 16,63 and Vitold Kreyer of the USSR took the bronze, with a last ditch effort of 16,43.

Twice Olympic champion in the **shot put**, Parry O'Brien of the United States was shooting for his third gold medal. However, he was up against a couple of big men in fellow Americans Bill Nieder and Dallas Long. Nieder was a nervous individual and Long a placid fellow, while O'Brien had the concentration and determination. In the first round of the final Nieder threw 18,67 metres for an Olympic record, but O'Brien topped his put with 18,77, with Mike Lindsay of Britain briefly holding third spot with 17,63. In the next round, Nieder equalled O'Brien's mark with 18,77 but Long beat it with 18,88, which motivated O'Brien into firing one off to 19,11. It was in the fifth round that Nieder, the world record holder, steadied his nerve and blasted to 19,68 for the gold and an Olympic record. O'Brien took the silver with 19,11 and Long the bronze, throwing 19,01 with his last put.

Al Oerter of the USA, the defending champion in the **discus throw**, was up against the co-world record holders, Edmund Piatkowski of Poland and another American, Rink Babka. In the preliminaries Oerter set a new Olympic record with 58,43 metres, but the first round saw Babka lead him with 58,02 to 57,64, with Viktor Kompaneyets of the USSR third at 55,06. Nothing changed until the fourth round, when Jozsef Szecsenyi of Hungary moved up to third with 55,22. In the next round, however, Oerter threw a big one and launched it to 59,18 for a Games record and the gold. Babka took silver with his earlier 58,02 and the bronze went to the USA's Dick Cochran who threw 57,16 in the

Lying third and waiting to pounce in a heat of the 1,500 metres, the favourite, Herb Elliott of Australia, eased his way to the final where he triumphed in style.

Rising to the partisan Italian crowd, Livio Berruti, the local hero, wins the 200 metres amid wild enthusiasm.

All-Sport Photographic Ltd.

Glenn Davis

Glenn Davis was the first of only two athletes to win the Olympic 400m hurdles title twice, the other being Edwin Moses, also an American (1976 and 1984).

Davis, who was born in Wellsburg, West Virginia, on 12 September 1934, made a meteoric rise to the top in the one-lap low hurdles, because he had raced in less than a dozen competitions before going to Melbourne. Originally a sprinter, he was no faster than 54·4 sec on his first attempt at hurdling the 400 m course, but when the American Olympic trials were held, he set a world record of 49·5 sec. He won in Melbourne with 50·1 sec.

His world records were not only confined to the hurdles. Twice in 1958 he improved the world best time for 440 yards flat, first with 45·8 sec, and then 45·7 sec. That year he also improved the 400m hurdles mark to 49·2 sec.

The Rome Games of 1960 saw him still at the top of his form and he not only retained his hurdles title with an Olympic record 49·3 sec, but ran the third leg in the United States 4 × 400m world record-breaking winning team.

Davis was also capable of racing the 100m in 10·3 sec, the 200m in 21·0 sec and of long jumping 24ft (7,32m).

He finished his sporting career as an American footballer.

Herb Elliott

No athlete has achieved a more sweeping victory in an Olympic track final than Herb Elliott's 20-yard 1,500m win, which produced a world record time of 3-35·6 at the 1960 Rome Games. He was never beaten over 1,500m or a mile throughout his racing career.

Elliott was born in Perth, Western Australia, on 25 February 1938 and his prowess as a youngster came to the fore in 1957, when he started breaking world junior records. Like Emil Zatopek, of Czechoslovakia, in earlier years he developed strength through rigourous interval training, wearing heavy boots and surging up seaside sand dunes. All this was encouraged by his elderly coach Percy Cerutty, who masterminded Elliott's great triumph in Rome.

Approaching the 1,000m in that 1,500m final, Elliott staggered his opposition by bursting into a 20-yard lead and continuing the exceptional pace right through to the finish. When reaching the back straight on the final lap he saw Cerutty standing by the side of the track frantically waving a white towel. That was a signal for Elliott that he was on course for a world record and to give everything he had left in him. He responded by smashing the world mark he had set two years previously to ecstatic applause from the packed Rome stadium.

Ralph Boston

Ralph Boston was the man who finally cracked Jesse Owens's world long jump record of 26ft 8¼in (8,13m), which had stood for 25 years. He did so at Walnut, California, in August 1960 when he reached 26ft 11¼in (8,21m). Twelve months later he became the first to clear 27ft with 27ft 0½in (8,24m) and subsequently he improved this mark four more times to ultimately achieve an all-time best of 27ft 5in (8,35m) in 1965.

The youngest of ten children, born in Laurel, Mississippi, on 9 May 1939, Boston began showing his prowess as a long jumper when only 14. By the age of 20 he was landing beyond 25ft (7,62m). Being a student at Tennessee State University provided Boston with the opportunity to put the polish to his jumping skills and it came as no surprise at the Rome Olympics in 1960, to see him take the long jump gold with a Games record of 26ft 7½in (8,12m).

So consistent was his form during the seasons between, he was generally expected to keep his Olympic title in Tokyo, but Lynn Davies of Britain provided the big upset by winning with 26ft 5½in (8,07m), just an inch and a half ahead of Boston. The popular American was still jumping close to 27ft (8,23m) four years later and in Mexico he finished with the bronze in spite of achieving a personal Olympic best, 26ft 9¼in (8,16m).

fifth round.

In the **hammer throw**, Hal Connolly of the USA was not only the defending champion, but also the world record holder. The standard had jumped since the last Games and three throwers beat the old record in the preliminaries, Mike Ellis of Britain with 63,21 metres, the USSR's Anatoliy Samotsvetov with 64,67 and his countryman Valiliy Rudenkov with 67,03. Rudenkov took the lead in the first round of the final with 65,60 from Tadeusz Rut of Poland on 64,51, but in the second round the Pole improved to 64,64 while Zvenko Bezjak of Yugoslavia threw 64,21. It was then that Rudenkov made his winning throw of 67,10. Gyula Zsivotsky of Hungary clinched the silver medal with a throw of 65,79, while Rut got the bronze. Connolly, troubled by injury, was eighth.

Javelin throwers are often erratic. Bill Alley of the USA, who held the world record, and the defending champion, Egil Danielsen of Norway, did not get by the qualifying competition, while three quality throwers bowed out after three throws in the final: Janusz Sidlo of Poland, the European champion, who had thrown 85,15 metres in the preliminaries, Carlo Lievore of Italy and Al Cantello of the USA, who qualified in the prelims with 79,72. The medals were decided in the first round: Viktor Tsibulenko of Russia winning the gold with 84,64, Germany's Walter Krueger the silver with 79,36 and Gergely Kulcsar of Hungary, the bronze.

Competing in the Olympic **decathlon**, were Rafer Johnson of the USA, the world record holder, and his great rival, Formosa's Chuan-Kwang Yang. Yang got off to a good start in the 100 metres with 10·7 sec to Johnson's 10·9, and increased his lead by long jumping 7,46 metres, before Johnson produced a great 15,82 metres shot to go ahead. Then the heavens opened and it poured with rain, which delayed the competition. Back in harness, Yang had the better high jump with 1,90 metres and pulled back some points with a 48·1 sec hurdles, but Johnson immediately snatched it back with a fine 48,49 metres discus. The Formosan later clawed back points in the pole vault with 4,30 metres but lost a few in the javelin, when Johnson threw 69,76 metres. Coming up to the last event, the 1,500 metres, Johnson had 67 points in hand and he shadowed his great rival throughout the race, which Yang completed in 4-48·5. The gold went to Johnson with 8,392, an Olympic record, and Yang scored 8,334 for the silver, while Vasiliy Kuznyetsov of Russia, who had a good second day, won the bronze.

Women's Events

On paper, the fastest girls prior to Rome over **100 metres** were Wilma Rudolph of the USA, Catherine Capdevielle of France, Giuseppina Leone of Italy and Maria Itkina of the USSR, all having run 11·4 sec, while Betty Cuthbert of Australia had clocked 10·4 for the 100 yards. In the first semi-final, Rudolph won convincingly in a world record time of 11·3, while Dorothy Hyman of Britain took the second in 11·5 from Itkina. The final was run with a following wind and after one false start, Itkina led for 25 metres, until Rudolph swept past to win in 11·0, with Hyman coming through to take second in 11·3, just beating Leone, who was given the same time. (Automatic timings: Rudolph 11·18, Hyman 11·43 and Leone 11·48).

In the **200 metres**, Wilma Rudolph not only came to the Games as world record holder, but had created a tremendous impression with her stunning performances in the short sprints. The best times came in the heats, where wind conditions were favourable and both Dorothy Hyman and Giuseppina Leone of Italy clocked 23·7 sec, while Rudolph set a new Olympic record of 23·2. In the final there was a strong adverse wind, but Rudolph soon took the lead to stride home in 24·0 and win the gold. A desperate battle was going on behind her, with Hyman and Maria Itkina fighting it out along the straight, but Jutta Heine of Germany came with a late rush to claim second place in 24·4 from Hyman in 24·7. (Automatic timings: Rudolph 24·13, Heine 24·58 and Hyman 24·82).

After 32 years, the **800 metres** was reinstated as an Olympic event and in the heats the existing Olympic record of 2-16·8 was beaten by all except one runner. The world record holder for the event was Lyudmila Shevtzova-Lysenko of the USSR, but her great rival, Sin-Kim Dan of Korea was not present. Dixie Willis of Australia was the fastest qualifier at 2-05·9, but in the final things were to go horribly wrong for her. Willis was in the lead until 150 metres to go, when Shevtzova-Lysenko drew level and they sprinted down the home straight together, with Australia's Brenda Jones and Ursula Donath of Germany in close attendance. Suddenly, Willis stepped off the track with 30 metres to go, leaving Shevtzova-Lysenko to fight off Jones and win in 2-04·3 to equal her own world record. The Australian finished second in 2-04·4 and third was Donath in 2-05·6. (Automatic timings: Shevtzova-Lysenko 2-04·50, Jones 2-04·58).

The **80 metres hurdles** world record holder was Gisela Birkemeyer of Germany, but it was Irina Press of the USSR who was on form, and she set a new Olympic record of 10·6 sec in the semi-final. In the final, Press was swiftly away and used her basic speed to great effect, but Carole Quinton of Britain was a more polished hurdler and ran her close. Press won in 10·8 from Quinton in 10·9, with Birkemeyer third in 11·0. (Automatic timings: Press 10·93, Quinton 10·99 and Birkemeyer 11·13).

A new world and Olympic record was set in the first round of the **4 × 100 metres relay** when America finished in 44·4 sec. The final was a close race between the USA, Germany, Russia and Poland for three legs until America's Wilma Rudolph got hold of the baton. She began a metre down, but won by three metres in 44·5, from Germany in 44·8 and Poland in 45·0. The US team was Martha Hudson, Lucinda Williams, Barbara Jones and Wilma Rudolph. (Automatic timings: USA 44·72, Germany 45·0 and Poland 45·19).

Iolanda Balas, the world record holder in the **high jump**, was head and shoulders above everyone else. Fifteen girls qualified at 1,65 metres and all of them repeated their performance in the final, but when the bar went to 1,68 only five cleared. At 1,71 Balas, Dorothy Shirley of Britain, Jaroslawa Jozwiakowska of Poland and Galina Dolya of the USSR all succeeded, but only Balas went on to clear 1,73, 1,77, 1,81 and 1,85 for a new Olympic record. The minor medals were decided on the count-back rule and Shirley and Jozwiakowska each received a silver medal, while Dolya was fourth.

Nineteen girls qualified for the final of the **long jump**, the best of them being Mary Bignal of Britain with a leap of 6,33, but her nerves let her down in the final and she could only finish ninth. Hildrun Claus of Germany, the world record holder, was the early leader with 6,21 metres, but then Vyera Krepkina of the USSR had successive jumps of 6,22 and 6,37 to win the title. Elzbieta Krzesinska of Poland, the defending champion, jumped 6,27 for the silver and Claus got the bronze.

Russia's Tamara Press was in a class of her own in the **shot put**. In the second round of the final. Press pushed the iron ball out to a new Olympic record of 17,32 metres and it was then purely a matter of who would win the silver and bronze. The last round was the decider, as Johanna Luettge of Germany exploded to 16,61 for the silver position and Earlene Brown of the USA hit 16,42 for the bronze.

Tamara Press also headed the rankings for the **discus throw** before Rome. Against her was the 1952 winner, Nina Romashkova-Ponomaryeva of the USSR and the 1956 winner, Olga Connolly (née Fikotova) of the USA In the first round of the final, Lia Manoliu of Rumania led with 52,36 metres from Press on 51,64 and

Germany's Kriemhild Hausmann on 51,47. Romashkova-Ponomaryeva moved into first place in the next round with 52,42 and in the following extended her lead to 53,39, and then 55,10 to win the Olympic title again after eight years Press took second with her last throw of 52,59, from Manoliu, third with her first-round 52.36.

The world record holder for the **javelin throw** was Elvira Ozolina of the USSR, and against her was Dana Zatopkova of Czechoslovakia, the winner from eight years previously. Ozolina ultimately won the final competition with her very first throw of 55,98 metres, an Olympic record, but there was still a very keen fight for the other two medals During the third round with Urszula Figwer of Poland and Anna Pazera of Australia leading her, Zatopkova whipped her javelin out to 53,78 for the silver medal. Russia's Birute Kaledene on 53,45 eventually won the bronze with Peskova of Czechoslovakia in fourth place.

Four athletes in contention during the final stages of the 10,000 metres, which was won by Pyotr Bolotnikov of the USSR, seen here in second place.

COMPETITOR	COUNTRY CODE	EVENT	ROUND	HEAT	PLACE	TIME & DISTANCE	MEDAL
MALES							
Abdelfattah, A.	UAR	Long jump	Q		DNQ	6,94	
Abdelkader, M.	UAR	100m	1	9	6	11·34	
Abdullah, M.	IRQ	Pole vault	Q		DNQ	0	
Aceituno, J.	CHI	5000m	1	1	DNF		
Addeche, H.	FRA	10000m	F		23	30-25·4	
Addy, J.	GHA	4×400m relay	1	4	2	3-10·66	
			SF	2	5	3-11·03	
Ado, G.	UGA	4×100m relay	1	2	DIS		
		400m	1	4	4	49·12	
Ahmed, Y.Z.A.	AFG	4×100m relay	1	4	4	44·53	
Ahrendt, E.	GER	Javelin throw	Q		DNQ	73,29	
Akraka, S.	NIG	4×100m relay	1	2	2	40·25	
			SF	1	DIS		
Alander, P.	FIN	800m	1	7	5	1-52·20	
Alard, P.	FRA	Discus throw	Q		DNQ	51,02	
Albarran, J.	ESP	100m	1	8	7	11·2	
Ali, R.	PAK	Long jump	Q		DNQ	0	
		4×100m relay	1	3	3	42·67	
			SF	2	6	42·99	
Al-Jamali, N.	IRQ	110m hurdles	1	3	6	15·99	
		400m hurdles	1	5	6	58·0	
Allen, J.	USA	50k walk	F		24	5:03-15·2	
Alley, W.	USA	Javelin throw	Q		DNQ	68,66	
Allonsius, E.	BEL	5000m	1	4	6	14-37·20	
Almeida, P.	POR	Long jump	Q		DNQ	7,10	
Alsop, F.	GBR	Long jump	F		13	7,25	
		Triple jump	F		12	15,49	
Altan, D.	TUR	Pole vault	Q		DNQ	0	
Ameur, H.	FRA	5000m	1	2	5	14-14·17	
		10000m	F		22	30-12·4	
Amu, A.	NIG	400m	1	8	1	46·93	
			2	4	3	46·76	
			SF	2	4	46·74	
		4×100m relay	1	2	2	40·25	
			SF	1	DIS		
Amukun, E.	UGA	100m	1	4	3	10·80	
			2	3	4	10·75	
		200m	1	5	2	21·38	
			2	1	4	21·47	
		4×100m relay	1	2	DIS		
Andersen, B.	DEN	Pole vault	Q		DNQ	4,00	
Anentia, A.	KEN	10000m	F		19	30-01·0	
Aniset, J.	LUX	5000m	1	4	11	15-17·0	
Antao, S.	KEN	100m	1	2	1	10·64	
			2	4	3	10·61	
			SF	2	6	10·72	
		200m	1	11	1	21·44	
			2	2	4	21·43	
		110m hurdles	1	1	5	15·13	
Antonelli, F.	ITA	10000m	F		27	30-39·4	
Antwi, J.A.	GHA	400m	1	1	5	47·81	
		4×400m relay	1	4	2	3-10·66	
			SF	2	5	3-11·03	
Anyfantakis, M.	GRE	Javelin throw	Q		DNQ	69,53	
Areta, L.	ESP	Long jump	Q		DNQ	7,04	
		Triple jump	Q		DNQ	14,93	
Ariel, G.	ISR	Shot put	Q		DNQ	14,65	
Arjaveekul, B.	THA	4×100m relay	1	1	5	42·19	
Arkhipchuk, V.	URS	200m	1	1	2	21·67	
			2	2	5	21·58	
Arnoux, J.	FRA	50k walk	F		28	5:20-22·0	
Artinyuk, A.	URS	5000m	1	2	3	14-09·92	
			F		9	14-08·45	
Asensio, M.	ESP	200m	1	11	5	22·45	
Asplund, B.	SWE	Hammer throw	Q		DNQ	57,27	
Astroth, H.	GER	50k walk	F		16	4:50-57·0	
Awori, A.	UGA	100m	1	3	5	11·09	
		110m hurdles	1	6	4	15·36	
			2	3	4	14·94	
		4×100m relay	1	2	DIS		
Babka, R.	USA	Discus throw	F		2	58,02	S
Bachvarov, M.	BUL	100m	1	1	5	10·95	
		200m	1	10	5	22·36	
Back, L.	SWE	20k walk	F		6	1:37-17·0	
Bagdonas, E.	USA	Hammer throw	Q		DNQ	59,48	
Baguley, J.	AUS	Long jump	Q		DNQ	6,96	
		Triple jump	F		13	15,22	
Bahrouni, K.	TUN	20k walk	F		27	1:47-09·6	
Baker, B.	AUS	Long jump	Q		DNQ	6,43	
Bakir, B.	MOR	Marathon	F		8	2:21-21·4	
Balajcza, T.	HUN	20k walk	F		DNF		
Balke, J.	GER	800m	1	5	2	1-53·72	
			2	4	3	1-48·98	
			SF	2	4	1-47·63	
Barabas, A.	RUM	1500m	1	2	9	3-47·71	
		5000m	1	4	9	15-11·2	
Baraldi, G.	ITA	800m	1	8	5	1-52·15	

COMPETITOR	COUNTRY CODE	EVENT	ROUND	HEAT	PLACE	TIME & DISTANCE	MEDAL
Barra, J.	BEL	200m	1	8	4	22·43	
Barras, G.	SUI	Pole vault	Q		DNQ	4,00	
Barris, T.	ESP	1500m	1	1	11	3-56·10	
Bartholome, B.	GER	Marathon	F		28	2:28-39·0	
Bartenyev, L.	URS	200m	1	4	2	21·89	
			2	3	5	21·65	
		4×100m relay	1	1	2	40·39	
			SF	2	3	40·30	
			F		2	40·24	S
Battista, E.	FRA	Triple jump	Q		DNQ	15,22	
Bautista, E.	PHI	200m	1	8	5	23·16	
		4×100m relay	1	2	4	41·55	
Beatty, J.	USA	5000m	1	1	9	14-44·40	
Beckert, L.	GER	Marathon	F		56	2:40-10·0	
Begier, Z.	POL	Discus throw	F		14	53,18	
Berezutskiy, N.	URS	110m hurdles	1	2	2	14·50	
			2	1	3	14·57	
			SF	1	6	14·69	
Bernard, M.	FRA	1500m	1	2	1	3-42·34	
			F		7	3-41·5	
		5000m	1	3	2	14-04·82	
			F		7	14-04·68	
Berruti, L.	ITA	200m	1	7	1	21·14	
			2	4	1	20·91	
			SF	2	1	20·65*	
			F		1	20·62*	G
		4×100m relay	1	2	1	40·16	
			SF	2	2	40·29	
			F		4	40·33	
Berthelsen, R.	NOR	Long jump	Q		DNQ	7,09	
Bertrand, C.	BWI	200m	1	9	3	21·51	
			2	1	6	21·57	
Beucher, T.	USA	Javelin throw	Q		DNQ	68,11	
Bezjak, Z.	YUG	Hammer throw	F		6	64,21	
Bhatia, R.	IND	5000m	1	2	11	15-06·6	
		Marathon	F		60	2:57-06·0	
Bikila, A.	ETH	Marathon	F		1	2:15-16·2*	G
Birrell, R.	GBR	110m	1	3	3	14·82	
			2	4	5	14·78	
Bisson, F.	ITA	Triple jump	Q		DNQ	14,76	
Bitan, S.	TUN	High jump	Q		DNQ	0	
Bizim, A.	RUM	Javelin throw	Q		DNQ	68,92	
Bjoergvin, H.	ISL	Decathlon	F		14	6261	
Blue, A.	AUS	800m	1	4	1	1-50·82	
			2	3	3	1-50·05	
			SF	1	5	1-47·97	
Bock, M.	GER	Decathlon	F		10	6894	
Bofferding, R.	LUX	4×400m relay	1	2	5	3-21·87	
		200m	1	10	6	23·36	
Bogey, R.	FRA	Marathon	F		13	29-22·53	
Bohaty, J.	TCH	5000m	1	3	7	14-30·34	
		10000m	F		DNF		
Bolotnikov, P.	URS	10000m	F		1	28-32·18*	G
Bolshov, V.	URS	High jump	F		4	2,14	
Bommarito, G.	ITA	400m	1	5	3	48·79	
			2	4	5	47·71	
		4×400m relay	1	2	3	3-10·00	
			SF	1	4	3-07·83	
Bonas, C.	VEN	Long jump	Q		DNQ	0	
Bondada, S.	IND	Long jump	Q		DNQ	7,08	
Bondarenko, D.	URS	Long jump	F		8	7,58	
Boston, R.	USA	Long jump	F		1	8,12*	G
Bouchaib, E.	MOR	100m	1	4	6	10·11	
		200m	1	7	5	22·34	
Boyes, M.	GBR	400m hurdles	1	1	4	52·32	
Bozek, E.	POL	4×400m relay	1	2	2	3-09·67	
			SF	2	4	3-10·88	
Bragg, D.	USA	Pole vault	F		1	4,70	G
Brakchi, A.	FRA	Long jump	Q		DNQ	7,20	
Bravi, A.	ITA	Long jump	F		10	7,47	
Breckenridge, A.	USA	Marathon	F		30	2:29-38·0	
Brightwell, R.	GBR	400m	1	2	2	48·58	
			2	3	2	46·31	
			SF	1	4	46·25	
		4×400m relay	1	3	3	3-20·47	
			SF	1	3	3-07·67	
			F		5	3-08·47	
Brlica, V.	TCH	3000m steeplechase	1	1	6	9-00·07	
Brodnik, J.	YUG	Decathlon	F		9	6918	
Bruder, H.	SUI	4×400m relay	1	3	1	3-10·79	
			SF	2	3	3-09·77	
			F		6	3-09·55	
Brumel, V.	URS	High jump	F		2	2,16*	S
Buchel, A.	LIE	Decathlon	F		DNF		

Left table:

COMPETITOR	COUNTRY CODE	EVENT	ROUND	HEAT	PLACE	TIME & DISTANCE	MEDAL
Budd, F.	USA	100m	1	9	2	10·55	
			2	3	1	10·52	
			SF	1	3	10·55	
			F		5	10·46	
		4×100m relay	1	4	1	39·87	
			SF	2	1	39·67	
			F			D S	
Buhl, H.	GER	3000m steeplechase	1	3	4	8-49·56	
Bukhantsev, K.	URS	Discus throw	F		8	53,61	
Bulatov, V.	URS	Pole vault	Q		DNQ		
Bullard, H.	BAH	400m	1	3	6	51·20	
Bulyshev, V.	URS	800m	1	1	1	1-51·83	
			2	3	5	1-50·74	
Bumroongpruck, M.	THA	400m	1	7	6	49·85	
Bunaes, C.	NOR	100m	1	1	2	10·80	
			2	2	5	10·69	
		200m	1	9	2	21·46	
			2	4	5	21·50	
Burleson, D.	USA	1500m	1	1	3	3-42·40	
			F		6	3-40·9	
Calhoun, L.	USA	110m hurdles	1	4	1	14·37	
			2	1	1	14·16	
			SF	2	1	13·88	
			F		1	13·98	G
Camacho, P.	PUR	Triple jump	Q		DNQ	14,21	
Cantello, A.	USA	Javelin throw	F		10	74,70	
Carlsson, L.	SWE	20k walk	F		14	1:40-25·0	
Carney, L.	USA	200m	1	2	1	21·31	
			2	3	1	21·06	
			SF	1	3	21·24	
			F		2	20·69	S
Catola, E.	ITA	400m hurdles	1	5	4	51·94	
			SF	1	5	52·44	
Cavalli, E.	ITA	Triple jump	Q		DNQ	15,48	
Cazzola, P.	ITA	4×100m relay	1	2	2	40·16	
			SF	2	2	40·29	
			F		4	40·33	
Chapman, D.	GBR	3000m steeplechase	1	2	6	8-53·24	
Charriere, R.	SUI	50k walk	F		27	5 09-00·8	
Cherbina, A.	URS	50k walk	F	4	4	31-44·0	
Chevichalov, G.	URS	400m hurdles	1	4	1	51·97	
			SF	1	4	52·14	
Chistyakov, V.	URS	110m hurdles	1	3	2	14·45	
			2	4	2	14·51	
			SF	2	3	14·46	
			F		6	14·71	
Chittick, J.	AUS	110m hurdles	1	2	5	14·86	
Chromik, J.	POL	3000m steeplechase	1	3	7	9-06·63	
Cieply, D.	POL	Hammer throw	F		5	64,57	
Cihak, Z.	TCH	Discus throw	F		13	53,29	
Clark, D.	USA	Pole vault	Q		DNQ	4,20	
Close, P.	USA	1500m	1	3	9	3-50·69	
Cochran, R.	USA	Discus throw	F		3	57,16	B
Coleman, P.	USA	3000m steeplechase	1	1	5	8-56·72	
Collardot, C.	FRA	Long jump	F		6	7,68	
Connolly, H.V.	USA	Hammer throw	F		8	63,59	
Consolini, A.	ITA	Discus throw	F		17	52,44	
Conti, L.	ITA	5000m	1	1	2	14-01·55	
			F		12	14-34·45	
Cornacchia, G.	ITA	110m hurdles	1	1	3	14·77	
			2	1	4	14·68	
Corsaro, G.	ITA	20k walk	F		26	1:46-47·2	
Crawford, R.	AUS	20k walk	F		11	1:39-16·2	
		50k walk	F		DIS		
Cruz, R.	PUR	Pole vault	F		4	4,55	
Csermak, J.	HUN	Hammer throw	Q		DNQ	59,72	
Csutoras, C.	HUN	200m	1	5	3	21·90	
		400m	1	3	5	48·31	
Cullmann, B.	GER	4×100m relay	1	3	1	39·61	
			SF	1	1	39·88	
			F		1	39·66	G
Cushman, C.	USA	400m hurdles	1	3	1	51·98	
			SF	2	1	50·89	
			F		2	49·77	S
Cunliffe, E.	USA	800m	1	3	3	1-48·95	
			2	3	2	1-49·83	
			SF	2	6	1-50·92	
Da Conceicao, J.T.	BRA	200m	1	8	2	21·48	
			2	2	6	21·63	
Dalkilic, M.	TUR	1500m	1	2	10	3-48·18	
		5000m	1	4	10	15-13·6	
Danielsen, E.	NOR	Javelin throw	Q		DNQ	72,93	
Dargouth, A.	TUN	800m	1	6	6	1-54·87	
Da Silva, A.C.	BRA	100m	1	4	4	10·98	
Da Silva, A. Ferraz	BRA	400m	1	3	4	48·10	
		400m hurdles	1	1	3	52·25	

Right table:

COMPETITOR	COUNTRY CODE	EVENT	ROUND	HEAT	PLACE	TIME & DISTANCE	MEDAL
Da Silva, A.F.	BRA	Triple jump	F		14	15,07	
Davis, E.	SAF	400m	1	1	2	47·31	
			2	1	5	48·18	
		4×400m relay	1	3	2	3-16·32	
			SF	1	1	3-06·53	
			F		4	3-05·18	
Davis, G.	USA	400m hurdles	1	2	2	52·41	
			SF	1	2	51·20	
			F		1	49·51*	G
		4×400m relay	1	4	1	3-10·58	
			SF	2	1	3-08·57	
			F		1	3-02·37*	G
Davis, I.	USA	Triple jump	F		4	16,41	
Davis, O.	USA	400m	1	9	1	46·91	
			2	4	1	46·02*	
			SF	1	1	45·62*	
			F		1	45·07*	G
		4×400m relay	1	4	1	3-10·58	
			SF	2	1	3-08·57	
			F		1	3-02·37*	G
Day, G.	SAF	400m	1	8	2	47·22	
			2	3	3	46·47	
			SF	1	5	46·84	
		4×400m relay	1	3	2	3-16·32	
			SF	1	1	3-06·53	
			F		4	3-05·18	
De Andres, A.	ESP	Javelin throw	Q		DNQ	60,84	
Declerck, L.	BEL	400m	1	3	3	48·00	
			2	4	7	48·51	
		4×400m relay	1	2	4	3-15·26	
De Florentiis, S.	ITA	Marathon	F		38	2:31-54·0	
De Gaetano, A.	ITA	50k walk	F		10	4:41-01·6	
Delany, R.	IRL	800m	1	8	3	1-51·19	
			2	3	6	1-51·42	
De La Quadra, M.	ESP	Discus throw	Q		DNQ	0	
Delecour, J.	FRA	100m	1	4	2	10·75	
			2	1	4	10·87	
		200m	1	10	2	21·48	
			2	3	4	21·64	
		4×100m relay	1	4		DIS	
Delerue, H.	FRA	20k walk	F		12	1:39-37·6	
Dellinger, W.	USA	5000m	1	3	4	14-08·72	
Depastas, E.	GRE	1500m	1	3	8	3-48·77	
De Peana, G.	GUY	5000m	1	4	13	15-54·2	
Deprez, J.	FRA	110m hurdles	1	6	5	17·24	
De Rosso, L.	ITA	20k walk	F		22	1:45-04·2	
Deseano, J.	PUR	4×400m relay	1	1	5	3-13·91	
Desyatchikov, A.	URS	10000m	F		4	28-39·72	
De Terlizzi	ITA	Marathon	F		DNF		
Dhaoui	TUN	Marathon	F		DNF		
Diaz, L.	CEY	Marathon	F		39	2:32-12·0	
Dickson, G.	CAN	Marathon	F		55	2:38-46·0	
Dienesz, B.	HUN	50k walk	F		DNF		
Ditta, A.	PAK	Pole vault	Q		DNQ	4,00	
Dolezal, J.	TCH	50k walk	F		17	4:51-18·6	
Donazar, W.	URU	Long jump	Q		DNQ	7,24	
Donner, H.	AUT	High jump	Q		DNQ	1,95	
Dordoni, G.	ITA	50k walk	F		7	4:33-27·2	
Dumas, C.	USA	High jump	F		6	2,03	
Dunne, W.	IRL	Marathon	F		42	2:33-08·0	
Du Plessis, S.	SAF	Discus throw	Q		DNQ	51,86	
Duriez, M.	FRA	110m hurdles	1	1	4	14·90	
			2	4	6	15·19	
Dyachkov, Y.	URS	Decathlon	F		DNF		
Ebina, J.	JPN	Long jump	Q		DNQ	6,83	
Edlund, D.	SWE	Discus throw	Q		DNQ	51,76	
Edstrom, D.	USA	Decathlon	F		DNF		
Einarsson, V.	ISL	Triple jump	F		5	16,37	
		Long jump	Q		DNQ	6,76	
Eli, I.	SUD	110m hurdles	1	4		DNF	
Elliott, H.	AUS	1500m	1	1	1	3-41·50	
			F		1	3-35·6*	G
El-Jisr, S.	LEB	Shot put	Q		DNQ	13,82	
Ellis, M.	GBR	Hammer throw	F		15	54,22	
El-Tayeb, M.	SUD	100m	1	8	6	11·1	
Enitropoulos, P.	GRE	Decathlon	F		23	4737	
Erickson, S.	SWE	Triple jump	F		11	15,49	
Essalhi	TUN	Marathon	F		DNF		
Esteves, H.	VEN	100m	1	3	1	10·62	
			2	1	1	10·71	
			SF	2	5	10·57	
		4×100m relay	1	1	3	41·11	
			SF	1	2	40·49	
			F		5	40·83	

COMPETITOR	COUNTRY CODE	EVENT	ROUND	HEAT	PLACE	TIME & DISTANCE	MEDAL
Eves, L.	CAN	100m	1	3	4	11·01	
		200m	1	10	4	22·02	
		4×100m relay	1	4	2	42·27	
			SF	1	4	41·27	
Fahmi, F.	IRQ	4×100m relay	1	1	4	41·87	
Fairbrother, C.	GBR	High jump	Q		DNQ	1,95	
Falcon, J.	ESP	Hammer throw	Q		DNQ	57,24	
Falih, F.	IRQ	200m	1	12	4	22·77	
Farrell, T.	GBR	800m	1	2	1	1-49·05	
			2	4	5	1-50·84	
Faust, J.	USA	High jump	F		17	1,95	
Feinberg, B.	ISR	Javelin throw	Q		DNQ	68,24	
Fernandez, J.	ESP	3000m steeplechase	1	2	8	9-12·8	
Ferreira, J.	POR	3000m steeplechase	1	1	11	9-30·2	
Fevzi, P.	TUR	10000m	F		29	32-06·2	
Figuerola, E.	CUB	100m	1	1	1	10·57	
			2	3	2	10·53	
			SF	1	2	10·58	
			F		4	10·44	
Fischer, W.	GER	400m hurdles	1	4	4	53·35	
Flores, V.	VEN	400m hurdles	1	6	4	52·79	
Flossbach, H.	GER	5000m	1	2	1	14-09·25	
			F		8	14-07·03	
Folk, M.	POL	100m	1	8	1	10·5	
			2	2	3	10·48	
			SF	1	4	10·66	
		200m	1	10	1	21·28	
			2	4	2	21·02	
			SF	1	2	21·15	
			F		4	20·90	
		4×100m relay	1	3	DIS		
Foreman, P.	BWI	Long jump	F		12	7,26	
Fossati, N.	ITA	4×400m relay	1	2	3	3-09·67	
			SF	1	4	3-07·83	
Fournier, M.	FRA	High jump	F		14	2,00	
Fraschini, M.	ITA	4×400m relay	1	2	3	3-09·67	
			SF	1	4	3-07·83	
Fredriksson, K.	SWE	Javelin throw	F		6	78,33	
Freeman, N.	AUS	20k walk	F		2	1:34-16·4	S
		50k walk	F		DIS		
Galliker, B.	SUI	400m hurdles	1	1	1	51·20	
			SF	2	3	51·47	
			F		6	51·11	
Gardner, K.	BWI	110m hurdles	1	5	1	14·46	
			2	2	2	14·45	
			SF	1	3	14·32	
			F		5	14·55	
		4×400m relay	1	2	1	3-09·28	
			SF	2	2	3-09·34	
			F		3	3-04·13	B
Gatti, P.	ITA	Triple jump	F		DNF	0	
Genevay, P.	FRA	200m	1	1	1	21·33	
			2	4	3	21·26	
			SF	2	6	21·17	
		4×100m relay	1	4	DIS		
Geneve, P.	FRA	Marathon	F		35	2:31-20·0	
Georgopopoulos, N.	GRE	100m	1	9	5	11·12	
		200m	1	3	2	22·18	
			2	2	7	22·15	
		4×100m relay	1	3	2	41·81	
			SF	2	5	41·90	
Gerbig, K.	GER	110m hurdles	1	3	4	14·87	
			2	3	5	14·97	
Germar, M.	GER	100m	1	8	5	11·0	
		200m	1	11	3	21·76	
Ghafar, G.A.	AFG	4×100m relay	1	4	4	44·53	
Ghanim, M.	IRQ	4×100m relay	1	1	4	41·87	
Giannone, S.	ITA	200m	1	12	6	21·61	
			2	3	7	21·95	
		4×100m relay	1	2	1	40·16	
			SF	2	2	40·29	
			F		4	40·33	
Gierajewski, B.	POL	4×400m relay	1	2	2	3-09·67	
			SF	2	4	3-10·88	
Glasgow, C.	GUY	200m	1	3	3	22·75	
		400m	1	5	5	50·84	
Golubnichy, V.	URS	20k walk	F		1	1:34-07·2	G
Gomes, R.	GUY	800m	1	9	2	1-53·06	
			2	2	5	1-52·47	
Gomez, G.	ARG	Marathon	F		15	2:23-00·0	
Gomez, I.	PHI	4×100m relay	1	2	4	41·55	
		100m	1	2	5	11·19	
Gomez, J.	ESP	800m	1	8	6	1-53·90	
Goryayev, V.	URS	Triple jump	F		2	16,63	S
Gosal, J.	INA	100m	1	8	4	10·9	

COMPETITOR	COUNTRY CODE	EVENT	ROUND	HEAT	PLACE	TIME & DISTANCE	MEDAL
Gosper, R.	AUS	400m	1	4	2	47·20	
			2	2	2	46·64	
			SF	1	6	47·28	
Goudge, C.	GBR	400m hurdles	1	3	4	52·75	
Gouider, M.	TUN	1500m	1	1	12	3-58·52	
Grachev, K.	URS	400m	1	2	3	49·44	
			2	3	6	47·78	
		4×400m relay	1	4	5	3-12·31	
Grecescu, C.	RUM	10000m	F		20	30-03·0	
Grelle, J.	USA	1500m	1	2	2	3-43·65	
			F		8	3-45·0	
Grieser, M.	GER	Discus throw	F		16	52,69	
Grodotzki, H.	GER	5000m	1	1	1	14-01·29	
			F		2	13-45·01	S
		10000m	F		2	28-37·22	S
Grodzinowsky, A.	ISR	100m	1	1	6	11·19	
		200m	1	9	4	21·99	
		400m	1	9	6	49·03	
Grogorenz, K.	GER	Decathlon	F		8	7032	
Gronowski, J.	POL	Pole vault	Q		DNQ	4,20	
Grossi, F.	ITA	Discus throw	Q		DNQ	50,43	
Gruber, A.	AUT	Marathon	F		52	2:37-40·0	
Grujic, M.	YUG	4×400m relay	1	1	3	3-10·75	
			SF	1	6	3-10·34	
Guenard, G.	PUR	400m	1	5	1	47·39	
			2	2	5	47·39	
		4×400m relay	1	1	5	3-13·91	
Gulbrandsen, J.	NOR	400m hurdles	1	2	1	52·39	
			SF	1	6	52·56	
Habib, Z.S.	AFG	4×100m relay	1	4	4	44·53	
Hadi, S.A.	AFG	4×100m relay	1	4	4	44·53	
Hafner, F.	YUG	3000m steeplechase	1	3	6	8-55·68	
Halberg, M.	NZL	5000m	1	4	2	14-04·28	
			F		1	13-43·76	G
		10000m	F		5	28-49·11	
Hall, A.	USA	Hammer throw	F		14	59,76	
Hall, E.	GBR	20k walk	F		10	1:38-54·0	
Haluza, R.	USA	20k walk	F		24	1:45-11·0	
Hamarsland, A.	NOR	1500m	1	2	3	3-44·63	
			F		9	3-45·0	
Hamid, N.	IRQ	Shot put	Q		DNQ	13,65	
		Discus throw	Q		DNQ	39,37	
Hannemann, A.	GER	1500m	1	1	8	3-47·57	
Hary, A.	GER	100m	1	2	2	10·74	
			2	2	1	10·32*	
			SF	2	1	10·41	
			F		1	10·32*	G
		4×100m relay	1	3	1	39·61	
			SF	1	1	39·88	
			F		1	39·66	G
Haugen, S.	NOR	Discus throw	F		11	53,36	
Haupert, N.	LUX	4×400m relay	1	2	5	3-21·87	
		800m	1	6	4	1-54·83	
Havenstein, G.	GER	Marathon	F		57	2:41-14·0	
Hayase, H.	JPN	200m	1	12	3	22·44	
		400m	1	1	6	49·13	
		4×100m relay	1	4	3	42·60	
			SF	1	5	42·39	
Hazle, G.	SAF	20k walk	F		13	1:40-16·2	
		50k walk	F		12	4:43-18·8	
Hecker,	AUT	Marathon	F		DNF		
Hecker, G.	HUN	3000m steeplechase	1	3	9	9-12·4	
Hellsten, V.	FIN	400m	1	8	4	48·52	
		4×400m relay	1	4	4	3-11·90	
Hewson, B.	GBR	800m	1	1	4	1-54·73	
Hildreth, P.	GBR	110m hurdles	1	4	4	14·90	
			2	1	4	14·78	
Hinze, M.	GER	Triple jump	F		7	15,93	
Hiotis, C.	GRE	5000m	1	3	9	15-01·2	
Hiroshima, K.	JPN	Marathon	F		31	2:29-40·0	
Hoeger, X.	GER	10000m	F		17	29-50·2	
Hoenicke, G.	GER	10000m	F		12	29-20·14	
Hoey, M.	IRL	5000m	1	1	10	15-00·52	
Howard, R.	USA	400m hurdles	1	1	2	51·32	
			SF	2	2	50·91	
			F		3	49·90	B
Howell, J.	GBR	Long jump	Q		DNQ	7,19	
Hoykinpuro, R.	FIN	5000m	1	1	5	14-21·92	
Huang, S.-T.	FOR	100m	1	7	5	11·37	
		200m	1	4	5	23·08	
Hueneke, H.	GER	3000m steeplechase	1	1	3	8-50·59	
			F		DNF		
Huertz, F.	LUX	4×400m relay	1	2	5	3-21·87	
		400m	1	2	4	50·34	
Humbert, R.	LUX	4×400m relay	1	2	5	3-21·87	
Husson, G.	FRA	Hammer throw	Q		DNQ	59,83	
Hyman, M.	GBR	10000m	F		9	29-05·11	
Idriss, M.	FRA	High jump	F		12	2,03	

COMPETITOR	COUNTRY CODE	EVENT	ROUND	HEAT	PLACE	TIME & DISTANCE	MEDAL
Igun, S.	NIG	High jump	Q		DNQ	1,90	
		Triple jump	Q		DNQ	14,74	
Iharos, S.	HUN	5000m	1	2	2	14-09-38	
			F	.	10	14-11-91	
		10000m	F		11	29-16-07	
Ingolic, B.	YUG	800m	1	7	4	1-51-51	
Iqbal, M.	PAK	Hammer throw	F		12	61,79	
Jackson, B.	GBR	4×400m relay	1	3	3	3-20-47	
			SF	-	3	3-07-67	
			F		5	3-08-47	
James, K.	SAF	Marathon	F		13	2:22-53-6	
Janke, F.	GER	5000m	1	3	-	14-02-58	
			F		4	13-47-14	
Janz, H.	GER	400m hurdles	1	5	1	51-30	
			SF	1	3	51-55	
			F		4	50-05	
Jarembowski, J.	POL	4×100m relay	1	3	DIS		
Jaskolski, J.	POL	Triple jump	Q		DNQ	15,04	
Jassim, K.	IRQ	4×100m relay	1	1	4	41-87	
Jazy, M.	FRA	1500m	1	3	2	3-45-03	
			F		2	3-38-4	S
Jefferys, E.	SAF	100m	1	8	2	10-6	
			2	1	5	10-89	
		200m	1	12	1	21-18	
			2	1	2	21-22	
			SF	1	4	21-46	
		4×400m relay	1	3	2	3-16-32	
			SF	1	1	3-06-53	
			F		4	3-05-13	
Jegathesan, M.	MAL	400m	1	6	4	48-56	
Jerome, H.	CAN	100m	1	4	1	10-72	
			2	4	1	10-58	
			SF	1	DNF		
		4×100m relay	1	4	2	42-27	
			SF	1	4	41-27	
Jirasek, J.	TCH	4×400m relay	1	4	3	3-11-33	
Jochman, M.	POL	5000m	1	2	8	14-31-29	
Johansson, H.	SWE	4×400m relay	1	4	3	3-10-91	
			SF	2	6	3-11-05	
Johnson, A.	GBR	50k walk	F		DIS		
Johnson, D.	BWI	100m	1	3	2	10-66	
			2	2	4	10-51	
		200m	1	8	1	21-35	
			2	3	3	21-25	
			SF	2	5	21-16	
Johnson, G.H.	LIB	400m	1	5	6	51-54	
		800m	1	1	6	1-56-04	
Johnson, R.	USA	Decathlon	F		1	8392*	G
Johnson, S.	USA	200m	1	3	1	21-81	
			2	1	1	21-08	
			SF	2	3	20-93	
			F		5	20-93	
		4×100m relay	1	4	1	39-87	
			SF	2	1	39-67	
			F		DIS		
Jones, C.	USA	3000m steeplechase	1	3	2	8-49-32	
			F		7	9-18-22	
Jones, D.	GBR	100m	1	7	1	10-69	
			2	3	3	10-68	
			SF	2	4	10-48	
		200m	1	6	2	21-29	
			2	4	4	21-33	
		4×100m relay	1	1	1	40-27	
			SF	1	3	40-63	
			F		3	40-32	B
Jones, H.	USA	110m hurdles	1	2	1	14-32	
			2	4	1	14-19	
			SF	1	2	14-22	
			F		3	14-17	B
Jonsson, L.	SWE	200m	1	9	6	22-41	
		4×400m	1	4	3	3-10-91	
			SF	2	6	3-11-05	
Joshi Tilak, R.	IND	100m	1	1	7	11-43	
Jost, H.	SUI	Hammer throw	Q		DNQ	59,82	
Julian, I.	NZL	Marathon	F		18	2:24-50-6	
Jurek, M.	TCH	5000m	1	4	5	14-31-53	
Juskowiak, J.	POL	4×100m relay	1	3	DIS		
Kahma, M.	FIN	Decathlon	F		7	7112	
Kaiser, J.	GER	4×400m relay	1	1	1	3-10-58	
			SF	1	2	3-07-60	
			F		2	3-02-84	S
Kamaruddin, M.	MAL	Long jump	Q		DNC	6,74	
Kamerbeek, E.	HOL	Decathlon	F		5	7236	
Kammermann, W.	SUI	3000m steeplechase	1	1	9	9-11-8	
Kantorek, P.	TCH	Marathon	F		14	2:22-59-8	
Karabi, B.	TUN	400m	1	4	7	52-12	
Karim, J.	IRQ	400m	1	8	5	49-35	
Karvonen, P.	FIN	3000m steeplechase	1	2	7	9-04-91	
Kaufmann, K.	GER	400m	1	3	1	47-42	
			2	1	1	46-67	
			SF	2	1	45-88	
			F		2	45-08	S
		4×400m relay	1	1	1	3-10-58	
			SF	1	2	3-07-60	
			F		2	3-02-84	S
Keily, A.	GBR	Marathon	F		25	2:27-00-0	
Kelley, J.	USA	Marathon	F		19	2:24-58-0	
Kent-Smith, B.	GBR	1500m	1	2	4	3-46-21	
Kerr, G.	BWI	800m	1	7	1	1-51-11	
			2	3	1	1-49-58	
			SF	1	1	1-47-26*	
			F		3	1-47-25	B
		4×400m relay	1	2	1	3-09-28	
			SF	2	2	3-09-34	
			F		3	3-04-13	B
Khaliq, A.	PAK	100m	1	2	7	11-34	
		200m	1	4	6	23-24	
		4×100m relay	1	3	3	42-67	
			SF	2	6	42-99	
Khan, H.	PAK	Shot put	Q		DNQ	13,53	
		Discus throw	Q		DNQ	46,57	
Khan, M.	PAK	Triple jump	Q		DNQ	14,43	
Khlebarov, D.	BUL	Pole vault	F		11	4,30	
Khudir, Z.	IRQ	4×100m relay	1	1	4	41-87	
Kilty, B.	GBR	Marathon	F		29	2:28-55-0	
Kim, Jong	KOR	100m	1	5	6	11-63	
Kim, Y.-B.	KOR	Marathon	F		DNF		
Kinder, M.	GER	400m	1	1	1	46-84	
			2	3	3	46-82	
			SF	1	3	46-13	
			F		5	46-04	
		4×400m relay	1	1	1	3-10-58	
			SF	1	2	3-07-60	
			F		2	3-02-84	S
Klaban, R.	AUT	800m	1	8	1	1-50-96	
			2	4	4	1-50-32	
		1500m	1	1	7	3-47-24	
Klics, F.	HUN	Discus throw	F		10	53,37	
Klimov, G.	URS	50k walk	F		DIS		
Knuts, P	SWE	800m	1	5	2	1-51-36	
			2	2	7	1-52-91	
Kocak, E.	TUR	800m	1	9	3	1-59-12	
			2	4	7	1-52-66	
Koch, C.	HOL	Discus throw	F		22	49,21	
Koch, H.	GER	20k walk	F		16	1:41-53-4	
Koeppen, F.	GER	Long jump	Q		DNQ	7,32	
Kolnik, M.	YUG	Decathlon	F		DNF		
Kompaneyets, V.	URS	Discus throw	F		6	55,06	
Konov, A.	URS	3000m steeplechase	1	2	3	8-50-19	
			F		8	9-18-23	
Konovalov, Y.	URS	100m	1	1	3	10-83	
			2	2	6	10-69	
		200m	1	6	3	21-50	
			2	1	5	21-52	
		4×100m relay	1	1	2	40-39	
			SF	2	3	40-30	
			F		2	40-24	S
Kormalis, L	GRE	4×100m relay	1	3	2	41-81	
			SF	2	5	41-90	
Komitoudis, J.	GRE	4×100m relay	1	3	2	41-81	
			SF	2	5	41-90	
Kosanov, G.	URS	100m	1	6	2	10-90	
			2	3	6	10-87	
		4×100m relay	1	1	2	40-39	
			SF	2	3	40-30	
			F		2	40-24	S
Kotei, R.	GHA	High jump	F		10	2,03	
Kounadis, A.	GRE	Discus throw	F		18	52,42	
Kouveloyannis, A.	GRE	Hammer throw	Q		DNQ	55,18	
Kovac, D.	YUG	4×400m relay	1	1	3	3-10-75	
			SF	1	6	3-10-34	
Kovacs, J	HUN	10000m	F		15	29-34-71	
Kovacs, L	HUN	800m	1	6	3	1-51-45	
			2	2	6	1-52-55	
		1500m	1	3	5	3-46-20	
Kowalski, J.	POL	400m	1	5	2	48-49	
			2	4	4	46-82	
		4×400m relay	1	2	2	3-09-67	
			SF	2	4	3-10-88	
Krasovskis, J.	URS	Pole vault	F		13	4,30	
Krayer, V	URS	Triple jump	F		3	16,43	B
Krstensen, T.	DEN	20k walk	F		15	1:41-07-6	
Krstov, K.	BUL	Pole vault	F		10	4,40	

COMPETITOR	COUNTRY CODE	EVENT	ROUND	HEAT	PLACE	TIME & DISTANCE	MEDAL
Krivosheyev, A.	URS	800m	1	5	1	1-53·49	
			2	2	2	1-51·40	
			SF	2	5	1-48·25	
Krol, W.	POL	400m hurdles	1	1	5	52·52	
Kropidlowski, K.	POL	Long jump	Q		DNQ	7,33	
Krueger, W.	GER	Javelin throw	F		2	79,36	S
Kryunov, B.	URS	400m hurdles	1	6	3	52·66	
		4×400m relay	1	4	5	3-12·31	
Krzesinski, A.	POL	Pole vault	F		12	4,30	
Krzyszkowiak, Z.	POL	10000m	F		7	28-52·75	
		3000m steeplechase	1	2	2	8-49·92	
			F		1	8-34·30*	G
Kuehl, F.	GER	Shot put	Q		DNQ	15,71	
		Discus throw	Q		DNQ	50,40	
Kuisma, V.	FIN	Javelin throw	F		4	78,40	
Kulcsar, G.	HUN	Javelin throw	F		3	78,57	B
Kumiszcze, Z.	POL	400m hurdles	1	6	5	53·47	
Kunauer, E.	AUT	100m	1	7	4	11·13	
		200m	1	5	5	22·34	
Kunen, F.	HOL	Marathon	F		36	2:31-25·0	
Kushnir, D.	ISR	Long jump	Q		DNQ	7,20	
Kutyenko, D.	URS	Decathlon	F		4	7567	
Kuznyetsov, Vasiliy	URS	Decathlon	F		3	7809	B
Kvachakidze, R.	URS	Long jump	Q		DNQ	6,82	
Kwiatkowski, E.	POL	Shot put	Q		DNQ	16,71	
Kyle, D.	CAN	5000m	1	2	7	14-25·36	
		10000m	F		24	30-27·2	
Labidi, D.	TUN	Marathon	F		49	2:35-43·0	
Laeng, P.	SUI	200m	1	2	3	21·75	
		4×100m relay	1	1	3	40·92	
			SF	2	4	41·06	
Lahcen, M.	MOR	3000m steeplechase	1	3	11	9-29·4	
Laipenieks, J.	CHI	Decathlon	F		19	5865	
Laird, R.	USA	50k walk	F		19	4:53-21·6	
Lal, C.N.	IND	Marathon	F		40	2:32-13·0	
Lambrechts, J.	BEL	800m	1	2	3	1-49·24	
			2	1	DNF		
		4×400m relay	1	2	4	3-15·26	
Lambrechts, M.	BEL	400m	1	4	5	49·66	
		4×400m relay	1	2	4	3-15·26	
		400m hurdles	1	2	5	53·67	
Landstroem, E.	FIN	Pole vault	F		3	4,55	B
Lansky, J.	TCH	High jump	F		=7	2,03	
Larsen, L.	DEN	20k walk	F		25	1:46-35·8	
Lauer, M.	GER	110m hurdles	1	1	1	14·45	
			2	2	1	14·06	
			SF	2	2	14·13	
			F		4	14·20	
		4×100m relay	1	3	1	39·61	
			SF	1	1	39·88	
			F		1	39·66	G
Laufer, P.	GER	Pole vault	Q		DNQ	4,20	
Lauridsen, J.	DEN	Marathon	F		41	2:32-32·0	
Lawlor, J.	IRL	Hammer throw	F		4	64,95	
Lawrence, A.	AUS	5000m	1	2	4	14-10·71	
		10000m	F		DNF		
		Marathon	F		54	2:38-46·0	
Lazhar, B.-M.	TUN	20k walk	F		DNF		
		50k walk	F		26	5:07-57·4	
Lazreg, A.	MOR	800m	1	4	6	1-55·91	
Lee, C.H.	KOR	Marathon	F		20	2:25-02·2	
Lee, S.-C.	KOR	Marathon	F		47	2:35-14·0	
Leenaert, H.	BEL	5000m	1	1	6	14-25·81	
Lefanczik, S.	GER	20k walk	F		DNF		
Leiser, A.	SUI	50k walk	F		25	5:06-55·0	
Lemos, W.	ARG	Marathon	F		50	2:36-55·0	
Lenoir, P.Y.	FRA	800m	1	2	4	1-49·41	
Leps, E.	CAN	800m	1	4	2	1-50·93	
			2	4	6	1-52·13	
		4×400m relay	1	1	2	3-10·65	
			SF	1	5	3-08·37	
Lesek, R.	YUG	Pole vault	Q		DNQ	4,20	
Lewandowski, S.	POL	800m	1	6	4	1-51·75	
		1500m	1	3	11	3-59·75	
Li, P.-T.	FOR	400m	1	5	4	49·69	
		400m hurdles	1	6	6	54·23	
Lievore, C.	ITA	Javelin throw	F		9	75,21	
Lincoln, M.	AUS	1500m	1	3	7	3-47·18	
Lindner, D.	GER	20k walk	F		4	1:35-33·8	
Lindroos, C.	FIN	Discus throw	Q		DNQ	51,07	
Lindsay, M.	GBR	Shot put	F		5	17,80	
		Discus throw	Q		DNQ	50,15	
Lingnau, H.	GER	Shot put	F		12	16,98	
Lipsnis, V.	URS	Shot put	F		4	17,90	
Ljunggren, J.	SWE	20k walk	F		7	1:37-59·0	
		50k walk	F		2	4:25-47·0	S
Lolos, C.	GRE	4×100m relay	1	3	2	41·81	
			SF	2	5	41·90	
Long, D.	USA	Shot put	F		3	19,01	B
Lopez, R.	CUB	Triple jump	Q		DNQ	14,53	
Lorenz, S.	GER	Hammer throw	Q		DNQ	59,06	
Lorger, S.	YUG	110m hurdles	1	5	2	14·56	
			2	3	3	14·56	
			SF	2	5	14·83	
Losch, M.	GER	Hammer throw	Q		DNQ	59,38	
Lowry, P.	IRL	100m	1	3	6	11·11	
		200m	1	6	5	22·30	
Lucking, M.	GBR	Shot put	F		8	17,43	
Lukman, L.	YUG	Pole vault	F		9	4,40	
MacDonald, B.	USA	50k walk	F		23	5:00-47·6	
McIntyre, G.	IRL	Marathon	F		22	2:26-03·0	
McKenzie, G.	USA	Marathon	F		48	2:35-16·0	
Macquet, M.	FRA	Javelin throw	Q		DNQ	73,74	
Magee, B.	NZL	10000m	F		26	30-35·8	
		Marathon	F		3	2:17-18·2	B
Maglaras, D.	GRE	Long jump	F		11	7,45	
Mahlendorf, W.	GER	100m	1	6	4	10·98	
		4×100m relay	1	3	1	39·61	
			SF	1	1	39·88	
			F		1	39·66	G
Maiyoro, N.	KEN	5000m	1	1	4	14-06·29	
			F		6	13-53·25	
Majid, S.	IRQ	Javelin throw	Q		DNQ	57,52	
Majtan, D.	YUG	High jump	Q		DNQ	1,95	
Makomaski, Z.	POL	800m	1	1	3	1-52·70	
			2	2	4	1-51·72	
Malcher, G.	GER	Pole vault	F		5	4,50	
Malcherczyk, R.	PCL	Triple jump	F		6	16,01	
Malik, A.	PAK	110m hurdles	1	5	6	15·52	
		4×100m relay	1	1	3	42·67	
			SF	2	6	42·99	
Mandlik, V.	TCH	200m	1	6	DNF		
Manninen, E.	FIN	Long jump	Q		DNQ	7,34	
Manninen, O.	FIN	Marathon	F		23	2:26-33·0	
Manyagas, S.	THA	100m	1	1	4	10·87	
		4×100m relay	1	1	5	42·19	
Marien, L.	BEL	Decathlon	F		18	5919	
Markusson, S.	ISL	800m	1	6	5	1-52·88	
		1500m	1	2	7	3-47·20	
Marquis, L.	SUI	20k walk	F		17	1:41-59·6	
		50k walk	F		22	5:00-13·0	
Marsellos, G.	GRE	110m hurdles	1	4	5	14·92	
Martini, M.	ITA	400m hurdles	1	6	2	52·26	
			SF	1	7	52·57	
Martins, E.	POR	Hammer throw	Q		DNQ	54,92	
Massaquoi, A.	LBR	Marathon	F		62	3:43-18·0	
Matsulevich, A.	URS	4×400m relay	1	4	5	3-12·31	
		400m hurdles	1	2	3	53·00	
Matthews, K.	GBR	20k walk	F		DNF		
Matthews, V.	GBR	110m hurdles	1	5	4	15·07	
			2	3	6	15·12	
Matthias, W.	GER	400m hurdles	1	3	2	52·23	
			SF	2	5	51·95	
Matuschewski, M.	GER	800m	1	4	3	1-51·17	
			2	1	3	1-48·24	
			SF	1	3	1-47·54	
			F		6	1-52·21	
Maurer, R.	SUI	High jump	Q		DNQ	1,95	
May, W.	USA	110m hurdles	1	3	1	14·16	
			2	3	1	13·91	
			SF	1	1	13·87	
			F		2	13·99	S
Meconi, S.	ITA	Shot put	F		13	16,73	
Meier, W.	GER	Decathlon	F		16	6000	
Merawi, G.	ETH	10000m	F		DNF		
		5000m	1	1	8	14-41·22	
Merriman, J.	GBR	10000m	F		8	28-52·89	
Messitt, B.	IRL	Marathon	F		DNF		
Metcalf, J.	GBR	400m hurdles	1	6	1	52·24	
			SF	2	7	52·72	
Mihalic, F.	YUG	Marathon	F		12	2:21-52·6	
Mijares, R.	MEX	Decathlon	F		21	5413	
Mikhailov, A.	URS	110m hurdles	1	6	1	14·53	
			2	3	2	14·02	
			SF	2	DNF		
Mikhailov, Y.	URS	Triple jump	F		10	15,67	
Milde, L.	GER	Discus throw	F		12	53,33	
Miller, G.	GBR	High jump	F		16	2,00	
Mills, L.	NZL	Shot put	F		11	17,06	
		Discus throw	Q		DNQ	50,77	
Mimm, R.	USA	20k walk	F		23	1:45-09·0	
Mimoun, A.	FRA	Marathon	F		34	2:31-20·0	
Misson, T.	GBR	50k walk	F		5	4:33-03·0	

COMPETITOR	COUNTRY CODE	EVENT	ROUND	HEAT	PLACE	TIME & DISTANCE	MEDAL
Moc, L.	TCH	20k walk	F		8	1:38-32·4	
		50k walk	F		11	4:42-33·6	
Moceidreke, S.	FIJ	100m	1	5	3	10·92	
			2	2	7	10·85	
		200m	1	5	4	21·97	
Moens, R.	BEL	4×400m relay	1	2	4	3-15·26	
		800m	1	6	1	1-50·73	
			2	4	1	1-48·59	
			SF	2	2	1-47·49	
			F		2	1-46·55	S
Molins, J.	ESP	5000m	1	2	9	14-51·2	
Molzberger, M.	GER	Long jump	F		9	7,49	
Momotkov, E.	URS	1500m	1	1	5	3-43·80	
Morale, S.	ITA	400m hurdles	1	4	2	52·13	
			SF	2	4	51·48	
Morayemos, C.	GRE	800m	1	4	5	1-54·60	
Morris, R.	USA	Pole vault	F		2	4,60	S
Muchitsch, H.	AUT	Decathlon	F		17	5950	
Mueller, H.	SUI	100m	1	2	3	10·94	
			2	1	7	10·95	
		4×100m relay	1	1	3	40·92	
			SF	2	4	41·06	
Mueller, L.	GER	3000m steeplechase	1	2	1	8-49·86	
			F		6	9-01·57	
Mukhtar, K.	IRQ	1500m	1	3	13	4-00·33	
		5000m	1	1	11	15-00·97	
Mulkey, P.	USA	Decathlon	F		DNF		
Mullins, J.	CAN	800m	1	8	4	1-51·46	
		1500m	1	1	10	3-53·45	
		4×400m relay	1	1	2	3-10·65	
			SF	1	5	3-08·37	
Murad, L.	VEN	100m	1	5	5	10·82	
			2	4	5	10·97	
		200m	1	7	3	21·36	
		4×100m relay	1	1	3	41·11	
			SF	1	2	40·49	
			F		5	40·83	
Murphy, T.	USA	800m	1	9	1	1-52·30	
			2	1	1	1-48·12	
			SF	1	6	1-48·29	
Muzyk, R.	POL	110m hurdles	1	6	3	14·94	
			2	4	4	14·68	
Myitung, N.	BUR	Marathon	F		27	2-28-17·0	
Nagy, S.	HUN	Shot put	F		14	16,67	
Navarro, M.	ESP	Marathon	F		17	2-24-17·4	
Nawaz, M.	PAK	Javelin throw	Q		DNQ	70,06	
Negousse, R.	ETH	100m	1	3	7	11·47	
Nemec, Z.	TCH	Discus throw	F		19	52,14	
Netopilik, J.	TCH	Long jump	Q		DNQ	7,26	
Nieder, W.	USA	Shot put	F		1	19,68*	G
Nikulin, Y.	URS	Hammer throw	F		10	63,10	
Nilsson, K.	SWE	High jump	F		=7	2,03	
Norris, D.	NZL	Long jump	D		DNQ	7,04	
		Triple jump	Q		DNQ	14,30	
Norton, R.	USA	100m	1	6	1	10·88	
			2	1	3	10·78	
			SF	2	3	10·47	
			F		6	10·50	
		200m	1	6	1	21·27	
			2	2	2	21·14	
			SF	2	2	20·81	
			F		6	21·09	
		4×100m relay	1	4	1	39·87	
			SF	2	1	39·67	
			F			DIS	
Noszaly, S.	HUN	High jump	F		13	2,03	
Ntiforo, G.	GHA	100m	1	2	2	11·15	
Nyberg, E.	SWE	Marathon	F		53	2-42-59·0	
Oakley, A.	CAN	20k walk	F		9	1:38-46·0	
		50k walk	F		6	4:33-08·6	
O'Brien, P.	USA	Shot put	F		2	19,11	S
Oehri, E.	LIE	800m	1	5	6	2-00·49	
		1500m	1	1	DNF		
Oerter, A.	USA	Discus throw	F		1	59,18*	G
O'Gorman, D.	GBR	Marathon	F		16	2-24-16·2	
Ogushi, K.	JPN	400m hurdles	1	3	3	52·58	
		4×100m relay	1	4	3	42·60	
			SF	1	5	42·39	
Ohlemann, S.	CAN	800m	1	9	4	2-07·4	
		4×400m relay	1	1	2	3-10·65	
			SF	1	5	3-08·37	
Okamoto, N.	JPN	Hammer throw	F		13	60,08	
Okantey, M.	GHA	200m	1	4	3	21·91	
Okazaki, T.	JPN	Long jump	F		DNS		
		4×100m relay	1	4	3	42·60	
			SF	1	5	42·39	

COMPETITOR	COUNTRY CODE	EVENT	ROUND	HEAT	PLACE	TIME & DISTANCE	MEDAL
Okello, J.	UGA	4×100m relay	1	2	DIS		
		110m hurdles	1	1	2	14·59	
			2	1	2	14·48	
			SF	1	5	14·59	
Oksanen, E.	FIN	Marathon	F		24	2:26-38·0	
Okundaye, O.	NIG	Pole vault	Q		DNQ	0	
Oladapo, A.	NIG	4×100m relay	1	2	2	40·25	
			SF	1		DIS	
Oladitan, J.	NIG	Long jump	Q		DNQ	7,38	
Oliveira, M.	POR	5000m	1	2	6	14-16·14	
Oloko, S.	NIG	110m hurdles	1	3	5	15·04	
Omagbemi, J.	NIG	200m	1	1	3	26·40	
		4×100m relay	1	2	2	40·25	
			SF	1		DIS	
Onel, C.	TUR	3000m steeplechase	1	3	10	9-14·6	
Onur, A.	TUR	100m	1	6	6	11·45	
		200m	1	11	6	22·61	
O'Reilly, F.	IRL	50k walk	F		20	4:54-40·0	
Orywal, Z.	POL	1500m	1	1	DNF		
		800m	1	7	6	1-55·89	
Ota, T.	JAP	Triple jump	Q		DNQ	15,42	
Owusu, F.	GHA	800m	1	5	5	1-55·41	
		4×400m relay	1	4	2	3-10·66	
			2	4	5	3-11·03	
Ozguden, F.	TUR	400m hurdles	1	5	5	55·43	
		400m	1	8	6	50·87	
Ozog, S.	POL	10000m	F		18	29-58·0	
Ozolin, E.	URS	100m	1	9	3	10·86	
			2	1	6	10·90	
		4×100m relay	1	1	2	40·39	
			SF	2	3	40·30	
			F		2	40·24	
Paama, M.	URS	Javelin throw	F		11	74,56	
Paccagnella, L.	ITA	Decathlon	F		13	6283	
Pagda, Y.	TUR	Triple jump	Q		DNQ	14,11	
Palmer, M.	GBR	3000m steeplechase	1	3	8	9-10·68	
Pamich, A.	ITA	50k walk	F		3	4:27-55·4	B
Panciera, R.	ITA	4×400m relay	1	2	3	3-10·00	
			SF	1	4	3-07·83	
Pantilat, Y.	ISR	800m	1	1	5	1-54·86	
		1500m	1	3	12	4-00·14	
Papavasiliou, G.	GRE	3000m steeplechase	1	1	4	8-51·46	
Parsch, P.	HUN	800m	1	7	3	1-51·34	
			2	1	DNF		
		1500m	1	2	DNF		
Patarinski, D.	BUL	Triple jump	Q		DNQ	15,37	
Pedersen, T.	NOR	Javelin throw	F		DNS		
Pellosis, C.	PHI	400m	1	6	6	51·51	
Perez, C.	ESP	10000m	F		25	30-31·6	
Perrone, F.	ITA	Marathon	F		37	2:31-32·0	
Peter, K.	GER	Hammer throw	Q		DNQ	59,83	
Petrenko, I.	URS	Pole vault	F		=6	4,50	
Petrusic, M.	YUG	110m hurdles	1	2	3	14·74	
			2	2	5	14·71	
Pettersson, A.	SWE	400m	1	2	1	48·44	
			2	2	DNS		
		4×400m relay	1	4	3	3-10·91	
			SF	2	6	3-11·05	
Pettersson, S.	SWE	High jump	F		5	2,09	
Pfeil, W.	GER	High jump	Q		DNQ	1,95	
Phiphormongkol, D.	THA	1500m	1	2	11	4-24·4	
Piatkowski, E.	POL	Discus throw	F		5	55,12	
Piquemal, C.	FRA	100m	1	8	3	10·7	
			2	3	5	10·76	
		4×100m relay	1	4	DIS		
Pirie, G.	GBR	5000m	1	3	8	14-43·6	
		10000m	F		10	29-15·49	
Pjetursson, J.	ISL	High jump	Q		DNQ	1,95	
Plaza, S.	MEX	100m	1	6	3	10·95	
			2	3	7	10·93	
		200m	1	4	4	22·17	
Plihal, J.	TCH	Shot put	F		10	17,36	
Polianichev, V.	URS	4×400m relay	1	4	5	3-12·31	
Popov, S.	URS	Marathon	F		5	2:19-18·8	
Porter, C.	AUS	High jump	Q		DNQ	1,95	
Porumb, C.	RUM	High jump	F		11	2,03	
Pote, R.	BEL	100m	1	6	5	11·19	
		200m	1	11	4	22·27	
		Long jump	Q		DNQ	6,92	
Power, D.	AUS	5000m	1	4	1	14-03·9	
			F		5	13-52·38	
		10000m	F		3	28-37·65	B
Preussger, M.	GER	Pole vault	Q		DNQ	4,20	
Procel, R.	MEX	Long jump	Q		DNQ	7,23	
Puckett, R.	NZL	Marathon	F		51	2:37-36·0	
Puell, T.	GER	High jump	F		=7	2,03	

COMPETITOR	COUNTRY CODE	EVENT	ROUND	HEAT	PLACE	TIME & DISTANCE	MEDAL
Putu, E.	LIB	100m	1	5	5	11·34	
Quaye, W.	GHA	4×400m relay	1	4	2	3-10·66	
			SF	2	5	3-11·03	
Racic, K.	YUG	Hammer throw	Q		DNQ	57,27	
Radford, P.	GBR	100m	1	9	1	10·51	
			2	4	1	10·60	
			SF	1	1	10·57	
			F		3	10·42	B
		200m	1	5	1	21·25	
			2	3	2	21·12	
			SF	2	4	21·04	
		4×100m relay	1	1	1	40·27	
			SF	1	3	40·63	
			F		3	40·32	B
Rado, C.	ITA	Discus throw	F		7	54,00	
Radziwonowicz, Z.	POL	Javelin throw	F		7	77,31	
Ragho, J.	IND	Marathon	F		45	2:35-01·0	
Rahkamo, K.	FIN	Triple jump	F		8	15,84	
Rahmani, R.	IRN	Triple jump	Q		DNQ	14,70	
Rakuro, M.	FIJ	Discus throw	Q		DNQ	47,18	
Rantala, H.	FIN	Triple jump	Q		DNQ	15,11	
Rasmussen, W.	NOR	Javelin throw	F		5	78,36	
Raziq, G.	PAK	110m hurdles	1	4	3	14·68	
			2	2	3	14·51	
			SF	2	4	14·49	
		4×100m relay	1	3	3	42·67	
			SF	2	6	42·99	
Razzak, A.	IRQ	High jump	Q		DNQ	0	
		Long jump	Q		DNQ	6,37	
		Triple jump	Q		DNQ	14,56	
Read, N.	NZL	20k walk	F		5	1:36-59–2	
		50k walk	F		DNF		
Reed, L.	GBR	1500m	1	1	9	3-48·24	
Rekola, P.	FIN	4×400m relay	1	1	4	3-11·90	
		200m	1	7	4	22·27	
Repo, P.	FIN	Discus throw	F		9	53,44	
Reske, J.	GER	400m	1	8	3	47·38	
			2	3	4	47·43	
		4×400m relay	1	1	1	3-10·58	
			SF	1	2	3-07·60	
			F		2	3-02·84	
Reymond, G.	SUI	20k walk	F		DNF		
Rhadi, A.	MOR	10000m	F		14	29-32·00	
		Marathon	F		2	2:15-41·6	S
Ribas, J.	ESP	50k walk	F		18	4:51-20·0	
Riebensham, P.	GER	High jump	Q		DNQ	1,95	
Riintamaeki, J.	FIN	400m hurdles	1	5	3	51·70	
			SF	1	1	51·20	
			F		5	50·98	
		4×400m relay	1	1	4	3-11·90	
Rizzo, A.	ITA	1500m	1	2	8	3-47·56	
Roberson, B.	USA	Long jump	F		2	8,11	S
Roberts, J.	LIB	100m	1	9	7	11·37	
		200m	1	3	4	23·22	
Robinson, B.	NZL	200m	1	9	5	22·35	
		400m	1	3	2	47·70	
			2	4	6	48·44	
Robinson, T.	BAH	100m	1	5	1	10·68	
			2	1	2	10·76	
			SF	1	5	10·69	
		200m	1	7	2	21·56	
			2	1	3	21·32	
			SF	1	5	21·67	
Rodriguez, I.	PUR	400m	1	6	5	49·74	
Roegnvaldsson, P.	ISL	110m hurdles	1	4	6	15·38	
Roelants, G.	BEL	3000m steeplechase	1	3	3	8-49·52	
			F		4	8-47·85	
Rogelio, O.	PHI	4×100m relay	1	2	4	41·55	
Romero, E.	VEN	4×100m relay	1	2	3	41·11	
			SF	1	2	40·49	
			F		5	40·83	
Romero, R.	VEN	100m	1	7	3	10·89	
			2	4	6	11·23	
		200m	1	11	2	21·60	
			2	1	7	21·58	
		4×100m relay	1	2	3	41·11	
			SF	1	2	40·49	
			F		5	40·83	
Rotich, B.	KEN	400m	1	7	3	47·89	
			2	3	7	47·97	
		400m hurdles	1	5	2	51·39	
			SF	2	6	51·97	
Roubanis, G.	GRE	Pole vault	Q		DNQ	4,30	
Roudnitska, E.	FRA	110m hurdles	1	4	2	14·53	
			2	2	4	14·66	
Rowe, A.	GBR	Shot put	Q		DNQ	16,68	

COMPETITOR	COUNTRY CODE	EVENT	ROUND	HEAT	PLACE	TIME & DISTANCE	MEDAL
Rozsavoelgyi, I.	HUN	800m	1	3	4	1-49·51	
		1500m	1	1	2	3-42·15	
			F		3	3-39·2	B
Rudenkov, V.	URS	Hammer throw	F		1	67,10*	G
Rumiancev, N.	URS	Marathon	F		11	2:21-49·4	
Rut, T.	POL	Hammer throw	F		3	65,64	B
Rzhishchin, S.	URS	3000m steeplechase	1	3	1	8-48·11	
			F		3	8-42·34	B
Sadanaga, N.	JPN	Marathon	F		46	2:35-11·0	
Sahiner, C.	TUR	110m hurdles	1	1	6	15·75	
		High jump	Q		DNQ	0	
Said, M.	ETH	400m	1	9	5	48·30	
		800m	1	2	6	1-50·49	
Said, M.	MOR	5000m	1	2	10	14-53·6	
Sakowski, K.	GER	50k walk	F		DIS		
Sakurai, K.	JPN	Triple jump	Q		DNQ	14,59	
Salminen, E.	FIN	High jump	Q		DNQ	1,95	
Salomon, H.	GER	Javelin throw	F		12	74,11	
Salonen, O.	FIN	1500m	1	1	6	3-46·57	
Saloranta, S.	FIN	5000m	1	3	6	14-15·35	
		10000m	F		21	30-04·8	
Salvat, F.	GBR	5000m	1	1	7	14-33·64	
Samotsvetov, A.	URS	Hammer throw	F		7	63,60	
Santos, J.	POR	Decathlon	F		DNF		
Saoudi, A.	MOR	Marathon	F		61	2:59-41·0	
Sar, F.	ITA	Decathlon	F		6	7195	
Sardi, A.	ITA	200m	1	10	3	21·81	
		4×100m relay	1	2	1	40·16	
			SF	2	2	40·29	
			F		4	40·33	
Savic, S.	YUG	4×400m relay	1	1	3	3-10·75	
			SF	1	6	3-10·34	
Savinkov, V.	URS	800m	1	4	4	1-51·49	
Schaufelberger, W.	SUI	4×100m relay	1	1	3	40·92	
			SF	2	4	41·06	
Schlosser, G.	SUI	Long jump	Q		DNQ	7,27	
Schmidt, J.	POL	Triple jump	F		1	16,81*	G
		4×100m relay	1	3	DIS		
Schmidt, P.	GER	800m	1	8	2	1-50·97	
			2	2	1	1-51·38	
			SF	2	3	1-47·95	
			F		4	1-47·82	
Schnellmann, S.	SUI	200m	1	8	3	21·59	
			2	3	6	21·66	
		4×100m relay	1	1	3	40·92	
			SF	2	4	41·06	
Schottes, K.-E.	GER	110m hurdles	1	6	2	14·90	
			2	1	6	14·81	
Schwarte, A.	GER	1500m	1	3	4	3-45·46	
Segal, D.	GBR	200m	1	2	2	21·48	
			2	2	3	21·21	
			SF	1	DIS		
		4×100m relay	1	1	1	40·27	
			SF	1	3	40·63	
			F		3	40·32	B
Selvey, W.	AUS	Shot put	F		15	16,18	
		Discus throw	F		21	49,34	
Serchinich, S.	ITA	20k walk	F		21	1:43-58·6	
Seye, A.	FRA	100m	1	7	2	10·75	
			2	4	4	10·64	
		200m	1	9	1	21·21	
			2	2	1	20·95	
			SF	1	1	21·00	
			F		3	20·83	B
		4×100m relay	1	4	DIS		
Sfikas, C.	GRE	Triple jump	Q		DNQ	14,32	
Shah, M.	PAK	5000m	1	4	12	15-43·0	
		3000m steeplechase	1	2	9	9-20·0	
Shahrudin, A.	MAL	100m	1	4	5	11·11	
		200m	1	2	4	22·40	
Sharpe, W.	USA	Triple jump	Q		DNQ	15,44	
Shavlakadze, R.	URS	High jump	F		1	2,16*	G
Shekaib, A.	AFG	100m	1	6	7	11·79	
Shepherd, G.	CAN	400m hurdles	1	2	4	53·05	
Shibata, H.	JPN	Triple jump	Q		DNQ	14,93	
		4×100m relay	1	4	3	42·60	
			SF	1	5	42·39	
Shirley, E.	GBR	3000m steeplechase	1	1	10	9-14·8	
Short, G.	CAN	100m	1	5	4	11·04	
		4×100m relay	1	4	2	42·27	
			SF	1	4	41·27	
Sidlo, J.	POL	Javelin throw	F		8	76,46	
Siebert, J.	USA	800m	1	2	2	1-49·08	
			2	2	3	1-51·53	
			SF	2	4	1-48·20	
Sillon, V.	FRA	Pole vault	Q		DNQ	4,30	

COMPETITOR	COUNTRY CODE	EVENT	ROUND	HEAT	PLACE	TIME & DISTANCE	MEDAL
Silva, J.	CHI	Marathon	F		33	2:31-18·0	
Sime, D.	USA	100m	1	3	3	10·75	
			2	2	2	10·37	
			SF	2	2	10·46	
			F		2	10·35	S
		4×100m relay	1	4	1	39·87	
			SF	2	1	39·67	
			F		DIS		
Simon, A.	HUN	3000m steeplechase	1	1	7	9·02·79	
Sinfield, I.	AUS	Marathon	F		43	2:34-16·0	
Singh, A.	IND	20k walk	F		DNF		
		50k walk	F		15	4:47-23·4	
Singh, G.R.	IND	High jump	Q		DNQ	1,90	
		Decathlon	F		DNF		
Singh, J.	IND	110m hurdles	1	5	5	15·34	
Singh, Milkha	IND	400m	1	6	2	47·72	
			2	2	2	46·71	
			SF	1	2	46·08	
			F		4	45·73	
Singh, V.	IND	Long jump	Q		DNQ	6,70	
Singh, Z.	IND	20k walk	F		20	1:43-19·8	
		50k walk	F		8	4:37-44·6	
Sivoplyasov, I.	URS	Javelin throw	Q		DNQ	73,85	
Skobla, J.	TCH	Shot put	F		9	17,39	
Skourtis, D.	GRE	400m hurdles	1	4	5	53·85	
Skrinjar, F.	YUG	Marathon	F		10	2:21-40·2	
Slegr, J.	TCH	4×400m relay	1	4	4	3-11·33	
		800m	1	2	5	1-50·23	
Smith, D.	NZL	800m	1	1	2	1-51·86	
			2	1	4	1-48·52	
Snajder, V.	YUG	4×400m relay	1	1	3	3-10·75	
			SF	1	6	3-10·34	
Snell, P.	NZL	800m	1	3	1	1-48·22	
			2	4	2	1-48·84	
			SF	2	1	1-47·34	
			F		1	1-46·48*	G
Sobota, P.	POL	High jump	F		15	2,00	
Soederland, A.	SWE	50k walk	F		DNF		
Soederland, E.	SWE	50k walk	F		DNF		
Sokolov, N.	URS	3000m steeplechase	1	1	1	8-43·56	
			F		2	8-36·55	S
Solodov, G.	URS	20k walk	F		DNF		
Sosgornik, A.	POL	Shot put	F		6	17,57	
Soth, R.	USA	5000m	1	4	7	14-40·85	
Sowa, C.	LUX	20k walk	F		18	1:42-43·8	
		50k walk	F		3	4:57-00·4	
Spence, Malcolm B.	SAF	400m	1	4	1	46·79	
			2	4	2	46·21	
			SF	2	2	46·0?	
			F		3	45·60	B
		4×400m relay	1	3	2	3-16·32	
			SF	1	1	3-06·53	
			F		4	3-05·18	
Spence, Malcolm A.	BWI	400m	1	7	1	47·77	
			2	1	3	47·00	
			SF	2	5	46·99	
		4×400m relay	1	2	1	3-09·28	
			SF	2	2	3-09·34	
			F		3	3-04·13	B
Srisombati, S.	THA	5000m	1	3	11	15-32·6	
Steinbach, M.	GER	Long jump	F		8	8,00	
Stokes, H.	USA	Triple jump	Q		DNQ	14,74	
Strand, B.	FIN	4×400m relay	1	1	4	3-11·90	
Strandli, S.	NOR	Hammer throw	F		11	63,05	
Stulac, G.	CAN	Decathlon	F		22	5198	
Suarez, O.	ARG	Marathon	F		9	2:21-26·6	
Sugawara, T.	JPN	Hammer throw	Q		DNQ	59,32	
Sugioka, K.	JPN	High jump	Q		DNQ	1,95	
Suh, Y.-J.	KOR	Long jump	Q		DNQ	6,98	
Sullivan, T.	RHO	800m	1	7	2	1-51·26	
			2	1	5	1-50·01	
		1500m	1	1	4	3-42·96	
Sum, K.	KEN	Marathon	F		59	2:46-55·0	
Sutinen, M.	FIN	Pole vault	F		=6	4,50	
Suutari, S.	FIN	Decathlon	F		12	6751	
Svara, N.	ITA	110m hurdles	1	5	3	15·03	
			2	4	3	14·59	
			SF	1	4	14·50	
Swatowski, S.	POL	400m	1	6	3	48·23	
			2	3	5	47·56	
		4×400m relay	1	2	2	3-09·67	
			SF	2	4	3-10·88	
Sykora, S.	TCH	50k walk	F		14	4:46-14·6	
Syllis, V.	GRE	400m	1	7	5	48·56	
Syrovatski, L.	FRA	Javelin throw	Q		DNQ	71,59	
Szabo, M.	HUN	5000m	1	4	8	14-51·99	
Szecsenyi, J.	HUN	Discus throw	F		4	55,79	
Szekeres, B.	HUN	5000m	1	1	DNF		

COMPETITOR	COUNTRY CODE	EVENT	ROUND	HEAT	PLACE	TIME & DISTANCE	MEDAL
Tedenby, L.	SWE	3000m steeplechase	1	3	5	8-52·94	
Teran, J.	MEX	400m	1	4	6	49·75	
Ter-Ovanesyan, I.	URS	Long jump	F		3	8,04	B
Texereau, G.	FRA	3000m steeplechase	1	1	8	9-04·23	
Thierfelder, K.	GER	Triple jump	Q		DNQ	15,08	
Thomas, A.	AUS	1500m	1	2	5	3-46·95	
		5000m	1	3	3	14-06·27	
			F		11	14-20·88	
Thomas, H.	VEN	Decathlon	F		20	5753	
Thomas, J.	USA	High jump	F		3	2,14	B
Thompson, D.	GBR	50k walk	F		1	4:25-30·0*	G
Thorbjoernsson, H.	ISL	100m	1	9	4	11·05	
Thorlaksson, V.	ISL	Pole vault	Q		DNQ	4,20	
Thun, H.	AUT	Hammer throw	F		9	63,53	
Timme, H.	HOL	Decathlon	F		15	6206	
Tinoco, A.	MEX	3000m steeplechase	1	2	10	9-38·0	
Tipping, D.	AUS	100m	1	2	6	11·30	
		200m	1	12	5	23·09	
Tjoernebo, G.	SWE	3000m steeplechase	1	1	2	8-48·77	
			F		5	8-58·87	
Tobacco, T.	CAN	400m	1	4	3	48·52	
			2	1	4	47·61	
		4×100m relay	1	4	2	42·27	
			SF	1	4	41·27	
		4×400m relay	1	1	2	3-10·65	
			SF	1	5	3-08·37	
Todorov, T.	BUL	Discus throw	F		20	52,12	
Toegersen, T.	DEN	Marathon	F		6	2:21-03·4	
Tomasek, R.	TCH	Pole vault	F		8	4,50	
Tomlinson, I.	AUS	Long jump	Q		DNQ	7,03	
		Triple jump	F		9	15,71	
Tongaram, S.	THA	800m	1	8	7	1-57·24	
Torgersen, T.	NOR	Marathon	F		26	2:27-30·0	
Trollsaes, P.-O.	SWE	400m hurdles	1	4	3	52·49	
		400m relay	1	4	3	3-10·91	
			SF	2	6	3-11·05	
Trousil, J.	TCH	400m	1	1	4	47·53	
		4×400m relay	1	4	4	3-11·05	
Truex, M.	USA	10000m	F		6	28-50·34	
Trusenyev, V.	URS	Discus throw	F		15	52,93	
Tsakanikas, G.	GRE	Shot put	Q		DNQ	16,44	
Tseriwa, C.	RHO	5000m	1	3	10	15-02·8	
		10000m	F		28	30-47·8	
Tsibulenko, V.	URS	Javelin throw	F		1	84,64	G
Tulloh, M.B.S.	GBR	5000m	1	4	4	14-17·30	
Uddebom, E.	SWE	Shot put	Q		DNQ	16,31	
		Discus throw	Q		DNQ	50,87	
Ulivell, L.	ITA	Long jump	Q		DNQ	0	
Unsal, Y.	TUR	Long jump	Q		DNQ	6,97	
Urbach, D.	GER	Shot put	F		7	17,47	
Vacharabhan, P.	THA	4×100m relay	1	1	5	42·19	
Vaide, A.	SWE	Marathon	F		21	2:25-40·2	
Valentin, S.	GER	1500m	1	2	6	3-46·99	
Valkama, J.	FIN	Long jump	F		5	7,69	
Vamos, Z.	RUM	1500m	1	3	3	3-45·07	
			F		5	3-40·8	
Vana, Z.	TCH	4×400m relay	1	4	4	3-11·33	
		400m	1	7	4	48·48	
Vandendriessche, A.	BEL	Marathon	F		DNF		
Van Dyck, R.	BEL	Pole vault	Q		DNQ	4,00	
Vedjakov, A.	URS	20k walk	F		DNF		
		50k walk	F		9	4:39-57·6	
Vega, R.	PUR	4×400m relay	1	1	5	3-13·91	
		200m	1	6	4	21·94	
Vickers, S.	GBR	20k walk	F		3	1:34-56·4	B
Villalonga, J.	PUR	4×400m relay	1	1	5	3-13·91	
Viskari, A.	FIN	Marathon	F		53	2:38-06·0	
Visser, H.	HOL	Long jump	F		7	7,66	
Vista, R.	PHI	4×100m relay	1	2	4	41·55	
Vogelsang, F.	SUI	Decathlon	F		11	6767	
Von Wartburg, U.	SUI	Javelin throw	Q		DNQ	71,56	
Vorobyev, K.	URS	Marathon	F		4	2:19-06·6	
Vuorisalo, O.	FIN	1500m	1	3	10	3-52·68	
Waegli, C.	SUI	800m	1	3	2	1-48·88	
			2	1	2	1-48·15	
			SF	1	2	1-47·40	
			F		5	1-48·19	
		4×400m relay	1	3	1	3-10·79	
			SF	2	3	3-09·77	
			F		6	3-09·55	
Waern, D.	SWE	1500m	1	3	1	3-44·18	
			F		4	3-40·0	
Wakgira, A.	ETH	Marathon	F		7	2:21-09·4	
Wardak, A.	AFG	110m hurdles	1	2	DNF		
		Javelin throw	Q		DNQ	54,20	

COMPETITOR	COUNTRY CODE	EVENT	ROUND	HEAT	PLACE	TIME & DISTANCE	MEDAL
Watanabe, K.	JPN	Marathon	F		32	2:29-45.0	
Watson, A.	USA	Long jump	Q		DNQ	7,32	
Weber, M.	GER	50k walk	F		13	4:44-47.4	
Weber, R.	SUI	4×400m relay	1	3	1	3-10.79	
			SF	2	3	3-09.77	
			F		6	3-09.55	
		400m	1	9	4	47.73	
Wedderburn, J.	BWI	400m	1	9	2	47.56	
			2	2	4	47.22	
		4×400m relay	1	2	1	3-09.28	
			SF	2	2	3-09.34	
			F		3	3-04.13	B
Weller, G.	ARG	50k walk	F		DIS		
Wendelin, M.	GER	200m	1	4	1	21.71	
			2	4	6	21.71	
Wenk, J.	GBR	800m	1	6	3	1-54.27	
			2	3	4	1-50.13	
Whitehead, N.	GBR	4×100m relay	F	1	1	40.27	
			SF	1	3	40.63	
			F		3	40.32	B
Wiggs, M.	GBR	1500m	1	3	6	3-46.61	
William, P.	FRA	Triple jump	Q		DNQ	13,29	
Wischmeier, J.	GER	Triple jump	Q		DNQ	15,23	
Wittwer, A.	SUI	Marathon	F		44	2:34-42.0	
Wongsuwan, P.	THA	Long jump	Q		DNQ	6,78	
		4×100m relay	1	1	5	42.19	
Wrighton, J.	GBR	400m	1	9	3	47.60	
			2	2	6	48.09	
		4×400m relay	1	3	3	3-20.47	
			SF	1	3	3-07.67	
			F		5	3-08.47	
Yang, C.-K.	FOR	Decathlon	F		2	8334	S
Yaqub, N.	PAK	400m hurdles	1	3	5	52.91	
Yardley, H.M.	GBR	400m	1	1	3	47.38	
			2	1	6	48.93	
		4×400m relay	1	3	3	3-20.47	
			SF	1	3	3-07.67	
			F		5	3-08.47	
Yasuda, N.	JPN	Pole vault	Q		DNQ	4,20	
Yasuma, Y.	JPN	Long jump	Q		DNQ	7,34	
Yefimov, B.	URS	5000m	1	3	5	14-14.68	
Yerman, J.	USA	400m	1	6	1	47.37	
			2	2	1	46.54	
			SF	2	6	48.96	
		4×400m relay	1	4	1	3-10.58	
			SF	2	1	3-08.57	
			F		1	3-02.37*	G
Young, E.	USA	400m	1	7	2	47.79	
			2	3	1	46.25	
			SF	2	3	46.29	
			F		6	46.07	
		4×400m relay	1	4	1	3-10.58	
			SF	2	1	3-08.57	
			F		1	3-02.37*	G
Young, G.	USA	3000m steeplechase	1	2	4	8-50.93	
Yusuf Zaid, A.	AFG	200m	1	8	6	23.22	
Zakharov, Y.	URS	5000m	1	1	4	14-10.41	
Zalata, K.	IRQ	100m	1	7	6	11.50	
Zamboni, P.	ITA	110m hurdles	1	2	4	14.82	
			2	2	6	15.02	
Zareef Sayed, H.	AFG	400m	1	1	7	53.91	
Zarrouki, M.	TUN	400m hurdles	1	3	6	54.34	
Zaugg, E.	SUI	4×400m relay	1	3	1	3-10.79	
			SF	2	3	3-09.77	
			F		6	3-09.55	
Zhanal, B.	TCH	3000m steeplechase	1	2	5	8-53.01	
Zhukov, Y.	URS	10000m	F		16	29-42.2	
Zimny, K.	POL	5000m	1	4	3	14-07.75	
			F		3	13-45.09	B
		10000m	F		DNF		
Zinn, R.	USA	20k walk	F		19	1:42-47.0	
Zlassi, N.	TUN	20k walk	F		28	1:55-21.0	
		50k walk	F		DNF		
Zouaki, M.	MOR	400m hurdles	1	1	6	55.65	
Zsivotzky, G.	HUN	Hammer throw	F		2	65,79	S

FEMALES

COMPETITOR	COUNTRY CODE	EVENT	ROUND	HEAT	PLACE	TIME & DISTANCE	MEDAL
Adir, I.	ISR	100m	1	5	6	13.04	
Ahrens, M.	CHI	Javelin throw	F		12	47,53	
Allday, S.	GBR	Shot put	Q		DNQ	13,15	
		Discus throw	Q		DNQ	41,12	
Almqvist, I.	SWE	Javelin throw	Q		DNQ	47,67	
Antal, M.	HUN	Javelin throw	F		9	50,25	
Archer, B.	GUY	High jump	Q		DNQ	1,55	
Bacskai, M.	HUN	4×100m relay	1	1	4	47.54	
Badana, V.	PHI	Long jump	Q		DNQ	5,59	
Balas, I.	RUM	High jump	F		1	1,85*	G

COMPETITOR	COUNTRY CODE	EVENT	ROUND	HEAT	PLACE	TIME & DISTANCE	MEDAL
Ballod, V.	URS	High jump	F		15	1,65	
Becker, I.	GER	High jump	F		=9	1,65	
Bergh, W.	SWE	Discus throw	F		12	43,96	
Bertoni, L.	ITA	30m hurdles	1	6	3	11.54	
		4X100m relay	1	1	3	46.76	
			F		5	45.80	
Bibro, M.	POL	Long jump	F		13	5,86	
Biechl, A.	GER	4×100m relay	1	1	2	45.96	
			F		2	45.00	S
Bignal, M.	GBR	80m hurdles	1	2	1	11.40	
			SF	1	1	11.16	
			F		4	11.22	
		Long jump	F		9	6,01	
		4×100m relay	1	1	1	45.92	
			F		DIS		
Bijleveld, J.	HOL	Long jump	F		7	6,11	
Birkemeyer, G.	GER	100m	1	5	2	12.31	
			2	1	4	12.26	
		200m	1	2	1	24.32	
			SF	2	4	25.05	
		80m hurdles	1	4	1	11.31	
			SF	2	2	11.01	
			F		3	11.13	B
Bistrova, G.	URS	80m hurdles	1	6	2	11.26	
			SF	1	2	11.16	
			F		5	11.26	
Bortoluzzi, M.	ITA	High jump	Q		DNQ	1,55	
Brierre, S.	FRA	80m hurdles	1	5	3	11.75	
Broemmel, A.	GER	Javelin throw	Q		DNQ	45,52	
Brown, B.	USA	High jump	Q		DNQ	1,50	
Brown, E.	USA	Shot put	F		3	16,42	B
		Discus throw	F		6	51,29	
Capdevielle, C.	FRA	100m	1	6	2	11.94	
			2	3	2	12.16	
			SF	2	3	11.82	
			F		5	11.64	
		200m	1	2	2	24.46	
			SF	1	7	25.04	
Celesnik, M.	YUG	Discus throw	Q		DNQ	30,84	
Cerna, V.	TCH	Shot put	F		11	15,06	
Charles, D.	GBR	800m	1	1	5	2-14.24	
Chenchik, T.	URS	High jump	F		5	1,68	
Chi, C.	FOR	80m hurdles	1	6	5	12.71	
Chojnacka, M.	POL	Long jump	F		11	5,98	
Ciray, G.	TUR	800m	1	4	6	2-11.55	
Claus, H.	GER	Long jump	F		3	6,21	B
Crowder, S.	USA	80m hurdles	1	6	4	12.43	
Csoka, G.	HUN	800m	1	3	2	2-09.77	
			F		7	2-08.11	
Cuthbert, B.	AUS	100m	1	4	2	12.21	
			2	4	4	12.18	
Daniels, B.	USA	800m	1	2	DNF		
Diaz, B.	CUB	80m hurdles	1	2	4	11.83	
Diti, M.	RUM	Javelin throw	F		10	49,56	
Dolya, G.	URS	High jump	F		4	1,71	
Donath, U.	GER	800m	1	2	1	2-07.92*	
			F		3	2-05.6	B
Dos Santos, W.	BRA	80m hurdles	1	2	5	11.84	
Doynikova, Z.	URS	Shot put	F		5	16,13	
Duggan, P.	AUS	100m	1	2	1	12.18	
			2	2	4	12.32	
		200m	1	1	4	24.80	
		4×100m relay	1	2	DIS		
Dunn, L.	PAN	4×100m relay	1	2	4	46.66	
Dupureur, M.	FRA	800m	1	1	4	2-12.42	
Figwer, U.	POL	Javelin throw	F		5	52,33	
Fikotova-Connolly, O.	USA	Discus throw	F		7	50,95	
Fleming, N.	AUS	200m	1	3	2	24.35	
			SF	1	4	24.44	
		Long jump	F		15	5,82	
		4×100m relay	1	2	DIS		
Frith, H.	AUS	High jump	F		=6	1,65	
		Long jump	F		17	5,62	
Fukuda, A.	JPN	Long jump	Q		DNQ	5,78	
Gaertner, J.	USA	High jump	Q		DNQ	1,50	
Garisch, R.	GER	Shot put	F		6	15,94	
Gere, O.	YUG	High jump	F		=9	1,65	
Gerhards, A.	GER	Javelin throw	F		11	49,27	
Gleichfield, A.	GER	800m	1	1	3	2-11.05*	
			F		5	2-06.63	
Gooden, C.	PAN	100m	1	3	4	12.36	
			2	3	6	12.70	
		4×100m relay	1	2	4	46.66	
Gouilleux, N.	FRA	800m	1	3	7	2-13.53	
Grecescu, F.	RUM	800m	1	2	3	2-10.10	

COMPETITOR	COUNTRY CODE	EVENT	ROUND	HEAT	PLACE	TIME & DISTANCE	MEDAL
Guenard, D.	FRA	80m hurdles	1	3	2	11·37	
			SF	2	6	11·51	
Halkier, K.	DEN	Discus throw	Q		DNQ	43,99	
Haslam, E.	CAN	100m	1	1	3	12·21	
			2	1	5	12·46	
		200m	1	5	3	24·63	
		800m	1	3	4	2-10·1?	
		4×100m relay	1	1	5	48·05	
Hatzroni, A.	ISR	Shot put	Q		DNC	?2,59	
Hausmann, K.	GER	Discus throw	F		4	51,47	
Heine, J.	GER	200m	1	3	1	24·04	
			SF	1	2	24·15	
			F		2	24·58	S
		4×100m relay	1	1	2	45·96	
			F		2	45·00	S
Heldt, E.	HUN	200m	1	6	6	25·50	
		4×100m relay	1	1	4	47·54	
Hendrix, B.	GER	100m	1	7	2	11·99	
			2	2	2	12·02	
			SF	1	5	11·99	
		4×100m relay	1	1	2	45·96	
			F		2	45·00	
Hiscock, J.	GBR	200m	1	2	4	24·85	
Hobers, E.	HOL	High jump	Q		DNQ	1 60	
Hoffman, H.	GER	Long jump	F		6	6 11	
Hoffmann, W.	GER	Shot put	F		8	15,14	
Hofrichter, D.	AUT	Discus throw	Q		DNQ	44,94	
Holmes, J.	PAN	100m	1	5	3	12·52	
			2	2	5	12·39	
		4×100m relay	1	2	4	46 66	
Hudson, M.	USA	100m	1	7	4	12 33	
			2	3	4	12·30	
		4×100m relay	1	2	1	44·50*	
			F		1	44·72	G
Hunte, S.	PAN	4×100m relay	1	2	4	46·66	
Hyman, D.	GBR	100m	1	5	1	11·98	
			2	4	1	11·77	
			SF	2	1	11·65	
			F		2	11·43	S
		200m	1	5	2	23·82	
			SF	2	2	24·78	
			F		3	24·82	B
		4×100m relay	1	1	1	45·92	
			F		DIS		
Iannaccone, G.	ITA	800m	1	2	5	2-13·72	
Ignatyeva, L.	URS	200m	1	3	4	24·90	
Itkina, M.	URS	100m	1	3	1	11·83	
			2	2	1	11·83	
			SF	2	2	11·78	
			F		4	11·54	
		200m	1	4	2	24·20	
			SF	2	3	24·8?	
			F		4	24·85	
		4×100m relay	1	2	2	45·15	
			F		4	45·39	
Ito, F.	JPN	Long jump	F		12	5,98	
Janiszewska, B.	POL	200m	1	4	1	24·08	
			SF	1	3	24·36	
			F		5	24·96	
		4×100m relay	1	2	3	45·40	
			F		3	45·19	B
Jenner, A.	GBR	100m	1	1	4	12·39	
			2	2	6	12·4	
Jerome, V.	CAN	100m	1	5	4	12·58	
			2	4	5	12·50	
		4×100m relay	1	1	5	48·05	
Jesionowska, C.	POL	200m	1	5	2	24·45	
			SF	2	6	25·45	
		4×100m relay	1	2	3	45·40	
			F		3	45·19	B
Johansson, B.	FIN	Long jump	F		18	5 57	
Jonas, I.	HUN	4×100m relay	1	1	4	47·54	
Jones, Barbara	USA	100m	1	1	2	11·91	
			2	4	2	12·02	
			SF	2	4	11·84	
		4×100m relay	1	2	1	44·50*	
			F		1	44 72	G
Jones, Brenda	AUS	800m	1	1	2	2-11·14	
			F		2	2-04·58	S
Jordan, J.	GBR	800m	1	4	2	2-07·29	
			F		6	2-07·95	
Jozwiakowska, J.	POL	High jump	F		=2	1,71	S
Junker, R.	GER	Long jump	F		4	6,19	
Kaledene, B.	URS	Javelin throw	F		3	53,45	B
Karashik, I.	ISR	Long jump	Q		DNQ	5,08	
		200m	1	2	5	26·69	
Kazi, A.	HUN	800m	1	2	4	2-11·07	
Kerkova, S.	BUL	100m	1	4	4	12·66	
			2	2	7	12·80	
		80m hurdles	1	2	3	11·73	
Kimura, Y.	JPN	Long jump	Q		DNQ	5,45	
Klimaj, J.	POL	Shot put	F		10	14,66	
Kock, L.	DEN	Javelin throw	Q		DNQ	43,01	
Konvur, C.	TUR	High jump	Q		DNQ	1,50	
Kopp, Z.	GER	80m hurdles	1	6	1	11·10	
			SF	2	4	11·09	
Koshelyeva, R.	URS	80m hurdles	1	3	1	11·26	
			SF	1	3	11·22	
			F		6	11·28	
Kraan, G.	HOL	800m	1	3	6	2-10·71	
Krasteva, T.	BUL	Shot put	Q		DNQ	13,99	
Krepkina, V.	URS	100m	1	7	1	11·97	
			2	1	2	12·14	
			SF	1	6	12·08	
		Long jump	F		1	6,37*	G
		4×100m relay	1	2	2	45·15	
			F		4	45·39	
Krzesirska, E.	POL	Long jump	F		2	6,27	S
Kulhava, B.	TCH	800m	1	3	5	2-10·23	
Kummerfeldt, V.	GER	800m	1	4	3	2-07·34	
			F		4	2-06·07	
Kurrell, P.	USA	Discus throw	Q		DNQ	43,23	
Kuzneyetsova, E.	URS	Discus throw	F		5	51,43	
Kyle, N.	IRL	100m	1	5	5	12·59	
		200m	1	6	5	25·06	
Langbein, M.	GER	4×100m relay	1	1	2	45·96	
			F		2	45·00	S
Lee, H.-J.	KOR	800m	1	1	7	2-28·4	
Lenzke, K.	GER	High jump	Q		DNQ	1,60	
Leone, G.	ITA	100m	1	1	1	11·87	
			2	3	1	12·11	
			SF	1	2	11·71	
			F		3	11·48	B
		200m	1	1	1	23·90	
			SF	2	1	24·69	
			F		6	25·01	
		4×100m relay	1	1	3	46·76	
			F		5	45·80	
Lewington, N.	CAN	100m	1	2	4	12·67	
			2	3	7	13·23	
		4×100m relay	1	1	5	48·05	
Lin, C.-T.	FOR	Long jump	Q		DNQ	5,51	
Lorentzon, B.	SWE	High jump	F		=6	1,65	
Luettge, J.	GER	Shot put	F		2	16,61	S
McCallum, S.	CAN	80m hurdles	1	4	4	11·90	
		Long jump	Q		DNQ	5,22	
		4×100m relay	1	1	5	48·05	
Manoliu, L.	RUM	Discus throw	F		3	52,36	B
Markussen, V.	DEN	100m	1	2	3	12·53	
			2	4	6	12·56	
Maslovskaya, V.	URS	200m	1	6	3	24·12	
			SF	1	6	24·77	
		4×100m relay	1	2	4	45·15	
			F		4	45·39	
Matistovich, Z.	URS	800m	1	1	3	2-11·57	
Matsuda, Y.	JPN	Shot put	Q		DNQ	13,51	
Mertova, S.	TCH	Discus throw	F		11	48,28	
Mitchell, S.	AUS	Long jump	Q		DNQ	5,60	
Morgan, V	NZL	100m	1	4	3	12·61	
			2	1	7	12·66	
		200m	1	3	5	25·39	
Mueller, D	GER	Discus throw	Q		DNQ	0	
Munkacsi, A.	HUN	200m	1	4	3	24·53	
		4×100m relay	1	1	4	47·54	
Murauer, F	AUT	80m hurdles	1	4	5	12·08	
Nemcova, J.	TCH	Discus throw	F		8	50,12	
Nowakowska, K.	POL	800m	1	3	3	2-09·81	
Nutting, P.	GBR	80m hurdles	1	4	3	11·65	
Oldham, K.	USA	Javelin throw	F		13	46,52	
Onel, A.	TUR	100m	1	7	5	13·59	
		Long jump	Q		DNQ	4,97	
Oxvang, M.	DEN	High jump	Q		DNQ	1,60	
Ozolina, E.	URS	Javelin throw	F		1	55,98*	G
Parlyuk, E.	URS	800m	1	4	4	2-07·71	
Paternoster, P.	ITA	Discus throw	Q		DNQ	43,11	
Pazera, A.	AUS	Javelin throw	F		6	51,15	
Perkins, P.	GBR	800m	1	2	6	2-15·41	
Persighetti, C.	GBR	Long jump	F		19	5,57	
Peskova, V.	TCH	Javelin throw	F		4	52,56	
Petry-Amiel, F.	FRA	High jump	F		=9	1,65	
Platt, S.	GBR	Javelin throw	F		7	51,01	
Pollards, E.	USA	200m	1	5	4	24·64	

COMPETITOR	COUNTRY CODE	EVENT	ROUND	HEAT	PLACE	TIME & DISTANCE	MEDAL
Press, I.	URS	80m hurdles	1	1	1	10·91*	
			SF	2	1	10·77*	
			F		1	10·93	G
		4x100m relay	1	2	2	45·15	
			F		4	45·39	
Press, T.	URS	Discus throw	F		2	52,59	S
		Shot put	F		1	17,32*	G
Prikrylova, L.	TCH	Long jump	Q		DNQ	5,64	
Quinton, C.	GBR	80m hurdles	1	1	2	11·07	
			SF	2	3	11·07	
			F		2	10·99	S
		4x100m relay	1	1	1	45·92	
			F		DIS		
Radchenko, L.	URS	Long jump	F		5	6,16	
Raepke, H.	GER	100m	1	6	4	12·45	
		200m	1	1	3	24·32	
Ricci, E.	ITA	Discus throw	Q		DNQ	45,86	
Richert, K.	GER	80m hurdles	1	5	1	11·40	
			SF	1	4	11·27	
Richter, H.	POL	100m	1	6	3	12·13	
			2	2	3	12·10	
			SF	1	4	11·93	
		200m	1	6	4	24·31	
		4x100m relay	1	2	3	45·40	
			F		3	45·19	B
Robertson, I.	USA	80m hurdles	1	1	5	11·69	
Rogers, N.	USA	High jump	F		14	1,65	
Romashkova-Ponomaryeva, N	URS	Discus throw	F		1	55,10*	G
Rudolph, W.	USA	100m	1	6	1	11·65*	
			2	1	1	11·70	
			SF	1	1	11·41*	
			F		1	11·18*	G
		200m	1	6	1	23·30*	
			SF	1	1	23·79	
			F		1	24·13	G
		4x100m relay	1	2	1	44·50*	
			F		5	44·72	G
Rusin, E.	POL	Shot put	F		11	14,55	
Rykowska, K.	POL	Discus throw	Q		DNQ	46,75	
Schmitz-Porz, M.	GER	High jump	F		=9	1,65	
Schuch, I.	GER	Discus throw	F		9	49,86	
Shaprunova, V.	URS	Long jump	F		8	6,01	
Sharamovich, L.	BUL	Shot put	Q		DNQ	14,09	
Shastitko, A.	URS	Javelin throw	F		8	50,92	
Shevtsova-Lysenko, L.	URS	800m	1	3	1	2-09.31	
			F		1	2-04.50*	G
Shirley, D.	GBR	High jump	F		=2	1,71	S
Sikovec, O.	YUG	100m	1	3	3	12·24	
			2	3	5	12·61	
		200m	1	5	5	24·95	
Slaap, F.	GBR	High jump	F		=6	1,65	
Sloper, V.	NZL	Shot put	F		4	16,39	
		Discus throw	F		10	48,41	
Smart, J.	GBR	100m	1	4	1	12·04	
			2	3	3	12·17	
			SF	1	3	11·89	
			F		6	11·72	
		200m	1	6	3	24·12	
			SF	1	5	24·74	
		4x100m relay	1	1	1	45·92	
			F		DIS		

COMPETITOR	COUNTRY CODE	EVENT	ROUND	HEAT	PLACE	TIME & DISTANCE	MEDAL
Smith, A.	USA	Long jump	Q		DNQ	0	
Solaiman, M.	PHI	100m	1	2	2	12·40	
			2	1	6	12·54	
		200m	1	4	4	25·98	
Sosgornik, B.	POL	30m hurdles	1	4	2	11·56	
			SF	1	5	11·44	
Stamejcic, D.	YUG	80m hurdles	1	1	3	11·47	
Stolzova, A.	TCH	200m	1	3	3	24·85	
		80m hurdles	1	3	4	11·59	
Strasser, E.	AUT	Javelin throw	Q		DNQ	43,80	
Stroessenreuther, E.	GER	Javelin throw	Q		DNQ	46,85	
Ter-Laak-Spik, G.	HOL	800m	1	4	5	2-10.36	
Terry, J.	USA	80m hurdles	1	3	3	11·58	
Thetu, M.	FRA	Long jump	F		14	5,85	
Thompson, J.	NZL	Discus throw	Q		DNQ	46,74	
Thorvaldsen, U.	NOR	Javelin throw	Q		DNQ	41,99	
Thrower, N.	AUS	80m hurdles	1	2	2	11·54	
			SF	1	6	11·46	
		4x100m relay	1	2	DIS		
Tizzoni, P.	ITA	Long jump	Q		DNQ	5,65	
		4x100m relay	1	1	3	46·76	
			F		5	45·80	
Uchida, H.	JPN	Discus throw	Q		DNQ	43,78	
Usenik, M.	YUG	Shot put	F		12	14,19	
Valenti, S.	ITA	4x100m relay	1	1	3	46·76	
			F		5	45·80	
Walasek, Z.	POL	800m	1	1	6	2-16.44	
Weigel, B.	NZL	Long jump	F		10	5,98	
White, W.	USA	Long jump	F		16	5,77	
Wieczorek, T.	POL	100m	1	7	3	12·25	
			2	4	3	12·14	
			SF	2	5	12·05	
		80m hurdles	1	5	2	11·46	
			SF	2	5	11·40	
		4x100m relay	1	2	3	45·40	
			F		3	45·19	B
Wieslander, U.	SWE	200m	1	2	3	24·82	
		80m hurdles	1	1	4	11·60	
Wigney, G.	AUS	80m hurdles	1	5	4	11·89	
Willard, M.	AUS	100m	1	3	3	12·10	
			2	1	3	12·25	
			SF	2	6	12·05	
		4X100m relay	1	2	DIS		
Williams, A.	GBR	Javelin throw	Q		DNQ	42,44	
Williams, L.	USA	200m	1	1	2	24·10	
			SF	2	5	25·14	
		4x100m relay	1	2	1	44·50*	
			F		1	44·72	G
Willis, D.	AUS	800m	1	4	1	2-06.03*	
			F		DNF		
Wu, J.-Y.	FOR	Shot put	Q		DNQ	11,76	
		Discus thorw	Q		DNQ	0	
Zatopkova, D.	TCH	Javelin throw	F		2	53,78	S
Zbikowsksa, B.	POL	800m	1	2	2	2-09.57	
			F		8	2-11.8	
Zibina, G.	URS	Shot put	F		7	15,56	
Zwier, N.	HOL	High jump	F		=9	1,65	

1964

Telstar Brings Tokyo's Stars to Millions

After Melbourne, Tokyo registered another first in 1964: the first Games to be held in Asia. The Japanese spent vast sums on the Games, which were beautifully organised and enjoyed by all who took part.

The track and field events were of a high standard, with some notable firsts: USA athletes won both the 5,000 and 10,000 metres, no American athlete having won either before. For Great Britain, there were victories in the men's and women's long jumps, the first gold medals in either event. Other outstanding efforts were by Bikila, this time wearing shoes, who recovered from having his appendix out in time (five weeks!) to become the first man to win the marathon twice; Bob Hayes, who equalled the world 100 metres record, and not least Peter Snell, whose 800 and 1,500 metres double was the first for 44 years.

All this was watched by the world through Telstar, the new television satellite. Tokyo staged a very happy games.

Men's Track Events

Bob Hayes of the USA, built like a tank, was the 100 yards record holder at 9·1 sec and was the **100 metres** favourite. The times in the preliminary races had been variable due to changing winds, but Hayes startled the spectators in the first semi-final with a wind-blown 9·9. In the final he appeared momentarily to lag behind the rest as they came out of the blocks, but at 40 metres was ahead of Enrique Figuerola of Cuba, who was just up on Harry Jerome of Canada. Hayes kept powering away and won in a world record equalling 10·0, while

Figuerola, who was fading fast, just made second, a fraction up on Jerome in third, both recording 10·2. (Automatic timings: Hayes 10·06, Figuerola 10·25 and Jerome 10·27).

Henry Carr of the USA was the man of the moment in the **200 metres**, having run a stunning world record of 20·2 over the longer 220 yards. And in the final, Livio Berruti of Italy, defending his title, drew the unpopular tight inside lane with Carr in the wide sweeping seventh lane. This was the first Games at which eight finalists contested the sprints and hurdles. Paul Drayton of the USA tore around the bend, but Carr with his long legs swept past him off the bend and majestically strode down the straight to win in 20·3 for an Olympic record. Drayton kept ahead of the other six finalists for second in 20·5, whilst Ed Roberts of Trinidad and Tobago took third at 20·6, with the rest in a line just behind. (Automatic timings: Carr 20·36, Drayton 20·58 and Roberts 20·63).

In the **400 metres** there were two ultra fast men from America, Mike Larrabee, who had equalled the world record of 44·9 sec and Ulis Williams, who was just behind him in that race. Larrabee was in the advantageous fifth lane for the final, with Williams in eight. Wendell Mottley of Trinidad and Tobago went off fast and reached 200 in 21·6, with Andrzej Badenski of Poland, Robbie Brightwell of Britain and Williams at his heels. Coming into the straight, Larrabee was four metres down on Mottley, but put in a blistering finish and caught him with ten metres to go, winning in 45·1. Mottley was second in 45·2 and Badenski third in 45·6, just holding off Brightwell on 45·7. (Automatic timings:

Mark Shearman

Betty Cuthbert

Dubbed 'The Beaut'' by her fellow Australians because of her particularly good looks, Betty had the joy of collecting three gold medals from the 1956 Games in Melbourne and another in Tokyo eight years later.

Her Melbourne successes came in the 100m, 200m and 4 × 100 metre relay, when she was a shy 18-year-old. But there was certainly no shyness about her racing stride, for after setting an Olympic record of 11·4 sec in her heat of the 100m, she won the final with two yards to spare in 11·5 sec. Her 200m title win in 23·4 sec was even more decisive and on the final day of the Games she anchored Australia's sprint relay team to a world-breaking 44·5 sec.

At the Rome Olympics in 1960 she was forced to withdraw from her events after one race because of a pulled hamstring. But by 1964, having established herself as a world record-breaking quarter-miler, she chose to concentrate on the new women's 400m event, and won the thrilling final by a stride from Ann Packer, of Britain, in 52·0 sec.

Betty was born at Merrylands, Sydney, on 20 April 1938, and much credit for her achievements are due to June Ferguson, a relay silver medallist at the London Olympics, who coached her right through to Olympic stardom and 14 world records.

Larrabee 45·15, Mottley 45·24 and Badenski 45·64).

With the world record under his belt, the holder of the Olympic **800 metres** title, Peter Snell, was expected to repeat his 1960 victory. But opposition was expected in the form of George Kerr of Jamaica, who broke the Olympic record with 1-46·1 in the semi-finals, and Wilson Kiprugut of Kenya, with the same time. The first 130 metres of the final was in lanes and when they broke, Kiprugut was leading and passed the 400 in 52·0, closely followed by Jacques Pennewaert of Belgium, Kerr, America's Tom Farrell and Bill Crothers of Canada, with Snell boxed in in seventh place. With 250 metres to go Snell went to the front and was round the final bend before the other runners knew what was happening. Kerr, Kiprugut and Crothers made a determined effort to catch him, but it was of no use and Snell won in 1-40·1, an Olympic record. Crothers won the battle of the chasing group in 1:45·6 for silver, with Kiprugut in 1-45·9 taking the bronze from Kerr, fourth with the same time.

Snell was also the one mile world record holder and had his eyes on an **800** and **1,500 metres** double. The first three laps in the final were of moderate pace, with Michel Bernard of France and then John Davies of New Zealand leading. Snell was content to follow the pace until about 250 metres from home when he threw in a devastating spurt, entering the home straight six metres ahead, to win by twice this margin in 3-38·1. The race for the silver medal centred around five runners: Davies, Josef Odlozil of Czechoslovakia, Britain's Alan Simpson, Daryl Burleson of America and Witold Baran of Poland. Odlozil just edged past Davies for the silver, both credited with 3-39·6 and Simpson was a shade back in fourth at 3-39·7.

The top competitors for the **5,000 metres** were all of a similar standard, with Ron Clarke of Australia being the most consistent but lacking a finishing kick. Clarke won the fastest heat in 13-48·4, while Murray Halberg of New Zealand, the winner four years previously, was eliminated. After a slow start in the final, Clarke took up the running with Michel Jazy of France on his shoulder. He was followed closely by Harold Norpoth of Germany, Russia's Nikolai Dutov and Bill Baillie of New Zealand. Clarke then tried surging to shake off his opponents but it did not work and there was a pack of

nine at the bell jostling for position. Bill Dellinger took the lead and the pace hotted up, but Jazy jumped him and tore to the front with Bob Schul of the USA following. Schul pulled him back slowly but surely and went on to win in 13-48·8 with a 54·8 last lap. Norpoth and Dellinger both caught Jazy just before the tape, the German winning the battle for second in 13-49·6 to 13-49·8.

Ron Clarke of Australia was the favourite to win the **10,000 metres**, a straight final with 38 running. Once away, the runners settled down to a fast but steady pace, dictated by Clarke. Billy Mills of America was in the lead at 5km in 14-04·6 with Clarke second, Mamo Wolde of Ethiopia third and Mohamed Gammoudi of Tunisia fourth, then a gap to the next runner. These four kept together until with two laps to go Wolde started dropping back. Gammoudi then took off around the final curve, with Clarke chasing hard. But Mills held back until the finishing straight, when he let rip and sailed past the other two to win in 28-24·4, a new Olympic record, from Gammoudi in 28-24·8 and Clarke in 28-25·8.

Basil Heatley of Britain was the fastest **marathon** runner prior to the Olympics with a fine 2:13-55·0 and was among the favourites for the race where Abebe Bikila of Ethiopia was defending his title. Ron Clarke of Australia was the early leader, passing 10km in a fast 30-04, but shortly after 15km Bikila took up the running with Jim Hogan of Ireland hanging onto him. At 30km Bikila had Hogan still closely trailing him, but Clarke was fading fast as Kokichi Tsuburaya of Japan moved into third place, with Heatley fourth. The result became a foregone conclusion as Bikila ran into the stadium without any sign of distress and won in 2:12-11·2 for a new world best and Olympic record, to become the first man to retain his title. And while he was exercising on the grass, the local Tsuburaya came into view, accompanied by roars of approval, with Heatley only ten metres behind him. Heatley spurted the last 180 metres and took the silver in 2:16-19·2 from Tsuburaya, who made do with the bronze in 2:16-22·8.

With Hayes Jones in such great form, the Americans looked set to make a clean sweep of the medals in the **110 metres hurdles**. His leading challengers, Anatoliy Mikhailov of the USSR and the USA's Blaine Lindgren

Mark Shearman

Iolanda Balas

Iolanda Balas was a high jumper *extraordinaire*. Between 1956 and 1961 she either broke or equalled the women's world high jump record no fewer than 14 times. Few men at the time were capable of clearing her world mark of 1,91m (6ft 3¼in).

Using the old-fashioned scissors style, Iolanda became the first woman to clear 6ft in 1960 and ten years later only five other women had jumped this height, while the Rumanian champion had repeated the performance more than 50 times.

Iolanda Balas was born in Timisoara, Transylvania, on 12 December 1936, and set her initial world record in the summer of 1956 with 1,75m (5ft 8¾in). She was expected to capture the Olympic title that same year in Melbourne, but managed only 1,67m (5ft 5¾in), and finished back in fifth place.

It was a different story however at Rome in 1960 and Tokyo in 1964. In both cities she was a decisive winner, with 1,85m (6ft 0¾in) in Rome and 1,90m (6ft 2¾in) in Tokyo. Tendon trouble ended her career in 1967.

Few have dominated an event so completely as did the long-legged 1,85m (6ft 0¾in) tall Balas, who following her Melbourne disappointment, won 140 consecutive competitions over a period of ten years. Iolanda married her coach Ion Soeter, the Rumanian men's high jump champion, in 1967.

Britain's silver medal hero, Paul Nihill, strides out in the 50 kilometres walk.

Mark Shearman

Mark Shearman

Abebe Bikila

Born at Mout, on 7 August 1932, Bikila, a 28-year-old member of the Ethipian Imperial Bodyguard, became black Africa's first Olympic athletics gold medal winner and the first to win the marathon at two successive Games. His victory in Rome 1960 came after a tense race with Morocco's Ben Abdesselem Rhadi with whom he ran shoulder to shoulder from 18km. Superior finishing strength brought Bikila home the winner in a world best 2:15-16·2. It was his third marathon, and he shocked the world's press by running in bare feet.

More experience in distance running by the time he was chosen to defend the title in the Tokyo Games of 1964, Bikila, now running in shoes, was in complete command of the race at half-way and pressed on to win his second Olympic gold by more than four minutes, with a new world best mark of 2:12-11·2. Later, he made a third attempt to take the title in Mexico City, 1968, but a broken bone in a leg forced him to stop running after 17km.

Bikila's successes led to his being presented with a car by his government and in 1969 he was involved in a crash which left him paralysed from the waist downwards. Alas, he became confined to a wheelchair until his death from a brain haemorrhage on 25 October 1973.

Mark Shearman

Valeriy Brumel

Brumel is one of the most remarkable high jumpers in athletics history. When he broke the world record for the sixth time with 7ft 5¾in (2,28m) in 1963, he jumped 17 inches above his own height.

Born on 14 April 1942 in Tolbuzino, Siberia, he was showing exceptional promise in the event when only 14 and by the time he was 18, was tieing the European record of 7ft 2½in (2,19m). This height amounted to a seven-inch improvement in a season and selection for the Rome Olympics the same year was a heartening reward. There, he cleared the same height as the winner, Robert Shavlakadze, the Soviet first choice, with an Olympic record 7ft 1in (2,16m), but he had to be content with the silver on the count-back of failures.

It was the following year that Brumel became firmly established as the world's leading jumper, when raising the world record to 7ft 4in (2,23m) and improving it yet again with 7ft 4½in. Brumel was a strong tip to take the Tokyo Games gold, but he only just qualified for the final.

Although again feeling the pressure Brumel managed to salvage the gold with a new Olympic record 7ft 1¾in (2,18m), which John Thomas of the United States also cleared but was relegated to second place on a count-back.

Mark Shearman

Peter Snell

Bursting on to the international scene as a surprise winner of the 800m at the Rome Olympics in 1960, Peter Snell became a dominating force in world middle distance running.

He was born in Opunake on 17 December 1938, and lawn tennis was his sport until the noted athletics coach, Arthur Lydiard, spotted him as an 18-year-old with potential to become an outstanding track athlete. Once taking him under his wing, Lydiard had Snell building deep strength in his strong body with 100-mile-a-week training runs. It was his super strength that brought him his victory in Rome.

By 1962 the popular Kiwi had taken over the world record from Moens with 1-44·3, on his way to setting new world figures for 880 yards. That same year also saw him become the world's all-time fastest miler with 3-54·4 and also achieve an 880 yards mile "double" at the Commonwealth Games in Perth, Australia. Clearly he was going to be an extremely hard man to beat at the 1964 Olympics in Tokyo. And so it proved, with Snell becoming the first since Antwerp in 1920 to win both the 800m and 1,500m finals at one Olympic Games. Before 1964 was out he had shown his mastery yet again in improving his world mile record to 3-54·1 and also setting new world figures for 1,000m of 2-16·6.

Gold and silver for America in the 200 metres, in the shapes of Henry Carr, the winner, and Paul Drayton.

Mark Shearman

looked good in the semi-finals, although Willie Davenport of the USA was eliminated, being troubled by an injury. In the final, Jones was away fastest but Lindgren had caught him by the seventh flight. However, Jones' superior speed on the run-in got him the gold in 13·6 sec from Lindgren in 13·7, with Mikhailov closing up fast for the bronze medal, also in 13·7. (Automatic timings: Jones 13·67, Lindgren 13·74 and Mikhailov 13·78).

Warren Cawley of the USA had recently set a world record over **400 metres hurdles** and was favoured to win, but there was also the European champion and record holder Salvatore Morale of Italy to consider. Cawley won the first semi-final in 49·8 sec and John Cooper of Britain took the second in 50·4 in a close finish. With the final underway, the Italians Morale and Roberto Frinolli led over the first five flights, followed by Cooper and the USA's Jay Luck with Cawley fifth. Cawley started a wind-up finish with 150 metres to go and passed his opponents between the seventh and ninth hurdles, going on to victory in 49·6. Meanwhile, Frinolli had run himself out, while Luck hit hurdle eight, and it was Cooper who was just that bit stronger. He took the silver, with Morale the bronze, although they both received the same time of 50·1.

As the world record holder, and European champion, Gaston Roelants of Belgium was tipped to win the **3,000 metres steeplechase**. In the final, he quickly took command, leading Adolf Alexeiunas of the USSR with the rest of the field closely grouped behind and when he later put more pressure on, his rivals began to lose ground. Roelants continued to stretch his lead, although George Young of the USA vainly tried to catch him, with the main pack 50 metres adrift. But with a lap to go, Maurice Herriott of Britain made his challenge and passed Young with 200 metres left. However, he could not catch the tiring Roelants, who won in 8-30·8 for an Olympic record, and had to settle for the silver with a time of 8-32·4. Ivan Beliaev of the USSR was third in 8-33·8.

Ken Matthews of Great Britain, the European champion, was the most likely winner of the **20 kilometres walk**, with Vladimir Golubnichy, the defending champion and best of the Russians, the danger. Matthews virtually led the race from start to finish, passing the half distance in 44-23·0 and taking the gold in 1:29-34·0. The other medallists who also assumed their silver and bronze positions early, were Dieter Lindner of Germany who was second in 1:31-13·2 and the defending champion, Golubnichy, with third place in 1:31-59·4.

In the **50 kilometres walk**, Abdon Pamich, the European champion, was favoured for the gold, but there was also some strong competition from Britain, Russia and Germany. Following an early burst by Gennadiy Agapov of the USSR, Pamich took the lead over Chris Hohne of Germany with Britain's Paul Nihill and the Russian in joint third place. Pamich passed the half-way stage in 2:03-09·0, with Hohne and Nihill only a couple of steps behind and by then Agapov had found the pace too hot. Hohne was the next to ease off and Pamich and Nihill strode along together for another 15km, until the Italian gradually drew away to win in 4:11-12·4, for a new world best and Olympic record. Nihill took the silver medal in 4:11-31·2 and Ingvar Pettersson of Sweden came through to take third in 4:14-17·4.

The **4 × 100 metres relay** reached a new high standard at Tokyo with all eight finalists breaking the magic 40·0 second mark. In the first semi-final, the USA only just won from France and Jamaica to equal the Olympic record of 39·5 sec, while in the second, Italy pipped Poland and Venezuela all being timed at 39·6. In the first leg of the final, Poland went ahead, when the USA lost two metres with a bad change-over. The next two American runners only managed to hold their own, also due to indifferent passing, but Bob Hayes, the anchor man stormed past Marian Dudziak of Poland to win in 39·0 for a new world record, with Poland taking the silver in 39·3. France took third in 39·3, with Britain eighth and last in 39·6, in a very close race. The US team was Paul Drayton, Gerry Ashworth, Dick Stebbins and Bob Hayes. (Automatic timings: USA 39·06, Poland 39·36 and France 39·36).

As well as the USA, Britain, Jamaica and Trinidad had great teams in the **4 × 400 metres relay**. In the final, Tim Graham gave Britain a slight lead over the USA's Ollan Cassell and Trinidad's Ed Skinner, but at the end of the second lap, the American Mike Larrabee handed over first. Then America's Ulis Williams and Trinidad's Ed Roberts both did 45·4 on the third lap, with Jamaica and Britain being just behind Trinidad. But on the final leg, Henry Carr had no problem running 44·5 and setting a new world record for the USA of 3-00·7, while behind them a tremendous tussle was going on. Britain's Robbie Brightwell just pushed his chest in front of Trinidad's Wendell Mottley to take the silver position in 3-01·6, Trinidad being given third in 3-01·7.

Men's Field Events

In the **high jump** four years previously, John Thomas of the USA had been the favourite and had lost to Russia's Valeriy Brumel. This time however, Brumel was the record holder and Thomas was seeking revenge. Once the competitors sorted themselves out, the field was narrowed to five and the bar was elevated to 2,12 metres. Brumel and his fellow Russian Robert Shavlakadze cleared first time with the other three doing likewise at the second time of asking. At 2,14 America's John Rambo made it with his first effort and Stig Pettersson of Sweden at his second, but Brumel, Thomas and Shavlakadze needed three. Pettersson and Shavlakadze both failed at 2,16, to take fourth and fifth places respectively. At the new Olympic record height of 2,18 Rambo failed and took bronze, while Brumel and Thomas got over first time but could not make 2,20. Brumel was declared the winner and Thomas took the silver.

This was the beginning of the fibre-glass era and Fred Hansen of the USA, the master of the flexible pole, was expected to win the **pole vault** hands down. The Olympic record stood at 4,70 metres, but at 4,90 seven went clear. However, only four surmounted the magic 5,00 metres: Hansen and three Germans, Wolfgang Reinhardt, Klaus Lehnertz and Manfred Preussger, all at their first attempt. At 5,05 Hansen had the audacity to pass, and Reinhardt cleared to lead the competition, while Lehnertz and Preussger failed. With the bar at 5,10, only Hansen cleared (on his last try!) to take the gold medal and Olympic record, while Reinhardt took the silver and Lehnertz the bronze.

The defending champion in the **long jump**, the USA's Ralph Boston, had recently raised his world record and after making the best qualifying jump of 8,03 metres, seemed likely to win. The final started in low key with

"The Golden Girl", Mary Rand, née Bignall, produced a stunning long jump series in Tokyo, where she broke the world record on her way to winning the event.

Mark Shearman

Igor Ter-Ovanesyan of Russia leaping 7,78 to Boston's 7,76 and Wariboko West of Nigeria holding third with 7,56. The fourth round saw Boston take the lead at 7,88, from Ter-Ovanesyan 7,80 and Lynn Davies of Britain now on 7,78. On a wet, drizzly and cold day, familiar to the Welsh, Davies exploded off the board to land at a surprising 8,07 in the fifth round, while Ter-Ovanesyan responded with 7,99 and Boston with a foul. Boston had to do something in his last jump, and giving it everything reached 8,03. Thus, Davies took the gold with his 8,07, Boston the silver with 8,03 and Ter-Ovanesyan the bronze with 7,99.

Jozef Schmidt of Poland, the defending champion and world record holder in the **triple jump**, had been plagued with leg injuries all season, but was still expected to go well. But it was Britain's Fred Alsop who led the first round of the final with 16,46 metres from Schmidt on 16,37, and Viktor Kravchenko of the USSR with 16,14. In the second round, Schmidt improved to 16,65 and Kravchenko to 16,38. Russia's Olyeg Fedoseev bounded into second place with 16,58 in the fifth round and Schmidt saved his last leap to gain a new Olympic record

of 16,85 and the gold medal. Kravchenko, with a fourth round 16,57, collected the bronze.

In the **shot put**, Dallas Long of the USA was the top thrower in the competition, having recently broken the world record. His compatriot Randy Matson appeared his biggest rival, while the double gold medallist, Parry O'Brien, was competing in his fourth Olympics. In the first round Long threw 19,61 metres, with European champion Vilmos Varju of Hungary reaching 19,23 and O'Brien 18,95. Matson then tossed the ball 19,19 in the second round, before taking the lead and the Olympic record with his next throw of 19,88. The two top places were ultimately decided in the fourth round, as Matson again beat the record with 20,20, only for Long to hammer out a 20,33 put for the gold medal. Matson took silver while Varju secured the bronze medal with a heave of 19,39.

The question in the **discus throw** was: would Al Oerter of the USA win his third consecutive gold medal? Doctors had advised him not to compete with an injured rib cage, as he was in pain each time he threw, but Ludvik Danek of Czechoslovakia had recently broken

Mark Shearman

Ann Packer

Ann was born in Reading on 8 March 1942, and gained her first national colours for long jumping in 1960 after winning the Women's AAA title for the event. Later she became eager for variety and ventured into sprints, hurdling and high jumping with a measure of success.

Not until scoring an exciting victory over the Russian European champion, Maria Itkina, at 400m did Ann consider tackling this event more seriously. And to help her develop strength for the distance she took to racing an occasional 800m.

Then came the 1964 team selection for Tokyo and she found herself nominated for the 800m as well as the 400m. The shorter distance was her main target and it was not until she was edged into second place in Betty Cuthbert's Olympic record-breaking 400m run that the British girl began to think seriously about the 800m. And nobody was more surprised than Ann by her ultimate victory, enhanced by the fact that she had reduced the world record to 2-01·1 sec.

The inspiration behind her racing was her fiancé, the British team captain, Robbie Brightwell, who came home from the same Games with a silver, won in the 4 × 400 relay. They are now married with a son, Ian, who is making quite a name for himself as a professional footballer with Manchester City.

Irina Press pictured in action.

Mark Shearman

Irina and Tamara Press

The most remarkable pair of sisters world athletics has ever known, both Irina and Tamara Press were gold medal winners in the 1960 Rome Games, Irina in the 80m hurdles and Tamara in the shot. They won golds again at Tokyo in 1954, Irina in the pentathlon and Tamara, the shot and the discus.

Between them they achieved 23 world records. Irina was responsible for 11: five of them for 80m hurdles (she also three times tied existing records) and six for pentathlon. Tamara put the shot a world record distance six times between 1959 and 1965 and also produced a world best for the discus six times.

They were powerful girls, and like the runners Kuts and Borzov came from the Ukraine. They were born in Kharkov, Tamara on 10 May 1937 and Irina on 10 March 1939. The German invasion during the Second World War led to their fleeing the country (they were Jewish). Tamara was the first to become interested in athletics and by 1957 she had entered the world rankings for shot and discus, which encouraged Irina to enter the sport.

Both retired in 1966 because of their mother's ill-health. By coincidence, the European championships in Budapest that year, saw female competitors being called upon for the first time to undergo sex tests.

American Red Indian, Billy Mills, dashes through the tape to win the 10,000 metres, ahead of Mohamed Gammoudi and Ron Clarke.   Mark Shearman

his world record and the American wanted to win badly. In the preliminary rounds Oerter actually broke his Olympic record with 60,54 metres. With the final under way, he opened with 57,65 to Danek's 59,73 and Jay Silvester's 56,99. Another American, Dave Weill, took the second spot in the next round with 59,49, while Oerter improved to 58,34. Danek then skimmed out a beautiful throw in the fourth round to take the lead and the Olympic record with 60,52, but Oerter topped this with 61,00 for the gold medal and the Olympic record in the next round. Danek took the silver with his 60,52 and Weill the bronze with 59,49.

Although Hal Connolly of the USA held the world record for the **hammer throw**, there were at least six athletes nearly as good. The Olympic record went three times in the preliminaries with first Romuald Klim of the USSR throwing 67,10 metres, then Connolly 67,40, and finally Hungary's Gyula Zsivotzky 67,99. It was Zsivotzky who led the first round in the final with 69,09, for another new record with Uwe Beyer of Germany at 68,09 and Klim at 67,19. Klim then improved to 68,59 in the next, before throwing 69,74 in the fourth round for the gold medal and the Olympic record. Zsivotzky won the silver with his 69,09 and Beyer the bronze with 68,09.

Terje Pedersen of Norway became history's first 90,00 metres **javelin throw**er during the 1964 season and was joint favourite with Janusz Sidlo of Poland and Russia's Janis Lusis, but surprisingly he was eliminated in the preliminaries. In the first round of the final, Sidlo threw 80,17, Urs von Wartburg of Switzerland 78,72 and Pauli Nevala of Finland 76,42. Lusis picked up the lead in the second round with 80,57, but the competition was decided in the fourth round, when Nevala floated his javelin out to 82,66 in poor atmospheric conditions to win the gold medal. Gergely Kulcsar of Hungary lofted an 82,32 effort to take the silver medal while Lusis' earlier 80,57 took the bronze.

New tables had been introduced for the **decathlon** and Chuan-Kwang Yang of Taiwan (previously Formosa), the world record holder, had had his world record reduced from 9,121 to 8,089 points. The fastest 100 metres times of 10·7 sec were recorded by Willi Holdorf of Germany and Hector Thomas of Venezuela, and in the long jump both Holdorf and Thomas leaped 7,00 metres to lead. The shot saw Mikhail Storozhenko of the USSR throw an excellent 16,37 metres to take over the lead from Holdorf, and after the high jump he still led, but Hans-Joachim Walde of Germany was now second by virtue of a 1,96 metres jump. In the 400, Holdorf ran 48·2 sec to finish the first day with 4,090 points with Walde on 4,074 points and Rein Aun of the USSR third. The positions of the top three changed little during the second day, when despite a constant drizzle, Holdorf won the gold with a total of 7,887 points, Aun the silver with 7,842 and Walde the bronze with 7,809, while an injured Yang was fifth.

Women's Events

The **100 metres** saw the emergence of another great sprinter in the shape of Wyomia Tyus of the USA, who equalled the world record in the second round of the heats. The final was run against the wind, and after one false start Tyus was quickest into her sprinting, with Miguelina Cobian of Cuba and Edith McGuire of the USA, away the slowest. Tyus led from start to finish and won in 11·4 sec, while McGuire took the silver medal in 11·6. Ewa Klobukowska of Poland came through in the latter half of the race to take third, also in 11·6. (Automatic timings: Tyus 11·49, McGuire 11·62 and Klobukowska 11·64).

Edith McGuire of the USA was favourite for the **200 metres** and substantiated this with fast runs in all three rounds. McGuire had a perfect start in the final and although Marilyn Black of Australia ran a very swift bend to lead her into the straight, she simply flowed down the finishing stretch to win in a new Olympic record time of 23·0 sec. Irena Kirszenstein of Poland, with a slow bend, had the fastest finish of all to take the silver with 23·1, just pipping Black who was also timed in 23·1. (Automatic timings: McGuire 23·05, Kirszenstein 23·13 and Black 23·18).

Sin-Kim Dan of North Korea had run 51·4 sec, but she was not competing in the **400 metres**, a new event introduced to the Olympic Games. Among the pre-race favourites were Ann Packer of Britain, Betty Cuthbert of Australia and the European champion, Maria Itkina of the USSR. Packer easily produced the fastest times in the preliminaries and was looked upon as a sure thing. In the final, Cuthbert went off very fast having a clear lead

Mark Shearman

Lynn Davies

Lynn Davies, born in Nantymoel, Glamorgan, on 20 May 1942, cleared over 21 feet in his first long jump at 18. Four seasons of dedicated endeavour to become an Olympic champion were rewarded when he won the long jump title in Tokyo. With such famed opposition as the world record-holder, Ralph Boston, of the United States, Russia's perfectionist, Igor Ter-Ovanesyan and the Nigerian champion Wariboko West, few expected Davies to emerge as the champion.

Conditions were all against the competitors achieving peak performances. Rain and a cold wind were causing problems for all the finalists and at the time of his fifth jump the Welshman was back in third place. Davies looked for the flag at the top of stadium to assess the strength of the headwind and for a moment it dropped. Instantly the British champion started his run and made the finest jump of his athletic career, 26ft 5½in (8,07m).

Ter-Ovanesyan followed with 8,04m. With only Boston to worry about now with his last jump, Davies could not watch the American's final bid to keep his title. But Boston's leap fell four centimetres short of the Welsh leader.

Davies's dream of retaining that title in Mexico City were shattered the moment Bob Beamon made his incredible world record leap of 29ft 2½in (8,90m) with his first jump there.

from Packer and Itkina at 200 metres and was well ahead coming into the finishing straight. At this stage Packer made supreme efforts to get on terms with the leader, but Cuthbert got to the tape first in 52·0 for an inaugural record, with the English girl taking the silver medal in 52·2. As Itkina faded, Australia's Judy Amoore came through to take the bronze medal in 53·4. (Automatic timings: Cuthbert 52·01, Packer 52·20).

Because North Korea were not affiliated to the IAAF, Sin-Kim Dan who had run 1-58·0 against the listed world record for the **800 metres**, was not competing. However, eight women lined up for the final with Marise Chamberlain of New Zealand having a best time of 2-01·4, while Maryvonne Dupureur of France had 2-03·9 and Laine Erik of the USSR 2-04·1. The slowest girl in the race was Ann Packer of Britain at 2-05·3. Zsuzsa Szabo of Hungary immediately went into the lead followed by Dupureur, who took over the running after 200 and passed the 400 in an astonishing 58·6 with five other girls in contention. Dupureur passed the 600 in

1-29·8 followed by Chamberlain and Packer, who came through like an express and swept past the tiring Dupureur 30 metres from the finish to win in 2-01·1, a new Olympic record. Dupureur was second in 2-01·9 and Chamberlain third in 2-02·8.

The **80 metres hurdles** sported a field that included three ladies who had hurdled a world record 10·5: Karin Balzer of Germany, Irina Press of Russia and Draga Stamejcic of Yugoslavia. Ikuko Yoda of Japan was quickest away in the final, with Rosie Bonds of the USA close behind, and led for the first three flights until Balzer, Kilborn and Press overtook her. Over the last few hurdles, Press faded while Teresa Ciepla of Poland caught the leaders. A photo-finish picture was needed to decide that Balzer had got the gold, Ciepla the silver and Pam Kilborn of Australia the bronze, all being given 10·5 with the wind reading a fraction over the limit for a world record. (Automatic timings: Balzer 10·54, Ciepla 10·55 and Kilborn 10·56).

Poland, as world record holders, came to the Games

The Pole, Josef Schmidt, added a new dimension to the triple jump event when he retained his title in great style.   Mark Shearman

with a reputation for having a swift **4 × 100 metres relay** team, and they won the first heat in 44·6 while the USA took the second in 44·8. In the final, Teresa Ciepla of Poland established a lead over Willye White of the USA, which was reduced to a narrow margin in the second leg when Wyomia Tyus nearly caught Irena Kirszenstein. But Poland's baton changing was superb, and Halina Gorecka and Ewa Klobukowska built up a lead to win in 43·6, a new world record, with America second in 43·9 and Britain third with 44·0. (Automatic timings: Poland 43·69, USA 43·92 and Britain 44·09).

In the **high jump** Iolanda Balas of Rumania held the world record at 1,91 metres. Fifteen competed in the final, but at 1,74 only four were left and at 1,76 Aida dos Santos of Brazil also failed. Taisia Chenchik of the USSR cleared 1,78 and received the bronze medal, while Michele Brown of Australia surmounted 1,80 on her second attempt for the silver. Balas went on to jump 1,82, 1,86 and 1,90 for an Olympic record before failing at a new world's best of 1,92.

All the top jumpers were present in the **long jump**, including the world record holder, Tatyana Schelkanova of the USSR. During the qualifying rounds, Helga Hoffmann of Germany had jumped 6,44 for an Olympic record, but this was soon exceeded by Mary Rand of Britain with 6,52. In the first round of the competition proper, Rand led with a record 6,59 from Diana Jorgova of Bulgaria on 6,24 and Schelkanova 6,21. The second round saw Irena Kirszenstein of Poland leap 6,43 and Viorica Viscopoleanu of Rumania achieve 6,35. In the next round Kirszenstein improved to 6,56 and Schelkanova to 6,42 which ultimately gave her the bronze medal. The fourth trial saw Rand extend her lead to 6,63 and then in the fifth she leaped to a super world record of 6.76 and the gold medal. Kirszenstein responded with 6,60 to take home the silver.

The **shot put** world record holder was Tamara Press of the USSR, who in the very first round of the final exceeded her old Olympic record with 17,51. Her second throw reached 17,72, but her last effort, again an Olympic record, travelled 18,14 to win the gold. There was keen rivalry for the silver position between Renate Garisch-Culmberger of Germany and the veteran champion from 1952 and 1956, Galina Zybina of Russia. Garisch-Culmberger threw 17,41, Zybina responded with 17,45 but the German girl came back with 17,61 to take the silver medal, leaving Zybina with the bronze.

Tamara Press, apart from her prowess in other events, was again the leading **discus throw**er of the year. The defending Olympic champion, Nina Romashkova-Ponomaryeva was also throwing, as was the bronze medallist from Rome, Lia Manoliu of Rumania. Ingrid Lotz of Germany took the lead in the first round of the final with 57,21, which she held until Press finally pulled out a big one with 57,27 in the fifth round, to win the gold medal. Lotz won the silver, while the 56,97 throw by Manoliu, also achieved in the fifth round, was good enough for the bronze.

Prior to the Games the favourite for the **javelin throw**ing competition was Elvira Ozolina of the USSR, who held the world record at 61,38 metres, but that all changed in the preliminaries, when her compatriot Elena Gorchakova arched her spear to a new world record distance of 62,40. In the final, Gorchakova could not repeat this performance and made only 57,06 for the bronze medal. Antal Rudas of Hungary collected the silver award with a distance of 58,27, while Mihaela Penes of Rumania, on her very first throw, took the title and the gold medal with 60,54.

A new event at the Olympics, the **pentathlon**, consisted of 80 metres hurdles, shot and high jump on the first day, and long jump and 200 metres on the second day. Irina Press, the younger sister of Tamara, won the competition with 5,246 points, a world and Olympic record. Mary Rand of Britain scored 5,035, while the USSR's Galina Bystrova totalled 4,956. Press' performances were 10·7 sec in the hurdles, a massive 17,16 metres shot, a 1,63 metres high jump, a 6,24 metres long jump and 24·67 sec in the 200 metres.

In the final of the 100 metres, the American Bob Hayes (extreme right), powered to a decisive win.

Mark Shearman

MALES

COMPETITOR	COUNTRY CODE	EVENT	ROUND	HEAT	PLACE	TIME & DISTANCE	MEDAL
Abdallah, O.	TAN	Marathon	F		47	2:40-06-0	
Abramov, N.	URS	Marathon	F		26	2:27-09-4	
Abugattas, R.	PER	High Jump	Q		DNQ	1,95	
Addy, E.C.O.	GHA	4×100m relay	1	3	5	40·85	
			SF	1	8	40·7	
Addy, J.A.	GHA	400m	1	5	3	47·27	
			2	4	4	47·37	
			SF	2	8	47·6	
		4×400m relay	1	3	5	3-10·4	
Agapov, G.	URS	50k walk	F		12	4:24-34-0	
Aguilar, F.	ESP	5000m	1	2	12	14-19·2	
Ahey, M.K.	GHA	100m	1	3	3	10·61	
			2	4	7	10·67	
		4×100m relay	1	3	5	40·85	
			SF	1	8	40·7	
		Long jump	F		7	7,30	
Akika, E.	NGR	110m hurdles	1	5	7	14·70	
Akotkar, B.	IND	Marathon	F		33	2:29-27·4	
Akpata, S.	NGR	Long jump	Q		DNQ	7,34	
Aksenov, V.	URS	Javelin throw	Q		DNQ	69,46	
Aldegalega, A.R.	POR	Marathon	F		44	2:38-02·2	
Alexeiunas, A.	URS	3000m steeplechase	1	3	1	8-31·8*	
			F		7	8-39·0	
Allonsius, E.	BEL	1500m	1	4	4	3-43·3	
			SF	2	6	3-41·9	
		5000m	1	2	6	13-55·0	
Allotey, S.F.	GHA	100m	1	4	2	10·62	
			2	3	7	10·73	
		4×100m relay	1	3	5	40·85	
			SF	1	8	40·7	
Allsopp, E.J.	AUS	50k walk	F		17	4:31-07·8	
Alsop, F.J.	GBR	Long jump	Q		DNQ	7,26	
		Triple jump	F		4	16,46	
Amano, Y.	JPN	4×400m relay	1	1	5	3-12·3	
Ambu, A.	ITA	Marathon	F		40	2:34-37·6	
Amevor, E.D.	GHA	1500m	1	4	11	3-58·4	
Amu, A.	NGR	4×100m relay	1	1	5	40·44	
Amukun, E.	UGA	200m	1	2	5	21·55	
		4×100m relay	1	3	6	41·4	
Aniset, J.	LUX	Marathon	F		34	2:29-52·6	
Anisimov, V.	URS	400m hurdles	1	4	2	51·72	
			SF	2	4	50·72	
			F		7	51·1	
		4×400m relay	1	1	2	3-07·4	
			F		7	3-05·9	
Ankio, R.A.	FIN	Pole vault	F		12	4,70	
Antao, S.	KEN	100m	1	6	4	10·79	
		200m	1	3	2	21·52	
			2	1	3	22·11	
Areta, L.F.	ESP	Long jump	F		5	7,34	
		Triple jump	Q		DNQ	15,41	
Aritmendi, F.	ESP	5000m	1	4	4	14-05·0	
Arjtaweekul, T.	THA	4×100m relay	1	2	7	41·8	
Arkhipchuk, V.	URS	400m	1	2	3	47·70	
			2	3	8	47·9	
		4×400m relay	1	1	2	3-07·4	
			F		7	3-05·9	
Arntong, T.K.	THA	1500m	1	2	10	4-08·7	
Asai, K.	JPN	4×100m relay	1	2	6	41·0	
			SF	2	8	40·6	
Ashworth, G.H.	USA	4×100m relay	1	2	1	39·83	
			SF	1	1	39·50*	
			F		1	39·06*	G
Asiodu, S.	NGR	4×100m relay	1	1	5	40·44	
			SF	1	6	40·19	
Asplund, K.B.	SWE	Hammer throw	Q		DNQ	61,15	
Aun, R.	URS	Decathlon	F		2	7842	S
Awan, M.U.H.	PAK	400m hurdles	1	3	8	55·3	
Awori, A.S.	UGA	200m	1	6	7	22·2	
		110m hurdles	1	1	5	14·68	
		4×100m relay	1	3	6	41·4	
Ayachi, L.	TUN	3000m steeplechase	1	2	9	9-02·0	
Babakhanlou, A.	IRN	100m	1	6	8	11·14	
Babb, W.D.	RHO	110m hurdles	1	1	7	14·80	
Badenski, A.	POL	400m	1	3	1	46·46	
			2	2	1	46·51	
			SF	2	2	46·21	
			F		3	45·64	B
		4×400m relay	1	2	2	3-07·2	
			F		6	3-05·3	
Baidiuk, S.	URS	5000m	1	1	2	14-00·2	
			F		10	14-11·2	
Baikov, V.	URS	Marathon	F		DNF		
Baillie, W.D.	NZL	5000m	1	1	2	13-55·4	
			F		6	13-51·0	

COMPETITOR	COUNTRY CODE	EVENT	ROUND	HEAT	PLACE	TIME & DISTANCE	MEDAL
Bakarinov, Y.	URS	Hammer throw	F		5	66,72	
Bambuck, R.	FRA	100m	1	10	3	10·62	
			2	4	6	10·60	
		200m	1	2	1	21·29	
			2	3	3	21·47	
			SF	2	5	21·09	
Barabas, A.	RUM	5000m	1	1	4	14-00·2	
Baran, W.	POL	1500m	1	1	1	3-45·3	
			SF	1	2	3-38·9	
			F		6	3-40·3	
Barandun, M.	SUI	100m	1	9	6	10·79	
Barkovsky, L.	URS	Long jump	Q		DNQ	7,39	
Battista, E.	FRA	Triple jump	Q		DNQ	15,04	
Beche, D.A.	CIV	1500m	1	1	7	3-53·5	
Beer, K.	GER	Long jump	Q		DNQ	7,27	
Begier, Z.	POL	Discus throw	F		6	57,06	
Behm, J.J.	FRA	400m hurdles	1	5	4	52·20	
Beliaev, I.	URS	3000m Steeplechase	1	1	2	8-42·0	
			F		3	8-33·8	B
Belitsky, I.	URS	1500m	1	4	8	3-46·7	
Bello, S.	ITA	400m	1	2	2	47·54	
			2	1	6	46·93	
		4×400m relay	1	2	3	3-07·6	
Benaissa, B.	MAR	Marathon	F		12	2:22-27·0	
Ben Boubaker, H.	TUN	Marathon	F		DNF		
Ben Messaoud, N.	TUN	50k walk	F		DIS		
Benum, P.	NOR	10000m	F		19	30-00·8	
Berger, R.	GER	4×100m relay	1	2	3	40·21	
			SF	2	5	40·16	
Bernard, K.	TRI	400m	1	2	1	46·80	
			2	3	2	46·73	
			SF	2	7	47·08	
		4×400m relay	1	2	1	3-05·0	
			F		3	3-01·7	B
Bernard, M.	FRA	1500m	1	2	1	3-43·4	
			SF	1	4	3-39·7	
			F		7	3-41·2	
Berruti, L.	ITA	200m	1	8	1	21·11	
			2	1	2	21·24	
			SF	2	2	20·78	
			F		5	20·83	
		4×100m relay	1	1	1	39·74	
			SF	2	1	39·63	
			F		7	39·54	
Bertoia, D.R.	CAN	800m	1	4	7	1-52·2	
Bertrand, C.	TRI	200m	1	1	3	21·39	
			2	3	5	21·69	
Betancourt, L.	CUB	110m hurdles	1	4	2	14·67	
			SF	1	6	14·23	
Beyer, H.	GER	Decathlon	F		6	7647	
Beyer, U.	GER	Hammer throw	F		3	68,09	B
Bezabih, T.	ETH	200m	1	5	6	22·03	
		400m	1	4	3	46·73	
			2	4	3	47·23	
			SF	1	7	47·1	
Bhakdikul, K.	THA	High jump	Q		DNQ	0	
Bhupendra, E.K.C.	NEP	Marathon	F		DNF		
Bianchi, B	ITA	4×400m relay	1	2	3	3-07·6	
Bianchi, F.	ITA	800m	1	6	5	1-50·2	
		1500m	1	2	7	3-47·9	
Bigby, E.J.	AUS	4×100m relay	1	3	4	40·64	
			SF	1	5	40·19	
Bikila, A.	ETH	Marathon	F		1	2:12-11·2*	G
Blek, A.	TCH	20k walk	F		11	1:33-45·0	
		50k walk	F		20	4:34-54·2	
Birlenbach, H.	GER	Shot put	Q		DNQ	17,77	
Bliznetsov, G.	URS	Pole vault	F		5	4,95	
Blue, A.A.C.	AUS	800m	1	5	3	1-49·7	
			SF	3	7	1-49·6	
Boase, G.	AUS	Triple jump	9		DNQ	0	
Boccardo, J.P.	FRA	400m	1	1	3	46·63	
			2	1	3	46·34	
			SF	1	8	47·1	
		4×400m relay	1	1	3	3-07·5	
			F		8	3-07·4	
Boekaerts, P.	BEL	800m	1	6	6	1-50·9	
Bogatzki, P.	GER	800m	1	2	1	1-50·3	
			SF	2	3	1-46·9	
			F		7	1-47·2	
Bogliatto, M.	ITA	High jump	F		16	2,06	
Boguszewicz, L.	POL	5000m	1	2	4	13-52·8	
Boletnikov, P.	URS	10000m	F		25	30-52·8	
Bosshard, H.	SUI	4×400m relay	1	3	4	3-09·3	
Boston, R.H.	USA	Long jump	F		2	8,03	S
Boulter, J.P.	GBR	800m	1	5	1	1-48·9	
			SF	2	4	1-47·1	

COMPETITOR	COUNTRY CODE	EVENT	ROUND	HEAT	PLACE	TIME & DISTANCE	MEDAL
Brightwell, R.I.	GBR	400m	1	1	2	46·13	
			2	3	3	47·15	
			SF	1	1	45·79	
			F		4	45·75	
		4×400m relay	1	3	1	3-04·7	
			F		2	3-01·6	S
Brodie, M.W.	USA	50k walk	F		29	4:57-41·0	
Brumel, V.	URS	High jump	F		1	2,18*	G
Buchel, A.	LIE	Decathlon	F		14	6849	
Bugri, S.Z.	GHA	4×400m relay	1	3	5	3-10·4	
Bukhantsov, K.	URS	Discus throw	F		9	54,38	
Bullivant, M.J.	GBR	10000m	F		21	30-12·0	
Bulyshev, V.	URS	800m	1	1	3	1-48·6	
			SF	1	5	1-47·5	
Bumroon-spruek, M.	THA	4×400m relay	1	3	7	3-18·4	
Burke, E.A.	USA	Hammer throw	F		7	65,66	
Burleson, D.	USA	1500m	1	1	3	3-45·6	
			SF	2	1	3-41·5	
			F		5	3-40·0	
Bychkov, V.	URS	400m	1	5	5	47·32	
			2	4	7	47·91	
		4×400m relay	1	1	2	3-07·4	
			F		7	3-05·9	
Camara, S.	MLI	100m	1	1	7	11·3	
Campbell, W.M.	GBR	200m	1	3	1	21·33	
			2	3	6	21·74	
		4×100m relay	1	1	3	40·13	
			SF	1	4	40·13	
			F		8	39·69	
Carr, H.	USA	200m	1	7	2	21·12	
			2	2	1	21·02	
			SF	2	1	20·69	
			F		1	20·36*	G
		4×400m relay	1	1	1	3-05·3	
			F		1	3-00·7*	G
Carroll, N.	IRL	800m	1	5	5	1-51·1	
Carter, C.S.	GBR	800m	1	2	3	1-51·0	
			SF	3	4	1-49·1	
Caruthers, E.J.	USA	High jump	F		8	2,09	
Cassell, O.C.	USA	400m	1	5	6	46·81	
			2	1	2	46·24	
			SF	2	5	46·69	
		4×400m relay	1	1	1	3-05·3	
			F		1	3-00·7*	G
Cavero, J.	PER	400m hurdles	1	4	6	53·7	
Cawley, W.J.	USA	400m hurdles	1	2	1	50·88	
			SF	1	1	49·89	
			F		1	49·6	G
Cervan, F.	YUG	5000m	1	3	7	14-16·6	
		10000m	F		10	29-21·0	
Chabbanga, M.H.	TAN	800m	1	6	8	1-54·9	
Chatelet, F.	FRA	800m	1	1	5	1-48·9	
Chiflta, L.D.	RHO	Marathon	F		57	2:51-53·2	
Chinh, Ho Thanh	VNM	100m	1	4	7	11·9	
Chistiakov, V.	URS	110m hurdles	1	4	3	14·75	
			SF	1		DIS	
Chu, Ming	HKG	Long jump	Q		DNQ	6,41	
		Triple jump	Q		DNQ	13,50	
Chudomel, V.	TCH	Marathon	F		18	2:24-46·8	
Chung, Ki-Sun	KOR	100m	1	2	6	11·08	
		200m	1	8	7	22·3	
Chung, Kyo-Mo	KOR	800m	1	4	6	1-51·8	
		1500m	1	3	9	3-53·0	
Cieply, O.	POL	Hammer throw	F		8	64,83	
Ciochina, S.	RUM	Triple jump	F		5	16,23	
Clarke, R.W.	AUS	5000m	1	4	1	13-48·4	
			F		9	13-58·0	
		10000m	F		3	28-25·8	B
		Marathon	F		9	2:20-26·8	
Clayton, W.K.	JAM	Long jump	Q		DNQ	7,28	
Clerckx, H.	BEL	5,000m	1	4	10	14-40·0	
		10000m	F		12	29-29·6	
Clifford, B.	IRL	1,500m	1	1	8	3-54·9	
Cochard, J.	FRA	Long jump	F		5	7,44	
Collie, G.R.	BAH	100m	1	4	5	10·90	
		200m	1	6	5	21·91	
Connolly, H.V.	USA	Hammer throw	F		6	66,65	
Cook, A.	AUS	5000m	1	1	5	14-02·4	
		10000m	F		8	29-15·8	
		Marathon	F		52	2:42-03·6	
Cooper, J.H.	GBR	400m hurdles	1	1	1	50·58	
			SF	2	1	50·40	
			F		2	50·1	S
		4×400m relay	1	3	1	3-04·7	
			F		2	3-01·6	S
Coppejans, P.	BEL	Pole vault	Q		DNQ	4,20	

COMPETITOR	COUNTRY CODE	EVENT	ROUND	HEAT	PLACE	TIME & DISTANCE	MEDAL
Cornacchia, G.	ITA	110m hurdles	1	3	2	14·25	
			SF	2	2	14·06	
			F		7	14·12	
Coulibaly, Y.D.F.	CIV	400m	1	5	7	48·8	
Coutinho, A.F.	IND	4×100m relay	1	2	5	40·68	
			SF	2	7	40·5	
Covelli, F.G.	USA	Javelin throw	Q		DNQ	68,08	
Crawford, R.J.	AUS	20k walk	F		22	1:38-47·0	
		50k walk	F		11	4:24-19·6	
Crothers, W.F.	CAN	400m	1	5	2	46·86	
			2	2	2	46·73	
			SF	2	6	46·96	
		800m	1	6	1	1-49·3	
			SF	3	1	1-47·3	
			F		2	1-45·6	S
Cruz, D.S.	PUR	Long jump	Q		DNQ	6,74	
Cruz, H.	PUR	110m hurdles	1	2	6	14·93	
Cruz, R.	PUR	Pole vault	Q		DNQ	4,50	
Csutoras, C.	HUN	100m	1	2	4	10·72	
		200m	1	3	3	21·54	
			2	2	6	21·50	
		4×100m relay	1	1	4	40·32	
			SF	1	7	40·31	
Czernik, E.	POL	High jump	F		11	2,06	
Dalkilic, M.	TUR	5000m	1	1	7	14-12·0	
Dam, J.N.	DEN	5000m	1	2	10	14-20·4	
Danek, L.	TCH	Discus throw	F		2	60,52	S
Daour, G.	SEN	4×400m relay	1	1	6	3-12·5	
Da Rocha, J.F.	POR	100m	1	7	4	11·02	
		200m	1	8	5	21·79	
Davenport, W.	USA	110m hurdles	1	1	2	14·44	
			SF	1	7	14·28	
Davies, J.L.	NZL	1500m	1	1	2	3-45·5	
			SF	2	3	3-41·9	
			F		3	3-39·6	B
Davies, L.	GBR	100m	1	3	6	10·78	
		4×100m relay	1	1	3	40·13	
			SF	1	4	40·13	
			F		8	39·69	
		Long jump	F		1	8,07	G
Davis, I.S.	USA	Triple jump	F		9	16,00	
Dean, G.A.	GBR	800m	1	4	5	1-49·6	
Defevre, A.	FRA	Long jump	Q		DNQ	7,24	
Delecour, J.	FRA	200m	1	7	3	21·38	
			2	1	4	21·58	
			SF	2	7	21·26	
		4×100m relay	1	3	1	39·84	
			SF	1	2	39·66	
			F		3	39·36	B
Delerue, H.	FRA	20k walk	F		13	1:34-58·0	
		50k walk	F		15	4:27-47·6	
Dellinger, W.S.	USA	5000m	1	2	2	13-52·2	
			F		3	13-49·8	B
Demin, S.	URS	Pole vault	F		15	4,40	
D'Encausse, H.	FRA	Pole vault	F		15	4,40	
Descloux, J.L.	SUI	200m	1	1	5	21·52	
		4×400m relay	1	3	4	3-09·3	
Dia, M.	SEN	Triple jump	F		13	15,44	
Dilbagh, S.K.	MAL	3000m steeplechase	1	3	10	9-18·8	
Dionisi, R.	ITA	Pole vault	Q		DNQ	4,20	
Diop, M.	SEN	4×100m relay	1	2	4	40·55	
			SF	2	6	40·26	
Di Tolla, G.	PER	100m	1	3	7	10·99	
		200m	1	1	9	22·1	
Doring, F.	GER	3000m steeplechase	1	2	6	8-43·2	
Dorner, R.	GER	3000m Steeplechase	1	3	6	8-55·0	
Doumya, B.	SEN	100m	1	7	5	11·02	
		4×100m relay	1	2	4	40·55	
			SF	2	6	40·26	
Drayton, O.P.	USA	200m	1	1	1	20·70	
			2	1	1	20·98	
			SF	1	1	20·58*	
			F		2	20·58	S
		4×100m relay	1	2	2	39·83	
			SF	1	1	39·50*	
			F		1	39·06*	G
Drecoll, R.	GER	High jump	F		6	2,09	
Dudziak, M.	POL	100m	1	4	6	10·60	
			2	1	6	10·52	
		4×100m relay	1	1	2	39·96	
			SF	2	2	39·63	
			F		1	39·36	S
Dukom, J.	MAL	4×100m relay	1	1	6	41·4	
Dulam, A.	MGL	800m	1	2	7	1-56·3	

COMPETITOR	COUNTRY CODE	EVENT	ROUND	HEAT	PLACE	TIME & DISTANCE	MEDAL
Du Preez, J.	RHO	100m	1	2	5	10·79	
		200m	1	1	4	21·45	
			2	2	8	21·87	
Duriez, M.	FRA	110m hurdles	1	5	1	14·22	
			SF	1	4	14·10	
			F		6	14·09	
Dutov, N.	URS	5000m	1	4	3	13·50·6	
			F		7	13·53·8	
Duttweiler, W.	SUI	Pole vault	Q		DNQ	4,40	
		Decathlon	F		DNF		
Dyrzka, J.C.P.	ARG	400m	1	3	6	48·3	
		110m hurdles	1	2	7	15·2	
		400m hurdles	1	2	2	51·17	
			SF	2	8	53·1	
Earle, W.J.	AUS	100m	1	6	3	10·79	
			2	1	8	10·60	
		4×100m relay	1	3	4	40·64	
			SF	1	5	40·19	
Ebreo, M.I.	PHI	4×100m relay	1	3	7	41·7	
Eckschmidt, S.	HUN	Hammer throw	F		11	63,83	
Eddy, G.J.	AUS	400m	1	1	4	46·92	
			2	3	6	47·65	
		4×400m relay	1	2	4	3-08·2	
Edgington, J.W.	GBR	20k walk	F		8	1:32-46·0	
Edelen, L.C.	USA	Marathon	F		6	2:18-12·4	
Ejiri, T.	JPN	50k walk	F		22	4:37-31·8	
Ejoke, D.	NGR	200m	1	6	4	21·48	
Elende, H.	CGO	High jump	F		20	1,90	
El Ghazi, B.A.	MAR	3000m steeplechase	1	1	3	8-42·8	
			F		9	8-43·6	
El Maachi, B.	MAR	100m	1	2	3	10·70	
			2	2	6	10·57	
		200m	1	3	4	21·58	
			2	3	4	21·66	
			SF	1	8	21·61	
El Marghni, C.	TUN	20k walk	F		24	1 41-11·0	
		50k walk	F		30	4 59-13·0	
Emberger, R.J.	USA	Decathlon	F		10	7292	
Erbstoesser, H.	GER	200m	1	5	5	21·40	
		4×100m relay	1	2	3	40·2?	
			SF	2	5	40·16	
Erinle, F.	NGR	110m hurdles	1	1	4	14·57	
		4×100m relay	1	1	5	40·44	
			SF	1	6	40·19	
Eskola, P.K.	FIN	Long jump	Q		DNQ	7,43	
Etcheverry, P.	CHI	Javelin throw	Q		DNQ	60,77	
Fahsl, H.	GER	Hammer throw	Q		DNQ	62,35	
Farrell, T.F.	USA	800m	1	1	2	1-48·6	
			SF	3	2	1-47·8	
			F		5	1-46·6	
Fayolle, J.	FRA	5000m	1	3	10	14-44·6	
		10000m	F		13	29-30·8	
Fedoseev, O.	URS	Triple jump	F		2	16,58	S
Feld, I.	URS	Pole vault	F		9	4,80	
Field, P.M.M.	HKG	800m	1	6	7	1-54·0	
		1500m	1	4	12	4-02·6	
Figuerola, E.	CUB	100m	1	10	1	10·50	
			2	2	1	10·31	
			SF	2	3	10·48	
			F		2	10·25	S
Filipiuk, M.	POL	4×400m relay	1	2	2	3-07·2	
			F		6	3-05·3	
Fishback, J.M.	USA	3000m steeplechase	1	3	4	8-50·2	
Floerke, K.L.	USA	Triple jump	Q		DNQ	15,36	
Foik, M.	POL	200m	1	4	1	21·11	
			2	4	2	21·08	
			SF	1	4	20·94	
			F		6	20·83	
		4×100m relay	1	1	2	39·95	
			SF	2	2	39·63	
			F		2	39·36	S
Fornes, A.	PUR	Marathon	F		55	2:46-22·6	
Forssander, B.E.O.	SWE	110m hurdles	1	3	3	14·35	
			SF	2	5	14·21	
Fournet, B.	FRA	110m hurdles	1	3	5	14·83	
Francis, P.	KEN	800m	1	3	5	1-50·?	
Freeman, N.F.	AUS	20k walk	F		4	1:32-06·8	
Frinolli, R.	ITA	400m hurdles	1	1	3	51·23	
			SF	1	2	50·28	
			F		6	50·7	
		4×400m relay	1	2	3	3-07·6	
Funai, T.	JPN	10000m	F		14	29-33·2	
Gairdner, W.D.	CAN	400m hurdles	1	1	5	53·8	
		Decathlon	F		11	7·47	
Gakou, A.	SEN	400m	1	3	7	50·1	
Gammoudi, M.	TUN	5000m	1	3	1	14-10·2	
			F		DNS		
		10000m	F		2	28-24·8	S
Ganga, B.T.	NEP	Marathon	F		DNF		
Gardiner, R.C.	AUS	20k walk	F		DNF		
		50k walk	F		5	4:17-06·8	
Garriga, L.M.	ESP	High jump	Q		DNQ	2,03	
Geeroms, W.	BEL	400m hurdles	1	3	1	51·24	
			SF	1	4	51·00	
			F		8	51·4	
Genevay, P.	FRA	200m	1	5	3	21·08	
			2	4	3	21·35	
			SF	1	5	21·00	
		4×100m relay	1	3	1	39·84	
			SF	1	2	39·66	
			F		3	39·36	B
Ghafourizadeh, H.	IRN	400m	1	7	8	50·8	
Giani, I.	ITA	100m	1	8	4	10·69	
Giannattasio. P.	ITA	4×100m relay	1	1	1	39·74	
			SF	2	1	39·63	
			F		7	39·54	
Gierajewski, B.	POL	400m hurdles	1	2	5	52·8	
Gieseler, H.	GER	400m hurdles	1	1	DNF		
Gilad, A.	ISR	800m	1	5	DIS		
Golubnichy, V.	URS	20k walk	F		3	1:31-59·4	B
Gori, I.	HUN	20k walk	F		15	1:35-38·0	
Graham, D.A.	GBR	5000m	1	4	7	14-21·6	
Graham, T.J.M.	GBR	400m	1	2	4	48·4	
			2	2	3	46·83	
			SF	2	4	46·53	
			F		6	46·08	
		4×400m relay	1	3	1	3-04·7	
			F		2	3-01·6	S
Grajales, P.A.	COL	200m	1	6	3	21·48	
			2	3	7	21·78	
		400m	1	5	4	47·28	
			2	4	6	47·86	
Grecescu, C.	RUM	Marathon	F		36	2:30-42·6	
Groth, M.A.	USA	800m	1	3	6	1-51·4	
Gurgushinov, L.N.	BUL	Triple jump	Q		DNQ	14,75	
Gustafsson, L.-E.	SWE	3000m steeplechase	1	2	2	8-34·2	
			F		8	8-41·8	
Gutierrez, F.J.	COL	100m	1	7	6	11·03	
		200m	1	?	6	21·88	
Gyulai, I.	HUN	400m	1	?	6	48·0	
Haas, F.	GER	400m hurdles	1	4	3	52·2	
			SF	1	6	51·6	
Hagen, H.	GER	Marathon	F		24	2:26-39·8	
Haglund, L.G.	SWE	Discus throw	Q		DNQ	0	
Haid, H.	AUT	400m hurdles	1	1	6	54·6	
Halberg, M.G.	NZL	5000m	1	3	4	14-12·0	
		10000m	F		7	29-10·8	
Hall, A.W.	USA	Hammer throw	F		12	63,82	
Hannachi, M.H.	TUN	Marathon	F		DNF		
Hannemann, A.	GER	10000m	F		27	30-56·6	
Hansen, F.M.	USA	Pole vault	F		1	5,10*	G
Harbanslal, H.	IND	Marathon	F		43	2:37-05·8	
Hardin, W.F.	USA	400m hurdles	1	5	1	51·37	
			SF	2	6	50·90	
Hartmann, D.	GER	3000m steeplechase	1	1	8	9-09·2	
Havasi, I.	HUN	50k walk	F		19	4:34-14·0	
Hayase, H.	JPN	400m	1	7	6	48·5	
		4×400m relay	1	1	5	3-12·3	
Hayes, R.L.	USA	100m	1	8	1	10·41	
			2	4	1	10·37	
			SF	1	1	9·91	
			F		1	10·06*	G
		4×100m relay	1	2	1	39·83	
			SF	1	1	39·50*	
			F		1	39·06*	G
Haynes, T.S.A.	RHO	Marathon	F		54	2:45-08·6	
Headley, L.W.	JAM	100m	1	10	2	10·57	
			2	4	3	10·50	
			SF	2	6	10·59	
		4×100m relay	1	3	2	40·11	
			SF	1	3	39·68	
			F		4	39·49	
Heatley, B.B.	GBR	Marathon	F		2	2:16-19·2	S
Helland, T.	NOR	5000m	1	2	3	13-52·4	
			F		8	13-57·0	
Hellen, J.H.	FIN	High jump	Q		DNQ	2,00	
Herings, R.	GER	Javelin throw	F		7	74,72	
Herman, P.I.	USA	Decathlon	F		4	7787	

COMPETITOR	COUNTRY CODE	EVENT	ROUND	HEAT	PLACE	TIME & DISTANCE	MEDAL
Herrera, A.	VEN	100m	1	7	2	10·59	
			2	4	2	10·43	
			SF	1	7	10·42	
		200m	1	2	2	21·38	
			2	2	4	21·29	
			SF	1	6	21·07	
		4×100m relay	1	2	2	40·10	
			SF	2	3	39·65	
			F		6	39·53	
Herrera, H.	VEN	400m	1	7	5	47·95	
		4×100m relay	1	2	2	40·10	
			SF	2	3	39·65	
			F		6	39·53	
Herrmann, S.	GER	10000m	F		11	29-27·0	
Herring, J.B.	GBR	5000m	1	1	6	14-07·2	
Herriott, M	GBR	3000m steeplechase	1	2	1	8-33·0*	
			F		2	8-32·4	S
Hiblot, M.	FRA	4×400m relay	1	1	3	3-07·5	
			F		8	3-07·4	
Hill, R.	GBR	10000m	F		18	29-53·0	
		Marathon	F		19	2:25-34·4	
Hill, W.	HKG	200m	1	6	8	22·5	
		400m	1	7	7	48·7	
Hinze, M.	GER	Triple jump	F		6	16,15	
Hodge, R.A.	USA	Decathlon	F		9	7325	
Hoffmann, D.	GER	Shot put	F		12	17,11	
Hogan, J.J.	IRL	Marathon	F		DNF		
Hogan, J.M.W.	GBR	400m hurdles	1	4	4	52·5	
Hohne, C.	GER	50k walk	F		6	4:17-41·6	
Hoilette, R.L.	JAM	400m	1	3	4	47·50	
			2	3	5	47·60	
Holdorf, W.	GER	Decathlon	F		1	7887	G
Holdsworth, G.A.	AUS	100m	1	9	5	10·69	
		200m	1	8	6	21·65	
			2	4	7	22·13	
		4×100m relay	1	3	4	40·64	
			SF	1	5	40·19	
Hollingsworth, R.A.	GBR	Discus throw	F		10	53,87	
Holtz, W.D.	GER	1500m	1	3	2	3-46·6	
			SF	1	6	3-42·3	
Honda, T.	JPN	4×400m relay	1	1	5	3-12·3	
Honicke, G.	GER	Marathon	F		38	2:33-23·0	
Hopkins, G.P.	USA	Long jump	F		DIS		
Houvion, M.	FRA	Pole vault	Q		DNQ	0	
Husson, G.	FRA	Hammer throw	Q		DNQ	60,04	
Hwang, C.D.	KOR	Triple jump	Q		DNQ	13,98	
Idriss, M.	CHA	High jump	F		9	2,09	
Igun, S.	NGR	High jump	F		15	2,06	
Iijima, H.	JPN	100m	1	1	1	10·40	
			2	3	3	10·50	
			SF	2	7	10·63	
		4×100m relay	1	2	6	41·0	
			SF	2	8	40·6	
Iijima, K.	JPN	400m hurdles	1	5	5	52·8	
Ishiguro, N.	JPN	20k walk	F		23	1:39-40·0	
Issa, A.	CHA	800m	1	3	2	1-49·7	
			SF	3	6	1-49·4	
Itokawa, T.	JPN	Shot put	Q		DNQ	15,84	
Ivanov, L.	URS	10000m	F		5	28-53·2	
Iwashita, S.	JPN	5000m	1	4	6	14-18·4	
Jackson, T.	USA	100m	1	2	1	10·53	
			2	1	2	10·41	
			SF	1	8	10·66	
Jackson, W.	TRI	100m	1	3	5	10·70	
Jaskolski, J.	POL	Triple jump	F		12	15,82	
Jazmin, A.L.	PHI	400m	1	2	5	49·9	
Jazy, M.	FRA	5000m	1	1	1	13-55·4	
			F		4	13-49·8	
Jegathesan, M.	MAL	100m	1	7	3	10·60	
			2	3	5	10·62	
		200m	1	5	2	20·99	
			2	1	3	21·40	
			SF	2	8	21·26	
		4×100m relay	1	1	6	41·4	
Jegher, G.	ITA	Marathon	F		17	2:24-45·2	
Jelinek, R.	SUI	800m	1	5	6	1-54·6	
		1500m	1	3	7	3-51·2	
Jerome, H.	CAN	100m	1	5	1	10·51	
			2	1	1	10·32	
			SF	2	1	10·37	
			F		3	10·27	B
		200m	1	5	1	20·95	
			2	3	1	21·23	
			SF	2	4	21·01	
			F		4	20·79	

COMPETITOR	COUNTRY CODE	EVENT	ROUND	HEAT	PLACE	TIME & DISTANCE	MEDAL
John, H.	GER	110m hurdles	1	2	3	14·39	
			SF	1	5	14·14	
Johnson, D.O.	JAM	100m	1	6	2	10·61	
			2	1	5	10·51	
		4×100m relay	1	3	2	40·11	
			SF	1	3	39·68	
			F		4	39·49	
Johnson, W.	LBR	100m	1	9	DNF		
		200m	1	3	6	24·7	
Jones, H.W.	USA	110m hurdles	1	5	2	14·24	
			SF	2	3	14·06	
			F		1	13·67*	G
Jones, R.	GBR	4×100m relay	1	1	3	40·13	
			SF	1	4	40·13	
			F		8	39·69	
Joo, H.K.	KOR	Marathon	F		50	2:41-08·2	
Jordanov, E.Y.	BUL	High jump	F		12	2,06	
Juettner, J.	GER	400m	1	3	3	47·06	
			2	3	4	47·22	
			SF	1	5	46·78	
		4×400m relay	1	3	2	3-04·9	
			F		5	3-04·3	
Julian, J.L.	NZL	Marathon	F		29	2:27-57·6	
Jurca, V.	RUM	200m	1	8	6	21·82	
		400m hurdles	1	3	6	52·7	
Juutilainen, P.K.	FIN	800m	1	2	4	1-51·0	
			SF	2	8	1-50·3	
Kahn, L.G.	JAM	400m	1	7	3	47·25	
			2	2	4	46·97	
			SF	1	6	47·0	
		4×400m relay	1	3	3	3-05·3	
			F		4	3-02·3	
Kalfelder, J.	GER	400m	1	5	6	47·77	
Kalocsai, H.	HUN	Long jump	Q		DNQ	6,99	
		Triple jump	Q		DNQ	15,53	
Kamata, M.	JPN	100m	1	4	6	10·94	
		4X100m relay	1	2	6	41·0	
			SF	2	8	40·6	
Kamerbeek, E.	HOL	Decathlon	F		DNF		
Kanai, H.	JPN	Javelin throw	Q		DNQ	65,85	
Kanda, M.	RHO	Marathon	F		51	2:41-09·0	
Kaneko, S.	JPN	Discus throw	Q		DNQ	46,46	
Kanitasut, C.	THA	4×100m relay	1	2	7	41·8	
Kantorek, P.	TCH	Marathon	F		25	2:26-47·2	
Kapambwe, C.	RHO	Marathon	F		46	2:39-28·4	
Karasiov, N.	URS	Discus throw	F		6	18,86	
Karlsson, R.S.T.	SWE	20k walk	F		20	1:37-07·0	
Karunananda, R.J.	CEY	5000m	1	3	12	16-22·2	
		10000m	F		29	34-21·2	
Kasahara, S.	JPN	Hammer throw	Q		DNQ	61,87	
Kawazu, K.	JPN	Long jump	Q		DNQ	7,28	
Keats, I.	NZL	Marathon	F		42	2:36-16·8	
Keino, K.	KEN	1500m	1	3	1	3-45·8	
			SF	2	5	3-41·9	
		5000m	1	4	2	13-49·6	
			F		5	13-50·4	
Keocanta, S.	THA	5000m	1	3	11	16-08·8	
Kerr, G.E.	JAM	800m	1	5	2	1-48·9	
			SF	2	1	1-46·1*	
			F		4	1-45·9	
		4×400m relay	1	3	3	3-05·3	
			F		4	3-02·3	
Khan, A.	PAK	800m	1	2	8	1-56·4	
		1500m	1	3	11	3-56·7	
Khlebarov, D.P.	BUL	Pole vault	Q		DNQ	0	
Khrolovich, B.	URS	20k walk	F		7	1:32-45·4	
Kidd, B.	CAN	5000m	1	1	9	14-21·8	
		10000m	F		26	30-56·4	
Kilby, B.L.	GBR	Marathon	F		4	2:17-02·4	
Kim, B-K.	KOR	Discus throw	Q		DNQ	42,73	
Kim, Y-B.	KOR	Marathon	F		16	2:24-40·6	
Kimihara, K.	JPN	Marathon	F		8	2:19-49·0	
Kinder, M.	GER	800m	1	3	1	1-49·5	
			SF	3	3	1-47·9	
		4×400m relay	1	3	2	3-04·9	
			F		5	3-04·3	
Kinnunen, J.V.P.	FIN	Javelin throw	F		6	76,94	
Kiprop, K.	KEN	Decathlon	F		17	6707	
Kiprugut, W.	KEN	400m	1	7	2	47·04	
			2	3	7	47·7	
		800m	1	1	1	1-47·8	
			SF	2	2	1-46·1	
			F		3	1-45·9	B
Kiss, A.	HUN	20k walk	F		21	1:38-27·0	
Klaban, R.	AUT	800m	1	6	4	1-49·9	
			SF	2	5	1-47·4	
Klein, W.	GER	Long jump	F		10	7,15	

COMPETITOR	COUNTRY CODE	EVENT	ROUND	HEAT	PLACE	TIME & DISTANCE	MEDAL
Kler, D.S.	MAL	3000m steeplechase	1	3	10	9-18-8	
Klim, R.	URS	Hammer throw	F		1	69,74*	G
Kluczek, I.	POL	400m	1	7	4	47.35	
		4×400m relay	1	2	2	3-07.2	
			F		6	3-05.3	
Knickenberg, M.	GER	100m	1	10	4	10.74	
Knill, H.-R.	SUI	1500m	1	1	6	3-47.2	
Knoke, G.J.	AUS	400m hurdles	1	1	2	50.94	
			SF	1	3	50.63	
			F		4	50.4	
		4×400m relay	1	2	4	3-08.2	
Koch, C.	HOL	Discus throw	Q		DNQ	52,57	
Kogo, B.	KEN	3000m steeplechase	1	3	5	8-51-0	
Komar, W.	POL	Shot put	F		9	18,20	
Kompaneets, V.	URS	Discus throw	F		12	51,96	
Kone, G.	CIV	100m	1	3	1	10-50	
			2	1	4	10-45	
			SF	2	2	10.48	
			F		=6	10.47	
Kontarev, A.	URS	110m hurdles	1	2	2	14.26	
			SF	2	6	14.27	
Koppen, R.	GER	High jump	F		19	2,00	
Kosanov, G.	URS	100m	1	5	5	10.94	
		4×100m relay	1	3	3	40.19	
			SF	2	4	39.70	
			F		5	39.50	
Kovac, P.	YUG	400m hurdles	1	4		DIS	
Kragbe, S.D.	CIV	Shot put	Q		DNQ	16,59	
		Discus throw	Q		DNQ	46,43	
Kravchenko, V.	URS	Triple jump	F		3	16,57	B
Kreer, V.	URS	Triple jump	Q		DNQ	15,71	
Kristensen, T.	DEN	20k walk	F		14	1:35-30.0	
Krivec, G.	GER	Triple jump	Q		DNQ	15,78	
Krivosheev, A.	URS	800m	1	4	4	1-49-5	
			SF	2	6	1-47-5	
Kuda, D.	MAL	110m hurdles	1	4	6	15.17	
		4×400m relay	1	3	6	3-17.6	
Kuehl, F.	GER	Discus throw	Q		DNQ	53,53	
Kuklich, I.	URS	400m hurdles	1	5	8	53.3	
Kulcsar, G.	HUN	Javelin throw	F		2	82,32	S
Kunalan, C.	MAL	4×100m relay	1	1	6	41.4	
Kuraishi, J.K.	IRQ	200m	1	4	5	22.6	
		400m	1	6	7	49.5	
		4×100m relay	1	1		DIS	
Kuribayashi, K.	JPN	20k walk	F		25	1:43-07-0	
Kuznetsov, Vasiliy	URS	Decathlon	F		7	7569	
Kuznetsov, Vladimir	URS	Javelin throw	F		8	74,26	
Laeng, P.	SUI	400m	1	6	3	47.12	
			2	1	5	46.72	
		4×400m relay	1	3	4	3-09.3	
Laidebeur, B.	FRA	100m	1	1	2	10.51	
			2	1	7	10.59	
		4×100m relay	1	3	1	39.84	
			SF	1	2	39.66	
			F		3	39.36	B
Laird, R.O.	USA	20k walk	F		DIS		
Laitinen, T.R.	FIN	Pole vault	F		14	4,60	
Lambrechts, J.	BEL	800m	1	1	4	1-48-9	
			SF	3	8	1-52-8	
Langer, R.	GER	Shot put	F		11	17,29	
Larrabee, M.D.	USA	400m	1	8	1	46.88	
			2	3	1	46.57	
			SF	2	1	46.02	
			F		1	45.15	G
		4×400m relay	1	1	1	3-05.3	G
			F		1	3-00-7*	G
Larrieu, G.R.	USA	10000m	F		24	30-42-6	
Larsson, S.-O. M.	SWE	5000m	1	4	5	14-10-2	
Lawlor, J.F.	IRL	Hammer throw	Q		DNQ	59,12	
Lay, R.W.	AUS	100m	1	8	3	10.53	
			2	2	3	10.42	
			SF	1	5	10.35	
		200m	1	6	2	21.34	
			2	2	5	21.49	
		4×100m relay	1	3	4	40.64	
			SF	1	5	40.19	
Lazim, K.T.	IRQ	4×100m relay	1	1	DIS		
Lee, A.R. Tu.	TAI	100m	1	3	8	11-2	
		200m	1	4	6	23.0	
Lee, S.-H.	KOR	Marathon	F		11	2:22-02-8	
Lehnertz, K.	GER	Pole vault	F		3	5,00	B
Leps, E.	CAN	1500m	1	1	4	3-46-4	
			SF	1	8	3-51-2	
Lesek, R.	YUG	Pole vault	F		13	4,70	
Letzerich, M.	GER	5000m	1	2	8	14-06-2	
Leupi, O.	SUI	Marathon	F		41	2:35-05-4	
Leuschke, B.	GER	50k walk	F		4	4:15-26-8	

COMPETITOR	COUNTRY CODE	EVENT	ROUND	HEAT	PLACE	TIME & DISTANCE	MEDAL
Lievore, C.	ITA	Javelin throw	Q		DNQ	70,88	
Lindback, S.	SWE	800m	1	2	2	1-50-8	
			SF	1	8	1-49-8	
		1500m	1	3	5	3-47-1	
Lindgren, G.P.	USA	10000m	F		9	29-20.6	
Lindgren, H.B.	USA	110m hurdles	1	2	1	14.20	
			SF	2	1	13.95	
			F		2	13.74	S
Lindmer, D.	GER	20k walk	F		2	1:31-13-2	S
Lindsay, M.R.	GBR	Shot put	Q		DNQ	17,23	
Lipsnis, V.	URS	Shot put	F		10	18,11	
Liungin, E.	URS	50k walk	F		18	4:32-01-6	
Ljunggren, J.A.	SWE	20k walk	F		19	1:37-03-0	
		50k walk	F		16	4:29-09-2	
Loffler, V.	GER	4×100m relay	1	2	3	40.21	
			SF	1	4	40.16	
Long, D.C.	USA	Shot put	F		1	20,33*	G
Lorenzo, C.	MEX	100m	1	4	4	10.74	
		200m	1	2	6	21-60	
Losch, H.	GER	Discus throw	F		11	52,08	
Lotz, M.	GER	Hammer throw	Q		DNQ	61,88	
Luck, J.E.	USA	400m hurdles	1	3	3	51.77	
			SF	2	2	50.43	
			F		5	50.5	
Lucking, M.T.	GBR	Shot put	Q		DNQ	17,67	
Luitjes, F.J.	HOL	100m	1	3	4	10.69	
		200m	1	5	4	21.13	
			2	4	4	21.40	
			SF	1	7	21.16	
Lurot, M.	FRA	800m	1	6	2	1-49-8	
			SF	1	7	1-49-7	
Lusis, J.	URS	Javelin throw	F		3	80,57	B
Ly, N-V.	VNM	5000m	1	3	13	17-28-0	
		Marathon	F		DNF		
McArdle, P.J.	USA	Marathon	F		23	2:26-24-4	
McCarthy, C.	USA	50k walk	F		21	4:35-41-6	
McCleane, D.G.	IRL	800m	1	3	3	1-49-9	
			SF	2	7	1-48-4	
MacDonald, B.D.	USA	50k walk	F		26	4:45-10-4	
McKim, W.	GBR	1500m	1	1	5	3-46-8	
McNeil, P.S.	JAM	100m	1	3	3	10.60	
			2	3	4	10.54	
			SF	1	6	10.39	
		4×100m relay	1	3	2	40.11	
			SF	2	3	39.68	
			F		4	39.49	
Macquet, M.	FRA	Javelin throw	Q		DNQ	69,35	
Macsai, J.	HUN	3,000m steeplechase	1	1	7	9-08-8	
Magee, A.B.	NZL	10000m	F		23	30-32-0	
Maki, S.D.	CIV	110m hurdles	1	2	8	15.3	
Maldonado, V.	VEN	400m	1	4	7	47.7	
		400m hurdles	1	5	2	51.64	
			SF	2	7	51.19	
Mane, M.	SEN	4×100m relay	1	2	4	40.55	
			SF	2	6	40.26	
Manglaras, D.	GRE	Long jump	Q		DNQ	7,21	
Maniak, W.J.	POL	100m	1	7	1	10.57	
			2	2	2	10.35	
			SF	1	2	10.15	
			F		4	10.42	
		4×100m relay	1	1	2	39.96	
			SF	2	2	39.63	
			F		2	39.36	S
Manyakass, S.	THA	100m	1	10	7	10.98	
		4×100m relay	1	2	7	41.8	
Marien, L.	BEL	110m hurdles	1	4	4	14.93	
Marsellos, G.	GRE	110m hurdles	1	4	5	14.97	
Martin, B.	FRA	4×400m relay	1	1	3	3-07-5	
			F		8	3-07-4	
Matousek, J.	TCH	Hammer throw	F		9	64,59	
Matson, J.R.	USA	Shot put	F		2	20,20	S
Matthews, K.J.	GBR	20k walk	F		1	1:29-34-0*	G
Matuschewski, M.	GER	800m	1	5	4	1-50-0	
			SF	1	4	1-47-3	
May, J.	GER	1500m	1	2	2	3-44-2	
			SF	2	8	3-46-8	
Mazlan, H.	MAL	4×100m relay	1	1	6	41.4	
Mazza, G.	ITA	110m hurdles	1	1	1	14.26	
			SF	1	3	14.06	
			F		8	14.17	
Meakin, A.	GBR	100m	1	6	6	10.91	
Meconi, S.	ITA	Shot put	Q		DNQ	17,29	
Mecser, L.	HUN	5000m	1	3	9	14-35-4	
Medinger, M.	LUX	800m	1	2	6	1-52-6	
		1500m	1	3	8	3-51-8	
Mejia, D.	MEX	400m	1	1	7	48-1	
Mejia, A.	COL	5000m	1	2	13	14-41-4	

COMPETITOR	COUNTRY CODE	EVENT	ROUND	HEAT	PLACE	TIME & DISTANCE	MEDAL
Mensah, B.	GHA	4×400m relay	1	3	5	3-10.4	
Metcalfe, A.P.	GBR	400m	1	3	2	46.79	
			2	4	5	47.81	
		4×400m relay	1	3	1	3-04.7	
			F		2	3-01.6	S
Middleton, R.C.	GBR	50k walk	F		13	4:25-49.2	
Mihalyfi, L.	HUN	100m	1	9	4	10.65	
		4×100m relay	1	1	4	40.32	
			SF	1	7	40.31	
Mikhailov, A.	URS	110m hurdles	1	3	1	14.13	
			SF	1	1	13.90	
			F		3	13.78	B
Miki, T.	JPN	Javelin throw	Q		DNQ	68,70	
Milde, L.	GER	Discus throw	Q		DNQ	53,39	
Miller, G.A.	GBR	High jump	F		18	2,03	
Mills, L.R.	NZL	Shot put	F		7	18,52	
		Discus throw	Q		DNQ	51,70	
Mills, W.M.	USA	10000m	F		1	28-24.4*	G
		Marathon	F		14	2:22-55.4	
Mirzamolimadail, K.S.J.	IRN	Discus throw	Q		DNQ	45,24	
Miwa, S.	JPN	50k walk	F		27	4:52-00.6	
Miyazaki, K.	JPN	High jump	Q		DNQ	1,90	
Moore, O.W.	USA	5000m	1	4	8	14-24.0	
Morale, S.	ITA	400m hurdles	1	4	1	51.17	
			SF	2	3	50.48	
			F		3	50.1	B
		4×400m relay	1	2	3	3-07.6	
Morbey, J.M.	GBR	Long jump	F		11	7,09	
Moreno, I.	CHI	100m	1	9	2	10.59	
			2	3	6	10.69	
		200m	1	7	4	21.55	
			2	2	7	21.74	
Morimoto, M.	JPN	800m	1	6	3	1-49.9	
			SF	1	6	1-47.7	
Morita, H.	JPN	Pole vault	Q		DNQ	4,40	
Moro, G.	CAN	Pole vault	F		10	4,70	
		Decathlon	F		16	6716	
Mortland, J.E.	USA	20k walk	F		17	1:36-35.0	
Mottley, W.	TRI	400m	1	1	1	45.94	
			2	1	1	45.88	
			SF	1	2	45.96	
			F		2	45.24	S
		4×400m relay	1	2	1	3-05.0	
			F		3	3-01.7	B
Mrombe, R.	RHO	Marathon	F		56	2:49-30.8	
Murad, L.	VEN	100m	1	5	3	10.86	
			2	3	8	10.77	
		4×100m relay	1	2	2	40.10	
			SF	2	3	39.65	
			F		6	39.53	
Muro, Y.	JPN	4×100m relay	1	2	6	41.0	
			SF	2	8	40.6	
Murray, A.F.	GBR	10000m	F		22	30-22.4	
Myton, N.F.	JAM	800m	1	2	5	1-52.4	
		1500m	1	1	9	3-57.0	
Nagy, Z.	HUN	Shot put	F		5	18,88	
Naito, Y.	JPN	20k walk	F		DIS		
Najde, B.	SWE	5000m	1	3	6	14-13.4	
Naroditsky, L.	URS	3000m steeplechase	1	2	5	8-43.0	
Nashathar, S.S.	MAL	Javelin throw	Q		DNQ	51,63	
Naumann, M.	GER	Marathon	F		39	2:33-42.0	
Ndiaye, A.	SEN	100m	1	5	6	11.06	
Ndiaye, Mamadou	SEN	4×400m relay	1	1	6	3-12.5	
Ndiaye, Mambaye	SEN	4×400m relay	1	1	6	3-12.5	
Negrete, F.	MEX	Marathon	F		21	2:26-07.0	
Neira, J.G.	COL	800m	1	3	7	1-55.6	
Nelzy, G.	FRA	4×400m relay	1	1	3	3-07.5	
			F		8	3-07.4	
Nevala, P.L.	FIN	Javelin throw	F		1	82,66	G
Nihill, V.P.	GBR	50k walk	F		2	4:11-31.2	S
Nikiciuk, W.	POL	Javelin throw	F		9	73,11	
Nikula, P.K.	FIN	Pole vault	F		7	4,90	
Nikulin, Y.	URS	Hammer throw	F		4	67,69	
Nilsson, K-A.	SWE	High jump	F		6	2,09	
Njitock, D.	CMR	100m	1	6	7	11.13	
		200m	1	3	5	22.5	
Norpoth, H.	GER	5000m	1	3	3	14-11.6	
			F		2	13-49.6	S
Nuttall, C.R.	CAN	110m hurdles	1	3	4	14.82	
Nyakwayo, C.	KEN	Marathon	F		45	2:38-38.6	
Oakley, A.H.	CAN	20k walk	F		DNF		
		50k walk	F		14	4:27-24.6	
Obersiebrasse, F.	GER	100m	1	9	1	10.47	
			2	1	3	10.44	
			SF	2	8	10.68	
O'Brien, W.P.	USA	Shot put	F		4	19,20	
Ochana, J.	USA	400m hurdles	1	3	4	52.4	
Odlozil, J.	TCH	1500m	1	4	3	3-43.2	
			SF	1	3	3-39.3	
			F		2	3-39.6	S
Oduka, J.O.	UGA	100m	1	5	4	10.91	
		4×100m relay	1	3	6	41.4	
Oerter, A.A.	USA	Discus throw	F		1	61,00*	G
Ogan, G.	NGR	Triple jump	Q		DNQ	15,35	
Ogushi, K.	JPN	400m hurdles	1	4	5	53.6	
O'Hara, T.M.	USA	1500m	1	3	3	3-46.7	
			SF	2	7	3-43.4	
Ohiri, C.	NGR	Triple jump	Q		DNQ	15,08	
Okamoto, N.	JPN	Hammer throw	Q		DNQ	61,51	
Okantey, M.F.	GHA	200m	1	7	6	21.97	
		4×100m relay	1	3	5	40.85	
			SF	1	8	40.7	
Okazaki, T.	JPN	Triple jump	F		10	15,90	
Okiring, V.	UGA	110m hurdles	1	3	7	15.5	
Okorafor, L.	NGR	4×100m relay	SF	1	6	40.19	
Oksanen, E.I.	FIN	Marathon	F		13	2:22-36.0	
Okuzawa, Z.	JPN	3000m steeplechase	1	1	5	8-50.0	
Olafsson, J.T.	ISL	High jump	Q		DNQ	2,00	
Olofsson, K.U.	SWE	1500m	1	2	5	3-44.8	
			SF	1	7	3-44.8	
Oliveira, M.F.	POR	3000m steeplechase	1	1	1	8-40.8	
			F		4	8-36.2	
Omagbemi, J.	NGR	4×100m relay	1	1	5	40.44	
			SF	1	6	40.19	
Omolo, A.	UGA	400m	1	3	5	47.65	
		4×100m relay	1	3	6	41.4	
Onel, C.	TUR	3000m steeplechase	1	1	10	9-15.6	
Onofre, R.P.	PHI	100m	1	8	5	10.78	
		200m	1	7	7	22.17	
		4×100m relay	1	3	7	41.7	
Orentas, K.	URS	5000m	1	2	6	13-54.0	
O'Riordan, T.B.M.	IRL	5000m	1	2	9	14-08.8	
Ota, T.	JPN	Triple jump	Q		DNQ	0	
Otsubo, M.	JPN	Pole vault	Q		DNQ	4,20	
Ottolina, S.	ITA	200m	1	4	2	21.27	
			2	2	2	21.16	
			SF	1	2	20.76	
			F		8	20.94	
		4×100m relay	1	1	1	39.74	
			SF	2	1	39.63	
			F		7	39.54	
Ottoz, E.	ITA	110m hurdles	1	4	1	14.63	
			SF	1	4	14.12	
			F		4	13.84	
Owiti, J.	KEN	100m	1	4	3	10.64	
			2	2	7	10.64	
Ozolin, E.	URS	100m	1	2	5	10.52	
			2	2	5	10.48	
		200m	1	4	3	21.32	
			2	4	5	21.47	
		4×100m relay	1	3	4	40.19	
			SF	2	4	39.70	
			F		5	39.50	
Paddick, J.C.	GBR	20k walk	F		10	1:33-28.4	
Pal, A.	IND	110m hurdles	1	5	7	53.3	
		4×400m hurdles	1	1	3	3-08.8	
Pamich, A.	ITA	50k walk	F		1	4:11-12.4*	G
Papanikolaou, C.	GRE	Pole vault	F		18	4,40	
Park, S.-K.	KOR	Javeline throw	Q		DNQ	62,50	
Parker, J.M.	GBR	110m hurdles	1	5	3	14.26	
			SF	2	8	14.65	
Payne, A.H.	GBR	Hammer throw	Q		DNQ	61,90	
Peckham, L.W.	AUS	High jump	F		10	2,09	
Pedersen, T.O.	NOR	Javelin throw	Q		DNQ	72,10	
Pellosis, C.A.	PHI	4×100m relay	1	3	7	41.7	
Pemelton, W.G.	USA	Pole vault	F		8	4,80	
Pender, M.	USA	100m	1	3	2	10.53	
			2	3	2	10.44	
			SF	2	4	10.49	
			F		=6	10.47	
Pennel, J.T.	USA	Pole vault	F		11	4,70	
Pennewaert, J.	BEL	400m	1	4	8	47.7	
		800m	1	4	2	1-49.2	
			SF	1	3	1-47.0	
			F		8	1-50.5	
Pensuvabharp, N.	THA	800m	1	1	8	1-58.8	
		4×400m relay	1	3	7	3-18.4	
Peralta, V.	MEX	Marathon	F		53	2:44-23.6	
Pettersson, I.A.	SWE	50k walk	F		3	4:14-17.4	B
Pettersson, S.	SWE	High jump	F		4	2,14	
Philipp, L.	GER	5000m	1	1	8	14-15.2	
Piatkowski, E.	POL	Discus throw	F		7	55,81	

COMPETITOR	COUNTRY CODE	EVENT	ROUND	HEAT	PLACE	TIME & DISTANCE	MEDAL
Pichaya, R.	IND	4×100m relay	1	2	5	40·68	
			SF	2	7	40·5	
Pierrakos, C.	GRE	Javelin throw	F		10	72,65	
Pinter, J.	HUN	5000m	1	1	10	14-41·0	
		Marathon	F		37	2:30-50·2	
Piquemal, C.	FRA	100m	1	5	2	10·58	
			2	2	5	10·48	
			SF		5	10·56	
		4×100m relay	1	3	1	39·84	
			SF	1	2	39·66	
			F		3	39·36	B
Poirier, R.	FRA	400m hurdles	1	3	5	52·6	
Pomfret, E.	GBR	3000m steeplechase	1	3	3	8-45·2	
			F		10	8-43·8	
Popa, I.	RUM	50k walk	F		28	4:57-40·8	
Powell, K.L.	IND	100m	1	1	4	10·74	
		200m	1	6	6	21·94	
		4×100m relay	1	2	5	40·68	
			SF	2	7	40·5	
Preatoni, E.	ITA	4×100m relay	1	1	1	39·74	
			SF	2	1	39·63	
			F		7	39·54	
Preussger, M.	GER	Pole vault	F		4	5,00	
Psawkin, L.	ISR	100m	1	5	7	11·13	
Puckett, R.L.	NZL	Marathon	F		27	2:27-34·0	
Pystynen, P.K.	FIN	Marathon	F		20	2:26-00·6	
Quartey, E.Q.	GHA	400m	1	8	2	47.12	
			2	1	7	47·06	
		4×400m relay	1	3	5	3-10·4	
Rabai, G.	HUN	4×100m relay	1	1	4	40·32	
			SF	1	7	40·31	
Rabemila, M.	MAD	Triple jump	Q		DNQ	14,62	
Radford, P.F.	GBR	100m	1	2	2	10·69	
			2	4	5	10·59	
		200m	1	2	4	21·52	
			2	4	6	21·53	
		4×100m relay	1	1	3	40·13	
			SF	1	4	40·13	
			F		8	39·39	
Radosevic, D.	YUG	Discus throw	Q		DNQ	52,71	
Rahman, M.O.	MAL	4×400m relay	1	3	6	3-17·6	
Rajan	BUR	50k walk	F		DNF		
Ralph, M.	GBR	Triple jump	Q		DNQ	15,57	
Rambo, J.B.	USA	High jump	F		3	2,16	B
Ravdrianjatovo, J.	MAD	5000m	1	1	11	15-50·4	
Rasmussen, W.L.	NOR	Javelin throw	Q		DNQ	68,43	
Ravelomanantsoa, J.	MAD	100m	1	1	6	10·89	
		200m	1	8	8	22·4	
Raziq, G.	PAK	110m hurdles	1	2	5	14·76	
Red, W.E.	USA	Javelin throw	F		11	71,52	
Reimann, H.-G.	GER	20k walk	F		12	1:34-51·0	
Reinhardt, W.	GER	Pole vault	F		2	5,05	S
Reinosa, I.	PUR	Discus throw	Q		DNQ	46,36	
Repo, P.	FIN	Discus throw	Q		DNQ	52,93	
Rim, D.-S.	KOR	Hammer throw	Q		DNQ	56,43	
Rim, H.-K	KOR	Shot put	Q		DNQ	13,64	
Rivas, R.	ESP	100m	1	10	8	11·12	
Roberts, E.	TRI	200m	1	6	1	20·89	
			2	4	1	20·90	
			SF	2	3	20·86	
			F		3	20·63	E
		4×400m relay	1	2	1	3-05·0	
			F		3	3-01·7	B
Robinson, P.D.	JAM	4×100m relay	1	3	2	40·11	
			SF	1	3	39·68	
			F		4	39·49	
Robinson, T.A.	BAH	100m	1	8	2	10·50	
			2	3	1	10·38	
			SF	1	3	10·22	
			F		8	10·57	
Roche, K.J.	AUS	400m	1	6	5	47·43	
			2	2	7	48·0	
		400m hurdles	1	3	2	51·52	
			SF	2	5	50·86	
		4×400m relay	1	2	4	3-08·2	
Roderfeld, F.	GER	200m	1	8	3	21·58	
			2	3	8	22·29	
Roelants, G.	BEL	3000 steeplechase	1	3	2	8-33·8	
			F		1	8-30·8*	G
Romero, R.	VEN	4×100m relay	1	2	2	40·10	
			SF	2	3	39·65	
			F		6	39·53	
Rothe, S.	GER	10000m	F		20	30-04·6	
Rozsnyai, H.	HUN	100m	1	6	5	10·84	
		4×100m relay	1	1	4	40·32	
			SF	1	7	40·31	
Ruckborn, H.-J.	GER	Triple jump	F		8	16,09	

COMPETITOR	COUNTRY CODE	EVENT	ROUND	HEAT	PLACE	TIME & DISTANCE	MEDAL
Rut, T.	POL	Hammer throw	F		10	64,52	
Rutyna, M.	POL	20k walk	F		26	1:48-41·0	
		50k walk	F		DIS		
Ryan, M.A.B.	AUS	400m hurdles	1	2	8	58·0	
Ryan, J.R.	USA	1500m	1	2	4	3-44·4	
			SF	1	9	3-55·0	
Sabater, A.	PUR	110m hurdles	1	1	6	14·69	
Sadiq, M.	PAK	400m	1	4	6	47·3	
			2	1	8	48·0	
Sahiner, C.	TUR	110m hurdles	1	3	6	15·12	
Sainte-Rose, R.	FRA	High jump	Q		DNQ	2,00	
Saito, K.	JPN	50k walk	F		25	4:43-01·0	
Sakowski, K.	GER	50k walk	F		8	4:20-31·0	
Sakurai, K.	JPN	Triple jump	Q		DNQ	15,59	
Salomon, H.	GER	Javelin throw	Q		DNQ	71,92	
Salonen, O.V.K.	FIN	1500m	1	2	6	3-46·8	
Saloranta, S.S.	FIN	5000m	1	3	8	14-24·6	
Samsam, L.	MAR	Shot put	Q		DNQ	17,24	
Sar, F.	ITA	Decathlon	F		13	7054	
Sarr, M.	SEN	400m hurdles	1	5	6	53·2	
Saruwatari, T.	JPN	3000m steeplechase	1	2	7	8-46·6	
Saunders, H.C.	BAH	Triple jump	Q		DNQ	14,59	
Savchuk, B.	URS	200m	1	5	DIS		
		4×100m relay	1	3	3	40·19	
			SF	2	4	39·70	
			F		5	39·50	
Schenk, H.	GER	Javelin throw	F		12	69,82	
Schillkowski, W.	GER	High jump	F		17	2,06	
Schmidt, J.	POL	Triple jump	F		1	16,85*	G
Schmitt, J.	GER	400m	1	4	5	46·90	
			2	2	6	47·24	
		4×400m relay	1	3	2	3-04·9	
			F		5	3-04·3	
Schul, R.K.	USA	5000m	1	3	2	14-11·4	
			F		1	13-48·8	G
Schulz, H-U.	GER	4×400m relay	1	3	2	3-04·9	
			F		5	3-04·3	
Schumann, H.	GER	100m	1	6	1	10·52	
			2	4	4	10·55	
			SF	1	4	10·30	
			F		5	10·46	
		200m	1	7	1	21·09	
			2	2	3	21·25	
			SF	2	6	21·18	
Scott, N.I.	NZL	5000m	1	4	11	15-01·0	
Selvaratnam, K.	MAL	400m hurdles	1	4	7	53·8	
		4×400m relay	1	3	6	3-17·6	
Selvey, W.P.	AUS	Discus throw	Q		DNQ	51,96	
Sereme, D.	MLI	Decathlon	F		18	5917	
Sebsibe, M.	ETH	800m	1	4	8	1-52·8	
		1500m	1	4	7	3-45·8	
Shah, I.	PAK	100m	1	7	7	11·49	
		Long jump	Q		DNQ	0	
Shankhorenejao, A.	IRN	200m	1	5	7	22·3	
Sharpe, W.J.	USA	Triple jump	F		11	15,84	
Shavlakadze, R.	URS	High jump	F		5	2,14	
Shinnick, P.K.	USA	Long jump	Q		DNQ	7,26	
Sidlo, J.	POL	Javelin throw	F		4	80,17	
Siebert, J.F.	USA	800m	1	4	2	1-49·2	
			SF	1	2	1-47·0	
			F		6	1-47·0	
Sil, W.-C	KOR	High jump	Q		DNQ	0	
Silvester, L.J.	USA	Discus throw	F		4	59,09	
Simon, A.	HUN	1500m	1	4	9	3-49·1	
		3000m steeplechase	1	3	7	8-57·9	
Simpson, A.	GBR	1500m	1	4	1	3-42·8	
			SF	2	2	3-41·5	
			F		4	3-39·7	
Singer, J.	GER	400m hurdles	1	2	4	52·1	
Singh, A.	IND	4×400m relay	1	-	4	3-08·8	
Singh, L.	IND	Triple jump	Q		DNQ	14,95	
Singh, Makhan	IND	4×100m relay	1	2	5	40·68	
			SF	2	7	40·5	
		4×400m relay	1	1	4	3-08·8	
Singh, Milkha	IND	4×400m relay	1	1	4	3-08·8	
Singh, R.G.	IND	110m hurdles	1	5	4	14·37	
			SF	2	1	14·04	
			F		5	14·09	
Sirirangsri, C.	THA	Marathon	F		58	2:59-25·6	
Skinner, E.	TRI	400m	1	4	2	46·50	
			2	4	1	46·90	
			SF	2	3	46·50	
			F		8	46·8	
		4×400m relay	1	2	1	3-05·0	
			F		3	3-01·7	B
Skvortsov, V.	URS	High jump	F		14	2,06	

COMPETITOR	COUNTRY CODE	EVENT	ROUND	HEAT	PLACE	TIME & DISTANCE	MEDAL
Smith, J.I.	RHO	100m	1	9	7	10·86	
		200m	1	4	4	21·77	
			2	1	7	22·05	
Smolinski, Z.	POL	Hammer throw	F		14	62,90	
Sneazwell, A.H.	AUS	High jump	F		13	2,06	
Snell, P.G.	NZL	800m	1	4	1	1-49·0	
			SF	1	1	1-46·9	
			F		1	1-45·1*	G
		1500m	1	3	4	3-46·8	
			SF	1	1	3-38·8	
			F		1	3-38·1	G
So, K.T.	HKG	50k walk	F		31	5:07-53·2	
Soderlund, A.W.	SWE	20k walk	F		18	1:36-53·0	
Soi, A.	KEN	Marathon	F		DNF		
Sokolowski, W.	POL	Pole vault	Q		DNQ	0	
Sola, I.	ESP	Pole vault	F		15	4,40	
Solodov, G.	URS	20k walk	F		5	1:32-33·0	
Songok, K.	KEN	400m hurdles	1	3	7	54·5	
Sosgornik, A.	POL	Shot put	Q		DNQ	17,75	
Soudek, E.	AUT	Discus throw	Q		DNQ	51,78	
Sow, A.	SEN	200m	1	7	5	21·91	
		4×100m relay	1	2	4	40·55	
			SF	2	6	40·26	
Sowa, C.	LUX	20k walk	F		16	1:36-16·0	
		50k walk	F		9	4:20-37·2	
Span, S.	YUG	3000m steeplechase	1	1	6	8-57·6	
Spence, Malcolm	JAM	4×400m relay	1	3	3	3-05·3	
			F		4	3-02·3	
Spence, Melville	JAM	4×400m Relay	1	3	3	3-05·3	
			F		4	3-02·3	
Sperling, G.	GER	20k walk	F		9	1:33-15·8	
Stalmach, A.	POL	Long jump	F		8	7,26	
Stebbins, R.V.	USA	200m	1	8	2	21·17	
			2	3	2	21·28	
			SF	1	3	20·88	
			F		7	20·89	
		4×100m relay	1	2	1	39·83	
			SF	1	1	39·50*	
			F		1	39·06*	G
Stevenson, D.D.	GBR	Pole vault	Q		DNQ	4,50	
Storozhenko, M.	URS	Decathlon	F		8	7464	
Stoykovski, G.I.	BUL	Triple jump	F		7	16,10	
Stoytchev, R.Z.	BUL	Long jump	Q		DNQ	7,33	
Stutz, E.	SUI	50k walk	F		23	4:40-45·0	
Suarez, O.R.	ARG	Marathon	F		DNF		
Subramaniam, R.	MAL	800m	1	3	8	1-58·5	
		1500m	1	1	10	3-59·4	
Suetoe, J.	HUN	10000m	F		16	29-43·0	
		Marathon	F		5	2:17-55·8	
Sugawara, T.	JPN	Hammer throw	F		13	63,69	
Sugioka, K.	JPN	High jump	Q		DNQ	2,00	
Sumbwegam	BIR	Marathon	F		35	2:30-35·8	
Suzuki, S.	JPN	Decathlon	F		15	6838	
Sverbetov, G.	URS	400m	1	6	4	47·37	
			2	2	8	48·0	
		4×400m relay	1	1	2	3-07·4	
			F		7	3-05·9	
Swatowski, S.	POL	400m	1	1	5	47·6	
		4×400m relay	1	2	2	3-07·2	
			F		6	3-05·3	
Syka, Z.	POL	100m	1	1	5	10·79	
Syversson, M.R.	SWE	50k walk	F		24	4:41-47·6	
Szecsenyi, J.	HUN	Discus throw	F		5	57,23	
Szklarczyk, E.I.	POL	3000m steeplechase	1	2	8	8-48·0	
Taitt, J.L.	GBR	110m hurdles	1	2	4	14·52	
Takayanagi, S.	JPN	Pole vault	Q		DNQ	7,15	
Tanaka, A.	JPN	110m hurdles	1	5	6	14·58	
Telp, R.	URS	800m	1	3	4	1-50·0	
			SF	3	5	1-49·1	
Temu, N.	KEN	Marathon	F		49	2:40-46·6	
Terasawa, T.	JPN	Marathon	F		15	2:23-09·0	
Ter-Ovanesyan, I.	URS	Long jump	F		3	7,99	B
Texereau, G.	FRA	3000m steeplechase	1	2	4	8-34·6	
			F		6	8-38·6	
Theiler, M.	SUI	4×400m relay	1	3	4	3-09·3	
Thiaw, D.A.	SEN	4×400m relay	1	1	6	3-12·5	
Thomas, A.G.	AUS	1500m	1	2	9	3-54·9	
		5000m	1	2	11	14-27·8	
Thomas, D.	TAN	400m	1	3	8	50·4	
Thomas, H.	VEN	Decathlon	F		DNF		
Thomas, J.C.	USA	High jump	F		2	2,18*	S
Thompson, D.J.	GBR	50k walk	F		10	4:22-39·4	
Thorlaksson, V.	ISL	Decathlon	F		12	7135	
Thun, H.	AUT	Hammer throw	F		15	62,76	
Tikhomirov, N.	URS	Marathon	F		22	2:26-07·4	
Tipton, L.E.	USA	Javelin throw	Q		DNQ	70,74	
Toffey, J.E.	CIV	3000m steeplechase	1	1	9	9-47·4	
Tomas, J.	TCH	5000m	1	3	5	14-12·6	
		10000m	F		17	29-46·4	
Tomasek, R.	TCH	Pole vault	F		6	4,90	
Tomlinson, I.R.	AUS	Long jump	Q		DNQ	7,07	
		Triple jump	Q		DNQ	15,76	
Tongsuke, S.	THA	200m	1	1	8	22·6	
		400m	1	6	6	48·9	
		4×400m relay	1	3	7	3-18·4	
Torii, Y.	JPN	Pole vault	Q		DNQ	4,40	
Torres, A.S.	DOM	100m	1	10	6	10·93	
Trense, H.H.	GER	Long jump	Q		DNQ	7,30	
Trousil, J.	TCH	400m	1	7	1	47·04	
			2	2	5	47·22	
Trusenev, V.	URS	Discus throw	F		8	54,78	
Trzmiel, W.	GER	110m hurdles	1	5	5	14·38	
Tsakanikas, G.	GRE	Shot put	F		13	16,87	
		Discus throw	Q		DNQ	51,03	
Tsuburaya, K.	JPN	10000m	F		6	28-59·4	
		Marathon	F		3	2:16-22·8	B
Tulzer, V.	AUT	1500m	1	3	6	3-49·0	
Tuna, A.	TUR	Triple jump	Q		DNQ	15,21	
Tuominen, J.A.U.	FIN	400m hurdles	1	5	3	51·88	
			SF	1	8	54·0	
Vagg, R.A.	AUS	Marathon	F		31	2:28-41·0	
Vaillant, J.	FRA	5000m	1	2	7	14-05·8	
		10000m	F		15	29-33·6	
Valentin, S.	GER	1500m	1	4	6	3-44·9	
Valle, E.O.	FIN	Marathon	F		28	2:27-34·4	
Valles, A.V.	PHI	100m	1	2	7	11·21	
		4×100m relay	1	3	7	41·7	
Van Dendriessche, A.	BEL	Marathon	F		7	2:18-42·6	
Varanauskas, A.	URS	Shot put	F		8	18,41	
Varju, V.	HUN	Shot put	F		3	19,39	B
Vassella, P.F.	AUS	400m	1	4	4	46·77	
			2	1	4	46·55	
			SF	1	4	46·52	
			F		7	46·32	
		4×400m relay	1	2	4	3-08·2	
Vaupshas, A.	URS	Long jump	Q		DNQ	7,43	
Vazic, S.	YUG	1500m	1	4	5	3-43·7	
			SF	2	9	3-48·3	
		5000m	1	4	9	14-33·8	
Vediakoiv, A.	URS	50k walk	F		7	4:19-55·8	
Venkata, S.-B	IND	Long jump	Q		DNQ	6,76	
Victor, A.	MAL	4×100m relay	1	3	6	3-17·6	
Vidal, R.	CHI	Marathon	F		30	2:28-01·6	
Vilaikit, M.	THA	4×100m relay	1	2	7	41·8	
Vincent, S.A.	IRQ	110m hurdles	1	4	8	16·2	
		400m hurdles	1	2	6	54·0	
		4×100m relay	1	1	DIS		
		Triple jump	Q		DNQ	13,85	
Vincent, T.A.	AUS	3000m steeplechase	1	3	8	8-58·8	
Vitsudhamakul, A.	THA	4×400m relay	1	3	7	3-18·4	
Voegele, G.	SUI	Marathon	F		32	2:29-17·8	
Voigt, C.	GER	110m hurdles	1	4	7	15·19	
Von Wartburg, U.	SUI	Javelin throw	F		5	78,72	
Wadoux, J.	FRA	1500m	1	4	2	3-43·0	
			SF	2	4	3-41·9	
			F		9	3-45·4	
Walde, H-J.	GER	Decathlon	F		3	7809	B
Wallach, P.	GER	4×100m relay	1	2	3	40·21	
			SF	2	5	40·16	
Walser, H.	LIE	800m	1	1	7	1-57·5	
		1500m	1	3	10	3-53·3	
Warden, P.	GBR	400m hurdles	1	2	3	51·61	
			SF	1	5	51·2	
Watanabe, K.	JPN	10000m	F		28	31-00·6	
Weill, D.L.	USA	Discus throw	F		3	59,49	B
West, W.	GER	Long jump	F		4	7,60	
Whetton, J.	GBR	1500m	1	2	3	3-44·2	
			SF	1	5	3-39·9	
			F		8	3-42·4	
Wiggs, M.E.	GBR	5000m	1	2	1	13-51·0	
			F		11	14-20·8	
Williams, U.C.	USA	400m	1	4	1	46·20	
			2	4	2	46·96	
			SF	1	3	46·29	
			F		5	46·01	
		4×400m relay	1	1	1	3-05·3	
			F		1	3-00·7*	G
Wolde, D.	ETH	Marathon	F		10	2:21-25·2	
Wolde, M.	ETH	10000m	F		4	28-31·8	
		Marathon	F		DNF		
Wu, A.-M.	TAI	Decathlon	F		DNF		
Yamada, H.	JPN	Long jump	F		9	7,16	

COMPETITOR	COUNTRY CODE	EVENT	ROUND	HEAT	PLACE	TIME & DISTANCE	MEDAL
Yamaguchi, T.	JPN	1500m	1	4	0	3-56.7	
Yang, C.-K.	TAI	Pole vault	F		DNS		
		Decathlon	F		5	7650	
Yasuda, H.	JPN	110m hurdles	1	1	3	14.53	
			SF	2	7	14.30	
Yazdanpanah-Barughi, E.	IRN	800m	1		6	1-54.7	
		1500m	1	2	8	3-54.8	
Yokomizo, S.	JPN	3000m steeplechase	1	3	9	9-04.6	
Yombe, L.	CGO	100m	1	10	5	10.87	
Yoshida, M.	JPN	4×400m relay	1	1	5	3-12.3	
Young, G.L.	USA	3000m steeplechase	1	2	3	8-34.2	
			F		5	8-38.2	
Yui, K.	JPN	400m hurdles	1	2	7	54.7	
Yusaf, M.	PAK	Marathon	F		43	2:40-46.0	
Zageris, E.	URS	400m hurdles	1	1	4	51.59	
			SF	1	7	52.2	
Zalada, K.	IRQ	100m	1	8	6	11.17	
		4×100m relay	1	1		DIS	
Zemba, J.	TCH	Discus throw	Q		DNQ	52.13	
Zielinski, A.	POL	200m	1	1	2	21.24	
			2	1	5	21.59	
		4×100m relay	1	1	2	39.96	
			SF	2	2	39.63	
			F		2	39.35	S
Zinn, R.L.	USA	20k walk	F		6	1:32-43.0	
Zsivotzky, G.	HUN	Hammer throw	F		2	69.09	S
Zubov, B.	URS	200m	1	2	3	21.46	
			2	1	6	21.86	
		4×100m relay	1	3	3	40.19	
			SF	2	4	39.70	
			F		5	39.50	
Zwolak, V.A.	USA	3000m steeplechase	1	1	4	8-43.6	

FEMALES

COMPETITOR	COUNTRY CODE	EVENT	ROUND	HEAT	PLACE	TIME & DISTANCE	MEDAL
Ahanotu, C.	NGR	100m	1	4	4	11.95	
			2	2	7	11.8	
Aigner, I.	AUT	100m	1	2	5	12.05	
			2	3	7	12.0	
		200m	1	2	4	24.77	
		80m hurdles	1	4	6	11.27	
Amoore, J.F.	AUS	400m	1	3	2	53.85	
			SF	2	1	53.39	
			F		3	53.4	B
Anderson, J.	DEN	800m	1	1	7	2-15.2	
Angelova, V.M.	BUL	Discus throw	F		4	56.70	
Anum, A.	GHA	Long jump	Q		DNQ	5.45	
Arden, D.	GBR	100m	1	1	2	11.55	
			2	4	2	11.5	
			SF	1	6	11.84	
		200m	1	6	2	24.21	
			SF	1	4	24.01	
			F		8	24.01	
		4×100m relay	1	1	2	44.96	
			F		3	44.09	B
Bair, R.J.	USA	Javelin throw	Q		DNQ	46.89	
Balas, I.	RUM	High jump	F		1	1.90*	G
Balzer, K.	GER	80m hurdles	1	1	1	10.71*	
			SF	2	1	10.65	
			F		1	10.54*	G
Barcenas, L.A.	PHI	4×100m relay	1	2	7	48.8	
Baskerville, E.	USA	High jump	Q		DNQ	1.65	
Becker, I.	GER	Long jump	F		4	6.40	
		Pentathlon	F		8	4717	
Bennett, J.E.	AUS	200m	1	1	3	24.34	
			SF	1	7	24.7	
		4×100m relay	1	1	4	45.28	
			F		6	45.0	
Berthelsen, B.	NOR	Long jump	F		9	6.19	
Biatmaku, F.-N.	IRN	High jump	Q		DNQ	0	
Bieda, J.	POL	High jump	F		10	1.71	
Bijleveld, J.C.A.	HOL	100m	1	4	6	12.35	
		Long jump	F		15	5.93	
Black, M.M.	AUS	100m	1	6	1	11.58	
			2	2	1	11.4	
			SF	1	2	11.63	
			F		6	11.73	
		200m	1	5	2	23.78	
			SF	2	1	23.42	
			F		3	23.18	B
		4×100m relay	1	1	4	45.28	
			F		6	45.0	
Boateng, C.A.	GHA	100m	1	5	8	12.9	
Bognar, J.	HUN	Shot put	F		11	15.65	
Bonds, R.	USA	80m hurdles	1	4	1	10.64*	
			SF	1	4	10.8	
			F		8	10.8	

COMPETITOR	COUNTRY CODE	EVENT	ROUND	HEAT	PLACE	TIME & DISTANCE	MEDAL
Bowering, D.M.	AUS	100m	1	1	4	11.83	
			2	3	5	11.7	
		4×100m relay	1	1	4	45.28	
			F		6	45.0	
Brown, E.D.	USA	Shot put	F		12	14.80	
Brown, M.M.	AUS	High jump	F		2	1.80	S
Brown, T.	USA	High jump	F		NP	0	
Brown, V.D.	USA	200m	1	4	3	24.17	
			SF	2	8	24.39	
Burvill, M.A.	AUS	100m	1	5	4	11.68	
			2	4	4	11.7	
			SF	2	8	11.85	
		200m	1	3	1	24.22	
			SF	1	5	24.3	
		4×100m relay	1	1	4	45.28	
			F		6	45.0	
Buscher, M.	GER	400m	1	2	2	55.32	
			SF	1	7	55.2	
Bystrova, G.	URS	80m hurdles	1	1	2	10.96	
			SF	2	6	10.89	
		Pentathlon	F		3	4956	B
Cadic, C.	FRA	100m	1	2	3	12.00	
			2	4	6	12.0	
Canguio, M.	FRA	80m hurdles	1	2	6	11.09	
		4×100m relay	1	2	4	46.0	
			F		8	46.1	
Catarama, O.	RUM	Discus throw	F		8	53.08	
Charanggool, S.	THA	400m	1	2	8	64.0	
		4×100m relay	1	2	8	50.3	
Charton, V.B.	JAM	4×100m relay	1	1	5	46.0	
Chamberlain, A.M.	NZL	800m	1	2	2	2-06.8	
			SF	2	1	2-04.6	
			F		3	2-02.8	B
Chenchik, T.	URS	High jump	F		3	1.78	B
Chi, Cheng	TAI	80m hurdles	1	2	7	11.18	
		Long jump	Q		DNQ	5.67	
		Pentathlon	F		17	4229	
Chuiko, A.	URS	Long jump	F		11	6.13	
Ciepla, T.B.	POL	80m hurdles	1	4	3	10.73	
			SF	1	2	10.77	
			F		2	10.55	S
		4×100m relay	1	1	1	44.62	
			F		1	43.69*	G
Cobb, V.M.	GBR	100m	1	6	6	12.01	
Cobian, M.	CUB	100m	1	6	2	11.67	
			2	3	3	11.5	
			SF	1	1	11.62	
			F		5	11.72	
		200m	1	2	1	23.89	
			SF	1		DIS	
Cuthbert, B.	AUS	400m	1	1	3	56.0	
			SF	1	2	53.8	
			F		1	52.01*	G
Daniel, M.	PAN	100m	1	2	6	12.60	
		200m	1	4	7	26.6	
		4×100m relay	1	1	6	47.6	
Dashzeveg, N.	MEL	Discus throw	Q		DNQ	44.55	
Dechdamrong, P.	THA	4×100m relay	1	2	8	50.3	
De La Vina, J.H.	PHI	Discus throw	Q		DNQ	42.27	
Demys, M.	FRA	Javelin throw	F		10	47.25	
Diaconescu, M.	ROM	Javelin throw	F		6	53.71	
Diel, E.	GER	80m hurdles	1	2	4	10.94	
			SF	1	7	11.05	
Dos Santos, A.	BRA	High jump	F		4	1.74	
D'Souza, S.	IND	400m	1	1	6	58.0	
Dunn, L.	PAN	80m hurdles	1	1	5	11.53	
		4×100m relay	1	1	6	47.6	
Dupureur, M.	FRA	800m	1	1	1	2-04.5	
			SF	1	1	2-04.1*	
			F		2	2-01.9	S
Erik, L.	URS	800m	1	3	3	2-08.3	
			SF	1	3	2-04.7	
			F		6	2-05.1	
Ezoe, R.	JPN	4×100m relay	1	2	6	47.0	
Farina, E.M.	ARG	4×100m relay	1	2	5	46.7	
		Long jump	Q		DNQ	5.57	
Farkas, G.	YUG	800m	1	3	4	2-08.7	
			SF	2	7	2-09.9	
Fikotova-Connolly, O.	USA	Discus throw	F		12	51.58	
Flegel, J.	AUT	High jump	F		NP	0	
		Pentathlon	F		20	3476	
Formeinc, M.M.	ARG	100m	1	6	7	12.20	
		4×100m relay	1	2	5	46.7	
Frisch, K.	GER	4×100m relay	1	2	2	45.01	
			F		5	44.7	

COMPETITOR	COUNTRY CODE	EVENT	ROUND	HEAT	PLACE	TIME & DISTANCE	MEDAL
Frith, H.A.R.	AUS	Long jump	Q		DNQ	5,83	
		Pentathlon	F		11	4557	
Gaida, G.	URS	100m	1	6	4	11·94	
			2	4	7	12·0	
		200m	1	3	3	24·45	
		4×100m relay	1	1	3	44·98	
			F		4	44·44	
Garisch-Culmberger, R.	GER	Shot put	F		2	17,61	S
Gerace, D.R.	CAN	High jump	F		5	1,71	
		Pentathlon	F		15	4445	
Gerhards, A.	GER	Javelin throw	F		8	52,37	
Geverkof, J.	IRN	Shot put	Q		DNQ	9,17	
		Discus throw	Q		DNQ	30,05	
Giron, E.E.	MEX	100m	1	5	6	12·21	
		200m	1	1	6	25·3	
Gleichfeld, A.	GER	800m	1	3	2	2-08·2	
			SF	1	2	2-04·6	
			F		5	2-03·9	
Gorchakova, E.	URS	Javelin throw	F		3	57,06	B
Gorecka, H.	POL	100m	1	5	2	11·56	
			2	3	2	11·5	
			SF	1	4	11·74	
			F		7	11·83	
		4×100m relay	1	1	1	44·62	
			F		1	43·69*	G
Grieveson, E.J.	GBR	400m	1	1	4	56·8	
			SF	1	5	54·8	
Grissom, J.J.	USA	Long jump	Q		DNQ	5,91	
Guenard, D.	FRA	4×100m relay	1	2	4	46·0	
			F		8	46·1	
		Pentathlon	F		12	4548	
Gueneau, D.	FRA	100m	1	3	3	12·02	
			2	2	6	11·8	
		4×100m relay	1	2	4	46·0	
			F		8	46·1	
Han, J.-H.	KOR	Long jump	Q		DNQ	5,45	
Han, M.-H.	KOR	400m	1	3	7	58·7	
		800m	1	3	8	2-22·7	
		4×100m relay	1	1	7	50·1	
Hansen, N.E.D.	DEN	Long jump	Q		DNQ	5,89	
		Pentathlon	F		9	4611	
Hart, R.	GHA	100m	1	1	5	11·98	
			2	3	6	11·9	
		80m hurdles	1	1	3	11·34	
			SF	2	8	11·16	
Heine, J.	GER	200m	1	5	DIS		
		4×100m relay	1	2	2	45·01	
			F		5	44·7	
Helmbold, M.	GER	Shotput	F		5	16·91	
Heldt, E.	HUN	100m	1	1	6	12·01	
		200m	1	1	5	24·90	
		4×100m relay	1	2	3	45·9	
			F		7	45·2	
Hinten, A.A.J.	HOL	Pentathlon	F		14	4466	
Hodson, M.	GBR	800m	1	2	1	2-08·5	
			SF	1	7	2-07·1	
Hoffman, A.	CAN	400m	1	2	7	55·98	
		800m	1	1	8	2-17·4	
Hoffmann, H.	GER	Long jump	F		8	6,23	
		Pentathlon	F		6	4737	
Hokland, O.H.	NOR	Long jump	F		16	5,68	
		Pentathlon	F		16	4429	
Huebner, J.	GER	Shot put	F		9	15,77	
Hyman, D.	GBR	100m	1	4	1	11·64	
			2	1	2	11·54	
			SF	2	4	11·66	
			F		8	11·90	
		200m	1	4	2	24·02	
			SF	2	5	23·95	
		4×100m relay	1	1	2	44·96	
			F		3	44·09	B
Inokuchi, T.	JPN	4×100m relay	1	2	6	47·0	
Itkina, M.	URS	400m	1	2	1	54·99	
			SF	2	2	53·50	
			F		5	54·6	
Izawa, M.	JPN	200m	1	6	5	25·4	
Jacob, H.	GER	100m	1	6	5	11·96	
			2	2	5	11·9	
		200m	1	3	2	24·23	
			SF	2	7	24·1	
Jamieson, L.A.	GBR	Long jump	F		17	5,65	
Jorgova, D.H.	BUL	Long jump	F		6	6,24	
Kaarna, L.K.	FIN	High jump	F		13	1,65	
Kaledene, B.	URS	Javelin throw	F		4	56,31	
Katayama, M.	JPN	Javelin throw	F		11	46,87	

COMPETITOR	COUNTRY CODE	EVENT	ROUND	HEAT	PLACE	TIME & DISTANCE	MEDAL
Kaufmanas, A.A.	ARG	4×100m relay	1	2	5	46·7	
		Long jump	Q		DNQ	5,29	
Kaufmann, W.	GER	800m	1	1	6	2-14·6	
Kazi, O.	HUN	400m	1	3	5	56·5	
		800m	1	3	6	2-12·1	
			SF		8	2-10·2	
Kerkova, S.A.	BUL	80m hurdles	1	1	4	11·50	
			SF	1	8	11·41	
Khristova, I.M.	BUL	Shot put	F		10	15,69	
Kilborn, P.	AUS	80m hurdles	1	3	2	10·79	
			SF	1	1	10·69	
			F		3	10·56	B
Kippax, P.A.	GBR	400m	1	2	6	55·57	
			SF		5	54·4	
Kirszenstein, I.	POL	200m	1	6	1	23·82	
			SF	1	2	23·62	
			F		2	23·13	S
		4×100m relay	1	1	1	44·62	
			F		1	43·69*	G
		Long jump	F		2	6,60	S
Kisaki, M.	JPN	800m	1	3	7	2-18·6	
Kishimoto, S.	JPN	Long jump	Q		DNQ	5,87	
Kispal, S.E.	HUN	Long jump	Q		DNQ	5,69	
Kitipongpitaya, P.	THA	Discus throw	Q		DNQ	38,73	
Kleiber, K.J.	HUN	Shot put	Q		DNQ	14,52	
		Discus throw	F		6	54,87	
Klobukowska, E.	POL	100m	1	3	1	11·45	
			2	4	1	11·4	
			SF	2	2	11·42	
			F		3	11·64	B
		4×100m relay	1	1	1	44·62	
			F		1	43·69*	G
Knott, S.P.	USA	800m	1	2	6	2-12·2	
Knowles, L.Y.	GBR	High jump	Q		DNQ	1,60	
Kostenko, G.	URS	High jump	Q		DNQ	1,65	
Koumaru, E.	JPN	Long jump	Q		DNQ	5,66	
Kraan, G.M.	HOL	800m	1	2	4	2-09·8	
			SF	2	4	2-06·2	
			F		7	2-05·8	
Kupferschmied, G.	GER	High jump	F		12	1,68	
Kuznetsova, E.	URS	Discus throw	F		5	55,17	
Kyle, M.E.E.	IRL	400m	1	2	4	55·42	
			SF	2	7	55·3	
		800m	1	2	5	2-11·3	
			SF	2	8	2-12·9	
Lace, R.	URS	100m	1	1	3	11·70	
			2	2	3	11·6	
			SF	2	6	11·76	
		4×100m relay	1	1	3	44·98	
			F		4	44·44	
Lagrosas, L.R.	PHI	High jump	Q		DNQ	1,55	
		Long jump	Q		DNQ	5,52	
Lamdani, M.	ISR	High jump	Q		DNQ	1,65	
Langer, D.	GER	High jump	Q		DNQ	0	
Laufer, H.	GER	Long jump	F		7	6,24	
		Pentathlon	F		DNF		
Lebret, E.	FRA	400m	1	3	3	54·8	
			SF	1	4	54·5	
			F		8	55·5	
Lee, Hak-Ja	KOR	4×100m relay	1	1	7	50·1	
		Pentathlon	F		19	3649	
Lee, He-Ja	KOR	Javelin throw	Q		DNQ	34,95	
Leenasen, T.	THA	High jump	Q		DNQ	0	
Lehocka, E.	TCH	100m	1	6	3	11·89	
			2	4	3	11·6	
			SF	1	7	11·91	
		200m	1	1	2	24·30	
			SF	1	6	24·5	
Limberg, K.	GER	Discus throw	F		7	53,81	
Lorenz, D.	GER	Discus throw	F		14	45,63	
Lotz, I.	GER	Discus throw	F		2	57,21	S
Lurot, M.	FRA	100m	1	1	4	24·75	
		4×100m relay	1	2	4	46·0	
			F		8	46·1	
McCredie, N.C.	CAN	Shot put	F		7	15,89	
		Discus throw	Q		DNQ	47,27	
McGuire, E.M.	USA	100m	1	2	1	11·47	
			2	3	1	11·4	
			SF	1	3	11·67	
			F		2	11·62	S
		200m	1	5	1	23·47	
			SF	1	1	23·37	
			F		1	23·05*	G
		4×100m relay	1	2	1	44·83	
			F		2	43·92	S

COMPETITOR	COUNTRY CODE	EVENT	ROUND	HEAT	PLACE	TIME & DISTANCE	MEDAL
McIntosh, A.	NZL	100m	1	3	4	12·06	
			2	1	6	12·06	
		80m hurdles	1	2	5	10·84	
			SF	1	5	10·90	
Mair, A.V.	JAM	200m	1	4	5	25·0	
		4×100m relay	1	1	5	46·0	
Maisack, E.	GER	400m	1	1	*7	58·6	
Manoliu, L.	RUM	Discus throw	F		3	56·57	B
Matthews, G.M.	GBR	High jump	Q		DNQ	1·65	
Meyer, R.	GER	100m	1	2	4	12·01	
			2	3	8	12·7	
Mitchell, J.	PAN	4×100m relay	1	1	6	47·6	
Miyamoto, E.	JPN	4×100m relay	1	2	6	47·0	
Molinos, A.D.	PHI	4×100m relay	1	2	7	48·8	
Montgomery, E.I.	USA	High jump	F		8	1·71	
Morris, U.L.	JAM	200m	1	5	3	24·24	
			SF	2	3	23·7	
			F		4	23·5	
		400m	1	2	3	55·39	
			SF	1	6	54·9	
		4×100m relay	1	1	5	46·0	
Mukhanova, V.	URS	800m	1	1	4	2-08·3	
			SF	1	5	2-04·8	
Munkacsi, A.	HUN	400m	1	1	1	54·42*	
			SF	1	3	54·0	
			F		4	54·4	
		4×100m relay	1	2	3	45·9	
			F		7	45·2	
Musani, M.	ITA	80m hurdles	1	4	5	12·9	
Muyanga, I.P.M.	UGA	100m	1	4	5	12·05	
			2	1	7	12·24	
		200m	1	3	5	27·6	
Nemcova, J.	TCH	Discus throw	F		9	52·80	
Nemeshazi, M.	HUN	100m	1	3	2	11·73	
			2	3	4	11·5	
			SF	2	7	11·77	
		4×100m relay	1	2	3	45·9	
			F		7	45·2	
Norrlund, S.M.	FIN	80m hurdles	1	2	8	11·23	
Oakley, D.L.	PAN	100m	1	4	7	12·38	
		200m	1	6	6	26·2	
		4×100m relay	1	-	6	47·6	
Obonai, S.	JPN	Shot put	Q		DNQ	13·70	
Ogawa, K.	JPN	400m	1	1	5	57·6	
			SF	1	8	57·1	
Okoli, A.	NGR	High jump	Q		DNQ	1·65	
O'Neal, L.	USA	80m hurdles	1	3	4	10·93	
			SF	2	7	10·99	
Ozolina, E.	URS	Javelin throw	F		5	54·81	
Packer, A.E.	GBR	400m	1	3	1	53·18*	
			SF	1	1	52·77*	
			F		2	52·20	S
		800m	1	1	5	2-12·6	
			SF	2	3	2-06·0	
			F		1	2-01·1*	G
Park, H.-S.	KOR	4×100m relay	1	1	7	50·1	
Park, Y.-S.	KOR	Discus throw	Q		DNQ	37·50	
Parkin, S.	GBR	Long jump	F		13	6·04	
Pazera, A.	AUS	Javelin throw	Q		DNQ	44·87	
Penes, M.	RUM	Javelin throw	F		1	60·54	G
Pensberger, M.	GER	4×100m relay	1	2	2	45·01	
			F		5	44·7	
Peters, M.E.	GBR	Shot put	Q		DNQ	14·46	
		Pentathlon	F		4	4797	
Piatkowska, M.	POL	80m hurdles	1	3	1	10·67*	
			SF	2	4	10·75	
			F		6	10·76	
Piotrowski, I.M.	CAN	100m	1	5	3	11·59	
			2	1	4	11·63	
			SF	2	5	11·74	
		200m	1	2	3	24·47	
Platt, S.M.	GBR	Javelin throw	F		9	48·59	
Pollmann, E.	GER	100m	1	3	DIS		
		200m	1	6	4	24·44	
		4×100m relay	1	2	2	45·01	
			F		5	44·7	
Popova, G.	URS	100m	1	4	3	11·82	
			2	1	3	11·54	
			SF	1	5	11·83	
		4×100m relay	1	1	3	44·98	
			F		4	44·44	
Porter, D.H.	NZL	100m	1	4	2	11·77	
			2	4	5	11·8	
		200m	1	6	3	24·24	
			SF	2	6	24·03	
Press, I.	URS	80m hurdles	1	2	1	10·77	
			SF	1	3	10·85	
			F		4	10·62	
		Shot put	F		6	16·71	
		Pentathlon	F		1	5246*	G
Press, T.	URS	Shot put	F		1	18·14*	G
		Discus throw	F		1	57·27*	G
Pryce, P.A.	GBR	80m hurdles	1	2	2	10·82	
			SF	2	5	10·75	
Pulis, O.	YUG	High jump	F		7	1·71	
Rajamani, M.	MAL	400m	1	3	6	57·8	
Ramazan, A.	MGL	400m	1	1	8	60·8	
		800m	1	2	7	2-21·1	
Rand, M.D.	GER	4×100m relay	1	1	2	44·96	
			F		3	44·09	B
		Long jump	F		1	6·76*	G
		Pentathlon	F		2	5035	S
Restar, N.R.	PHI	4×100m relay	1	2	7	48·8	
Ritchie, S.I.	ARG	200m	1	2	5	24·79	
		4×100m relay	1	2	5	46·7	
Romashkova-Ponomaryeva, N	URS	Discus throw	F		11	52·48	
Rudas, A.M.	HUN	Javelin throw	F		2	58·27	S
Ruger, K.	GER	High jump	F		9	1·71	
Safa-Mehr, S.	RN	100m	1	2	7	13·2	
		Long jump	Q		DNQ	5·06	
Salagean, A.	RUM	Shot put	F		8	15·83	
Samotesova, L.	URS	200m	1	4	1	23·86	
			SF	2	2	23·74	
			F		5	23·59	
		4×100m relay	1	1	3	44·98	
			F		4	44·44	
Sato, H.	JPN	Javelin throw	F		7	52·48	
Schelkanova, T.	URS	Long jump	F		3	6·42	B
Schmidt, G.	GER	400m	1	3	4	55·1	
			SF	2	4	54·2	
			F		7	55·4	
Schubert, R.	GER	Javelin throw	F		12	46·50	
Schwalbe, I.	GER	Javelin throw	Q		DNQ	45·55	
Sherrard, C.	USA	80m hurdles	1	2	5	11·00	
Simpson, J.M.	GBR	200m	1	1	1	24·06	
			SF	1	3	23·75	
			F		7	23·98	
		4×100m relay	1	1	2	44·96	
			F		3	44·09	B
Siziakova, M.	URS	Pentathlon	F		10	4580	
Skobtsova, Z.	URS	800m	1	2	3	2-08·6	
			SF	2	6	2-07·4	
Slaap, F.	GBR	High jump	F		6	1·71	
Smith, A.R.	GBR	800m	1	3	1	2-08·0	
			SF	1	4	2-04·8	
			F		8	2-05·8	
Smith, C.L.	JAM	100m	1	5	5	11·79	
			2	2	4	11·7	
			SF	1	8	11·99	
		80m hurdles	1	3	5	11·8	
		4×100m relay	1	1	5	46·0	
Smith, J.L.	USA	400m	1	2	5	55·56	
			SF	2	6	54·5	
Snider, A.M.	CAN	80m hurdles	1	1	DIS		
Sobotta, B.	POL	100m	1	2	2	11·89	
			2	2	5	11·84	
		200m	1	2	2	24·19	
			SF	2	4	23·78	
			F		6	23·97	
Song, Yang-Ja	KOR	100m	1	6	8	12·7	
		200m	1	5	5	26·5	
		4×100m relay	1	1	7	50·1	
Soraja, K.	THA	100m	1	5	7	12·6	
		200m	1	4	6	26·1	
		4×100m relay	1	2	8	50·3	
Stamejcic, D.	YUG	80m hurdles	1	4	4	10·84	
			SF	2	3	10·73	
			F		7	10·86	
		Pentathlon	F		5	4790	
Stugner, J.	HUN	Discus throw	F		10	52·52	
Such, I.	HUN	4×100m relay	1	2	3	45·9	
			F		7	45·2	
Sulaiman, M.	PHI	100m	1	1	7	12·01	
		200m	1	5	4	25·4	
		4×100m relay	1	2	7	48·8	
Sydranski, L.M.	ISR	100m	1	3	6	12·16	
		200m	1	4	4	24·68	
Sykora, L.	AUT	High jump	Q		DNQ	1·65	
Szabo, Z.	HUN	800m	1	1	3	2-07·7	
			SF	2	2	2-05·1	
			F		4	2-03·5	

COMPETITOR	COUNTRY CODE	EVENT	ROUND	HEAT	PLACE	TIME & DISTANCE	MEDAL
Takahashi, M.	JPN	Pentathlon	F		18	3914	
Talysheva, T.	URS	80m hurdles	1	3	3	10·92	
			SF	1	6	10·98	
		Long jump	F		10	6,18	
Thompson, D.A.	USA	200m	1	3	4	24·62	
Torii, M.	JPN	High jump	Q		DNQ	1,60	
Trio, M.V.	ITA	Long jump	F		14	5,98	
Tyus, W.	USA	100m	1	5	1	11·35	
			2	1	1	11·23*	
			SF	2	1	11·40	
			F		1	11·49	G
		4×100m relay	1	2	1	44·83	
			F		2	43·92	S
Van Der Zwaard, M.C.	HOL	400m	1	1	2	54·86	
			SF	2	3	54·19	
			F		6	55·2	
Van Eyck-Vos, J.	HOL	300m	1	3	5	2-09·1	
			SF	1	6	2-05·7	
Viscopoleanu, V.	RUM	Long jump	F		5	6,35	
Watson, M.R.	USA	Long jump	Q		DNQ	5,94	
White, M.E.	USA	100m	1	1	1	11·50	
			2	2	2	11·5	
			SF	2	3	11·51	
			F		4	11·67	
		4×100m relay	1	2	1	44·83	
			F		2	43·92	S

COMPETITOR	COUNTRY CODE	EVENT	ROUND	HEAT	PLACE	TIME & DISTANCE	MEDAL
White, W.B.	USA	4×100m relay	1	2	1	44·83	
			F		2	43·92	S
		Long jump	F		12	6,07	
Weislander, U.-B.	SWE	100m	1	3	5	12·10	
			2	2	8	11·9	
Wingerson, J.A.	CAN	80m hurdles	1	4	5	11·16	
		Pentathlon	F		13	4514	
Winslow, B.P.	USA	Pentathlon	F		7	4724	
Woodhouse, R.	AUS	High jump	F		11	1,71	
Worner, A.	GER	800m	1	2	2	2-08·6	
			SF	2	5	2-07·1	
Yeh, Chu-Mei.	TAI	200m	1	6	7	27·1	
		80m hurdles	1	3	6	12·1	
Yimploy, B.	THA	4×100m relay	1	2	8	50·3	
Yoda, I.	JPN	80m hurdles	1	4	2	10·71	
			SF	2	2	10·72	
			F		5	10·72	
		4×100m relay	1	2	6	47·0	
Yokoyama, M.	JPN	Discus throw	Q		DNQ	47,18	
Young, I.M.	NZL	Shot put	F		4	17,26	
		Discus throw	F		13	49·59	
Zybina, G.	URS	Shot put	F		3	17,45	B

Peter Snell of New Zealand, comes home for the 800 metres gold medal, ahead of Bill Crothers (57), Wilson Kiprugut (386) and George Kerr (375).

Mark Shearman

1968

Bob Beamon Leaps into the Record Books

Mexico City was a controversial choice for the 1968 Olympics because of the unknown effects of the altitude of 2,240 metres above sea-level. Just before the Games were due to be held, students at the University of Mexico began riots which were ruthlessly put down by the police and army, many dying and being injured in Mexico City itself.

After Enriqueta Basilio had become the first woman to light the Olympic flame, the altitude queries were answered. Distance runners, particularly those who had not trained at altitude, suffered severe distress. Ron Clarke, one of the greatest runners not to win a gold medal, collapsed and was unconscious for ten minutes after finishing sixth in the 10,000 metres, where he was beaten by five runners from higher altitudes.

In the explosive events, on the other hand, the thin air helped, and Bob Beamon produced a long jump world record so far in advance of anything done before, that some predicted it would last 100 years.

Men's Track Events

The **100 metres** times were most decidedly affected by the high altitude of Mexico City as sprinters consistently ran a tenth of a second faster than they had under normal conditions. In the first semi-final, Jim Hines of the USA won in 10·0 sec from Roger Bambuck of France, while his great rival and compatriot, Charlie Greene, triumphed in the second with 10·1 over Lennox Miller of Jamaica. After one false start in the final, the 5ft 5in Mel Pender of the USA was immediately ahead with Hines, Miller and Greene in a line just behind. At 50 metres these four were abreast, but Hines flowed away to win by a metre in 9·9 and equal the world record. Greene tied up in the latter stages and Miller was second in 10·0, a mere fraction up on Greene in third. (Automatic timings: Hines 9·95, Miller 10·04 and Greene 10·07).

Altitude also played its part in the **200 metres**. A pre-Olympic meeting at altitude had seen the American John Carlos run a fantastic 19·7 sec, but the record had been disallowed because he had worn the new brush spikes which consisted of 68 tiny needles in the sole of each shoe. Americans Carlos and Tommie Smith, the world record holder, were tipped as Olympic victors, and won their respective semi-finals in 20·1, well inside the Olympic record. From the gun in the final, it was Carlos who shot around the bend at amazing speed and was up on Smith coming off the curve. But the long striding Smith swept past Carlos with 30 metres left and raising his arms above his head, won in 19·8 for a new world record. Carlos was demoralised and eased off, allowing a fast finishing Peter Norman of Australia to pip him for second place, both clocking 20·0. (Automatic timings: Smith 19·83, Norman 20·06 and Carlos 20·10).

Even more than in the two shorter sprints, the rarefied air affected the times of the **400 metres**. Running at altitude in illegal spikes before the Games, the American Lee Evans had clocked 44·0 sec, while his compatriot, Larry James, did 44·1 in regular footwear. Heat times were unprecedented with the slowest being won in 46·6 and in the semi-finals Evans ran 44·8 to break the Olympic record. Evans, in lane six, started fast in the final and had made up two staggers by 200 metres. He then poured it on around the final bend and was four metres up on James entering the finishing straight with America's Ron Freeman a similar distance behind. The smooth-flowing James slowly began catching his teammate, but could not quite make it as Evans hit the tape in a mind boggling 43·8 for the gold and world record. James was only just behind in 43·9, while Freeman took the bronze in 44·4. (Automatic timings: Evans 43·86, James 43·97 and Freeman 44·41).

The favourite for the **800 metres** was Wilson Kiprugut, who came from high altitude Kenya. Walter Adams of West Germany won the first semi-final in 1-46·4 from East Germany's Dieter Fromm, while Ralph Doubell of Australia beat Kiprugut in 1-45·7 to 1-45·8 in the second. The final was a straightforward race with Kiprugut racing into the lead and passing the 400m in 51·0, while Doubell stayed a little off the pace with the field grouped behind him. Kiprugut was still forcing at 600m, but Doubell kicked in the straight and passed him with 40 metres remaining to win, and equal the world record, in a time of 1-44·3. Kiprugut finished in 1-44·5 for the silver and Tom Farrell of the USA beat off the chasing group to take the bronze in 1-45·4. (Automatic timings: Doubell 1-44·40, Kiprugut 1-44·57 and Farrell 1-45·46).

Jim Ryun of the USA was the world record holder in the **1,500 metres**, but the altitiude man Kip Keino of Kenya was considered the better bet for the title. In the heats the runners were cautious and times were slow. Ben Jipcho of Kenya, however, cut out a terrific pace in the final and ran the 400 in 56·0 with Keino second and the field strung out behind. Keino then led at 800 in 1-55·3, followed by Boco Tuemmler and Harold Norpoth, both of West Germany, Britain's John Whetton and Ryun. The order was the same at the bell, reached in 2-39·0. with Ryun 2·6 sec adrift. But the Kenyan kept going and although the American raced to the head of the chasing group with Tuemmler in pursuit, he had left it far too late, and Keino won in 3-34·9, an Olympic record. Ryun was second in 3-37·8 and Tuemmler third in 3-39·0. (Automatic timings: Keino 3-34·91, Ryun 3-37·89 and Tuemmler 3-39·08).

Kip Keino was also favoured to win the **5,000 metres** with the main opposition coming from his fellow Kenyan Naftali Temu and world record holder Ron Clarke of Australia. Thirteen ran in the final where Clarke set an early moderate pace, before Keino went to the front at

2km and slowed it further. Nikolai Sviridov of the USSR was not having this, and took up the lead, passing 3km in 8-38·2. Just before 4km, Clarke speeded the pace up a little, but with 600 to go Mohamed Gammoudi of Tunisia took command and sprinted the final lap in 60·2 to win in 14-05·0. Keino chased him home in 14-05·2 for the silver and Temu was third with a time of 14-06·4. (Automatic timings: Gammoudi 14-05·01, Keino 14-05·16 and Temu 14-06·41).

As predicted, the **10,000 metres** turned out to be a slow race, with 37 competing in a straight final that saw the lead change 13 times. Juan Martinez of Mexico led for five laps, but after the halfway mark, Mamo Wolde of Ethiopia injected some pace, taking with him Naftali Temu of Kenya, Mohamed Gammoudi of Tunisia and Ron Clarke of Australia. At the bell Wolde sprinted away followed by Temu, while Clarke virtually gave up. Temu then made a determined sprint with 50 metres to go, and won in 29-27·4 from Wolde in 29-28·0. Meanwhile, Gammoudi was holding off a fast finishing Martinez to take the bronze in 29-34·2. (Automatic timings: Temu 29-27·40 and Wolde 29-27·15).

At altitude, everyone feared the **marathon**, but the rarefied air had less effect in this competition than in the middle-distance events. The race commenced at an easy pace and at 20km Tim Johnston of Britain and Gaston Roelants of Belgium were together in 66-02·0, with 11 others also close at hand. But by 30km, Mamo Wolde of Ethiopia had a 65 sec lead over Japan's Kenji Kimihara, with a group of four in third spot: Mike Ryan of New Zealand, Ismail Akcay of Turkey, Johnston and Ethiopia's Merawai Gebrou. At 40km, the top nine runners were running in their eventual finishing positions and Wolde stretched his lead to win the gold in 2:20-26·4 with Kimihara tottering in for the silver in 2:23-31·0 and Ryan the bronze in 2:23-45·0.

All the heats of the **110 metres hurdles** were run in fast times with Eddy Ottoz of Italy equalling the Olympic record of 13·5 sec. Erv Hall of the USA won the first semi-final in a new Games record of 13·3, while in the second Willie Davenport of the USA was first in 13·5. Davenport was keyed up for the final and he was out of his blocks like the shot of a gun, while Ottoz got off poorly. Hall could never get on even terms with his great rival, but Ottoz finally came good and caught Leon

Aided by altitude, the American Bill Toomey, produced a set of fine sprint times to win the decathlon.   Mark Shearman

Coleman of the USA as he brushed his sixth hurdle. Davenport won in 13·3 to equal the Olympic record and Hall was second, but was nearly beaten by Ottoz's dive for the finish, both being timed at 13·4. (Automatic timings: Davenport 13·33, Hall 13·42 and Ottoz 13·46).

Geoff Vanderstock had recently broken the **400 metres hurdles** world record with 48·8 sec and the heats were fast as Ron Whitney of the USA broke the Olympic record with 49·0 in the third race. In the final, Reiner Schubert of Germany and David Hemery of Great Britain rose to the first barrier together. Hemery, in lane

Mark Shearman

Willie Davenport

Of the 21 Olympic 110m hurdles finals raced since the start of the Modern Olympic Games in 1896 only on four occasions have the Americans failed to collect the gold medal, such is the ever high standard of high hurdling in the States. And it was never more difficult to get into the United States team than in 1968, when 19 of the world's best 25 for the event were American born.

Among that number was Willie Davenport, who was born in May 1943 in Warren, Ohio, and who had been kept out of the Tokyo final because of a leg injury. He had recovered well to rekindle a hope that perhaps Mexico City would provide him with the opportunity to win a place on that victor's rostrum. Then injury struck again, but not for long, and by the time the American trials were due, Davenport was as sharp as a needle again and won convincingly to be the US first string for Mexico.

This time he was on the mark for the final and away to a brilliant start from which he was never caught. The long-awaited gold was his, and the Olympic record also at 13·3 sec.

He received tempting offers to become an American footballer, but declined them all until after he had brought the world record down to 13·2 sec in 1969.

six, passed Whitney in lane seven to clock an unprecedented 23·0 at the half-way stage, and came off the bend five metres ahead of Vanderstock and Roberto Frinolli of Italy. He continued to stride majestically over the barriers and won in the outstanding time of 48·1 for a new world record. Behind, there was a fierce struggle as Frinolli faded and Whitney made a gallant attempt to get among the medals. At the tape there were five in a line and it took a photo-finish to award Gerhard Hennige of West Germany the silver and John Sherwood of Britain the bronze, both in 49·0. (Automatic timings: Hemery 48·12, Hennige 49·02 and Sherwood 49·03).

Nobody wanted to lead in the final of the **3,000 metres steeplechase** until the fifth lap when Gaston Roelants of Belgium injected some pace, passing 2km in 6-03·2. He was followed by Ben Kogo of Kenya, Bulgaria's Mikhail Zhelev, Russia's Alex Morozov, Kerry O'Brien of Australia and George Young of America. It was Kogo who hit the bell first, with Amos Biwott of Kenya, who always took the water jump without getting his feet wet, at the tail end of the leading six. Young then made his move and was chased by O'Brien, before Kogo went to the front and looked every inch the winner. This was until Biwott appeared from nowhere to win the gold in 8-51·0 to Kogo's 8-51·6, with Young third at 8-51·8. (Automatic timings: Biwott 8-51·02, Kogo 8-51·56 and Young 8-51·86).

Russia, whose big two were Nikolai Smaga and the 1960 Olympic champion, Vladimir Golubnichy, were favoured for a double in the **20 kilometres walk**. Soon after 5km Golubnichy and Smaga forced the pace and they passed 10km in 46-54 with a group of five trying to hang on. The two leaders were timed at 1:10-19 for 15km, with Rudolph Haluza of the USA third 23 seconds down and Mexico's Jose Pedraza fourth. Golubnichy came into the stadium five seconds in front of Smaga with Pedraza a similar distance adrift. The Mexican, to the applause of the crowd, quickly overtook the second Russian but could not quite reach Golubnichy, who won in 1:33-58·4 to Pedraza's 1:34-00·0 and Smaga's 1:34-03·4.

There was a leading group of 13 at 5km in the **50 kilometres walk**, led by Paul Nihill of Britain. This was reduced to six at 15km and four at 20km: Christoph Hoehne of East Germany, Nihill, and Russia's Gennadiy Agapov and Sergei Grigoryev. After 25km Nihill faded, and Hoehne went on to win in 4:20-13·6. Antil Kiss of Hungary assumed second position when Nihill dropped out at 40km and took the silver in 4:30-17·0, while Larry Young of the USA moved into third spot over the last 10km to finish in 4:31-55·4.

In the **4 × 100 metres relay**, nine teams beat the previous Olympic record of 39·0 sec, due to the fast conditions. Cuba did it first in heat one of the preliminaries with 38·7, which was improved by Jamaica in heat two at 38·6, to equal the world record, and again in the first semi-final with 38·3 to beat it. The final was very close over the first three legs between the USA, Cuba, France, Jamaica and East Germany. At the final exchange, Cuba were leading nearly a metre up on East

A ding-dong struggle ensued in the closing stages of the women's 400 metres, culminating in Colette Besson snatching the gold medal for France from Britain's favourite girl, Lillian Board.

Mark Shearman

Germany, with the USA nearly two metres down and France and Jamaica, who did some bad passing, just behind. Then, amid great excitement, Jim Hines tore through the field and clocked up a win in world record time for the USA of 38·2. Cuba were second in 38·3 and France just edged out Jamaica for the bronze, both recording 38·4. The US team was Charlie Greene, Mel Pender, Ron Smith and Jim Hines. (Automatic timings: USA 38·24, Cuba 38·40 and France 38·43).

The **4 × 400 metres relay** was also the scene of some dramatic competition and record breaking, as the USA set a new Olympic record in the heats with 3-00·7 over Kenya in 3-00·8. Kenya took the lead in the first leg of the final, with Daniel Rudisha running 44·6 to America's Vince Matthew's 45·0, but Ron Freeman put the USA back in the lead on the next stage with a fantastic 43·2. Larry James then extended the gap by running 43·8, and Lee Evans motored the anchor leg in 44·1, giving 2-56·1, for the gold medal and a superlative world record. Kenya also dipped under the magic three minutes with 2-59·6 while West Germany were third in 3-00·5, but nearly lost out on the line. (Automatic timings: 2-56·16, Kenya 2-59·64 and West Germany 3-00·57).

Men's Field Events

Each time Dick Fosbury of the USA prepared for the **high jump**, there was a buzz of anticipation. Fosbury had invented a new form of jumping that involved arching over the bar on his back, which became known as the "Fosbury flop". At 2,14 metres in the final, seven cleared, but at 2,18 both the USA's Reynaldo Brown, who had passed the previous height, and Valeriy Skvortsov of the USSR failed, placing them fifth and fourth respectively. Fosbury cleared first time to equal the Olympic record, while Ed Caruthers of the USA needed three attempts and Valentin Gavrilov of the USSR passed. The bar was now at 2,20 and all succeeded, but only Fosbury made it first time at 2,22, while Caruthers needed two jumps and Gavrilov failed, taking the bronze position. At 2,24 Fosbury flopped over on his third attempt and the gold was his with the silver going to Caruthers. Fosbury tried for a new world record of 2,29, but was unsuccessful.

Eleven vaulters exceeded the Olympic **pole vault** record of 5,10 metres, but only five remained at 5,40, a fraction below Bob Seagren's world record. All five failed on their first try, but Seagren of the USA and Claus Schiprowski of West Germany made it on their next attempts and East Germany's Wolfgang Nordwig did it on his third. The two who failed were Chris Papanicolau of Greece who was placed fourth and the USA's John Pennel, a previous world record holder, fifth. At the world record height of 5,45 all had near misses. The count-back scorecard revealed that Seagren had won the gold, Schiprowski the silver and Nordwig the bronze.

Ralph Boston, the champion of 1960 in the **long jump**, fully expected to regain his title, and Lynn Davies, the defending champion, had similar hopes, but a drama awaited them both. In the qualifying rounds things looked good for Boston with an Olympic record of 8,27 metres, while his fellow-American Bob Beamon was having trouble with his run-up and fouled twice. Beamon's third jump yielded a mighty 8,19. The first round of the finals saw the first three jumpers foul. It was now Beamon's turn to go and the uninhibited jumper sped down the run-way and launched himself

Mamo Wolde made it three marathons in a row for Ethiopia when he picked up the mantle from the great Abebe Bikila. Mark Shearman

into space beyond 27 feet, beyond 28 and even beyond 29 feet to land at 8,90 metres (29ft 2½in) for a new world record. The rest of the competition was an anticlimax, but Klaus Beer of East Germany jumped a life-time best to take the silver at 8,19 and Boston reached 8,16 to take the bronze.

As with the long jump, the thin air did wonders for the **triple jump**, with five men exceeding the old world record. In the preliminaries, Giuseppe Gentile of Italy bounded out to 17,10 metres for a new world best and in the competition proper he improved on this in the first round to 17,22. Second at this stage was the USSR's Victor Saneyev with 16,49. In the next round Nelson Prudencio of Brazil joined the 17-metre club with 17,05, while Saneyev improved to 16,84. On his very next trial Saneyev went into the lead with 17,23 and consolidated this in the last round with a winning jump of 17,39. Prudencio took the silver with a fifth round 17,27 and Gentile the bronze with his 17,22.

The **shot put** went as predicted with the world record holder, Randy Matson of the USA, breaking the Olympic record in the preliminaries with 20,68 metres. In the final rounds he won with his very first put of 20,54. Strangely, eight of the 12 finalists produced their best throws with their very first put, including all the medal winners. The USA's George Woods was second with 20,12 and Eduard Gushchin of the USSR third with

The fastest one lap sprinter ever, Lee Evans of America, surges towards the finishing line to win.

Mark Shearman

20,09, a little short of his European record.

It was inconceivable that the three-time Olympic **discus throw**ing champion could win a fourth time but that is exactly what he did. Jay Silvester of the USA, the world record holder, was the favourite and he looked good in the qualifying round, throwing 63,34 metres for an Olympic record. Al Oerter of the USA, the three-times champion, opened steadily with 61,78 but in the third round spun his discus into the atmosphere to land at the Olympic record distance of 64,78 to win the competition. East Germany's Lothar Milde commenced well with 62,44 and on his next throw attained 63,08 for the silver medal. Ludvik Danek needed three tries to reach 62,92 for the bronze position, while Silvester could only finish fifth with 61,78.

In the **hammer throw** Romuald Klim of the USSR, the defending Olympic champion, and Hungary's Gyula Zsivotzky, the latest world record holder, were the favourites. Zsivotzky let rip in the qualifying rounds with a new Olympic record of 72,60 metres and in the very first round of the competition proper backed this up with 72,26 to Klim's 72,24. In the next round Zsivotzky threw 72,46 and then 72,54, but Klim came back at him with 72,82, while Lazar Lovasz of Hungary did 69,78, which ultimately won him the bronze medal. In the fourth round Klim extended his lead to 73,28, but in the fifth Zsivotzky sent the ball and wire to 73,36 for the gold medal and Olympic record, with Klim taking the silver.

Mark Shearman

Wyomia Tyus

Born in Griffin, Georgia, on 29 August 1948, Wyomia Tyus was one of the famous "Tennessee Tigerbelles" developed at the Tennessee State University. And to this day she is the only person to have won an Olympic 100m final twice.

Tyus was inspired to become a sprinter when as a 15-year-old she saw the televised pictures of Wilma Rudolph winning three gold medals in Rome. By the time the Tokyo Games were due in 1964, she had progressed so well that she merited her selection for the American team as a 100m sprinter. So sharp had become her pace that not even a strong headwind could stop her winning the title in 11·4 sec.

Confirmation of her supremacy in women's sprinting was soon forthcoming in the summer of 1965, when she equalled the world record for 100 yards (10·3 sec) and 100m (11·1 sec) in the space of a fortnight. But her crowning performance came in the 100m final at the 1968 Games in Mexico City. There she sped the course in a new world record of 11·0 sec flat. And another gold medal was rewarded for more outstanding sprinting over the final leg of the 4 × 100m relay in which the American team reduced the world record to 42·8 sec.

Janis Lusis of the USSR was a prolific **javelin throw**er and held the world record at 91,98 metres. The Finns, with their long tradition in the event, pinned their hopes on Jorma Kinnunen, who opened his account with 86,30 to lead from Ake Nilsson of Sweden on 83,48. Lusis took the lead in the next round with 86,34, before Gergely Kulcsar of Hungary produced 87,06 with his fourth trial, which eventually won him the bronze medal. The two big throws came in the last round, as Lusis whipped his javelin above the heads of the vast crowd to 90,10 for the gold medal and Olympic record, inspiring Kinnunen to throw 88,58 for the silver.

Bill Toomey of the USA had set his heart on winning a gold in the **decathlon**, but he was up against Kurt Bendlin of West Germany, the world record holder. Toomey had a brilliant first day and ran the fastest 100m in 10·4 sec, jumped furthest with 7,87m and ran an unbelievable 45·6 sec for the 400m. His first day total was 4,499 points, with his nearest rival, Joachim Kirst of East Germany, on 4,384 and Hans-Joachim Walde of West Germany, on 4,299. Toomey's second day was weaker and his rivals closed up event by event until with only the 1,500m to go Walde just needed a 14-second advantage to win, while Bendlin required 12. Toomey made sure of the outcome in the rarefied air of Mexico City by running 4-57·1 to beat both his rivals. Result: Toomey 8,193 points, a new Olympic record, for gold, Walde 8,111 for silver and Bendlin 8,064 for bronze.

Women's Events

Wyomia Tyus of the USA was favoured to retain her title in the **100 metres**, but she had up against her an array of formidable sprinters in Lyudmila Samotyesova of the USSR, Margaret Bailes of the USA, Irena Szewinska of Poland and Barbara Ferrell of the USA, all of whom had run a world record 11·1. In the second round both Ferrell and Szewinska equalled the world record, and the scene was set for a great final. Tyus and Ferrell were both charged with false starts, but, at the third attempt, were the fastest to leave the blocks, with Szewinska the slowest. Tyus powered the course and won in a new world record of 11·0. Ferrell could not hold her, finishing abreast with Raelene Boyle of Australia and the fast-finishing Szewinska. The photo showed

Ferrell to have won the silver, and Szewinska the bronze, with Boyle fourth, all in 11·1. (Automatic timings: Tyus 11·08, Ferrell 11·15 and Szewinska 11·19).

The **200 metres** world record holder, Irena Szewinska of Poland, was firm favourite to win as, on paper, her opponents were several metres slower. In heat one Raelene Boyle of Australia equalled the Olympic record of 23·0 sec and in the next race Barbara Ferrell broke the record with 22·9. The semi-finals saw Boyle run 22·9 in the first and Ferrell and Australia's Jenny Lamy 22·8 in the second. In the final, Wyomia Tyus of the USA got an excellent start and ran a good bend to lead by a metre into the straight over Ferrell, with Boyle and Szewinska just behind. With 75m to go, Boyle went past Tyus but was in turn overtaken by Szewinska, who went on to win in 22·5 for the gold and a new world record. Boyle was second in 22·7, while Lamy came strong in the straight and took third with 22·8. (Automatic timings: Szewinska 22·58, Boyle 22·74 and Lamy 22·88).

Lillian Board of Britain was tipped to win the **400 metres** and she looked all set to do so, with a semi-final win in 52·2 sec. Jarvis Scott of the USA went off fast in the final followed by Board and they passed the 200 in 24·4 and 24·5 respectively. Around the final turn, Board overtook Scott and led her and Aurelia Penton of Cuba by one metre with the others three metres back. Then Colette Besson of France and Natalya Pyechenkina of the USSR came with late sprints and the French girl passed Board with five metres to go to win in 52·0, equalling the Olympic record. Board took the silver in 52·1 and Pyechenkina and bronze with 52·2. (Automatic timings: Besson 52·03, Board 52·12 and Pyechenkina 52·25).

Vera Nikolic of Yugoslavia, the world record holder, was tipped to win the **800 metres**, but she failed to finish in the semi-finals, pulling up after 300 metres. She walked off towards the dressing rooms and was reported to have had a mental breakdown. In the final, Madeline Manning of the USA and Ileana Silai of Rumania set off at a terrific pace and Silai reached the bell in 59·1, followed by Manning, Pat Lowe of Britain and America's Doris Brown. Lowe moved up into second place, but coming off the bend Manning kicked hard and won in 2-00·9 for a new Olympic record. Lowe tied up and Sheila Taylor of Britain, Maria Gommers of

Action from the women's 800 metres final depicts Madeline Manning of America (centre), the eventual winner, sandwiched between two British girls, Pat Lowe (left) and Sheila Taylor.

Mark Shearman

Holland and Silai tussled for a while with Silai winning the silver in 2-02·5 and Gommers the bronze in 2-02·6. (Automatic timings: Manning 2-00·92, Silai 2-02·58 and Gommers 2-02·63).

In the **80 metres hurdles** Pam Kilborn of Australia broke the Olympic record with 10·4 as did her countrywoman Maureen Caird. Kilborn did 10·4 again in the semi-finals when Vyera Korsakova, the Russian world record holder, was eliminated. The start in the final was very even and the hurdlers were all together at the fourth flight. Caird moved ahead followed by Kilborn and Chen Chi of Formosa and they finished in that order, Caird, with 10·3, an Olympic record, taking gold, Kilborn in 10·4 the silver and Chi in 10·4 the bronze. (Automatic timings: Caird 10·39, Kilborn 10·46 and Chi 10·51).

America, who had the four fastest individuals, were expected to win the **4 × 400 metres relay** and they duly won the first heat in a world record time of 43·4 sec from Australia in 43·7. Holland surprised in the second heat with another 43·4, beating the USSR at 43·6, with Poland dropping the baton. But in the final, the USA employed good baton exchanges and won without trouble, their time of 42·8 being a new world record. Cuba's well drilled team finished second in 43·3, while the USSR took the bronze position in 43·4. The Australians, who had the capability to run America close, disappointed in fifth place. The winning team was Barbara Ferrell, Margaret Bailes, Mildrette Netter and Wyomia Tyus. (Automatic timings: USA 42·88, Cuba 43·36 and USSR 43·41).

In the **high jump** Rita Schmidt of East Germany was favoured to win, while Ilona Gusenbauer of Austria was competing only two months after giving birth to a child. Eight jumpers cleared 1.76 metres, including Gusenbauer, while six jumped 1,78, but three could go no higher. Valya Kozyr of the USSR jumped 1,80 on her third attempt and won the bronze medal, while Tonya Okorokova of the USSR cleared the same height with her first try to take the silver. Finally, Milena Rezkova of Czechoslovakia cleared 1.82 on her third jump to win the gold but her attempts at 1,84 were unsuccessful.

There were no particular favourites for the **long jump** and it came as a surprise when the world record was broken. The best of the qualifiers was Heide Rosendahl of West Germany with 6,54 metres. In the first round proper, Viorica Viscopoleanu of Rumania jumped 6,82 for a new world record, while Sheila Sherwood of Britain cleared 6,60 and Tanya Talysheva of the USSR reached 6,55 to hold the medal positions. Talysheva improved to 6,66 in the next round and Sherwood responded with 6,68 on her fifth jump. Viscopoleanu took the gold with 6,82, Sherwood the silver with 6,68 and Talysheva the bronze with 6,66.

Margitta Gummel of East Germany was the world record holder in the **shot put** and her very first throw of the competition broke the Olympic record with 18,53 metres. She improved in the third round to 19,07 and again in the fifth to 19,61, breaking the world record twice to win the gold. Maritta Lange of East Germany took the silver medal with 18,78, while Nadyezhda Chizhova of the USSR also only needed one throw to take the bronze medal with 18,19.

West Germany's Liesel Westermann had achieved a

Dick Fosbury of America, stunned spectators and judges alike with his unique backward flop, when winning the high jump. <small>Mark Shearman</small>

Mark Shearman

David Hemery

Past performances had not prepared the specialists for the astonishing world record victory Hemery scored for Britain in the 400m hurdles final in Mexico City.

Hemery was born on 18 July 1944 in Cirencester, Gloucestershire, but while based in Boston — he studied at the University there — he made a detailed study of each of the likely US candidates for the Mexico Games, raced them whenever posssible, and meanwhile concentrated on improving his own technique and strength.

When the Games fell due he knew he was in his best-ever form, but was not prepared to show his hand in the preliminary rounds. He was satisfied just to qualify for the final. Not till then was the greatness of Hemery exposed. He raced like a man inspired and pulverised the opposition to such an extent that his world record time of 48·1 sec left him well clear of the whole field.

Hemery's endeavour to repeat the performance in Munich four years later was thwarted by the arrival on the 400m hurdles scene of Uganda's John Akii-Bua, who lowered the world record to 47·82 sec. The Englishman's 48·52 sec earned him the bronze to which he added a silver from Britain's second place in the 4 × 400m relay.

"Black Power" supporter, Tommie Smith of America, glides down the finishing straight for an expected victory in the 200 metres.   Mark Shearman

Ralph Doubell, the Australian 800 metres runner, raised his game to new heights when he beat the more fancied athletes for the gold medal.
Mark Shearman

world best of 62,54 prior to the Games, but never hit top form in the **discus throw**ing competition, which was notable only for the interruptions for medal ceremonies. Lia Manoliu of Rumania threw 58,28 in the first round for an Olympic record and ultimately the gold medal. The silver medal went to Westermann who achieved 57,76 and the bronze to Jolan Kleiber of Hungary who hurled 54.90 in the first round.

The **javelin throw**ing competition was a very open contest with any one of half-a-dozen women capable of capturing the title, including Mihaele Penes of Rumania, the defending champion. Penes opened with a big throw of 59,92 metres but Angela Nemeth of Hungary responded in the next round with 60,36, the winning throw of the competition, while Penes took the silver. The bronze medal position was held by Marta Rudas of Hungary with 56,38 right until the last round, when Eva Janko of Austria took it from her with a cast of 58,04.

Four women had exceeded 5,000 points in the **pentathlon** leading up to the Games: Heide Rosendahl and Ingrid Becker, both of West Germany, and Galina Sofina and Valentina Tikhomirova, both of the USSR. Unfortunately, Rosendahl pulled a muscle in the warm-up and could not compete. In the 80 metres hurdles Meta Antenan of Switzerland ran 10·7 before Mary Peters of Britain put the shot 15,09 metres to take over the lead. Later, Liesel Prokop of Austria high jumped 1,68 metres to total 3,061 points at the end of the first day, with Tikhomirova on 3,000 and Peters on 2,965. Prokop still led after the long jump, but Becker crept up into second place with a 6,43 metres long jump, and won the event with 23·5 sec in the 200 metres to total 5,098 points. Prokop on 4,966 took silver and Annamaria Toth of Hungary, on 4.959, collected the bronze.

Amos Biwot, the Kenyan steeplechaser, is shown making an extravagant clearance at the water jump on his way to winning the gold medal.
Mark Shearman

Head and shoulders above contemporary shot putters, the American Randy Matson, won as he pleased.

Mark Shearman

Mark Shearman

Al Oerter

A legend of the Games. Al Oerter achieved the seemingly impossible feat of winning *four* successive discus finals.

He was born in Astoria, New York, on 19 September 1936, and was American high-school record holder in 1954. His first Olympic gold was presented to him in the 1956 Melbourne Games, when he was only 20, after establishing a Games record of 56,36m (184ft 10½in). In Rome four years later, he improved the record still further, to 59,18m (194ft 1½in).

Few believed he could possibly win a third gold in Tokyo, especially as he was having to wear a surgical brace to relieve severe pain caused by a slipped disc. Oerter also experienced the misfortune of tearing a rib cage cartilage a few days before the final. But determined not to surrender his title without a fight, he discarded the brace and went into the competition with his right side taped and packed with ice. With just one throw remaining, the plucky American was back in fourth place. Then came his winning strike: 61,00m (200ft 1½in) to extend the Olympic record once more.

But surely, it was thought, he could not succeed a fourth time. Oerter was convinced otherwise and the confidence in himself led to his increasing the Games record still further in the 1968 Mexico Games to 64,78m (212ft 6in), his lifetime best.

COMPETITOR	COUNTRY CODE	EVENT	ROUND	HEAT	PLACE	TIME & DISTANCE	MEDAL
Kunisch, H.	SUI	Marathon	F		44	2:50-58·2	
Kunz, H.	SUI	Decathlon	F		DNF		
Kutschinski, R.	USA	800m	1	2	3	1-47·61	
			SF	1	5	1-47·39	
Kvalheim, A.	NOR	1500m	1	4	4	3-47·50	
			SF	1	8	3-55·32	
Labadie, E.	MEX	4×100m relay	1	2	7	40·09	
Ladany, S.	ISR	50k walk	F		24	5:01-06·0	
Laird, R.	USA	20k walk	F		25	1:44-38·0	
Lanka, J.	URS	Decathlon	F		14	7227	
Laris, T.	USA	10000m	F		16	30-26·2	
Larsen, G.	DEN	800m	·	3	6	1-51·98	
Lee, M.-J.	KOR	Marathon	F		29	2:38-52·2	
Lee, S.-H.	KOR	Marathon	F		46	2:52-46·2	
Lehnertz, K.	GER	Pole vault	Q		DNQ	4,75	
Lemonis, G.	GRE	Shot put	Q		DNQ	16,43	
Lepik, T.	URS	Long jump	F		5	8,09	
Lerwill, A.	GBR	Long jump	Q		DNQ	7,62	
Lespagnard, R.	BEL	Decathlon	F		17	7125	
Letzerich, M.	GER	10000m	F		18	30-48·6	
Leuschke, B.	GDR	50k walk	F		DNF		
Lewis, G.	AUS	100m	1	8	6	10·55	
		200m	1	7	1	20·71	
			2	1	=2	20·81	
			SF	2	5	20·53	
Liani, S.	ITA	110m hurdles	1	5	=3	14·01	
			SF	2	7	14·09	
Liga, V.	FIJ	Javelin throw	Q		DNQ	62,32	
Lightman, S.	GBR	50k walk	F		18	4:52-20·0	
Lindberg, S.	SWE	20k walk	F		15	1:40-03·0	
		50k walk	F		5	4:34-05·0	
Liquori, M.	USA	1500m	1	5	1	3-52·78	
			SF	2	4	3-52·17	
			F		12	4-18·22	
L'Oficial, J.	DOM	400m	1	6	7	47·93	
		800m	1	4	7	1-55·66	
		4×400m relay	1	1	5	3-19·42	
Longe, C.	GBR	Decathlon	F		13	7338	
Losch, M.	GDR	Discus throw	F		4	62,12	
Lovasz, L.	HUN	Hammer throw	F		3	69,78	B
Lundmark, K.	SWE	High jump	Q		DNQ	2,06	
Lusis, J.	URS	Javelin throw	F		1	90,10*	G
McKenzie, D.	NZL	Marathon	F		37	2:43-36·6	
Mackenzie, R.	CAN	400m	1	4	4	47·05	
			2	1	4	46·15	
			SF	2	8	49·28	
		4×400m relay	1	3	7	3-09·70	
Maclaren, B.	CAN	4×400m relay	1	3	7	3-09·70	
McLaren, R.	CAN	400m hurdles	1	1	6	51·84	
McMahon, P.	IRL	Marathon	F		12	2:29-21·0	
McNeil, P.	JAM	100m	1	7	6	10·62	
Maddaford, R.	NZL	5000m	1	3	4	14-20·82	
			F		10	14-39·72	
		10000m	F		12	30-17·2	
Magarinos, R.	ESP	400m	1	3	5	46·92	
Maggard, D.	USA	Shot put	F		5	19,43	
Magnor, H.	GER	50k walk	F		11	4:39-43·2	
Maguire, E.	NZL	10000m	F		DNF		
Majekodunmi, B.	NGR	4×100m relay	1	1	5	39·47	
			SF	2	DNF		
Makama, M.	NGR	400m	1	6	3	46·49	
			2	4	7	46·41	
		4×400m relay	1	2	3	3-05·78	
Maki, S.	CIV	110m hurdles	1	3	6	14·32	
Maldonado, V.	VEN	400m hurdles	1	1	4	51·46	
			SF	1	8	52·29	
		4×400m relay	1	3	5	3-07·65	
Maluski, J.	POL	1500m	1	5	9	3-54·83	
Malyutin, A.	URS	Pole vault	F		12	5,00	
Mandl, H.	AUT	Decathlon	F		DNF		
Maniak, W.	POL	100m	1	1	4	10·49	
		4×100m relay	1	3	4	40·27	
			SF	1	4	38·99	
			F		8	39·22	
Martinez, C.	CUB	400m	1	5	6	47·28	
		4×400m relay	1	3	4	3-05·28	
Martinez, J.	MEX	5000m	1	3	2	14-20·06	
			F		4	14-10·76	
		10000m	F		4	29-35·0	
Martinez, J.	ESP	Hammer throw	Q		DNQ	63,40	
Maslakov, V.	URS	200m	1	1	5	21·07	
			2	4	6	20·96	
Masresha, W.	ETH	5000m	1	2	3	14-26·99	
			F		6	14-17·70	
		10000m	F		8	29-57·0	
Massaquoi, A.	SLE	10000m	F		DNF		
		Marathon	F		45	2:52-28·0	

COMPETITOR	COUNTRY CODE	EVENT	ROUND	HEAT	PLACE	TIME & DISTANCE	MEDAL
Matson, R.	USA	Shot put	F		1	20,54	G
Matthews, V.	USA	4×400m relay	1	1	1	3-00·71*	
			F		1	2-56·16*	G
May, P.	AUS	Triple jump	F		6	17,02	
Mays, C.	USA	Long jump	F		NP	0	
M'Baye, D.	SEN	4×400m relay	1	2	4	3-06·94	
Mecser, L.	HUN	10000m	F		22	30-54·8	
		Marathon	F		DNF		
Mederos, G.	CUB	Discus throw	Q		DNQ	52,30	
Medina, S.	MEX	4×400m relay	1	3	6	3-08·19	
Meighan, O.	HBR	Long jump	Q		DNQ	6,06	
Mejia, A.	COL	10000m	F		10	30-10·6	
Mendoza, R.	NCA	Shot put	Q		DNQ	13,33	
		Discus throw	Q		DNQ	39,62	
Menet, H.	SUI	3000m steeplechase	1	2	13	10-02·06	
Menocal, F.	NCA	400m	1	3	7	49·14	
		800m	1	5	8	1-58·96	
Merschenz, K.	CAN	20k walk	F		18	1:40-11·0	
		50k walk	F		9	4:37-57·4	
Metz, G.	GER	100m	1	9	4	10·55	
		200m	1	7	5	21·24	
		4×100m relay	1	2	3	39·16	
			SF	1	3	38·93	
			F		6	38·76	
Mikityenko, L.	URS	5000m	1	3	7	14-44·35	
		10000m	F		17	30-46·0	
Milde, L.	GDR	Discus throw	F		2	63,08	S
Milek, P.	YUG	High Jump	Q		DNQ	2,00	
Miller, Lennox	JAM	100m	1	6	6	10·15	
			2	1	1	10·11	
			SF	2	2	10·15	
			F		2	10·04	S
		4×100m relay	1	2	1	38·65*	
			SF	1	1	38·39*	
			F		4	38·47	
Miller, Leslie	BAH	400m	1	7	7	46·99	
Mills, L.	NZL	Shot put	F		11	18,18	
Miranda, P.	MEX	3000m steeplechase	1	1	11	9-25·95	
Miura, N.	JPN	3000m steeplechase	1	2	8	9-32·95	
Molders, G.	GER	3000m steeplechase	1	3	10	9-32·22	
Molloy, M.	IRL	Marathon	F		41	2:48-13·6	
Monsegue, R.	TRI	100m	1	6	5	10·56	
Monsels, E.	SUR	100m	1	8	5	10·48	
			2	4	8	10·45	
Montes, P.	CUB	100m	1	4	1	10·14	
			2	3	1	10·16	
			SF	2	3	10·19	
			F		4	10·14	
		4×100m relay	1	1	1	38·76*	
			SF	2	1	38·64	
			F		2	38·40	S
Moore, K.	USA	Marathon	F		14	2:29-49·4	
Mora, R.	DOM	110m hurdles	1	5	7	16·85	
		4×400m relay	1	1	5	3-19·42	
Morales, C.	HON	5000m	1	2	14	18-40·13	
Morales, G.	NCA	Hammer throw	Q		DNQ	45,76	
Morales, J.	CUB	110m hurdles	1	3	3	13·94	
			SF	1	7	14·08	
		4×100m relay	1	1	1	38·76*	
			SF	2	1	38·64	
			F		2	38·40	S
Moreno, I.	CHI	100m	1	3	2	10·53	
			2	1	4	10·37	
			SF	2	6	10·37	
		200m	1	5	1	20·93	
			2	2	4	20·83	
			SF	1	5	20·84	
Morgan, G.	SUD	100m	1	7	8	11·09	
		200m	1	3	7	22·70	
Morozov, A.	URS	3000m steeplechase	1	3	4	9-08·45	
			F		5	8-55·61	
Moses, P.	KEN	Marathon	F		49	2:55-17·0	
Mueller, H.	GER	400m	1	5	4	45·98	
			2	4	3	45·78	
			SF	1	=6	46·22	
		4×400m relay	1	3	1	3-03·90	
			F		3	3-00·57	B
Mueller, J.	GER	20k walk	F		DNF		
Mueller, W.	GDR	400m	1	8	=1	46·66	
			2	2	4	46·32	
			SF	1	8	48·37	
		4×400m relay	1	1	4	3-07·00	
Muraki, Y.	JPN	Triple jump	Q		DNQ	15,83	
Murphy, F.	IRL	1500m	1	5	10	3-54·85	
Murro, M.	USA	Javelin throw	F		9	80,08	
Mustakari, E.	FIN	Pole vault	F		NP	0	

Head and shoulders above contemporary shot putters, the American Randy Matson, won as he pleased.

Mark Shearman

Mark Shearman

Al Oerter

A legend of the Games, Al Oerter achieved the seemingly impossible feat of winning *four* successive discus finals.

He was born in Astoria, New York, on 19 September 1936, and was American high-school record holder in 1954. His first Olympic gold was presented to him in the 1956 Melbourne Games, when he was only 20, after establishing a Games record of 56,36m (184ft 10½in). In Rome four years later, he improved the record still further, to 59,18m (194ft 1½in).

Few believed he could possibly win a third gold in Tokyo, especially as he was having to wear a surgical brace to relieve severe pain caused by a slipped disc. Oerter also experienced the misfortune of tearing a rib cage cartilage a few days before the final. But determined not to surrender his title without a fight, he discarded the brace and went into the competition with his right side taped and packed with ice. With just one throw remaining, the plucky American was back in fourth place. Then came his winning strike: 61,00m (200ft 1½in) to extend the Olympic record once more.

But surely, it was thought, he could not succeed a fourth time. Oerter was convinced otherwise and the confidence in himself led to his increasing the Games record still further in the 1968 Mexico Games to 64,78m (212ft 6in), his lifetime best.

In a thrilling finish, the top three pole vaulters tied at 5,40 metres, but the American, Bob Seagren, won the competition under the count-back ruling.

Mark Shearman

Mark Shearman

Bob Beamon

Britain's reigning Olympic long jump champion, Lynn Davies, commenting on the eve of the defence of his title at the 1968 Games in Mexico City said: "It only needs Bob Beamon to hit the board right once and we can all go home."

How prophetic those words proved. Beamon, with his first jump in the final, leapt from the board with such power and speed that he landed in the pit at 8,90m (29ft 2½in) to add an incredible 55cm (21½in) to the world record. Not surprisingly that record stands to this day.

And yet the gangling Beamon, who was born in Jamaica, New York, on 29 August 1946, nearly failed to qualify for the final. Two preliminary round no-jumps left him with just one final attempt to achieve the qualifying distance of 7,65m (25ft 1¼in). Taking the precaution of reducing his run-up speed he managed to get beyond the mark, in spite of taking off well before the board.

So the stage was set for the never-to-be-forgotten final. "Tell me I'm not dreaming", Beamon was heard to say when the distance of his title winning jump was announced.

As a sprinter capable of 9·5 sec for the 100 yards, with spring and height, he also had the advantage of the altitude in Mexico.

A keen basketball player, he became a professional in 1973.

"Always the bridesmaid, never the bride", Ron Clarke the Australian world record holder for the 5,000 metres, leads Mohamed Gammoudi of Tunisia (781), the eventual winner. Clarke finished in fifth place.

Mark Shearman

A giant among javelin specialists, Janis Lusis of the USSR, won his event with yet another 90 metre throw.

Mark Shearman

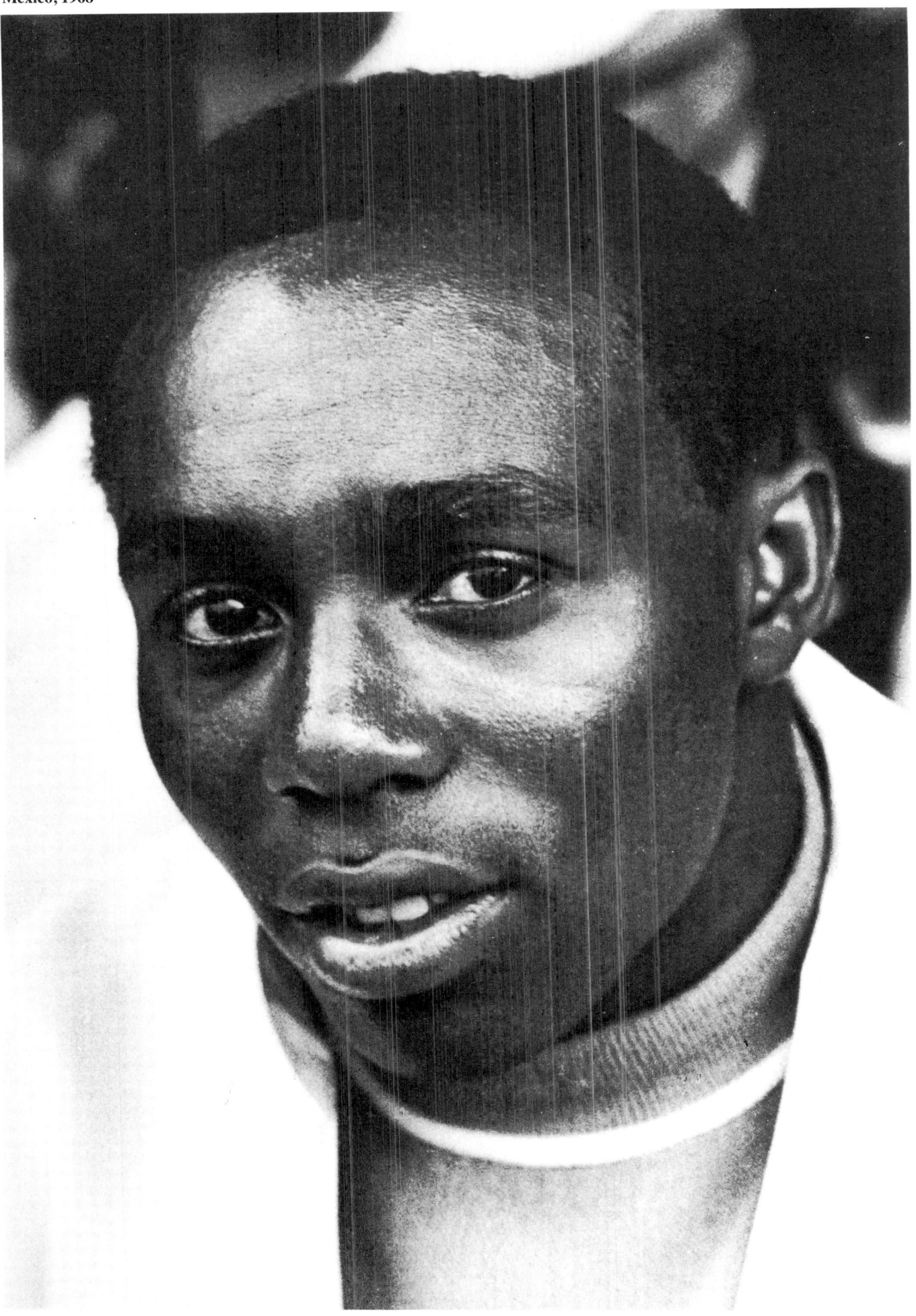

The first man to break the 10·00 sec barrier for the 100 metres, using automatic timing, Jim Hines of the States, was the winner of that event in Mexico City.

Mark Shearman

COMPETITOR	COUNTRY CODE	EVENT	ROUND	HEAT	PLACE	TIME & DISTANCE	MEDAL
MALES							
Abdulai, K.	NGR	100m	1	7	4	10·45	
			2	2	7	10·38	
		4×100m relay	1	1	5	39·47	
			SF	2		DNF	
Abe, N.	JPN	Long jump	Q		DNQ	7,58	
		4×100m relay	1	2	6	40·02	
Abugattas, F.	PER	High jump	Q		DNQ	2,03	
Abugattas, R.	PER	High jump	Q		DNQ	2,00	
Acevedo, F.	PER	200m	1	5	4	21·02	
			2	2	3	20·78	
			SF	1	8	20·91	
Adams, W.	GER	800m	1	3	1	1-48·50	
			SF	1	1	1-46·41	
			F		4	1-45·83	
Adcocks, W.	GBR	Marathon	F		5	2:25-33·0	
Addy, J.	GHA	200m	1	5	3	21·00	
			2	4	5	20·91	
		4×100m relay	1	1	6	39·87	
			SF	2	5	39·96	
Ade Nji, E.	KHM	5000m	1	1	12	15-46·21	
Agapov, G.	URS	50k walk	F		DNF		
Ahey, M.	GHA	100m	1	5	3	10·59	
			2	2	8	10·49	
		Long jump	F		13	7,71	
		4×100m relay	1	1	6	39·87	
			SF	2	5	39·96	
Ahmed, I.	MAL	110m hurdles	1	2	6	14·36	
Akcay, I.	TUR	Marathon	F		4	2:25-18·8	
Akhwari, J.	TAN	Marathon	F		57	3:25-17·0	
Aktas, H.	TUR	Marathon	F		25	2:35-09·6	
Alanov, V.	URS	10000m	F		24	31-01·0	
Alarotu, A.	FIN	Pole vault	F		14	5,00	
Alder, J.	GBR	Marathon	F		DNF		
Alexa, J.	TCH	High jump	Q		DNQ	2,09	
Alsop, F.	GBR	Triple jump	Q		DNQ	15,71	
Alvarez, J.	ESP	3000m steeplechase	1	1	2	9-03·74	
			F		11	9-24·51	
Amaizon, D.	ARG	3000m steeplechase	1	1	12	9-43·06	
Ambu, A.	ITA	Marathon	F		21	2:33-19·6	
Ametepey, J.	GHA	800m	1	4	4	1-50·78	
Ammann, E.	SUI	Hammer throw	Q		DNQ	62,40	
Amoah, J.	GHA	Triple jump	Q		DNQ	15,65	
Ande, M.	NGR	Marathon	F		54	3:03-47·6	
Andersson, S.	SWE	20k walk	F		21	1:41-58·0	
		50k walk	F		13	4:40-42·6	
Angelo, H.	SUD	800m	1	5	6	1-53·43	
Anyamah, C.	FRA	Decathlon	F		DNF		
Archer, C.	TRI	4×100m relay	1	1	3	38·86	
			SF	1	6	39·52	
Arese, F.	ITA	1500m	1	1	5	3-51·86	
			SF	1	7	3-54·85	
Areta, L.	ESP	Triple jump	F		12	15,75	
Arguello, J.	NCA	100m	1	9	8	11·18	
		200m	1	4	7	22·80	
Arrechea, H.	COL	110m hurdles	1	2	5	14·09	
Arzhanov, Y.	URS	800m	1	6	3	1-48·46	
			SF	1		DNS	
Asati, C.	KEN	100m	1	3	6	10·63	
		200m	1	2	2	20·66	
			2	2	5	20·84	
		4×400m relay	1	1	2	3-00·84	
			F		2	2-59·64	S
Asirvatham, V.	MAL	400m	1	2	6	48·02	
Asswai, M.	LBA	400m hurdles	1	1	8	54·34	
Astacio, J.	SAL	200m	1	6	6	23·13	
		400m	1	4	7	52·92	
Aun, R.	URS	Decathlon	F		DNF		
Avilov, N.	URS	Decathlon	F		4	7909	
Ayachi, L.	TUN	3000m steeplechase	1	2	7	9-24·62	
Ayed-Mansoor, M.	KUW	Marathon	F		DNF		
Bacheler, J.	USA	5000m	1	2	4	14-31·00	
			F		DNS		
Badenski, A.	POL	400m	1	2	1	45·52	
			2	4	2	45·60	
			SF	1	3	45·50	
			F		=6	45·42	
		4×400m relay	1	2	1	3-03·02	
			F		4	3-00·58	
Baez, C.	PUR	800m	1	6	8	1-52·70	
Baeza, E.	CHI	Marathon	F		36	2:43-15·6	
Bailey, D.	CAN	1500m	1	1	6	3-52·11	
Balachowski, J.	POL	400m	1	7	2	46·23	
			2	2	5	46·33	
		4×400m relay	1	2	1	3-03·02	
			F		4	3-00·58	
Balfour, A.	BAH	High jump	Q		DNQ	1,95	
Balikhin, V.	URS	110m hurdles	1	5	1	13·82	
			SF	1	8	14·13	
Bambuck, R.	FRA	100m	1	5	1	10·18	
			2	2	3	10·17	
			SF	1	2	10·11	
			F		5	10·16	
		200m	1	6	2	20·61	
			2	4	3	20·63	
			SF	1	4	20·47	
			F		5	20·51	
		4×100m relay	1	2	2	39·03	
			SF	2	3	38·83	
			F		3	38·43	B
Banthorpe, R.	GBR	200m	1	7	2	20·73	
			2	4	4	20·83	
			SF	2	7	20·88	
		4×100m relay	1	2	4	39·33	
			SF	1	5	39·46	
Barahona, E.	HON	1500m	1	1	11	4-56·08	
Barkovskly, L.	URS	Long jump	F		11	7,90	
Barney, E.	ARG	Pole vault	Q		DNQ	4,80	
Barreneche, H.	COL	Marathon	F		DNF		
Barrett, T.	BAH	Triple jump	Q		DNQ	15,79	
Bartsch, O.	URS	20k walk	F		6	1:36-16·8	
Baumann, H.	GDR	Hammer throw	F		8	68,26	
Beamon, R.	USA	Long jump	F		1	8,90*	G
Becquer, F.	MEX	100m	1	8	7	10·72	
		4×100m relay	1	2	7	40·09	
Beer, A.	FRA	Shot put	Q		DNQ	18,72	
Beer, K.	GDR	Long jump	F		2	8,19	S
Bell, W.	USA	800m	1	1	5	1-51·52	
Bello, S.	ITA	400m	1	6	4	46·54	
			2	1	8	46·84	
		4×400m relay	1	1	3	3-04·93	
			F		7	3-04·64	
Bendlin, K.	GER	Decathlon	F		3	8064	B
Ben Haddou, H.	MOR	1500m	1	4	2	3-47·01	
			SF	1	12	4-01·70	
Benn, M.	GBR	1500m	1	4	8	3-56·43	
Berg, O.	SWE	1500m	1	2	7	4-00·42	
Berruti, L.	ITA	200m	1	1	4	21·06	
			2	2	6	21·01	
		4×100m relay	1	3	5	41·59	
			SF	2	4	39·46	
			F		7	39·22	
Bertould, G.	FRA	400m	1	7	4	46·31	
			2	3	7	48·91	
		4×400m	1	3	3	3-04·69	
			F		8	3-07·51	
Beyer, U.	GER	Hammer throw	Q		DNQ	65,44	
Bezabeh, T.	ETH	400m	1	3	2	45·60	
			2	3	3	46·02	
			SF	1	4	45·60	
			F		=6	45·42	
Biedermann, F.	LIE	Decathlon	F		19	6323	
Bikila, A.	ETH	Marathon	F		DNF		
Birbilis, G.	GRE	400m hurdles	1	4	8	52·62	
Birlenbach, H.	GER	Shot put	F		8	18,80	
Biwott, A.	KEN	3000m steeplechase	1	3	1	8-49·39	
			F		1	8-51·02	G
Blinston, J.A.	GBR	5000m	1	2	7	15-06·28	
Bliznyetsov, G.	URS	Pole vault	F		6	5,30	
Blomkvist, J.	SWE	Pole vault	Q		DNQ	4,75	
Blyden, F.	ISV	110m hurdles	1	1	5	14·74	
Bobb, E.	TRI	4×400m relay	1	3	2	3-04·55	
			F		6	3-04·52	
Boccardo, J.	FRA	4×400m relay	F		8	3-07·51	
Bolshov, V.	URS	High jump	Q		DNQ	2,09	
Bon, N.	KEN	400m	1	7	1	46·21	
			2	1	7	46·39	
		4×400m relay	1	1	2	3-00·84	
			F		2	2-59·64	S
Boosey, D.	GBR	Triple jump	Q		DNQ	16,01	
Boschert, R.	GER	Long jump	F		12	7,89	
Boston, R.	USA	Long jump	F		3	8,16	B
Boulter, J.	GBR	1500m	1	1	3	3-51·63	
			SF	1	9	3-56·13	
Boxberger, J.	FRA	1500m	1	3	5	3-47·55	
			SF	1	2	3-54·00	
			F		6	3-46·65	
Boyce, P.	AUS	High jump	Q		DNQ	2,06	
Boychuk, A.	CAN	Marathon	F		10	2:28-40·2	
Bristol, A.	PUR	110m hurdles	1	2	3	13·92	
			SF	2	8	14·13	
Brooker, W.	CAN	400m hurdles	1	2	5	51·68	
		4×400m relay	1	3	7	3-09·70	
Brooks, V.	JAM	Long jump	F		15	7,51	

Mexico

COMPETITOR	COUNTRY CODE	EVENT	ROUND	HEAT	PLACE	TIME & DISTANCE	MEDAL
Brosius, K.	GER	3000m steeplechase	1	1	9	9-23·98	
Brown, R.	USA	High jump	F		5	2,14	
Bruch, R.	SWE	Discus throw	F		8	59,28	
Bryan-Jones, G.	GBR	3000m steeplechase	1	3	7	9-16·86	
Buehler, R.	SUI	Javelin throw	Q		DNQ	61,06	
Bugri, S.	GHA	400m	1	4	4	45·88	
			2	3	4	46·08	
			SF	1	5	45·92	
Bull, M.	GBR	Pole vault	F		13	5,00	
Buniak, P.	CAN	Marathon	F		DNF		
Burgher, L.	JAM	Triple jump	Q		DNQ	15,29	
Burke, E.	USA	Hammer throw	F		12	65,72	
Burnham, E.	BAR	400m	1	1	6	47·94	
Busca, P.	ITA	20k walk	F		12	1:37-32·0	
Busch, J.	GDR	Marathon	F		15	2:30-42·6	
Calonge, A.	ARG	100m	1	9	2	10·44	
			2	1	5	10·39	
		200m	1	1	2	20·81	
			2	3	6	21·03	
Calzado, E.	CUB	20k walk	F		27	1:49-27·0	
Campbell, C.	GBR	400m	1	8	=1	46·66	
			2	1	6	46·35	
		4×400m relay	1	2	2	3-03·67	
			F		5	3-01·21	
Campos, E.	MEX	20k walk	F		20	1:41-52·0	
Candan, N.	TUR	High jump	Q		DNQ	1,95	
Cappella, F.	CAN	50k walk	F		23	4:58-31·6	
Carette, J.	FRA	200m	1	5	2	20·97	
			2	1	5	21·15	
		4×400m relay	1	3	2	3-04·69	
			F		8	3-07·51	
Carlos, J.	USA	200m	1	1	1	20·54	
			2	1	1	20·69	
			SF	1	-	20·12*	
			F		3	20·10	B
Carlsen, G.	USA	Discus throw	F		6	59,46	
Carmona, R.	MEX	Decathlon	F		DNF		
Carrigan, C.	USA	Pole vault	Q		DNQ	4,60	
Carroll, N.	IRL	400m	1	6	6	46·83	
		800m	1	3	3	1-49·01	
Carter, C.	GBR	800m	1	4	6	1-52·99	
Caruthers, E.	USA	High jump	F		2	2,22	S
Caspers, L.	GER	Hammer throw	Q		DNQ	65,54	
Castellanos, R.	SAL	20k walk	F		29	1:58-48·0	
Castro, C.	MEX	4×400m relay	1	3	6	3-08·19	
Cayenne, B.	TRI	800m	1	6	2	1-48·22	
			SF	1	4	1-46·83	
			F		8	1-54·40	
		4×400m relay	1	3	2	3-04·55	
			F		6	3-04·52	
Charankov, I.	BUL	Marathon	F		30	2:39-49·6	
Charland, M.	CAN	Long jump	Q		DNQ	7,35	
Chen, C.-S.	FOR	Decathlon	F		DNF		
		100m	1	4	6	10·91	
Chen, M.-C.	FOR	Long jump	Q		DNQ	6,71	
		Triple jump	Q		DNQ	15,29	
Chihota, N.	TAN	100m	1	9	4	10·57	
		200m	1	1	6	21·28	
Clochina, S.	RUM	Triple jump	F		13	15,62	
Clark, F.	AUS	20k walk	F		16	1:40-06·0	
		50k walk	F		12	4:40-13·8	
Clarke, R.	AUS	5000m	1	2	2	14-20·78	
			F		5	14-12·45	
		10000m	F		6	29-44·8	
Clayton, D.	AUS	Marathon	F		7	2:27-23·8	
Clayton, W.	JAM	Long jump	Q		DNQ	7,57	
Cochard, J.	FRA	Long jump	Q		DNQ	6,11	
Coleman, L.	USA	110m hurdles	1	4	1	13·77	
			SF	2	2	13·54	
			F		4	13·67	
Colin, P.	MEX	50k walk	F		25	5:01-30·0	
Colnard, P.	FRA	Shot put	F		9	18,79	
Combes, R.	FRA	Marathon	F		DNF		
Connolly, H.	USA	Hammer throw	Q		DNQ	65,00	
Cooper, J.	GBR	400m hurdles	1	2	3	51·43	
			SF	1	7	50·82	
Cordero, E.	SAL	3000m steeplechase	1	2	14	11-19·23	
Cordova, L.	HON	1500m	1	5	12	5-18·92	
Cornacchia, G.	ITA	110m hurdles	1	1	4	14·13	
Corrales, C.	HON	200m	1	7	7	23·93	
Covelli, F.	USA	Javelin throw	Q		DNQ	73,04	
Crawley, A.	AUS	Long jump	F		6	8,02	
Cropper, D.	GBR	800m	1	6	1	1-47·96	
			SF	2	8	1-47·67	
Crosa, G.	ITA	High jump	F		6	2,14	
Crothers, W.	CAN	4×400m relay	1	3	7	3-09·70	
Cruz, R.	SAL	50k walk	F		28	5:56-22·0	

COMPETITOR	COUNTRY CODE	EVENT	ROUND	HEAT	PLACE	TIME & DISTANCE	MEDAL
Csermak, J.	HUN	50k walk	F		DNF		
Cubias, A.	SAL	800m	1	4	8	2-08·72	
		1500m	1	3	10	4-32·58	
Cuello, G.	ARG	800m	1	2	DNF		
Cuque, C.	GUA	Marathon	F		39	2:45-20·4	
Cych, J.	POL	3000m steeplechase	1	2	12	9-50·78	
Cziffra, Z.	HUN	Triple jump	Q		DNQ	15,04	
Danek, L.	TCH	Discus throw	F		3	62,92	B
Davenport, W.	USA	110m hurdles	1	2	1	13·65*	
			SF	2	1	13·53	
			F		1	13·33*	G
Davies, H.	GBR	400m	1	4	5	47·30	
Davies, L.	GBR	Long jump	F		9	7,94	
Daws, R.	USA	Marathon	F		22	2:33-53·0	
Day, R.	USA	5000m	1	3	6	14-23·23	
Degeufu, F.	ETH	5000m	1	3	5	14-21·66	
			F		8	14-18·98	
		10000m	F		14	30-19·4	
De Hertoghe, A.	BEL	1500m	1	2	2	3-59·33	
			SF	2	6	3-52·57	
			F		11	3-53·63	
Del Buono, G.	ITA	800m	1	6	6	1-50·23	
		1500m	1	4	6	3-48·41	
Delecour, J.	FRA	100m	1	9	3	10·45	
			2	4	6	10·36	
		4×100m relay	1	2	2	39·03	
			SF	2	3	38·83	
			F		3	38·43	B
Delerue, H.	FRA	50k walk	F		21	4:57-40·2	
Della-Rossa, I.	URS	50k walk	F		DNF		
D'Encausse, H.	FRA	Pole vault	F		7	5,25	
De Noorlander, E.	HOL	Decathlon	F		9	7554	
De Palma, G.	ITA	Marathon	F		31	2:39-58·2	
Deza, A.	PER	110m hurdles	1	5	6	14·38	
Dia, M.	SEN	Triple jump	F		8	16,73	
Diaz, R.	CUB	400m	1	3	4	46·48	
			2	2	6	46·38	
		4×400m relay	1	3	4	3-05·28	
Diby, B.	CIV	4×100m relay	1	2	5	39·68	
			SF	1	7	39·69	
Diessl, W.	AUT	Decathlon	F		12	7465	
Diessner, B.	GDR	5000m	1	1	6	14-41·03	
Dogon Yaro, M.	NGR	400m	1	7	3	46·24	
			2	1	5	46·19	
		4×400m relay	1	1	3	3-05·78	
Domansky, E.	CAN	400m	1	7	5	46·46	
Dome, R.	VEN	4×400m relay	1	3	5	3-07·65	
Dominguez, R.	DOM	4×100m relay	1	1	7	41·48	
Dooley, T.	USA	20k walk	F		17	1:40-08·0	
Dosza, C.	RUM	High jump	Q		DNQ	2,03	
Doubell, R.	AUS	800m	1	4	1	1-47·24	
			SF	2	1	1-45·78	
			F		1	1-44·40*	G
Dralu, S.	UGA	200m	1	5	6	21·38	
Duckin, N.	URS	Triple jump	F		5	17,09	
Dudziak, M.	POL	100m	1	8	3	10·46	
			2	3	5	10·32	
		4×100m relay	1	3	3	40·27	
			SF	1	4	38·99	
			F		8	39·22	
Dufresne, J.	FRA	800m	1	1	2	1-47·61	
			SF	1	6	1-51·89	
Duriez, M.	FRA	110m hurdles	1	5	2	14·00	
			SF	2	4	13·73	
			F		7	13·77	
Duttweiler, W.	SUI	Decathlon	F		DNF		
Dyce, B.	JAM	800m	1	6	4	1-48·58	
			SF	2	6	1-47·30	
		1500m	1	5	8	3-54·65	
Dyrzka, J.	ARG	400m	1	7	4	47·02	
			2	2	7	46·85	
		400m hurdles	1	2	1	49·82	
			SF	1	5	49·86	
Dzhurov, S.	BUL	Decathlon	F		16	7173	
Eckschmidt, S.	HUN	Hammer throw	F		5	69,46	
Eggers, H.	GDR	100m	1	7	3	10·38	
			2	4	4	10·25	
			SF	1	7	10·29	
		4×100m relay	1	3	1	38·93	
			SF	1	2	38·72	
			F		5	38·66	
Egwunyenga, A.	NGR	400m	1	3	6	47·37	
		4×400m relay	1	2	3	3-05·78	

COMPETITOR	COUNTRY CODE	EVENT	ROUND	HEAT	PLACE	TIME & DISTANCE	MEDAL
Kunisch, H.	SUI	Marathon	F		44	2:50-58·2	
Kunz, H.	SUI	Decathlon	F		DNF		
Kutschinski, R.	USA	800m	1	2	3	1-47·61	
			SF	1	5	1-47·39	
Kvalheim, A.	NOR	1500m	1	4	4	3-47·50	
			SF	1	8	3-55·32	
Labadie, E.	MEX	4×100m relay	1	2	7	40·09	
Ladany, S.	ISR	50k walk	F		24	5:01-06·0	
Laird, R.	USA	20k walk	F		25	1:44-38·0	
Lanka, J.	URS	Decathlon	F		14	7227	
Laris, T.	USA	10000m	F		16	30-26·2	
Larsen, G.	DEN	800m	1	3	6	1-51·98	
Lee, M.-J.	KOR	Marathon	F		29	2:38-52·2	
Lee, S.-H.	KOR	Marathon	F		46	2:52-46·2	
Lehnertz, K.	GER	Pole vault	Q		DNQ	4,75	
Lemonis, G.	GRE	Shot put	Q		DNQ	16,43	
Lepik, T.	URS	Long jump	F		5	8,09	
Lerwill, A.	GBR	Long jump	Q		DNQ	7,62	
Lespagnard, R.	BEL	Decathlon	F		17	7125	
Letzerich, M.	GER	10000m	F		18	30-48·6	
Leuschke, B.	GDR	50k walk	F		DNF		
Lewis, G.	AUS	100m	1	8	6	10·55	
		200m	1	7	1	20·71	
			2	1	=2	20·81	
			SF	2	5	20·53	
Liani, S.	ITA	110m hurdles	1	5	=3	14·01	
			SF	2	7	14·09	
Liga, V.	FIJ	Javelin throw	Q		DNQ	62,32	
Lightman, S.	GBR	50k walk	F		18	4:52-20·0	
Lindberg, S.	SWE	20k walk	F		15	1:40-03·0	
		50k walk	F		5	4:34-05·0	
Liquori, M.	USA	1500m	1	5	1	3-52·78	
			SF	2	4	3-52·17	
			F		12	4-18·22	
L'Oficial, J.	DOM	400m	1	6	7	47·93	
		800m	1	4	7	1-55·66	
		4×400m relay	1	1	5	3-19·42	
Longe, C.	GBR	Decathlon	F		13	7338	
Losch, M.	GDR	Discus throw	F		4	62,12	
Lovasz, L.	HUN	Hammer throw	F		3	69,78	B
Lundmark, K.	SWE	High jump	Q		DNQ	2,06	
Lusis, J.	URS	Javelin throw	F		1	90,10*	G
McKenzie, D.	NZL	Marathon	F		37	2:43-36·6	
Mackenzie, R.	CAN	400m	1	4	4	47·05	
			2	1	4	46·15	
			SF	2	8	49·28	
		4×400m relay	1	3	7	3-09·70	
Maclaren, B.	CAN	4×400m relay	1	3	7	3-09·70	
McLaren, R.	CAN	400m hurdles	1	1	6	51·84	
McMahon, P.	IRL	Marathon	F		12	2:29-21·0	
McNeil, P.	JAM	100m	1	7	6	10·62	
Maddaford, R.	NZL	5000m	1	3	4	14-20·82	
			F		10	14-39·72	
		10000m	F		12	30-17·2	
Magarinos, R.	ESP	400m	1	3	5	46·92	
Maggard, D.	USA	Shot put	F		5	19,43	
Magnor, H.	GER	50k walk	F		11	4:39-43·2	
Maguire, E.	NZL	10000m	F		DNF		
Majekodunmi, B.	NGR	4×100m relay	1	1	5	39·47	
			SF	2	DNF		
Makama, M.	NGR	400m	1	6	3	46·49	
			2	4	7	46·41	
		4×400m relay	1	2	3	3-05·78	
Maki, S.	CIV	110m hurdles	1	3	6	14·32	
Maldonado, V.	VEN	400m hurdles	1	1	4	51·46	
			SF	1	8	52·29	
		4×400m relay	1	3	5	3-07·65	
Maluski, J.	POL	1500m	1	5	9	3-54·83	
Malyutin, A.	URS	Pole vault	F		12	5,00	
Mandl, H.	AUT	Decathlon	F		DNF		
Maniak, W.	POL	100m	1	1	4	10·49	
		4×100m relay	1	3	3	40·27	
			SF	1	4	38·99	
			F		8	39·22	
Martinez, C.	CUB	400m	1	5	6	47·28	
		4×400m relay	1	3	4	3-05·28	
Martinez, J.	MEX	5000m	1	3	2	14-20·06	
			F		4	14-10·76	
		10000m	F		4	29-35·0	
Martinez, J.	ESP	Hammer throw	Q		DNQ	63,40	
Maslakov, V.	URS	200m	1	1	5	21·07	
			2	4	6	20·96	
Masresha, W.	ETH	5000m	1	2	3	14-26·99	
			F		6	14-17·70	
		10000m	F		8	29-57·0	
Massaquoi, A.	SLE	10000m	F		DNF		
		Marathon	F		45	2:52-28·0	

COMPETITOR	COUNTRY CODE	EVENT	ROUND	HEAT	PLACE	TIME & DISTANCE	MEDAL
Matson, R.	USA	Shot put	F		1	20,54	G
Matthews, V.	USA	4×400m relay	1	1	1	3-00·71*	G
			F		1	2-56·16*	G
May, P.	AUS	Triple jump	F		6	17,02	
Mays, C.	USA	Long jump	F		NP	0	
M'Baye, D.	SEN	4×400m relay	1	2	4	3-06·94	
Mecser, L.	HUN	10000m	F		22	30-54·8	
		Marathon	F		DNF		
Mederos, G.	CUB	Discus throw	Q		DNQ	52,30	
Medina, S.	MEX	4×400m relay	1	3	6	3-08·19	
Meighan, O.	HBR	Long jump	Q		DNQ	6,06	
Mejia, A.	COL	10000m	F		10	30-10·6	
Mendoza, R.	NCA	Shot put	Q		DNQ	13,33	
		Discus throw	Q		DNQ	39,62	
Menet, H.	SUI	3000m steeplechase	1	2	13	10-02·06	
Menocal, F.	NCA	400m	1	3	7	49·14	
		800m	1	5	8	1-58·96	
Merschenz, K.	CAN	20k walk	F		18	1:40-11·0	
		50k walk	F		9	4:37-57·4	
Metz, G.	GER	100m	1	9	4	10·55	
		200m	1	7	5	21·24	
		4×100m relay	1	2	3	39·16	
			SF	1	3	38·93	
			F		6	38·76	
Mikityenko, L.	URS	5000m	1	3	7	14-44·35	
		10000m	F		17	30-46·0	
Milde, L.	GDR	Discus throw	F		2	63,08	S
Milek, P.	YUG	High Jump	Q		DNQ	2,00	
Miller, Lennox	JAM	100m	1	6	6	10·15	
			2	1	1	10·11	
			SF	2	2	10·15	
			F		2	10·04	S
		4×100m relay	1	2	1	38·65*	
			SF	1	1	38·39*	
			F		4	38·47	
Miller, Leslie	BAH	400m	1	7	7	46·99	
Mills, L.	NZL	Shot put	F		11	18,18	
Miranda, P.	MEX	3000m steeplechase	1	1	11	9-25·95	
Miura, N.	JPN	3000m steeplechase	1	2	8	9-32·95	
Molders, G.	GER	3000m steeplechase	1	3	10	9-32·22	
Molloy, M.	IRL	Marathon	F		41	2:48-13·6	
Monsegue, R.	TRI	100m	1	6	5	10·56	
Monsels, E.	SUR	100m	1	8	5	10·48	
			2	4	8	10·45	
Montes, P.	CUB	100m	1	4	1	10·14	
			2	3	1	10·16	
			SF	2	3	10·19	
			F		4	10·14	
		4×100m relay	1	1	1	38·76*	
			SF	2	1	38·64	
			F		2	38·40	S
Moore, K.	USA	Marathon	F		14	2:29-49·4	
Mora, R.	DOM	110m hurdles	1	5	7	16·85	
		4×400m relay	1	1	5	3-19·42	
Morales, C.	HON	5000m	1	2	14	18-40·13	
Morales, G.	NCA	Hammer throw	Q		DNQ	45,76	
Morales, J.	CUB	110m hurdles	1	3	3	13·94	
			SF	1	7	14·08	
		4×100m relay	1	1	1	38·76*	
			SF	2	1	38·64	
			F		2	38·40	S
Moreno, I.	CHI	100m	1	3	2	10·53	
			2	1	4	10·37	
			SF	2	6	10·37	
		200m	1	5	1	20·93	
			2	2	4	20·83	
			SF	1	5	20·84	
Morgan, G.	SUD	100m	1	7	8	11·09	
		200m	1	3	7	22·70	
Morozov, A.	URS	3000m steeplechase	1	3	4	9-08·45	
			F		5	8-55·61	
Moses, P.	KEN	Marathon	F		49	2:55-17·0	
Mueller, H.	GER	400m	1	5	4	45·98	
			2	4	3	45·78	
			SF	1	=6	46·22	
		4×400m relay	1	3	1	3-03·90	
			F		3	3-00·57	B
Mueller, J.	GER	20k walk	F		DNF		
Mueller, W.	GDR	400m	1	8	=1	46·66	
			2	2	4	46·32	
			SF	1	8	48·37	
		4×400m relay	1	1	4	3-07·00	
Muraki, Y.	JPN	Triple jump	Q		DNQ	15,83	
Murphy, F.	IRL	1500m	1	5	10	3-54·85	
Murro, M.	USA	Javelin throw	F		9	80,08	
Mustakari, E.	FIN	Pole vault	F		NP	0	

COMPETITOR	COUNTRY CODE	EVENT	ROUND	HEAT	PLACE	TIME & DISTANCE	MEDAL
Mustapha, M.	UGA	5000m	1	2	9	15-10·24	
		10000m	F		21	30-54·2	
		Marathon	F		55	3:04-53·8	
Myton, N.	JAM	800m	1	3	DNF		
Nadenicek, L.	TCH	110m hurdles	1	5	5	14·18	
Nagai, J.	JPN	800m	1	5	5	1-51·27	
Nallet, J.-C.	FRA	400m	1	5	3	45·93	
			2	4	4	45·80	
			SF	2	7	49·01	
		4×400m relay	1	3	3	3-04·69	
			F		8	3-07·51	
N'Diaye, P.	SUI	800m	1	1	4	1-51·31	
		4×400m relay	1	2	4	3-06·94	
Nelson, V.	USA	10000m	F		28	31-40·2	
Nemeth, M.	HUN	Javelin throw	Q		DNQ	75,50	
Neri, J.	MEX	1500m	1	3	6	3-47·88	
Nermerich, B.N.	GER	50k walk	F		DNF		
Neu, H.-D.	GER	Discus throw	F		9	58,66	
Neumann, K.	GDR	Triple jump	Q		DNQ	15,16	
Nevala, P.	FIN	Javelin throw	Q		DNQ	77,90	
Niare, N.	MLI	Discus throw	Q		DNQ	56,60	
Nicolas, C.	FRA	1500m	1	2	4	3-59·35	
			SF	2	11	4-04·47	
Nicolau, C.	FRA	400m	1	1	3	45·77	
			2	2	DNS		
		4×400m relay	1	3	3	3-04·69	
Nightingale, C.	USA	3000m steeplechase	1	1	6	9-13·23	
Nihill, V.P.	GBR	50k walk	F		DNF		
Nikiciuk, W.	POL	Javelin throw	F		4	85,70	
Nikolaidis, P.	GRE	Pole vault	Q		DNQ	4,80	
Nilsson, K.	SWE	Javelin throw	F		6	83,48	
Niwa, K.	JPN	Pole vault	F		11	5,15	
Nordwig, W.	GDR	Pole vault	F		3	5,40*	B
Norman, P.	AUS	200m	1	6	1	20·23*	
			2	2	1	20·44	
			SF	1	2	20·22	
			F		2	20·06	S
Norpoth, H.	GER	1500m	1	3	3	3-47·00	
			SF	1	5	3-54·34	
			F		4	3-42·57	
		5000m	1	3	3	14-20·59	
			F		DNF		
Nottage, B.	BAH	100m	1	5	4	10·64	
		200m	1	4	4	21·31	
			2	4	8	21·53	
		4×100m relay	1	1	4	39·45	
			SF	2	DNF		
Nowosz, Z.	POL	100m	1	3	5	10·57	
		4×100m relay	1	3	3	40·27	
			SF	1	4	38·99	
			F		8	39·22	
Nunez, M.	DOM	1500m	1	2	10	4-23·67	
Nwemba, E.	ZAM	Marathon	F		56	3:06-16·0	
Nyakvoon, A.	MAL	Long jump	Q		DNQ	7·29	
Nyamau, M.	KEN	400m	1	5	2	45·91	
			2	2	3	46·12	
			SF	2	6	46·37	
		4×400m relay	1	1	3	3-03·84	
			F		2	2-59·64	S
O'Baid-Daifallah, S.	KUW	Marathon	F		DNF		
O'Brien, K.	AUS	3000m steeplechase	1	2	2	9-01·49	
			F		4	8-52·08	
Odlozil, J.	TCH	1500m	1	3	4	3-47·49	
			SF	2	5	3-52·53	
			F		8	3-48·69	
Oerter, A.	USA	Discus throw	F		1	64,78*	G
Ogura, S.	JPN	Long jump	Q		DNQ	7,57	
		4×100m relay	1	2	6	40·02	
Ojo, R.	NGR	100m	1	6	4	10·47	
			2	3	8	10·58	
		4×100m relay	1	1	5	39·47	
			SF	2	DNF		
Olafsson, J.	ISL	High jump	Q		DNQ	2,06	
Oliveira, M.	POR	3000m steeplechase	1	1	8	9-19·22	
Olivera, M.	CUB	400m hurdles	1	1	7	51·98	
		4×100m relay	1	3	4	3-05·28	
Oliveros, J.	MEX	20k walk	F		13	1:38-17·0	
Olsen, G.	DEN	Marathon	F		34	2:42-24·6	
Omolo, A.	UGA	100m	1	2	4	10·50	
			2	3	7	10·45	
		400m	1	5	1	45·85	
			2	2	1	45·33	
			SF	2	4	45·52	
			F		8	47·61	
Onofre, R.	PHI	110m hurdles	1	4	6	15·01	
		100m	1	6	6	10·58	

COMPETITOR	COUNTRY CODE	EVENT	ROUND	HEAT	PLACE	TIME & DISTANCE	MEDAL
Ortiz, J.	GUA	20k walk	F		28	1:54-48·0	
Ottolina, S.	ITA	400m	1	8	3	46·78	
			2	3	DNS		
		4×100m relay	1	3	5	41·59	
			SF	2	4	39·46	
			F		7	39·22	
		4×400m relay	1	1	3	3-04·93	
			F		7	3-04·64	
Ottoz, E.	ITA	110m hurdles	1	3	1	13·61*	
			SF	1	2	13·53	
			F		3	13·46	B
Oukada, L.	MAR	3000m steeplechase	1	1	DNF		
Ouko, R.	KEN	800m	1	4	3	1-47·65	
			SF	2	5	1-47·15	
Owusu, E.	GHA	4×400m relay	1	1	6	39·87	
			SF	2	5	39·96	
Oyebami, T.	NGR	4×100m relay	1	1	5	39·47	
			SF	2	DNF		
Paama, M.	URS	Javelin throw	Q		DNQ	77,26	
Palacios, T.	GUA	High jump	Q		DNQ	2,06	
Pamich, A.	ITA	50k walk	F		DNF		
Pani, J.	FRA	Long jump	F		7	7,97	
Papanicolau, C.	GRE	Pole vault	F		4	5,35	
Parker, M.	GBR	110m hurdles	1	4	4	14·16	
Pascoe, A.	GBR	110m hurdles	1	5	=3	14·01	
Patirez, V.	VEN	4×400m relay	1	3	5	3-07·65	
Payne, A.	GER	Hammer throw	F		10	67,62	
Payne, J.	BER	1500m	1	4	10	4-18·92	
Peckham, L.	AUS	High jump	F		8	2,12	
Pedraza, J.	MEX	20k walk	F		2	1:34-00·0	S
		50k walk	F		8	4:37-51·4	
Peiren, M.	BEL	Marathon	F		20	2:32-49·0	
Pektor, W.	AUT	Javelin throw	F		10	77,40	
Penaloza, A.	MEX	Marathon	F		13	2:29-48·8	
Penner, M.	USA	100m	1	4	2	10·35	
			2	2	2	10·16	
			SF	1	4	10·21	
			F		7	10·17	
		4×100m relay	1	1	2	38·86	
			SF	2	2	38·69	
			F		1	38·24*	G
Pernel, J.	USA	Pole vault	F		5	5,35	
Pennewaert, J.	BEL	400m	1	4	6	48·55	
		800m	1	5	7	1-53·81	
Perera, W.	CEY	Marathon	F		51	2:59-05·8	
Perez, C.	ESP	Marathon	F		DNF		
Perez, J.	CRC	5000m	1	2	12	15-41·37	
		10000m	F		30	32-14·6	
Persson, B.	SWE	3000m steeplechase	1	1	3	9-06·43	
			F		10	9-20·61	
Peyter, I.	AUT	Pole vault	Q		DNQ	0	
Pfister, R.	SUI	20k walk	F		23	1:43-36·0	
Philipp, L.	GER	10000m	F		23	30-57·0	
Piatkowski, E.	POL	Discus throw	F		7	59,40	
Pina, M.	MEX	400m	1	7	6	46·81	
		4×400m relay	1	3	6	3-08·19	
Piquemal, C.	FRA	4×100m relay	1	2	2	39·03	
			SF	2	3	38·83	
			F		3	38·43	B
Plachy, J.	TCH	800m	1	3	2	1-48·65	
			SF	2	3	1-45·96	
			F		5	1-45·99	
Planchart, M.	VEN	100m	1	2	8	10·80	
Plasket, C.	ISV	200m	1	7	6	21·29	
Poirier, R.	FRA	400m hurdles	1	4	3	50·51	
			SF	2	6	51·23	
Pollemis, W.	BEL	10000m	F		DNF		
Portmann, M.	SUI	High jump	Q		DNQ	2,06	
Pousi, P.	FIN	Long jump	Q		DNQ	7,63	
		Triple jump	Q		DNQ	15,84	
Prealori, E.	ITA	100m	1	5	5	10·65	
		4×100m relay	1	3	5	41·59	
			SF	2	4	39·46	
			F		7	39·22	
Prowell, H.	GUY	Marathon	F		50	2:57-01·4	
Prudencio, N.	BRA	Triple jump	F		2	17,27	S
Puce, C.	CAN	Discus throw	Q		DNQ	57,34	
Puttemans, E.	BEL	5000m	1	1	5	14-34·58	
			F		12	14-59·56	
Puosi, G.	ITA	4×400m relay	1	1	3	3-04·93	
			F		7	3-04·64	
Quaye, W.	GHA	400m hurdles	1	2	6	55·54	
		4×100m relay	1	1	6	39·87	
			SF	2	5	39·96	

COMPETITOR	COUNTRY CODE	EVENT	ROUND	HEAT	PLACE	TIME & DISTANCE	MEDAL
Questad, L.	USA	200m	1	3	1	20·75	
			2	4	2	20·54	
			SF	2	3	20·48	
			F		6	20·62	
Quevedo, J.	GUA	1500m	1	1	9	4-03·13	
		5000m	1	3	9	15-23·03	
		3000m steeplechase	1	3	12	9·48·37	
Radutorahalahy, D.	MAD	Decathlon	F		DNF		
Raiko, O.	URS	1500m	1	3	2	3-46·84	
			SF	2	7	3-52·73	
Rajalingam, G.	MAL	200m	1	6	4	21·58	
			2	2	8	21·52	
		4×100m relay	1	3	4	40·69	
			SF	1	8	40·89	
Ramasamy, S.	MAL	800m	1	2	4	1-50·87	
		1500m	1	2	9	4-06·49	
Ramirez, H.	CUB	100m	1	9	1	10·30	
			2	2	1	10·10	
			SF	1	6	10·25	
		4×100m relay	1	1	1	38·76*	
			SF	2	1	38·64	
			F		2	38·40	S
Ravelomanantsoa, J.-L.	MAD	100m	1	2	2	10·30	
			2	4	2	10·18	
			SF	2	4	10·26	
			F		8	10·28	
		200m	1	3	5	21·53	
Reed, P.	GBR	Long jump	Q		DNQ	0	
Reilly, W.	USA	3000m steeplechase	1	3	5	9-10·35	
Reimann, H.	GDR	20k walk	F		7	1:36-31·14	
Reimers, J.	GER	Discus throw	Q		DNQ	54,02	
Reinitzer, H.	AUT	Discus throw	Q		DNQ	53,52	
Riedo, D.	SUI	110m hurdles	1	1	3	14·10	
			SF	1	6	14·07	
Riesner, H.	GER	Marathon	F		33	2:41-29·0	
Rios, W.	PUR	1500m	1	4	10	4-14·47	
Risa, A.	NOR	3000m steeplechase	1	1	4	9-07·31	
			F		8	9-08·98	
Risi, U.	ITA	3000m steeplechase	1	3	11	9-43·97	
Roberts, E.	TRI	200m	1	2	=3	20·69	
			2	3	2	20·50	
			SF	2	2	20·44	
			F		4	20·34	
		4×100m relay	1	1	3	38·97	
			SF	1	6	39·52	
		4×400m relay	1	3	2	3-04·55	
			F		6	3-04·52	
Robinson, T.	BAH	100m	1	6	DNF		
		4×100m relay	1	1	4	39·45	
			SF	2	DNF		
Roelants, G.	BEL	Marathon	F		11	2:29-04·8	
		3000m steeplechase	1	3	3	9-08·29	
			F		7	8-59·50	
Romanowski, E.	POL	200m	1	3	3	20·95	
			2	3	3	20·85	
			SF	2	6	20·80	
		4×100m relay	1	3	3	40·27	
			SF	1	4	38·99	
			F		8	39·22	
Romansky, S.	USA	50k walk	F		26	5:38-03·4	
Rudisha, D.	KEN	400m	1	2	4	46·96	
			2	3	6	47·68	
		4×400m relay	1	1	2	3-00·84	
			F		2	2-59·64	S
Rummakko, P.	FIN	Marathon	F		DNF		
Rushmer, A.	GBR	5000m	1	3	8	15-05·17	
Rutyna, M.	POL	20k walk	F		26	1:47-29·0	
		50k walk	F		22	4:58-03·8	
Ryan, M.	NZL	Marathon	F		3	2:23-45·0	B
Ryun, J.	USA	1500m	1	4	1	3-45·80	
			SF	2	1	3-51·25	
			F		2	3-37·89	S
Saavedra, P.	CHI	110m hurdles	1	4	5	14·47	
Sagna, C.	SEN	Long jump	Q		DNQ	7,31	
Sagna, E.	SEN	1500m	1	1	10	4-04·12	
Sainte-Rose, R.	FRA	High jump	F		9	2,09	
Saisi, T.	KEN	800m	1	1	1	1-46·99	
			SF	1	3	1-46·64	
			F		7	1-47·59	
Saito, K.	JPN	50k walk	F		17	4:47-29·6	
		20k walk	F		DNF		
Salomon, H.	GER	Javelin throw	F		12	73,50	
Salve, E.	BEL	1500m	1	4	3	3-47·11	
			SF	1	10	3-58·16	
Sanchez, A.	MEX	400m hurdles	1	4	6	51·62	

COMPETITOR	COUNTRY CODE	EVENT	ROUND	HEAT	PLACE	TIME & DISTANCE	MEDAL
Sanchez, J.	ESP	100m	1	9	7	10·69	
Saneyev, V.	URS	Triple jump	F		1	17,39*	G
Sang, J.	KEN	100m	1	2	6	10·64	
		200m	1	3	2	20·90	
			2	1	5	21·04	
Santos, E.	HON	10000m	F		DNF		
Santos, R.	SAL	100m	1	8	8	11·22	
Sapeya, V.	URS	100m	1	8	4	10·46	
			2	1	8	10·51	
		4×100m relay	1	3	2	39·03	
			SF	2	DNF		
Sardo, F.	MEX	4×400m relay	1	3	6	3-08·19	
Sarr, L.	SEN	Long jump	Q		DNQ	7,61	
Sarr, M.	SEN	400m hurdles	1	2	4	51·58	
			SF	2	8	52·20	
		4×400m relay	1	2	4	3-06·94	
Sasaki, S.	JPN	Marathon	F		DNF		
Sauer, M.	GER	Triple jump	Q		DNQ	16,02	
Sawaki, K.	JPN	5000m	1	1	9	15-00·86	
		10000m	F		27	31-25·2	
Schaumburg, G.	GDR	Discus throw	F		10	58,62	
Schelter, H.	GDR	100m	1	6	2	10·34	
			2	3	2	10·29	
			SF	2	=7	10·40	
		4×100m relay	1	3	1	38·93	
			SF	2	2	38·72	
			F		5	38·66	
Schenk, H.	GDR	Triple jump	Q		DNQ	15,61	
Schiprowski, C.	GER	Pole vault	F		2	5,40*	S
Schmidt, J.	POL	Triple jump	F		7	16,89	
Schmidtke, K.	GER	100m	1	7	2	10·38	
			2	1	7	10·48	
		4×100m relay	1	2	3	39·16	
			SF	1	3	38·93	
			F		6	38·76	
Schneiter, W.	SUI	5000m	1	2	8	15-08·24	
Schoebel, P.	FRA	110m hurdles	1	1	2	13·83	
			SF	1	4	13·78	
			F		8	14·02	
Schubert, R.	GER	400m hurdles	1	3	2	49·15	
			SF	1	4	49·38	
			F		7	49·30	
Schwabe, H.	GDR	4×400m relay	1	1	4	3-07·00	
Scott, L.	USA	5000m	1	1	11	15-13·69	
Seagren, R.	USA	Pole vault	F		1	5,40*	G
Sebsibe, M.	ETH	800m	1	6	5	1-49·75	
Selzer, P.	GDR	50k walk	F		4	4:33-09·8	
Senoussi, A.	CHA	High jump	F		12	2,09	
Serate, H.	PUR	Triple jump	Q		DNQ	15,09	
Sguazzero, A.	ITA	4×100m relay	1	3	5	41·59	
			SF	2	4	39·46	
			F		7	39·22	
Shakirov, M.	URS	Marathon	F		DNF		
Sharafetdinov, R.	URS	5000m	1	1	7	14-44·41	
Sherwood, J.	GBR	400m hurdles	1	3	4	50·31	
			SF	1	3	49·37	
			F		3	49·03	B
		4×400m relay	1	2	2	3-03·67	
			F		5	3-01·21	
Short, W.	TRI	200m	1	4	2	21·00	
			2	2	7	21·51	
		4×100m relay	1	1	3	38·97	
			SF	1	6	39·52	
Shuplyakov, A.	URS	Hammer throw	F		9	67,74	
Sibon, G.	FRA	800m	1	4	5	1-50·87	
Sidlo, J.	POL	Javelin throw	F		7	80,58	
Sieghart, I.	GER	High jump	F		10	2,09	
Sierra, J.	COL	100m	1	3	7	10·88	
Sievers, K.	GER	Marathon	F		23	2:34-11·8	
Silva, R.	MEX	800m	1	3	5	1-50·49	
Silva-Netto, B.	PHI	5000m	1	2	13	17-10·15	
		10000m	F		31	32-35·2	
		Marathon	F		49	2:56-19·4	
Silvester, J.	USA	Discus throw	F		5	61,78	
Simeonov, N.	BUL	Marathon	F		42	2:48-30·4	
Simon, G.	TRI	400m	1	8	5	47·95	
		4×400m relay	1	3	2	3-04·55	
			F		6	3-04·52	
Simon, R.	BEL	800m	1	1	DNF		
		1500m	1	5	11	4-06·97	
Singh, B.	IND	High jump	Q		DNQ	2,09	
Singh, N.	MAL	Javelin throw	Q		DNQ	70,70	
Sinkala, D.	ZAM	Marathon	F		35	2:42-51·0	
Sinyayev, Y.	URS	100m	1	3	4	10·56	
		4X100m relay	1	3	2	39·03	
			SF	2	DNF		

COMPETITOR	COUNTRY CODE	EVENT	ROUND	HEAT	PLACE	TIME & DISTANCE	MEDAL
Skomorokhov, V.	URS	400m hurdles	1	1	3	50·72	
			SF	2	4	49·61	
			F		5	49·12	
Skvortsov, V.	URS	High jump	F		4	2.16	
Sloan, R.	USA	Decathlon	F		7	7692	
Smaga, N.	URS	20k walk	F		3	1:34-03·4	B
Smid-Jensen, S.	DEN	Decathlon	F		8	7648	
Smith, D.	USA	Triple jump	Q		DNQ	15,75	
Smith, R.	USA	4×100m relay	1	1	2	38·86	
			SF	2	2	38·69	
			F		1	38·24*	G
Smith, Tommie	USA	200m	1	2	1	20·37	
			2	3	1	20·28	
			SF	2	1	20·14	
			F		1	19·83*	G
Smith, Tracy	USA	10000m	F		11	30-14·6	
Sneazwell, A.	AUS	High jump	Q		DNQ	2,06	
Sola, I.	ESP	Pole vault	F		9	5,20	
Songkok, K.	KEN	110m hurdles	1	1	6	14·76	
		400m hurdles	1	4	5	50·66	
Soriano, D.	DOM	4×400m relay	1	1	5	3-19·42	
Soriano, L.	DOM	4×100m relay	1	1	7	41·48	
Sowa, C.	LUX	20k walk	F		19	1:40-17·0	
		50k walk	F		16	4:44-45·2	
Speake, J.	GBR	4×100m relay	1	2	4	39·33	
			SF	1	5	39·46	
Sperling, G.	GDR	20k walk	F		5	1:35-27·2	
Spielvogel, G.	GER	High jump	F		7	2,14	
Stalmach, A.	POL	Long jump	F		8	7,94	
Stawiarz, E.	POL	5000m	1	2	10	15-13·87	
		10000m	F		DNF		
Steane, R.	GBR	200m	1	6	3	20·66	
			2	1	=2	20·81	
			SF	1	6	20·85	
Steffny, M.	GER	Marathon	F		7	2:31-23·8	
Stenlund, G.	USA	Javelin throw	Q		DNQ	73,52	
Stewart, E.	JAM	4×100m relay	1	2	1	38·65*	
			SF		1	38·39*	
			F		4	38·47	
Steylen, A.	HOL	Marathon	F		27	2:37-42·0	
Stolle, M.	GDR	Javelin throw	F		5	84.42	
Storey, S.	GBR	110m hurdles	1	3	5	14·20	
Stoykovski, G.	BUL	Triple jump	F		9	16,46	
Stubbs, N.	BAH	100m	1	4	5	10·67	
		200m	1	3	6	21·64	
Stutz, E.	SUI	50k walk	F		20	4:53-33·8	
Styepanenko, O.	URS	110m hurdles	1	2	4	13·95	
			SF	2	5	13·83	
Su, P.-T.	FOR	110m hurdles	1	2	7	15·11	
Su, W.-H.	SWI	Long jump	Q		DNQ	7,30	
		100m	1	5	7	10·81	
Sugawara, T.	JPN	Hammer throw	F		4	69,78	
Sugioka, K.	JPN	High jump	Q		DNQ	2,09	
Suhkarkov, A.	URS	Marathon	F		23	2:38-07·4	
Sumbwegam	BUR	Marathon	F		13	2:32-22·0	
Surawatari, T.	JPN	3000m steeplechase	1	3	9	9-26·30	
Suzuki, T.	JPN	10000m	F		19	30-52·0	
Sviridov, N.	URS	5000m	1	2	5	14-38·70	
			F		7	14-18·40	
		10000m	F		5	29-43·2	
Sy, N.	SEN	100m	1	1	5	10·61	
Szabo, J.	HUN	3000m steeplechase	1	1	10	9-25·82	
Szerenyi, J.	HUN	10000m	F		20	30-53·6	
Szordykowski, H.	POL	800m	1	4	2	1-47·48	
			SF	1		DNS	
		1500m	1	2	3	3-59·34	
			SF	1	4	3-54·24	
			F		7	3-46·69	
Tagg, M.	GBR	10000m	F		13	30-13·0	
Tait, R.	NZL	Discus throw	F		12	57,68	
Tancred, W.	GBR	Discus throw	Q		DNQ	51,74	
Tate, N.	USA	Triple jump	Q		DNQ	15,84	
Taylor, R.	GBR	5000m	1	1	8	14-46·52	
Teale, J.	GBR	Shot put	F		10	18,65	
Tegla, F.	HUN	Discus throw	F		11	58,36	
Tellez, E.	CUB	400m	1	6	5	46·30	
		4×400m relay	1	3	4	3-05·28	
Temu, N.	KEN	5000m	1	2	1	14-20·38	
			F		3	14-06·41	B
		10000m	F		1	29-27·40	G
		Marathon	F		19	2:32-36·0	
Ter-Ovanesyan, I.	URS	Long jump	F		4	8,12	
Texereau, G.	FRA	3000m steeplechase	1	3	DNF		
		Marathon	F		DNF		
Theimer, R.	GDR	Hammer throw	F		7	68,84	
Thein, H.	BUR	Marathon	F		47	2:54-03·6	
Thorkaksson, V.	ISL	Decathlon	F		DNF		
Thurton, C.	HON	200m	1	5	7	22·14	
Tiectke, M.	GDR	Decathlon	F		10	7551	
Todosijevic, M.	YUG	High jump	F		13	2,06	
Toomey, W.	USA	Decathlon	F		1	8193*	G
Torres, A.	DOM	200m	1	6	5	21·99	
		4×100m relay	1	1	7	41·48	
Toth, G.	HUN	Marathon	F		24	2:34-49·0	
Towndray, F.	MAD	110m hurdles	1	3	7	15·00	
		High jump	Q		DNQ	2,03	
Trautmann, U.	SUI	Decathlon	F		18	7044	
Travis, D.	GBR	Javelin throw	Q		DNQ	74,36	
Trerise, N.	CAN	1500m	1	4	5	3-47·67	
			SF	2	10	3-57·30	
Trzmiel, W.	GER	110m hurdles	1	3	2	13·87	
			SF	2	3	13·60	
			F		5	13·68	
Tuemmler, B.	GER	1500m	1	1	2	3-51·59	
			SF	1	1	3-53·66	
			F		3	3-39·08	B
Tuna, A.	TUR	Triple jump	Q		DNQ	15,65	
Tuominen, J.	FIN	400m hurdles	1	4	4	50·63	
Turay, M.	SLE	High jump	Q		DNQ	1,95	
Ugolini, G.	FRA	Long jump	F		16	7,44	
Usami, A.	JPN	Marathon	F		9	2:28-06·2	
Valadares, J.	HON	5000m	1	1	14	18-21·52	
Vale, E.	NCA	20k walk	F		DNF		
Van Butsele, R.	BEL	3000m steeplechase	1	2	11	9-38·79	
Vanderstock, G.	USA	400m hurdles	1	1	2	50·62	
			SF	1	2	49·22	
			F		4	49·07	
Vanegas, C.	NCA	20k walk	F		DNF		
Van Manshoven, G.	BEL	800m	1	2	3	1-52·32	
Vaju, V.	HUN	Shot put	Q		DNQ	18,86	
Vasala, P.	FIN	1500m	1	4	9	4-08·51	
Velez, D.	NCA	Long jump	Q		DNQ	6,63	
		Javelin throw	Q		DNQ	61,32	
		Decathlon	F		20	5943	
Veras, P.	DOM	100m	1	2	5	10·51	
		200m	1	4	6	21·53	
		4×100m relay	1	1	7	41·48	
Villain, J.	FRA	3000m steeplechase	1	2	1	9-01·12	
			F		9	9-16·27	
Virtilis, I.	GRE	1500m	1	3	8	3-55·57	
Visini, V.	ITA	50k walk	F		6	4:36-33·2	
Vizcarrondo, J.	PUR	100m	1	2	7	10·71	
Vlassis, E.	GRE	Triple jump	Q		DNQ	15,71	
Von Moltke, W.	GER	Decathlon	F		DNF		
Von Ruden, T.	USA	1500m	1	2	1	3-59·15	
			SF	1	3	3-54·12	
			F		9	3-49·27	
Von Wartburg, U.	SUI	Javelin throw	F		8	80,56	
Waddell, T.	USA	Decathlon	F		6	7720	
Waroux, J.	FRA	5000m	1	3	1	14-19·80	
			F		9	14-20·73	
Wagner, W.	GER	3000m steeplechase	1	2	6	9-24·49	
Walde, H.-J.	GER	Decathlon	F		2	8111	S
Walker, J.	USA	Triple jump	F		4	17,12	
Watson, P.	AUS	1500m	1	4	7	3-55·41	
Webb, J.	GBR	20k walk	F		22	1:42-51·0	
Weemann, W.	CAN	High jump	Q		DNQ	2,00	
Weidner, G.	GER	50k walk	F		14	4:43-26·2	
Weinstand, W.	POL	400m hurdles	1	3	5	50·71	
Welsh, P.	NZL	3000m steeplechase	1	3	6	9-13·80	
Werner, J.	POL	400m	1	6	1	45·97	
			2	3	1	45·63	
			SF	2	5	45·75	
		4×400m relay	1	2	1	3-03·02	
			F		4	3-00·58	
Wessel, H.	GDR	Decathlon	F		DNF		
Weum, K.	NOR	110m hurdles	1	4	3	14·08	
			SF	2	6	14·04	
Whetton, J.	GBR	1500m	1	5	3	3-53·04	
			SF	2	3	3-52·05	
			F		5	3-43·90	
Whitney, R.	USA	400m hurdles	1	3	1	49·06*	
			SF	2	2	49·29	
			F		6	49·27	
Wiegner, H.	SWI	100m	1	5	6	10·75	
		200m	1	4	3	21·06	
			2	3	7	21·42	
Wieser, T.	SUI	High jump	Q		DNQ	2,03	
Winbolt Lewis, M.	GBR	400m	1	6	2	46·27	
			2	4	5	45·91	
		4×400m relay	1	2	2	3-03·67	
			F		5	3-01·21	

COMPETITOR	COUNTRY CODE	EVENT	ROUND	HEAT	PLACE	TIME & DISTANCE	MEDAL
Wisdom, G.	BAH	Long jump	Q		DNQ	6,99	
		4×100m relay	1	1	4	39·45	
			SF	2	DNF		
Wolde, M.	ETH	5000m	1	1	3	14-29·85	
			F		DNS		
		10000m	F		2	29-27·75	S
		Marathon	F		1	2:20-26·4	G
Woldemedhin, T.	ETH	3000m steeplechase	1	1	7	9-13·24	
Wolfermann, K.	GER	Javelin throw	Q		DNQ	75,78	
Woods, G.	USA	Shot put	F		2	20,12	S
Wu, A. Min	FOR	Pole vault	Q		DNQ	4,50	
		Decathlon	F		15	7209	
Wuecherer, G.	FRG	100m	1	8	2	10·42	
			2	2	6	10·33	
		4×100m relay	1	2	3	39·16	
			SF	1	3	38·93	
			F		6	38·76	
Wyns, L.	BEL	Javelin throw	Q		DNQ	73,68	
Wyss, H.	SUI	Pole vault	Q		DNQ	4,50	
Yamada, H.	JPN	Long jump	F		10	7,93	
		4×100m relay	1	2	6	40·02	
Young, G.	USA	Marathon	F		16	2:31-15·0	
		3000m steeplechase	1	2	2	9-02·31	
			F		3	8-51·86	B
Young, L.	USA	50k walk	F		3	4:31-55·4	B
Yoyaga, C.	CIV	440m	1	7	8	50·11	
Yui, K.	JPN	400m hurdles	1	1	5	51·56	
Zabiah, C.	SAL	Hammer throw	Q		DNQ	37,46	
Zacharias, T.	GER	High jump	Q		DNQ	2,09	
Zambrose, A.	MAL	400m hurdles	1	3	8	53·23	
Zammel, A.	TUN	5000m	1	2	6	14-54·02	
Zerbes, M.	GDR	400m	1	4	3	46·84	
			2	4	6	46·19	
		4×400m relay	1	1	4	3-07·00	
Zhelev, M.	BUL	3000m steeplechase	1	3	2	9-00·96	
			F		6	8-58·41	
Zhelobovski, M.	URS	1500m	1	5	5	3-53·23	
			SF	1	11	3-59·08	
Zolotaryev, A.	URS	Triple jump	Q		DNQ	15,41	
Zsivotzky, G.	HUN	Hammer throw	F		1	73,36*	G

FEMALES

COMPETITOR	COUNTRY CODE	EVENT	ROUND	HEAT	PLACE	TIME & DISTANCE	MEDAL
Ackermans, M.	HOL	Pentathlon	F		17	4650	
Aigner, I.	AUT	80m hurdles	1	4	4	10·83	
			SF	1	8	11·12	
Akindele, O.	NGR	100m	1	3	5	11·70	
			2	3	7	11·75	
		200m	1	4	4	23·91	
		4×100m relay	1	1	6	45·23	
Alayrangues, M.	FRA	4×100m relay	1	1	4	44·32	
			F		8	44·30	
Ammann, S.	SUI	Long jump	Q		DNQ	0	
		Pentathlon	F		23	4414	
Antenen, M.	SUI	80m hurdles	1	4	5	10·95	
		Pentathlon	F		8	4848	
Anum, A.	GHA	200m	1	3	7	23·95	
		Long jump	Q		DNQ	5,61	
Bailes, M.	USA	100m	1	2	1	11·30	
			2	3	2	11·34	
			SF	2	3	11·53	
			F		5	11·37	
		200m	1	1	2	23·17	
			SF	2	3	22·95	
			F		7	23·18	
		4×100m relay	1	1	1	43·50*	
			F		1	42·88*	G
Bair, R.	USA	Javelin throw	F		11	53,14	
Bakker, C.	HOL	4×100m relay	1	2	1	43·49*	
			F		4	43·44	
Balogh, G.	HUN	100m	1	6	5	11·80	
			2	4	6	11·78	
		200m	1	1	6	24·15	
		4×100m relay	1	2	5	44·65	
Balzer, K.	USA	80m hurdles	1	5	1	10·72	
			SF	1	4	10·83	
			F		5	10·61	
Bantegny, M.	FRA	Pentathlon	F		15	4697	
Barnay, G.	FRA	High jump	F		9	1,71	
Barton, M.	GBR	Long jump	F		12	5,95	
Basilio, E.	MEX	400m	1	1	5	55·47	
		80m hurdles	1	1	6	11·20	
		4×100m relay	1	1	7	47·09	
Baskerville, E.	USA	High jump	Q		DNQ	0	
Bauer, I.	GDR	Pentathlon	F		7	4849	

COMPETITOR	COUNTRY CODE	EVENT	ROUND	HEAT	PLACE	TIME & DISTANCE	MEDAL
Becker, I.	GER	Long jump	F		6	6,43	
		4×100m relay	1	1	3	44·18	
			F		6	43·70	
		Pentathlon	F		1	5098	G
Bennett, J.	AUS	400m	1	1	6	56·56	
		4×100m relay	1	1	2	43·77	
			F		5	43·50	
Berendonk, B.	GER	Discus throw	F		8	52,80	
Berthelsen, B.	NOR	Long jump	F		7	6,40	
		Pentathlon	F		18	4649	
Berto, S.	CAN	100m	1	5	5	11·81	
			2	2	DNS		
		4×100m relay	1	1	5	44·73	
Besson, C.	FRA	400m	1	1	1	53·11	
			SF	1	2	53·62	
			F		1	52·03*	G
Blagoeva, Y.	BUL	High jump	Q		DNQ	1,68	
Board, L.	GBR	200m	1	2	4	23·49	
			SF	1	6	23·52	
		400m	1	2	2	53·00	
			SF	2	1	52·56	
			F		2	52·12	S
		4×100m relay	1	2	3	43·98	
			F		7	43·78	
Bodunrin, O.	NGR	100m	1	6	4	11·71	
			2	4	DNS		
		400m	1	4	8	57·09	
		4×100m relay	1	1	6	45·23	
Bognar, J.	HUN	Shot put	F		4	17,78	
Bonci, V.	RUM	High jump	Q		DNQ	1,65	
Bornholdt, M.	GER	Long jump	Q		DNQ	6,27	
		Pentathlon	F		5	4890	
Boy, R.	GDR	Shot put	F		5	17,72	
Boyle, R.	AUS	100m	1	4	2	11·44	
			2	3	1	11·29	
			SF	2	2	11·41	
			F		4	11·20	
		200m	2	1	1	23·09*	
			SF	1	1	22·95*	
			F		2	22·74	S
		4×100m relay	1	1	2	43·77	
			F		5	43·50	
Brown, D.	USA	800m	1	3	2	2-09·54	
			SF	2	2	2-05·23	
			F		5	2-03·98	
Brown, S.	AUS	400m	1	3	6	55·43	
Bufanu, V.	RUM	80m hurdles	1	2	2	10·92	
			SF	1	7	11·08	
Bukharina, G.	URS	4×100m relay	1	2	2	43·67	
			F		3	43·41	B
Burge, D.	AUS	100m	1	3	1	11·53	
			2	4	2	11·33	
			SF	1	3	11·46	
			F		6	11·44	
		200m	1	4	2	23·69	
			SF	1	7	23·65	
		4×100m relay	1	1	2	43·77	
			F		5	43·50	
Burneleit, K.	GDR	800m	1	1	4	2-07·13	
			SF	1	5	2-08·41	
Caird, M.	AUS	80m hurdles	1	4	1	10·48	
			SF	1	1	10·59	
			F		1	10·39*	G
Callaghan, S.	USA	High jump	Q		DNQ	1,60	
Catarama, O.	RUM	Discus throw	F		13	50,20	
Cederstrom, G.	SWE	Long jump	Q		DNQ	5,72	
		Pentathlon	F		DNF		
Charlton, V.	JAM	100m	1	3	6	11·71	
		200m	1	2	6	24·39	
		4×100m relay	1	1	DIS		
Chemabwai, T.	KEN	400m	1	3	5	54·05	
Chesire, E.	KEN	800m	1	1	6	2-10·92	
Chi, Cheng	FOR	100m	1	4	3	11·45	
			2	2	2	11·31	
			SF	1	4	11·49	
			F		7	11·53	
		4×100m relay	1	2	6	47·24	
		80m hurdles	1	4	2	10·53	
			SF	2	2	10·56	
			F		3	10·51	B
Chizhova, N.	URS	Shot put	F		3	18,19	B
Chmelkova, A.	TCH	400m	1	2	6	54·91	

COMPETITOR	COUNTRY CODE	EVENT	ROUND	HEAT	PLACE	TIME & DISTANCE	MEDAL
Cobian, M.	CUB	100m	1	2	3	11.48	
			2	1	4	11.41	
			SF	2	4	11.63	
			F		8	11.61	
		200m	1	5	2	23.50	
			SF	2	6	23.39	
		4×100m relay	1	2	4	44.15	
			F		2	43.36	S
Connolly, O.	USA	Discus throw	F		6	52.96	
Covell, A.	CAN	400m	1	2	5	54.34	
Csabi, K.	HUN	High jump	F		10	1,71	
Cypriano, M.	BRA	High jump	F		11	1,71	
Dahlgren, J.	CAN	Javelin throw	F		13	51,34	
Damm-Olesen, A.	DEN	800m	1	4	5	2-09.01	
Dashzeve, N.	MOA	Discus throw	F		12	50,76	
De La Vina, J.	PHI	Discus throw	F		15	46,56	
Denise, N.	FRA	High jump	Q		DNQ	1,69	
Dos Santos. A.	BRA	Pentathlon	F		20	4578	
Drinkwater, L.	USA	400m	1	4	4	54.56	
			SF	2	8	57.39	
Dupureur, M.	FRA	800m	1	3	1	2-09.55	
			SF	2	4	2-05.58	
			F		8	2-08.28	
Dyer, J.	USA	80m hurdles	1	5	3	10.94	
			SF	2	6	10.84	
Elejarde, M.	CUB	80m hurdles	1	2	4	10.99	
		4×100m relay	1	2	4	44.15	
			F		2	43.36	S
Emonts-Gast, R.	BEL	80m hurdles	1	4	7	11.50	
		Pentathlon	F		30	3654	
Erik, L.	URS	800m	1	1	2	2-06.52	
			SF	2	5	2-06.09	
Evert, V.	URS	Javelin throw	F		14	51,16	
Faithova, M.	TCH	High jump	F		6	1,78	
Ferrell, B.	USA	100m	1	6	1	11.28	
			2	1	1	11.12*	
			SF	1	2	11.37	
			F		2	11.15	S
		200m	1	3	1	22.94*	
			SF	2	1	22.87*	
			F		4	22.93	
		4×100m relay	1	1	1	43.50*	
			F		1	42.88*	G
Fisher, J.	CAN	400m	1	1	4	54.62	
			SF	1	8	55.37	
Focic, D.	YUG	Pentathlon	F		29	3814	
Friedrich, B.	USA	Javelin throw	F		9	53,44	
Fuchs, M.	GER	Shot put	F		7	17,11	
Garbey, M.	CUB	Long jump	Q		DNQ	6,14	
Giron, E.	MEX	100m	1	1	7	12.30	
		200m	1	5	7	25.32	
		4×100m relay	1	1	7	47.03	
Gleskova, E.	TCH	100m	1	5	1	11.62	
			2	1	2	11.29	
			SF	2	6	11.80	
		200m	1	1	5	24.03	
Golomazova, L.	URS	100m	1	5	3	11.74	
			2	2	4	11.54	
			SF	1	8	11.71	
		200m	1	3	6	23.73	
Gommers, M.	HOL	800m	1	2	1	2-04.06	
			SF	2	1	2-05.13	
			F		3	2-02.63	B
Govoni, D.	ITA	400m	1	4	5	54.77	
Green, M.	GBR	400m	1	4	2	54.00	
			SF	2	5	53.64	
Grushkina, V.	URS	High jump	F		12	1,71	
Gummel, M.	GDR	Shot put	F		1	19,61*	G
Gusenbauer, I.	AUT	High jump	F		8	1,76	
Haimi, E.	FIN	400m	1	4	6	55.01	
			1	3	5	2-09.67	
Hamblin, C.	USA	Pentathlon	F		24	4330	
Hansen, N.	DEN	Pentathlon	F		13	4738	
Hendry, J.	CAN	Long jump	Q		DNQ	0	
		4×100m relay	1	1	5	44.73	
Henning, H.	GER	400m	1	1	3	53.58	
			SF	1	1	53.33	
			F		7	52.89	
Hennipman, G.	HOL	100m	1	5	4	11.76	
			2	1	7	11.59	
		200m	1	2	3	23.43	
			SF	2	8	23.60	
		4×100m relay	1	2	1	43.49*	
			F		4	43.44	
Herrmann, H.	GER	100m	1	6	6	11.88	
		200m	1	4	6	24.62	

COMPETITOR	COUNTRY CODE	EVENT	ROUND	HEAT	PLACE	TIME & DISTANCE	MEDAL
Hoffman, A.	CAN	800m	1	4	2	2-08.94	
			SF	1	4	2-07.03	
			F		7	2-06.99	
Hrepevnik, S.	YUG	High jump	F		14	1,68	
Illgen, K.	GDR	Discus throw	F		10	52,18	
Inkpen, B.	GBR	High jump	F		13	1,68	
Ivelreva, L.	URS	80m hurdles	1	5	4	10.97	
Jahn, R.	GER	200m	1	5	6	24.02	
		4×100m relay	1	1	3	44.18	
			F		6	43.70	
James, D.	GBR	100m	1	4	4	11.78	
			2	1	3	11.36	
			SF	1	7	11.68	
Janko, E.	AUT	Javelin throw	F		3	58,04	B
Jaworska, D.	POL	Javelin throw	F		5	56,06	
Jehlickova, J.	TCH	800m	1	4	3	2-08.96	
			SF	2	8	2-13.59	
Jinadu, M.	NGR	4×100m relay	1	1	6	45.23	
Jones, P.	GBR	80m hurdles	1	4	6	11.03	
Jozwik, U.	POL	4×100m relay	1	2	7	53.02	
Kaumanas, A.	ARG	100m	1	2	6	11.90	
		200m	1	4	5	24.57	
Keizer, I.	HOL	800m	1	4	4	2-08.96	
			SF	1	7	2-14.88	
Khristova, I.	BUL	Shot put	F		6	17,25	
Kilborn, P.	AUS	100m	1	2	4	11.62	
			2	1	6	11.50	
		80m hurdles	1	2	1	10.41*	
			SF	2	1	10.44	
			F		2	10.46	S
Kispal, E.	HUN	Long jump	Q		DNQ	5,98	
		4×100m relay	1	2	5	44.65	
Kiss, M.	HUN	100m	1	4	6	12.10	
		80m hurdles	1	2	3	10.93	
			SF	2	8	11.22	
Kleiber, J.	HUN	Discus throw	F		3	54,90	B
Koleska, A.	GER	Javelin throw	F		7	55,20	
Korsakova, V.	URS	80m hurdles	1	1	2	10.74	
			SF	1	5	10.86	
Kozyr, V.	URS	High jump	F		3	1,80	B
Kraker, F.	USA	800m	1	1	5	2-07.34	
Krawcewicz, L.	POL	Javelin throw	F		12	51,54	
Lagrosas, L.	PHI	Pentathlon	F		25	4131	
Lamy, J.	AUS	200m	1	3	2	23.19	
			SF	2	2	22.89	
			F		3	22.88	B
		4×100m relay	1	1	2	43.77	
			F		5	43.50	S
Lance, M.	GDR	Shot put	F		2	18,78	S
Laurela, Kaisa	FIN	Javelin throw	F		8	53,96	
Lazova K.	BUL	High jump	Q		DNQ	1,68	
Lin, C.-Y.	FOR	Long jump	Q		DNQ	5,59	
		4×100m relay	1	2	6	47.24	
		Pentathlon	F		26	4104	
Loehnert, B.	GDR	Long jump	F		14	4,49	
Lowe, P.	GER	800m	1	3	3	2-09.57	
			SF	1	3	2-06.62	
			F		6	2-04.25	
Lubej, M.	YUG	100m	1	1	4	11.68	
			2	2	5	11.61	
		200m	1	1	4	23.96	
		80m hurdles	1	2	5	11.02	
		Pentathlon	F		12	4764	
Mair A.	JAM	4×100m relay	1	1	DIS		
Manning, M.	USA	800m	1	4	1	2-08.74	
			SF	1	1	2-05.82	
			F		1	2-00.92*	G
Manoliu, L.	RUM	Discus throw	F		1	58,28*	G
Martinez, A.	MEX	4×100m relay	1	1	7	47.09	
Martinez, R.	SAL	Shot put	F		14	10,18	
Meldrum, J.	CAN	80m hurdles	1	3	5	11.17	
		Pentathlon	F		11	4774	
Meyer, G.	FRA	100m	1	2	5	11.65	
		4×100m relay	1	1	4	44.32	
			F		8	44.30	
Meyer, R.	GER	100m	1	5	2	11.71	
			2	3	6	11.67	
		4×100m relay	1	1	3	44.18	
			F		6	43.70	
Miller, D.	CAN	100m	1	1	5	11.71	
			2	2	7	11.64	
		4×100m relay	1	1	5	44.73	
Molina, R.	CHI	Shot put	F		12	12,85	

COMPETITOR	COUNTRY CODE	EVENT	ROUND	HEAT	PLACE	TIME & DISTANCE	MEDAL
Montandon, N.	FRA	200m	1	1	3	23·34	
			SF	2	4	23·02	
			F			23·08	
		4×100m relay	1	1	4	44·32	
			F		8	44·30	
Montgomery, E.	USA	High jump	Q		DNQ	1,68	
Morris, U.	JAM	200m	1	5	3	23·80	
			SF	2	7	23·59	
		400m	1	2	4	54·19	
			SF	1	6	54·63	
		4×100m relay	1	1	DIS		
Moseke, C.	USA	Discus throw	F		14	48,28	
Munkacsi, A.	HUN	400m	1	2	7	55·61	
Muravyeva, L.	URS	Discus throw	F		9	52,26	
Neil, A.	GBR	100m	1	3	4	11·70	
			2	2	6	11·61	
		4×100m relay	1	2	3	43·98	
			F		7	43·78	
Nemeshazi, M.	HUN	100m	1	5	6	12·00	
		4×100m relay	1	2	5	44·65	
Nemeth, A.	HUN	Javelin throw	F		1	60,36	G
Netter, M.	USA	4×100m relay	1	1	1	43·50*	
			F		1	42·88*	G
Nikolic, V.	YUG	800m	1	1	1	2-05·78	
			SF	1		DNF	
Noirot, M.	FRA	400m	1	3	4	53·67	
			SF	2	7	54·30	
Odogwu, V.	NGR	Long jump	F		9	6,23	
Okorokova, T.	URS	High jump	F		2	1,80	S
Omorogbe, J.	NGR	4×100m relay	1	1	6	45·23	
Otto, A.	GER	Discus throw	F		4	54,40	
Page, J.	GBR	800m	1	4	6	2-10·21	
Paik, O.-J.	KOR	Shot put	F		13	12,67	
Panerai, C.	ITA	80m hurdles	1	1	5	11·10	
Peat, V.	GBR	100m	1	1	2	11·52	
			2	3	3	11·39	
			SF	2	8	11·81	
Penes, M.	RUM	Javelin throw	F		2	59,92	S
Penton, A.	CUB	400m	1	2	1	52·86	
			SF	1	4	54·08	
			F		5	52·75	
Peters, M.	GBR	Pentathlon	F		9	4803	
Pigni, P.	ITA	800m	1	1	3	2-06·72	
			SF	2	7	2-07·82	
Piotrowski, I.	CAN	100m	1	2	2	11·40	
			2	4	3	11·41	
			SF	1	6	11·55	
		200m	1	2	5	23·74	
		4×100m relay	1	1	5	44·73	
Platt, S.	GBR	Javelin throw	F		15	48,52	
Popescu, C.	RUM	Pentathlon	F		22	4435	
Popkova, V.	URS	200m	1	2	2	23·40	
			SF	2	5	23·28	
		4×100m relay	1	2	2	43·67	
			F		3	43·41	B
Popova, A.	URS	Discus throw	F		5	53,42	
Potts, S.	NZL	800m	1	3	4	2-09·63	
			SF	2	6	2-07·27	
Prokop, L.	AUT	Pentathlon	F		2	4966	S
Pryce, P.	GBR	80m hurdles	1	3		DNF	
Pyechenkina, N.	URS	400m	1	4	1	53·73	
			SF	2	3	52·83	
			F		3	52·25	B
Quesada, V.	CUB	100m	1	1	3	11·67	
			2	3	5	11·65	
		4×100m relay	1	2	4	44·15	
			F		2	43·36	S
Rallins, M.	USA	80m hurdles	1	1	1	10·69	
			SF	2	5	10·70	
Reichert, K.	GER	100m	1	4	5	11·95	
			2	1	8	11·70	
Reid, A.	JAM	High jump	Q		DNQ	1,71	
Rezkova, M.	TCH	High jump	F		1	1,82	G
Ringa, E.	URS	Long jump	Q		DNQ	5,84	
Roberts, J.	AUS	Discus throw	F		16	46,26	
Robotham, G.	CRC	Long jump	Q		DNQ	4,75	
		Pentathlon	F		32	2909	
Robotham, J.	CRC	400m	1	2	8	58·25	
Roman, M.	MEX	Long jump	Q		DNQ	5,75	
		4×100m relay	1	1	7	47·09	
		Pentathlon	F		31	3604	
Romay, F.	CUB	100m	1	3	2	11·53	
			2	4	4	11·47	
			SF	1	5	11·52	
		200m	1	4	2	23·71	
		4×100m relay	1	2	4	44·15	
			F		2	43·36	S
Rosendahl, H.	GER	Long jump	F		8	6,40	
Rudas, M.	HUN	Javelin throw	F		4	56,38	
Samotyesova, L.	URS	100m	1	3	3	11·57	
			2	3	4	11·45	
			SF	2	5	11·67	
		200m	1	1	1	23·16	
			SF	1	5	23·52	
		4×100m relay	1	2	2	43·67	
			F		3	43·41	B
Sarna, M.	POL	Long jump	F		5	6,47	
		4×100m relay	1	2	7	53·02	
Schaefer, G.	GER	Shot put	F		10	15,26	
Schell, I.	GER	80m hurdles	1	1	3	10·77	
			SF	2	7	10·84	
Schmidt, R.	GDR	High jump	F		5	1,78	
Schulze, K.	GDR	High jump	F		7	1,76	
Scott, J.	USA	400m	1	1	2	53·53	
			SF	2	4	53·22	
			F		6	52·79	
Scott, S.	GBR	Pentathlon	F		10	4786	
Seidler, M.	USA	Shot put	F		11	14,86	
Sherwood, S.	GBR	Long jump	F		2	6,68	S
Shezifi, H.	ISR	400m	1	3	8	56·38	
		800m	1	2	6	2-09·23	
Shirley, D.	GBR	High jump	Q		DNQ	1,68	
Silai, I.	RUM	800m	1	2	2	2-04·11	
			SF	1	2	2-05·94	
			F		2	2-02·58	S
Simpson, J.	GBR	400m	1	3	3	53·63	
			SF	1	3	54·01	
			F		4	52·57	
		4×100m relay	1	2	3	43·98	
			F		7	43·78	
Smith, C.	JAM	80m hurdles	1	1	4	11·09	
		100m	1	2	7	11·94	
		4×100m relay	1	1	DIS		
Sofina, G.	URS	Pentathlon	F			DNF	
Solontsova, I.	URS	Shot put	F		9	15,88	
Sosa, C.	SAL	80m hurdles	1	5	6	12·90	
Sosa, V.	SAL	100m	1	6	7	13·76	
Spielberg, C.	GDR	Discus throw	F		7	52,86	
Stephens, L.	KEN	100m	1	4		DNF	
Sterk, M.	HOL	200m	1	5	5	24·01	
		4×100m relay	1	2	1	43·49*	
			F		4	43·44*	
Stoeck, J.	GER	200m	1	3	3	23·37	
			SF	1	4	23·41	
			F		8	23·25	
		4×100m relay	1	1	3	44·18	
			F		6	43·70	
Strasser, E.	AUT	Javelin throw	Q		DNQ	0	
Straszynska, D.	POL	80m hurdles	1	4	3	10·72	
			SF	2	3	10·60	
			F		6	10·66	
		4×100m relay	1	2	7	53·02	
Stroy, E.	USA	400m	1	3	2	53·58	
			SF	1	5	54·35	
Stugner, J.	HUN	Discus throw	F		11	52,08	
Sukniewicz, T.	POL	80m hurdles	1	3	2	10·72	
			SF	1	6	11·00	
Szewinska, I.	POL	100m	1	4	1	11·32	
			2	4	1	11·20	
			SF	1	1	11·30	
			F		3	11·19	B
		200m	1	5	1	23·21	
			SF	1	3	23·21	
			F		1	22·58*	G
		Long jump	Q		DNQ	6,19	
		4×100m relay	1	2	7	53·02	
Talysheva, T.	URS	80m hurdles	1	3	3	10·81	
			SF	1	3	10·80	
			F		8	10·72	
		Long jump	F		3	6,66	B
Taylor, S.	GBR	800m	1	2	3	2-04·17	
			SF	2	3	2-05·29	
			F		4	2-03·81	
Telliez, S.	FRA	100m	1	1	6	12·10	
		200m	1	5	4	23·84	
		4×100m relay	1	1	4	44·32	
			F		6	44·30	
Tien, A.-M.	FOR	200m	1	1	7	25·53	
		4×100m relay	1	2	6	47·24	
		Pentathlon	F		27	3899	
Tikhomirova, V.	URS	Pentathlon	F		4	4927	
Toth, A.	HUN	Pentathlon	F		3	4959	B
		4×100m relay	1	2	5	44·65	

COMPETITOR	COUNTRY CODE	EVENT	ROUND	HEAT	PLACE	TIME & DISTANCE	MEDAL
Tranter, M.	GBR	200m	1	3	5	23-58	
		4×100m relay	1	2	3	43-98	
			F		7	43-78	
Tsimozh, L.	URS	Javelin throw	F		10	53.40	
Tyus, W.	USA	100m	1	1	1	11-21*	
			2	2	1	11-08*	
			SF	2	1	11.35	
			F		1	11-08*	G
		200m	1	4	1	23-46	
			SF	1	2	23-14	
			F		5	23-08	
		4×100m relay	1	1	1	43-50*	
			F		1	42-88*	G
Uhlemann, G.	GDR	Pentathlon	F		19	4644	
Ulloa, C.	CHI	80m hurdles	1	3	4	11-13	
Urbancic, N.	YUG	Javelin throw	F		6	55,42	
Valentova, J.	TCH	High jump	F		4	1,78	
Van Den Berg, W.	HOL	100m	1	6	3	11-60	
			2	2	3	11-45	
			SF	2	7	11-81	
		200m	1	3	4	23-54	
		4×100m relay	1	2	1	43-43*	
			F		4	43-44	
Van Der Hoeven	HOL	400m	1	3	-	53-17	
			SF	2	2	52-69	
			F		8	53-02	
Van Der Made, M.	HOL	800m	1	3	6	2-10-59	
Van Noorduyn, E.	HOL	Shot put	F		8	16,23	
Van Wolvelaere, P.	USA	80m hurdles	1	3	1	10-65	
			SF	1	2	10-72	
			F		4	10-60	
Verbele, I.	URS	400m	1	2	3	54-07	
			SF	1	7	54-67	
Vettorazzo, M.	ITA	Pentathlon	F		21	4504	
Vicent, J.	URU	100m	1	5	7	12-53	
		200m	1	2	7	24-89	
		400m	1	4	7	56-34	
Viscopoleanu, V.	RUM	Long jump	F		1	6,82*	G
Waerness, A.	NOR	High jump	Q		DNQ	1,60	
Wallgren, K.	SWE	200m	1	3	8	24-23	
		400m	1	4	3	54-30	
			SF	2	6	53-93	
Watson, M.	USA	Long jump	F		10	6,20	
Westermann, L.	GER	Discus throw	F		2	57,76	S
White, W.	USA	Long jump	F		11	6,08	
Wieck, B.	GDR	800m	1	2	5	2-08-18	
Wieczorek, B.	GDR	Long jump	F		4	6,48	
Wieslander, U.	SWE	100m	1	3	7	11-86	
		80m hurdles	-	1	7	11-24	
Wilson, A.	GBR	80m hurdles	1	2	7	11-19	
		Long jump	F		13	5,90	
		Pentathlon	F		16	4688	
Winslow, P.	USA	Pentathlon	F		6	4877	
Yeh, C.-N.	FOR	200m	1	2	8	25-55	
		80m hurdles	1	5	5	11-77	
		4×100m relay	1	2	6	47-24	
Yurukova, S.	BUL	80m hurdles	1	2	6	11-07	
		Pentathlon	F		14	4728	
Zebrowska, E.	POL	80m hurdles	1	5	2	10-83	
			SF	2	4	10-70	
			F		7	10-66	
Zharkova, L.	URS	100m	1	6	2	11-54	
			2	1	5	11-43	
		4×100m relay	1	2	2	43-67	
			F		3	43-41	B
Zimina, A.	URS	800m	1	2	4	2-04-48	
			SF	1	6	2-08-54	

In the semi-finals of the 400 metres hurdles, David Hemery of Britain (402), the eventual gold medallist, was content to glide home in third place behind Gerhard Hennige of West Germany and America's Ron Whitney (316).

Victor Saneyev, the great USSR triple jumper, won the first of three consecutive gold medals in Mexico.

Mark Shearman

1972

Viren Gets Up to Win — Then Wins Again

The 1972 Munich Olympics are forever linked with tragedy. The West Germans built a magnificent complex and the Games were the most widely reported, there being over 4,000 of the world's media present. But they presented an obvious stage for terrorism, and the world had a close-up view as eight Arab terrorists killed two and held hostage nine of the Israeli team. The terrorists were allowed to go to the airport, where a rescue attempt was made, but all the hostages were killed and most of their captors died, too. The Games were suspended for a memorial service, and continued later in a sombre atmosphere.

There were good performances in track and field, the best being by Lasse Viren, who won the 10,000 metres in world record time, despite falling over during the race, and then added the 5,000 metres to his collection. Lia Manoliu of Rumania, already the oldest discus gold medallist (1968), set a "long-service" record by competing in her sixth Olympics.

Men's Track Events

In the **100 metres**, Valeriy Borzov of Russia and the three Americans Eddie Hart, Ray Robinson and Bob Taylor were among those tipped to take the medals at Munich. This was the first Games at which automatic timing had been officially used and also saw the introduction of an automatic false-start device to aid the starter. In the second round, the coach to the three American sprinters had unfortunately misconstrued the starting time as 6·15 instead of 16·15. The athletes raced to the track as soon as the event was announced on TV, but only Taylor was in time to run in heat three, where Borzov clocked 10·07 sec and the American, without a warm-up, was second in 10·16. The final produced superb starts by Jobst Hirscht of West Germany and Alek Kornelyuk of the USSR. These two were slightly ahead of Borzov, while Trinidad's Hasely Crawford pulled a muscle in his acceleration phase. Borzov then built up a metre lead over the first half of the course and won by that much in 10·14 from Taylor in 10·24, with the slow starting Lennox Miller of Jamaica taking bronze in 10·33.

Valeriy Borzov was also favoured to win the **200 metres** but Larry Black of the USA and Italy's Pietro Mennea showed up well in the preliminary rounds. Don Quarrie of Jamaica was another tipped sprinter, but he pulled a muscle in the semi-finals. Black, in lane one, was best away at the gun in the final, with Borzov in lane six, the next best. The first 100 was run in 10·4 with Borzov and Black level coming off the bend. At this stage Borzov powered away and won in 20·00 sec from Black 20·19, while Mennea led the chasing group to finish third in 20·30.

The US **400 metres** trials winner, Wayne Collett, had run the fastest time of the year in 44·1 sec and was

Following the banning of the newly introduced catapole, Wolfgang Nordwig of East Germany, fully avenged his Mexico City defeat, when winnning the pole vault.   Mark Shearman

looked upon as an obvious winner. The final saw the USA's John Smith take his marks with his thigh heavily strapped, due to a muscle strain, and after running the first bend he dropped out. Vince Matthews of the USA powered the backstraight with Collett chasing and held his position to win in 44·66 to his rival's 44·80. Meanwhile, Julius Sang and Charles Asati, both of Kenya, were finishing fast. Sang proved the stronger and took the bronze in 44·92.

Dave Wottle of the USA and Pekka Vasala of Finland were the fastest men of the year over **800 metres**, but the latter had elected to run in the 1,500. Mike Boit and his fellow Kenyan, Robert Ouko, led the final at a fine lick to cover the first 200m in 24·7. The pace abruptly slackened at 300 and Ouko led through the bell in 52·3, with Wottle at the rear of the eight man field in 53·5. With 300m to go, Russia's Evgeniy Arzhanov dashed to the front and was two metres ahead of Ouko entering the home straight with Boit and Wottle behind him. Quickly seeing the danger, Wottle kicked and caught Arzhanov on the line to win in 1-45·86 to 1-45·89 with Boit, a shade back, third in 1-46·01.

America's **1,500 metres** world record holder, Jim Ryun, tripped up in his heat and was eliminated. The first lap of the final saw Brendan Foster of Britain in the lead in 61·4, but at 600 Kip Keino of Kenya went to the front, followed by Pekka Vasala of Finland, Foster, Mike Boit of Kenya, and Rod Dixon and Tony Polhill, both of New Zealand. Keino passed the 800 in 2-01·4 and then winding up the pace with a 55·1 third lap, he went even faster on the final circuit, with Vasala, Boit, Foster and Dixon close behind. Vasala struck off the last bend and ran home the winner in 3-36·33 from the chasing Keino in 3-36·81, with Dixon third in 3-37·46.

There was no clear favourite in the **5,000 metres** and the final started off at a mediocre pace with 3km being passed in 8-20·2 by Javier Alvarez of Spain. Steve Prefontaine of the USA then hotted up the tempo, followed by Lasse Viren of Finland, Emil Puttemans of Belgium, Mohamed Gammoudi of Tunisia and Ian Stewart of Britain. Approaching the bell, Viren swept into the lead with Gammoudi fighting him hard. Viren held first place with ease and won in 13-26·42 for a new Olympic record with Gammoudi second in 13-27·33. Stewart came with a determined sprint in the straight and finished a close-up third in 13-27·61, with Prefontaine fourth.

Dave Bedford of Britain, the European record holder, was expected to do well in the **10,000 metres**, but Finland's Lasse Viren was also highly rated. Emil Puttemans of Belgium and Bedford ran an extravagant first heat with Puttemans winning in 27-53·28, an Olympic record. In the final, Bedford immediately took the lead and set off at a storming pace, passing 5km in 13-44·0. At this point the following group was Miruts Yifter of Ethiopia, Puttemans, Mariano Haro of Spain, Viren, Frank Shorter of the USA, Mohamed Gammoudi of Tunisia, Abdelkader Zaddem of Tunisia and Dane Korica of Yugoslavia. Suddenly, Viren fell and Gammoudi sprawled over him. Viren leapt to his feet at once and continued running while Gammoudi, who was still dazed, gave up. Meanwhile, Viren steadily regained lost ground and at 6km went into the lead, to dictate the pace for the rest of the race. Viren won in 27-38·4, a world record, with Puttemans holding on to take silver with 27-39·88 and Yifter bronze in 27-40·96.

The 74 starters in the **marathon** ran 900 metres of the track before taking to the Munich roads, and a third of the runners were still close behind the leader Derek Clayton of Australia at the 10km stage, passed in 31-15. Frank Shorter of the USA started to draw away from the field after 15km and was 31 seconds in front of Karel Lismont of Belgium and four others at 20km in 61-30·0. Shorter then went two minutes up on Lismont, who now headed Mamo Wolde of Ethiopia by eight seconds, nearly a minute ahead of Ken Moore of the USA. The crowd rose to applaud the winner as a demonstrator ran nearly a whole lap protesting against over-solemnity of the Games. Shorter duly arrived and won in 2:12-19·8. Lismont finished second at 2:14-31·8 with Wolde catching up fast in 2:15-08·4.

Rod Milburn of the USA was the **110 metres hurdles** king of the moment. In the semi-finals his countryman Tom Hill won the first heat in 13·47 from France's Guy Drut and Milburn took the second in 13·44 from Frank Siebeck of East Germany. With the final under way, Lubomir Nadenicek of Czechoslovakia exploded from the blocks first, but Hill, Milburn and Willie Davenport, the defending champion, reached the first flight together, and Milburn with his faster hurdling technique was leading from thereon. Drut was off poorly but by the half-way stage was up with Hill and Davenport, who hit the eighth hurdle and ruined his chance of a medal. Milburn won in 13·24, a new world record, but Drut chased him hard to record 13·34 for the silver with Hill third in 13·48.

Ralph Mann of the USA was the man most expected to win the **400 metres hurdles**, but he was in for a big surprise. A year before, John Akii-Bua of Uganda had been just a raw athlete, but he had made his mark by winning the first semi-final in 49·25 sec, beating Mann and the defending champion David Hemery of Britain. In the other semi, America's Jim Seymour won with a time of 49·33 from Evgeniy Gavrilenko of the USSR.

Ludvik Danek

Nobody would begrudge Ludvik Danek his winning the discus title at the Munich Games in 1972. For two successive Olympics he had been overshadowed by the great Al Oerter, of the USA, with throws inferior to the Czech's world-best figures. Danek had an extraordinary habit of failing to produce his best when it mattered most — except in 1972. There he left nobody in doubt as to who was the master by winning with 211ft 3in (64,40m), well ahead of the American champion, Jay Silvester.

Danek, who was born on 6 January 1937 at Horice, Czechoslovakia, had taken the silver when Oerter produced a late winning throw in 1964 and the bronze behind Oerter and the East German, Lotha Milde at Mexico City in 1968.

Before going to Tokyo in 1964 the Czech had taken the world record from Oerter with 211ft 9½in (64,55m) and a year later increased this to 213ft 11½ft (65,22m). But by 1972 Jay Silvester had six times broken the world record and looked likely to deprive Danek of the gold once and for all. However, to the delight of his followers, the Czech rose magnificently to the occasion and took the title that had evaded him for so long.

The world record holder, and favourite for the women's 100 metres hurdles, Annelie Erhardt of East Germany, takes the event in her stride.

Mark Shearman

With the gun starting the final, Akii-Bua stormed off in lane one, while Hemery in five also went out fast. At the eighth flight, just coming off the bend, they were level, with Mann and Seymour just behind, but Akii-Bua just strode on and won in 47·82 for a new world record. Mann caught Hemery on the tape and was second in 48·51, with the Briton taking bronze in 48·52.

It was not clear from the heats of the **3,000 metres steeplechase** who the most likely winner might be, but already Anders Garderud of Sweden, a prospective medallist, had been eliminated. In the final, Amos Biwott of Kenya, the defending champion, trotted out the first lap in 70·8, before Poland's Bronisław Malinowski injected some more pace in the third lap. He was followed by Kenya's three athletes, Ben Jipcho, Biwott and Kip Keino, with Tapio Kantanen of Finland, Dusan Moravcik of Czechoslovakia and Russia's Romualdas Bitte also in attendance. But in the penultimate lap, Keino made his bid for gold and raced into the lead, followed by Jipcho and Kantanen. Keino won with a last lap of 59·2 in 8-23·64 for a new Games record, with Jipcho second in 8-24·62 and Kantanen third in 8-24·66.

Race conditions were good, as 24 heel and toe experts ambled out of the stadium at the start of the **20 kilometres walk**, among them Paul Nihill of Britain who had clocked a world best of 1:24-50·0 over the distance. When the 15km marker was reached, four men were spearheading the field: Peter Frenkel and Hans Reimann of East Germany, Vladimir Golubnichy of the USSR, the defending champion, and East Germany's Gerhard Sperling. The battle hotted up in the last kilometre, when Golubnichy tried to get away from Frenkel, but could not shake him off and the East German arrived at the stadium first to win in 1:26-42·4, an Olympic record. Golubnichy strolled home in 1:26-55·2 for silver and Reimann collected the bronze with a time of 1:27-16·6.

Bernd Kannenberg of West Germany was by far the fastest man at the **50 kilometres walk**, having set a world test of 3:52-45·0. The weather was ideal as 36 men set out on their long march and Kannenberg, followed by the Russians Veniamin Soldatenko and Sergei Grigoriev, set a hot pace until the latter found the speed too stiff for him and dropped back. The two leaders powered on to 35km, when Soldatenko slowed a little at a feeding station and Kannenberg took the opportunity to forge ahead. At 40km, Kannenberg had a 21-second advantage and went on to win in 3:56-11·6 from a slowing Soldatenko in 3:58-24·0, while Larry Young of the USA, who had assumed the bronze medal position shortly after the half-way stage, stayed on in 4:00-46·0.

The heats in the 4 × **100 metres** were not remarkable and the same applied in the semi-finals, where the USA won the first and France took the second. In the final, the Russian lead-off runner Alek Korneliuk, took half a metre out of the USA's Larry Black on the first leg, but America's Bob Taylor had two metres lead at the half-way point over Russia, with West Germany third, Poland fourth and East Germany fifth. This lead was increased and Gerald Tinker handed Eddie Hart a four-metre advantage for the USA to win in 38·19, a new world record. The USSR with Valeriy Borzov on the anchor leg, finished second in 38·50, with West Germany third in 38·79.

On paper, the USA had an invincible team for the **4 × 400 metres relay**, but John Smith had a pulled thigh muscle, whilst Vince Matthews and Wayne Collett were suffering disciplinary action following a black rights protest at the 400 metres medal ceremony. With only three other athletes, the USA was forced to withdraw. In the final, Kenya led on the first leg, but in the second were demoted to third, when West Germany's Horst Schloeske stormed a 44·2 stint to lead with Poland in attendance. The positions remained the same at the end of the third leg, where Britain's Hemery ran the quickest lap in 45·1, but there were only twelve metres between the first and last teams. Karl Honz of West Germany was away on the last leg like a demon possessed, but Julius Sang of Kenya was nearly as fast. He went past Andrzej Badenski of Poland on the bend and past Honz with 75m to go, to win in 2-59·83 with a fantastic leg time of 43·5. Meanwhile, David Jenkins for Britain came past the dying Honz to take the silver in 3-00·46 with a 44·1 leg. Third place went to France in 3-00·65, while West Germany came home in 3-00·88.

Men's Field Events

Forty of the best competed in the **high jump**, 12 of whom were floppers and the rest straddle exponents. Nineteen qualified for the final at 2,15 metres and only five managed to jump any higher. The last three, 18-year-old Dwight Stones of the USA, Stefan Junge of East Germany and Yuri Tarmak of the USSR, all attempted 2,21 and all failed on their first trial. Tarmak and Junge went across the bar on their second trys while Stones needed three attempts. Tarmak was the only jumper to elevate himself over 2,23 and this he did at his second attempt, before coming out at 2,26, to win the gold medal. Junge took the silver under the count-back rule from Stones, who won the bronze.

The **pole vault** was surrounded by controversy. A new fibreglass pole had been developed in America and had come into use earlier in the year, with the effect that the world record had shot up from 5,49 metres to 5,63. The IAAF ruled that as the pole had not been available by 31 August, 1971, it could not be used as it would put certain countries at a disadvantage. Four years earlier, Wolfgang Nordwig of East Germany and Bob Seagren of America had met in the final, the lattter being the victor, and now there was a re-match. Seven vaulters achieved 5,20, but only four cleared 5,30 and West Germany's Reinhard Kuretzky ultimately failed at that height. At 5,35 the two leading rivals Nordwig and Seagren cleared first time, but the USA's Jan Johnson needed two attempts. The bar then went up to the Olympic record height of 5,40 and Johnson could not make it. At 5,45 Nordwig flipped over first time, while Seagren failed and took the silver. Nordwig cleared 5,50 on his last try and then tried 5,56 without success. He collected the gold, however.

In the **long jump** Randy Williams of the USA laid aside his teddy bear mascot for the preliminaries and jumped 8,34 metres, just to qualify. And fellow American Preston Carrington also had a big one with 8,22. In the competition proper, Williams jumped 8,24 in the first round, which eventually was good enough for the gold medal, while Carrington cleared 7,99 to hold second spot. But in the third round, West Germany's Hans Baumgartner jumped 8,18 to secure the silver position. The bronze medal was still up for grabs and in the fifth trials, Arnie Robinson of the USA extended his legs to 8,03, which was good enough.

Viktor Saneyev of the USSR was the defending champion in the **triple jump**, where the new world record holder, Pedro Perez of Cuba, suffered leg problems and had to withdraw from the preliminaries. The first round of the finals saw Saneyev ultimately win the event with his jump of 17,35, while the silver medallist from Mexico City, Nelson Prudencio, reached 16,87. In the next round, Jorg Drehmel, of East Germany dropped into second place with 17,02, and then produced some mighty bounds to close on the leader with 17,31, which was good enough for the silver medal. Meanwhile, Prudencio improved to 17,05 on his last attempt to take home a bronze medal.

The Americans and East Germany had a stranglehold on the **shot put** and it was expected that the winner would come from one of them. A surprise in the preliminaries, however, was the elimination of Alek Baryshnikov of the USSR, who used the rotational technique, while the best qualifying throw came from Wladyslaw Komar of Poland, who let out a yell every time he released the iron ball, with 20,60. In the first round of the final, amidst great excitement, East Germany's Hartmut Briesenick threw 20,97 to break the Olympic record. This was improved by his fellow countryman Hans-Peter Gies, to 21,14, while Komar exceeded it in the next round with 21,18. In the third round, Briesenick improved to 21,02 and then to 21,14 in the next, but was overtaken when George Woods of the USA exploded, to drop his shot at 21,17. The result was: Komar 21,18 for the gold, Woods 21,17 for the silver, and Briesenick 21,14 for the bronze.

For the **discus throw**ing competition, the big three were Ludvik Danek of Czechoslovakia, the European

Mark Shearman

Kipchoge Keino

Kipchoge Keino was the first of black Africa's Olympic track champions and competed in the 1964, 1968 and 1972 Games.

Keino, born in Kipsano on 17 January 1940, had outstanding natural ability, which was helped by his living and training at high altitude. In spite of this he met with considerably mixed fortunes when stepping on the track for Olympic competition.

In Tokyo, two years after establishing himself in international class, his best performance was to finish fifth in the 5,000m. A year later he bettered the world records for 3,000m and 5,000m and also clocked 3-54·2 for a mile.

At the 1968 Games in Mexico City, he was daring enough to tackle the 10,000m, the 5,000m and the 1,500m. But the pace of the 10,000m forced him to withdraw before the finish.

Much of his confidence was restored when he captured the silver in the 5,000m, only 0·2 sec behind Gammoudi, of Tunisia. His persistence in trying to strike gold was finally rewarded in the 1,500m when he outpaced the favourite, Jim Ryun, for the title and set an Olympic record of 3-34·9.

While in Munich four years later, he was forced to be satisfied with the silver in the 1,500m, but sprung a surprise by winning the 3,000m steeplechase, an event he had never taken seriously before.

Britain's Brendan Foster (284) leads the 1,500 metres field, with the eventual winner, Pekka Vasala of Finland, tucked in behind (third right).

Mark Shearman

champion, Ricky Bruch of Sweden, who had a share of the world record and Jay Silvester of the USA, who had the other share. Danek impressed his rivals in the preliminaries by throwing 64,32 metres, but he had to build up in the competition proper from 58,12 on his first throw to a winning 64,40 with his last. Jay Silvester won the silver medal with his third throw of 63,50, while Bruch also needed a build-up series before reaching 63,40 in the fifth round for the bronze.

Anatoliy Bondarchuk of the USSR headed the year's rankings in the **hammer throw** with 75,76 metres and was the best in the qualifying rounds with 72,88. He opened his account in the final with 75,50 for a new Olympic record and ultimately the gold medal. Second at this stage was Jochen Sachse of East Germany and third the defending champion Gyula Zsivotzky of Hungary. In the next round, Vasiliy Khmelevski of the USSR threw 71,62 and improved to 74,04 in the next round, where Sachse threw 73,70, before landing his last effort at 74,96 to take the silver medal.

Janis Lusis of the USSR was fully expected to retain his **javelin throw**ing title and he would have done so had it not been for one man. The preliminaries saw West Germany's Klause Wolfermann throw 86,22 to qualify and then 86,68 in the first round of the finals, to stand second behind Lusis' 88,88, with Hannu Siitonen of Finland sitting in third spot with 84,32. Bill Schmidt of the USA took the bronze medal in the next round with 84,42, while Lusis improved to 89,54 in the third round and Wolfermann to 88,40 in the fourth. Wolfermann responded in the next with a mighty 90,48 to win the gold and although Lusis countered on his last throw with 90,46, he failed by two centimetres, having to settle for the silver.

The **decathlon** promised to be a low key event but nothing could have been further from the truth. At the end of the first day, Joachim Kirst of East Germany led with 4,364 points from Nikolai Avilov of the USSR with 4,345. Kirst achieved his total with help of a big shot put of 16,09 metres and long jump of 7,59 metres, while Avilov scored highly in the high jump with 2,12 metres and had a long jump of 7,68 metres. Kirst pulled a muscle next day and Avilov won the competition with a surprising world record of 8,454 points. He excelled in four of the five events on the second day: a 14·31 sec hurdles, a 46,98 metres discus, 4,55 metres pole vault and a 61,66 metres javelin. Meanwhile, Leonid Litvinenko of the USSR lifted himself from a lowly 16th to a silver medal, with the aid of a 47,84 metres discus, a 4,40 metres pole vault and a 58,94 metres javelin. Also, another late starter, Ryszard Katus of Poland, clawed his way from 11th position on the first day to a bronze medal with 7,984 points following an impressive hurdles of 14·41 sec, vault of 4,50 metres, javelin of 59,96 metres and a fantastic 1,500m of 4·05·91.

Women's Events

Favourite for the **100 metres** was Renate Stecher of East Germany who had a share in the world record but the great surprise in the heats was the elimination of Ellen Stropahl of East Germany, who also had a share. Silvia Chivas of Cuba ran 11·18 in the heats, while Stecher and Raelene Boyle of Australia won the semi-finals in 11·18 and 11·32. In the final there was a very even start, but Stecher moved with rugged power, being clear of the field at 40 metres, and went on to win in 11·07, a world record for automatic timing. Boyle was second in 11·23, while Chivas tied up, but still clocked 11·24 for third.

Renate Stecher was the firm favourite for the **200 metres**, after triumphing in her semi-final, even though the defending champion Irene Szewinska of Poland was competing. The final saw Stecher come out of her blocks fast, but Raelene Boyle of Australia ran a superb bend to lead into the straight. Slowly, Stecher pulled back the leeway and finished first in 22·40, a world record. Boyle recorded 22·45, while Szewinska, after a slow bend, came through strongly in the straight, for third place in 22·74.

In the **400 metres** heats, Gyorgyi Balogh of Hungary set a new Olympic record of 51·71 sec. Two days later in the semi-finals, Helga Seidler of East Germany improved the record to 51·68, while Monika Zehrt later broke the record again with 51·47. In the final, Balogh sprinted around the bend and held the lead until passed by Zehrt of East Germany at 200 metres, with Rita Wilden of West Germany just behind. Zehrt pushed on strongly to win in 51·08 for a new record. Wilden finished second in 51·21, while Kathy Hammond of the USA came with a late burst to secure the bronze position in 51·64.

Hildegard Falck was the world record holder for the **800 metres** and was fully expected to strike gold, even though Svetla Zlateva of Bulgaria set a new Olympic record of 1·58·93 in the heats. In the final, Zlateva, Vera Nikolic of Yugoslavia and Rumania's Ilena Silai vied with each other for the lead, and the Rumanian passed the bell first in 58·31, with the rest of the field bunched behind her. Down the backstraight, Zlateva led a charge, followed closely by Nikolic, Gunhild Hoffmeister of East Germany and Falck. But coming off the final bend Falck struck and sustained her momentum to win in 1·58·55, for an Olympic record. Meanwhile, Niola Sabaite of the USSR, made a bid from well back and closed fast on the leaders to finish second in 1·58·65, with Hoffmeister third in 1·59·19.

The **1,500 metres** was an event new to the Olympics. Lyudmila Bragina of the USSR held the world record at 4·06·9 but this was expected to be beaten and in the very first heat she shaved it to 4·06·47. Later, in her semi-final Bragina won in 4·05·07 to reduce the record once again. In the final Bernie Boxem and Ilja Keizer, both of Holland, led the field, but just before 800m Bragina went into the lead and immediately speeded matters up to arrive at 1,200 in 3·14·6 with East Germany's Karin Burneleit lying second in 3·17·1 and five others bunched behind her. Around the bend the chasing group began to pull back on the leader but their final sprint was too late as Bragina crossed the line in 4·01·38, another world record. Second was Gunhild Hoffmeister of East Germany in 4·02·83, just holding off Paola Cacchi of Italy, who did 4·02·85.

In previous years hurdling for women had been held over 80 metres, but for the first time it was to be a **100 metres hurdle** event, run over ten flights instead of eight. Annelie Ehrhardt of East Germany was the favourite and world record holder at 12·5 sec and, as did Valeria Bufanu of Rumania, she won her semi-final. In the final Ehrhardt and Pam Ryan of Australia were quickest out of the blocks and led over the first hurdle but the East German girl drew ahead at the second flight. Thirty-four-year-old Karin Balzer of East Germany passed Ryan and Bufanu overtook them both, but Ehrhardt won in 12·59 for a new record. Bufanu was second in 12·84 and Balzer third in 12·90.

Cuba won the first heat of the **4 × 100 metres relay**, in 43·67 sec from the USSR in 43·77, while East Germany

Mark Shearman

John Akii-Bua

John Akii-Bua was Uganda's first winner of an Olympic gold medal. A tall, powerfully built police instructor, he gained the prized award in the 400m hurdles in the 1972 Munich Games. Having heard that he had been drawn in the inside lane for the final, the worst possible draw for him with his long legs, Akii-Bua could not sleep properly overnight. He was concerned over the advantage he thought David Hemery, Britain's holder of the title, and the American champion, Ralph Mann, would have. with less tight bends to contend with. But racing like a man inspired the Ugandan whipped round the 400m circuit in a new world record 47·82 sec, leaving Mann (48·51 sec) and Hemery (48·52 sec) six metres behind.

The new champion was born in Kampala on 3 December 1949, one of a family of 43 children, his father having had eight wives. Though still in world class form at the time of the 1976 Games in Montreal, Akii-Bua was not given the chance to defend his crown because of the African boycott.

A year later he fled Uganda, following the overthrow of Idi Amin and was subsequently imprisoned in Kenya for a month until it was discovered who he was.

Mark Shearman

Mary Peters

A competitor of immense charm and personality, Mary Peters could become a tigress when the chips were down in a major pentathlon championship.

She finished fourth in her first Olympic pentathlon at Tokyo in 1964, but an ankle injury kept her below her best in the 1968 Mexico Games, where she finished ninth. She was then 29-years-old, having been born on 6 July 1939 in Halewood, Lancashire, and most thought she might retire from the sport. But not Mary. With typical determination she trained hard to improve and at her fourth Commonwealth Games in 1970 she won both the shot and the pentathlon titles for Northern Ireland, having long since moved to live in Belfast.

Mary chose a more restful season for 1971 but in 1972, with the Munich Olympics coming, she got down to training more seriously than ever and what a shock she provided for her rivals at those Games! After the first day of competition the British girl was 97 points in the lead. Producing personal best performances the following day in the long jump and 200m, she clinched the gold medal with a world record score of 4,801 points — and all at the age of 33.

These days, Mary still retains exceptional fitness, supervising her own health centre in Belfast.

Mark Shearman

Valeriy Borzov

Valeriy Borzov is the only non-American to win both the 100m and 200m at an Olympic Games. He achieved the feat in the Munich Games of 1972, with extreme confidence and power.

A tall, blond-haired and blue-eyed Ukrainian, born near Lvov on 20 October 1949. he first attracted international attention in 1968 when winning the same two titles at the European junior championships. Carefully developed in Kiev by physiologists and coaches, he equalled the European senior record for 100m a year later, to establish himself as a real threat to the leading US sprinters for the coming Games.

Any chance of Borzov competing against either of the two fastest Americans disappeared when Eddie Hart and Reynaud Robinson arrived too late to go to their marks for the 100m quarter-finals when they misread the starting time of their races. But there were doubts whether either could have checked the success of Borzov, so strong and swift were his starts, only climaxed by his finishing speed. He was a clear winner in both finals and also received a silver medal as anchorman in the Russian's unsuccessful chase after the USA's world record-breaking 4 × 100m relay team.

Borzov has since married the famous Soviet gymnast, Lyudmila Turischeva.

won the second in 42·88 from West Germany in 42·95. However, the final turned out to be a duel between the two Germany's. On the first leg the two teams were even but West Germany had the edge in both the second and third, leaving Heide Rosendahl a metre up on Renate Stecher at the final change-over. Rosendahl had an inspired run for West Germany to win in 42·81, equalling the manual 42·8 world record. East Germany clocked 42·95 for second place and Cuba was third in 43·36. The winning team was Christiane Krause, Ingrid Mickler, Anegret Richter and Heide Rosendahl.

The **4 × 400 metres relay** was another new event for women and in the first heat West Germany won in 3-29·32 from France, while East Germany took the second in 3-28·48 for a new world record from the USA. At the end of the first leg in the final, Mable Fergerson of the USA led from Dagmar Kaesling of East Germany, while on the second circuit Rita Kuehne ran brilliantly to put East Germany in front. That is the way they stayed with Helga Seidler running the third leg and Monika Zehrt the anchor, for a superb 3-22·95 and a new world record. The USA came second in 3-25·15 and West Germany third in 3-26·51.

For the **high jump** event, the top three women were Rita Schmidt of East Germany, the European indoor champion, Ilona Gusenbauer of Austria, the world record holder, and Bulgaria's Yordanka Blagoeva. From a field of 40, there were 23 who qualified for the final, of which seven jumpers scaled 1,85 metres, but four of these failed at the next height. Over the bar first time at 1,88 were 17-year-old flop jumper Ulrike Meyfarth of West Germany and Blagoeva, while Gusenbauer needed two attempts. The bar was then raised to 1,90, but all three failed at their first attempts, before Meyfarth arched over to win the competition. Blagoeva took the silver on the count-back, with Gusenbauer the bronze. Meyfarth now tried 1,92 and snapped over first time to equal the world record, but could not make it at 1,94.

In the **long jump** qualifying rounds, Angelika Liebsch of East Germany had the leading jump with 6,69 metres, but in the competition proper, Heide Rosendahl, the world record holder from West Germany, quickly set the pace with a winning 6,78 on her first jump. Second at this stage was Eva Suranova of Czechoslovakia on 6,51, who improved to 6,60 in the next round. The third round saw Diana Yorgova of Bulgaria leap 6,62 and she later took the silver medal with 6.77, while Suranova sailed to 6,67 for the bronze.

Nadyezhda Chizhova of the USSR towered above everyone else in the **shot put**, although she had up against her Margitta Gummel of East Germany, the defending Olympic champion. Ivankka Khristova, of Bulgaria was the best of the qualifiers with 19,20 metres but Chizhova put paid to everybody in the final with a first round explosion of 21,03, a new world record and the winning put. Khristova did come up with 19,35 to hold second spot, but Gummel threw 19,55 in the third round for the silver medal, which was extended to 20,22 in the next, leaving Khristova with bronze.

Faina Melnik was tipped to win the **discus throw** as she had recently taken over the world record, but she had to watch for Argentina Menis of Rumania and Liesel Westermann of West Germany. No less than four women broke the old Olympic record in the preliminaries, with Menis achieving the best at 61,58 metres, whilst in the finals no fewer than eight exceeded the old mark. Russia's Tamara Danilova threw 62,64 in the first round, but was quickly overhauled by Menis

with 64,28; both being record throws. In the third round Vasilka Stoeva of Bulgaria floated one out to 64,20 to put pressure on the leader. But the big ones came in the next round, when Melnik launched a tremendous throw of 66,62 for a Games record, and just short of her world mark, while Menis threw an impressive 65,06 for the silver. Stoeva then hurled 64,34 for the bronze medal with her fifth trial.

Ruth Fuchs of East Germany was the emerging star in the **javelin throw**ing event and she had the world record to prove it. She qualified with a useful 60,88 metres and then improved throughout the competition, finally throwing 63,88 in the fifth round to win the gold medal. Her fellow countrywoman, Jaqueline Todten, was equally progressive, starting with 55,44 and improving in stages to 62,54 on her last throw, to take the silver medal. Conversely, the bronze medallist, Kathy Schmidt of the USA produced her big throw with a first round effort of 59,94.

The best of the **pentathlon** women was Burglinde Pollak of East Germany, but the margin over her competitors was not that great. After the 100m hurdles, Christine Bodner of East Germany was leading with 13·25 from Britain's Mary Peters at 13·29. But in the shot, Peters threw a fine 16,20 metres to lead Pollak with 16,04 and then increased her lead over the East German girl after the high jump, with an excellent 1,82 metres to 1,76. The position at the end of the first day was Peters 2,969 points. Pollak 2,872 and Russia's Valentina Tikhomirova 2,744. Pollak pulled up in the long jump with 6,21 metres to Peters' 5,98 and everything depended on the 200 metres. Peters ran 24·08 to Pollak's 23·93, but it was Heide Rosendahl of West Germany who was the new danger girl, as she had crept up following a 6,83 metres long jump and the 200m was a good event for her. She won in in 22·96, but Peters' 24·08 was good enough by one-tenth of a second for the gold. The result: Peters with a world record of 4,801 points was first, with Rosendahl 4,791 in silver position and Pollak, 4,768, in bronze position.

The great West German all-rounder, Heide Rosendahl, hangs in the air for a magnificent long jump victory; Heide also gained a silver medal from the pentathlon.   Mark Shearman

A few strides from victory in the 800 metres, Dave Wottle of America, wearing the hat, leads with Arzhanov of Russia (extreme right), in close attendance.

Mark Shearman

Frank Shorter (1014), the American marathon runner, led the pack out of the stadium and shortly after two hours later, returned alone to win the gold medal.

Mark Shearman

MALES

COMPETITOR	COUNTRY CODE	EVENT	ROUND	HEAT	PLACE	TIME & DISTANCE	MEDAL
Abba-Kimet, G.	CHA	100m	1	8	5	10·89	
Abdallah, O.	TAN	4×400m relay	1	2	6	3-10·12	
Abdelgalil, I.	SUD	200m	1	7	6	22·41	
		4×400m relay	1	2	8	3-14·51	
Abdulai, K.	NGR	100m	1	5	2	10·57	
			2	4	4	10·41	
		4×100m relay	1	2	3	39·66	
			SF	1	6	39·73	
Abehi, J.	CIV	Javelin throw	Q		DNQ	72,20	
Abeti, P.	ITA	200m	1	1	5	21·17	
			2	3	6	21·00	
Abidoye, J.	NGR	800m	1	8	6	1-52·00	
		1500m	1	6	9	3-48·77	
Aboker, M.	SOM	800m	1	1	DIS		
		1500m	1	6	10	3-59·54	
Aboyade-Cole, A.	NGR	110m hurdles	1	1	5	14·16	
Accambray, J.	FRA	Hammer throw	F		19	65,06	
Acerbi, M.	ITA	110m hurdles	1	4	1	13·99	
			SF	2	8	14·45	
Acevedo, F.	PER	400m	1	6	3	45·80	
			2	5	DNS		
Adams, W.	GER	800m	1	5	DNF		
Addy, J.	GHA	200m	1	8	3	21·06	
			2	3	DIS		
		4×100m relay	1	3	2	39·46	
			SF	1	7	39·99	
Ade, N.	CMR	5000m	1	1	10	15-19·6	
		3000m steeplechase	1	2	11	9-34·4	
Adouna, M.	TOG	Long jump	Q		DNQ	7,25	
Afonin, V.	URS	5000m	1	2	7	14-08·6	
Agbamu, G.	NGR	400m hurdles	1	5	7	53·58	
Ahey, M.	GHA	Long jump	Q		DNQ	7,39	
Akcay, I.	TUR	Marathon	F		DNF		
Akhmetov, R.	URS	High jump	F		8	2,15	
Akii-Bua, J.	UGA	400m hurdles	1	4	1	50·35	
			SF	1	1	49·25	
			F		1	47·82*	G
Ala-Leppilampi, M.	FIN	3000m steeplechase	1	2	2	8-31·8	
			F		10	8-41·03	
Alah-Djaba, S.	CHA	100m	1	9	2	10·65	
			2	4	7	10·51	
		200m	1	8	DNF		
Aldegalega, A.	POR	Marathon	F		41	2:28-24·6	
Aldosary, G.	ARS	4×100m relay	1	1	6	43·35	
Aldosary, S.	ARS	200m	1	6	7	22·56	
		4×100m relay	1	1	6	43·35	
Alebic, J.	YUG	400m	1	1	6	47·01	
		4×400m relay	1	1	5	3-05·70	
Alers, L.	PUR	100m	1	1	8	11·09	
		4×100m relay	1	1	5	41·34	
Alexa, J.	TCH	High jump	Q		DNQ	2,09	
Algegd, M.	ARS	100m	1	3	7	11·23	
		4×100m relay	1	1	6	43·35	
Alkahtani, S.	ARS	Javelin throw	Q		DNQ	53,06	
Almabrouk, A.	ARS	5000m	1	3	13	15-51·0	
Alsafraa, A.N.	ARS	1500m	1	3	8	4-14·47	
Alvarez, J.	ESP	5000m	1	2	4	13-36·6	
			F		10	13-41·83	
		10000m	1	1	3	28-08·58	
			F		12	28-56·38	
Amakdouf, M.	MAR	1500m	1	3	7	3-48·38	
Amoah, J.	GHA	Triple jump	Q		DNQ	15,84	
Amuke, D.	KEN	100m	1	1	5	10·76	
		200m	1	8	4	21·53	
			2	4	DNS		
Andersen, K.	DEN	Discus throw	Q		DNQ	53,52	
Anderson, J.	USA	10000m	1	3	8	28-34·2	
Andrade, D.	SEN	800m	1	3	7	1-53·89	
		1500m	1	1	9	3-59·22	
Andreev, P.	URS	10000m	1	3	3	28-20·97	
			F		11	28-46·27	
Angenvoorth, P.	GER	Marathon	F		16	2:20-19·0	
Araujo, N.	ARG	Marathon	F		DNF		
Arese, F.	ITA	1500m	1	2	1	3-43·99	
			2	3	7	3-41·08	
Ariyamongkol, P.	THA	4×100m relay	1	3	6	41·04	
Ariyamongkol, S.	THA	4×100m relay	1	3	6	41·04	
Armstrong, A.	TRI	100m	1	10	5	10·56	
			2	1	3	10·47	
		200m	1	4	3	21·12	
			2	2	3	21·00	
			SF	2	6	21·13	
Armstrong, G.	GBR	400m	1	6	7	46·48	
			2	4	7	47·10	
Aroche, P.	MEX	20k walk	F		12	1:33-05·0	

COMPETITOR	COUNTRY CODE	EVENT	ROUND	HEAT	PLACE	TIME & DISTANCE	MEDAL
Arza, D.	PAN	800m	1	8	4	1-51·64	
		1500m	1	1	5	3-41·73	
Arzhanov, E.	URS	800m	1	5	1	1-48·26	
			2	3	2	1-46·32	
			F		2	1-45·89	S
Asati, C.	KEN	400m	1	6	1	45·16	
			2	5	1	46·04	
			SF	1	4	45·47	
			F		4	45·13	
		4×400m relay	1	1	2	3-01·27	
			F		1	2-59·83	G
Ashaba, V.	UGA	1500m	1	4	8	3-45·15	
		3000m steeplechase	1	1	10	8-45·0	
Atamas, V.	URS	100m	1	12	4	10·51	
			2	5	8	10·83	
Avila, I.	MEX	20k walk	F		22	1:45-45·4	
Avilov, N.	URS	Decathlon	F		1	8454*	G
Awil, J.	SOM	Marathon	F		DNF		
Ayoo, S.	UGA	400m	1	1	7	47·04	
Azzouzi, A.	ALG	800m	1	1	3	1-49·38	
			2	1	6	1-49·42	
		1500m	1	7	7	3-46·37	
Ba, O.	SEN	4×400m relay	1	2	7	3:11·19	
Babu, S.	IND	High jump	Q		DNQ	1,90	
Bacheler, J.	USA	Marathon	F		9	2:17-38·2	
Badel, A.	SUI	50k walk	F		DNF		
Badenski, A.	POL	400m	1	1	1	46·21	
			2	5	2	46·19	
			SF	1	8	46·38	
		4×400m relay	1	3	1	3-02·52	
			F		5	3-01·05	
Badrankov, A.	URS	10000m	1	1	6	28-35·84	
Bahadur, B.	NEP	Marathon	F		60	2:57-58·8	
Bahadur, J.	NEP	Marathon	F		DNF		
Baird, M.	AUS	110m hurdles	1	3	6	14·55	
Bakai, J.	HUN	Decathlon	F		DNF		
Balachowski, J.	POL	4×400m relay	1	3	1	3-02·52	
			F		5	3-01·05	
Ballati, G.	ITA	400m hurdles	1	2	5	50·90	
Bannister, J.	USA	Decathlon	F		20	7022	
Baranov, A.	URS	Marathon	F		15	20:20-10·4	
Barch, O.	URS	50k walk	F		4	4:01-35·4	
Bariban, M.	URS	Triple jump	F		9	16,30	
Barkovski, L.	URS	Long jump	F		8	7,75	
Barrett, T.	BAH	Triple jump	Q		DNQ	15,51	
Barreneche, H.	COL	Marathon	F		29	2:23-40·0	
Barrionuevo, L.	ARG	High jump	Q		DNQ	1,90	
Baryshnikov, A.	URS	Shot put	Q		DNQ	18,65	
Bashir, A.	PAK	110m hurdles	1	1	8	15,38	
Bassegela, J.-P.	CGO	200m	1	3	6	21·72	
		4×100m relay	1	4	4	39·86	
			SF	2	8	39·97	
Baumgartner, H.	GER	Long jump	F		2	8,18	S
Bayi, F.	TAN	1500m	1	2	6	3-45·44	
		3000m steeplechase	1	2	9	8-41·4	
Bazunu, R.	NGR	4×100m relay	1	2	3	39·66	
			SF	1	6	39·73	
Bedane, L.	ETH	Marathon	F		10	2:18-36·8	
Bedasso, K.	ETH	4×100m relay	1	4	DNF		
Bedford, D.	GBR	5000m	1	1	2	13-49·8	
			F		12	13-43·22	
		10000m	1	1	2	27-53·64	
			F		6	28-05·44	
Beer, A.	FRA	Shot put	Q		DNQ	18,74	
Beers, J.	CAN	High jump	F		=6	2,15	
Belay, S.	ETH	200m	1	1	6	21·73	
		4×100m relay	1	4	DNF		
Bello, S.	ITA	4×400m relay	1	2	5	3-09·71	
Bendixen, F.	NDR	Long jump	Q		DNQ	7,61	
Benedetti, L.	ITA	4×100m relay	1	4	2	39·29	
			SF	2	4	39·21	
			F		8	39·14	
Bennett, J.	USA	Decathlon	F		4	7974	
Benson, A.	AUS	5000m	1	3	7	13-42·8	
Benti, A.	ETH	4×400m relay	1	2	4	3-08·59	
Bergaoui, H.	TUN	400m hurdles	1	3	7	53·70	
Berkes, E.	GER	110m hurdles	1	1	4	14·14	
Bernhard, R.	SUI	Long jump	Q		DNQ	7,68	
Bertould, G.	FRA	400m	1	4	4	46·36	
			2	4	4	46·14	
		4×400m relay	1	1	3	3-03·13	
			F		3	3-00·65	B
Bessonov, G.	URS	Triple jump	Q		DNQ	16,18	
Beyer, H.	GER	Decathlon	F		DNF		
Beyer, U.	GER	Hammer throw	F		4	71,52	

COMPETITOR	COUNTRY CODE	EVENT	ROUND	HEAT	PLACE	TIME & DISTANCE	MEDAL
Bezabeh, T.	ETH	400m	1	5	1	45.88	
			2	2	3	45.97	
			SF	1	6	45.98	
		4×400m relay	1	2	4	3-08.59	
Bicaba, A.	VOL	100m	1	6	5	10.71	
Bicourt, J.	GBR	3000m steeplechase	1	3	8	8-33.8	
Birlenbach, H.	GER	Shot put	F		7	20.37	
Bitte, R.	URS	3000m steeplechase	1	3	2	8-30.2	
			F		7	8-34.64	
Biwott, A.	KEN	3000m steeplechase	1	4	1	8-23.73*	
			F		6	8-33.48	
Bjambajav, E.	MGL	100m	1	1	6	10.93	
Bjoerkgren, D.	SWE	50k walk	F		13	4:22-00.0	
Black, L.	USA	200m	1	5	1	20.79	
			2	4	1	20.58	
			SF	2	1	20.36	
			F		2	20.19	S
		4×100m relay	1	4	1	38.95	
			SF	1	1	38.54	
			F		1	38.19*	S
Blackman, C.	CAN	4×400m relay	1	1	4	3-04.22	
Boeroe, K.	NOR	5000m	1	4	10	14-15.8	
Bogdanov, P.	URS	High jump	Q		DNQ	2.12	
Bohman, L.	TCH	100m	1	2	3	10.71	
			2	5	5	10.52	
		4×100m relay	1	2	2	39.31	
			SF	1	4	39.01	
			F		4	38.52	
Boit, M.	KEN	800m	1	7	1	1-47.25	
			2	3	1	1-45.87	
			F		3	1-46.0	B
		1500m	1	7	1	3-42.16	
			2	1	1	3-41.3x	
			F		4	3-38.4x	
Bombach, H-J.	GDR	100m	1	1	3	10.65	
			2	3	3	10.64	
		4×100m relay	1	4	3	39.17	
			SF	2	3	39.06	
			F		5	38.90	
Bondarchuk, A.	URS	Hammer throw	F		1	75.50*	G
Boontud, S.	THA	4×100m relay	1	3	6	41.04	
Born, H.	SUI	Decathlon	F		19	7217	
Borth, B.	GDR	100m	1	8	2	10.48	
			2	1	3	10.44	
			SF	1	7	10.60	
		4×100m relay	1	1	3	39.17	
			SF	2	3	39.06	
			F		5	38.90	
Borzov, V.	URS	100m	1	2	1	10.47	
			2	3	1	10.07	
			SF	1	1	10.21	
			F		1	10.14	G
		200m	1	3	1	20.64	
			2	1	1	20.30	
			SF	1	1	20.74	
			F		1	20.00	G
		4×100m relay	1	1	1	39.15	
			SF	2	2	39.00	
			F		2	38.50	S
Bouboud, M.	MAR	4×400m relay	1	1	6	3-05.92	
Bourbeillon, J.-P.	FRA	4×100m relay	1	2	1	39.01	
			SF	2	1	39.00	
			F		7	39.14	
Boxberger, J.	FRA	1500m	1	7	4	3-42.60	
			2	2	2	3-42.36	
Boyd, R.	AUS	Pole vault	Q		DNQ	4.80	
Brabec, J.	TCH	Shot put	F		10	19.86	
Briesenick, H.	GDR	Shot put	F		3	21.14	B
Brinkworth, N.	PAK	400m hurdles	1	2	7	54.67	
Bristol, A.	PUR	110m hurdles	1	1	6	14.61	
Brooks, C.	BAR	Decathlon	F		DNF		
Brouzet, Y.	FRA	Shot put	F		13	19.61	
Brown, D.	USA	3000m steeplechase	1	3	9	8-41.2	
Broz, J.	TCH	Long jump	Q		DNQ	7.76	
Bruch, R.	SWE	Discus throw	F		3	63.40	B
Bruggeman, R.	USA	400m hurdles	1	4	6	54.36	
Brutti, A.	ITA	Marathon	F		21	2:22-12.0	
Bryde, K.	CAN	Pole vault	Q		DNQ	0	
Buchheit, G.	FRA	3000m steeplechase	1	1	8	8-41.2	
Buciarski, W.	POL	Pole vault	F		10	5.00	
Buettner, D-W.	GER	400m hurdles	1	1	1	49.78	
			SF	2		DNF	
Bugri, S.	GHA	400m	1	3	4	47.83	
			2	1	8	47.34	
Bull, M.	GBR	Pole vault	Q		DNQ	4.80	

COMPETITOR	COUNTRY CODE	EVENT	ROUND	HEAT	PLACE	TIME & DISTANCE	MEDAL
Burton, L.	USA	200m	1	9	1	20.80	
			2	3	1	20.68	
			SF	1	2	20.78	
			F		4	20.37	
Buttari, G.	ITA	110m hurdles	1	3	DIS		
Byrame, A.	FRA	100m	1	12	6	10.64	
Cabrera, R.	ARG	Marathon	F		55	2:42-37.2	
Caero, L.	BOL	100m	1	8	7	11.19	
		Long jump	Q		DNQ	6.77	
Calhern, G.	ISV	100m	1	4	5	10.90	
Callander, W.	BAH	100m	1	4	4	10.78	
		4×100m relay	1	4	5	40.48	
Calonge, A.	ARG	100m	1	9	4	10.73	
		200m	1	2	3	21.39	
			2	2	6	21.11	
Campbell, C.	GBR	800m	1	2	6	1-54.81	
Campbell, T.	JAM	4×400m relay	-	3	4	3-03.83	
Capes, G.	GBR	Shot put	Q		DNQ	18.94	
Carballo, H.	ESP	4×100m relay	1	4	DNF		
Carette, J.	FRA	4×400m relay	1	3	3	3-03.13	
			F		3	3-00.65	B
Carlgren, E.	SWE	4×400m relay	1	1	3	3-03.05	
			F		7	3-02.57	
Carpentieri, D.	ITA	50k walk	F		23	4:33-10.6	
Carrington, P.	USA	Long jump	F		5	7.99	
Carter, A.	GBR	800m	1	7	3	1-47.64	
			2	3	3	1-46.45	
			F		6	1-46.55	
Carvalho, J.	POR	400m hurdles	1	3	6	52.64	
		4×400m relay	1	1	7	3:10-00	
Casanas, A.	CUB	110m hurdles	1	4	DNF		
Cech, P.	TCH	110m hurdles	1	5	3	14.04	
			SF	1	4	13.82	
			F		8	13.86	
Cefan, G.	RUM	3000m steeplechase	1	1	4	8-33.8	
Cellerino, L.	ITA	4×400m relay	1	2	5	3-09.71	
Charlotin, M.	HAI	Marathon	F		62	3:29-21.0	
Chauvelot, D.	FRA	100m	1	11	2	10.66	
			2	3	7	10.54	
Chen Chin-Lung	CHN	Long jump	Q		DNQ	6.79	
		4×100m relay	1	2	7	41.78	
Chen Ming-Chih	CHN	4×100m relay	1	2	7	41.78	
		Triple jump	Q		DNQ	14.73	
Cherrier, B.	FRA	200m	1	1	2	20.79	
			2	4	3	20.62	
			SF	2	7	21.15	
		4×100m relay	1	2	1	39.01	
			SF	2	1	39.00	
			F		7	39.14	
Chiheta, N.	TAN	100m	1	7	5	10.79	
		4×100m relay	1	4	6	41.07	
Chokimane, O.	MAR	200m	1	5	4	21.29	
			2	1	6	21.00	
		4×400m relay	1	1	6	3-05.92	
Cikic, M.	YUG	4×400m relay	1	1	5	3-05.70	
Cindolo, G.	ITA	10000m	1	1	16	33-03.4	
Claude, A.	CAN	Javelin throw	Q		DNQ	75.56	
Clayton, D.	AUS	Marathon	F		13	2:19-49.6	
Clerc, P.	SUI	100m	1	6	2	10.58	
			2	1	4	10.45	
		200m	1	9	4	21.32	
			2	3	4	20.82	
Collett, W.	USA	400m	1	4	2	46.00	
			2	1	1	45.80	
			SF	2	3	45.77	
			F		2	44.80	S
Colon, A.	PUR	1500m	1	5	7	3-44.62	
Condori, R.	BOL	Marathon	F		58	2:56-11.4	
Conway, P.	IRL	Shot put	Q		DNQ	16.69	
Cooper A.	TRI	400m	1	9	3	47.15	
			2	2	7	48.29	
		4×400m relay	1	2	2	3-03.48	
			F		8	3-03.60	
Corbu, C.	RUM	Long jump	Q		DNQ	7.54	
		Triple jump	F		4	16.85	
Corval, J-P.	FRA	400m hurdles	1	1	3	50.15	
			SF	1	8	50.75	
Craft, J.	USA	Triple jump	F		5	16.83	
Cramerotti, R.	ITA	Javelin throw	Q		DNQ	71.12	
Crampton, J.	BIR	800m	1	7	6	1-54.23	
		1500m	1	7	10	4-06.86	
Crawford, H.	TRI	100m	1	7	1	10.50	
			2	3	3	10.18	
			SF	1	2	10.36	
			F		DNF		
Cropper, D.	GBR	800m	1	3	2	1-47.45	
			2	1	3	1-48.42	

COMPETITOR	COUNTRY CODE	EVENT	ROUND	HEAT	PLACE	TIME & DISTANCE	MEDAL
Csik, J.	HUN	Javelin throw	F		12	76,14	
Cuch, T.	POL	100m	1	2	5	10·89	
		4×100m relay	1	3	1	39·11	
			SF	1	3	38·90	
			F		6	39·03	
Cusack, N.	IRL	10000m	1	2	10	28-45·8	
Cuttell, R.	CAN	High jump	Q		DNQ	2·09	
Cybulski, G.	POL	Long jump	F		12	7,58	
Czerbniak, J.	POL	4×100m relay	1	3	1	39·11	
			SF	1	3	38·90	
			F		6	39·03	
Da Cunha-Silva, F.	POR	400m	1	5	6	47·67	
		4×400m relay	1	1	7	3-10·00	
Dahlgren, J.	SWE	High jump	F		11	2,15	
Daley, A.	JAM	4×100m relay	1	3	4	3-03·83	
Dal Forno, E.	ITA	High jump	F		10	2,15	
Dalmati, J.	HUN	50k walk	F		23	4:31-23·2	
Dalurzo, C.	ARG	800m	1	5	5	1-50·58	
Danek, L.	TCH	Discus throw	F		1	64,40	G
Daniels, G.	GHA	100m	1	6	4	10·65	
		200m	1	7	3	21·05	
			2	2	5	21·10	
		4×100m relay	1	3	2	39·46	
			SF	1	7	39·99	
Danis, I.	TCH	400m hurdles	1	4	3	50·62	
			SF	1	6	50·01	
D'Arcy, L.	NZL	100m	1	9	5	10·77	
Da Silva L Gonzaga	BRA	100m	1	3	5	10·63	
		200m	1	5	5	21·81	
Davenport, W.	USA	110m hurdles	1	1	2	13·97	
			SF	2	3	13·73	
			F		4	13·50	
Davies, L.	GBR	Long jump	Q		DNQ	7,64	
Dear, B.	GBR	4×100m relay	1	4	3	39·63	
			SF	2	6	39·47	
Decosse, J-C.	FRA	50k walk	F		DNF		
De Hertoghe, A.	BEL	1500m	1	3	5	3-44·62	
Del Buono, G.	ITA	1500m	1	4	5	3-40·78	
			2	1	6	3-41·99	
Demec, J.	TCH	100m	1	5	4	10·66	
		4×100m relay	1	2	2	39·31	
			SF	1	4	39·01	
			F		4	38·82	
De Menego, F.	ITA	Marathon	F		38	2:26-52·2	
D'Encausse, H.	FRA	Pole vault	F		NP	0	
De Vincentis, A.	ITA	Discus throw	Q		DNQ	0	
Dia, M.	SEN	Triple jump	F		6	16,83	
Dieye, S.	SEN	4×400m relay	1	2	7	3-11·19	
Dinneen, W.	PUR	Hammer throw	Q		DNQ	62,02	
Dionisi, R.	ITA	Pole vault	Q		DNQ	0	
Dixon, R.	NZL	1500m	1	4	2	3-40·03	
			2	3	1	3-37·91	
			F		3	3-37·46	B
Djoudi, Sid-Ali	ALG	800m	1	2	5	1-50·41	
Doessegger, W.	SUI	10000m	1	1	8	28-36·4	
Dogon-Yaro, M.	NGR	4×400m relay	1	2	3	3-04·31	
Do Matos, A.F.	POR	4×400m relay	1	1	7	3-10·00	
Dooley, T.	USA	20k walk	F		15	1:34-58·8	
Do Rosario, C.	SEN	4×100m relay	1	3	5	40·95	
Dowswell, R.	CAN	Javelin throw	Q		DNQ	77,42	
Dralu, W.	UGA	100m	1	6	7	10·92	
		200m	1	9	6	21·87	
Drehmel, J.	GDR	Triple jump	F		2	17,31	S
Drut, G.	FRA	110m hurdles	1	5	1	13·78	
			SF	1	2	13·49	
			F		2	13·34	S
Dufresne, J.-P.	FRA	1500m	1	1	3	3-40·75	
			2	3	8	3-41·62	
Dunn, C.	USA	High jump	Q		DNQ	2,12	
Dyce, B.	JAM	800m	1	7	4	1-47·95	
		1500m	1	5	6	3-45·87	
Ebba, H.	ETH	1500m	1	5	1	3-41·61	
			2	1	10	3-43·69	
Eckschmidt, S.	HUN	Hammer throw	F		6	71,20	
Ehl, K.	FRG	100m	1	11	3	10·67	
			2	3	5	10·44	
		4×100m relay	1	1	2	39·17	
			SF	1	2	38·86	
			F		3	38·79	B
Eisenberg, F.	GDR	5000m	1	3	2	13-38·4	
			F		9	13-40·84	
Ekman, G.	SWE	1500m	1	4	3	3-40·40	
			2	3	5	3-39·44	
Elliott, H.	FRA	High jump	F		15	2,10	
Elmer, K.	CAN	1500m	1	7	8	3-46·56	
Embleton, P.	GBR	20k walk	F		14	1:33-22·2	
Encsi, I.	HUN	Hammer throw	F		11	70,06	
Entezari, R.	IRN	400m	1	8	4	47·89	
			2	2	8	48·69	
		800m	1	1	5	1-50·54	
Evele, H.	CMR	High jump	Q		DNQ	1,90	
Faager, A.	SWE	400m	1	2	2	46·29	
			2	4	4	46·54	
		4×400m relay	1	1	3	3-03·05	
			F		7	3-02·57	
Farah, D.	SUD	1500m	1	1	10	4-02·94	
		4×400m relay	1	2	8	3-14·51	
Faustin, J.-M.	HAI	400m	1	3	6	52·33	
Fava, F.	ITA	3000m steeplechase	1	4	5	8-35·0	
Fejer, G.	HUN	Discus throw	F		5	62,62	
Feldmann, A.	SUI	3000m steeplechase	1	1	6	8-35·8	
Feleke, S.	ETH	4×100m relay	1	4	DNF		
Fenouil, G.	FRA	4×100m relay	1	2	1	39·01	
			SF	2	1	39·00	
			F		7	39·14	
Fernandez, A.	ESP	800m	1	5	DIS		
Fernandez, A.	ESP	Marathon	F		39	2:27-24·2	
Ferrer, J.	PUR	400m hurdles	1	4	7	54·83	
Ferrer, P.	PUR	400m	1	4	6	47·90	
		4×100m relay	1	1	5	41·34	
Fettouh, S.	MAR	4×400m relay	1	1	6	3-05·92	
Feuerbach, A.	USA	Shot put	F		5	21,01	
Field, B.	AUS	400m hurdles	1	4	4	51·46	
		Long jump	Q		DNQ	7,76	
Finlay, R.	CAN	5000m	1	5	6	13-44·0	
Fiser, V.	TCH	Triple jump	Q		DNQ	15,96	
Fisher, C.	AUS	1500m	1	4	4	3-42·50	
			2	1	5	3-41·96	
Fitinsa, T.	ETH	5000m	1	3	9	13-50·4	
Floegstad, K.	NOR	Triple jump	F		8	16,44	
Flores, A.	GUA	Decathlon	F		DNF		
Fongang, E.	CMR	1500m	1	7	9	3-54·12	
		10000m	1	1	13	31-32·6	
Fordjour, B.	GHA	1500m	1	4	10	4-08·24	
Fossander, B.	SWE	110m hurdles	1	2	6	14·56	
Foster, B.	GBR	1500m	1	1	4	3-40·79	
			2	2	3	3-38·20	
			F		5	3-39·02	
Foster, J.	NZL	Marathon	F		8	2:16-56·2	
Francis, C.	CAN	100m	1	9	3	10·68	
			2	4	8	10·51	
Fraquelli, S.	ITA	Pole vault	Q		DNQ	4,80	
Fray, M.	JAM	100m	1	10	3	10·47	
			2	4	3	10·28	
			SF	1	4	10·48	
			F		5	10·40	
Frederique	MAD	400m	1	9	6	48·72	
Frenkel, P.	GDR	20k walk	F		1	1:26-42·4*	G
Frenn, G.	USA	Hammer throw	Q		DNQ	62,14	
Frinolli, R.	ITA	400m hurdles	1	1	7	51·69	
Fromm, D.	GDR	800m	1	6	1	1-46·94	
			2	1	2	1-48·06	
			F		8	1-47·96	
Gabbett, P.	GBR	Decathlon	F		DNF		
Gabre, E.	ETH	100m	1	7	6	10·89	
		4×100m relay	F	4	DNF		
Gaetjens, P.-R.	HAI	100m	1	7	7	11·50	
Gage, T.	USA	Hammer throw	F		12	69,50	
Gakou, A.	SEN	400m	1	9	4	47·68	
			2	3	7	46·96	
Galea, H.	VEN	4×100m relay	1	2	4	39·74	
			SF	2	7	39·74	
Galloway, J.	USA	10000m	1	1	11	29-35·0	
Gammoudi, M.	TUN	5000m	1	1	1	13-49·8	
			F		2	13-27·33	S
		10000m	1	2	1	27-54·69	
			F		DNF		
Gamski, I.	URS	Hammer throw	F		18	66,26	
Garcia, F.	ESP	200m	1	7	2	20·89	
			2	5	5	20·77	
		4×100m relay	1	4	DNF		
Garderud, A.	SWE	5000m	1	1	4	13-57·2	
		3000m steeplechase	1	3	5	8-30·8	
Gardiaby, A.	SEN	Pole vault	Q		DNQ	0	
Garshol, A.	NOR	100m	1	8	3	10·49	
			2	1	7	10·55	
		200m	1	4	6	21·16	
			2	4	7	25·30	
Gauthier, B.	FRA	High jump	F		14	2,15	
Gavrilas, R.	RUM	Decathlon	F		16	7417	
Gavrilenko, E.	URS	400m hurdles	1	5	1	49·73	
			SF	2	2	49·34	
			F		=6	49·66	

COMPETITOR	COUNTRY CODE	EVENT	ROUND	HEAT	PLACE	TIME & DISTANCE	MEDAL
Gayoso, M.	ESP	800m	1	6	3	1-47.52	
			2	3	5	1-47.73	
Gebre, E.	ETH	100m	1	7	6	10.89	
Gentile, G.	ITA	Triple jump	Q		DNQ	15.04	
Georges, G.	HAI	200m	1	4	7	22.97	
Georgiadis, G.	GRE	Hammer throw	Q		DNQ	63.58	
Ghesquiere, R.	BEL	Decathlon	F		11	7677	
Ghiasi, T.	IRN	High jump	Q		DNQ	2.12	
Ghipu, G.	RUM	800m	1	5	4	1-50.06	
Ghizlat, O.	MAR	400m	1	2	4	46.37	
			2	1	7	46.84	
		4×400m relay	1	1	6	3-05.92	
Gies, H.-P.	GDR	Shot put	F		4	21.14	
Giovanardi, D.	ITA	4×400m relay	1	2	5	3-09.71	
Glasauer, G.	GER	Javelin throw	Q		DNQ	73.12	
Gloeckler, T.	GER	Shot put	F		18	18.35	
Gloerfeld, A.	GER	Long jump	Q		DNQ	7.50	
Golubnichy, V.	URS	20k walk	F		2	1:26-55.2	S
Gomez, R.	NIC	Marathon	F		DNF		
Gonzales, F.	FRA	800m	1	6	5	1-48.77	
Gonzalez, G.	PUR	100m	1	7	4	10.73	
		200m	1	4	4	21.22	
			2	1	7	21.0	
		4×100m relay	1	1	5	41.34	
Gonzalez, R.	MEX	50k walk	F		20	4:26-13.4	
Gordon, I.	CAN	4×400m relay	1	1	4	3-04.22	
Goris, R.	BEL	5000m	1	1	6	13-57.8	
Grahn, B.	FIN	Shot put	Q		DNQ	18.20	
Green, B.	GBR	100m	1	4	2	10.41	
			2	2	2	10.38	
			SF	2	8	10.52	
		200m	1	5	3	21.25	
			2	5	7	21.41	
		4×100m relay	1	4	3	39.63	
			SF	2	5	39.47	
Gres, J-P.	FRA	4×100m relay	1	2	1	39.0	
			SF	2	1	39.0	
			F		7	39.14	
Grigoriev, S.	URS	50k walk	F		DS		
Grimnes, B.	NOR	Javelin throw	F		5	83.08	
Guerini, V.	ITA	4×100m relay	1	4	2	39.25	
			SF	2	4	39.21	
			F		8	39.14	
Guerreros, A.	PAR	100m	1	4	7	11.12	
Guettaya, M.	TUN	800m	1	1	2	1-49.33	
			2	2	7	1-49.75	
		1500m	1	7	5	3-43.90	
Gunawardene, S.	CEY	100m	1	11	6	11.00	
		200m	1	6	3	21.60	
			2	2	8	21.31	
Gushiken, K.	JPN	Triple jump	Q		DNQ	16.19	
Gustafsson, E.	FIN	100m	1	7	3	10.68	
			2	2	6	10.78	
		4×100m relay	1	3	3	39.54	
			SF	2	5	39.30	
Gysin, R.	SUI	800m	1	3	3	1-47.46	
			2	3	6	1-48.17	
Hackman, R.	GHA	3000m steeplechase	1	3	12	8-57.6	
Halle, P.	NOR	5000m	1	3	3	13-38.6	
			F		7	13-34.38	
Halliday, D.	GBR	100m	1	7	2	10.58	
			2	5	6	10.50	
		4×100m relay	1	4	3	39.63	
			SF	2	6	39.47	
Hamdi, M.	SUD	110m hurdles	1	4	7	15.80	
Hamze, K.	LIB	400m	1	5	7	49.20	
		800m	1	6	7	1-52.54	
Hansen, T.B.	DEN	1500m	1	6	2	3-41.08	
			2	1	3	3-41.64	
			F		10	3-46.58	
Hardware, R.	JAM	200m	1	3	3	21.09	
			2	5	3	20.75	
			SF	2	8	21.24	
Haro, M.	ESP	5000m	1	4	3	13-35.4	
			F		DNS		
		10000m	1	2	2	27-56.0	
			F		4	27-48.2	
Hart, E.J.	USA	100m	1	11	1	10.47	
			2	2	DNS		
		4×100m relay	1	4	1	38.96	
			SF	1	1	38.54	
			F		1	38.19*	G
Hartnett, J.	IRL	5000m	1	3	12	14-34.6	
Hawkins, J.	CAN	High jump	F		9	2.15	
Hayden, S.	USA	50k walk	F		27	4:36-07.2	
Hedmark, L.	SWE	Decathlon	F		DNF		
Hemery, D.	GBR	400m hurdles	1	2	1	49.72	
			SF	1	3	49.66	
			F		3	48.52	B
		4×400m relay	1	1	1	3-01.26	
			F		2	3-00.46	S
Hennig, K.-P.	GER	Discus throw	Q		DNQ	58.64	
Hensgens, S.	HOL	800m	1	8	4	1-51.18	
Herbrand, F.	BEL	Decathlon	F		6	7947	
Hernandez, G.	MEX	50k walk	F		8	4:12-09.0	
Herrmann, B.	GER	4×400m relay	1	2	1	3-03.27	
			F		4	3-00.88	
Hidalgo, J.	VEN	400m hurdles	1	2	6	54.00	
		4×100m relay	1	3	5	3-06.99	
Hill, R.	GBR	Marathon	F		6	2:16-30.6	
Hill, T.	USA	110m hurdles	1	2	1	13.62	
			SF	1	1	13.47	
			F		3	13.48	B
Hilton, L.	USA	5000m	-	4	8	14-07.2	
Hirscht, J.	GER	100m	1	12	2	10.36	
			2	1	1	10.25	
			SF	1	3	10.36	
			F		6	10.40	
		4×100m relay	1	1	2	39.17	
			SF	1	2	38.86	
			F		3	38.79	B
Hla, T.	BIR	Marathon	F		57	2:48-53.2	
Hoegberg, U.	SWE	1500m	1	6	5	3-41.45	
			2	1	9	3-43.57	
Hoehne, C.	GDR	50k walk	F		14	4:20-01.0	
Holden, A.	GBR	3000m steeplechase	1	1	5	8-33.8	
Hollings, S.	GBR	3000m steeplechase	1	4	4	8-35.0	
Holt, D.	GBR	10000m	1	2	11	28-46.8	
Homziuk, J.	POL	Long jump	Q		DNQ	7.63	
Honz, K.	GER	400m	1	7	4	46.77	
			2	4	1	45.87	
			SF	1	2	45.32	
			F		7	45.68	
		4×400m relay	1	2	1	3-03.27	
			F		4	3-00.88	
Horcic, J.	TCH	1500m	1	2	7	3-45.72	
		3000m steeplechase	1	3	4	8-30.6	
Howe, T.	LBR	800m	1	2	8	2-00.70	
Hussein, A.N.	SUD	400m	1	5	3	47.01	
			2	3	8	47.33	
		800m	1	5	3	1-48.94	
			2	2	8	1-51.05	
		4×400m relay	1	2	8	3-14.51	
Idrissou, I.	DAH	400m	1	7	6	48.50	
Igun, S.	NGR	Triple jump	F		11	16.03	
Ijirigho, B.	NGR	400m	1	2	5	46.59	
			2	3	5	46.81	
		4×400m relay	1	2	3	3-04.31	
Ingvarsson, S.	SWE	50k walk	F		15	4:21-01.0	
Inoue, T.	JPN	Triple jump	F		12	15.88	
Ioan, S.	RUM	High jump	F		16	2.10	
Isaksson, K.	SWE	Pole vault	Q		DNQ	0	
Ishida, Y.	JPN	Hammer throw	Q		DNQ	63.82	
Ivancic, I.	YUG	Shot put	Q		DNQ	18.95	
Ivanov, B.	URS	Decathlon	F		13	7657	
Ivanov, I.	URS	800m	1	8	1	1-51.02	
			2	2	5	1-49.61	
		1500m	1	1	6	3-42.27	
Ivchenko, E.	URS	20k walk	F		DIS		
Jackson, H.	JAM	Long jump	Q		DNQ	7.50	
		Triple jump	Q		DNQ	0	
Jaman, M.	ARS	400m	1	8	6	49.67	
James, T.	TRI	200m	1	6	4	21.83	
			2	5	6	21.34	
Janczenko, T.	POL	Decathlon	F		8	7861	
Jansky, J.	TCH	5000m	1	5	3	13-39.2	
		10000m	1	1	5	28-23.15	
					9	28-23.59	
Jaremski, Z.	POL	400m	1	9	2	46.20	
			2	4	3	46.52	
			SF	2	DNS		
		4×400m relay	1	3	1	3-02.52	
			F		5	3-01.05	
Jellinghaus, M.	GER	200m	1	2	2	21.10	
			2	3	2	20.70	
			SF	2	4	20.75	
			F		7	20.65	
Jenkins, D.	GBR	400m	1	2	1	46.15	
			2	3	1	45.99	
			SF	1	5	45.91	
		4×400m relay	1	1	1	3-01.26	
			F		2	3-00.46	S
Jenner, B.	USA	Decathlon	F		10	7722	

COMPETITOR	COUNTRY CODE	EVENT	ROUND	HEAT	PLACE	TIME & DISTANCE	MEDAL
Jensen, D.	DEN	50k walk	F		29	4:57-13-8	
Jensen, J.	DEN	Marathon	F		30	2:24-00-2	
Jernberg, I.	SWE	Pole vault	F		10	5,10	
Jipcho, B.	KEN	5000m	1	1	3	13-56-8	
		3000m steeplechase	1	2	1	8-31-6	
			F		2	8-24-62	S
Joachimowski, N.	POL	Triple jump	F		7	16,69	
Johnson, J.	USA	Pole vault	F		3	5,35	B
Johnson, K.	BAH	100m	1	3	6	10-91	
		200m	1	7	5	21-70	
Johnson, R.	NZL	400m hurdles	1	5	4	50-48	
Joseph, A.	HAI	10000m	1	3	DNF		
Joseph, C.	TRI	400m	1	1	2	46-38	
			2	1	5	46-14	
		4×400m relay	1	2	2	3-03-48	
			F		8	3-03-60	
Jourdan, R.	USA	High jump	Q		DNQ	2,12	
Jozwik, M.	POL	110m hurdles	1	4	2	14-06	
			SF	2	5	14-06	
Juantorena, A.	CUB	400m	1	4	1	45-94	
			2	1	2	45-96	
			SF	2	5	46-07	
Juhola, M.	FIN	200m	1	4	2	20-98	
			2	2	7	21-19	
		4×100m relay	1	3	3	39-54	
			SF	2	5	39-30	
Juma, R.	KEN	10000m	1	3	11	29-13-0	
		Marathon	F		DNF		
Junge, S.	GDR	High jump	F		2	2,21	S
Justus, K.-P.	GDR	1500m	1	4	4	3-40-44	
			2	3	9	3-44-64	
Kaerlin, G.	DEN	5000m	1	2	10	14-39-2	
Kahma, P.	FIN	Discus throw	F		9	59,66	
Kaiser, G.	SUI	3000m steeplechase	1	4	9	8-45-4	
Kalliomaeki, A.	FIN	Pole vault	F		NP	0	
Kamanya, C.	TAN	400m	1	4	3	46-18	
			2	5	4	46-55	
		4×100m relay	1	4	6	41-07	
		4×100m relay	1	2	6	3-10-12	
Kambale, M.	MAW	Marathon	F		56	2:45-50-0	
Kangni, R.	TOG	800m	1	4	7	1-52-09	
Kannenberg, B.	GER	20k walk	F		DNF		
		50k walk	F		1	3:56-11-6*	G
Kantanen, T.	FIN	5000m	1	3	6	13-42-0	
		3000m steeplechase	1	1	1	8-24-8*	
			F		3	8-24-66	B
Kaonga, E.	MAW	200m	1	5	6	22-18	
Kar, E.	LBR	1500m	1	5	10	4-21-41	
Karikari, O.	GHA	4×100m relay	1	3	2	39-46	
			SF	1	7	39-99	
Karttunen, O.	FIN	4×400m relay	1	3	2	3-02-97	
			F		6	3-01-12	
Kasmi, M.	ALG	1500m	1	1	8	3-45-16	
Katona, G.	HUN	Long jump	Q		DNQ	7,68	
		Triple jump	Q		DNQ	16,19	
Katus, R.	POL	Decathlon	F		3	7984	B
Kawagoe, T.	JPN	Long jump	Q		DNQ	7,47	
Keino, K.	KEN	1500m	1	4	1	3-39-97	
			2	2	1	3-41-15	
			F		2	3-36-81	S
		3000m steeplechase	1	1	2	3-27-6	
			F		1	8-23-64*	G
Kemper, F.-J.	GER	800m	1	3	1	1-47-34	
			2	2	2	1-48-83	
			F		4	1-46-50	
Keogh, M.	IRL	5000m	1	1	5	13-57-8	
Kerbiriou, F.	FRA	400m	1	3	3	47-01	
			2	4	5	46-63	
		4×400m relay	1	3	3	3-03-13	
			F		3	3-00-65	B
Khamis, A.	EGY	10000m	1	2	15	30-19-2	
Khmelevski, V.	URS	Hammer throw	F		3	74-04	B
Kim Chang Son	PRK	Marathon	F		37	2:26-45-6	
Kimatyo, F.	KEN	400m hurdles	1	1	6	51-23	
Kimihara, K.	JPN	Marathon	F		5	2:16-27-0	
King, B.	GBR	Decathlon	F		15	7468	
Kinnunen, J.	FIN	Javelin throw	F		6	82,08	
Kirkbride, J.	GBR	1500m	1	2	5	3-45-34	
Kirkham, C.	GBR	Marathon	F		20	2:21-54-8	
Kirst, J.	GDR	Decathlon	F		DNF		
Kiss, A.	HUN	50k walk	F		26	4:34-45-0	
Klauss, M.	GDR	Long jump	F		6	7,96	
Klein, E.	GER	Hammer throw	F		7	71,14	
Klopfer, G.	USA	20k walk	F		19	1:38-33-6	
Klotz, H.	GER	4×100m relay	1	1	2	39-17	
			SF	1	2	38-86	
			F		3	38-79	B
Knoke, G.	AUS	400m hurdles	1	2	2	50-10	
			SF	2	6	52-79	
Kocuvan, M.	YUG	4×400m relay	1	1	5	3-05-70	
Koehler, H.	GER	4×400m relay	1	2	1	3-03-27	
			F		4	3-00-88	
Kokot, M.	GDR	100m	1	3	1	10-49	
			2	4	6	10-44	
		4×100m relay	1	1	3	39-17	
			SF	2	3	39-06	
			F		5	38-90	
Kolbeck, F.	FRA	Marathon	F		28	2:23-01-2	
Komar, W.	POL	Shot put	F		1	21,18*	G
Komenan, K.	CIV	100m	1	4	3	10-50	
			2	2	3	10-60	
			SF	1	6	10-57	
		4×100m relay	1	2	5	39-81	
Kone, G.	CIV	4×100m relay	1	2	5	39-81	
Kontossoros, S.	GRE	3000m steeplechase	1	4	8	8-41-0	
Korica, D.	YUG	10000m	1	3	4	28-22-24	
			F		7	28-15-18	
Korneliuk, A.	URS	100m	1	5	1	10-38	
			2	4	1	10-23	
			SF	2	3	10-35	
			F		4	10-36	
		4×100m relay	1	1	1	39-15	
			SF	2	2	39-00	
			F		2	38-50	S
Koskei, W.	KEN	400m hurdles	1	2	4	50-58	
Kotu, T.	ETH	5000m	1	4	4	13-46-2	
Koussoulas, I.	GRE	High jump	Q		DNQ	2,12	
Koyama, T.	JPN	5000m	1	1	8	14-12-6	
		3000m steeplechase	1	1	3	8-29-8	
			F		9	8-37-66	
Krishnan, T.	MAL	400m	1	9	5	48-31	
		4×400m relay	1	3	6	3-13-51	
Kriz, L.	TCH	200m	1	2	4	21-58	
			2	3	7	21-46	
Kukkoaho, M.	FIN	400m	1	9	1	46-05	
			2	3	3	46-11	
			SF	2	4	46-02	
			F		6	45-49	
		4×400m relay	1	3	2	3-02-97	
			F		6	3-01-12	
Kulcsar, G.	HUN	Javelin throw	Q		DNQ	77,24	
Kulczycki, T.	POL	400m hurdles	1	1	4	50-19	
			SF	2	5	50-80	
Kumar, P.	IND	Discus throw	Q		DNQ	53,12	
Kupczyk, A.	POL	800m	1	5	2	1-48-52	
			2	3	4	1-46-69	
			F		7	1-47-10	
Kuretzky, R.	GER	Pole vault	F		4	5,30	
Kynos, J.	TCH	200m	1	1	3	20-95	
			2	1	3	20-68	
			SF	2	5	20-88	
		4×100m relay	1	2	2	39-31	
			SF	1	4	39-01	
			F		4	38-82	
Ladani, S.	ISR	50k walk	F		19	4:24-38-6	
Lagerqvist, H.	SWE	Pole vault	F		7	5,20	
Lamitie, B.	FRA	Triple jump	F		10	16,27	
Lang, H.	AUT	4×100m relay	1	1	4	40-49	
			SF	1	DIS		
Larsen, G.	DEN	1500m	1	2	4	3-44-66	
			2	3	10	3-59-44	
Lauenbourg, J.	DEN	5000m	1	4	11	14-18-8	
Leddy, E.	IRL	3000m steeplechase	1	2	9	8-47-4	
Lee Chung-Ping	CHN	100m	1	2	8	14-98	
		400m hurdles	1	5	6	52-61	
		4×100m relay	1	2	7	41-78	
Le Roy, Y.	FRA	Decathlon	F		12	7675	
Lerwill, A.	GBR	Long jump	F		7	7,91	
Lespagnard, R.	BEL	Decathlon	F		14	7519	
Lesse, L.	GDR	Marathon	F		25	2:22-49-6	
Letzerich, M.	GER	10000m	1	3	14	29-37-8	
Liani, S.	ITA	110m hurdles	1	5	2	13-95	
			SF	1	5	13-90	
Lismont, K.	BEL	10000m	1	2	9	28-41-8	
		Marathon	F		2	2:14-31-8	S
Litvinenko, L.	URS	Decathlon	F		2	8035	S
Lockhart, H.	BAH	4×100m relay	1	4	5	40-48	
Loennqvist, S.	FIN	4×400m relay	1	3	2	3-02-97	
			F		6	3-01-12	
Lopes, C.	POR	5000m	1	1	9	14-29-6	
		10000m	1	3	9	28-53-6	
		Marathon	F		43	2:28-37-0	
Lopez, C.C.	GUA	5000m	1	2	11	15-53-4	
Lopez, H.	VEN	800m	1	5	6	1-50-76	
Losch, H.	GDR	Discus throw	Q		DNQ	56,54	

COMPETITOR	COUNTRY CODE	EVENT	ROUND	HEAT	PLACE	TIME & DISTANCE	MEDAL
Louka, L.	GRE	Shot put	Q		DNQ	17,48	
Lovetski, V.	URS	200m	1	6	2	20·99	
			2	4	4	21·83	
		4×100m relay	1	1	1	39·15	
			SF	2	2	39·00	
			F		2	38·50	S
Lubiejewski, S.	POL	Hammer throw	Q		DNQ	64,80	
Luke, F.	USA	Javelin throw	F		8	80,06	
Lund, K.	NOR	50k walk	F		24	4:34-23·4	
Lupan, P.	RUM	1500m	1	3	5	3-44·78	
Lusis, J.	URS	Javelin throw	F		2	90,46	S
McCafferty, I.	GBR	5000m	1	3	1	13-38·2	
			F		11	13-43·20	
McDaid, D.	IRL	Marathon	F		23	2:22-25·2	
MacDonald, R.	CAN	110m hurdles	1	3	3	14.36	
			SF	1	6	14.22	
McGann, D.	IRL	Marathon	F		42	2:28-31·6	
McGrath, M.	AUS	Triple jump	Q		DNQ	15,90	
Macgregor, D.	GBR	Marathon	F		7	2:16-34·4	
McKenzie, D.	NZL	Marathon	F		22	2:22-19·2	
MacLaren, B.	CAN	400m	1	6	7	47·55	
		4×400m relay	1	1	4	3-04·22	
McLaren, G.	CAN	5000m	1	2	5	13-43·8	
McLaren, P.	CAN	4×400m Relay	1	1	4	3-04·2	
McSweeney, F.	IRL	400m	1	5	5	47·07	
Mabuza, M.	SWZ	1000m	1	2	DNF		
Mabuza, R.	SWZ	Marathon	F		17	2:20-39·6	
Mageri, H.	FRG	High jump	F		4	2,18	
Magnor, H.-R.	GER	50k walk	F		16	4:21-63·4	
Maier, W.	GER	3000m steeplechase	1	2	4	8-37·6	
Maipambe, N.	ZAM	100m	1	4	7	48·84	
Maisonave, W.	PUR	Triple jump	Q		DNC	15,38	
		Long jump	Q		DNQ	7,58	
Majekodumni, B.	NGR	100m	1	11	4	10·70	
		4×100m relay	1	2	3	39·66	
			SF	1	6	39·73	
Major, I.	HUN	High jump	F		=6	2,15	
Makama, M.	NGR	4×400m relay	1	2	3	3-04·31	
Maki, S.	CIV	110m hurdles	1	3	7	14·59	
Makki, H.	ARS	Shot put	Q		DNQ	11,57	
Malam, G.	CMR	100m	1	11	5	10·85	
		200m	1	4	6	21·77	
Malinowski, B.	POL	5000m	1	5	8	13-48·2	
		3000m steeplechase	1	4	2	8-28·2	
			F		4	8-27·92	
Mamede, F.	POR	800m	1	2	4	1-48·59	
		1500m	1	7	6	3-45·07	
		4×400m relay	1	1	7	3-10·00	
Mandonda, A.	CGO	800m	1	1	7	1-51·17	
Mane, M.	SEN	4×100m relay	1	3	5	40·95	
Mangish, R.	SUI	Decathlon	F		DNF		
Mango, J.-P.	SEN	4×400m relay	1	2	7	3-11·19	
Manley, M.	USA	3000m steeplechase	1	4	10	8-50·4	
Mann, R.	USA	400m hurdles	1	3	2	50·18	
			SF	1	2	49·53	
			F		2	48·51	S
Manners, T.	NZL	Marathon	F		34	2:25-29·2	
Manolov, T.	BUL	Hammer throw	Q		DNQ	65·62	
Maranda, K.	POL	3000m steeplechase	1	2	10	8-50·4	
Marchan, A.	VEN	4×100m relay	1	2	4	39·74	
			SF	2	7	39·74	
Marlow, P.	GBR	20k walk	F		17	1:35-38·8	
Marshall, P.	TRI	4×400m relay	1	2	2	3-03·48	
			F		8	3-03·60	
Martinez, J.-M.	MEX	10000m	1	3	5	28-23·14	
			F		10	28-44·08	
Martini, R.	ITA	Marathon	F		24	2:22-41·4	
Marzouk, G.	ARS	Triple jump	Q		DNQ	13,82	
Masresha, W.	ETH	10000m	1	2	7	28-26·02	
Mata, F.	VEN	100m	1	5	5	10·73	
		4×100m relay	1	2	4	39·74	
			SF	2	7	39·74	
Matola, M.	MAW	100m	1	12	6	11·31	
Matos, A.	POR	110m hurdles	1	2	7	14·74	
Matos, M.	CUB	Long jump	Q		DNQ	7,47	
Matousek, J.	TCH	100m	1	4	1	10·37	
			2	1	2	10·35	
			SF	2	7	10·51	
		200m	1	7	1	20·70	
			2	2	1	20·65	
			SF	1	5	20·99	
		4×100m relay	1	2	2	39·37	
			SF	1	4	39·01	
			F		4	38·82	

COMPETITOR	COUNTRY CODE	EVENT	ROUND	HEAT	PLACE	TIME & DISTANCE	MEDAL
Matthews, V.	USA	400m	1	5	2	45·94	
			2	2	2	45·62	
			SF	1	1	44·94	
			F		1	44·66	G
Matupe, M.	MAW	Triple jump	Q		DNQ	13,57	
May, J.	GER	5000m	1	5	9	14-06·6	
Mayr, H.	GER	20k walk	F		13	1:33-13·8	
Medani, S.	SUD	10000m	1	3	13	29-32·8	
		Marathon	F		DNF		
Medjimurec, L.	YUG	800m	1	2	2	1-48·13	
			2	2	4	1-49·01	
		1500m	1	5	8	3-52·10	
Meier, W.	SUI	1500m	1	4	6	3-43·19	
Meite, A.	CIV	100m	1	1	2	10·51	
			2	5	4	10·52	
		4×100m relay	1	2	5	39·81	
Meja, A.	COL	Marathon	F		48	2:31-56·4	
Menet, H.	SUI	3000m steeplechase	1	2	8	8-45·4	
Mennea, P.	ITA	200m	1	4	1	20·53	
			2	5	1	20·47	
			SF	2	2	20·52	
			F		3	20·30	B
		4×100m relay	1	4	2	39·29	
			SF	2	4	39·21	
			F		8	39·14	
Menocal, F.	NCA	400m	1	2	8	50·95	
		800m	1	2	7	1-58·64	
Merschenz, K.	CAN	50k walk	F		DNF		
Metz, R.	FRA	200m	1	5	2	21·08	
			2	1	4	20·83	
Miasnikov, V.	URS	110m hurdles	1	2	5	14.13	
Mielke, G.	GER	10000m	1	1	DNF		
Mignon, H.	BEL	800m	1	7	2	1-47·50	
			2	2	6	1-49·71	
		1500m	1	2	2	3-44·22	
			2	2	2	3-41·72	
			F		6	3-39·05	
Milassin, L.	HUN	110m hurdles	1	5	5	14·21	
Milburn, R.	USA	110m hurdles	1	3	1	13·57	
			SF	2	1	13·44	
			F		1	13·24*	G
Miller, L.	JAM	100m	1	1	1	10·45	
			2	5	1	10·33	
			SF	2	1	10·31	
			F		3	10·33	B
Mills, L.	NZL	Shot put	Q		DNQ	18,38	
		Discus throw	F		14	55,86	
Miranda, P.	MEX	5000m	1	2	6	13-45·2	
		10000m	1	2	8	28-35·8	
Mkandawire, D.	MAW	High jump	Q		DNQ	1,90	
Mobarak, I.	MAL	110m hurdles	1	1	7	14·78	
Mobarak, M.	KUW	400m	1	8	5	49·61	
Mogaka, E.	KEN	5000m	1	4	12	14-37·2	
Mohamed Y'Moh	ETH	3000m steeplechase	1	3	11	8-52·6	
Mokalam, T.	PHI	100m	1	11	7	11·02	
		200m	1	9	5	21·81	
Molina, F.	AFG	Marathon	F		53	2:38-18·6	
Monsals, S.	SLR	100m	1	6	3	10·61	
			2	5	7	10·64	
		200m	1	4	5	21·26	
			2	5	DNF		
Montes, P.	CUB	4×100m relay	1	3	4	39·65	
			SF	1	5	39·04	
Moore, K.	USA	Marathon	F		4	2:15-39·8	
Moorosi, M.	LES	100m	1	6	6	10·74	
		200m	1	3	4	21·15	
			2	4	5	20·90	
Mora, V.	COL	Marathon	F		52	2:37-34·6	
Morales, J.	CUB	4×100m relay	1	3	4	39·65	
			SF	1	5	39·04	
Moravnik, D.	TCH	5000m	1	3	4	13-40·4	
		3000m steeplechase	1	4	3	8-33·4	
			F		5	8-29·06	
Moravec, R.	TCH	High jump	Q		DNQ	2,12	
Moro, G.	CAN	Decathlon	F		DNF		
Mose, P.	KEN	5000m	1	3	5	13-41·4	
		10000m	1	2	5	28-18·74	
			F		13	29-02·87	
Moser, A.	SUI	10000m	1	3	10	29-05·8	
Moutaftsidis, S.	GRE	Hammer throw	F		16	68,30	
Msiska, W.	MAW	400m	1	7	7	48·81	
Mukonde, L.	ZAM	100m	1	9	6	11·16	
Mulomba, B.	ZAM	800m	1	7	5	1-53·38	
Munabi, A.	UGA	Triple jump	Q		DNQ	15,82	
Muraki, Y.	JPN	Triple jump	Q		DNQ	15,59	
Muranyi, J.	HUN	Discus throw	F		12	57,92	
Murei, M.	KEN	400m hurdles	1	5	5	51·63	

COMPETITOR	COUNTRY CODE	EVENT	ROUND	HEAT	PLACE	TIME & DISTANCE	MEDAL
Murofushi, S.	JPN	Hammer throw	F		8	70,88	
Murphy, F.	IRL	800m	1	8	3	1-51-12	
			2	1	5	1-49-15	
		1500m	1	5	5	3-43-38	
Murray, G.	JAM	110m hurdles	1	5	4	14-16	
Musa, M.	SUD	4×400m relay	1	2	8	3-14-51	
Musonda, H.	ZAM	5000m	1	4	13	14-37-4	
Mwalwanda, W.	MAW	Decathlon	F		21	6227	
Mwanga, O.	TAN	4×100m relay	1	4	6	41-07	
		4×400m relay	1	2	6	3-10-12	
Mwebi, J.	KEN	100m	1	3	4	10-60	
Nadenicek, L.	TCH	110m hurdles	1	3	2	13-93	
			SF	2	4	13-89	
			F		7	13-76	
Nakopoulos, P.	GRE	3000m steeplechase	1	3	10	8-48-4	
Navab, F.	IRN	100m	1	4	6	11-02	
N'Dao, M.	SEN	4×100m relay	1	2	5	40-95	
Ndee, H.	TAN	200m	1	3	7	21-74	
		4×100m relay	1	4	6	41-07	
		4×400m relay	1	2	6	3-10-12	
N'dri, K.	CIV	4×100m relay	1	2	5	39-81	
Nelson, A.	CAN	110m hurdles	1	5	7	14-73	
Nemeth, M.	HUN	Javelin throw	F		7	81,98	
Nepraunik, A.	AUT	100m	1	12	5	10-61	
		4×100m relay	1	1	4	40-49	
			SF	1		DIS	
Neu, H-D.	GER	Discus throw	Q		DNQ	58,10	
Niare, N.	MLI	Discus throw	F		13	56,48	
Nickel, G.	GER	110m hurdles	1	2	3	13-95	
			SF	2	6	14-23	
Nihill, P.	GBR	20k walk	F		6	1:28-44-4	
		50k walk	F		9	4:14-09-4	
Nikkari, S.	FIN	Marathon	F		11	2:18-49-4	
Nkanza, L.	CGO	4×100m relay	1	4	4	39-86	
			SF	2	8	39-97	
Nkopeka, H.	MAW	800m	1	6	8	1-57-71	
		1500m	1	5	9	4-00-88	
Nkounkou, T.	CGO	400m	1	2	7	47-86	
		4×100m relay	1	4	4	39-86	
			SF	2	8	39-97	
Nma, T.	LBR	400m	1	3	5	49-73	
Nor, A.	SIN	High jump	Q		DNQ	2,00	
Nordwig, W.	GDR	Pole vault	F		1	5,50*	G
Norpoth, H.	GER	5000m	1	2	3	13-33-4	
			F		6	13-32-58	
Nowosz, Z.	POL	100m	1	12	3	10-36	
			2	3	4	10-40	
			SF	2	4	10-42	
			F		7	10-46	
		4×100m relay	1	3	1	39-11	
			SF	1	3	38-90	
			F		6	39-03	
Ntsana, A.N.	CGO	4×100m relay	1	4	4	39-86	
			SF	2	8	39-97	
Nueckles, G.	GER	400m	1	3	1	46-64	
			2	5	3	46-30	
			SF	1	7	46-28	
Nusrat, I.	PAK	200m	1	8	5	22-07	
		400m	1	1	8	49-47	
Nyamau, H.	KEN	400m	1	2	3	46-33	
			2	3	4	46-80	
		4×400m relay	1	1	2	3-01-27	
			F		1	2-59-83	G
Oakley, A.	CAN	50k walk	F		21	4:28-42-6	
O'Brien, K.	AUS	3000m steeplechase	1	2	DNF		
Oehman, K.	SWE	4×400m relay	1	1	3	3-03-05	
			F		7	3-02-57	
Ohl, V.	GER	Pole vault	F		6	5,20	
Ojo, R.	NGR	400m	1	5	4	47-03	
			2	1	6	46-73	
		4×400m relay	1	2	3	3-04-31	
Okonkwo, C.	NIG	Shot put	Q		DNQ	16,51	
Olakunle, H.	NGR	4×100m relay	1	2	3	39-66	
			SF	1	6	39-73	
Oldfield, B.	USA	Shot put	F		6	20,91	
Oliveros, J.	MEX	20k walk	F		9	1:32-40-6	
		50k walk	F		DNF		
Ommer, M.	GER	200m	1	8	1	20-80	
			2	1	2	20-53	
			SF	1	6	21-08	
Onissiforou, K.	GRE	400m	1	8	3	46-94	
			2	4	8	47-22	
Onyango, P.	KEN	Triple jump	Q		DNQ	14,74	
Ornoch, J.	POL	20k walk	F		7	1:32-01-6	
		50k walk	F		DNF		

COMPETITOR	COUNTRY CODE	EVENT	ROUND	HEAT	PLACE	TIME & DISTANCE	MEDAL
Osei-Agyemang, S	GHA	100m	1	3	2	10-52	
			2	5	5	10-66	
		4×100m relay	1	3	2	39-46	
			SF	1	7	39-99	
Osman, H.	MAL	4×400m relay	1	3	6	3-13-51	
Ouko, R.	KEN	800m	1	2	1	1-47-44	
			2	1	1	1-47-61	
			F		5	1-46-53	
		4×400m relay	1	1	2	3-01-27	
			F		1	2-59-83	G
Owusu, J.	GHA	Long jump	F		4	8,01	
Paeivaerinta, P.	FIN	1500m	1	3	4	3-44-38	
			2	2	8	3-45-13	
		3000m steeplechase	1	3	1	8-29-0	
			F		8	8-37-17	
Palomares, R.	MEX	Marathon	F		51	2:35-48-4	
Pamich, A.	ITA	50k walk	F		DIS		
Pantelei, V.	URS	1500m	1	7	3	3-42-27	
			2	1	2	3-41-60	
			F		8	3-40-24	
Papadimitriou, V.	GRE	High jump	F		=12	2,15	
Papanikolaou, C.	GRE	Pole vault	F		11	5,00	
Papageorgo-poulos, V.	GRE	100m	1	10	1	10-24*	
			2	5	3	10-45	
			SF	1		DNS	
Park Sang-Soo	COR	High jump	Q		DNQ	2,00	
Pascoe, A.	GBR	110m hurdles	1	4	3	14-08	
			SF	2	7	14-24	
		4×400m relay	1	1	1	3-01-26	
			F		2	3-00-46	S
Patry, M.	SUI	High jump	D		DNQ	2,09	
Paukkonen, R.	FIN	Marathon	F		19	2:21-06-4	
Payne, H.	GBR	Hammer throw	Q		DNQ	64,56	
Pecar, Z.	YUG	Discus throw	Q		DNQ	57,84	
Peckham, L.	AUS	High jump	F		18	2,10	
Pedersen, W.	DEN	3000m steeplechase	1	1	12	9-03-0	
Penaloza, A.	MEX	Marathon	F		45	2:29-51-0	
Perez, C.	ESP	Marathon	F		50	2:33-22-6	
Perez, F.	VEN	4×400m relay	1	3	5	3-06-99	
Perez, M.	MEX	5000m	1	4	7	13-58-2	
Perez, P.	CUB	Triple jump	Q		DNQ	15,72	
Perez, R.	CRC	10000m	1	2	13	29-36-6	
Perk, H.-J.	GER	Decathlon	F		DNF		
Perrinelle, J.-P.	FRA	400m hurdles	1	3	5	51-81	
Peyadesa, P.	MAL	4×400m relay	1	3	6	3-13-51	
Pfister, B.	SUI	110m hurdles	1	4	6	14-33	
Philipp, L.	GER	Marathon	F		32	2:24-25-4	
Phillips, E.	VEN	400m	1	4	5	46-74	
			2	5	7	46-97	
		4×400m relay	1	3	5	3-06-99	
Pierre, F.	HAI	800m	1	7	7	2-01-47	
Piggot, L.	GBR	100m	1	3	3	10-54	
			2	3	6	10-53	
		4×100m relay	1	4	3	39-66	
			SF	2	6	39-47	
Pineyrua, D.	URU	Hammer throw	Q		DNQ	59,84	
Pirnie, B.	CAN	Shot put	F		17	18,90	
Plachy, J.	TCH	800m	1	6	2	1-47-06	
			2	2	3	1-48-91	
Plunge, R.	URS	Shot put	F		14	19,30	
Podluzhnyi, V.	URS	Long jump	F		9	7,72	
Polhill, T.	NZL	1500m	1	7	2	3-42-25	
			2	2	3	3-41-81	
			F		9	3-41-82	
Polleunis, W.	BEL	5000m	1	4	5	13-52-6	
		10000m	1	3	2	28-19-71	
			F		14	29-10-15	
Pomaney, M.	GHA	Triple jump	Q		DNQ	15,72	
Powell, J.	USA	Discus throw	F		4	62,82	
Powell, T.	CAN	4×400m relay	1	1	4	3-04-22	
Preatoni, E.	ITA	4×100m relay	1	4	2	39-29	
			SF	2	4	39-21	
			F		8	39-14	
Prefontaine, S.	USA	5000m	1	1	2	13-32-6	
			F		4	13-28-25	
Price, B.	GBR	110m hurdles	1	2	2	13-94	
			SF	1	7	14-37	
Priestley, L.	JAM	400m	1	2	6	45-75	
			2	2	6	47-76	
		4×400m relay	1	3	4	3-03-83	
Prikhodko, V.	FRA	Hammer throw	Q		DNQ	61,78	
Prudencio, N.	BRA	Triple jump	F		3	17,05	B
Puklakov, N.	URS	5000m	1	4	6	13-57-6	
Puosi, G.	ITA	4×400m relay	1	2	5	3-09-71	
Pusa, L.	FIN	Javelin throw	Q		DNQ	0	

COMPETITOR	COUNTRY CODE	EVENT	ROUND	HEAT	PLACE	TIME & DISTANCE	MEDAL
Puttemans, E.	BEL	5000m	1	2	1	13-31·8*	
			F		5	13-30·82	
		10000m	1	1	1	27-53·28*	
			F		2	27-39·58	S
Quarrie, D.	JAM	200m	1	2	-	21·04	
			2	4	2	20·43	
			SF	1	DNF		
Quax, R.	NZL	5000m	1	2	9	14-05·2	
Quevedo, J.	GUA	3000m steeplechase	1	4	13	9-23·4	
		10000m	1	2	14	30-08·4	
		Marathon	F		54	2:40-33·6	
Quispe, C.	BOL	Marathon	F		61	3:07-22·8	
		10000m	1	1	15	32-31·8	
Rabee, Y.	KUW	100m	1	5	7	11·20	
Rabenja, A.	MAD	4×100m relay	1	2	6	40·58	
Rafaralahy, H.	MAD	4×100m relay	1	2	6	40·58	
Rahming, F.	BAH	400m	1	7	5	48·30	
Rahoui, B.	ALG	5000m	1	3	8	13-45·0	
		3000m steeplechase	1	4	7	8-41·0	
Rajamaeki, A.	FIN	100m	1	10	4	10·52	
			2	4	5	10·43	
		4×100m relay	1	3	3	39·54	
			SF	2	5	39·30	
Ralaincasolo	MAD	4×100m relay	1	2	6	40·58	
Ramirez, H.	CUB	4×100m relay	1	3	4	39·55	
			SF	1	5	39·04	
Randrianalijaono, J.	MAD	400m hurdles	1	1	8	52·75	
Rasoanaiuo, E.	MAD	800m	1	1	6	1-50·79	
		1500m	1	1	3	3-48·45	
Ratanapol, A.	THA	4×100m relay	1	3	6	41·04	
Ravelomanantsoa, J.	MAD	100m	1	10	2	10·29	
			2	2	1	10·47	
			SF	2	6	10·46	
		4×100m relay	1	2	6	40·58	
Rebmann, L.	SUI	Long jump	Q		DNQ	7,25	
Regassa S.	ETH	800m	1	8	8	1-53·32	
		1500m	1	3	1	3-43·61	
			2	2	4	3-41·83	
Regner, G.	AUT	4×100m relay	1	1	4	40·49	
			SF	1	DIS		
Reichenbach, R.	GER	Shot put	F		13	19,48	
Reid, R.	TRI	100m	1	1	4	10·74	
Reimann, H.	GDR	20k walk	F		3	1:27-16·6	B
Reinitzer, H.	AUT	Discus throw	Q		DNQ	52,56	
Reynolds, M.	GBR	400m	1	7	2	46·46	
			2	1	4	46·11	
			SF	2	7	46·71	
		4×400m relay	1	1	1	3-01·26	
			F		2	3-00·46	S
Rico, J.	VEN	4×100m relay	1	2	4	39·74	
			SF	2	7	39·74	
Riehm, K.-H.	GER	Hammer throw	F		10	70,12	
Riesinger, W.	GER	5000m	1	4	9	14-15·2	
Rinne, E.	FIN	Triple jump	Q		DNQ	15,98	
Rinne, J.	FIN	Discus throw	F		11	59,22	
Risa, A.	NOR	5000m	1	1	7	14-01·6	
		10000m	1	3	7	28-31·74	
Roberts, E.	TRI	200m	1	3	2	20·95	
			2	3	5	20·99	
		4×400m relay	1	2	2	3-03·48	
			F		8	3-03·60	
Robinson, A.	USA	Long jump	F		3	8,03	B
Robinson, R.	USA	100m	1	6	1	10·56	
			2	1	DNS		
Rocha, J.	BOL	Marathon	F		DNF		
Roelants, G.	BEL	Marathon	F		DNF		
Roenner, V.	SWE	4×400m relay	1	1	3	3-03·05	
			F		7	3-02·57	
Rojas-Soto, E.	PAR	400m	1	6	6	47·43	
Rolstad, J.	NOR	20k walk	F		11	1:33-03·2	
Roost, A.	CAN	Discus throw	Q		DNQ	56,58	
Rootham, G.	AUS	800m	1	4	4	1-48·17	
Rosa, L.	CEY	Marathon	F		DNF		
		10000m	1	2	16	30-20·2	
Rothenburg, H.-J.	GDR	Shot put	F		11	19,74	
Rousseau, J.	FRA	Long jump	F		10	7,65	
Rowe, K.	JAM	4×400m relay	1	3	4	3-03·83	
Rudolph, C.	GDR	400m hurdles	1	3	1	50·00	
			SF	2	DNF		
Ruegsegger, F.	SUI	5000m	1	5	12	14-54·4	
Rwabu, F.	UGA	Marathon	F		59	2:57-04·4	
Ryu Man-Hyong	PRK	Marathon	F		49	2:32-29·4	
Ryun, J.	USA	1500m	1	4	9	3-51·52	
Sabapathy, S.	MAL	4×400m relay	1	3	6	3-13·5	
Sabinal, J.	MEX	Marathon	F		26	2:22-56·6	

COMPETITOR	COUNTRY CODE	EVENT	ROUND	HEAT	PLACE	TIME & DISTANCE	MEDAL
Sachse, J.	GDR	Hammer throw	F		2	74,96	S
Said, B.	ARS	Long jump	Q		DNQ	6,32	
		4×100m relay	1	1	6	43·35	
Saidu, D.	LBR	200m	1	6	6	22·48	
Sainte-Rose, L.	FRA	200m	1	9	2	21·09	
			2	5	4	20·76	
			SF	1	7	21·42	
Saisi, T.	KEN	800m	1	3	5	1-48·50	
Salin, A.	FIN	400m hurdles	1	3	4	50·45	
		4×400m relay	1	3	2	3-02·97	
			F		6	3-01·12	
Salve, E.	BEL	1500m	1	6	6	3-42·12	
Samphon, M.	KHM	100m	1	1	7	10·95	
Samsam, L.	MAR	Shot put	F		15	19,11	
Sanchez, J.	ESP	4×100m relay	1	4	DNF		
Sanchez, R.	FRA	800m	1	3	4	1-47·93	
Sanos, M.	BAH	100m	1	2	2	10·67	
			2	1	6	10·50	
		200m	1	2	5	21·61	
		4×100m relay	1	4	5	40·48	
Saneyev, V.	URS	Triple jump	F		1	17,35	G
Sang, J.	KEN	400m	1	7	1	45·24	
			2	4	2	45·92	
			SF	2	1	45·30	
			F		3	44·92	B
		4×400m relay	1	1	2	3-01·27	
			F		1	2-59·83	G
Samhouse, R.	VEN	4×400m relay	1	3	5	3-06·99	
Sans, A.	FRA	800m	1	1	1	1-49·19	
			2	1	7	1-49·55	
Sarr, A.	SEN	110m hurdles	1	4	4	14·12	
Sarria, L.	ESP	4×100m relay	1	4	DNF		
Sartee, L.	LBR	100m	1	2	8	11·09	
Sarteur, A.	FRA	100m	1	9	1	10·42	
			2	5	2	10·40	
			SF	1	5	10·51	
Savage, S.	USA	3000m steeplechase	1	1	7	8-39·0	
Savchenko, V.	URS	400m hurdles	1	1	2	49·90	
			SF	1	7	50·28	
Savin, C.	KHM	400m	1	9	7	48·82	
Sawaki, K.	JPN	5000m	1	5	7	13-44·8	
		10000m	1	2	12	29-29·0	
Scharn, H.	HOL	1500m	1	6	4	3-41·41	
			2	2	7	3-44·41	
Schenk, H.-G.	GDR	Triple jump	Q		DNQ	15,91	
Schenke, S.	GDR	200m	1	1	1	20·66	
			2	3	3	20·79	
			SF	1	4	20·97	
			F		6	20·56	
		4×100m relay	1	1	3	39·17	
			SF	2	3	39·06	
			F		5	38·90	
Schivo, M.	ITA	High jump	F		17	2,10	
Schloeske H-R.	GER	400m	1	8	1	45·27	
			2	2	1	45·41	
			SF	2	2	45·62	
			F		5	45·31	
		4×400m relay	1	2	1	3-03·27	
			F		4	3-00·88	
Schmid, J.	GER	800m	1	4	3	1-47·75	
			2	1	4	1-48·84	
Schmidt, W.	USA	Javelin throw	F		3	84,42	B
Schoebel, J.	FRA	Decathlon	F		18	7273	
Schoterman, A.	USA	Hammer throw	Q		DNQ	65,18	
Schreyer, S.	GDR	Decathlon	F		5	7950	
Schubert, R.	GER	400m hurdles	1	3	3	50·23	
			SF	1	4	49·80	
			F		5	49·65	
Schulten H-D.	GER	3000m steeplechase	1	4	6	8-39·8	
Schumann, M.	GER	110m hurdles	1	4	5	14·13	
Schwarz, J.	GER	Long jump	Q		DNQ	7,63	
Scorza A.	ARG	50k walk	F		28	4:42-41·4	
Seagren, R.	USA	Pole vault	F		2	5,40	S
Seediq M.	PAK	800m	1	8	7	1-52·58	
Selzer, P.	GDR	50k walk	F		5	4:04-05·4	
Sen, H.	TUR	5000m	1	5	11	14-26·0	
		10000m	1	3	15	29-51·8	
Senoussi, A.	CHA	High jump	Q		DNQ	2,00	
Sequeira, E.	IND	5000m	1	3	11	14-01·4	
Seymour, J.	USA	400m hurdles	1	5	2	49·81	
			SF	2	1	49·33	
			F		4	48·64	
Shapka, K.	URS	High jump	F		=12	2,15	
Sharafeldirov, R.	URS	10000m	1	2	6	28-24·64	
Sherbak, I.	URS	Marathon	F		35	2:25-37·4	
Sherwood, J.	GBR	400m hurdles	1	5	DNF		

COMPETITOR	COUNTRY CODE	EVENT	ROUND	HEAT	PLACE	TIME & DISTANCE	MEDAL
Shorter, F.	USA	10000m	1	2	3	27-58-23	
			F		5	27-51-32	
		Marathon	F		1	2:12-19-8	G
Sidler, A.	SUI	Marathon	F		44	2:29-09-2	
Siebeck, F.	GDR	110m hurdles	1	1	1	13-83	
			SF	2	2	13-58	
			F		5	13-71	
Sieghart, I.	GER	High jump	Q		DNQ	2,12	
Sierra, J.	COL	200m	1	7	4	21-10	
			2	1	5	20-87	
Siitonen, H.	FIN	Javelin throw	F		4	84,32	
Silei, C.	KEN	1500m	1	5	7	3-51-95	
Silovs, Y.	URS	4×100m relay	1	1	1	39-15	
			SF	2	2	39-00	
			F		2	38-50	S
Silvester, J.	USA	Discus throw	F		2	63,50	S
Simeon, S.	ITA	Discus throw	F		10	59,34	
Simola, S.	FIN	Shot put	F		16	19,06	
Simpson, B.	CAN	Pole vault	F		5	5,20	
Singh, C.V.	IND	Decathlon	F		17	7378	
Singh Gill, M.	IND	Long jump	Q		DNQ	7,30	
		Triple jump	Q		DNQ	0	
Singh, J.	IND	Shot put	Q		DNQ	17,15	
Singh, S.R.	IND	800m	1	6	4	1-47-72	
Sitta, S.	KHM	High jump	Q		DNQ	1,90	
Skripka, S.	URS	3000m steeplechase	1	2	6	8-41-4	
Skowronek, R.	POL	Decathlon	F		DNF		
Slusarski, T.	POL	Pole vault	F		NP	0	
Smaga, N.	URS	20k walk	F		5	1:28-16-6	
Smart, W.	CAN	1500m	1	2	8	3-49-23	
Smedley, R.	GBR	1500m	1	5	3	3-42-12	
			2	2	9	3-45-78	
Smidt-Jensen, S.	DEN	Decathlon	F		7	7947	
Smith, B.	NZL	200m	1	9	3	21-17	
			2	2	4	21-04	
Smith, C.	USA	200m	1	6	1	20-79	
			2	2	2	20-66	
			SF	1	3	20-86	
			F		5	20-55	
Smith, D.	BAH	110m hurdles	1	3	4	14-46	
		4×100m relay	1	4	5	40-48	
Smith, D.	USA	Triple jump	Q		DNQ	14,55	
Smith, J.	USA	400m	1	8	2	46-00	
			2	3	2	46-04	
			SF	1	3	45-46	
			F		DNF		
Smith, S.	USA	Pole vault	Q		DNQ	4,80	
Soernes, S.	NOR	3000m steeplechase	1	4	11	8-54-8	
Soldatenko, V.	URS	50k walk	F		2	3:58-24-0	S
Sonsky, M.	USA	Javelin throw	F		10	77,94	
Soo Wen-Ho	CHN	100m	1	8	4	10-59	
			2	2	7	10-82	
		200m	1	3	5	21-55	
			2	4	6	21-47	
		4×100m relay	1	2	7	41-78	
Soriano, M.	ESP	400m hurdles	1	1	5	50-88	
Sotutu, U.	FIJ	5000m	1	5	13	15-24-2	
		10000m	1	1	DNF		
		3000m steeplechase	1	4	12	9-12-0	
Sow, A.	SEN	4×100m relay	1	2	7	3-11-19	
Sowa, C.	LUX	20k walk	F		18	1:36-23-8	
		50k walk	F		10	4:14-21-2	
Spasojevic, M.	YUG	Triple jump	Q		DNQ	15,69	
Sperling, G.	GDR	20k walk	F		4	1:27-55-0	
Springer, C.	BAR	400m	1	6	DNF		
Stradtmueller, K.	GDR	50k walk	F		11	4:14-28-8	
Stawiarz, E.	POL	Marathon	F		40	2:28-12-4	
Stefansson, B.	ISL	100m	1	5	6	10-99	
		400m	1	1	6	46-76	
			2	5	6	46-92	
Steffny, M.	GER	Marathon	F		31	2:24-25-4	
Sternad, P.	AUT	Hammer throw	F		17	66,64	
Stewart, I.	GBR	5000m	1	4	2	13-33-0	
			F		3	13-27-61	B
Stewart, L.	GBR	10000m	1	3	6	28-31-33	
Stewart, L.	TRI	800m	1	4	5	1-48-74	
Stiglic, S.	YUG	Hammer throw	F		15	68,34	
Stolle, M.	GDR	Javelin throw	F		9	79,32	
Stones, D.	USA	high jump	F		3	2,21	B
Sugawara, T.	JPN	Hammer throw	F		20	64,70	
Sugioka, K.	JPN	High jump	Q		DNQ	2,06	
Suppiah, P.	SIN	5000m	1	1	11	15-36-6	
		10000m	1	1	14	31-59-2	
Sviridov, N.	URS	5000m	1	5	2	13-38-4	
			F		8	13-39-31	
Swenson, K.	USA	800m	1	8	2	1-51-06	
			2	3	DNF		

COMPETITOR	COUNTRY CODE	EVENT	ROUND	HEAT	PLACE	TIME & DISTANCE	MEDAL
Sy, B.	SEN	100m	1	8	1	10-30	
			2	4	2	10-27	
			SF	2	5	10-42	
		4×100m relay	1	3	5	40-95	
Szekeres, F.	HUN	Marathon	F		33	2:25-17-6	
Szepesi, A.	HUN	High jump	F		5	2,18	
Szordykowsi, H.	POL	1500m	1	3	3	3-44-16	
			2	2	6	3-42-49	
Tadesse, M.	ETH	400m	1	1	3	46-38	
			2	5	5	46-85	
		800m	1	4	1	1-47-10	
			2	3	7	1-48-87	
		4×400m relay	1	2	4	3-08-59	
Tait, R.	NZL	Discus throw	Q		DNQ	56,60	
Takeuchi, A.	JPN	3000m steeplechase	1	2	5	8-40-4	
Tancred, W.	GBR	Discus throw	Q		DNQ	57,24	
Tarmak, Y.	URS	High jump	F		1	2,23	G
Tayler, R.	NZL	5000m	1	3	10	13-56-2	
Taylor, R.	USA	100m	1	12	1	10-32	
			2	3	2	10-16	
			SF	2	1	10-30	
			F		2	10-24	S
		4×100m relay	1	4	1	38-96	
			SF	1	1	38-54	
			F		1	38-19	G
Tegla, F.	HUN	Discus throw	F		7	60,60	
Temu, N.	KEN	10000m	1	1	12	30-19-6	
Tenggren, H.	SWE	50k walk	F		12	4:16-37-6	
Ter-Ovanesyan, I.	URS	Long jump	Q		DNQ	7,77	
Theimer, R.	GDR	Hammer throw	F		13	69,16	
Thijs, P.	BEL	3000m steeplechase	1	3	7	8-35-0	
Thorith, D.	GDR	Discus throw	F		6	62,42	
Thorley, G.	NZL	5000m	1	5	10	14-11-6	
		10000m	1	3	DNF		
Thorsteinsson, T.	ISL	800m	1	4	6	1-50-78	
Tibaduiza, D.	COL	10000m	1	3	12	29-24-0	
Tihanyi, J.	HUN	High jump	Q		DNQ	2,09	
Tiihonen, P.	FIN	Marathon	F		DNF		
Tijou, N.	FRA	10000m	1	1	7	28-36-08	
Timms, H.	GBR	50k walk	F		25	4:34-43-8	
Tinker, G.	USA	4×100m relay	1	4	1	38-96	
			SF	1	1	38-54	
			F		1	38-19	G
Toerring, J.	DEN	110m hurdles	1	3	5	14-50	
		Long jump	Q		DNQ	0	
Tomizawa, H.	JPN	High jump	F		19	2,05	
Tomonaga, Y.	JPN	400m	1	3	2	47-01	
			2	4	6	46-92	
Toth, G.	HUN	Marathon	F		27	2:22-59-8	
Toure, H.	ETH	20k walk	F		20	1:43-11-6	
Tourkey, F.	ARS	Discus throw	Q		DNQ	33,78	
Tourret, C.	FRA	Long jump	Q		DNQ	7,55	
Tracanelli, F.	FRA	Pole vault	F		8	5,10	
Travis, D.	GBR	Javelin throw	Q		DNQ	74,68	
Triana, J.	CUB	4×100m relay	1	3	4	39-65	
			SF	1	3	39-04	
Tuemkan, M.	TUR	800m	1	6	6	1-49-50	
		1500m	1	1	7	3-43-97	
Tuemmler, B.	GER	1500m	1	2	3	3-44-53	
			2	2	10	3-50-01	
Tuita, L.	FRA	Javelin throw	F		11	76,34	
Tziortzis, S.	GRE	400m hurdles	1	4	2	50-54	
			SF	2	4	50-06	
			F		=6	49-66	
Ubori, L.	YUG	4×400m relay	1	1	5	3-05-70	
Unetani, Y.	JPN	Marathon	F		36	2:25-59-0	
Usami, A.	JPN	10000m	1	1	10	29-24-8	
		Marathon	F		12	2:18-58-0	
Vaatainen, J.	FIN	5000m	1	4	1	13-32-8	
			F		13	13-53-84	
Vaeaenaenen, A.	FIN	Long jump	F		11	7,62	
Valdimarsson, E.	ISL	Discus throw	Q		DNQ	55,38	
Valle, E.	NCA	20k walk	F		21	1:45-09-4	
Vallejo, J.	ARG	Hammer throw	Q		DNQ	60,08	
Van Renterghem, W.	BEL	Marathon	F		46	2:29-58-4	
Varju, V.	HUN	Shot put	F		8	20,10	
Vasala, P.	FIN	1500m	1	6	1	3-40-86	
			2	3	2	3-37-91	
			F		1	3-36-33	G
Vecchiato, M.	ITA	Hammer throw	F		9	70,58	
Velasquez, D.	FRA	400m	1	7	3	46-70	
			2	2	6	46-91	
		4×400m relay	1	3	3	3-03-13	
			F		3	3-00-65	B
Velez, D.	NCA	Javelin throw	Q		DNQ	63,74	
Velikorodnykh, Y.	URS	Marathon	F		14	20:20-02-2	

COMPETITOR	COUNTRY CODE	EVENT	ROUND	HEAT	PLACE	TIME & DISTANCE	MEDAL
Vilen, R.	FIN	100m	1	8	6	11·00	
		4×100m relay	1	1	3	39·54	
			SF	2	5	39·30	
Villain, J.-P.	FRA	3000m steeplechase	1	3	3	8-30·4	
			F		11	8-45·72	
Viren, L.	FIN	5000m	1	5	1	13-38·4	
			F		1	13-26·42*	G
		10000m	1	2	4	28-04·41	
			F		1	27-38·35*	G
Visini, V.	ITA	20k walk	F		8	1:32-30·0	
		50k walk	F		7	4:08-31·4	
Vizcarrondo, J.	PUR	100m	1	10	6	10·79	
		4×100m relay	1	1	5	41·34	
Vlk, J.	TCH	Shot put	F		9	20·09	
Voje, J.	NOR	3000m steeplechase	1	2	7	8-42·0	
Volkov, E.	URS	800m	1	2	3	1-48·57	
			2	1	8	1-50·05	
Vollmer, T.	USA	Discus throw	F		8	60·24	
Von Wartburg, U.	SUI	Javelin throw	Q		DNQ	76,36	
Wagner, S.	POL	100m	1	5	3	10·62	
			2	2	4	10·51	
		4×100m relay	1	3	1	39·11	
			SF	1	3	38·90	
			F		6	39·03	
Wagner, W.	GER	3000m steeplechase	1	3	6	8-34·0	
Wahab, Z.	MAL	100m	1	10	7	10·90	
		200m	1	6	5	21·87	
Wakachu, J.	TAN	Marathon	F		DNF		
Walde, J.	GER	Decathlon	F		DNF		
Walker, A.	USA	Triple jump	Q		DNQ	15,23	
Walsh, D.	IRL	Marathon	F		47	2:31-12·0	
Warhurst, J.	GBR	50k walk	F		18	4:23-21·6	
Warnke, E.	CHI	5000m	1	5	5	13-43·6	
Wasughe, A.	SOM	High jump	Q		DNQ	2,00	
Watts, J.	GBR	Discus throw	Q		DNQ	53,86	
Weidner, G.	GER	50k walk	F		6	4:03-28·0	
Weigle, W.	USA	50k walk	F		17	4:22-52·2	
Wellmann, P.-H.	GER	1500m	1	5	2	3-41·83	
			2	3	4	3-38·42	
			F		7	3-40·03	
Werner, J.	POL	400m	1	6	4	45·93	
			2	1	3	46·02	
			SF	2	6	46·26	
		4×400m relay	1	3	1	3-02·52	
			F		5	3-01·05	
Wesch, W.	GER	20k walk	F		16	1:35-20·6	
Wessinghage, T.	GER	1500m	1	1	1	3-41·56	
			2	1	7	3-43·39	
Wheeler, R.	USA	1500m	1	6	3	3-41·34	
			2	3	6	3-40·36	
Williams, B.	GBR	Hammer throw	F		16	68,18	
Williams, R.	USA	Long jump	F		1	8,24	G
Wilson, B.	GBR	110m hurdles	1	5	6	14·31	
Wimaladase, W.	CEY	400m	1	1	4	46·62	
			2	2	5	46·50	
Wipperman, D.	GER	Discus throw	Q		DNQ	58,10	
Wirz, H.	SUI	400m hurdles	1	4	5	52·34	
Wodzynski, L.	POL	110m hurdles	1	1	3	14·03	
			SF	1	3	13·81	
			F		6	13·72	
Wodzynski, M.	POL	110m hurdles	1	2	4	14·02	
			SF	1	8	14·63	
Wolhunter, R.	USA	800m	1	1	4	1-49·43	
Wolde, D.	ETH	Marathon	F		18	2:20-44·0	
Wolde, M.	ETH	Marathon	F		3	2:15-08·4	B
Wolde, T.M.	ETH	10000m	1	1	9	28-45·4	
Wolfermann, K.	GER	Javelin throw	F		1	90,48*	G
Woods, G.	USA	Shot put	F		2	21,17	S
Worku, S.	ETH	4×400m relay	1	2	4	3-08·59	
Wottle, D.	USA	800m	1	4	2	1-47·64	
			2	2	1	1-48·68	
			F		1	1-45·86	G
		1500m	1	1	2	3-40·69	
			2	2	4	3-41·64	
Wucherer, G.	GER	100m	1	2	4	10·82	
		4×100m relay	1	1	2	39·17	
			SF	1	2	38·86	
			F		3	38·79	B
Wuerfel, G.	AUT	4×100m relay	1	1	4	40·49	
			SF	1	DIS		
Yanghat, A.	CGO	100m	1	2	7	10·95	
Yavala, S.	FIJ	400m	1	2	6	47·78	
Yeo, Kian Chyne	SIN	100m	1	2	6	10·92	
		200m	1	2	6	21·89	
Yifter, M.	ETH	10000m	1	3	1	28-18·11	
			F		3	27-40·96	B
Young, G.	USA	5000m	1	5	4	13-41·2	

COMPETITOR	COUNTRY CODE	EVENT	ROUND	HEAT	PLACE	TIME & DISTANCE	MEDAL
Young, L.	USA	20k walk	F		10	1:32-53·4	
		50k walk	F		3	4:00-46·0	B
Younis, M.	PAK	1500m	1	4	7	3-44·06	
Zacharopoulos, S.	GRE	1500m	1	3	2	3-43·83	
			2	1	8	3-43·47	
Zaddem, A.	TUN	10000m	1	1	4	28-14·70	
			F		8	28-18·17	
Zeilbauer, J.	AUT	Decathlon	F		9	7741	
Zembri, R.	FRA	5000m	1	2	8	14-34·4	
Zenk, H.-J.	GDR	200m	1	8	2	20·93	
			2	5	2	20·59	
			SF	2	3	20·63	
			F		8	21·05	
Zhelev, M.	BUL	3000m steeplechase	1	2	3	8-35·8	
			F		12	9-02·59	
Ziegler, R.	GER	400m hurdles	1	5	3	50·17	
			SF	1	5	49·88	
Zielinski, T.	POL	3000m steeplechase	1	1	11	8-49·8	
Zorin, Y.	URS	400m hurdles	1	2	3	50·35	
			SF	2	3	49·60	
			F		8	50·25	
Zsinska, A.	HUN	800m	1	3	6	1-48·96	
Zsivotzky, G.	HUN	Hammer throw	F		5	71,38	
FEMALES							
Acosta, A.	CUB	400m	1	1	6	54·52	
		4×400m relay	SF	1	5	3-32·44	
Adam, M.	GDR	Shot put	F		5	18,94	
Afriyie, H.	GHA	100m	1	4	4	11·90	
			2	2	7	12·04	
		200m	1	3	4	24·38	
			2	3	7	24·47	
Ahlers, R.	HOL	High jump	F		=16	1,79	
Alanes, A.	PHI	100m	1	4	7	12·37	
		200m	1	2	4	25·28	
			2	1	7	24·98	
		4×100m relay	SF	1	DIS		
Albertus, K.	GDR	Long jump	Q		DNQ	6,01	
Allison, J.	GBR	1500m	1	1	7	4-14·89	
Allwood, R.	JAM	100m	1	4	2	11·46	
			2	2	=3	11·52	
			SF	1	8	11·58	
		200m	1	1	3	23·56	
			2	2	2	23·33	
			SF	1	4	23·14	
			F		8	23·11	
		4×400m relay	SF	2	5	3-31·89	
Al Nasser, M.	SYR	800m	1	3	DNF		
Aman, J.	MAL	400m	1	2	6	57·36	
Ammann, S.	SUI	Long jump	Q		DNQ	6,26	
Amzina, V.	BUL	800m	1	4	5	2-05·95	
		1500m	1	2	2	4-12·85	
			SF	1	5	4-09·12	
Andersen, G.	NOR	1500m	1	2	6	4-16·00	
Andre, J.	FRA	100m hurdles	1	4	3	13·33	
			SF	2	5	13·30	
Anghelova, N.	BUL	Pentathlon	F		6	4496	
Annum, A.	GHA	100m	1	3	2	11·54	
			2	3	3	11·45	
			SF	1	4	11·47	
			F		6	11·41	
		200m	1	1	1	23·15	
			2	2	2	22·95	
			SF	2	4	23·30	
			F		7	22·99	
Antenen, M.	SUI	100m hurdles	1	3	4	13·61	
			SF	1	DNF		
		Long jump	F		6	6,49	
Attlesey, K.	USA	Long jump	Q		DNQ	5,80	
Ayaa, J.	UGA	400m	1	1	4	52·85	
			2	2	3	52·68	
			SF	1	7	52·91	
Babosek, B.	YUG	High jump	Q		DNQ	1,73	
Bach, M.	GER	100m hurdles	1	2	3	13·46	
			SF	1	6	13·31	
Bakulin, E.	POL	4×100m relay	SF		4	44·19	
			F		8	44·20	
Balogh, G.	HUN	400m	1	4	2	52·75	
			2	3	1	51·71*	
			SF	1	3	51·90	
			F		8	52·39	
Bazer, K.	GDR	100m hurdles	1	4	1	13·10	
			SF	1	3	12·97	
			F		3	12·90	B
Becker, M.	RUM	Javelin throw	Q		DNQ	50,74	
Berendonk, B.	GER	Discus throw	F		11	56,58	

COMPETITOR	COUNTRY CODE	EVENT	ROUND	HEAT	PLACE	TIME & DISTANCE	MEDAL
Bernard, V.	GBR	400m	1	7	4	53·31	
			2	4	5	53·29	
		4×400m relay	SF	2	4	3-30·05	
			F		5	3-28·74	
Besfamilnaia, N.	URS	200m	1	2	3	23·62	
			2	1	2	23·20	
			SF		5	23·31	
		4×100m relay	SF	1	2	43·77	
			F		5	43·59	
Besson, C.	FRA	400m	1	5	3	53·41	
			2	2	5	53·39	
		4×400m relay	SF	1	2	3-30·02	
			F		4	3-27·52	
Bisang, D.	SUI	High jump	Q		DNQ	1,65	
Bishop, B.	BAR	400m	1	1	7	56·35	
		4×400m relay	SF	1	7	3-44·45	
Blagoeva, Y.	BUL	High jump	F		2	1,88	S
Bochkova, S.	BUL	Discus throw	F		10	56,72	
Bodner, C.	GDR	Pentathlon	F		4	4671	
Boedding, I.	GER	4×400m relay	SF	1	1	3-29·32*	
			F		3	3-26·51	B
Bognar, J.	HUN	Shot put	F		11	18,23	
Boxem, B.	HOL	1500m	1	2	3	4-13·83	
			SF	2	5	4-08·81*	
			F		9	4-13·10	
Boyle, R.	AUS	100m	1	5	1	11·37	
			2	1	2	11·30	
			SF	2	1	11·32	
			F		2	11·23	S
		200m	1	2	2	23·58	
			2	4	1	23·06	
			SF	1	2	22·92	
			F		2	22·45	S
		4×100m relay	SF	1	3	44·03	
			F		6	43·61	
		4×400m relay	SF	2	3	3-29·99	
			F		6	3-28·84	
Bragina, L.	URS	1500m	1	1	1	4-06·47*	
			SF	2	1	4-05·07*	
			F		1	4-01·38*	G
Brill, D.	CAN	High jump	F		8	1,82	
Brown, R.	USA	Javelin throw	Q		DNQ	47,88	
Bruce, A.	JAM	High jump	F		9	1,82	
Bruzsenyak, I.	HUN	Pentathlon	F		8	4419	
		Long jump	F		10	6,39	
Bufanu, V.	RUM	100m hurdles	1	2	1	12·94	
			SF	1	1	12·84	
			F		2	12·84	S
		Long jump	Q		DNQ	0	
Bukharina, G.	URS	100m	1	2	5	11·69	
			2	3	8	11·81	
		4×100m relay	SF	1	2	43·77	
			F		5	43·59	
Burneleit, K.	GDR	1500m	1	3	2	4-10·83	
			SF	2	2	4-05·78	
			F		4	4-04·11	
Byfield, D.	JAM	4×100m relay	SF	2	DIS		
Cacchi, P.	ITA	1500m	1	2	1	4-09·53	
			SF	1	2	4-07·83	
			F		3	4-02·85	B
Caird, M.	AUS	100m hurdles	1	3	5	13·63	
		4×100m relay	SF	1	3	44·03	
			F		6	43·61	
Calvert, S.	USA	Javelin throw	Q		DNQ	51,38	
Carey, S.	GBR	1500m	1	4	3	4-13·01	
			SF	2	4	4-07·41	
			F		5	4-04·81	
Carrero, R.	NCA	100m	1	2	8	13·45	
		200m	1	5	5	28·02	
			2	3	DNS		
Casapicola, C.	AUT	4×400m relay	SF	2	6	3-42·19	
Castillo, B.	CUB	4×100m relay	SF	1	5	3-32·44	
Charlton, V.	JAM	4×100m relay	SF	2	DIS		
Chemabwai, T.	KEN	400m	1	3	4	53·38	
			2	2	7	53·54	
Chewinska, L.	POL	Shot put	F		10	18,24	
Chibas, M.	CUB	4×400m relay	SF	1	5	3-32·44	
Chikani, A.	ZAM	Long jump	Q		DNQ	5,17	
Chistiakova, N.	URS	400m	1	2	4	53·81	
			2	2	8	54·58	
		4×400m relay	SF	1	3	3-30·23	
			F		8	3-31·89	
Chitty, M.	GBR	Long jump	Q		DNQ	6,26	

COMPETITOR	COUNTRY CODE	EVENT	ROUND	HEAT	PLACE	TIME & DISTANCE	MEDAL
Chivas, S.	CUB	100m	1	1	1	11·18	
			2	1	1	11·22	
			SF	2	2	11·33	
			F		3	11·24	B
		4×100m relay	SF	1	1	43·67	
			F		3	43·36	B
Chizhova, N.	URS	Shot put	F		1	21,03*	G
Chizunga, E.	MAW	800m	1	3	7	2-19·22	
		1500m	1	3	8	4-41·47	
Cioltan, V.	RUM	Shot put	F		13	16,62	
Connolly, O.	USA	Discus throw	Q		DNQ	51,58	
Coomber, M.	GBR	800m	1	3	6	2-02·99	
Critchley, M.	GBR	200m	1	6	6	24·04	
			2	4	6	24·05	
Cropper, P.	GBR	800m	1	4	4	2-03·55	
Cummings, C.	JAM	4×100m relay	SF	2	DIS		
Damm Olesen, A.	DEN	800m	1	4	2	2-01·77	
			2	1	6	2-04·19	
Danilova, T.	URS	Discuss throw	F		4	62,86	
Davis, I.	USA	100m	1	3	1	11·34	
			2	4	1	11·27	
			SF	1	2	11·36	
			F		4	11·32	
		4×100m relay	SF	2	3	43·07	
			F		4	43·39	
Debourse, M-C.	FRA	Pentathlon	F		17	4239	
Dela Vina, J.	PHI	Discus throw	Q		DNQ	53,92	
Dimmock, P.	GBR	High jump	Q		DNQ	1,70	
Dolzhenko, E.	URS	Shot put	F		4	19,24	
Ducas, O.	FRA	Pentathlon	F		22	4101	
		Long jump	Q		DNQ	6,16	
Duclos, N.	FRA	400m	1	4	1	52·69	
			2	4	4	52·96	
			SF	2	6	52·18	
		4×400m relay	SF	1	2	3-30·02	
			F		4	3-27·52	
Duvivier, M.	FRA	800m	1	1	5	2-04·87	
		4×400m relay	SF	1	2	3-30·02	
			F		4	3-27·52	
Edet, E.	NGR	100m	1	5	7	12·06	
		100m hurdles	1	4	7	14·67	
		4×100m relay	SF	1	7	45·15	
Edwards, D.	USA	400m	1	3	5	54·43	
Ehrhardt, A.	GDR	100m hurdles	1	1	1	12·70*	
			SF	2	1	12·73	
			F		1	12·59*	G
Eisler, B.	CAN	Long jump	Q		DNQ	6,10	
Ejstrup, G.	DEN	High jump	F		=12	1,82	
Eklund, M.	FIN	400m	1	2	3	53·81	
			2	2	6	53·50	
		4×100m relay	SF	1	6	44·68	
		4×400m relay	SF	1	4	3-30·84	
			F		7	3-29·44	
Elejarde, M.	CUB	4×100m relay	SF	1	1	43·67	
			F		3	43·36	B
El Faquir, F.	MAR	100m	1	2	7	12·56	
		200m	1	6	7	25·27	
Ellenberger, G.	GER	800m	1	3	4	2-01·92	
			2	2	7	2-02·97	
Eppinger, M.	GER	Pentathlon	F		12	4313	
Falck, H.	GER	800m	1	1	1	2-01·52	
			2	2	1	2-01·41	
			F		1	1-58·55*	G
		4×400m relay	SF	1	1	3-29·32*	
			F		3	3-26·51	B
Fergerson, M.	USA	400m	1	1	3	52·05	
			2	4	3	52·93	
			SF	2	4	51·91	
			F		5	51·96	
		4×400m relay	SF	2	2	3-28·63	
			F		3	3-25·15	S
Ferrell, B.	USA	100m	1	4	3	11·47	
			2	1	3	11·38	
			SF	1	4	11·49	
			F		7	11·45	
		200m	1	1	2	23·38	
			2	1	4	23·30	
			SF	1	7	23·39	
Few, R.	GBR	High jump	Q		DNQ	1,73	
Fibingerova, H.	TCH	Shot put	F		7	18,81	
Fitzgerald, G.	USA	Pentathlon	F		9	4206	
Fitzner, I.	ARG	100m	1	3	8	12·51	
Focic, D.	YUG	Pentathlon	F		11	4332	
Forde, L.	BAR	4×400m relay	SF	1	7	3-44·45	
Franzoti, R.	YUG	Long jump	Q		DNQ	6,02	
Frederick, J.	USA	Pentathlon	F		21	4167	

COMPETITOR	COUNTRY CODE	EVENT	ROUND	HEAT	PLACE	TIME & DISTANCE	MEDAL
Frese, C.	GER	400m	1	6	1	52·39	
			2	2	4	53·01	
			SF	1		DNF	
Fuchs, R.	GDR	Javelin throw	F		1	63·88*	G
Gaertner, R.	GER	High jump	F		14	1,82	
Garbey, M.	CUB	Long jump	F		4	6·52	
Gerhards, A.	GER	Javelin throw	F		9	55·84	
Gilbert, C.	USA	High jump	Q		DNQ	1·70	
Gildemeister, R.	GDR	High jump	F		=12	1·82	
Gillies, P.	AUS	100m hurdles	1	2	6	13·82	
Gleskova, E.	TCH	100m	1	2	3	11·50	
			2	3	2	11·43	
			SF	1	3	11·43	
			F		8	12·48	
Goldsberry, S.	USA	High jump	Q		DNQ	1,90	
Gooding, H.	BAR	800m	1	2	8	2-19·69	
		4×400m relay	SF	1	7	3-44·45	
Govoni, D.	ITA	400m	1	5	5	53·93	
			2	3	8	53·78	
		800m	1	1	6	2-05·24	
Grassano, M.	ITA	4×100m relay	SF	1	5	44·62	
Greene, P.	USA	200m	1	4	2	23·38	
			2	3	5	23·35	
Gryziecka, E.	POL	Javelin throw	F		7	57·00	
Gummel, M.	GDR	Shot put	F		2	20,22	S
Gusenbauer, I.	AUT	High jump	F		3	1,88	B
Haden, S.	NZL	800m	1	5	4	2-04·86	
Hadky, M.	MAR	800m	1	5	7	2-12·43	
Haglund, L.	SWE	100m	1	3	6	11·97	
		4×100m relay	SF	2		DIS	
Hammond, K.	USA	400m	1	2	1	53·45	
			2	3	4	52·44	
			SF	1	4	51·92	
			F		3	51·64	B
		4×400m relay	SF	2	2	3-28·65	
			F		2	3-25·5	S
Hanna, L.	CAN	High jump	Q		DNQ	1,73	
Heinich, C.	GDR	200m	1	6	3	23·90	
			2	1	3	23·23	
			SF	1	3	23·28	
			F		=5	22·89	
		4×100m relay	SF	2	1	42·88	
			F		2	42·95	S
Hess, M.	SUI	1500m	1	4	7	4-19·67	
Hinzmann, G.	GDR	Discus throw	F		6	61,72	
Hodges, L.	JAM	4×100m relay	SF	2		DIS	
Hoffman, A.	CAN	800m	1	3	2	2-01·57	
			2	1	3	2-01·37	
			F		8	2-00·17	
Hoffman, M.	AUS	100m	1	1	7	11·68	
			2	3	7	11·78	
		4×100m relay	SF	1	3	44·03	
			F		6	43·61	
Hoffmeister, G.	GDR	800m	1	5	2	2-03·15	
			2	1	2	2-01·21	
			F		3	1-59·19	B
		1500m	1	4	2	4-12·80	
			SF	1	3	4-07·94	
			F		2	4-02·83	S
Hrepevnik, S.	YUG	High jump	F		20	1,76	
Huebnerova, M.	TCH	High jump	F		15	1,82	
Hunt, P.	NZL	400m	1	7	2	52·92	
			2	3	6	52·56	
Ilina, L.	URS	Long jump	Q		DNQ	6,25	
Inaoka, M.	JPN	High jump	Q		DNQ	1,65	
Inkpen, B.	GBR	High jump	F		4	1,85	
Ionescu, C.	RUM	Discus throw	F		7	60,42	
Ivanova, A.	URS	Shot put	F		9	18,28	
Janko, E.	AUT	Javelin throw	F		6	58,56	
Jaworska, D.	POL	Javelin throw	Q		DNQ	52,40	
Jedrejek, D.	POL	4×100m relay	SF	1	4	44·19	
			F		8	44·20	
Jehlickova, J.	TCH	1500m	1	1	5	4-08·39	
			SF	2	9	4-18·16	
Johnson, P.	USA	100m hurdles	1	4	2	13·23	
			SF	1	5	13·26	
Jones, D.	CAN	Pentathlon	F		10	4349	
Joseph M.	HAI	100m	1	5	8	13·84	
Jozwik, U.	POL	4×100m relay	SF	1	4	44·19	
			F		8	44·20	
Kacperczyk, K.	POL	400m	1	2	5	53·85	
			2	4	8	54·39	
		4×400m relay	SF	2		DNF	

COMPETITOR	COUNTRY CODE	EVENT	ROUND	HEAT	PLACE	TIME & DISTANCE	MEDAL
Kaefer, K.	AUT	200m	1	5	4	24·42	
			2	3	6	23·92	
		400m	1	1	5	53·60	
			2	1	5	52·82	
		4×400m relay	SF	2	6	3-42·19	
Kaesling, D.	GDR	400m	1	6	2	52·99	
			2	4	1	52·33	
			SF	1	2	51·73	
			F		7	52·19	
		4×400m relay	SF	2	1	3-28·48*	
			F		1	3-22·95*	G
Kalpakian, A.	LIB	400m	1	5	7	65·18	
Kapler, H.	AUT	4×400m relay	SF	2	6	3-42·19	
Karbanova, M.	TCH	High jump	F		22	1,76	
Kaufer, E.	GDR	100m	1	2	4	11·59	
			2	4	7	11·55	
		4×100m relay	SF	2	1	42·88	
			F		2	42·95	S
Kazachkova, T.	URS	1500m	1	4	8	4-20·15	
Keizer, I.	HOL	1500m	1	1	3	4-08·00	
			SF	1	4	4-08·25	
			F		6	4-05·13	
Kerner, H.	POL	4×100m relay	SF	1	4	44·19	
			F		8	44·20	
Kheng, M.	KHM	100m	1	4	8	12·72	
		200m	1	3	7	25·86	
Khristova, I.	BUL	Shot put	F		3	19,35	B
Knutsson, I.	SWE	1500m	1	3	5	4-11·32	
			SF	1	9	4-14·97	
Koenig, W.	USA	800m	1	5	6	2-08·71	
Kolesnikova, N.	URS	400m	1	4	3	53·20	
			2	1	3	52·30	
			SF	2	7	52·29	
		4x400m relay	SF	1	3	3-30·23	
			F		8	3-31·89	
Koloska, A.	GER	Javelin throw	Q		DNQ	48,42	
Komka, M.	HUN	High jump	F		23	1,71	
Koroleva, S.	URS	Javelin throw	F		8	56,36	
Kraker, F.	USA	1500m	1	2	4	4-14·73	
			2	1	8	4-12·76	
Krause, C.	GER	200m	1	5	2	23·51	
			2	2	4	23·22	
			SF	1	5	23·17	
		4×100m relay	SF	2	2	42·97	
			F		1	42·81*	G
Kroniger, A.	GER	200m	1	3	1	23·37	
			2	4	2	23·14	
			SF	2	2	23·03	
			F		=5	22·89	
Krumpholz, A.	GDR	100m hurdles	1	3	2	13·31	
			SF	2	3	13·24	
			F		7	13·27	
Kucserka, M.	HUN	Javelin throw	F		10	54,40	
Kuehne, R.	GDR	4×400m relay	SF	2	1	3-28·48*	
			F		1	3-22·95*	G
Kulcsar, M.	HUN	800m	1	4	3	2-02·35	
			SF	1		DNS	
		1500m	1	3		DNF	
Lange, M.	GDR	Shot put	F		6	18,85	
Langkilde, S.	DEN	High jump	F		21	1,76	
Lanraman, S.	GER	100m	1	6	4	11·45	
			2	2	5	11·72	
Lard, K.	SU	Pentathlon	F		26	3788	
Larrieu, F.	USA	1500m	1	3	3	4-11·18	
			SF	2	8	4-15·26	
Larsson, A.	SWE	4×100m relay	SF	1	6	3-32·62	
Lazareva, A.	URS	High jump	Q		DNQ	1,73	
Lee, Chiu-Hsia	CHN	800m	1	4	8	2-11·81	
		1500m	1	1	9	4-37·15	
Leiser, V.	SUI	400m	1	7	6	54·65	
Liebsch, A.	GDR	Long jump	F		14	6,23	
Ligethuti, S.	HUN	1500m	1	2	7	4-16·08	
Lin, Chun-Yu	CHN	Pentathlon	F		28	3676	
		Long jump	Q		DNQ	5,50	
Lundgren, K.	SWE	400m	1	4	4	53·70	
			2	4	7	53·87	
		4×100m relay	SF	2		DIS	
		4x400m relay	SF	1	6	3-32·62	
Lungu B.	ZAM	100m	1	2	6	12·42	
		200m	1	6	6	25·11	
Lynch, A.	GBR	100m	1	1	4	11·52	
			2	3	4	11·57	
			SF	2	7	11·64	
		4×100m relay	SF	2	4	43·76	
			F		7	43·71	
Mack, K.	GER	Pentathlon	F		7	4449	
Maiyo, C.	KEN	800m	1	5	9	2-04·86	
		1500m	1	4	9	4-20·91	

COMPETITOR	COUNTRY CODE	EVENT	ROUND	HEAT	PLACE	TIME & DISTANCE	MEDAL
Malstroem, C.	SWE	4x400m relay	SF	1	6	3-32·62	
Manning, M.	USA	800m	1	1	2	2-02·63	
			2	2	5	2-02·39	
		4x400m relay	SF	2	2	3-28·63	
			F		2	3-25·15	S
Manoliu, L.	RUM	Discus throw	F		9	58,50	
Mantawel, A.	PHI	400m	1	4	7	57·91	
		4×100m relay	SF	1	DIS		
Marakina, N.	URS	Javelin throw	Q		DNQ	51,06	
Martin, B.	FRA	4x400m relay	SF	1	2	3-30·02	
			F		4	3-27·52	
Martin-Jones, R.	GBR	Long jump	Q		DNQ	5,93	
Massing, C.	AUT	4x400m relay	SF	2	6	3-42·19	
Matthews, B.	NZL	100m	1	6	5	11·77	
			2	1	8	11·87	
		100m hurdles	1	2	5	13·81	
Mei, G.	MAL	Pentathlon	F		DNF		
Melnik, F.	URS	Discus throw	F		1	66,62*	G
Menis, A.	RUM	Discus throw	F		2	65,06	S
Merten, C.	GER	1500m	1	1	6	4-12·60	
Meyfarth, U.	GER	High jump	F		1	1,92*	G
Mickler, I.	GER	100m	1	5	3	11·55	
			2	2	=3	11·52	
			SF	1	7	11·53	
		4×100m relay	SF	2	2	42·97	
			F		1	42·81*	G
Misomali, M.	MAW	100m	1	1	8	11·68	
Molina, R.	CHI	Shot put	Q		DNQ	14,61	
Molinari, C.	ITA	100m	1	3	4	11·61	
			2	1	7	11·63	
		4×100m relay	SF	1	5	44·62	
Mollova, L.	BUL	Javelin throw	F		4	59,36	
Morgunova, N.	URS	800m	1	5	1	2-02·64	
			2	2	8	2-04·93	
Morris, U.	JAM	200m	1	4	3	23·99	
			2	1	5	23·62	
		4x400m relay	SF	2	5	3-31·89	
Moser, M.	SUI	1500m	1	1	8	4-24·94	
Mosquera, J.	COL	100m	1	1	6	11·64	
			2	4	8	11·66	
		200m	1	1	5	24·20	
			2	2	6	24·00	
Mundinger, E.	GER	High jump	F		10	1,82	
Muneene, G.	ZAM	400m	1	7	7	57·71	
Muraviova, L.	URS	Discus throw	F		8	59·00	
Murphy, M.	IRL	100m hurdles	1	3	6	15·89	
		Penathlon	F		27	3770	
Murray, D.	GBR	200m	1	1	4	23·76	
			2	3	4	23·69	
			SF	2	8	24·03	
Musani, R.	UGA	200m	1	4	5	25·37	
			2	2	8	25·28	
Nadolna, K.	POL	Discus throw	Q		DNQ	52,52	
Nappi, L.	ITA	100m	1	4	5	12·02	
			2	2	8	12·13	
		4×100m relay	SF	1	5	44·62	
Neil, A.	GBR	100m	1	3	3	11·55	
			2	1	6	11·58	
		4×100m relay	SF	2	4	43·76	
			F		7	43·71	
Nenzell, A.	SWE	1500m	1	4	6	4-16·67	
Netter, M.	USA	4×100m relay	SF	2	3	43·07	
			F		4	43·39	
Neuenschwander, E.	SUI	800m	1	1	7	2-06·89	
Nicholls, F.	BAR	100m	1	3	7	12·16	
Nikolic, V.	YUG	800m	1	2	2	1-59·62	
			2	1	4	2-01·49	
			F		5	1-59·98	
		1500m	1	2	9	4-23·36	
Nixon, E.	AUS	Long jump	Q		DNQ	6,27	
Njoku, N.	NGR	High jump	Q		DNQ	0	
		Shot put	Q		DNQ	10,63	
Noeding, E.	PER	Pentathlon	F		24	3870	
Nowak, T.	POL	100m hurdles	1	1	3	13·16	
			SF	1	4	13·10	
			F		5	13·17	
Nygrynova, J.	TCH	Long jump	F		12	6,24	
Obi, A.	NGR	4×100m relay	SF	1	7	45·15	
Olaye, H.	NGR	200m	1	2	5	25·30	
			2	4	8	25·09	
		4×100m relay	SF	1	7	45·15	
Olfert, M.	GDR	Long jump	F		8	6,46	
Olsson, A.	SWE	4×100m relay	SF	2	DIS		
Olsson, G.	SWE	100m hurdles	1	4	6	14·37	
		4×100m relay	SF	2	DIS		

COMPETITOR	COUNTRY CODE	EVENT	ROUND	HEAT	PLACE	TIME & DISTANCE	MEDAL
O'Neal, L.	USA	100m Hurdles	1	2	4	13·78	
			SF	2	7	13·89	
Orosz, I.	HUN	400m	1	5	6	54·83	
Orr, J.	AUS	800m	1	2	5	2-04·46	
		1500m	1	1	4	4-08·06	
			SF	2	6	4-08·86	
			F		8	4-12·15	
Orselli, A.	ITA	4×100m relay	SF	1	5	44·62	
Oshikoya, M.	NGR	Pentathlon	F		14	4279	
		Long jump	Q		DNQ	6,22	
		4×100m relay	SF	1	7	45·15	
Paik, Ok-Ja	KOR	Shot put	Q		DNQ	15,78	
Pangelova, T.	URS	1500m	1	3	1	4-10·75	
			SF	1	1	4-07·66	
			F		7	4-06·45	
Papp, M.	HUN	Pentathlon	F		23	4074	
Pascoe, D.	GBR	200m	1	3	3	23·97	
			2	2	5	23·72	
		4×100m relay	SF	2	4	43·76	
			F		7	43·71	
Paulanyi, M.	HUN	Javelin throw	F		11	52,36	
Payne, R.	GBR	Discuss throw	F		12	56,50	
Peasley, C.	AUS	800m	1	1	3	2-03·11	
			2	1	7	2-04·56	
		4x400m relay	SF	2	3	3-29·99	
			F		6	3-28·84	
Peikert, M.	GDR	Pentathlon	F		18	4232	
Penton, A.	CUB	400m	1	6	3	53·25	
			2	3	3	52·02	
			SF	1	5	52·15	
		4x400m relay	SF	1	5	3-32·44	G
Peters, M.	GBR	Pentathlon	F		1	4801*	G
Petrova, T.	BUL	1500m	1	4	5	4-14·95	
Piecyk, D.	POL	400m	1	7	3	53·08	
			2	3	5	52·62	
		4x400m relay	SF	2	DNF		
Pierre, L.	TRI	200m	1	4	6	26·32	
Politz, M.	GDR	800m	1	3	5	2-02·40	
Pollak, B.	GDR	Pentathlon	F		3	4768	B
Popescu, C.	RUM	High jump	F		19	1,76	
Powell, C.	BAH	100m	1	6	7	12·01	
Prokop, L.	AUT	Pentathlon	F		DNF		
Proskova, A.	TCH	High jump	F		18	1,79	
Rabsztyn, G.	POL	100m hurdles	1	3	1	13·29	
			SF	2	4	13·24	
			F		8	13·44	
Rallins, M.	USA	100m hurdles	1	3	3	13·51	
			SF	1	7	13·75	
Randerz, E.	SWE	4x400m relay	SF	1	6	3-32·62	
Ranky, A.	HUN	Javelin throw	Q		DNQ	53,48	
Ranz, G.	GER	1500m	1	2	8	4-18·60	
Rautanen, T.	FIN	100m	1	5	6	11·89	
		4×100m relay	SF	1	6	44·68	
		4x400m relay	SF	1	4	3-30·84	
			F		7	3-29·44	
Rechner, B.	SUI	High jump	Q		DNQ	1,73	
Reid, A.	JAM	High jump	F		11	1,82	
Reiser, G.	CAN	1500m	1	1	2	4-06·71	
			SF	1	7	4:09·51	
Render, M.	USA	100m	1	1	5	11·60	
			2	3	6	11·67	
		4×100m relay	SF	2	3	43·07	
			F		4	43·39	
Rendina, C.	AUS	400m	1	1	1	51·94*	
			2	1	1	51·96	
			SF	2	3	51·90	
			F		6	51·99	
		4x400m relay	SF	2	3	3-29·99	
			F		6	3-28·84	
Richter, A.	GER	100m	1	1	2	11·30	
			2	3	1	11·33	
			SF	2	3	11·39	
			F		5	11·38	
		4×100m relay	SF	2	2	42·97	
			F		1	42·81*	G
Rieuwpassa, C.	INA	100m	1	4	6	12·23	
		200m	1	1	6	24·68	
			2	4	7	25·03	
Rivas, E.	COL	400m	1	6	7	56·33	
Rodriquez, M.	CUB	High jump	Q		DNQ	1,73	
Romay, F.	CUB	4×100m relay	SF	1	1	43·67	
			F		3	43·36	B
Roscoe, J.	GBR	400m	1	2	2	53·67	
			2	1	6	53·01	
		4x400m relay	SF	2	4	3-30·05	
			F		5	3-28·74	

COMPETITOR	COUNTRY CODE	EVENT	ROUND	HEAT	PLACE	TIME & DISTANCE	MEDAL
Rosendahl, H.	GER	Pentathlon	F		2	4791	S
		Long jump	F		1	6,78	G
		4×100m relay	SF	2	2	42.97	
			F		1	42.81*	G
Ross-Edwards, A.	AUS	400m	1	5	4	53.48	
			2	4	5	53.60	
		4x400m relay	SF	2	3	3-23.99	
			F		6	3-23.84	
Rudolf, E.	HUN	High jump	F		=16	1.79	
Rueckes, A.	GER	400m	1	7	5	53.92	
			2	1	7	53.22	
		4x400m relay	SF	1	1	3-29.32*	
			F		3	3-26.51	B
Runtso, L.	URS	4x400m relay	SF	1	3	3-30.23	
			F		3	3-31.89	
Ruth, T.	HOL	400m	1	3	3	53.16	
			2	1	4	52.45	
			SF	2	8	53.02	
Ruus, R.	URS	800m	1	4	7	2-11.18	
Ryan, P.	AUS	100m	1	3	5	11.73	
			2	2	6	11.85	
		100m hurdles	1	1	2	12.93	
			SF	1	2	12.95	
			F		4	12.98	
		4×100m relay	SF	1	3	44.03	
			F		6	43.51	
Sabaite, N.	URS	800m	1	3	1	2-01.50	
			2	1	1	2-00.30	
			F		2	1-58.65	S
Sadowick, J.	CAN	400m	1	6	6	54.53	
Saeluzika, M.	MAW	200m	1	2	6	28.29	
Salao, L.	PHI	100m hurdles	1	1	6	15.15	
		4×100m relay	SF	1		DIS	
Sandhu, K.	IND	400m	1	6	8	57.74	
Saunders, Y.	JAM	400m	1	5	1	52.38	
			2	2	1	52.15	
			SF	2	5	51.95	
		4x400m relay	SF	2	5	3-31.89	
Schenk, S.	GER	800m	1	6	3	2-02.23	
			2	1	5	2-01.50	
Schittenhelm, E.	GER	100m	1	6	1	11.32	
			2	4	2	11.42	
			SF	1	5	11.49	
Schmidt, K.	USA	Javelin throw	F		3	59.94	B
Schmidt. R.	GDR	High jump	F		5	1.85	
Schueller, H.	GER	100m hurdles	1	4	4	13.50	
			SF	2	6	13.33	
		Long jump	F		5	6,51	
Seidler, H.	GDR	400m	1	5	2	52.79	
			2	1	2	51.97	
			SF	1	1	51.68*	
			F		4	51.86	
		4x400m relay	SF	2	1	3-28.48*	
			F		1	3-22.95*	G
Seidler, M.	USA	Shot put	Q		DNQ	16,18	
Shakhamorov, E.	ISR	100m	1	2	1	11.45	
			2	1	4	11.46	
			SF	1	4	11.49	
		100m hurdles	1	1	4	13.17	
			SF	2		DNS	
Sherwood, S.	GBR	Long jump	F		9	6,41	
Sidorova, M.	URS	200m	1	6	1	23.46	
			2	4	4	23.33	
			SF	1	7	23.40	
		4×100m relay	SF	1	2	43.77	
			F		5	43.59	
Silai, I.	RUM	800m	1	4	1	2-01.42	
			2	2	3	2-01.85	
			F		6	2-00.04	
Simeoni, S.	ITA	High jump	F		6	1,85	
Simpson, J.	GBR	400m	1	6	5	54.13	
		4x400m relay	SF	2	4	3-30.05	
			F		5	3-28.74	
Skowronska, E.	POL	800m	1	2	4	2-03.23	
		4x400m relay	SF	2		DNF	
Smith, J.	GBR	1500m	1	3	4	4-11.27	
			SF	1	6	4-09.37	
Soerum, W.	NOR	1500m	1	4	4	4-14.10	
			SF	2	7	4-09.70	

COMPETITOR	COUNTRY CODE	EVENT	ROUND	HEAT	PLACE	TIME & DISTANCE	MEDAL
Stecher, R.	GDR	100m	1	4	1	11.31	
			2	2	1	11.27	
			SF	1	1	11.18	
			F		1	11.07*	G
		200m	1	2	1	22.96	
			2	3	1	23.31	
			SF	2	1	22.83	
			F		1	22.40*	G
		4×100m relay	SF	2	1	42.88	
			F		2	42.95	S
Stirling, R.	GBR	800m	1	5	3	2-03.64	
			2	2	4	2-02.36	
			F		7	2-00.15	
		4x400m relay	SF	2	4	3-30.05	
			F		5	3-28.74	
Stoyanova, E.	BUL	Shot put	F		8	18,34	
Stoeva, V.	BUL	Discus throw	F		3	64,34	B
Strandvall, M.-L.	FIN	400m	1	4	2	52.85	
			2	4	2	52.53	
			SF	1	6	52.23	
		4×100m relay	SF	1	6	44.68	
		4x400m relay	SF	1	4	3-30.84	
			F		7	3-29.44	
Straszynska, D.	POL	100m hurdles	1	2	2	13.03	
			SF	2	2	12.91	
			F		6	13.18	
Stropahl, E.	GDR	100m	1	5	5	11.63	
			2	1	5	11.48	
		200m	1	4	1	23.54	
			2	2	1	22.93	
			SF	1	1	22.90	
			F		4	22.75	
Struppert, B.	GDR	4×100m relay	SF	2	1	42.88	
			F		2	42.95	S
Suranova, E.	TCH	Long jump	F		3	6,67	B
Svendsen, J.	USA	Shot put	Q		DNQ	14,96	
Svensdottir, L.	ISL	High jump	Q		DNQ	1,60	
Sykora, M.	AUT	400m	1	3	6	54.46	
		800m	1	3	3	2-01.82	
			2	2	6	2-02.44	
Syrovatskaia, O.	URS	400m	1	6	4	53.62	
			2	3	7	53.42	
		4x400m relay	SF	1	3	3-30.23	
			F		8	3-31.89	
Szewinska, I.	POL	100m	1	6	2	11.33	
			2	2	2	11.49	
			SF	1	6	11.54	
		200m	1	5	1	23.37	
			2	1	1	22.79	
			SF	1	3	22.92	
			F		3	22.74	B
Telliez, S.	FRA	110m	1	6	3	11.36	
			2	3	5	11.64	
		200m	1	6	2	23.51	
			2	3	3	23.69	
			SF	2	6	23.34	
Thompson, J.	USA	200m	1	5	3	23.67	
			2	4	3	23.22	
			SF	1	6	23.18	
Tikhomirova, V.	URS	Pentathlon	F		5	4597	
Tillett, L.	AUS	Pentathlon	F		16	4258	
		Long jump	Q		DNQ	5,99	
Tittel, E.	GER	1500m	1	4	1	4-12.12	
			SF	2	3	4-06.65	
			F			DNF	
Tkachenko, N.	URS	Pentathlon	F		9	4370	
Todten, J.	GDR	Javelin throw	F		2	62,54	S
Torres, C.	PHI	4×100m relay	SF	1		DIS	
Toussaint, C.	USA	800m	1	2	6	2-08.90	
		4x400m relay	SF	2	2	3-28.63	
			F		2	3-25.15	S
Tracey, M.	IRL	800m	1	1	4	2-04.18	
		1500m	1	3	6	4-16.43	
Trotman, M.	BAR	200m	1	6	5	24.06	
			2	1	6	24.00	
		4x400m relay	SF	1	7	3-44.45	
Truse, C.	CUB	400m	1	7	1	52.80	
			2	1		DNS	
Tyynelae, S.	FIN	1500m	1	3	7	4-21.41	
Urbancic, N.	YUG	Javelin throw	F		5	59,06	
Vaamonde, L.	VEN	Pentathlon	F		25	3794	
Valdes, C.	CUB	100m	1	5	2	11.53	
			2	4	3	11.46	
			SF	1	6	11.52	
		4×100m relay	SF	1	1	43.67	
			F		3	43.36	B

COMPETITOR	COUNTRY CODE	EVENT	ROUND	HEAT	PLACE	TIME & DISTANCE	MEDAL
Valkova, I.	BUL	100m	1	2	2	11·49	
			2	4	6	11·48	
		4×100m relay	SF	2	5	43·95	
Van Gool, W.	HOL	100m	1	1	3	11·43	
			2	4	5	11·47	
		200m	1	3	2	23·86	
			2	2	3	23·22	
			SF	1		DNS	
Van Kiekebelt, D.	CAN	Pentathlon	F		15	4272	
		Long jump	Q		DNQ	6,07	
Vassekova, R.	BUL	Shot put	F		12	17,86	
		Disc throw	Q		DNQ	53,86	
Venkova, I.	BUL	4×100m relay	SF	2	5	43·95	
Verheuen, M.	BEL	800m	1	4	6	2-09·13	
Vernon, J.	GBR	100m hurdles	1	1	5	13·37	
		4×100m relay	SF	2	4	43·76	
			F		7	43·71	
Vicent, J.	URU	200m	1	3	6	25·09	
			2			DNS	
		400m	1	3	7	55·33	
Vilca, M.	PER	100m	1	6	6	11·85	
		200m	1	3	5	24·46	
			2	2	7	24·48	
Vintila, E.	RUM	Pentathlon	F		20	4199	
		Long jump	F		14	6,13	
Viscopoleanu, V.	RUM	Long jump	F		7	6,48	
Vulescu, R.	RUM	High jump	Q		DNQ	1,65	
Walsh, C.	IRL	800m	1	2	7	2-08·98	
Watson, M.	USA	Long jump	Q		DNQ	6,09	
		4×100m relay	SF	2	3	43·07	
			F		4	43·39	
Wauters, M.	BEL	Discus throw	Q		DNQ	49,62	
Westermann, L.	GER	Discus throw	F		5	62,18	
White, W.	USA	Long jump	F		11	6,27	
Wilden, R.	GER	400m	1	1	2	51·97	
			2	3	2	51·91	
			SF	2	2	51·76	
			F		2	51·21	S
		4x400m relay	SF	1	1	3-29·32*	
			F		3	3-26·51	B

COMPETITOR	COUNTRY CODE	EVENT	ROUND	HEAT	PLACE	TIME & DISTANCE	MEDAL
Williams, R.	JAM	400m	1	4	6	55·72	
		4x400m relay	SF	2	5	3-31·89	
Wilmi, P.	FIN	200m	1	4	4	24·16	
			2	4	5	23·68	
		4×100m relay	SF	1	6	44·68	
		4x400m relay	SF	1	4	3-30·84	
			F		7	3-29·44	
Wilson, A.	GBR	100m hurdles	1	4	5	13·53	
		Pentathlon	F		13	4279	
Wilson, D.	USA	High jump	Q		DNQ	1,70	
Witschas, R.	GDR	High jump	F		7	1,85	
Wright, T.	CAN	1500m	1	2	5	4-15·43	
Wu, Yu-Chih	CHN	High jump	Q		DNQ	0	
Yama, M.	JPN	High jump	Q		DNQ	1,65	
Yamashita, H.	JPN	Long jump	Q		DNQ	6,14	
Yankova, Y.	BUL	4×100m relay	SF	2	5	43·95	
Yorgova, D.	BUL	Long jump	F		2	6,77	S
		4×100m relay	SF	2	5	43·95	
Zehrt, M.	GDR	400m	1	3	1	52·49	
			2	2	2	52·33	
			SF	2	1	51·47*	
			F		1	51·08*	G
		4x400m relay	SF	2	1	3-28·48*	
			F		1	3-22·95*	G
Zharkova, L.	URS	100m	1	5	4	11·56	
			2	4	4	11·46	
			SF	1	8	11·67	
		4×100m relay	SF	1	2	43·77	
			F		5	43·59	
Zientarska, B.	POL	400m	1	4	5	54·20	
		4x400m relay	SF	2		DNF	
Zlateva, S.	BUL	800m	1	2	1	1-58·93*	
			2	2	2	2-01·66	
			F		4	1-59·72	
Zorgo, E.	RUM	Javelin throw	F		NP	0	

In a very close 800 metres finish, Hildegard Falck of West Germany (159), just edges out Niola Sabaite of Russia, in an Olympic record.   Mark Shearman

1976
White Lightning Strikes Twice

Something went wrong in the arrangements for the Montreal Olympics, which cost four and a half times the initial estimate. Despite strikes, all was eventually ready in time, and there was to be no repeat of the Munich tragedy. However there was the first of the last-minute boycotts which had now become fashionable — this one by African nations upset at the presence of New Zealand, which had enjoyed rugby links with South Africa.

There were some pleasant stories arising from the track and field events. Miklos Nemeth of Hungary, the men's javelin throwing winner, followed his father onto the top step of the podium, Imre having won the hammer throw in 1948 in London. Irena Szewinska of Poland won her seventh Olympic medal, a gold in the 400m, in her fourth Games (she was to appear at Moscow, too).

Two outstanding doubles were achieved by Lasse Viren, who repeated his 1972 Munich victories in the 5,000m and 10,000m (and then finished fifth in the marathon) and by Alberto Juantorena of Cuba, who became the first man (excluding the 1906 Intercalated Games) to win both the 400m and 800m. A tall figure in white vest and trunks and long white socks, he earned the nickname "White Lightning", although the Spanish-speaking Cubans preferred "El Caballo", the horse.

Men's Track Events

Harvey Glance of the USA won the first semi-final of the **100 metres** in 10·24 sec from defending champion Valeriy Borzov of the USSR, while Hasely Crawford of Trinidad took the other in 10·22 with Don Quarrie of Jamaica second. The final needed two starts before the sprinters left their blocks, with Glance perceptibly in front over the first few metres and Borzov second. At 50 metres Quarrie had recovered from his slowish start and was abreast of Glance and Borzov and at 75 metres he led, but Crawford was powering along and he took the Jamaican on the tape to win with 10·06 to 10·08. Borzov was third in 10·14.

Don Quarrie of Jamaica was the favourite for the **200 metres** and showed some sharp sprinting in the second round when winning in 20·28 sec. He also won his semi-final in 20·48, while Pietro Mennea of Italy took the other. In the final, Quarrie and Dwayne Evans of the USA were quickest away at the gun. Into the home straight Quarrie led with another American, Millard Hampton, just behind with Evans and Mennea next Down the straight the two leaders pulled away and Quarrie won in 20·23 from Hampton second in 20·29, while Evans held off Mennea to take third in 20·43.

Alberto Juantorena of Cuba was favoured to take the **400 metres** title, though he had already won the 800 metres and the pundits felt he looked too tired for the double. In the first semi-final he started very slowly but finished fast to win in 45·10 sec from Belgium's Fons Brijdenbach in 45·28, while in the second, the USA's Fred Newhouse clocked 44·89 in defeating Britain's David Jenkins. Newhouse went out fast in the final as did fellow American Herman Frazier, and he led at 200 metres with Frazier a metre down and Juantorena, Brijdenbach and Maxie Parks of the USA a good two metres further adrift. Juantorena then began to motor and he caught Newhouse 20 metres from home to win in 44·26, the fastest time ever recorded at non-altitude. Newhouse was second in 44·40 and Frazier third with 44·95.

A galaxy of stars like Alberto Juantorena of Cuba, Rick Wohlhuter of the USA, Carlo Grippo of Italy and Belgium's Ivo van Damme lined up for the **800 metres**. Juantorena took the first semi-final in 1-45·88 from Van Damme and Wohlhuter the second in 1-46·72 from Grippo, but not without being first disqualified for elbowing and then reinstated. Eight runners lined up in their lanes with the break being at 330 metres instead of 130. Juantorena, Wohlhuter and Sri Ram Singh of India led at the break, but Juantorena was in front soon after half-way and strode strongly onwards to win in 1-43·50, a new world record. With 30 metres to go Wohlhuter tied up and van Damme edged past him to take the silver in 1-43·86. Wohlhuter collected the bronze with a time of 1-44·12.

The absence, due to the African boycott, of Kenya's Mike Boit and Tanzania's Filbert Bayi diminished the **1,500 metres**. Nine runners lined up for a rain-soaked final, but as nobody wished to take the lead, the field trailed through three slow laps with Eamonn Coghlan of Ireland in front at that point. John Walker of New Zealand then broke away and his sprint for the tape won him the gold medal in 3-39·17. Behind Walker the rest were sprinting madly with Ivo van Damme of Belgium snatching the silver in 3-39·27 and West Germany's Paul-Heinz Wellmann taking the bronze in 3-39·33.

In the **5,000 metres** Lasse Viren of Finland was defending his title but few believed that he would succeed. Heat three was extremely fast, caused by Brendan Foster of Great Britain trying to run everyone off their feet and succeeding with a new Olympic record of 13-20·34, with eight others under 13-30·0. The final started off at a moderate pace, but Foster picked up the lead at 600 metres and took the field to 2km in 5-26·6, before Viren went to the front and promptly slowed the pace down. Dick Quax of New Zealand became the reluctant leader and others took turns until with three laps to go Viren wound up the pace. At the bell a group of six were bunched behind him, but he accelerated again and reached the tape to win in 13-24·76, having run the last 400 in 55·4 sec. Second was Quax in 13-25·16 and third Klaus-Peter Hildenbrand of West Germany in 13-25·38.

The prospective gold and silver medal winners, Lasse Viren of Finland and Dick Quax, the New Zealander, are pictured together in the 5,000 metres.

Mark Shearman

Mark Shearman

Alberto Juantorena

Albert Juantorena, born in Orente on 11 November 1950, became the only man in Olympic Games history to win the 400m and 800m finals, a feat for long thought to be impossible. A giant of a man with matching stride, he first gave indication of being Olympic potential when winning the 400m gold medal at the 1973 World Student Games. By 1976 he had firmly established himself as an extraordinary athlete and proved it by winning the Olympic 400m title in Montreal, with a time of 44·26 sec, a performance considered comparable to the American Lee Evans' world mark of 43·8 sec run at altitude in Mexico.

Then, despite all the arduous preliminary rounds of the 800m, the Cuban dominated the final with a world record-shattering 1-43·5.

Juantorena won both races over these distances in the World Cup the following year before Achilles tendon strain started to give him trouble. This prevented his making a successful defence of his titles in the 1980 Moscow Games. Cuban sources said that Juantorena shed 11lb in weight when competing in his 11 races at Montreal.

As in the 5,000 metres, Lasse Viren was also the defending champion for the **10,000 metres**. The early pace was slow in the final, with 3km passed in 8-33-4, after which Carlos Lopes of Portugal speeded things up to pass 5km in 14–08·9 and reduce the leading group from ten to six. At 7km Lopes led Viren and Brendan Foster of Britain with the next runner, Rumania's Ilie Floroiu, ten metres back. A further kilometre on and Foster dropped off the pace, while Viren waited until 600 metres to go before making his strike for home. He won in 27-40·38 with Lopes trailing in 27-45·17 and Foster getting bronze in 27-54·92.

Frank Shorter of the USA was a confident defending champion in the **marathon**, where 67 runners trotted out of the stadium led by Britain's Barry Watson. Bill Rogers of the USA led at 20km in 61-24·0 heading a bunch of nine: Shorter, Lasse Viren of Finland, Shivnath Singh of India, Karel Lismont of Belgium, Waldemar Cierpinski of East Germany, Jerome Drayton of Canada, Goran Bengtsson of Sweden and Australia's Chris Wardlaw. But just before 25km Shorter got away from the pack. Within four minutes Cierpinski had joined the American and at 40km, he was 32 seconds in front of Shorter, going on to win in 2:09-55·0 for a new Olympic record. Shorter won the silver in 2:10-45·8 and Lismont took the bronze with 2:11-12·6.

For the first time ever it was not an American-based hurdler who was favourite for the **110 metres hurdles**, as France's Guy Drut, the European champion, had a fast 13·1 sec under his belt. Charlie Foster of the USA won the first semi-final in 13·45 from East Germany's Thomas Munkelt, and Alejandro Casanas of Cuba took the second in 13·34 from Drut. In the final, however, Drut got off to a brilliant start with Willie Davenport of the USA second best and Casanas almost last. The Frenchman had a slight advantage at the third hurdle from Davenport, James Owens of the USA, and Munkelt, but increased his lead from the eighth flight, with Casanas coming through fast. Drut just made it to the line in 13·30 with Casanas second with 13·33 and Davenport third in 13·38.

Ed Moses of the USA was co-favourite with the defending champion John Akii-Bua for the **400 metres hurdles**, until the African boycott deprived the Ugandan of the opportunity to run. In the first semi-final, Mike Shine of the USA won in 49·40 sec from Jose Carvalho of Portugal, while Moses took the second in an extravagant 48·29 from Evgeniy Gavrilenko of Russia. With the final underway, Moses flew from the blocks like a man possessed. Gavrilenko also went off hard with Britain's Alan Pascoe and Mike Shine trying not to lose contact. Moses was clear of Gavrilenko by the seventh hurdle and strode majestically. 13 strides between hurdles, all the way to win in 47·63 for a world record. Shine overtook a tiring Gavrilenko in the final stretch to take the silver medal in 48·69 with Gavrilenko's 49·45 earning the bronze.

The **3,000 metres steeplechase** heats saw some very brisk times with Bronislaw Malinowski of Poland taking the first in 8-18·56 from East Germany's Frank Baumgartl, and Dennis Coates of Britain the second in 8-18·95 from Finland's Tapio Kantanen. Antonio Campos of Spain led off in the final with Coates and Malinowski following but with four laps left, the Pole went to the front with Anders Garderud of Sweden, the world record holder, Baumgartl and Kantanen in attendance. With 300 metres to go, Garderud struck Racing like mad, with Malinowski hanging on like grim

Arnie Robinson of America, the long jump bronze medallist from 1972, improved to take the gold in Montreal.   Mark Shearman

death, he gained two metres at the last water jump. Baumgartl chased hard and closed up the straight, but clipped the last hurdle and sprawled to the ground, leaving Garderud to win in 8-08·02 for a new world record. Malinowski had to jump over the fallen East German and finished in a creditable 8-09·11 for the silver medal, while the unlucky Baumgartl got up to take the bronze in 8-10·36.

Daniel Bautista of Mexico, the new world record holder, was up against all the medallists from four years before in the **20 kilometres walk**; Peter Frenkel and Hans Reimann of East Germany and Russia's Vladimir Golubnichy. The course was over eight laps of the local roads and 38 heel and toe men strolled out of the tunnel to commence their task. At 5km Frenkel led followed by the Mexicans Bautista, Raul Gonzales and Domingo Colin, Reimann and East Germany's Karl-Heinz

Mark Shearman

Irena Szewinska

This great athlete was born as Irena Kirszenstein in Leningrad, Russia, on 24 May 1946, of Polish parents. She became an exceptional Olympic competitor, winning seven medals in five different events from five Games.

Her first award was a silver for finishing runner-up to Britain's Mary Rand as an 18-year-old in the long jump in the 1964 Tokyo Games. She won a silver again with second place in the 200m and capped the week with a gold as a member of the Polish world record-breaking 4 × 100m relay team.

At her second Games in Mexico City, where she competed under her married name of Szewinska, Irena took a bronze in the 100m and then produced a world record in the 200m final with 22·5 sec.

In Munich four years later she was in the action again, following the birth of her son, and received a bronze for her third place in the 200m. The following season she switched to 400m and in only her second race at the distance became the first woman to break 50 sec. And at the 1976 Montreal Games she added to her medal collection with a gold at 400m in a time of 49·29 sec, another world record.

While competing in Moscow, a muscle injury in the 400m semi-final put a finish to her magnificent Olympic career.

Mark Shearman

Lasse Viren

To win the 5,000m and 10,000m at one Olympic Games is a remarkable feat in itself. But to do so *twice* must go down in Olympic history as one of the most outstanding achievements of the Games.

What a sensation Viren, born in Myrskyla on 22 July 1949, provided in his bid for the first of those four titles — the 10,000m in Munich in 1972. When lying in fifth position during the final he stumbled and fell, then smartly picked himself and gave chase after the leaders. He was in the hunt again by the 6,000m mark. And with a lap-and-a-half to go the "Flying Finn" struck for victory — and got it in a time of 27-38·4, which broke the seven-year-old world record held by Ron Clarke.

Keeping on his feet throughout Viren was again in tremendous form in the 5,000m, when he broke the Olympic record with 13-26·4.

Only occasionally did he appear in major championships over the next four years, so he was far from being the favourite when the 10,000m gold was at stake again in Montreal, but in winning again, he was only 2 sec slower than in Munich.

Following his second 5,000m success there were questions raised as to whether Viren had been involved in blood boosting, which he strongly denied.

Ruth Fuchs

Ruth Fuchs was born in Egelin on 14 December 1946. In 1972 she broke the world javelin record for the first time, and she went on to transform the scene of women's javelin throwing. This first throw, made in Potsdam, was the forerunner of her raising the world figures by 7 metres over the next eight years.

When winning the first of her two gold medals, in the 1972 Munich Games, she reached more than 3 metres beyond the previous Games best with 209ft 7in (63,88m) and her winning throw in Montreal, four years later, landed another 2 metres beyond this mark. She is the only woman to have succesfully defended the Olympic javelin title.

By a remarkable coincidence, on the very same day in 1972 (11 June), Ewa Gryzieka, of Poland, had thrown 205ft 8½in (62,70m) in Bucharest to break the world record which had stood since the Tokyo Olympics of 1964. Imagine the astonishment expressed when the ticker tapes informed the world later that day that Fuchs had raised the mark to an incredible 213ft 5½in (65,06m).

In 1977 Kate Schmidt of the United States took over the world record but Fuchs won it back two years later in Dresden with 228ft 1in (69,52m) and the following year improved it to 229ft 6½in (69,96m).

East beats West Germany in the women's 200 metres. Barbel Eckert (far right) wins from Annegret Richter, with Renate Stecher in third position.

Stadtmuller. Frenkel still led at 10km from the same group except that Gonzales had dropped back, and shortly after, Colin was red-flagged and dropped out. Only three remained at 15km: Reimann, Frenkel and Bautista. Two kilometres later Bautista changed gear and quickly opened a gap which he extended to win in 1:24-40·6, an Olympic record, while Reimann got away from Frenkel to finish second in 1:25-13·8 to 1:25-29·4.

Wet conditions were the order of the day for the **4 × 100 metres relay** final. At the first exchange, the USSR, East Germany and the USA were on a par, but from thereon the Americans never looked back, extending their lead by a metre on each of their subsequent legs to win in 38·33 sec. East Germany were a trifle up on Russia and Poland at the final exchange and with the help of an excellent pass, won the silver medal in 38·66 with Russia taking the bronze in 38·78. The winning team was Harvey Glance, John Jones, Millard Hampton and Steve Riddick.

In the first heat of the **4 × 400 metres relay**, Britain's Alan Pascoe had the baton knocked out of his hand and a team with a real medal chance were eliminated. The USA were never headed in the final, with Herman Frazier running the lead leg in 45·3 sec, Benny Brown the second at 44·6, Fred Newhouse the third at 43·8 and Maxie Parks the anchor at 45·0, for a winning time of 2-58·65. Poland took the silver medal, mainly due to Jan Werner's 44·0 sec leg, in 3-01·43 and West Germany was third with 3-01·98.

Men's Field Events

Dwight Stones of the USA was the favourite to win the **high jump** as he had recently set a new world record. Fourteen high jumpers qualified at 2,16 metres to enter the final jump-off, ten of whom successfully cleared the bar at 2,18 but only four did so at 2,21: Jack Wszola of Poland, Greg Joy of Canada, Stones and Russia's Sergei Budalov. At 2,23 Wszola cleared on his first attempt, and Joy made it on his third, but Stones failed, due in part to the wet conditions underfoot. Budalov missed once and reserved his two remaining attempts for 2,25 at which he failed and under the count-back rule he was placed fourth and Stones third. Wszola flopped over 2,25 at his second attempt, but Joy, after one miss at this height, elected to take his next two attempts at 2,27 at which he failed, to be placed second. Wszola, the gold medallist, then made two unsuccessful attempts at 2,27 and one at 2,29.

Twenty vaulters qualified for the **pole vault** final by vaulting 5,10 metres and seven of them were still jumping when the bar was elevated to the Olympic record height of 5,50. Jean-Michel Bellot of France failed at this height after clearing 5,40 and Earl Bell of the USA, Wojciech Buciarski of Poland and France's Patrick Abada also failed at 5,50, but with 5,45 under their belts. Tadeusz Slusarski of Poland, Finland's Antti Kalliomaeki and USA's Dave Roberts, the world record holder, all cleared the bar at their first try and at 5,55 all

Mark Shearman

Victor Saneyev

It is doubtful if we shall ever see a more thrilling triple jump final at an Olympic Games than the action in the event in Mexico City in 1968. Three jumpers between them broke the world record five times, and Saneyev finished up with the best mark of 17,39m (57ft 0¾in).

Born in Sukhumi on 3 October 1945, Saneyev began his athletics career as a long jumper, but by the time he was 18 he had become proficient also at the triple jump, as was shown when he captured the silver medal for both events at the European Junior championships. Not until three years later, however, did he make his mark as a world-class competitor. Then for the 1968 Games he was faced with the decision of whether he should go for both, or concentrate on one event.

In the light of the strength of the opposition in the long jump, which included the famed Americans Ralph Boston and Bob Beamon, he opted for the triple jump and justified his decision by winning the gold.

Saneyev retained his Olympic title in Munich, four years later, and again at Montreal in 1976, and even won the silver for the event in Moscow, 1980. Although Joao de Silva of Brazil has since deprived him of his world record, Saneyev's 1968 clearance remains the Olympic Games all-time best.

failed with the exception of Roberts who passed, which proved to be a tactical error. He attempted 5,60 but also failed and got the bronze, with Kalliomaeki taking the silver and Slusarski the gold, all at 5,50, the count-back rule deciding the positions.

In the **long jump**, Arnie Robinson of the USA, the bronze medallist from Munich, and Yugoslavia's Nenad Stekic were favourites for top honours. With the very first jump of the competition proper, Robinson leapt 8,35 metres which was good enough for the gold medal. Four of the top five all produced their best jumps in the first round, the exception being the bronze medallist Frank Wartenberg of East Germany. Robinson won with 8,35, Randy Williams of the USA, the defending champion, took the silver with 8,11 and Wartenberg the bronze with 8,02.

Viktor Saneyev of the USSR was trying to retain his title in the **triple jump** against the world record holder, Joao de Oliveira of Brazil and two good Americans in James Butts and Tommy Haynes. There were two big jumps in the qualifying rounds, from de Oliveira with 16,81 and Saneyev with 16,77. Pedro Perez of Cuba led the first round of the final with 16,81 and Butts took over with 16,76 in the next. Saneyev then came good and jumped 17,06 in the third to take the lead, while de Oliveira shifted into second place with 16,85. In the fourth trials, Butts regained pole position with 17,18 only for Saneyev to respond in the next with 17,29, the winning jump. De Oliveira's best came in the last round, but 16,90 was good only for the bronze medal.

Rotating **shot put** expert Alek Baryshnikov of the USSR was the new world record holder, but the tricky technique was unpredictable. Things looked good in the preliminaries as he set a new Olympic record of 21,32 metres and his first round put of 20,53 looked promising. Then Al Feuerbach of the USA hit the mark at 20,55 to take the lead, but in the third round Baryshnikov appeared to have got it all sown up with a whirl of 21,00. However, the fifth trials were the telling ones, as Udo Beyer of East Germany launched 21,05 for the gold and Evgeniy Mironov of Russia clicked with 21,03 for the silver, leaving Baryshnikov at 21,00 having to be satisfied with the bronze.

As the holder of the world's best **discus throw**, Mac Wilkins of the USA, stamped his mark on the

Bruce Jenner, of the USA, is seen winning the 1,500 metres event in the decathlon, to become Olympic champion.   Mark Shearman

competition when qualifying with a new Olympic record of 68,28 metres. In the competition proper, Wolfgang Schmidt of East Germany led the first round with 63,68, but in the second, first America's John Powell overtook him with 64,24 and then Wilkins with 67,50. The third round saw two more big throws with Powell spinning his disc to 65,70 and Schmidt scaling his to 65,15, which was further improved with his last round throw to 66,22. Result: Wilkins 67,50, Schmidt 66,22 and Powell 65,70.

The Russian camp had a trio of **hammer throw**ers of which any one could win: Anatoliy Bondarchuk, the defending champion, Yuri Sedykh their record holder, Alek Spiridonov, the world's third best. There were four 75-metre throws in the first round of the competition as

The eventual winner of the 3,000 metres steeplechase, Anders Gärderud of Sweden (812), is seen in the early stages behind Malinowski of Poland, who took the silver.

Mark Shearman

Bondarchuk, first of all, threw 75,48, within two centimetres of his Olympic record, then Sedykh achieved 75·64 to break the record, followed by Spiridonov with 75,74 and finally West Germany's Karl-Hans Riehm at 75,00 to improve it further. In the second round, Sedykh rotated his wire and ball three times in the circle and whipped it away for a 77,52, an Olympic record, which won the gold medal. In the fourth round, Riehm improved to 75,46 and the last trials yielded a 76,08 throw from Spiridonov, which took the silver.

Seppe Hovinen of Finland was the leader in the qualifying rounds of the **javelin throw** with 89,78 metres, but Hungary's Miklos Nemeth, son of the 1948 hammer victor, was close behind with 89,28. In the very first round of the final Nemeth launched his javelin with a satisfied grunt, and it seemed to sail on forever until landing beyond the little flag that marked the world record. Nemeth jumped for delight at his 94,58 throw that ultimately won him the gold medal. Inspired by Nemeth's success the next thrower, Hannu Siitonen of Finland, deliberated a little and sent his spear wafting into the sky to land at 87,92 and several throws later Gheorge Megelea of Rumania threw 87,16. These two throws were good enough for the lesser medal placings, resulting in Siitonen with the silver and Megelea the bronze.

In the American trials Bruce Jenner had missed the world record in the **decathlon** by just ten points, and a good contest was in prospect with the world record holder and defending champion, Nikolai Avilov of the USSR. Fastest time in the 100m came from Guido Kratschmer of West Germany who ran 10·66 sec and he held his lead in the long jump after leaping 7,39 metres. The shot saw him still in front, but Jenner was now second, after throwing 15,35. Next came the high jump, and Avilov moved into second place following a 2,14 jump, and Jenner dropped down to third. The first day ended after the 400m with Kratschmer scoring a total of 4,333 points, Avilov on 4,315 and Jenner, who ran 47·51 sec, on 4,298. In the hurdles, Avilov went into the lead with 14·20 sec, followed by Kratschmer, but after the discus, where he threw 50,04, Jenner had moved up to second place in the competition. For the first time Jenner led, pole vaulting 4,80 metres and he extended his lead with a 68,52 metres throw in the javelin. The situation at the 1,500 was that Kratschmer would need to beat Jenner by over 12 seconds to win and Avilov would have to beat him by 20. The outcome was that Jenner chased the world record and ran a fast 4-12·61. He succeeded with a world best score of 8,618 points to take the gold, while Kratschmer ran 4-29·09 for 8,411 and silver and Avilov 4-26·6 for 8,369 and bronze.

Women's Events

Annegret Richter, of West Germany set a new Olympic record of 11·05 sec in the second round of the **100 metres** and then broke the world record with 11·01 in the first semi-final when defeating the USA's Evelyn Ashford. Renate Stecher of East Germany won the other semi-final in 11·10 from Inge Helten, the West German world record holder. The girls were away very evenly in the final, but by 20 metres Richter, Helten and Stecher were clear of the rest. At 50 metres Helten was perceptibly leading from the other two, with Chandra Cheeseborough fourth, but Richter gained momentum over the latter stages and won in 11·08, from Stecher who took the silver in 11·13 and Helten the bronze in 11·17.

Renate Stecher of East Germany and West Germany's Annegret Richter were the top women in the **200 metres**, as Szewinska was concentrating on the 400 metres. Stecher won the first semi-final in 22·68 sec, Raelene Boyle of Australia, the silver medallist of Munich, being eliminated for two false starts. And Barbel Eckert of East Germany won the second in 22·71, defeating Richter. At the gun to start the final, Inge Helten of West Germany was into her sprinting quickest, but Eckert came off the turn first, followed by Richter then Stecher. There was little to choose between them until 30 metres from home when Stecher weakened and Eckert nosed ahead to win in 22·37 for an Olympic record, with Richter a fraction behind in 22·39. Stecher was third with 22·47.

Leading lights in the **400 metres** were Irena Szewinska of Poland and East Germany's Christina Brehmer. In the first semi-final Szewinska clocked 50·48 sec for a new Games record, while Rosalyn Bryant of the USA took

Mark Shearman

John Walker

A man with an exceptional track running record, nobody has run more miles under four minutes than John Walker. Born in Papukura on 12 January 1952, he first hit the international headlines when pressing Filbert Bayi, of Tanzania, to a world record 1,500m of 3-32·2 in the 1974 Commonwealth Games in Christchurch.

The following year he himself joined the world record-breakers with a mile run of 3-49·4 in Gothenburg — the first time any athlete had broken the 3-50·0 barrier.

Maintaining his superb tactical form Walker went to the 1976 Olympics in Montreal fitter than he had ever been, and reaped the reward by becoming the 1,500m champion with a run of 3-39·17. The same season saw him crack the world mark for 2,000m with 4-51·4.

A nagging Achilles tendon strain troubled him for a lengthy spell, but he recovered well, and in the late 1980s could still be seen competing on indoor and outdoor tracks around the world for the sheer pleasure of it. Though past his best he could still dip inside four minutes for the mile.

the second in 50·62 from the co-favourite Brehmer. In the final Brehmer and Bryant tore into the lead, but Szewinska caught up, with her long strides eating up the ground, to win in 49·28, for a brilliant world record. Meanwhile, Brehmer and Bryant were paying the price of their fast start, as Ellen Streidt of East Germany and Pirjo Haggman of Finland were catching up fast. Brehmer just took the silver in 50·51 from Streidt third in 50·55, a mere fraction up on Haggman.

The **800 metres** semi-finals were very fast, the first being won by East Germany's Anita Weiss in 1-56·53, leading all the way to smash the previous Olympic record, with Tatyana Kazankina of the USSR second in 1-57·49. Svetlana Styrkina of the USSR won the second race in a fast 1-57·28, beating Nikolina Shtereva of Bulgaria in 1-57·35. The final was awaited with anticipation and at the gun Weiss shot straight into the lead, but Styrkina overtook her before the bell in 55·1 and at 600 had stretched the field with her fast pace. But around the final bend it was Weiss who led followed by Shtereva, Elfi Zinn of East Germany and Kazarkina. The Russian girl then kicked hard in the straight to go on and win in the amazing new world record time of 1-54·94 from Shtereva, second in 1-55·42 and Zinn, third with

1-55·60.

Tatyana Kazankina of the USSR, the winner of the 800 metres, was really a **1,500 metres** runner, and held the world record at 3-56·0. The first semi-final was a good race, won by Ulrike Klapezynski of East Germany in 4-02·13 with the fifth finisher only half a second behind and two further deserving girls shut out from the final. The final started off at a crawl with the Finn Nina Holmen leading through 900 metres. Italy's Gabriella Dorio took it up for another 200, at which point the defending champion, Lyudmila Bragina of the USSR, made a long run for home. Then, with 250 metres left, the East Germans Gunhild Hoffmeister and Klapezynski shot to the front. But off the final bend Kazankina swept by them to win in 4-05·48, with Hoffmeister second in 4-06·02 and Klapezynski third in 4-06·09.

While Annelie Ehrhardt, the defending champion in the **100 metres hurdles**, was suffering with a back injury, Johanna Schaller, her East German compatriot, was the sharpest in the semi-finals, winning in 12·93 sec. The USSR's Tatyana Anisimova actually took the second in 12·91, but a protest was made as her countrywoman Lyubov Kononova had tripped over a hurdle and fallen into the path of Rumania's Valeria Stefanescu. The jury

Mark Shearman

Don Quarrie

Don Quarrie was born in Kingston, Jamaica, on 25 February 1951, and his track career spanned two decades, during which time he had his full share of misfortune.

Selected as a 17-year-old for the Mexico City Olympics in 1968 he was injured while training there and forced to miss his sprinting events. Fully recovered by 1970, he won both the 100m and 200m at the Commonwealth Games in Edinburgh. The following season he joined the world record-holders when tieing Tommie Smith's 200m best time of 19·8 sec but injury was to thwart his Olympic chances again the following year in Munich. By 1975 he was racing at top speed again, repeating his 19·8 sec for the 200m, twice in the space of a fortnight.

But the run that gave him his biggest lift as he prepared for the Montreal Olympics in 1976, was to join the world record-holders for the 100m as well, by sprinting the distance in 9·9 sec at Modesto. This set him up for the approaching Games where he became the first Jamaican to win the 200m final (20·23 sec). He also collected the silver behind Hasely Crawford, of Trinidad in the 100m.

Quarrie was in lively action, four years later, in Moscow, this time taking the bronze in the 200m behind Pietro Mennea, of Italy, and Britain's Allan Wells.

The last of the great woman straddle jumpers, Rosemary Ackermann, of East Germany, wraps herself around the bar for victory.

Mark Shearman

ruled that the race be re-run without Kononova, and Anisimova won, this time in 13·08. The final saw Grazyna Rabsztyn of Poland with East Germany's Schaller and Gunrun Berend away fastest with Anisimova a shade behind, alongside another Russian, Natalya Lebedeva. Rabsztyn hit the ninth hurdle, and at the tenth Anisimova and Schaller were neck and neck. However, Schaller had the stronger finish and won in 12·77 from Anisimova in 12·78, with Lebedeva third in 12·80.

In the **4 × 100 metres relay**, West Germany won the first semi-final in a fast 42·61 sec from the USSR in 43·33 and in the other, East Germany clocked 43·00 to the USA's 43·46. The final was a contest between the slightly better passing of West Germany and the greater speed of East Germany. Marlies Oelsner gave the East Germans a slight lead over West Germany's Elvira Possekel, which was lost at the exchange. On the next leg Renate Stecher for East and Inge Helten for West were equal, but Annegret Richter gave her team a metre lead over the East's Carla Bodendorf. Barbel Eckert then sped home to win for East Germany in 42·55, an Olympic record, with Annegret Kroniger finishing second for West Germany in 42·59. The USSR was third with 43·09.

The **4 × 400 metres relay** world record came under severe pressure in the heats when East Germany recorded 3-23·28. The final saw East Germany's Doris Maletzki run 50·5 on the first leg to stack up a good lead, while Brigitte Rohde on the second and Ellen Streidt on the third each ran a blistering 49·5. The anchor girl, Christina Brehmer, then completed her leg in 49·7 to shatter the world record with 3-19·23 and win the gold medals. In second place came the USA with the help of a 49·5 run by Rosalyn Brant for an elapsed time of 3-22·81 and the USSR was third in 3-24·24.

East Germany's Rosemarie Ackermann had just set a new world best for the **high jump** of 1·96 metres and was the firm favourite. Twenty-one women surmounted the qualifying height of 1,80 and after three hours of jumping there were still 11 attempting 1,89. At 1,91, Maria Mracnova of Czechoslovakia and Joni Huntley of America failed and were placed fourth and fifth

respectively. The bar then went up to the Olympic record height of 1,93 and Ackermann rotated around the bar at her second attempt with her straddle technique to win the gold medal, while Sara Simeoni of Italy received the silver under the count-back rule and Yordanka Blagoeva of Bulgaria got the bronze. Ackermann failed at a world record attempt of 1,97.

Two East Germans, Sigun Siegl and Angela Voigt, were vying for **long jump** honours. The first round saw Voigt leap 6,72 metres, which was eventually good enough to take the gold medal, while Siegl and Ildiko Szabo of Hungary jumped 6,51. Although they both improved to 6,59 and 6,57 respectively, Lidiya Alfeyeva of the USSR sailed out to 6,60 in the fourth round for the bronze, while in the fifth, the USA's Kathy McMillan exploded to 6,66 for the silver.

Eastern Europe continued their stranglehold of the **shot put** with world record holder Ivanka Christova of Bulgaria expected to take home gold. The competition was a straight final with only 13 competitors throwing. The leader in the first round was Nadyezhda Chizhova of the USSR with 20,84 from East Germany's Marianne Adam on 20,55 and Ilona Schoknect on 20,52. In the next round Chizhova moved on to 20,96 and Christova reached 20,88, which she further improved in the fifth round when she blasted one out to 21,16 for the Olympic record and gold medal. Chizhova's 20,96 was good for the silver position, while Czechoslovakia's Helena Fibingerova was ensured the bronze medal with 20,67.

Russia's Faina Melnik was history's first 70-metre girl in the **discus throw**ing event and had high hopes for a gold medal. In the first round of the finals, Gabrielle Hinzmann of East Germany threw 66,84, for an Olympic record, but it was short-lived as her compatriot Evelyn Schlaak soared her disc to 69,00, to set a new mark and win the gold medal. Unfortunately for her, Melnik could achieve only 65,42 and did not get among the remaining medals. Maria Vergova of Bulgaria who spun a 67,30 effort, collected the silver medal while Hinzmann's first round throw was good enough for the bronze.

Prior to the Games, **javelin throw**ers, Ruth Fuchs of East Germany, the defending champion, had been in excellent form and had thrown a new world best of 69,12 metres. However, in the preliminaries, Marion Becker of West Germany surprised with an Olympic record of 65,14, but Fuchs in the first round of the finals exceeded this with 65,94, the winning throw of the competition. Becker progressed to 64,70 in the third round for the silver award, and Sabine Sebrowski of East Germany who hurled 63,08, held the bronze medal position until the USA's Kate Schmidt notched up 63,96.

The **pentathlon** turned out to be a very close contest indeed. Nadeshda Tkachenko of Russia led the first day after three events with a total of 3,788 points, following a 13·40 sec hurdles, 14,90 metres shot and 1,80 metres high jump, whilst compatriot Ludmilla Popovskaya lay second with 3,772 and Burglinde Pollak of East Germany, the world record holder, third with 3,768. On the second day, the East Germans came up with good long jumps and fast 200 metres. Siegrun Siegl jumped 6,49 and sprinted 23·08 and moved from seventh on day one to first with 4,745 points. Then Christine Laser did 6,27 and 23.48 and moved from fifth to second, also with 4,754 points. Third place went to Pollak with 4,740 points. Siegl won the gold through having beaten Laser by three events to two. Had Pollak run the 200 metres six-hundredths of a second faster, she would have won gold, not bronze.

A rare defeat for the Americans in the high hurdles came when Guy Drut, the Frenchman, was followed home by Alejandro Casanas of Cuba.
Mark Shearman

COMPETITOR	COUNTRY CODE	EVENT	ROUND	HEAT	PLACE	TIME & DISTANCE	MEDAL
MALES							
Abada, P.	FRA	Pole vault	F		4	5,45	
Abdulkareem, A.	KUW	200m	1	3	4	22·44	
			2	3	8	22·34	
		4×100m relay	1	2	6	41·61	
Abehi, J.	CIV	Javelin throw	Q		DNQ	73·40	
Abhunza, C.	NCA	High jump	Q		DNQ	0	
Abrahams, G.A.	PAN	100m	1	4	2	10·40	
			2	2	1	10·35	
			SF	1	4	10·37	
			F		5	10·25	
		200m	1	4	1	20·95	
			2	1	2	20·72	
			SF	2	5	21·15	
Accambray, J.	FRA	Hammer throw	F		9	70,54	
Adams, B.	GBR	20k walk	F		11	1:30-46·2	
Adams F.	TRI	4×100m relay	1	3	2	40·08	
			SF	1	6	39·88	
Ahmad, R.	MAL	100m	1	8	6	10·93	
		200m	1	5	5	21·92	
Aksinin, A.	URS	100m	1	5	3	10·60	
			2	1	4	10·55	
			SF	2	7	10·50	
		4×100m relay	1	2	3	39·63	
			SF	2	3	39·36	
			F		3	38·78	B
Aktas, H.	TUR	Marathon	F		37	2 24-30·0	
Al-Abbasi, K.	ARS	400m hurdles	1	4	5	55·00	
		4×400m relay	1	1	7	3-17·53	
Alawad, A.	KUW	100m	1	3	6	11·27	
		4×100m relay	1	2	6	41·61	
Al-Bishy, S.	ARS	Shot put	Q		DNQ	11,58	
Al-Zabramauji, M.	ARS	Discus throw	Q		DNQ	35,94	
Alebic, J.	YUG	400m	1	5	3	47·03	
			2	4	5	46·94	
Aletti, J.	FRA	High jump	Q		DNQ	2,05	
Alfaro E.	COL	20k walk	F		19	1:53-13·3	
Alfonso, D.	CUB	400m hurdles	1	1	2	50·76	
			SF	2	3	49·84	
			F		7	50·19	
		4×400m relay	1	2	3	3-05·19	
			F		7	3-03·81	
Ali, H.	ARS	200m	1	1	5	23·37	
		4×100m relay	1	2	7	42·00	
		4×400m relay	1	1	7	3-17·53	
Al Malky, A.	ARS	4×100m relay	1	2	7	42·00	
Almen, R.	SWE	High jump	F		10	2·18	
Almstrom, H.	SWE	Shot put	Q		DNQ	18,76	
Alrabee'Ah, I.	KUW	4×100m relay	1	2	6	41·61	
Al Shaibani, A.	ARS	1500m	1	3	8	4-03·70	
Al Shalawi, R.	ARS	10000m	1	2	DNF		
Alvarez, C.	CUB	4×400m relay	1	2	3	3-05·19	
			F		7	3-03·81	
Alzinkawi, M.	KUW	Shot put	Q		DNC	13,17	
Amoureux, J.C.	FRA	100m	1	3	5	10·75	
		4×100m relay	1	3	2	39·71	
			SF	2	2	39·33	
			F		7	39·16	
Angus, K.	GBR	Marathon	F		31	2:22-18·6	
Anohin, T.	URS	800m	1	1	6	1-46·81	
			SF	2	7	1-47·71	
		4×400m relay	1	2	6	3-07·72	
Arame, J.	FRA	200m	1	5	3	21·34	
			2	3	3	21·04	
			SF	2	6	21·29	
		4×100m relay	1	3	2	39·71	
			SF	2	2	39·33	
			F		7	39·16	
Armstrong, A.	TRI	100m	1	2	3	10·59	
			2	4	4	10·46	
			SF	1	6	10·52	
		200m	1	2	DNF		
Asgeirsson, A.	ISL	1500m	1	3	7	3-45·47	
		3000m steeplechase	1	1	11	8-53·95	
Asiry, A.	ARS	400m	1	2	8	49·72	
		4×400m relay	1	1	7	3-17·53	
Avilov, N.	URS	Decathlon	F		3	8369	3
Ba, I.	SEN	Long jump	Q		DNQ	6,96	
Backman, R.	SWE	Decathlon	F		20	7319	
Baird, D.	AUS	Pole vault	F		12	5,25	
Ballbe, A.	ESP	800m	1	2	4	1-48·38	
Balli, V.	TUR	Marathon	F		38	2:24-47·0	
Banos, A.	ESP	Marathon	F		51	2:31-01·6	
Barch, O.	URS	20k walk	F		13	1:31-12·4	
Barrineau. J.	URA	High jump	F		11	2,14	
Baryshnikov, A.	URS	Shot put	F		3	21,00	B
Barrineau, J.	USA	High jump	F		11	2·14	
Bastians, W.	GEF	100m	1	2	7	11·17	
Baumgartl, F.	GDF	3000m steeplechase	1	1	2	8-21·25	
			F		3	8-10·36	B
Baumgartner, H.	GER	Long jump	F		8	7,84	
Bautista, D.	MEX	20k walk	F		1	1:24-40·6*	G
Beilschmidt, R.	GDR	High jump	F		7	2,18	
Bell, E.	USA	Pole vault	F		6	5,45	
Bellot, J.M.	FRA	Pole vault	F		7	5,40	
Benedetti, L.	ITA	4×100m relay	1	1	2	39·35	
			SF	2	4	39·39	
			F		6	39·08	
Bengtsson, C.	SWE	Marathon	F		14	2:17-39·6	
Bennett, A.	GBR	200m	1	6	1	21·26	
			2	2	3	21·07	
			SF	2	8	21·52	
		4×400m relay	1	1	DNF		
Bergamo, R.	ITA	High jump	F		6	2,18	
Berger, H.-J.	GER	Long jump	Q		DNQ	7,70	
Bernhard, R.	SUI	Long jump	F		9	7,74	
Beyer, U.	GDR	Shot put	F		1	21,05	G
Bicourt, J.	GBR	3000m steeplechase	1	1	8	8-35·71	
Bielczyk, P.	POL	Javelin throw	F		4	86,50	
Bieler, K.-D.	GER	100m	1	8	2	10·58	
			2	3	7	10·80	
		4×100m relay	1	2	2	39·63	
			SF	2	5	39·58	
Binnington, M.	AUS	110m hurdles	1	2	DNF		
		4×400m relay	1	2	5	3-05·75	
Biskupsi, E.	POL	Triple jump	F		7	16,49	
Bjorklund, G.	USA	10000m	1	3	2	28-12·24	
			F		13	28-38·08	
Black, C.	GBR	Hammer throw	F		7	73,18	
Black, D.	GBR	5000m	1	1	9	13-39·37	
Blancuer, R.	ESP	Long jump	Q		DNQ	6,19	
Bobin, P.	FRA	Decathlon	F		14	7580	
Bocaghi, A.	IRN	100m	1	3	7	11·39	
		200m	1	7	6	22·47	
Bogue, G.	CAN	400m	1	4	5	47·42	
			2	1	8	48·98	
Bohari, M.	ARS	Triple jump	Q		DNQ	13,85	
Boller, W.	GER	High jump	Q		DNQ	2,13	
Bombardella, R.	LUX	100m	1	7	5	10·76	
		200m	1	8	1	21·18	
			2	4	3	21·03	
			SF	1	6	21·16	
Boncarchuk, A.	URS	Hammer throw	F		3	75,48	B
Boontud, S.	THA	4×100m relay	1	2	5	40·53	
			SF	1	8	40·68	
Borchert, R.	GER	4×100m relay	1	2	2	39·63	
			SF	2	5	39·58	
Boro, K.	NOR	10000m	1	2	3	28-23·07	
			F		DNF		
Boros, S.	HUN	Javelin throw	Q		DNQ	77,60	
Borzov, V.	URS	100m	1	6	2	10·53	
			2	3	2	10·39	
			SF	1	2	10·30	
			F		3	10·14	B
		4×100m relay	1	2	3	39·68	
			SF	2	3	39·36	
			F		3	38·78	B
Botse, R.	SUR	800m	1	3	7	1-49·85	
Boxberger, J.	FRA	5000m	1	3	10	13-36·94	
Boyd, R.	AUS	Pole vault	Q		DNQ	5,00	
Brabec, J.	TCH	Shot put	F		11	19,62	
Bradford, C.	JAM	100m	1	5	4	10·64	
			2	2	7	10·62	
		200m	1	1	3	21·57	
			2	1	3	21·03	
			SF	1	4	21·09	
			F		7	21·17	
		4×400m relay	1	1	3	3-03·86	
			F		5	3-02·84	
Bratanov, Y.	BUL	400m hurdles	1	3	4	51·84	
			SF	1	3	50·11	
			F		6	50·03	
Brathwaite, C.	TRI	100m	1	9	4	10·71	
		4×100m relay	1	3	4	40·08	
			SF	1	6	39·88	
Brijdenbach, A.	BEL	400m	1	4	1	46·73	
			2	1	2	46·56	
			SF	1	2	45·28	
			F		4	45·04	
Bristol, A.	PUR	110m hurdles	1	2	4	14·04	
			SF	2	6	13·98	
Brokken, B.	BEL	High jump	Q		DNQ	0	
Brou, K.	CIV	Long jump	Q		DNQ	7,20	
Brouzet, Y.	FRA	Shot put	Q		DNQ	19,14	

COMPETITOR	COUNTRY CODE	EVENT	ROUND	HEAT	PLACE	TIME & DISTANCE	MEDAL
Brown, B.	USA	4×400m relay	1	1	1	2-59·52	
			F		1	2-58·65	G
Brown, D.	USA	3000m steeplechase	1	2	8	8-33·25	
Bruch, R.	SWE	Discus throw	Q		DNQ	58,06	
Buccione, R.	ITA	20k walk	F		10	1:30-40·0	
Buchanan, J.	CAN	Long jump	Q		DNQ	7,49	
Buciarski, W.	POL	Pole vault	F		5	5,45	
Budalov, S.	URS	High jump	F		4	2,21	
Buerkle, R.	USA	5000m	1	3	9	13-29·01	
Buttari, G.	ITA	110m hurdles	1	3	3	13·88	
			SF	2	7	14·06	
Butts, J.	USA	Triple jump	F		2	17,18	S
Callendar, W.	BAH	200m	1	7	4	21·79	
			2	4	6	21·78	
		4×100m relay	1	3	5	40·47	
			SF	2	7	40·53	
Campos, A.	ESP	3000m steeplechase	1	1	4	8-24·53	
			F		8	8-22·65	
Candelo, J.	COL	400m hurdles	1	4	DNF		
Capes, G.	GBR	Shot put	F		6	20,36	
Caravani, L.	ITA	100m	1	1	3	10·66	
			2	1	7	10·81	
		4×100m relay	1	1	2	39·35	
			SF	2	4	39·39	
			F		6	39·08	
Cardozo, E.	PAR	Marathon	F		43	2:27-22·8	
Carrasco, J.	ESP	High jump	Q		DNQ	2,05	
Cartas, J.	MEX	110m hurdles	1	2	7	14·56	
Carvalho, J.	POR	400m	1	6	7	48·47	
		400m hurdles	1	1	4	50·99	
			SF	1	2	49·97	
			F		5	49·94	
Casanas, A.	CUB	110m hurdles	1	2	2	13·73	
			SF	2	1	13·34	
			F		2	13·33	S
		4×100m relay	1	3	1	39·54	
			SF	1	2	39·25	
			F		5	39·01	
Cefan, G.	RUM	3000m steeplechase	1	2	12	8-57·22	
Centrowitz, M.	USA	1500m	1	1	6	3-45·02	
Cerrada, F.	ESP	5000m	1	1	12	13-43·89	
Chambul, B.	CAN	Discus throw	Q		DNQ	55,86	
Charles, O.	HAI	10000m	1	1	13	42-00·11	
Chauvelot, D.	FRA	100m	1	2	5	10·79	
		4×100m relay	1	3	2	39·71	
			SF	2	2	39·33	
			F		7	39·16	
Cheater, M.	NZL	Hammer throw	Q		DNQ	67,38	
Chedid, I.	BRA	High jump	Q		DNQ	0	
Chettle, D.	AUS	Marathon	F		DNF		
Choe, C.S.	PRK	Marathon	F		12	2:16-33·2	
Chong, K.B.	MAL	20k walk	F		32	1:40-16·8	
Cid, R.	ESP	Triple jump	Q		DNQ	16,00	
Cierpinski, W.	GDR	Marathon	F		1	2:09-55·0*	G
Cindolo, G.	ITA	Marathon	F		DNF		
Civil, L.	CUB	800m	1	1	3	1-45·88	
			SF	2	6	1-47·31	
Clarke, R.	BAR	200m	1	3	5	22·75	
		4×100m relay	1	3	6	41·15	
Clement, F.	GBR	800m	1	2	1	1-47·51	
			SF	1	8	1-48·28	
		1500m	1	3	2	3-37·53	
			SF	2	4	3-38·92	
			F		5	3-39·65	
Coates, D.	GBR	3000m steeplechase	1	2	1	8-18·95	
			F		9	8-22·99	
Coghlan, E.	IRL	1500m	1	5	1	3-39·87	
			SF	2	1	3-38·60	
			F		4	3-39·51	
Cohen, G.	GBR	400m	1	6	2	47·77	
			2	3	7	47·67	
		4×400m relay	1	1	DNF		
Colin, D.	MEX	20k walk	F		DIS		
Colon, A.	PUR	1500m	1	4	5	3-43·51	
Colson, S.	USA	Javelin throw	F		5	86,16	
Commons, C.	AUS	Long jump	Q		DNQ	7,46	
Conrath, J.-M.	FRA	5000m	1	1	5	13-34·39	
Coombs, J.	TRI	4×400m relay	1	2	2	3-03·54	
			F		6	3-03·46	
Corbu, C.	RUM	Triple jump	F		8	16,43	
Cornelius, E.	ANT	4×100m relay	1	1	7	41·84	
Corval, J.-P.	FRA	110m hurdles	1	1	4	14·00	
			SF	1	7	13·97	
Craig, P.	CAN	1500m	1	3	4	3-38·00	
			SF	2	7	3-41·02	

COMPETITOR	COUNTRY CODE	EVENT	ROUND	HEAT	PLACE	TIME & DISTANCE	MEDAL
Crawford, H.	TRI	100m	1	1	1	10·42	
			2	3	1	10·29	
			SF	2	1	10·22	
			F		1	10·06	G
		200m	1	2	3	22·35	
			2	4	1	20·95	
			SF	1	3	20·99	
			F		8	1-19·6	
Crouch, G.	AUS	1500m	1	3	3	3-37·97	
			SF	1	2	3-39·86	
			F		8	3-41·80	
Cubillo, J.	COL	Marathon	F		48	2:29-44·4	
Cuevas, M.	MEX	Marathon	F		18	2:18-08·8	
Cusack, N.	IRL	Marathon	F		55	2:35-47·2	
Cybulski, G.	POL	Long jump	Q		DNQ	7,71	
Cyriaque, W.	HAI	400m	1	1	8	51·49	
Daley, A.	JAM	400m	1	6	4	48·04	
			2	1	7	48·46	
Danek, L.	TCH	Discus throw	F		9	61·28	
Da Silva, D.	BRA	400m	1	3	2	47·21	
			2	4	4	46·48	
			SF	1	8	46·69	
Da Silva, R.	BRA	100m	1	3	3	10·61	
			2	3	4	10·57	
			SF	1	7	10·54	
		200m	1	7	2	20·99	
			2	1	3	20·76	
			SF	2	3	21·01	
			F		5	20·84	
Davenport, W.	USA	110m hurdles	1	2	1	13·70	
			SF	2	3	13·55	
			F		3	13·38	B
De Jesus, H.	POR	1500m	1	1	2	3-44·20	
			SF	2	9	3-47·37	
De Jesus, J.	PUR	Marathon	F		23	2:19-34·8	
Dejonckheere, G.	BEL	20k walk	F		25	1:35-03·8	
De Oliveira, J.C.	BRA	Long jump	F		5	8,00	
		Triple jump	F		3	16,90	B
De Roche, P.	FRA	Long jump	Q		DNQ	7,38	
Desruelles, R.	BEL	Long jump	Q		DNQ	7,60	
De Vincentiis, A.	ITA	Discus throw	F		15	55,86	
Dezart, T.	HAI	Marathon	F		DNF		
Dickenson, P.	GBR	Hammer throw	Q		DNQ	68,52	
Dieye, C.	SEN	400m	1	5	6	47·98	
Diguida, A.	ITA	400m	1	2	4	46·52	
			2	1	4	47·07	
			SF	1	7	46·50	
Dill, C.	BER	200m	1	2	4	22·38	
			2	2	6	21·40	
		4×100m relay	1	1	4	39·90	
			SF	1	5	39·78	
Dixon, F.	USA	Decathlon	F		23	6754	
Dixon, R.	NZL	5000m	1	3	2	13-20·48	
			F		4	13-25·50	
Djonev, V.	BUL	Javelin throw	F		14	73,88	
Dolegiewicz, B.	CAN	Discus throw	Q		DNQ	0	
Domansky, D.	CAN	400m	1	2	6	47·24	
			2	3	DNS		
		4×400m relay	1	1	4	3-03·89	
			F		4	3-02·64	
Dorosario, C.	SEN	200m	1	4	6	21·96	
		4×100m relay	1	2	4	40·40	
			SF	2	6	40·37	
Drayton, J.	CAN	Marathon	F		6	2:13-30·0	
Drut, G.	FRA	110m hurdles	1	2	3	14·04	
			SF	2	2	13·49	
			F		1	13·30	G
Duda, B.	POL	20k walk	F		21	1:33-53·4	
Dukowski, A.	CAN	4×100m relay	1	3	3	39·72	
			SF	1	4	39·46	
			F		8	39·47	
Dupree, R.	USA	Triple jump	F		12	16,23	
Durkin, M.	USA	1500m	1	2	5	3-38·89	
Echevin, G.	GER	100m	1	8	1	10·53	
			2	1	8	12·00	
Egger, J.-P.	SUI	Shot put	Q		DNQ	18,13	
Ehl, K.	GER	4×100m relay	1	2	3	39·63	
			SF	1	5	39·58	
El-Khashaami, A.	ARS	800m	1	5	7	1-57·67	
Enyeart, M.	USA	800m	1	6	3	1-47·96	
Etienne, P.	HAI	100m	1	6	7	11·05	
		200m	1	6	5	22·57	
Evans, D.	USA	200m	1	3	1	20·96	
			2	1	1	20·56	
			SF	1	2	20·83	

COMPETITOR	COUNTRY CODE	EVENT	ROUND	HEAT	PLACE	TIME & DISTANCE	MEDAL
Faber, L.	LUX	20k walk	F		28	1:36-21·0	
Faddoul, G.	LIB	Long jump	Q		DNQ	0	
		Javelin throw	Q		DNQ	54.92	
Falkum, L.R.	NOR	High jump	F		14	2,10	
Fall, A.	SEN	100m	1	7	3	10·72	
			2	3	5	10·60	
		4×100m relay	1	2	4	40·40	
			SF	2	6	40·37	
Faraj, S.	KUW	110m hurdles	1	3	8	15·57	
Farago, J.	HUN	Discus throw	F		14	57,48	
Farina, P.	ITA	200m	1	4	3	21·32	
			2	1	7	21·31	
Farmer, P.	AUS	Hammer throw	F		12	68,00	
Farrelly, P.	CAN	20k walk	F		33	1:41-35·2	
Fava, F.	ITA	10000m	1	2	5	28-24·30	
		Marathon	F		8	2:14-24·6	
Fernandez, A.	ESP	Marathon	F		46	2:28-37·8	
Ferragne, C.	CAN	High jump	F		12	2,14	
Ferrer, J.	PUR	400m hurdles	1	4	4	52·45	
			SF	2	8	51·04	
		4×400m relay	1	1	6	3-06·03	
Ferrer, P.	PUR	100m	1	5	5	10·76	
		200m	1	6	3	21·50	
			2	4	5	21·33	
		4×400m relay	1	1	6	3-06·08	
Feuerbach, A.	USA	Shot put	F		4	20,55	
Fitzgerald, P.	AUS	100m	1	4	6	10·87	
		200m	1	3	2	21·35	
			2	4	4	21·07	
			SF	1	8	21·29	
Fitzsimons, D.	AUS	10000m	1	1	5	28-16·43	
			F		14	29-17·74	
Fleschen, K.	GER	1500m	1	5	4	3-42·09	
Floroiu, I.	RUM	5000m	1	1	7	13-37·09	
		10000m	1	2	4	28-23·40	
			F		5	27-59·93	
Flynn, O.	GBR	20k walk	F		14	1:31-42·4	
Fonseca, S.	HON	20k walk	F		27	1:36-07·0	
Ford, B.	GBR	10000m	1	1	6	28-17·26	
			F		8	28-7·78	
Forget, R.	CAN	High jump	Q		DNQ	2,05	
Fortini, R.	ITA	High jump	Q		DNQ	2,05	
Foster, B.	GER	5000m	1	3	1	13-20·34*	
			F		5	13-26·19	
		10000m	1	2	2	28-22·19	
			F		3	27-54·92	B
Foster, C.	USA	110m hurdles	1	1	1	13·68	
			SF	1	1	13·45	
			F		4	13·41	
Foster, J.	NZL	Marathon	F		17	2:17-53·4	
Fraehmke, G.	GER	3000m steeplechase	1	1	DNF		
Fraser, H.	CAN	200m	1	8	4	21·54	
			2	1	8	21·57	
		4×100m relay	1	3	3	39·72	
			SF	1	4	39·46	
			F		8	39·47	
Frazier, H.	USA	400m	1	1	1	46·09	
			2	1	1	46·52	
			SF	2	3	45·24	
			F		3	44·95	B
		4×400m relay	1	1	1	2-59·52	
			F		1	2-58·65	G
Frenkel, P.	GDR	20k walk	F		3	1:25-29·4	B
Fukura, K.	JPN	High jump	Q		DNQ	2,13	
Galusic, V.	YUG	20k walk	F		24	1:34-46·8	
Garcia, F.	ESP	4×100m relay	1	1	5	39·93	
			SF	2	DIS		
Garderud, A.	SWE	3000m steeplechase	1	1	3	8-21·43	
			F		1	8-08·02*	G
Garpenborg, C.	SWE	100m	1	3	4	10·64	
			2	2	8	10·63	
Gavrilenko, E.	URS	400m hurdles	1	3	2	50·93	
			SF	2	2	49·73	
			F		3	49·45	B
		4×400m relay	1	2	6	3-07·72	
Geis, P.	USA	5000m	1	1	2	13-32·36	
			F		12	13-42·51	
Gemise-Fareau, G.	FRA	Decathlon	F		17	7486	
George, R.	USA	Javelin throw	C		DNQ	78,32	
Gesicki, M.	POL	800m	1	1	4	1-46·36	
			SF	1	6	1-47·06	
Ghesquiere, R.	BEL	Decathlon	F		DNF		
Ghiassi, T.	IRN	High jump	Q		DNQ	2.10	
Ghipu, G.	RUM	1500m	1	2	6	3-39·20	
Gies, H.-P.	GDR	Shot put	F		5	20,47	
Glance, H.	USA	100m	1	5	1	10·37	
			2	4	1	10·23	
			SF	1	1	10·24	
			F		4	10·19	
		4×100m relay	1	1	1	38·76	
			SF	1	1	38·51	
			F		1	38·33	G
Glans, D.	SWE	3000m steeplechase	1	2	3	8-23·73	
			F		7	8-21·53	
Godwin, G.	BER	High jump	Q		DNQ	2,05	
Goh, C.S.	PRK	Marathon	F		52	2:31-54·8	
Golubnichy, V.	URS	20k walk	F		7	1:29-24·6	
Gomez, E.	NCA	800m	1	3	8	1-57·97	
Gomez, F.	CUB	100m	1	6	4	10·68	
			2	4	5	10·49	
		4×100m relay	1	1	1	39·54	
			SF	1	2	39·25	
			F		5	39·01	
Gomez, J.-P.	FRA	10000m	1	1	2	28-10·52	
			F		9	28-24·07	
Gomez, R.	MEX	5000m	1	2	5	13-46·23	
		10000m	1	2	11	30-05·19	
		Marathon	F		19	2:18-21·2	
Gonzalez, F.	FRA	1500m	1	3	5	3-38·59	
			SF	2	6	3-40·73	
Gonzalez, R.	MEX	20k walk	F		5	1:28-18·2	
Gooding, V.	BAR	4×400m relay	1	2	7	3-08·13	
Gotsky, A.	URS	Marathon	F		9	2:15-34·0	
Grant, P.	AUS	400m	1	1	4	47·03	
			2	1	6	47·69	
		400m hurdles	1	2	5	51·07	
		4×400m relay	1	2	5	3-05·75	
Grebeniuk, A.	URS	Decathlon	F		9	7803	
Greenaway, C.	ANT	Long jump	Q		DNQ	6,96	
		4×100m relay	1	1	7	41,84	
Greene, O.	BAR	800m	1	5	6	1-51.43	
		4×400m relay	1	2	7	3-08·13	
Grimes, H.	BAR	400m	1	1	7	49·24	
		4×100m relay	1	3	6	41·15	
		4×400m relay	1	2	7	3-08·13	
Grimes, B.	NOR	Javelin throw	F		13	74,88	
Grippo, C.	ITA	800m	1	4	2	1-47·21	
			SF	2	2	1-46·95	
			F		8	1-48·39	
Gros, J.	POL	Marathon	F		47	2:28-45·8	
Grzejsczazak, B.	POL	200m	1	6	2	21·35	
			2	4	2	21·02	
			SF	2	4	21·14	
			F		6	20·91	
		4×100m relay	1	1	3	39·41	
			SF	2	1	39·09	
			F		4	38·83	
Guachalla, L.	BUL	Marathon	F		60	2:45-31·8	
Guerini, V.	ITA	4×100m relay	1	1	2	39·35	
			SF	2	4	39·39	
			F		6	39·08	
Gueye, I.	SEN	Discus throw	Q		DNQ	52,82	
Gutierrez, E.	CUB	400m	1	3	5	47·89	
			2	3	6	46·65	
		4×400m relay	1	2	3	3-05·19	
			F		7	3-03·81	
Gutteridge, J.	GBR	Pole vault	Q		DNQ	4,80	
Gysin, R.	SUI	800m	1	6	4	1-48·69	
		1500m	1	5	5	3-42·69	
Haapakoski, T.	FIN	Pole vault	F		15	5,20	
Hall, A.	USA	Javelin throw	F		15	71,70	
Halldorsson, H.	ISL	Shot put	Q		DNQ	18,93	
Hampton, M.	USA	200m	1	1	1	21·11	
			2	3	2	20·83	
			SF	1	2	20·69	
			F		2	20·29	S
		4×100m relay	1	1	1	38·76	
			SF	1	1	38·51	
			F		1	38·33	G
Hanly, D.	AUS	400m hurdles	1	1	5	51·90	
		4×400m relay	1	2	5	3-05·75	
Harichand, H.	IND	10000m	1	2	8	28-48·72	
Haro, M.	ESP	10000m	1	1	3	28-11·66	
			F		6	28-00·28	
Hart, L.	USA	Hammer throw	Q		DNQ	67,74	
Hashem, A.A.	KUW	4×100m relay	1	2	6	41·61	
		400m hurdles	1	3	5	53·06	
Hasler, G.	LIE	800m	1	3	5	1-48·83	
		1500m	1	2	7	3-39·34	
Hatzistathis, P.	GRE	Long jump	Q		DNQ	7,33	
Haynes, T.	USA	Triple Jump	F		5	16,78	

COMPETITOR	COUNTRY CODE	EVENT	ROUND	HEAT	PLACE	TIME & DISTANCE	MEDAL
Haywood, R.	AUS	20k walk	F		12	1:30-59·2	
		Marathon	F		DNF		
Hedmark, L.	SWE	Decathlon	F		8	7974	
Heerenveen, R.	AHO	400m	1	4	6	47·44	
			2	4	8	48·88	
Hegedis, J.	ESP	Triple Jump	Q		DNQ	16,03	
Hermens, J.	HOL	10000m	1	1	4	28-16·07	
			F		10	28-25·04	
		Marathon	F		25	2:19-48·2	
Hernandez, L.	MEX	5000m	1	1	6	13-36·42	
		10000m	1	3	8	28-44·17	
Herrera, A.	CUB	Triple jump	Q		DNQ	15,98	
Herrman, B.	GER	400m	1	5	2	46·99	
			2	3	4	46·07	
			SF	1	5	45·94	
		4×400m relay	1	1	2	3-03·24	
			F		3	3-01·98	B
Hessam, S.	IRN	Discus throw	Q		DNQ	52,40	
Hewelt, J.	POL	400m hurdles	1	3	3	51·39	
			SF	2	7	50·57	
Hildenbrand, K.-P.	GER	5000m	1	2	3	13-45·85	
			F		3	13-25·38	B
Hill, D.	CAN	1500m	1	5	3	3-41·24	
			SF	1	DNF		
Hjeltnes, K.	NOR	Discus throw	F		7	63,06	
Hofmeister, F.-P.	GER	400m	1	4	3	47·17	
			2	4	3	46·20	
			SF	2	6	46·05	
		4×400m relay	1	1	2	3-03·24	
			F		3	3-01·98	B
Hogberg, U.	SWE	1500m	1	4	6	3-47·96	
Hoglund, H.	SWE	Shot put	F		8	20,17	
Honz, K.	GER	400m	1	3	4	47·47	
			2	1	3	46·94	
			SF	2	8	46·63	
Hooper, B.	GBR	Pole vault	F		16	5,00	
Hope, L.	CAN	4×400m relay	1	1	4	3-03·89	
			F		4	3-02·64	
Hovinen, S.	FIN	Javelin throw	F		7	84,26	
Hoving, E.	HOL	800m	1	3	6	1-48·99	
		1500m	1	1	5	3-45·00	
Howard, T.	CAN	Marathon	F		30	2:22-08·8	
Husbands, A.	TRI	4×100m relay	1	3	4	40·08	
			SF	1	6	39·88	
Idava, V.	PHI	Marathon	F		57	2:38-23·2	
Ierissiotis, K.	GRE	Hammer throw	Q		DNQ	65,50	
Inoue, T..	JPN	Triple jump	Q		DNQ	16,06	
Isakov, Y.	URS	Pole vault	Q		DNQ	0	
Isaksson, K.	SWE	Pole vault	F		NP	0	
Ivancic, I.	YUG	Shot put	Q		DNQ	18,88	
Iwama, Y.	JPN	Pole vault	Q		DNQ	0	
Jaakola, J.	FIN	Javelin throw	F		DNS		
Jacobs, C.	ANT	200m	1	1	2	21·50	
			2	3	6	21·33	
		4×400m relay	1	2	8	3-09·66	
Jairsuraparp, S.	THA	100m	1	7	4	10·75	
		4×100m relay	1	2	5	40·53	
			SF	1	8	40·68	
Jakobsson, O.	ISL	Javelin throw	Q		DNQ	72,78	
Janicijevic, D.	YUG	10000m	1	1	9	28-48·87	
Jankunis, W.	USA	High jump	F		13	2,10	
Jaremski, Z.	POL	400m	1	1	3	46·68	
			2	4	6	47·10	
		4×400m relay	1	2	1	3-03·03	
			F		2	3-01·43	S
Jenkins, D.	GBR	400m	1	5	1	46·60	
			2	4	2	46·18	
			SF	2	2	45·20	
			F		7	45·57	
		4×400m relay	1	1	DNF		
Jenner, B.	USA	Decathlon	F		1	8618*	G
Jensen, J.P.	DEN	Marathon	F		28	2:20-44·6	
Jernberg, I.	SWE	Pole vault	Q		DNQ	0	
Jervis, L.	BAH	100m	1	5	7	10·87	
		4×100m relay	1	3	5	40·47	
			SF	2	7	40·53	
Jinno, H.	JPN	100m	1	6	6	10·94	
Joachimowski, M.	POL	Triple jump	Q		DNQ	16,29	
Jobin, M.	CAN	20k walk	F		23	1:34-33·4	
Johansson, T.	SWE	200m	1	4	2	21·05	
			2	2	5	21·08	
John, T.	NGY	10000m	1	3	14	32-26·96	
		Marathon	F		56	2:38-04·6	

COMPETITOR	COUNTRY CODE	EVENT	ROUND	HEAT	PLACE	TIME & DISTANCE	MEDAL
Jones, J.	USA	100m	1	2	1	10·43	
			2	2	2	10·46	
			SF	2	3	10·30	
			F		6	10·27	
		4×100m relay	1	1	1	38·76	
			SF	1	1	38·51	
			F		1	38·33	G
Jordan, P.	BAR	100m	1	9	6	10·95	
		4×100m relay	1	3	6	41·15	
Joseph, C.	TRI	400m	1	5	5	47·72	
			2	2	8	46·61	
		4×100m relay	1	3	4	40·08	
			SF	1	6	39·88	
		4×400m relay	1	2	2	3-03·54	
			F		6	3-03·46	
Joseph, W.	HAI	800m	1	2	7	2-15·26	
Joy, G.	CAN	High jump	F		2	2,23	S
Juantorena, A.	CUB	400m	1	6	3	47·89	
			2	2	2	45·92	
			SF	1	1	45·10	
			F		1	44·26	G
		800m	1	4	1	1-47·15	
			SF	1	1	1-45·88	
			F		1	1-43·50*	G
		4×400m relay	1	2	3	3-05·19	
			F		7	3-03·81	
Kablan, D.	CIV	200m	1	3	2	21·57	
			2	2	2	20·91	
			SF	1	5	21·14	
		4×100m relay	1	1	6	40·23	
			SF	1	7	40·64	
Kahma, P.	FIN	Discus throw	F		6	63,12	
Kali, W.	NGY	200m	1	7	7	22·64	
		400m	1	4	7	48·85	
Kalliomaeki, A.	FIN	Pole vault	F		2	5,50*	S
Kamata, T.	JPN	5000m	1	1	8	13-38·22	
		10000m	1	3	7	28-36·21	
Kannenberg, B.	GER	20k walk	F		DNF		
Kantanen, T.	FIN	3000m steeplechase	1	2	2	8-20·82	
			F		4	8-12·60	
Kardong, D.	USA	Marathon	F		4	2:11-15·8	
Karst, M.	GER	3000m steeplechase	1	2	4	8-25·02	
			F		5	8-20·14	
Karttunen, O.	FIN	400m	1	4	4	47·22	
			2	1	5	47·45	
		4×400m relay	1	1	5	3-05·02	
			F		8	3-06·51	
Kathiniotis, A.	GRE	Triple jump	Q		DNQ	14,13	
Katus, R.	POL	Decathlon	F		12	7616	
Kaupang, L.M.	NOR	1500m	1	5	7	3-44·59	
Keating, M.	CAN	Hammer throw	Q		DNQ	65,68	
Kelemen, E.	HUN	High jump	Q		DNQ	2,13	
Kerbiriou, F.	FRA	4×400m relay	1	2	4	3-05·48	
Khalifa, S.	ARS	4×100m relay	1	2	7	42·00	
Killing, W.	GER	High jump	Q		DNQ	2,05	
Kim, C.S.	PRK	Marathon	F		44	2:27-38·8	
Kishkun, V.	URS	Pole vault	F		13	5,20	
Klein, E.	GER	Hammer throw	F		8	71,34	
Klein, H.	ISV	20k walk	F		36	1:50-50·4	
Kokinai, J.	NGY	5000m	1	2	11	14-58·33	
		Marathon	F		59	2:41-49·0	
Kokot, M.	GDR	4×100m relay	1	2	1	39·42	
			SF	1	3	39·43	
			F		2	38·66	S
Kolbeck, F.	FRA	Marathon	F		34	2:22-56·8	
Kolesnikov, N.	URS	200m	1	4	4	21·33	
			2	2	4	21·08	
			SF	1	7	21·25	
		4×100m relay	1	2	3	39·68	
			SF	2	3	39·36	
			F		3	38·78	B
Kolmsee, W.	GER	Triple jump	F		6	16,68	
Konan, K.	CIV	4×100m relay	1	1	6	40·23	
			SF	1	7	40·64	
Koshikawa, K.	JPN	High jump	Q		DNQ	2,13	
Kouadio, G.	CIV	4×100m relay	1	1	6	40·23	
			SF	1	7	40·94	
Kousis, M.	GRE	Marathon	F		29	2:21-42·0	
Koyama, T.	JPN	3000m steeplechase	1	2	9	8-37·28	
Kozakiewicz, W.	POL	Pole vault	F		11	5,25	
Kratschmer, G.	GER	Decathlon	F		2	8411	S
Krieg, L.	GER	4×400m relay	1	1	2	3-03·24	
			F		3	3-01·98	B
Kukkoaho, M.	FIN	400m	1	5	4	47·67	
			2	3	5	46·24	
		4×400m relay	1	1	5	3-05·02	
			F		8	3-06·51	

COMPETITOR	COUNTRY CODE	EVENT	ROUND	HEAT	PLACE	TIME & DISTANCE	MEDAL
Kulebyakin, V.	URS	110m hurdles	1	1	3	13·99	
			SF	1	4	13·59	
			F		7	13·93	
Kurrat, K.-D.	GDR	100m	1	6	1	10·37	
			2	4	2	10·29	
			SF	1	3	10·30	
			F		7	10·31	
		4×100m relay	1	2	1	39·42	
			SF	1	3	39·43	
			F		2	38·66	S
Kuukasjarvi, P.	FIN	Triple jump	F		10	16,20	
Kuznetsov, B.	URS	5000m	1	1	3	13-32·78	
			F		DNF		
Kvalheim, K.	NOR	5000m	1	3	3	13-20·60	
			F		9	13-30·63	
Kyteas, D.	GRE	Pole vault	Q		DNQ	5,00	
Lahti, J.	FIN	Decathlon	F		11	7711	
Laine, M.	FIN	1500m	1	2	8	3-45·32	
Laird, R.	USA	20k walk	F		20	1:33-27·6	
Lamitie, B.	FRA	Triple jump	F		11	16,23	
Lamothe, D.	HAI	5000m	1	1	13	18-50·07	
Larios, A.	NCA	400m	1	4	3	50·52	
Larkins, P.	AUS	3000m steeplechase	1	1	10	8-46·89	
Lauterbach, H.	GDR	High jump	Q		DNQ	2,13	
Leddy, E.	IRL	5000m	1	1	11	13-40·54	
		10000m	1	2	9	28-55·29	
Lelievre, G.	FRA	20k walk	F		9	1:29-53·6	
Leonard, S.	CUB	100m	1	9	2	10·62	
			2	2	5	10·59	
		4×100m relay	1	3	1	39·54	
			SF	1	2	39·25	
			F		5	39·01	
Lepik, T.	URS	Long jump	Q		DNQ	7 49	
Lepold, E.	HUN	100m	1	9	5	10·82	
		200m	1	7	3	21·50	
			2	2	7	21·68	
Leppanen, H.	FIN	Decathlon	F		DNF		
Lespagnard, R.	BEL	Decathlon	F		19	7322	
Levisse, P.	FRA	10000m	1	2	12	32-07·84	
Lewis, F.	BAH	Long jump	F		11	7,61	
Licznerski, Z.	POL	100m	1	3	2	10·60	
			2	4	6	10·52	
		4×100m relay	1	1	3	39·41	
			SF	2	1	39·09	
			F		4	38·83	
Lismont, K.	BEL	10000m	1	1	7	28-17·45	
			F		11	28-26·48	
		Marathon	F		3	2:11-12·6	3
Litvinenko, L.	URS	Decathlon	F		7	8025	
Llatser, H.	FRA	4×400m relay	1	2	4	3-05·48	
Loennqvist, S.	FIN	4×400m relay	1	1	5	3-05·02	
			F		8	3-06·51	
Lohre, G.	GER	Pole vault	F		9	5,35	
Loikkanen, A.	FRA	1500m	1	1	7	3-45·32	
Lopes, C.	POR	10000m	1	1	1	28-04·53	
			F		2	27-45·17	S
Lopez, H.	HON	Marathon	F		41	2:26-00·0	
Lusis, J.	URS	Javelin throw	F		8	80,26	
Lutz, M.	USA	200m	1	4	5	21·50	
McAndrew, J.	CAN	Long jump	Q		DNQ	7,48	
McCubbins, M.	CAN	10000m	1	1	12	33-22·35	
McDaid, D.	IRL	Marathon	F		42	2:27-07·2	
Macdonald, D.	USA	5000m	1	2	7	13-47·14	
McLaren, G.	CAN	5000m	1	2	6	13-46·40	
McNamara, J.	IRL	Marathon	F		39	2:24-57·2	
Magnani, M.	ITA	Marathon	F		13	2:16-56·4	
Maier, W.	GER	3000m steeplechase	1	1	9	8-44·82	
Mainwaring, C.	ANT	110m hurdles	1	1	8	15·54	
		400m hurdles	1	3	6	54·67	
Major, I.	HUN	High jump	Q		DNQ	2 05	
Makela, H.	FIN	4×400m relay	1	1	5	3-05·02	
			F		8	3-06·51	
Malinowski, B.	POL	1500m	1	3	6	3-41·67	
		3000m steeplechase	1	1	1	8-18·56*	
			F		2	8-09·11	S
Mamede, F.	POR	800m	1	2	5	1-49·58	
		1500m	1	2	3	3-37·98	
			SF	1	8	3-42·59	
Manandhar, B.	NEP	Marathon	F		50	2:30-07·0	
Mangual, I.	PUR	400m	1	3	3	47·39	
			2	2	7	46·56	
		4×400m relay	1	1	6	3-06·08	
Manguan, S.	ESP	Marathon	F		DNF		
Marajo, J.	FRA	800m	1	5	5	1-49·60	
Marek, C.	GER	Decathlon	F		10	7767	
Marsh, H.	USA	3000m steeplechase	1	1	6	8-31·46	
			F		10	8-23·99	
Martinez, J.	ESP	4×100m relay	1	1	5	39·93	
			SF	2	DIS		
Masallam, H.	ARS	4×400m relay	1	1	7	3-17·53	
Matos, M.	CUB	Long jump	Q		DNQ	7,57	
Mayer, J.	FRA	200m	-	8	3	21·25	
			2	4	8	24·27	
Medina, L.	CUB	800m	1	6	6	1-50·15	
		1500m	1	5	6	3-42·71	
Megelea, G.	RUM	Javelin throw	F		3	87,16	B
Meita, A.	CIV	100m	1	2	2	10·53	
			2	3	3	10·45	
			SF	1	6	10·46	
		4×100m relay	1	1	6	40·23	
			SF	1	7	40·64	
Mendoza, E.	USA	10000m	1	1	10	29-02·97	
Mendoza, R.	CUB	Marathon	F		33	2:22-43·2	
Mennea, P.	ITA	200m	1	5	1	20·93	
			2	2	1	20·70	
			SF	1	1	20·67	
			F		4	20·54	
		4×100m relay	1	1	2	39·35	
			SF	2	4	39·39	
			F		6	39·08	
Menocal, F.	NCA	1500m	1	2	9	4-12·47	
Micha, L.	BEL	100m	1	1	4	10·69	
		200m	1	8	2	21·25	
			2	3	4	21·09	
			SF	2	7	21·46	
Mielke, G.	GER	Marathon	F		54	2:35-44·8	
Mignon, H.	BEL	1500m	1	2	4	3-38·32	
			SF	1	7	3-40·92	
Milanesio, V.	ITA	200m	1	8	6	21·94	
Mironov, E.	URS	Shot put	F		2	21,03	S
Mitchell, R.	AUS	200m	1	2	1	21·91	
			2	2	DNS		
		400m	1	2	2	46·11	
			2	2	1	45·76	
			SF	1	4	45·69	
			F		6	45·40	
		4×400m relay	1	2	5	3-05·75	
Mitchell, R.	GBR	Long jump	Q		DNQ	7,69	
Mizukami, M.	JPN	Marathon	F		21	2:18-44·2	
Mobarak, I.A.	MAL	110m hurdles	1	2	5	14·27	
			SF	2	8	14·21	
Monsels, S.	SUR	100m	1	9	1	10·58	
			2	2	6	10·61	
		200m	1	5	4	21·60	
			2	3	5	21·29	
Moorcroft, D.	GBR	1500m	1	5	2	3-40·69	
			SF	1	3	3-39·88	
			F		7	3-40·94	
Moore, A.	FIJ	100m	1	9	7	11·16	
		200m	1	5	4	21·82	
			2	3	7	21·75	
		Long jump	Q		DNQ	6,81	
Moore, A.	GBR	Triple jump	Q		DNQ	0	
Moore, R.	CUB	Pole vault	F		NP	0	
Mora, P.	COL	Marathon	F		DNF		
Mora, V.M.	COL	10000m	1	1	11	30-26·57	
Morales A.	PUR	Javelin throw	F		12	75,54	
Moravcik, D.	TCH	3000m steeplechase	1	2	11	8-41·95	
Moreau, G.	BEL	High jump	Q		DNQ	2,13	
Morikawa, Y.	JPN	20k walk	F		34	1:42-20·6	
Morillas, F.	ESP	High jump	Q		DNQ	2,05	
Morrison J.	CUB	Discus throw	Q		DNQ	59,92	
Moseev, L.	URS	Marathon	F		7	2:13-33·4	
Moses, E.	USA	400m hurdles	1	4	1	49·95	
			SF	2	1	48·29	
			F		1	47·63*	G
Munkelt, T.	GDR	110m hurdles	1	3	1	13·69	
			SF	1	2	13·48	
			F		5	13·44	
Murofushi S.	JPN	Hammer throw	F		11	68,88	
Muster, P.	SUI	200m	1	2	2	22·33	
			2	1	5	21·09	
Myasnikov, V.	URS	110m hurdles	1	3	2	13·81	
			SF	1	3	13·70	
			F		6	13·94	
Myricks, L.	USA	Long jump	F		DNS		
Nagy, I.	RUM	Discus throw	Q		DNQ	57,28	
Nallet, J.C.	FRA	400m hurdles	1	1	3	50·77	
			SF	2	5	50·08	

COMPETITOR	COUNTRY CODE	EVENT	ROUND	HEAT	PLACE	TIME & DISTANCE	MEDAL
Nash, M.	CAN	100m	1	4	3	10·59	
			2	1	3	10·48	
			SF	1	5	10·52	
		4×100m relay	1	3	3	39·72	
			SF	1	4	39·46	
			F		8	39·47	
Ndao, M.	SEN	100m	1	8	5	10·74	
		4×100m relay	1	2	4	40·40	
			SF	2	6	40·37	
Nemeth, M.	HUN	Javelin throw	F		1	94,58*	G
Neu, H.-D.	GER	Discus throw	F		12	60,46	
Nevens, M.	BEL	1500m	1	1	1	3-44·18	
			SF	2	8	3-41·52	
Newhouse, F.	USA	400m	1	2	1	45·42	
			2	4	1	45·97	
			SF	2	1	44·89	
			F		2	44·40	S
		4×400m relay	1	1	1	2-59·52	
			F		1	2-58·65	G
Newman, S.	JAM	300m	1	3	2	1-48·46	
			SF	2	5	1-47·22	
		4×400m relay	1	1	3	3-03·86	
			F		5	3-02·84	
Nihill, P.	GBR	20k walk	F		30	1:36-40·4	
Nogboun, A.	CIV	400m	1	6	6	48·24	
Norman. J.	GBR	Marathon	F		26	2:20-04·8	
Norona, C.	CUB	400m	1	1	6	48·46	
Nowosz, Z.	POL	200m	1	5	2	21·29	
			2	1	6	21·22	
Oakley, A.	CAN	20k walk	F		35	1:44-08·8	
Obaid, R.	ARS	Pole vault	Q		DNQ	0	
Olsen, P.	CAN	Javelin throw	F		11	77,70	
Orimus, L.	FIN	5000m	1	3	7	13-23·43	
Ornoch, J.	POL	20k walk	F		17	1:32-19·2	
Ortis, V.	ITA	5000m	1	2	9	13-52·40	
Ortiz, J.	PUR	800m	1	4	5	1-51·38	
		4×400m relay	1	1	6	3-06·08	
Orzel, K.	POL	Marathon	1		15	2-17-43·4	
O'Shaughnessy, N.	IRL	800m	1	6	5	1-49·29	
		1500m	1	4	4	3-40·12	
Ovett, S.	GBR	800m	1	3	1	1-48·27	
			SF	1	3	1-46·14	
			F		5	1-45·44	
		1500m	1	2	1	3-37·89	
			SF	1	6	3-40·34	
Owens, J.	USA	110m hurdles	1	3	5	14·03	
			SF	1	4	13·76	
			F		6	13·73	
Pachale, S.	GDR	Discus throw	F		5	64,24	
Padilla, A.	NCA	100m	1	2	8	11·52	
		200m	1	1	4	23·07	
			2	4	7	22·74	
Paeivaerinta, P.	FIN	5000m	1	2	2	13-45·77	
			F		13	13-46·61	
		10000m	1	2	DNF		
Papageorgo-poulos, V.	GRE	100m	1	5	6	10·82	
Paragi, F.	HUN	Javelin throw	Q		DNQ	77,48	
Paratanavong, S.	THA	4×100m relay	1	2	5	40·53	
			SF	1	8	40·68	
Parks, M.	USA	400m	1	3	1	46·12	
			2	3	3	45·99	
			SF	1	3	45·61	
			F		5	45·24	
		4×400m relay	1	1	1	2-59·52	
			F		1	2-58·65	G
Parr, J.	AUS	110m hurdles	1	3	4	14·02	
			SF	1	6	13·88	
Parris, G.	GRE	400m hurdles	1	4	3	51·91	
			SF	1	DNF		
Pascoe, A.	GBR	400m hurdles	1	4	2	51·66	
			SF	2	4	49·95	
			F		8	51·29	
		4×400m relay	1	1	DNF		
Pereverzev, A.	URS	Long jump	F		10	7,66	
Perez, P.	CUB	Triple jump	F		4	16,81	
Pernica, L.	TCH	Decathlon	F		13	7602	
Perrinelle, J.-P.	FRA	400m hurdles	1	2	=3	50·78	
			SF	1	6	50·82	
Peters, M.	ANT	Triple jump	Q		DNQ	14,94	
Petrov, P.	BUL	100m	1	3	1	10·46	
			2	4	3	10·30	
			SF	2	4	10·30	
			F		8	10·35	

COMPETITOR	COUNTRY CODE	EVENT	ROUND	HEAT	PLACE	TIME & DISTANCE	MEDAL
Pfeifer, J.	GDR	4×100m relay	1	2	1	39·42	
			SF	1	3	39·43	
			F		2	38·66	S
Philippe, M.	FRA	800m	1	6	7	1-50·81	
Pietrzyk, J.	POL	400m	1	4	2	46·92	
			2	2	3	46·30	
			SF	2	5	45·65	
		4×400m relay	1	2	1	3-03·03	
			F		2	3-01·43	S
Pihl, R.	SWE	Decathlon	Q		4	8218	
Pinto, A.	POR	Marathon	F		22	2:18-53·4	
Pirnie, B.	CAN	Shot put	Q		DNQ	17,82	
Plachy, J.	TCH	800m	1	3	4	1-48·63	
Poaniewa, P.	FRA	High jump	Q		DNQ	2,05	
Podberschek, E.	ITA	Hammer throw	Q		DNQ	66,56	
Podlas, R.	POL	4×400m relay	1	2	1	3-03·03	
			F		2	3-01·43	S
Podluzhny, V.	URS	Long jump	F		7	7,88	
Polleunis, W.	BEL	5000m	1	2	1	13-45·24	
			F		6	13-26·99	
Ponomarev, V.	URS	300m	1	5	3	1-48·59	
		4×400m relay	1	2	6	3-07·72	
Porter, T.	USA	Pole vault	F		14	5,20	
Powell, J.	USA	Discus throw	F		3	65,70	B
Price, B.	GBR	110m hurdles	1	1	2	13·82	
			SF	1	5	13·78	
Priestley, L.	JAM	400m	1	2	5	46·74	
			2	2	5	46·45	
		4×400m relay	1	1	3	3-03·86	
			F		5	3-02·84	
Prohorenko, Y.	URS	Pole vault	F		10	5,25	
Prudencio, N.	BRA	Triple jump	Q		DNQ	16,22	
Puttemans, E.	BEL	5000m	1	1	DNF		
		10000m	1	3	4	28-15·52	
			F		DNF		
Quarrie, D.	JAM	100m	1	4	1	10·38	
			2	1	1	10·33	
			SF	2	2	10·26	
			F		2	10·08	S
		200m	1	7	1	20·85	
			2	3	1	20·28	
			SF	2	1	20·48	
			F		1	20·23	G
		4×400m relay	1	1	3	3-03·86	
			F		5	3-02·84	
Quax, D.	NZL	5000m	1	1	1	13-30·85	
			F		2	13-25·16	S
		10000m	1	3	9	28-56·92	
Rabbi, H.	IRN	5000m	1	2	10	14-47·12	
		10000m	1	3	13	31-44·27	
Raise, O.	ITA	High jump	Q		DNQ	2,05	
Ramirez, H.	CUB	100m	1	8	4	10·72	
		4×100m relay	1	3	1	39·54	
			SF	1	2	39·25	
			F		5	39·01	
Ratanapol, A.	THA	100m	1	8	3	10·71	
			2	1	6	10·65	
		4×100m relay	1	2	5	40·53	
			SF	1	8	40·68	
Raudales, L.A.	HON	Marathon	F		49	2:29-25·0	
Rault, L.	FRA	10000m	1	3	11	29-40·76	
Regales, S.	AHO	100m	1	6	8	11·11	
Reichenbach, R.	GER	Shot put	Q		DNQ	19,31	
Reimann, H.	GDR	20k walk	F		2	1:25-13·8	S
Richards, P.	ANT	4×100m relay	1	1	7	41·84	
		4×400m relay	1	2	8	3-09·66	
Riddick, S.	USA	100m	1	7	1	10·43	
			2	1	2	10·36	
			SF	2	5	10·33	
		4×100m relay	1	1	1	38·76	
			SF	1	1	38·51	
			F		1	38·33	
Riehm, K.-H.	GER	Hammer throw	F		4	75,46	
Roberts, D.	USA	Pole vault	F		3	5,50*	B
Robertson, E.	NZL	3000m steeplchase	1	2	5	8-26·31	
			F		6	8-21·08	
Robins, P.	BAH	Triple jump	Q		DNQ	0	
Robinson, A.	USA	Long jump	F		1	8,35	G
Robinson, J.	USA	800m	1	2	2	1-47·56	
			SF	1	5	1-46·43	
Roche, M.	USA	3000m steeplechase	1	2	10	8-37·36	
Rock, R.	CAN	Long jump	Q		DNQ	7,57	
Rodgers, W.	USA	Marathon	F		40	2:25-14·8	
Roger, H.	FRA	4×400m relay	1	2	4	3-05·48	
Romersa, M.	LUX	High jump	Q		DNQ	2,05	
Roncini, G.	ITA	110m hurdles	1	1	6	14·10	
			SF	1	8	13·97	

COMPETITOR	COUNTRY CODE	EVENT	ROUND	HEAT	PLACE	TIME & DISTANCE	MEDAL
Roost, A.	CAN	Discus throw	Q		DNQ	55,56	
Rothenburg, H.-J.	GDR	Shot put	F		10	19,79	
Rousseau, J.	FRA	Long jump	F		4	8 00	
Ruiz, J.L.	ESP	10000m	1	3	*2	31-03-43	
Russell, R.	ISV	100m	1	4	7	11-22	
Ryan, K.	NZL	Marathon	F		DNF		
Ryffel, M.	SUI	5000m	1	3	11	13-46-07	
Saar, A.	SEN	110m hurdles	1	1	7	14-20	
Sachse, J.	GDR	Hammer throw	F		6	74 30	
Saint-Hilaire, E.	HAI	1500m	1	4	8	4-23-41	
Sainte-Rose, L.	FRA	4×100m relay	1	3	2	39 71	
			SF	2	2	39-33	
			F		7	39-16	
Saleh, G.	ARS	High jump	Q		DNQ	C	
Samara, F.	USA	Decathlon	F		15	7504	
Sanchez, J.L.	ESP	4×100m relay	1	1	5	39-33	
			SF	2	DIS		
Sanchez, R.	FRA	800m	1	4	DIS		
Sands, C.	BAH	100m	1	7	6	10-52	
		200m	1	5	DNF		
		4×100m relay	1	3	5	40-47	
			SF	2	7	40-53	
Sands, M.	BAH	100m	1	4	4	10-55	
			2	3	DNS		
		400m	1	1	2	46-52	
			2	2	6	46-43	
Saneyev, V.	URS	Triple jump	F		1	17,29	G
Sarria, L.	ESP	4×100m relay	1		5	39-93	
			SF	2	DIS		
Saunders, B.	CAN	400m	1	1	5	47-24	
			2	2	4	46-42	
			SF	1	6	46-48	
		4×400m relay	1	1	4	3-03-89	
			F		4	3-02-64	
Savic, M.	YUG	800m	1	4	4	1-47-73	
Schmid, H.	GER	400m hurdles	1	2	2	50-57	
			SF	1	DIS		
		4×400m relay	1	1	2	3-03-24	
			F		3	3-01-98	B
Schmidt, W.	GDR	Discus throw	F		2	66,22	S
Schmidt, W.	GER	Hammer throw	F		5	74,72	
Schoofs, H.	BEL	Marathon	F		10	2:15-52-4	
Schroeder, G.	BEL	Shot put	Q		DNQ	18 33	
		Discus throw	Q		DNQ	54,80	
Schutter, E.	HOL	Decathlon	F		DNF		
Scully, C.	USA	20k walk	F		29	1:36-37-4	
Seale, I.	CAN	4×400m relay	1	1	4	3-03-89	
			F		4	3-02-64	
Seidel, M.	GDR	Hammer throw	F		10	70,02	
Sedykh, Y.	URS	Hammer throw	F		1	77,52*	G
Sehly, M.	ARS	100m	1	2	6	11-10	
		4×100m relay	1	2	7	42-00	
Sellik, E.	URS	5000m	1	3	4	13-20-81	
			F		11	13-36-72	
Semenov, V.	URS	20k walk	F		15	1:31-59-0	
Seniukov, S.	URS	High jump	F		5	2,18	
Serrano, V.	PUR	Marathon	F		53	2:34-53-6	
Sharpe, M.	BER	100m	1	2	4	10-70	
		4×100m relay	1	1	4	39-90	
			SF	1	5	39-78	
Shaughnessy, D.	CAN	10000m	1	3	10	29-26-96	
Shevchenko, V.	URS	Triple jump	Q		DNQ	16,15	
Shine, M.	USA	400m hurdles	1	3	1	50-91	
			SF	1	1	49-90	
			F		2	48-69	S
Shmock, P.	USA	Shot put	F		9	19,89	
Shorter, F.	USA	Marathon	F		2	2:10-45 8	S
Siddique, M.	PAK	1500m	1	5	9	3-45-59	
Siebeck, F.	GDR	110m hurdles	1	1	5	14-01	
			SF	2	5	13-74	
Siitonen, H.	FIN	Javelin throw	F		2	87,92	S
Silhavy, J.	TCH	Discus throw	F		13	58,42	
Silovs, Y.	URS	100m	1	9	3	10-70	
			2	4	DNS		
		4×100m relay	1	2	3	39-68	
			SF	2	3	39-36	
			F		3	38-78	B
Silvester, L.J.	USA	Discus throw	F		8	61,98	
Simeon, S.	ITA	Discus throw	Q		DNQ	59,06	
Simmons, A.	GBR	10000m	1	3	1	28-01-82	
			F		4	27-56-26	
Simoes, A.	POR	5000m	1	3	6	13-21-93	
			F		8	13-29-38	
Simons, G.	BER	100m	1	1	5	10-76	
		4×100m relay	1	1	4	39-90	
			SF	1	5	39-78	
Simonsen, B,	SWE	20k walk	F		26	1:35-31-8	

COMPETITOR	COUNTRY CODE	EVENT	ROUND	HEAT	PLACE	TIME & DISTANCE	MEDAL
Simpson, B.	CAN	Pole vault	F		NP	0	
Singh, S.	IND	Marathon	F		11	2:16-22-0	
Singh, S.R.	IND	800m	1	1	2	1-45-86	
			SF	1	4	1-46-42	
			F		7	1-45-77	
Skowronek, R.	POL	Decathlon	F		5	8113	
Slusarski, T.	POL	Pole vault	F		1	5,50*	G
Smet, M.	BEL	5000m	1	3	8	13-23-76	
		10000m	1	2	1	28-22-07	
			F		7	28-02-80	
Smith, D.	BAH	110m hurdles	-	3	6	14-13	
		4×100m relay	1	3	5	40-47	
			SF	2	7	40-53	
So, S.	JPN	Marathon	F		20	2:18-26-0	
Solis, F.	DOM	800m	1	2	6	1-55-56	
Solomon, M.	TRI	400m	1	6	1	47-29	
			2	3	1	45-83	
			SF	2	7	46-20	
		4×400m relay	1	2	2	3-03-54	
			F		6	3-03-46	
Sontag, A.	POL	Triple jump	Q		DNQ	15,82	
Sorenson, R.	DEN	1500m	1	1	8	3-45-39	
Sowerby, F.	ANT	400m	1	6	5	48-12	
			2	4	7	48-03	
		4×400m relay	1	2	8	3-09-66	
Spencer, R.	CUB	High jump	Q		DNQ	2,05	
Spik, H.	FIN	Marathon	F		16	2:17-50-6	
Spir, P.	CAN	1500m	1	4	7	3-59-60	
Spiridonov, A.	URS	Hammer throw	F		2	76,08	S
Spooner, H.	CAN	4×100m relay	1	3	3	39-72	
			SF	1	4	39-46	
			F		8	39-47	
Stadtmuller, K.-H.	GDR	20k walk	F		4	1:26-50-6	
Stahlberg, R.	FIN	Shot put	F		12	18,99	
Stankevics, I.	HUN	20k walk	F		16	1:32-06-6	
Start, S.	GDR	Decathlon	F		6	8048	
Staynings, A.	GBR	3000m steeplechase	1	2	6	8-29-21	
			F		11	8-33-66	
Stefansson, B.	ISL	100m	1	1	6	11-28	
		400m	1	5	7	48-34	
Steiner, T.	ARG	Decathlon	F		22	7052	
Steinmann, D.	GER	100m	1	6	3	10-68	
			2	4	7	10-67	
		4×100m relay	1	2	2	39-63	
			SF	2	5	39-58	
Stekic, N.	YUG	Long jump	F		6	7,89	
Sterrad, P.	AUT	Hammer throw	Q		DNQ	66,14	
Stewart, I.	GBR	5000m	1	2	4	13-45-94	
			F		7	13-27-65	
Stones, D.	USA	High jump	F		3	2,21	B
Stroot, E.	GER	Decathlon	F		21	7063	
Stukalov, D.	URS	400m hurdles	1	2	=3	50-78	
			SF	2	5	50-47	
		4×400m relay	1	2	6	3-07-72	
Susanj, L.	YUG	800m	1	6	2	1-47-82	
			SF	2	3	1-47-03	
			F		6	1-45-75	
Sveinsson, E.	ISL	Decathlon	F		DNF		
Svensson, A.	SWE	800m	1	5	4	1-48-86	
		1500m	1	1	4	3-44-42	
Swan, Renelda	BER	400m	1	3	6	49-13	
Swan, Raymond	BER	Marathon	F		58	2:39-18-4	
Swanston, G.	TRI	Long jump	Q		DNQ	7,40	
Swierczynski, A.	POL	100m	1	7	2	10-62	
			2	3	5	10-59	
		4×100m relay	1	1	3	39-41	
			SF	2	1	39-09	
			F		4	38-83	
Sy, B.	SEN	100m	1	6	5	10-81	
		200m	1	8	5	21-54	
		4×100m relay	1	2	4	40-40	
			SF	2	6	40-37	
Taillon, D.	CAN	110m hurdles	1	3	7	14-23	
Takanezawa, I.	JPN	Pole vault	F		8	5,40	
Tancred, P.	GBR	Discus throw	Q		DNQ	55,50	
Tegla, F.	HUN	Discus throw	F		11	60,54	
Temim, D.	YUG	High jump	Q		DNQ	2,10	
Thiede, N.	GDR	Discus throw	F		4	64,30	
Thieme, A.	GDR	100m	1	1	2	10-64	
			2	2	3	10-50	
			SF	2	8	10-50	
		4×100m relay	1	2	1	39-42	
			SF	1	3	39-43	
			F		2	38-66	S
Thijs, P.	BEL	3000m steeplechase	1	2	7	8-31-55	
Thompson, D.	GBR	Decathlon	F		18	7434	
Thorslund, T.	NOR	Javelin throw	F		10	78,24	

COMPETITOR	COUNTRY CODE	EVENT	ROUND	HEAT	PLACE	TIME & DISTANCE	MEDAL
Thurton, C.	BIZ	100m	1	6	7	11·03	
Thurton, E.	BIZ	400m	1	2	7	48·91	
Tibaduiza, D.	COL	5000m	1	2	8	13-49·49	
		10000m	1	2	10	29-28·17	
Toivola, J.	FIN	Marathon	F		27	2:20-26·6	
Torring, J.	DEN	High jump	F		8	2,18	
Totland, T.	NOR	High jump	F		9	2,18	
Toukonen, I.	FIN	3000m steeplechase	1	1	5	8-27·96	
			F		12	8-42·74	
Tracanelli, F.	FRA	Pole vault	F		NP	0	
Trotman, P.	BAR	4×100m relay	1	3	6	41·15	
Trott, D.	BER	100m	1	4	5	10·67	
			2	1	5	10·64	
		4×100m relay	1	1	4	39·90	
			SF	1	5	39·78	
Tuitt, H.	TRI	800m	1	5	2	1-48·48	
			SF	1		DNF	
		4×400m relay	1	2	2	3-03·54	
			F		6	3-03·46	
Tuokko, M.	FIN	Discus throw	Q		DNQ	59,80	
Turner, E.	ANT	4×100m relay	1	1	7	41·84	
		4×400m relay	1	2	8	3-09·66	
Turri, J.A.	ARG	Shot put	Q		DNQ	17,76	
Tziortzis, S.	GRE	400m hurdles	1	1	1	50·42	
			SF	2	6	50·30	
Uhlemann, D.	GER	5000m	1	3	5	13-21·08	
			F		10	13-31·07	
		10000m	1	3	6	28-29·28	
Urlando, G.P.	ITA	Hammer throw	Q		DNQ	68,54	
Usami, A.	JPN	Marathon	F		32	2:22-29·6	
Vainio, M.	FIN	10000m	1	1	8	28-26·60	
Van Damme, I.	BEL	800m	1	6	1	1-47·80	
			SF	1	2	1-46·00	
			F		2	1-43·86	S
		1500m	1	4	2	3-39·33	
			SF	2	3	3-38·75	
			F		2	3-39·27	S
Vasilou, E.	GRE	110m hurdles	1	2	6	14·33	
Vega, R.	COL	20k walk	F		31	1:37-27·4	
Veglia, R.	ITA	Long jump	Q		DNQ	7,48	
Velasquez. R.	FRA	4×400m relay	1	2	4	3-05·48	
Velev, V.	BUL	Discus throw	F		10	60,94	
Velikorodnyh, V.	URS	Marathon	F		24	2:19-45·6	
Vikhor, N.	URS	Discus throw	Q		DNQ	57,50	
Villain, J.-P.	FRA	3000m steeplechase	1	1	7	8-35·03	
Viren, L.	FIN	5000m	1	1	4	13-33·39	
			F		1	13-24·76	G
		10000m	1	3	3	28-14·95	
			F		1	27-40·38	G
		Marathon	F		5	2:13-10·8	
Virgin, C.	USA	10000m	1	2	5	28-30·22	
Visini, V.	ITA	20k walk	F		8	1:29-31·6	
Von Wartburg, U.	SUI	Javelin throw	Q		DNQ	0	
Vycichlo, J.	TCH	Triple jump	F		9	16,28	
Walker, J.	NZL	800m	1	2	3	1-47·63	
		1500m	1	3	1	3-46·87	
			SF	1	1	3-39·65	
			F		1	3-39·17	G
Walker, L.	USA	20k walk	F		22	1:34-19·4	
Wardlaw, C.	AUS	10000m	1	3	5	28-17·52	
			F		12	28-29·91	
		Marathon	F		35	2:23-56·8	
Warnke, E.	CHI	5000m	1	1	10	13-39·69	
		10000m	1	2	7	28-43·63	
Wartenberg, F.	GDR	Long jump	F		3	8,02	B
Wason, H.	BAR	4×400m relay	1	2	7	3-08·13	
Watson, B.	GBR	Marathon	F		45	2:28-32·2	
Weidner, G.	GER	20k walk	F		18	1:32-56·8	
Wellman, P.-H.	GER	800m	1	3	1	1-48·47	
		1500m	1	4	1	3-39·86	
			SF	2	5	3-38·99	
			F		3	3-39·33	B
Wenman, K.	CAN	Pole vault	Q		DNQ	5,00	
Werner, J.	POL	400m	1	2	3	46·19	
			2	3	2	45·88	
			SF	2	4	45·44	
			F		8	45·63	
		4×400m relay	1	2	1	3-03·03	
			F		2	3-01·43	S
Werthner, G.	AUT	Decathlon	F		16	7493	
Wessing, M.	GER	Javelin throw	F		9	79,06	
Wessinghage, T.	GER	800m	1	1	5	1-46·56	
			SF	1	7	1-48·18	
		1500m	1	2	2	3-37·93	
			SF	1	5	3-40·06	

COMPETITOR	COUNTRY CODE	EVENT	ROUND	HEAT	PLACE	TIME & DISTANCE	MEDAL
Wheeler, Q.	USA	400m hurdles	1	2	1	50·32	
			SF	1	4	50·22	
			F		4	49·86	
Wilkins, M.	USA	Discus throw	F		1	67,50	G
Williams, R.	USA	Long jump	F		2	8,11	S
Wohlhuter, R.	USA	800m	1	1	1	1-45·71	
			SF	2	1	1-46·72	
			F		3	1-44·12	B
		1500m	1	4	3	3-39·94	
			SF	2	2	3-38·71	
			F		6	3-40·64	
Wolodko, S.	POL	Discus throw	Q		DNQ	59,42	
Woods, G.	USA	Shot put	F		7	20,26	
Woronin, M.	POL	100m	1	5	2	10·56	
			2	2	4	10·53	
			SF	1	8	10·69	
		200m	1	7	5	21·90	
		4×100m relay	1	1	3	39·41	
			SF	2	1	39·09	
			F		4	38·83	
Wszola, J.	POL	High jump	F		1	2,25*	G
Wuelbeck, W.	GER	800m	1	5	1	1-48·47	
			SF	2	4	1-47·18	
			F		4	1-45·26	
Yershov, V.	URS	Javelin throw	F		6	85,26	
Yetman, W.	CAN	Marathon	F		36	2:24-17·4	
Yohanan, T.	IND	Long jump	Q		DNQ	7,67	
Younis, M.	PAK	800m	1	1	7	1-48·50	
Zambaldo, A.	ITA	20k walk	F		6	1:28-25·2	
Zaxaropoulos, S.	GRE	1500m	1	5	8	3-45·12	
Zeilbauer, J.	AUT	Decathlon	F			DNF	
Zemen, J.	HUN	800m	1	4	3	1-47·40	
		1500m	1	1	3	3-44·27	
			SF	1	4	3-39·94	
			F		9	3-43·02	
FEMALES							
Ackermann, R.	GDR	High jump	F		1	1,93*	G
Adam, M.	GDR	Shot put	F		4	20,55	
Ahlers, R.	HOL	High jump	F		=12	1,84	
Aksenova, L.	URS	400m	1	5	3	52·90	
			2	1	4	51·73	
			SF	1	6	51·55	
		4×400m relay	'F	1	1	3-24·54	
			F		3	3-24·24	B
Alaerts, L.	BEL	100m	1	5	5	11·63	
			2	3	7	11·71	
		200m	1	4	5	23·53	
			2	1	6	23·80	
		4×400m relay	SF	2	6	3-32·87	
Alexander, A.	CUB	Long jump	Q		DNQ	6,20	
Alfeeva, L.	URS	Long jump	F		3	6,60	B
Allwood, R.	JAM	100m	1	1	3	11·35	
			2	1	3	11·34	
			SF	1	5	11·32	
		200m	1	1	3	23·34	
			2	2	5	23·40	
		4×100m relay	SF	2	4	43·88	
			F		6	43·24	
Andrianova, O.	URS	Discus throw	F		10	60,80	
Anisimova, T.	URS	100m hurdles	1	1	1	12·98	
			SF	1	1	13·08	
			F		2	12·78	S
Anisimova, V.	URS	100m	1	4	2	11·37	
			2	4	4	11·47	
			SF	1	6	11·39	
		4×100m relay	SF	1	2	43·33	
			F		3	43·09	B
Armstrong, D.	USA	200m	1	4	1	23·18	
			2	1	2	23·20	
			SF	1	6	23·16	
		4×100m relay	SF	2	2	43·46	
			F		7	43·35	
Ashford, E.	USA	100m	1	6	3	11·25	
			2	3	1	11·28	
			SF	1	2	11·21	
			F		5	11·24	
		4×100m relay	SF	2	2	43·46	
			F		7	43·35	
Awara, S.	JPN	Long jump	Q		DNQ	6,04	
Babich, S.	URS	Javelin throw	F		6	59,42	

COMPETITOR	COUNTRY CODE	EVENT	ROUND	HEAT	PLACE	TIME & DISTANCE	MEDAL
Bailey, M.	CAN	100m	1	1	4	11-46	
			2	4	3	11-44	
			SF	1	8	11-47	
		200m	1	1	4	23-36	
			2	3	3	23 24	
			SF	1	5	23 06	
		4×100m relay	SF	2	3	43 53	
			F		4	43 17	
Barnes, E.	GBR	800m	1	3	5	2-01-70	
		4×400m relay	SF	2	3	3-27-09	
			F		7	3-25-01	
Barsuk, L.	URS	Long jump	Q		DNQ	5,98	
Barth, E.	GER	4×400m relay	SF	1	4	3-26-31	
			F		5	3-25-71	
Becker, M.	GER	Javelin throw	F		2	64-70	S
Berend, G.	GDR	100m hurdles	1	4	1	13-03	
			SF	1	2	12-96	
			F		4	12-92	
Berg, R.	BEL	400m	1	2	4	53-66	
			2	4	7	53-74	
		4×400m relay	SF	2	6	3-32-87	
Besfamilnaya, N.	URS	100m	1	5	4	11-52	
			2	1	5	11-53	
		200m	1	3	2	23-39	
			2	1	4	23-45	
			SF	2	8	23-33	
		4×100m relay	SF	1	2	43-33	
			F		3	43-09	B
Betancourt, M.	CUB	Discus throw	F		7	63,86	
Betioli, M.L.	BRA	High jump	Q		DNQ	1,75	
Blagoeva, Y.	BUL	High jump	F		3	1,91	B
Blake, H.	JAM	400m	1	2	6	53-90	
		4×400m relay	SF	1	DIS		
Blos, M.	GDR	100m	1	4	6	11-70	
Bodendorf, C.	GDR	200m	1	5	1	22-95	
			2	1	1	23-20	
			SF	1	2	22-84	
			F		4	22-64	
		4×100m relay	SF	2	1	43-00	
			F		1	42-55*	G
Bonova, I.	BUL	4×400m relay	SF	2	5	3-31-08	
Boothe, L.	GBR	100m hurdles	1	3	4	13-69	
			SF	1	8	13-73	
Bottiglieri, R.	ITA	400m	1	6	6	53-37	
			2	4	6	52-51	
Boyle, R.	AUS	100m	1	3	1	11-39	
			2	3	2	11-29	
			SF	2	3	11-22	
			F		4	11-23	
		200m	1	3	1	23-12	
			2	2	1	22-97	
			SF	1	DIS		
		4×100m relay	SF	1	4	43-57	
			F		5	43-18	
Bradacova, V.	TCH	High jump	Q		DNQ	1,75	
Bradley, S.	CAN	100m hurdles	1	2	6	14-07	
Brady, R.	USA	100m hurdles	1	3	5	13-84	
Bragina, L.	URS	1500m	1	2	1	4-07-11	
			SF	1	3	4-02-41	
			F		5	4-07-20	
Brehmer, C.	GDR	400m	1	1	1	52-45	
			2	2	2	51-67	
			SF	2	2	50-86	
			F		2	50-51	S
		4×400m relay	SF	2	1	3-23-38	
			F		1	3-19-23*	G
Brill, D.	CAN	High jump	Q		DNQ	0	
Brown, D.	GBR	High jump	Q		DNQ	0	
Bruce, A.	JAM	Pentathlon	F		15	4198	
Bruzsenyak, I.	HUN	Long jump	Q		DNQ	6,02	
		Pentathlon	F		16	4193	
Bryant, R.	USA	400m	1	5	1	52-01	
			2	4	2	51-74	
			SF	2	1	50-62	
			F		5	50-65	
		4×400m relay	SF	1	2	3-25-15	
			F		2	3-22-81	S
Bulfoni, D.	ITA	High jump	Q		DNQ	1,75	
Burnard, V.	AUS	400m	1	6	2	52-10	
			2	2	3	51-79	
			SF	2	6	51-71	
		4×400m relay	SF	2	2	3-25-98	
			F		4	3-25-56	
Calvert, S.	USA	Javelin throw	Q		DNQ	53,08	
Campbell, R.	CAN	400m	1	1	5	54-54	
			2	1	8	54-16	
		4×400m relay	SF	2	4	3-28-81	
			F		8	3-28-91	

COMPETITOR	COUNTRY CODE	EVENT	ROUND	HEAT	PLACE	TIME & DISTANCE	MEDAL
Canty, J.	AUS	400m	1	3	3	52-88	
			2	1	6	52-65	
		4×400m relay	SF	2	2	3-25-98	
			F		4	3-25-56	
Castelein, S.	BEL	1500m	1	3	4	4-12-95	
			SF	1	9	4-13-46	
Cerchlanova, J.	TCH	800m	1	2	4	2-02-36	
Cheeseborough, C.	USA	100m	1	4	1	11-28	
			2	2	2	11-36	
			SF	1	3	11-26	
			F		6	11-31	
		200m	1	1	1	23-17	
			2	3	2	23-19	
			SF	2	6	23-20	
		4×100m relay	SF	2	2	43-46	
			F		7	43-35	
Chivas, S.	CUB	100m	1	4	3	11-43	
			2	3	4	11-42	
			SF	1	7	11-43	
		4×100m relay	SF	2	5	44-29	
Chizhova, N.	URS	Shot put	F		2	20,96	S
Christova, I.	BUL	Shot put	F		1	21,16*	G
Clarke, W.	GBR	4×100m relay	SF	1	3	43-44	
			F		8	43-79	
Colyear, S.	GBR	100m	1	1	5	11-47	
			2	3	5	11-51	
		100m hurdles	1	1	3	13-18	
			SF	2	7	17-32	
		4×100m relay	SF	1	3	43-44	
			F		8	43-79	
Cornejaud, C.	FRA	4×100m relay	SF	1	5	43-95	
Creamer, A.	GBR	800m	1	4	4	2-03-48	
Crosiata, S.	ITA	1500m	1	4	8	4-16-78	
Cummings, C.	JAM	100m	1	1	6	11-69	
			2	2	7	11-75	
		200m	1	6	5	23-50	
			2	4	4	23-45	
			SF	1	7	23-41	
		4×100m relay	SF	2	4	43-88	
			F		6	43-24	
		4×400m relay	SF	1	DIS		
Davy, F.	BAR	200m	1	2	4	24-45	
			2	4	7	24-27	
Debourse, M.C.	FRA	High jump	F		=15	1,84	
Delachanal, C.	FRA	200m	1	4	2	23-38	
			2	3	5	23-65	
		4×100m relay	SF	1	5	43-95	
Dell, G.	AUS	100m hurdles	1	2	5	13-68	
Desewici, A.M.	URU	Pentathlon	F		19	3628	
Donnelly, P.	USA	100m hurdles	1	1	5	13-71	
Dorio, G.	ITA	800m	1	2	3	2-01-63	
			SF	1	8	2-02-46	
		1500m	1	1	1	4-10-84	
			SF	2	4	4-07-61	
			F		6	4-07-27	
Droese, M.	GDR	Shot put	F		6	19,79	
Eckert, B.	GDR	200m	1	2	1	23-78	
			2	4	1	22-85	
			SF	2	1	22-71	
			F		1	22-37*	G
		4×100m relay	SF	2	1	43-00	
			F		1	42-55*	G
Ehrhardt, A.	GDR	100m hurdles	1	2	3	13-49	
			SF	2	5	13-71	
Elder, W.	GBR	400m	1	1	2	52-60	
			2	3	5	52-70	
		4×400m relay	SF	2	3	3-27-09	
			F		7	3-28-01	
Engel, S.	GDR	Discus throw	F		5	65,88	
Eppinger, M.	GER	Pentathlon	F		10	4352	
Estrella, D.	DOM	100m	1	5	6	12-12	
		200m	1	6	6	24-95	
Ferguson, S.	BAH	100m	1	3	6	12-26	
		Long jump	Q		DNQ	5,62	
Fibingerova, H.	TCH	Shot put	F		3	20,67	B
Filtatova, G.	URS	High jump	F		=15	1,84	
Fitzgerald, G.	USA	Pentathlon	F		13	4263	
Focic, D.	YUG	Pentathlon	F		11	4314	
Forde, L.	BAR	100m	1	1	7	12-02	
		400m	1	1	4	53-93	
			2	1	7	53-62	
Francoti, R.	YUG	Long jump	Q		DNQ	5,83	
Frederick, J.	USA	Pentathlon	F		7	4566	
Freitas, E.	BRA	100m	1	2	4	11-80	
			2	1	7	11-77	
Fuchs, R.	GDR	Javelin throw	F		1	65,94*	G

COMPETITOR	COUNTRY CODE	EVENT	ROUND	HEAT	PLACE	TIME & DISTANCE	MEDAL
Fuhrmann, D.	GER	400m	1	6	3	52·58	
			2	1	5	52·02	
		4×400m relay	SF	1	4	3-26·31	
			F		5	3-25·71	
Gargaro, M.	ITA	1500m	1	3	7	4-15·94	
Garrett, A.	NZL	800m	1	4	7	2-05·78	
		1500m	1	4	7	4-10·68	
Gauthier, A.	HAI	100m	1	6	7	13·11	
Gauthier, R.	HAI	400m	1	6	7	1-13·27	
Gerasimova, V.	URS	800m	1	3	2	1-59·68	
			SF	2	6	2-01·00	
Girven, P.	USA	High jump	F		18	1,84	
Gisladottir, P.	ISL	High jump	Q		DNQ	0	
Gluth, D.	GDR	800m	1	1	3	2-00·70	
			SF	1	4	1-59·32	
			F		7	1-58·99	
Goddard, B.	GBR	200m	1	1	6	23·64	
			2	2	6	23·74	
Golden, H.	GBR	200m	1	4	6	23·77	
			2	4	6	23·94	
Gomis, J.	SEN	100m hurdles	1	1	6	14·57	
Gorbacheva, N.	URS	Discus throw	F		8	63,46	
Gudmundsdottir, L.	ISL	800m	1	1	7	2-07·26	
		1500m	1	4	9	4-20·27	
Grassi, G.	SMR	High jump	Q		DNQ	0	
Haggman, P.	FIN	400m	1	6	4	52·73	
			2	1	3	51·35	
			SF	2	3	51·03	
			F		4	50·56	
		4×400m relay	SF	1	3	3-26·30	
			F		6	3-25·87	
Haglund, L.	SWE	100m	1	3	2	11·40	
			2	2	4	11·48	
			SF	2	8	11·41	
Haist, J.	CAN	Discus throw	F		11	59,74	
Hein, J.	GDR	Javelin throw	F		4	63,84	
Helten, I.	GER	100m	1	1	1	11·26	
			2	2	1	11·20	
			SF	2	2	11·18	
			F		3	11·17	B
		200m	1	4	3	23·40	
			2	2	2	23·09	
			SF	1	3	22·97	
			F		5	22·68	
		4×100m relay	SF	1	1	42·61*	
			F		2	42·59	S
Hendricks, R.	ISV	100m	1	2	6	13·51	
Hinzmann, G.	GDR	Discus throw	F		3	66,84	B
Hocking, I.	PUR	400m	1	2	7	57·85	
		800m	1	4	6	2-08·46	
Hodges, L.	JAM	100m	1	2	3	11·54	
			2	4	6	11·58	
		4×100m relay	SF	2	4	43·88	
			F		6	43·24	
Hoffman, A.	CAN	800m	1	1	5	2-05·32	
Hoffmeister, G.	GDR	1500m	1	4	2	4-08·23	
			SF	1	4	4-02·45	
			F		2	4-06·02	S
Hollman, S.	GER	400m	1	2	5	53·73	
			2	3	7	53·77	
Holmen, N.	FIN	1500m	1	2	3	4-07·14	
			SF	2	2	4-07·53	
			F		9	4-09·55	
Holzapfel, B.	GER	High jump	F		11	1,87	
Howe, M.	CAN	100m	1	3	5	11·83	
			2	3	8	11·96	
		4×100m relay	SF	2	3	43·53	
			F		4	43·17	
Hrepevnik, S.	YUG	High jump	F		=12	1,84	
Hunt, C.	AUS	Javelin throw	Q		DNQ	0	
Huntley, J.	USA	High jump	F		5	1,89	
Ilyina, N.	URS	400m	1	6	1	51·97	
			2	3	2	51·32	
			SF	2	5	51·42	
		4×400m relay	SF	1	1	3-24·54	
			F		3	3-24·24	B
Ingram, S.	USA	400m	1	4	1	51·83	
			2	1	1	51·31	
			SF	1	3	50·90	
			F		6	50·90	
		4×400m relay	SF	1	2	3-25·15	
			F		2	3-22·81	S
Ivanova, Y.	BUL	4×400m relay	SF	2	5	3-31·08	
Jackson, M.	USA	800m	1	5	2	2-00·62	
			SF	2	8	2-07·25	
Janko, E.	AUT	Javelin throw	F		9	57,20	

COMPETITOR	COUNTRY CODE	EVENT	ROUND	HEAT	PLACE	TIME & DISTANCE	MEDAL
Janssen, C.	HOL	Long jump	Q		DNQ	6,10	
Jiles, P.	USA	4×400m relay	SF	1	2	3-25·15	
			F		2	3-22·81	S
Jones, D.	BER	100m	2	1	5	11·84	
			2	1	DNF		
Jones, D.	CAN	Pentathlon	F		6	4582	
		Long jump	F		11	6,13	
Jowett, S.	NZL	100m	1	3	3	11·70	
			2	2	8	11·81	
		200m	1	2	2	24·12	
			2	1	8	24·23	
Karbanova, M.	TCH	High jump	F		19	1,81	
Katiukova, R.	URS	1500m	1	1	2	4-10·88	
			SF	1	6	4-03·20	
Kazankina, T.	URS	800m	1	5	1	2-00·15	
			SF	1	2	1-57·49	
			F		1	1-54·94*	G
		1500m	1	3	2	4-12·10	
			SF	2	1	4-07·37	
			F		1	4-05·48	G
King, M.	USA	Pentathlon	F		17	4165	
Kirst, R.	GDR	High jump	Q		DNQ	1,78	
Klapezynski, U.	GDR	1500m	1	3	1	4-11·62	
			SF	1	1	4-02·13	
			F		3	4-06·09	B
Klimovicha, I.	URS	4×400m relay	SF	1	1	3-24·54	
			F		3	3-24·24	B
Knudson, W.	USA	800m	1	3	3	1-59·91	
			SF	1	7	2-02·31	
Koch, M.	GDR	400m	1	2	3	52·78	
			2	4	3	51·87	
			SF	1	DNS		
Kononova, L.	URS	100m hurdles	1	4	3	13·36	
			SF	2	DNS		
Krachevskaya, E.	URS	Shot put	F		9	18,36	
Kraus, B.	GER	1500m	1	4	1	4-07·79	
			SF	1	7	4-04·21	
Kroniger, A.	GER	200m	1	1	5	23·43	
			2	3	DNS		
		4×100m relay	SF	1	1	42·61*	
			F		2	42·59	S
Lambrou, M.	GRE	Long jump	Q		DNQ	6,13	
Laplante, D.	USA	100m hurdles	1	2	4	13·51	
			SF	1	6	13·36	
Larrieu, F.	USA	1500m	1	2	6	4-07·21	
			SF	2	9	4-09·07	
Laser, C.	GDR	Pentathlon	F		2	4745	S
Lazar, M.	HUN	800m	1	4	5	2-04·05	
		1500m	1	1	9	4-23·30	
Lebedeva, N.	URS	100m hurdles	1	3	1	12·94	
			SF	1	3	13·03	
			F		3	12·80	B
Lindholm, M.	FIN	400m	1	4	6	53·64	
			2	2	6	54·07	
		4×400m relay	SF	1	3	3-26·30	
			F		6	3-25·87	
Longden, S.	GBR	Pentathlon	F		12	4276	
Loverock, P.	CAN	100m	1	2	2	11·47	
			2	4	1	11·50	
			SF	2	7	11·40	
		200m	1	6	3	23·34	
			2	4	2	23·03	
			SF	2	5	23·09	
		4×100m relay	SF	2	3	43·53	
			F		4	43·17	
Lynch, A.	GBR	100m	1	5	2	11·40	
			2	2	3	11·36	
			SF	2	4	11·28	
			F		7	11·32	
		4×100m relay	SF	1	3	43·44	
			F		8	43·79	
McMeekin, C.	GBR	800m	1	5	6	2-04·54	
McMillan, K.	USA	Long jump	F		2	6,66	S
McTaggart, J.	CAN	200m	1	2	3	24·35	
			2	2	8	24·47	
		4×100m relay	SF	2	3	43·53	
			F		4	43·17	
Maletzki, D.	GDR	4×400m relay	SF	2	1	3-23·38	
			F		1	3-19·23*	G
Marasescu, N.	RUM	1500m	1	4	3	4-08·31	
			SF	2	7	4-07·92	
Marinenko, N.	URS	High jump	Q		DNQ	1,70	

COMPETITOR	COUNTRY CODE	EVENT	ROUND	HEAT	PLACE	TIME & DISTANCE	MEDAL
Maslakova, L.	URS	100m	1	1	2	11.30	
			2	3	3	11.37	
			SF	2	5	11.34	
		200m	1	4	5	23.51	
			2	4	5	23.63	
		4×100m relay	SF	1	2	43.33	
			F		3	43.09	B
Matay, A.	HUN	High jump	F		9	1.67	
Melnik, F.	URS	Shot put	F		10	18.07	
		Discus throw	F		4	66.40	
Menis, A.	RUM	Discus throw	F		6	65.38	
Merrill, J.	USA	1500m	1	1	3	4-10.92	
			SF	1	5	4-02.61	
			F		8	4-08.54	
Meyfarth, U.	GER	High jump	Q		DNQ	1.73	
Milassin, A.	HUN	Long jump	F		10	6.13	
Moreau, L.	CAN	Shot put	F		13	15.48	
		Discus throw	F		13	55.88	
Morehead, B.	USA	100m	1	2	1	11.35	
			2	4	2	11.30	
			SF	2	6	11.38	
Mracnova, M.	TCH	High jump	F		4	1.89	
Murray, D.	GBR	400m	1	2	2	52.75	
			2	4	5	52.39	
		4×400m relay	SF	2	3	3-27.09	
			F		7	3-28.01	
Nail, B.	AUS	400m	1	5	4	52.98	
			2	3	3	51.71	
			SF	1	5	51.44	
		4×400m relay	SF	2	2	3-25.98	
			F		4	3-25.56	
N'Drin, C.	CIV	400m	1	4	7	54.13	
		800m	1	3	6	2-04.54	
Nedeva, E.	BUL	Long jump	Q		DNQ	6.15	
Neufville, M.	JAM	400m	1	3	4	52.93	
			2	2	DNS		
Niang, N.	SEN	800m	1	4	7	2-09.52	
		1500m	1	2	9	4-44.64	
Nimmo, M.	GBR	Long jump	Q		DNQ	5.94	
Noeding, E.	PER	100m hurdles	1	4	5	14.14	
		Pentathlon	F		DNF		
Nowakowska, B.	POL	100m hurdles	1	2	1	13.05	
			SF	1	5	13.04	
Nygrynova, J.	TCH	Long jump	F		6	6.54	
Oelsner, M.	GDR	100m	1	5	1	11.36	
			2	1	2	11.27	
			SF	1	4	11.29	
			F		8	11.34	
		4×100m relay	SF	2	1	43.00	
			F		1	42.55*	G
Ongar, I.	ITA	100m hurdles	1	2	2	13.37	
			SF	2	3	13.41	
			F		8	13.51	
Panayotova, L.	BUL	200m	1	6	4	23.49	
			2	1	7	23.87	
		Long jump	F		NP	0	
Papp, M.	HUN	Pentathlon	F		8	4535	
Pavlicic, J.	YUG	400m	1	3	6	54.11	
Peeva, Y.	BUL	Javelin throw	F		12	52.24	
Pekhlivanova, R.	BUL	1500m	1	1	6	4-13.11	
Pereira, S.	BRA	200m	1	3	6	24.00	
		Long jump	Q		DNQ	6.13	
Pfister, R.	SUI	Discus throw	F		12	57.24	
Pierre, M.L.	HAI	200m	1	4	8	28.19	
Pira, A.	BEL	High jump	F		17	1.84	
Pollak, B.	GBR	Pentathlon	F		3	4740	B
Pollock, J.	AUS	800m	1	1	2	2-00.66	
			SF	1	5	1-59.93	
		1500m	1	1	7	4-14.22	
Poor, C.	USA	1500m	1	4	6	4-08.89	
Popa, C.	RUM	High jump	F		8	1.87	
Popovskaya, L.	URS	Pentathlon	F		4	4700	
Possekel, E.	FRA	100m	1	4	4	11.48	
			2	3	6	11.58	
		4×100m relay	SF	1	1	42.61*	
			F		2	42.59	S
Prevost, N.	FRA	100m hurdles	1	1	4	13.70	
			SF	2	6	13.95	
Prorochenko, T.	URS	200m	1	6	2	23.21	
			2	2	3	23.11	
			SF	1	4	22.97	
			F		6	23.03	
		4×100m relay	SF	1	2	43.33	
			F		3	43.09	B
Puica, M.	RUM	1500m	1	1	5	4-12.62	
Purcell, M.	IRL	1500m	1	4	5	4-08.63	
Pursianen, M.-L.	FIN	100m	1	6	6	11.62	
			2	4	7	11.72	
		200m	1	5	5	24.52	
			2	2	7	24.10	
		4×400m relay	SF	1	3	3-26.30	
			F		6	3-25.87	
Pusey, J.	JAM	200m	1	5	2	23.56	
			2	3	4	23.42	
			SF	2	7	23.31	
		4×100m relay	SF	2	4	43.88	
			F		6	43.24	
		4×400m relay	SF	1	DIS		
Rabsztyn, C.	POL	100m hurdles	1	1	2	13.09	
			SF	2	2	13.35	
			F		5	12.96	
Ramsden, D.	GBR	4×100m relay	SF	1	3	43.44	
			F		8	43.79	
Reeve, S.	GBR	Long jump	F		9	6.27	
Rega, C.	FRA	200m	1	3	4	23.54	
			2	2	4	23.33	
			SF	2	4	23.00	
			F		8	23.09	
		4×100m relay	SF	1	5	43.95	
Reid, A.	JAM	High jump	F		21	1.78	
Rendina, C.	AUS	800m	1	4	2	2-01.76	
			SF	2	5	2-00.29	
		4×400m relay	SF	2	2	3-25.98	
			F		4	3-25.56	
Richter, A.	GER	100m	1	6	1	11.19	
			2	1	1	11.05*	
			SF	1	1	11.01*	
			F		1	11.08	G
		200m	1	3	3	23.47	
			2	1	3	23.35	
			SF	2	2	22.90	
			F		2	22.39	S
		4×100m relay	SF	1	1	42.61*	
			F		2	42.59	S
Rieuwpassa, C.	INA	100m	1	4	7	11.98	
			1	3	7	24.86	
Ritter, H.	LIE	200m	1	4	7	26.15	
		400m	1	5	6	58.52	
Ritter, M.	LIE	800m	1	3	7	2-14.39	
Robertson, D.	AUS	100m	1	4	6	11.50	
			2	2	6	11.56	
		200m	1	1	2	23.23	
			2	4	3	23.12	
			SF	2	3	22.91	
			F		7	23.05	
		4×100m relay	SF	1	4	43.67	
			F		5	43.18	
Rohde, B.	GDR	4×400m relay	SF	2	1	3-23.38	
			F		1	3-19.23*	G
Romay, F.	CUB	4×100m relay	SF	2	5	44.29	
		200m	1	6	DNF		
Romero, C.	CUB	Discus throw	F		9	61.18	
Rosani, D.	POL	Discus throw	Q		DIS		
Rot, E.	ISR	100m hurdles	1	4	2	13.06	
			SF	1	4	13.04	
			F		6	13.04	
Sakorafa, S.	GRE	Javelin throw	Q		DNQ	0	
Salin, R.	FIN	400m	1	5	2	52.57	
			2	4	1	51.62	
			SF	1	4	51.26	
			F		7	50.98	
		4×400m relay	SF		3	3-26.30	
			F		6	3-25.87	
Sanderson, T.	GBR	Javelin throw	F		10	57.00	
Santini, G.	SMR	Long jump	Q		DNQ	4.90	
Sapenter, D.	USA	400m	1	2	1	52.33	
			2	3	1	51.23	
			SF	2	4	51.34	
			F		8	51.66	
		4×400m relay	SF	1	2	3-25.15	
			F		2	3-22.81	S
Sarria, M.	CUB	Shot put	F		11	16.31	
Saunders, V.	CAN	800m	1	5	4	2-03.54	
		4×400m relay	SF	2	4	3-28.81	
			F		8	3-28.91	
Schaller, J.	GDR	100m hurdles	1	3	2	13.02	
			SF	1	1	12.93	
			F		1	12.77	G
Schinzel, S.	AUT	200m	1	3	5	23.74	
			2	3	6	23.95	
Schlaak, E.	GDR	Discus throw	F		1	69.00*	G
Schmidt, K.	USA	Javelin throw	F		3	63.96	B
Schoknecht, I.	GDR	Shot put	F		5	20.54	
Sebrowski, S.	GDR	Javelin throw	F		5	63.08	

COMPETITOR	COUNTRY CODE	EVENT	ROUND	HEAT	PLACE	TIME & DISTANCE	MEDAL
Seidler, M.	USA	Shot put	F		12	15,60	
Shlyahkto, T.	URS	High jump	F		6	1,87	
Shtereva, N.	BUL	800m	1	2	2	2-01·02	
			SF	2	2	1-57·35	
			F		2	1-55·42	S
		1500m	1	4	4	4-08·38	
			SF	1	2	4-02·33	
			F		4	4-06·57	
Siegl, S.	GDR	Long jump	F		4	6,59	
		Pentathlon	F		1	4745	G
Silai, I.	RUM	800m	1	4	3	2-02·82	
			SF	1	6	2-02·22	
		1500m	1	3	6	4-13·61	
Simeoni, S.	ITA	High jump	F		2	1,91	S
Simpson, R.	JAM	400m	1	5	5	54·07	
			2	3	8	53·88	
		4×400m relay	SF	1	DIS		
Smith, K.	USA	Javelin throw	F		8	57,50	
Sokolova, N.	URS	400m	1	4	2	52·45	
			2	2	1	51·63	
			SF	2	8	51·95	
		4×400m relay	SF	1	1	3-24·54	
			F		3	3-24·24	B
Sokolova, P.	BUL	100m hurdles	1	3	3	13·52	
			SF	1	7	13·67	
		Pentathlon	F		9	4394	
Sone, M.	JPN	High jump	Q		DNQ	1,70	
Spencer, P.	USA	High jump	Q		DNQ	1,70	
Spinu, D.	RUM	Long jump	Q		DNQ	6,06	
Stecher, R.	GDR	100m	1	6	2	11·21	
			2	4	1	11·22	
			SF	2	1	11·10	
			F		2	11·13	S
		200m	1	6	1	22·75	
			2	3	1	23·04	
			SF	1	1	22·68	
			F		3	22·47	B
		4×100m relay	SF	2	1	43·00	
			F		1	42·55	G
Stefanescu, V.	RUM	100m hurdles	1	4	4	13·60	
			SF	2	4	13·59	
			F		7	13·35	
Steger, C.	FRG	4×400m relay	SF	1	4	3-26·31	
			F		5	3-25·71	
Stewart, M.	GBR	1500m	1	1	4	4-11·10	
			SF		5	4-07·65	
Stoll, C.	GDR	1500m	1	2	2	4-07·13	
			SF	2	8	4-08·28	
Stoyanova, E.	BUL	Shot put	F		8	18,89	
Streidt, E.	GDR	400m	1	3	1	52·56	
			2	1	2	51·33	
			SF	1	2	50·51	
			F		3	50·55	B
		4×400m relay	SF	2	1	3-23·38	
			F		1	3-19·23*	G
Stride, M.	CAN	400m	1	6	5	53·21	
			2	4	8	53·14	
		4×400m relay	SF	2	4	3-28·81	
			F		8	3-28·91	
Striezel, C.	FRG	Long jump	Q		DNQ	6,09	
Styrkina, S.	URS	800m	1	1	1	2-00·12	
			SF	2	1	1-57·28	
			F		5	1-56·44	
Suman, M.	RUM	800m	1	3	4	2-00·00	
			SF	2	4	2-00·01	
			F		8	2-02·21	
Sundkvist, S.	FIN	High jump	F		=15	1,84	
Suranova, E.	TCH	Long jump	Q		DNQ	0	
Szabo, I.	HUN	200m	1	5	4	24·35	
			2	4	DNS		
		Long jump	F		5	6,57	
		400m	1	4	3	52·75	
			2	4	4	52·00	
			SF	1	1	50·48*	
			F		1	49·28*	G
Tannander, A.	SWE	High jump	F		7	1,87	
Taylor, G.	GBR	400m	1	4	5	53·46	
			2	2	5	53·71	
		4×400m relay	SF	2	3	3-27·09	
			F		7	3-28·01	
Taylor, I.	CUB	100m	1	3	4	11·73	
			2	4	8	11·92	
		4×100m relay	SF	2	5	44·29	

COMPETITOR	COUNTRY CODE	EVENT	ROUND	HEAT	PLACE	TIME & DISTANCE	MEDAL
Telliez, S.	FRA	100m	1	5	3	11·47	
			2	1	6	11·64	
		4×100m relay	SF	1	5	43·95	
Thijs, R.	BEL	800m	1	1	4	2-04·39	
		4×400m relay	SF	2	6	3-32·87	
Tkachenko, N.	URS	Pentathlon	F		5	4669	
Tomova, L.	BUL	800m	1	5	2	2-00·54	
			SF	2	7	2-01·97	
		4×400m relay	SF	2	3	3-31·08	
Tuisorisori, M.	FIJ	Long jump	Q		DNQ	5,79	
		Pentathlon	F		18	3827	
Tveit, A.	NOR	High jump	Q		DNQ	1,70	
Vaamonde, L.	VEN	100m hurdles	1	4	6	19·17	
Valdes, C.	CUB	100m	1	6	5	11·47	
			2	2	5	11·52	
		200m	1	2	DNF		
		4×100m relay	SF	2	5	44·29	
Valero C.	ESP	800m	1	1	6	2-06·14	
		1500m	1	3	8	4-17·65	
Van Nuffel, A.	BEL	800m	1	5	5	2-04·09	
		4×400m relay	SF	2	6	3-32·87	
Vanroy, B.	BEL	1500m	1	1	8	4-16·27	
Vergova, M.	BUL	Discus throw	F		2	67,30	S
Vintila, E.	RUM	Long jump	F		8	6,38	
Voigt, A.	GDR	Long jump	F		6	6,72	G
Vorohobko, T.	URS	Pentathlon	F		14	4245	
Waitz, G.	NOR	1500m	1	2	4	4-07·20	
			SF	1	8	4-04·80	
Walker, L.	CAN	High jump	F		20	1,78	
Walker, S.	USA	Long jump	Q		DNQ	6,20	
Wallez, R.	BEL	400m	1	3	5	52·94	
			2	3	6	53·04	
Walls, M.	GBR	High jump	Q		DNQ	1,70	
Watson, M.	USA	Long jump	Q		DNQ	5,93	
		4×100m relay	SF	2	2	43·46	
			F		7	43·35	
Weiss, A.	GDR	800m	1	2	1	2-00·48	
			SF	1	1	1-56·53*	
			F		4	1-55·74	
Wellmann, E.	GER	1500m	1	2	5	4-07·20	
			SF	1	3	4-07·54	
			F		7	4-07·91	
Wells, D.	AUS	100m	1	6	4	11·47	
			2	4	5	11·51	
		200m	1	5	3	23·78	
			2	1	5	23·65	
		4×100m relay	SF	1	4	43·67	
			F		5	43·18	
Wenzel, J.	CAN	800m	1	2	6	2-03·62	
Werthner, P.	CAN	1500m	1	3	9	4-18·19	
Weston, K.	USA	800m	1	2	5	2-03·31	
White, J.	CAN	High jump	F		10	1,87	
Wilden, R.	GER	400m	1	1	3	53·08	
			2	2	4	52·41	
			SF	2	7	51·82	
		4×400m relay	SF	1	4	3-26·31	
			F		5	3-25·71	
Wildschek, C.	AUT	400m	1	3	2	52·65	
			2	3	4	52·25	
			SF	1	7	52·20	
Wilms, E.	GER	Shot put	F		7	19,29	
Wilson, B.	AUS	4×100m relay	SF	1	4	43·67	
			F		5	43·18	
Winbigler, M.L.	USA	Discus throw	Q		DNQ	48,22	
Wright, T.	CAN	1500m	1	2	8	4-15·23	
Wycisk, H.	GDR	Long jump	F		7	6,39	
Yakubovich, N.	URS	Javelin throw	F		7	59,16	
Yakubowich, J.	CAN	400m	1	4	4	53·35	
			2	2	7	55·02	
		4×400m relay	SF	2	4	3-28·81	
			F		8	3-28·91	
Yatzinska, V.	BUL	1500m	1	3	3	4-12·72	
			SF	2	6	4-07·89	
Yule, P.	GBR	1500m	1	3	5	4-13·36	
Zinn, E.	GDR	800m	1	4	1	2-01·54	
			SF	2	3	1-57·56	
			F		3	1-55·60	B
Zlateva, S.	BUL	800m	1	3	1	1-59·24	
			SF	1	3	1-57·93	
			F		6	1-57·21	
		4×400m relay	SF	2	5	3-31·08	
Zorgo, E.	RUM	Javelin throw	F		11	55,60	
Zorn, D.	NZL	1500m	1	2	7	4-12·81	

1980

Coe and Ovett Shine in Moscow

The invasion of Afghanistan by the Soviet Union led to a boycott of the Moscow Olympic Games by many nations, the US President Jimmy Carter taking the initiative. The three most powerful nations missing were the USA, West Germany and Japan. Nations whose governments supported Carter but who, for one reason or another, were unable or unwilling to restrict the freedom of their athletes included Great Britain and Australia. Some competitors from these countries took part, while others did not.

The most eagerly anticipated events of the Games were the 800 metres and 1,500 metres, where Great Britain had two outstanding runners who had been exchanging world records for some time while avoiding each other in actual head-to-head competition. These two were Seb Coe and Steve Ovett, and the 1980 Olympics were seen as the showdown between them.

Men's Track Events

There were three favourites for the **100 metres**, Allar Wells of Britain, Marian Woronin of Poland and Silvio Leonard of Cuba, with the latter having an all-time best of 9·98 sec. Wells had to re-learn his start for Olympic year as it was his normal practice not to use blocks, but the IAAF had insisted that blocks must be used. The reason for this ruling was that blocks were now wired to the starter to detect false starts. Wells was tipped to win the final, following his hot 10·11 in the preliminaries, although Petar Petrov of Bulgaria caused a surprise when recording 10·13. The finalists were away first time at the gun with Alek Aksinin of Russia quickest into his stride and Leonard only a fraction behind. After 30 metres there were only four sprinters in it with Aksinin in front and Leonard, Wells and Osvaldo Lara of Cuba dead level. At 60 metres Lara was fading and at 80, Wells and Leonard were neck and neck. Seven metres from the finish, Wells went into an extended lean which took him to the line a fraction ahead of Leonard with both clocking 10·25. Coming up fast was Petrov, who took the bronze medal in 10·39.

In the **200 metres**, the world record holder, Pietro Mennea of Italy was tipped to win, but had suffered an early season injury and was short of racing, while many were looking for on-form Allan Wells to produce a sprint double. Nothing outstanding occured in the preliminary heats and the expected athletes qualified for the final. The draw for the medal race saw Silvio Leonard on the inside, Don Quarrie, the defending champion, in lane four, Wells in lane seven and Mennea on the outside. Wells was off at the gun, blasting around the easy turn of lane seven and had pulled back the stagger on Mennea in the first 70 metres. He was two metres up entering the straight with Mennea and Quarrie together. But with 75 metres left, Mennea moved into overdrive, gliding along behind the powerful Wells. Mennea inched ahead and despite Wells' lean won in 20·19 to 20·21 with Quarrie holding off Leonard for the bronze medal with 20·29.

The pre-race favourites in the **400 metres** were Fons Brijdenbach of Belgium, Bert Cameron of Jamaica and the defending champion, Alberto Juantorena of Cuba, who earlier in the year had undergone an operation on his Achilles tendon. The semi-finals brought other possible winners to light. A little-known East German, Frank Schaffer, clocked 45·47 sec and a virtually unknown Russian from Siberia, Victor Markin, did 45·60, while Rick Mitchell of Australia achieved 45·48. In the final, Brijdenbach was off like a rocket and passed 200 in 21·1 with Schaffer and Markin hanging on to him in 21·2. Into the home straight and Brijdenbach still led from David Jenkins of Britain, but these two started to tie-up. Markin and Schaffer then took over with Mitchell and Juantorena just behind. With 80 metres to go Markin edged in front to win with 44·60, while Mitchell came up fast to take the silver in 44·84 from a tiring Schaffer in 44·87.

Seb Coe of Britain was the world record holder and was head and shoulders above everyone else in the **800 metres**. It was inconceivable that he could be beaten, but he was. The press made great play that Seb was the good man and his rival Steve Ovett, the hard man of middle distance running, but the latter's tactics paid off. The fastest athletes qualified for the final, in which the first 130 metres was run in lanes. It was a slow start with the runners bunching and Ovett trapped in the middle, trying to elbow his way out, while Coe was on the outside, out of trouble, but running further than anyone else. Agberto Guimaraes of Brazil led at 400 metres in a slow 54·3 and Nikolai Kirov of Russia was first to break followed by Ovett, leaving Coe at the rear. Ovett sped towards the finish and won in 1-45·4, while Coe made a superhuman effort to take the silver with 1-45·9, just in front of Kirov, 1-46·0, and Guimaraes, who was fourth.

Although Seb Coe of Britain was the world record holder in the **1,500 metres**, his rival and compatriot, Steve Ovett, was expected to win, especially after his 800 metres success. Other possible contenders like Steve Scott of America, John Walker of New Zealand and Tom Wessinghage of West Germany were among the boycotting nations and were not competing. Nine contestants from two semi-finals came under starter's orders and once away, Jurgen Straub of East Germany dictated the pace, taking the field around the first circuit in a slow 61·6 and through 800 metres in 2-04·9, with Coe stuck to his shoulder. The fireworks came on the third lap when Straub injected some terrific pace to cover the ground in 54·2, with Coe and the others strung out behind him. Off the final bend both Coe and Ovett closed up on the still speeding Straub, but Coe was always better poised to strike. Coe made his effort from

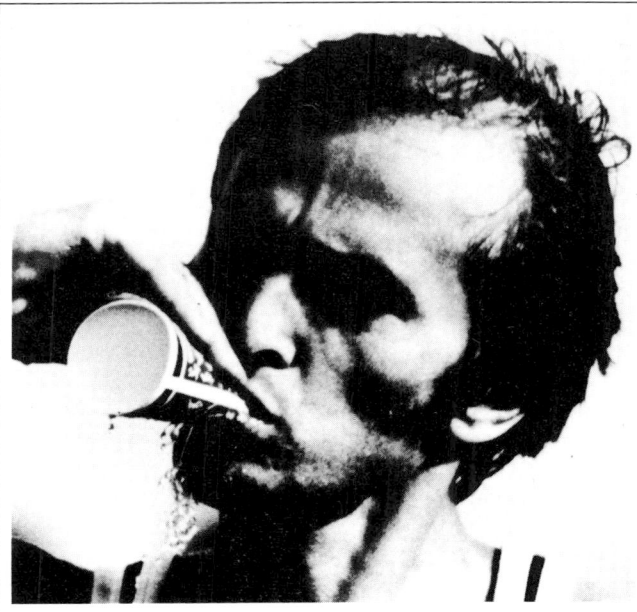
Mark Shearman

Waldermar Cierpinski

It was unfortunate for Cierpinski that his country decided to boycott the 1984 Olympics in Los Angeles. The absence of the East Germans deprived him of a chance of achieving a record three successive Olympic marathon wins.

He won his first Games gold in the event at Montreal in 1976, with a time that improved the previous fastest Olympic mark set by Ethiopia's Abebe Bikila by more than 2 minutes with 2:9-55. The East German was again faster than Bikila's best when equalling the Ethiopian's achievement of successfully defending the title in Moscow four years later.

Trained to perfection, Cierpinski ran each of his races with sound judgement. He knew his own capabilities and paced himself accordingly, ignoring any pressures the opposition might try to put on him.

Born in Nugattersleben on 3 August 1950, Cierpinski was originally a steeplechaser, but was encouraged by coaches to try the marathon in 1974. In the same year he was running the course in around 2:20. His performance before Montreal had not particularly excited the tipsters, but it was a different story prior to the Moscow Games.

Mark Shearman

Miruts Yifter

Dubbed "Yifter the Shifter" because of the exceptionally fast finishes he could produce in 5,000m and 10,000m races, this Ethiopian Air Force officer had a sequence of unlucky experiences where the Olympics were concerned. Winner of the bronze in the 10,000m at Munich in 1972, he was expected to be among the medallists in the 5,000m, but for a reason that remains a mystery he failed, though qualified, to reach the start of the final. Then Ethiopia boycotted the Montreal Games in 1976.

Yifter found ample consolation in the 1980 Moscow Games. Arriving there with a tremendous feeling of confidence, having won the World Cup 5,000m and 10,000m the previous year, he proved unbeatable and returned home with the Olympic gold medals for both these distances, setting an Olympic record 13-21·0 over the shorter course.

Although 36, this Ethiopian marvel ran the last 200m of the 5,000m in 27·2 sec and was even faster with 26·8 sec for the final 200m of the 10,000m, which he won in 27-42·7.

Born on 15 May 1944, Yifter is only 5ft 4in and the father of six.

Mark Shearman

Yuri Sedykh

Yuri Sedykh is one of the finest hammer throwers ever to be produced by the Soviet Union. Born in Nova Cherkassk on 11 June 1955, he showed skill in the hammer event as a junior, and caught the eye of Anatoliy Bondarchuk, the Russian 1972 Olympic champion. Bondarchuk took the young protege under his wing for coaching and so successful was the partnership that by 1973 Sedykh was setting a world junior record of 226ft 6in (69,04m) and winning the European junior title.

Sedykh thrived to such an extent under Bondarchuk's guidance that although only 21 years of age, he succeeded his mentor as Olympic champion in Montreal 1976 with a close to world record throw of 254ft 4in (77,52m), Bondarchuk being left to collect the bronze.

The new champion by now had become a super technician and with increased body strength was consistently making world-class throws. In 1980, months prior to the Olympic Games, he twice broke the world record, first with 263ft 8½in (80,38m) and then with 264ft 6½in (80,64m), to give ample warning to his title challengers. Came the Moscow Games and he did his followers truly proud by not only winning the gold medal again but extending the world record even further, to 268ft 4½in (81,80m).

In a lack-lustre field for the 110 metres hurdles, Thomas Munkelt of East Germany won, leaving Casanas, the Cuban, with silver yet again.

Mark Shearman

100 metres from the tape to win handily in 3-38·4 from Straub 3-38·8, having covered the last 800 of the race in 1-49·6. Meanwhile, Ovett did not quite manage to reach Straub, and gave him best some metres from the tape, to record 3-39·0 for the bronze medal.

Ethiopians were a force in the **5,000 metres**, with Mohammed Kedir and Miruts Yifter, who had been credited with a 48·0 sec 400 metres, so was considered a real danger man. Twelve runners made the final, which commenced with Yifter and Kedir controlling the pace at a moderate speed. There were still nine in contention with three laps to go, but Kedir and Yifter hotted up the pace over the last kilometre, taking it in turns to lead. Eamonn Coghlan of Ireland was the first to make his final effort with 300 metres to go, and this started an almighty sprint for the finish. Within 40 metres Yifter had gained the lead, and he went on to win in 13-21·0, running the last kilometre in 2-29·6 and the last 400 in 54·9. Suleiman Nyambui of Tanzania and Kaarlo Maaninka of Finland both overtook Coghlan in the final stretch to be placed second and third respectively in 13-21·6 and 13-22·0.

Lasse Viren of Finland had won the **10,000 metres** at the last two games and there were those that thought he would do the hat trick. In the final, Brendan Foster of Britain led the first lap in 70·0 sec, before the three Ethiopians Tolossa Kotu, Miruts Yifter and Mohammed Kedir took charge and not only alternated the lead, but varied the pace to reach the half-way stage in 14-03 0. Just over half a lap later they made a sustained surge and after 18 laps, the only athletes in contention with them were Viren and Kaarlo Maanika of Finland. With two to go, Viren made a break, but he crumbled at the bell, leaving Yifter racing away into the lead to win in 27-42 7 from Maanika in 27-44·3 and Kedir in 27-44·7, with Kotu fourth.

Gerard Nijboer of Holland was the hot name in the **marathon**, having run the second best time ever. Waldemar Cierpinski of East Germany was the defending champion, but only the great Abebe Bikila had ever achieved the distinction of winning twice. On a hot day at 27°C (71°F), Jorn Lauenborg of Denmark was the early leader, but at 10km he had given way to the top Russian runner, Vladimir Kotov, who fronted a group of 25 runners at 20km. Rodolfo Gomez of Mexico soon took over and strung out the field with a suicidal 5km in 14-13·0, but he was still 23 seconds in front at the 35km stage. The chasing group of nine included Cierpinski, Nijboer, Dereje Nedi of Ethiopia and the Russian trio of Satymkul Dzhumanazarov, Leonid Moseyev and Kotov. Finally, at 36km, Cierpinski took command, and followed by Nijboer, reached the stadium first to finish with a 200 metres sprint in 33·4 to record 2:11-03 for his second win. Nijboer was second only 17 seconds later, while Dzhumanazarov won the battle of the Russians to take third place in 2:11-35·0.

Two of the hot favourites for the **110 metres hurdles** were missing, Renaldo Nehemiah and Greg Foster, the American and world top two. The strongest contenders were Thomas Munkelt of East Germany and Alejandro Casanas of Cuba, who was the new favourite. Three inspired Russians made the final alongside Casanas, Munkelt, Jan Pusty of Poland, Arto Bryggare of Finland and Javier Moracho of Spain. Casanas was first out of the blocks, but lost his advantage by hitting the first and second hurdles very hard. This allowed Munkelt and two Russians, Alek Puchkov and Andrey Prokofyev, to move ahead of Casanas. Although Casanas steadily pulled back the leaders, he was a fraction short of Munkelt when they crossed the line in 13·39 and 13·40. Munkelt, a dentist by profession said: "I told you I would drill through the opposition." Puchkov finished third in 13·44.

When the "certain" gold medallist Ed Moses, of the USA, and Harald Schmid, of West Germany, the "certain" silver medallist, did not compete, the **400 metres hurdles** lost some of its lustre. The Russians were the favourites to provide the winner with either Vasiliy Arkhipenko or Nikolai Vasilev and although John Akii-Bua, the gold medalist from 1972, was a competitor, he did not make the finals. Gary Oakes of Britain was the revelation of the final as he took an

Ecstacy is etched on the face of Marlies Gohr, as she comes home for East Germany in a 4 × 100 metres relay best time of 41·6 sec.

Mark Shearman

immediate lead and held on to it for 250 metres, when Volker Beck of East Germany and Arkhipenko came up to him. He fought them all the way until the ninth hurdle, when tiredness hit him. Beck looked relaxed in the home straight and strode through the finish with arms aloft in 48·70, from Arkhipenko, who attempted to win with his exaggerated lean, but had to be content with second in 48·86. Oakes hung on well to secure the bronze in 49·11.

Bronislaw Malinowski of Poland, the silver medallist four years previously, was the firm favourite to win the **3,000 metres steeplechase**, but against him was Filbert Bayi of Tanzania, a previous holder of the 1,500 metres world record and a committed front runner. In the final,

Bayi was off at a terrific lick, completing the first kilometre in 2-38·8, which is 7-56·4 pace. He did not let up much and was timed at 5-20·3 for two kilometres, a world's best. Four seconds behind trailed Ashetu Tura of Ethiopia, followed by Malinowski and Domingo Ramon of Spain, then a gap to another Spaniard, Francisco Sanchez. With three laps to go, Bayi was tiring and becoming ragged over the water jumps. Malinowski caught Tura with 600 metres to go and started to make inroads on Bayi's big lead. At the final water jump he passed the tiring Bayi and romped up the straight to finish in 8-09·7. Bayi struggled to keep going and finished in 8-12·5 from Tura in 8-13·6, with Ramon back in fourth.

The world record holder and defending Olympic champion, Daniel Bautista of Mexico, was expected to walk away with the **20 kilometres walk** and he nearly did so. Under hot and humid conditions, Bautista led the walkers over the roads of Moscow, passing the 5km in 20:35 and the half-way stage in a fast 41-25·0, with a stream of heel-and-toe men behind. But with less than 2km left, Bautista was disqualified for lifting, one of seven disqualifications, 38 warnings and 136 cautions. Maurizio Damilano of Italy was left in the lead, and he finished in fine style with 1:23-35·5 for a new Olympic record. Over a minute later Pyotr Pochinchuk of the USSR strolled across the finish for the silver medal in 1:24-45·4, while Roland Wieser of East Germany was a similar distance back in 1:25-58·2.

Under the blazing sun with temperatures over 30°C (88°F), the **50 kilometres walk** was a test of endurance. Raul Gonzalez of Mexico, the world record holder, was tipped for the gold, but there were several other strong contenders in the field including three Russians and two Spaniards, Jorge Llopart and Jose Marin. Hartwig Gauder of East Germany controlled the race from the very start. He passed 10km in 44-41·0 with the 42-year-old Russian, Yevgeniy Ivchenko, at his shoulder and at 20km he led Llopart and six others in 1:29-35. At this stage the leading group of eight became three as Gauder took Gonzales and Boris Yakovlyev with him. But at 34km Yakovlyev was disqualified and after 40km Gonzalez dropped out. Gauder passed 40km in 3:01-47·0, and strode on to set a new Olympic record of 3:49-24·0 to win the gold medal, while Llopart held his

Mark Shearman

Steve Ovett

Britain was fortunate to have three of the greatest middle-distance runners of the 1970s and 1980s: Steve Ovett, Seb Coe and Steve Cram. Ovett, born on 9 October 1955 in Brighton, is the oldest, nearly a year older than Coe.

Outstanding from schooldays, he won the European Cup 800m in 1975, then ran in the 800m and 1,500m in the 1976 Olympic Games, finishing fifth in the 800m. After losing his first race over 1,500m in 1977, he remained unbeaten over that distance or a mile until the Olympic 1,500m final in Moscow in 1980. He was beaten by Coe, but took the gold in the 800m.

In 1980 he broke the world mile record and first equalled, then beat, Coe's 1,500m record. In 1981 he lost his world mile record to Coe, regained it and lost it again, all in the space of nine days. He suffered a bad leg injury in 1982 when he ran into a railing, and this upset his programme. He appeared at Los Angeles for the Olympics but had only just recovered from bronchitis. He finished last in the 800m final, went to hospital, but bravely forced himself into the 1,500m final four days later. With 350 metres to run, he led with Coe and Cram, but was forced to drop out distressed while the other two finished first and second. He continued his career, but did not dominate world middle distance running as before.

Jurgen Straub of East Germany, (far right) leads the 1,500 metres field, with Sebastian Coe (254) poised to strike for the gold.

Mark Shearman

position to take the silver in 3:51-25 from the ageing Russian, Ivchenko, in 3:56-32·0.

Cuba were unlucky in the heats of **4 × 110 metres relay** when their anchor runner, Tomas Gonzalez, started prematurely and Silvio Leonard could not make contact. In the first leg of the final the USSR, Poland and East Germany all came into their exchange boxes pretty level, but East Germany had Eugen Ray on the second leg and he put his country two metres ahead. For the third leg the USSR had Alek Aksinin, who blasted around the turn into the lead with Poland also heading East Germany. Although Poland's Marian Woronin made up some ground on Russia's anchor, it was not quite enough and Andrey Prokoyev dived over the line at the finish to win in 38·26, a new European record. Poland was a fraction behind in 38·33, while France came through in 38·53 to beat Britain and a disappointing East Germany for the bronze.

In the absence of the USA and West Germany in the **4 × 400 metres relay**, East Germany appeared to have the best chance of taking the title with the USSR and Great Britain also in the medal hunt. The first leg in the final saw East Germany's Andreas Knebel in close attendance to Russia's Mikhail Linge, with Trinidad lying handily. On the second stage, East Germany showed ahead of Russia with Trinidad still third. With the race hotting up, Frank Schaffer ran 44·8 for East Germany on the penultimate leg, but he was matched by Russia's Nikolai Chernetsky and they handed over together with France now third. Not having any leeway to make up, the individual 400 metres winner, Viktor Markin, gave East Germany's Volker Beck no chance and romped home in 3-01·1 to 3-01·3. Italy, France and Britain were all there with an opportunity for the bronze

medal on the final exchange, but Britain muffed theirs and did not finish, leaving Pietro Mennea who clocked 45·2, to deliver the goods for Italy in 3-04·3.

Men's Field Events

Jack Wszola of Poland the world **high jump** record holder. and defending Olympic champion, was one of the 16 men who jumped 2,21 metres and qualified for the final. Only 11 of them sailed over the bar at 2,21 and a mere six at the next height of 2,24. At the Olympic record height of 2,27, there were four successful jumpers, Wszola of Poland with three East Germans, Jorg Freimuth, Gerd Wessig and Henry Lauterbach. The next height was 2,29 and all got over it first time except Wessig, who needed two attempts. Now the bar was elevated to 2,31 which Wessig cleared at his first attempt while Wszola and Freimuth needed two tries. At this stage Lauterbach failed and was placed fourth. The next height of 2,33 saw only Wessig over and then, amid great excitement, he went clear for a new world record of 2,36. The silver medal went to Wszola on the count-back rule and Freimuth salvaged the bronze.

Pole vault standards in 1980 had been shooting up. Wladyslaw Kozakiewicz of Poland set a new world best in May with 5,72 metres. The Frenchman Thierry Vigneron soared to 5,75 in June and his compatriot, Philipe Houvion, topped this with 5,77 in July. No less than nine vaulters were attempting the new Olympic record height of 5,55 and only three of them failed, with Vigneron among them. The bar was now raised to the crunch height of 5,65 and just one man jack-knifed over the bar at his first attempt, Kozakiewicz. His compatriot, Tadausz Slusarski, the defending Olympic champion, sidled over on his third trial, while Konstantin Volkov, the leading Russian, and Houvion both cleared well on their last attempts. The predominantly Russian crowd were now hissing whenever Kozakiewicz jumped and the Poles among the spectators did likewise to Volkov. At 5,70 the bar was promptly vaulted by Kozakiewicz, with the rest failing. Volkov, who saved one of his jumps for the next height of 5,75 at which he failed, shared the silver medal with Slusarski, while Houvion was fourth. After surmounting 5,70 and a new world record of 5,78 for the gold, Kozakiewicz tried 5,82, but his concentration had gone.

European **long jump** record holder, Lutz Dombrowski of East Germany, had been injured in the early part of the season, but had made a miraculous recovery to jump 8,45 metres in July. In the very first leap of the final, Valery Podiuzhny of Russia landed at 8,07, while two jumps later Lazlo Szalma of Hungary reached 8,13. But Dombrowski had the last word in round one with 8,15. East Germany's Frank Paschek then led with 8,21 but Dombroski later responded with 8,32. Podiuzhny moved into third place with 8,18 in the next round, while the fifth round saw Dombrowski psyche himself up for a major effort. It certainly was and he landed at 8,54 for the gold medal, with Paschek taking the silver at 8,21 and Podiuzhny the bronze at 8,18.

"The champ still reigns" chanted the Russians, referring to Victor Saneyev, three times Olympic victor in the **triple jump**, but he had strong opposition, not only from his own countrymen, but from Keith Connor of Great Britain and from the reigning world record holder, Joao de Oliveira of Brazil. Best of the qualifiers was Ken Lorraway of Australia with 17,02 metres. In round one of the final the first big jump came from Oliveira at 16,96 and Saneyev responded with 16,85. There was drama in the third round when Ian Campbell of Australia bounded to 17,50, but the judges decided that he dragged his toe on the ground and it was disallowed. Strangely, the video camera did not pick up the infringement. Jaak Uudmae of the USSR now took the lead with 17,35 and Oliveira improved in second position on 17,22, while Saneyev also improved to 17,02. In the next round Connor leapt into the fourth spot with 16,87. The final round saw Saneyev make one mighty last ditch effort to retain his title with 17,24, before Campbell

sailed well over 17,00 for the fourth time and for the fourth time a foul was called. Oliveira saved his biggest jump for last, a tremendous hop, step and jump which landed at about 17,80, but again the red flag went up, so Uudmae won the gold, Saneyev the silver and Oliveira the bronze.

Prior to the Games only one man was spoken of as becoming the winner of the **shot put** and that was Udo Beyer of East Germany, the world record holder. Geoff Capes of Britain was expected to win a medal and he momentarily went into the lead in the first round with a 20,50 put, but the very next attempt saw the amazingly fast Vladimir Kiselyev of the USSR throw 21,10. In the next round his compatriot, Alek Baryshnikov, using the difficult rotational technique, came within two centimetres of the leader with 21,08 and Beyer in the following round lobbed one out to 21,06. With his final throw, Kiselyev put the matter beyond all doubt with an impressive 21,35 to take the gold medal, while Baryshnikov took the silver and Beyer the bronze.

With the absence of Mac Wilkins of the USA in the **discus throw**, it looked a certainty that the world record holder, Wolfgang Schmidt of East Germany, would secure the gold medal. Yuri Dumchev of the USSR got off the first big throw in the final of 64,78 metres, but the improving Imrich Bugar of Czechoslovakia with the very next throw, edged him with 65,14. Two rounds later Schmidt sailed his platter out to 65,30 only to be quickly overtaken by Dumchev with 65,58. The big throws came in the fourth round, first by Schmidt at 65,64, then by Bugar 66,38 and finally a mighty heave from the unkown Victor Raschupkin of the USSR which landed at 66,64. With their final throws, Luis Delis of Cuba reached 66,32 and Dumchev 67,00, which landed outside the sector. Raschupkin took the gold, Bugar the silver and Delis the bronze.

In the **hammer throw**ing competition, Yuri Sedykh, the defending champion, was up against fellow-Russian Sergei Litvinov, the new world record holder. Only one notable thrower was absent, the consistent Karl-Hans Riehm of West Germany. The old Olympic record went in the qualifying rounds when Sedykh launched one out to 78,22 metres, but in the final there was another story to tell. On his opening throw, Sedykh dispirited his opponents with a new world record of 81,80 and

Mark Shearman

Allan Wells

Allan Wells was the first Briton for 52 years to win the Olympic 100m sprint final, his success coming at the 1980 Games in Moscow. Born on 3 May 1952 in Edinburgh, it was not until he was 26 that the strongly built Scot took seriously to sprinting. Previously he had been far more interested in long jumping and it was only when becoming rather bored with the leaping that he decided to switch to the 100m. The result was dramatic, for within a year he was equalling the 100m British record.

By 1978 he had proved himself in the top bracket of international sprinters by finishing sixth in the 100m European championship final and winning a gold (200m) and silver (100m) at the Commonwealth Games in Edmonton, Canada. In 1979 he also won World Cup 100m and European Cup 200m gold medals.

So expectations ran high that he could reach the gold standard again at the Moscow Olympic Games the following year. There he won the 100m by a hair's breadth from Silvio Leonard, of Cuba, with both recording 10·25 sec. Wells looked set to repeat the victory in the 200m final only to be caught in the very last stride by the Italian Pietro Mennea, finishing strongly in the outside lane.

An elated Allan Wells delights in his 100 metres victory for Scotland and Britain. Mark Shearman

ultimately the gold medal. Litvinov tried to retaliate immediately, but it did not come off, although he threw 80,64. The third string Russian, Juri Tamm, reached 78,96 for the bronze medal and a clean sweep, with Roland Steuk of East Germany not far behind with 77,54 in fourth position.

The **javelin throw** is an unpredictable event, and world record holder Ferenc Paragi of Hungary, who led the qualifiers, could not finish in the first eight in the final, while his compatriot, the defending champion Miklos Nemeth, could finish only eighth. Wolfgang Hansich of East Germany led the first round throwers in the final with 86,72, followed by Heino Puuste of the USSR, 86,10, and his compatriot Alek Makarov with 85,84. The third Russian thrower, Danis Kula, their big hope, logged two no throws and was in danger of being eliminated. But on his third attempt, the javelin landed tail first, as seen by thousands of eye witnesses, and the judges calmly measured the throw at 88,88. As though to

redeem the situation, Kula's next throw was a legitimate 91,20, which won him the gold medal. Makarov's final throw of 89,64 secured him the silver, while Hanisch's earlier effort of 86,72 gave him the bronze.

Twice, leading up to the Games, the **decathlon** world record was broken. First Daley Thompson of Great Britain scored 8,622 points in May, beating Guido Kratschmer of West Germany. Kratschmer improved the top score to 8,649 in June, would not be competing at the Olympics due to his country's boycott. The first day was brilliant for Thompson as he ran three metres faster than anyone else in the 100 metres with 10·62 sec. His long jump was a phenomenal 8,00 metres against the wind. His shot was more than adequate at 15,18 metres and better than any of his nearest rivals. And his 2,08 metres high jump was beaten only by the Russian Sergei Zhelanov, with a superb 2,18. Nobody could touch him in the 400 metres, where he ran 48·01 sec for a first day total of 4,542 and on schedule for a world record. Yuri

Kutsenko of the USSR scored 4,278 and fellow Russian Valeriy Kachanov 4,265. The second day was wet and dreary which reflected in the performances. Kachanov hurdled 14·40 sec, but Thompson was only a fraction behind with 14·47 and in the discus the Briton threw a creditable 42,24 metres. But he was below par in the pole vault with 4,70 metres, where Kachanov withdrew injured. Thompson's javelin throw was good at 64,16 metres and he had an unassailable lead of 280 points entering the 1,500 metres, where he was content to stroll home in 4-39·9 for the gold. His winning total was 8,495 points while Kutsenko held on to second place with 8,331 and Zhelanov took third with 8,135.

Women's Events

Marlies Gohr of East Germany was favourite for the **100 metres** with her 10·88 sec world record and consistent form, but Lyudmila Kondratyeva of the USSR had shown recent startling form. And it was clear in the semi-finals that Kondratyeva would take some beating when she handily defeated Gohr. In the final, the starter held the girls in the set position for an extraordinarily long time, but even so Linda Haglund of Sweden was away like a flash with Kondratyeva and Romy Muller of East Germany at her heels. At 60 metres both Gohr and Kondratyeva passed Haglund, with the East German girl slightly to the front. But with great determination Kondratyeva forced herself over the line to win in 11·06 from Gohr in 11·07, with East Germany's Ingrid Auerswald coming through to snatch the bronze with 11·14.

The **200 metres** was thought to be in the hands of Barbel Wockel of East Germany, the defending champion. Lyudmila Kondratyeva of the USSR was out with a strained hamstring sustained in the 100 metres and Marita Koch, of East Germany, the world record holder, was concentrating on the 400 metres. The danger girl, Natalya Bochina of the USSR, broke the Olympic record with 22·26 in the heats, while Merlene Ottey of Jamaica was also under the old mark of 22·37 in the semi-finals. In the final both Bochina and Ottey were quickly into their running and led into the straight, but not for long, as Wockel soon accelerated past them and won without trouble in 22·03. Meanwhile, Bochina and

Ottey were racing neck and neck, and the former's strength got her second place in 22·19 to the Jamaican girl's 22·20.

Marita Koch of East Germany was the only woman to have run under 49·00 sec for the **400 metres**, but she had suffered an early season thigh injury and was short of racing. Five of the semi-finalists dipped under 51·0 and the lane draw for these five was Nina Zyuskova of the USSR in three, with outside her Koch, Christina Lathan of East Germany, Jarmila Kratochvilova of Czechoslovakia and Irina Nazarova of the USSR in lane eight. Straight from the gun Koch blasted away and took up the stagger on Lathan in the first 100 metres. Coming into the finishing straight, Koch was nearly 10 metres clear of the heavily built Kratochvilova with Lathan a further four metres back, and she swept on to win in

Tatyana Kazankina of the USSR (10), the winner of the 1,500 metres.
Mark Shearman

Mark Shearman

Marita Koch

Marita Koch was probably the greatest of all the great East German women track champions. Three times she broke the world record for 200m and six times set world figures for 400m. In so doing she became the first woman to race 200m in under 22 sec, when establishing her present world 200m best of 21·79 sec at Dresden in 1973; and the first to break 49 sec for 400m with 48·94 sec at Prague in 1978, before producing her all-time best of 47·60 sec — a time faster than all the male Olympic winners at the distance before Eric Liddell produced 47·6 sec in 1924.

The elegant Marita, born at Wismar on 18 February 1957, first competed in the Olympics at Montreal in 1976 but had to withdraw from her semi-final because of injury. However, she savoured Olympic glory in Moscow when she won the 400m gold with a then Games best of 48·88 sec. The East German boycott of the Games there prevented Marita defending the title.

Over a period of six years starting in 1977, she was beaten only four times in major competitions. She won gold medals for individual and relay events at world and European championships and even set a world best mark for 60m indoors.

48·88, a new Olympic record. Both Kratochvilova and Lathan pulled back some of the ground, with the former taking the silver in 49·46 and Lathan the bronze with 49·66.

When it came to the **800 metres**, the three Russian girls were superior to the opposition, with world record holder, Nadezhda Olizarenko, at their head. The semi-finals were fast, but the final proved to be even faster. Olizarenko assumed the lead and made things hot from the front, completing lap one in the fast time of 56·2 sec, with only 0·6 between first and last runners. Olizarenko increased the pace yet further with Mineyeva and Providokhina chasing hard, and finally drew away to win with a world record of 1-53·5. Mineyeva equalled the old world record in 1-54·9 for the silver medal, while Providohkina took the bronze in 1-55·5. The first of the non-Russians was Martina Kampfert, of East Germany, in a creditable 1-56·3.

In the **1,500 metres** Tatyana Kazankina of the USSR was the phenomenon of her age, being both Olympic champion and world record holder in 1976 at 800 and 1,500. She knew her speed was waning so elected only to defend her 1,500 title, and prepared with a new world best of 3-55·0. Kazankina then made sure the first of the two heats was fast by winning in 3-59·2, which drew the sting from some of her chief rivals. In the final, Nadezhda Olizarenko of the USSR set a moderate pace, with all the field bunched, but with 700 metres to go, Kazankina had had enough and spurted away to win in a new Olympic record of 3-56·6. She was followed home by Christianne Wartenberg of East Germany, in 3-57·8. Meanwhile, Gabriella Doria of Italy and Ulrike Bruns of East Germany were battling it out for third, until Olizarenko came with a last minute spurt to take the bronze in 3-59·6.

There were only two athletes favoured for the **100 metres hurdles**, Grazyna Rabsztyn of Poland, the world record holder, and her rival and fellow countrywoman Lucyna Langer. Rabsztyn looked the likely winner in the semi-finals, where she was fastest with 12·64 sec, but the final was another story. The East German girls, Johanna Klier and Bettina Gartz got beautiful starts, with Vera Komisova of the USSR also getting away well. Rabsztyn, however, had lost metres and was trailing the field. At mid-way, Komisova and Klier were flying along together with Langer and Kerstin Claus of East Germany just behind. Komisova took the race on the run-in with an Olympic record of 12·56 from Klier, 12·63, and Langer 12··65, while Rabsztyn could finish only fifth in 12·74.

Only seven countries entered the **4 × 100 metres relay** and a straight final was run. The indisputable champions of the event, East Germany, gave an appalling display of baton changing, yet broke the world record with ease! Romy Muller was their lead off and actually ran past the second leg runner, Barbel Wockel and handed the baton backwards. Wockel and the next runner Ingrid Auerswald must have been impressed with this technique for the same thing happened again! The exchange between Auerswald and Marlies Gohr was more conventional and the East Germans romped home in 41·60 sec for a best-ever mark. The USSR had an excellent run and with slick baton passing clocked 42·10 for the silver position, while Britain also excelled themselves in third place with a creditable 42.43.

Eleven teams competed in the **4 × 400 metres relay**. The USSR employed the same trick in the women's race as the men's, resting Nina Zyuskova and Irna Nazarova,

Sara Simeoni, the Italian silver medallist in the Montreal high jump, went one better in 1980, winning the gold.   Mark Shearman

and this probably gave them the edge they needed for the final. East Germany started the favourites and Gabi Lowe led off for them against Tatyana Prorochenko of the USSR, who completed her leg in 50·2, 0·4 up. Then, Barbara Krug took over for East Germany and raced into the lead with a 50·5 stint against Tatyana Goischik's 51·5. In the third leg, Nina Zyuskova of the USSR chased Christina Lathan hard, but the East German girl trod on the kerb coming off the final bend and twisted her ankle, limping home after Zyuskova, who ran 49·7. With a deficit of only six metres, Marita Koch seemed certain to catch Irina Nazarova, but the latter ran an inspired race to win for the USSR in 3-20·2 to East Germany's 3-20·4.

Sara Simeoni of Italy was the **high jump** world record holder, and favourite to take the title, as the defending champion Rosemarie Ackermann of East Germany was beset by injuries. Six jumpers cleared the bar at 1,91 metres, but only Simeoni, Urszula Kielan of Poland and Jutta Kirst of East Germany succeeded at 1·94. Ackermann was one of those who failed and she was placed fourth. At 1,97 both Kielan and Kirst failed three times with Kielan getting the silver medal on the count-back rule and Kirst the bronze. Simeoni cleared on her second attempt at the Olympic record height of 1,97 and took the gold.

In the **long jump**, Lidia Alfeyeva of the USSR led the qualifiers with a leap of 6,78 metres. The first round saw the Olympic record broken well and truly by Tatiana Skachko of the USSR with 6.96 and two other jumpers also exceeded the old mark of 6,82. Skachko improved her lead to 7,01 in the third round, but was overtaken first by Tatiana Kolpakova of the USSR with 7,06 for the gold medal and then by Brigitte Wujak of East Germany with 7,04 for the silver.

All the top **shot put** exponents were competing, with

Pietro Mennea, the Italian 200 metres world record holder, achieved a lifetime ambition when he came home fractionally ahead of Britain's Allan Wells.   Mark Shearman

the single exception of Helena Fibingerova of Czechoslovakia, who had suffered a shoulder tear. The favourite was Ilona Slupianek of East Germany, who held the world record, but who three years before had been caught taking steriods and banned from international competition for a year. It was a straight final and the fourth throw of the competition by Margitta Pufe of East Germany went 21,20 metres and cracked the Olympic record. But it was not long before Slupianek stepped into the circle and settled it with a throw of 22,41. In fact any five of her six throws would have won her the title. Svetlana Krachevskaya of the

USSR threw 21,42 in the third round for the silver medal, leaving the bronze to Pufe.

With the defending champion and world record holder Evelin Jahl of East Germany on form, the **discus throw**ing competition was another one-horse-race. Best of the rest were thought to be Maria Petkova of Bulgaria and Faina Melnik of the USSR, the 1972 champion. The big surprise in the prelims, was that Melnik failed to qualify. The bulky Petkova led the first round with 67,68 metres, but Jahl had things her way in the next with an Olympic record of 69,76. She then improved on this to 69,96 with her third throw to take the gold medal, while Petkova took the silver with 67,90. Gisela Beyer remained in third position with 67,08 for five rounds, but Tatyana Lesovaya of the USSR overtook her with her final throw of 67,40, to secure the bronze medal.

Of the three top ranked girls for the **javelin throw**, Tessa Sanderson of Britain fluffed her throws in the preliminaries, Ruth Fuchs, the defending champion and twice Olympic champion, could do no better than eighth and the new world record holder, Tatyana Biryulina of Russia, had to be satisfied with sixth. The Olympic record went in the qualifying rounds when Ute Richter of East Germany threw her spear 66,66 metres. In the first round of the finals, Maria Colon of Cuba launched her weapon 68,40 to better the new Olympic mark and win the competition. With her second throw, Saida Gunba of the USSR threw 67,76 for the silver medal, while Ute Hommola of East Germany took the bronze with 66,56, just two centimetres in front of Richter.

The one-day **pentathlon** competition had been reorganised by replacing the 200 metres with an 800 metres and Olga Kuragina of the USSR had recently scored 4,856 for a new world record. Russia provided all the medal winners and Nadyezhda Tkachenko dominated the competition, winning with a new world and Olympic record of 5,083. Her shot of 16,84 metres and long jump of 6,74 metres contributed most to her victory. The silver medal went to Olga Rukavishnikova who produced a 1,88 metres high jump and a 6,79 metres long jump to score 4,937. Kuragina, who hurdled in 13·26 sec and ran the 800 in 2-03·60, took the bronze medal with 4,875 points and was the third athlete to beat the old world record.

Left table

COMPETITOR	COUNTRY CODE	EVENT	ROUND	HEAT	PLACE	TIME & DISTANCE	MEDAL
MALES							
Abascal, J.-M.	ESP	1500m	1	1	6	3-44·7	
Abdenouz, E.	ALG	5000m	1	2	1	13-42·1	
			SF	2	12	14-15·9	
Abdulsada, F.	IRQ	4×400m relay	1	3	4	3-10·5	
Abramov, V.	URS	5000m	1	2	3	13-42·9	
			SF	1	6	13-40·7	
Adams, F.	TRI	100m	1	9	5	10·30	
Adamus, D.	POL	Javelin throw	Q		DNQ	76·82	
Adio, H.	NGR	100m	1	3	4	10·58	
			2	2	7	10·67	
		200m	1	6	4	21·79	
		4×100m relay	1	2	=4	39·48	
			F		7	39·12	
Agathine, A.	SEY	Triple jump	Q		DNQ	14,21	
Agbo, F.	FRA	High jump	Q		DNQ	2,15	
Aho, A.	BEN	200m	1	5	5	22·09	
Aho, A.	FIN	Javelin throw	F		9	80,58	
Aho, P.	BEN	100m	1	4	5	11·01	
Aldet, M.	ALG	800m	1	6	3	1-50·4	
			SF	1	8	1-48·2	
		1500m	1	1	2	3-43·9	
			SF	1	9	3-44·9	
Akabi-Davis, W.	SLE	400m	1	6	6	50·80	
		4×100m relay	1	2	8	42·53	
		4×400m relay	1	2	8	3-25·0	
Akii-Bua, J.	UGA	400m hurdles	1	1	5	50·87	
			SF	2	7	51·10	
		4×400m relay	1	2	5	3-07·0	
Aksinin, A.	URS	100m	1	3	1	10·26	
			2	3	1	10·29	
			SF	1	3	10·45	
			F		4	10·42	
		4×100m relay	1	1	1	38·68	
			F		1	38·26	G
Alebic, J.	YUG	400m	1	6	1	47·61	
			2	1	6	46·60	
		4×400m relay	1	1	3	3-05·3	
Alemayehu, M.	ETH	Marathon	F		24	2:18-40	
Alface, D.	MOZ	10000m	1	3	DNF		
Alfaro, E.	COL	20k walk	F		19	1:42-19·7	
		50k walk	F		15	4:46-23	
Ali, M.	TAN	100m	1	3	6	10·86	
		200m	1	9	5	21·83	
Alimi, A.	BEN	5000m	1	3	12	15-44·0	
Alli, Y.	NGR	Long jump	Q		DNQ	7,43	
Al-Mosawi, A.	KUW	100m	1	8	7	11·28	
Al-Shammari, K.	KUW	1500m	1	1	8	3-57·6	
Al-Zinkawi, M.	KUW	Shot put	Q		DNQ	17,15	
Andonov, A.	BUL	Decathlon	F		7	7927	
Angelopoulos, N.	GRE	200m	1	1	4	21·98	
Anikin, Y.	URS	Triple jump	F		9	16·12	
Antipov, A.	URS	10000m	1	1	DNF		
Anton, E.	ESP	Marathon	F		22	2:18-16	
Aquino, E.	MEX	5000m	1	1	8	13-48·9	
			SF	1	12	14-01·4	
		10000m	1	2	7	29-21·3	
Arame, J.	FRA	200m	1	3	2	21·24	
			2	2	2	20·95	
			SF	2	6	21·05	
Araujo, A.S.	BRA	200m	1	3	4	21·49	
			2	2	7	21·22	
		4×100m relay	1	2	=4	39·43	
			F		8	39·54	
Arkhipenko, V.	URS	400m hurdles	1	3	1	50·22	
			SF	2	1	49·80	
			F		2	48·86	S
Arop, J.	UGA	Javelin throw	F		12	77·34	
Assimi, A.	BEN	800m	1	5	6	1-59·9	
Austin, S.	AUS	5000m	1	2	7	13-43·2	
			SF	2	11	13-47·6	
		10000m	1	1	5	29-45·2	
Ayoo, S.	UGA	400m	1	2	3	47·78	
			2	3	5	47·03	
		4×400m relay	1	1	5	3-07·0	
Babaci, L.	ALG	3000m steeplechase	1	3	7	8-38·7	
			SF	1	6	8-25·5	
			F		11	8-31·8	
Babaly, L.	HUN	4×100m relay	1	2	6	39·97	
Bakosi, B.	HUN	Long jump	Q		DNQ	7,29	
		Triple jump	F		7	16,47	
Balcha, Kassa	ETH	1500m	1	4	6	3-43·1	
Balcha, Kebede	ETH	Marathon	F		DNF		
Balkis, A.	SYR	High jump	Q		DNQ	2,05	
Barbosa, L.	COL	Marathon	F		34	2:22-58	

Right table

COMPETITOR	COUNTRY CODE	EVENT	ROUND	HEAT	PLACE	TIME & DISTANCE	MEDAL
Barie, Z.	TAN	5000m	1	2	9	13-49·9	
			SF	1	7	13-44·9	
		10000m	1	1	DNF		
Barre, Pascal	FRA	4×100m relay	1	1	2	39·01	
			F		3	38·53	B
Barre, Patrick	FRA	4×100m relay	1	1	2	39·01	
			F		3	38·53	B
Barrett, G.	AUS	Marathon	F		DNF		
Baryshnikov, A.	URS	Shot put	F		2	21,08	S
Basnet, L.	NEP	5000m	1	1	11	16-11·7	
Bassegela, J.-P.	CGO	4×100m relay	1	2	7	40·09	
Bautista, D.	MEX	20k walk	F		DIS		
		50k walk	F		DIS		
Bayi, F.	TAN	3000m steeplechase	1	1	1	8-21·4	
			SF	1	1	8-16·2	
			F		2	8-12·5	S
Beck, V.	GDR	400m hurdles	1	1	3	50·35	
			SF	1	1	50·36	
			F		1	48·70	G
		4×400m relay	1	2	1	3-03·4	
			F		2	3-01·3	S
Bekele, N.	ETH	800m	1	6	4	1-51·1	
		1500m	1	3	7	3-45·8	
Belfaa, O.	ALG	High jump	Q		DNQ	2,05	
Belkov, G.	URS	High jump	F		10	2,21	
Bell, A.	GBR	400m	1	8	4	47·38	
			2	2	4	46·17	
			SF	2	8	48·50	
		4×400m relay	1	3	2	3-05·9	
			F		DNF		
Bellot, J.-M.	FRA	Pole vault	F		5	5,60	
Belsky, V.	URS	Long jump	F		6	8,10	
Bencik, J.	TCH	20k walk	F		DIS		
		50k walk	F		13	4:27-39	
Bermudez, M.	MEX	50k walk	F		DNF		
Bernhard, R.	SUI	Long jump	F		9	7,88	
Beusekom, P.	HOL	4×400m relay	1	1	5	3-06·0	
Beyer, O.	GDR	800m	1	5	1	1-48·9	
			SF	2	4	1-47·6	
Beyer, U.	GDR	Shot put	F		3	21,06	B
Bezabeh, A.	ETH	800m	1	6	5	1-52·7	
		4×400m relay	1	2	7	3-18·2	
Bichea, V.	RUM	3000m steeplechase	1	3	3	8-35·4	
			SF	2	3	8-24·3	
			F		9	8-23·9	
Black, C.	GBR	Hammer throw	Q		DNQ	66,74	
Black, D.	GBR	Marathon	F		DNF		
Blango, C.	SLE	Decathlon	F		16	5080	
Blazek, P.	TCH	20k walk	F		14	1:35-30·8	
		50k walk	F		10	4:16-26	
Boehni, F.	SUI	Pole vault	Q		DNQ	5,15	
Boima, S.	SLE	100m	1	5	6	11·08	
		200m	1	9	6	22·93	
		4×100m relay	1	2	8	42·53	
Borghi, F.	ITA	High jump	Q		DNQ	2,18	
Borlee, J.	BEL	400m	1	5	4	47·77	
			2	3	8	47·73	
Bradford, C.	JAM	200m	1	5	1	21·17	
			2	2	6	21·04	
		4×100m relay	1	1	4	39·71	
		4×400m relay	1	3	DNF		
Branche, G.	SLE	800m	1	2	7	1-54·6	
		1500m	1	2	10	4-03·9	
		4×400m relay	1	1	8	3-25·0	
Brandt, A.	SWE	20k walk	F		13	1:34-44·0	
Bratanov, Y.	BUL	400m hurdles	1	3	5	50·56	
			SF	2	5	50·17	
			F		8	56·35	
Brathwaite, C.	TRI	100m	1	1	3	10·44	
			2	2	4	10·37	
			SF	2	8	10·54	
		200m	1	8	2	21·13	
			2	3	5	21·02	
		4×100m relay	1	1	5	39·74	
Brecka, F.	TCH	200m	1	7	2	21·49	
			2	2	7	21·47	
		4×400m relay	1	2	2	3-03·5	
					7	3-07·0	
Brijdenbach, A.	BEL	400m	1	4	2	47·72	
			2	1	2	45·88	
			SF	1	1	45·46	
			F		5	45·10	
		4×400m relay	1	2	DNF		
Brogini, A.	ITA	Decathlon	F		DNF		
Brouwer, H.	HOL	200m	1	3	6	21·96	

COMPETITOR	COUNTRY CODE	EVENT	ROUND	HEAT	PLACE	TIME & DISTANCE	MEDAL
Bruce, A.	TRI	200m	1	6	1	21·36	
			2	4	4	20·94	
			SF	1	7	21·16	
		4×100m relay	1	1	5	39·74	
Bryggare, A.	FIN	110m hurdles	1	3	2	13·77	
			SF	2	3	13·78	
			F		6	13·76	
Bugar, I.	TCH	Discus throw	F		2	66,38	S
Bulakowski, B.	POL	20k walk	F		7	1:28-36·3	
		50k walk	F		DNF		
Burakov, V.	URS	400m	1	7	2	46·41	
			2	3	3	46·23	
			SF	2	5	45·97	
		4×400m relay	1	1	1	3-01·8	
Busse, A.	GDR	800m	1	3	1	1-47·4	
			SF	1	2	1-46·9	
			F		5	1-46·9	
		1500m	1	2	1	3-44·3	
			SF	1	3	3-43·5	
			F		4	3-40·2	
Cabrejas, R.	ESP	High jump	F		16	2,10	
Camara, S.	GUI	800m	1	6	5	1-58·9	
Cameron, B.	JAM	400m	1	2	1	47·54	
			2	3	6	47·31	
		4×400m relay	1	3	DNF		
Campbell, I.	AUS	Triple jump	F		5	16,72	
Campos, J.	POR	1500m	1	3	5	3-41·3	
			SF	1	7	3-44·4	
Capes, G.	GBR	Shot put	F		5	20,50	
Carew, J.	SLE	100m	1	1	6	11·11	
Carlsson, A.	SWE	3000m steeplechase	1	1	10	9-01·8	
Casabona, J.	ESP	4×400m relay	1	1	6	3-06·9	
		400m hurdles	1	2	5	51·26	
Casali, S.	SMR	20k walk	F		24	1:49-21·3	
Casanas, A.	CUB	110m hurdles	1	3	1	13·46	
			SF	1	1	13·44	
			F		2	13·40	S
		4×100m relay	1	1	DNF		
Castro, M. de	BRA	100m	1	6	5	10·74	
		4×100m relay	1	2	=4	39·48	
			F		8	39·54	
Centelles, J.	CUB	High jump	Q		DNQ	2,10	
Chalchisa, M.	ETH	Javelin throw	Q		DNQ	51,04	
Chamrad, J.	TCH	Hammer throw	F		12	68,16	
Chand, H.	IND	10000m	1	3	10	29-45·8	
		Marathon	F		31	2:22-08	
Chanthaphone, T.	LAO	20k walk	F		25	2:20-22·0	
Charbonnel, J.-M.	FRA	Marathon	F		DNF		
Chauhan, B.	IND	Shot put	Q		DNQ	17,05	
Chernetsky, N.	URS	400m	1	8	1	47·04	
			2	4	4	46·30	
			SF	1	6	45·94	
		4×400m relay	1	1	1	3-01·8	
			F		1	3-01·1	G
Chervanev, Y.	URS	110m hurdles	1	1	1	13·75	
			SF	1	3	13·78	
			F		8	15·80	
Chideka, R.	BOT	5000m	1	1	10	14-47·2	
Chiwala, P.	ZAM	Marathon	F		DNF		
Chochev, A.	BUL	Triple jump	F		6	16,56	
Choe, C.S.	NKO	Marathon	F		33	2:22-42	
Choueiry, N.	LEB	Marathon	F		DNF		
Cid, R.	ESP	Triple jump	Q		DNQ	16,20	
Cierpinski, W.	GDR	Marathon	F		1	2:11-03	G
Coe, S.	GBR	800m	1	4	1	1-48·5	
			SF	3	1	1-46·7	
			F		2	1-45·9	S
		1500m	1	3	2	3-40·1	
			SF	2	1	3-39·4	
			F		1	3-38·4	G
Coelho, I.	ANG	100m	1	4	7	11·42	
Coghlan, E.	IRL	5000m	1	3	3	13-45·4	
			SF	2	2	13-28·8	
			F		4	13-22·8	
Cohen, G.	GBR	400m	1	4	4	48·35	
			2	3	7	47·35	
		4×400m relay	1	3	3	3-05·9	
			F		DNF		
Colin, D.	MEX	20k walk	F		DIS		
Confait, V.	SEN	4×100m relay	1	1	6	40·25	
		4×400m relay	1	3	7	3-19·2	
Connor, K.	GBR	Triple jump	F		4	16,87	

COMPETITOR	COUNTRY CODE	EVENT	ROUND	HEAT	PLACE	TIME & DISTANCE	MEDAL
Coombs, J.	TRI	400m	1	3	2	46·55	
			2	2	2	45·81	
			SF	2	4	45·96	
			F		8	46·33	
		4×400m relay	1	2	4	3-04·3	
			F		6	3-06·6	
Copu, P.	RUM	3000m steeplechase	1	2	7	8-45·6	
			SF	1	11	8-45·0	
Corgos, A.	ESP	Long jump	F		7	8,09	
Correia, P.R.	BRA	200m	1	9	3	21·27	
			2	4	6	21·01	
		4×400m relay	1	1	2	3-04·9	
			F		5	3-05·9	
Costa, E.	MOZ	100m	1	2	5	11·02	
Cram, S.	GBR	1500m	1	1	4	3-44·1	
			SF	1	4	3-43·6	
			F		8	3-42·0	
Craveirinha, S.	MOZ	Long jump	Q		DNQ	6,94	
Crawford, H.	TRI	100m	1	5	2	10·42	
			2	1	5	10·28	
		4×100m relay	1	1	5	39·74	
Dagba, H.	BEN	Triple jump	Q		DNQ	14,71	
Dagher, R.	LEB	100m	1	5	5	11·01	
		200m	1	5	6	22·27	
Dahal, N.	NEP	10000m	1	3	13	31-19·8	
Dalhauser, R.	SUI	High jump	F		5	2,24	
Damilano, G.	ITA	20k walk	F		11	1:33-26·2	
Damilano, M.	ITA	20k walk	F		1	1:23-35·5*	G
Dangou, I.	BEN	Javelin throw	Q		DNQ	63,56	
Da Oliveira, J.C.	BRA	Long jump	F		DNS		
		Triple jump	F		3	17,22	B
Davis, M.	JAM	4×100m relay	1	1	4	39·71	
Deble, A.	ETH	400m	1	1	6	49·77	
		4×400m relay	1	2	7	3-18·2	
De Castella, R.	AUS	Marathon	F		10	2:14-31	
De Castro, M.C.	BRA	100m	1	6	5	10·74	
		4×100m relay	1	2	=4	39·48	
			F		8	39·54	
Degboe, D.	BEN	1500m	1	2	11	4-15·3	
De Leeuw, E.	BEL	400m	1	1	4	47·59	
			2	2	6	46·47	
		4×400m relay	1	2	DNF		
Deleze, P.	SUI	1500m	1	2	5	3-44·8	
Delifotis, D.	GRE	Long jump	Q		DNQ	7,74	
Delis, L.	CUB	Discus throw	F		3	66,32	B
Demarthon, F.	FRA	400m	1	1	3	47·43	
			2	1	5	46·38	
		4×400m relay	1	3	1	3-05·4	
			F		4	3-04·8	
Demyanyuk, A.	URS	High jump	F		11	2,21	
Deroche, P.	FRA	Long jump	F		10	7,77	
Desruelles, P.	BEL	Pole vault	Q		DNQ	0	
Diab, E.	LBA	400m	1	3	6	49·89	
		4×400m relay	1	2	6	3-16·7	
Diakite, M.	GUI	400m	1	4	6	49·59	
Diallo, A.	SEN	Triple jump	Q		DNQ	15,68	
Diallo, B.	SEN	100m	1	6	6	10·75	
		200m	1	7	4	21·56	
			2	4	7	21·10	
		4×100m relay	1	1	7	41·71	
Dickenson, P.	GBR	Hammer throw	Q		DNQ	64,22	
Didriksson, J.	ISL	800m	1	2	6	1-51·01	
		1500m	1	4	7	3-44·4	
Dimov, A.	URS	3000m steeplechase	1	3	2	8-33·2	
			SF	1	2	8-24·9	
			F		8	8-19·8	
Diouf, C.	SEY	4×100m relay	1	1	7	41·71	
Diouf, C.T.	SEN	100m	1	3	5	21·89	
Dittrich, T.	GDR	110m hurdles	1	3	5	13·93	
			SF	1	5	13·90	
Dombrowski, L.	GDR	Long jump	F		1	8,54	G
Dos Santos, N.R.	BRA	100m	1	3	3	10·51	
			2	1	7	10·45	
		4×100m relay	1	2	=4	39·48	
			F		8	39·54	
Dramiga, C.	UGA	400m	1	1	5	48·69	
		4×400m	1	2	5	3-07·0	
Dubois, J.	FRA	400m	1	2	2	47·57	
			2	3	4	46·60	
			SF	2	6	46·72	
		4×400m relay	1	3	1	3-05·4	
			F		4	3-04·8	
Duginets, I.	URS	Discus throw	F		6	64,04	
Dumchev, Y.	URS	Discus throw	F		5	65,58	

COMPETITOR	COUNTRY CODE	EVENT	ROUND	HEAT	PLACE	TIME & DISTANCE	MEDAL
Dunecki, L.	POL	100m	1	3	2	10-42	
			2	3	5	10-40	
		200m	1	5	2	21-30	
			2	4	3	20-87	
			SF	2	3	20-82	
			F		6	20-68	
		4×100m relay	1	1	2	38-83	
			F		2	38-33	S
Dunkel, U.	GDR	50k walk	F		DIS		
Duong, D.	VNM	Triple jump	Q		DNQ	14-59	
Dupont, P.	FRA	800m	1	1	3	1-43-6	
			SF	3	6	1-43-7	
During, W.	SLE	200m	q	5	7	23-12	
		4×100m relay	1	2	8	42-53	
Dyulgerov, E.	BUL	Hammer throw	F		6	74,04	
Dzhumanazarov, S	URS	Marathon	F		3	2:11-35	B
Eberding, J.	GDR	Marathon	F		21	2:15-04	
Egan, S.	IRL	Hammer throw	Q		DNQ	63.94	
Egger, J.P.	SUI	Shot put	F		12	18.90	
Ekblom, T.	FIN	3000m steeplechase	1	1	6	8-27-8	
			SF	2	4	8-24-3	
			F		12	8-41-9	
Elabed, M.	SYR	400m	1	5	5	50-17	
Elali, S.	SYR	5000m	1	2	12	15-08-2	
Elegbede, K.	NGR	4×100m relay	1	2	=4	39-48	
			F		7	39-12	
		Long jump	F		11	7,49	
Elias, J.L.	PER	100m	1	9	8	13-66	
Elmarghani, E.	LBA	Marathon	F		49	2:42-27	
Elmargini, S.	LBA	800m	1	5	4	1-50-0	
		4×400m relay	1	2	6	3-15-7	
Ezeigbo, H.	GBR	400m	1	5	3	47-46	
			2	4	6	46-88	
		4×400m relay	1	3	5	3-14-1	
Fabeure, L.	LUX	20k walk	F		DNF		
Fall, I.	SEN	4×100m relay	1	1	7	41-71	
Fall, M.	SEN	High jump	Q		DNQ	2,10	
Farmer, P.	AUS	Hammer throw	Q		DNQ	59,16	
Fedotkin, A.	URS	5000m	1	1	6	13-45-6	
			SF	2	8	13-31-9	
			F		8	13-24-1	
Fellah, A.	LBA	4×400m relay	1	2	6	3-16-7	
Fellice, J.	FRA	4×400m relay	1	3	1	3-05-4	
			F		4	3-04-8	
Ferreira, A.	BRA	400m hurdles	1	2	7	50-14	
			SF	1	7	52-31	
		4×400m relay	1	1	2	3-04-9	
			F		5	3-05-9	
Fituma, K.	ETH	4×400m relay	1	2	7	3-18-2	
Fitzsimmons, D.	AUS	5000m	1	1	7	13-46-4	
			SF	1	10	13-58-3	
Floroiu, I.	RUM	10000m	1	3	5	29-03-1	
			F		10	28-16-3	
Flynn, R.	IRL	1500m	1	3	6	3-42-0	
Fontanella, V.	ITA	1500m	1	3	1	3-40-1	
			SF	2	2	3-40-1	
			F		5	3-40-4	
Ford, B.	GBR	Marathon	F		DNF		
Foster, B.	GBR	10000m	1	2	3	28-55-2	
			F		11	28-22-6	
Freimuth, J.	GDR	High jump	F		3	2,31	B
Freire, C.	BRA	High jump	Q		DNQ	2,05	
Froissart, R.	FRA	4×400m relay	1	3	1	3-05-4	
			F		4	3-04-8	
Fuhrmann, D.	GDR	Javelin throw	F		7	83,50	
Fursov, V.	URS	50k walk	F		5	3:58-32	
Gardenkrans, K.	SWE	Discus throw	F		12	60,24	
Gauder, H.	GDR	50k walk	1	1	1	3:49-24*	G
George, R.	SLE	100m	1	3	7	11-37	
		200m	1	6	6	23-20	
		4×100m relay	1	2	8	42-53	
Gerbi, G.	ITA	3000m steeplechase	1	3	6	8-37-1	
			SF	2	5	8-27-2	
			F		6	8-18-5	
Gerstenberg, D.	GDR	Hammer throw	F		5	74,60	
Gessese, A.	ETH	Long jump	Q		DNQ	6,66	
Gibicsar, I.	HUN	High jump	Q		DNQ	2,15	
Gilkes, J.	GUY	100m	1	8	1	10-34	
			2	4	1	10-26	
			SF	2	5	10-44	
		200m	1	7	1	21-07	
			2	3	2	20-83	
			SF	1	5	20-87	
Girat, D.	CUB	Long jump	Q		DNQ	7,57	
Gisler, R.	SUI	4×400m relay	1	3	3	3-07-2	
Golda, I.	POL	Hammer throw	F		8	73,74	
Gomez, J.	MEX	10000m	1	2	8	29-53-6	
Gomez, R.	MEX	10000m	1	3	8	29-25-7	
		Marathon	F		6	2:12-39	
Gonzalez, A.	FRA	1500m	1	2	4	3-44-6	
			SF	1	8	3-44-7	
Gonzalez, B.	ESP	4×400m	1	1	6	3-06-9	
Gonzalez, J.L.	ESP	1500m	1	3	4	3-40-9	
			SF	2	8	3-42-6	
Gonzalez, R.	MEX	20k walk	F		6	1:27-48-6	
		50k walk	F		DNF		
Gonzalez, R.	CUB	Marathon	F		DNF		
Gonzalez, T.	CUB	100m	1	6	3	10-65	
			2	3	7	10-44	
		200m	1	1	2	21-64	
			2	4	8	21-19	
		4×100m relay	1	1	DNF		
Gopal, A.	SEY	110m hurdles	1	3	8	16-36	
Greaves, W.	GBR	110m hurdles	1	2	4	13-85	
			SF	1	6	13-98	
Grigoriev, A.	URS	High jump	F		8	2,21	
Grippo, C.	ZAM	800m	1	4	4	1-48-9	
			SF	2	6	1-48-7	
Grummt, S.	GDR	Decathlon	F		8	7892	
Guimaraes, A.C.	BRA	800m	1	3	3	1-48-2	
			SF	1	3	1-46-9	
			F		4	1-46-2	
		4×400m relay	1	1	2	3-04-9	
			F		5	3-05-9	
Gullstrand, C.	SWE	400m hurdles	1	1	6	50-95	
Gustafsson, B.	SWE	20k walk	F		DIS		
		50k walk	F		DNF		
Haapakoski, T.	FIN	Pole vault	F		9	5,45	
Haas, P.	SUI	4×400m relay	1	3	3	3-07-2	
Haba, P.	GUI	100m	1	8	6	11-19	
		200m	1	3	7	22-70	
Habchaoui, R.	ALG	5000m	1	3	9	13-59-9	
		10000m	1	2	6	29-12-9	
Hackney, R.	GBR	3000m steeplechase	1	3	5	8-36-4	
			SF	2	7	8-29-2	
Hadfield, P.	AUS	Decathlon	F		13	7709	
Hagelsteens, A.	BEL	5000m	1	1	5	13-44-9	
			SF	2	10	13-46-7	
		10000m	1	1	6	29-47-6	
Halldorsson, H.	ISL	Shot put	F		10	19,55	
Halwand, B.	ZAM	Marathon	F		43	2:36-51	
Hamdan, A.	SYR	10000m	1	1	9	31-12-9	
Hamilton, O.	JAM	800m	1	5	3	1-49-3	
			SF	1	4	1-47-6	
Hanisch, W.	GDR	Javelin throw	F		3	86,72	B
Harrek, D.	ALG	800m	1	3	5	1-49-9	
			SF	3	8	1-51-9	
		1500m	1	4	8	3-45-3	
Hashem, E.	KUW	Long jump	Q		DNQ	0	
Hashem, A.	KUW	400m hurdles	1	3	8	53-31	
Herrera, Al.	CUB	Triple jump	Q		DNQ	0	
Herrera, Ar.	CUB	Triple jump	F		11	16,03	
Heyer, W.	GDR	20k walk	F		DIS		
Hlasa, K.	LES	800m	1	1	7	1-56-1	
		Marathon	F		DNF		
Hoff, B.	GDR	200m	1	7	3	21-53	
			2	2	3	20-96	
			SF	1	2	20-69	
			F		5	20-50	
		4×100m relay	1	2	1	38-65	
			F		5	38-73	
Hoffman, Z.	POL	Triple jump	Q		DNQ	15,35	
Hogberg, G.	SWE	Marathon	F		DNF		
Holtom, M.	GBR	110m hurdles	1	3	3	13-83	
			SF	2	5	13-94	
Honey, G.	AUS	Long jump	Q		DNQ	7,44	
Hooper, B.	GBR	Pole vault	F		11	5,35	
Hooper, P.	IRL	Marathon	F		42	2:30-28	
Hooper, R.	IRL	Marathon	F		38	2:23-53	
Hornillos, I.	ESP	400m	1	8	6	47-45	
		4×400m relay	1	1	6	3-06-9	
Hossfeld, H.	GDR	Discus throw	F		11	61,14	
Hounkanrin, L.	BEN	400m	1	2	6	51-04	
Hounnou, T.	BEN	Long jump	Q		DNQ	7,07	
Houry, A.	SYR	Discus throw	Q		DNQ	47,52	
Houvion, P.	FRA	Pole vault	F		4	5,65	
Hreitani, M.	SYR	110m hurdles	1	1	7	15-45	
Huhtala, H.	FIN	Hammer throw	F		9	71,96	
Illorson, G.	CAM	100m	1	9	1	10-34	
			2	4	2	10-29	
			SF	1	8	10-60	
		200m	1	1	5	22-21	
Imadiyi, F.	NGR	4×400m relay	1	3	5	3-14-1	
Inacio, R.	ANG	200m	1	1	6	22-52	

COMPETITOR	COUNTRY CODE	EVENT	ROUND	HEAT	PLACE	TIME & DISTANCE	MEDAL
Ismail, A.	MOZ	110m hurdles	1	3	7	15·18	
Ivan, J.	TCH	110m hurdles	1	1		DNF	
Ivanov, V.	BUL	200m	1	8	4	21·28	
			2	4	5	20·96	
		4×100m relay	1	1	3	39·25	
			F		6	38·99	
Ivchenko, Y.	URS	50k walk	F		3	3:56-32	B
Jacobi, H.J.	GDR	Shot put	F		6	20,32	
Jakobsson, O.	ISL	Shot put	F		11	19,07	
		Discus throw	Q		DNQ	0	
Jansky, J.	TCH	Marathon	F		DNF		
Jaskulka, S.	POL	Long jump	F		5	8,13	
Jenkins, D.	GBR	400m	1	1	1	46·67	
			2	4	1	45·99	
			SF	1	3	45·59	
			F		7	45·56	
Jokinen, E.	FIN	Decathlon	F		9	7826	
Jonga, T.	ZIM	Marathon	F		51	2:47-17	
Joseph, C.	TRI	4×400m relay	1	2	4	3-04·3	
			F		6	3-06·6	
Josiah, L.	BOT	100m	1	2	6	11·15	
		200m	1	7	6	22·45	
Joumaa, A.	SYR	3000m steeplechase	1	2	10	9-29·4	
Juantorena, A.	CUB	400m	1	7	3	46·69	
			2	3	2	46·23	
			SF	2	3	45·95	
			F		4	45·09	
Kachanov, V.	URS	Decathlon	F		DNF		
Kachenjela, C.	ZAM	100m	1	1	5	11·03	
Kadhum, A.	IRQ	4×400m relay	1	3	4	3-10·5	
Kalliomaki, A.	FIN	Pole vault	Q		DNQ	0	
Kamber, U.	SUI	4×400m relay	1	3	3	3-07·2	
Kanza, I.	CGO	4×100m relay	1	2	7	40·09	
Karageorgos, A.	GRE	20k walk	F		15	1:36-53·4	
Karageorgos, C.	GRE	50k walk	F		12	4:24-36	
Karaniotov, I.	BUL	100m	1	7	4	10·66	
		4×100m relay	1	1	3	39·25	
			F		6	38·99	
Kareng, W.	ESP	400m hurdles	1	2		DNF	
Kedir, M.	ETH	5000m	1	2	2	13-42·7	
			SF	2	1	13-28·6	
			F		12	13-34·2	
		10000m	1	1	1	28-16·4	
			F		3	27-44·7	B
Kefalas, L.	GRE	100m	1	2	2	10·70	
			2	1	8	10·62	
Kendor, S.	SLE	400m	1	5	6	52·98	
		800m	1	6	7	2-06·5	
		4×400m relay	1	1	8	3-25·0	
Khalifa, M.	IRQ	Triple jump	Q		DNQ	15,86	
Kharlov, A.	URS	400m hurdles	1	2	4	50·79	
			SF	1	5	50·64	
Khemanith, P.	LAO	400m	1	3	7	53·74	
Khin, S.	BIR	Marathon	F		47	2:41-41	
Khristov, N.	BUL	Shot put	Q		DNQ	19,01	
Kiakouama, A.	CGO	100m	1	6	4	10·69	
		4×100m relay	1	2	7	40·09	
Kio, J.	NGR	Long jump	Q		DNQ	7,77	
Kirov, N.	URS	800m	1	2	2	1-47·5	
			SF	2	1	1-46·6	
			F		3	1-46·0	B
Kiselyov, V.	URS	Shot put	F		1	21,35*	G
Kiss, F.	HUN	200m	1	2	2	21·34	
			2	1	4	21·24	
			SF	1	8	21·17	
		4×100m relay	1	2	6	39·97	
Klarenbeek, M.	HOL	400m	1	8	3	47·37	
			2	2	8	46·81	
		4×400m relay	1	1	5	3-06·0	
Klimaszewski, A.	POL	Long jump	Q		DNQ	7,76	
Klimczyk, M.	POL	Pole vault	F		6	5,55	
Knapic, Z.	YUG	4×400m relay	1	1	3	3-05·3	
Knebel, A.	GDR	4×400m relay	1	2	1	3-03·4	
			F		2	3-01·3	S
Koh, C.S.	NKO	Marathon	F		27	2:20-08	
Kolar, K.	CZE	400m	1	1	2	47·26	
			2	4	3	46·27	
			SF	1	8	46·11	
		4×400m relay	1	2	2	3-03·5	
			F		7	3-07·0	
Kolev, B.	BUL	800m	1	4	3	1-48·7	
			SF	3	3	1-47·3	
Komnenic, V.	YUG	High jump	F		6	2,24	
Kone, S.	MLI	100m	1	9	7	11·07	
Konrad, W.	AUT	3000m steeplechase	1	1	4	8-25·0	
			SF	2	10	8-51·6	

COMPETITOR	COUNTRY CODE	EVENT	ROUND	HEAT	PLACE	TIME & DISTANCE	MEDAL
Kopitar, R.	YUG	400m hurdles	1	3	3	50·34	
			SF	1	2	50·55	
			F		5	49·67	
		4×400m relay	1	1	3	3-05·3	
Kortelainen, J.	FIN	Marathon	F		DNF		
Kotov, V.	URS	Marathon	F		4	2:12-05	
Kotu, T.	ETH	10000m	1	3	1	28-55·3	
			F		4	27-46·5	
Koussis, M.	GRE	Marathon	F		20	2:18-02	
Kozakiewicz, W.	POL	Pole vault	F		1	5,78*	G
Krastev, P.	BUL	110m hurdles	1	1	3	13·95	
			SF	2	6	13·99	
Kula, D.	URS	Javelin throw	F		1	91,20	G
Kulibaba, S.	URS	Pole vault	F		8	5,45	
Kuma, Y.	ETH	Triple jump	Q		DNQ	13,60	
Kumar, S.	IND	1500m	1	2	8	3-55·6	
Kunze, H.J.	GDR	5000m	1	1	2	13-44·4	
			SF	1	11	14-00·3	
Kurrat, K.-D.	GDR	100m	1	1	4	10·53	
			2	4	6	10·54	
Kutsenko, Y.	URS	Decathlon	F		2	8331	S
Lahti, J.	FIN	Decathlon	F		11	7765	
Lara, O.	CUB	100m	1	4	3	10·39	
			2	1	3	10·21	
			SF	2	2	10·34	
			F		5	10·43	
		200m	1	8	1	21·06	
			2	1	3	21·01	
			SF	2	4	20·93	
			F		8	21·19	
		4×100m relay	1	1		DNF	
Larose, M.	SEY	100m	1	1	7	11·27	
		4×100m relay	1	1	6	40·25	
		4×400m relay	1	3	7	3-19·2	
Lauenborg, J.	DEN	Marathon	F		DNF		
Laukkanen, V.	FIN	3000m steeplechase	1	2	6	8-38·4	
			SF	1	10	8-33·3	
Lauterbach, H.	GDR	High jump	F		4	2,29	
Lawrence, A.	JAM	4×100m relay	1	1	4	39·71	
Lee, Q.-K.	VNM	1500m	1	3	10	4-06·8	
Leitner, J.	TCH	Long jump	Q		DNQ	7,68	
Lelievre, G.	FRA	50k walk	F		DNF		
Lemme, A.	GDR	Discus throw	Q		DNQ	59,44	
Leonard, S.	CUB	100m	1	1	1	10·33	
			2	2	1	10·16	
			SF	1	2	10·40	
			F		2	10·25	S
		200m	1	9	1	20·95	
			2	2	1	20·93	
			SF	1	1	20·61	
			F		4	20·30	
		4×100m relay	1	1		DNF	
Letseka, J.	LES	100m	1	4	6	11·21	
		200m	1	7	5	22·31	
Li, J.-H.	NKO	Marathon	F		29	2:21-10	
Licznerski, Z.	POL	200m	1	9	4	21·36	
			2	2	5	21·22	
		4×100m relay	1	1	2	38·83	
			F		2	38·33	S
Linge, M.	URS	4×400m relay	1	1	1	3-01·8	
			F		1	3-01·1	G
Lishebo, D.	ZAM	400m hurdles	1	1	7	51·73	
		4×400m relay	1	1	7	3-14·9	
Lismont, K.	BEL	Marathon	F		9	2:13-27	
Litvinov, S.	URS	Hammer throw	F		2	80,64	S
Llopart, J.	ESP	50k walk	F		2	3:51-25	S
Lloveras, J.	ESP	400m hurdles	1	3	4	50·48	
			SF	2	8	51·86	
Loikkanen, A.	FIN	1500m	1	3	3	3-40·5	
			SF	1	6	3-44·0	
Lomicky, J.	TCH	4×400m relay	1	2	2	3-03·5	
			F		7	3-07·0	
Lorraway, K.	AUS	Triple jump	F		8	16,44	
Ludwig, D.	POL	Decathlon	F		6	7978	
Lukuba, D.	TAN	100m	1	8	5	10·74	
		200m	1	5	4	21·76	
Luliga, M.	TAB	800m	1	2	5	1-49·6	
			SF	3	7	1-51·5	
Lupiya, C.	ZAM	400m	1	2	4	48·49	
			2	1	7	47·67	
		4×400m relay	1	1	7	3-14·9	
Maaninka, K.	FIN	5000m	1	3	6	13-45·8	
			SF	1	3	13-40·2	
			F		3	13-22·0	B
		10000m	1	1	2	28-31·0	
			F		2	27-44·3	S
Maaraoui, A.	SYR	400m hurdles	1	1	7	53·26	

COMPETITOR	COUNTRY CODE	EVENT	ROUND	HEAT	PLACE	TIME & DISTANCE	MEDAL
Mabikana, B.	CGO	110m hurdles	1	1	6	15·12	
Mabruk, M.	LBA	1500m	1	4	9	3-54·5	
McFarlane, M.	GBR	200m	1	2	4	21·43	
			2	1	6	21·33	
		4×100m relay	1	2	3	39·20	
			F		4	38·62	
McLeod, M.	GBR	10000m	1	3	2	28-57·5	
			F		12	28-40·8	
McMaster, A.	GBR	100m	1	5	3	10·43	
			2	3	6	10·42	
		4×100m relay	1	2	3	39·20	
			F		4	38·62	
McStravick, B.	GBR	Decathlon	F		15	7616	-
Mada, A.	ALG	10000m	1	1	3	30-23·5	
		Marathon	F		DNF		
Magnani, M.	ITA	Marathon	F		8	2:13-12	
Mahmoud, K.	KUW	800m	1	3	7	1-51·4	
Makarov, A.	URS	Javelin throw	F		2	89,64	S
Makhlouf, M.	SYR	800m	1	4	6	1-52·3	
		1500m	1	4	10	4-00·3	
Malekwa, Z.	TAN	Javelin throw	Q		DNQ	71,58	
Malinowski, B.	POL	3000m steeplechase	1	1	1	8-29·5	
			SF	2	1	8-21·2	
			F		1	8-09·7	G
Malinverni, S.	ITA	400m	1	6	2	47·63	
			2	1	8	47·79	
		4×400m relay	1	2	3	3-03·5	
			F		3	3-04·3	B
Malovec, D.	TCH	4×400m relay	1	2	2	3-03·5	
			F		7	3-07·0	
Malozemlin, V.	URS	1500m	1	4	4	3-38·7	
			SF	1	5	3-43·6	
Maminski, B.	POL	3000m steeplechase	1	1	3	8-24·0	
			SF	1	3	8-18·8	
			F		7	8-19·5	
Manandhar, B.	NEP	Marathon	F		37	2:23-51	
Manuel, B.	ANG	5000m	1	2	11	14-51·4	
Marajo, J.	FRA	800m	1	6	1	1-49·6	
			SF	2	3	1-47·3	
			F		7	1-47·3	
		1500m	1	1	1	3-43·9	
			SF	2	3	3-39·6	
			F		7	3-41·5	
Marchei, M.	ITA	Marathon	F		35	2:23-21	
Marczak, R.	POL	Marathon	F		DNF		
Marie, A.	SEY	3000m steeplechase	1	3	10	9-19·7	
		Marathon	F		DNF		
Marin, J.	ESP	20k walk	F		5	1:26-45·6	
		50k walk	F		6	4·03·08	
Markin, V.	URS	400m	1	5	1	46·88	
			2	2	1	45·58	
			SF	2	2	45·60	
			F		1	44·60	G
		4×400m relay	F		1	3-01·1	G
Martin, L.	TAN	10000m	1	3	11	30-33·4	
		Marathon	F		23	2:18-21	
Massallay, J.	SLE	800m	1	4	7	2-04·4	
		4×400m	1	1	8	3-25·0	
		400m	1	3	5	49·68	
Matei, S.	RUM	High jump	F		13	2,18	
Meier, F.	SUI	400m hurdles	1	3	2	50·32	
			SF	2	4	50·12	
			F		7	50·0	
Meisch, D.	GDR	50k walk	F		DIS		
Mennea, P.	ITA	100m	1	2	1	10·56	
			2	1	4	10·27	
			SF	1	6	10·58	
		200m	1	2	1	21·26	
			2	4	1	20·60	
			SF	2	1	20·70	
			F		1	20·19	G
		4×400m relay	1	2	3	3-03·5	
			F		3	3-04·3	B
Mhaladi, I.	BOT	1500m	1	2	9	3-59·1	
Michel, D.	GDR	Javelin throw	Q		DNQ	78·34	
Milhau, R.	FRA	800m	1	4	2	1-48·5	
			SF	1	6	1-49·1	
Milic, V.	YUG	Shot put	F		8	20,07	
Millonig, D.	AUT	5000m	1	3	4	13-45·7	
			SF	1	4	13-29·4	
			F		6	13-23·3	
Mills, R.	GBR	20k walk	F		10	1:32-37·8	
Milne, R.	GBR	4×400m relay	1	3	2	3-05·9	
			F		DNF		

COMPETITOR	COUNTRY CODE	EVENT	ROUND	HEAT	PLACE	TIME & DISTANCE	MEDAL
Minshid, A.	IRQ	4×400m relay	1	3	4	3-10·5	
Mitchell, R.	AUS	400m	1	3	3	46·63	
			2	1	1	45·73	
			SF	1	2	45·48	
			F		2	44·84	S
Mitiku, T.	ETH	20k walk	F		23	1:45-45·7	
Mladenov, A.	BUL	High jump	Q		DNQ	2,10	
Mohammed, R.	TRI	4×400m relay	1	2	4	3-04·3	
			F		6	3-06·6	
Mohammed, Y.	ETH	5000m	1	3	5	13-45·8	
			SF	1	4	13-39·4	
			F		10	13-28·4	
Molomo, P.	MOZ	5000m	1	3	11	15-11·9	
Mokopo, M.	LES	1500m	1	1	7	3-55·5	
Moorcroft, D.	GBR	5000m	1	2	5	13-43·0	
			SF	1	9	13-58·2	
Moracho, J.	ESP	110m hurdles	1	2	3	13·72	
			SF	7	4	13·80	
			F		7	13·78	
Moravcik, D.	TCH	3000m steeplechase	1	2	2	8-33·4	
			SF	2	6	8-28·0	
			F		10	8-29·1	
Morcelli, A.	ALG	1500m	1	2	7	3-46·0	
Moreau, G.	BEL	High jump	F		14	2,18	
Morris, D.	JAM	High jump	Q		DNQ	2,10	
Moseyev, L.	URS	Marathon	F		5	2:12-14	
Mosweu, G.	BOT	10000m	1	3	12	30-38·8	
Mpioh, E.	CGO	Marathon	F		52	2:48-14	
Msube, Z.	ZIM	5000m	1	3	10	14-06·7	
Mudongo, L.	BOT	800m	1	1	6	1-52·5	
Munkelt, T.	GDR	110m hurdles	1	2	1	13·55	
			SF	2	1	13·49	
			F		1	13·39	G
		4×100m relay	1	2	1	38·65	
			F		5	38·73	
Murad, K.	KUW	Hammer throw	Q		DNQ	47,40	
Muravyov, V.	URS	100m	1	4	2	10·37	
			2	4	3	10·34	
			SF	2	3	10·42	
			F		6	10·44	
		4×100m relay	1	1	1	38·68	
			F		1	38·26	G
Musaanga, B.	ZAM	Triple jump	Q		DNQ	14,79	
Musango, A.	ZAM	800m	1	4	5	1-51·6	
		1500m	1	3	8	3-53·7	
		4×400m relay	1	1	7	3-14·9	
Muziyo, A.S.	ZAM	200m	1	3	5	22·47	
		4×400m relay	1	1	7	3-14·9	
Mwita, P.	TAN	100m	1	9	6	11·07	
Nagy, I	HUN	100m	1	8	4	10·68	
		200m	1	4	2	21·80	
			2	2	6	21·38	
		4×100m relay	1	2	6	39·97	
Nagy, L.	RUM	Discus throw	Q		DNQ	59,34	
Nahri, N.	SYR	100m	1	3	5	10·67	
		200m	1	2	5	22·14	
Najem, N.	KUW	Discus throw	Q		DNQ	39,26	
Nakaia, K.	BRA	100m	1	2	3	10·72	
			2	2	8	10·70	
		4×100m relay	1	2	=4	39·48	
			F		8	39·54	
Naylor, N.	GBR	High jump	F		9	2,21	
Ndao, M.	SEN	100m	1	2	4	10·73	
		4×100m relay	1	1	7	41·71	
Ndiaye, D.	SEN	Long jump	Q		DNQ	7,66	
Ndiemandoi, E.	TAN	Marathon	F		14	2:16-47	
Ndyabagye, F.	UGA	Long jump	Q		DNQ	0	
Nedi, D.	ETH	Marathon	F		7	2:12-44	
Nemeth, M.	HUN	Javelin throw	F		8	82,40	
Nemeth, F.	AUT	1500m	1	4	3	3-38·3	
			SF	2	6	3-40·8	
Nenov, S.	BUL	3000m steeplechase	1	3	9	8-43·8	
			SF	1	12	8-50·2	
Nguyen, Q.	VNM	Marathon	F		50	2:44-37	
Ngwila, D.	ZAM	Marathon	F		48	2:42-11	
		10000m	1	2	9	30-29·2	
Niare, N.	MLI	Discus throw	Q		DNQ	57,34	
Nijboer, G.	HOL	Marathon	F		2	2:11-20	S
Niklaus, S.	SUI	Decathlon	F		12	7762	
Nkhoma, A.	ZIM	Marathon	F		53	2:53-35	
Nkounkou, T.	CGO	100m	1	8	3	10·53	
			2	2	6	10·59	
		4×100m relay	1	2	7	40·09	
Noel, E.	TRI	4×100m relay	1	1	5	39·74	
Nsayyif, H.A.	IRQ	400m	1	6	4	48·03	
			2	4	8	48·50	
		4×400m relay	1	3	4	3-10·5	

COMPETITOR	COUNTRY CODE	EVENT	ROUND	HEAT	PLACE	TIME & DISTANCE	MEDAL
Nyambui, S.	TAN	5000m	1	3	2	13-45.4	
			SF	2	5	13-30.2	
			F		2	13-21.6	S
Oakes, G.	GBR	400m hurdles	1	2	3	50.39	
			SF	2	3	50.07	
			F		3	49.11	B
Okodogbe, P.	NGR	100m	1	1	2	10.39	
			2	3	4	10.34	
			SF	2	7	10.51	
		200m	1	3	3	21.42	
			2	3	3	20.89	
			SF	1	6	21.03	
		4×100m relay	1	2	=4	39.48	
			F		7	39.12	
Olizarenko, S.	URS	3000m steeplechase	1	2	3	8-34.2	
			SF	2	DNF		
Olowo, P.	UGA	4×400m relay	1	2	5	3-07.0	
Onta, R.	NEP	100m	1	5	7	11.61	
Orozco, G.	CUB	Hammer throw	F		11	68,68	
O'Shea, M.	IRL	5000m	1	2	10	14-03.0	
Ottley, D.	GBR	Javelin throw	Q		DNQ	77,20	
Ovett, S.	GBR	800m	1	1	1	1-49.4	
			SF	1	1	1-46.6	
			F		1	1-45.4	G
		1500m	1	4	1	3-36.8	
			SF	1	1	3-43.1	
			F		3	3-39.0	B
Oyeledun, S.	NGR	100m	1	9	4	10.59	
			2	4	8	10.73	
		4×100m relay	1	2	=4	39.48	
			F		7	39.12	
Paez, A.	ESP	800m	1	1	2	1-49.5	
			SF	2	5	1-47.8	
Panzo, H.	FRA	100m	1	6	2	10.53	
			2	3	3	10.29	
			SF	1	4	10.45	
			F		8	10.49	
		4×100m relay	1	1	2	39.01	
			F		3	38.53	B
Paragi, F.	HUN	Javelin throw	F		10	79,52	
Paroczai, A.	HUN	800m	1	2	3	1-47.5	
			SF	2	7	1-48.8	
Paschek, F.	GDR	Long jump	F		2	8,21	S
Pavlov, P.	BUL	200m	1	1	3	21.78	
			2	3	8	21.35	
		4×100m relay	1	1	3	39.25	
			F		6	38.99	
Pawlowicz, J.	POL	4×400m relay	1	1	4	3-05.8	
Pegado, G.J.	BRA	400m	1	7	6	48.71	
		4×400m relay	1	1	2	3-04.9	
			F		5	3-05.9	
Pena, E.	COL	20k walk	F		17	1:38-00.0	
		50k walk	F		14	4:29-27	
Perarnau, M.	ESP	High jump	Q		DNQ	2,15	
Pereira, C.	SEY	200m	1	1	7	22.59	
		4×100m relay	1	1	6	40.25	
		4×400m relay	1	3	7	3-19.2	
Perera, N.	CEY	4×400m relay	1	3	6	3-14.4	
Persson, T.	SWE	Marathon	F		30	2:21-11	
Perumal, S.	IND	200m	1	6	5	22.39	
Peter, J.	GDR	10000m	1	2	2	28-50.0	
			F		6	28-05.6	
		Marathon	F		40	2:24-53	
Petitbois, B.	FRA	200m	1	9	2	21.16	
			2	1	5	21.32	
Petrov, P.	BUL	100m	1	4	1	10.32	
			2	1	2	10.13	
			SF	1	1	10.39	
			F		3	10.39	B
		200m	1	5	3	21.59	
			2	1	8	21.89	
		4×100m relay	1	1	3	39.25	
			F		6	38.99	
Peynado, D.	JAM	400m	1	4	1	47.37	
			2	2	7	46.50	
		4×400m relay	1	3	DNF		
Phongsavanh, V.	LAO	800m	1	6	6	2-05.5	
Pierzynka, Z.	POL	Marathon	F		26	2:20-03	
Pietrzyk, J.	POL	400m	1	7	5	47.18	
		4×400m relay	1	1	4	3-05.8	
Pinto, A.	POR	Marathon	F		16	2:17-04	
Pisic, B.	YUG	110m hurdles	1	2	5	14.13	
			SF	1	7	14.16	
Plachy, J.	TCH	1500m	1	2	3	3-44.4	
			SF	2	5	3-40.4	
			F		6	3-40.7	
Pochinchuk, P.	URS	20k walk	F		2	1:24-45.4	S

COMPETITOR	COUNTRY CODE	EVENT	ROUND	HEAT	PLACE	TIME & DISTANCE	MEDAL
Podiuzhny, V.	URS	Long jump	F		3	8,18	B
Ponitzsch, R.	GDR	3000m steeplechase	1	2	9	8-56.5	
Pontes Campos, J.	POR	1500m	1	3	5	3-41.3	
			SF	1	7	3-44.4	
Popovic, A.	YUG	200m	1	6	3	21.65	
			2	1	7	21.66	
Pottel, R.	GDR	Decathlon	F		DNF		
Pousi, O.	FIN	Triple jump	Q		DNQ	0	
Premachandra, A.	CEY	4×400m relay	1	3	6	3-14.4	
Prenzler, O.	GDR	200m	1	2	3	21.35	
			2	3	4	20.89	
			SF	2	5	21.00	
Pribilinec, J.	TCH	20k walk	F		20	1:42-52.4	
Prieto, A.	ESP	10000m	1	2	5	29-12.8	
			F		DNF		
Prokhorenko, Y.	URS	Pole vault	Q		DNQ	0	
Prokofyev, A.	URS	110m hurdles	1	2	2	13.61	
			SF	2	2	13.59	
			F		4	13.49	
		4×100m relay	1	1	1	38.68	
			F		1	38.26	G
Proteasa, A.	RUM	High jump	F		7	2,21	
Puchkov, A.	URS	110m hurdles	1	3	4	13.84	
			SF	1	2	13.50	
			F		3	13.44	B
Pudas, R.	FIN	Pole vault	F		12	5,25	
Puranen, A.	FIN	Javelin throw	F		5	85,12	
Pusty, J.	POL	110m hurdles	1	1	2	13.84	
			SF	2	4	13.81	
			F		5	13.68	
Puttemans, E.	BEL	5000m	1	2	4	13-43.0	
			SF	1	8	13-50.2	
Puuste, H.	URS	Javelin throw	F		4	86,10	
Quarrie, D.	JAM	100m	1	7	2	10.37	
			2	3	2	10.29	
			SF	1	5	10.55	
		200m	1	3	1	20.87	
			2	1	1	20.89	
			SF	2	2	20.76	
			F		3	20.29	B
		4×100m relay	1	1	4	39.71	
Raborg, R.	PER	Long jump	Q		DNQ	6,85	
Raise, O.	ITA	High jump	Q		DNQ	2,18	
Rakabaele, V.	LES	Marathon	F		36	2:23-29	
Rakotoarisoa, T.	MAD	800m	1	3	6	1-50.5	
		1500m	1	3	9	3-55.9	
Ramon, D.	ESP	3000m steeplechase	1	3	1	8-31.9	
			SF	2	2	8-22.0	
			F		4	8-15.8	
Ramotshabe, J.	BOT	400m	1	2	7	51.49	
Randrianari, J.	MAD	10000m	1	2	11	31-18.4	
		Marathon	F		25	2:19-23	
Ranjit, S.	IND	20k walk	F		18	1:38-27.2	
Rashchupkin, V.	URS	Discus throw	F		1	66,64	G
Ray, E.	GDR	100m	1	5	1	10.38	
			2	3	3	10.30	
			SF	2	6	10.47	
		4×100m relay	1	2	1	38.65	
			F		5	38.73	
Rea, W.	AUT	Long jump	Q		DNQ	7,74	
Reis, C.	MOZ	200m	1	7	DNF		
Reitz, C.	GBR	3000m steeplechase	1	2	4	8-35.3	
			SF	1	8	8-29.8	
Reshetnyak, A.	URS	800m	1	3	2	1-47.9	
			SF	3	5	1-48.2	
Rhaima, J.	IRQ	110m hurdles	1	2	7	14.89	
Richard, A.	FRA	100m	1	4	4	10.51	
			2	4	5	10.45	
		4×100m relay	1	1	2	39.01	
			F		3	38.53	B
Richards, I.	GBR	50k walk	F		11	4:22-57	
Rieger, P.	GDR	Long jump	Q		DNQ	7,59	
Roelandt, D.	BEL	4×400m relay	1	2	DNF		
Rola, S.	POL	50k walk	F		7	4:07-07	
Ronac, M.	PER	Decathlon	F		DNF		
Rose, N.	GBR	5000m	1	1	3	13-44.7	
			SF	1	5	13-40.6	
Ryffel, M.	SUI	5000m	1	3	1	13-45.0	
			SF	2	3	13-29.3	
			F		5	13-23.1	
		10000m	1	3	DNF		
Sacpraseuth, S.	LAO	200m	1	9	7	24.28	
Sahabandu, K.	CEY	4×400m relay	1	3	6	3-14.4	
Sahil, A.	ALG	High jump	Q		DNQ	2,18	
Saini, G.	IND	5000m	1	1	9	14-06.6	
Sajkowski, A.	POL	Marathon	F		DNF		

COMPETITOR	COUNTRY CODE	EVENT	ROUND	HEAT	PLACE	TIME & DISTANCE	MEDAL
Sala, C.	ESP	110m hurdles	1	3	6	14.23	
			SF	2	7	14.00	
Salonen, R.	FIN	20k walk	F		9	1:31-32.0	
		50k walk	F		DNF		
Samararatne, D.	CEY	4×400m relay	1	3	6	3-14.4	
Sanchez, F.	ESP	3000m steeplechase	1	1	5	8-27.5	
			SF	1	4	8-19.0	
			F		5	8-18.0	
Sanyeyev, V.	URS	Triple jump	F		2	17,24	S
Santa Cruz, J.	CUB	Discus throw	F		10	61,52	
Sarr, A.	SEN	110m hurdles	1	2	6	14.57	
Sator, L.	HUN	50k walk	F		9	4:10-53	
Savic, M.	YUG	800m	1	5	2	1-49.2	
			SF	1	5	1-47.6	
		4×400m relay	1	1	3	3-05.3	
Sawall, W.	AUS	50k walk	F		8	4.08-25	
Schaffer, F.	GDR	400m	1	7	1	46.13	
			2	3	1	46.15	
			SF	2	1	45.47	
			F		3	44.87	B
		4×400m relay	1	2	1	3-03.4	
			F		2	3-01.3	S
Schildhauer, W.	GDR	10000m	1	1	3	28-32.1	
			F		7	28-11.0	
Schlegel, S.	GDR	100m	1	6	1	10.44	
			2	1	6	10.28	
		4×100m relay	1	2	1	38.65	
			F		5	38.73	
Schlisske, A.	GDR	110m hurdles	1	1	4	14.18	
			SF	1	8	14.60	
Schmidt, W.	GDR	Discus throw	F		4	65,64	
Schoofs, R.	BEL	Marathon	F		18	2:17-28	
Schulting, H.	HOL	400m	1	6	5	48.53	
		400m hurdles	1	2	1	50.01	
			SF	1	4	50.61	
		4×400m relay	1	1	5	3-06.0	
Scott, W.	AUS	10000m	1	3	3	28-58.8	
			F		9	28-15.1	
Sedykh, Y.	URS	Hammer throw	F		1	81,80*	G
Sellik, E.	URS	5000m	1	3	8	13-52.4	
		10000m	1	2	4	29-12.1	
			F		8	28-13.8	
Seluma, A.	LBA	200m	1	2	6	22.88	
		4×400m relay	1	2	6	3-16.7	
Sena, J.	POR	3000m steeplechase	1	2	DNF		
Shahanga, G.	TAN	Marathon	F		15	2:16-47	
Sharp, C.	GBR	100m	1	8	2	10.33	
			2	4	4	10.38	
			SF	1	7	10.60	
		200m	1	1	4	21.51	
			2	2	4	21.16	
			SF	2	8	21.24	
		4×100m relay	1	2	3	39.20	
			F		4	38.62	
Shesterov, V.	URS	10000m	1	3	9	29-32.4	
Shetewi, E.	LBA	Marathon	F		44	2:38-01	
Shlyapnikov, A.	URS	100m	1	9	3	10.43	
			2	2	5	10.41	
Shrestha, M.	NEP	Marathon	F		45	2.38-52	
Sidorov, N.	URS	200m	1	8	3	21.15	
			2	4	2	20.83	
			SF	2	7	21.17	
		4×100m relay	1	1	1	38.68	
			F		1	38.26	G
Siegele, J.	AUT	20k walk	F		22	1:45-17.8	
Siegele, W.	AUT	20k walk	F		DNF		
Sigurdsson, O.	ISL	100m	1	7	7	10.94	
		400m	1	8	5	47.39	
Simonsen, B.	SWE	50k walk	F		4	3.57-08	
Sinersaari, P.	FIN	Javelin throw	F		6	84,34	
Singh, Sriram	IND	800m	1	1	4	1-49.8	
			SF	2	8	1-49.0	
Singh, Shivnath	IND	Marathon	F		DNF		
Slusarski, T.	POL	Pole vault	F		=2	5,65	S
Smedegaard, J.	DEN	400m	1	3	4	47.01	
			2	1	3	45.89	
			SF	2	7	47.00	
Smet, M.	BEL	Marathon	F		13	2:16-00	
Smith, B.	GBR	5000m	1	3	7	13-46.3	
			SF	2	9	13-36.7	
Smith, D.	AUS	20k walk	F		DIS		
		50k walk	F		DNF		
Smith, G.	GBR	10000m	1	1	7	30-00.1	
Solanas, A.	ESP	Long jump	Q		DNQ	7,73	
Solomin, A.	URS	20k walk	F		DIS		
Solomon, M.	TRI	400m	1	5	2	47.24	
			2	4	2	46.12	
			SF	1	4	45.61	
			F		6	45.55	
		4×400m relay	1	2	4	3-04.3	
			F		6	3-06.6	
Somminhom, S.	LAO	100m	1	2	7	11.69	
Spasojevic, M.	YUG	Triple jump	F		10	16,09	
Spok, H.	FIN	Marathon	F		32	2:22-24	
Stadtmueller, K.-H	GDR	20k walk	F		8	1:29-21.7	
Stahl, K.-E.	SWE	Marathon	F		19	2:17-44	
Stahlberg, R.	FIN	Shot put	F		4	20,82	
Stapleton, I.	JAM	400m	1	6	3	47.97	
			2	4	7	47.64	
		4×400m relay	1	3	DNF		
Stark, S.	GDR	Decathlon	F		DNF		
Starostka, A.	POL	4×400m relay	1	1	3	3-05.8	
Stasevich, A.	URS	200m	1	4	DNF		
Staynings, A.	GBR	3000m steeplechase	1	1	8	8-47.5	
			SF	2	11	8-52.3	
Steiner, J.	AUT	Marathon	F		39	2:24-24	
Stekic, N.	YUG	Long jump	Q		DNQ	5,75	
Stepien, A.	POL	400m	1	4	3	47.99	
			2	2	5	46.31	
		4×400m relay	1	1	1	3-05.8	
Steuk, R.	GDR	Hammer throw	F		4	77,54	
Stoev, V.	BUL	Shot put	Q		DNQ	0	
Stoikov, S.	BUL	Javelin throw	F		11	79,04	
Straub, J.	GDR	1500m	1	4	2	3-37.0	
			SF	2	2	3-39.4	
			F		2	3-38.8	S
Strittmatter, R.	SUI	4×400m relay	1	3	3	3-07.2	
Suero, G.	DOM	100m	1	5	4	10.53	
			2	3	8	10.57	
		200m	1	4	3	22.16	
			2	2	8	21.75	
Suma-Keita, B.	SLE	Marathon	F		46	2:41-20	
Sumariwalla, A.	IND	100m	1	6	7	11.04	
Sykora, J.	TCH	5000m	1	2	6	13-43.1	
			SF	2	7	13-31.0	
			F		9	13-25.0	
		10000m	1	3	7	29-19.8	
Szalai, J.	HUN	400m hurdles	1	2	2	50-23	
			SF	1	6	51.06	
Szalas, J	HUN	20k walk	F		12	1:34-10.5	
Szalma L.	HUN	Long jump	F		4	8,13	
Szczerkowski, J.	POL	Decathlon	F		10	7822	
Szekeres, F.	HUN	Marathon	F		12	2:15-18	
Szparak, R.	POL	400m hurdles	1	-	4	50.45	
			SF	2	6	50.41	
Tamberi, M.	ITA	High jump	F		15	2,15	
Tamm, J.	URS	Hammer throw	F		3	78,96	B
Tarev, A.	BUL	Pole vault	Q		DNQ	5,25	
Tarsi, Z	HUN	High jump	Q		DNQ	2,18	
Tatar, I.	HUN	100m	1	7	5	10.69	
		4×100m relay	1	2	6	39.97	
Tebroke, G.	HOL	10000m	1	3	6	29-05.8	
			F		14	28-50.1	
Teller, L.	NCA	400m hurdles	1	2	DNF		
Tembo, K.	ZIM	10000m	1	2	10	30-53.8	
Thabana, M.	LES	10000m	1	1	10	34-01.5	
Thiele, K.	GDR	4×400m relay	1	2	1	3-03.4	
			F		2	3-01.3	S
Thompson, D.	GBR	Decathlon	F		1	8495	G
Thompson, .	GBR	Marathon	F		DNF		
Tiainen, .	FIN	Hammer throw	F		10	71,38	
Tibaduiza, D.	COL	10000m	1	2	DNF		
		Marathon	F		17	2:17-06	
Tishchenko, V.	URS	1500m	1	2	2	3-44.4	
			SF	2	7	3-41.5	
Toboc, H.	RUM	400m	1	1	6	49.90	
		400m hurdles	1	1	6	50.89	
			SF	1	3	50.58	
			F		6	49.84	
Toporek, M.	AUT	20k walk	F		21	1:44-56.0	
Tore, H.	ETH	20k walk	F		16	1:37-16.6	
Tozzi, R.	ITA	400m	1	7	4	47.01	
			2	4	5	46.73	
		4×400m relay	1	2	3	3-03.5	
			F		3	3-04.3	B
Trabado, C.	ESP	800m	1	2	4	1-47.9	
			SF	1	7	1-48.1	
		4×400m relay	1	1	6	3-06.9	
Tranquille, R.	SEY	400m	1	4	5	49.34	
		4×100m relay	1	1	6	40.25	
		4×400m relay	1	3	7	3-19.2	

COMPETITOR	COUNTRY CODE	EVENT	ROUND	HEAT	PLACE	TIME & DISTANCE	MEDAL
Treacy, J.	IRL	5000m	1	1	4	13-44·8	
			SF	1	4	13-40·3	
			F		7	13-23·7	
		10000m	1	1	DNF		
Truppel, J.	GDR	Marathon	F		11	2:14-55	
Trzepizur, J.	POL	High jump	F		12	2,18	
Tuffa, B.	ETH	100m	1	4	8	11·55	
		200m	1	8	6	23·18	
		4×400m relay	1	2	7	3-18·2	
Tuokko, M.	FIN	Discus throw	F		9	61,84	
Tuparov, I.	BUL	Long jump	Q		DNQ	7,46	
Tura, A.	ETH	3000m steeplechase	1	1	2	8-23·8	
			SF	1	2	8-16·2	
			F		3	8-13·6	B
Udo, D.	NGR	400m	1	3	1	46·48	
			2	1	4	46·18	
			SF	1	5	45·88	
		4×400m relay	1	3	5	3-14·1	
Urlando, G.	ITA	Hammer throw	F		7	73,90	
Uti, S.	NGR	4×400m relay	1	3	5	3-14·1	
Uudmae, J.	URS	Triple jump	F		1	17,35	G
Vainio, M.	FIN	5000m	1	2	8	13-45·2	
			SF	2	6	13-30·4	
			F		11	13-32·1	
		10000m	1	3	4	28-59·9	
			F		13	28-46·3	
Valetudie, C.	FRA	Triple jump	F		12		
Valiulis, R.	URS	4×400m relay	1	1	1	3-01·8	
			F		1	3-01·1	G
Vandenberghe, R.	BEL	4×400m relay	1	2	DNF		
Vanous, J.	TCH	50k walk	F		DIS		
Vasilev, N.	URS	400m hurdles	1	1	1	50·09	
			SF	2	2	49·87	
			F		4	49·34	
Velev, V.	BUL	Discus throw	F		8	63,04	
Vicente, S.	MOZ	1500m	1	1	9	3-58·07	
Vigneron, T.	FRA	Pole vault	F		7	5,45	
Viren, L.	FIN	10000m	1	1	4	28-45·0	
			F		5	27-50·5	
		Marathon	F		DNF		
Vladimirov, E.	BUL	Discus throw	F		7	63,18	
Vlk, J.	TCH	Shot put	F		7	20,24	
Voicu, N.	RUM	3000m steeplechase	1	1	9	8-49·0	
Volkov, K.	URS	Pole vault	F		=2	5,65	S
Volpi, R.	ITA	3000m steeplechase	1	2	5	8-35·6	
			SF	1	7	8-29·7	
Vorobei, A.	URS	3000m steeplechase	1	1	7	8-42·6	
			SF	2	9	8-44·3	
Vriend, C.	HOL	Marathon	F		41	2:26-41	
Vukicevic, P.	YUG	110m hurdles	1	1	5	14·19	
			SF	2	8	14·12	
Wagenknecht, D.	GDR	800m	1	2	1	1-47·5	
			SF	3	2	1-46·7	
			F		6	1-47·0	
Wardlaw, C.	AUS	Marathon	F		28	2:20-42	
Warren, D.	GBR	800m	1	6	2	1-49·9	
			SF	2	2	1-47·2	
			F		8	1-49·3	
Weber, A.	GDR	Pole vault	Q		DNQ	5,15	
Wells, A.	GBR	100m	1	7	1	10·35	
			2	1	1	10·11	
			SF	2	1	10·27	
			F		1	10·25	G
		200m	1	6	2	21·57	
			2	3	1	20·59	
			SF	1	4	20·75	
			F		2	20·21	S
		4×100m relay	1	2	3	39·20	
			F		4	38·62	
Werthner, G.	AUT	Decathlon	F		4	8050	
Wesolowski, K.	POL	3000m steeplechase	1	3	4	8-35·6	
			SF		9	8-33·1	
Wessig, G.	GDR	High jump	F		1	2,36*	G
Westbroek, M.	HOL	100m	1	7	6	10·91	
		4×400m relay	1	1	5	3-06·0	
Whitehead, T.	GBR	4×400m relay	1	3	2	3-05·9	
			F		DNF		
Wieser, R.	GDR	20k walk	F		3	1:25-58·2	B
Woldehana, G.	ETH	3000m steeplechase	1	2	8	8-54·6	
Woldetsadik, H.	ETH	3000m steeplechase	1	3	8	8-41·0	
			SF	2	8	8-35·0	

COMPETITOR	COUNTRY CODE	EVENT	ROUND	HEAT	PLACE	TIME & DISTANCE	MEDAL
Woronin, M.	POL	100m	1	9	2	10·35	
			2	2	2	10·27	
			SF	2	4	10·43	
			F		7	10·46	
		200m	1	4	1	21·63	
			2	1	2	20·97	
			SF	1	3	20·75	
			F		7	20·81	
		4×100m relay	1	1	2	38·83	
			F		2	38·33	S
Wszola, J.	POL	High jump	F		2	2,31	S
Wuycke, W.	VEN	800m	1	3	4	1-48·5	
			SF	3	4	1-47·4	
Yakovlyev, B.	URS	50k walk	F		DIS		
Yakovlyev, P.	URS	1500m	1	1	5	3-44·2	
Yanev, Y.	BUL	Long jump	F		8	8,02	
Yankov, R.	BUL	Decathlon	F		14	7624	
Yanchev, I.	BUL	Pole vault	Q		DNQ	0	
Yarosh, A.	URS	Shot put	F		9	19,93	
Yevsyukov, Y.	URS	20k walk	F		4	1:26-28·3	
Yifter, M.	ETH	5000m	1	1	1	13-44·4	
			SF	1	2	13-40·0	
			F		1	13-21·0	G
		10000m	1	2	1	28-41·7	
			F		1	27-42·7	G
Zalar, M.	SWE	Pole vault	F		10	5,35	
Zdravkovic, D.	YUG	1500m	1	1	3	3-44·0	
			SF	1	2	3-43·4	
			F		9	3-43·1	
Zeilbauer, J.	AUT	Decathlon	F		5	8007	
Zerihun, A.	ETH	800m	1	1	5	1-50·3	
Zerkowski, M.	POL	1500m	1	4	5	3-39·2	
			F	2	9	3-48·2	
Zeru, H.	ETH	1500m	1	2	6	3-45·7	
Zhelanov, S.	URS	Decathlon	F		3	8135	B
Zuliani, M.	ITA	400m	1	8	2	47·16	
			2	2	3	45·93	
			SF	1	7	46·01	
		4×400m relay	1	2	3	3-03·5	
			F		3	3-04·3	B
Zwiefelhofer, V.	TCH	Marathon	F		DNF		
Zwolinski, K.	POL	100m	1	7	3	10·60	
			2	4	7	10·54	
		4×100m relay	1	2	2	38·83	
			F		2	38·33	S
FEMALES							
Abashidze, N.	URS	Shot put	F		4	21,15	
Ackermann, R.	GDR	High jump	F		4	1,91	
Akhrimenko, N.	URS	Shot put	F		7	19,74	
Akinyemi, M.	NGR	400m	1	4	4	52·64	
		4×400m relay	1	2	6	3-36·0	
Alaerts, L.	BEL	200m	1	4	5	24·51	
		4×400m relay	1	2	5	3-30·7	
			F		7	3-31·6	
Alfeyeva, L.	URS	Long jump	F		8	6,71	
Ali, M.	TAN	100m	1	3	7	12·19	
		200m	1	3	5	24·99	
Allwood, R.	JAM	100m	1	1	3	11·68	
			2	2	8	11·69	
		4×100m relay	F		6	43·19	
Ancheva, G.	BUL	200m	1	6	3	23·35	
			2	2	5	23·37	
			SF	1	8	23·27	
Andonova, M.	BUL	400m	1	4	6	53·30	
		4×400m relay	1	1	2	3-28·7	
			F		DNF		
Anisimova, T.	URS	100m hurdles	1	3	3	13·31	
Anisimova, V.	URS	100m	1	3	2	11·53	
			2	3	4	11·33	
			SF	1	5	11·51	
		4×100m relay	F		2	42·10	S
Auerswald, I.	GDR	100m	1	1	1	11·32	
			2	3	1	11·12	
			SF	1	2	11·27	
			F		3	11·14	B
		4×100m relay	F		1	41·60*	G
Ayanlaja, G.	NGR	400m	1	5	6	53·55	
		4×400m relay	1	2	6	3-36·0	
Bancole, E.	BEN	100m	1	2	7	13·19	
Barlag, S.	HOL	Pentathlon	F		10	4333	
Bartonova, Z.	TCH	Shot put	F		10	18,40	
		Discus throw	F		11	57,78	
Beckles, L.	FRA	100m	1	5	4	11·59	
			2	2	5	11·54	
			SF	1	8	11·70	

COMPETITOR	COUNTRY CODE	EVENT	ROUND	HEAT	PLACE	TIME & DISTANCE	MEDAL
Benedetic, L.	YUG	High jump	Q		DNQ	1,30	
Berg, R.	BEL	4×400m relay	1	2	5	3-30·7	
			F		7	3-31·6	
Besliu, D.	RUM	800m	1	1	3	2-01·9	
			SF	1	5	2-00·8	
Betancourt, M.	CUB	Discus throw	Q		DNQ	57,32	
Beyer, G.	GDR	Discus throw	F		4	67,08	
Bielczyk, Z.	POL	100m hurdles	1	2	3	13·21	
			SF	1	4	13·09	
			F		8	13·08	
		4×100m relay	F		7	43·59	
Biryulina, T.	URS	Javelin throw	F		6	65,08	
Blagoeva, Y.	BUL	High jump	Q		DNQ	1,80	
Blechacz, B.	POL	Javelin throw	F		9	61,46	
Bochina, N.	URS	100m	1	5	3	11·38	
			2	2	3	11·30	
			SF	2	5	11·33	
		200m	1	3	1	23·24	
			2	3	1	22·26*	
			SF	2	2	22·75	
			F		2	22·19	S
		4×100m relay	F		2	42·10	S
Bolivar, C.	PER	100m	1	5	7	12·07	
		200m	1	2	4	25·33	
Boothe, L.	GBR	100m hurdles	1	3	6	13·86	
Boungnavong, B.	LAO	200m	1	4	6	30·42	
Boxer, C.	GBR	800m	1	1	4	2-02·1	
			SF	2	8	2-00·9	
Boyd, D.	AUS	100m	1	2	2	11·56	
			2	1	4	11·35	
			SF	2	8	11·44	
		200m	1	4	2	23·36	
			2	3	5	22·91	
			SF	2	3	22·80	
			F		7	22·76	
Boye, M.	SEN	100m	1	2	6	12·42	
		400m	1	3	7	55·16	
Bozhkova, S.	BUL	Discus throw	F		8	63,14	
Brasil, C.	BRA	Pentathlon	F		14	4263	
Bruns, U.	GDR	1500m	1	1	4	4-01·6	
			F		5	4-00·7	
Buerki, C.	SUI	1500m	1	1	7	4-05·5	
Bukis, A.	POL	800m	1	3	4	1-58·9	
			SF	2	7	2-00·3	
		1500m	1	2	5	4-06·0	
Bulkowska, D.	POL	High jump	Q		DNQ	1,85	
Bykova, T.	URS	High jump	F		9	1,88	
Chernova, L.	URS	400m	1	5	5	51·57	
			SF	1	5	51·30	
		4×400m relay	1	1	1	3-25·3	
Claus, K.	GDR	100m hurdles	1	1	3	12·75	
			SF	2	4	12·99	
			F		4	12·66	
Colon, M.	CUB	Javelin throw	F		1	63,40*	G
Csoke, K.	HUN	Discus throw	Q		DNQ	57,38	
Damado, F.O.	SEN	100m	1	3	6	12·16	
		200m	1	6	5	24·45	
			2	1	8	24·80	
Damianova, S.	BUL	400m	1	1	4	52·23	
		4×400m relay	1	1	2	3-28·7	
			F		DNF		
De Letourdie, B.	SEY	100m	1	1	7	13·04	
		200m	1	5	6	26·91	
Dimitrova, V.	BUL	Pentathlon	F		7	4458	
Dimova, B.	BUL	4×400m relay	1	1	2	3-28·7	
			F		DNF		
Donkova, Y.	BUL	100m hurdles	1	1	6	13·24	
			SF	1	6	13·39	
Dorio, G.	ITA	800m	1	1	1	2-01·4	
			SF	1	5	1-59·0	
			F		8	1-59·2	
		1500m	1	2	3	4-05·0	
			F		4	4-00·3	
Dunecka, M.	POL	400m	1	5	4	51·81	
			SF	1	7	51·93	
		4×400m relay	1	2	2	3-29·7	
			F		6	3-27·9	
Elloy, L.	FRA	100m hurdles	1	3	5	13·60	
			SF	1	5	13·33	
Elmoughrabi, H.	SYR	400m	1	2	6	59·33	
		800m	1	4	6	2-17·6	
Emmanuel, M.	TAN	1500m	1	1	11	4-26·8	
Enang, R.	CAM	100m	1	5	8	12·40	
		200m	1	5	5	25·46	
Encheva, C.	BUL	4×100m relay	F		4	42·67	
Forgacs, J.	HUN	400m	1	3	6	53·06	
		4×400m relay	1	2	3	3-29·7	
			F		5	3-27·9	
Fuchs, R.	GDR	Javelin throw	F		8	63,94	
Gartz, B.	GDR	100m hurdles	1	2	2	13·06	
			SF	1	3	13·04	
			F		7	12·93	
Gillies, P.	AUS	100m hurdles	1	2	6	13·86	
Goddard, B.	GBR	200m	1	4	1	23·35	
			2	2	3	22·97	
			SF	1	4	22·73	
			F		6	22·72	
		4×100m relay	F		3	42·43	B
Gohr, M.	GDR	100m	1	3	2	11·41	
			2	2	1	11·12	
			SF	2	2	11·18	
			F		2	11·07	S
		4×100m relay	F		1	41·60*	G
Govshchik, T.	URS	4×400m relay	1	1	1	3-25·3	
			F		1	3-20·2	G
Grandrieux, V.	FRA	4×100m relay	F		5	42·84	
Guerrero, P.	PER	Javelin throw	Q		DNQ	45,42	
Gunba, S.	URS	Javelin throw	F		2	67,76	S
Gusheva, L.	BUL	Long jump	F		12	6,24	
Guzowska, M.	POL	Pentathlon	F		12	4326	
Haggman, P.	FIN	400m	1	3	2	52·56	
			SF	1	3	51·02	
			F		7	51·35	
Haglund, L.	SWE	100m	1	4	3	11·37	
			2	3	3	11·31	
			SF	2	3	11·36	
			F		4	11·16	
		200m	1	5	3	23·85	
			2	3	4	22·90	
			SF	1	6	23·11	
		4×100m relay	F		DNF		
Hartley, D.	GBR	4×400m relay	1	1	3	3-29·0	
			F		3	3-27·5	B
Hearnshaw, S.	GBR	Long jump	F		9	6,50	
Heimann, S.	GDR	Long jump	F		7	6,71	
Herczeg, A.	HUN	Discus throw	F		12	55,06	
Hodges, L.	JAM	100m	1	2	5	11·79	
		4×100m relay	F		6	43·19	
Hommola, U.	GDR	Javelin throw	F		3	66,56	B
Hoyte-Smith, J.	GBR	400m	1	4	1	52·24	
			SF	1	6	51·47	
		4×400m relay	1	1	3	3-29·0	
			F		3	3-27·5	B
Hunte, H.	GBR	100m	1	4	3	11·40	
			2	1	3	11·25	
			SF	1	4	11·36	
			F		8	11·34	
		4×100m relay	F		3	42·43	B
Innis, J.	GUY	100m	1	4	6	11·79	
		Long jump	F		13	6,10	
Jahl, E.	GDR	Discus throw	F		1	69,96*	G
Janak, M.	HUN	Javelin throw	Q		DNQ	57,80	
Januchta, J.	POL	800m	1	2	2	1-59·7	
			SF	2	3	1-58·9	
			F		6	1-58·3	
		4×400m relay	1	2	2	3-29·7	
			F		6	3-27·9	
Kafer, K.	AUT	400m	1	3	4	52·82	
Kampfert, M.	GDR	800m	1	3	2	1-58·8	
			SF	1	2	1-58·1	
			F		4	1-56·3	
Karlsson, A.-E.	SWE	High jump	Q		DNQ	1,80	
Katolik, E.	POL	800m	1	4	4	2-01·2	
			SF	1	7	2-01·1	
		4×400m relay	1	2	2	3-29·7	
			F		6	3-27·9	
Kazankina, T.	URS	1500m	1	1	1	3-59·2*	
			F		1	3-56·6*	G
Khampaseuth	LAO	100m	1	2	8	14·62	
Kielan, U.	POL	High jump	F		2	1,94	S
Kirst, J.	GDR	High jump	F		3	1,94	B
Klier, J.	GDR	100m hurdles	1	3	2	13·03	
			SF	2	2	12·77	
			F		2	12·63	S
Koblasova, M.	TCH	Pentathlon	F		11	4328	
Koch, M.	GDR	400m	1	5	2	51·06	
			SF	1	1	50·57	
			F		1	48·88*	G
		4×400m relay	1	2	1	3-28·7	
			F		2	3-20·4	S
Kolpakova, T.	URS	Long jump	F		1	7,06*	G

COMPETITOR	COUNTRY CODE	EVENT	ROUND	HEAT	PLACE	TIME & DISTANCE	MEDAL
Komisova, V.	URS	100m hurdles	1	1	1	12·67	
			SF	1	1	12·78	
			F		1	12·56*	G
		4×100m relay	F		2	42·10	S
Kondratyeva, L.	URS	100m	1	4	1	11·13	
			2	1	1	11·06	
			SF	2	1	11·11	
			F		1	11·06	G
Korodi, I.	RUM	4×400m relay	1	2	4	3-29·8	
			F		4	3-27·7	
Krachevskaya, S.	URS	Shot put	F		2	21,42	S
Kratochvilova, J.	TCH	400m	1	5	1	51·04	
			SF	1	3	50·79	
			F		2	49·46	S
Krawczuk, E.	POL	High jump	Q		DNQ	1,85	
Krug, B.	GDR	4×400m relay	1	2	1	3-28·7	
			F		2	3-20·4	S
Kunova, E.	BUL	Pentathlon	F		8	4431	
Kuragina, O.	URS	Pentathlon	F		3	4875	B
Kyomo, N.	TAN	100m	1	5	6	11·77	
		200m	1	5	4	24·22	
			2	3	8	24·59	
Laihorinne, H.	FIN	100m	1	1	5	11·70	
Lambrou, M.	GRE	Long jump	Q		DNQ	6,37	
Langer, L.	POL	4×100m relay	F		7	43·59	
		100m hurdles	1	1	2	12·75	
			SF	1	2	12·91	
			F		3	12·65	B
Lannaman, S.	GBR	100m	1	2	3	11·58	
			2	3	2	11·20	
			SF	2	5	11·38	
		200m	1	3	2	23·55	
			2	3	3	22·84	
			SF	2	4	22·82	
			F		8	22·80	
		4×100m relay	F		3	42·43	B
Larios, X.	NCA	400m	1	2	7	1-01·50	
Laser, C.	GDR	Pentathlon	F		DNF		
Lathan, C.	GDR	400m	1	1	1	51·33	
			SF	2	1	50·16	
			F		3	49·66	B
		4×400m relay	1	2	1	3-28·7	
			F		2	3-20·4	S
Lazarciuc, N.	RUM	400m	1	1	5	52·52	
		4×400m relay	1	2	4	3-29·8	
			F		4	3-27·7	
Lebeau, L.	FRA	100m hurdles	1	1	4	13·18	
			SF	1	7	13·54	
Lesovaya, T.	URS	Shot put	F		3	67,40	B
Lia, N.	RUM	200m	1	6	6	24·54	
Liebich, B.	GDR	1500m	1	2	6	4-06·8	
Lillak, T.	FIN	Javelin throw	Q		DNQ	56,26	
Litovchenko, I.	JRS	100m hurdles	1	2	1	12·97	
			SF	2	3	12·84	
			F		6	12·84	
Littlewood, A.	GBR	Shot put	F		13	17,53	
Livermore, J.	GBR	Pentathlon	F		13	4304	
Lombardo, R.	ITA	4×400m relay	1	1	5	3-46·2	
Longden, S.	GBR	Pentathlon	F		15	4234	
Lorentzon, S.	SWE	High jump	Q		DNQ	1,85	
Lovin, F.	RUM	800m	1	4	2	2-00·2	
			SF	2	4	1-59·2	
Lowe, G.	GDR	400m	1	4	2	52·43	
			SF	1	2	50·85	
			F		6	51·33	
		4×400m relay	1	2	1	3-28·7	
			F		2	3-20·4	S
Ludovina, O.	MOZ	Discus throw	Q		DNQ	0	
Macdonald, L.	GBR	400m	1	2	2	52·57	
			SF	2	4	51·60	
			F		8	52·40	
		4×400m relay	1	1	3	3-29·0	
			F		3	3-27·5	B
Malbranque, S.	FRA	400m	1	2	5	53·46	
Marasescu, N.	RUM	1500m	1	2	4	4-05·9	
			F		9	4-04·8	
Marlow, J.	GBR	1500m	1	1	9	4-15·9	
Maslakova, L.	URS	200m	1	5	1	23·49	
			2	1	2	23·24	
			SF	1	7	23·27	
		4×100m relay	F		2	42·10	S
Masullo, M.	ITA	100m	1	2	4	11·77	
			2	1	8	11·57	
		200m	1	3	4	24·00	
			2	2	7	23·74	
Matai, A.	HUN	High jump	F		10	1,85	
Mate, A.	MOZ	400m	1	4	8	1-00·90	
		800m	1	4	7	2-19·7	
Matthews, P.	AUS	Javelin throw	Q		DNQ	55,72	
Meheux, E.	SLE	100m	1	4	7	13·22	
		200m	1	3	6	26·77	
		100m hurdles	1	3	7	15·61	
Melnik, F.	URS	Discus throw	Q		DNQ	53,76	
Michel, A.	BEL	400m	1	4	7	54·22	
		4×400m relay	1	2	5	3-30·7	
			F		7	3-31·6	
Miller, L.	GBR	High jump	F		11	1,85	
Mineyeva, O.	URS	800m	1	1	2	2-01·5	
			SF	1	1	1-57·5	
			F		2	1-54·9	S
		4×400m relay	1	1	1	3:25·3	
Moller, L.	SWE	4×100m relay	F		DNF		
Morel, M.	SEY	800m	1	2	7	2-17·0	
		1500m	1	1	13	4-37·9	
Mulhall, G.	AUS	Shot put	F		12	18,00	
		Discus throw	Q		DNQ	54,90	
Muller, R.	GDR	100m	1	2	1	11·41	
			2	1	2	11·09	
			SF	1	1	11·22	
			F		5	11·16	
		200m	1	1	1	23·11	
			2	3	2	22·55	
			SF	2	1	22·72	
			F		4	22·47	G
		4×100m relay	F		1	41·60*	G
Murashova, G.	URS	Discus throw	F		7	63,84	
Mwanjala, M.	TAN	800m	1	1	5	2-05·2	
		1500m	1	2	10	4-20·9	
Naigre, R.	FRA	200m	1	4	3	23·50	
			2	3	6	23·10	
			SF	2	7	23·18	
		4×100m relay	F		5	42·84	
Nazarova, I.	URS	400m	1	3	1	51·66	
			SF	2	2	50·18	
			F		4	50·07	
		4×400m relay	F		1	3-20·2	G
Nedeva, E.	BUL	Long jump	Q		DNQ	5,83	
Neubert, R.	GDR	Pentathlon	F		4	4698	
Ngambi, C.	CAM	Pentathlon	F		17	3832	
Nguyen, T.	VNM	Long jump	Q		DNQ	5,35	
Nsenu, O.	NGR	100m	1	3	5	11·72	
			2	2	6	11·55	
Nygrynova, J.	TCH	Long jump	F		6	6,83	
Nyiti, L.	TAN	800m	1	4	5	2-11·1	
Oliszewska, G.	POL	400m	1	4	3	52·62	
			SF	2	7	52·36	
		4×400m relay	F		2	3-29·7	
			F		6	3-27·9	
Olizarenko, N.	URS	800m	1	2	1	1-59·3	
			SF	2	1	1-57·7	
			F		1	1-53·5*	G
		1500m	1	1	2	3-59·5	
			F	5	3	3-59·6	B
Orosz, I.	HUN	200m	1	3	3	23·69	
			2	1	6	23·68	
		4×400m relay	1	2	3	3-29·7	
			F		5	3-27·9	
Osho-Williams, E.	SLE	100m	1	3	8	12·95	
		200m	1	1	5	25·87	
		400m	1	1	8	1-00·44	
		800m	1	4	8	2-33·4	
Ottey, M.	JAM	200m	1	6	1	22·70	
			2	2	1	22·86	
			SF	1	1	22·32	
			F		3	22·20	B
		4×100m relay	F		6	43·19	
		4×400m relay	1	1	4	3-31·5	
Pal, I.	HUN	400m	1	1	2	51·99	
			SF	2	6	51·99	
		4×400m relay	1	2	3	3-29·7	
			F		5	3-27·9	
Panayotova, L.	BUL	200m	1	1	2	23·17	
			2	1	3	23·29	
			SF	2	6	23·07	
		4×100m relay	F		4	42·67	
Pap, M.	HUN	Long jump	Q		DNQ	6,41	
Papp, M.	HUN	Long jump	Q		DNQ	6,32	
		Pentathlon	F		5	4562	
Peralta, M.	DOM	100m hurdles	1	1	7	14·18	
Pergar, B.	YUG	1500m	1	2	8	4-13·2	
Petkova, M.	BUL	Discus throw	F		2	67,90	S
Petrova, I.	BUL	Shot put	F		11	18,34	

COMPETITOR	COUNTRY CODE	EVENT	ROUND	HEAT	PLACE	TIME & DISTANCE	MEDAL
Petrova, T.	BUL	800m	1	4	3	2-00·6	
			SF	2	6	2-00·0	
		1500m	1	1	8	4-13·8	
Petrucci, C.	ITA	Shot put	F		14	17,27	
Picaut, F.	FRA	Pentathlon	F		9	4424	
Pihl, H.	SWE	100m hurdles	1	3	4	13·46	
			SF	1	8	13·58	
		4×100m relay	F		DNF		
Pollak, B.	GDR	Pentathlon	F		6	4583	
Popa, C.	RUM	High jump	F		8	1,88	
Popova, S.	BUL	100m	1	5	1	11·35	
			2	2	4	11·42	
			SF	2	7	11·44	
		4×100m relay	F		4	42·67	
Porcelli, D.	ITA	800m	1	2	5	2-10·7	
		4×400m relay	1	1	5	3-46·2	
Possamai, A.	ITA	800m	1	3	5	2-04·1	
		1500m	1	2	9	4-14·7	
		4×400m relay	1	1	5	3-46·2	
Probert, M.	GBR	400m	1	1	3	52·16	
			SF	2	5	51·89	
		4×400m relay	1	1	3	3-29·8	
			F		3	3-27·5	B
Prorochenko, T.	URS	4×400m relay	1	1	1	3-25·3	
			F		1	3-20·2	G
Providokhina, T.	URS	800m	1	3	1	1-58·5	
			SF	1	3	1-58·3	
			F		3	1-55·5	B
Pufe, M.	GDR	Shot put	F		3	21,20	B
		Discus throw	F		5	66,12	
Puica, M.	RUM	1500m	1	1	5	4-01·7	
			F		7	4-01·3	
Pusey, J.	JAM	200m	1	2	1	23·39	
			2	1	4	23·35	
			SF	2	5	22·90	
		4×100m relay	F		6	43·19	
		4×400m relay	1	1	4	3-31·5	
Putiniene, J.	URS	Javelin throw	F		11	59,94	
Quintavalla, F.	ITA	Javelin throw	F		12	57,52	
Rabsztyn, G.	POL	100m hurdles	1	3	1	12·72	
			SF	2	1	12·64	
			F		5	12·74	
		4×100m relay	F		7	43·59	
Raduly-Zorgo, E.	RUM	Javelin throw	F		7	64,08	
Raheliarisoa, A.	MAD	800m	1	2	6	2-11·7	
		1500m	1	1	12	4-30·8	
Rattray, C.	JAM	4×400m relay	1	1	4	3-31·5	
Reeve, S.	GBR	Long jump	F		10	6,46	
Rega, C.	FRA	100m	1	1	2	11·53	
			2	3	5	11·40	
			SF	2	4	11·36	
			F		7	11·32	
		200m	1	2	2	23·49	
			2	2	4	23·29	
			SF	1	5	22·87	
		4×100m relay	F		5	42·84	
Reichenbach, I.	GDR	Shot put	F		8	19,66	
Reichstein, A.	GDR	High jump	F		6	1,91	
Richter, U.	GDR	Javelin throw	F		4	66,54	
Ritchie, M.	GBR	Discus throw	F		9	61,16	
Rivers, P.	AUS	Javelin throw	Q		DNQ	55,80	
Romero, C.	CUB	Discus throw	F		10	60,86	
Rossi, E.	ITA	400m	1	3	5	52·98	
		4×400m relay	1	1	5	3-46·2	
Rukavishnikova, O.	URS	Pentathlon	F		2	4937	S
Sakorafa, S.	GRE	Javelin throw	Q		DNQ	0	
Samungi, M.	RUM	400m	1	2	4	52·89	
		4×400m relay	1	2	4	3-29·8	
			F		4	3-27·7	
Sanderson, T.	GBR	Javelin throw	Q		DNQ	48,76	
Sarria, M.	CUB	Shot put	F		9	19,37	
Scott, D.	JAM	Long jump	Q		DNQ	5,83	
Senglaub, B.	SUI	100m	1	1	4	11·69	
			2	1	7	11·56	
		200m	1	1	4	23·62	
			2	2	8	23·84	
Serkova, M.	URS	High jump	Q		DNQ	1,80	
Shishkova, M.	BUL	100m	1	3	3	11·57	
			2	1	5	11·47	
			SF	1	7	11·65	
		4×100m relay	F		4	42·67	
Shtereva, N.	BUL	800m	1	3	3	1-58·9	
			SF	1	4	1-58·9	
			F		7	1-58·8	
		1500m	1	2	7	4-03·3	
Siegl, S.	GDR	Long jump	F		5	6,87	

COMPETITOR	COUNTRY CODE	EVENT	ROUND	HEAT	PLACE	TIME & DISTANCE	MEDAL
Silai, I.	RUM	1500m	1	2	2	4-04·7	
			F		8	4-03·0	
Simeoni, S.	ITA	High jump	F		1	1,97*	G
Simpson, R.	JAM	400m	1	5	7	55·59	
		4×400m relay	1	1	4	3-31·5	
Sirak, F.	ETH	800m	1	1	7	2-08·7	
Siska, X.	HUN	100m hurdles	1	1	5	13·23	
			SF	1	DNF		
Skachko, T.	URS	Long jump	F		3	7,01	B
Skoglund, A.-L.	SWE	400m	1	1	6	52·78	
		4×100m relay	F		DNF		
Slupianek, I.	GDR	Shot put	F		1	22,41*	G
Smallwood, K.	GBR	100m	1	5	2	11·37	
			2	2	2	11·24	
			SF	1	3	11·30	
			F		6	11·28	
		200m	1	6	2	23·15	
			2	1	1	22·95	
			SF	1	3	22·65	
			F		5	22·61	
		4×100m relay	F		3	42·43	B
Smolka, L.	URS	1500m	1	2	1	4-04·4	
			F		6	4-01·3	
Soetewey, K.	BEL	High jump	F		12	1,80	
Stachurska, E.	POL	100m	1	1	DIS		
		200m	1	4	4	23·58	
			2	3	7	23·11	
		4×100m relay	F		7	43·59	
Stamenova, R.	BUL	400m	1	2	3	52·71	
			SF	1	8	52·96	
		4×400m relay	1	1	2	3-28·7	
			F		DNF		
Stanton, C.	AUS	High jump	F		=6	1,91	
Stoyanova, E.	BUL	Shot put	F		6	20,22	
Strong, S.	GBR	100m hurdles	1	2	4	13·21	
			SF	1	5	13·12	
Sulter, E.	FRA	100m	1	4	4	11·56	
			2	1	6	11·48	
			SF	1	6	11·63	
		4×100m relay	F		5	42·84	
Sysoyeva, M.	URS	High jump	F		5	1,91	
Szewinska, I.	POL	400m	1	3	3	52·57	
			SF	2	8	53·13	
Tacu, F.	RUM	Discus throw	F		6	64,38	
Tarita, E.	RUM	400m	1	4	5	52·96	
		4×400m relay	1	2	4	3-29·8	
			F		4	3-27·7	
Tchuinte, A.	CAM	Javelin throw	Q		DNQ	55,36	
Tkachenko, N.	URS	Pentathlon	F		1	5083*	G
Todorova, A.	BUL	Javelin throw	F		10	60,66	
Toth, E.	HUN	4×400m relay	1	3	3	3-29·7	
			F		5	3-27·9	
Toure, F.	MLI	800m	1	3	6	2-19·8	
Toutounji, D.	SYR	High jump	Q		DNQ	0	
Tran, T.N.A.	VNM	200m	1	2	5	26·83	
		400m	1	5	8	1-00·62	
Tran, T V.	VNM	100m	1	4	8	13·23	
Trinh, T.-B.	VNM	1500m	1	2	11	4-38·6	
Uba, R.	NGR	100m	1	4	5	11·75	
			2	3	6	11·60	
		200m	1	1	3	23·36	
			2	2	6	23·55	
Ullrich, H.	GDR	800m	1	4	1	2-00·1	
			SF	2	2	1-58·7	
			F		5	1-57·2	
Usha, P.T.	IND	100m	1	1	6	12·27	
		200m	1	6	7	25·16	
Vader, E.	HOL	100m	1	3	4	11·61	
		200m	1	6	4	23·50	
			2	1	4	23·67	
			SF	2	8	23·44	
Valkova, D.	BUL	100m hurdles	1	2	5	13·66	
			SF	1	6	13·79	
Vallecilla, N.	ECU	Pentathlon	F		DNF		
Vancheva, I.	BUL	Javelin throw	F		5	65,38	
Van Nuffel, A.-M.	BEL	800m	1	2	4	2-00·1	
			SF	1	8	2-02·0	
Vaughan, K.	NGR	400m	1	1	7	53·54	
		4×400m relay	1	2	6	3-36·0	
Verguts, K.	BEL	200m	1	2	3	23·89	
			2	1	7	24·00	
Veselinova, V.	BUL	Shot put	F		5	20,72	
Wallez, R.	BEL	400m	1	5	5	52·00	
		4×400m relay	1	2	5	3-30·7	
			F		7	3-31·6	
Wartenberg, C.	GDR	1500m	1	1	3	4-00·4	
			F		2	3-57·8	S

COMPETITOR	COUNTRY CODE	EVENT	ROUND	HEAT	PLACE	TIME & DISTANCE	MEDAL
Wells, D.	AUS	100m	1	5	5	11·72	
			2	2	7	11·66	
Whitbread, F.	GBR	Javelin throw	Q		DNQ	49,74	
Wlodarczyk, A.	POL	Long jump	F		4	6,95	
Wockel, B.	GDR	200m	1	5	2	23·55	
			2	2	2	22·86	
			SF	1	2	22·54	
			F		1	22·03*	G
		4×100m relay	F		1	41·60*	G
Wojnar-Baran, B.	POL	Long jump	F		11	6,33	
Woldegibriel, A.	ETH	1500m	1	1	10	4-25·3	

COMPETITOR	COUNTRY CODE	EVENT	ROUND	HEAT	PLACE	TIME & DISTANCE	MEDAL
Woy, A.	NGR	4×400m relay	1	2	6	3-36·0	
Wray, Y.	GBR	Pentathlon	F		16	4159	
Wujak, B.	GDR	Long jump	F		2	7,04	S
Yatsinska, V.	BUL	800m	1	2	3	1-59·9	
			SF	2	5	1-59·9	
		1500m	1	1	6	4-04·7	
Zutshi, G.	IND	800m	1	1	6	2-06·6	
Zyuskova, N.	URS	400m	1	2	1	51·42	
			SF	1	4	51·12	
			F		5	50·17	
		4×400m relay	F		1	3-20·2	G

A young Steve Cram, of Britain, made his Olympic debut in 1980 and reached the final of the 1,500 metres.

Mark Shearman

1984

Carl Lewis Leads the American Celebrations

The 1984 Olympic Games were boycotted by most of the Eastern Communist countries, ostensibly on the grounds of inadequate security, but with no doubt a hint of revenge for 1980 in their decision. The other Eastern block countries followed suit, only Rumania sending a team.

Because of the huge losses made by Montreal in 1976, there was only one candidate to host the Games in 1984: Los Angeles. The IOC were forced to give California capitalism its head, with the result that the Games were well organised. However, a huge commercial bonanza for one of the richest parts of the world was not really in the Olympic spirit.

The USA enjoyed a sporting carnival, with many of the events falling to home athletes. Outstanding was Carl Lewis, and his four gold medals equalled those of the legendary Jesse Owens, whose grand-daughter carried the torch into the stadium.

Men's Track Events

There was only one favourite for the **100 metres**, Carl Lewis, since Mel Lattany the only other sub 10·0 man had not made the American team and Lewis obliged by running a very fast second round heat in 10·04 sec, the best non-altitude time ever run at the Olympics. The sprinters were away first time in the final with Sam Graddy of America in the lead just heading Canada's Ben Johnson. Lewis was slow in picking up his speed, but came through to lead at 80 metres and appeared to be accelerating right to the finish in an outstanding 9·99, without any aiding wind. Johnson relaxed over the latter part of the race as he felt his leg cramping, which allowed Graddy to take the silver in 10·19 from Johnson 10·22. Lewis's winning margin of 0·2 sec was one of the widest in Olympic history.

"King" Carl Lewis of America was naturally the undisputed favourite for the **200 metres** and the other likely medallists were seen as his fellow American, Kirk Baptiste, and the defending champion, Pietro Mennea of Italy. Lewis and Baptiste were fastest in the semi-finals with times of 20·27 and 20·29 sec respectively. In the final, Lewis was in lane seven, and purred around the curve, hitting the 100 metres timer in 10·23, followed by Baptiste, 10·41, Tom Jefferson of the USA, 10·43 and Joao da Silva of Brazil, 10·47. He just glided along the home straight in 9·57 to finish easing up in 19·80 for the gold medal. It was the third fastest time ever, despite being run against the wind. Baptiste actually closed a little on Lewis to collect the silver medal with 19·96, while Jefferson fought off da Silva to take the bronze in 20·26.

During the second semi-final of the **400 metres**, Bert Cameron of Jamaica, momentarily leapt in the air with cramp at 130 metres and lost an estimated 10 metres, yet he chased after the field and qualified in 45·10.

Unfortunately, he could not run in the final as his hamstring had stiffened up too much. Darren Clark of Australia committed himself from the gun and ran the first 200 in 21·2, to lead Sunder Nix of the USA. At 300 in 32·3, Clark was a metre in advance of Gabriel Tiacoh of the Ivory Coast with Nix, Antonio McKay and Alonzo Babers, all of America, well in contention. The Australian eventually paid the price for his fast pace and Babers powered up the straight to win in 44·27 from Tiacoh in 44·54, while McKay was strong enough to salvage third in 44·71. The silver won by Tiacoh, provided the Ivory Coast with its first-ever Olympic medal.

In the **800 metres** Seb Coe of Britain was tipped as the winner. The preliminaries were full of fast times with the first round heats being won in the 1-45·0 to 1-47·0 range, and the second rounds even faster. In the first semi-final, Ed Koech of Kenya ran the first lap in 49·6, which precipitated the extraordinary time of 1-43·82 by Joaquim Cruz of Brazil, from Koech in 1-44·12 and Earl Jones of the USA in 1-44·51. The defending champion, Steve Ovett of Britain, had to dive across the line in order to qualify in fourth place in 1-44·81. Coe took the other semi-final in 1-45.51. In the final, Koech took up the lead, passing the 400 in 51·1 and 600 in 1-17·8 with Cruz, Coe, Jones and Billy Konchellah of Kenya close up. Off the final bend it was Cruz who struck first with Jones and Coe trying to respond, but Cruz had the measure of his opponents and won in a new Olympic record of 1-43·00. Coe took the silver position, yet again, in 1-43·64 and Jones the bronze at 1-43·83. Ovett was in a bad condition and finished last, suffering from bronchitis and later went to hospital.

The talk of the **1,500 metres** was whether Seb Coe of Britain could make it two in a row. He had another Briton, Steve Cram, the world champion, to contend with, but Said Aouita of Morocco had opted for the 5,000 metres and America's Sidney Maree was out with a hamstring tear. The semi-finals were fast, and Jose Abascal of Spain and Steve Scott of America looked nippy, while against all advice, the ailing Steve Ovett of Britain ran and qualified in 3-36·55. In the final, Joseph Chesire of Kenya and Omar Khalifa of Sudan took the pack through the 400 in 58·9, while Scott led at 800 in a steady 1-56·9. Scott and Abascal then increased the pace, and at the bell, reached in 2-53·3, Abascal led, closely shadowed by Coe, Cram and Ovett. Midway round the bend, Ovett stepped off the track, gasping for oxygen. The two remaining Britons overtook Abascal around the final bend and Coe strode away to win in 3-32·53, an Olympic record. Cram took the silver in 3-33·40 and Abascal the bronze, just holding off Chesire in 3-34·30 to 3-34·52.

Said Aouita of Morocco was considered a certainty for the **5,000 metres**. The world record holder, David Moorcroft of Great Britain, ran well in the heats, but

The American, Joan Benoit, won the first woman's marathon and quite rightly celebrates.
Mark Shearman

Morocco's second winner at the Games, Said Aouita, romps home in the 5,000 metres, having chosen that event in preference to the 1,500.
Mark Shearman

was suffering from a groin injury and Martti Vainio of Finland was stopped from running the final, when a drug test was found to be positive. In the final, Ezequiel Canario of Portugal set a stiff pace for the first kilometre, then his team-mate Antonio Leitao took over and passed 3km in 7-59·3, with most of the field bunched behind. The pace quickened and the leading group was soon down to six: Leitao, Aouita, Tim Hutchings of Britain, Paul Kipkoech and Charles Cheruiyot, both of Kenya, and Markus Ryffel of Switzerland. With 500 metres left, Aouita, Leitao and Ryffel broke away, and the former struck with 250 to go and won as he pleased in 13-05·59, for an Olympic record. Ryffel came in second in 13-07·54 and Leitao third in 13-09·20.

Although Fernando Mamede of Portugal was the **10,000 metres** world record holder, the man everyone was talking about was Italy's Alberto Cova, who had won the European championship in 1982 and the world championship in 1983, with late sprints. The final started steadily with Musa Gouda of Sudan leading in the early stages, before John Treacy of Ireland took over at 5km in 14-19·9. At this point Mamede ran off the track. In the sixth kilometre, Martti Vainio of Finland increased the pace and took Cova with him, while Mike McLeod of Britain led the following group. Cova took off with 150 metres to go and romped home in 27-47·54, having run the second 5,000 in 13-27·0, while Vainio finished second in 27-51·10. The third place was fiercely fought out by a group of five, but McLeod held a slight lead to complete the course in 28-06·22 from Mike Musyoki of Kenya in 28-06·46. Following Vainio's disqualification in the 5,000 metres, he was stripped of his silver medal in the 10,000, which was given to McLeod, with the bronze going to Musyoki.

Rob de Castella of Australia, the world championship winner of 1983, his runner-up, Carlo Lopes of Portugal and Toshihiko Seko of Japan were all regarded as possible **marathon** winners. Soon after the start, Cor Lambregts of Holland went into the lead, which by 10km was in the hands of Ahmed Ismail of Somalia. At 20km, Joseph Nzau of Kenya passed the check point in 61-26·0 with Lopes on his shoulder, followed by John Treacy of Ireland, Charlie Spedding of Britain, De Castella, and Djama Robleh of Djibouti. At 35km Lopes took off and passed 40km in 2-02·56, and he went on to win in 2-09·21, an Olympic record. Coming up to the stadium entrance, Treacy and Spedding were side by side. But Treacy did not wait until he was on the track to sprint and grabbed a short lead, which he never relinquished, to secure the silver in 2:09-56. Spedding's 2:09-58 was good enough for the bronze and Takeshi Soh of Japan came in fourth.

Greg Foster was the top **110 metres hurdles** exponent leading up to the Games and he equalled the Olympic record of 13·24 in both the heats and semi-finals. Tonie Campbell of the USA caused a false start in the final, but on the second attempt the hurdlers were away. Canada's Mark McKoy had his usual explosive start and grabbed a short lead. Meanwhile, Foster had hesitated at the off, thinking he had made a false start, which probably cost him the race. McKoy hit the first hurdle hard, which let Roger Kingdom of the USA and Arto Bryggare of Finland into the lead. At the second flight, Foster was up with the leaders and at the next both he and Kingdom were leaving Bryggare behind. Kingdom hit hurdles four and five while Foster did likewise with six and seven. Both men were sprinting desperately fast, but raggedly, and despite clouting the last two flights, Kingdom

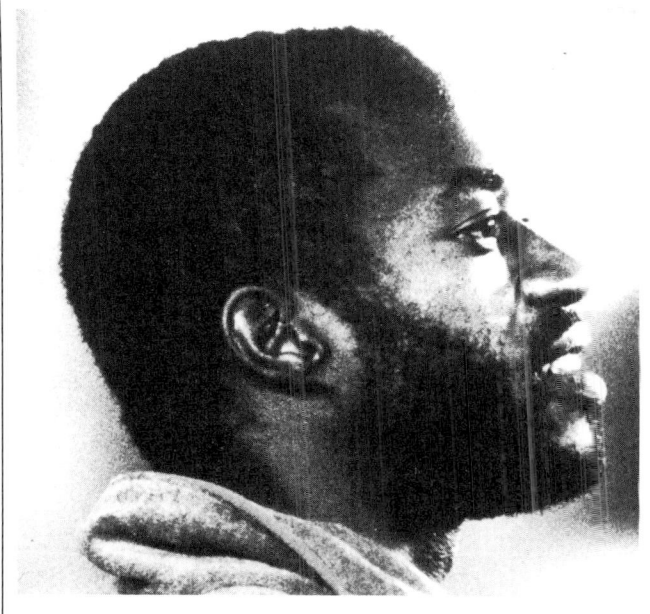

Mark Shearman

Edwin Moses

Born in Dayton, Ohio, on 31 August 1955, he showed real class potential as a schoolboy for both 400m flat and 110m hurdles. The coaches convinced Moses he would be wise to make the 400m hurdles his special event because of the combination of his staying power for the 400m and his ability to hurdle well.

How right the advice was is shown in the remarkable sequence of successes Moses has since achieved in the event: two Olympic gold medals and bringing the world record down to the present day 47·02 sec. Over a period of ten years he has run more than 90 400m hurdles races and been beaten in only two of them.

There was much disappointment when the African boycott prevented Uganda's reigning Olympic champion, Akii-Bua, defending his title in the 1976 Montreal Games, as a terrific race between them was envisaged. The spectators, however, were still treated to the American breaking Akii-Bua's record with 47·64 sec, a full second faster than the runner-up.

There can be no doubting that the phenomenal Moses would have won again in Moscow, four years later, had the United States team not been withdrawn from the action.

He collected his second gold for the event in Los Angeles in 1984 and began looking forward to adding a third in Seoul.

Mark Shearman

Carl Lewis

The finest sprinter/long jumper since Jesse Owens, whose home town was also Birmingham, Alabama, Lewis stole the show in the athletics at Los Angeles in 1984 by winning the 100m (9·99 sec), 200m (19·80 sec, an Olympic record), long jump 28ft 0¼in (8,54m) and 4 × 100m relay (37·83 sec, a world record). And by doing so he equalled the feat of Owens 48 years previously.

Lewis was born on 1 July 1961 and first began to attract attention when as a 17-year-old he ran the 100 yards in 9·3 sec and leapt 25ft 9in (7,85m) in the long jump.

Coming under the guidance of the noted coach, Tom Tellez, when he became an undergraduate at the University of Houston in 1979, Lewis was soon landing in the 27 feet (8,23m) area of the long jump pits and the following year touched down on one occasion at 28ft 3½in (8,62m), a performance bettered only by Bob Beamon's world record 29ft 2½in (8,90m).

At the US trials before going to Europe for the 1983 world championships in Helsinki, Lewis continued his formidable long jumping form by reaching 28ft 10¼in (8,79m), and in addition won the 100m and set a US record 19·75 sec in the 200m, all of which, not surprisingly, made him a hot favourite for these events at the Los Angeles Olympics.

Mark Shearman

Sebastian Coe

The greatness of Coe as a middle distance runner was never more demonstrated than, when, in the space of 41 days in the summer of 1979, he broke three world records: 800m with 1-42·4, the mile with 3-49, and then the 1,500m with 3-32·03.

Here indeed was gold medal material for the following year's Olympics in Moscow. Yet his winning prospects were by no means assured by the time the Games arrived, because of another Englishman, Steve Ovett, tieing Coe's 1,500m record in Oslo prior to going to the Games. The feeling then was that maybe Coe would win the 800m and Ovett the 1,500m. To everyone's surprise the reverse was the outcome, Ovett taking the gold over the shorter course and Coe the 1,500m in 3-38·4.

The following year Coe improved his world record for 800m to 1-41·73, and in 1983 Ovett the 1,500 world figures to 3-30·77. So Coe again became favourite for the 800m at Los Angeles in 1984 and Ovett likewise for the 1,500m. When the strain of the pressure racing proved too much for Ovett's body in Los Angeles, a golden double looked likely for Coe. But again Coe was left to receive the silver for the 800m behind Brazil's new-found star, Joaquim Cruz. There was still satisfaction for Coe, however, for he kept his 1,500m crown to become the first man to win the event at successive Games.

snatched the gold in 13·20 for a new Olympic record from Foster in 13·23. Bryggare held off McKoy to take the bronze in 13·40.

Had it not been for the American boycott in 1980 at Moscow, Ed Moses would probably have been looking for his third consecutive win in the **400 metres hurdles**. His two nearest competitors were the 18-year-old American, Danny Harris, who had only run his first hurdles race in March of that year and Harald Schmid of West Germany. Moses was stationed in lane six in the final and he simply blasted away and caught Amadou Dia Ba of Senegal in lane seven by the third flight. At the fifth, Moses touched down in 21·1 sec with his closest competitor, Schmid, half a second adrift. Moses then strode majestically around the bend and along the home straight to win in 47·75. Behind him, Harris caught the West German at the last barrier and went on to collect the silver in 48·13, from Schmid in 48·19.

It was a pity that Boguslaw Maminski of Poland was not allowed to compete in the **3,000 metres steeplechase**, but he would have had a hard time winning. Twelve ran in the final and Peter Renner of New Zealand cut out the pace. A 13th runner joined the steeplechasers at the end of the first lap carrying a flag and attempted to leap the water jump with the Olympians, while holding his flag aloft. The message on the flag read: "Our Earth Our Peace One Human Family". He was eventually cornered and marched away. Renner continued to lead through one kilometre in 2·47·4 and 2km in 5·32·6, with Kenya's Julius Korir second and the USA's Brian Diemer third. At the bell, Korir led from Henry Marsh of the USA, who had moved up from the back of the leading bunch. And with 200 metres to go, Korir struck, storming to the finish in 8·11·80. Half-way along the home straight, Marsh was overtaken by Joseph Mahmoud of France, who ran on to take the silver medal in 8·13·31 and within a few metres of the line Diemer also edged past him for the bronze in 8·14·06.

Ernesto Canto of Mexico had recently set a world record in the **20 kilometres walk**, but was up against his legendary countryman, Raul Gonzales, and the defending Olympian, Maurizio Damilano of Italy. The competition commenced with five laps of the track and the troupe of walkers left the stadium headed by Canada's Guillaume Leblanc, who reached 5km in 20·48 followed by a group of nine, some ten seconds behind. Damilano was leading at 10km, which was passed in 41·33 with Canto, Gonzales, Leblanc and Carlo Mattioli of Italy in attendance. The Italian broke up this group at 15km, reached in 62·14, and only Canto and Gonzalez managed to hang on. But it was Canto who appeared first from the tunnel with Gonzalez 30 metres behind and Damilano a further 25 adrift. Canto clocked up a new Olympic record of 1:23·13 to win from Gonzalez in 1:23·20 and Damilano in 1:23·26.

In the **50 kilometres walk**, Raul Gonzalez of Mexico was competing in his fourth Olympics and was one of the best stylists around. Missing from the line-up because of the boycott were several good East Germans and Russians. It was a very hot day, which caused nine walkers to drop out as Gonzalez set a blistering pace from the start and led through 10km in 45·59. The leading group was down to three at 30km, passed in 2:16·24: Gonzalez, Maurizio Damilano of Italy and Erling Andersen of Norway. By 40km Gonzalez was out on his own from Damilano, who soon dropped out. Gonzalez went on to win in 3:47·26 for an Olympic record from Bo Gustafsson of Sweden in 3:53·19 and

Sandro Bellucci of Italy in 3:53·45.

Twenty teams contested the **4 × 110 metres relay**, but it was considered unlikely that any would trouble the United States. In the final, the lane draw was, from the inside: Jamaica, West Germany, Italy, Britain, USA, Canada, France and Brazil. At the gun Ben Johnson for Canada was away like a streak of lightning and was a metre up on Sam Graddy of America, with Jamaica a further metre behind. On the second leg, Tony Sharpe for Canada raced along the back straight chased by the USA's Ron Brown, who caught him at the changeover. A good exchange gave America's Calvin Smith the lead and when Carl Lewis took the baton for the USA on the anchor stage, he stormed home to break the world record with 37·83 sec. Jamaica, with Ray Stewart on the last leg, clocked 38·62 for the silver medal, while Canada recorded 38·70 for the bronze.

The **4 × 400 metres relay** was another "certainty" for the USA. In the semi-finals, the team had violated the rules when Walter McKoy on the second leg, cut to the inside immediately after he had taken the baton, instead of running the bend in lanes, and was lucky not to be disqualified. In the final, Australia's Bruce Frayne went out fast but was overtaken at the first exchange by Sunday Uti of Nigeria, with America's Sunder Nix third 45·59 and Britain's Kriss Akabusi fourth. On the second leg, Darren Clark of Australia took over with America's Ray Armstead running him close. However, America drew away through Alonzo Babers on the penultimate leg, but a close battle was developing between the next three teams. And while the USA anchor man, Antonio McKay, came home in the overall time of 2·57·91 for the gold medal, Britain's Phil Brown pulled out all the stops with 2·59·13 for the silver. The bronze went to Nigeria in 2·59·32.

Men's Field Events

China was back into Olympic competition after nearly three decades with Jianhua Zhu their world record holder in the **high jump**. At 2,29 metres there were still eight jumpers active on the apron. Shu Cai of China had already made one unsuccessful attempt, but reserved his next two for 2,31 at which he failed. Then Doug Nordquist of the USA, Milt Ottey of Canada and Yupeng Liu of China were also eliminated when unable to clear 2,31, being placed fifth to seventh respectively. With the bar now at 2,33, both Zhu and Dwight Stones failed and the count-back rule gave the former third and Stones fourth. The two remaining jumpers, Dietmar Mogenburg of West Germany and Patrik Sjoberg of Sweden, both went over 2,33. Sjoberg received the silver as Mogenburg went on to clear 2,35 for the gold before failing at a world best height of 2,40.

It was widely expected that the **pole vault** would be a contest between the American and French atheletes, as the Russians, with their world record holder Sergei Bubka, were boycotting the Games. The vaulters played a cat and mouse game with each other, alternatively passing as the bar was raised and thereby trying to obtain an advantage over each other. Kimmo Pallonen of Finland cleared 5,45 metres for fifth place, while American Mike Tully got over 5,55 and missed out 5,60. Both Earl Bell of the USA and Thierry Vigneron of France soared above 5,60, but could advance no higher, and tied for the bronze medal. Tully came back in at 5,65 and cleared on his third attempt, which ultimately gained him the silver medal. Then, Pierre Quinon of France, who had failed once at this height, gambled on clearing 5,70, which he did, and also 5,75 to win gold. Meanwhile, Tully had waited to see how high Quinon would go before rejoining the competition at 5,80, at which he failed.

Carl Lewis was head and shoulders above everyone else in the **long jump**. particularly with the Russians and Lutz Dombrowski of East Germany not competing. Giovanni Evangelisti of Italy led off the competition in the first round of the finals with 8,09 metres. This was followed by Myricks of the USA jumping 8,06, but his fellow American, Carl Lewis, the king of jumpers, hitch-kicked his way to 8,54, his winning jump. Lewis had just one more attempt, which was a foul. then picked up his bag and left the competition. The crowd booed, but Lewis claimed that he was tired after two 200-metres runs in the morning. The silver went to Gary Honey of Australia with 8,24 and the bronze to Evangelisti, also with 8,24, his second best jump being behind Honey's.

Without the Russians, Lazara Betancourt of Cuba and Christov Makov of Bulgaria competing in the **triple jump** at Los Angeles, the event appeared to lack lustre, and the Americans Willie Banks and Mike Conley were strongly favoured for the gold medals. Zen Xian Zou of China began the finals with 16,83 metres and Al Joyner, with the aid of the wind, bounded to 17,26. On the second round Keith Connor of Britain leapt to 16,87 to take second place. Conley, who was nursing a strained ankle, progressed to 17,18 with his third jump, but produced a foul of about 17,60 on his last attempt. Joyner took the gold, Conley the silver and Connor the bronze.

Some of the big guns were missing in the **shot put**, notably Brian Oldfield, the reinstated amateur, his fellow American John Brenner, who came only fourth in his domestic trials, and Udo Beyer, the world record holder from East Germany. Alessandro Andrei of Italy was the best thrower on the day and improved from 20,71 to 20,97 and finally to 21,26 for the premier position. Mike Carter of the USA led the first round with 20,63 and later threw 21,09 for the silver spot, while his fellow American, Dave Laut, had a last round duel with his colleague, August Wolf, to take third place with 20,97 to 20,93.

The Americans John Powell and Mac Wilkins were the favourites for the **discus throw**, but the still air conditions in the stadium mitigated against long throws and the competition was very close. Round one of the finals saw Rolf Danneberg of West Germany throw 64,74 metres, only to have Wilkins top his mark with 65,96. Third at this point was Knut Hjeltnes of Norway at 64,72 and Powell, fourth with 64,68. In the next session Wilkins launched a mighty throw of over 68 metres, but trod on the circle rim, while Hjeltnes threw 65,28 in the third round to move up to second spot. Danneberg's fourth toss placed him head of the list with 66,60 and Wilkins' sixth effort of 66,30 consolidated his second position. Powell edged up to 65,12 and his final blast of 65,46 got him a medal. Result: Danneberg 66,60 took the gold; Wilkins 66,30 the silver, and Powell 65,46 the bronze.

By being absent, the Russians probably missed a clean sweep in the **hammer throw**ing competition and left the field open to Finland's Juha Tiainen. Klaus Ploghaus of West Germany was an early leader in the competition with his first round throw of 75,50 metres, which he improved to 75,96 in the next session. Then, with his third attempt, Tiainen took command with 78,08, to win the gold medal. Meanwhile, Karl-Hans Riehm of West Germany registered 77,98 for the silver. Giampaolo Uriando of Italy and fellow countryman Orlando Bianchini both threw 75.96 and caught up with Ploghaus, who on his final effort improved to 76,68 to make sure of the bronze.

Uwe Hohn of East Germany was the only man in history who had a **javelin throw** that exceeded 100 metres and he was denied the chance of an Olympic medal due to the boycott. In the final, Britain's David Ottley had led the competition for three rounds with an opening launch of 85.74, until the Finn, Arto Harkonen, responded with 86,76. That throw was good enough for the gold medal and Ottley had to be content with silver. The bronze went to Kenth Eldebrink of Sweden with a 83,72 effort in the fifth round.

Britain's Daley Thompson, the king of the **decathlon**, had won Commonwealth, European, world and Olympic titles and was now shooting for a second Olympic title, a feat that only America's Bob Mathias had achieved. Thompson was always in command and led the first day with a world best total of 4,633 points from his great rival Jurgen Hingsen of West Germany, who had 4,519 points, and his compatriot, Siggi Wentz on 4,332. Hingsen's downfall was the pole vault, where he performed below expectations and lost over 100 points. Daley Thompson's winning performances were 100m: 10·44 sec; long jump: 8·01 metres; shot put: 15,72 metres; high jump: 2,03 metres; 400m: 46·97 sec; 110m hurdles: 14·34 sec; discus: 46,56 metres; pole vault: 5,00 metres; javelin: 65,24 metres; 1,500m: 4-35·00. Result: Thompson 8,798 points, an Olympic record: Hingsen 8,673; Wentz 8,412. Thompson missed Hingsen's world record by one point. but as the tables were changed in 1985, he rescored at 8,847 against Hingsen's 8,832 and recaptured his world record.

Women's Events

America's queen of the sprints, Evelyn Ashford, was favourite for the **100 metres** particularly without East Germany's Marlies Gohr, the world champion, in the field. Alice Brown reacted first to the starter's pistol in the final and held everyone at bay until Ashford caught up with her at 20 metres. America's Jeanette Bolden was also pressing Brown, but Ashford strode away to win in a new Olympic record of 10·97 sec. In the battle for the other medals. Merlene Ottey-Page of Jamaica had come up hard and passed Bolden, then tried to out-lean Brown at the finish, but failed. Brown won the silver with a time of 11·13, while Ottey-Page collected the bronze, finishing in 11·16.

The East German duo of Marita Koch and Barbel Wockel, the reigning Olympic champion, were all powerful in Europe over **200 metres**, but in their absence, Valerie Brisco-Hooks of America and Merlene Ottey-Page of Jamaica were the best bets for the medals. Even without some of the "big guns" from Europe there was some snappy sprinting in the heats and semi-finals. Florence Griffith of the USA was swiftly into her sprinting in the final and haring around the turn. Brisco-Hooks had a hesitant start, but caught Griffith as they came into the straight and just flowed down the finishing straight to win in an outstanding 21·81 for an Olympic record. Ottey-Page and Kathy Cook of Britain were catching up on Griffith rapidly in the closing stages,

Mark Shearman

Valerie Brisco-Hooks

Valerie Brisco-Hooks is a perfect example of a female athlete achieving a new high standard of performance after becoming a mother. She married the professional American footballer Alvin Hooks in 1981.

Born in Greenwood, Mississippi, on 6 July 1960, she represented the United States in the Pan-American Games as a 19-year-old in 1979 without being placed, and the following season her best for 400m was only in the 52 sec class.

Returning to competition in 1983 after her son was born, she soon began to show improved form for 100m and 200m. By this time she was building up strength with the aid of weight training and running long distances. When the 1984 US Olympic trials duly arrived, she was beautifully trained, and proved the value of all her hard preparatory work when achieving a new personal best for the 200m of 22·16 sec and also getting inside 50·0 sex for 400m for the first time with 43·83 sec.

Thus her Olympic places were assured. But few expected Mrs Hooks to bring off a magnificent individual gold medal double at the Games. But she did, winning the 200m in an Olympic record of 21·81 sec and the 400m in another Olympic best time of 48·83 sec. She also received a third gold for another superb run in the US 4 × 400m relay team.

but Griffith took the silver in 22·04 from Ottey-Page 22·09, who had a better lean than Cook in 22·10. The winner's opening 100 was timed at 11·20 and closing 100, 10·61.

Marita Koch of East Germany and Tatana Kochembova of Czechoslovakia were the noticeable absentees from the **400 metres** and Chandra Cheeseborough was the considered favourite, on the strength of her national record in the American trials. It was the British girl, Kathy Cook, who was away the fastest in the final and running in lane six she passed the 200 in 23·4. But Valerie Brisco-Hooks of the USA in lane five was only a metre down, with Americans Cheeseborough and Lillie Leatherwood and Canada's Marita Payne off the pace some six or seven metres back. Cheeseborough now began powering down the straight and went past Cook, but Brisco-Hooks held on to win in 48·83 for an Olympic record, to Cheeseborough's 49·05. Cook was wilting, but managed to keep striding to take the bronze in 49·43 from a fast-closing Payne in 49·91.

Doina Melinte from Rumania, the only eastern bloc country to compete at Los Angeles, was the best of the European girls over **800 metres**. The preliminaries were rather pedestrian by world standards and the final shaped up for a US-Rumania duel. The pace in the final was brisk, with Kim Gallagher of the USA and Melinte leading at first, before Gabriella Dorio of Italy took over at 400 metres. Melinte made her break with 250 to go, and won handily in 1-57·60 from Gallagher in 1-58·63 and Fita Lovin of Rumania in 1-58·83, with Dorio a close up fourth.

Even with the Russians missing and Mary Decker of the USA electing to run the 3,000 metres, there were still some top class performers entered in the **1,500 metres**, such as the Rumanians, Doina Melinte and Maricica Puica, and Gabriella Dorio of Italy. In the final, Christina Boxer of Britain took up the running, leading the pack though 400 in 62·2 and 800 in 2-14·7. But with 600 to go, Dorio had seen enough of the slow pace, and struck out with Melinte on her shoulder, followed by Boxer, Roswitha Gerdes of West Germany and Christine Benning of Britain, with Rumania's Puica caught napping. Melinte went to the front with 200 to go, but Dorio struck back coming off the final bend and held

her lead to win in 4-03·25 from Melinte in 4-03·76. Puica finished fast to grab the bronze medal in 4-04·15.

This was the first time the **3,000 metres** had been included in the Olympics, and two of the world's top three runners, Maricica Puica of Rumania and Mary Decker of the USA, were in action. Missing was the Russian phenomenon, Tatyana Kazankina. In the final, Decker set a smart pace, covering the first 400 in 66·9 and one kilometre in 2-50·5, with Zola Budd and Wendy Sly of Britain and Puica in a tight group. At 1,600 metres, passed in 4-35·9, Budd slipped into the lead, running in her bare feet, but off the bend she collided with Decker, who was trying to come up on the inside, sending the American girl sprawling onto the infield and out of the race. Budd continued to lead, passing 2km in 5-44·1, but with 500 to go, Sly led Puica past her. With 250 to go, Puica made her break and went away to win in 8-35·96 to Sly's 8-39·47. Lynn Williams won the fight for the bronze medal, passing Budd with 200 metres left to finish in 8-42·14.

Although the **marathon** was another new event for women at the Olympics, it had great appeal, with the Norwegians Grete Waitz and Ingrid Kristiansen and the world record holder, Joan Benoit of the USA, in contention for medals. It was a particularly hot day and Benoit took a gamble by setting a very stiff pace: 10km in 35-24; 20km in 68-32; 30km in 1:42-23 and 40km in 2:17-14, finishing in a final 2:24-52 to win the race. Meanwhile, Waitz, Kristiansen, Rosa Mota of Portugal and Lorraine Moller of New Zealand, were running in a stretched group behind. Eventually, Waitz pushed the pace with Kristiansen and Mota falling back to finish second in 2:26-18. And Mota, seeing Kristiansen weaken, overtook her for the bronze with a time of 2:26-57.

In the absence of the East Europeans, Shirley Strong of Britain was considered to be the most likely Olympic champion in the **100 metres hurdles** and she confirmed her favouritism with the fastest time in the heats. In the final, Ulrike Denk of West Germany was quickest into her running, and led Strong, and the Americans Benita Fitzgerald-Brown and Kim Turner. The English girl took a slight lead at the sixth hurdle from Fitzgerald-Brown, who then turned the tables by the ninth flight and went on to win in 12·84 to Strong's 12·88, with Turner

Tessa Sanderson became Britain's first ever javelin gold medallist, while her team-mate Fatima Whitbread took the bronze.   Mark Shearman

Two of Britain's leading lights, Steve Cram (left) and Steve Ovett (centre), seen in the second semi-final of the 1,500 metres. Cram took silver in the final.   Mark Shearman

apparently tieing with France's Michele Chardonnet, in 13·06. As the girls moved towards the medal ceremony it was announced that Turner was third and Chardonnet fourth at which the latter broke down in tears. Three months after the Games Chardonnet was also awarded a medal and a tie for third place by the IAAF Council.

Ann-Louise Skoglund of Sweden was thought to be a likely winner in the **400 metres hurdles**, another new Olympic event, and she recorded the fastest time in the heats of 55·17, to vindicate her supporters. The clear surprise of the semi-finals were the qualifications of Pillavulakandi Usha of India and Nawal El Moutawakel of Morocco, who rose well above their past achievements. In the final, El Moutawakel, in lane three, went off at a cracking pace. She was never headed and sprinted the last ten metres with her hands above her head to win this inaugural event in 54·61 sec. Judy Brown of the USA ran an uninspired race to finish second in 55·20, while Skoglund, in third place, hit the last hurdle, which allowed Cristina Cojocaru of Rumania to claim the bronze medal in 55·41.

Eleven teams competed in the **4 × 100 metres relay**, with the USA and Jamaica locking certain of collecting medals. Alice Brown for the US set off at a great lick in the final and was a metre up on Canada's Angela Bailey at the first exchange, while the other leading contender, Jamaica, fouled up when Grace Jackson knocked the baton out of the hand of Juliette Cuthbert, the lead-off runner. America then also had a bad exchange and Jeanette Bolden went off to hand over slightly up on Canada's Marita Payne. But another bad pass for America, saw Canada's Angela Taylor in the lead, with America's Cheeseborough chasing hard. Cheeseborough finally took a three metres lead over Canada and Ashford went away to win in an excellent 41·65 from Canada in 42·77, while Britain outkicked France for third in 43·11.

The **4 × 400 metres relay** proved to be of a better

Mark Shearman

Carlos Lopes

The pride of Portuguese athletics, Carlos Lopes excelled both in cross country running and on the track. The 5ft 6in (1,68m), deep-chested stayer twice won the world cross country championship, but, great as were these successes for him, his most satisfactory achievement must have been winning the marathon at the 1984 Los Angeles Games, in an Olympic record time of 2:09·21.

Lopes was born in Viseu on 18 February 1947 and that victory was the culmination of 18 years of racing. It was not until 1975, when the Portuguese Government offered their best athletes the opportunity to have jobs, with plenty of time off for training, that Lopes began to show world class pace. The following year he won the world cross country championship by a runaway margin on Chepstow racecourse and also took the silver medal behind Finland's Lasse Viren in the Olympic 10,000m in Montreal.

Portugal boycotted the Moscow Olympics in 1980, which was around the time Lopes was having acute Achilles tendon trouble. But winning the world cross country championship again in New Jersey in 1984, eight years after his first success, showed him to be right back in peak form. And how he proved it in the Los Angeles Games later in the year.

standard than expected. The first leg was very close between Canada's Charmaine Crooks, clocking 50·30, and the USA's Lillie Leatherwood's 50·50. But, in the second stage, Sherri Howard for the USA, ran a brilliant 48·83 to take the lead over Canada and Valerie Brisco-Hooks then increased the gap with a 49·23 third lap. Chandra Cheeseborough ran home for the US in 49·73, for an overall time of 3-18·29, an Olympic record, from Canada in 3-21·21. West Germany maintained third position throughout and recorded 3-22·98.

Ulrike Meyfarth of West Germany, the **high jump** winner of 1972, and the defending champion, Sara Simeoni of Italy, were the two to be watched in the absence of the world record holder, Tamara Bykova of the USSR. Six athletes cleared 1,94 metres, including Debbie Brill of Canada, who introduced the Brill bend back in 1968. At 1,97, the Olympic record height, three jumpers cleared: Meyfarth, Simeoni and Joni Huntley of America, all on their second attempts. The bar was then raised to 2,00 and Meyfarth and Simeoni went over first time leaving Huntley to collect the bronze medal. At 2,02 only Meyfarth succeeded, with Simeoni taking the silver. The winner tried three times at a world best of 2,07, but she was not even close.

All of the top **long jump** proponents of the day came from Russia, East Germany and Rumania, and only the Rumanians competed at Los Angeles. In the first round, two girls jumped 6,80 metres, Anisoara Stanciu of Rumania and Sue Hearnshaw of Britain, with Vali Ionescu of Rumania holding down third at 6,59. In the next round Jackie Joyner of the USA moved into third position with 6,72 and in the fourth improved to 6,77. Stanciu then made the gold medal jump of 6,96, before Ionescu leapt 6,81 for the silver, leaving Hearnshaw in the bronze medal position with 6,80.

In the absence of the top throwers from Russia, East Germany and Czechoslovakia, the **shot put** was between Claudia Losch of West Germany and Mihaela Loghin of Rumania. Losch commenced the final with 19,97 metres and then improved to 20,31 with her next throw. Loghin took over the lead in the fourth round with 20,47, which seemed to inspire Losch to greater concentration, for she launched the winning put of 20,48 in the last round, much to the dismay of her rival. Judith Oakes of Britain briefly held third spot before Gael Martin of Australia

got going to throw 19,19 for the bronze medal.

Ria Stalman of Holland was the most accomplished of the **discus throwers** in the absence of most of the eastern bloc countries, and she quickly asserted her authority with her first throw of 64,50 metres. However, in the fifth round, Leslie Deniz of the USA, flipped the platter to 64,86, but Stalman responded in the last round with 65,36 to win the competition, leaving the American girl with the silver. Meanwhile, Ulla Lundholm of Finland who had thrown 62,84 at her first attempt, was relegated into fourth place, when Florenta Craciunescu of Rumania superseded that mark with 63,64 for the bronze medal.

Prior to the Games there were four main contenders for the **javelin throw**, the two British girls Tessa Sanderson and Fatima Whitbread, Anna Verouli of Greece, who did not qualify for the final, and the world record holder, Tiina Lillak of Finland, who had an injured ankle. Of the great throwers, only Petra Felke of East Germany was not competing. Sanderson produced her best throw of 69,56 in the first round and broke the Olympic record, with Trine Solberg of Norway and Whitbread lying equal second on 64,52, but the latter improved to 65,40 with her next attempt. Lillak produced 69,00 in the second round and then retired injured, while Whitbread improved twice more to 65,82 and finally to 67,14. Result: Sanderson the gold, Lillak the silver and Whitbread the bronze.

The **heptathlon** had now replaced the previous pentathlon and was held over two days instead of one. The big names in this event were not competing and any one of half-a-dozen girls had a reasonable chance of gold. The lead changed throughout the competition, with Glynis Nunn of Australia winning the 100m hurdles in 13·02 sec, then Judy Simpson of Great Britain taking over the lead with a 1,86 metre high jump. She held on to it through the shot and 200 metres to finish with 3,759 points at the end of the first day, from Jackie Joyner of the USA on 3,739 and Nunn on 3,731. Sabine Everts of West Germany led after her long jump of 6,71 metres, while Joyner came back into the reckoning with a javelin throw of 44,52 metres. But Nunn's 800m in 2-10·57 was sufficient to hoist her to a win and a gold medal with 6,390 points. Joyner took the silver with 6,385 and Everts the bronze with 6,363.

Daley Thompson won the decathlon for Britain in Los Angeles, following up his 1980 Moscow success. He goes for the hat-trick in Seoul.

Daley Thompson

Without doubt Daley Thompson is the world's all-time greatest decathlete. Successes in world, European and Commonwealth championships have been capped by his being only the second man — Bob Mathias in 1948 and 1952 was the first — to win the Olympic title twice.

He was born in Notting Hill, London, on 30 July 1958. Being sent at the age of 18 to contest the event in the Montreal Games of 1976, where he finished eighth, fired Thompson with a tremendous determination to become an Olympic champion. This led to his setting a world Junior record the following year and becoming a decisive winner of the Commonwealth title in Canada in 1978.

Before going to Moscow in 1980, where he won the first of his Olympic gold medals, he broke the world record for the first time with 8,662 points. Three times he lost and regained the world record after it had been taken from him by the Germans Guido Kratschmer and then Jurgen Hingsen (twice). But Thompson left them in no doubt as to who was the world's best when he retained his Olympic title in Los Angeles with a new world mark of 8,798 points.

Mark Shearman

Evelyn Ashford

The only woman to break 11 sec in an Olympic 100m final, Evelyn Ashford achieved this feat in Los Angeles.

From Shreveport, Louisiana, where she was born on 15 April 1957, her first attempt to gain Olympic honours in Montreal saw her placed fifth in the 100m.

By 1979 she had really begun to blossom and that season she won the 100m and 200m at the Pan-American Games with the impressive times of 11·07 sec and 22·24 sec respectively. The same year she won the same two events in the World Cup finals with 11·06 sec and 21·83 sec.

The American boycott of the Moscow Games in 1980, robbed her of the chance of collecting a cherished Olympic medal, but she continued her winning ways in the World Cup again a year later, getting down to 11·02 sec over the 100m and taking the 200 in 22·18 sec.

So her form was looking good for the Olympics in Los Angeles. Just how well the East German girls could have matched her pace there can only be a matter for conjecture, but the star of American women's sprinting sped with such power and control that she looked unbeatable by anybody on the day the gold medal was at stake. She was also a member of the United States winning sprint relay team.

Mark Shearman

Ulrike Meyfarth

West German coaches have an uncanny skill for producing world class high jumpers among their women as well as their men and in Miss Meyfarth they found a remarkable performer for the event. Born at Frankfurt on 4 May 1956, she was only 16 when to the delight of all West Germany she won the women's title at the 1972 Munich Games. Her clearance of 6ft 3½in (1.92m) tied the world record at that time.

From then on the East German challenge hotted up considerably with Rosemary Ackermann taking the world record in seven stages from 6ft 4½in (1,94m) in 1974 to 6ft 6¾in (2,0m) in 1977.

While Ulrike was always lurking in the wings it was not until ten years after her Olympic triumph in Munich that she became a world record holder again, with a 6ft 7½in (2,02m) clearance in Athens. The following season, in the European Cup final at the Crystal Palace, London, she improved even this to 6ft 8in (2,03m).

In 1983 Bykova added another centimetre to this mark in Pisa, but when it came to the Olympic Games in Los Angeles a year later, the West German girl was in world-beating form again. She won back the Olympic title she had previously won 12 years earlier, with a Games record 6ft 7½in (2,02m).

Mark Shearman

Joaquim Cruz

Born in Rio de Janeiro on 12 March 1963, Cruz revealed himself a youngster of exceptional talent when in his teens he broke the world junior record for 800m. Standing 6ft 1½in (6·87m) with a smooth rhythmic stride, he soon developed into a senior racer to respect, especially after beating the Cuban Olympic champion, Alberto Juantorena, in the South American trials for the 1981 World Cup tournament, where he set up a South American record of 1-44·30.

The following year found Cruz more interested in learning English than racing round tracks because of his wish to be accepted for a sports scholarship, which was granted when he obtained entry to the University of Oregon, Eugene.

There he became a strong front runner, and in 1983 he succeeded in winning the 800m bronze medal at the world championships.

Obviously his steady progress had made him one to note for the Los Angeles Olympics in 1984, but few were prepared for the strength of the run which gave him victory over Sebastian Coe in the 800m final in a Games record 1-43·00.

Coe was unstinting in his praise for the 21-year-old Brazilian's success and was, no doubt, somewhat relieved when Cruz decided to pull out of the 1,500m.

The winner of the women's 800 metres in Los Angeles, Doina Melinte of Rumania, also gained a silver in the 1,500. Mark Shearman.

A scene prior to the collision between the front two, Mary Decker and Zola Budd. Also pictured are the eventual gold and silver medallists, Maricica Puica of Rumania (left) and Wendy Sly of Britain.

Mark Shearman.

COMPETITOR	COUNTRY CODE	EVENT	ROUND	HEAT	PLACE	TIME & DISTANCE	MEDAL
MALES							
Abascal, J.	ESP	1500m	1	5	1	3-37·68	
			SF	1	1	3-35·70	
			F		3	3-34·30	B
Abdilahi, C.	DJI	Marathon	F		32	2:19-11	
Abdulla, F.	QAT	100m	1	10	5	10·78	
		4×100m relay	1	1	6	40·60	
			SF	2	8	40·43	
Abdulla, M.	UAE	100m	1	2	8	11·11	
Abossolo, J.-P.	CMR	400m hurdles	1	4	7	52·85	
		4×400m relay	1	2	7	3-16·00	
Abrahams, G.	CRC	100m	1	10	7	11·31	
		200m	1	2	8	22·75	
Achia, W.	UGA	Marathon	F		DNF		
Acosta, L.	ECU	800m	1	2	7	1-54·06	
Adamson, M.	JAM	Marathon	F		52	2:25-02	
Adegbeingbe, L.	NGR	4×100m relay	1	2	4	39·94	
Aden, J.	SOM	800m	1	3	4	1-48·64	
		1500m	1	2	5	3-46·80	
Adeyanju, I.	NGR	4×100m relay	1	2	4	39·94	
			SF	2	5	38·98	
Agbebaku, A.	NGR	Triple jump	F		7	16,67	
Agosta, M.	LUX	Marathon	F		54	2:27-41	
Aguiar, R.	ARG	Marathon	F		59	2:31-18	
Aguilar, F.	PAN	200m	1	3	4	21·50	
Aguilar, O.	CHI	10000m	1	1	7	28-29·6	
		5000m	1	4	6	13-51·53	
			SF	1	11	13-51·13	
		Marathon	F		DNF		
Ahmed, A.	SOM	Marathon	F		73	2:44-39	
Ahmed, S.	DJI	Marathon	F		20	2:15-59	
Aidet, M.	ALG	1500m	1	3	7	3-53·92	
Akabusi, K.	GBR	400m	1	10	1	45·64	
			2	1	3	45·43	
			SF	1	7	45·69	
		4×400m relay	1	2	1	3-06·10	
			SF	1	2	3-02·98	
			F		2	2-59·13	S
Akonniemi, A.	FIN	Shot put	F		9	18,98	
Al-Abdulla, J.	QAT	200m	1	4	4	21·10	
			2	4	7	21·44	
		4×100m relay	1	1	6	40·60	
			SF	2	8	40·43	
Alakbary, A.	OMA	3000m steeplechase	1	1	12	10-22·96	
Alakbary, S.	OMA	100m	1	3	6	10·86	
		4×400m relay	1	4	5	3-15·87	
Alcalde, M.	ESP	50k walk	F		9	4:05-47	
Alcala, G.	MEX	5000m	1	3	9	13-50·60	
			SF	1	8	13-45·98	
Al-Duaillah, J.	KUW	400m hurdles	1	6	5	51·45	
Algadi, A.	YAR	800m	1	8	8	2-05·90	
Algadi, A.-S.	YAR	10000m	1	2	DNF		
		5000m	1	4	13	16-06·58	
Alheshimi, A.	OMA	200m	1	6	6	22·83	
		4×400m relay	1	4	5	3-15·87	
Ali, H.	UAE	110m hurdles	1	4	6	15·75	
Allassane, M.	NIG	1500m	1	4	9	3-56·43	
Alli, Y.	NGR	Long jump	F		9	7,78	
Almaliki, M.	OMA	400m	1	3	6	47·61	
		4×400m relay	1	4	5	3-15·87	
Alonso, J.	ESP	400m hurdles	1	6	DNF		
Alonzo, J.-V.	GUA	20k walk	F		34	1:35-32	
		50k walk	F		17	4:36-35	
Alouini, M.	TUN	800m	1	8	3	1-47·20	
			2	4	5	1-45·78	
		1500m	1	2	6	3-49·78	
Al-Rahim, I.	QAT	4×100m relay	1	1	6	40·60	
			SF	2	8	40·43	
Alsameer, A.	OMA	Marathon	F		DNF		
Alsharji, A.	OMA	1500m	1	1	8	4-12·76	
		800m	1	8	7	2-00·38	
Alsharji, B.	OMA	4×400m relay	1	4	5	3-15·87	
Altun, A.	TUR	Marathon	F		DNF		
Amakye, W.	GHA	800m	1	6	6	1-54·80	
Ambowode, A.	CAF	Marathon	F		71	2:41-26	
Amike, H.	NGR	400m hurdles	1	5	2	50·11	
			SF	2	4	49·36	
			F		8	53·78	
Andersen, E.	NOR	20k walk	F		8	1:25-54	
		50k walk	F		DIS		
Andre, D.	MRI	100m	1	3	8	11·19	
		200m	1	10	6	22·16	
		400m	1	2	7	49·09	
Andrei, A.	ITA	Shot put	F		1	21,26	G
Annijs, E.	BEL	High jump	Q		DNQ	2,21	

COMPETITOR	COUNTRY CODE	EVENT	ROUND	HEAT	PLACE	TIME & DISTANCE	MEDAL
Antibo, S.	ITA	10000m	1	1	2	28-22·57	
			F		4	28-06·50	
		5000m	1	3	6	13-46·32	
			SF	2	13	13-47·53	
Anzarah, J.	KEN	400m	1	8	2	46·12	
			2	1	5	45·67	
		4×400m relay	1	4	2	3-06·07	
			SF	2	7	3-04·74	
Aouita, S.	MAR	5000m	1	2	4	13-45·66	
			SF	2	1	13-28·39	
			F		1	13-05·59*	G
Araouzos, D.	CYP	Long jump	Q		DNQ	5,67	
Archer, D.	TRI	4×400m relay	1	1	3	3-06·81	
			SF	2	DIS		
Armstead, R.	USA	4×400m relay	1	4	1	3-01·44	
			F		1	2-57·91	G
Arnold, M.	SUI	400m	1	2	3	46·46	
			2	2	6	46·10	
Arop, J.	UGA	Javelin throw	Q		DNQ	69,76	
Arques, J.	ESP	100m	1	2	3	10·42	
			2	4	4	10·52	
Ashoush, M.	EGY	Shot put	Q		DNQ	18,11	
Asumi, B.E.	GEQ	800m	1	7	7	2-17·29	
Atkinson, J.	AUS	High jump	Q		DNQ	2,21	
Attipoe, P.	GHA	100m	1	5	5	10·60	
			2	3	7	10·78	
		4×100m relay	1	2	5	40·20	
			SF	1	5	40·19	
Atwood, D.	USA	Javelin throw	F		11	78,10	
Atuti, J.	KEN	400m	1	7	5	47·04	
Avila, C.	HON	Marathon	F		71	2:42-03	
Ayaz, N.	TUR	5000m	1	2	11	14-36·89	
Ayaz, N.	TUR	10000m	1	3	DNF		
Aziz, I.	UAE	800m	1	4	6	1-54·86	
		1500m	1	5	DNF		
		4×400m relay	1	1	7	3-19·90	
Babers, A.	USA	400m	1	5	1	45·81	
			2	3	1	44·75	
			SF	1	2	45·17	
			F		1	44·27	G
		4×400m relay	1	4	1	3-01·44	
			F		1	2-57·91	G
Babits, L.	CAN	Javelin throw	F		8	80,68	
Baccouche, F.	TUN	3000m steeplechase	1	1	3	8-27·49	
			SF	2	6	8-18·70	
			F		12	8-43·40	
		5000m	1	2	DNF		
Badinelli, D.	ITA	Triple jump	Q		DNQ	16,13	
Badra, H.	EGY	Triple jump	F		11	16,07	
Bainimoli, I.-D.	FIJ	100m	1	3	7	11·15	
		200m	1	1	6	22·16	
Baker, S.	AUS	20k walk	F		14	1:27-43	
Bakhta, A.	ALG	200m	1	8	4	21·15	
			2	1	8	21·35	
Balotihanji, K.	BOT	1500m	1	2	8	3-58·69	
Banks, W.	USA	Triple jump	F		6	16,75	
Baptiste, K.	USA	200m	1	8	1	20·63	
			2	4	1	20·48	
			SF	1	1	20·29	
			F		2	19·96	S
Barbosa, J.-L.	BRA	800m	1	9	3	1-47·12	
			2	2	4	1-46·87	
			SF	2	8	1-48·70	
		4×400m relay	1	3	5	3-05·08	
			SF	2	5	3-03·99	
Barella, M.	ITA	Pole vault	F		8	5,30	
Barie, Z.	TRI	10000m	1	3	3	28-15·18	
			F		13	28-32·28	
		5000m	1	4	8	13-53·00	
			SF	1	7	13-43·49	
Barr, O.	GUY	800m	1	5	3	1-47·65	
			2	4	7	1-46·97	
		1500m	1	2	DNF		
Barre, P.	FRA	200m	1	5	1	20·88	
			2	1	6	20·95	
Barroso, L.	POR	100m	1	8	4	10·76	
			1	7	6	22·03	
Barry, S.	GBR	20k walk	F		24	1:30-46	
Beattie, P.	GBR	400m hurdles	1	1	8	51·27	
Bechard, D.	MRI	Hammer throw	Q		DNQ	0	
		Discus throw	Q		DNQ	41,10	
Becker, U.	GER	1500m	1	5	3	3-37·76	
			SF	2	6	3-37·28	
Belkessam, A.	ALG	800m	1	6	4	1-47·51	
			2	2	7	1-48·11	
Bell, E.	USA	Pole vault	F		=3	5,60	B
Bellucci, S.	ITA	50k walk	F		3	3:53-45	B

COMPETITOR	COUNTRY CODE	EVENT	ROUND	HEAT	PLACE	TIME & DISTANCE	MEDAL
Bemou, J.-D.	CGO	400m	1	4	5	47·26	
		4×100m relay	1	3	6	40·74	
Ben Haddad, M.-R.	ALG	110m hurdles	1	1	5	14·44	
Benjamin, I.	SLE	100m	1	9	6	11·13	
		200m	1	9	5	21·54	
		4×100m relay	1	2	6	40·77	
Benjamin, L.	ANT	Long jump	Q		DNC	7,57	
		4×100m relay	1	3	5	40·70	
			SF	2	6	40·14	
Bennett, T.	GBR	400m	1	3	3	46·09	
			2	3	5	45·51	
		4×400m relay	1	2	1	3-06·10	
			SF	1	2	3-02·98	
			F		2	2-59·13	S
Bermudez, M.	MEX	50k walk	F		DIS		
Bethune, T.	CAN	400m	1	5	5	46·98	
		4×400m relay	1	1	2	3-04·47	
			2	1	3	3-03·93	
			F		8	3-02·82	
Bianchini, O.	ITA	Hammer throw	F		4	75,94	
Bile, A.	SOM	800m	1	1	2	1-46·92	
			2	3	5	1-46·49	
		1500m	1	6	4	3-40·72	
			SF	1	DIS		
Bitanga, E.	CMR	200m	1	1	DNF		
Bitok, S.	KEN	10000m	1	3	1	28-12·17	
			F		6	28-09·01	
Bodjona, B.	TOG	Long jump	Q		DNQ	6,82	
Boehni, F.	SUI	Pole vault	F		7	5,30	
Boffi, F.	ITA	3000m steeplechase	1	2	7	8-32·26	
			SF	1	10	8-30·82	
Boileau, A.	CAN	Marathon	F		44	2:22·43	
Bongiorni, G.	ITA	4×100m relay	1	2	3	39·87	
			SF	1	2	39·32	
			F		4	38·87	
Boonprasert, P.	THA	4×100m relay	1	1	5	40·58	
			SF	1	8	40·33	
Boraboti, S.	GEQ	400m	1	3	DIS		
Bordeleau, A.	CAN	Marathon	F		65	2:34·27	
Boreham, A.	GBR	Decathlon	F		20	7485	
Borromeo, C.	IND	800m	1	9	5	1-51·52	
Bounour, A.	ALG	5000m	1	4	5	13-51·52	
			SF	1	13	13-57·43	
Bouschen, P.	GER	Triple jump	F		5	16,77	
Boussemart, J.-J.	FRA	200m	1	9	2	20·82	
			2	3	2	20·54	
			SF	1	4	20·55	
			F		6	20·55	
		4×100m relay	1	1	3	40·04	
			SF	2	4	38·91	
			F		6	39·10	
Boxberger, L.	FRA	Marathon	F		42	2:22·00	
Bradstock, R.	GBR	Javelin throw	F		7	81,22	
Briggs, M.	GBR	400m hurdles	1	5	4	50·80	
Bright, T.	USA	Decathlon	F		12	7862	
Brobby, R.	GHA	4×100m relay	1	2	5	40·20	
			SF	1	5	40·19	
Brown, P.	GBR	400m	1	5	3	46·26	
			2	2	7	46·63	
		4×400m relay	1	2	1	3-06·10	
			SF	1	2	3-02·98	
			F		2	2-59·13	S
Brown, R.	USA	100m	1	9	1	10·58	
			2	3	2	10·40	
			SF	1	4	10·34	
			F		4	10·26	
		4×100m relay	1	1	1	38·89	
			SF	1	1	38·44	
			F		1	37·83*	G
Browne, A.	ANT	400m	1	6	5	47·29	
		4×100m relay	1	3	5	40·70	
			SF	2	6	40·14	
		4×400m relay	1	2	5	3-10·95	
Brunel, G.	FRA	400m hurdles	1	1	6	50·99	
Bryggare, A.	FIN	110m hurdles	1	1	1	13·35	
			SF	2	3	13·52	
			F		3	13·40	B
Buechel, M.	LIE	100m	1	5	7	10·98	
		200m	1	4	7	22·14	
Burke, E.	USA	Hammer throw	Q		DNQ	67,52	
Burns, A.	USA	Discus throw	F		5	64,98	
Butera, F.	RWA	400m hurdles	1	5	7	54·35	
		400m	1	2	8	51·41	
Caban, C.	PUR	Marathon	F		53	2:27·16	
Caceres, P.	ARG	3000m steeplechase	1	1	10	8-50·02	
Caetano, C.	POR	Marathon	F		DNF		
Cai, S.	ROC	High jump	F		8	2·27	
Camacho, J.	BOL	Marathon	F		38	2:21·04	
Cameron, B.	JAM	400m	1	4	1	46·14	
			2	3	3	45·16	
			SF	2	4	45·10	
Campbell, A.	USA	110m hurdles	1	2	1	13·53	
			SF	1	2	13·56	
			F		5	13·55	
Campos, J.	POR	5000m	1	3	5	13-46·27	
			SF	2	9	13-34·46	
Campos, L.	ESA	20k walk	F		37	1:48·45	
Carario, E.	POR	5000m	1	1	1	13-43·28	
			SF	2	8	13-32·64	
			F		9	13-26·50	
Canovic, N.	YUG	High jump	Q		DNQ	2,15	
Canti, A.	FRA	400m	1	6	2	46·14	
			2	2	4	45·64	
			SF	1	5	45·59	
		4×400m relay	1	2	4	3-08·33	
Canto, E.	MEX	20k walk	F		1	1:23·13*	G
		50k walk	F		10	4:01·59	
Caristan, S.	FRA	110m hurdles	1	4	2	13·45	
			SF	1	3	13·62	
			F		6	13·71	
Carter, M.	USA	Shot put	F		2	21,09	S
Casali, S.	SMR	20k walk	F		35	1:35·48	
Castillo, M.	DOM	110m hurdles	1	4	5	14·05	
Castro, E.	MEX	5000m	1	4	3	13-51·46	
			SF	2	10	13-42·04	
Catalano, M.	CAN	Shot put	Q		DNQ	17,24	
Ceesay, P.	GAM	800m	1	9	7	1-55·35	
		1500m	1	1	7	3-59·14	
Chae, H.-N.	KOR	Marathon	F		48	2:23·33	
Chaparro, N.	PAR	400m hurdles	1	3	8	56·98	
		110m hurdles	1	1	6	15·51	
Chen, C.-M.	TPE	Marathon	F		=56	2:29·53	
Chen, H.-Y.	TPE	Javelin throw	Q		DNQ	71,48	
Cheruiyot, C.	KEN	5000m	1	3	1	13-45·99	
			SF	2	4	13-28·56	
			F		6	13-18·41	
Cheruiyot, K.	KEN	1500m	1	6	5	3-41·96	
Chesire, J.	KEN	1500m	1	1	1	3-38·51	
			SF	1	=4	3-35·83	
			F		4	3-34·52	
Chevalier, W.	FRA	110m hurdles	1	2	5	14·32	
Ciofani, W.	FRA	Hammer throw	F		7	73,46	
Clark, D.	AUS	400m	1	10	2	45·68	
			2	1	2	44·77	
			SF	1	3	45·26	
			F		4	44·75	
		4x400m relay	1	-	1	3-03·72	
			SF	2	2	3-03·79	
			F		4	2-59·70	
Clary, D.	USA	5000m	1	2	3	13-44·97	
			SF	2	11	13-46·02	
Coe, S.	GBR	800m	1	2	1	1-45·71	
			2	2	3	1-46·75	
			SF	2	1	1-45·51	
			F		2	1-43·64	S
		1500m	1	2	2	3-45·30	
			SF	1	3	3-35·81	
			F		1	3-32·53*	G
Colin, M.	MEX	20k walk	F		17	1:28·26	
Confait, V.	SEY	400m hurdles	1	3	7	53·62	
		400m	1	10	DIS		
Conley, M.	USA	Triple jump	F		2	17,18	S
Connor, K.	GBR	Triple jump	F		3	16,87	B
Coocherd, V.	THA	4x100m relay	1	1	5	40·58	
			SF	1	8	40·83	
Cook, G.	GBR	4x400m relay	1	2	1	3-06·10	
			SF	1	2	3-02·98	
			F		2	2-59·13	S
Cooper, B.	BAH	Discus throw	Q		DNQ	53,70	
Coralie, V.	MRI	Decathlon	F		25	6084	
Corgos, A.	ESP	Long jump	F		10	7,69	
Cornielle, R.	DOM	10000m	1	1	DNF		
		5000m	1	2	14	17-16·77	
Correia, P.	BRA	100m	1	6	4	10·45	
			2	4	7	10·54	
		4x100m relay	1	2	2	39·27	
			SF	1	4	39·52	
			F		8	39·40	
Cova, A.	ITA	10000m	1	2	1	28-26·10	
			F		1	27-47·54	G
Cram, S.	GBR	1500m	1	6	1	3-40·33	
			SF	2	1	3-36·30	
			F		2	3-33·40	S

COMPETITOR	COUNTRY CODE	EVENT	ROUND	HEAT	PLACE	TIME & DISTANCE	MEDAL
Crawford, H.	TRI	100m	1	1	4	10·48	
			2	1	4	10·56	
Crist, J.	USA	Decathlon	F		6	8130	
Cruden, S.	SUR	800m	1	5	8	1-53·31	
		400m	1	6	7	50·07	
Cruz, J.	BRA	800m	1	5	1	1-45·66	
			2	3	1	1-44·84	
			SF	1	1	1-43·82	
			F		1	1-43·00*	G
		1500m	1	4	1	3-41·01	
Cruz, M.-A.	MEX	Marathon	F		DNF		
Cummings, P.	USA	10000m	1	2	9	29-09·82	
Daenens, P.	BEL	3000m steeplechase	1	3	3	8-28·26	
			SF	2	7	8-21·77	
Dahl, O.	NOR	Marathon	F		33	2:19-28	
D'Aleo, G.	ITA	Marathon	F		35	2:20-12	
Dalhauser, R.	SUI	High jump	F		11	2,10	
Damilano, M.	ITA	20k walk	F		3	1:23-26	B
		50k walk	F		DNF		
Daniel, V.	MOZ	100m	1	1	6	10·81	
Daniels, O.	LBR	100m	1	6	6	10·76	
		4x100m hurdles	1	3	7	42·05	
Danneberg, R.	GER	Discus throw	F		1	66,60	G
Da Silva, A.	BRA	200m	1	8	5	21·24	
		4×100m relay	1	2	2	39·27	
			SF	1	4	39·52	
			F		8	39·40	
Da Silva, J.B.	BRA	200m	1	4	3	20·70	
			2	2	4	20·61	
			SF	2	2	20·61	
			F		4	20·30	
		4×400m relay	1	3	5	3-05·08	
			SF	2	5	3-03·99	
Da Silva, R.	BRA	200m	1	1	3	21·08	
			2	3	4	20·88	
			SF	1	6	20·80	
		4×100m relay	1	2	2	39·27	
Davies-Hale, P.	GBR	3000m steeplechase	1	1	7	8-31·97	
			SF	1	8	8-26·15	
Dawn, S.	BAN	100m	1	8	8	11.25	
		200m	1	1	7	22·59	
Debacker, P.	FRA	3000m steeplechase	1	1	6	8-30·35	
			SF	1	2	8-20·34	
			F		8	8-21·51	
De Bruin, E.	HOL	Shot put	F		8	19,65	
		Discus throw	F		9	62,32	
De Castella, R.	AUS	Marathon	F		5	2:11-09	
De La Garza, J.	MEX	Javelin throw	Q		DNQ	78,80	
De La Parte, S.	ESP	Marathon	F		DNF		
Del Prado, A.	PHI	400m	1	8	3	46·82	
			2	4	8	46·71	
Deleze, P.	SUI	1500m	1	3	DNF		
Denou, K.	TOG	Triple jump	Q		DNQ	14,44	
Desruelles, R.	BEL	100m	1	8	1	10·46	
Dia Ba, A.	SEN	400m hurdles	1	5	1	49·94	
			SF	1	3	49·44	
			F		5	49·28	
		4x400m relay	1	3	DIS		
Diallo, B.	SEN	400m	1	1	4	46·73	
		4x400m relay	1	3	DIS		
Diallo, M.	SEN	Triple jump	F		12	15,99	
Diawara, H.	SEN	4x100m relay	1	1	4	40·15	
			SF	1	7	40·63	
Diaz, A.	GUA	Decathlon	F		24	6342	
Diemer, B.	USA	3000m steeplechase	1	1	1	8-25·92	
			SF	2	3	8-18·36	
			F		3	8-14·06	B
Diesel, O.	PAR	Triple jump	Q		DNQ	14,19	
		Long jump	Q		DNQ	6,78	
Dixon, R.	NZL	Marathon	F		10	2:12-57	
Djan, M.	GHA	4x100m relay	1	2	5	40·20	
			SF	1	5	40·19	
Dodoo, F.	GHA	Triple jump	Q		DNQ	15,55	
Dolegiewicz, B.	CAN	Shot put	F		11	18,39	
Donovan, P.	IRL	1500m	1	2	4	3-45·70	
Dos Santos, N.	BRA	100m	1	9	3	10·70	
			2	2	4	10·53	
		4×100m relay	SF	1	4	39·52	
			F		8	39·40	
Dubois, D.	FRA	4x400m relay	1	2	4	3-08·33	
Ducceschi, R.	ITA	50k walk	F		5	3:59-26	
Duhaime, J.	CAN	3000m steeplechase	1	2	5	8-31·54	
			SF	1	9	8-26·32	
Dupont, P.	FRA	800m	1	4	3	1-48·09	
			2	4	8	1-48·95	
Ebrahim, K.	UAE	400m hurdles	1	5	8	55·50	
		4x400m relay	1	1	7	3-19·90	

COMPETITOR	COUNTRY CODE	EVENT	ROUND	HEAT	PLACE	TIME & DISTANCE	MEDAL
Edge, D.	CAN	Marathon	F		DNF		
Edwards, C.	BAR	4x100m relay	1	3	4	40·47	
			SF	2	7	40·18	
		4x400m relay	1	3	1	3-03·31	
			SF	2	4	3-03·89	
			F		6	3-01·60	
Edwards, N.	JAM	100m	1	10	5	10·57	
			2	2	3	10·44	
			SF	2	7	10·63	
		4x100m relay	1	3	1	38·93	
Egbunike, I.	NGR	400m	1	3	1	46·63	
			2	2	1	45·26	
			SF	1	1	45·16	
			F		7	45·35	
		4x400m relay	1	4	3	3-06·34	
			SF	2	1	3-02·22	
			F		3	2-59·32	B
Einarsson, S.	ISL	Javelin throw	Q		DNQ	69,82	
Ekblom, T.	FIN	3000m steeplechase	1	3	6	8-29·45	
			SF	1	3	8-20·54	
			F		9	8-23·95	
Eldebrink, K.	SWE	Javelin throw	F		3	83,72	B
Elliott, P.	GBR	800m	1	9	2	1-46·98	
			2	1	4	1-45·49	
Emordi, P.	NGR	Triple jump	Q		DNQ	15,88	
Erazo, N.	PUR	200m	1	10	4	21·72	
Eriksson, T.	SWE	High jump	Q		DNQ	2,21	
		Triple jump	Q		DNQ	15,97	
Erixson, M.	SWE	5000m	1	2	1	13-44·45	
			SF	2	7	13-29·72	
			F		12	13-41·64	
Escauriza, C.	PAR	Decathlon	F		22	6546	
Evangelisti, G.	ITA	Long jump	F		3	8,24	B
Evers, J.	GER	100m	1	5	3	10·54	
			2	5	8	10·69	
		200m,	1	3	3	21·12	
			2	2	5	20·95	
		4x100m relay	1	1	2	39·04	
			SF	2	3	38·70	
			F		5	38·99	
Evoniuk, M.	USA	20k walk	F		7	1:25-42	
		50k walk	F		DNF		
Fall, I.	SEN	4x100m relay	SF	1	7	40·63	
Fall, M.	SEN	800m	1	3	2	1-47·91	
			2	4	4	1-45·71	
			SF	1	6	1-45·03	
		4x400m relay	1	3	DIS		
Fawair, M.	JOR	800m	1	4	5	1-53·89	
		1500m	1	3	8	3-59·85	
Fellice, J.	FRA	4x400m relay	1	2	4	3-08·33	
Ferguene, A.	ALG	20k walk	F		26	1:31-24	
Fernandez, D.	VEN	Decathlon	F		18	7553	
		20k walk	F		26	1:31-24	
Ferner, H.-P.	GER	800m	1	7	2	1-47·55	
			2	4	2	1-45·52	
			SF	2	5	1-46·16	
Fernholm, S.	SWE	Discus throw	F		8	63,22	
Ferreira, A.	BRA	400m hurdles	1	1	2	49·85	
			SF	1	8	50·70	
		4x400m relay	1	3	5	3-05·08	
Ferreira, S.	FRA	Pole vault	F		13	5,30	
Fesselier, M.	FRA	20k walk	F		20	1:29-46	
Figueredo, F.	PAR	800m	1	5	7	1-52·22	
Fizuleto, N.	YUG	High jump	Q		DNQ	2,18	
Flowers, D.	BIZ	200m	1	10	5	21·72	
Flynn, R.	IRL	5000m	1	1	3	13-46·84	
			SF	1	4	13-40·74	
			F		11	13-34·50	
Folseca, S.	HON	20k walk	F		31	1:34-53	
Fong, W.	SAM	110m hurdles	1	4	DNF		
Fontecchio, M.	ITA	110m hurdles	1	1	3	13·75	
			SF	2	6	13·86	
Forde, E.	BAR	400m	1	7	2	45·47	
			2	2	3	45·60	
			SF	2	6	45·32	
		4x400m relay	1	3	1	3-03·31	
			SF	2	4	3-03·89	
			F		6	3-01·60	
Foster, G.	USA	110m hurdles	1	4	1	13·24*	
			SF	2	1	13·24*	
			F		2	13·23	S
Frayne, B.	AUS	400m	1	6	1	46·08	
			2	3	4	45·35	
			SF	2	5	45·21	
		4x400m relay	1	1	1	3:03·72	
			SF	2	2	3-03·79	
			F		4	2-59·70	

COMPETITOR	COUNTRY CODE	EVENT	ROUND	HEAT	PLACE	TIME & DISTANCE	MEDAL
Froude, D.	NZL	Marathon	F		34	2:19-44	
Futterknecht, T.	AUT	400m hurdles	1	1	4	50·25	
Fuwa, H.	JPN	100m	1	5	6	10·56	
			2	3	6	10·75	
		200m	1	5	5	21·37	
		4x400m relay	1	1	5	3-08·18	
			SF	1	8	3-10·72	
Fye, O.	GAM	100m	1	8	6	10·87	
		200m	1	3	5	21·56	
		4x100m relay	1	1	7	40·73	
Gambke, W.	GER	Javelin throw	F		4	82,46	
Gamliel, A.	ISR	10000m	1	2	10	29-31·32	
		5000m	1	3	10	14-02·95	
Ganunga, I.	MAW	800m	1	5	6	1-51·25	
		1500m	1	5	8	3-53·86	
Garcia, J.	ESP	5000m	1	1	8	14-12·15	
Garcia, H.-A.	GUA	3000m steeplechase	1	2	11	9-02·41	
		1500m	1	5	9	3-57·59	
Gasparoni, M.	FRA	100m	1	2	4	10·47	
			2	3	3	10·56	
			SF	1	7	10·49	
		4x100m relay	1	1	3	40·04	
			SF	2	4	38·91	
			F		6	39·10	
Geirnaert, J.	BEL	Marathon	F		41	2:21-35	
Georgakopulos, K.	GRE	Discus throw	F		11	60,30	
Ghanem, A.	EGY	400m hurdles	1	1	7	51·08	
Ghesini, A.	ITA	Javelin throw	Q		DNQ	72·96	
Giessing, T.	GER	4x400m relay	1	3	2	3-03·33	
Gillingham, M.	GBR	400m hurdles	1	3	6	52·15	
Girvan, M.	GBR	Hammer throw	F		9	72,32	
Glass, J.	CAN	110m hurdles	1	2	4	14·07	
			SF	1	4	13·88	
			F		8	14·15	
Gloor, R.	SUI	Long jump	Q		DNQ	7,71	
Gomez, J.	MEX	10000m	1	1	6	28-28·50	
Gomez, J.-C.	ARG	10000m	1	3	12	29-58·06	
		5000m	1	1	10	14-28·48	
Gomez, R.	MEX	Marathon	F		DNF		
Goncalo, P.	MOZ	4x400m relay	1	1	6	3-08·95	
Gonzalez, A.	FRA	1500m	1	4	3	3-42·84	
Gonzalez, B.	ESP	800m	1	5	4	1-48·01	
		4x400m	1	4	4	3-08·79	
Gonzalez, J.	PUR	Marathon	F		13	2:14-00	
Gonzalez, J.-L.	ESP	1500m	1	1	5	3-47·01	
Gonzalez, M.	ESP	4x400m relay	1	4	4	3-08·79	
Gonzalez, R.	MEX	20k walk	F		2	1:23-20	S
		50k walk	F		1	3:47·26*	G
Goode, M.	USA	High jump	F		11	2,10	
Gouda, M.	SUD	10000m	1	3	8	28-20·26	
			F		10	28-29·43	
		5000m	1	2	9	13-59·41	
Gouile, J.	UGA	200m	1	10	2	21·59	
			2	3	7	21·55	
		4x400m relay	1	2	3	3-08·05	
			SF	1	4	3-04·02	
			F		7	3-02·09	
Graddy, S.	USA	100m	1	5	1	10·29	
			2	2	1	10·15	
			SF	1	2	10·27	
			F		2	10·19	S
		4x100m relay	1	1	1	38·89	
			SF	1	1	38·44	
			F		1	37·83*	G
Gray, J.	USA	800m	1	6	1	1-47·19	
			2	3	3	1-45·82	
			SF	2	3	1-45·82	
			F		7	1-47·89	
Gray, K.	JAM	400m hurdles	1	5	3	50·46	
Gray, R.	CAN	Discus throw	Q		DNQ	59,34	
Greaves, W.	GBR	110m hurdles	1	2	3	14·04	
			SF	2	5	13·86	
Green, B.	USA	Hammer throw	F		5	75,60	
Greenaway, D.	IVB	400m	1	1	5	47·33	
		4x400m relay	1	2	6	3-11·89	
Gregorek, J.	USA	3000m steeplechase	1	2	8	8-38·43	
			SF	2	11	8-38·19	
Griffiths, S.	JAM	4x400m relay	1	3	4	3-03·85	
			SF	2	6	3-04·24	
Grimes, H.	BAR	4x100m relay	1	3	4	40·47	
			SF	2	7	40·18	
Gubey, D.	FRA	50k walk	F		12	4:13-34	
Guimaraes, A.	BRA	800m	1	7	3	1-47·72	
			2	1	3	1-45·18	
			SF	2	6	1-46·60	
		1500m	1	3	2	3-43·26	
			SF	1		DNF	
Gullstrand, C.	SWE	400m hurdles	1	4	6	51·27	
		4x400m relay	1	1	4	3-07·32	
			SF	1	7	3-09·40	
Gunthor, W.	SUI	Shot put	F		5	20,28	
Gurung, J.	NEP	800m	1	1	8	1-56·72	
Guss, L.	CAN	400m hurdles	1	6	3	51·02	
Gustafsson, B.	SWE	50k walk	F		2	3:53-19	S
Gutteridge, J.	GBR	Pole vault	F		11	5,10	
Gun, J.-S.	TPE	Decathlon	F		16	7629	
Guy, G.	JAM	1500m	1	3	5	3-52·04	
Haas, C.	GER	100m	1	11	1	10·41	
			2	1	3	10·51	
			SF	1	6	10·41	
Hackney, R.	GBR	3000m steeplechase	1	2	2	8-30·31	
			SF	1	5	8-20·77	
			F		10	8-27·10	
Hadfield, P.	AUS	Decathlon	F		14	7683	
Halsteinsson, V.	ISL	Discus throw	Q		DNQ	59,58	
Haley, E.	GUY	100m	1	7	4	10·74	
		200m	1	1	5	21·52	
Hamada, A.	BRN	400m hurdles	1	4	4	50·62	
Hamed, M.	EGY	Discus throw	Q		DNQ	0	
Hamilton, O.	JAM	800m	1	3	1	1-46·95	
			2	3	6	1-46·74	
Handelsman, M.	ISR	800m	1	7	4	1-47·90	
		1500m	1	4	6	3-45·05	
		400m	1	9	6	48·17	
Hanna, S.	BAH	Triple jump	Q		DNQ	16,14	
		Long jump	Q		DNQ	7,10	
Hardarson, K.	ISL	Long jump	Q		DNQ	7,09	
Harkonen, A.	FIN	Javelin throw	F		1	86,76	G
Harries, A.	GER	800m	1	4	4	1-48·92	
Harris, D.	USA	400m hurdles	1	6	1	49·81	
			SF	2	1	48·92	
			F		2	48·13	S
Hartmann, G.	AUT	Marathon	F		DNF		
Hartmann, W.	GER	Discus throw	Q		DNQ	59,92	
Harvey, M.	AUS	50k walk	F		11	4:09-18	
Hassan, E.	SUD	400m	1	6	DNF		
Hassane, I.	CHA	400m	1	1	8	49·64	
Hawkins, T.	USA	400m hurdles	1	4	1	49·51	
			SF	1	2	48·94	
			F		6	49·42	
Hegarty, D.	IRL	Hammer throw	Q		DNQ	70,56	
Heiring, J.	USA	20k walk	F		23	1:30-20	
Henry, A.	ANT	100m	1	8	7	10·99	
		4x100m relay	1	3	5	40·70	
			SF	2	6	40·14	
Heras, A.	ESP	400m	1	9	2	46·06	
			2	2	5	45·88	
		4x400m relay	1	4	4	3-08·79	
Herbert, J.	GBR	Triple jump	F		10	16,40	
Herle, C.	GER	10000m	1	2	4	28-30·28	
			F		5	28-08·21	
		5000m	1	2	6	13-46·35	
			SF	2	DNF		
Herrera, J.	MEX	Marathon	F		36	2:30-33	
Hill, G.	IVB	100m	1	11	6	11·11	
		4x400m relay	1	2	6	3-11·89	
Hillardt, M.	AUS	1500m	1	4	3	3-41·18	
			SF	1	8	3-38·12	
Hinds, D.	CAN	400m	1	4	3	46·42	
			2	3	8	46·19	
		4x400m relay	1	1	2	3-04·47	
			SF	1	3	3-03·93	
			F		8	3-02·82	
Hinds, S.	CAN	4x100m relay	1	2	1	39·20	
			SF	1	3	39·39	
			F		3	38·70	B
Hingsen, J.	GER	Decathlon	F		2	8673	S
Hintnaus, T.	BRA	Pole vault	F		12	5,40	
Hjeltnes, K.	NOR	Discus throw	F		4	65,28	
Hlawe, S.	SWZ	Marathon	F		45	2:22-45	
Hodge, L.	IVB	200m	1	6	5	22·28	
		4x400m relay	1	2	6	3-11·89	
Hodge, N.	ISV	100m	1	4	3	10·58	
			2	2	7	10·69	
		200m	1	8	3	21·12	
Holtom, M.	GBR	110m hurdles	1	1	DIS		
Honey, G.	AUS	Long jump	F		2	8,24	S
Hoogewerf, S.	CAN	800m	1	8	4	1-47·74	
Hooper, R	IRL	Marathon	F		51	2:24-51	
Hufane, A.	SOM	5000m	1	1	DNF		
Huhtala, H.	FIN	Hammer throw	F		6	75,28	
Husby, S.-R.	NOR	Marathon	F		DNF		

COMPETITOR	COUNTRY CODE	EVENT	ROUND	HEAT	PLACE	TIME & DISTANCE	MEDAL
Hutchings, T.	GBR	5000m	1	1	2	13-46·01	
			SF	2	5	13-28·60	
			F		4	13-11·50	
Idun, J.	GHA	200m	1	2	7	22·55	
Igohe, J.	TAN	1500m	1	5	6	3-39·62	
			SF	1	10	3-41·57	
Ikangaa, J.	TAN	Marathon	F		6	2:11-10	
Ikpoto, E.	NGR	4×100m relay	1	2	4	39·94	
			SF	2	5	38·98	
Illut, J.	PHI	Marathon	F		77	2:49-39	
Imo, C.	NGR	100m	1	3	2	10·39	
			2	5	5	10·42	
		4×100m relay	1	2	4	39·94	
			SF	2	5	38·98	
Ingraham, A.	BAH	400m	1	1	3	46·72	
			2	1	7	46·14	
Inthachai, R.	THA	4×100m relay	1	1	5	40·58	
			SF	1	8	40·83	
Ismail, A.-M.	SOM	Marathon	F		47	2:23-27	
Ismail, M.	UAE	4×400m relay	1	1	7	3-19·90	
Issakhouri, G.	LIB	Long jump	Q		DNQ	6,80	
Jachno, A.	AUS	50k walk	F		DNF		
Jadi, N.	MAL	400m	1	2	5	47·12	
		200m	1	2	5	21·88	
Jallow, A.	GAM	4×100m relay	1	1	7	40·73	
Jallow, D.	GAM	400m	1	5	7	48·36	
		4×100m relay	1	1	7	40·73	
Jang, J.-K.	KOR	200m	1	10	1	21·32	
			2	2	6	21·14	
Jarju, B.	GAM	100m	1	11	4	10·68	
		4×100m relay	1	1	7	40·73	
Jaros, R.	GER	Triple jump	Q		DNQ	16,02	
Jaspers, S.	HOL	5000m	1	2	8	13-58·51	
Jefferson, T.	USA	200m	1	4	1	20·63	
			2	3	1	20·47	
			SF	1	2	20·40	
			F		3	20·26	B
Jerbeh, R.	UAE	400m	1	6	6	48·71	
		4×400m relay	1	1	7	3-19·90	
Jimeno, R.	ESP	Hammer throw	Q		DNQ	66,38	
Jobin, M.	CAN	20k walk	F		21	1:29-49	
		50k walk	F		DNF		
Johansson, T.	SWE	400m	1	2	6	47·77	
		4×400m relay	1	1	4	3-07·32	
			SF	1	7	3-09·40	
Johnsen, T.	NOR	Hammer throw	Q		DNQ	65,72	
Johnson, B.	CAN	100m	1	7	1	10·35	
			2	1	1	10·41	
			SF	2	2	10·42	
			F		3	10·22	B
		4×100m relay	1	2	1	39·20	
			SF	1	3	39·39	
			F		3	38·70	B
Jones, A.	BAR	100m	1	6	5	10·69	
		4×100m relay	1	3	4	40·47	
			SF	2	7	40·18	
Jones, D.	ANT	800m	1	9	6	1-51·52	
		1500m	1	2	7	3-55·65	
		4×400m	1	2	5	3-10·95	
Jones, E.	USA	800m	1	4	1	1-47·75	
			2	4	1	1-45·44	
			SF	1	3	1-44·51	
			F		3	1-43·83	B
Jones, H.	GBR	Marathon	F		12	2:13-57	
Jones, S.	GBR	10000m	1	3	4	28-15·22	
			F		8	28-28·08	
Jonga, T.	ZIM	800m	1	8	5	1-49·59	
		1500m	1	5	7	3-40·42	
			SF	2	11	3-41·80	
Jonot, F.	FRA	400m hurdles	1	3	5	51·39	
Jorgensen, H.	DEN	Marathon	F		19	2:15-55	
Josjoe, E.	SWE	4×400m relay	1	1	4	3-07·32	
			SF	1	7	3-09·40	
Joyner, A.	USA	Triple jump	F		1	17,26	G
Kablan, D.	CIV	200m	1	1	4	21·39	
		4×400m relay	1	3	3	3-03·50	
			SF	1	6	3-04·87	
Kalogiannis, A.	GRE	400m hurdles	1	6	4	51·27	
Kambale, M.	MAW	10000m	1	2	12	30-47·73	
		Marathon	F		DNF		
Kanai, Y.	JPN	10000m	1	3	2	28-14·67	
			F		7	28-27·06	
Kardioni, J.	INA	4×100m relay	1	3	3	40·43	
			SF	1	6	40·37	
Kariuki, J.	KEN	3000m steeplechase	1	3	6	8-19·45	
			SF	1	6	8-21·07	
			F		7	8-17·47	

COMPETITOR	COUNTRY CODE	EVENT	ROUND	HEAT	PLACE	TIME & DISTANCE	MEDAL
Kassianidis, M.	CYP	10000m	1	3	10	29-06·08	
		Marathon	F		62	2:32-51	
Kattis, D.	GRE	High jump	Q		DNQ	2,15	
Kechtouche, B.	ALG	20k walk	F		30	1:34-12	
Kemobe, D.	CHA	Long jump	Q		DNQ	7,37	
Kere, J.	SOL	100m	1	9	7	11·57	
Khalifa, O.	SUD	800m	1	2	2	1-45·81	
			2	2	2	1-46·33	
			SF	1	5	1-44·87	
		1500m	1	1	2	3-38·93	
			SF	2	5	3-36·76	
			F		8	3-37·11	
Khumoyarona, K.	BOT	100m	1	4	7	11·49	
Kiakouama, A.	CGO	200m	1	5	7	21·64	
		4×100m relay	1	3	6	40·74	
Kiernan, G.	IRL	Marathon	F		9	2:12-20	
Kilani, B.	JOR	10000m	1	1	13	30-43·54	
		5000m	1	1	12	15-20·58	
Kim, B.-J.	KOR		1	4	DIS		
		1500m	1	5	10	4-02·63	
Kim, J.-I.	KOR	Long jump	F		8	7,81	
Kim, J.-Y.	KOR	3000m steeplechase	1	3	10	8-43·50	
Kim, W.-S.	KOR	Marathon	F		58	2:30-57	
Kingdom, R.	USA	110m hurdles	1	3	1	13·53	
			SF	1	1	13·24*	
			F		1	13·20*	G
Kio, J.	NGR	Long jump	F		12	7,57	
Kipkoech, P.	KEN	5000m	1	4	7	13-51·54	
			SF	2	6	13-29·08	
			F		5	13-14·40	
Kitur, D.	KEN	400m	1	2	2	46·25	
			2	4	2	45·78	
			SF	2	4	45·62	
		4×400m relay	SF	2	7	3-04·74	
Kitur, S.	KEN	400m hurdles	1	4	2	49·70	
			SF	1	5	49·80	
		4×400m relay	1	4	2	3-06·07	
Kivina, I.	TAN	10000m	1	1	12	30-29·50	
Kiyai, M.	KEN	Triple jump	Q		DNQ	15,90	
		Long jump	Q		DNQ	7,51	
Klein, P.	GER	4×100m relay	1	1	2	39·04	
			SF	2	3	38·70	
			F		5	38·99	
Koech, E.	KEN	800m	1	7	1	1-47·11	
			2	1	1	1-44·74	
			SF	1	2	1-44·12	
			F		6	1-44·86	
Koeleman, H.	HOL	3000m steeplechase	1	2	4	8-31·34	
			SF	2	10	8-32·29	
Koffler, J.	GER	4×100m relay	SF	2	3	38·70	
			F		5	38·99	
Konchellah, B.	KEN	800m	1	9	1	1-46·27	
			2	2	1	1-46·15	
			SF	2	2	1-45·67	
			F		4	1-44·03	
Korir, J.	KEN	3000m steeplechase	1	2	1	8-29·08	
			SF	2	1	8-12·40	
			F		1	8-11·80	G
Kouadio, O.	CIV	100m	1	10	3	10·72	
			2	3	8	10·80	
Koussis, M.	GRE	Marathon	F		26	2:17-38	
Koutsoukis, D.	GRE	Shot put	Q		DNQ	18,74	
Kratschmer, G.	GER	Decathlon	F		4	8326	
Krdzalic, S.	YUG	Javelin throw	Q		DNQ	76,52	
Kulmiye, M.-M.	SOM	10000m	1	2	11	29-37·93	
Kyeswa, M.	UGA	400m	1	5	4	46·78	
		4×400m relay	1	3	2	3-08·05	
			SF	1	4	3-04·02	
			F		7	3-02·09	
Lacy, S.	USA	5000m	1	3	3	13-46·16	
			SF	1	10	13-46·65	
Lafranchi, B.	SUI	Marathon	F		50	2:24-38	
Lahbi, F.	MAR	800m	1	4	2	1-47·81	
			2	1	5	1-45·67	
		1500m	1	1	6	3-47·54	
Lakafia, J.-P.	FRA	Javelin throw	F		12	70,86	
Lam, T.-S.	HKG	High jump	Q		DNQ	2,10	
Lambregts, C.	HOL	Marathon	F		DNF		
Lamothe, D.	HAI	Marathon	F		78	2:52-19	
Lanzoni, R.	CRC	Marathon	F		DNF		
Lapointe, F.	CAN	20k walk	F		11	1:27-06	
		50k walk	F		DIS		
Laut, D.	USA	Shot put	F		3	20,97	B
Lawrence, A.	JAM	4×100m relay	1	3	1	38·93	
			SF	2	1	38·67	
			F		2	38·62	S
Lazare, A.	FRA	Marathon	F		28	2:17-52	

COMPETITOR	COUNTRY CODE	EVENT	ROUND	HEAT	PLACE	TIME & DISTANCE	MEDAL
Lazarus, T.	ZIM	Marathon	F		DNF		
Leblanc, G.	CAN	20k walk	F		4	1:24-29	
		50k walk	F		DNF		
Lee, F.-A.	TPE	Long jump	Q		DNQ	7,23	
		Decathlon	F		19	7541	
Lee, H.-Y.	KOR	Marathon	F		37	2:20-56	
Leitao, A.	POR	5000m	1	4	1	13-51 33	
			SF	1	2	13-39 76	
			F		3	13-09 20	B
Lelievre, G.	FRA	20k walk	F		5	1 27-50	
		50k walk	F		DNF		
Leveille, P.	CAN	400m hurdles	1	5	5	51-47	
Lewis, C.	USA	100m	1	1	1	10-32	
			2	5	1	10-04	
			SF	2	1	10-14	
			F		1	9-99	G
		200m	1	7	1	21-02	
			2	1	1	20-48	
			SF	2	1	20-27	
			F		1	19-80	G
		Long jump	F		1	8,54	G
		4×100m relay	1	1	1	38-89	
			SF	1	1	38-44	
			F		1	37 83*	G
Li, J.	ROC	110m hurdles	1	3	4	14-29	
			SF	2	8	14-15	
Lightbourne, A.	BAH	100m	1	4	4	10-64	
			2	4	8	10-59	
Lindner, J.	AUT	Hammer throw	Q		DNQ	71,28	
Lindsay, H.	ANT	4×400m relay	1	2	5	3-10-95	
Lishebo, D.	ZAM	400m	1	1	1	46 20	
			2	1	4	45-57	
			SF	2	8	45-97	
Lismont, K.	BEL	Marathon	F		24	2:17-07	
Liu, C.-C.	TPE	High jump	Q		DNQ	2,10	
Liu, Y.-H.	ROC	Long jump	F		5	7,99	
Liu, Y.-P.	ROC	High jump	F		7	2,29	
Llatser, H.	FRA	400m	1	4	6	47.30	
Llopart, J.	ESP	50k walk	F		7	4:04-42	
Loforte, L.	MOZ	400m	1	8	4	47-07	
		4×400m relay	1	1	6	3-08-95	
Logan, J.	USA	Hammer throw	Q		DNQ	71,18	
Loikkanen, A.	FIN	5000m	1	4	4	13-51-47	
			SF	1	14	13-58 74	
		1500m	1	1	DNF		
Lopes, C.	POR	Marathon	F		1	2:09-21*	G
Lopez, R.	PAR	10000m	1	1	DNF		
		3000m steeplechase	1	2	12	9-36-36	
		5000m	1	3	13	15-16-64	
Lopez, A.	GUA	800m	1	3	6	1-54-19	
		400m	1	4	8	52-21	
Lopez, R.	SAL	400m	1	5	8	48-71	
Lorentzen, R.	NOR	Javelin throw	Q		DNQ	76,62	
Lorraway, K.	AUS	Triple jump	Q		DNQ	15,92	
Louis, R.	BAR	400m	1	4	4	46-70	
		4x400m relay	1	3	1	3-03-31	
			SF	2	4	3-03-89	
			F		6	3-01-60	
Lozano, D.	GEQ	1500m	1	6	10	4-34-71	
Lubke, R.	GER	100m	1	9	4	10-70	
		200m	1	2	2	20-88	
			2	4	2	20-57	
			SF	2	4	20-67	
			F		5	20-51	
		4x100m relay	1	1	2	39-04	
			SF	2	3	38-70	
			F		5	38-99	
Lytle, D.	USA	Pole vault	F		6	5 40	
McCalla, E.	GBR	Triple jump	F		8	16 66	
McCombie, I.	GBR	20k walk	F		19	1:28-53	
McCoy, W.	USA	4x400m relay	1	4	1	3-01-44	
			SF	1	1	3-00-19	
McCullough, C.	IRL	Hammer throw	Q		DNQ	65 56	
McFarlane, M.	GBR	100m	1	1	3	10 47	
			2	5	4	10-36	
			SF	2	3	10-45	
			F		5	10-27	
		4x100m relay	1	3	2	39-00	
			SF	2	2	38-53	
			F		7	39-13	
McKay, A.	USA	400m	1	8	1	45 55	
			2	1	1	44-72	
			SF	2	3	44-92	
			F		3	44-71	B
		4x400m relay	SF	1	1	3-00-19	
			F		1	2-57-91	G

COMPETITOR	COUNTRY CODE	EVENT	ROUND	HEAT	PLACE	TIME & DISTANCE	MEDAL
McKoy, M.	CAN	110m hurdles	1	1	2	13-58	
			SF	2	2	13-30	
			F		4	13-45	
McLeod, M.	GBR	10000m	1	1	5	28-24-92	
			F		2	28-06-22	S
McRae, M.	USA	Long jump	F		11	7,63	
McSravick, B.	GBR	Decathlon	F		11	7890	
Maddocks, C.	GBR	50k walk	F		16	4:26-33	
Madzokere, C.	ZIM	400m	1	9	7	48-49	
		200m	1	7	7	22-75	
Mafe, A.	GBR	200m	1	6	2	21-24	
			2	2	3	20-55	
			SF	2	3	20-63	
			F		8	20-85	
Mahmoud, I.	JOR	Marathon	F		64	2:33-30	
Mahmoud, J.	FRA	3000m steeplechase	1	2	3	8-30-85	
			SF	2	5	8-18-62	
			F		2	8-13-31	S
Mahorn, A.	CAN	200m	1	7	2	21-42	
			2	1	3	20-69	
			SF	1	5	20-77	
Maisiba-Otieno, M.	KEN	Marathon	F		49	2:24-13	
Malekwa, Z.	TAN	Javelin throw	Q		DNQ	75,18	
Mallat, J.-Y.	LIB	100m	1	5	6	10-83	
		200m	1	6	8	22-91	
Mamba, C.	SWZ	100m	1	5	8	11-24	
		200m	1	3	8	22-76	
Mamposasa, G.	MAW	5000m	1	1	11	14-48-08	
		Marathon	F		74	2:46-14	
Mamede, F.	POR	10000m	1	1	1	28-21-87	
			F		DNF		
Manandhar, B.	NEP	Marathon	F		46	2:22-51	
Manninen, R.	FIN	Javelin throw	Q		DNQ	79,26	
Mansaray, A.	SLE	4x100m relay	1	2	6	40-77	
Marchei, M.	ITA	Marathon	F		43	2:22-38	
Marie, A.	SEY	10000m	1	3	14	32-04-11	
		3000m steeplechase	1	3	11	9-32-30	
Marie-Fose, B.	FRA	100m	1	7	3	10-59	
			2	1	6	10-60	
		4x100m relay	1	1	3	40-04	
			SF	2	4	38-91	
			F		6	39-10	
Marin, J.	ESP	20k walk	F		6	1:25-32	
Marsh, H.	USA	3000m steeplechase	1	3	4	8-29-23	
			SF	1	4	8-20-57	
			F		4	8-14-25	
Marshall, J.	USA	800m	1	3	3	1-47-99	
			2	2	5	1-47-18	
Martin, E.	GBR	5000m	1	3	2	13-46-16	
			SF	1	5	13-41-70	
			F		13	13-53-34	
Martin, F.	AUS	100m	1	8	3	10-64	
			2	6	7	10-61	
		200m	1	6	2	20-98	
Martino, M.	ITA	Discus throw	F		NP	0	
Masong, A.	TAN	Marathon	F		21	2:16-25	
Matlapeng, B.	BOT	Marathon	F		DNF		
Materazzi, R.	ITA	800m	1	2	4	1-46-03	
			2	2	6	1-47-90	
		1500m	1	5	4	3-37-95	
			SF	1	7	3-36-51	
			F		11	3-40-74	
Mattioli, C.	ITA	20k walk	F		5	1:25-07	
Mayers, J.	BAR	200m	1	10	3	21-70	
			2	2	7	21-46	
		4x100m relay	1	3	4	40-47	
			SF	2	7	40-18	
Mayr, M.	SUI	800m	1	6	3	1-47-36	
			2	2	8	1-48-30	
Mbangiwa, J.	BOT	Marathon	F		76	2:48-12	
Mbazira, D.	UGA	100m	1	2	7	11-03	
Mbela, G.	GEQ	100m	1	8	5	10-79	
		200m	1	8	7	22-14	
Meghoo, G.	JAM	4x100m relay	1	3	1	38-93	
			SF	2	1	38-67	
			F		2	38-62	S
Mei, S.	ITA	1500m	1	1	3	3-39-25	
			SF	2	7	3-37-96	
Meier, F.	SUI	400m hurdles	1	2	3	49-81	
			SF	2	6	49-89	
Mekin, H.	EGY	110m hurdles	1	2	6	14-67	
Meledje, F.	CIV	400m hurdles	1	3	3	50-27	
		4x400m relay	1	3	3	3-03-50	
			SF	1	6	3-04-69	
Mendes, D	MOZ	400m hurdles	1	4	8	54-52	

COMPETITOR	COUNTRY CODE	EVENT	ROUND	HEAT	PLACE	TIME & DISTANCE	MEDAL
Mennea, P.	ITA	200m	1	1	1	20·70	
			2	2	2	20·50	
			SF	1	3	20·47	
			F		7	20·55	
		4x100m relay	1	2	3	39·87	
			SF	1	2	39·32	
			F		4	38·87	
		4x400m relay	F		5	3-01·44	
Mensah, C.	GHA	100m	1	9	5	10·92	
		4x100m relay	1	2	5	40·20	
			SF	1	5	40·19	
Mercado, M.	PUR	Marathon	F		31	2:19-09	
Mersal, N.	EGY	400m	1	6	4	46·46	
Messomo, B.	CMR	100m	1	2	6	10·98	
		4x400m re ay	1	2	7	3-16·00	
Metellus, A.	CAN	High jump	Q		DNQ	2,18	
Miangoto, O.	CHA	800m	1	9	8	1-56·02	
Mihas, D.	GRE	Triple jump	Q		DNQ	16,15	
Mileham, M.	GBR	Hammer throw	F		NP	0	
Miller, A.	FIJ	Decathlon	F		DNF		
Miller, L.	ANT	200m	1	4	6	21·93	
		4x100m relay	1	3	5	40·70	
			SF	2	6	40·14	
		4x400m relay	1	2	4	3-10·95	
Minihan, G.	AUS	400m	1	2	4	46·93	
		4x400m relay	1	1	1	3-03·72	
			SF	2	1	3-03·79	
			F		4	2-59·70	
Mitchell, R.	AUS	4x400m relay	1	1	1	3-03·72	
			F		4	2-59·70	
Mizogushi, K.	JPN	Javelin throw	Q		DNQ	74,82	
Moen, L.-O.	NOR	50k walk	F		13	4:15-12	
Mogenburg, D.	GER	High jump	F		1	2,35	G
Mohammad, M.	PAK	100m	1	6	7	10·87	
		200m	1	3	6	22·04	
Mohammad, R.	PAK	Javelin throw	Q		DNQ	74,58	
Molinari, M.	SMR	800m	1	2	8	1-57·09	
Moluh, M.	CMR	400m	1	10	7	48·90	
		4x400m relay	1	2	7	3-16·00	
Molyneaux, J.	IVB	800m	1	7	5	1-53·23	
		4x400m relay	1	2	6	3-11·89	
Monkemeyer, U.	GER	5000m	1	3	8	13-48·66	
			SF	1		DNF	
Montelatici, M.	ITA	Shot put	F		6	19,98	
Moorcroft, D.	GBR	5000m	1	4	2	13-51·40	
			SF	2	2	13-28·44	
			F		14	14-16·61	
Mora, O.	CRC	10000m	1	2	13	30-49·43	
		5000m	1	4	11	14-33·49	
Moracho, J.	ESP	110m hurdles	1	3	2	14·05	
			1	1	5	13·89	
Morales, L.	PUR	100m	1	9	2	10·60	
			2	5	3	10·35	
			SF	2	5	10·54	
		200m	1	8	2	21·05	
			2	1	4	20·82	
			SF	1	8	21·22	
Morceli, A.	ALG	1500m	1	4	7	3-45·09	
Moreira, D.	POR	Marathon	F		DNF		
Morejon, O.	BOL	20k walk	F		36	1:44-42	
		50k walk	F		DNF		
Moreno, J.	COL	20k walk	F		12	1:27-12	
Moreno, Q.	COL	20k walk	F		9	1:26-04	
		50k walk	F		DNF		
Morris, Desmond	JAM	High jump	Q		DNQ	2,15	
Morris, Devon	JAM	400m	1	10	4	45·80	
			2	1	6	46·14	
		4x400m relay	1	3	4	3-03·85	
			SF	2	6	3-04·24	
Morrisette, J.	ISV	Pole vault	Q		DNQ	5,20	
Moses, C.	GHA	400m	1	8	7	50·39	
Moses, E.	USA	400m hurdles	1	1	1	49·33	
			SF	1	1	48·51	
			F		1	47·75	G
Motti, W.	FRA	Decathlon	F		5	8266	
Moulton, A.	LBR	200m	1	4	8	22·94	
		4x100m relay	1	3	7	42·05	
Moussa, D.	NIG	800m	1	7	DIS		
Moutsanas, S.	GRE	800m	1	1	4	1-47·32	
			2	1	7	1-46·34	
Mpio, M.	CGO	3000m steeplechase	1	1	11	9-05·58	
Mubarak, N.	KUW	110m hurdles	1	3	5	14·56	
Mubarak, S.	UAE	Long jump	Q		DNQ	6,98	
Mulenga, M.	ZAM	High jump	Q		DNQ	2,05	
Munyasia, P.	KEN	20k walk	F		32	1:34-53	
Munyoro, M.	KEN	400m hurdles	1	5	6	51·99	
Muraya, J.	KEN	1500m	1	3	4	3-51·61	

COMPETITOR	COUNTRY CODE	EVENT	ROUND	HEAT	PLACE	TIME & DISTANCE	MEDAL
Murofushi, S.	JPN	Hammer throw	Q		DNQ	70,92	
Musango, A.	ZAM	800m	1	2	6	1-48·84	
		1500m	1	4	8	3-46·99	
Muslar, E.	BIZ	5000m	1	2	12	15-05·78	
Musyoki, M.	KEN	10000m	1	1	3	28-24·24	
			F		3	28-06·46	B
Mwawsegha, A.	MAW	400m	1	8	6	49·12	
Myricks, L.	USA	Long jump	F		4	8,16	
Nagel, C.	GER	High jump	Q		DNQ	2,18	
Nakaia, K.	BRA	100m	1	11	3	10·55	
			2	3	5	10·69	
		4x100m relay	1	2	2	39·27	
			SF	1	4	39·52	
			F		8	39·40	
Narracott, P.	AUS	100m	1	4	2	10·55	
		200m	1	4	5	21·20	
			2	1	7	10·60	
Naylor, M.	GBR	High jump	Q		DNQ	2,18	
Ncube, Z.	ZIM	10000m	1	2	2	28-28·53	
			F		11	28-31·61	
		5000m	1	3	7	13-46·33	
			SF	1	12	13-53·25	
Nding, H.	CGO	100m	1	3	5	10·66	
		4x100m relay	1	3	6	40·74	
Ndiwa, J.	KEN	800m	1	8	1	1-46·73	
			2	4	2	1-45·59	
			SF	2	7	1-48·06	
Nenepath, C.	INA	100m	1	3	4	10·66	
		200m	1	3	7	22·20	
		4x100m relay	1	3	3	40·43	
			SF	1	6	40·37	
Newhouse, I.	CAN	400m hurdles	1	4	5	51·14	
Ngeny, K.	KEN	Marathon	F		68	2:37-19	
Ngoawe, H.	ZAM	100m	1	1	7	10·94	
		200m	1	5	6	21·58	
Niang, B.	SEN	800m	1	1	1	1-46·90	
			2	1	6	1-45·71	
		4x400m relay	1	3	DIS		
Niemi, D.	FIN	High jump	F		9	2,24	
Nijboer, G.	HOL	Marathon	F		DNF		
Nilsson, R.	SWE	50k walk	F		DIS		
Nix, S.	USA	400m	1	7	1	45·42	
			2	2	2	45·31	
			SF	1	3	45·41	
			F		5	44·75	
		4x400m relay	SF	1	1	3-00·19	
			F		1	2-57·91	G
Nkounkou, T.	CGO	4x100m relay	1	3	6	40·74	
Nocco, E.	ITA	4x400m relay	1	2	2	3-06·28	
			SF	2	3	3-03·87	
			F		5	3-01·44	
Nogboum, A.	CIV	4x400m relay	1	3	3	3-03·50	
			SF	1	6	3-04·69	
Nordquist, D.	USA	High jump	F		5	2,29	
Ntaole, F.	LES	10000m	1	3	13	30-18·71	
		Marathon	F		40	2:21-09	
Nyambariro-Nhauro, P.	ZIM	Marathon	F		67	2:37-18	
Nyberg, T.	SWE	400m hurdles	1	1	5	50·47	
Nylander, S.	SWE	400m hurdles	1	3	1	49·88	
			SF	2	2	49·03	
			F		4	48·97	
		4x400m relay	1	1	4	3-07·32	
			SF	1	7	3-09·40	
Nyambane, A.	KEN	200m	1	5	4	21·35	
Nzau, J.	KEN	10000m	1	2	3	28-28·71	
			F		14	28-32·57	
		Marathon	F		7	2:11-28	
Obey, W.-O.	LBR	4x100m relay	1	3	7	42·05	
O'Brien, L.	IRL	3000m steeplechase	1	3	8	8-31·89	
			SF	1	11	8-34·90	
O'Connor, D.	USA	20k walk	F		33	1:35-12	
O'Donoghue, P.	NZL	1500m	1	6	3	3-40·69	
			SF	2	8	3-38·71	
Ojha, P.-R.	NEP	400m	1	7	8	52·12	
Okot, M.	UGA	400m	1	10	5	46·68	
		4x400m relay	1	2	3	3-08·05	
			SF	1	4	3-04·02	
			F		7	3-02·09	
Olamini, V.	SWZ	800m	1	3	DIS		
Oliver, C.	SOL	800m	1	8	6	1-53·22	
Olsen, P.-E.	NOR	Javelin throw	F		9	78,98	
Omar, I.-O.	SOM	400m	1	1	7	47·91	
O'Mara, F.	IRL	1500m	1	4	4	3-41·76	
Omori, S.	JPN	400m hurdles	1	2	5	50·14	
		4x400m relay	1	1	5	3-08·16	
			SF	1	8	3-10·73	

COMPETITOR	COUNTRY CODE	EVENT	ROUND	HEAT	PLACE	TIME & DISTANCE	MEDAL
Opicho, J.	KEN	4x100m relay	1	4	2	3-05.07	
			SF	2	7	3-04.74	
O'Rourke, M.	NZL	Javelin throw	Q		DNQ	0	
Ortega, O.	ARG	1500m	1	6	DNF		
O'Sullivan, M.	IRL	800m	1	2	5	1-46.85	
			2	4	6	1-46.21	
		1500m	1	3	3	3-49.65	
			SF	2	9	3-39.40	
O'Sullivan, V.	USA	50k walk	F		4	4 22-51	
Ottey, M.	CAN	High jump	F		6	2,29	
Ottley, D.	GBR	Javelin throw	F		2	85,74	S
Ovett, S.	GBR	800m	1	5	2	1-46.66	
			2	3	2	1-45.72	
			SF	1	4	1-44.81	
			F		8	1-52.28	
		1500m	1	3	-	3-49.23	
			SF	2	2	3-36.55	
			F		DNF		
Oyeledun, S.	NGR	4x100m relay	SF	2	5	33.93	
Padilla, D.	USA	5000m	1	1	5	13-52.56	
			SF	1	6	13-41.73	
			F		7	13-23.56	
Pallonen, K.	FIN	Pole vault	F		5	5,45	
Pandit, A.	NEP	Marathon	F		63	2:32-53	
Panetta, F.	ITA	3000m steeplechase	1	1	8	8-37.05	
			SF	2	9	8-31.24	
		10000m	1	3	9	29-00.78	
Park, Y.-J.	KOR	Triple jump	Q		DNQ	15,54	
Parker, D.	BAH	100m	1	10	2	10.65	
			2	5	6	10.58	
		200m	1	3	2	21.12	
			2	1	7	21.10	
Parmentier, A.	BEL	Marathon	F		30	2:18-10	
Parsons, G.	GBR	High jump	Q		DNQ	2,21	
Patrignani, C.	ITA	1500m	1	3	6	3-52.63	
Paul, M.	TRI	400m	1	5	2	46.18	
			2	4	3	45.34	
			SF	1	6	45.60	
		4x400m relay	1	1	3	3-06.81	
			SF	2	DIS		
Pavoni, P.	ITA	100m	1	10	4	10.72	
Pearless, P.	NZL	800m	1	3	5	1-49.95	
Peltier, D.	BAR	400m	1	1	2	46.57	
			2	1	8	46.48	
		4x400m relay	1	3	1	3-03.31	
			SF	2	4	3-03.89	
			F		6	3-01.60	
Pereira, H.	MOZ	200m	1	7	5	21.87	
		4x400m relay	1	1	6	3-08.95	
Persson, T.	SWE	Marathon	F		DNF		
Peters, R.	NGR	4×400m relay	1	4	3	3-06.34	
			SF	2	1	3-02.22	
			F		3	2-59.32	B
Petranoff, T.	USA	Javelin throw	F		10	78,40	
Pezzatini, A.	ITA	20k walk	F		28	1 32-27	
Pfitzinger, P.	USA	Marathon	F		11	2:13-53	
Philippou, F.	CYP	3000m steeplechase	1	3	7	8-30.09	
			SF	1	12	8-39.47	
		Marathon	F		DNF		
Pinto, J.	POR	20k walk	F		25	1:30-54	
		50k walk	F		8	4:04-02	
Pipersburg, P.	BIZ	400m	1	4	7	48.04	
Pitayo, M.	MEX	10000m	1	2	8	28-59.19	
Pitters, A.	PAN	100m	1	11	2	10.50	
			2	1	8	10.63	
Ploghaus, K.	GER	Hammer throw	F		3	76,68	B
Porter, P.	USA	10000m	1	3	7	28-19.94	
			F		15	28-34.59	
Powell, J.	USA	Discus throw	F		3	65,46	B
Prieto, A.	ESP	10000m	1	2	7	23-57.78	
Promna, S.	THA	100m	1	4	1	10.52	
			2	3	4	10.61	
		200m	1	6	4	21.53	
		4×100m relay	1	1	5	40.58	
			SF	1	8	40.83	
Puckerin, M.	TRI	4×400m relay	1	1	3	3-06.81	
			SF	2	DIS		
Purnomo	INA	100m	1	2	2	10.40	
			2	4	3	10.43	
			SF	1	8	10.51	
		200m	1	9	3	21.01	
			2	1	5	20.93	
		4×100m relay	1	3	3	40.43	
			SF	1	6	40.37	
Quarrie, D.	JAM	200m	1	6	1	20.84	
			2	3	3	20.57	
			SF	2	7	20.77	
		4×100m relay	1	3	1	38.93	
			SF	2	1	38.67	
			F		2	38.62	S
Quentrec, Y.	FRA	400m	1	9	4	46.94	
		4×400m relay	1	2	4	3-08.33	
Quinon, P.	FRA	Pole vault	F		1	5,75	G
Rajakumar, B.	MAL	800m	1	5	5	1-48.19	
		1500m	1	6	7	3-55.19	
Rakabaele, V.	LES	Marathon	F		61	2:32-15	
Ram, C.	IND	20k walk	F		22	1:30-06	
Ramirez, M.	COL	400m	1	3	4	47.17	
		200m	1	7	4	21.71	
Ramon, D.	ESP	3000m steeplechase	1	1	2	8-26.04	
			SF	1	1	8-19.08	
			F		6	8-17.27	
Ramutshabi, J.	BOT	800m	1	1	5	1-48.17	
		400m	1	5	6	48.11	
Randriamahaza-man, A.	MAD	400m	1	9	8	48.86	
Randrianarie-velo, J.	MAD	Marathon	F		72	2:43-05	
Reid, D.	GBR	100m	1	5	2	10.41	
			2	1	2	10.47	
			SF	1	3	10.32	
			F		7	10.33	
		4×100m relay	1	3	2	39.00	
			SF	2	2	38.63	
			F		7	39.13	
Reid, L.	JAM	200m	1	2	1	20.62	
			2	2	DNF		
Reitz, C.	GBR	3000m steeplechase	1	3	5	8-29.33	
			SF	2	4	8-18.62	
			F		5	8-15.48	
Reneau, P.	BIZ	100m	1	1	8	10.96	
Renner, P.	NZL	3000m steeplechase	1	3	2	8-22.95	
			SF	2	2	8-18.12	
			F		11	8-29.81	
Ribaud, R.	ITA	4×400m relay	SF	2	3	3-03.87	
			F		5	3-01.44	
Richard, A.	FRA	100m	1	6	2	10.35	
			2	4	6	10.53	
		4×100m relay	1	1	3	40.04	
			SF	2	4	38.91	
			F		6	39.10	
Riehm, K.-H.	GER	Hammer throw	F		2	77,98	S
Rios, C.	PUR	3000m steeplechase	1	2	6	8-31.88	
			SF	2	12	8-44.70	
Rivera, E.	PUR	Pole vault	Q		DNQ	5,10	
Rizvi, M.	PAK	400m	1	3	7	49.58	
		800m	1	6	5	1-51.29	
Roberts, B.	CAN	800m	1	9	4	1-47.56	
			2	3	8	1-49.72	
Robleh, D.	DJI	Marathon	F		8	2:11-39	
Rodan, J.	FIJ	400m	1	8	5	49.00	
Rodrigues, A.	BRA	Triple jump	Q		DNQ	16,12	
Rodrigues, T.	SUR	1500m	1	4	10	4-02.87	
Rogers, A.	NZL	1500m	1	1	4	3-39.78	
			SF	1	6	3-36.46	
			F		9	3-38.98	
Rolle, E.	MAH	400m hurdles	1	6	2	50.41	
			SF	1	7	50.16	
Roller, S.	USA	Javelin throw	Q		DNQ	75,50	
Rono, K.	KEN	3000m steeplechase	1	1	9	8-41.75	
Rose, D	SEY	100m	1	7	7	11.04	
		200m	1	9	7	21.87	
Rose, N.	GBR	10000m	1	2	5	28-31.13	
			F		12	28-31.73	
Rousseau, V.	BEL	5000m	1	1	6	13-57.96	
Rudasingwa, J.	RWA	800m	1	7	6	1-53.23	
		1500m	1	6	8	3-57.62	
Rufenacht, M.	SUI	Decathlon	F		10	7924	
Ruguja, V.	UGA	Marathon	F		29	2:17-54	
Ruiz, A.	ESP	Pole vault	F		9	5,20	
Russell, R.	ISV	100m	1	7	6	11.02*	
Rutiginga, M.	TAN	5000m	1	1	9	14-27.78	
Fwamuhanda, P.	UGA	400m hurdles	1	3	4	50.55	
		4×400m relay	1	2	3	3-08.05	
			SF	1	4	3-04.02	
			F		7	3-02.09	
Ryffel, M.	SUI	5000m	1	3	4	13-46.16	
			SF	1	3	13-40.08	
			F		2	13-07.54	S

COMPETITOR	COUNTRY CODE	EVENT	ROUND	HEAT	PLACE	TIME & DISTANCE	MEDAL
Sabia, D.	ITA	800m	1	1	3	1·47·04	
			2	1	2	1·44·90	
			SF	2	4	1·45·96	
			F		5	1·44·53	
		4×400m relay	1	2	2	3·06·28	
			SF	2	3	3·03·87	
Sahner, C.	GER	Hammer throw	F		NP	0	
St. Louis, A.	TRI	400m	1	8	DNF		
Sakamoto, T.	JPN	High jump	Q		DNQ	2,21	
Sala, C.	ESP	110m hurdles	1	2	2	14·02	
			SF	2	4	13·85	
			F		7	13·80	
Salandra, A.	SAL	100m	1	11	7	11·31	
		200m	1	6	7	22·90	
Salazar, A.	USA	Marathon	F		15	2:14·19	
Saleh, M.	QAT	Decathlon	F		21	6589	
Salem, W.	QAT	4×100m relay	1	1	6	40·60	
			SF	2	8	40·43	
Salonen, R.	FIN	50k walk	F		4	3:58·30	
Salzmann, R.	GER	Marathon	F		18	2:15·29	
Samayoa, E.	GUA	100m	1	2	5	10·84	
		200m	1	8	8	22·19	
		400m	1	7	3	46·03	
Sanchez, A.	ESP	400m	2	3	6	45·79	
		4×400m relay	1	4	4	3·08·79	
Sands, L.	BAH	Long jump	Q		DNQ	7,32	
Sandy, F.	SLE	4×100m relay	1	2	6	40·77	
Santos, W.	BRA	400m	1	9	5	47·55	
		4×400m relay	SF	2	5	3·03·99	
Sarkpa, S.	LBR	400m	1	10	6	47·65	
Saunders, B.	CAN	400m	1	3	5	47·40	
		4×400m relay	1	1	2	3·04·47	
			SF	1	3	3·03·93	
			F		8	3·02·82	
Saunders, N.	BER	High jump	Q		DNQ	2,18	
Savadogo, M.	MLI	200m	1	9	6	21·72	
Saviniemi, T.	FIN	Javelin throw	Q		DNQ	76,46	
Sawall, W.	AUS	20k walk	F		16	1:28·24	
		50k walk	F		DNF		
Sawny, S.	GRN	800m	1	1	7	1·53·08	
Sawyerr, D.-P.	SLE	200m	1	9	4	21·29	
		4×400m relay	1	2	6	40·77	
Scammell, P.	AUS	800m	1	6	2	1·47·24	
			2	3	7	1·47·40	
		1500m	1	5	5	3·39·18	
			SF	2	10	3·40·83	
Schleder, E.	BRA	Marathon	F		23	2:16·35	
Schmid, H.	GER	400m hurdles	1	2	1	49·34	
			SF	2	3	49·04	
			F		3	48·19	B
Schmitt, U.	GER	400m hurdles	1	4	3	49·77	
			SF	1	6	50·08	
		4×400m relay	1	3	2	3·03·33	
			SF	1	5	3·04·69	
Schuler, C.	USA	50k walk	F		6	3:59·46	
Scott, S.	USA	1500m	1	4	2	3·41·02	
			SF	1	2	3·35·71	
			F		10	3·39·86	
Seck, C.-L.	SEN	100m	1	3	3	10·45	
			2	2	5	10·54	
		4×100m relay	1	1	4	40·65	
			SF	1	7	40·63	
Seck, S.	SEN	4×100m relay	1	1	4	40·15	
Seko, T.	JPN	Marathon	F		14	2:14·13	
Selvaggio, A.	ITA	5000m	1	4	9	13·55·73	
Selvaggio, P.	ITA	5000m	1	2	10	14·04·74	
Sene, M.	SEN	4×100m relay	1	1	4	40·15	
			SF	1	7	40·63	
Senior, M.	JAM	400m	1	3	2	46·73	
			2	4	6	46·50	
		4×400m relay	1	3	4	3·03·85	
			SF	2	6	3·04·24	
Serrani, L.	ITA	Hammer throw	Q		DNQ	70,64	
Shahanga, G.	TAN	10000m	1	2	6	28·42·92	
		Marathon	F		22	2:16·27	
Sharpe, T.	CAN	100m	1	1	2	10·38	
			2	2	2	10·33	
			SF	2	4	10·52	
			F		8	10·35	
		200m	1	6	3	21·31	
			2	3	6	21·46	
		4×100m relay	1	2	1	39·20	
			SF	1	3	39·39	
			F		3	38·70	B
Shata, A.	EGY	Shot put	Q		DNQ	18,58	
Shemtov, S.	ISR	Marathon	F		60	2:31·34	
Shijie, W.	ROC	Long jump	Q		DNQ	7,36	
Shintaku, M.	JPN	10000m	1	1	4	28·24·30	
			F		16	28·55·54	
Sigurdsson, I.	ISL	400m	1	4	2	46·30	
			2	3	7	46·07	
Silva, A.	CHI	Marathon	F		=56	2:29·53	
Silva, E.R.	BRA	400m	1	1	6	47·55	
Silva, J.-J.	BRA	10000m	1	1	10	29·10·52	
		5000m	1	1	7	14·03·44	
Silweya, O.	MAW	100m	1	10	6	11·22	
		200m	1	5	8	22·46	
Sim, D.-S.	KOR	100m	1	11	5	10·72	
Simionato, C.	ITA	200m	1	3	1	21·06	
			2	4	4	20·86	
			SF	2	8	20·92	
Simons, G.	BER	200m	1	2	6	21·88	
Simonsen, B.	SWE	50k walk	F		DIS		
Singh, G.	IND	Javelin throw	Q		DNQ	70,08	
Sinon, P.	SEY	800m	1	6	7	2·04·89	
		1500m	1	6	9	4·25·80	
Situ, K.	ZAI	5000m	1	4	12	15·02·52	
		Marathon	F		DNF		
Sjoberg, P.	SWE	High jump	F		2	2,33	S
Skamrahl, E.	GER	400m	1	9	1	45·94	
			2	4	5	46·39	
		4×400m relay	1	3	2	3·03·33	
			SF	1	5	3·04·69	
Skerritt, A.	TRI	400m	1	7	4	46·30	
			2	2	8	46·93	
		4×400m relay	1	1	3	3·06·81	
			SF	2		DIS	
Skramstad, T.	NOR	Decathlon	F		17	7579	
Slaney, R.	GBR	Discus throw	Q		DNQ	57,66	
Smith, C.	USA	4×100m relay	1	1	1	38·89	
			SF	1	1	38·44	
			F		1	37·83*	G
Smith, D.	AUS	20k walk	F		10	1:26·48	
Smith, G.	GBR	Marathon	F		DNF		
Smith, H.	SAM	Discus throw	Q		DNQ	51,90	
		Shot put	Q		DNQ	16,09	
Smith, K.	JAM	400m hurdles	1	2	2	49·66	
			SF	2	5	49·58	
		4×400m relay	SF	2	6	3·04·24	
Smith, W.	USA	4×400m relay	1	4	1	3·01·44	
			SF	1	1	3·00·19	
Sogomo, E.	KEN	4×400m relay	1	4	2	3·06·07	
			SF	2	7	3·04·74	
Soh, S.	JPN	Marathon	F		17	2:14·38	
Soh, T.	JPN	Marathon	F		4	2:10·55	
Sokolowski, M.	CAN	4×400m relay	1	1	2	3·04·47	
			SF	1	3	3·02·98	
			F		8	3·02·82	
Soler, R.	PER	5000m	1	4	10	14·28·26	
Solorzano, F.	ECU	Long jump	Q		DNQ	6,93	
		Decathlon	F		23	6519	
Souza, G.	BRA	400m	1	3	3	47·02	
			2	4	7	46·65	
		4×400m relay	1	3	5	3·05·08	
			SF	2	5	3·03·99	
Spedding, C.	GBR	Marathon	F		3	2:09·58	B
Spence, E.	CAN	110m hurdles	1	3	6	14·93	
Spivey, J.	USA	1500m	1	6	2	3·40·58	
			SF	2	2	3·36·53	
			F		5	3·36·07	
Stahl, K.-E.	SWE	Marathon	F		DNF		
Steen, D.	CAN	Decathlon	F		8	8047	
Stekic, N.	YUG	Long jump	Q		DNQ	7,60	
Stewart, R.	JAM	100m	1	6	1	10·24	
			2	4	1	10·30	
			SF	1	1	10·26	
			F		6	10·29	
		4×100m relay	SF	2	1	38·67	
			F		2	38·62	S
Stock, K.	GBR	Pole vault	Q		DNQ	5,20	
Stolz, K.	GER	Shot put	F		12	18.31	
Stones, D.	USA	High jump	F		4	2,31	
Swai, A.	TAN	5000m	1	3	11	14·22·20	
Tafelmeier, K.	GER	Javelin throw	Q		DNQ	73,52	
Taiwo, J.	NGR	Triple jump	F		9	16,64	
Takahashi, T.	JPN	Pole vault	F		14	5,10	
Takano, S.	JPN	400m	1	6	3	46·26	
			2	4	4	45·91	
			SF	1	8	45·88	
		4×400m relay	1	1	5	3·08·16	
			SF	1	8	3·10·73	
Tall, H.	LBR	4×100m relay	1	3	7	42·05	
Tallheim, S.	SWE	Shot put	F		7	19,81	

COMPETITOR	COUNTRY CODE	EVENT	ROUND	HEAT	PLACE	TIME & DISTANCE	MEDAL
Tamean, L.	GUI	200m	1	8	6	21·97	
		400m	1	7	7	47·50	
Tarore, A.	MLI	Long jump	Q		DNQ	6,92	
Tawalbeh, A.	JOR	20k walk	F		38	1:49·35	
Tche Noubossie, E.	CMR	Triple jump	Q		DNQ	14,39	
		Long jump	Q		DNQ	6,75	
		4×400m relay	1	2	7	3-16·00	
Terzi, M.	TUR	Marathon	F		16	2:14·20	
Theleso, T.	BOT	Marathon	F		55	2:29·20	
Thiebault, P.	FRA	1500m	1	2	1	3-45·18	
			SF	1	9	3-40·96	
Thode, J.	AHO	100m	1	7	5	10·95	
		200m	1	7	3	21·62	
			2	3	5	21·45	
Thompson, D.	GBR	Decathlon	F		1	8798	G
		4×100m relay	1	3	2	39·00	
			SF	2	2	33·65	
			F		7	39·13	
Thranhardt, C.	GER	High jump	F		10	2,15	
Tiacoh, G.	CIV	400m	1	2	1	45·96	
			2	4	1	45·15	
			SF	2	1	44·64	
			F		2	44·54	S
		4×400m relay	1	3	3	3-03·50	
			SF	1	6	3-04·69	
Tiainen, J.	FIN	Hammer throw	F		1	78,08	G
Tiainen, P.	FIN	Marathon	F		27	2:17·43	
Tibaduiza, D.	COL	10000m	1	3	11	29-07·19	
		Marathon	F		DNF		
Tilli, S.	ITA	100m	1	8	2	10·48	
			2	3	1	10·39	
			SF	2	6	10·55	
		200m	1	9	1	20·72	
			2	1	2	20·64	
			SF	2	6	20·72	
		4×100m relay	1	2	3	39·87	
			SF	1	2	39·32	
			F		4	38·37	
Tipan, L.	ECU	10000m	1	1	11	30-07·49	
		5000m	1	3	12	14-52·43	
Titos, A.	MOZ	800m	1	1	6	1-51·73	
		4×400m relay	1	1	6	3-08·95	
Tokwepota, T.	GUI	10000m	1	2	14	31-29·14	
		5000m	-	2	13	15-24·68	
		Marathon	F		66	2:36-36	
Tommelein, R.	BEL	400m hurdles	1	2	4	50·05	
			SF	2	8	50·06	
Toporek, M.	AUT	20k walk	F		29	1:33·58	
Torres, J.	ESP	3000m steeplechase	1	2	9	8-40·76	
Toumi, H.	ALG	Hammer throw	Q		DNQ	67,63	
Tozzi, R.	ITA	4×400m relay	1	2	2	3-06·28	
			SF	2	3	3-03·87	
			F		5	3-01·44	
Traore, A.	MLI	Triple jump	Q		DNQ	15,32	
Trabado, C.	ESP	800m	1	2	3	1-46·00	
Traspaderne, J.	ESP	Marathon	F		DNF		
Treacy, J.	IRL	10000m	1	3	5	28-18·13	
			F		9	28-28·68	
		Marathon	F		2	2:09·56	S
Trott, W.	BER	100m	1	4	6	10·76	
Tully, M.	USA	Pole vault	F		5	5,65	S
Tuttle, J.	USA	Marathon	F		DNF		
Twegbe, N.	LBR	5000m	1	1	13	17-36·69	
		Marathon	F		DNF		
Ueta, P.	JPN	Triple jump	Q		DNQ	15,66	
Ugbusie, M.	NGR	4×400m relay	1	4	3	3-06·34	
			SF	2	1	3-02·22	
			F		3	2-59·32	B
Ullo, A.	ITA	100m	1	6	3	10·36	
			2	1	5	10·57	
		4×100m relay	1	2	3	39·87	
			SF	1	2	39·32	
			F		4	38·37	
Ulloa, E.	CHI	3000m steeplechase	1	1	5	8-29·71	
			SF	2	3	8-28·99	
Urlando, G.	ITA	Hammer throw	F		DIS		
Usui, J.	JPN	Long jump	F		7	7,87	
Uti, S.	NGR	400m	1	10	3	45·74	
			2	3	2	45·01	
			SF	2	2	44·83	
			F		6	44·93	
		4×400m relay	1	4	3	3-06·34	
			SF	2	1	3-02·22	
			F		3	2-59·32	B
Vaihinger, J.	GER	4×400m relay	SF	1	5	3-04·69	

COMPETITOR	COUNTRY CODE	EVENT	ROUND	HEAT	PLACE	TIME & DISTANCE	MEDAL
Vainio, M.	FIN	10000m	1	3	6	28-19·25	
			F	2	DIS		
		5000m	1	1	DIS		
			SF	2	DIS		
Vamvakas, G.	GRE	400m hurdles	1	2	6	50·39	
Van Dijck, W.	BEL	3000m steeplechase	1	1	4	8-29·68	
			SF	1	7	8-23·08	
Van Miltenberg, P.	AUS	100m	1	1	5	10·55	
			2	4	5	10·52	
		200m	1	1	2	21·06	
			2	4	5	21·09	
		4×400m relay	SF	2	2	3-03·79	
Vargas F.	COL	20k walk	F		18	1:28-46	
Verbeeck, R.	BEL	5000m	1	2	5	13-46·27	
			SF	2	12	13-46·03	
Vera, A.	ESP	1500m	1	2	3	3-45·44	
			SF	2	3	3-36·55	
			F		7	3-37·02	
Verzy, F.	FRA	High jump	Q		DNQ	2,15	
Vesty, P.	GBR	20k walk	F		13	1:27-28	
Vetterli, P.	SUI	Decathlon	F		13	7739	
Vigneron, T.	FRA	Pole vault	F		=3	5,60	B
Vignon, A.-A.	TOG	400m	1	7	6	47·43	
Vilhjalmsson, E.	ISL	Javelin throw	F		6	81·58	
Virgin, C.	USA	10000m	1	1	9	28-37·58	
Vriend, C.	HOL	Marathon	F		39	2:21-08	
Wagner, A.	GER	Discus throw	F		6	64,72	
Wahlander, Y.	SWE	Shot put	Q		DNQ	18,28	
Waigwa, W.	KEN	5000m	1	1	4	13-48·84	
			SF	1	1	13-38·59	
			F		10	13-27·34	
Walker, J.	NZL	5000m	1	2	2	13-44·75	
			SF	2	3	13-28·48	
			F		8	13-24·46	
Walker, N.	GBR	110m hurdles	1	3	3	14·07	
			SF	1	DNF		
Wallace, D.	JAM	4×400m relay	1	3	4	3-03·85	
Walsh, S.	NZL	Long jump	Q		DNQ	0	
Wandu-Namonge, S.	TAN	1500m	1	6	6	3-45·55	
Watson, B.	GBR	200m	1	2	3	21·26	
			2	4	6	21·14	
Weil, G.	CHI	Shot put	F		10	18,69	
Weimin, Y.	ROC	Pole vault	F		10	5,10	
Weir, R.	GBR	Hammer throw	F		8	72·62	
		Discus throw	F		10	61,36	
Weitzl, E.	AUT	Shot put	Q		DNQ	18.96	
Wells, A.	GBR	100m	1	2	1	10·32	
			2	4	2	10·33	
			SF	2	8	10·71	
		4×100m relay	1	3	2	39·00	
			SF	2	2	38·63	
			F		7	39·13	
Wells, J.	BAH	Long jump	F		6	7,97	
Weng, K.	ROC	Decathlon	F		15	7662	
Wentz, S.	GER	Decathlon	F		3	8412	B
Weppler, M.	GER	4×400m relay	1	3	2	3-03.33	
			SF	1	5	3-04·69	
Werthner, G.	AUT	Decathlon	F		9	8012	
Wilkins, M	USA	Discus throw	F		2	66,30	S
Williams, D.	CAN	100m	1	3	1	10.35	
			2	5	2	10·27	
			SF	1	5	10·34	
		200m	1	4	2	20·70	
			2	2	1	20·40	
			SF	2	5	20·70	
		4×100m relay	1	2	1	39·20	
			SF	1	3	39·39	
			F		3	38·70	B
Williams, M.	ISV	Marathon	F		75	2:46-50	
Williams, P.	CAN	10000m	1	1	8	28-36·15	
		5000m	1	2	7	13-47·56	
			SF	1	9	13-46·34	
Wirz, P.	SUI	1500m	1	5	2	3-37·75	
			SF	1	4	3-35·83	
			F		6	3-36·97	
Witarsa, E.	INA	4×100m relay	1	3	3	40·43	
			SF	1	6	40·37	
Wolf, A.	USA	Shot put	F		4	20,93	
Wooding, J.	USA	Decathlon	F		7	8091	
Wray, S.	BAH	High jump	Q		DNQ		
Wright, D.	AUS	110m hurdles	1	4	4	14·00	
			SF	2	2	13·93	
Wu, C.-J.	TPE	110m hurdles	1	4	3	13·91	
			SF	1	6	14·21	

COMPETITOR	COUNTRY CODE	EVENT	ROUND	HEAT	PLACE	TIME & DISTANCE	MEDAL
Wuycke, W.	VEN	800m	1	8	2	1-46·88	
			2	3	4	1-46·17	
			SF	1	7	1-47·32	
Yadav, A.-P.	NEP	Marathon	F		69	2:38-10	
Yoshida, M.	JPN	Javelin throw	F		5	81,98	
Yoshida, R.	JPN	400m hurdles	1	3	2	50·24	
			SF	2	7	49·92	
		4×400m relay	1	1	5	3-08·16	
			SF	1	8	3-10·73	
Young, G.	JAM	100m	1	4	5	10·64	
		200m	1	5	3	21·14	
			2	4	3	20·75	
			SF	1	7	21·17	
Yu, Z.-C.	ROC	110m hurdles	1	1	4	14·20	
			SF	1	7	14·26	
Yu, Z.-H.	ROC	100m	1	7	2	10·53	
			2	2	6	10·59	
		200m	1	2	4	21·48	
Yurdadon, M.	TUR	Marathon	F		DNF		
Zachariasen, A.	DEN	Marathon	F		25	2:17-10	
Zadok, Y.	ISR	3000m steeplechase	1	3	9	8-42·28	
Zalar, M.	SWE	Pole vault	Q		DNQ	0	
Zea, O.	VEN	400m hurdles	1	2	7	51·44	
Zebiao, J.I.	ROC	Pole vault	Q		DNQ	5,10	
Zerbini, L.	ITA	Discus throw	F		7	63,50	
Zhang, F.-I.	ROC	20k walk	F		27	1:32-10	
		50k walk	F		15	4:23-29	
Zhu, J.	ROC	High jump	F		3	2,31	B
Zimmerman, M.	BEL	400m hurdles	1	1	3	49·90	
			SF	1	4	49·79	
			F		7	50·69	
Zirkelbach, C.	GER	4×100m relay	1	1	2	39·04	
Zou, Z.-X.	ROC	Triple jump	F		4	16,83	
Zuliani, M.	ITA	4×400m relay	1	2	2	3-06·28	

FEMALES

COMPETITOR	COUNTRY CODE	EVENT	ROUND	HEAT	PLACE	TIME & DISTANCE	MEDAL
Abdallah, R.	JOR	3000m	1	1	10	10-48·00	
Abraham, S.K.	IND	800m	1	3	4	2-04·69	
			SF	2	8	2-05·42	
		4×400m relay	1	1	4	3-33·85	
			F		7	3-32·49	
Addy, M.	GHA	400m	1	2	7	58·91 *	
		4×400m	1	2	5	3-40·38	
Adiru, E.	UGA	800m	1	3	6	2-07·39	
Agront, L.	PUR	High jump	Q		DNQ	1,80	
Aksu, S.	TUR	100m	1	1	6	11·86	
		200m	1	1	5	24·27	
			2	4	5	24·03	
		100m hurdles	1	3	5	13·96	
Andersen-Schiess, G.	SUI	Marathon	F		37	2:48-42	
Anderson, J.	LSA	Heptathlon	F		DNF		
Appiah, M.	GHA	4×400m relay	1	2	5	3-40·38	
Arigoni, L.	ARG	High jump	Q		DNQ	1,80	
Armah, G.	GHA	4×100m relay	1	2	5	45·20	
Ashford, E.	USA	100m	1	3	1	11·06	
			2	1	1	11·21	
			SF	1	1	11·03	
			F		1	10·97 *	G
		4×100m relay	1	2	1	42·59	
			F		1	41·65	G
Audain, A.	NZL	Marathon	F		DNF		
Bacoul, R.-A.	FRA	100m	1	1	2	11·36	
			2	2	2	11·37	
			SF	2	5	11·58	
		200m	1	5	2	23·11	
			2	1	1	22·57	
			SF	2	4	22·53	
			F		7	22·78	
		4×100m relay	1	1	3	43·64	
			F		4	43·15	
Bailey, A.	CAN	100m	1	4	3	11·56	
			2	1	2	11·47	
			SF	2	4	11·54	
			F		6	11·40	
		200m	1	1	4	24·15	
			2	1	3	22·97	
			SF	2	5	22·75	
		4×100m relay	1	2	2	43·53	
			F		2	42·77	S
Bakari, G.	GHA	800m	1	2	6	2-14·50	
		4×400m relay	1	2	5	3-40·38	
Baker, L.	GBR	800m	1	2	3	2-01·73	
			SF	2	4	2-00·66	
			F		5	2-00·03	

COMPETITOR	COUNTRY CODE	EVENT	ROUND	HEAT	PLACE	TIME & DISTANCE	MEDAL
Baptiste, J.	GBR	200m	11	1	2	23·31	
			2	4	2	23·11	
			SF	1	5	22·86	
Barksdale, S.	USA	400m hurdles	1	2	2	56·89	
			SF	1	6	56·19	
Barnett, H.	GBR	400m	1	3	3	52·94	
			SF	2	8	52·26	
		4×400m relay	1	1	2	3-27·68	
			F		4	3-25·51	
Bartholomew, J.	GRN	Long jump	Q		DNQ	6,07	
Beaugeant, C.	FRA	Heptathlon	F		DNF		
Bechard, C.	MRI	Discus throw	Q		DNQ	37,94	
Benning, C.	GBR	1500m	1	1	1	4-10·48	
			F		5	4-04·70	
Benoit, J.	USA	Marathon	F		1	2:24-52 *	G
		Long jump	Q		DNQ	6,07	
Bentzur, M.	ISR	100m	1	5	6	12·30	
Bernard, J.	TRI	4×100m relay	1	2	4	44·78	
			F		7	44·23	
Beurskens, C.	HOL	Marathon	F		22	2:37-51	
Blackman, C.	BAR	400m	1	4	6	54·26	
		400m hurdles	1	4	6	61·19	
Bolden, J.	USA	100m	1	1	1	11·25	
			2	4	2	11·42	
			SF	2	2	11·48	
			F		4	11·25	
		4×100m relay	1	2	1	42·59	
			F		1	41·65	G
Borralho, R.	POR	Marathon	F		38	2:50-58	
Boxer, C.	GBR	1500m	1	2	4	4-07·40	
			F		6	4-05·53	
Braun, S.	GER	Heptathlon	F		6	6236	
Bremser, C.	USA	3000m	1	3	2	8-43·97	
			F		4	8-42·78	
Brill, D.	CAN	High jump	F		5	1,94	
Brisco-Hooks, V.	USA	400m	1	4	1	51·42	
			SF	1	1	51·14	
			F		1	48·83 *	G
		200m	1	3	1	23·30	
			2	1	2	22·28	
			SF	2	1	22·78	
			F		1	21·81 *	G
		4×400m	F		1	3-18·29 *	G
Brown, A.	USA	100m	1	4	1	11·15	
			2	3	1	11·35	
			SF	2	1	11·31	
			F		2	11·13	S
		4×100m relay	1	2	1	42·59	
			F		1	41·65	G
Brown, Julie	USA	Marathon	F		36	2:47-33	
Brown, Judi	USA	400m hurdles	1	1	1	55·97 *	
			SF	2	2	55·97	
			F		2	55·20	S
Browne, V.	AUS	High jump	F		6	1,94	
Bryan, L.	ANT	800m	1	4	6	2-11·44	
		1500m	1	1	11	4-21·97	
		4×400m relay	1	2	4	3-39·32	
Buala, E.	GUI	400m	1	2	6	56·82	
		200m	1	6	5	24·82	
			2	3	7	24·87	
Budd, Z.	GBR	3000m	1	3	3	8-44·62	
			F		7	8-48·80	
Burke, J.	JAM	200m	1	5	5	23·75	
			2	2	6	23·56	
		4×100m relay	1	1	5	43·05	
Buerki, C.	SUI	3000m	1	3	4	8-45·82	
			F		5	8-45·20	
Bussmann, G.	GER	400m	1	2	1	52·42	
		4×400m relay	1	2	2	3-33·63	
			F		3	3-22·98	B
Cady, C.	USA	Shot put	F		7	17,23	
Callender, B.	GBR	4×100m relay	1	1	2	43·47	
			F		3	43·11	B
Campana, C.	ITA	4×400m relay	1	2	1	3-32·55	
			F		6	3-30·82	
Campbell, R.	USA	800m	1	2	2	2-01·72	
			SF	2	5	2-01·21	
Candelario, F.	DOM	100m	1	5	4	12·12	
Capotosto, B.	ARG	100m hurdles	1	4	4	13·90	
Cardenas, M.	MEX	Marathon	F		40	2:51-03	
Chardonnet, M.	FRA	100m hurdles	1	1	2	13·32	
			SF	2	2	13·09	
			F		=3	13·06	B
Charles, R.	ANT	100m	1	6	7	12·04	
		4×400m relay	1	2	4	3-39·32	

COMPETITOR	COUNTRY CODE	EVENT	ROUND	HEAT	PLACE	TIME & DISTANCE	MEDAL
Cheeseborough, C.	USA	400m	1	1	1	50·94	
			SF	2	1	50·32	
			F		2	49·05	S
		4×100m relay	1	2	1	42·59	
			F		1	41·65	G
		4×400m relay	F		1	3-18·29?	G
Chepchirchir, L.	KEN	1500m	1	1	10	4-21·97	
Chirchir, S.	KEN	800m	1	2	5	2-07·17	
Cirulli, G.	ITA	400m hurdles	1	3	4	57·49	
			SF	1	6	56·45	
		4×400m relay	1	2	1	3-32·55	
Clark, R.	CAN	800m	1	1	4	2-04·67	
			SF	1	8	2-05·42	
Clarke, E.	BAH	100m	1	6	4	11·61	
			2	3	5	11·85	
		4×100m relay	1	1	4	44·15	
			F		6	44·18	
Cojocaru, C.	RUM	400m hurdles	1	3	2	56·94	
			SF	1	2	55·24	
			F		3	55·41	B
Commandeur, O.	HOL	400m hurdles	1	3	2	56·67	
			SF	2	6	57·01	
Cook, K.	GBR	400m	1	2	2	52·64	
			SF	1	2	51·49	
			F		3	49·43	B
		200m	1	6	1	23·71	
			2	2	3	23·02	
			SF	2	3	22·38	
			F		4	22·10	
		4×100m relay	1	1	2	43·47	
			F		3	43·11	B
Craciunescu, F.	RUM	Shot put	F		8	17,23	
		Discus throw	F		3	63,54	B
Crooks, C.	CAN	400m	1	1	2	52·04	
			SF	1	3	51·53	
			F		7	50·45	
		4×400m relay	1	2	3	3-33·78	
			F		2	3-21·21	S
Cunha, A.	POR	3000m	1	1	4	3-46·38	
			F		6	3-46·37	
Cuthbert, J.	JAM	100m	1	2	2	11·83	
			2	3	4	11·71	
			SF	2	8	11·80	
		4×100m relay	F		8	53·54	
Dancetovic, S.	YUG	Long jump	F		12	5,88	
Danville, S.	GBR	100m hurdles	1	1	3	13·46	
			SF	2	5	13·35	
Davis, P.	BAH	100m	2	1	1	11·5?	
			2	4	4	11·6?	
			SF	2	7	?1·70	
		200m	1	2	2	23·37	
			2	1	4	22·97	
			SF	2	8	23·02	
		4×100m relay	1	1	4	44·15	
			F		6	44·18	
De Cano, L.P.	HON	Marathon	F		DNF		
De Jesus, M.	PUR	Long jump	Q		DNQ	5,63	
		4×400m relay	1	1	5	3-37·89	
De La Cruz, A.	PHI	400m hurdles	1	3	7	62·70	
De Vega, L.	PHI	100m	1	6	6	11·85	
			2	2	6	11·97	
		200m	1	1	6	25·10	
DeSnoo, L.	USA	Discus throw	F		10	54,84	
Decker, M.	USA	3000m	1	1	1	8-44·38*	
			F		DNF		
Decker, V.	GAM	4×100m relay	1	2	6	47·18	
Denk, U.	GER	100m hurdles	1	3	1	13·32	
			SF	2	4	13·20	
			F		7	13·32	
Deniz, L.	USA	Discus throw	F		2	64,86	S
Dinkins, G.-A.	LBR	100m	1	5	7	12·35	
Dixon, D.	USA	4×400m relay	1	1	1	3-22·82	
Dorio, G.	ITA	800m	1	4	2	2-01·41	
			SF	2	2	1-59·53	
			F		4	1-59·05	
		1500m	1	2	1	4-04·51	
			F		1	4-03·25	G
Dressel, B.	GER	Heptathlon	F		9	6082	
Durbrook, M.-C.	BEL	Marathon	F		24	2:38·01	
Dwyer-Brown, O.	JAM	400m hurdles	1	3	5	58·42	
Egger, R.	SUI	Javelin throw	Q		DNQ	57,88	
El Moutawakel, N.	MAR	400m hurdles	1	2	1	56·49	
			SF	1	3	55·65	
			F		1	54·6?*	G
Elliott, D.	GBR	High jump	F		=9	1,88	
Elloy, L.	FRA	100m hurdles	1	4	5	13·93	
Emmanuel, G.	TRI	400m	1	2	5	54·0?	

COMPETITOR	COUNTRY CODE	EVENT	ROUND	HEAT	PLACE	TIME & DISTANCE	MEDAL
Enang-Mesode, R.	CMR	100m	1	1	5	11·81	
			2	4	7	12·02	
		200m	1	2	4	24·39	
			2	4	6	24·25	
Ernstrom, E.	SWE	3000m	1	2	6	9-06·54	
Estrella, D.	DOM	100m	1	4	8	12·25	
		200m	1	6	4	24·72	
			2	4	7	24·98	
Everts, S.	GER	Heptathlon	F		3	6363	B
Ewanje-Epee, M.	FRA	High jump	F		4	1,94	
Farmer, S.	JAM	400m hurdles	1	2	3	57·06	
			SF	1	5	56·05	
			F		8	57·15	
Farrell, E.	AHO	100m	1	4	6	11·94	
Ferguson, S.	BAH	Long jump	F		8	6,44	
Ferreira, M.	POR	Marathon	F		39	2:50·58	
Findlay, V.	JAM	4×100m relay	1	1	1	43·05	
			F		8	53·54	
Fitch, G.	CAN	3000m	1	3	6	9-07·18	
Fitzgerald-Brown, B.	USA	100m hurdles	1	1	1	13·13	
			SF	2	1	12·98	
			F		1	12·84	G
Flintoff, D.	AUS	400m hurdles	1	1	3	57·20	
			SF	2	3	56·24	
			F		6	56·21	
Fogli, L.	ITA	Marathon	F		9	2:29·28	
Forde, G.	TRI	100m	1	1	4	11·76	
			2	2	5	11·86	
		4×100m relay	1	2	4	44·78	
			F		7	44·23	
Fowler, O.	BAH	4×100m relay	1	1	4	44·15	
			F		6	44·18	
Freeman, G.	GAM	4×100m relay	1	2	6	47·18	
French, S.	CAN	3000m	1	2	8	9-24·66	
Fukumitsu, H.	JPN	High jump	Q		DNQ	1,87	
Furniss, J.	GBR	3000m	1	1	6	8-48·00	
Gallagher, K.	USA	800m	1	4	1	2-00·37	
			SF	1	1	2-00·48	
			F		2	1-58·63	S
Garcia, E.	BRA	100m	1	4	4	11·63	
			2	4	6	11·82	
		Long jump	Q		DNQ	6,01	
Garcia, K.-L.	SAL	3000m	1	3	9	9-42·28	
		1500m	1	1	12	4-38·00	
Garden, L.	AUS	Long jump	F		11	6,30	
Gareau, F.	CAN	100m	1	3	5	11·66	
			2	3	6	11·88	
		4×100m relay	1	2	2	43·53	
			F		2	42·77	S
Gareau, J.	CAN	Marathon	F		DNF		
Gaschet, L.	FRA	100m	1	4	2	11·42	
			2	?	4	11·51	
			SF	1	7	11·68	
		200m	1	4	3	23·32	
			2	2	2	22·87	
			SF	1	4	22·73	
			F		8	22·86	
		4×100m relay	1	1	3	43·64	
			F		4	43·15	
Gaugel, H.	GER	100m	1	6	2	11·38	
			2	1	3	11·50	
			SF	2	6	11·62	
		200m	1	2	3	23·37	
			2	4	3	23·19	
			SF	2	7	23·02	
		4×100m relay	1	2	3	44·30	
			F		5	43·57	
		4×400m relay	F		3	3-22·98	B
Gerdes, R.	GER	1500m	1	1	4	4-10·64	
			F		4	4-04·41	
Geremias, C.	BRA	Heptathlon	F		DNF		
		Long jump	Q		DNQ	6,04	
Gibson, S.	GBR	Javelin throw	F		9	59,66	
Gisladottir, T.	ISL	High jump	Q		DNQ	1,80	
Givens, R	USA	200m	1	5	1	22·88	
			2	3	2	22·81	
			SF	1	3	22·69	
			F		6	22·36	
Gongora, L.-M.	ARG	3000m	1	2	9	9-41·14	
		1500m	1	2		4-28·02	
Gordon, Y.	HKG	Marathon	F		34	2:46·12	
Gould, D.	AUS	3000m	1	2	5	9-05·66	
Green, C.	JAM	400m	1	4	5	53·61	
		4×400m relay	F		5	3-27·51	
Greene, D.	BAH	4×100m relay	1	1	4	44·15	
			F		6	44·18	

COMPETITOR	COUNTRY CODE	EVENT	ROUND	HEAT	PLACE	TIME & DISTANCE	MEDAL
Greiner, C.	USA	Heptathlon	F		4	6281	
Griffin, L.	USA	Shot put	F		9	17,00	
		Discus throw	F		12	50,16	
Griffith, F.	USA	200m	1	1	1	22·56	
			2	4	1	23·33	
			SF	1	1	22·27	
			F		2	22.04	S
Griffith, J.	GUY	400m	1	1	4	52·27	
			SF	1	5	52·39	
Grime, L.	NZL	400m hurdles	1	2	5	58·02	
Gronfeldt, L.	ISL	Javelin throw	Q		DNQ	48,70	
Guevara, E.	PER	Marathon	F		35	2:46-50	
Hagger, K.	GBR	Heptathlon	F		8	6127	
Hamrin, M.-L.	SWE	Marathon	F		18	2:36-41	
Hansen, J.	USA	3000m	1	2	2	8-58·64	
			F		8	8-51·53	
Head, V.	GBR	Shot put	F		6	17,90	
		Discus throw	F		7	58,18	
Hearnshaw, S.	GBR	Long jump	F		3	6,80	B
Helander, T.	FIN	400m hurdles	1	1	4	57·22	
			SF	2	4	56·59	
			F		7	56·55	
Hidding, T.	HOL	Heptathlon	F		7	6147	
Holzapfel, B.	GER	High jump	F		=11	1,85	
Hope-Washington, E.	TR	4×100m relay	1	2	4	44·78	
			F		7	44·23	
Howard, D.	USA	4×400m relay	1	1	1	3-22·82	
Howard, S.	USA	4×400m relay	1	1	1	3-22·82	
			F		1	3-18·29*	G
Hoyte-Smith, J.	GBR	4×400m relay	1	1	3	3-27·68	
			F		4	3-25·51	
Hunter, S.	JAM	100m hurdles	1	2	4	13·44	
			SF	1	8	13·84	
Huntley, J.	USA	High jump	F		3	1,97	B
Ingiro, B.	GUI	100m	1	1	7	12·19	
		100m hurdles	1	1	6	15·39	
Inniss, J.	GUY	Long jump	Q		DNQ	6,17	
Ionesco, C.	CAN	Shot put	F		12	15,25	
		Discus throw	Q		DNQ	52,28	
Ionescu, V.	RUM	Long jump	F		2	6,81	S
Isphording, J.	USA	Marathon	F		DNF		
Jackson, G.	JAM	100m	1	3	2	11·24	
			2	4	1	11·38	
			SF	1	3	11·27	
			F		5	11.39	
		200m	1	2	1	22·70	
			2	3	1	22·52	
			SF	2	2	22·32	
			F		5	22·20	
		4×400m relay	1	1	2	3-26·56	
			F		5	3-27·51	
		4×100m relay	1	1	1	43·05	
			F		8	53·54	
Jacobs, S.	GBR	4×100m relay	1	1	2	43·47	
			F		3	43·11	B
Jambane, B.	MOZ	100m	1	2	5	12·55	
			2	1	8	12·57	
		200m	1	5	6	25·14	
Jawo, J.	GAM	100m	1	3	7	12·10	
		4×100m relay	1	2	6	47·18	
Jiao, Y.-X.	ROC	Discus throw	F		11	53,32	
Joseph, J.	ANT	400m	1	1	7	53·63	
		4×400m relay	1	2	4	3-39·32	
Joyce, M.	IRL	3000m	1	3	5	8-54·34	
Joyce, R.	IRL	Marathon	F		23	2:37-57	
Joyner, J.	USA	Heptathlon	F		2	6385	S
		Long jump	F		5	6,77	
Kameli, S.	CAN	100m hurdles	1	4	3	13·72	
			SF	2	8	13·65	
Kane, M.	USA	1500m	1	1	7	4-11·86	
Keskitalo, S.	FIN	Marathon	F		15	2:35-15	
Killingbeck, M.	CAN	400m	1	2	3	52·77	
			SF	2	5	51·72	
		4×400m relay	F		2	3-21·21	S
Kimajo, H.	KEN	3000m	1	1	7	8-57·21	
Klinger, M.	GER	800m	1	1	2	2-03·66	
			SF	2	3	2-00·00	
			F		7	2-00·65	
Kraus, B.	GER	3000m	1	2	1	8-57·53	
			F		DNF		
Kristiansen, I.	NOR	Marathon	F		4	2:27-34	
Kyalisma, R.	UGA	400m hurdles	1	3	3	57·38	
			SF	2	7	57·02	

COMPETITOR	COUNTRY CODE	EVENT	ROUND	HEAT	PLACE	TIME & DISTANCE	MEDAL
Kyomo, N.	TAN	100m	1	5	5	12·26	
			2	4	8	12·53	
		200m	1	2	5	24·68	
			2	2	8	25·11	
Laaksalo, T.	FIN	Javelin throw	F		4	66,40	
Lai, L.-J.	TPE	400m hurdles	1		5	58·54	
Laine, F.	FIN	Javelin throw	F		11	58,18	
Lapajne, L.	YUG	High jump	Q		DNQ	1,87	
Launa, I.	GUI	Heptathlon	F		19	5146	
Leatherwood, L.	USA	400m	1	3	1	52·05	
			SF	2	2	50·83	
			F		5	50·25	
		4×400m relay	1	1	1	3-22·82	
			F		1	3-18·29*	G
Lee, H.-C.	TPE	Javelin throw	Q		DNQ	52,46	
Lee, Y.-S.	KOR	100m	1	4	7	12·06	
Leisten-schneider, N.	GER	4×400m relay	1	2	2	3-33·63	
Lewis, C.	USA	Long jump	F		9	6,43	
Lewis, M.	JAM	Discus throw	Q		DNQ	49,00	
Li, M.-S.	ROC	Shot put	F		5	17,96	
Liao, W.	ROC	Long jump	Q		DNQ	6,16	
Lillak, T.	FIN	Javelin throw	F		2	69,00	S
Lind, A.	PUR	800m	1	2	4	2-01·84	
			SF	1	6	2-03·27	
		4×400m relay	1	1	5	3-37·39	
Liu, H.-J.	ROC	100m hurdles	1	2	5	13·64	
			SF	2	7	13·57	
Liu, Y.-C.	TPE	High jump	Q		DNQ	1,70	
Loghin, M.	RUM	Shot put	F		2	20,47	S
Lombardo, P.	ITA	4×400m relay	1	2	1	3-32·55	
			F		6	3-30·82	
Lorraway, R.	AUS	Long jump	F		6	6,67	
Losch, C.	GER	Shot put	F		1	20,48	G
Loval, M.-F.	FRA	100m	1	6	3	11·51	
			2	4	3	11·56	
			SF	1	6	11·64	
		4×100m relay	1	1	3	43·64	
			F		4	43·15	
Lovin, F.	RUM	800m	1	2	1	2-01·51	
			SF	2	1	1-59·29	
			F		3	1-58·83	B
		1500m	1	1	3	4-10·58	
			F		9	4-09·11	
Lundholm, U.	FIN	Discus throw	F		4	62,84	
McCabe, J.	SWE	800m	1	1	3	2-04·16	
			SF	2	6	2-02·20	
		1500m	1	2	7	4-16·48	
MacDougall, L.	GBR	1500m	1	2	5	4-09·08	
			F		11	4-10·58	
Machado, M.	POR	800m	1	4	5	2-05·74	
		3000m	1	2	4	9-01·77	
McRoberts, B.	CAN	1500m	1	1	5	4-10·64	
			F		7	4-05·98	
Malgadey-Forgrave, S.	CAN	100m hurdles	1	3	4	13·47	
			SF	1	6	13·42	
Malone, A.	CAN	Marathon	F		17	2:36-33	
Manecke, M.	GER	Discus throw	F		6	58,56	
Marjamaa, H.	FIN	100m	1	5	2	11·43	
			2	3	2	11·51	
			SF	1	5	11·37	
		200m	1	6	2	24·10	
			2	4	4	23·51	
			SF	1	6	23·12	
Martha, S.	AHO	200m	1	2	6	25·56	
Martin, G.	AUS	Shot put	F		3	19,19	B
		Discus throw	F		8	55,88	
Martin, L.	AUS	Marathon	F		7	2:29-03	
Marxer, M.	LIE	Heptathlon	F		20	4913	
Masuda, A.	JPN	Marathon	F		DNF		
Masullo, M.	ITA	200m	1	4	2	23·30	
			2	2	4	23·19	
			SF	2	6	22·88	
		4×400m relay	F		6	3-30·82	
Mathieu, E.	PUR	4×400m relay	1	1	5	3-37·39	
Mathieu, M.-L.	PUR	400m	1	3	4	53·27	
			SF	1	7	53·69	
		4×400m relay	1	1	5	3-37·39	
Matsui, E.	JPN	Javelin throw	Q		DNQ	55,92	
May, C.	IRL	Marathon	F		28	2:41-27	
Mbanugo, I.	NGR	Marathon	F		DNF		
Meighan, Z.	GUA	400m	1	1	8	55·64	
		800m	1	3	7	2-14·17	

COMPETITOR	COUNTRY CODE	EVENT	ROUND	HEAT	PLACE	TIME & DISTANCE	MEDAL
Melinte, D.	RUM	800m	1	3	1	2-02.77	
			SF	1	2	2-01.42	
			F		1	1-57.60	G
		1500m	1	1	=1	4-10.48	
			F		2	4-03.76	S
Medonca, E.	BRA	Marathon	F		44	2:52-19	
Mensah, M.	GHA	4×400m relay	1	2	5	3-40.38	
		4×100m relay	1	2	5	42.20	
Meyfarth, U.	GER	High jump	F		1	2,02*	G
Milana, A.	ITA	Marathon	F		12	2.33-01	
Mina, Z.	LIB	400m	1	4	7	59.56	
Mistoul, O.	GAB	Shot put	F		13	14,59	
Mo, M.-O.	KOR	200m	1	3	4	24.86	
			2	2	6	24.70	
Moe, B.	NOR	Marathon	F		26	2:40-52	
Moller, L.	NZL	Marathon	F		5	2:28-34	
Mori, M.	JPN	Javelin throw	Q		DNQ	55,60	
Morley, S.	GBR	400m	1	4	3	53.71	
			SF	1	7	56.67	
Moro, M.	ITA	Marathon	F		20	2:37-06	
Mota, R.	PIR	Marathon	F		3	2:26-57	B
		3000m	1	3	DNF		
Mozun, I.	ESP	High jump	Q		DNQ	1,75	
Mpika, F.	CGO	100m	1	2	4	12.54	
			2	2	8	12.60	
		200m	1	6	6	25.05	
			2	1	7	24.97	
Mukamurenzi, M.	RWA	3000m	3	3	7	9-27.03	
		1500m	1	2	10	4-31.56	
Muros, E.	PHI	Long jump	Q		DNQ	5,54	
Mwanjala, H.	TAN	3000m	1	2	10	9-42.66	
Naigre, R.	FRA	200m	1	1	3	23.50	
			2	3	5	23.54	
		4×100m relay	1	1	3	43.64	
			F		4	43.15	
Nazario, N.	PUR	Marathon	F		33	2:45-49	
Ndow, A.	GAM	200m	1	3	5	25.41	
			2	3	8	25.24	
		4×100m relay	1	2	6	47.18	
N'drin, C.	CIV	800m	1	1	5	2-06.06	
Nelson, K.	CAN	100m hurdles	1	1	5	13.77	
Ng, L.-C.	HKG	Marathon	F		31	2:42-38	
Ngambi, C.	CMR	100m	1	4	5	11.67	
			2	2	4	11.82	
			SF	1	8	11.91	
		100m hurdles	1	1	4	13.54	
			SF	1	7	13.70	
Ngo-Nack, A.	CMR	Discus throw	Q		DNQ	38,32	
Nunn, G.	AUS	Heptathlon	F		1	6390	G
		100m hurdles	1	2	3	13.29	
			SF	2	3	13.14	
			F		5	13.20	
		Long jump	F		7	6,53	
Oakes, H.	GBR	100m	1	3	3	11.32	
			2	3	3	11.54	
			SF	2	4	11.57	
			F		7	11.43	
		4×100m relay	1	1	2	43.47	
			F		3	43.11	B
Oakes, J.	GBR	Shot put	F		4	18,14	
O'Connor, M.	NZL	Marathon	F		27	2:41-22	
Oker, E.	GER	100m hurdles	1	2	2	13.14	
			SF	1	5	13.37	
		4×100m relay	1	2	3	44.30	
			F		5	43.57	
Oliver, I.	JAM	400m	1	1	3	52.19	
			SF	2	7	52.14	
		4×400m relay	1	1	2	3-26.56	
			F		5	3-27.51	
Ongollo, G.	GAB	100m	1	5	3	12.40	
O'Shea, C.	IRL	800m	1	3	2	2-03.60	
			SF	1	4	2-02.70	
			F		8	2-00.77	
Osh-Williams, E.	SLE	100m	1	1	8	12.83	
Ottey-Page, M.	JAM	100m	1	6	1	11.26	
			2	2	1	11.21	
			SF	1	2	11.17	
			F		3	11.16	B
		200m	1	4	1	22.90	
			2	2	1	22.53	
			SF	1	2	22.57	
			F		3	22.09	B
		4×100m relay	1	1	1	43.05	
			F		8	53.54	
Pace, J.	MLT	Javelin throw	Q		DNQ	47,92	
Page, A.	CAN	400m hurdles	1	4	4	59.09	
			SF	1	8	57.89	
Page, P.	USA	100m hurdles	1	4	1	13.32	
			SF	1	4	13.36	
			F		8	13.40	
Pagel, R.	USA	Shot put	F		11	16,06	
Pantazi, E.	GRE	100m hurdles	1	2	6	14.20	
Panyapuek, W.	THA	4×400m relay	1	1	5	45.62	
Parr, M.	IRL	400m hurdles	1	4	7	61.66	
Patarach, J.	THA	4×100m relay	1	1	5	45.62	
Payne, M.	CAN	400m	1	3	2	52.89	
			SF	2	3	50.94	
			F		4	49.91	
		4×400m relay	1	2	3	3-33.78	
			F		2	3-21.21	S
		4×100m relay	1	2	2	43.53	
			F		2	42.77	S
Peeters, F.	BEL	Marathon	F		29	2:42-22	
Peters, B.	GER	Javelin throw	F		7	62,34	
Phenglaor, S.	THA	Long jump	Q		DNQ	5,51	
Picaut, F.	FRA	Heptathlon	F		13	5914	
Ping, G.E.	ROC	High jump	Q		DNQ	1,84	
Polmar-Tuin, C.	CAN	Heptathlon	F		16	5648	
Possamai, A.	ITA	3000m	1	1	3	8-45.84	
			F		10	9-10.82	
Puica, M.	RUM	3000m	1	3	2	8-43.32*	
			F		1	8-35.96*	G
		1500m	1	2	2	4-05.30	
			F		3	4-04.15	B
Quartey, C.	GHA	4×100m relay	1	2	5	45.20	
Quintavalla, F.	ITA	Javelin throw	Q		DNQ	56,48	
Ramos, A.	CHI	800m	1	3	5	2-05.77	
		1500m	1	2	8	4-22.03	
Rao, V.	IND	4×400m relay	1	4	4	3-33.85	
			F		7	3:32-49	
Rasmussen, D.	DEN	Marathon	F		13	2:33-40	
Rattray, C.	JAM	400m	1	2	4	52.78	
			SF	1	6	53.23	
		4×400m relay	1	1	2	3-26.56	
			F		5	3-27.51	
Redetzky, H.	GER	High jump	F		=11	1,85	
Regonesi, M.	CHI	Marathon	F		32	2:44-44	
		3000m	1	3	DNF		
Reid, B.	CAN	High jump	Q		DNQ	1,70	
Richardson, J.	CAN	4×400m relay	1	2	3	3-33.78	
			F		2	3-21.21	S
Richburg, D.	USA	1500m	1	1	8	4-13.25	
Rione, T.	ESP	100m	1	3	4	11.55	
			2	4	5	11.76	
		200m	1	3	3	24.48	
			2	3	6	23.78	
Ritchie, M.	GBR	Discus throw	F		5	62,58	
Ritter, H.	LIE	1500m	1	-	9	4-19.39	
Ritter, L.	CAN	High jump	F		8	1,91	
Rivers, P.	AUS	Javelin throw	F		12	56,20	
Rodger, D.	NZL	3000m	1	1	5	8-47.90	
			F		9	8-56.43	
Ronquillo, M.	MEX	Marathon	F		41	2:51-04	
Ross-Green, J.	CAN	Heptathlon	F		15	5904	
Rossi, E.	ITA	400m	1	1	6	53.04	
		4×400m relay	1	2	1	3-32.55	
			F		6	3-30.82	
Rougeron, M.	FRA	High jump	Q		DNQ	1,84	
Rowell, S.	GBR	Marathon	F		14	2:34-08	
Ruegger, S.	CAN	Marathon	F		8	2:29-09	
Sanderson, T.	GBR	Javelin throw	F		1	69,56*	G
Sasaki, M.	JPN	Marathon	F		19	2:37-04	
Sato, M.	JPN	High jump	Q		DNQ	1,84	
Savigny, M.-N.	FRA	100m hurdles	1	3	3	13.36	
			SF	1	3	13.30	
			F		6	13.28	
Schabinger, M.	GER	200m	1	6	3	24.12	
			2	2	5	23.84	
		4×100m relay	1	2	3	44.30	
			F		5	43.57	
Schneider, C.	SUI	Heptathlon	F		10	6042	
Schulte-Mattler, H.	GER	400m	1	1	5	52.77	
		4×400m relay	1	2	2	3-33.63	
			F		3	3-22.98	B
Schumann, C.	GUA	100m	1	2	3	12.04	
			2	3	7	12.23	
		200m	1	4	5	24.91	
			2	2	7	24.90	
Scott, D.	CAN	1500m	1	2	6	4-09.16	
			F		10	4-10.41	
Scott, D.	JAM	Long jump	F		10	6.40	

COMPETITOR	COUNTRY CODE	EVENT	ROUND	HEAT	PLACE	TIME & DISTANCE	MEDAL
Scutt, M.	GBR	400m	1	4	4	52·89	
			SF	2	6	52·07	
		4×400m relay	1	1	3	3-27·68	
			F		4	3-25·51	
Senghor, C.	SEN	High jump	Q		DNQ	1,70	
Sergent, A.	FRA	3000m	1	2	7	9-15·82	
Shmueli, Z.	ISR	Marathon	F		30	2:42-27	
Simeoni, S.	ITA	High jump	F		2	2,00	S
Simpson, J.	GBR	Heptathlon	F		5	6280	
		High jump	Q		DNQ	1,84	
Skoglund, A.-L.	SWE	400m hurdles	1	4	1	55·75*	
			SF	1	1	55·17*	
			F		5	55·43	
Sly, W.	GBR	3000m	1	2	3	8-58·66	
			F		2	8-39·47	S
Slythe, C.	CAN	800m	1	3	3	2-04·17	
			SF	1	7	2-04·95	
Smellie, D.	CAN	Heptathlon	F		17	5638	
Smith, J.	GBR	Marathon	F		11	2:32-48	
Smith, K.	USA	Javelin throw	F		8	62,06	
Smith, S.	BER	Javelin throw	Q		DNQ	52,74	
Smyth, R.	IRL	3000m	1	1	9	9-01·69	
Soeteway, M.-C.	BEL	High jump	Q		DNQ	1,80	
Solberg, T.	NOR	Javelin throw	F		5	64,52	
Spencer, P.	USA	High jump	F		=11	1,85	
Stalman, R.	HOL	Discus throw	F		1	65,36	G
Stanciu, A.	RUM	Long jump	F		1	6,96	G
Stanton, C.	AUS	High jump	F		=11	1,85	
Stevens, M.	CAN	4×400m relay	1	2	4	3-39·32	
Stripet, P.	THA	4×100m relay	1	1	5	45·62	
Strithoa, R.	THA	400m	1	3	6	58·11	
Strong, S.	GBR	100m hurdles	1	2	1	12·86	
			SF	1	2	13·16	
			F		2	12·88	S
Sulinski, C.	USA	Javelin throw	F		10	58,38	
Sussiek, C.	GER	4×400m relay	1	2	2	3-33·63	
Sutfin, L.	USA	Javelin throw	Q		DNQ	55,92	
Tahapari, E.	INA	400m	1	3	5	55·82	
		200m	1	4	6	25·07	
Tangjitnusorn, W.	THA	100m	1	3	8	12·18	
		4×100m relay	1	1	5	45·62	
Tannander, A.	SWE	Heptathlon	F		14	5908	
		Long jump	Q		DNQ	6,16	
Tannander, K.	SWE	Heptathlon	F		12	5985	
Taylor, A.	CAN	100m	1	5	1	11·23	
			2	2	3	11·42	
			SF	1	4	11·36	
			F		8	11·62	
		4×100m relay	1	2	2	43·53	
			F		2	42·77	S
Taylor, G.	GBR	400m hurdles	1	2	4	57·64	
			SF	2	5	56·72	
		4×400m relay	1	1	3	3-27·68	
			F		4	3-25·51	
Tchuinte, A.	CMR	Javelin throw	Q		DNQ	55,94	
Teske, C.	GER	Marathon	F		16	2:35-56	
Thacker, A.	USA	Long jump	F		4	6,78	
Thimm, U.	GER	400m	1	4	3	52·53	
			SF	2	4	51·03	
			F		6	50·37	
		4×100m relay	1	2	3	44·30	
			F		5	43·57	
		4×400m relay	F		3	3-22·98	B
Thomas, A.	JAM	4×400m relay	1	1	2	3-26·56	
Thomas, S.	GBR	100m	1	5	3	11·91	
			2	2	7	12·13	
Thyssen, I.	GER	Javelin throw	F		6	63,26	
Toivonen, T.	FIN	Marathon	F		10	2:32-07	
Trujillo, M.	MEX	Marathon	F		25	2:38-50	
Tsai, L.-J.	TPE	Heptathlon	F		18	5447	
Tuisorisori, M.	FIJ	100m	1	2	6	13·04	
		200m	1	1	7	26·82	
Turner, K.	USA	100m hurdles	1	3	2	13·33	
			SF	1	1	13·11	
			F		=3	13·06	B
Ungu, B.	ZAI	800m	1	1	6	2-18·79	
Usha, P.	IND	400m hurdles	1	1	2	56·81	
			SF	2	1	55·54	
			F		4	55·42	
		4×400m relay	1	1	4	3-33·85	
			F		7	3-32·49	
Usifo, M.	NGR	400m hurdles	1	4	2	57·78	
			SF	2	8	58·55	
		100m hurdles	1	4	2	13·54	
			SF	2	6	13·52	
Vader, E.	HOL	100m	1	1	3	11·43	
			2	1	5	11·56	
		200m	1	3	2	23·65	
			2	3	3	23·31	
			SF	1	7	23·43	
Valsamma, M.	IND	400m hurdles	1	4	5	60·03	
		4×400m relay	1	1	4	3-33·85	
			F		7	3-32·49	
Van Heerden, M.	ZIM	Discus throw	Q		DNQ	50,54	
Van Hulst, E.	HOL	800m	1	4	3	2-03·38	
			SF	1	5	2-03·25	
		1500m	1	1	6	4-10·69	
			F		12	4-11·58	
Van Landeghem, R.	BEL	Marathon	F		21	2:37-11	
Vasile, N.	RUM	High jump	F		=11	1,85	
Vazquez, A.	MEX	400m hurdles	1	1	6	60·86	
Verbeek, G.	CAN	800m	1	4	4	2-04·16	
			SF	2	7	2-03·28	
Verouli, A.	GRE	Javelin throw	Q		DNQ	57,72	
Wagaki, M.	KEN	Marathon	F		43	2:52-00	
Waithera, R.	KEN	400m	1	4	2	52·53	
			SF	1	4	52·21	
			F		8	51·56	
		200m	1	5	4	23·42	
			2	3	4	23·37	
			SF	1	8	23·45	
Waitz, G.	NOR	Marathon	F		2	2:26-18	S
Walsh, P.	IRL	Discus throw	F		9	55,38	
Welch, P.	GBR	Marathon	F		6	2:28-54	
Whitbread, F.	GBR	Javelin throw	F		3	67,14	B
Whittaker, S.	GBR	200m	1	5	3	23·22	
			2	1	5	22·98	
Wijnsma, M.	HOL	Heptathlon	F		11	6015	
Williams, A.	TRI	100m	1	6	5	11·74	
			2	1	6	11·89	
		200m	1	4	4	23·88	
		4×100m relay	1	2	4	44·78	
			F		7	44·23	
Williams, L.	CAN	3000m	1	1	2	8-45·77	
			F		3	8-42·14	B
Wiredu, D.	GHA	100m	1	3	6	11·85	
			2	1	7	12·00	
		4×100m relay	1	2	5	45·20	
Wirtz, M.-A.	SEY	100m	1	6	8	12·61	
		200m	1	2	7	25·88	
		Long jump	Q		DNQ	5,21	
Wright, D.	CAN	400m hurdles	1	2	6	58·17	
		4×400m relay	1	2	3	3-33·78	
Wright, N.	BOL	Marathon	F		42	2:51-35	
Wright-Scott, A.	USA	400m hurdles	1	3	6	59·77	
Wysocki, R.	USA	800m	1	1	2	2-04·05	
			SF	1	6	2-02·31	
			F		6	2-00·34	
		1500m	1	2	3	4-06·65	
			F		8	4-08·92	
Yang, W.-Q.	ROC	High jump	F		=9	1,88	
Yang, Y.-Q.	ROC	Shot put	F		10	16,97	
Zheng, D.	ROC	High jump	F		7	1,91	
Zhu, H.-Y.	ROC	Javelin throw	Q		DNQ	53,18	
Zutshi, G.	IND	3000m	1	3	8	9-40·63	

1988

Flo Jo Adds Glamour Plus Speed

It took a return to the Orient to produce the most peaceful Games since 1964. The only major track and field countries to boycott the celebrations were Ethiopia and Cuba, over the North Korean claim that the festival should have been a shared venture. Money now rules, with the Games making a reported £210 million profit, £75 million up on Los Angeles. With payments to athletes now legalised, it was reported that a gold medal was worth £100,000 in benefits, which undoubtedly drove some athletes to take illegal drugs, while injuries reached their highest level yet. There was the sad case of Ben Johnson to reflect upon, stripped of his medal and disgraced in front of the world. The glamour girl of the Games was Florence Griffith-Joyner, who collected three golds and a silver, a feat even Carl Lewis could not attain this time around.

Men's Track Events

Leading up to the Games, the question on everyone's lips was, would Canada's Ben Johnson repeat his defeat of America's Carl Lewis in the **100 metres**, as he had done at the world championships in 1987. Johnson ran cannily in the preliminaries, finishing third in his second round heat to Britain's Linford Christie, the European champion. Meanwhile, Lewis was blazing the track with 9·99 and 9·97 timings and looked set to take gold. The final saw Johnson power out of his blocks and quickly build up a one metre advantage over fellow Canadian Desai Williams, who was slightly up on the rest of the field. But at 60 metres the pattern was set; Johnson holding a metre lead over Lewis, with Christie half a metre back, just fending off the Americans, Calvin Smith and Dennis Mitchell. Helped by a slight following wind of 1·1 metres per second, Johnson smashed the world record in 9·79, with Lewis second in 9·92. A dipping Christie came third in 9·97 and Smith was outleaned in 9·99. This historic race resulted in an unprecedented four sprinters running under the magic 10·00 barrier. However, there was no gold medal for Johnson, because two days later he was disqualified for taking drugs! The gold went to Lewis, silver to Christie and bronze to Smith.

Carl Lewis, the reigning **200 metres** Olympic champion, was fully expected to bring home the bacon again and he looked all set in the heats to fulfill this promise. That was until his training partner, fellow American Joe DeLoach, looked just as good running 20·06 in his semi-final. The final saw DeLoach fractionally better away from his mark, with Lewis and Britain's Linford Christie also getting good starts. Lewis then took control coming off the bend, with Robson Da Silva of Brazil just heading Christie and DeLoach. But it was the latter who finished fastest, sweeping past his rivals 30 metres from the finish, to win in 19·75 for a new Olympic record. Lewis took second place with 19·79 and Da Silva held off Christie to record 20·04 for the bronze.

Prior to the Games, a new king of the one lap had appeared in the form of Henry "Butch" Reynolds of America. He had sliced a sizeable piece off the world **400 metres** record and along with two other Americans he dominated the preliminary rounds when running in the low 44·0's. In the final, Innocent Egbunike of Nigeria was out of his blocks and around the track like a "bolt from the blue", but America's Steve Lewis drew ahead of him and passed the 200 in 21·1. Entering the home straight, fellow American Danny Everett joined Lewis with Mohamed Al-Malki from Oman, two metres back, followed by Darren Clark of Australia and Reynolds. The race favourite then made his famous late surge over the final 100 metres, but could not reach Lewis, who won in 43·87 from Reynolds 43·93 and Everett 44·09.

The **800 metres** was considered to be a very open event. Joaquim Cruz of Brazil, the defending champion, had not shown much form since 1985, while Morocco's Said Aouita and Britain's Steve Cram were stepping down a distance to seek a medal. Prior to the Games, America's Johnny Gray looked to have the best chance of winning, having won some very fast races on his European tour, especially when Cram ran poorly in the second round and was eliminated. In the final, Nixon Kiprotich set off at an alarming rate and passed the 200 in 23·5, closely followed by the Brazilians, Jose Barbosa and Cruz. Kiprotich took the 400 in a speedy 49·54, with Barbosa one and a half metres down, Cruz a further metre behind and Britain's Peter Elliott another five metres adrift. At this stage Paul Ereng of Kenya was some seven metres down on Elliott, but he and Aouita accelerated with 250 to go. Coming into the final straight, Cruz led from Elliott, Ereng and Aouita, with the others falling back. With 50 metres left, Ereng struck off at a hot pace and won in 1-43·45 from Cruz 1-43·90, while Aouita overtook Elliott for the bronze in 1-44·06 to the latter's 1-44·12.

What a race the **1,500 metres** was going to be, with Morocco's Said Aouita matched with Britain's Steve Cram. The first hiccup came when Aouita did not start in the semi-finals and the second when Cram did not hit top form. Ireland's Marcus O'Sullivan was the early leader in the final, recording 59·65 over the first 400, with Omar Khalifa of the Sudan, and Britain's Cram and Peter Elliott following closely. Kenya's Peter Rono eventually took up the running, recording 2-00·31 at the end of the second lap and 2-56·69 at 1,200, with Elliott, America's Jeff Atkinson, Cram and Jens-Peter Herold of East Germany, hot on his tail. Off the final bend, Atkinson was dropped and Herold sprinted past Cram and Elliott. The two Britains retaliated, but at the finish it was Rono who came first in 3-35·96, Elliott second 3-36·15, Herold third 3-36·21 and Cram fouth 3-36·24.

Without Morocco's Said Aouita, the **5,000 metres** was wide open. Stefano Mei of Italy took the initiative from the gun for a couple of laps with the pack at his heels, before Bulgaria's Evgeni Ignatov led for a short while.

But it was Kenya's John Ngugi who took command just before the one kilometre mark, passed in 2-42·75. A 59·6 lap by Ngugi opened up a 12 metres gap, which was increased to 50 by two kilometres in 5-14·96 and he kept his speed going to reach four kilometres in 10-36·21. Meanwhile, Ireland's John Doherty led the chasing group, but with eight laps to go, Portugal's Domingos Castro surged away from the pack and started to close on Ngugi. With two laps left, Ngugi was 30 metres up on Castro, who was a similar distance ahead of West Germany's Dieter Baumann and East Germany's Hans Kunze. But the latter pair started to speed up and overtook Castro down the finishing straight with a 55·00 last lap. However, they could not reach Ngugi, who ran 60·08 and took the gold in 13-11·70, from Baumann 13-15·52 and Kunze 13-15·73.

Any one of half a dozen runners appeared quite capable of snatching victory in the **10,000 metres**. Among the more fancied athletes was Hans Kunze of East Germany, Salvatore Antibo from' Italy and Eamonn Martin of Britain, with the Kenyan's half expected to spring a surprise. In the final, Antibo dashed off at an alarming pace, showing 62·0 at 400 and 2-41·74 at one kilometre. Close behind him came Brahim Boutayeb of Morocco, the Kenyan's Kipkembui Kimeli and Moses Tanui, and someway off the pace, Mexico's Marcus Barreto, leading the chasing group. At the half way stage, reached in 13-36·52, the leading group looked set to threaten the world record. A lap and a half later Boutayeb was in the van and at 18 he held a lead of 15 metres, which he had increased considerably following 21 laps, with Tanui dropping further back. With less than two to go, Antibo made his effort and overtook Kimeli in an effort to catch the leader, but Boutayeb's final surge was too much for him and the Moroccan crossed the line in 27-21·46, for an Olympic record and gold medal. Antibo claimed the silver in 27-23·55 and Kimeli the bronze with 27-25·16.

With Ethiopia not attending the Games, there was a great loss to the **marathon**, with both Belayneh Dinsamo, the world's fastest marathoner and Wodajo Buti, absent. Some 120 hopefuls lined up for the start and after three laps of the stadium Vincent Ruguga of Uganda was in the lead. Soon after 5km, Juma Ikangaa of Tanzania hotted up the pace and went through 10km in 30-39 with a group of about 35. This was reduced to about 25 at the half-way

stage, passed in 64-50, with Mexico's Martin Mondragon in front. The next 4km saw the leading group down to 13 and then to seven at 30km in 1:32-49, comprising, Ikangaa, Gelindo Bordin of Italy, Douglas Wakiihuri of Kenya, Ahmed Saleh from Djibouti, Charlie Spedding of Britain and the two Japs, Takeyuki Nakayama and Toshikiko Seko. Seko soon dropped off the pack and at 35km Spedding and Ikangaa also went, followed by Nakayama at 37km. At this stage Saleh pressed ahead and at 40km was 50 metres up on Wakiihuri, with Bordin 80 metres further adrift. But within a kilometre, the two leaders had weakened and Bordin took up the running to win in a time of 2:10-32. Wakiihuri took the silver 2:10-47 and Saleh the bronze with 2:10-59.

In the early part of the year, America's Greg Foster was being hailed as the next Olympic **110 metres hurdles** champion, but he broke an arm and the plaster cast was too big a handicap for him to get through the American trials. Following two lean years, Roger Kingdom, the reigning Olympic champion, became only the second man to hurdle below 13 seconds. In the second round, Kingdom broke his own Olympic record, before taking his place in the line-up for the final. After one false start, Art Blake of America appeared to get away with a flyer, but hit the first hurdle with Colin Jackson of Britain, Vladimir Shishkin of Russia and Kingdom less than half a metre behind. By the third flight, Kingdom was away in front, followed by Jackson and Tonie Campbell of America, in that order. Kingdom increased his lead throughout to win in the stunning time of 12·98, for a new Olympic record, with Jackson taking silver 13·28 and Campbell bronze 13·38.

One of the all-time greats of track and field, Ed Moses, was hoping to lay claim to his third Olympic gold medal in the **400 metres hurdles** . He appeared to have a tough time on his hands, fending off the rising stars in this event, but his semi-final win looked impressive. In the final he looked good, setting off at a fast pace with only fellow American Andre Phillips staying with him. The surprise came at 180 metres when Phillips surged ahead and put him under pressure. Moses fought tooth and nail all the way around the final bend and into the straight, but two hurdles from home Phillips increased his lead. It was then the turn of the hurdling revelation, El Hadjdia Dia Ba from remote Senegal, who spurted past Moses in the last

Mark Shearman

Roger Kingdom

An American from Vienna, Georgia, born on 26 August 1962, he is hardly a household name, but has now won two Olympic gold medals at the high hurdles in successive Games.

Roger started out at the Vienna High School as an all-rounder, winning the state school titles for the discus, high jump and hurdles, even having notions of taking up the decathlon. Three years later this 1,83 tall, 86kg athlete, was tasting big success, winning the National Collegiate 110 metres hurdles and then taking the Pan American Games gold.

The Los Angeles Olympic trials saw him scrape into the USA team in third position. It came as a great shock to many when Kingdom won the cherished Olympic title, despite having a slow start and a tendency to knock hurdles over. When he did get things right, he simply went like the wind, as his slightly wind assisted 13·00 run at Sacramento had already proved. Although Roger had a good season in 1985, his racing record over the next two years was poor, due to injury.

All credit to him for his terrific come-back in 1988, when he won his second Olympic gold in 12·98, being only the second man ever to dip under the magic 13·00 seconds.

The Canadian Ben Johnson, shown in action prior to the Seoul Games, where he broke the world record when winning the 100 metres final, before being disqualified two days later for drug taking.

Mark Shearman

The finish of the sensational 100 metres shows the disgraced Canadian Ben Johnson (159), the winner Carl Lewis of the USA (1102), second placed Linford Christie of Britain (413) and the bronze winning Calvin Smith, also of America (1130).   Mark Shearman

20 metres. The result: Phillips the gold in an Olympic record of 47·19, second Dia Ba 47·23 and third Moses 47·56.

Although Italy's Francesco Panetta was favoured to win the **3,000 metres steeplechase**, any one of a dozen athletes had the ability to strike gold, as the semi-finals had shown. Right from the beginning of the final, Panetta attempted to stretch the pace, reeling off 400 in 68·1, one kilometre in 2-42·93 and two in 5-28·29. He was followed by William Van Dijck of Belgium and Peter Koech of Kenya. A lap later and Panetta was faltering, so Koech took command, chased by Britain's Mark Rowland, Kenya's Patrick Sang and Italy's Alessandro Lambruschini. With 450 to go, Julius Kariuki of Kenya came up to the leaders and took off over the last lap, with Koech and Rowland not far behind. But Kariuki drew further away with 200 to go and won in 8-05·51 for a new Olympic record, with Koech taking the silver in 8-06·79 and Rowland recording 8-07·96 for the bronze.

Italy's Maurizo Damilano was most people's favourite to win the **20 kilometres walk**, following his win in the world championships of the previous year. Against him were some formidable opponents, like East Germany's Ronald Weigel, the Czech Jozef Pribilinec and Russia's Mikhail Schennikov, who had recently set a world's best. Ernesto Canto of Mexico led in the early stages at the head of a group of 18, which was whittled down to three at 15km; Canto, Weigel and Pribilinec. Shortly after this, the fast pace caused Canto to be disqualified and Pribilinec finally got away from the East German. But Weigel hauled him back over the latter stages, although being chased hard himself by Damilano. Pribilinec held onto his lead to take the gold medal in 1:19-57, for a new Olympic record, with Weigel gaining the silver in 1:20-00 and the consistant Damilano the bronze in 1:20-14.

Hartwig Gauder and Ronald Weigel of East Germany,

had dominated the **50 kilometres walk** in the important competitions during 1987 and were highly fancied for the top medals. However, in the early part of the race, Martin Bermudez of Mexico set the pace, but was overtaken by his compatriot, Herman Andrade, later pulled out for lifting, who passed 20km in 1:29-47. Andrade in turn was overhauled by the trio Gauder, Weigel and Russia's Vyacheslav Ivanenko, who were battling along at the head of a group, which was down to seven at 35km. The pace really hotted up over the last 15km and Ivanenko, looking almost fresh, won in a new Olympic record of 3:38-29, with Weigel taking the silver in 3:38-56 and Gauder the bronze in 3:39-45.

A big surprise in the **4 × 100 metres relay** was the elimination of America in the first round heats on technical grounds. Calvin Smith, running the third leg, three times tried to pass to Mark McNeil and, when he did, the baton was outside the exchange zone. The final saw Russia's Victor Bryzgin build up a metre lead on the first leg over Jamaica and West Germany and with Vladimir Krylov and Vladimir Muravyov, maintaining the momentum, Russia gave their final sprinter, Vitaliy Savin, a two metre advantage at the final exchange. Behind them came France and West Germany abreast, with Canada a further metre adrift, followed by Britain. Russia stormed to victory in 38·19, with Linford Christie bringing up Britain into the silver position in 38·28 and France clocking 38·40 for the bronze.

It was not a question of who would win the **4 × 400 metres relay**, but by how much. The final saw America's Danny Everett complete his lap, with Jamaica alongside and Nigeria in third place. Steve Lewis then ran away from the opposition to record 43·4, which gave the USA a two second advantage over Nigeria and East Germany, with Jamaica lying fourth. Kevin Robinzine increased America's lead on the third lap, leaving Jamaica way off

Mark Shearman

Jozef Pribilinec

There has been more than a 50 year tradition of race walking in Czechoslovakia and it is no real surprise to find one of the all-time greats, Jozef Pribilinec, coming from that country. Jozef was born at Kremnica, on 6 July 1960 and is by profession a soldier.

He was 17 when he first emerged on the walking scene. Within two years he had made a name for himself by setting world junior track records at 3km of 11-13·2, 10km 40-55·4 and winning the European junior 10km championships.

As a senior walker, he was blooded at the 1980 Olympic Games and his first success came the following year when he broke the world record over 5km with 18-51·2. In 1982 Jozef was placed second at the European championships in the 20km event and a year later he finished a close second to Mexico's Ernesto Canto over the same distance in the world championships. The Olympic year of 1984 was a lean one, with Czechoslovakia boycotting the Games, but he bounced back in 1985 to set world records at 3km of 11-00·2 and 10km of 38-02·6.

In 1986 he pushed the world hour record to 15,447 km and in the world indoor championships of 1987, was second over 5km. Jozef's most recent triumph came when he won the gold medal at Seoul for the 20km.

pace in second spot, followed by West Germany, East Germany and Britain. The order never changed and "Butch" Reynolds brought home the USA in 2-56·16, to equal the world and Olympic record, with Jamaica's 3-00·30, good enough for the silver in a tight finish with West Germany, who recorded 3-00·56.

Men's Field Events

Javier Sotomayor of Cuba hit form at the right time with a world record, a couple of weeks before the Olympic **high jump** competition, but unfortunately, Cuba was boycotting the Games. Sweden's Patrick Sjoberg was rated to win and he was in there jumping among the final six, with the bar at 2,36, a height which he cleared on his second attempt, as did Russia's Rudolf Povarnitsyn. America's Hollis Conway and Gennadiy Avdeyenko of Russia who got over at their first attempt, while Nick Saunders of Bermuda and West Germany's Dietmar Mogenburg, each failed. Only Avdeyenko managed to arch over 2,38, for a new Games record and gold medal, on his second try. He then took one attempt at 2,40,

before asking for the height to be raised to 2,44, at which he was unsuccessful with his further two jumps. Conway gained the silver on the count-back rule, while Povarnitsyn and Sjoberg were equal third for the bronze.

Had the firm favourite in the **pole vault**, Sergei Bubka of Russia, failed to have won the supreme title, it would have come as a great surprise. The Russians, French and Americans, were all out in full force in the final, with three competitors each, but it was the Russians who completely dominated the proceedings. Russia's Grigoriy Yegorov cleared 5,80 for the Olympic record and went out at 5,90, which gave him the bronze medal. His compatriot, Radion Gataulin, in his third attempt, went over 5,85 for another record, which was good enough for the silver medal. The winner of the event, Bubka, had two failures at 5,90 for the gold and Olympic record, before clearing with 20 centimetres to spare. He then asked for the bar to be raised to 6,10 in an attempt on his world record, but interruptions by two medal presentations left him off the boil and he declined to jump.

Interest in the **long jump** was stoked up by the expected duel between the reigning champion, Carl Lewis and

Mark Shearman

Florence Griffith-Joyner

Perfectly relaxed in her running, Florence has well earned the nick-name "Flo Jo". Born on 21 December 1959 and one of 11 children, she was brought up in a tough area of Los Angeles, a background that has given her determination and grit.

A smart runner right from the age of seven, Florence took to sprinting seriously at college in 1978 and three years later entered the international scene, gaining second place in the world Cup 200.

In 1983 she came fourth in the world championships and the Los Angeles Olympics the following year saw her win a silver medal for the 200. Unfortunately, the next two season were on a lower note; only third in the Grand Prix in 1985 and nearly giving up a year later.

The turning point came in 1987, when coach Bob Kersee inspired her to sprint the 100 in 10·96 and the 200, at the world championships for second place, in 21·96, where she wore a one-piece ski suit. Florence was truly transformed and at the American trials she tore to a fantastic world record 100 in 10·49, before running the 200 in 21·77. Her feats in the Seoul Olympics were superb; the 100 in 10·54 and a 200 world record in 21·34, with a further gold and silver for the two relays.

fellow American Larry Myricks, whose superb jumping had landed him within two centimetres of Lewis in the American trials. The preliminaries saw the American third string, Mike Powell leap 8,34, with Myricks on 8,19. In round one of the final, Powell led off with a distance of 8,23 and Myricks recorded 8,14. The last jumper was Lewis, who hitch-kicked his way to 8,41 and in his next trial cut the sand at 8,56, with Myricks improving to 8,27. Things hotted up in the third round when Powell extended himself to a lifetime best of 8,49, but Lewis, now under threat, soared to 8,72 with his fourth jump. Myricks was also fired up and with his fifth effort he launched himself to the 8,70's, but his take-off foot was well over the mark and he had to settle for bronze, with Powell taking the silver and Lewis a unique gold; the only man ever to retain a long jump title.

The big guns in the **triple jump** were Willie Banks of America, the world record holder, who had leapt beyond his universal record in the American trials, with a windy 18,20 and Christov Markov of Bulgaria, the European record holder and current world champion. Always a threat were a clutch of Russian jumpers, Igor Lapshin, 17,37, Alek Kovalenko 17,24 and Oleg Protsenko 17,00, who led the qualifiers and were ever ready to grab a few medals if the chance arose. In the final, Ivan Slanar of Czechoslovakia took the lead with 16,58, but was quickly displaced by Lapshin with 16,75, then Kovalenko at 17,42, for a new Olympic record. Protsenko's first jump

was not far behind with 17,38, but Markov attacked the ground so vigorously that he bounded to 17,61 for the Olympic record and gold medal. In the sixth and final round, Lapshin moved into the silver position with 17,52, while bronze medallist Kovalenko fouled a 17,80 effort. Banks, the pre-Games favourite, could only manage 17,03 and was beaten into sixth position by his American team-mate, Charlie Simpkins.

Earlier in the year, East Germany's Ulf Timmermann had set a new world record of 23,06 in the **shot put**. His closest rivals were fellow countryman Udo Beyer, America's up-and-coming star, Randy Barnes and the world and European champion, Werner Guenthoer from Switzerland. In the preliminaries, Timmermann came dangerously close to the Olympic record with 21,27. However, the first round of competition proper soon saw the record tumble. Guenthoer threw 21,45, only to be overtaken by Timmermann at 22,02, who then raised it to 22,16 in the third round and to 22,29 in the fifth. Meanwhile, Guenthoer had improved to 21,99 and Beyer recorded 21,40. An unexpected turn of events came in the final round when Barnes finally perfected his rotational throwing technique and launched the shot out to 22,39. Unperturbed, the 1,98 metre tall, Timmermann, dug deep with his final throw and responded with a gold medal winning 22,47, the sixth record of the event. Barnes took the silver and Guenthoer the bronze.

World record holder for the **discus throw**, Juergen

Portugal's Rosa Mota (460) leaves the stadium on her golden way in the women's marathon, with Lisa Martin (17), Australia's silver girl, in close attendance.   Mark Shearman

Mark Shearman

Tatyana Samolenko

Samolenko's greatest forte has been her tactical racing brain, coupled with an excellent sprint finish. She was born in Sekretarka, near Orenburg, Russia, on 12 August 1961, as Tatyana Khamitova and took seriously to middle distance running at the age of 16.

Tatyanaya's progress was slow over both the 800 and 1500, until after her marriage, when she became the Russian champion over the latter distance in 1986 and finished second in the 1500 and fifth in the 3000 at the European championships.

However, 1987 was a great year, with a silver in the world indoor 1500, followed by gold in the 3000. That same year she also won the world Cup 1500 and the European Cup 800. It was the world championships that made her favourite for the Olympics, where she won as she pleased in both the 1500 and 3000, using her, by now, famous sprint finish.

In the Seoul Olympic Games, 1500, Rumania's Ivan ran away from her to win and she was pipped by a compatriot for the silver, but she triumphed in the 3000, where her strength and kick finish gave her the gold.

Schult of East Germany, had become a most constant competitor and was expected to be a tough nut to beat, especially in still air conditions prevailing. The preliminaries saw another excellent thrower, West German Ralf Danneberg, chuck 65,70, to lead the qualifiers. In the final, Schult commenced with an Olympic record of 68,82, which was to prove his gold medal throw, even though he had two others just short of his best at 68,18 and 68,26. Romas Ubartas of Russia, a most steady discus man, threw 66,86, before launching 67,48 with his final effort, to gain the silver. The bronze medal was won by Danneberg, who made 67,38 with his fifth throw.

Eight years previously, Yuri Sedykh, Yuri Tamm and Sergei Litvinov had won the three Olympic medals for Russia in the **hammer throw**. In 1984 they were denied defending their titles, but uniquely they came back to Seoul and all but duplicated their earlier feat. The challenge from up and coming throwers like East Germany's Ralf Haber and West Germany's Heinz Weis did not materialise and Litvinov was the best of the qualifiers with 81,24, a little short of the Olympic record. The first round of the final saw Tamm lead off with 80,94, but several throws later the fast turning Litvinov unleashed a mighty 84,76, for a new Games record, while Sedykh replied with a modest 80,96. In the next round, Tamm upped his best to 81,16, to win the bronze medal and Sedykh improved to 83,62, which he subsequently increased to 83,76 for the silver. But in the fifth round, Litvinov hurled his missile to 84,80 for the gold, thus reversing his 1980 placing with Sedykh.

This was the first **javelin throwing** competition at an Olympic Games for which the new specification spear, with its forward centre of gravity, had been used. Prior to Seoul, Jan Zelezny of Czechoslvakia, had set the world record of 87,66 with the new javelin, against 104,80 for the old and was tipped to take the gold medal. And it was Zelezny, who zoomed the javelin with his fast arm to an Olympic record of 85,90, in the preliminaries. The first round of the final saw Finland's Seppo Raty throw 80,00, but this was quickly superseded by Gerald Weiss of East Germany with 80,66. Towards the end of the round, Russia's Viktor Yesyukov took the lead with 81,42 and with the very next attempt, Tapio Korjus of Finland,

arced his spear to 82,74. In the second round both Yesyukov and Zelezny reached 82,32, but Raty regained the lead with his third effort of 83,26, which eventually gained him the bronze. This inspired Zelenzy to throw 83,46 in the fourth and 84,12 in the last round. However, Korjus produced his gold medal effort of 84,28 with his final fling, leaving Zelezny with the silver, while Klaus Tafelmeier of West Germany improved from sixth to fourth, his last throw sailing out to 82,72.

Daley Thompson of Britain was shooting for his third consecutive **decathlon** Olympic gold, but his fitness was in question. Shortly before the start of the competition, West Germany's Siggy Wentz had to drop out through an injury and his fellow West Germany Jurgen Hingsen, another of Thompson's rivals, suffered three false starts in the 100m and withdrew. Thompson powered to 10·62 in his heat and led the competition, but in the long jump Christian Plaziat of France leapt 7,62 to Thompson's 7,38 and took the lead. Christian Schenk of East Germany

Sergei Bubka

There are few athletes who can lay claim to an unbeaten championship record once reaching top international class, but Sergei Bubka is one of them. He was born in Donyetsk, Russia, on 4 December 1963 and with an elder brother, now a 5,85 vaulter, he took up pole vaulting when a mere 11 years old.

His first international experience was at the European junior championships, 1981, where he disappointed by placing equal seventh. Two years later, however, he surprised many when winning the world title and in 1984 began his onslaught on the world records, both indoor and out. Sergei raised the indoor mark three times and the outdoor four, but he missed out on the Los Angeles Olympics. The next season saw him triumph in the world indoor championships and later he topped the magic 6,00. In 1986 he took the European title, won the IAAF Grand Prix, improved his indoor record four times to 5,95 and also pushed the outdoor ceiling up to 6,01.

The following year was just as astonishing, as he won the world indoor title and twice improved the under-cover record to 5,87, before switching outdoors, where he upped his universal mark to 6,03. Yet again this year, Sergei was to the fore, winning the Seoul Olympic vault and posting a new world standard with 6,06. He is now shooting for 6,10 (20 feet).

then took charge and ended the first day with 4,470 points, from Plaziat 4,375 and Thompson 4,332, who was nursing an injured leg. Schenk's performances were 11·25 for the 100, 7,43 long jump, 15,48 shot, a superb 2,27 high jump and a 48·90 400. On the second day, the East German Torsten Voss became the danger to Schenk, but the latter held his lead with marks of 15·13 in the 110 hurdles, 49,28 discus, 4,70 vault, 61,32 javelin and 4-28·95 1,500, to total 8,488 points and win the gold medal. Voss took the silver with 8,399 and Daley Thompson, who was lying third with just the 1,500 to go, was beaten out of a medal position when Canada's Dave Steen ran a lifetime best and took the bronze with 8,328 to the Englishman's 8,306.

Women's Events

Every so often there appears a special athlete who hoists standards to a new high level. Florence Griffith-Joyner of America, affectionally known as "Flo Jo", is one such lady. Griffith-Joyner in the very first round of the **100 metres** lowered the Olympic record from 10·97 to 10·88, a time equalled by fellow American Evelyn Ashford in the second round, where Griffith-Joyner clocked a scintillating 10·62. Following this, she coasted to a 10·70 semi-final before making her supreme effort in the final. From the gun, there were four sprinters leading the field, Griffith-Joyner, fellow American Gwen Torrence, Bulgaria's Anelia Vetchernikova and Heike Drechsler from East Germany. At the half-way stage, the race was still close, with Griffith-Joyner leading by 30 centimetres from Vetchernikova and Torrence, a shade further behind. Increasing her lead at ever stride, Griffith-Joyner strode to victory, with a big grin on her face, in the startling time of 10·54, for yet another Olympic record. Three metres behind, Ashford came through to clock 10·83, holding off Drechsler in 10·85.

Before bursting upon the world as the fastest woman over 100 metres, Florence Griffith-Joyner had been a **200 metres** specialist and with her new found speed over the shorter distance, the world record was expected to go. First she obliged with an Olympic record of 21·76 in the second round and then, in the semi-finals, she broke the world record with 21·56. In the final, however, it was the long-legged Grace Jackson of Jamaica who was quickest out of her blocks, but off the bend, Griffith-Joyner was in front, with Jackson less than a metre behind and East Germany's Silke Moeller third. With swift, but rangy strides, Griffith-Joyner just flowed away from the opposition to hit the electric beam in 21·34, a new world and Olympic record. Jackson crossed the line, a comfortable second in 21·72, while Merlene Ottey of Jamaica looked to have the third spot, but eased up a few yards from the line, letting East Germany's Heike Drechsler in for the bronze with 21·95.

Two possible medal contenders were not competing in the **400 metres**, Russia's Aelita Yurchenko and Cuba's Anna Quirot. And another favourite, East Germany's Kirsten Emmelmann went out in the semi-final. After a false start by Valerie Brisco-Hooks, the defending champion, the field got away to a swift start with Australia's Denise Howard leading at 200 in 23·4. The Soviets, Olga Bryzgina and Olga Nazarova, together with East Germany's Petra Mueller and Brisco-Hooks, were close up on the leader. Coming into the final straight, Bryzgina was forging the way home, one metre ahead of Nazarova and stretched her lead to win in a new Olympic record time of 48·65. Mueller came with a late rush to secure the silver medal in 49·45, with Nazarova the bronze in 49·90.

As is becoming usual, the two East German **800 metres** runners, Christine Wachtel and Sigrun Wodars, peaked to perfection for the premier race of the calendar. The fancied Russian, Nadezhda Olizarenko, went out in the semi-finals, but her dangerous compatriot, Inna Yevseyeva, lined up for the final race. From the gun, Wachtel and Wodars went into the lead and hotted up the pace, with the latter taking the bell in a fast 56·3. At 500 metres they led from Yevseyeva, Slobodanka Colovic of Yugoslavia and America's Kim Gallagher, with the other three contestants off the pace. Wachtel struck with 200 to go, but Wodars timed her spurt perfectly to wrest the gold from her fellow countrywomen in 1-56·10 to 1-56·64, while Gallagher closed rapidly to pick up the bronze medal in 1-56·91.

In a slowish **1,500 metres** race, Tatyana Samolenko of Russia was regarded as having a finishing sprint of no equal, but the final did not turn out that way. Into the lead from the gun went the rising star, Paula Ivan of Rumania, followed closely by America's Mary Decker-Slaney. In the second lap, Ivan started to open up a gap which grew,

Mark Shearman

Jackie Joyner-Kersee

Jackie is one of the super women athletes and in the heptathlon she is head and shoulders above everyone else at present. Born in East St Louis, Illinois, on 3 March 1962, she stands 1,78 tall and weighs 70kg.

Back in 1974 she started out as a long jumper and had gained national prominence by 1982, with long jump wins in the Track Athletic Congress and National Collegiate championships. By this time Jackie had already taken up the heptathlon and two years later she competed in the world championships.

She finally hit the big time in 1984, when runner-up in the Olympic heptathlon and fifth in the long jump. In 1985 she won the IAAF Grand Prix competition and the following year married her coach Bob Kersee, while blossoming in the heptathlon, with two world records.

Nineteen eighty-seven was even better, with a double first at the world championships in the long jump and heptathlon, breaking the world record in the former. Jackie duplicated her double in the 1988 Olympics and also set two heptathlon world records during the course of the year. Her next ambition is to attack the world 400 metres hurdles record.

The eventual winner, Rumania's Paula Ivan (466), sets a furious pace in the women's 1,500 metres, with compatriot Doina Melinte (467), Mary Decker-Slaney of the USA (496) and Russia's Tatyana Samolenko (548), hanging on.

Mark Shearman

stride by stride, leaving compatriot Doina Melinte to head the chasing group. In the third lap, Samolenko took up the chase, followed by Melinte, East Germany's Andrea Hahmann and Britain's Chris Cahill. With 200 to go, Ivan was more than 60 metres ahead and she won comfortably in a new Olympic record time of 3-53·96, with splits of 62·52, 63·24, 62·49 and 45·71. Meanwhile, Samolenko was leading a charge along the finishing straight, with Cahill at her heels and these two looked likely medallists, until in a startling burst of speed, Russia's Lailoute Baikauskaite snatched the silver, in 4-00·24. Samolenklo, who recorded 4-00·30, had to be satisfied with the bronze and Cahill was a creditable fourth in 4-00·64.

There were no clear favourites for the **3,000 metres**, but Tatyana Samolenko of Russia, Mary Decker-Slaney of America and Maricica Puica of Rumania, were considered possibilities. Strangely, Puica dropped out of her semi-final heat, 200 metres before the finish, while among the leaders. Decker-Slaney, as usual, took up her front running stance in the final and led through 400 in 64·0, with the pack scuttling behind her. Shortly after two kilometres, America's Vicki Huber went to the front, followed by Yvonne Murray of Britain and Rumania's Paula Ivan. With 450 to go, Murray made a break for home, which was covered by Ivan and Samolenko and 200 metres further on, both girls strode past the British girl, who gamely stuck to her task. Samolenko then timed her sprint to a nicety from 50 metres out and won in an Olympic record time of 8-26·53, from Ivan 8-27·15 and Murray 8-29·02.

A new event to the Olympic programme, the **10,000 metres** for women, was expected to by won by Ingrid Kristiansen of Norway, who held the world record. The final saw Lyudmila Matveyeva of Russia lead through the first lap in 3-09·79 and one kilometre in 9-09·8. By two kilometres, Kristiansen was in front, hotting up the pace with a 69·0 lap. She was followed by East Germany's Kathrin Ullrich, then a small gap, and Britain's Liz McColgan, the Russians Olga Bondarenko and Yelena Zhupieva, with the rest off the pace. After seven laps, Kristiansen dropped out in agony with an injured foot and Ullrich built up a 40 metres lead. But in lap 12, McColgan and the two Russians caught up with Ullrich and the 5,000 was passed in 15-37·89. McColgan pressed on and Ullrich was dropped after ten more laps, followed by Zhupieva, with three to go. Bondarenko sprinted the final 200 to win in 31-05·21, for an inaugural Olympic record, while McColgan took the silver in 31-08·44 and Zhupieva the bronze with 31-19·82.

Top contenders for the **marathon** were the silver and bronze winners from 1984, Norway's Grete Waitz and Portugal's Rosa Mota, together with Katrin Doerre of East Germany and Lisa Martin from Australia, all proven sub 2:26-00 marathon runners. The world's fastest, Ingrid Kristiansen, had selected to concentrate on the 10,000 track event and it was without her that 72 runners representing 40 nations, left the stadium, led by Martin. Soon, Waitz, Mota and Martin were spearheading the leading group, which was reduced to 18 at 18km. By the half-way stage, which was passed in 1:12-40, there were only 12 left in contention and it was here that Mota made several determined efforts to drop the field. Martin, Russia's Tatyna Polovinskaya and Doerre held on, but Waitz dropped back and retired with badly strained legs around 30km. At 37km, Polovinskaya found the pace too hot and Mota gradually drew away to win in 2:25-40, from Martin 2:25-53 and Doerre 2:26-21.

The **100 metres hurdles** was considered to be a duel between the two Bulgarians, Ginka Zagorcheva, the current world record holder, and Yordanka Donkova, who had a world mark pending. Unfortunately, the former dropped out in the first round, but Donkova set a new Olympic record of 12·47 in the second trials. After a false start, East Germany's Cornelia Oschkenat was the quickest away, with Julie Rocheleau of Canada and Donkova, leaving West Germany's Claudia Zaczkiewicz a trifle behind. At the third hurdle, Donkova was clear of the rest and at the fifth, another East German, Siebert, was second, with Zaczkiewicz and Oschkenat following in that order. Donkova's winning time of 12·38 set a new Olympic record, while Siebert took the silver with 12·61 and Zazckiewicz the bronze with 12·75, although it was a close run thing with Russia's Natalya Grigorieva gaining fast.

On past performances Sabine Busch of East Germany was the favourite for the **400 metres hurdles**, but her early season form had not been outstanding. In the first round heats, Ellen Fiedler of East Germany swept away the old record with a snappy 54·58 timing, but Australia's Debbie Flintoff-King later put this mark to shame with 54·00. In the final, Russia's Tatyana Ledovskaya shot out of her blocks to reach the first hurdle one metre up on the rest of the field, which she increased to two metres on entering the finishing stretch in front of Fiedler and Busch, while Flintoff-King was a metre or so further back. The Australian dug deep. With 50 metres to go, she was in second position, hauling Ledovskaya back stride by stride and at the tape they appeared to arrive in a dead heat. Flintoff-King was announced the victor in the new Olympic record time of 53·17, from Ledovskaya 53·18 and Fiedler third with 53·63.

Russia was quickest in the preliminaries of the **4 × 100 metres relay** with 42·01 and along with East Germany and America, were expected to take the medals. Alice Brown, for the United States, ran a swift first leg to lead by nearly two metres over East Germany and Russia, but a poor exchange to Sheila Echols lost most of that advantage. An excellent second baton pass by East Germany and they were neck and neck with America, with Russia only half a metre behind. On the third leg, America's Florence Griffith-Joyner built up a lead, but then fumbled when handing over to Evelyn Ashford, while East Germany streaked away with Russia on her shoulder. Ashford then pulled back a three metre deficit and as she drew level with her rivals, the Russian girl pulled a muscle, allowing America home first in 41·98 and East Germany second in 42·09. Russia were lucky to salvage the bronze medal with 42·75 from a fast closing West Germany.

East Germany had long been superior in the **4 × 400 metres relay**, but her leading athletes had retired and Russia took on the roll as favourites. For some strange reason, Spain was not allowed to compete in the heats, but were offered an apology. The final saw Russia's Tatyana Ledovskaya build up a useful lead over America during the first lap, which Olga Nazarova then extended in the second, before handing over to Maria Pigigina. It was in this leg that America's Valerie Brisco-Hooks ran 48·4, bringing the States within three metres of Russia. The last lap runners were Olga Brygina, for Russia, and Florence Griffith-Joyner, representing America, and they both clocked 48·1. Russia won in a new world and Olympic record of 3-15·18, to America's 3-15·51, with the bronze going to East Germany 3-18·29, who ran third all the way.

Bulgaria was highly confident that their world champion and record holder in the **high jump**, would have no difficulty in taking the Olympic title. Stefka Kostadinova commenced jumping at 1,80 and cleared all the heights up to and including 2,01, at her first attempt. America's Louise Ritter did likewise, but both failed three times at 2,03. The rules now called for a fourth attempt at 2,03 before lowering of the bar began. And it was Kostadinova who jumped first and failed, while Ritter cleared for the gold medal and Olympic record. Kostadinova took the silver with 2,01, while the bronze position was more clear cut, with only Russia's Tamara Bykova surmounting 1,99.

Olga Bondarenko of the USSR, makes history, when winning the first ever women's 10,000 metres from Britain's Liz McColgan. Mark Shearman

There were four luminaries in the **long jump**, Galina Chistyakova of Russia, the new world record holder, her compatriot, Yelena Belevskaya, East Germany's Heike Drechsler and Jackie Joyner-Kersee from America. Belevskaya made a good start in the preliminaries when she jumped 7,06 to equal the Olympic record. In the first round of the final, first Drechsler leapt 6,92, then Joyner-Kersee 7,00 and finally Chistyakova, using a simple sail technique, landed at 7,11 for a new Games best. Drechsler next jumped 7,18 to secure the lead, which she increased to 7,22. Then Joyner-Kersee moved into second place with a 7,16 leap, before her fifth effort lifted the gold medal, with an Olympic record of 7,40.

Drechsler's 7,22 took silver and Chistyakova gained the bronze with 7,11, while Belevskaya logged 7,04 for fourth spot.

It was a forgone conclusion that Russia's world record holder in the **shot put**, Natalya Lisovskaya, would win the Olympic gold, but the lesser medals were up for grabs. Among the most likely contenders were two Chinese, Meisu Li and Zhihong Huang. West German's Claudia Losch with 20,39, headed the qualifiers, but it was Lisovskaya who took charge in the finals, by first throwing 21,69, then 21,74 and finally 22,24, for the gold medal. Although six other weight-girls exceeded 20 metres, only two broke the 21 metres barrier. East Germany's Kathrin Neimke won the silver medal on her last throw, with 21,07 and China's Li's put of 21,06, was only one centimetre less, for the bronze award.

Rumania's Daniela Costain was the only world class **discus thrower** missing from the event and the fight for gold was expected to be between the reigning world champion, Martina Hellmann of East Germany and her compatriot, Gabrielle Reinsch, who had set a new world record. The competition proper started with a bang as Hellmann soared the discus out to a new Olympic record of 71,84 and in the fourth round, improved to 72,30 for gold. Six other throwers were peppering 66 metres with their early attempts, until in the fifth round, East Germany's Diana Gansky, unleased a 71,88 metre heave to claim the silver spot. The old campainer, Tsvetanka Khristova of Bulgaria, with her fifth attempt, threw 69,74 for the bronze.

Sporting fans were looking forward to another titanic **javelin throw**ing battle between East Germany's Petra Felke and Britain's Fatima Whitbread, two of the greatest spear throwers ever seen. In the lead-up to the Games, Felke had set the world alight with the first ever 80 metre throw, while Whitbread was nursing an injury and Tina Lillak of Finland, a former world record holder, got herself back into form. Unfortunately, Lillak did not even survive the qualifying round, where Whitbread produced the best throw of 68,44. Beate Koch of East Germany threw 67,30 in the first round of the final, but this was soon eclipsed by Felke with an Olympic record of 72,62, which she improved to 74,68 following her next effort to take the gold medal. Whitbread secured second place in this round with 67,46, improving to 67,82 in the fifth and finally 70,32, in a competition fraught with swirling wind conditions. Koch took home the bronze medal with her early throw.

Barring injury, there was nobody going to stop Jackie Joyner-Kersee winning the **heptathlon**. Three times she had raised the world record and was now enjoying a 400 points advantage over her nearest competitor, Anke Behmer of East Germany. Joyner-Kersee led the competition from start to finish, beginning with a fast 100 metres hurdles in 12·69, followed by a 1,86 high jump, 15,80 shot and a speedy 200 in 22·56. Only East Germany's Sabine John bettered any of her marks on the first day, with a shot put of 16,23. Joyner-Kersee led after four events with 4,264 points, followed by John 4,083 and Behmer 3,986. The second day saw Joyner-Kersee long jump 7,27, which exceeded the Olympic record in the individual event. Then she threw 45,66 in the javelin against 47,50 by Switzerland's Corinne Schneider. Behmer set a fast pace in 800, recording 2-04·20, but Joyner-Kersee hung on to record a personal best of 2-08·51 and total 7,291 points for a new world and Olympic record. John won the silver with 6,897 and Behmer's 6,858 was good enough for the bronze.

MALES

COMPETITOR	COUNTRY CODE	EVENT	ROUND	HEAT	PLACE	TIME & DISTANCE	MEDAL
Abbas, M.	LEB	400m	1	5	7	51·29	
		800m	1	5	7	1-53·76	
Aboobakur, A.R.	MLD	4×100m relay	1	1	7	44·31	
Abdenouz, R.	ALG	800m	1	9	4	1-47·97	
			2	1	4	1-46·97	
			SF	2	7	1-45·95	
Abdillahi, T.	DJI	10000m	1	2	18	30-05·53	
Abellan, A.	ESP	Marathon	F		64	2:31-10	
Aboubacar, I.	NGR	Marathon	F		59	2:28-15	
Aboud, F.	LBA	Triple jump	Q		DNQ	5,13	
Abrantes, Antonio	POR	800m	1	3	4	1-49·01	
		4×400m relay	1	2	3	3-07·75	
			SF	1	7	3-07·75	
Abrantes, Arnaldo	POR	4×100m relay	1	4	3	39·61	
			SF	2	DIS		
Abshire, B.	USA	3000m steeplechase	1	3	4	8-36·56	
			SF	2	9	8-27·78	
Achouch, M.	EGY	Shot put	Q		DNQ	18,94	
Adam, H.	MEX	4×100m relay	1	4	4	40·31	
Adams, L.	STV	Triple jump	Q		DNQ	14,73	
Adamson, D.	JAM	Marathon	F		84	2:47-57	
Adani, A.-H.	SOM	5000m	1	1	13	14-37·98	
Aden, H.-Y.	DJI	1500m	1	1	12	3-51·56	
Adeniken, O.	NGR	100m	1	9	3	10·56	
			2	4	2	10·30	
			SF	1	6	10·33	
		200m	1	10	3	20·77	
			2	4	3	20·92	
			SF	2	6	20·67	
		4×100m relay	SF	1	6	39·05	
Adeyanju, I.	NGR	100m	1	11	2	10·45	
			2	5	3	10·32	
			SF	2	7	10·60	
		200m	1	2	3	21·10	
			2	5	6	21·01	
		4×100m relay	SF	1	6	39·05	
Afzal, M.	PAK	100m	1	7	6	10·91	
		200m	1	3	6	21·89	
		4×100m relay	1	3	6	3-08·54	
Agostinho, P.	POR	100m	1	6	DNF		
		4×100m relay	1	4	3	39·61	
			SF	2	DIS		
Aguilar, D.	CHI	Marathon	F		DNF		
Ahmad, B.	PAK	4×400m relay	1	3	6	3-08·54	
Ahmed, A.	LBA	200m	1	8	7	22·11	
		400m	1	5	5	48·89	
Akabusi, K.	GBR	400m hurdles	1	4	2	49·62	
			SF	1	4	49·22	
			F		6	48·69	
		4×400m relay	SF	1	3	3-04·60	
			F		5	3-02·00	
Akogyiram, E.	GHA	4×100m relay	1	2	3	39·13	
			SF	2	5	39·46	
Akonay, B.	TAN	10000m	1	1	15	29-19·06	
Akutsu, K.	JPN	10000m	1	1	8	28-16·43	
			F		14	28-09·70	
Al-Alawyat, A.-A.	ARS	Javelin throw	Q		DNQ	56,32	
Alam, A.	BAN	200m	1	1	8	22·52	
Alam, M.S.	BAN	4×100m relay	1	4	6	41·78	
Alassane Ousseni	BEN	200m	1	4	4	21·74	
		4×100m relay	1	4	5	41·52	
Albakheet, W.	KUW	Hammer throw	Q		DNQ	63,86	
Albentosa, J.-M.	ESP	10000m	1	1	DNF		
Al-Bishi, M.	ARS	100m	1	1	7	10·85	
		200m	1	3	7	22·09	
Al-Bulushi, M.	OMA	800m	1	1	7	1-51·03	
		4×400m relay	1	1	7	3-12·89	
Alcalde, M.	ESP	50k walk	F		25	3:59-13	
Al-Doseri, A.	BHR	3000m steeplechase	1	3	11	9-10·85	
Al-Dossary, Y.	ARS	110m hurdles	1	3	6	15·03	
Al-Dousari, H.	ARS	1500m	1	4	9	3-51·53	
		3000m steeplechase	1	3	10	8-45·24	
			SF	2	12	8-44·22	
Aldowaila, J.	KUW	400m hurdles	1	1	6	51·87	
Al-Habsi, S.	OMA	400m	1	6	5	48·30	
		4×400m relay	1	1	7	3-12·89	
Alharazi, A.	PRY	5000m	1	2	16	14-49·25	
Alhussein, H.	SYR	Javelin throw	Q		DNQ	63,34	
Ali, Y.	NGR	Long jump	Q		DNQ	7,73	
Ali Shah, H.	PAK	Triple jump	Q		DNQ	14,88	
Al-Khalidi, A.	OMA	100m	1	8	5	10·90	
		200m	1	6	6	21·82	
		4×400m relay	1	1	7	3-12·89	
Alkhudhur, Z.	KUW	110m hurdles	1	3	5	14·44	
			2	2	8	14·56	

COMPETITOR	COUNTRY CODE	EVENT	ROUND	HEAT	PLACE	TIME & DISTANCE	MEDAL
Al-Malki, M.-A.	OMA	400m	1	3	1	46·79	
			2	3	3	45·02	
			SF	2	3	44·69	
			F		8	45·03	
		4×400m relay	1	1	7	3-12·89	
Alonso, J.	ESP	400m hurdles	1	3	3	50·21	
			SF	1	6	49·57	
Alqahtani, H.	ARS	400m	1	4	6	48·53	
		800m	1	2	DIS		
Al-Semeer, A.	OMA	Marathon	F		83	2:46-59	
Altun, A.	TUR	Marathon	F		71	2:37-44	
Alyouhah, M.	KUW	Triple jump	Q		DNQ	15,72	
Ambowode, A.	CAF	Marathon	F		42	2:23-52	
Amike, H.	NGR	4×400m relay	1	3	3	3-06·59	
			SF	2	4	3-01·13	
			F		7	3-02·50	
Amores, J.	CRC	Marathon	F		45	2:24-49	
Andersen, E.	NOR	20k walk	F		22	1:22-30	
		50k walk	F		DNF		
Andersen, G.	NOR	Shot put	F		10	19,91	
Andrade, H.	MEX	50k walk	F		DIS		
Andrei, A.	ITA	Shot put	F		7	20,36	
Antibo, S.	ITA	5000m	1	2	2	13-58·08	
			SF	1	8	13-25·64	
		10000m	1	1	4	28-09·35	
			F		2	27-23·55	S
Anton, A.	ESP	5000m	1	2	7	13-58·59	
			SF	2	12	13-39·13	
Aoto, S.	JPN	4×100m relay	1	3	3	39·70	
			SF	1	5	38·90	
Aouita, S.	MAR	800m	1	5	1	1-49·67	
			2	3	1	1-45·24	
			SF	2	2	1-44·79	
			F		3	1-44·06	B
		1500m	1	2	4	3-42·18	
			SF	2	DNS		
Apostolov, V.	BUL	Hammer throw	Q		DNQ	71,10	
Arellano, R.	PAR	Discus throw	Q		DNQ	50,90	
Arop, J.	UGA	Javelin throw	Q		DNQ	69,10	
Arpin, P.	FRA	5000m	1	1	8	13-48·03	
			SF	2	7	13-24·82	
			F		14	14-13·19	
		10000m	1	2	6	28-25·56	
			F		7	27-39·36	
Arques, J.	ESP	100m	1	13	2	10·44	
			2	3	5	10·43	
		4×100m relay	1	3	DNF		
Ashurst, A.	GBR	Pole vault	Q		DNQ	0	
Asif, I.	MLD	100m	1	12	8	11.49	
		200m	1	6	8	23.17	
		4×100m relay	1	1	7	44.31	
Asinga, T.	SUR	100m	1	7	DIS		
Atkins, H.	BAR	100m	1	3	8	11·01	
		200m	1	5	5	21·98	
Atkinson, J.	USA	1500m	1	3	2	3-38·33	
			SF	1	5	3-39·12	
			F		10	3-40·80	
Avdeyenko, G.	URS	High jump	F		1	2,38*	G
Babapur, N.	IRN	Marathon	F		93	3:00-20	
Baccouche, F.	TUN	3000m steeplechase	1	3	7	8-38·67	
			SF	2	10	8-31·36	
Bagyula, I.	HUN	Pole vault	F		7	5,60	
Bah, A.	GUI	Marathon	F		96	3:06-27	
Baker, S.	AUS	20k walk	F		11	1:21-47	
		50k walk	F		6	3:44-07	
Bakos, G.	HUN	110m hurdles	1	6	4	13.94	
			2	3	8	18.02	
		4×100m relay	1	4	1	39.12	
			SF	2	3	38.84	
			F		8	39.19	
Ballard, R.	AUS	4×400m relay	1	1	4	3-05·93	
			SF	1	4	3-06·63	
			F		6	3-02·00	
Banks, W.	USA	Triple jump	F		6	17,03	
Barbosa, J.-L.	BRA	800m	1	8	2	1-46·32	
			2	2	3	1-46·20	
			SF	2	3	1-44·99	
			F		6	1-45·39	
		1500m	1	1	8	3-44·46	
Barnes, R.	USA	Shot put	F		2	22,39	S
Barr, O.	GUY	800m	1	9	7	1-55·95	
Barreto, M.	MEX	5000m	1	3	14	13-45·82	
			SF	1	14	13-53·93	
		10000m	1	2	14	29-18·14	
Barrios, A.	MEX	5000m	1	1	9	13-59·04	
		10000m	1	1	3	28-08·63	
			F		5	27-39·32	

COMPETITOR	COUNTRY CODE	EVENT	ROUND	HEAT	PLACE	TIME & DISTANCE	MEDAL
Barroso, L.	POR	200m	1	9	2	21·31	
			2	3	4	20·81	
		4×100m relay	1	4	3	39·61	
			SF	2	DIS		
Baskin, T.	USA	800m	1	5	4	1-50·38	
Basnyat, K.	NEP	Marathon	F		85	2:47·57	
Baumann, D.	GER	5000m	1	2	6	13-58·46	
			SF	1	3	13-22·71	
			F		2	13-15·52	S
Bednarek, J.	POL	50k walk	F		24	3:58-31	
Begeo, H.	PHI	3000m steeplechase	1	1	8	8-46·60	
			SF	1	12	8-35·09	
Belisle, P.	BIZ	Marathon	F		98	3:14·02	
Belkessam, A.	ALG	800m	1	7	5	1-47·96	
			2	4	5	1-46·93	
Bell, E.	USA	Pole vault	F		4	5,70	
Bellucci, S.	ITA	50k walk	F		32	4:04-56	
Bemou, J.	CGO	400m	1	5	4	48·46	
Bennett, T.	GBR	400m	1	1	-	46·37	
			2	2	6	45·96	
		4×400m relay	1	1	2	3-04·18	
			SF	1	3	3-04·60	
			F		5	3-02·00	
Berger, A.	AUT	100m	1	12	2	10·40	
			2	4	3	10.34	
		200m	1	5	4	21·29	
			2	3	7	21·40	
Bermudez, M.	MEX	50k walk	F		15	3:49·22	
Bertimon, C.	FRA	Javelin throw	Q		DNQ	70,84	
Bessi, G.	MON	100m	1	10	8	11·55	
Beyer, U.	GDR	Shot put	F		4	21.40	
Bickford, B.	USA	10000m	1	1	7	28-16·16	
			F		18	29-09·74	
Bimiakoumou, A.	CGO	4×100m relay	1	2	6	41·26	
Binns, S.	GBR	10000m	1	1	13	28-52·83	
Birch, S.	LBR	100m	1	6	7	11.68	
Blagg, P.	GBR	50k walk	F		28	4:00-07	
Blake, A.	USA	110m hurdles	1	6	1	13·66	
			2	4	2	13.65	
			SF	1	2	13.52	
			F		8	13·96	
Blazek, P.	TCH	20k walk	F		15	1:22-39	
		50k walk	F		12	3:47-31	
Blondel, A.	FRA	Decathlon	F		6	8263	
Boateng, N.	GHA	4×100m relay	SF	2	5	39·46	
Bodenmueller, K.	AUT	Shot put	Q		DNQ	18,89	
Bogate, T.	NEP	Marathon	F		66	2:31-49	
Boileau, A.	CAN	Marathon	F		28	2:18-20	
Bole, M.	FIJ	100m	1	3	7	11·19	
		200m	1	4	5	22.44	
Bonfirm, J.	BRA	100m	1	9	5	10·75	
Bordin, G.	ITA	Marathon	F		1	2:10-32	G
Borglund, P.	SWE	Javelin throw	F		9	78,22	
Bouhalla, M.	ALG	20k walk	F		34	1:27-10	
Boutayeb, M.	MAR	10000m	1	2	1	28-17·61	
			F		1	27-21·46*	G
Boye, C.	SEN	800m	1	5	3	1-49·89	
			2	1	3	1-46·62	
			SF	2	6	1-45·93	
Bradstock, R.	GBR	Javelin throw	Q		DNQ	75,96	
Brahm, T.	USA	5000m	1	3	13	13-45·28	
			SF	2	15	14-04·12	
Brahmi, A.	ALG	3000m steeplechase	1	2	3	8-35·59	
			SF	2	1	8-15·54	
			F		13	8-26·68	
Brankovic, S.	YUG	400m	1	9	5	46·59	
		4×400m relay	1	2	2	3-05·62	
			SF	2	5	3-01·59	
Braun, P.	GER	800m	1	6	1	1-47·32	
			2	4	4	1-46·86	
			SF	1	8	1-47·43	
Bravo, A.	MEX	50k walk	F		33	4:08-08	
Brige, B.	FRA	Long jump	F		7	7,97	
Bright, T.	USA	Decathlon	F		7	8216	
Brown, C.	CAN	200m	1	7	5	21·45	
			2	5	7	21·18	
Brown, P.	GBR	4×400m relay	1	1	2	3-04·18	
			SF	1	3	3-04·60	
			F		5	3-02·00	
Browne, A.	ANT	400m	1	8	8	48.92	
		4×100m relay	1	3	6	41·13	
		4×400m relay	1	2	6	3-11·04	
Browne, J.	ANT	Long jump	Q		DNQ	7,67	
Brunner, W.	GER	Discus throw	Q		DNQ	57,50	
Bryzgin, V.	URS	4×100m relay	1	2	1	38·82	
			SF	2	1	38·55	
			F		1	38-19	G

COMPETITOR	COUNTRY CODE	EVENT	ROUND	HEAT	PLACE	TIME & DISTANCE	MEDAL
Bubka, S.	URS	Pole vault	F		1	5,90*	G
Buchel, M.	LIE	100m	1	2	8	11.21	
		200m	1	1	7	22·02	
Buckner, J.	GBR	5000m	1	3	10	13-43-69	
			SF	1	7	13-23·17	
			F		6	13-23·85	
Buckner, R.	JAM	110m hurdles	1	6	3	13·89	
			2	4	3	13.91	
			SF	1	8	13·98	
Bugar, I.	TCH	Discus throw	F		12	60,88	
Buncic, M.	USA	Discus throw	F		10	62,46	
Bunney, E.	GBR	4×100m relay	1	4	2	39·17	
			SF	1	2	38·52	
			F		2	38·28	S
Bura, J.	TAN	Marathon	F		43	2:24-17	
Burnett, H.	JAM	4×400m relay	1	2	1	3-04·00	
Cai J.	PRC	100m	1	8	2	10·55	
			2	6	8	10.83	
		4×100m relay	1	2	4	39·67	
Cai, S.	PRC	Marathon	F		26	2:17-54	
Calizaya, P.	BOL	10000m	1	1	18	30-35.01	
Callender, C.	GBR	4×100m relay	1	4	2	39·17	
Camacho, B.	BOL	Marathon	F		69	2:34-41	
Cameron, B.	JAM	400m	1	8	1	46·24	
			2	2	4	45·16	
			SF	1	4	44·50	
			F		6	44·94	
		4×400m relay	SF	2	3	3-00·94	
			F		2	3-00·30	S
Camp, B.	AUS	Marathon	F		41	2:23-49	
Campbell, D.	CAN	1500m	1	2	7	3-42·97	
Campbell, J.	NZL	Marathon	F		12	2:14-08	
Campbell, T.	USA	110m hurdles	1	2	1	13·45	
			2	2	1	14·47	
			SF	1	2	13·47	
			F		3	13·38	B
Canario, E.	POR	10000m	1	2	9-	28-43·02	
Cannon, R.	USA	Triple jump	Q		DNQ	15,69	
Canti, D.	SMR	100m	1	12	7	11·11	
Canto, E.	MEX	20k walk	F		DIS		
Carisan, S.	FRA	110m hurdles	1	1	2	13·96	
			2	1	3	13·61	
			SF	1	5	13·71	
Carlowitz, J.	GDR	400m	1	5	2	45·64	
			2	1	2	45·09	
			SF	1	6	45·08	
		4×400m relay	1	2	2	3-08·13	
			SF	2	1	3-00·60	
			F		4	3-01·13	
Carmona, R.	MEX	110m hurdles	1	6	7	15·24	
Carvalho, J.	ANG	Marathon	F		74	2:40-45	
Castillo, M.	DOM	110m hurdles	1	2	5	14·40	
			2	4	6	14·21	
Castro, Dionsio	POR	10000m	1	1	DNF		
Castro, Domingos	POR	5000m	1	1	3	13-47·87	
			SF	1	1	13-22·44	
			F		4	13-16·09	
Caterino, P.	POR	Marathon	F		DNF		
Cha, H.-S.	KOR	3000m steeplechase	1	2	8	8-59·82	
Chang, J.-K.	KOR	200m	1	2	4	21·27	
			2	4	5	21·35	
		4×100m relay	1	1	4	39·61	
Charadia, A.	ARG	Hammer throw	Q		DNQ	68,26	
Chen, Y.	PRC	Triple jump	Q		DNQ	16,25	
Chen, Z	PRC	Long jump	Q		DNQ	7,66	
Cheng, H.-F.	POR	100m	1	1	3	10·48	
			2	4	7	10·54	
		4×100m relay	1	1	5	40·40	
Cheruiyo, C.	KEN	5000m	1	3	2	13-43·11	
			SF	1	10	13-38·44	
Cheruiyot, K.	KEN	1500m	1	2	1	3-39·98	
			SF	1	1	3-38·09	
			F		7	3-37·94	
Chesire, J.	KEN	1500m	1	1	4	3-41·72	
			SF	1	6	3-39·17	
			F		11	3-40·82	
Chipalo, J.	ZAM	400m	1	5	6	48·97	
		4×400m relay	1	2	7	3-11·35	
Chmara, M.	POL	Pole vault	F		NP	0	
Cho, H.-W.	KOR	High jump	Q		DNQ	2,22	
Cho, J.-S.	KOR	1500m	1	3	11	3-45·63	
		4×400m relay	1	1	8	3-14·71	

COMPETITOR	COUNTRY CODE	EVENT	ROUND	HEAT	PLACE	TIME & DISTANCE	MEDAL
Christie, L.	GBR	100m	1	5	1	10·19	
			2	1	1	10·11	
			SF	2	2	10·11	
			F		2	9·97	S
		200m	1	7	1	21·05	
			2	3	1	20·49	
			SF	2	2	20·33	
			F		4	20·09	
		4×100m relay	SF	1	2	38·52	
			F		2	38·28	S
Chung, P.-H.	KOR	20k walk	F		46	1:32-23	
Clark, D.	AUS	400m	1	7	1	45·93	
			2	3	2	44·96	
			SF	1	3	44·38	
			F		4	44·55	
		4×400m relay	SF	1	4	3-06·63	
			F		6	3-02·49	
Coghlan, E.	IRL	5000m	1	3	7	13-43·48	
			SF	1	15	14-02·16	
Collet, P.	FRA	Pole vault	F		=5	5,70	
Conover, M.	USA	Marathon	F		DNF		
Consiglio, D.	CAN	1500m	1	4	13	3-55·31	
Conway, H.	USA	High jump	F		2	2,36	S
Cooper, B.	BAH	Discus throw	Q		DNQ	59,74	
Cordero, D.	PUR	400m hurdles	1	2	7	51·26	
Corgos, A.	ESP	Long jump	F		5	8,03	
Cornet, C.	ESP	400m	1	2	2	46·16	
			2	3	5	45·39	
Corre, J.-C.	FRA	20k walk	F		20	1:23-09	
Couto, F.	POR	5000m	1	2	8	13-58·72	
Cova, A.	ITA	10000m	1	2	10	28-43·84	
Crabb, S.	GBR	1500m	1	4	3	3-41·12	
			SF	2	9	3-39·55	
Cram, S.	GBR	800m	1	2	2	1-47·77	
			2	3	6	1-46·47	
		1500m	1	1	1	3-40·89	
			SF	1	2	3-38·30	
			F		4	3-36·24	
Crouser, B.	USA	Javelin throw	Q		DNQ	72,72	
Cruz, J.	BRA	800m	1	9	1	1-47·16	
			2	1	1	1-46·10	
			SF	1	2	1-44·75	
			F		2	1-43·90	S
		1500m	1	3	7	3-40·92	
			SF	1	DNS		
Culbert, J.	AUS	Long jump	Q		DNQ	7,64	
Cunha, L.	POR	100m	1	11	5	10·80	
		200m	1	7	4	21·72	
Curvelo, Paulo	POR	4×400m relay	1	2	3	3-07·75	
			SF	1	7	3-07·75	
Curvelo, Pedro	POR	4×100m relay	1	4	3	39·61	
			SF	2	DIS		
Cuypers, A.	BEL	110m hurdles	1	4	4	13·89	
			2	4	4	13·97	
			SF	1	7	13·92	
		400m hurdles	1	2	3	50·42	
			SF	2	7	49·75	
Dallas, C.	ISV	Marathon	F		77	2:42-19	
Damilano, M.	ITA	20k walk	F		3	1:20-14	B
Daniels, O.	LBR	100m	1	11	4	10·68	
		200m	1	3	3	21·59	
			2	4	8	22·25	
Danielsson, J.	SWE	5000m	1	3	8	13-43·54	
			SF	1	8	13-25·25	
			F		10	13-30·44	
Danneberg, R.	GER	Discus throw	F		3	67,38	B
Da Silva, R.	BRA	100m	1	1	1	10·37	
			2	5	2	10·24	
			SF	2	4	10·24	
			F		5	10·11	
		200m	1	9	1	21·12	
			2	5	1	20·41	
			SF	1	2	20·28	
			F		3	20·04	B
Dasko, M.	URS	5000m	1	3	12	13-45·25	
			SF	2	13	14-43·65	
David, K.	TCH	Marathon	F		55	2:26-12	
Davis, H.	JAM	400m	1	6	2	45·97	
			2	4	4	45·40	
			SF	2	6	45·48	
		4×400m relay	1	2	1	3-04·00	
			SF	2	3	3-00·94	
			F		2	3-00·30	S
Dawod, A.	PRY	10000m	1	1	21	32-33·04	
Deady, M.	USA	1500m	1	2	2	3-41·91	
			SF	2	8	3-39·47	
Deal, L.	USA	Hammer throw	Q		DNQ	73,66	

COMPETITOR	COUNTRY CODE	EVENT	ROUND	HEAT	PLACE	TIME & DISTANCE	MEDAL
De Benedictis, G.	ITA	20k walk	F		9	1:21-18	
De Bruin, E.	HOL	Discus throw	F		9	63,06	
De Castella, R.	AUS	Marathon	F		8	2:13-07	
Dejonckheere, G.	BEL	20k walk	F		35	1:27-14	
		50k walk	F		DNF		
Deleze, P.	SUI	5000m	1	1	11	14-12·79	
Delice, P.	TRI	400m	1	9	4	46·14	
			2	4	7	45·75	
DeLoach, J.	USA	200m	1	5	1	20·98	
			2	4	1	20·56	
			SF	2	1	20·06	
			F		1	19·75*	G
D'Encausse, P.	FRA	Pole vault	F		8	5,60	
De Souza, B.	BEN	110m hurdles	1	1	7	15·05	
De Wit, R.	HOL	Decathlon	F		8	8189	
Dia Ba, E.	SEN	400m hurdles	1	1	1	49·41	
			SF	2	3	48·48	
			F		2	47·23	S
		4×400m relay	1	3	4	3-06·93	
			SF	2	7	3-07·19	
Diamini, T.	SWZ	Marathon	F		58	2:28-06	
Diarra, O.	MLI	100m	1	11	3	10·53	
			2	1	8	10·61	
		200m	1	8	6	21·55	
			2	1	8	21·46	
Diarra, O.	SEN	400m	1	3	3	46·86	
			2	2	7	46·23	
		4×400m relay	1	3	4	3-06·93	
			SF	2	7	3-07·19	
Diaz, J.	SEN	4×100m relay	1	2	DIS		
Diemer, B.	USA	3000m steeplechase	1	2	4	8-38·40	
			SF	2	7	8-23·89	
Di Napoli, G.	ITA	1500m	1	1	5	3-41·85	
			SF	2	11	3-43·58	
Dinh, M.	VIE	100m	1	11	7	11.09	
		200m	1	8	8	22·65	
Dobeleit, N.	GER	200m	1	8	4	20·86	
			2	4	4	20·98	
		4×400m relay	SF	2	2	3-00·66	
			F		3	3-00·56	B
Dodoo, F.	GHA	Triple jump	Q		DNQ	16,17	
Doehring, J.	USA	Shot put	F		11	19,89	
Doherty, J.	IRL	5000m	1	1	7	13-47·99	
			SF	2	5	13-24·61	
			F		9	13-27·71	
Domingues, A.	BRA	3000m steeplechase	1	1	5	8-32·77	
			SF	1	11	8-35·05	
Dossary, Y.	ARS	400m hurdles	1	5	7	53·51	
Douglas, T.	BER	200m	1	6	2	20·91	
			2	2	3	20·70	
			SF	2	8	20·84	
		400m	1	10	2	45·69	
			2	2	8	46·28	
Dove-Edwin, H.	SLE	100m	1	3	6	10·89	
		4×100m relay	1	3	7	41·19	
		4×400m relay	1	1	6	3-10·47	
Druppers, R.	HOL	800m	1	6	2	1-47·48	
			2	2	5	1-46·91	
Duan, X.	PRC	800m	1	7	6	1-52·17	
		1500m	1	2	9	3-44·88	
Ducceschi, R.	ITA	50k walk	F		8	3:45-43	
Dumchev, Y.	URS	Discus throw	F		4	66,42	
Dupnai, A.	NGU	10000m	1	2	20	32-50·63	
		Marathon	F		75	2:41-47	
Dusabe, T.	RWA	Marathon	F		78	2:42-52	
Dzekedzeke, K.	MAW	800m	1	3	6	1-50·60	
		1500m	1	2	13	4-02·61	
Ebong-Salle, F.	CMR	Long jump	Q		DNQ	7,65	
Ebrahimm-Warsama, A.	QAT	10000m	1	1	16	29-37·99	
Edet, V.	NGR	4×100m relay	1	1	2	39·15	
			SF	1	6	39·05	
Edge, D.	CAN	Marathon'	F		67	2:32-19	
Edwards, J.	GBR	Triple jump	Q		DNQ	15,88	
Edwards, P.	GBR	Shot put	Q		DNQ	17,28	
Egbunike, I.	NGR	400m	1	10	2	46·02	
			2	2	2	45·02	
			SF	2	4	44·74	
			F		5	44·72	
		4×400m relay	1	3	3	3-06·59	
			SF	2	4	3-01·13	
			F		7	3-02·50	
Ehrle, K.	AUT	400m hurdles	1	1	2	50·10	
			SF	1	7	51·04	
Einarsson, S.	ISL	Javelin throw	Q		DNQ	75,52	
Elizondo, M.	MEX	4×100m relay	1	4	4	40·31	
Elliott, N.	BAH	Triple jump	F		10	16·19	

COMPETITOR	COUNTRY CODE	EVENT	ROUND	HEAT	PLACE	TIME & DISTANCE	MEDAL
Elliott, P.	GBR	800m	1	7	1	1-46·83	
			2	4	2	1-46·61	
			SF	1	4	1-44·94	
			F		4	1-44·12	
		1500m	1	3	3	3-38·60	
			SF	1	3	3-38·56	
			F		2	3-36·15	S
Endo, T.	JPN	10000m	1	2	DNF		
Enweani, C.	CAN	200m	1	8		20·65	
			2		3	20·62	
			SF	2	5	20·57	
		4×100m relay	F		7	38·93	
Epacua, S.	GEQ	100m	1	11	8	11·52	
Ereng, P.	KEN	800m	1	8	1	1-46·14	
			2	1	2	1-46·38	
			SF	1	1	1-44·55	
			F		1	1-43·45	G
		4×400m relay	1	3	2	3-05·21	
			SF	1	2	3-03·24	
			F		8	3-04·69	
Esmail, A.	SOM	Marathon	F		DNF		
Evangelisti, G.	ITA	Long jump	F		4	8,08	
Everett, D.	USA	400m	1	9	1	45·63	
			2	2	1	44·83	
			SF	1	2	44·36	
			F		3	44·09	B
		4×400m relay	F		1	2-56·16*	G
Everett, M.	USA	800m	1	4	4	1-49·86	
Evoniuk, M.	USA	50k walk	F		22	3:56-55	
Eyestone, E.	USA	Marathon	F		29	2:19-09	
Ezinwa, D.	NGR	4×100m relay	1	1	2	39·15	
Falise, D.	BEL	Triple jump	F		11	16,17	
Fall, M.	SEN	800m	1	1	4	1-49·14	
		4×400m relay	1	3	4	3-06·93	
			SF	2	7	3-07·19	
Fanelli, G.	AMS	Marathon	F		51	2:25-35	
Faudet, A.	CHA	400m	1	2	6	48·69	
Faulkner, S.	GBR	Long jump	Q		DNQ	7,74	
Faulknor, C.	JAM	4×100m relay	1	3	3	39·53	
			SF	1	3	38·75	
			F		4	38·47	
Fehringer, H.	AUT	Pole vault	F		13	5,40	
Fell, G.	CAN	3000m steeplechase	1	2	7	8-51·25	
			SF	2	6	8-19·99	
			F		11	8-21·73	
Feraday, S.	CAN	Javelin throw	Q		DNQ	73,32	
Ferguene, A.	ALG	20k walk	F		32	1:26-33	
Fernandes, G.	ANG	200m	1	9	DIS		
Fesselier, M.	FRA	20k walk	F		16	1:22-43	
Fetter, G.	HUN	100m	1	7	4	10·54	
			2	4	8	10·55	
Fiaz, M.	PAK	400m	1	8	6	47·13	
		4×400m relay	1	3	7	3-08·54	
Firiam, P.	VAN	400m	1	2	7	51·77	
Flax, K.	USA	Hammer throw	Q		DNQ	72,80	
Flemming, J.	ISV	100m	1	10	6	10·70	
		200m	1	9	3	21·33	
			2	1	6	21·33	
Floreal, E.	CAN	Triple jump	Q		DNQ	16,11	
Floris, S.	ITA	4×100m relay	1	1	3	39·20	
			SF	2	2	38·65	
			F		4	38·65	
Fofana, L.	CIV	4×400m relay	1	3	5	3-07·40	
Folkes, C.	CAN	4×400m relay	1	2	5	3-09·52	
Fonseca, S.	HON	20k walk	F		40	1:27-41	
Forde, E.	BAR	400m	1	7	3	46·47	
			2	1	8	46·59	
		4×400m relay	1	1	5	3-06·03	
Forster, K.	GBR	Marathon	F		33	2:20-45	
Forsythe, M.	GBR	Long jump	F		12	7,54	
Francois, A.	STV	200m	1	6	7	21·88	
Freimuth, U.	GDR	Decathlon	F		18	7860	
Gaehwiler, B.	SUI	Decathlon	F		12	8114	
Garcia, J.	ESP	Pole vault	Q		DNQ	0	
Gariba, S.	GHA	4×100m relay	1	2	3	39·13	
			SF	2	5	39·46	
Garner, M.	AUS	200m	1	5	2	21·09	
			2	4	7	21·68	
		4×400m relay	1	1	4	3-05·93	
			SF	1	4	3-06·63	
			F		6	3-02·49	
Gaseitsiwe, K.	BOT	800m	1	6	4	1-48·08	
		4×400m relay	1	3	7	3-13·16	
Gaspar, A.	ANG	100m	1	9	8	10·92	
Gasuon, F.	ESP	4×100m relay	1	3	DNF		
Gataullin, R.	URS	Pole vault	F		2	5,85	S
Gauder, H.	GDR	50k walk	F		3	3:39-45	B
Gayaple, S.	CHA	1500m	1	4	14	3-58·46	
Gecsek, T.	HUN	Hammer throw	F		6	78,36	
Geoffroy, R.	FRA	1500m	1	1	3	3-41·68	
			SF	1	8	3-40·96	
Georgiev, G.	BUL	Discus throw	F		11	61-24	
Ghanem, A.	EGY	400m hurdles	1	2	4	50·44	
Gilbert, G.	CAN	Long jump	Q		DNQ	7,61	
Gloden, J.	LUX	Marathon	F		36	2:22-14	
Gnalo, A.	TOG	400m	1	3	6	51·46	
Goma, K.	ERN	100m	1	7	5	10·80	
Gombedza, J.	ZIM	Marathon	F		72	2:38-13	
Gomez, A.	ESP	5000m	1	1	9	13-51·60	
			SF	1	11	13-41·73	
Gong, G.	FRC	Decathlon	F		31	7231	
Gonzalez, A.	FRA	Marathon	F		37	2:22-24	
Gonzalez, M.	MEX	5000m	1	1	6	13-47·98	
			SF	2	10	13-32·52	
		10000m	1	2	8	28-36·66	
			F		11	27-59·90	
Goville, J.	UGA	400m	1	8	5	47·11	
		4×100m relay	1	1	6	41·39	
Grabarczyk, A.	POL	Triple jump	Q		DNQ	16,24	
Graells, J.	AND	800m	1	8	7	1-53·34	
		1500m	1	4	11	3-52·68	
Graham, J.	CAN	400m hurdles	1	1	3	50·30	
			SF	1	8	51·33	
		4×400m relay	1	2	5	3-09·52	
Graham, W.	JAM	400m hurdles	1	5	2	49·40	
			SF	2	2	48·37	
			F		5	48·04	
		4×400m relay	1	2	1	3-04·00	
			SF	2	3	3-00·94	
			F		2	3-00·30	S
Grant, B.	SLE	400m hurdles	1	4	7	51·73	
		4×100m relay	1	3	7	41·19	
		4×400m relay	1	1	6	3-10·47	
Grant, D.	GBR	High jump	F		=7	2,31	
Graudyn, V.	URS	800m	1	4	1	1-48·90	
			2	1	5	1-47·07	
Gray, I.	BIZ	5000m	1	1	17	15-33·24	
Gray, J.	USA	800m	1	3	1	1-48·83	
			2	2	1	1-45·96	
			SF	2	4	1-45·04	
			F		5	1-44·80	
Gudmundsson, P.	ISL	Shot put	Q		DNQ	19,21	
Guerthoer, W.	SU	Shot put	F		3	21,99	B
Gugler, C.	SU	Decathlon	F		22	7745	
Guilte, E.	PUR	200m	1	5	3	21·09	
			2	1	4	20·73	
			SF	2	7	20·77	
Guimaraes, A.	BRA	800m	1	6	5	1-48·49	
Guldberg, M.	DEN	1500m	1	2	3	3-42·01	
			SF	1	7	3-39·86	
Gustafsson, B.	SWE	50k walk	F		7	3:44-49	
Gustafsson, T.	SWE	Hammer throw	F		11	74,24	
Haas, C.	GER	100m	1	4	6	10·54	
			2	3	8	10·57	
		4×100m relay	1	2	2	39·01	
			SF	1	4	38·75	
			F		6	38·55	
Haber, R.	GDR	Hammer throw	F		4	80,44	
Hackrey, R.	GBR	3000m steeplechase	1	3	8	8-39·30	
			SF	1	DNF		
Hacksteiner, M.	SUI	1500m	1	3	4	3-39·05	
			SF	2	7	3-39·18	
Hadi, A.	MLD	Marathon	F		DNF		
Hafsteinsson, V.	ISL	Discus throw	Q		DNQ	58,94	
Haleem, H.	MLD	Marathon	F		DNF		
Halvorsen, J.	NOR	10000m	1	1	11	28-22·25	
			F		16	28-29·21	
Hamada, A.	BRN	400m hurdles	1	5	6	51·34	
Hampstead, C.	GUY	110m hurdles	1	6	6	14·88	
Han, M.-S.	KOR	Shot put	Q		DNQ	15,68	
Hanim, M.	MLD	4×100m relay	1	1	7	44·31	
Hanna, S.	BAH	Long jump	Q		DNQ	7,54	
Hannecker, A.	GER	Discus throw	F		8	63,28	
Harmsworth, P.	GBR	4×400m relay	1	1	2	3-04·18	
Harries, P.	GBR	400m hurdles	1	1	5	50·81	
Heer, F.	GER	4×100m relay	1	2	2	39·01	
			SF	1	4	38·75	
			F		6	38·55	
Heiring, J.	USA	20k walk	F		38	1:27-30	
Heisler, R.	USA	Discus throw	Q		DNQ	59,00	
Henrich, M.	GER	4×400m relay	1	1	1	3-03·90	
			SF	2	2	3-00·66	
Herbert, J.	GBR	Triple jump	Q		DNQ	16,18	
Hernandez, H.	ESP	Marathon	F		DNF		

COMPETITOR	COUNTRY CODE	EVENT	ROUND	HEAT	PLACE	TIME & DISTANCE	MEDAL
Hernandez, M.	MEX	800m	1	3	5	1-49·03	
Herold, J.-P.	GDR	1500m	1	4	1	3-40·87	
			SF	2	5	3-38·59	
			F		3	3-36·21	B
Herrera, J.	MEX	Marathon	F		11	2:13-58	
Hill M.	GBR	Javelin throw	Q		DNQ	77,20	
Hingsen, J.	GER	Decathlon	F		DNF		
Hjeltnes, K.	NOR	Discus throw	F		7	64,94	
Hlawe, S.	SWZ	Marathon	F		44	2:24-42	
Hodge, L.	BVI	100m	1	9	6	10·79	
		200m	1	6	5	21·78	
Hodge, N.	ISV	100m	1	3	5	10·73	
Homela, M.	ZIM	800m	1	9	3	1-47·36	
			2	4	8	1-46·62	
		1500m	1	1	11	3-47·38	
Hoogewerf, S.	CAN	800m	1	5	2	1-49·76	
			2	2	2	1-45·99	
			SF	1	7	1-47·30	
Hooper, D.	IRL	Marathon	F		24	2:17-16	
Hosaka, T.	JPN	20k walk	F		47	1:32-46	
Howard, J.	USA	High jump	F		10	2,31	
Hraban, R.	TCH	Decathlon	F		20	7781	
Hudec, J.	TCH	110m hurdles	1	4	2	13·78	
			2	1	4	13·65	
			SF	2	5	13·73	
Huhtala, H.	FIN	Hammer throw	F		9	75,38	
Hurlston, P.	CAY	Javelin throw	Q		DNQ	62,34	
Hussein, I.	KEN	Marathon	F		DNF		
Hwang, H.-C.	KOR	400m hurdles	1	1	4	50·52	
		4×400m relay	1	1	8	3-14·71	
Hyde, D.	BIZ	Triple jump	Q		DNQ	14,09	
Ignatov, E.	BUL	5000m	1	3	5	13-43·42	
			SF	2	6	13-24·76	
			F		8	13-26·41	
		10000m	1	1	5	28-15·63	
			F		12	28-09·32	
Ikangaa, J.	TAN	Marathon	F		7	2:13-06	
Imo, C.	NGR	100m	1	6	1	10·62	
			2	2	8	11·44	
Ince, A.	BAR	400m hurdles	1	3	6	52·76	
		4×400m relay	1	1	5	3-06·03	
Ismael, H.	DJI	5000m	1	1	14	14-45·40	
Ismael, Y.	CHA	10000m	1	1	19	30-47·29	
Itt, E.	GER	400m hurdles	1	3	2	50·10	
			SF	2	4	48·86	
			F		8	48·78	
Ivanenko, V.	URS	50k walk	F		1	3:38-29*	G
Ivanov, L.	BUL	20k walk	F		43	1:28-43	
Jachno, A.	AUS	20k walk	F		28	1:24-52	
		50k walk	F		19	3:53-23	
Jackson, C.	GBR	110m hurdles	1	1	1	13·50	
			2	4	1	13·37	
			SF	1	3	13·55	
			F		2	13·28	S
Jadi, N.	MAL	400m	1	6	6	49·52	
Jalal, M.	BAN	100m	1	8	6	10·94	
		4×100m relay	1	4	6	41·78	
Jallow, D.	GAM	400m	1	8	3	46·91	
			2	1	7	46·35	
James, I.	CAN	Long jump	Q		DNQ	7,52	
Jarrett, A.	GBR	110m hurdles	1	3	2	13·45	
			2	3	1	13·59	
			SF	2	4	13·56	
			F		6	13·54	
Jedrusik, T.	POL	400m	1	9	3	46·12	
			2	1	4	45·27	
			SF	1	8	46·17	
Jensen, E.	DEN	110m hurdles	1	5	3	13·91	
			2	2	5	14·02	
Jeremiah, J.	VAN	100m	1	1	8	10·96	
		200m	1	10	7	22·01	
Joda, M.	SUD	10000m	1	2	13	29-03·87	
Johansson, S.	SWE	20k walk	F		25	1:23-51	
		50k walk	F		20	3:53-34	
John, H.	NGU	100m	1	4	7	10·96	
Johnson, B.	CAN	100m	1	8	1	10·37	
			2	1	3	10·17	
			SF	2	1	10·03	
			F		DIS		
Johnson, D.	USA	Decathlon	F		9	8180	
Johnson, P.	BAH	Triple jump	Q		DNQ	16,03	
Jonah, M.-D.	SLE	1500m	1	1	14	3-55·15	
Jones, D.	ANT	800m	1	9	5	1-49·31	
		1500m	1	4	8	3-51·22	
Jones, M.	GBR	Hammer throw	Q		DNQ	70,38	
Jorgensen, H.	DEN	Marathon	F		22	2:16-40	
Journod, P.	FRA	Discus throw	Q		DNQ	58,94	

COMPETITOR	COUNTRY CODE	EVENT	ROUND	HEAT	PLACE	TIME & DISTANCE	MEDAL
Jung, M.-O.	KOR	20k walk	F		49	1:40-09	
Just, P.	CAN	Pole vault	Q		DNQ	5,30	
Kachapov, R.	URS	Marathon	F		10	2:13-49	
Kaestner, A.	USA	50k walk	F		34	4:12-49	
Kaida, L.	ALG	Long jump	Q		DNQ	7,10	
		Triple jump	Q		DNQ	15,68	
Kalboussi, M.	TUN	1500m	1	4	7	3-43·72	
Kalembo, D.	ZAM	400m	1	3	4	47·44	
		4×400m relay	1	2	7	3-11·35	
Karaffa, L.	HUN	4×100m relay	1	4	1	39·12	
			SF	2	3	38·84	
			F		8	39·19	
Karaulic, B.	YUG	400m hurdles	1	3	5	51·32	
		4×400m relay	1	2	2	3-05·62	
			SF	2	5	3-01·59	
Karimou, H.	NIG	Marathon	F		80	2:43-51	
Kariuki, J.	KEN	3000m steeplechase	1	2	2	8-33·42	
			SF	2	4	8-18·53	
			F		1	8-05·51*	G
Karna, J.	FIN	Long jump	F		10	7,82	
Kasahara, T.	JPN	100m	1	10	5	10·62	
		4×100m relay	1	3	3	39·70	
Kate, M.	HOL	Marathon	F		15	2:14-53	
Katombi, E.	ANG	1500m	1	1	13	3-54·25	
Kawasumi, H.	JPN	4×400m relay	1	1	3	3-05·63	
			SF	2	6	3-03·80	
Kearns, T.	IRL	110m hurdles	1	2	4	14·17	
			2	1	7	14·30	
Keita, F.	SLE	Long jump	Q		DNQ	6,87	
		4×100m relay	1	3	7	41·19	
Keita, S.	SLE	Marathon	F		95	3:04-00	
Kemp, T.	BAH	High jump	Q		DNQ	2,19	
Keskitalo, P.	FIN	Decathlon	F		11	8143	
Kgarametso, B.	BOT	200m	1	9	6	22.79	
		4×400m relay	1	3	7	3-13·16	
Khalifa, M.-O.	MTN	5000m	1	2	17	15-18·64	
Khalifa, O.	SUD	1500m	1	4	5	3-41·46	
			SF	2	3	3-38·40	
			F		12	3-41·07	
Khan, M.	FIJ	1500m	1	3	13	4-03·20	
Kharitse, M.	LES	100m	1	6	5	10·97	
Khellil, A.	ALG	Marathon	F		35	2:21-12	
Kidikas, V.	URS	Discus throw	Q		DNQ	60,88	
Kim, B.-S.	KOR	4×100m relay	1	1	4	39·61	
Kim, C.-K.	KOR	Pole vault	Q		DNQ	5,30	
Kim, J.-I.	KOR	Long jump	Q		DNQ	7,70	
Kim, J.-T.	KOR	110m hurdles	1	5	5	14·06	
			2	4	5	14·00	
Kim, W.-T.	KOR	Marathon	F		18	2:15-44	
Kim, Y.-G.	KOR	5000m	1	2	13	14-09·45	
Kimeli, K.	KEN	10000m	1	1	1	28-00·39	
			F		3	27-25·16	B
Kinder, G.	USA	Decathlon	F		DNF		
King, J.	GBR	Long jump	Q		DNQ	7,57	
Kingdom, R.	USA	110m hurdles	1	3	1	13·40	
			2	1	1	13·17*	
			SF	2	1	13·37	
			F		1	12·98*	G
Kinnunen, K.	FIN	Javelin throw	F		10	78,04	
Kipkemboi, S.	KEN	400m	1	7	2	46·15	
			2	2	5	45·44	
		4×100m relay	1	3	4	40·30	
		4×400m relay	1	3	2	3-05·21	
			SF	1	2	3-03·24	
			F		8	3-04·69	
Kiprotich, N.	KEN	800m	1	1	2	1-48·68	
			2	3	4	1-45·68	
			SF	2	1	1-44·71	
			F		8	1-49·55	
Kipsang, J.	KEN	Marathon	F		DNF		
Kitur, S.	KEN	400m hurdles	1	2	2	49·88	
			SF	2	6	49·74	
Klein, P.	GER	4×100m relay	1	2	2	39·01	
			SF	1	4	38·75	
			F		6	38·55	
Knowles, G.	BAH	110m hurdles	1	3	4	14·22	
			2	3	6	14·30	
Koech, P.	KEN	3000m steeplechase	1	1	3	8-31·66	
			SF	1	2	8-15·68	
			F		2	8-06·79	S
Koeleman, H.	HOL	3000m steeplechase	1	1	7	8-35·20	
			SF	1	8	8-21·86	
Koike, H.	JPN	4×400m relay	1	1	3	3-05·63	
			SF	2	6	3-03·80	
Koji, K.	ZAI	10000m	1	2	DNF		
		Marathon	F		73	2:38-34	
Kolasa, M.	POL	Pole vault	F		NP	0	

COMPETITOR	COUNTRY CODE	EVENT	ROUND	HEAT	PLACE	TIME & DISTANCE	MEDAL
Kopitar, R.	YUG	400m hurdles	1	4	5	50·54	
Korjus, T.	FIN	Javelin throw	F		1	84,28	G
Kosaka, T.	JPN	50k walk	F		31	4:03-12	
Kovacs, A.	HUN	100m	1	2	2	10·39	
			2	2	3	10·27	
			SF	2	5	10·31	
		200m	1	6	3	20·93	
			2	2	5	21·19	
		4×100m relay	1	4	1	39·12	
			SF	2	3	38·84	
			F		8	39·19	
Kovalenko, A.	URS	Triple jump	F		3	17,42	B
Kpidi, A.	CIV	4×400m relay	1	3	5	3-07·40	
Kram, R.	ALG	1500m	1	3	6	3-39·90	
			SF	1	9	3-41·39	
Krawczyk, K.	POL	High jump	F		12	2,31	
Krdzalic, S.	YUG	Javelin throw	F		12	73,28	
Krieger, H.	POL	Shot put	F		12	19,51	
Kruger, A.	GBR	Decathlon	F		24	7623	
Krylov, V.	URS	100m	1	10	4	10·34	
			2	2	3	10·26	
			SF	2	DNS		
		4×100m relay	1	2	1	38·82	
			SF	2	1	38·55	
			F		1	38·19	G
Kubista, J.	TCH	1500m	1	3	12	3-46·41	
Kucej, J.	TCH	400m hurdles	1	4	4	49·89	
Kuhn, B.	GER	4×400m relay	1	1	1	3-03·90	
Kulker, H.	HOL	1500m	1	4	2	3-40·90	
			SF	1	4	3-39·06	
			F		6	3-37·08	
Kulmiye, M.	SOM	Marathon	F		91	2:58-10	
Kulvet, V.	URS	Decathlon	F		DNF		
Kunwar, D.	NEP	110m hurdles	1	4	7	16·51	
		400m hurdles	1	1	7	56·80	
		Decathlon	F		34	5339	
Kunze, H.	GDR	5000m	1	3	11	13-44·34	
			SF	1	6	13-23·04	
			F		3	13-15·73	B
		10000m	1	2	3	28-22·09	
			F		6	27-39·35	
Kurihara, K.	JPN	100m	1	4	2	10·46	
			2	5	6	10·49	
		4×100m relay	1	3	3	39·70	
			SF	1	5	38·90	
Kuya, Z.	CIV	4×400m relay	1	3	7	3-07·40	
Kvernmo, G.	NOR	Marathon	F		DNF		
Kwon, S.-L.	KOR	Marathon	F		DNF		
Lachal, M.	MAR	1500m	1	3	5	3-39·20	
			SF	2	12	3-45·65	
Lafranchi, B.	SUI	Marathon	F		DNF		
Lahbi, F.	MAR	800m	1	1	11	1-47·82	
			2	2	7	1-47·32	
Lambruschini, A.	ITA	3000m steeplechase	1	1	4	8-32·59	
			SF	2	2	8-16·92	
			F		4	8-12·17	
Lamothe, D.	HAI	Marathon	F		20	2:16-15	
Lanzoni, R.	CRC	Marathon	F		40	2:23-45	
Lapointe, F.	CAN	50k walk	F		14	3:48-15	
Laporte, S.	FRA	Javelin throw	Q		DNQ	69 40	
Lapshin, I.	URS	Triple jump	F		2	17 52	S
Lauret, T.	FRA	100m	1	4	6	10 56	
			2	2	6	10 51	
Laventure, C.	FRA	5000m	1	2	3	13-58·19	
			SF	1	9	13-29·92	
Lawson, B.	TOG	100m	1	1	5	10·59	
Lazare, A.	FRA	Marathon	F		DNF		
Lazazzera, M.	ITA	100m	1	10	3	10·47	
			2	2	5	10·50	
Lazdins, R.	CAN	Discus throw	Q		DNC	57,94	
Leblanc, G.	CAN	20k walk	F		10	1:21-29	
Lee, F.-A.	FOR	Decathlon	F		25	7579	
Lee, J.-B.	KOR	Pole vault	Q		DNQ	0	
Lee, j.-H.	KOR	Hammer throw	Q		DNQ	55,98	
Lee, K.-I.	KOR	Decathlon	F		33	6917	
Lee, S.-K.	KOR	10000m	1	2	16	29-37·14	
Lee, S.-L.	FOR	100m	1	5	6	10·69	
		200m	1	2	5	21·53	
			2	2	6	21·34	
		4×100m relay	1	1	5	40·40	
Lee, W.-J.	KOR	Javelin throw	Q		DNQ	78,10	
Lefevre, P.	FRA	Javelin throw	Q		DNQ	76,42	
Lefou, J.	MRI	110m hurdles	1	2	6	14·73	
Leitao, J.	POR	Long jump	Q		DNQ	6,99	
		Triple jump	Q		DNQ	15,50	
Lemercier, A.	FRA	50k walk	F		16	3:50-28	
Le Stum, B.	FRA	3000m steeplechase	1	3	6	8-36·95	
			SF	1	9	8-26·69	
Leung, W.K.	HKG	100m	1	1	6	10·82	
		200m	1	3	6	21·69	
Lewis, C.	USA	100m	1	13	1	10·14	
			2	5	1	9·99	
			SF	1	1	9·97	
			F		1	9·92*	G
		200m	1	10	1	20·72	
			2	1	1	20·57	
			SF	1	1	20·23	
			F		2	19·79	S
		Long jump	F		1	8,72	G
Lewis, S.	USA	400m	1	5	1	45·31	
			2	3	1	44·41	
			SF	1	1	44·35	
			F		1	43·87	G
		4×400m relay	1	3	1	3-02·16	
			SF	1	1	3-02·84	
			F		1	2-56·16*	G
Lewis, T.	USA	20k walk	F		44	1:31-00	
Li, B.	PRC	20k walk	F		41	1:27-57	
		50k walk	F		29	4:00-07	
Li, F.	PRC	200m	1	8	5	21·33	
			2	4	6	21·38	
		4×100m relay	1	2	4	39·67	
Li, T.	PRC	100m	1	5	4	10·47	
			2	1	6	10·53	
		4×100m relay	1	2	4	39·67	
Lima, J.	POR	110m hurdles	1	5	6	14·73	
Lin K.-L.	FOR	800m	1	3	7	1-52·95	
		400m	1	4	4	48·18	
Lindner, J.	AUT	Hammer throw	F		10	75,36	
Lindsay, H.	ANT	200m	1	10	6	21·78	
		4×100m relay	1	3	6	41·18	
		4×400m relay	1	2	6	3-11·04	
Linley, E.	STV	800m	1	2	6	1-51·71	
Litvinov, S.	URS	Hammer throw	F		1	84,89*	G
Llopart, J.	ESP	50k walk	F		13	3:48-09	
Lloyd, A.	AUS	5000m	1	1	4	13-47·91	
			SF	1	12	13-42·49	
		10000m	1	1	DNF		
Logan, J.	USA	Hammer throw	Q		DNQ	72,64	
Lomba, F.	POR	400m	1	2	5	47·57	
		4×400m relay	1	2	3	3-07·75	
			SF	1	7	3-07·75	
Lombocko, H.-M.	CGO	4×100m relay	1	2	6	41·26	
Long, D.	GER	Marathon	F		21	2:16-18	
Longiross, B.	UGA	Marathon	F		62	2:30-29	
Lopez, L.	CRC	Marathon	F		68	2:32-43	
Lopez, R.	PAR	1500m	1	2	12	3-53·31	
		3000m steeplechase	1	1	9	8-56·06	
			SF	2	13	8-52·62	
Lopez, R.	HON	20k walk	F		48	1:37-09	
Loua, F.	GUI	100m	1	6	6	11·20	
		200m	1	5	6	22·78	
Lous, R.	BAR	400m	1	1	4	46·80	
		4×400m relay	1	1	5	3-06·03	
Lubensky, Z.	TCH	Pole vault	F		11	5,50	
Luebke, R.	GER	200m	1	3	2	20·81	
			2	3	3	20·80	
			SF	1	8	21·23	
		4×400m relay	1	1	1	3-03·90	
			SF	1	2	3-00·66	
			F		3	3-00·56	B
McCloy, P.	CAN	10000m	1	2	15	29-34·07	
McCombie, I.	GBR	20k walk	F		13	1:22-03	
McCullagh, C.	IRL	Hammer throw	Q		DNQ	68,66	
McDonald, J.	IRL	20k walk	F		17	1:22-45	
McFarlane, M.	GBR	4×100m relay	1	4	2	39·17	
			SF	1	2	38·52	
			F		2	38·28	S
McHugh T.	IRL	Javelin throw	Q		DNQ	76,46	
McKay, A.	USA	4×400m relay	1	3	1	3-02·16	
			SF	1	1	3-02·84	
McKean, T.	GBR	800m	1	9	2	1-47·24	
			2	2	DIS		
McKoy, M.	CAN	110m hurdles	1	4	1	13·78	
			2	1	2	13·56	
			SF	2	3	13·54	
			F		7	13·61	
McLeod, M.	GBR	10000m	1	1	DNF		
McNeill, L.	USA	4×100m relay	1	4	DIS		
Ma, Y.-F.	PRC	Shot put	Q		DNQ	18,27	
Mabrouk, G.	KUW	Javelin throw	Q		DNQ	65,84	

COMPETITOR	COUNTRY CODE	EVENT	ROUND	HEAT	PLACE	TIME & DISTANCE	MEDAL
Macev, I.	YUG	400m	1	10	5	46·37	
		4×400m relay	1	2	2	3-05·62	
			SF	2	5	3-01·59	
Machura, R.	TCH	Shot put	F		5	20,57	
Maddocks, C.	GBR	20k walk	F		24	1:23-46	
Madonia, E.	ITA	100m	1	1	2	10·40	
			2	6	4	10·38	
		4×100m relay	1	1	3	39·20	
			SF	2	2	38·65	
			F		4	38·65	
Maeke, J.	SOL	10000m	1	2	22	35-16·93	
		Marathon	F		DNF		
Maher, P.	CAN	Marathon	F		46	2:24-49	
Mahorn, A.	CAN	200m	1	3	1	20·55	
			2	3	2	20·59	
			SF	1	3	20·43	
			F		5	20·39	
		4×100m relay	1	3	1	39·41	
			SF	2	4	38·94	
			F		7	38·93	
Mahoulikponto, P.	BEN	4×100m relay	1	4	5	41·52	
Mahovlich, M.	CAN	Javelin throw	Q		DNQ	69,44	
Mahua, G.	GEQ	200m	1	9	5	22·33	
		400m	1	1	6	48·11	
Mai, H.-F.	FOR	4×100m relay	1	1	5	40·40	
Mair, J.	JAM	100m	1	13	4	10·44	
			2	1	4	10·41	
		4×100m relay	1	3	2	39·53	
			SF	1	3	38·75	
			F		4	38·47	
Makok, K.	ZAI	800m	1	7	DIS		
Malekwa, Z.	TAN	Javelin throw	Q		DNQ	67,56	
Mambosasa, G.	MAW	5000m	1	2	15	14-30·01	
		Marathon	F		DNF		
Maminski, B.	POL	3000m steeplechase	1	2	6	8-45·72	
			SF	1	6	8-18·28	
			F		8	8-15·97	
Manandhar, B.	NEP	Marathon	F		54	2:25-57	
Mandebele, S.	ZIM	5000m	1	2	12	14-03·97	
		10000m	1	2	17	29-50·99	
Manderson, F.	GBR	High jump	Q		DNQ	2,19	
Manik, I.	MLD	4×100m relay	1	1	7	44·31	
Mansoor, T.	QAT	100m	1	3	1	10·42	
			2	4	5	10·38	
		4×100m relay	1	2	5	40·05	
Mardi, M.	INA	100m	1	2	3	10·40	
			2	6	2	10·32	
			SF	1	7	10·39	
		4×100m relay	1	2	DNF		
Mardle, P.	GBR	Discus throw	Q		DNQ	58,28	
Maree, S.	USA	5000m	1	1	2	13-47·58	
			SF	1	2	13-22·61	
			F		5	13-23·69	
Marie-Rose, B.	FRA	200m	1	7	2	21·11	
			2	2	1	20·48	
			SF	2	3	20·50	
			F		8	20·58	
		4×100m relay	1	1	1	38·87	
			SF	1	1	38·49	
			F		3	38·40	B
Marin, J.	ESP	20k walk	F		4	1:20-34	
		50k walk	F		5	3:43-03	
Marios, H.	CYP	Triple jump	Q		DNQ	15.95	
Maritim, J.	KEN	400m hurdles	1	5	3	49·64	
			SF	1	5	49·50	
Markin, A.	URS	110m hurdles	1	2	3	14·17	
			2	2	7	14·19	
Markov, K.	BUL	Triple jump	F		1	17·61*	G
Marsh, H.	USA	3000m steeplechase	1	1	6	8-33·89	
			SF	1	7	8-18·94	
			F		6	8-14·39	
Marshall, B.	CAN	High jump	Q		DNQ	2,22	
Martin, E.	GBR	5000m	1	2	1	13-58·00	
			S	2	9	13-26·26	
		10000m	1	2	5	28-25·46	
			F		DNF		
Martin, R.	USA	200m	1	1	1	20·65	
			2	2	2	20·54	
			SF	1	6	20·62	
Marzouq, A.F.	QAT	4×100m relay	1	2	5	40·05	
Marzouq Al-Abdulla, R.	QAT	110m hurdles	1	1	6	14·69	
			2	1	8	14·47	
		4×100m relay	1	2	5	40·05	
Massad, A.-E.	SUD	5000m	1	1	18	15-50·91	
Matei, S.	RUM	High jump	Q		DNQ	2,19	

COMPETITOR	COUNTRY CODE	EVENT	ROUND	HEAT	PLACE	TIME & DISTANCE	MEDAL
Matete, S.	ZAM	400m hurdles	1	2	6	51·06	
		4×400m relay	1	2	7	3-11·35	
Matiapeng, B.	BOT	Marathon	F		34	2:20-51	
Matsubara, K.	JPN	4×100m relay	1	3	3	39·70	
Matthes, S.	GDR	100m	1	5	3	10·35	
			2	3	3	10·36	
Mattioli, C.	ITA	20k walk	F		19	1:22-58	
Maude, A.	NGR	800m	1	5	5	1-50·48	
Maweni, S.	BOT	400m	1	6	4	47·97	
		4×400m relay	1	3	7	3-13·16	
Maziya, F.	SWZ	100m	1	5	8	11·52	
Mbaye, A.	SEN	100m	1	3	3	10·64	
			2	3	6	10·45	
		4×100m relay	1	2	DIS		
Mbaye, H.	SEN	400m hurdles	1	4	6	50·58	
Meghoo, G.	JAM	4×100m relay	1	3	2	39·53	
			SF	1	3	38·75	
			F		4	38·47	
Mehdi, S.	YAR	200m	1	2	8	22·95	
Mei, S.	ITA	5000m	1	3	1	13-42·96	
			SF	2	1	13-24·30	
			F		7	13-26·17	
Meisch, D.	GDR	50k walk	F		9	3:46-31	
Mellaard, E.	HOL	Long jump	F		11	7,71	
Mellado, S.	SAL	Decathlon	F		26	7517	
Melzer, H.	GDR	3000m steeplechase	1	3	3	8-36·45	
			SF	1	3	8-16·27	
			F		10	8-19·82	
Mendez, P.	PAR	800m	1	1	6	1-50·72	
Mennea, P.	ITA	200m	1	6	4	21·10	
			2	2	DNS		
Merande, B.	KEN	10000m	1	1	10	28-21·84	
			F		DNF		
Mercenario, C.	MEX	20k walk	F		7	1:20-53	
Miakakem, R.	CHA	5000m	1	3	19	15-42·73	
Michel, D.	GDR	Javelin throw	Q		DNQ	77,70	
Mileham, M.	GBR	Hammer throw	Q		DNQ	62,42	
Miller, A.	FIJ	110m hurdles	1	5	7	14·86	
		Decathlon	F		32	7016	
Miller, L.	AUS	400m hurdles	1	3	4	50·53	
		4×400m relay	1	1	4	3-05·93	
Miller, L.	ANT	4×100m relay	1	3	6	41·18	
		4×400m relay	1	2	6	3-11·04	
Millonig, D.	AUT	5000m	1	1	10	14-01·92	
Milzerhossain, M.	BAN	400m	1	3	5	48·76	
		800m	1	8	6	1-51·16	
		4×100m relay	1	4	6	41·78	
Min, S.-H.	KOR	Discus throw	Q		DNQ	47,84	
Minev, P.	BUL	Hammer throw	Q		DNQ	74,46	
Missioulla, E.	URS	20k walk	F		27	1:24-39	
Mitchell, D.	USA	100m	1	11	1	10·37	
			2	1	2	10·13	
			SF	2	3	10·23	
			F		4	10·04	
		4×100m relay	1	4	DIS		
Mizoguchi, K.	JPN	Javelin throw	Q		DNQ	77,46	
Mnyampanda, J.	TAN	5000m	1	3	15	14-05·09	
Moeller, F.	GDR	4×400m relay	SF	2	1	3-00·60	
			F		4	3-01·13	
Mogenburg, D.	GER	High jump	F		6	2,34	
Mohammed, A.	NGR	Marathon	F		70	2:35-26	
Mohamud Aden, J.	SOM	1500m	1	2	11	3-49·84	
Mohloli, M.	LES	Marathon	F		82	2:44-44	
Mohsin, N.	IRQ	110m hurdles	1	6	5	14·46	
			2	3	7	14·47	
Moli, Y.	CHA	800m	1	1	8	1-57·97	
Molico, B.-E.	GEQ	1500m	1	2	14	4-16·40	
Molinari, M.	SMR	800m	1	4	7	1-52·35	
Moncif, A.	MAR	1500m	1	4	6	3-41·73	
			SF	1	DNF		
Mondragon, M.	MEX	Marathon	F		57	2:27-10	
Moneghetti, S.	AUS	Marathon	F		5	2:11-49	
Monzo, A.	NIG	Marathon	F		47	2:25-05	
Moracho, J.	ESP	110m hurdles	1	4	5	13·96	
			2	1	6	13·88	
Moreno, C.	CHI	100m	1	8	4	10·70	
		200m	1	7	5	22·13	
Moreno, H.	COL	20k walk	F		33	1:27-06	
		50k walk	F		30	4:01-31	
Moreno, Q.	COL	20k walk	F		DNF		
Morgan, G.	USA	20k walk	F		37	1:27-26	
Moriniere, M.	FRA	100m	1	5	2	10·34	
			2	6	3	10·37	
		4×100m relay	1	1	1	38·87	
			SF	1	1	38·49	
			F		3	38·40	B

COMPETITOR	COUNTRY CODE	EVENT	ROUND	HEAT	PLACE	TIME & DISTANCE	MEDAL
Morris, D.	JAM	400m	1	9	2	45·95	
			2	3	4	45·30	
			SF	2	7	45·68	
		4×400m relay	1	2	1	3-04·00	
			SF	2	3	3-00·94	
			F		2	3-00·30	S
Morris, I.	TRI	400m	1	4	1	45·84	
			2	1	1	44·70	
			SF	2	2	44·60	
			F		7	44·95	
Morrisson, B.	CAN	4×100m relay	1	3	1	39·41	
			SF	2	4	38·94	
			F		7	38·93	
Morton, L.	GBR	50k walk	F		27	3:59-30	
Moser, S.	SUI	Decathlon	F		27	7502	
Moses, E.	USA	400m hurdles	1	3	1	49·38	
			SF	1	1	47·89	
			F		3	47·56	B
Moussa, O.	DJI	Marathon	F		49	2:25-25	
Mrazek, R.	TCH	20k walk	F		5	1:20-43	
		50k walk	F		17	3:50-46	
Mthembu, G.	SWZ	Marathon	F		53	2:25-56	
Muavesi, L.	FIJ	800m	1	2	7	1-54·48	
Mowatt, A.	CAN	4×100m relay	1	3	1	39·41	
			SF	2	4	38·94	
Muftahmubarak, S.	QAT	4×100m relay	1	2	5	40·05	
Muravyov, V.	URS	4×100m relay	1	2	1	38·32	
			SF	2	1	38·55	
			F		1	38·19	G
Murphy, M.	AUS	400m	1	1	2	46·38	
			2	1	6	45·93	
		4×400m relay	1	1	4	3-05·93	
			SF	1	4	3-06·63	
			F		6	3-02·49	
Muslar, E.	BIZ	Marathon	F		79	2:43-29	
Musonda, E.	ZAM	400m	1	4	7	49·21	
		4×400m relay	1	2	7	3-11·35	
Musonge, M.	UGA	4×100m relay	1	1	6	41·39	
Mutoke, K.	ZAI	5000m	1	1	16	14-56·33	
		Marathon	F		89	2:55-21	
Muyaba, F.	ZIM	100m	1	2	6	10·75	
		200m	1	1	6	21·66	
Mwathiwa, J.	MAW	Marathon	F		87	2:51-43	
Myles-Mills, J.	GHA	100m	1	12	1	10·31	
			2	6	1	10·21	
			SF	1	8	10·43	
		200m	1	10	4	21·04	
			2	3	6	20·95	
		4×100m relay	1	2	3	39·13	
			SF	2	5	39·46	
Myricks, L.	USA	Long jump	F		3	8,27	B
Nabunone, E.	INA	5000m	1	2	14	14-19·40	
		10000m	1	1	17	29-55·23	
Nagi, E.	YAR	100m	1	4	8	11·53	
Nai, H.-F.	FOR	Long jump	Q		DNQ	7,45	
		Triple jump	Q		DNQ	15,74	
Nakayama, T.	JPN	Marathon	F		4	2:11-05	
Nava, E.	MEX	100m	1	9	4	10·68	
		4×100m relay	1	4	4	40·31	
Naveko, C.	MAW	10000m	1	1	20	31-23·53	
Ndagijimana, E.	RWA	800m	1	5	6	1-52·08	
		1500m	1	4	10	3-51·61	
Ndinga, H.	CGO	100m	1	2	5	10·74	
		200m	1	1	5	21·66	
		4×100m relay	1	2	6	41·26	
Ndinga, P.	CGO	4×100m relay	1	2	6	41·26	
Ndiwa, J.	KEN	800m	1	7	3	1-47·11	
			2	2	6	1-47·27	
Nechchadi, E.	MAR	Marathon	F		DNF		
Neff, J.-M.	FRA	50k walk	F		D S		
Neisse, E.	FRA	50k walk	F		DIS		
Nelson, C.	CAN	5000m	1	1	12	14-15·94	
Nenadal, Z.	TCH	Javelin throw	Q		DNQ	75,56	
Ngadjadoum, P.	CHA	High jump	Q		DNQ	2,15	
Ngugi, J.	KEN	5000m	1	1	5	13-47·93	
			SF	2	2	13-24·43	
			F		1	13-11·70	G
Nharimue, J.	MOZ	400m	1	7	6	47·33	
Niang, B.	SEN	800m	1	2	1	1-47·65	
			2	3	3	1-45·38	
			SF	1	5	1-45·09	
		4×400m relay	1	3	4	3-06·93	
			SF	2	7	3-07·19	
Nijboer, G.	HOL	Marathon	F		13	2:14-40	
N'jie, M.	GAM	800m	1	6	7	1-55·57	
Nkala, E.	ZIM	400m	1	7	4	46·60	
Noack, A.	GDR	20k walk	F		8	1:21-14	

COMPETITOR	COUNTRY CODE	EVENT	ROUND	HEAT	PLACE	TIME & DISTANCE	MEDAL
Noronha, P.	MOZ	Triple jump	Q		DNQ	14,71	
Noubossie, E.	CMR	400m	1	4	5	48·31	
Ntawulikura, M.	RWA	5000m	1	3	17	14-08·84	
Nteso, N.	LES	Marathon	F		61	2:29-44	
N'tyamba, J.	ANG	800m	1	9	6	1-52·23	
Nurez, J.	DOM	100m	1	3	2	10·47	
			2	3	2	10·33	
			SF	2	6	10·35	
Nyangau, E.	KEN	400m	1	10	4	46·25	
			2	3	7	46·09	
		4×100m relay	1	3	4	40·30	
O'Connell, C.	IRL	Decathlon	F		29	7310	
Ogouchi, F.	BEN	4×100m relay	1	4	5	41·52	
Ogweng, J.	UGA	Marathon	F		92	2:59-35	
Okot, M.	UGA	4×100m relay	1	1	6	41·39	
Olander, M.	SWE	Decathlon	F		17	7869	
Oliveira, H.	POR	20k walk	F		39	1:27-39	
Olobia, O.	NGR	4×100m relay	1	1	2	39·15	
			SF	1	6	39·05	
Olson, W.	USA	Pole vault	F		12	5,50	
Olukoju, A.	NGR	Discus throw	Q		DNQ	54,44	
Olweny, S.	UGA	200m	1	3	5	21·79	
Omar I.	SOM	800m	1	3	3	1-48·97	
			2	2	4	1-46·55	
			SF	2	8	1-46·62	
O'Mara, F.	IRL	5000m	1	2	10	13-59·46	
Ondiek, K.	KEN	100m	1	10	4	10·51	
			2	1	7	10·57	
		200m	1	6	1	20·79	
			2	2	4	20·79	
		4×100m relay	1	3	4	40·30	
Ondieki, Y.	KEN	5000m	1	2	4	13-58·24	
			SF	1	5	13-22·85	
			F		12	13-52·01	
O'Reilly, G.	IRL	1500m	1	3	10	3-43·23	
Ortiz, A.	ESP	High jump	F		14	2,25	
Ortiz, E.	DOM	100m	1	11	6	11·01	
Ortiz, P.	COL	10000m	1	1	14	29-08·25	
		Marathon	F		39	2:34-40	
Osawa, T.	JPN	100m	1	2	6	10·71	
Osland, P.	CAN	800m	1	8	5	1-47·16	
			2	1	6	1-48·02	
		4×400m relay	1	2	5	3-09·52	
Ostrowski, R.	POL	800m	1	1	3	1-49·04	
			2	4	6	1-47·72	
O'Sullivan, M.	IRL	1500m	1	1	6	3-42·01	
			SF	2	6	3-38·84	
			F		8	3-38·39	
Ottey, M.	CAN	High jump	Q		DNQ	2,22	
Ottley, D.	GBR	Javelin throw	F		11	76,96	
Ould Khayar, M.	MTN	1500m	1	1	15	4-12·18	
Ousseni I.	BEN	100m	1	6	3	10·72	
			2	5	8	10·76	
Ovchinnikov, V.	URS	Javelin throw	F		7	79,12	
Ozturk, Z.	TUR	1500m	1	4	12	3-54·26	
Padilla, D.	USA	5000m	1	2	5	13-58·45	
			SF	2	11	13-37·11	
Paklin, L.	URS	High jump	F		=7	2,31	
Pale, H.	VOL	100m	1	13	5	10·76	
		200m	1	1	3	21·22	
			2	2	7	21·35	
Palma, M.	BRA	20k walk	F		45	1:41-42	
Pambudi, K E.	INA	4×100m relay	1	2	DNF		
Panetta, F.	ITA	3000m steeplechase	1	2	1	8-29·75	
			SF	1	5	8-17·23	
			F		9	8-17·79	
Pang, Y.	PRC	Long jump	F		9	7,86	
Pannier, R.	FRA	3000m steeplechase	1	1	1	8-30·94	
			SF	2	5	8-19·39	
			F		12	8-23·80	
Park, Y.-J.	KOR	Triple jump	Q		DNQ	15,86	
Parker, A	JAM	110m hurdles	1	1	3	14·00	
			2	2	6	14·05	
Parsons, G.	GBR	High jump	F		16	2,15	
Partyka, A.	POL	High jump	Q		DNQ	2,19	
Pastoriza F.	ARG	High jump	Q		DNQ	2,10	
Pastusinski, J.	POL	Triple jump	F		8	16,72	
Pavoni, P.	ITA	100m	1	7	2	10·36	
			2	5	4	10·33	
		4×100m relay	1	1	3	39·20	
			SF	2	2	38·65	
			F		4	38·65	
Peltoniemi A.	FIN	Pole vault	F		9	5,60	
Penalver, A.	ESP	Decathlon	F		23	7743	
Perchin, A	URS	20k walk	F		14	1:22-32	
Perricelli, G.	ITA	50k walk	F		11	3:47-14	
Peter, J.	GDR	Marathon	F		DNF		

COMPETITOR	COUNTRY CODE	EVENT	ROUND	HEAT	PLACE	TIME & DISTANCE	MEDAL
Petranoff, T.	USA	Javelin throw	Q		DNQ	77,48	
Pfitzinger, P.	USA	Marathon	F		14	2:14-44	
Phillips, A.	USA	400m hurdles	1	5	1	49-34	
			SF	2	1	48-19	
			F		1	47-19*	G
Pinto, A.	POR	10000m	1	1	6	28-15-63	
			F		13	28-09-53	
Pinto, J.	POR	20k walk	F		31	1:26-33	
		50k walk	F		21	3:55-57	
Pizzolato, O.	ITA	Marathon	F		16	2:15-20	
Plasencia, S.	USA	10000m	1	2	DNF		
Plaza, D.	ESP	20k walk	F		12	1:21-53	
Plaziat, C.	FRA	Decathlon	F		5	8272	
Poelman, S.	NZL	Decathlon	F		16	8021	
Poli, G.	ITA	Marathon	F		129	2:16-07	
Ponce, J.	HON	400m	1	9	6	51-11	
		400m hurdles	1	2	8	55-38	
Popovic, S.	YUG	800m	1	8	3	1-46-49	
			2	3	2	1-45-30	
			SF	1	6	1-45-11	
		4×400m relay	1	2	2	3-05-62	
			SF	2	5	3-01-59	
Popovich, V.	URS	50k walk	F		26	3:59-23	
Porter, P.	USA	10000m	1	2	11	28-45-04	
Potachev, A.	URS	50k walk	F		4	3:41-00	
Pouye, B.	SEN	4×100m relay	1	2	DIS		
Povarnitsyn, R.	URS	High jump	F		=3	2,36	B
Powell, M.	USA	Long jump	F		2	8,49	S
Prasad, B.	FIJ	10000m	1	2	21	33-30-43	
		Marathon	F		76	2:41-50	
Prianon, J.-L.	FRA	10000m	1	1	2	28-08-38	
			F		4	27-36-43	
Pribilinec, J.	TCH	20k walk	F		1	1:19-57*	G
Prieto, A.	ESP	10000m	1	2	4	28-22-52	
			F		10	27-52-78	
Protsenko, O.	URS	Triple jump	F		4	17,38	
Pueyo, R.	ESP	20k walk	F		23	1:23-40	
Queneherve, G.	FRA	200m	1	2	1	20-55	
			2	4	2	20-77	
			SF	1	4	20-54	
			F		6	20-40	
		4×100m relay	1	1	1	38-87	
			SF	1	1	38-49	
			F		3	38-40	B
Quinaliza, J.	ECU	Triple jump	Q		DNQ	15,86	
Quinn, B.	IRL	3000m steeplechase	1	3	9	8-40-87	
			SF	2	11	8-43-34	
Ramotshabi, J.	BOT	4×400m relay	1	3	7	3-13-16	
Rapp, M.	SUI	1500m	1	2	6	3-42-64	
Raty, S.	FIN	Javelin throw	F		3	83,26	B
Razine, A.	URS	100m	1	2	4	10-58	
Regalo, J.	POR	5000m	1	3	9	13-43-59	
			SF	2	3	13-24-48	
			F		DNF		
Regis, J.	GBR	100m	1	6	4	10-76	
		200m	1	4	1	20-90	
			2	1	2	20-61	
			SF	1	7	20-69	
		4×100m relay	1	4	2	39-17	
			SF	1	2	38-52	
			F		2	38-28	S
Reiterer, W.	AUS	Discus throw	Q		DNQ	59,78	
Retiz, C.	MEX	Marathon	F		50	2:25-34	
Reynolds, H.	USA	400m	1	2	3	46-28	
			2	4	1	44-46	
			SF	2	1	44-33	
			F		2	43-93	S
		4×400m relay	F		1	2-56-16*	G
Richards, G.	GBR	Decathlon	F		30	7237	
Ridgeon, J.	GBR	110m hurdles	1	6	2	13-75	
			2	2	3	13-74	
			SF	1	4	13-68	
			F		5	13-52	
Rizvi, S.	PAK	800m	1	4	6	1-51-58	
Robertson, M.	GBR	400m hurdles	1	5	5	50-67	
Robinson, A.	USA	4×100m relay	1	4	DIS		
Robinzine, K.	USA	4×400m relay	1	3	1	3-02-16	
			SF	1	1	3-02-84	
			F		1	2-56-16*	G
Rocandio, V.	ESP	4×100m relay	1	3	DNF		
Rodan, J.	FIJ	400m	1	1	7	48-69	
		400m hurdles	1	4	8	54-66	
Rodehau, G.	GDR	Hammer throw	F		12	72,36	
Rodrigues, A.	BRA	Triple jump	Q		DNQ	15,13	
Rodrigues, I.	BRA	Marathon	F		56	2:26-27	

COMPETITOR	COUNTRY CODE	EVENT	ROUND	HEAT	PLACE	TIME & DISTANCE	MEDAL
Rokaya, H.	NEP	1500m	1	4	15	4-01-17	
		5000m	1	1	15	14-53-75	
		10000m	1	2	19	30-48-16	
Roku, M.-R.	GEQ	5000m	1	1	19	16-44-13	
Rono, P.	KEN	1500m	1	3	1	3-37-65	
			SF	2	2	3-38-25	
			F		1	3-35-96	G
Rosswess, M.	GBR	200m	1	1	2	20-95	
			2	5	3	20-74	
			SF	2	4	20-51	
			F		7	20-51	
Roumain, C.	HAI	100m	1	7	7	11-22	
		200m	1	4	6	22-60	
Rousseau, V.	BEL	5000m	1	3	4	13-43-38	
			SF	2	14	14-03-74	
Rowland, M.	GBR	3000m steeplechase	1	1	2	8-31-40	
			SF	2	3	8-18-31	
			F		3	8-07-96	B
Ruffini, R.	TCH	High jump	F		15	2,20	
Ruguga, V.	UGA	Marathon	F		63	2:31-04	
Ruiz, A.	MEX	4×100m relay	1	4	4	40-31	
Rutherford, F.	BAH	Triple jump	Q		DNQ	15,84	
Ryu, T.-K.	KOR	800m	1	2	5	1-48-61	
		4×400m relay	1	1	8	3-14-71	
Sabia, D.	ITA	800m	1	2	3	1-47-84	
			2	4	1	1-46-58	
			SF	1	3	1-44-90	
			F		7	1-48-03	
Sadqat, M.	PAK	4×400m relay	1	3	6	3-08-54	
Saeed, F.-A.	YAR	5000m	1	3	18	15-11-20	
Sahere, A.	MAR	3000m steeplechase	1	1	DIS		
Sahner, C.	GER	Hammer throw	Q		DNQ	75,84	
Sakai, H.	JPN	20k walk	F		26	1:24-08	
Sala, C.	ESP	110m hurdles	1	5	4	14-00	
			2	3	4	13-77	
			SF	1	6	13-85	
Salame, J.	LIB	100m	1	10	7	11-49	
Saleh, A.	PRY	800m	1	6	6	1-55-24	
		1500m	1	3	14	4-03-86	
Saleh, A.	DJI	Marathon	F		3	2:10-59	B
Salom, I.	TAN	3000m steeplechase	1	2	9	9-10-36	
Salonen, R.	FIN	20k walk	F		42	1:28-25	
		50k walk	F		18	3;51-36	
Salzmann, R.	GER	Marathon	F		23	2:16-54	
Samarasinghe, V.	SRI	Marathon	F		65	2:31-29	
Samuel-Kaya, N.	CMR	100m	1	5	5	10-60	
		200m	1	1	4	21-45	
			2	5	8	21-39	
Samuels, V.	GBR	Triple jump	Q		DNQ	16,28	
Sanchez, A.	ESP	400m	1	7	5	47-18	
Sanchez, J.	MEX	20k walk	F		DIS		
Sandy, F.	SLE	100m	1	1	5	10-82	
		4×100m relay	1	3	7	41-19	
		4×400m relay	1	1	6	3-10-47	
Sang, L.	KEN	400m	1	3	2	46-85	
			2	4	6	46-72	
		4×400m relay	1	3	2	3-05-21	
			SF	1	2	3-03-24	
			F		8	3-04-69	
Sang, P.	KEN	3000m steeplechase	1	3	1	8-36-11	
			SF	1	4	8-16-70	
			F		7	8-15-22	
Sangouma, D.	FRA	200m	1	8	2	20-70	
			2	5	4	20-81	
		4×100m relay	1	1	1	38-87	
			SF	1	1	38-49	
			F		3	38-40	
Santos, D.	BRA	Marathon	F		48	2:25-13	
Saunders, N.	BER	High jump	F		5	2,34	
Savin, V.	URS	100m	1	3	10	10-52	
			2	5	5	10-36	
		4×100m relay	1	2	1	38-82	
			SF	2	1	38-55	
			F		1	38-19	
Sawe, T.	KEN	4×400m relay	1	3	2	3-05-21	
			SF	1	2	3-03-24	
			F		8	3-04-69	
Sawe, W.	KEN	50k walk	F		35	4:25-24	
Sawyer, D.	SLE	800m	1	5	8	1-57-88	
		4×400m relay	1	1	6	3-10-47	
Scammell, P.	AUS	1500m	1	2	10	3-45-21	
Schenk, C.	GDR	Decathlon	F		1	8488	G
Schennikov, M.	URS	20k walk	F		6	1:20-47	
Schersing, M.	GDR	4×400m relay	1	2	4	3-08-13	
			SF	2	1	3-00-60	
			F		4	3-01-13	
Schimmer, M.	GDR	4×400m relay	1	2	4	3-08-13	

COMPETITOR	COUNTRY CODE	EVENT	ROUND	HEAT	PLACE	TIME & DISTANCE	MEDAL
Schmid, H.	GER	400m hurdles	1	2	1	49·77	
			SF	1	3	49·93	
			F		7	48·76	
Schoenlebe, T.	GDR	400m	1	4	2	47·07	
			2	2	3	45·09	
			SF	2	5	44·90	
		4×400m relay	1	2	4	3-08·13	
			SF	2	1	3-00·60	
			F		4	3-01·13	
Schueler, C.	USA	50k walk	F		23	3-57·44	
Schult, J.	GDR	Discus throw	F		1	68,32*	G
Schumann, F.	GUM	Marathon	F		86	2:49·52	
Schwarthoff, F.	GER	110m hurdles	1	1	4	14·13	
			2	1	5	13·67	
Schweisfurth, D.	GER	4×100m relay	1	2	2	39·01	
			SF	1	4	38·75	
			F		6	38·55	
Scott, S.	USA	1500m	1	1	2	3-41·57	
			SF	2	1	3-38·20	
			F		5	3-36·99	
Seck, C.	SEN	100m	1	6	2	10·64	
			2	1	5	10·42	
Sedykh, Y.	URS	Hammer throw	F		2	83,76	S
Seko, T.	JPN	Marathon	F		9	2:13·41	
Selkridge, O.	ANT	400m hurdles	1	3	7	54·44	
		4×400m relay	1	2	6	3-11·04	
Selmi, M.	ALG	100m	1	2	7	11·08	
		200m	1	10	5	21·24	
			2	1	7	21·26	
Sermsiri, A.	THA	4×100m relay	1	3	5	40·57	
Serrani, L.	ITA	Hammer throw	Q		DNQ	70,50	
Serrano, A.	ESP	10000m	1	2	12	29-01·13	
Seyba, Y.	MLI	400m	1	8	7	48·33	
Seynou, C.	VOL	High jump	Q		DNQ	0	
Shageef, A.	MLD	400m	1	4	8	50·61	
Shahanuddin, C.	BAN	4×100m relay	1	4	6	41·78	
Shatta, A.	EGY	Shot put	Q		DNQ	17,61	
Shibata, H.	JPN	Long jump	Q		DNQ	7,48	
Shim, D.-S.	KOR	100m	1	8	3	10·56	
			2	6	6	10·55	
		4×100m relay	1	1	4	39·61	
Shintaku, H.	JPN	Marathon	F		17	2:15·42	
Shirley, S.	AUS	Decathlon	F		15	8036	
Shishkin, V.	URS	110m hurdles	1	5	1	13·75	
			2	3	2	13·60	
			SF	1	1	13·46	
			F		4	13·51	
Siguria, J.	NGU	800m	1	4	8	1-56·12	
		1500m	1	3	15	4-07·04	
Silva, A.	BRA	100m	1	10	2	10·44	
			2	2	2	10·25	
			SF	1	5	10·32	
Silva, A.	POR	800m	1	4	3	1-49·09	
			2	4	3	1-46·65	
			SF	2	5	1-45·12	
		4×400m relay	1	2	3	3-07·75	
			SF	1	7	3-07·75	
Silva, J.	POR	Marathon	F		27	2:18·05	
Silva, J.	BRA	Triple jump	Q		DNQ	15,95	
Silva, M.	POR	1500m	1	2	5	3-42·24	
			SF	2	4	3-38·56	
			F		9	3-38·77	
Silweya, O.	MAL	200m	1	7	6	22·24	
		400m	1	1	8	49·73	
Simkina, T.	TOG	Triple jump	Q		DNQ	13,92	
Simpkins, C.	USA	Triple jump	F		5	17,29	
Singh, D.	FIJ	3000m steeplechase	1	1	10	9-23·50	
Sjoberg, P.	SWE	High jump	F		=3	2,36	B
Skerritt, A.	CAN	400m	1	1	3	46·64	
			2	3	6	46·08	
		4×400m relay	1	2	5	3-09·52	
Slanar, I.	TCH	Triple jump	F		7	16,75	
Smirnov, S.	URS	Shot put	F		8	20,36	
Smith, A.	JAM	100m	1	4	3	10·49	
			2	6	7	10·63	
Smith, C.	USA	100m	1	2	1	10·28	
			2	4	1	10·16	
			SF	1	2	10·15	
			F		3	9·99	B
		4×100m relay	1	4	DIS		
Smith, D.	GBR	Hammer throw	Q		DNQ	69,12	
Smith, H.	SAM	Discus throw	Q		DNQ	49,40	
Smith, M.	CAN	Decathlon	F		14	8083	
Sobhi, N.	MAR	Marathon	F		30	2:19·56	
Soleyne, St C.	ANT	100m	1	8	8	11·17	
		4×100m relay	1	3	6	41·18	
Solorzano, F.	ECU	Decathlon	F		DNF		

COMPETITOR	COUNTRY CODE	EVENT	ROUND	HEAT	PLACE	TIME & DISTANCE	MEDAL
Souza, G.	BRA	400m	1	6	1	45·90	
			2	4	3	45·35	
			SF	1	7	45·27	
Sowa, M.	LUX	20k walk	F		DIS		
Spedding, C.	GBR	Marathon	F		6	2:12·19	
Spyrou, S.	CYP	800m	1	1	5	1-49·84	
		1500m	1	3	9	3-42·32	
			SF	1	10	3-43·49	
Squella, P.	CHI	800m	1	4	2	1-48·99	
			2	3	5	1-46·45	
Ssali, J.	UGA	100m	1	8	7	10·95	
		4×100m relay	1	1	6	41·39	
Staaf, J.	SWE	20k walk	F		30	1:24·59	
		50k walk	F		DNF		
Staines, G.	GBR	5000m	1	1	1	13-47·81	
			SF	2	4	13-24·51	
			F		13	13-55·00	
Stanton, B.	USA	High jump	F		11	2,31	
Steen, D.	CAN	Decathlon	F		3	8328	B
Steiner, A.	AUT	Long jump	Q		DNQ	7,61	
Steiner, R.	SUI	Javelin throw	Q		DNQ	76,02	
Steirmayr, T.	AUT	Long jump	Q		DNQ	7,36	
Stephens, D.	USA	Javelin throw	Q		DNQ	78,42	
Stevens, P.	BEL	100m	1	12	4	10·51	
			2	4	6	10·50	
		200m	1	8	3	20·84	
			2	3	5	20·94	
Stewart, R.	JAM	100m	1	7	1	10·22	
			2	3	1	10·25	
			SF	1	3	10·18	
			F		7	12·26	
Stone, R.	AUS	400m	1	8	2	46·52	
			2	4	8	46·04	
Straughn, S.	BAR	400m	1	2	4	47·37	
		4×400m relay	1	1	5	3-06·03	
Stroeme, L.-O.	NOR	5000m	1	2	DNF		
Suhonen, A.	FIN	800m	1	3	2	1-48·90	
			2	1	DNF		
		1500m	1	1	7	3-43·61	
Suli, P.	TON	100m	1	13	6	10·94	
		200m	1	7	7	22·49	
Sulinan, M.	QAT	1500m	1	2	8	3-44·43	
Sung, N.-K.	KOR	4×100m relay	1	1	4	39·61	
Surin, B.	CAN	Long jump	Q		DNQ	7,73	
Szabo, D.	HUN	Decathlon	F		13	8093	
Szalma, L.	HUN	Long jump	F		6	8,00	
Sziapkin, Z.	POL	20k walk	F		36	1:27·23	
Szikora, P.	TCH	50k walk	F		10	3:47·04	
Szitas, I.	HUN	Hammer throw	F		7	77,04	
Tadjire, N.	ALG	110m hurdles	1	1	5	14·36	
			2	4	8	14·35	
Tafelmeier, K.	GER	Javelin throw	F		4	82,72	
Tafralis, G.	USA	Shot put	F		9	20,16	
Taitano, R.	GUM	Marathon	F		94	3:03·19	
Taiwo, J.	NGR	Triple jump	F		9	16,46	
Takano, S.	JPN	400m	1	10	1	45·42	
			2	4	2	45·00	
			SF	1	5	44·90	
		4×100m relay	SF	1	5	38·90	
		4×400m relay	1	1	3	3-05·63	
			SF	2	6	3-03·80	
Talavera, E.	ESP	100m	1	12	5	10·61	
		4×100m relay	1	3	DNF		
Tamba, I.	SEN	200m	1	4	3	21·68	
			2	3	8	21·93	
		4×100m relay	1	2	DIS		
Tamm, Y.	URS	Hammer throw	F		3	81,16	B
Tanev, I.	BUL	Hammer throw	F		8	76·08	
Tarui, M.	KEN	10000m	1	2	2	28-20·98	
			F		8	27-47·23	
Taramai, W.	CKI	800m	1	9	8	1-58·80	
Tarev, A.	BUL	Pole vault	Q		DNQ	0	
Tarnovetskiy, P.	URS	Decathlon	F		10	8167	
Tarpenning, K.	USA	Pole vault	F		10	5,50	
Tatar, I.	HUN	100m	1	4	5	10·52	
			2	5	7	10·68	
		4×100m relay	1	4	1	39·12	
			SF	2	3	38·84	
			F		8	39·19	
Ten Kate, M.	HOL	10000m	1	1	12	28-23·23	
			F		9	27-50·20	
Teresa, T.	ESP	800m	1	7	4	1-47·32	
			2	3	8	1-48·01	
Terzi, M.	TUR	Marathon	F		32	2:20·12	
Tetengi, A.	NGR	4×100m relay	1	1	2	39·15	
Thee, M.	BOT	1500m	1	3	8	3-41·97	
			SF	2	10	3-42·62	

COMPETITOR	COUNTRY CODE	EVENT	ROUND	HEAT	PLACE	TIME & DISTANCE	MEDAL
Thiebaut, P.	FRA	5000m	1	3	3	13-43-28	
			SF		4	13-22-71	
			F		11	13-31-99	
Thompson, D.	GBR	Decathlon	F		4	8306	
Thraenhardt, C.	GER	High jump	Q		14	2,25	
			F		=7	2,31	
Tiacoh, G.	CIV	400m	1	5	3	47-19	
			2	4	5	45-49	
		4×400m relay	1	3	5	3-07-40	
Tianen, J.	FIN	Hammer throw	Q		DNQ	73,74	
Tilli, S.	ITA	200m	1	10	1	20-68	
			2	5	2	20-67	
			SF	1	5	20-59	
		4×100m relay	1	1	3	39-20	
			SF	2	2	38-65	
			F		4	38-65	
Timmermann, U.	GDR	Shot put	F		1	22,47*	G
Tiprod, S.	THA	4×100m relay	1	3	5	40-57	
Todman, W.	BVI	400m	1	10	7	50-11	
Todorov, G.	BUL	Shot put	Q		DNQ	19,68	
Tomov, T.	BUL	400m hurdles	1	5	4	50-67	
			SF	2	5	48-90	
Torres, E.	PUR	Triple jump	Q		DNQ	15,59	
Toso, L.	ITA	High jump	F		13	2,25	
Toumi, H.	ALG	Hammer throw	Q		DNQ	65,78	
Tourret, P.	FRA	110m hurdles	1	4	3	13-88	
			2	2	2	13-73	
			SF	2	7	13-96	
Toutain, T.	FRA	20k walk	F		18	1:22-55	
Trabado, C.	ESP	800m	1	8	4	1-46-76	
			2	4	7	1-48-12	
Treacy, J.	IRL	Marathon	F		DNF		
Trott, W.	BER	100m	1	5	7	10-69	
Trouabal, J.-C.	FRA	100m	1	13	2	10-39	
			2	3	4	10-41	
Tuffuor, E.	GHA	100m	1	4	1	10-31	
			2	4	4	10-37	
		4×100m relay	1	2	3	39-13	
Tuna, T.	NGU	200m	1	7	2	21-95	
		400m	1	6	3	47-87	
			2	3	8	47-48	
Twegbe, N.	LBR	800m	1	6	8	1-58-43	
Ubartas, R.	URS	Discus throw	F		2	67,48	S
Ugbisie, M.	NGR	4×400m relay	1	3	3	3-06-59	
			SF	2	4	3-01-13	
			F		7	3-02-50	
Ulloa, E.	CHI	3000m steeplechase	1	2	DNF		
Urbanik, S.	HUN	20k walk	F		21	1:23-18	
		50k walk	F		DNF		
Urbano, J.	POR	20k walk	F		29	1:24-56	
Urfaq, M.	PAK	Long jump	Q		DNQ	7,09	
Usher, C.	BIZ	400m	1	5	8	51-42	
Uti, S.	NGR	400m	1	4	3	47-08	
			2	1	5	45-33	
		4×400m relay	1	3	3	3-06-59	
			SF	2	4	3-01-13	
			F		7	3-02-50	
Vaihinger, J.	GER	4×400m relay	1	1	1	3-03-90	
			SF	2	2	3-00-66	
			F		3	3-00-56	B
Valent, G.	TCH	Discus throw	F		6	65,80	
Valenta, V.	TCH	Decathlon	F		28	7442	
Valiente, R.	PER	Long jump	Q		DNQ	6,92	
		Triple jump	Q		DNQ	15,59	
Valmon, A.	USA	4×400m relay	1	3	1	3-02-16	
			SF	1	1	3-02-84	
Valvik, S.-I.	NOR	Discus throw	Q		DNQ	60-64	
Van, T.	VNM	Marathon	F		97	3:10-57	
Vanderherten, D.	BEL	Marathon	F		DNF		
Van Dijck, W.	BEL	3000m steeplechase	1	3	5	8-36-80	
			SF	1	1	8-15-63	
			F		5	8-13-99	
Van Helden, R.	HOL	800m	1	7	2	1-46-99	
			2	3	7	1-46-61	
Vera, R.	ECU	10000m	1	1	9	28-17-88	
			F		15	28-17-64	
Viali, T.	ITA	800m	1	6	4	1-47-74	
			2	1	7	1-50-85	
Vida, J.	HUN	Hammer throw	Q		DNQ	74,30	
Vigneron, T.	FRA	Pole vault	F		=5	5,70	
Vignissy, D.G.M.	BEN	4×100m relay	1	4	5	41-52	
Vilhjalmsson, E.	ISL	Javelin throw	Q		DNQ	78,92	
Vindis, M.	YUG	Marathon	F		25	2:17-47	
Volkmann, J.	GER	3000m steeplechase	1	3	2	8-36-37	
			SF	2	8	8-25-19	
Voloshin, L.	URS	Long jump	F		8	7,89	
Voss, T.	GDR	Decathlon	F		2	8399	S
Vrabel, M.	TCH	10000m	1	2	DNF		
		Marathon	F		DNF		
Wakiihuri, D.	KEN	Marathon	F		2	2:10-47	S
Walker, J.	GUM	Marathon	F		90	2:56-32	
Wangganont, C.	THA	4×100m relay	1	3	5	40-57	
Warming, L.	DEN	Decathlon	F		19	7859	
Warsama, A.	QAT	5000m	1	3	16	14-06-20	
Warsoenke, S.	GDR	Javelin throw	Q		DNQ	78,22	
Watanasin, V.	THA	100m	1	9	7	10-88	
		4×100m relay	1	3	5	40-57	
Watson, M.	BER	800m	1	4	5	1-50-16	
		1500m	1	1	10	3-46-49	
Wattebosi, E.	INA	400m	1	10	6	47-10	
		4×100m relay	1	2	DNF		
Waziri, Y.	NGR	Marathon	F		60	2:29-14	
Wedderburn, E.	GBR	3000m steeplechase	1	2	5	8-83-90	
			SF	1	10	8-26-69	
Weigel, R.	GDR	20k walk	F		2	1:20-00	S
		50k walk	F		2	3:38-56	S
Weil, G.	CHI	Shot put	F		6	20,38	
Weis, H.	GER	Hammer throw	F		5	79,16	
Weiss, G.	GDR	Javelin throw	F		6	81,30	
Wekesa, P.	KEN	100m	1	9	2	10-50	
			2	6	5	10-43	
		4×100m relay	1	3	4	40-30	
Wellman, B.	BER	Triple jump	Q		DNQ	15,47	
Wennlund, D.	SWE	Javelin throw	F		8	78,30	
Werthner, G.	AUT	Decathlon	F		21	7753	
Whittle, B.	GBR	400m	1	2	1	46-07	
			2	1	3	45-22	
			SF	2	8	46-07	
		4×400m relay	1	1	2	3-04-18	
			SF	1	3	3-04-60	
			F		5	3-02-00	
Whymms, F.	BAH	100m	1	3	4	10-70	
Wilkins, M.	USA	Discus throw	F		5	65,90	
Williams, B.	GBR	100m	1	12	3	10-51	
			2	3	7	10-55	
Williams, D.	CAN	100m	1	9	11	10-24	
			2	2	1	10-16	
			SF	1	4	10-24	
			F		6	10-11	
		4×100m relay	1	3	1	39-41	
			SF	2	4	38-94	
			F		7	38-93	
Williams, M.	STV	400m	1	6	7	51-22	
Williams, M.	ISV	Marathon	F		88	2:52-06	
Williams, P.	CAN	5000m	1	3	6	13-43-43	
			SF	1	13	13-44-57	
		10000m	1	1	DNF		
Williams, W.	ISV	Marathon	F		81	2:44-40	
Wirz, P.	SUI	1500m	1	4	4	3-41-26	
			SF	1	DNF		
Woods, J.	IRL	Marathon	F		52	2:25-38	
Wright, C.	JAM	200m	1	4	2	20-94	
			2	5	5	20-87	
		4×100m relay	1	3	2	39-53	
			SF	1	3	38-75	
			F		4	38-47	
Wright, C.	CAN	Triple jump	Q		DNQ	16,09	
Wu, C.-J.	FOR	110m hurdles	1	4	6	14-11	
		4×100m relay	1	1	5	40-40	
Wynter, D.	ISV	400m	1	7	8	48-39	
Yamashita, N.	JPN	Triple jump	F		12	15,62	
Yamauchi, K.	JPN	200m	1	2	2	20-98	
			2	1	5	20-94	
		4×100m relay	SF	1	5	38-90	
		4×400m relay	1	1	3	3-05-63	
			SF	2	6	3-03-80	
Yang, G.	PRC	110m hurdles	1	3	3	14-01	
			2	4	7	14-24	
Yego, G.	KEN	400m hurdles	1	4	3	49-80	
			SF	2	DIS		
Yegorov, G.	URS	Pole vault	F		3	5,80	B
Yesyukov, V.	URS	Javelin throw	F		5	82,32	
Ylostalo, M.	FIN	110m hurdles	1	5	2	13-87	
			2	3	3	13-70	
			SF	2	8	14-09	
Yoneshige, S.	JPN	5000m	1	2	11	13-59-68	
		10000m	1	2	7	28-26-04	
			F		17	29-04-44	
Yoo, J.-S.	KOR	Marathon	F		31	2:20-11	
Yoon, N.-H.	KOR	400m	1	8	4	47-02	
		4×400m relay	1	1	8	3-14-71	
Yoshida, M.	JPN	Javelin throw	Q		DNQ	76,90	
Yoshida, R.	JPN	400m hurdles	1	2	5	50-49	

COMPETITOR	COUNTRY CODE	EVENT	ROUND	HEAT	PLACE	TIME & DISTANCE	MEDAL
Yougbare, A.	VOL	100m	1	3	7	10·90	
		200m	1	9	4	22·14	
Young, K.	USA	400m hurdles	1	4	1	49·35	
			SF	1	2	48·56	
			F		4	47·94	
Yousif, O.	IRQ	200m	1	2	6	21·88	
		400m	1	7	7	47·45	
Yousof, E.	QAT	800m	1	2	4	1-48·20	
Yu, Z.	PRC	110m hurdles	1	2	2	14·07	
			2	2	4	13·95	
			SF	2	6	13·94	
Yusuf, M.Y.	INA	4×100m relay	1	2		DNF	
Zankawi, M.	KUW	Shot put	Q		DNQ	15,92	
Zelezny, J.	TCH	Javelin throw	F		2	84,12	S
Zhang, G.	PRC	Marathon	F		38	2:22-49	
Zheng, C.	PRC	100m	1	4	4	10·51	
			2	4	7	10·72	
		4×100m relay	1	2	4	39·67	
Zhu, J.	PRC	High jump	Q		DNQ	2,19	
Zorko, B.	YUG	1500m	1	1	9	3-46·52	

FEMALES

COMPETITOR	COUNTRY CODE	EVENT	ROUND	HEAT	PLACE	TIME & DISTANCE	MEDAL
Abraham, S.	IND	800m	1	2	5	2-03·26	
		4×400m relay	1	1	7	3-33·46	
Abt, G.	GER	400m hurdles	1	5		55·72	
			SF	2	3	54·52	
			F		6	54·04	
		4×400m relay	1	1	3	3-27·75	
			F		2	3-22·49	
Acerenza, C.	URU	100m	1	5	7	12·11	
		200m	1	7	6	24·46	
Achuo-Bei, A.	CMR	400m	1	5	5	55·22	
		800m	1	1	7	2-07·10	
Acii, O.	UGA	200m	1	5	6	24·39	
		4×100m relay	1	3	6	46·55	
Adan, N.	PHI	400m hurdles	1	2	7	1-01·92	
Addy, M.	GHA	4×100m relay	1	3	5	44·12	
Aebi, R.	SUI	200m	1	5	4	23·22	
			2	1	4	22·88	
			SF	2	8	23·33	
Akhremenko, N.	URS	Shot put	F		7	20,13	
Aksu, S.	TUR	400m hurdles	1	5	6	57·20	
Alafrantti, P.	FIN	Javelin throw	F		10	58·20	
Almeida, A.	BRA	Marathon	F		44	2:43-40	
Alonso, A.	ESP	10000m	1	1	15	32-40·50	
Anderson, K.	CAN	4×100m relay	1	2	3	43·92	
			SF	2	5	43·82	
Andonova, L.	BUL	High jump	F		=5	1,93	
Angotzi, R.	ITA	200m	1	2	4	23·59	
			2	2	6	23·33	
		4×100m relay	1	2	5	44·33	
Aouam, F.	MAR	1500m	1	2	8	4-06·87	
			F		10	4-08·00	
		3000m	1	2		DNF	
Apiafi, G.	NGR	Shot put	Q		DNQ	15,06	
		Discus throw	Q		DNQ	49,84	
Appiah, M.	GHA	4×100m relay	1	3	5	44·12	
Araki, K.	JPN	Marathon	F		28	2:35-15	
Arendt, H.	GER	400m	1	7	2	52·69	
			2	2	3	52·08	
			SF	2	4	50·36	
			F		7	51·17	
		4×400m relay	1	1	3	3-27·75	
			F		4	3-22·49	
Artemova, N.	URS	3000m	1	2	6	8-44·30	
			F		5	8-31·67	
Asai, E.	JPN	Marathon	F		25	2:34-41	
Ashford, E.	USA	100m	1	5	1	11·10	
			2	2	1	10·88*	
			SF	1	1	10·99	
			F		2	10·83	S
		4×100m relay	1	3	1	42·39	
			SF	2	1	42·12	
			F		1	41·98	G
Astafei, G.	RUM	High jump	F		=5	1,93	
Audain, A.	NZL	10000m	1	1	12	32-10·73	
			F		11	32-10·47	
Augee, M.	GBR	Shot put	Q		DNQ	17·31	
Avdeyenko, L.	URS	High jump	Q		DNQ	1,87	
Avek, P.	NGU	3000m	1	2		DNF	
Avraam, A.	CYP	3000m	1	1	11	9-02·18	
		10000m	1	2	12	32-59·30	
Azarashvili, M.	URS	200m	1	6	2	22·98	
			2	1	2	22·37	
			SF	1	4	22·23	
			F		7	22·33	

COMPETITOR	COUNTRY CODE	EVENT	ROUND	HEAT	PLACE	TIME & DISTANCE	MEDAL
Eada, M.	BEN	100m	1	1	7	12·27	
		200m	1	1	6	25·42	
Baikauskaite, L.	URS	1500m	1	2	7	4-05·74	
			F		2	4-00·24	S
Bailey, A.	CAN	100m	1	7	3	11·61	
			2	1	5	11·29	
		4×100m relay	1	2	3	43·92	
			SF	2	5	43·82	
Bailey, S.	GBR	800m	1	1	3	2-02·36	
			SF	2	6	1-59·94	
		1500m	1	2	2	4-04·65	
			F		7	4-02·32	
Bakare, A.	NGR	400m	1	2	3	52·83	
			2	1	6	52·86	
		4×400m relay	1	1	6	3-30·21	
Bang, S.-H.	KOR	100m hurdles	1	4	7	13·84	
Bartczak, J.	POL	Long jump	Q		DNQ	6,30	
Bawuah, V.	GHA	4×100m relay	1	3	5	44·12	
Beaugeant, C.	FRA	Heptathlon	F		DNF		
		400m hurdles	1	5	3	56·03	
			SF	2	8	56·94	
Beaugendre, M.	FRA	High jump	Q		DNQ	1,84	
Beckford, P.	GBR	400m	1	1	5	54·39	
Behmer, A.	GDR	Heptathlon	F		3	6858	B
Behrendt, K.	GDR	4×100m relay	1	2	1	42·92	
			SF	1	2	42·23	
			F		2	42·09	S
Belanger, R.	CAN	800m	1	4	6	2-04·74	
Belevskaya, Y.	URS	Long jump	F		4	7,04	
Berkeley, M.	GBR	Long jump	Q		DNQ	5,04	
Beurskens, C.	HOL	Marathon	F		34	2:37-52	
Bily, L.	FRA	100m	1	3	3	11·34	
			2	3	6	11·35	
		4×100m relay	1	1	3	43·43	
			SF	2	4	43·66	
			F		7	44·02	
Bizicli, A.	ITA	Marathon	F		23	2:34-38	
Blaszak, G.	POL	400m hurdles	1	2	3	56·18	
			SF	1	7	56·76	
Boegman, N.	AUS	Long jump	F		5	6,73	
Bonapart, I.	SUR	100m	1	2	7	12·27	
		200m	2	5	6	24·95	
Bondarenko, O.	URS	10000m	1	1	2	31-47·67	
			F		1	31-05·21*	G
Bonnet, F.	FRA	Marathon	F		14	2:32-36	
Bouchonneau-Opoliger, M.	SUI	10000m	1	1	14	32-28·26	
Boulmerka, H.	ALG	800m	1	4	5	2-03·33	
		1500m	1	2	9	4-08·33	
Bowker, D.	CAN	1500m	1	1	12	4-07·06	
			F		12	4-17·95	
		3000m	1	2	8	8-43·81	
			F		15	9-11·95	
Boyle, J.	GBR	High jump	F		12	1,90	
Braun, S.	GER	Heptathlon	F		14	6109	
Breuer, G.	GDR	4×400m relay	1	1	1	3-27·37	
Brisco-Hooks, V.	USA	400m	1	6	1	51·96	
			2	4	2	51·24	
			SF	2	2	49·90	
			F		4	50·16	
		4×400m relay	F		2	3-15·51	S
Brown, A.	USA	4×100m relay	1	3	1	42·39	
			SF	2	1	42·12	
			F		1	41·98	G
Brown, W.	USA	Heptathlon	F		18	5982	
Browne, V.	AUS	High jump	Q		DNQ	1,90	
Brunet, R.	ITA	3000m	1	2	12	8-53·04	
Bryan, L.	ANT	800m	1	3	7	2-12·18	
		1500m	1	2	13	4-39·73	
Bryzgina, O.	URS	400m	1	6	1	51·94	
			2	1	1	51·90	
			SF	2	1	49·33	
			F		1	48·65*	G
		4×400m relay	1	2	3	3-27·14	
			F		1	3-15·18*	G
Buerki, C.	SUI	1500m	1	1	10	4-10·89	
		3000m	1	2	9	8-48·37	
			F		11	8-48·32	
Buraga, S.	URS	Heptathlon	F		10	6232	
Burzminski, M.	CAN	800m	1	2	5	2-02·85	
Busch, S.	GDR	400m hurdles	1	2	1	55·96	
			SF	2	4	54·71	
			F		4	53·69	
		4×400m relay	F		3	3-18·29	B
Bush, M.	CAY	Marathon	F		52	2:51-30	
Bussieres, L.	CAN	Marathon	F		26	2:35-03	
Buzu, G.	UGA	4×100m relay	1	3	6	46·55	

COMPETITOR	COUNTRY CODE	EVENT	ROUND	HEAT	PLACE	TIME & DISTANCE	MEDAL
Bykova, T.	URS	High jump	F		3	1,99	B
Cady, C.	USA	Discus throw	F		11	63,42	
Cahill, C.	GBR	1500m	1	2	6	4-05·33	
			F		4	4-00·64	
Caicedo, A.	COL	100m	1	3	4	11·59	
			2	2	8	11·65	
		4×100m relay	1	1	5	45·46	
		4×400m relay	1	2	DIS		
Caihua, Z.	PRC	100m	1	7	5	11·84	
Capriotti, A.	ITA	Long jump	Q		DNQ	6,31	
Carabali, N.	COL	200m	1	6	3	23·78	
			2	3	8	23·96	
		400m	1	5	3	53·27	
			2	3	3	51·76	
			SF	2	8	52·65	
		4×100m relay	1	1	5	45·46	
		4×400m relay	1	2	DIS		
Cazier-Ballo, M.	FRA	200m	1	7	5	23·50	
			2	1	8	23·63	
		4×100m relay	1	1	3	43·43	
Chala, L.	ECU	400m	1	1	4	53·74	
			2	3	7	53·83	
		400m hurdles	1	5	5	57·15	
Chalmers, A.	CAN	1500m	1	1	8	4-08·64	
		3000m	1	1	3	8-48·60	
			F		14	9-04·75	
Chang, F.-H.	FOR	400m	1	7	6	56·10	
		400m hurdles	1	4	7	1-00·16	
		4×100m relay	1	1	6	46·21	
Chartrand, C.	CAN	Javelin throw	Q		DNQ	54,10	
Chen, Q.-W.	PRC	3000m	1	2	11	8-51·53	
Chen, W.-I.	FOR	100m hurdles	1	3	5	14·01	
		4×100m relay	1	1	6	46·21	
Chen, Y.-L.	FOR	200m	1	7	7	25·03	
		4×100m relay	1	1	6	46·21	
Cheung, S.-Y	HKG	100m hurdles	1	4	8	14·26	
Chistyakova, G.	URS	Long jump	F		3	7,11	B
Choi, M.-J.	KOR	10000m	1	1	18	33-48·96	
Choi, M.-S.	KOR	Shot put	Q		DNQ	13,97	
Choi, S.-B.	KOR	800m	1	1	6	2-06·65	
		4×400m relay	1	2	5	3-51·09	
Clark, J.	USA	800m	1	2	2	2-00·83	
			SF	1	7	2-03·32	
Colle, F.	FRA	100m hurdles	1	1	4	13·32	
			2	1	5	13·00	
			SF	1	4	12·92	
			F		5	12·98	
Colovic, S.	YUG	800m	1	1	2	2-01·80	
			SF	1	3	1-58·49	
			F		4	1-57·50	
Cong, Y.	PRC	Shot put	F		9	19,69	
Cooman, N.	HCL	100m	1	2	2	11·22	
			2	2	4	11·08	
			SF	2	7	11·13	
		4×100m relay	1	3	3	43·96	
			SF	1	5	43·48	
Crehan, S.	GBR	Marathon	F		32	2:36-57	
Crooks, C.	CAN	400m	1	1	3	53·58	
			2	4	4	51·64	
			SF	2	7	51·63	
		4×400m relay	1	1	2	3-27·63	
			F		DNF		
Cruz, G.	ANA	100m	1	4	7	12·47	
		200m	1	5	7	25·62	
Curatola, M.	ITA	Marathon	F		8	2:30-14	
Cuthbert, J.	JAM	100m	1	4	1	11·14	
			2	3	2	11·03	
			SF	1	4	11·10	
			F		7	11·26	
		4×100m relay	SF	1	3	43·40	
			F		DNS		
Darami, E.	MAR	10000m	1	2	13	33-01·52	
Daruhi, O.	VAN	100m	1	8	7	13·00	
		200m	1	8	5	26·88	
Dasse, B.	USA	Shot put	F		12	17,60	
D'Avek, P.	NGU	1500m	1	1	14	4-46·49	
Davies, D.	GBR	High jump	F		=8	1,90	
Davis, P.	BAH	100m	1	2	1	11·20	
			2	1	4	11·21	
			SF	2	6	11·12	
		200m	1	7	2	23·08	
			2	4	3	22·92	
			SF	1	7	22·67	
Debois, N.	FRA	4×400m relay	1	1	5	3-29·95	

COMPETITOR	COUNTRY CODE	EVENT	ROUND	HEAT	PLACE	TIME & DISTANCE	MEDAL
Decker-Slaney, M	USA	1500m	1	2	2	4-03·61	
			F		8	4-02·49	
		3000m	1	2	4	8-44·15	
			F		10	8-47·13	
DeJesus, M.	PUR	Long jump	Q		DNQ	6,08	
Dela Cruz, A.	PHI	100m hurdles	1	3	6	14·36	
Demireva, V.	BUL	4×100m relay	1	1	4	43·92	
			SF	2	3	43·07	
			F		5	43·02	
Demsitz, L.	DEN	Long jump	F		12	6,38	
Dethier, S.	BEL	100m hurdles	1	2	DIS		
De Vega,L.	PHI	100m	1	4	6	11·67	
Devers-Roberts, G	USA	100m hurdles	1	4	3	13·18	
			2	3	4	13·22	
			SF	1	8	13·51	
Dewarder, M.	GUY	400m	1	4	5	54·76	
Diankolela-Missengui, J.	CGO	100m	1	5	8	12·14	
		200m	1	4	7	25·20	
Diarra, A.	MLI	100m	1	2	8	12·87	
		200m	1	6	7	25·81	
Dias, A.	POR	10000m	1	2	5	32-13·85	
			F		10	32-07·13	
Diba, D.	ZAI	3000m	1	2	16	10-32·88	
Dimitrova, S.	BUL	Heptathlon	F		12	6171	
Ditz, N.	USA	Marathon	F		17	2:33-42	
Dixon, D.	USA	400m	1	4	1	52·45	
			2	2	2	51·98	
			SF	1	3	49·84	
			F		5	50·72	
		4×400m relay	1	2	1	3-25·86	
			F		2	3-15·51	S
Doerre, K.	GDR	Marathon	F		3	2:26-31	B
Dong, Y.	PRC	Heptathlon	F		16	6087	
Donkova, Y.	BUL	100m hurdles	1	5	1	12·89	
			2	1	1	12·47*	
			SF	1	1	12·58	
			F		1	12·38*	G
		4×100m relay	1	1	4	43·92	
			SF	2	3	43·07	
			F		5	43·02	
Drechsler, H.	GDR	100m	1	6	2	11·15	
			2	1	1	10·96	
			SF	2	2	10·91	
			F		3	10·85	B
		200m	1	1	1	22·93	
			2	1	3	22·38	
			SF	2	2	22·27	
			F		3	21·95	B
		Long jump	F		2	7,22	S
Du, J.	PRC	100m hurdles	1	5	3	13·51	
			2	2	7	13·58	
Dube, G.	ZIM	100m	1	5	6	12·07	
		200m	1	6	5	24·42	
Dunn, P.	GBR	100m	1	1	3	11·39	
			2	4	5	11·37	
		200m	1	8	1	23·32	
			2	3	4	23·04	
			SF	2	6	23·14	
		4×100m relay	1	3	2	43·91	
			SF	1	6	43·50	
Duros, M.-P.	FRA	3000m	1	1	DNF		
Dzhygalova, L.	URS	4×400m relay	1	2	3	3-27·14	
Echols, S.	USA	Long jump	Q		DNQ	6,37	
		4×100m relay	1	3	1	42·39	
			SF	2	1	42·12	
			F		1	41·98	G
Edeh, R.	CAN	400m hurdles	1	2	5	56·59	
Edwards, D.	GBR	800m	1	4	2	2-01·79	
			SF	2	4	1-59·66	
			F		8	2-00·77	
Eichenmann, G.	SUI	Marathon	F		47	2:44-37	
Elien, E.	FRA	400m	1	4	4	52·90	
			2	2	6	53·36	
		4×400m relay	1	1	5	3-29·95	
Emmelmann, K.	GDR	400m	1	5	4	54·02	
			2	1	2	51·02	
			SF	2	5	50·39	
		4×400m relay	1	1	1	3-27·37	
			F		3	3-18·29	B
Escalante, O.	COL	4×100m relay	1	1	5	45·46	
		4×400m relay	1	2	DIS		
Eve, L.	BAH	Javelin throw	Q		DNQ	60·02	
Everts, S.	GER	Heptathlon	F		DNF		
Ewanje-Epee, Maryse	FRA	High jump	F		10	1,90	

COMPETITOR	COUNTRY CODE	EVENT	ROUND	HEAT	PLACE	TIME & DISTANCE	MEDAL
Ewanje-Epee, Monique	FRA	100m hurdles	1	4	4	13·13	
			2	2	4	13·10	
			SF	2	4	12·95	
			F		7	13·14	
Farrell, E.	ARU	100m	1	7	8	12·43	
		200m	1	4	8	25·74	
Fedyushina, V.	URS	Shot put	Q		DNQ	19,06	
Felke, P.	GDR	Javelin throw	F		1	74,68*	G
Ferguson, S.	BAH	Long jump	Q		DNQ	6,34	
Ferreira, C.	POR	Marathon	F		20	2:34-23	
Ferrian, D.	ITA	4×100m relay	1	2	5	44·33	
Ficher, F.	FRA	400m	1	2	4	53·42	
			2	4	7	52·95	
		4×400m relay	1	1	5	3-29·95	
Fiedler, E.	GDR	400m hurdles	1	3	1	54·58*	
			SF	2	1	54·28	
			F		3	53·63	B
Figueiredo, M.	BRA	200m	1	8	2	23·71	
			2	4	5	23·67	
		400m	1	3	1	51·74	
			2	1	5	51·32	
		4×400m relay	1	2	4	3-36·31	
Fink, C.	MEX	High jump	Q		DNQ	1,84	
Flemming, J.	AUS	100m hurdles	1	1	5	13·53	
			2		DNS		
		Heptathlon	F		7	6351	
Flintoff-King, D.	AUS	400m hurdles	1	4	1	54·99	
			SF	1	1	54·00*	
			F		1	53·17*	G
Floyd, D.	USA	800m	1	3	2	2-02·37	
			SF	2	2	1-58·82	
			F		5	1-57·80	
Fogli, L.	ITA	Marathon	F		6	2:27-49	
Gallagher, K.	USA	800m	1	4	1	2-01·70	
			SF	1	2	1-57·39	
			F		3	1-56·91	B
		1500m	1	1	4	4-07·22	
			F		11	4-16·25	
Gansky, D.	GDR	Discus throw	F		2	71,88	S
Garcia, K.	SAL	Marathon	F		58	3:04-21	
Georgieva, N.	BUL	200m	1	2	3	22·80	
			2	2	3	22·60	
			SF	2	5	22·67	
		4×100m relay	1	1	4	43·92	
			SF	2	3	43·07	
			F		5	43·02	
Geremias, C.	BRA	Heptathlon	F		22	5508	
Gibson, S.	GBR	Javelin throw	Q		DNQ	56,00	
Girard, P.	FRA	100m	1	7	4	11·65	
		4×100m relay	SF	2	4	43·66	
			F		7	44·02	
Goehr, M.	GDR	100m	1	2	3	11·22	
			2	2	3	10·99	
			SF	1	6	11·13	
		4×100m relay	1	2	1	42·92	
			SF	1	2	42·23	
			F		2	42·09	S
Greiner, C.	USA	Heptathlon	F		8	6297	
Griffith, A.	GRN	200m	1	2	7	24·79	
		400m	1	7	7	57·09	
Griffith-Joyner, F.	USA	100m	1	7	1	10·88*	
			2	3	1	10·62*	
			SF	2	1	10·70	
			F		1	10·54*	G
		200m	1	5	1	22·51	
			2	1	1	21·76*	
			SF	1	1	21·56*	
			F		1	21·34*	G
		4×100m relay	SF	2	1	42·12	
			F		1	41·98	G
		4×400m relay	F		2	3-15·51	S
Grigorieva, N.	URS	100m hurdles	1	1	1	12·95	
			2	2	2	12·89	
			SF	2	3	12·81	
			F		4	12·79	
Gronfeldt, I.	ISL	Javelin throw	Q		DNQ	54,28	
Groos, M.	USA	Marathon	F		29	2:40-59	
Grottenberg, S.	NOR	Marathon	F		36	2:38-17	
Gunnell, S.	GBR	100m hurdles	1	5	2	13·26	
			2	3	3	13·04	
			SF	2	6	13·13	
		400m hurdles	1	4	3	55·44	
			SF	1	4	54·48	
			F		5	54·03	
		4×400m relay	1	1	4	3-28·52	
Gurina, L.	URS	1500m	1	1	7	4-08·59	
Hagger, K.	GBR	Long jump	Q		DNQ	6,34	
		Heptathlon	F		17	5975	
Hahmann, A.	GDR	1500m	1	2	3	4-03·65	
			F		6	4-00·96	
Hall, L.	GBR	400m	1	3	4	53·13	
			2	1	7	53·42	
Halldorsdottir, H.	ISL	400m hurdles	1	3	6	58·99	
Hamilton-Fleming, S.	AUS	400m hurdles	1	5	4	56·08	
Hanson-Nortey, Y.	GBR	Shot put	Q		DNQ	15,13	
Hartwig, H.	GDR	Shot put	F		6	20,20	
Hasler, Y.	LIE	200m	1	6	6	24·91	
Hautenauve, J.	BEL	Heptathlon	F		20	5734	
Heggli, R.	SUI	100m hurdles	1	3	4	13·72	
			2	2	8	13·95	
Hellmann, M.	GDR	Discus throw	F		1	72,30*	G
Hitjding, T.	HOL	Heptathlon	F		DNF		
Holland, M.	AUS	400m	1	5	2	52·29	
			2	1	1	50·90	
			SF	2	3	50·24	
			F		8	51·25	
Hou, X.	PRC	Discus throw	F		8	65,94	
Howard, D.	USA	400m	1	7	1	52·26	
			2	1	3	51·02	
			SF	1	4	49·87	
			F		6	51·12	
		4×400m relay	1	2	1	3-25·86	
			F		2	3-15·51	S
Howard, S.	USA	4×400m relay	1	2	1	3-25·86	
Hsu. H.	FOR	Heptathlon	F		23	5290	
Huang, Z.	PRC	Shot put	F		8	19,82	
Huber, V.	USA	3000m	1	1	5	8-48·93	
			F		6	8-37·25	
Humphrey, J.	USA	100m hurdles	1	2	4	13·24	
			1	1	6	13·25	
			SF	2	7	13·59	
Hunter, J.	GBR	3000m	1	1	8	8-57·28	
Hunter, L.-E.	ZIM	Marathon	F		55	2:53·17	
Ikavuca, S.	TON	Discus throw	Q		DNQ	44,94	
Ilands, M.	BEL	Marathon	F		35	2:38-02	
Ilieva T.	BUL	4×100m relay	1	1	4	43·92	
			SF	2	3	43·07	
			F		5	43·02	
Issajenko A.	CAN	100m	1	8	3	11·42	
			2	2	5	11·27	
		4×100m relay	1	2	3	43·92	
			SF	2	5	43·82	
Ivan, P	RUM	1500m	1	2	1	4-03·33	
			F		1	3-53·96*	G
		3000m	1	2	1	8-43·10	
			F		2	8-27·15	S
Ivanova, Z.	URS	Marathon	F		9	2:30-25	
Jackson, G.	JAM	100m	1	1	2	11·18	
			2	4	3	11·13	
			SF	2	4	11·06	
			F		4	10·97	
		200m	1	6	1	22·66	
			2	3	1	22·24	
			SF	2	1	22·13	
			F		2	21·72	S
		4×100m relay	1	2	2	43·50	
			SF	1	3	43·30	
			F		DNS		
Jacobs, R.	USA	1500m	1	2	11	4-18·09	
Jacobs, S	GBR	100m	1	6	5	11·56	
			2	3	5	11·31	
		200m	1	7	4	23·37	
			2	4	5	23·38	
		4×100m relay	1	3	4	43·91	
			SF	1	6	43·50	
Jaime, B.	MEX	Marathon	F		43	2:43-00	
Janke, K.	GER	200m	1	8	3	23·83	
			2	4	7	23·87	
Janota, J.	POL	100m	1	2	4	11·71	
		200m	1	3	3	23·40	
			2	2	7	23·34	
		4×100m relay	1	3	4	43·98	
			SF	1	4	43·44	
			F		6	43·93	
Jawo, J.	GAM	100m	1	3	8	12·27	
Jeal, W.	GBR	100m hurdles	1	4	6	13·32	
			2	2	6	13·32	
Jennings, J.	GBR	High jump	Q		DNQ	1,90	
Jennings, L.	USA	10000m	1	2	8	32-18-44	
			F		6	31-39-93	
Ji, J.-M.	KOR	Heptathlon	F		24	5289	
Jin, L.	PRC	High jump	Q		DNQ	1,90	

COMPETITOR	COUNTRY CODE	EVENT	ROUND	HEAT	PLACE	TIME & DISTANCE	MEDAL
Jinadasa, T.	SRI	100m hurdles	1	5	DIS		
John, S.	GDR	Heptathlon	F		2	6897	S
		Long jump	F		8	6,55	
Johnson, B.	IRL	400m hurdles	1	4	6	58·61	
Johnson, K.	AUS	100m	1	7	6	11·44	
			2	4	6	11·42	
		200m	1	7	3	23·20	
			2	1	5	23·01	
Johnson, L.	JAM	4×100m relay	1	2	2	43·50	
Joseph, J.	ANT	200m	1	3	4	23·57	
			2	3	7	23·59	
Jousimaa, T.	FIN	Marathon	F		41	2:43-00	
Joyner-Kersee, J.	USA	Long jump	F		1	7,40*	G
		Heptathlon	F		1	7291*	G
Justin , M.	MRI	Marathon	F		51	2:50-00	
Kaber, D.	LUX	Marathon	F		7	2:29-23	
Karczmarek, A.	POL	Long jump	F		7	6,60	
Katewicz, R.	POL	Discus throw	Q		DNQ	60,34	
Keenan-Buckley, A	IRL	3000m	1	2	13	9-03·10	
Keough, L.	GBR	400m	1	6	2	52·26	
			2	3	5	51·91	
		4×400m relay	1	1	4	3-28·52	
Keskitalo, S.	FIN	Marathon	F		42	2:43-00	
Khinkhinhtwe	BIR	1500m	1	1	11	4-20·92	
		3000m	1	2	14	9-26·57	
Khristova, T.	BUL	Discus throw	F		3	69,74	B
Killingbeck, M.	CAN	4×400m relay	F		DNF		
Kim, C.-H.	KOR	Discus throw	Q		DNQ	45,88	
Kim, H.-S.	KOR	High jump	F		=8	1,90	
Kim, M.-K.	KOR	Marathon	F		DNF		
Kim, S.-J.	KOR	400m hurdles	1	3	7	59·78	
		4×400m relay	1	2	5	3-51·09	
Kinch, B.	GBR	4×100m relay	1	3	2	43·91	
			SF	1	6	43·50	
King, P.	USA	High jump	Q		DNQ	1,84	
Kinzel, G.	GER	4×400m relay	1	1	3	3-27·75	
Kleindl, U.	AUT	Long jump	Q		DNQ	6,13	
Klitzkie, L.	GUM	Marathon	F		63	3:35-32	
Knabe, K.	GDR	100m hurdles	1	1	2	13·13	
			2	1	3	12·81	
			SF	1	5	12·93	
Knoll, S.	GER	200m	1	4	3	23·51	
			2	1	6	23·15	
Koch, B.	GDR	Javelin throw	F		3	67,30	B
Kondratyeva, L.	URS	100m	1	3	2	11·19	
			2	3	3	11·05	
			SF	1	7	11·21	
		4×100m relay	1	1	1	42·88	
			SF	1	1	42·01	
			F		3	42·75	B
Kostadinova, S.	BUL	High jump	F		2	2,01	S
Kostiuchenkova, I.	URS	Javelin throw	F		4	67,00	
Krabbe, K.	GDR	200m	1	5	2	23·15	
			2	2	4	22·67	
			SF	1	6	22·59	
Kravetz, I.	URS	Long jump	F		10	6,46	
Kristiansen, I.	NOR	10000m	1	1	1	31-44·69*	
			F		DNF		
Kungu, B.	ZAI	400m	1	2	6	57·85	
		800m	1	1	8	2-11·00	
Kurochkina, T.	URS	400m hurdles	1	3	3	55·04	
			SF	2	2	54·46	
			F		7	54·39	
Kuttan, M.	IND	400m	1	6	5	53·41	
			2	3	8	53·93	
		4×400m relay	1	1	7	3-33·46	
Kyakutema, F.	UGA	100m	1	1	8	12·32	
		400m	1	2	5	56·00	
		4×100m relay	1	3	6	46·55	
Kyalisiina, R.	UGA	400m hurdles	1	2	5	59·62	
		4×100m relay	1	3	6	46·55	
Kytola, R.	FIN	Heptathlon	F		21	5686	
Laaksalo, T.	FIN	Javelin throw	Q		DNQ	60,64	
Lacambra, B.	ESP	400m	1	1	2	53·04	
			2	4	8	53·76	
Laidlow, S.	GBR	400m hurdles	1	5	7	59·28	
Lajbnerova, Z.	TCH	Heptathlon	F		9	6252	
Lange, I.	GDR	4×100m relay	1	2	1	42·92	
			SF	1	2	42·23	
			F		2	42·09	S
Lapierre, O.	CAN	Marathon	F		11	2:30-56	
Larrieu-Smith. F	USA	10000m	1	1	6	31-52·02	
			F		5	31-35·52	
Launa, I.	NGU	Heptathlon	F		25	4566	
Laurendet, J.	AUS	400m hurdles	1	2	4	56·44	
Lawrence, E.	CAN	4×400m relay	1	1	2	3-27·63	
Leatherwood, L.	USA	4×400m relay	1	2	1	3-25·86	

COMPETITOR	COUNTRY CODE	EVENT	ROUND	HEAT	PLACE	TIME & DISTANCE	MEDAL
Ledovskaya, T.	URS	400m hurdles	1	1	2	55·91	
			SF	1	2	54·01	
			F		2	53·18	S
		4×400m relay	F		1	3-15·18*	G
Lee, M.-O.	KOR	Marathon	F		15	2:32-51	
Lee, S.	CAN	10000m	1	1	5	31-51·42	
			F		8	31-50·51	
Lee, Y.-S.	KOR	4×100m relay	1	2	7	45·83	
Lelut, M.	FRA	Marathon	F		18	2:33-47	
Leroux, F.	FRA	100m	1	4	5	11·58	
			2	1	8	11·75	
		4×100m relay	1	1	3	43·43	
			SF	2	4	43·66	
			F		7	44·02	
Leroy, M.	FRA	200m	1	5	3	23·19	
			2	3	5	23·22	
		4×100m relay	1	1	3	43·43	
			SF	2	4	43·66	
			F		7	44·02	
Lesch, C.	GER	800m	1	2	3	2-00·95	
			SF	2	5	1-59·85	
Lewis, C.	USA	Long jump	Q		DNQ	6,47	
Li, B.	PRC	Javelin throw	Q		DNQ	58,92	
Li, C.-Y.	FOR	100m	1	7	7	12·16	
Li, J.	PRC	Marathon	F		54	2:53-08	
Li, M.	PRC	Shot put	F		3	21,06	B
Liao, W.	PRC	Long jump	Q		DNQ	6,44	
Lillak, T.	FIN	Javelin throw	Q		DNQ	60,06	
Lim, C.-A.	KOR	3000m	1	1	15	9-21·18	
		4×400m relay	1	2	5	3-51·09	
Lim, E.-J.	KOR	Marathon	F		37	2:38-21	
Lisovskaya, N.	URS	Shot put	F		1	22·24	G
Liu, H.	PRC	100m hurdles	1	4	2	13·02	
			2	3	6	14·37	
Liu, S.	PRC	Long jump	F		11	6,40	
		4×100m relay	1	2	4	44·29	
			SF	2	7	44·36	
Losch, C.	GER	Shot put	F		5	20,27	
Losch, S.	GDR	400m hurdles	1	1	1	55·90	
			SF	1	6	55·56	
McColgan, E.	GBR	10000m	1	2	1	32-11·95	
			F		2	31-08·44	S
McKernan, J.	GBR	Discus throw	Q		DNQ	50,92	
McLaughlin, E.	GBR	400m hurdles	1	1	3	56·11	
			SF	2	6	55·91	
McMiken, C.	NZL	10000m	1	2	10	32-20·39	
Machado, A.	POR	10000m	1	1	7	31-52·04	
			F		9	32-02·13	
Malovecz, Z.	HUN	Javelin throw	F		12	54,58	
Malchugina, G.	URS	200m	1	3	1	22·85	
			2	4	1	22·77	
			SF	2	4	22·55	
			F		8	22·42	
		4×100m relay	1	1	1	42·88	
			SF	1	1	42·01	
			F		3	42·75	B
Marshall, P.	USA	200m	1	8	DNF		
Martin, L.	AUS	Marathon	F		2	2:25-53	S
Martin, L.	USA	100m hurdles	1	1	3	13·20	
			2	2	5	13·20	
			SF	1	7	13·29	
Marxer, M.	LIE	100m hurdles	1	5	6	14·38	
Masullo, M.	ITA	100m	1	3	5	11·71	
		200m	1	3	5	23·58	
			2	3	6	23·52	
		4×100m relay	1	2	5	44·33	
Matsui, E.	JPN	Javelin throw	Q		DNQ	56·26	
Matsuno, A.	JPN	10000m	1	2	9	32-19·57	
Matussiavichene, D.	URS	800m	1	3	4	2-02·57	
			SF	2	7	2-00·15	
Matveyeva, L.	URS	10000m	1	2	2	32-12·87	
			F		12	32-12·27	
Maxie, L.	USA	400m hurdles	1	4	5	57·60	
May, F.	GBR	Long jump	F		6	6,62	
Mayhew, D.	USA	Javelin throw	F		7	61,78	
Mbuamangongo, R	GEQ	200m	1	8	6	31·12	
Melicherova, L.	TCH	Marathon	F		45	2:43-56	
Melinte, D.	RUM	1500m	1	1	1	4-06·87	
			F		9	4-02·89	
Melis, C.	ARU	Marathon	F		56	2:53-24	
Mexendez De Cox, M.-P.	GUA	Marathon	F		53	2:51-33	
Michallek, V.	GER	1500m	1	1	9	4-10·05	
		3000m	1	2	10	8-51·34	
Mikhalchenko, L.	URS	Discus throw	F		10	64,08	
Miles, H.	GBR	100m	1	8	6	11·88	

COMPETITOR	COUNTRY CODE	EVENT	ROUND	HEAT	PLACE	TIME & DISTANCE	MEDAL
Min, M.-M.	BIR	Marathon	F		DNF		
Minyemeck, J.	CMR	Shot put	Q		DNQ	12,73	
Miranda, T.	BRA	4×400m relay	1	2	4	3-36.81	
Mitkova, S.	BUL	Shot put	F		10	19.09	
		Discus throw	F		4	69.14	
Miyahara, M.	JPN	Marathon	F		29	2:35-26	
Moe, B.	NOR	Marathon	F		DNF		
Moeller, S.	GDR	100m	1	4	2	11-27	
			2	3	4	11-10	
			SF	1	5	11-12	
		200m	1	3	2	23-07	
			2	3	3	22-86	
			SF	1	3	22-75	
			F		5	22-09	
		4×100m relay	1	2	1	42-92	
			SF	1	2	42-23	
			F		2	42-09	S
Moller, L.	NZL	Marathon	F		33	2:37-52	
Montalvao, S.	BRA	4×400m relay	1	2	4	3-36-81	
Morris, R.	ISV	200m	1	2	6	24.5	
		400m	1	6	6	55-60	
Mota, R.	POR	Marathon	F		1	2:25-40	G
Mueller, I.	GDR	Shot put	F		4	20,37	
Mueller, P.	GDR	400m	1	3	2	51-33	
			2	3	1	51-45	
			SF	1	2	49-50	
			F		2	49-45	S
		4×400m relay	1	1	1	3-27-37	
			F		3	3-18-29	B
Mueller, R.	SUI	Marathon	F		48	2.47-31	
Mukamurenzi, M.	RWA	Marathon	F		38	2:40-12	
Mulliner, J.	GBR	Heptathlon	F		19	5746	
Munerotto, R.	ITA	10000m	1	1	9	32-06-37	
			F		14	32-29-34	
Murashova, G.	URS	Discus throw	F		NP	0	
Murphy-Rollins, M	IRL	Marathon	F		57	2:54-37	
Murray, Y.	GBR	3000m	1	2	2	8-43-73	
			F		3	8-29-02	B
Mutola, M.	MOZ	800m	1	2	7	2-04-36	
Myers, S.	ESP	100m	1	2	5	11-86	
Narozhilenko, L.	URS	100m hurdles	1	2	2	12-76	
			2	1	2	12-62	
			SF	2	DNF		
Nazarova, O.	URS	400m	1	1	1	52.18	
			2	4	1	50-26	
			SF	1	1	49-11	
			F		3	49-90	B
		4×400m relay	1	2	3	3-27-14	
			F		1	3-15-18*	G
N'da, L.	CIV	High jump	Q		DNQ	1,75	
Ndrin, C.	CIV	400m	1	6	4	52-48	
			2	4	5	52-04	
Neimke, K.	GDR	Shot put	F		2	21,07	S
Nelson, L.	USA	10000m	1	2	6	32-15-45	
			F		15	32-32-24	
Neubauer, D.	GDR	400m	1	2	1	52-51	
			2	4	3	51-48	
			SF	1	8	50-92	
		4×100m relay	1	1	1	3-27-37	
			F		3	3-18-29	B
Ng, K.-Y.	HKG	100m	1	3	7	12-18	
		200m	1	2	8	25-35	
Nkouka, L.-L.	CGO	400m	1	5	7	57-19	
Noh, H.-S.	KOR	1500m	1	1	12	4-26-05	
Nsang, O.-J.	GEQ	400m	1	1	7	1-07-58	
Nyinawabera, A.	RWA	Marathon	F		50	2:49-18	
Nyiramutuzo, D.	RWA	1500m	1	1	13	4-32-31	
		3000m	1	2	15	9-47-98	
Oakes, J.	GBR	Shot put	Q		DNQ	18,34	
O'Brien, C.	USA	Marathon	F		40	2:41-04	
Odhiambo, J.	KEN	100m	1	6	7	11-90	
		200m	1	4	5	24-26	
Ogborn, J.	GUM	Marathon	F		59	3:06-05	
Ogunkoya, F.	NGR	200m	1	1	3	23-12	
			2	2	5	22-88	
		4×400m relay	1	1	6	3-30-21	
Olizarenko, N.	URS	800m	1	4	3	2-01-81	
			SF	1	8	2-05-27	
Olyslager, M.	HOL	100m hurdles	1	3	1	13-04	
			2	2	3	13-02	
			SF	2	5	13-08	
		4×100m relay	1	3	3	43-96	
			SF	1	5	43-48	
Ongolio, G.	GAB	100m	1	7	6	11-85	
Onyali, M.	NGR	200m	1	2	2	22-82	
			2	4	2	22-89	
			SF	1	5	22-43	
		4×400m relay	1	1	6	3-30-21	
Oschkenat, C.	GDR	100m hurdles	1	4	1	12-72	
			2	2	1	12-69	
			SF	2	1	12-63	
			F		8	13-73	
Ottey, M.	JAM	100m	1	8	1	11-03	
			2	1	1	11-03	
			SF	2	DNS		
		200m	1	4	1	23-06	
			2	2	2	22-30	
			SF	1	2	22-07	
			F		4	21-99	
		4×100m relay	SF	1	3	43-30	
			F		DNS		
Ouiminga, M.	VOL	100m	1	6	8	12-62	
		200m	1	1	7	26-08	
Oumezdi, M.	MAR	100m	1	2	6	11-90	
Pagel, R.	USA	Shot put	Q		DNQ	18,55	
		Discus throw	Q		DNQ	57,50	
Pain, A.	GBR	Marathon	F		10	2:30-51	
Palm, E.	SWE	Marathon	F		24	2:34-41	
Pandey, R.	NEP	Marathon	F		60	3:10-31	
Panfil, M.	POL	Marathon	F		22	2:34-35	
Pardaens, A.	BEL	Marathon	F		DNF		
Park, M.-S.	KOR	4×100m relay	1	2	7	45-83	
Park, S.-J.	KOR	Long jump	Q		DNQ	5,90	
Patoucidou, P.	GRE	100m	1	1	5	11-85	
		4×100m relay	1	2	6	45-44	
Payne-Wiggins, M.	CAN	400m	1	2	2	52-70	
			2	3	2	51-73	
			SF	1	7	50-29	
		4×400m relay	1	1	2	3-27-63	
			F		DNF		
Perec, M.	FRA	200m	1	4	2	23-49	
			2	4	8	24-22	
Perez, C.	ESP	400m hurdles	1	4	2	55-29	
			SF	2	5	55-23	
Perkins, J.	AUS	3000m	1	1	10	9-01-82	
		10000m	1	2	14	33-45-22	
Peters, B.	GER	Javelin throw	Q		DNQ	60,20	
Petrovic, B.	YUG	High jump	Q		DNQ	1,80	
Pfitzinger, C.	NZL	3000m	1	1	9	9-01-30	
Phipps, A.	CAN	4×100m relay	1	2	3	43-92	
			SF	2	5	43-82	
Pinigina, M.	URS	4×400m relay	1	2	3	3-27-14	
			F		1	3-15-18*	G
Piquereau, A.	FRA	100m hurdles	1	5	4	13-56	
			2	3	DNF		
Pisiewicz, E.	POL	100m	1	3	6	11-84	
		4×100m relay	1	3	4	43-98	
			SF	1	4	43-44	
			F		6	43-93	
Plotzitzka, L.	GER	Shot put	Q		DNQ	19,06	
Plumer, P.	USA	3000m	1	2	7	8-45-21	
			F		13	8-59-17	
Polovinskaya, T.	URS	Marathon	F		4	2:27-05	
Pomoshchnikova, N.	URS	100m	1	6	1	11-11	
			2	2	2	10-98	
			SF	2	3	11-03	
			F		6	11-00	
		4×100m relay	1	1	1	42-88	
			SF	1	1	42-01	
			F		3	42-75	B
Powell, S.	JAM	800m	1	1	4	2-03-49	
		4×400m relay	1	2	2	3-26-83	
			F		5	3-23-13	
Pressler, K.	GER	Marathon	F		21	2:34-26	
Price, C.	USA	Shot put	Q		DNQ	17,09	
		Discus throw	Q		DNQ	57,04	
Protti, A.	SUI	400m hurdles	1	3	2	54-81	
			SF	1	5	54-56	
Puica, M.	ROM	3000m	1	1	DNF		
Pujol, M.	ESP	800m	1	1	5	2-03-73	
Rao, V.	IND	4×400m relay	1	1	7	3-33-46	
Rattray-Williams, C.	JAM	400m	1	6	3	52-39	
			2	3	4	51-81	
			SF	2	6	50-82	
		4×400m relay	1	2	2	3-26-83	
			F		5	3-23-13	
Rawat, M.	NEP	Marathon	F		61	3:11-17	
Redetzky, H.	GER	High jump	Q		DNQ	1,90	
Reinsch, G.	GDR	Discus throw	F		7	67,26	

COMPETITOR	COUNTRY CODE	EVENT	ROUND	HEAT	PLACE	TIME & DISTANCE	MEDAL
Renders, M.	BEL	10000m	1	1	13	32-11.49	
Renk, S.	GDR	Javelin throw	F		5	66,38	
Restrepo, X.	COL	200m	1	1	5	24.00	
		4×100m relay	1	1	5	45.46	
		4×400m relay	1	2	DIS		
Ribeiro, F.	POR	3000m	1	1	13	9-05.92	
Richards, S.	JAM	400m	1	3	3	52.19	
			2	2	5	52.90	
		4×400m relay	F		5	3-23.13	
Richardson, J.	CAN	400m	1	7	4	53.06	
			2	2	4	52.33	
			SF	1	5	49.91	
		4×400m relay	1	1	2	3-27.63	
Richter, S.	GER	100m	1	4	4	11.49	
			2	4	7	11.59	
		4×100m relay	1	1	2	42.99	
			SF	2	2	42.69	
			F		4	42.76	
Ritter, L.	USA	High jump	F		1	2,03*	G
Rochefort, E.	CAN	Marathon	F		31	2:36-44	
Rocheleau, J.	CAN	100m	1	5	5	11.60	
			2	4	8	11.75	
		100m hurdles	1	3	2	13.07	
			2	1	4	12.90	
			SF	1	3	12.91	
			F		6	12.99	
Rodriguez, A.	ESP	3000m	1	1	12	9-03.39	
Romanova, Y.	URS	3000m	1	1	1	8-48.47	
			F		4	8-30.45	
Ross, J.	STV	Long jump	Q		DNQ	5,50	
Rouillard, C.	CAN	10000m	1	1	10	32-09.08	
			F		16	32-41.43	
Ruotsalainen, S.	FIN	Heptathlon	F		15	6101	
Sablovskaite, R.	URS	Heptathlon	F		5	6456	
Saint-Phard, D.	HAI	Shot put	Q		DNQ	16,02	
Sakonninhom, M.	LAO	100m	1	8	8	15.12	
Samolenko, T.	URS	1500m	1	1	3	4-07.11	
			F		3	4-00.24	B
		3000m	1	2	5	8-44.18	
			F		1	8-26.53*	G
Sanderson, T.	GBR	Javelin throw	Q		DNQ	56,70	
Sardouk, M.	LIB	400m	1	4	6	1-00.01	
Sarvari, U.	GER	100m	1	8	2	11.26	
			2	1	3	11.16	
			SF	2	5	11.12	
		4×100m relay	1	1	2	42.99	
			SF	2	2	42.69	
			F		4	42.76	
Sato, M.	JPN	High jump	F		11	1,90	
Schabinger, M.	GER	4×400m relay	1	1	3	3-27.75	
Schneider, C.	SUI	Heptathlon	F		13	6157	
Schulz, I.	GDR	Heptathlon	F		6	6411	
Schuwalow, C.	AUS	10000m	1	1	11	32-10.05	
			F		17	32-45.07	
Seebaluck, S.	MRI	800m	1	2	8	2-08.93	
Selenska, A.	BUL	Javelin throw	F		11	56.78	
Selkridge, B.	ANT	400m	1	6	7	55.96	
Sergent, A.	FRA	3000m	1	2	8	8-45.94	
			F		12	8-49.14	
		10000m	1	2	4	32-13.45	
			F		19	33-17.38	
Shambagh, V.P.	IND	4×400m relay	1	1	7	3-33.46	
Shaomei, L.	PRC	100m	1	6	5	11.66	
Sheffield, L.	USA	400m hurdles	1	3	4	55.61	
			SF	1	3	54.36	
			F		8	55.32	
Shields, J.	GBR	10000m	1	2	11	32-46.07	
Short, S.	GBR	4×100m relay	1	3	2	43.91	
			SF	1	6	43.50	
Shubenkova, N.	URS	Heptathlon	F		4	6540	
Siebert, G.	GDR	100m hurdles	1	2	1	12.65	
			2	3	1	12.74	
			SF	1	2	12.60	
			F		2	12.61	S
Silhava, Z.	TCH	Shot put	F		11	18,86	
		Discus throw	F		6	67,84	
Simon, N.	FRA	400m	1	7	5	53.30	
		4×400m relay	1	1	5	3-29.95	
Simpson, J.	GBR	Heptathlon	F		DNF		
Singarayar, J.	MAL	400m	1	5	6	56.06	
Sirma, S.	KEN	1500m	1	2	10	4-10.13	
		3000m	1	1	14	9-06.90	

COMPETITOR	COUNTRY CODE	EVENT	ROUND	HEAT	PLACE	TIME & DISTANCE	MEDAL
Siwek, A.	POL	200m	1	1	2	23.10	
			1	4	4	22.96	
			SF	2	7	23.20	
		4×100m relay	1	3	4	43.98	
			SF	1	4	43.44	
			F		6	43.93	
Skeete, L.-A.	GBR	100m hurdles	1	3	3	13.38	
			2	1	7	13.27	
			SF	1	6	13.23	
Skordi, M.	GRE	200m	1	2	5	24.06	
		4×100m relay	1	2	6	45.44	
Slegers, L.	BEL	10000m	1	2	14	33-51.36	
Sly, W.	GBR	3000m	1	1	6	8-49.71	
			F		7	8-37.70	
Smekhnova, R.	URS	Marathon	F		16	2:33-19	
Smith, J.	GBR	4×400m relay	1	1	4	3-28.52	
Smith, K.	USA	Javelin throw	Q		DNQ	57,94	
Smolarek, J.	POL	100m	1	5	3	11.43	
			2	2	6	11.35	
		4×100m relay	1	3	4	43.98	
			SF	1	4	43.44	
			F		6	43.93	
Smyth, A.	IRL	Marathon	F		46	2:44-17	
Solberg, T.	NOR	Javelin throw	Q		DNQ	58,82	
Sommer, C.	USA	High jump	Q		DNQ	1,87	
Spence, V.	JAM	4×100m relay	1	2	2	43.50	
Stanton, C.	AUS	High jump	F		7	1,93	
Stewart, M.	CRC	800m	1	3	6	2-08.17	
Stoute, J.	GBR	4×400m relay	1	1	4	3-28.52	
Straughn, Y.	BAR	200m	1	6	4	23.81	
		400m	1	3	6	53.62	
			2	2	8	54.22	
Stuart, L.	GBR	200m	1	4	4	23.61	
			2	2	8	23.59	
Su, C.-Y.	FOR	High jump	Q		DNQ	1,80	
Sumei, S.	PRC	400m	1	3	5	53.46	
			2	2	7	53.58	
Sutfin, L.	USA	Javelin throw	Q		DNQ	56.12	
Szabo, K.	HUN	Marathon	F		13	2:32-26	
Tandian, A.	SEN	400m	1	7	3	52.95	
			2	5	6	52.33	
Tarolo, R.	ITA	100m	1	8	5	11.86	
		4×100m relay	1	2	5	44.33	
Tata-Muya, R.	KEN	400m hurdles	1	1	4	56.18	
Tate, E.	JAM	4×100m relay	1	2	2	43.50	
			SF	1	3	43.50	
			F		DNS		
Tate, M.	JAM	4×400m relay	1	2	2	3-26.83	
Tavares, S.	MEX	100m hurdles	1	1	6	13.81	
Telles, S.	BRA	800m	1	3	3	2-02.48	
			SF	1	6	2-01.86	
		4×400m relay	1	2	4	3-36.81	
Teloni, M.	CYP	Long jump	Q		DNQ	6,29	
Thiemard, D.	SUI	Javelin throw	F		9	58,54	
Thimm, U.	GER	400m	1	4	2	52.79	
			2	1	4	51.18	
			SF	1	6	50.28	
		4×100m relay	1	1	2	42.99	
			SF	2	2	42.69	
			F		4	42.76	
		4×400m relay	F		4	3-22.49	
Thomas, A.	GER	100m	1	5	4	11.46	
			2	3	7	11.37	
		200m	1	2	3	22.92	
			2	3	2	22.84	
			SF	1	8	22.91	
		4×100m relay	1	1	2	42.99	
			SF	2	2	42.69	
			F		4	42.76	
		4×400m relay	F		4	3-22.49	
Thomas, A.	JAM	4×400m relay	1	2	2	3-26.83	
			F		5	3-23.13	
Thompson, R.	SLE	1500m	1	2	14	5-31.42	
Thyssen, I.	GER	Javelin throw	F		8	60,76	
Tierney, E.	CKI	100m	1	4	8	12.52	
		200m	1	3	8	26.16	
Tinari, N.	CAN	10000m	1	2	7	32-16.27	
			F		13	32-14.05	
Tooby, A.	GBR	10000m	1	1	16	33-26.57	
Tooby, S.	GBR	Marathon	F		12	2:31.33	

COMPETITOR	COUNTRY CODE	EVENT	ROUND	HEAT	PLACE	TIME & DISTANCE	MEDAL
Torrence, G.	USA	100m	1	3	1	11·12	
			2	4	2	10·99	
			SF	1	3	11·02	
			F		5	10·97	
		200m	1	7	1	22·87	
			2	2	1	22·25	
			SF	2	3	22·53	
			F		6	22·17	
Trojer, I.	ITA	400m hurdles	1	4	4	55·74	
Tromp, G.	HOL	100m hurdles	1	4	6	13·48	
			2	3	5	13·42	
		400m hurdles	1	2	2	56·11	
			SF	1	8	57·57	
		4×100m relay	1	3	3	43·96	
			SF	1	5	43·48	
Tsomi, M.	GRE	4×100m relay	1	2	6	45·44	
Tukana, S.	FIJ	100m hurdles	1	1	7	15·50	
		Heptathlon	F		26	2560	
Turchak, O.	URS	High jump	F		4	1,96	
Ullrich, K.	GDR	10000m	1	1	4	31·51·40	
			F		4	31·29·27	
Urrutia, I.	COL	Shot put	Q		DNQ	15,13	
		Discus throw	Q		DNQ	53,82	
Usha, P.T.	IND	400m hurdles	1	1	7	59·55	
Usifo, M.	UGA	100m hurdles	1	2	5	13·50	
			2	3	DNF		
		400m hurdles	1	3	5	55·99	
Vader, E.	HOL	100m	1	4	3	11·38	
			2	1	6	11·51	
		4×100m relay	1	3	3	43·96	
			SF	1	5	43·48	
Vallecilla, N.	ECU	100m hurdles	1	5	5	13·97	
Van Dorp, Y.	HOL	400m	1	4	3	52·84	
			2	3	6	53·50	
Van Hulst, E.	HOL	1500m	1	1	5	4·07·40	
		3000m	1	1	2	3·48·54	
			F		9	8·43·92	
Vao Ikavuka, S.	TON	Shot put	Q		DNQ	12,31	
Vaughan, K.	NGR	4×400m relay	1	1	6	3·30·21	
Verouli, A.	GRE	Javelin throw	Q		DNQ	58,52	
Vetchernikova, A.	BUL	100m	1	1	1	11·09	
			2	4	1	10·96	
			SF	1	2	11·00	
			F		8	11·49	
Villeton, J.	FRA	Marathon	F		9	2·34·02	
Vincent, M.A.	GRN	Marathon	F		62	3·23·56	
Vriesde, L.	SUR	800m	1	4	4	2·01·83	
			SF	2	8	2·02·34	
		1500m	1	2	12	4·19·58	
Wachtel, C.	GDR	800m	1	2	1	2·00·52	
			SF	2	1	1·58·44	
			F		2	1·56·64	S
Wade, K.	GBR	800m	1	3	5	2·02·75	
			SF	1	5	2·00·86	
		1500m	1	1	6	4·08·37	
Waitz, G.	NOR	Marathon	F		DNF		
Wang, Q.-H.	PRC	10000m	1	1	8	32·04·52	
			F		18	32·49·86	
Wang, S.-H.	FOR	Long jump	Q		DNQ	5,87	
		4×100m relay	1	1	6	46·21	
Wang, X.	PRC	3000m	1	1	7	8·54·19	
		10000m	1	2	3	32·13·00	
			F		7	31·40·23	
Wangui, P.	KEN	Marathon	F		49	2·47·42	
Whitbread, F.	GBR	Javelin throw	F		2	70,32	S
Wijnsma, M.	HOL	Long jump	Q		DNQ	6,39	
		Heptathlon	F		11	6205	
Williams, A.	TRI	100m	1	6	4	11·62	
			2	2	7	11·45	
		200m	1	1	4	23·76	
			2	1	7	23·48	

COMPETITOR	COUNTRY CODE	EVENT	ROUND	HEAT	PLACE	TIME & DISTANCE	MEDAL
Williams, L.	CAN	1500m	1	2	4	4·04·20	
			F		5	4·00·86	
		3000m	1	1	4	8·48·70	
			F		8	8·38·43	
Williams, S.	USA	400m hurdles	1	5	2	55·98	
			SF	2	7	56·71	
Wodars, S.	GDR	800m	1	3	1	2·02·24	
			SF	1	1	1·57·21	
			F		1	1·56·10	G
Wolf, G.	GER	Marathon	F		27	2·35·11	
Womplou, M.	CIV	400m hurdles	1	1	5	57·35	
Woo, Y.-J.	KOR	200m	1	3	6	24·94	
		4×100m relay	1	2	7	45·83	
Wulah, M.	LBR	100m	1	1	6	12·16	
		200m	1	3	7	25·46	
		Long jump	Q		DNQ	5,23	
Wynn, C.	CAN	400m hurdles	1	1	6	58·00	
Xie, L.	PRC	10000m	1	1	17	33·28·13	
Xie, Z.	PRC	200m	1	8	4	24·01	
		4×100m relay	1	2	4	44·29	
			SF	2	7	44·36	
Xing, A.	PRC	Discus throw	Q		DNQ	59,26	
Xiong, Q.	PRC	Long jump	F		9	6,50	
Yang, K.-H.	KOR	400m	1	1	6	58·18	
		4×400m relay	1	2	5	3·51·09	
Yankey, D.	GHA	100m	1	8	4	11·64	
			2	3	8	11·63	
		100m hurdles	1	2	6	13·64	
		4×100m relay	1	3	5	44·12	
Yendork, J.	GHA	Long jump	Q		DNQ	5,40	
Yermolovich, N.	URS	Javelin throw	F		6	64·84	
Yevseyeva, I.	URS	800m	1	1	1	2·01·59	
			SF	2	3	1·59·10	
			F		6	1·59·37	
Yoo, C.-O.	KOR	Javelin throw	Q		DNQ	48,26	
Yeom, M.-K.	KOR	4×100m relay	1	2	7	45·83	
Young, D.	USA	4×100m relay	1	3	1	42·39	
Young, S.-L.	KOR	100m	1	6	6	11·74	
Ysrael, M.	GUM	Marathon	F		64	3·42·23	
Yu, H.	PRC	Discus throw	F		9	64·08	
Yumei, T.	PRC	100m	1	1	4	11·56	
			2	1	7	11·55	
Zaczkiewicz, C.	GER	100m hurdles	1	2	3	13·00	
			2	3	2	12·87	
			SF	2	2	12·75	
			F		3	12·75	B
Zagorcheva, G.	BUL	100m hurdles	1	3	DNF		
Zhang, C.	PRC	4×100m relay	1	2	4	44·29	
			SF	2	7	44·36	
Zhang, X.	PRC	200m	1	5	5	24·08	
		4×100m relay	1	2	4	44·29	
			SF	2	7	44·36	
Zhao, Y.-F.	PRC	Marathon	F		5	2·27·06	
Zhirova, M.	URS	100m	1	5	2	11·22	
			2	4	4	11·14	
			SF		8	11·24	
		4×100m relay	1	1	1	42·88	
			SF	1	1	42·01	
			F		3	42·75	B
Zhong, H.	PRC	Marathon	F		30	2·36·02	
Zhou, Y.-X.	PRC	Javelin throw	Q		DNQ	56,36	
Zhupieva, E.	URS	10000m	1	1	3	31·47·99	
			F		3	31·19·82	B
Zouganeli, G.	GRE	4×100m relay	1	2	6	45·44	
Zuniga, T.	ESP	800m	1	2	4	2·00·98	
			SF	1	4	1·58·85	
			F		7	1·59·82	
Zvereva, E.	URS	Discus throw	F		5	68,94	

Bibliography

Special mention must be given to two enthusiasts who have made a large contribution to Olympic track and field with their publications. Firstly, Ekkrhard Zur Megede of West Germany with his three volume work "Die Geschichte der Olympischen Leichtathletik", which attempts to record all Olympic competitors and America's Bill Mallon who has researched the early Games in his book, "The Olympic Games 1896, 1900, 1904 and 1906", Part I: Track and Field Athletics.

The following list comprises of books, magazines and newspapers, which were the main sources for the compilers:

Official Reports 1896, 1908. 1912, 1924-1984.
The Field, London (newspaper) 1896, 1906.
Sporting Life, London (newspaper) 1900.
Acropolis, Athens (newspaper) 1896.
The New York Herald (newspaper) 1896, 1900 & 1904.
Chicago Daily Tribune (newspaper) 1900 & 1904.
The New York Herald (newspaper) 1896, 1900 & 1904.
The Daily Messenger, Paris (newspaper) 1900.
1896 Olympics by D. Terry in Athletics Arena 1964.
The Olympic Games 1904 by C.J.P. Lucas & E.B. Woodward 1905.
Spaldings Olympic Games of 1906 by J.E. Sullivan 1906.
Olympic Games of London 1908 by Sporting Life 1908.
Olympiska Spelen by G.G. Uggla 1912.
De Olympika Spelen i Antwerpen 1920 by E. Bergvall.
Olympiaden VII 1920 by E. Bergvall.
US Olympic Committee Reports 1920-1964.
British Olympic Association Reports 1924-1976.
Olympialaiskisat, (Finnish Reports) 1924-1936.
Spaldings Official Athletic Almanacs 1903-1937.
Olympic Programmes 1912-1984.
Die Olympischen Spiele 1928 by J. Wagner, F. Klipstein & Dr. F. Messerli.
Olympiaden IV (Swedish Report) 1928.
Olympia 1932 & Olympia 1936 Band II.

Amateur Athlete (magazine) 1936-1960.
Athletics (magazine) 1948.
Athletics Weekly (magazine) 1952-1984.
Track & Field News (magazine) 1948-1984.
Leichtathletik (magazine) 1952-1984.
ATFS Olympic Handbook 1952, 1956, 1960, 1968, 1975 & 1979.
ATFS Annuals 1951-1988.
Handbook of Olympic Games Track & Field by R.L. Quercetani & D.H. Potts 1948.
Women's Track & Field World (magazine) 1968 and 1972.
Women's Track & Field Yearbook 1967-1976.
Encyclopedia of the Olympic Games by E. Kamper 1972.
Lexikon Der 12,000 Olympioniken by E. Kamper 1975.
Book of The Olympics by D. Walleschinsky 1984.
Athletics Arena Olympic Reports 1964, 1968 & 1972.
ATFS Track & Field Through the Years, Vol I 1929-1936.
Die Entwicklung der Leichtathletik Weltrekorde by E. Zur Megede 1972.
Race Walking Statistics 1963-1984.
Race Walking World Statistics 20km & Olympic Results by E. Rasmussen & P. Lassen 1977.
Race Walking World Statistics 50km & European Championships by E. Rasmussen & P. Lassen 1977.
World & National Leaders and Track & Field Athletics 1860-1972 by L. Mengoni, R. Magnusson, M. Sykota & D. Terry 1973.
The Games by M. Brant 1980.
Encyclopaedia of Athletics by M. Watman 1977.
The 1980 Olympics Track & Field by M. Shearman & M. Hannus 1980.
Los Angeles 1984 by D. Hedges, J. Robinson & J.V. Wigley.
Games of the XXIIIrd Olympiad Los Angeles 1984 Commemorative Book by International Sport Publications Ltd.